W9-ADW-679

HOMOSEXUALITY

GARLAND REFERENCE LIBRARY
OF SOCIAL SCIENCE
(VOL. 313)

HOMOSEXUALITY
A Research Guide

Wayne R. Dynes

GARLAND PUBLISHING, INC. • NEW YORK & LONDON
1987

Library of Congress Cataloging-in-Publication Data

Dynes, Wayne R.
Homosexuality : a research guide.

(Garland reference library of social science ;
vol. 313)
Includes indexes.
1. Homosexuality—Bibliography. I. Title.
II. Series: Garland reference library of social
science ; v. 313. [DNLM: 1. Homosexuality—abstracts.
ZWM 615 D997h]
Z7164.S42D96 1987 [HQ76.25] 016.3067'66 85–45109
ISBN 0-8240-8692-9 (alk. paper)

Cover design by Alison Lew

Printed on acid-free, 250-year-life paper
Manufactured in the United States of America

CONTENTS

CONTENTS

PREFACE

Criteria for inclusion of material in **Homosexuality: A Research Guide** are broad in order to reflect the interdisciplinary character of research. A glance at the Table of Contents reveals the range of categories. Moreover, many individual entries involve one or several disciplines or topics.

Within space limits every effort has been made to display the full spectrum of points of view. Such inclusiveness will not earn universal approval. Some would prefer that antihomosexual citations be omitted. Others will judge that there is too much material reflecting the concerns and concepts of the current gay and lesbian movements. Older bibliographies abound in psychiatric contributions, which are often negative and moralizing. While many of these items find their place here, no attempt has been made to record them en bloc. Generally speaking, when a subject or viewpoint is densely canvased in the literature, the **Guide** presents it selectively. Some less-studied topics, such as Economics and Music, are fleshed out with brief items providing signposts toward more comprehensive research. **Homosexuality: A Research Guide** seeks not only to mirror the remarkable roster of existing publications, but also to stimulate new work by pinpointing neglected themes and methods.

It is important to convey a sense of the history of the study of homosexual behavior--which goes back to the ancient Greeks. While some would assert that only the most recent publications matter, many of these will in course of time become dated. But like the older writings which preceded them, these texts will form part of the evolving history of the subject. To others the following pages will seem crowded with too much that reflects the passing preoccupations of the day. The AIDS section (XXIII.C) is a possible case in point. But even after medical progress renders current theories of the Acquired Immune Deficiency Syndrome obsolete, it will still be useful to chronicle and evaluate the stages of the crisis.

The **Guide** is not restricted to works in English. The major traditions of modern homosexual research began generations ago on the European continent. While much has been added in the last few decades--particularly in the social sciences--by English-speaking researchers, important publications continue to appear in Dutch, French, German, Italian, Portuguese, Spanish, and the Scandinavian languages. There are also significant contributions on Far Eastern themes in Chinese and Japanese. In its international coverage, the **Guide** looks forward to an emerging world history of homosexual behavior.

As a rule, creative works of fiction, poetry, and drama have been excluded. It is hard to determine valid principles of selection, inasmuch as a novel, say, may be of major importance in the history of literature, but have only a minor gay or lesbian character. At the other extreme are novels that are entirely gay or lesbian, but of slight literary merit. And to attempt to encompass the luxuriant productions of pulp pornography would trivialize the **Guide**. Fortunately, good bibliographies and critical histories exist, at least for creative writings available in English (see "Literary Studies," VI.H-J).

In order to find subjects in the **Guide** users are directed first to the Subject Index, where such topics as Japan, Labeling, and Music may be easily found. The Personal Names Index includes entries about persons as well as writings by specific authors. Connections are suggested by the topical arrangement of the Table of Contents. Turning to the main body of the work, the headnotes for the individual section offer an overview of the subject with indications of related subjects. Within the sections many entries contain references to, or citations of related works. For some topics it will be profitable to combine the use of the **Guide** with consultation of the appropriate articles in the **Encyclopedia of Homosexuality,** which is also being issued by Garland Publishing.

In order not to increase the bulk of this work beyond measure, it has been decided (in principle--there are a very few exceptions) to admit each item only once as a primary citation. The contributions of writers who appear in more than one section can be traced through the Personal Names Index. In many instances kindred items are supplied in the body of the annotation (embedded references). Inclusion of the item in the embedded position does not imply a judgment of inferior worth, but is simply intended to cluster related material and to save space. In some cases the embedded reference cites a work that appears elsewhere as a primary entry, serving as a cross reference. Moreover, the length of the annotation is not to be construed as a mark of value. Some first-rate works receive a relatively brief commentary because they are unproblematic--and in some instances the title and subtitle give much of the information required. Contributions of mixed character may need a longer annotation, assessing strengths and weaknesses. Moreover, books do not necessarily deserve a privileged position over articles and brochures. In such fields as psychology and medical research, journal articles are the primary vehicle of scientific communication. Since the late 1960s a plethora of journalistic material, most of it of current or local interest, has appeared in the gay and lesbian

press. Of necessity, this category appears here only very
selectively, but the major journals are covered on a current basis in the **Alternative Press Index** (1969-   ). As
a rule unpublished dissertations are not included; a few
exceptions have been made, however, for examples containing information not available in published sources.

Some items listed here will prove hard to find. This
rarity reflects the clandestinity that social taboos have
enforced until recently, the reluctance of many public and
university libraries to acquire and preserve the material,
and the inability of private collections to survive their
owners. Fortunately, the problem of access is being addressed by the gay and lesbian archives that have recently
emerged in North America and Europe. Inasmuch as this
work is a **Guide** and not a bibliography in the strict
sense, it has not been deemed appropriate to indicate the
history of editions of works cited. However, the editions
that are indicated are those that are believed to be the
fullest and most useful. Individual libraries, of course,
may contain editions other than the ones noted here.

Over the decade in which this work has been in progress, the writer has profited from the help of many persons and institutions. Two scholars of remarkable range
and critical acumen have monitored the whole work: Warren
Johansson, Senior Research Fellow, Gay Academic Union, New
York; and Stephen O. Murray, Director, Instituto Obregón,
San Francisco. At an early stage, Barbara Gittings, of
the American Library Association, offered both benevolent
advice and a courageous example. Stephen Wayne Foster has
been exceptionally generous in sharing his unique know-
ledge of little-known references. In special fields, par-
ticular help has been given by Claude Courouve, Paris;
Giovanni Dall'Orto, Milan; Jürgen Geisler, Frankfurt; Kent
Gerard, Berkeley; Júlio Gómes, Lisbon; David Greenberg,
New York; Paul Hardman, San Francisco; Gert Hekma, Amster-
dam; Manfred Herzer, Berlin; Arthur Leonard, New York; Jim
Levin, New York; Phoebe Lloyd, Philadelphia; João António
Mascarenhas, Rio de Janeiro; Luiz Mott, Bahia; Robert
Padgug, New York; Geoff Puterbaugh, Sunnyvale; Kathy D.
Schnapper, New York; Gary Simes, Sydney; the late Jack
Stafford; James Steakley, Madison; Leo Steinberg, New
York; and Arthur C. Warner, Princeton. Technical advice
has been provided by John Lauritsen. Other individuals,
too numerous to name, have contributed; may they find
traces of their good counsel in the entries below. The
following research institutions have been of indispensable
assistance: Canadian Gay Archives, Toronto; Columbia
University Libraries; Documentatiecentrum Homostudies,
University of Amsterdam; Gay Academic Union, New York;
Homosexual Information Center, Hollywood; International
Gay and Lesbian Archives, Hollywood; The New York Public
Library; ONE, Inc., Los Angeles; University of California
Libraries, Berkeley and Los Angeles.

ABBREVIATIONS

ARGOH	Anthropologists' Research Group on Homosexuality
col.	column
ed.	edition, edited by
esp.	especially
JfsZ	Jahrbuch fur sexuelle Zwischenstufen
JH	Journal of Homosexuality
NS	New Series
no.	number
vol.	volume

Homosexuality
A Research Guide

I. GENERAL

A. BIBLIOGRAPHY

The tentative beginnings of the task of gathering references about homosexual behavior ("sodomy") lie in the 17th
and 18th centuries, when savants--generally forensic
physicians, legal scholars, and theologians--began to
record such writings as they were able to discover. The
19th century saw two major advances: the creation of
erotic bibliographies (comprising what were sometimes
termed "curiosa") by collectors and booksellers; and the
compiling of systematic lists of references by homosexuals
themselves (e.g. Meienreis and Ulrichs). Much has been
accomplished in the present century, so that bibliographical control in the sphere of homosexuality is currently regarded as well developed by librarians at the
Kinsey Institute, who enjoy a panoramic command of the
fields of sex research. Yet problems persist. There is a
tendency, found particularly but not exclusively among
American scholars, to concentrate on work in one language
group, so that one's vision of the universe of research--
geographical and temporal--is narrowed. Moreover, there
is no current annual survey of progress in gay and lesbian
studies. Only recently, in fact, have some of the major
current subject bibliographies, such as **Art Index** and **MLA
Bibliography,** introduced homosexuality as a category. Entries in some existing retrospective bibliographies are
marred by misprints and incomplete references, faults
which may to some extent be excused because of the rarity
of many publications, which were often published semiclan-
destinely. In addition to the general bibliographies
cited below, more specialized ones will be found throughout this work under the appropriate subject categories.

1.   ASHBEE, HENRY SPENCER ("Pisanus Fraxi"). **Bibliog-
        raphy of Forbidden Books.** Introduction by Gershon
        Legman. New York: Jack Brussel, 1962. 3 vols.
Originally published in London under three titles: **Index librorum prohibitorum** (1877), **Centuria librorum
absconditorum** (1879), and **Catena librorum tacendorum**
(1885). Other reprints are known. In addition to
standard bibliographical data, entries frequently contain
an annotative essay summarizing the contents with liberal
quotations. Although these volumes cover the whole
field of erotica, they mention a considerable number
of works on homosexuality, some now neglected. Each
volume has an index of authors, titles, and subjects.

2.   AUGUST, EUGENE R. **Men's Studies: A Selected and
        Annotated Interdisciplinary Bibliography.** Little-

ton, CO: Libraries Unlimited, 1985. 233 pp.
Covers some 600 English-language books, arranged in 21
topical chapters, of which the last concerns homosexuality. Includes autobiographies and fiction, as well as
non-fiction.

3.   BEASLY, RUTH (ed.). **International Directory of Sex
        Research and Related Fields.** Boston: G. K. Hall,
        1976. 2 vols.
Lists over 1600 persons and groups in 48 countries, with
selected publications; derives from the files of the
Alfred C. Kinsey Institute, Indiana University.

4.   BELL, LOUIS NEWTON. **The Gay Seen, or 200+ Ap-
        proaches to the Fiction and Non-Fiction of the
        Other Sexual Minority.** Dominguez Hills: Edu-
        cational Resources Center of California State
        College, 1975. 147 pp. (Dominguez Hills Biblio-
        graphical Series, 11)
Select bibliography with annotations; indexed. Sometimes
idiosyncratic.

5.   BREWER, JOAN SCHERER, and ROD W. WRIGHT (eds.).
        **Sex Research: Bibliographies from the Institute for
        Sex Research.** Phoenix: Oryx Press, 1979. 212 pp.
Classified list of 4267 items, unannotated, selected from
the holdings of the Alfred C. Kinsey Institute, Indiana
University. Homosexuality has restricted coverage on the
grounds that it is well treated in other publications.
See "Sex Variations" (pp. 43-56) and "Pedophilia" (pp.
138-41). Author and subject indexes.

6.   BULLOUGH, VERN L., W. DORR LEGG, BARRETT W. ELCANO,
        and JAMES KEPNER (eds.). **An Annotated Bibliography
        of Homosexuality.** New York: Garland, 1976. 2 vols.
        (406; 468 pp.)
Despite some valid criticisms, this monumental work (almost 13,000 entries) opened a new era in research horizons
in its subject as the first attempt to cover, without
limitations of country or time period, the entire ensemble
of relevant fields--scholarly, scientific, and creative.
The title notwithstanding, only a few items are annotated; misprints abound (esp. in the numerous German
entries); and some items are incorrectly assigned to the
topical categories. Each volume has an author index,
but the absence of subject indexes hinders retrieval of
material on specific themes.

7.   **Catalogus van de Bibliotheek van het Nederlandsch
        Wetenschappelijk Humanitair Komitee.** The Hague:
        MWHK, 1922. 55 pp.
Catalogue of books (Dutch, German, French, and English)
kept in the house of Jacob Anton Schorer, a principal
figure in the Dutch Scientific-Humanitarian Committee.
An important reference for its time, the **Catalogus** had a
number of supplements, of which four were published: 1

(1926; 28 pp.); 2 (1930; 22 pp.); 3 (1932; 24 pp.); and
4 (1936; 28 pp.).

8.   COUROUVE, CLAUDE. **Bibliographie des homosexualités,**
      1478-1881. Third ed. Paris: The author, 1981.
A useful guide to French-language publications, fiction
and non-fiction. (This section is published together with
Fragments 4, by Courouve and Robert Kozérawski). It is
continued in **Bibliographie des homosexualités II, 1882-**
1924. Third ed. (Paris: The author, 1981). A new, more
comprehensive edition is in preparation.

9.   CRAWFORD, WILLIAM (ed.). **Homosexuality in Canada:**
      A Bibliography. New ed. Toronto: Canadian Gay
Archives, 1984. 378 cols. (CGA Publications, 9)
Useful classified list of material published in Canada or
by and about Canadians abroad. Less comprehensive for
French-language than English-language materials.

10.   DALL'ORTO, GIOVANNI. **Leggere omosessuale.** Turin:
      Edizioni Gruppo Abele, 1984. 108 pp.
Fundamental list of 749 Italian-language items published
between 1800 and 1983, annotated throughout. Includes
translations into Italian as well as original works.

11.   DYNES, WAYNE. "A Bibliography of Bibliographies of
      Homosexuality," **Cabirion and Gay Books Bulletin,**
      no. 10 (1984), 16-22.
About 180 items, annotated, in all major languages. In-
cludes some fugitive and minor items not cited here.
There is also a somewhat different version in Italian:
"Bibliografia di bibliografie sull'omosessualità," **Sodoma,**
2 (1985), 39-54.

12.   ELYSIAN FIELDS, BOOKSELLERS. **Gay Literature** [Title
      varies]. Elmhurst, NY: Elysian Fields, 1974ff.
About 25 catalogues in this series have appeared, which
are noteworthy for unusual and out-of-print items, which
are sold by mail order. A number of gay and lesbian
bookstores in the United States have also produced
noteworthy catalogues, including A Different Light (Los
Angeles), L'Androgyne (Montreal), Chosen Books (Detroit),
Giovanni's Room (Philadelphia), Lambda Rising (Washington,
DC), Oscar Wilde Memorial Bookshop (New York City), and
Womanbooks (New York City).

13.   FEUCHT, RAINER C. **Homosexualität und Randgebiete.**
      Ulm: BMCF Antiquariat, 1977. about 60 pp.
Carefully compiled bookseller's catalogue of 640 items in
several languages. Other useful European catalogues have
been produced by the bookstores Les Mots à la Bouche
(Paris), Prinz Eisenherz (Berlin), Sodom (Munich), and De
Woelrat (The Hague).

14.   GAY, JULES, "COMTE D'IÉNA." **Bibliographie des**
      ouvrages relatifs à l'amour. Fourth ed., revised

by J. Lemonnyer.   Paris: J. Lemonnyer, and Lille:
Stéphane Bécour, 1894-1900. 4 vols.
The most elaborate general erotic bibliography of the
19th century.   See also: Louis Perceau, **Bibliographie du
roman érotique au XIXe siècle** (Paris: Georges Fourdrin-
ier, 1930; 2 vols.).

15. **A Gay Bibliography: Eight Bibliographies on Lesbian
     and Male Homosexuality** [ed. by Jonathan Katz et
     al.]. New York: Arno Press, 1975.
Comprises five short bibliographies by Marion Zimmer
Bradley; Gene Damon [Barbara Grier] and Lee Stuart, **The
Lesbian in Literature, A Bibliography** (San Francisco,
1967); Noel I. Garde, **The Homosexual in Literature** (New
York, 1959); and William Parker, **Homosexuality: Selected
Abstracts and Bibliography** (San Francisco, 1966).

16. GITTINGS, BARBARA. **A Gay Bibliography.** Sixth ed.
     Philadelphia: Gay Task Force, American Library
     Association, 1980. 16 pp.
List of 563 current items selected to provide material
that is supportive of gay people and arranged in ten
major categories. In addition to books and some periodical citations (English language only), includes films
and filmstrips.

17. HANSEN, BENT (ed.). **Nordisk Bibliografi: Homosek-
     sualitet.** Copenhagen: Forlaget Pan, 1984. 32 pp.
Annotated list of original publications, fiction and
nonfiction, arranged by country (Denmark, Finland,
Iceland, Norway, and Sweden).

18. HERZER, MANFRED. **Bibliographie zur Homosexualität:
     Verzeichnis des deutschsprachigen nichtbelletrist-
     ischen Schrifttums zur weiblichen und männlichen
     Homosexualität aus den Jahren 1466 bis 1975 in
     chronologischer Reihenfolge.** Berlin: Verlag Rosa
     Winkel, 1982. 255 pp.
Exemplary bibliography (3404 items) of German-language
non-fiction material arranged in chronological order.
Subject and author indexes. A complementary volume,
admitting novels, short stories, poetry and plays, is in
preparation.

19. INDIANA UNIVERSITY. ALFRED C. KINSEY INSTITUTE FOR
     SEX RESEARCH. **Sex Studies Index, 1980.** Boston:
     G. K. Hall, 1982. 219 pp.
Classified list for the year by author and subject (see
esp. pp. 108-22). Apparently not continued. See also
R. Beasly; and J. S. Brewer and R. W. Wright, above; and
M. S. Weinberg and A. Bell, below.

20. KEARNEY, PATRICK J. **The Private Case: An Annotated
     Bibliography of the Private Case Erotica Collection
     in the British (Museum) Library.** London: Jay
     Landesman, 1981. 360 pp.

Definitive catalogue of the long-mysterious British
Library special collection, supplanting A. Rose (see
below) for the items that it contains. Only a small number of entries are directly pertinent.

21.   [MEIENREIS, RICHARD.] "Bibliographie der Homosex-
       ualität," **JfsZ**, 1 (1899), 215-38.
This list inaugurated the annual bibliographical coverage
of the **Jahrbuch für sexuelle Zwischenstufen**, published
under the auspices of the Berlin Scientific-Humanitarian
Committee, which set world standards for homosexual
bibliography. In the first ten years of compilation over
1000 contemporary publications were noted, some reviewed
in considerable detail by Eugen Wilhelm.

22.   MILLER, ALAN V. **Homosexuality in Specific Fields:**
       The Arts, the Military, Prisons, Sports, Teaching
       and Transsexuals: A Selected Bibliography. Toron-
       to: Ontario Ministry of Labour, Library, 1978. 58
       pp.
Something of an omnium gatherum, but sometimes useful for
out-of-the-way items. The author has since pursued more
defined bibliographical tasks in excellent work produced
under the auspices of the Canadian Gay Archives in
Toronto.

23.   MILLETT, ANTHONY PERCIVAL UPTON. **Homosexuality: A**
       Bibliography of Literature Published Since 1959 and
       Available in New Zealand. Wellington, NZ: Library
       School, 1967. 55 pp. (Bibliographical Series, 5)
Conscientious list, chiefly of interest for a few local
publications.

24.   PAOLELLA, EDWARD. "A Gay/Lesbian Studies Bibliog-
       raphy of Resources Selected from Non-Homosexual
       Periodical Literature," **Gay Books Bulletin**, no. 6
       (1981), 26-30.
Continued, with contributions from various researchers, in
Gay Books Bulletin, nos. 7-9.

25.   PARKER, WILLIAM. **Homosexuality: A Selective**
       Bibliography of Over 3000 Items. Metuchen,
       NJ: Scarecrow Press, 1971. 323 pp.
Emphasizes nonfiction, in English only, with the items
arranged by type of publication. Subject and author
indexes. Continued in his useful **Homosexuality Bibliog-**
raphy: Supplement 1970-1975 (Metuchen, NJ: Scarecrow
Press, 1977; 337 pp.); and **Homosexuality Bibliography:**
Second Supplement, 1976-1982 (Metuchen, NJ: Scarecrow
Press, 1985; 395 pp.).

26.   PIA, PASCAL. **Les livres de l'enfer du XVIème**
       siecle à nos jours. Paris: C. Coulet et A. Faure,
       1978. 2 vols.
Definitive **bibliographie raisonnée** of the famous Enfer
(private case) of the Bibliothèque Nationale, Paris. The

annotations contain much useful information on obscure
writers, editors, and publishers. Alphabetically arranged
by title, with author index.

27.   POTTER, CLARE.   The Lesbian Periodicals Index.
      Tallahassee, FL: Naiad Press, 1986.   413 pp.
Comprehensive index of 42 U.S. lesbian periodicals by
author and subject (1947ff.).   Does not include The
Ladder (which has its own index, included in the 1975
Arno Press reprint) or "mixed" periodicals with sub-
stantial lesbian content, such as Boston's Gay Community
News.

28.   [ROSE, ALFRED.]   "ROLF S. READE."   Registrum
      librorum eroticorum.   London: privately printed,
      1936.   2 vols.
Ambitious, occasionally disorganized and inaccurate list
of 5,061 erotic works in major European languages.   A
reprint appeared in 1965 (New York: Jack Brussel).

29.   SEROYA, FLORA C., et al.   Sex and Sex Education: A
      Bibliography. New York: Bowker, 1972.   336 pp.
A well-balanced selection for the period, with some
annotation.   Author, title, and analytic subject indexes.
"Homosexuality and Lesbianism" (pp. 94-104).

30.   [SFEIR-YOUNIS, LOUIS F., ed].   Vital Research on
      Homosexuality.   Ann Arbor, MI: University Micro-
      films International, 1982.   16 pp.
List of 214 M.A. and Ph.D. dissertations submitted to
U.S. universities, 1936-82, and available in xerox or
microfilm editions.

31.   SHARMA, UMESH D., and WILFRIED C. RUDY.   Homosex-
      uality: A Selected Bibliography.   Waterloo, Ont.:
      Waterloo Lutheran University, 1970.   114 pp.
A conscientious effort in its time, now largely obsolete.

32.   SHORE, DAVID A.   An Annotated Resource Guide to
      Periodicals in Human Sexuality.   Chicago: The
      author, 1978.   38 pp.
Discusses 53 periodicals.

33.   SLEUTJES, MARTIEN (ed.).   Catalogus van Leeuwen
      Bibliotheek: Historische Bibliotheek van de
      N.V.I.H.-C.O.C.   Amsterdam: N.V.I.H.-C.O.C., 1983.
      123 pp.
Catalogue of the collections of the leading Dutch homosexual organization (ca. 2177 titles).

34.   SURGEON GENERAL'S OFFICE.   UNITED STATES ARMY.
      Index-Catalogue of the Library.   Washington,
      D.C.: Government Printing Office, 1880-1955.   58
      vols. in 4 series.
Contains references to medical and psychiatric books and
articles in many languages, some not noticed elsewhere.

See "Sexual Instinct ..." as well as "Homosexuality."

35.   TASK FORCE ON LESBIAN AND GAY ISSUES. **An Annotated
       Bibliography of Lesbian and Gay Readings.** New
       York: Council on Social Work Education, 1983. 41
       pp.
About selected 350 entries, almost all annotated. Chiefly
nonfiction with a social-science emphasis, but including
a few novels and poetry collections.

36.   ULRICHS, KARL HEINRICH. **"Argonauticus." Zastrow
       und die Urninge des pietistischen, ultramontanen
       und freidenkenden Lagers.** Leipzig: Serbe, 1869.
       159 pp.
This pamphlet, ninth in the writer's series on Uranian
love, concludes with the first known attempt at a separate
bibliography on homosexuality (pp. 155-58). The list
("Schriften über Urningsliebe") begins with Ulrichs'
first eight pamphlets, followed by 27 works in ancient
and modern European languages. This bibliography is not
included in reprints of the pamphlet.

37.   WEIGEL, ADOLF. **Bibliographisches Verzeichnis der
       Bibliotheken von Professor Dr. Paul H. Brandt and
       Baron Werner v. Bleichroder.** Leipzig: The author,
       1930.
The first half of this book catalogues the scholarly
library of Paul H. Brandt ("Hans Licht"; 1875-1929), the
great German expert on homosexuality in classical antiquity.

38.   WEINBERG, MARTIN S., and ALAN P. BELL (eds.).
       Homosexuality: An Annotated Bibliography. New
       York: Harper and Row, 1972. 550 pp.
This large work, compiled under the auspices of the Kinsey
Institute of Indiana University, provides detailed but
uncritical abstracts for 1,263 books, pamphlets, and
articles published in the English language from 1940 to
1968. The book stresses psychiatric, medical, and
social-science contributions (many harshly negative), of
which only a selection is given in this **Guide.** This
compilation, which is conscientiously done within its
own terms of reference, will serve to reconstruct the
climate of opinion prevailing in the United States and
Britain through the late 1960s.

                          B. PIONEERS

For reasons that have not yet been fully explained, the
modern approach to the study of homosexual behavior--its
etiology, cultural history, psychology, and sociology--
originated in the 19th century, primarily in Germany.
Independent scholars such as Hoessli and Ulrichs, very

much aware of their outsider status, delved deeply into
the history of the subject. Their accomplishments laid
the foundations for the Berlin Scientific-humanitarian
Committee, begun in 1897 with the dual aim of promoting
legal reform and knowledge. The 19th century also saw
the rise of the modern psychiatric approach to the
subject. (For Freudian psychoanalysis, see XVII.B-C.)

39.   ALETRINO, ARNOLD. "Uranisme et dégénerescence,"
        Archives d'Anthropologie Criminelle, 23 (1908),
        633-67.
An early sympathetic overview by a Dutch physician and
novelist (1858-1916), who concludes that "degeneracy and
innate homosexuality are no more closely linked than
degeneracy and heterosexuality." The belief that homosexuality can occur in normal individuals was first enunciated by Aletrino in "Over uranisme en het laatste werk
van Raffalovich (Marc André)," Psychiatrische en Neurolog-
ische Bladen 1 (1897), 351-65, 452-83. See Maurice van
Lieshout, "Stiefkind der natuur: Het homobeeld bij Aletrino en Von Römer," Homojaarboek, 1 (1981), 75-105.

40.   BLOCH, IWAN. Das Sexualleben unserer Zeit in
        seinen Beziehungen zur modernen Kultur. Berlin:
        Marcus, 1907. 822 pp.
An early synthesis of the whole field of sexology by a
Berlin dermatologist and polymath (1872-1922). There is
an English translation by M. Eden Paul, The Sexual Life
of Our Time in Its Relations to Modern Civilization
(London: William Heinemann, 1908; 790 pp.); see Chapter
19, "The Riddle of Homosexuality" (pp.487-535) and
Chapter 20, "Pseudo-Homosexuality" (pp. 537-54). Among
the many learned works Bloch published, his masterwork
is probably Der Ursprung der Syphilis (Jena: Fischer,
1901-11; 2 vols.). Bloch sometimes wrote under the
pseudonym "Eugen Dühren."

41.   BLÜHER, HANS. Die Rede des Aristophanes: Proleg-
        omena zu einer Soziologie des Menschengeschlechts.
        Hamburg: Kala-Verlag, 1966. 166 pp.
An attempt, written towards the end of his life, by the
right-wing German homosexual theoretician (1888-1955), to
summarize his ideas. Blüher is best known for his stress
on the role of male bonding in the formation of states,
as seen in his: Die Rolle der Erotik in der männlichen
Gesellschaft (Jena: Diederichs, 1917-18; 2 vols.). See
Richard Mills in Gay Sunshine, no. 41-43 (1980, 41-45.

42.   BURTON, RICHARD, SIR. "Terminal Essay, Part IV,
        Social Conditions--Pederasty," in The Book of the
        Thousand Nights and a Night (London: privately
        printed, 1886), vol. 10, pp. 205-54.
In this learned essay, the English diplomat and oriental-
ist (1821-90) contends that there exists a "sotadic zone"
between the thirtieth and forty-third degrees, north

latitude, within which homosexual behavior is popular and
endemic. For some glosses on this text, see Stephen W.
Foster, "The Annotated Burton," in: Louie Crew (ed.), **The
Gay Academic** (Palm Springs, CA: ETC, 1978), pp. 92-101.
There is a biography, not altogether satisfactory, by Fawn
M. Brodie, **The Devil Drives: A Life of Sir Richard Burton**
(London: Penguin Books, 1971; 505 pp.).

43.   CARPENTER, EDWARD. **Homogenic Love and Its Place in
       a Free Society.** Manchester: Labour Press, 1894.
       51 pp.
An early defense of the dignity of homosexual love by an
English socialist and feminist (1844-1929). This book was
followed by several other notable publications, including
Ioläus: An Anthology of Friendship (London: Sonnenschein,
1902; 190 pp; the third edition of 1920 was reissued by
Pagan Press, New York, in 1982); **The Intermediate Sex: A
Study of Some Transitional Types of Men and Women** (London: Sonnenschein, 1908; 175 pp.); **Intermediate Types
among Primitive Folk** (London: George Allen and Unwin,
1918; 185 pp.). The fullest account of his life is: Tsu-
shichi Tsuzuki, **Edward Carpenter...** (Cambridge: Cambridge
University Press, 1980; 237 pp.). See also: **A Bibliography of Edward Carpenter** (Sheffield: Sheffield Central
Libraries, 1949; 83 pp.); and Jonathan Cutbill, **The
Writings of Edward Carpenter** ... (London: Gay's the Word,
1980; 9 pp.).

44.   CHEVALIER, JULIEN. **Une maladie de personnalité:
       l'inversion sexuelle: psycho-physiologie, socio-
       logie, tératologie, aliénation mentale, psychologie
       morbide, anthropologie, médecine judiciaire.**
       Lyon: Storck, 1893. 520 pp.
A major early work on sexual inversion, which treats it as
a chief symptom of a hereditary neuro-psychopathic condition that constitutes neither a distinct disease entity
nor an instinctive monomania. It is innate, appears from
earliest childhood, is stable, is accompanied by a significant phenomenology of mental or nervous disturbances, and
causes irrestistible impulses. The book is an expanded
version of an earlier work: **De l'inversion de l'instinct
sexuel au point de vue médico-legal** (Paris: O. Doin, 1885;
168 pp.).

45.   ELLIS, HAVELOCK. **Sexual Inversion.** New York: Arno
       Press, 1975. 299 pp.
The noted English sexologist and moralist (1859-1939)
viewed homosexuality sympathetically, as a congenital
variation. This issue reprints the first English edition
(London: 1897), which is quite rare. The book was ac-
tually first published in German as translated by Alfred
Kurella: **Das konträre Geschlechtsgefühl** (Leipzig: Georg
Wigand, 1896; 308 pp.), a version which bore the name of
Ellis's collaborator, John Addington Symonds, removed in
subsequent issues at the behest of Symonds's heirs.

46.   ELLIS, HAVELOCK. **Studies in the Psychology of Sex.**
       New York: Random House, 1936. 4 vols.
Ellis' collected books and papers on sexology. **Sexual In-**
version appears as vol. 2, part 2. See Phyllis Grosskurth, **Havelock Ellis: A Biography** (New York: Knopf, 1980;
492 pp.)

47.   FOREL, AUGUSTE HENRI. **The Sexual Question: A**
       Scientific, Psychologigical, Hygienic and Sociolog-
       ical Study. English adaptation from the second
       German edition by C. F. Marshall. Brooklyn: Phys-
       icians and Surgeons Book Co., 1932. 536 pp.
Forel (1848-1931) was a Swiss physician and administrator
who was important not so much for the originality of his
ideas, but for his activity in publicizing more enlightened concepts of human sexuality.

48.   FRAENKEL, EMANUEL. **De homosexuelle.** Copenhagen:
       Frimodt, 1908. 135 pp.
Antihomosexual exposition by a Danish physician and right-
wing politician, now forgotten. Interesting as evidence
of both the spread of, and resistance to German sex
research concepts in neighboring countries.

49.   FRIEDLAENDER, BENEDICT. **Renaissance des Eros**
       Uranios; die physiologische Freundschaft, ein nor-
       mal Grundbetrieb des Menschen und eine Frage der
       männlichen Gesellungsfreiheit in naturwissenschaft-
       licher, naturrechtlicher, culturgeschichtlicher und
       sittenkritischer Beleuchtung. Schmargendorf-Ber-
       lin: Verlag "Renaissance," 1904. 322, 88 pp.
Friedlaender (1866-1908), a homosexual opponent of the
Hirschfeld circle, attributed anti(homo)sexual attitudes
to the dominance of ascetic-Christian ideals and called
for a return to Hellenic values. See also his collected
papers: **Die Liebe Platons im Lichte der modernen Bio-**
logie (Treptow bei Berlin: Zack, 1909; 283 pp.).

50.   [GEIGEL, ALOIS.] **Das Paradoxon der Venus Urania:**
       Geschrieben fur Ärzte, Juristen, Geistliche und
       Erzieher, dann fur Freunde der Anthropologie und
       Psychologie. Würzburg: Stuber, 1869. 34 pp.
A critique of the ideas of Karl Heinrich Ulrichs (see
below). Although this essay was published anonymously,
the author is known to have been Geigel, a professor at
the University of Würzburg.

51.   GIDE, ANDRÉ. **Corydon.** New translation by Richard
       Howard. New York: Farrar, Straus and Giroux,
       1983. 135 pp.
Although Gide (1869-1951) intended his essay to be published in a shorter version in 1910, he postponed its
appearance until 1924, when it still caused a scandal.
Utilizing evidence from animal behavior, Gide insisted
that homosexuality was not biologically abnormal, unnatural or wrong. For some useful background information, see

Claude Courouve, in: **Gay Books Bulletin,** no. 5 (1981),
23-25; and in: **Cabirion,** no. 12 (1985), 30-31.

52.   GUYON, RENÉ. **Etudes d'éthique sexuelle.** Saint-
       Denis: Dardaillon, 1929-38. 6 vols.
Of the ten volumes originally projected by the French
jurist and adviser to the Thai government, only the
first six appeared. Guyon sought to work out the full
implications of the distinction between the sexual
instinct and the reproductive function. Two parts have
been translated into English: **The Ethics of Sexual Acts**
(New York: Knopf, 1934; 383 pp.); and **Sexual Freedom** (New
York: Knopf, 1939; 344 pp.).

53.   HEIMSOTH, KARL-GUENTHER. **Hetero- und Homophilie:
       eine neuorientierende An- und Einordnung der Er-
       scheinungsbilder, der "Homosexualität" und der
       "Inversion: in Berücksichtigung der sogenannten
       "normale Freundschaft" auf Grund der zwei ver-
       schiedenen erotischen Anziehungsgesetze und der
       bisexuellen Grundeinstellung des Mannes.** Dort-
       mund: Schmidt und Andernach, 1924. 33 pp.
Heimsoth, an eccentric right-wing German theorist, is
remembered for two things: (1) he introduced the term
homophilia; and (2) he advocated an astrological approach
to homosexuality (see **Charakterkonstellationen,** Munich:
Barth, 1928; 200 pp.).

54.   HILLER, KURT. **Paragraph 175: Die Schmach des Jahr-
       hunderts!** Hannover: P. Steegmann, 1922. 133 pp.
Essays and speeches by a German essayist, publicist and
advocate of gay rights (1885-1972), involved in several
avant-garde and independent left movements during the
period. See his autobiography: **Leben gegen die Zeit**
(Reinbek bei Hamburg: Rowohlt, 1969-73; 2 vols.); as well
as Lewis D. Wurgaft, **The Activists: Kurt Hiller and the
Politics of Action on the German Left, 1914-1933** (Transactions of the American Philosophical Society, 67:8,
1977; 114 pp.).

55.   HIRSCHFELD, MAGNUS. **Die Homosexualität des Mannes
       und des Weibes.** Berlin: Louis Marcus, 1914. 1067
       pp.
This encyclopedic, indeed monumental work sums up the
accomplishments of a decade and a half of intense activity
on the part of a team of scholars associated with the
Jahrbuch für sexuelle Zwischenstufen, published by the
Berlin Scientific-Humanitarian Committee. Of necessity
dated in the legal and psychiatric fields, it remains
worth consulting for the historical and cultural information it distills. Numerous footnotes and indexes of
names, and subjects. There are complete reprints of
1920 and 1985, but the 1963 issue (Köppern im Taunus:
Dithmar) is to be avoided inasmuch as it is drastically
abridged.

56.   HIRSCHFELD, MAGNUS. "Magnus Hirschfeld (Autobio-
      graphical Sketch)," in: Victor Robinson (ed.),
      Encyclopedia Sexualis. New York: Dingwall-Rock,
      1936, pp. 317-21.
Short account of the great scholar and activist's life
(1868-1935), completed just before his death in Nice. A
more detailed memoir (up to 1922) is **Von einst bis
jetzt: Geschichte einer homosexuellen Bewegung.** Edited
by James Steakley (Berlin: Verlag Rosa Winkel, 1986).
For his extensive writings see James D. Steakley, **The
Writings of Dr. Magnus Hirschfeld: A Bibliography** (Toronto: Canadian Gay Archives, 1985; 53 pp.). See also: **Magnus Hirschfeld: Leben und Werk: Eine Ausstellung aus
Anlass seines 50. Todestages** (Berlin: Verlag Rosa Winkel,
1985; 73 pp.); and the disappointing biography by Charlotte Wolff, **Magnus Hirschfeld: A Portrait of a Pioneer in
Sexology** (London: Quartet, 1986; 496 pp.).

57.   HOESSLI, HEINRICH. **Eros: die Männerliebe der
      Griechen: ihre Beziehungen zur Geschichte, Erzieh-
      ung, Literatur und Gesetzgebung aller Zeiten.**
      Glarus: The author, 1836-38. 2 vols.
The first major landmark in German-language studies of
male homosexuality. The first volume broke fresh ground
in considering parallels between the witchcraft delusion
and the persecution of homosexuals; the second provides a
copious anthology (with commentary) from world literature (chiefly poetry). The abridged issues of 1892 and
1924 are to be avoided. See Ferdinand Karsch-Haack, **Der
Putzmacher von Glarus, Heinrich Hoessli** (Leipzig: Max
Spohr, 1903; 112 pp.); reprinted in **Documents of the
Homosexual Rights Movement in Germany, 1836-1927** (New
York: Arno Press, 1975).

58.   HOHMANN, JOACHIM S., et al. **Sexualforschung und
      -aufklärung in der Weimarer Republik: Eine Über-
      sicht in Materialien und Dokumenten.** Berlin: Foer-
      ster, 1985. 300 pp.
Reprints German texts (1918-33) on sex education by such
figures as Karl Giese, Magnus Hirschfeld, Richard Linsert,
Helene Stöcker and others. There is an extensive interpretive essay by Hohmann (pp. 15-128), many reproductions of period documents, and a discussion of educational films. A broader canvas is painted by Marcus Wawer-
zonnek, **Implizite Sexualpädagogik in der Sexualwissenschaft 1886 bis 1939** (Cologne: Rugenstein, 1984; 286
pp.).

59.   HOHMANN, JOHANNES (ed.). **Der unterdrückte Sexus:
      historische Texte und Kommentare zur Homosexual-
      ität.** Lollar: Verlag Andreas Achenbach, 1977. 643
      pp.
An anthology of German-language texts from the early
forensic psychiatrists to the later 19th- and early 20th-
century writers, with useful introductory essays by
several hands.

60. JÄGER, GUSTAV. **Entdeckung der Seele.** Second
     ed. Leipzig: E. Guenther, 1880. 387 pp.
On pp. 245-54 and 264-66 of this now forgotten book, which
promoted an eccentric olfactory theory of sexual attraction, the new term "homosexual" was transmitted to the
medical and general public. Thereby Jager's informant
Kertbeny relayed his ideas and terms to the generation of
activists that emerged about 1900. See also his: "Ein
bisher ungedrücktes Kapitel über Homosexualität aus Der
Entdeckung der Seele," **JfsZ**, 2 (1900), 53-125.

61. [KERTBENY, KÁROLY MÁRIA.] **Paragraph 143 des
     Preussischen Strafgesetzbuches von 14. April 1851
     und seine Aufrechterhaltung als Paragraph 152 im
     Entwurfe eines Strafgesetzbuches für den Nord-
     deutschen Bund.** Leipzig: Serbe, 1869. 88 pp.
This pamphlet is a legal memoir by an Austrian-Hungarian
writer (born Karl Maria Benkert; 1824-1882), calling for
the abrogation of the penalty for male homosexual conduct
in the projected penal code. This text employed the word
"homosexual" for the first time. The memoir was supplemented by another: **Des Gemeinschädliche des Paragraph 143
des preussischen Strafgesetzbuches vom 14. April 1851 und
daher seine nothwendige Tilgung als Paragraph 152 im
Entwurfe eines Strafgesetzbuches fur den Norddeutschen
Bund** (Leipzig: Serbe, 1870; 75 pp.). The attribution
to Kertbeny, though likely, is not absolutely certain;
see Manfred Herzer, "Kertbeny and the Nameless Love," **JH**,
12 (1985), 1-26.

62. KRAFFT-EBING, RICHARD VON. **Psychopathia sexualis:
     eine klinisch-forensische Studie.** Stuttgart: Enke,
     1886. 110 pp.
The book that made the Austrian psychiatrist (1840-1902)
famous: the first best seller in modern sexology. Pages
56-72 and 102-08 deal with sexual inversion. The author
revised it repeatedly so that it attained 414 pp. by the
ninth ed. of 1894. The twelfth ed. (1903) was the last he
personally supervised. There are several English versions; see, e.g., that of Franklin S. Klaf, **Psychopathia
Sexualis, with Especial Reference to the Antipathic Sexual
Instinct: A Medico-Forensic Study** (New York: Stein and
Day, 1965; 434 pp.). See also his "Neue Studien auf dem
Gebiete der Homosexualität," **JfsZ**, 3 (1901), 1-36.

63. LOMBROSO, CESARE, and GUGLIELMO FERRERO. **La donna
     delinquente: la prostituta e la donna normale.**
     Turin: Roux, 1893. 640 pp.
Lombroso (1836-1909) was an influential Italian criminologist who advocated a congenital theory of criminal
behavior. He regarded same-sex behavior--in this case
lesbianism--as an aspect of degeneration. There is an
English version: **The Female Offender** (New York: Philosophical Library, 1958; 313 pp.). See also: **L'uomo
delinquente in rapporto all'antropologia, alla giurisprudenza e alla psichiatria.** Turin: Bocca, 1889; 3

vols.--see vol. 1, pp. 36, 233, 301, 452; vol. 2, pp.
235-38). The English translation of this work is
abridged. See Renzo Villa, **Il deviante e i suoi segni:
Lombroso e la nascita dell'antropologia criminale** (Milan:
Angeli, 1985; 293 pp.).

64.   MACKAY, JOHN HENRY. **Sagitta: Die Bücher der
       namenlosen Liebe.** Berlin: Verlag Rosa Winkel,
       1979. 2 vols.
New edition of the works written by Mackay (1864-1933), a
German anarchist poet, in defense of pederasty (boy love).
Because of the controversial nature of the subject, these
works (1905-26) were published under the pseudonym of
"Sagitta." There are Mackay Societies in Germany and the
United States. See esp. Hubert Kennedy, **Anarchist of
Love: The Secret Life of John Henry Mackay** (New York:
Mackay Society, 1983; 24 pp.).

65.   MAYNE, XAVIER (pseud. of Edward Irenaeus Prime-
       Stevenson). **The Intersexes.** New York: Arno Press,
       1975. 641 pp.
Originally issued by the author in a private edition of
125 copies printed in Italy in 1908. The first major work
on homosexuality by an American, it is primarily historical and literary in scope, though it does try to cover
recent sex research in Europe. Mayne (1868-1942) was
primarily a novelist, publishing his **Imre: A Memorandum**
also in 1908. See Noel I. Garde, "The Mysterious Father
of American Homophile Literature," **ONE Institute Quarterly,** 1:3 (1958), 94-98.

66.   MOLL, ALBERT. **Die kontrāre Geschlechtsempfindung.**
       Berlin: Fischer, 1891. 296 pp.
Moll (1862-1939), who regarded homosexuality as an illness, was nonetheless one of the first to write compre-
hensively about the subject from the standpoint of modern
sexology. From Moll Freud purloined the idea of infantile
sexuality. See the translation: **Perversions of the Sex
Instinct: A Study of Sex Inversion Based on Clinical
Data and Official Documents** (Newark: Julian Press, 1931;
237 pp.). Another important book by Moll is **Untersuchungen über die Libido sexualis** (vol. 1, parts 1 and 2;
Berlin: Fischer, 1897-98).

67.   MONTEIRO, ARLINDO CAMILLO. **Amor Sáfico e Socráti-
       co.** Lisbon: The author, 1922. 552 pp.
A major work by a Portuguese physician and historian,
covering research schools, historical evidence, medical
and psychiatric viewpoints, and legislation. Another
Portuguese work of erudition in this period is: Asdrúbal
António d'Aguiar, "Evolução da Pederastia e do Lesbismo
na Europa," **Arquivo da Universidade do Lisboa,** 11 (1926),
336-620.

68.   NIN FRÍAS, ALBERTO. **Alexis o el significado del
       temperamento urano.** Madrid: Javier Morata, 1932.

195 pp.
An essay by a Spanish novelist and literary critic
(1882-1937), intended as a complement to Gide's **Corydon**.
See also his work of literary criticism: **Homosexualismo
creador.** (Madrid: Javier Morata, 1933; 383 pp.).

69. RAFFALOVICH, MARC ANDRÉ. **Uranisme et unisexual-
     ité: étude sur différentes manifestations de
     l'instinct sexuel.** Lyon: Storck, 1896. 363 pp.
This substantial work by the Anglo-French-Polish writer
(1864-1934) offers a positive overview of the subject,
seeking to redirect the dominant medical discourse onto
a more humane path. Raffalovich, who frequently contributed articles on contemporary events and theories to the
French periodical **Archives d'Anthropologie Criminelle,**
showed a strong interest in the biographies of noted
homosexuals. See Philip W. J. Healy, "Uranisme et
Unisexualité: A Late Victorian View of Homosexuality,"
New Blackfriars, 59 (1978), 56-65; and "The Making of an
Edinburgh Salon," **Journal of the Eighteen Nineties Society,** no. 12-13 (1981-82), 25-39.

70. RAMDOHR, FRIEDRICH WILHELM BASIL VON. **Venus
     urania: über die Natur der Liebe, über ihre Ver-
     edelung und Verschönerung.** Leipzig: Göschen,
     1798. 4 vols.
A diffuse work in the Sturm und Drang mode on love and
friendship, with some guarded comments on emotional
relations between men as a Platonic counterpart of
heterosexual passion (vol. 3, 133-230).

71. SYMONDS, JOHN ADDINGTON. **Male Love: A Problem in
     Greek Ethics and other Writings.** Edited by John
     Lauritsen. New York: Pagan Press, 1983. 162 pp.
The Essay "A Problem in Greek Ethics," which has a
complicated publishing history, was written by Symonds in
1873 as a defense of homosexuality from the ancient
Greek example. This volume contains an appreciation of
Symonds (1840-93) by Robert Peters. See also Symonds,
The Letters. Edited by Herbert M. Schueller and Robert
Peters (Detroit: Wayne State University Press, 1967-69;
3 vols.) and the **Memoirs.** Edited by Phyllis Grosskurth
(New York: Knopf, 1985; 319 pp.). Some passages not
otherwise easily available are found in Percy Lancelot
Babington, **Bibliography of the Writings of John Addington
Symonds** (London: John Castle, 1925; 244 pp.).

72. TAMASSIA, ARRIGO. "Sull'inversione dell'istinto
     sessuale," **Rivista sperimentale di freniatria e di
     medicina legale,** 4 (1878), 93-117.
In an analysis deriving from the writings of J. L. Casper,
K. F. O. Westphal and R. von Krafft-Ebing, the Italian
psychiatrist introduced the term "sexual inversion" as the
equivalent of Westphal's "konträre Sexualempfindung,"
which earlier writers in the Romance languages had para-
phrased awkwardly at best. Inversion became the inter-

national psychiatric designation of the condition.

73.   TANDEM (pseud.). "Den kontraere Sexualfornem-
       melse: Fragmenter til Oplysning," **Bibliotek for
       Laeger,** 84 (1892), 205-22, 247-81.
The Danish author, a medical layman, surveys the entire
literature on sexual inversion that had appeared until
then in Western Europe and Scandinavia, ending with a
plea for enlightenment and tolerance.

74.   TARNOVSKIĬ, VENIAMIN MIKHAĬLOVICH. **Die krankhaften
       Erscheinungen des Geschlechtssinnes: eine foren-
       sisch-psychiatrische Studie.** Berlin: Hirschwald,
       1886. 152 pp.
Reviews the literature on sexual inversion that had appeared in Western Europe down to the time of publication,
adding material from the author's own practice in Russia.
The importance of the work lies in the fact that it made
available to European readers the finding of the Russian
psychiatrist Vladimir Fiodorovich Chizh, who in a paper
of 1882 had asserted that sexual inversion was not a clinical rarity, but was the explanation of many cases of
sodomy that came to the attention of the police and the
courts. There is an English translation by W. C. Costello
and Alfred Allinson, with a preface by Tarnovskii: **The
Sexual Instinct and Its Morbid Manifestations from the
Double Standpoint of Jurisprudence and Psychiatry** (Paris:
Charles Carrington, 1898; 239 pp.). On Tarnovskii, see
the biography by Sergeĭ Petrovich Arkhangel'skiĭ, **V. M.
Tarnovskii** (Leningrad: Meditsina, 1966; 98 pp.).

75.   ULRICHS, KARL HEINRICH. **Forschungen über das
       Rätsel der mannmännlichen Liebe.** New York: Arno
       Press, 1975.
Reprints a series of twelve pamphlets published by Ulrichs
(1825-1895), a courageous and learned defender of homosexual rights, between 1864 and 1880. Ulrichs held that
homosexuality results from the metensomatosis of a female
soul in a male body and vice versa. As a jurist, he was
concerned with the legal situation of male homosexuals,
which deteriorated in the Germany of his time. His
citations of classical and modern literature as evidence
for homosexual behavior constitute a mine of information
that is still being exploited. See also his "Vier
Briefe," **JfsZ,** 1 (1899), 36-70. See Hubert Kennedy, "The
'Third Sex' Theory of Karl Heinrich Ulrichs," **JH,** 6
(1980-81), 103-12.

76.   WEININGER, OTTO. **Geschlecht und Charakter.**
       Vienna: Wilhelm Braumüller, 1903. 599 pp.
A once-influential work that argues for a fundamental
relationship between sex and character. Every human being
is a blend of male and female elements. Man is the positive, productive, logical, conceptual, ethical, spiritual
force capable of genius, while woman is the negative
force, incapable of any of these virtues. Weininger's

key insight of universal bisexuality was further developed
by the psychoanalytic school. See the translation: **Sex
and Character** (New York: G. Putnam's Sons, 1906; 356 pp.).

77.   WESTERMARCK, EDWARD. **The Origin and Development of
      Moral Ideas.** London: Macmillan, 1906-08. 2 vols.
See Chapter 43, "Homosexual Love" (vol. 2, pp. 456-89).
From his field work and extensive reading, the Finnish
anthropologist Westermarck (1862-1939) produced a remarkable cross-cultural tableau, which implicitly demonstrated
the variability of same-sex relations. See Timothy Stroup
(ed.), **Edward Westermarck: Essays on His Life and Works**
(Acta Philosophica Fennica, Helsinki, 34, 1982; 299 pp.;
bibliography of his writings, pp. 274-92).

78.   WESTPHAL, KARL FRIEDRICH OTTO. "Die konträre Sex-
      ualempfindung: Symptom eines neuropathologischen
      (psychopathischen) Zustandes," **Archiv für Psychia-
      trie und Nervenkrankheiten,** 2 (1869), 73-108.
This paper is the starting point for the modern psychiatric approach. Westphal's observations are based largely
on one female case examined in the psychiatric ward of
the Charité (General Hospital) in Berlin, as well as a
male transvestite. He introduced the concept of "contrary sexual feeling"--later standardized as the Latin-
derived "sexual inversion."

                     C. TOWARD THE PRESENT

In the 1920s efforts were made in various countries to
diffuse sexual enlightenment--birth control, marriage
counseling, and a better understanding of what were still
called sexual anomalies. The Great Depression, beginning
in 1929, crippled these efforts toward popular education.
At the same time Hitler's rise to power radically transformed German sexology, undercutting its position of leadership in the world. Emigration from the European continent brought many psychoanalytically oriented psychiatrists to English-speaking countries, particularly to the
United States. With a few exceptions, these psychiatrists
generally regarded homosexuality as pathology, tended to
acquiesce in the indigenous penchant for "social engineering" as the answer to all human problems, and helped to
rationalize lingering religious opposition to homosexuality. At the end of the 1940s the homosexual movement
began in the United States, making contact with the
renascent but still stunted European groups. Only later,
in a changed social and intellectual climate, were open
homosexuals able to have a voice in their own self-definition.

79.   "ANOMALY." **The Invert.** Second, enlarged ed.

London: Baillere, Tindall and Cox, 1948.   290 pp.
Reflections of a tormented English Catholic on a range of
homosexual behavior and ethics, intended as a plea for
understanding. The first half--originally published in
1927--is a valuable indicator of the ambivalence then
widespread in the English-speaking world.

80.   ARTHUR, GAVIN. **The Circle of Sex.** San Francisco:
       Pan-Graphic Press, 1962. 86 pp.
A San Francisco homophile writer uses the face of a clock
to present twelve types of sexual identity/orientation,
ranging from exclusively heterosexual to exclusively
homosexual for both men and women.

81.   CHESSER, EUSTACE. **Odd Man Out: Homosexuality in
       Men and Women.** London: Victor Gollancz, 1959.   192
       pp.
A relatively liberal work for its time, showing the influence of Kinsey's findings and the Wolfenden Report.
Chesser assumes that homosexual behavior is created by a
faulty child-parent relationship, but society has complicated the matter by repressing deviant sexual behavior.
See also: Edward Glover (ed.), **The Problem of Homosexuality** (London: Institute for the Study of Treatment of
Delinquency, 1957; 40 pp.).

82.   CHURCHILL, WAINRIGHT. **Homosexual Behavior among
       Males: A Cross-Cultural and Cross-Species Inves-
       tigation.** New York: Hawthorne Books, 1967.   349
       pp.
A synthesis by a homosexual psychologist, discussing
the history of homosexuality (including Christian prohibitions) and theories of its causation.   Churchill
regards homosexual responsiveness as a component of
mammalian sexuality, increasing as the evolutionary
scale is ascended.   Decries the sex-negativism ("eroto-
phobia" and "homoerotophobia") that our civilization has
enshrined in its legislation.

83.   FISHER, PETER. **The Gay Mystique: The Myth and
       Reality of Male Homosexuality.** New York: Stein
       and Day 1972.   258 pp.
A representative document of the gay-liberation ferment
following the Stonewall Rebellion in 1969, discussing such
matters as variations in gay-male lifestyles, civil
rights, and self-esteem.   See also: John Murphy, **Homosexual Liberation: A Personal View** (New York: Praeger, 1971;
182 pp.).

84.   GROSS, ALFRED A. **Strangers in Our Midst: Problems
       of the Homosexual in American Society.** Washington,
       DC: Public Affairs Press, 1962.   182 pp.
Humane views for the time of the Director of the George W.
Henry Foundation, New York.   Criticizes the police and the
church for their tendencies to condemn rather than to
understand, but holds that homosexuals need psychotherapy

for their "disease." See also Gross's reminiscences of
his career: "American Experiment," **Man and Society: Journal of the Albany Trust,** no. 10 (Winter 1966), 12-22.

85. KARLEN, ARNO. **Sexuality and Homosexuality: A New
     View.** New York: W. W. Norton, 1971. 666 pp.
Parts 1 and 2 (pp. 1-235) are chiefly concerned with
historical data, from ancient Mesopotamia to the present.
The remainder of the work presents case studies and
interviews, framed by questionable psychoanalytic interpretations. While this large book is poorly organized and
often intrusively judgmental, so that it must be used
with caution, it does contain many references ("Critical
Bibliography," pp. 619-46). See Geoff Puterbaugh, "The
Mind of Arno Karlen," **Gay Books Bulletin,** no. 8 (1982),
20-22.

86. MAGEE, BRYAN. **One in Twenty: A Study of Homosex-
     uality in Men and Women.** London: Secker and
     Warburg, 1966. 192 pp.
BBC journalist's account of homosexual behavior in
Great Britain and the Netherlands, with discussions of
psychiatric attitudes, social patterns, and the legal
situation.

87. MERCER, JESSIE DECAMARRON. **They Walk in Shadow: A
     Study of Sexual Variations with Emphasis on the
     Ambisexual and Homosexual Components and Our
     Contemporary Sex Laws.** New York: Comet Press
     Books, 1959. 573 pp.
Turgid presentation of biological, psychological, medical,
socio-moral and legal aspects of sexual variation. Com-
mends the Wolfenden Report.

88. MIRABET I MULLOY, ANTONI. **Homosexualidad hoy.**
     Barcelona: Editorial Herder, 1985. 490 pp.
Comprehensive, positive work, reviewing (1) recent
scientific literature; (2) the history of repression
from the classical era through the Inquisition to modern
times; (3) the history of the gay movement from the turn
of the century onwards; (4) the achievements of gay and
lesbian organizations in Catalonia.

89. PLUMMER, DOUGLAS. **Queer People: The Truth about
     Homosexuals.** London: W. H. Allen, 1963. 122 pp.
A British homosexual describes his own life as well as
the difficulties faced by homosexuals in England in the
days prior to the law reform of 1967.

90. SAGHIR, MARCEL T. and ELI ROBINS. **Male and Female
     Homosexuality: A Comprehensive Investigation.**
     Baltimore: Williams and Wilkins, 1973. 341 pp.
Covers the whole area of male and female homosexuality
under a series of parallel chapter headings: childhood-
adolescent characteristics; sexual psychologic responses;
homosexual practices: statistical and behavioral consider-

ations; heterosexual practices; psychopathology; parental,
home and family relationships; and sociological considerations. Concludes that "treating homosexuality as a disease and homosexuals as patients is neither scientifically tenable nor actually feasible and practical."

91.   SANDERS, DENNIS. **Gay Source: A Catalog for Men.**
       New York: Coward, McCann and Geoghegan, 1977. 288
       pp.
A series of short pieces coordinated to show the panorama
of cultural, historical, lifestyle, and political aspects
of male homosexual experience. The lists of addresses of
organizations and the like are now largely out of date.

92.   STEARN, JESS. **The Sixth Man.** Garden City, NY:
       Doubleday, 1961. 286 pp.
A heterosexual journalist surveys the homosexual world
in the Eisenhower-Kennedy era, covering places of entertainment, professional interests, contacts, problems with
the police and blackmail, homosexual circles, aging, and
homosexual types.

93.   TRIPP, CLARENCE A. **The Homosexual Matrix.** New
       York: McGraw-Hill, 1975. 314 pp.
Stimulating, sometimes controversial discussion of
sexual behavior from a multi-disciplinary perspective
that owes much to the work of Alfred C. Kinsey. Strongly
criticizing psychoanalytic beliefs and therapy, Tripp
offers his own theories concerning the dynamics of
sexual relationships and the conditions that produce
eroticization of stimuli. He seeks to distinguish
homosexual behavior as such from effeminacy and inversion.

94.   WEINBERG, GEORGE. **Society and the Healthy Homosex-
       ual.** New York: St. Martin's Press, 1972. 147 pp.
Pro-homosexual arguments of a heterosexual psychologist.
Strongly condemning irrational antihomosexual prejudice,
Weinberg's book disseminated the term "homophobia."

95.   WEST, DONALD J. **Homosexuality Re-examined.**
       Minneapolis, MN: University of Minnesota Press,
       1977. 359 pp.
This volume--a revision of the author's 1968 book, **Homosexuality**--seeks to present an updated review of the
psychological, sociological, and popular literature
concerning the factors that determine sexual orientation,
the place of homosexuals in society, and the problems
they may encounter. The point of view is that of a
reasonable, though somewhat old-fashioned psychiatric
liberalism. See also his: "Homosexuality and Lesbianism,"
British Journal of Psychiatry, 143 (1983), 221-26.

96.   ZANE, DAVID. **Oh! Downtrodden.** Roslyn Heights,
       NY: Libra Publishing, 1976. 774 pp.
Autodidact's collage of quotation and opinion, focusing

in large part on the posited parallels of the stigmatization of homosexuals, Jews, blacks, cripples, and the
mentally ill.

D. SEX RESEARCH

The appearance of the first Kinsey Report in 1948, fifteen
years after the destruction of the Berlin Institut für
Sexualforschung, represents a major turning point in the
study of sex. The work of Kinsey and his associates
placed the subject in a positivistic and quantitative
framework that enhanced their authority in the Anglo-
Saxon mind. The Report also showed that the incidence
of homosexual behavior was much greater than had been
previously assumed, and that it could no longer be regarded as a rare anomaly. Moreover, the publications of
Kinsey and his associates also contributed to a movement
for homosexual law reform, which was to triumph in England
and Germany in the late 1960s, enjoying considerable,
though incomplete success in the United States. There was
much resistance to the Kinsey Reports (the second, female
one having appeared in 1953), and some serious flaws were
detected. However, no other research team succeeded in
rivaling these monuments of investigation. In the 1970s
the prestige of the Kinsey publications served as the
pretext for a tribe of illegitimate offspring--the journalistic "reports," which professed to offer large cross-
sectional studies of current sexual mores, but were often
little more than gossip.

97.   BANCROFT, JOHN. **Human Sexuality and Its Problems.**
        New York: Churchill Livingston, 1983. 447 pp.
A Scottish author attempts a digest of sexual research
up to 1980 for "health professionals specially interested in working with sexual problems." Clinically
oriented, the book's main focus is on research data and
their interpretation.

98.   BEACH, FRANK A. (ed.). **Human Sexuality in Four
        Perspectives.** Baltimore: Johns Hopkins Press,
        1977. 330 pp.
Eleven well-coordinated papers surveying the state of the
question from the developmental, sociological, physiological, and evolutionary points of view. See esp. "Homosexuality" by Martin Hoffman (pp. 164-89).

99.   BELL, ALAN P., and MARTIN S. WEINBERG. **Homosexual-
        ities: A Study of Diversity among Men and Women.**
        New York: Simon and Schuster, 1978. 505 pp.
This ambitious study, intended as a complement to the two
masterworks of A. C. Kinsey et al. (see below), examines
the various ways individuals have made social and psycho-

logical adjustments to their homosexuality. The monograph
is based on interviews conducted in the San Francisco
Bay area with 1500 individuals (including black men and
women, groups omitted from the two Kinsey studies) in
a project supported by the National Institute of Mental
Health. The book has attracted criticism on several
grounds: (1) the limitation to San Francisco makes
extrapolation to the rest of North America problematic;
(2) interviewing standards are unclear; (3) the proposed
typology of specific kinds of partnerships or lifestyles--
close-coupled, open-coupled, functional, dysfunctional,
and asexual--is of uncertain value.

100.   BELL, ALAN P., MARTIN S. WEINBERG, and SUE KIEFER
        HAMMERSMITH. **Sexual Preference: Its Development in
        Men and Women.** Bloomington: Indiana University
        Press, 1981. 242 pp.
Like the previous work, this monograph appears under the
sponsorship of the Alfred C. Kinsey Institute for Sexual
Research, Indiana University. Reviewing the existing
literature, the authors conclude that there is no significant correlation between early family experience and
adult sexual preference and therefore that sexual preference must be controlled essentially by biological-con-
stitutional factors. In addition to the expository
volume, there is also a **Statistical Appendix** (Bloomington: Indiana University Press, 1981; 321 pp.).

101.   DOWNEY, LOIS. "Intergenerational Change in Sex
        Behavior: A Belated Look at Kinsey's Males,"
        Archives of Sexual Behavior, 9 (1980), 307-17.
Five generations of respondents (5,460 white males) were
compared in terms of total frequency of sexual behavior.
Although homosexual contacts accounted for a constant
percentage of unmarried males over the five generations,
more males in each generation were actively engaging in
homosexual activity.

102.   GAGNON, JOHN H. "Sex Research and Social Change,"
        Archives of Sexual Behavior, 4 (1975), 111-41.
Argues that since the turn of the century there has been a
close relationship between sex research and general social
conditions. While the biological tradition is still
strong today, new emphasis is being placed on a cog-
nitive-social learning perspective.

103.   GEBHARD, PAUL, and ALAN B. JOHNSON. **The Kinsey
        Data: Marginal Tabulations of the 1938-1963
        Interviews Conducted by the Institute of Sex
        Research.** Philadelphia: W. B. Saunders, 1979.
        642 pp.
Permits the reexamination of certain questions covered in
the 1948 and 1953 volumes. Tables 432-569 contain data
pertinent to homosexual behavior. Responds in part to
questions posed by William G. Cochran et al., **Statistical
Problems in the Kinsey Report** (Washington, DC: American

Statistical Association, 1954; 338 pp.).

104.   GIESE, HANS. **Der homosexuelle Mann in der Welt.**
        Second ed. Stuttgart: F. Enke, 1964. 228 pp.
Liberal views, conditioned by existentialist philosophy,
of a closeted gay sex researcher (1920-70), who worked
chiefly in Hamburg. See his: "Differences in the Homosexual Relations of Man and Woman," **International Journal
of Sexology,** 7 (1954), 225-27. A contemporary synthesis
is Rudolf Klimmer, **Die Homosexualität als biologisch-
soziologische Zeitfrage** (Hamburg: Kriminalistik, Verlag
für kriminalistische Fachliteratur, 1965; 487 pp.).

105.   HAEBERLE, ERWIN J. **The Sex Atlas: A New Illustrat-
        ed Guide.** New York: Seabury Press, 1978. 509 pp.
A San Francisco researcher's handbook of the whole range
of human sexuality, with positive treatment of homosexual behavior.

106.   HITE, SHERRY. **The Hite Report: A Nationwide Study
        on Female Sexuality.** New York, NY: Macmillan,
        1976. 438 pp.
Summarizes the responses of 3000 American women to a
questionnaire concerning their own sexuality. This book
launched the fashion for a series of pop avatars of
Kinsey. As samples they are almost worthless, but they
reveal much of changing fashions--in this instance Hite's
own feminist concepts of sexuality. See also: **The Hite
Report on Male Sexuality** (New York: Knopf, 1981; 1129
pp.).

107.   HUNT, MORTON. **Sexual Behavior in the 1970s.** New
        York: Playboy, 1974. 388 pp.
Journalist's effort to update Kinsey's findings; as
such, it is methodologically inadequate. See pp. 303-27.

108.   JAY, KARLA, and ALLEN YOUNG. **The Gay Report.** New
        York: Summit Books, 1979. 861 pp.
Modeled on **The Hite Report** and its sequel, this compendium
of the results of questionnaires submitted by gay men and
lesbians is entertaining and sometimes instructive. It
does not reflect a serious effort to obtain a balanced
sample. See also: James Spada, **The Spada Report: The
Newest Survey of Gay Male Sexuality** (New York: New American Library, 1979; 339 pp.).

109.   KATCHADOURIAN, HERANT A. (ed.). **Human Sexuality: A
        Comparative and Developmental Perspective.**
        Berkeley: University of California Press, 1979.
        358 pp.
Seventeen new papers by established sex researchers, addressed to lay readers and summarizing the state of
research from evolutionary, biological, psychological, and
sociological perspectives.

110.   KINSEY, ALFRED C., et al. "Concepts of Normality

and Abnormality in Sexual Behavior," in: P. H. Hoch
and J. Zubin (eds.), **Psychological Development in
Health and Disease.** New York: Grune and Stratton,
1949, pp. 11-32.
Surveys the historical origins of sexual taboos as shapers
of current notions of "unnatural acts." Examining recent
data, concludes that prevailing concepts of normality and
abnormality in human sexual behavior are simply moral
evaluations. On Kinsey's (1894-1956) life, see Wardell
Pomeroy, **Dr. Kinsey and the Institute for Sex Research**
(New York: Harper and Row, 1972; 479 pp.).

111.   KINSEY, ALFRED C., WARDELL. B. POMEROY, CLYDE
       E. MARTIN, and PAUL. GEBHARD. **Sexual Behavior in
       the Human Female.** Philadelphia: W. B. Saunders,
       1953. 841 pp.
This sequel to Kinsey's first great study evaluates data
obtained in interviews with some 6,000 white women. Sexual orientation is presented on a scale similar to the
one used in the first volume; however, one to three percent of the sample were found to be essentially nonsexual.
Information is provided in relation to age, marital
status, educational level attained, parental occupation,
class, decade of birth, age at onset of adolescence,
rural-urban background, religion, techniques. and social
significance. The volume, which benefits from some
methodological refinements over the first one, contains a
comparison of male and female response with respect to
anatomy, physiology, psychological factors, neural mechanisms, and hormonal factors.

112.   KINSEY, ALFRED C., WARDELL B. POMEROY, A. and CLYDE
       E. MARTIN. **Sexual Behavior in the Human Male.**
       Philadelphia: W. B. Saunders, 1948. 804 pp.
Monumental presentation of data gathered by the Institute
of Sex Research, Indiana University, through interviews
with 5,300 white males, concerning sexual outlets and
the factors affecting the differential frequency of
these various outlets. Sexual orientation is treated in
the famous 0-6 scale, ranging from exclusive heterosexuality to exclusive homosexuality. Apart from its scientific
quality, the book had a major impact on the concept of
sex in the United States and throughout the world. The
finding that 37% of American men had had homosexual
experience to orgasm meant that the behavior could no
longer be viewed as a rare and exotic deviation, but was
a major facet of sexual experience. Some corrections to
the data regarding homosexuality appear in Paul H. Gebhard et al., **Sex Offenders** (New York: Harper and Row,
1965; 875 pp.).

113.   KRONHAUSEN, EBERHARD, and PHYLLIS KRONHAUSEN. **Sex
       Histories of American College Men.** New York: Bal-
       lantine, 1960. 313 pp.
Popularized account of the varieties of sexual behavior of
American college men based upon personal histories of

about 200 students at an all-male college. Findings,
including those for homosexuality, correspond with those
of Kinsey.

114.   LESTER, DAVID. **Unusual Sexual Behavior: The**
        Standard Deviations. Springfield, IL: Charles
        Thomas, 1975. 242 pp.
Summarizes a large body of research that tends to attribute sexual variation either to biology or to family
circumstances. See pp. 37-123.

115.   MASTERS, WILLIAM H., and VIRGINIA E. JOHNSON.
        Human Sexual Response. Boston: Little, Brown,
        1966. 366 pp.
This book, produced at Masters and Johnson's Reproductive
Biology Research Foundation, St. Louis, made the couple
famous. They supplemented Kinsey by producing more detailed accounts of the physiology of the sexual act. This
volume contains little on homosexuality, for which see
their **Homosexuality in Perspective** (Boston: Little, Brown,
1979; 450 pp.).

116.   ROBINSON, PAUL. **The Modernization of Sex: Havelock**
        Ellis, Alfred Kinsey, William Masters and Virginia
        Johnson. New York: Harper and Row, 1976. 200 pp.
Using an intellectual-history approach, Robinson seeks
to identify the assumptions, biases, tensions, and modes
of reasoning that characterize these four researchers,
who are probably the most influential ones produced by
the English-speaking world.

117.   SCHMIDT, GUNTER. "Allies and Persecutors: Science
        and Medicine in the Homosexuality Issue," **JH,**
        10:3-4 (1984), 127-40.
Traces research from the third-sex theory at the beginning
of the present century to some current hormonal approaches, concluding that the results can be used against
homosexuals and, in fact, have been.

                E. ESSAYS AND COLLECTIONS

This category comprises several types of publications: (a)
acts or proceedings of scholarly congresses, often
containing material of diverse scope and quality; (b)
essay collections presenting new material commissioned to
create a mosaic picture of a subject; (c) assemblages of
reprinted articles or excerpts (sometimes termed "case-
books"); (d) collected essays by a particular author.
Some collections pertaining to lesbianism appear in the
following chapter (II).

118.   ALBEE, GEORGE, et al. **Promoting Sexual Responsib-**

ility and Preventing Sexual Problems. Hanover, NH:
University Press of New England, 1983. 440 pp.
Twenty-two papers from a 1981 conference generally
supporting the claim that the sexist nature of our society
is the root cause of sexual problems.

119. BARNEY, NATALIE CLIFFORD. **Aventures de l'esprit.**
New York: Arno Press, 1975. 278 pp.
Reprint of the 1929 Paris edition of essays by the Amer-
ican expatriate lesbian writer on Djuna Barnes, Romaine
Brooks, Colette, Max Jacob, Marcel Proust, Renee Vivien
and others.

120. BENOÎT, LUC (ed.). **Sortir.** Montreal: L'Aurore,
1978. 303 pp.
Twenty-two essays and creative pieces on sexual variation
and liberation by Quebecois writers, some homosexual and
some heterosexual.

121. BIANCHI, HERMANUS, et al. **Der homosexuelle
Nächste.** Hamburg: Furche Verlag, 1963. 288 pp.
Nine papers by Dutch and German writers generally sym-
pathetic to homosexuality in the spheres of sociology,
law, religion, etc. Incorporates material from the
Dutch collection **De homoseksuele naaste** (Baarn: Bosch &
Keuning, 1961; 158 pp.). See also Theodor Bovet (ed.),
**Probleme der Homophilie in medizinischer, theologischer
und juristischer Sicht** (Bern: Haupt, 1965); and Wilhart
Siegmar Schlegel (ed.), **Der grosse Tabu** (Munich: Rutten
und Loening, 1967).

122. BULLOUGH, VERN L. (ed.). **The Frontiers of Sex
Research.** Buffalo, NY: Prometheus Books, 1979.
190 pp.
Eighteen essays by American scholars and activists on sex
roles, normality, transvestism, transsexualism, homosexuality, etc.

123. CHARDANS, JEAN-LOUIS. **History and Anthology of
Homosexuality--Histoire et anthologie de l'homosex-
ualité.** Paris: Centre d'Etudes et de Documentation
Pédagogiques, 1970. 381 pp.
Amateurish but extensive gathering of texts given parallel
in English and French; illustrated.

124. COOK, MARK, and GLENN WILSON (eds.). **Love and
Attraction: An International Conference.** Oxford:
Pergamon Press, 1979. 554 pp.
Papers on a wide variety of topics. See pp. 258-60, 263,
337, 381-86, 387-93, 497-535.

125. CORY, DONALD WEBSTER (pseud. of Edward Sagarin),
(ed.). **Homosexuality in Cross-Cultural Perspective.** New York: Julian Press, 1956. 440 pp.
Reprints older classic essays and chapters from books on
homosexuality by such writers as Richard Burton, Edward

Carpenter, Alfred C. Kinsey, Paolo Mantegazza, Voltaire, and Edward Westermarck.

126. COUROUVE, CLAUDE, and ROBERT KOZÉRAWSKI. **Fragments.** Paris: The authors, 1980-81. 4 brochures.
Collects about 200 pithy texts on the question of same-sex love, from Aragon to Zola.

127. CREW, LOUIE. **The Gay Academic.** Palm Springs, CA: ETC, 1978. 444 pp.
A collection of twenty-five essays exploring the status of homosexuals in the academic community and their contributions to traditional academic disciplines, including psychology, literature, history, religion, and philosophy.

127. D'ARCANGELO, ANGELO. **Inside the Sexual Revolution.** New York: Lancer Books, 1971. 381 pp.
Lightweight articles and essays by a gay journalist who captured some of the brash optimism of the "Stonewall mood" in New York City.

128. DUYVES, MATTIAS, et al. (eds.). **Among Men, among Women: Sociological and Historical Recognition of Homosocial Arrangements.** Amsterdam: University of Amsterdam, 1983. 611 pp.
Proceedings of an international conference held in Amsterdam on June 22-26, 1983, sponsored by the Gay Studies and Women's Studies Programs at the University of Amsterdam. All texts are in English. In addition to loose papers issued as supplements, however, there is a selection of fourteen revised texts in Dutch: **Onder mannen, onder vrouwen: studies van homosociale emancipatie** (Amsterdam: SUA, 1984).

129. GAGNON, JOHN H., and WILLIAM SIMON (eds.). **Sexual Deviance.** New York: Harper and Row, 1967. 310 pp.
With one exception, this is a collection of articles reprinted from other sources. Parts 3 and 4 contain pertinent articles by Nancy Achilles, Gagnon and Simon, Evelyn Hooker, Maurice Leznoff, Albert J. Reiss, and William A. Westley.

130. GAY, A. NOLDER (pseud. of William Koelsche). **The View from the Closet: Essays on Gay Life and Liberation, 1973-1977.** Boston: Union Park Press, 1978. 108 pp.
Urbane commentary on homosexual life and history by a Boston scholar and newspaper columnist.

131. GAY ACADEMIC UNION (ed.). **Universities and the Gay Experience: Proceedings of a Conference.** New York: Gay Academic Union, 1974. New York: Gay Academic Union, 1974. 105 pp.
Addresses, papers and discussions from the first GAU Conference held at John Jay College, New York, on Thanksgiving Weekend, 1973, and covering such topics as coming

out, the history of science, literature, and religion.
The acts of succeeding annual GAU conferences were not
published as such, though some individual papers were
printed in the periodicals **Gai Saber** and **Gay Books Bulletin**.

132.   HAHN, PIERRE (ed.). **Français encore un effort:**
        l'homosexualité et sa répression: Choix de textes.
        Paris: Martineau, 1970. 215 pp.
Anthology of short texts from ancient Greece to the
present, with commentary by Hahn, a French gay activist.

133.   HAIRE, NORMAN (ed.). **World League for Sexual**
        Reform: Congress, London, 1929. London: Kegan
        Paul, Trench, Trubner and Co., 1930. 670 pp.
Papers covering a wide spectrum of subjects addressed by
the sexual reform movement on the eve of the Great
Depression.

134.   **A Homosexual Emancipation Miscellany, c. 1835-**
        1952. New York: Arno Press, 1975. 172 pp.
Contains the poem "Don Leon," falsely attributed to Lord
Byron, as well as documents by Magnus Hirschfeld, the
British Society for the Study of Sex Psychology, and the
American gay rights pioneers Henry Gerber and Henry Hay.

135.   ITALIAANDER, ROLF (ed.). **Weder Krankheit noch**
        Verbrechen: Plädoyer für eine Minderheit.
        Hamburg: Gala Verlag, 1969. 332 pp.
Collection of short pieces by well-known German and
foreign writers, which are generally supportive of
homosexual rights, accompanied by historical and biographical notes.

136.   JAY, KARLA, and ALLEN YOUNG (eds). **Out of the**
        Closets: Voices of Gay Liberation. New York: Doug-
        las Books, 1972. 403 pp.
Collection of short articles, many experiential and militant, representing the radical phase of gay liberation
immediately following the Stonewall Rebellion. See also
their other collections: **After You're Out** (New York:
Links, 1975; 296 pp.); and **Lavender Culture** (New York:
Harcourt, Brace, Jovanovich, 1979; 493 pp.).

137.   JOHANSEN, ANETTE, and JORGEN JOHANSEN. **Rapport om**
        homofile. Copenhagen: Lindhart og Ringhof, 1973.
        187 pp.
Essays and interviews on social conditions of homosexuals.

138.   KEPNER, JAMES. **A Selection of Gay Liberation**
        Essays: 1953-1973. Torrance, CA: Kepner, 1973. 40
        pp.
A group of articles by a senior figure in the Los Angeles
gay movement, reprinted mainly from **ONE Magazine, HELP/**
Drummer, and the early **Advocate**.

139.   KLEINBERG, SEYMOUR. **Alienated Affections: Being
       Gay in America.** New York: St. Martin's Press,
       1980. 256 pp.
Somewhat astringent essays written from a radical-exist-
entialist perspective by a New York City professor, who
was one of the founders of the Gay Academic Union.

140.   KRICH, AARON M. (ed.). **The Homosexuals: As Seen by
       Themselves and Thirty Authorities.** New York: Cit-
       adel Press, 1954. 346 pp.
Part 1 consists of individual case histories of homosexuals and autobiographical accounts written by them.
Part 2 presents "an overview of major trends in treatment"
by physicians and psychoanalysts. This book is a characteristic document of a period in which the views and
experiences of "deviants" were treated as meaningful
only when interpreted and validated by judgmental psychiatric authorities.

141.   LORAINE, JOHN A. **Understanding Homosexuality: Its
       Biological and Psychological Bases.** New York: Am-
       erican Elsevier, 1974. 217 pp.
Nine articles treating such topics as psychological,
biological, and endocrinological factors in the etiology
of homosexuality; religious and legal aspects; and the
current role of homophile organizations.

142.   MARMOR, JUDD (ed.) **Sexual Inversion: The Multiple
       Roots of Homosexuality.** New York: Basic Books,
       1965. 358 pp.
Collection of papers in the fields of history, comparative zoology, genetics, endocrinology, sociology,
anthropology, law, psychology, and psychoanalytic psychiatry. This collection, still dominated by psychiatric
attitudes, should be compared with its more liberal
successor: Judd Marmor (ed.), **Homosexual Behavior: A
Modern Reappraisal** (New York: Basic Books, 1980; 416
pp.).

143.   REES, JOHN TUDOR, and HARLEY V. USILL (eds.). **They
       Stand Apart: A Critical Survey of the Problems of
       Homosexuality.** London: William Heinemann, 1955.
       220 pp.
A collection of articles from diverse points of view on
the legal situation, the nature of homosexuality, whether
it is harmful, and its moral status.

144.   RUITENBEEK, HENDRIK M. (ed.). **The Problem of
       Homosexuality in Modern Society.** New York: E. P.
       Dutton, 1963. 304 pp.
Reprints sixteen papers, several of them (such as those
by George Devereux, Evelyn Hooker, and Albert J. Reiss)
classics, generally in psychiatry and the social sciences.

145.   SCHWULENREFERAT IM ALLGEMEINEN STUDENTENAUSSCHUSS
       DER FU BERLIN (ed.). **Dokumentation der Vor-**

tragsreihe "Homosexualität und Wissenschaft."
Berlin: Verlag Rosa Winkel, 1985. 288 pp.
Papers by fifteen authors presented at the Free University, Berlin, on law, literature, politics, and the
history and future of the gay movement in Germany.

146. WARREN, CAROL (ed.). Sexuality: Encounters,
      Identities, and Relationships. Beverly Hills:
      Sage, 1976. 136 pp.
Reprints six papers on such topics as massage parlors; the
interrelation between sex, situation, and strategies in
the pairing ritual of homo ludens; secrecy in the lesbian
world; bisexuality in men; family attitudes and Mexican
male homosexuality; and meanings and process in erotic
aggression.

147. WELTGE, RALPH W. (ed.). The Same Sex: An Appraisal
      of Homosexuality. Philadelphia: Pilgrim Press,
      1969. 164 pp.
Eight of the essays in this book discuss homosexuality
(esp. in relation to religion, ethics, and the law)
fairly neutrally, while three reflect the point of view
of the emerging gay movement.

148. ZIEGLER, ALEXANDER. Kein Recht auf Liebe: Report-
      agen, Aufsätze, Stücke. Frankfurt am Main:
      Fischer, 1978. 278 pp.
Crusading essays on pederasty, homosexuals in the work
place and other subjects by a Swiss gay novelist.

         F. ENCYCLOPEDIAS AND DICTIONARIES

Until quite recently general encyclopedias, whose publishers were aware that the volumes were destined for the
shelves of secondary school and college libraries,
discretely shunned the whole subject of homosexuality or
dismissed it with a few evasive or uninformative remarks.
Hence the topic was treated only in specialized reference
works, which were, however, usually compiled by individuals working in the tradition of the sexual science that
had emerged in the early twentieth century. Their
treatments summarize what was then known (or simply
believed) by the major investigators of homosexual
behavior and psychology.

149.   ELLIS, ALBERT, and ALBERT ABARBANEL (eds.). The
       Encyclopedia of Sexual Behavior. New York: Haw-
       thorn Books, 1961. 2 vols.
Articles by various writers with a cross-cultural and
international emphasis. While attitudes are often
dated, the entries still convey useful information.
Bibliographies; index.

150.   GIESE, HANS. **Wörterbuch der Sexualwissenschaft.**
        Bonn: Instituts-Verlag, 1952. 216 pp.
Dictionary of sex research compiled by a (closeted) West
German homosexual scholar.

151.   HAIRE, NORMAN (ed.). **The Encyclopedia of Sexual
        Knowledge.** New York: Coward McCann, 1934. 636 pp.
Based in large measure on material assembled in France
by "Dr. Costler" (Arthur Koestler). Haire, an Australian
physician and leader of the sex reform movement in the
interwar period, was homosexual.

152.   HEGELER, INGE, and STEN HEGELER. **An ABZ of Love.**
        New York: Medical Press of New York, 1963. 288 pp.
Translation of a Danish work. About 600 entries, with 120
drawings; emphasizes sexual techniques.

153.   MARCUSE, MAX (ed.). **Handwörterbuch der Sexualwis-
        senschaft.** Bonn: A. Marcuse und E. Weber, 1923.
        481 pp.
An encyclopedic dictionary fusing sexological and psychiatric viewpoints. Contains several outstanding articles
by Hans Licht (Paul Brandt).

154.   ROBINSON, VICTOR (ed.). **Encyclopaedia Sexualis: A
        Comprehensive Encyclopaedia-Dictionary of the
        Sexual Sciences.** New York: Digwall-Rock, 1936.
        819 pp.
Reflects European sex research of the pre-1933 period,
though many articles are written by Americans. In
addition to the usual entries, see "Elmira Reformatory,
Sex in," "Hirschfeld, Magnus," and "Homosexual Twins."

155.   SANTA VICCA, EDMUND F. **The Treatment of Homosex-
        uality in Current Encyclopedias.** Ann Arbor: Uni-
        versity of Michigan, 1977. 323 pp. (unpublished
        dissertation).
Treats mainly general encyclopedias, rather than specialized ones.

                    G. LIBRARIES AND ARCHIVES

The emergence of gay and lesbian studies has posed special
problems for cataloguing and collection of materials, some
of which can be best solved in the special gay and lesbian
archives. As regards the profession, anecdotal evidence
suggests that a high proportion of male librarians are
homosexual, but the actual incidence and its sociopsychological grounding have not been elucidated.

156.   BERMAN, SANFORD. **The Joy of Cataloging.** Phoenix:
        Oryx Press, 1980. 242 pp.

Heterodox and stimulating reflections by a Minnesota
librarian who has championed the cause of adapting cataloguing practices to new social realities.

157.   BROOKS, JOAN, and HELEN C. HOFFER (eds.). **Sexual
        Nomenclature: A Thesaurus.** Boston: G. K. Hall,
        1976.
Computer printout of 2,000 descriptors (subject headings)
and their hierarchies, as well as 250 cross-references
from unused to used terms, documenting cataloguing
practice at the Kinsey Institute for Sex Research,
Indiana University.

158.   FRASER, JAMES A., and HAROLD A. AVERILL. **Organiz-
        ing an Archives: The Canadian Gay Archives Exper-
        ience.** Toronto: Canadian Gay Archives, 1983. 68
        pp. (CGA Publication no. 8)
Comprehensive, practical guide to planning and running a
gay/lesbian archive, presenting the CGA experience and
recommendations for use elsewhere. See also: Rick
Bébout, "Stashing the Evidence: The Canadian Gay Archives," **Body Politic,** no. 55 (August 1979), 21-22, 26.

159.   GELLATLY, PETER. **Sex Magazines in the Library
        Collection: A Scholarly Study of Sex in Serials and
        Periodicals.** New York: Haworth Press, 1981. 142
        pp.
Twelve papers on an important body of material not
adequately addressed, as a rule, in libraries. Note
esp. Frederick McEnroe, "A Select Bibliography of Gay
and Lesbian Periodicals" (pp. 87-97).

160.   GITTINGS, BARBARA. "Combatting the Lies in the
        Library," in: Louie Crew (ed.), **The Gay Academic**
        (Palm Springs: ETC, 1978), 107-20.
Lively account of experiences in the American Library
Association's Task Force on Gay Liberation, which she
heads. See also the brochure published by this task force
(subtitled: How to Get Gay Materials into Libraries: A
Guide to Library Selections Policies fy the Non-Librar-
ian): Stuart R. Miller, **Censored, Ignored, Overlooked, Too
Expensive?** (Philadelphia: ALA Gay Task Force, 1979; 10
pp.)

161.   GRECO, STEPHEN, and CHARLES FABER. "In Search of
        Our History: Archives, Libraries and Projects in
        History," **Advocate,** no. 330 (November 12, 1981),
        22-27.
On emerging institutions in New York City, San Francisco,
and Los Angeles.

162.   HANCKEL, FRANCES, and JOHN CUNNINGHAM. "Can Young
        Gays Find Happiness in YA Books?" **Wilson Library
        Bulletin,** 50 (1976), 528-34.
Positive advice on selecting fiction with gay themes and
characters for library collections serving young adults.

Since this article was written, there has been considerable improvement, both quantitatively and qualitatively;
see: Christine Jenkins and Julie Morris, **A Look at Gayness: An Annotated Bibliography of Gay Materials for
Young People.** Second ed. (Ann Arbor: Kindred Spirit
Press, 1982; 19 pp.).

163.   LEHMAN, J. LEE. "The Lesbian Herstory Archives,"
       Advocate, no. 264 (April 5, 1979), 14-17.
Account of the formation of the Archives in New York City
in 1973, its scope, acquisitions, and cataloguing prac-
tices. See also Beth Hodges, "Interview with Joan and
Deborah of the Lesbian Herstory Archives," **Sinister
Wisdom,** no.11 (Fall 1979), 3-13; and no. 13 (Spring
1980), 101-05. Bibliographies and information about
acquisitions are published in **Lesbian Herstory Archives
News.** See also: Clair Potter, **The Lesbian Periodicals
Index** (Tallahassee, FL: Naiad, 1986; 413 pp.)

164.   MICHEL, DEE. **Gay Studies Thesaurus.** Revised ed.
       Princeton, NJ: The author, 1985. 76 pp.
Contains a total of 1215 items, of which 911 are preferred
terms, to assist in "indexing and accessing materials of
relevance to gay culture, history, politics and psychology." This work, with a male emphasis, may be complemented by the **Lesbian Periodicals Index Thesaurus** and
the **Women's Studies Database.**

165.   TIMMONS, STUART. "Special Report: Gay/Lesbian
       Archives," **Advocate,** no. 447 (May 27. 1986), 30-33.
More than sixty gay and lesbian collections now exist.
They share poor finances and a growing concern about the
preservation of their holdings.

166.   WOLF, STEVE. "Sex and the Single Cataloguer,"
       in: Celeste West and Elizabeth Katz (eds.).
       Revolting Librarians. San Francisco: Bootlegger
       Press, 1972, pp. 39-44.
About prejudices in subject headings and classification
systems. In the same volume, see also Bianca Guttag,
"Homophobia in Library School" (pp. 37-38).

                     H.   PRESS AND MEDIA

The establishment of a large and viable gay and lesbian
press in North America has been a surprising and welcome
development of the post-Stonewall years--even if the
papers are more notable for their numbers than for
sustained quality of journalism. Pre-Hitler Germany
offers some precedent, and currently there are significant
gay presses in France, the Netherlands, Australia and a
few other countries. A different topic is the treatment
of homosexuality in the mainstream press, as well as the

newer media of radio and television. For a long time
these mainstream outlets drew a veil of silence over the
whole matter. Once this blackout was ended, they retained
a real potential for stereotypical and inadequate coverage. Concern for apparent imbalance has called into
being several homosexual groups to monitor coverage,
especially in television--where there has been some
resentment at the appearance of what others regard as yet
another pressure group.

167. ANDERSON, SCOTT. "The Gay Press Proliferates--and
      So Do Its Problems," **Advocate**, no. 282 (December 13,
      1979), 19-23.
This issue contains other relevant articles.

168. ARMSTRONG, DAVID. **A Trumpet to Arms: Alternative
      Media in America.** Boston: South End Press, 1981.
      359 pp.
An illustrated account of the rise of the "underground
press" in the 1960s and 1970s. See esp. pp. 230-53.

169. BRODY, MICHAL (ed.). **Are We There Yet? A Continu-
      ing History of Lavender Woman, A Chicago Lesbian
      Newspaper, 1971-1976.** Iowa City: Aunt Lute, 1985.
      188 pp.
Reprints of articles interspersed with interviews present
a composite picture of the paper and its times.

170. CHESMAN, ANDREA, and POLLY JOAN. **Guide to Women's
      Publishing.** Paradise, CA: Dustbooks, 1978. 304
      pp.
Includes data on lesbian presses, magazines, newspapers,
literary-cultural journals, print shops, bookstores,
and organizations.

171. CLARKE, LIGE, and JACK NICHOLS. **I Have More Fun
      with You Than Anybody.** New York: St. Martin's
      Press, 1972. 152 pp.
Memoirs of the gay activist lovers who edited the New
York City Newspaper **Gay.**

172. COLLYER, ROBIN, et al. "The Body Politic Trial,"
      Centerfold (Toronto), (February-March 1979),
      92-114.
Account of the prosecution of the distinguished Canadian
gay monthly for printing an article on pedophilia. Needless to say, the ongoing course of the trials is covered
in editorials and stories in **The Body Politic** itself.

173. COON, EARL O. "Homosexuality in the News," **Ar-
      chives of Criminal Dynamics,** 2 (1957), 843-65.
Purports to offer a method of reading between the lines of
news stories to detect homosexual situations that were not
explicitly mentioned in the press of that day.

174. CORZINE, HAROLD JAY. **The Gay Press.** St. Louis:
      Washington University, 1977. 277 pp. (unpublished
      dissertation)
Careful study of selected runs of gay newspapers.

175. **A Gay News Chronology, January 1969–May 1975.** New
      York: Arno Press, 1975. 156 pp.
Abstracts (562) of articles appearing in **The New York
Times.** May be supplemented for succeeding years by con-
sulting **The New York Times Index.**

176. "Gay News: How Good Are the Mainstream Media?" **Ad-
      vocate,** no. 347 (July 22, 1982), 25–27, 54.
Most gay reporters and editors remain closeted, and thus a
newsroom climate antagonistic to gays is allowed to thrive
and influence the choice and tone of stories.

177. GIROUARD, MICHEL. **Je vis mon homosexualité.** Mont-
      real: Québecor, 1980. 224 pp.
Autobiographical account of a French-Canadian television
personality.

178. GOULD, ROBERT E. "Homosexuality on Television,"
      Medical Aspects of Human Sexuality. 7 (October
      1973), 116–27.
An early article when offerings were indeed meager. Lists
of relevant television programs (of necessity incomplete)
may be found in William Parker, **Homosexuality Bibliography: Supplement, 1970–1975** (Metuchen, NJ: Scarecrow,
1977), pp. 274–76; and idem, **Homosexuality Bibliography:
Second Supplement, 1976–1982** (Metuchen, NJ: Scarecrow
Press, 1985), pp. 322–27.

179. GRIER, BARBARA, and COLETTA REID (eds.). **The
      Lavender Herring: Lesbian Essays from The Ladder.**
      Oakland, CA: Diana Press, 1976. 357 pp.
Writings selected from the leading lesbian monthly, **The
Ladder** (1956–72), which was itself reprinted in its
entirety, with a new index, by Arno Press, New York,
1975.

180. HANSCOMBE, GILLIAN, and ANDREW LUMSDEN. **Title
      Fight: The Battle for** Gay News. London: Brilliance
      Books, 1984. 264 pp.
Account of the complex maneuvers that resulted in the
demise of Britain's chief gay newspaper.

181. HEMMINGS, SUSAN. "Horrific Practices: How Lesbians
      Were Presented in the Newspapers of 1978," in: Gay
      Left Collective (ed.), **Homosexuality: Power and
      Politics.** London: Allison and Busby, 1980,
      pp. 157–71.
In 1978 British newspapers broke their habitual silence
on lesbianism in a series of sensational stories--on a
lesbian Member of Parliament; on artificial insemination; and on a teacher.

182.   HOFSESS, JOHN. "The Sexual Niggers," **Content: Can-
        ada's National News Media Magazine,**(August 1977),
        15, 18-19, 21-25.
Surveys treatment of homosexuals in major newspapers
and magazines of Canada.

183.   HOHMANN, JOACHIM S. (ed.). **Der Eigene: Ein Blatt
        für männliche Kultur.** Frankfurt am Main: Foerster,
        1981. 379 pp.
Selection of articles, fiction and illustrations from
the German magazine, which appeared in Berlin--with
interruptions-- from 1896 to 1931. See also the same
editor's selection from the Swiss magazine (1933-67) **Der
Kreis** (Frankfurt am Main: Foerster, 1980; 285 pp.)

184.   HOWES, KEITH, and JULIAN MELDRIM. **Declaring an
        Interest: A Projected Catalogue of Gay Images on
        Television in Britain.** Third ed. London: Hall-
        Carpenter Archives, 1983. 56 pp.
An alphabetical list of programs (including discussions,
documentaries, television plays, series, and films)
broadcast since 1954 on British public and commercial
television, with brief descriptive comments. Index of
persons.

185.   LAERMER, RICHARD. "The Televised Gay: How We're
        Pictured on the Tube," **Advocate,** no. 413 (February
        5, 1985), 20-25.
Well informed survey, with relevant quotations from network officials and producers.

186.   KPFA-FM (Radio Station, Berkeley, CA). **The
        Homosexual in Our Society: The Transcript of a
        Program Broadcast on November 24, 1958.** San
        Francisco: Pan-Graphic Press, 1959. 32 pp.
Two-hour program with gay and non-gay discussants, perhaps
the first of its kind. Text reprinted in **Mattachine
Review,** 6:7 (July 1960), 12-28; 6:8 (August 1960), 9-25.

187.   LESBIAN AND GAY MEDIA ADVOCATES. **Talk Back! The
        Gay Person's Guide to Media Action.** Boston: Al-
        yson, 1982. 119 pp.
How to get complaints about homophobic material in the
media taken seriously.

188.   LEVINE, RICHARD M. "How the Gay Lobby Has Changed
        Television," **TV Guide,** 29:22 (May 30, 1981), 2-6;
        and 29:23 (June 6, 1981), 47-52.
Objective presentation of the impact of the Gay Media Task
Force in pressing for positive images of gays and les-
bians, as well as in combatting stereotypes.

189.   MAURIAC, JEAN-PIERRE. "Arcadie, l'homophile et la
        presse," **Arcadie,** 243 (March 1974), 148-66.
The monthly **Arcadie,** at that time the only French gay
periodical, contrasts its role with that of the main-

stream press.

190. MAYNOR, JOE E. "Fundamentalist Ministers vs. Gay
      Rights Groups," **TV Guide**, 28:46 (November 15,
      1980), 16-20.
A clash in Charlotte, NC, presents problems for the
Federal Communications Commission.

191. MONTGOMERY, KATHRYN. "Gay Activists and the
      Networks," **Journal of Communication**, 31 (Summer
      1981), 49-57.
Gay activists have had success with the television
networks by adapting themselves to their structure,
geographical and operationally, while using techniques
of surveillance and feedback. See also her (unpublished) dissertation: **Gay Activists and the Networks: A
Case Study of Special Interest Pressure on the Networks**
(Los Angeles: University of Southern California, 1979;
243 pp.).

192. NICHOLSON, JOE. "Coming Out at the New York Post,"
      Columbia Journalism Review, 20 (March-April 1982),
      26-27.
Personal account of experiences at the controversial
New York City afternoon paper.

193. PARK, JAN CARL. "An Annotated Bibliography of Gay
      and Lesbian Communication Studies, **Alternative
      Communications**, 1:2 (May 1979). [entire issue]
Survey by the editor of **Alternative Communications**,
published by the Caucus of Gay Male and Lesbian Concerns
of the Speech Communication Association.

194. PEARCE, FRANK. "How to Be Immoral and Ill, Pathetic
      and Dangerous All at the Same Time," in: Stanley
      Cohen and Jack Young (eds.), **The Manufacture of
      the News**. London: Constable, 1973, pp. 284-301.
Analysis and critique of the treatment of homosexuals
in the British media.

195. PECK, ABE. **Uncovering the Sixties: The Life and
      Times of Underground Newspapers**. New York: Pan-
      theon, 1985. 304 pp.
Lively account by a participant of the rise, heyday, and
fall of the underground presses, 1964-1973, cast against
the culture and politics of the era. Only sporadic discussion of the gay/lesbian press, which is (perhaps
ironically) virtually the sole survivor of this once
flourishing phenomenon.

196. PIERSON, RANSDELL. "Uptight on Gay News," **Columbia
      Journalism Review** (March-April 1982), 25-33.
Concludes that, while papers frequently present gays in
a crime or drag-queen context and sporadically report on
their political activities, they almost never treat the
wider issues of how gays live.

197.   RADER, DOTSON. "An American Son," **Rolling Stone,**
        (April 27, 1973), 44-46.
On the brief fame of Lance Loud, a young man of Santa
Barbara who came out on the television documentary "An
American Family."

198.   SCHMIDT, WOLFGANG JOHANN (ed.). **Jahrbuch für**
        sexuelle Zwischenstufen. Frankfurt am Main: Qum-
        ran, 1983. 2 vols.
Selection of articles from the great German Yearbook,
which had been published by the Scientific-Humanitarian
Committee from 1899 to 1923. Includes Tables of Contents
for all issues.

199.   SPIEGELMAN, WILLARD. "The Progress of a Genre: Gay
        Journalism and Its Audience," **Salmagundi,** 58
        (1982), 308-25.
A not unsympathetic examination of some continuities in
gay male journalism, which yet concludes: "To define an
audience through sexual inclination alone is to appeal to
the lowest common denominator, the cravings of the flesh."

200.   WINTER, ALAN D. **The Gay Press: A History of the**
        Gay Community and Its Publications. Austin,
        TX: The author, 1977. 114 pp.
Perceives four phases in the American gay press: secre-
tive and conservative (1950s); open and moderate (1960s);
radical and militant (1969-71); seeking new directions
(1972ff.).

                    I. ADVERTISEMENTS

The existence of "personals" columns in middle-class newspapers opened a path for homosexuals to meet—at least
in a few newspapers willing to accept discreetly worded
notices. With the lifting of taboos in the 1960s, it was
possible to create explicit ads—though the franker ones
appeared mainly in the underground press and gay papers.
Sociologists have studied these ads as evidence of courtship patterns and concepts of desired sexual partners.

201.   ASCHAFFENBURG, GUSTAV. "Homosexuelle Werbeschrift-
        en," **Ärztliche Sachverständigenzeitung,** 34 (1928),
        351-54.
Homosexual advertisements in Weimar Germany.

202.   BERNAY, JÉRÔME. "Les homosexuels à travers les
        petites annonces du Nouvel Observateur," **Arcadie,**
        no. 298 (October 1978), 505-18.
Attitudes revealed by French personal advertisements.

203.   DEAUX, KAY, and RANDEL HANNA. "Courtship in the

Personals Column: The Influence of Gender and
Sexual Orientation," **Sex Roles,** 11:5/6 (1984),
353-75.
An analysis of 800 ads, equally balanced between men and
women, heterosexual and homosexual, shows that men were
more concerned with physical characteristics, while
women stressed psychological factors. Homosexuals were
more concerned with sexuality, while heterosexuala
specified a broader range of characteristics.

204.   KLIMMER, RUDOLF. "Annoncen in einer Zeitschrift
       für Homosexuelle," **Nervenarzt,** 40 (1969), 272-75.
Analysis of ads in a Danish gay magazine. See also his
article on S & M ads in: **Sexualmedizin,** 4 (1974), 585-
88.

205.   LANER, MARY R. "Media Mating II: 'Personals'
       Advertisements of Lesbian Women," **JH,** 4 (1978),
       41-61.
Advertisements were found to be more like those of nonlesbian women advertisers than like those of men of either
orientation.

206.   LANER, MARY R., and G. LEVI KAMEL. "Media Mating
       I: Newspaper 'Personals' Ads of Homosexual Men,"
       JH, 3 (1977), 149-62.
Homosexual ads were more frank than heterosexual ones, and
more specific about goals for desired relationships,
reflecting the "virilization" of the gay male subculture.

207.   LEE, JOHN A. "Meeting Males by Mail," in Louie
       Crew (ed.), **The Gay Academic.** Palm Springs, CA:
       ETC, 1978, pp. 415-27.
Besides attempting to characterize the differences between
Canadian and U.S. ads (based on analysis of the ads in
Body Politic and **The Advocate** respectively, Lee reports on
his own luck with ads he placed.

208.   LUMBY, MALCOLM E. "Men Who Advertise for Sex," **JH,**
       4 (1978), 63-72.
Based on a content analysis of 1,111 paid ads in **The
Advocate,** characterises differences between personal and
commercial (models, masseurs, and escorts) ads.

209.   NÄCKE, PAUL. "Angebot und Nachfrage von Homosex-
       uellen in Zeitungen," **Archiv für Kriminalanthro-
       pologie und Kriminalistik,** 8 (1902), 339-50; 9
       (1902), 217-18.
Together with "Päderastische Annoncen"--loc. cit., pp.
215-16--the first studies of gay "personals" advertisements.

210.   NÄCKE, PAUL. "Zeitungsannoncen von weiblichen
       Homosexuellen," **Archiv für Kriminalanthopologie und
       Kriminalistik,** 10 (1903), 225-29.
On turn-of-the-century lesbian advertisements.

211.   PRAETORIUS, NUMA (pseud. of Eugen Wilhelm).
        "Homosexuelle Inserate," **Anthropophyteia**, 6 (1909),
        167-77.
Study of personal ads in the Paris newspaper **Le Journal**.
Followed by another study on ads in **Le Supplement**, ibid.,
8 (1911), 231-43. Cf. also ibid., 8 (1911), 224-31.

212.   PRESTON, JOHN, and FREDERICK BRANDT. **Classified
        Affairs: A Gay Man's Guide to the Personal Ads.**
        Boston: Alyson, 1984. 120 pp.
How to write and interpret an ad, and where to place
it--with model examples.

213.   "Thirty-one Words," **Body Politic**, no. 113 (April
        1985), 29-32, 45.
Opinions by various members of the editorial board of the
Canadian gay monthly regarding the acceptability of a
racially explicit ad. Note an earlier contribution by a
reader (Allen Max), ibid., no. 55 (August 1979), 6.

                        J. PUBLIC OPINION

The concept of public opinion tends to oscillate between
two objects: (1) the views held by everyone who holds an
opinion, the public in the broad sense; and (2) the views
of "opinion-making" elites--professionals, politicians,
journalists, etc. Both concepts have been employed in
measuring attitudes regarding homosexual behavior. Apart
from their value in supporting legal and political efforts
to secure civil rights for homosexuals, public opinion
surveys provide information on myths and stereotypes
perpetuated by the masses.

214.   BOWMAN, RICHARD. "Public Attitudes toward Homosex-
        uality in New Zealand," **International Review of
        Modern Sociology**, 9 (1979), 224-243.
Interviews with 321 heterosexual adults in two New Zealand
cities found that the great majority did not express antihomosexual attitudes and supported removal of negative
sanctions against homosexuals.

214A.   CHAPPELL, DUNCAN, and PAUL R. WILSON. "Public
        Attitudes to the Reform of the Law Relating to
        Abortion and Homosexuality," **Australian Law
        Journal**, 42 (1968), 120-21, 175-79.
Shows the lingering of older attitudes. See also the
follow-up article, idem, "Changing Attitudes toward
Homosexual Law Reform," ibid., 46 (1972), 22-29; and
Hong Sung-Mooh, "Australian Attitudes towards Homosexu-
ality: A Comparison with College Students," **Journal of
Psychology**, 117 (1984), 89-96.

215. DE BOER, CONNIE. "The Polls: Attitudes toward Homo-
      sexuality," **Public Opinion Quarterly**, 44 (Summer
      1978), 266-76.
Offers some international comparisons.

216. "Les français et l'homosexualité: sondage realisé
      par l'I.F.O.P.," **Arcadie**, no. 304 (April 1979),
      283-68.
Results of a survey on homosexuality by the French Institute of Public Opinion, presented with commentary
by André Baudry, Marc Daniel, and others.

217. GALLUP OPINION INDEX, PRINCETON. "Homosexuality in
      America--Poll Findings," **The Gallup Report**, no. 147
      (October 1977), 1-24.
A majority held that homosexuals deserve equal rights in
jobs, but in general the poll discloses a mixed pattern.
Some minor advances are shown in the subsequent study,
ibid., no. 205, 3-19.

218. GLASSNER, BARRY, and CAROL OWEN. "Variations in
      Attitudes toward Homosexuality," **Cornell Journal of
      Social Relations**, 11 (1976), 161-76.
Reports on an attitude questionnaire given to 61 undergraduates at a St. Louis university. Being female, having
known homosexuals, and having parents perceived as having
an accepting attitude toward them were factors associated
with less social distance from homosexuals.

219. GROSS, ALAN E., et al. "Disclosure of Sexual
      Orientation and Impressions of Male and Female
      Homosexuals," **Personality and Social Psychology
      Bulletin**, 6 (1980), 307-14.
In a videotape test, homosexually identified targets were
judged more stereotypically by subjects of their own sex
than by those of the other sex.

220. HENLEY, NANCY, and FRED PINCUS. "Interrelationship
      of Sexist, Racist, and Antihomosexual Attitudes,"
      Psychological Reports, 42 (1978), 83-90.
Evaluating a questionnaire adminstered to 211 undergraduates, sexism and antihomosexual attitudes were negatively
correlated with father's and mother's education. Religious
and political orientation was also important.

221. "Homosexuality: Public Attitudes," **Drum**, no. 25
      (August 1967), 11-13, 29-31.
Reports on a CBS survey.

222. HONG, SUNG-MOOK. "Sex, Religion and Factor
      Analytically Derived Attitudes toward Homosexual-
      ity," **Australian Journal of Sex, Marriage and
      Family**, 4 (1983), 142-50.
Two factors were identified: Social-Personal Acceptance
and Perceived Normality, indicating that attitudes toward homosexuality involve multidimensional rather

than unidimensional concepts.

223.   IRWIN, PATRICK, and NORMAN L. THOMPSON. "Accep-
        tance of the Rights of Homosexuals: A Social
        Profile," **JH**, 3 (1977), 107-21.
Evaluating data from a nationwide survey, the authors
conclude that respondents who were willing to grant rights
to homosexuals tended to be well educated, young, Jewish
or nonreligious, from urban areas, raised in the Northeast
or Pacific states, and willing to provide freedom of
expression to people with nonconformist political ideas.

224.   LARSEN, KNUD S. et al. "Attitudes of Heterosexuals
        toward Homosexuality: A Likert-type Scale and
        Construct Validity," **Journal of Sex Research**, 16
        (1980), 245-57.
Reports on the development and testing with undergraduates
of a 20-item Heterosexual Attitudes Toward Homosexuality
(HATH) Scale. See also Larsen et al., "Anti-Black Attitudes, Religious Orthodoxy, Permissiveness, and Sexual Information: A Study of the Attitudes of Heterosexuals toward Homosexuality," ibid., 19 (1983), 105-18.

225.   LAURENS, ANDRÉ. **Les Français: Passions et tabous.**
        Paris: Editions Alain Moreau, 1985. 328 pp.
Correlates results of public opinion surveys conducted by
the Institut Français de Recherches Economiques et Sociales. French opinion on homosexuality is changing,
thanks to extensive discussion in the media. More tolerant views are held by young people and by Socialist Party
voters.

226.   LEVITT, EUGENE E., and ALBERT D. KLASSEN. "Public
        Attitudes toward Homosexuality: Part of the 1970
        National Survey by the Institute for Sex Research,"
        JH (1974), 29-43.
Based on a sample of 30,018 Americans, prsents data on
feelings of distrust and repugnance, rights of homosexuals, causes and cures of homosexuality, legal controls,
and homophobia.

227.   MCCLOSKY, HERBERT, and ALIDA BRILL. **Dimensions of
        Tolerance: What Americans Believe about Civil
        Liberties.** New York: Russell Sage Foundation,
        1983. 512 pp.
This major study compares the findings of two surveys
commissioned by the Russell Sage Foundation with others.
Concludes that tolerance must be learned, and the sophisticated arguments on which it is based make it much
harder to learn than intolerance. The surveys also
highlight the role of the elites, who tend to hold views
in advance of those of the population at large, and
thereby to serve to some extent as a bulwark against the
potential "tyranny of the majority." See esp. pp. 202-07.

228.   MILLHAM, JIM, et al. "A Factor-Analytic Concep-

tualization of Attitudes toward Male and Female
Homosexuals," **JH** 2 (1976), 3-10.
Evaluating a questionnaire administered to 785 male and
female heterosexuals, it was found that they make greater
distinctions in conceptualizing homosexuality than had
been previously recognized.

229.   MORIN, JEAN-PAUL, and GEORGETTE ST. ARNAUD. "Per-
       ceptions de l'homosexualité dans la societé qué-
       becoise contemporaine," **Service Social** (Canada),
       24 (July-December 1975), 47-89.
Includes comparison of opinions of homosexuals with a
random sample of the public.

230.   NEWMAN, GRAEME. **Comparative Deviance: Reception
       and Law in Six Cultures.** New York: Elsevier,
       1976. 332 pp.
Study of opinion and mores in India, Indonesia, Iran,
Italy, the United States, and Yugoslavia showed wide
variations with regard to abortion and homosexuality,
whereas murder, robbery, rape and the like were univer-
sally condemned.

231.   NYBERG, KENNETH L., and JON P. ALSTON. "Analysis
       of Public Attitudes toward Homosexual Behavior,"
       JH, 2 (1976-77), 99-107.
Data from a 1974 survey of 1,197 persons showed that more
favorable attitudes toward homosexuality were held by
those who were under 30, lived in larger urban centers,
and had college experience. See also Nyberg and Alston,
"Homosexual Labeling by University Youths," **Adolescence**,
12 (1977), 541-46.

232.   PRICE, JAMES H. "High School Students' Attitudes
       toward Homosexuals," **Journal of School Health**, 52
       (1982), 469-74.
Males generally held more negative views on homosexuality
than did females, though both agreed that is "unnatural."
The author discusses ways in which adolescents can become
more accepting of homosexuals.

233.   ROONEY, ELIZABETH A., and DON C. GIBBONS. "Social
       Reactions to 'Crimes without Victims.'" **Social
       Problems**, 13 (1966), 400-10.
Interprets answers of 353 San Francisco area residents
regarding abortion, drugs, and homosexuality--with very
mixed opinions expressed regarding the last.

234.   SCHNEIDER, WILLIAM, and I. A. LEWIS. "The Straight
       Story on Homosexuality and Gay Rights," **Public
       Opinion**, 7 (February-March 1984), 16-20, 59-60.
Interprets Los Angeles Times polls of September 1983
(national) and October 1983 (California), concluding that
"there are reasons to believe that sympathy for homosexuals will grow in time.... The gay rights movement,
however, faces a far more difficult situation that the

comparable movements for civil rights and women's rights."
See also: Schneider, "Homosexuality Still 'Wrong,' But
No Public Backlash on AIDS," **Los Angeles Times,** Opinion
section (January 5, 1986).

235. SHERRILL, KENNETH. "Homophobia: Illness or
      Disease?" **Gai Saber,** 1 (1977), 27-40.
Analyzes data on aversive attitudes to homosexuality
collected by the National Opinion Research Center (University of Chicago) in 1973. Concludes that support for
civil rights and liberties is linked to the trend toward
the youth culture and the "new morality."

236. SIMMONS, J. L. "Public Stereotypes of Deviants,"
      Social Problems, 13 (1965) 223-32.
In a survey studying the public perception of deviance,
homosexuality was the most frequent response to the
question of what constitutes deviance.

237. SMOLENAARS, A. J. "Analysis of Pick 3/8 Data on
      Attitudes toward Homosexuality, by the Compensatory
      Distance Model," **Nederlands Tijdschrift voor de
      Psychologie en haar Grensgebieden,** 29 (1974),
      631-47.
Reports on a survey of 385 Dutch subjects of different
professions, indicating that some professions were more
homogeneous in their opinions than others.

238. SOBEL, H. J. "Adolescent Attitudes toward Homosex-
      uality in Relation to Self Concept and Body
      Satisfaction," **Adolescence,** 11 (1976), 443-53.
Psychodynamic approach.

239. TURNBULL, DEBI, and MARVIN BROWN. "Attitudes
      towards Homosexuality and Male and Female Reactions
      to Homosexual and Heterosexual Slides," **Canadian
      Journal of Behavioural Science,** 9 (1977), 68-80.
Saskatchewan students were more antihomosexual than an
Ontario sample. Antihomosexual attitudes tended to
correlate with dislike of the slides as pornographic.

240. WARD, R. A. "Typifications of Homosexuals,"
      Sociological Quarterly, 20 (1979), 411-23.
Categorization as found in public opinion inquiries.

241. WEIS, CHARLES B., and ROBERT N. DAIN. "Ego
      Development and Sex Attitudes in Heterosexual and
      Homosexual Men and Women," **Archives of Sexual
      Behavior,** 8 (1979), 341-56.
More negative attitudes toward homosexuality were correlated with higher levels of personal guilt for heterosexual
and homosexual men and for heterosexual women.

242. WEST, WALTER G. "Public Tolerance of Homosexual
      Behavior," **Journal of Social Relations,** 12 (1977),
      25-36.

Tabulation of the answers of 1,504 respondents disclosed
that the less tolerant individual is older, less educated,
and attends church more frequently.

243.   YOUNG, MICHAEL, and JEAN WHIRTVINE. "Attitudes of
       Heterosexual Students toward Homosexual Behavior,"
       Psychological Reports, 51 (1982), 673-74.
Results from a required freshman course showed predominantly negative attitudes. See also: Randall G. Cuenot
and Stephen S. Fugita, "Perceived Homosexuality: Measuring
Heterosexual Attitudinal and Nonverbal Reactions,"**Per-**
sonality and Social Psychology Bulletin, 8 (1982),100-06.

                  K.   ATTITUDES OF PROFESSIONALS

Professional opinion, especially in the helping professions, is of consequence not merely for its influence on
the society as a whole, but also because of the contact of
professional individuals with homosexuals, including ones
who have problems exacerbated by their marginal and socially precarious lifestyles.

244.   AMERICAN PSYCHOLOGICAL ASSOCIATION, TASK FORCE ON
       THE STATUS OF LESBIAN AND GAY MALE PSYCHOLOGISTS.
       Removing the Stigma: Final Report of Board of
       Social and Ethical Responsibility. Washington,
       DC: American Psychological Association, 1980. 151
       pp. (Manuscript no. 2121)
Strongly positive statement.

245.   BARR, R. F., and S. V. CATTS. "Psychiatry Opinion
       and Homosexuality: A Short Report," **JH,** 1 (1974),
       213-15.
In a survey of about 200 psychiatric professionals, the
majority took the view either that homosexuality is a
developmental anomaly not necessarily associated with
neurotic symptoms or that it is a normal variant like
left-handedness. See also: Frances E. Baum, "Gay and
Lesbian Lifestyles: Implications for Social Workers,"
Australian Social Work, 36 (March 1983), 23-29; and Peter J. Blizzard and Murray S. Smith, "Medical Students;
Attitudes and Opinions about Human Sexual Behavior,"
Australian Journal of Social Issues, 10:4 (1975), 229-313.

246.   DAVISON, GERALD C., and G. TERRENCE WILSON. "Atti-
       tudes of Behavior Therapists toward Homosexuality,"
       Behavior Therapy, 4 (1973), 6830-96.
Responses to a questionnaire sent to British and American
behavior therapists reveal continuing strong support for
aversion therapy and for changing homosexual orientation.

247.   DRESSLER, JOSHUA. "Study of Law Student Attitudes

Regarding the Rights of Gay People to Be Teachers,"
JH, 4 (1979), 315-29.
From a survey of 528 students at 12 schools concludes that
law students, esp. women, are comparatively tolerant of
the right of homosexual persons to serve as teachers.

248.   FORT, JOEL, et al. "Attitudes of Mental Health
        Professionals toward Homosexuality and Its Treat-
        ment," **Psychological Reports,** 29 (1971), 347-50.
Survey of 163 professional therapists in the San Francisco
Bay area showed little support for mandatory treatment,
near unanimity on the need for liberalization of the
law, and widespread support for nonexclusionary employment practices.

249.   GAGNON, JOHN, et al. "Report of the American
        Sociological Association's Task Group on Homosex-
        uality," **American Sociologist,** 17 (1982), 164-80.
Consistent with previous stands by the Association, the
Report was strongly supportive.

250.   GARFINKLE, ELLEN M., and STEPHEN F. MORIN. "Psy-
        chologists' Attitudes toward Homosexual Psychother-
        apy Clients," **Journal of Social Issues,** 34 (1978),
        101-12.
In blind tests of a hypothetical client (presented as
either heterosexual or homosexual) attributions of psychological health were found to differ as a function of
sexual orientation of client and sex of therapist.

251.   GARTRELL, NANETTE, et al. "Psychiatrists' Atti-
        tudes toward Female Homosexuality," **Journal of
        Nervous and Mental Disease,** 159 (1974), 141-44.
Of 908 psychiatrists responding to a questionnaire, 66%
challenged the traditional belief that lesbianism equates
with sickness or inadequacy.

252.   GOCHROS, HARVEY L. "Teaching More or Less Straight
        Social Work Students to Be Helpful to More or Less
        Gay People," **Homosexual Counseling Journal,** 2:2
        (1975), 58-67.
Discomfort among social workers in dealing with homosexual
clients is often owing to inexperience with them, and can
be lessened through a program of learning experiences.
See also: Gochros: "Teaching Social Workers to Meet the
Needs of the Homosexually Oriented," **Journal of Social
Work and Human Sexuality,** 2 (1983-84), 137-56.

253.   GROSS, MARY J. "Changing Attitudes toward Homosex-
        uality--or Are They?" **Perspectives in Psychiatric
        Care,** 16 (1978), 70-75.
Some change for the better is found among medical and psychiatric professionals, but old attitudes linger among
many.

254.   MANOS, NIKOLAS. "Sexual Life, Problems, and

Attitudes of the Prospective Greek Physicians,"
Archives of Sexual Behavior, 12 (1983), 435-443.
Results of a questionnaire given to 82 male and 48 female
Greek medical students showed liberal trend.

255. MAY, EUGENE P. "Counselors', Psychologists', and
Homosexuals' Philosophies of Human Nature and
Attitudes toward Homosexual Behavior," **Homosexual
Counseling Journal**, 1 (1974). 35 pp.
Similarities and contrasts among the three groups based on
the Philosophies of Human Nature Scale of L. S. Wrights-
man.

256. MORRIS, PHILIP A. "Doctors' Attitudes to Homosexuality," **British Journal of Psychiatry**, 122 (1973),
435-36.
On more than 200 questionnaires returned, only a few
respondents considered homosexuality a disease, though a
large number regarded it as an aberrant behavior pattern.

257. SCHWARTZ, MICHAEL. "Military Psychiatry--Theory
and Practice in Noncombat Areas: The Role Conflicts
of the Psychiatrist," **Comprehensive Psychiatry**, 12
(1971), 520-25.
Protests that in the military the psychiatrist has been
forced to relinquish his role as helper therapist and to
become, instead, detective-interrogator for the institution. This creates distrust among those he should be
trying to help.

L. PORNOGRAPHY AND CENSORSHIP

In the English-speaking world virtually all writings on
homosexuality were long thought obscene. Only in recent
decades has the right to publish, distribute and sell
increasingly explicit materials with a homosexual content
been recognized by the courts and the police. The works
listed below deal with some of the problems occasioned by
homosexual and other pornography and by the feminist
backlash against the flood of what some women consider
offensive and even threatening publications. The struggle
for the freedom of the gay press is far from ended, as
is shown by recent cases in Canada and Great Britain.

258. ATHANASIOU, ROBERT, and PHILLIP SHAVER. "Correlates of Response to Pornography: A Comparison of
Male Heterosexuals and Homosexuals," **Proceedings of
the Annual Convention of the American Psychological
Association**, 5 (1970), 349-50.
In a survey of 20,000 Americans more monotonic relationships between response to pornography and behavior were
found for heterosexuals than for homosexuals.

48   HOMOSEXUALITY

259.   BLACHFORD, GREGG. "Looking at Pornography: Erotica
        and the Socialist Morality," **Gay Left**, 6 (1978),
        16-20.
Asks: Can we retain the erotic values of sexual images,
while eliminating the sexist and exploitative elements?

260.   BURGESS, ANN WOLBERT, and MARIEANNE LINDEQVIST
        CLARK (eds.). **Child Pornography and Sex Rings**.
        Lexington: Lexington Books, 1984. 227 pp.
Papers from a social-work perspective, some tending to
judgmental, even inflammatory attitudes.

261.   BURSTYN, VARDA (ed.). **Women against Censorship**.
        Vancouver: Douglas and McIntyre, 1985. 208 pp.
Papers by Canadian and U. S. feminists, arguing that women
have nothing to gain by allying themselves with censorship
advocates and politicians.

262.   CALIFIA, PAT. "Feminism vs. Sex: A New Conser-
        vative Wave?" **Advocate**, no. 286 (February 21,
        1980), 13-15.
Warns of the dangers of a de facto alliance of antiporn
feminists--some lesbian--and the New Right. See also
her: "Among Us, Against Us: The New Puritans," ibid.,
no. 290 (April 17, 1980), 14-18; "The Age of Consent: An
Issue and Its Effects on the Gay Movement," ibid., no.
303 (October 16, 1980), 19-23, 45, and no. 304 (October
30, 1980), 17-23, 45; and "See No Evil: The Antiporn
Movement," ibid., no. 428 (September 3, 1985), 35-39.

263.   CLAPP, JANE. **Art Censorship: A Chronology of
        Proscribed and Prescribed Art**. Metuchen, NJ:
        Scarecrow Press, 1972. 582 pp.
This rather dry compilation serves to focus attention
on censorship of the fine arts, which has been neglected
in recent controversies centering on printed matter and
film. Bibliography of 641 items; index.

264.   COPP, DAVID, and SUSAN WENDELL (eds.). **Pornography
        and Censorship**. Buffalo: Prometheus Books, 1983.
        414 pp.
Valuable collection of papers treating the problems from
several vantage points of philosophy, social science, and
law.

265.   DWORKIN, ANDREA. **Pornography: Men Possessing
        Women**. New York: Perigee (Putnam), 1981. 300 pp.
An impassioned polemic, which has proved an effective
vehicle for the propagation of Dworkin's militant views.
Unfortunately the treatment of gay-male erotica is tendentious and misleading.

266.   ENGLISH, DEIRDRE. "The Politics of Porn: Can
        Feminists Walk the Line?" **Mother Jones**, 5:3 (April
        1980), 20-23, 43-50.
Well-reasoned critique of the antipornography trend among

some feminists (including Dworkin), arguing that taking
men's pornography away will not alter how they think and
feel about women.

267.   FAUST, BEATRICE. **Women, Sex and Pornography.** New
       York: Macmillan, 1981. 239 pp.
Fair-minded, but properly critical examination of the
antipornography arguments.

268.   GOLDSTEIN, MICHAEL J., and HAROLD S. KANT. **Pornog-
       raphy and Sexual Deviance: A Report of the Legal
       and Behavioral Institute, Beverly Hills, Cal-
       ifornia.** Berkeley, CA: University of California
       Press, 1973. 194 pp.
Compared results of extensive interviews among atypical
groups (rapists, homosexuals, and heavy users of pornography) with two control samples, concluding that the
nondeviant groups had had significantly greater exposure
to pornographic materials during adolescence than the
deviants.

269.   GOODMAN, MICHAEL BARRY. **Contemporary Literary
       Censorship: The Case of Burroughs'** Naked Lunch.
       Methuen, NJ: Scarecrow Press, 1981. 330 pp.
Traces the controversy beginning in 1958, which was
ultimately settled in a successful court battle undertaken by Grove Press, with important consequences for
the freedom to read and publish. See also: Charles
Rembar, **The End of Obscenity: The Trials of** Lady Chatterley, Tropic of Cancer, **and** Fanny Hill (New York: Random
House, 1968; 528 pp.).

270.   JENKINSON, EDWARD B. **Censors in the Classroom.**
       New York: Avon, 1982. 184 pp.
Offers a number of case studies of recent campaigns in
the United States for censorship of textbooks and other
reading materials.

271.   LAURITSEN, JOHN. **Dangerous Trends in Feminism:
       Disruptions, Censorship, Bigotry.** New York: The
       author, 1977. 9 pp.
The author was one of the first to point out the problems
posed by the Susan Brownmiller-Andrea Dworkin trend in
feminism. See also his: **Rape, Hysteria, and Civil
Liberties** (New York: The author, 1979; 14 pp.).

272.   LEDERER, LAURA (ed.). **Take Back the Night: Women
       on Pornography.** New York: Morrow, 1980. 361 pp.
Collection of papers by a number of writers who argue
that pornography is causally linked to male aggressiveness and attacks on women.

273.   LEWIS, FELICE FLANNERY. **Literature, Obscenity and
       Law.** Carbondale: Southern Illinois University
       Press, 1976. 297 pp.
Lucid and scholarly portrayal of the interaction of

literary art, society's values and pressures, and the
legal system's response to changing conditions--chiefly
in 20th century American literature. See also: Dorothy
Ganfield Fowler, **Unmailable: Congress and the Post Office**
(Athens: University of Georgia Press, 1977; 266 pp.).

274. MCCOY, RALPH E. **Freedom of the Press: An Annotated
      Bibliography.** Carbondale: Southern Illinois
      University Press, 1968. about 500 pp.
An exemplary record of English-language materials from the
16th century to 1966. A **Ten Year Supplement (1967-1977)**
appeared in 1979 (557 pp.).

275. MALAMUTH, NEIL M., and EDWARD DONNERSTEIN (eds.).
      Pornography and Sexual Aggression. Orlando, FL:
      Academic Press, 1984. 333 pp.
Papers by various researchers grouped under the categories
of individual differences, experimental studies, correlational and cross-cultural factors, communicative factors,
and legal implications of the research. They tend to
the conclusion that pornography is harmful, though judgments vary as to the degree and character of the harm.

276. MASTERSON, JOHN. "The Effects of Erotica and
      Pornography on Attitudes and Behavior: A Review,"
      Bulletin of the British Psychological Society, 37
      (1984), 249-52.
Questions the reliability of data on availability and use
of pornography. Concludes that it in fact may be useful
barometer of the state of male-female relations in society.

277. PECKHAM, MORSE. **Art and Pornography: An Experiment
      in Explanation.** New York: Basic Books, 1969. 306
      pp.
Stimulating, though sometimes opaque discussion of current
theories of literary and visual erotica, with considerable
attention to homosexuality. Reaches a surprisingly positive conclusion: "European and American pornography
... has been as steadily innovative as science itself..."
(p. 298). Includes discussion of the concept of "porno-
topia," introduced by Stephen Marcus in **The Other Victorians** (New York: Basic, 1966).

278. **The Report of the Commission on Obscenity and
      Pornography.** New York: Random House, 1970. 700
      pp.
Main text of the the Report of a Presidential Commission
appointed in 1968. (There are also nine volumes of supplementary, "technical" material.) The Report generally
supports the liberal position that pornography has no
substantial harmful effects, a conclusion that is still
hotly debated. See also: Walter Barnett, "Corruption of
Morals: The Underlying Issue of the Pornography Commission Report," **Law and the Social Order** (1971), [part 2]
189-243.

279. THOMPSON, ANTHONY HUGH. **Censorship in Public
      Libraries in the United Kingdom during the Twen-
      tieth Century.** New York: Bowker, 1976. 236 pp.
Chronological survey citing numerous cases in the country
that is the source of our common "Anglo-Saxon" attitudes
in the matter.

280. VALSTAR, JOOP, et al. **Porno: analyzes van de
      verkeerde kant.** Boskoop, Netherlands: De Woerat,
      1982. (Homopolitieke teksten, 3)
Five papers analyzing the porno controversy from a gay-
liberation viewpoint, and arguing for the freeing of
fantasy.

281. WALKER, CHRIS. "Potentially Beneficial Aspects of
      Pornography," **Fag Rag**, no. 25 (1978), 8-10.
Images of beautiful bodies bring beauty to the homely,
memories to the old, and anticipation and dreams to the
young.

282. WILLIAMS, BERNARD. **Report of the Committee on
      Obscenity and Film Censorship.** London: Her
      Majesty's Stationery Office, 1979. 270 pp.
This British official commission recommends abandoning
such terms as "obscene" and "indecent." Holds that the
printed word deserves protection, but that restrictions
may be legitimately applied to visual and theatrical
works.

283. YAFFE, MAURICE, and EDWARD NELSON (eds.). **The
      Influence of Pornography on Behavior.** New York:
      Academic Press, 1982. 276 pp.
Assesses the current debate in which substantial harmful
influence has been argued, in contrast to earlier skepticism.

II. WOMEN'S STUDIES

A. LESBIAN STUDIES

Although men have shown a certain prurient interest in
lesbian behavior since the 16th century, it is only in
recent decades that the subject has received attention
from women and men that begins to compare with that
bestowed on male homosexuality. Even today, there is
uncertainty about the scope of the field, with some
stipulating lesbian sexual relations as a defining
feature, while others broaden the definition to include
affectionate, not necessarily genital relations and the
"woman-identified woman." Needless to say, the "second
wave" of the women's movement, from the 1960s on, and
women's studies programs, have greatly promoted the study
of lesbianism--though sometimes at the cost of melding the
subject with others which are akin to it, but still
distinct. Apart from the entries in this general section,
there are studies on particular aspects of lesbianism in
the appropriate sections of this work.

284. ABBOTT, SIDNEY, and BARBARA LOVE. **Sappho Was a
     Right On Woman: A Liberated View of Lesbianism.**
     New York: Stein and Day, 1972. 251 pp.
This statement by two New York City activists presents the
lesbian experience in two parts: What It Was Like, and
Living in the Future. Includes discussion of open identity, activism, and links with the feminist movement.

285. ALBRO, JOYCE C., and CAROL TULLY. "A Study of
     Lesbian Lifestyles in the Homosexual Micro-Culture
     and the Heterosexual Macro-Culture," **JH**, 4 (1979),
     331-44.
In a survey of 91 lesbians, it was found that they reported a sense of isolation from the heterosexual macro-
culture and turned to the homosexual microculture,
for friends, emotional support, and social interaction.

286. ALDRICH, ANN. **We Walk Alone.** New York: Fawcett,
     1955. 143 pp.
A lesbian novelist shows that the lesbian is "many women,"
with a wide range of backgrounds and psychological
characteristics. See also Aldrich (ed.), **Carol in a
Thousand Cities** (Greenwich, CT: Fawcett, 1960; 256 pp.).

287. ARNUP, KATHERINE, and AMY GOTTLIEB. "Annotated
     Bibliography," **Resources for Feminist Research,**
     12:1 (March 1983), 90-100.
This issue is entirely devoted to lesbian topics. There
are also indices to several lesbian periodicals, a

film- and videography (pp. 87-89), and a bibliography of
lesbian mothers and custody (pp. 106-09). Some Canadian
emphasis.

288. BAETZ, RUTH (ed.). **Lesbian Crossroads: Personal
      Stories of Lesbian Struggle and Triumph.** New
      York: William Morrow, 1980. 273 pp.
Statements by a number of women on self-realization,
interpersonal relations, religion, and lesbian commun-
ity--as well as interviews with parents and siblings.

289. BONNET, MARIE-JO. **Un choix sans équivoque: re-
      cherches historiques sur les relations amoureuses
      entre les femmes, XVIe-XXe siècle.** Paris: Denoël,
      1981. 296 pp.
Scholarly study of lesbian history, chiefly from French
literary sources. In addition to recording known facts,
treats the character of the sources, with particular
reference to elements of reticence and concealment. This
remarkable work contains an extensive bibliography, pp.
253-93.

290. BRAUCKMANN, JUTTA. **Weiblichkeit, Männlichkeit, und
      Antihomosexualität: Zur Situation der lesbischen
      Frau.** Berlin: Verlag Rosa Winkel, 1981. 94 pp.
Divides into four sections: (1) Female Homosexuality and
Heterosexuality; (2) Heterosexuality and Sexual Identities; (3) Antihomosexuality and Sexual Roles; and (4)
Feminine Roles and Lesbian Life. Contends that as long
as there are stringent definitions of "femininity" and
"masculinity," discrimination against lesbians will
continue. Extensive notes and bibliography.

291. BROOKS, VIRGINIA. **Minority Stress and Lesbian
      Women.** Lexington, MA: Heath, 1981. 219 pp.
Systematic presentation of a new model of stress and
stress management. Revised version of a doctoral dissertation in sociology, University of California, Berkeley,
1977.

292. CAVIN, SUSAN. **Lesbian Origins.** San Francisco: Ism
      Press, 1985. 288 pp.
A lesbian feminist analysis of the origins of human
society (reflecting in part the ideas of Frederick
Engels); sources of women's and lesbian oppression; and
new perspectives in women's liberation. Sometimes
speculative, this book offers insights into a number of
little studied areas.

293. CHAFETZ, JANET S., et al. "A Study of Homsosexual
      Women," **Social Work**, 19 (1974), 714-23.
Based on a sample of 51 Houston women, the article exlores
their lifestyles, problems, views of themselves, relationships with others, and their perceptions of society's
reactions to them. See also: Wayne L. Cotton, "Social and
Sexual Relationships of Lesbians," **Journal of Sex Re-**

search, 11 (1975), 139-48.

294.   CORY, DONALD WEBSTER (pseud. of Edward Sagarin).
       The Lesbian in America. New York: Citadel Press,
       1964. 288 pp.
An ethnographic study of lesbianism by a well-known male
homosexual writer, who holds that lesbianism is a learned
condition, established when experience proves it to be
pleasurable. Also covered are lesbians' attitudes toward
men, incidence, "butch" and "femme" styles, bisexuality,
family relations, passing, legal problems, and organizations for lesbians.

295.   CRONIN, DENISE M. "Coming Out among Lesbians,"
       in: Erich Goode and Richard R. Troiden (eds.),
       Sexual Deviance and Sexual Deviants. New York:
       Morrow, 1974, pp. 268-77.
From interviews and questionnaires, concludes that adopting a homosexual identity has a less drastic effect on the
lives of lesbians than it does on the lives of gay men.
Lesbians are women first and homosexuals second.

296.   CRUIKSHANK, MARGARET (ed.). **Lesbian Studies: Pres-
       ent and Future.** Old Westbury, NY: Feminist Press,
       1982. 286 pp.
Twenty-eight articles by lesbian scholars, some experien-
tial, others more strictly academic. Among the useful
reference features provided are "Sample Syllabi from
Courses in Lesbianism" (pp. 217-35); "Bibliography: Books"
by Lyndell MacCowan (pp. 237-60); and "Articles" by
Margaret Cruikshank (pp. 261-73). See also: Cruikshank
(ed.), **The Lesbian Path: 37 Lesbian Writers Share Their
Personal Experiences, Viewpoints, Traumas and Joys**
(Monterey, CA: Angel Press, 1980; 248 pp.).

297.   DARTY, TRUDY, and SANDEE POTTER (ed.). **Women-Iden-
       tified Women.** Palo Alto, CA: Mayfield, 1984. 316
       pp.
Nineteen essays, some previously published, emphasizing
the plurality of lesbian identities, problems engendered
by social intolerance, and lesbian culture. This informative collection also cites many useful references.

298.   DOMINY, MICHELE D. "Lesbian-Feminist Gender Concep-
       tions: Separatism in Christchurch, New Zealand,"
       Signs, 11 (1986), 274-89.
Field study showing the contrast between activist groups
and cultural lesbian-feminists who are seeking to achieve
an "ethos of natural purity."

299.   ETTORE, ELIZABETH M. **Lesbians, Women and Society.**
       Boston: Routledge and Kegan Paul, 1980. 208 pp.
Employing data gathered from interviews and participant
observation, an American lesbian residing in Britain
offers a quasi-Marxist theory of stages of emergent lesbian political consciousness. Sometimes opaque.

300. FARLEY, PAMELLA. "Lesbianism and the Social
      Function of Taboo," in: Hester Eisenstein and Alice
      Jardine (eds.), **The Future of Difference** (Boston:
      G. K. Hall, 1980), 267-73.
"[B]y definition heterosexuality denies homosexuality; but
it both requires and suppresses the scapegoat.... Not
only are the oppressed made to disappear, rendered invisible and even obliterated. So too are the means of oppression made to disappear."

301. FERGUSON, K. D., and DEANA C. FINKLER. "A Involve-
      ment and Overtness Measure for Lesbians: Its De-
      velopment and Relation to Anxiety and Social Zeit-
      geist," **Archives of Sexual Behavior,** 7 (1978), 211-
      27.
Interpreting a battery of tests, finds that anxiety was
not related to degree of homosexual involvement, while it
reflected degree of overtness in low- but not high-status
lesbians.

302. GALANA, LAUREL, and GINA COVINA. **The New Les-
      bians: Interviews with Women across the U.S. and
      Canada.** New York: Random House, 1977. 223 pp.
Presents interviews with twenty-one women of diverse backgrounds and situations.

303. GARTRELL, NANETTE. "The Lesbian as a 'Single'
      Woman," **American Journal of Psychotherapy,** 35
      (1981), 502-09.
Presents the process of coming out as a means of working
through the conflicts that social definitions of the
"single woman" create for lesbians. See rebuttal by
Charles W. Socarides, ibid., 510-15.

304. GOLDSTEIN, MELVIN. "Some Tolerant Attitudes toward
      Female Homosexuality throughout History," **Journal
      of Psychohistory,** 9 (1982), 437-60.
Offers psychohistorical speculations as to why lesbianism
has historically been tolerated, accepted and even encouraged. See comment by Robert J. Saunders, ibid., 10
(1983), 520-21. See also Wardell B. Pomeroy, "Why We
Tolerate Lesbians," **Sexology,** 31 (1965), 652-55.

305. GOODE, ERICH, and LYNNE HABER. "Sexual Correlates
      of Homosexual Experience: An Exploratory Study of
      College Women," **Journal of Sex Research,** 13 (1977),
      12-21.
A small group of college women who had had lesbian contacts were found to be in general more sexually experienced than a larger group without such contacts.

306. GOODMAN, BERNICE. **The Lesbian: A Celebration of
      the Difference.** Brooklyn, NY: Out and Out, 1977.
      69 pp.
Political essays, with emphasis on the situation of lesbian mothers.

307. GREGORY-LEWIS, SASHA. **Sunday's Women: A Report on
      Lesbian Life Today.** Boston: Beacon Press, 1979.
      217 pp.
A journalist's report, competent and non-sensationalized,
on the state of lesbian America at the time of writing.
Shows a political spectrum ranging from traditionalists,
through liberationists and radicals to authoritarians.

308. HALLIDAY, CAROLINE, et al. **Hard Words and Why
      Lesbians Have to Say Them.** London: Onlywoman,
      1978. 16 pp.
Contrasts self-understanding with environing stereotypes.

309. HASSELL, JULIE, and EDWARD W. SMITH. "Female
      Homosexuals' Concepts of Self, Men, and Women,"
      Journal of Personality Assessment, 39 (1975),
      154-59.
From a battery of tests given to 48 women, concludes that
the lesbian may be more independent, changeable, and
sexually preoccupied, and less well adjusted than her
heterosexual counterpart.

310. HEDBLOM, JACK H. "Dimensions of Lesbian Sexual
      Experience," **Archives of Sexual Behavior,** 2 (1973),
      329-41.
In a study of 65 Philadelphia lesbians, find that early
sexual experiences were consensual, refuting seduction
stereotypes. Also examines coming out, awareness of
lesbianism, and heterosexual involvements. See also:
Hedblom, "The Female Homosexual: Social and Attitudinal
Dimensions," in J. A. McCaffrey (ed.), **The Homosexual
Dialectic.** Englewood Cliffs, NJ: Prentice-Hall,1972,
pp. 31-64; as well as Hedblom and John J. Hartman,
"Research on Lesbianism: Selected Effects of Time,
Geographic Location and Data Collection Technique,"
Archives of Sexual Behavior, 9 (1980), 217-34.

311. HESS, ELIZABETH P. "Feminist and Lesbian Develop-
      ment: Parallels and Divergencies," **Journal of
      Humanistic Psychology,** 23 (1983), 67-78.
Explores the means by which an identity as a "feminist" or
"lesbian" becomes a positive one, as well as the interaction between the two identities.

312. HOGAN, ROBERT A. et al. "Attitudes, Opinions, and
      Sexual Development of 205 Homosexual Women," **JH,** 3
      (1977), 123-36.
Results show a high rate of only-child status among
lesbian women, a tendency towards ambivalence of opinion
on many issues, and a lack of insight into self and
others.

313. HOJGARD, GUNNA. **Kaere foraeldre: Lesbiske fortael-
      ler om deres forhold til familien.** Copenhagen:
      Demos, 1978. 124 pp.
Presents inverviews with lesbian women concerning their

relations with their families.

314.   HOPKINS, JUNE H.   "The Lesbian Personality," **British Journal of Psychiatry**, 115 (1969), 1433-36.
In place of the descriptor "neurotic," the following terms
are suggested as describing lesbians: more independent,
more resilient, reserved, dominant, bohemian, self-sufficient, and more composed.

315.   HUGHES, NYM, et al.   **Stepping Out of Line.** Vancouver, BC: Press Gang, 1985. 208 pp.
Essays for study and teaching on lesbianism and feminism,
coming out, parenting, reorganizing the law, religion, and
the medical system. Canadian emphasis; references.

316.   JOHNSTON, JILL.   **Lesbian Nation: The Feminist Solution.** New York: Simon & Schuster, 1973. 283 pp.
A militant writer advocates lesbian separatism. The text
is adapted from columns in **The Village Voice** (New York).
In a more tranquil mode, see her: "Lesbian/Feminism Reconsidered," **Salmagundi**, no. 58-59 (1982-83), 10-24.

316A. KEHOE, MONICA (ed.).   **Historical, Literary and Erotic Aspects of Lesbianism.** New York: Haworth Press, 1986. 182 pp.
Thirteen papers corresponding to JH, 12:3-4 (May 1986).

317.   KITZINGER, CELIA, and REX S. ROGERS.   "A Q-Methodological Study of Lesbian Identities," **European Journal of Social Psychology**, 15 (1985), 167-87.
English data from 41 women revealed identity factors explicated as Personal Fulfillment, Special Person, Individualistic, Radical Feminist and Traditional identities.

318.   KLEMESRUD, JUDY.   "Lesbians: The Disciples of Sappho, Updated," **New York Times Magazine** (March 28, 1971), 38-39, 41-52.
Journalistic apercus of interest chiefly for the date of
their appearance in a mainstream publication. Discussion
in issues of April 11 (pp. 5, 55) and May 9 (pp. 79-80).

319.   KOKULA, ILSE.   **Formen lesbischer Subkultur: Vergesellschaftung und soziale Bewegung.** Berlin: Verlag Rosa Winkel, 1983. 168 pp.
The writer, a German lesbian sociologist and activist,
portrays the structure of dynamic of lesbians in three
spheres: the bar, the clique, and the activist group.

320.   KRIEGER, SUSAN.   "Lesbian Identity and Community: Recent Social Science Literature," **Signs**, 8 (1982), 91-108.
Recent studies view lesbianism as a product of multiple
influences, and the examine the lesbian in terms of her
relationships in couples, institutions, communities, and
society rather than as an isolated individual or in
relation to her family of origin. Integration in such

communities may threaten as well as support the growth of
individual identity.

321.   KRIEGER, SUSAN. The Mirror Dance: Identity in a
        Woman's Community. Philadelphia: Temple University
        Press, 1983. 199 pp.
Ethnography of a midwestern lesbian community, where lesbian relationships are complex because they pose fundamental challenges to the individual's sense of self.

322.   KUDA, MARIE JAYNE. Women Loving Women: A Selected
        and Annotated Bibliography. Chicago: Lavender
        Press, 1975. 28 pp.
List of about 200 entries, largely superseded by M. Cruikshank, above, and by Barbara Grier, The Lesbian in Literature (Tallahassee: Naiad Press, 1981; 168 pp.).

323.   LANER, MARY R., and ROY H. LANER. "Sexual Prefer-
        ence or Personal Style? Why Lesbians are Disliked,"
        JH, 5 (1980), 339-56.
As in the case of homosexual men, the authors found that
lesbians are disliked both for sexual preference and for
personal style (departure from expected gender-role
models).

324.   LANNING, LEE, and VERNETTE HART. Ripening: An
        Almanac of Lesbian Lore and Vision. Minneapolis:
        Word Weavers, 1982. 160 pp.
Free-form work expressing oneness with nature. See also
their: Dreaming: An Almanac of Lesbian Lore and Vision
(Minneapolis: Word Weavers, 1983; 153 pp.).

325.   LATORRE, RONALD A., and KRISTINA WENDENBURG.
        "Psychological Characteristics of Bisexual,
        Heterosexual and Homosexual Women," JH, 9 (1983),
        87-97.
Of 125 women, feminine subjects were under-represented
among homosexual and bisexual women. Otherwise, the
three groups showed similar profiles.

326.   LE GARREC, EVELYNE. Des femmes qui s'aiment. Par-
        is: Seuil, 1984. 286 pp.
Sociological study of French lesbians in relation to
society; includes personal testimonies. See also: Marie
Lago and France Paramelle, La femme homosexuelle (Tour-
nai: Casterman, 1976; 203 pp.); and Nella Nobili and
Edith Zha, Les femmes et l'amour (Paris: Hachette, 1979;
318 pp.).

327.   LYNCH, JEAN M., and MARY ELLEN REILLY. "Relation-
        ships: Lesbian Perspectives," JH, 12:2 (1986),
        53-69.
A study of 70 largely middle-class and upper-middle-class
lesbian couples finds that most achieve partnerships
characterized by equality and freedom from traditional
butch-femme role playing.

328. MANNION, KRISTIANN. **Female Homosexuality: A
      Comprehensive Review of Theory and Research.**
      Washington: American Psychological Association,
      1976. 95 pp. (Catalogue of Selected Documents,
      6:44)
The empirical research involves three major areas of
investigation: assessment of the lesbian personality by
projective techniques; personality assessment studies
using nonprojective personality inventories and clinical
interviews; and biographical variables derived from
projective tests designed to measure attitudes toward
the family, as well as from biographical questionnaires.

329. MARTIN, DEL, and PHYLLIS LYON. **Lesbian/Woman.** San
      Francisco: Glide Foundation, 1972. 283 pp.
Forthright account of lesbians in America by two founders
of Daughters of Bilitis in San Francisco--about which organization the book gives considerable information. The
lesbian is defined as "a women whose primary erotic,
psychological, emotional and social interest is in a
member of her own sex, even though that interest may not
be overtly expressed." The revised edition (New York:
Bantam, 1983) has a ten-year update (1972-82).

330. NEWTON, ESTHER. "The Mythic Mannish Lesbian: Rad-
      clyffe Hall and the New Woman," **Signs,** 9 (1984),
      557-75.
Historically, the trend of cross-dressing for women initially signaled an asexual desire for autonomy, but
gradually became linked to lesbian sexual expression as
feminists sought to break out of the asexual model of
romantic friendships with other women.

331. PACZENSKY, SUSANNE VON. **Verschweige Liebe: Zur
      Situation der lesbischen Frau in der Gesellschaft.**
      Munich: Bertelsmann, 1984. 206 pp.
Interviews with 75 Hamburg lesbians and analysis of their
responses.

332. PASTRE, GENEVIEVE. **De l'amour lesbien.** Paris:
      Pierre Horay, 1980. 298 pp.
Somewhat subjective reflections by a French lesbian theorist.

333. PEPLAU, LETITIA A. et al. "Loving Women: Attach-
      ment and Autonomy in Lesbian Relationships," **Jour-
      nal of Social Issues,** 34 (1978), 7-27.
In a questionnaire study of 127 lesbians, the majority
said that their current relationship was extremely
close, personally satisfying, and egalitarian. See
also: Peplau et al., "Satisfaction in Lesbian Relationships," **JH,** 8 (1982), 23-35.

334. PONSE, BARBARA. "Secrecy in the Lesbian World,"
      Urban Life, 5 (1976), 313-38.
In fear of disapproval and sanctions, lesbians tend to

hide their identity behind a heterosexual facade. Life
is compartmentalized into gay and straight spheres. Under
the influence of women's and gay liberation this situation
is changing. See also her: **Identities in the Lesbian
World: The Social Construction of the Self** (Westport, CT:
Greenwood Press, 1978; 228 pp.).

335. POOLE, KENNETH. "The Etiology of Gender Identity
      and the Lesbian," **Journal of Social Psychology,** 87
      (1972), 51-57.
Finds support for a hypothesis that the childhood socialization experience of heterosexual females differs, in
certain role-learning aspects, from that of homosexual
females.

336. PRIETO, ENRIQUE. **La homosexualidad feminina.**
      Madrid: Uve, 1982. 116 pp.
This popularizing work, though primarily designed to
satisfy sexual curiosity, offers some glimpses of Spanish
lesbian life.

337. RICH, ADRIENNE. "Compulsory Heterosexuality and
      Lesbian Existence," **Signs,** 5 (1980), 631-60.
Controversial article criticizing perceived heterosexist
bias in much current feminist scholarship. "The denial of
reality and visibility to women's passion for women,
women's choice of women as allies, life companions, and
community, the forcing of such relationships into dissim-
ulation and their disintegration under intense pressure
have meant an incalculable loss to the power of all
women to change the social relations of the sexes, to
liberate ourselves and each other." See responses by Anne
Ferguson et al., ibid., 7 (1981), 158-99.

338. RIESS, BERNARD F. et al. "Psychological Test Data
      on Female Homosexuality: A Review of the Liter-
      ature," **JH,** 1 (1974), 71-85.
Critical and comparative review of existing studies on
responses by female homosexuals to projective and nonpro-
jective tests. See also: Riess, "New Viewpoints on the
Female Homosexual," in: V. Franks and V. Burtle (eds.),
**Women in Therapy: New Psychotherapies for a Changing
Society** (New York: Brunner/Mazel, 1974), pp. 191-214.

339. ROSEN, DAVID H. **Lesbianism: A Study of Female
      Homosexuality.** Springfield, IL: Charles C. Thomas,
      1974. 123 pp.
Presents a review of the literature on lesbianism and
results of a research study of 26 women.

340. RUPP, LEILA J. "'Imagine My Surprise': Women's
      Relationships in Historical Perspective," **Fron-
      tiers: A Journal of Women's Studies,** 5:3 (Fall
      1980), 61-70.
Reviews the conflicting approaches scholars have taken,
presents examples of different kinds of relationships

from the American women's movement in the 1940s and 50s,
and proposes a conceptual approach that recognizes the
diversity of women's relationships without denying their
common bond.

341.   SCHÄFER, SIGRID. "Sexual and Social Problems of
       Lesbians," **Journal of Sex Research**, 12 (1976),
       50-69.
From questionnaire data collected from 151 West German
lesbians, discusses the coming out period, the meaning of
their heterosexual experiences, and the social and
psychological challenges lesbian life poses.

342.   SCHWARZ, JUDITH. "Lesbians," in: Sarah M. Pritch-
       ard, **The Women's Annual Number 4, 1983-1984.**
       Boston: G. K. Hall, 1984, pp. 107-24
Bibliographical essays of work in recent years (emphasizing 1983), including such themes as third-world lesbians,
sexuality, history, and lesbian lives.

343.   SEGREST, MAB. **My Mama's Dead Squirrel: Lesbian
       Essays on Southern Culture.** Ithaca, NY: Firebrand
       Books, 1985. 237 pp.
Region, family, personality and self examined by an
articulate Southern lesbian.

344.   SHACHAR, SANDRA A., and LUCIA A. GILBERT. "Working
       Lesbians: Role Conflicts and Coping Strategies,"
       Psychology of Women Quarterly, 7 (1983), 244-56.
The most frequently reported interrole conflicts among 70
Texas women studied were bewteen the work and lover roles,
and the most frequent interrole conflicts involved the
work and daughter roles.

345.   SIMON, WILLIAM, and JOHN H. GAGNON. "Femininity in
       the Lesbian Community," **Social Problems**, 15 (1967),
       212-21.
Contends that lesbians tend to conform to rather than
deviate from the female gender role. Within relationships
lesbian sexuality is typically feminine, resulting in
the stability of couple bonds. See also their: "The
Lesbians: A Preliminary Overview," in: Gagnon and Simon
(eds.), **Sexual Deviance** (New York: Harper and Row, 1967),
pp. 247-82.

346.   SIMPSON, RUTH. **From the Closet to the Courts: The
       Lesbian Transition.** New York: Penguin, 1977. 180
       pp.
New York lesbian activist discusses oppression of homosexuals by the church, psychiatric profession, police, and
media--as well as the women's movement and common myths
about lesbians.

347.   SOPHIE, JOAN. "A Critical Examination of Stage
       Theories of Lesbian Identity Development," **JH**, 12:2
       (1986), 39-51.

Repeated interviews with 14 women were used to test
existing stage theories and to formulate a new general
theory.

348.   STANLEY, JULIA PENELOPE, and SUSAN J. WOLFE
        (eds.). **The Coming Out Stories.** Watertown, MA:
        Persephone Press, 1980. 252 pp.
Forty-two personal narratives emphasizing diversity and
pride. See also M. Cruikshank (ed.), above.

349.   STEARN, JESS. **The Grapevine.** New York: Mcfadden-
        Bartell, 1965. 320 pp.
Journalistic expose, typical for the period, discussing
types of lesbians, their private and social lives, and
organizations.

350.   VETERE, VICTORIA A. "The Role of Friendship in the
        Development and Maintenance of Lesbian Love
        Relationships," **JH,** 8 (1982), 51-65.
Finds that friendship was a key factor in the formation of
women's first same-sex relationship, and that it remains a
prime developmental and maintenance factor in current relationships. See also: Jean Weber,"Lesbian Networks,"
Christopher Street, 3:9 (April 1979), 51-54.

351.   VIDA, GINNA (ed.). **Our Right to Love: A Lesbian
        Resource Book.** Englewood Cliffs, NJ: Prentice-
        Hall, 1978. 318 pp.
A well-coordinated collective work dealing with many
aspects of lesbian life and with the lesbian feminist
movement. Bibliography by Carol D. Lightner (pp. 284-88).

352.   WILSON, M. LEE. "Female Homosexual's Need for
        Dominance and Endurance," **Psychological Reports,** 55
        (1984), 79-82.
The lack of a unique pattern for lesbians supports the
contention that homosexuals can have many personalities
within normal limits.

353.   WOLFF, CHARLOTTE. **Love between Women.** New
        York: St. Martin's Press, 1971. 230 pp.
Psychoanalytic approach by a London-based therapist.
Sympathetic in intent, it nonetheless presents a model of
lesbian existence as one marred by conflict and impair-
ment.

354.   WOLF, DEBORAH GOLEMAN. **The Lesbian Community.**
        Berkeley: University of California Press, 1979.
        196 pp.
An ethnography of a lesbian feminist community based on
field work in San Francisco. Finds that the impact of
women's liberation has profoundly altered lesbian culture,
creating a community centering on collective principles
and autonomous institutions.

355.   WYSOR, BETTIE. **The Lesbian Myth.** New York: Random

House, 1974. 438 pp.
Seeks to expose misconceptions found in religion, science,
psychiatry, and literature--and offers discussions by
lesbians on motherhood, lifestyles, sexuality, and activism.

B. LESBIAN-FEMINIST THEORY

The rise of the contemporary feminist movement produced a
considerable interest in theory, some of it informed by
Marxist or other leftist concerns. In some instances,
especially during the radical period of the early 1970s it
was suggested that the only true feminist is a lesbian--
hence the phenomenon of the "political lesbian," that is
one who adopts this position essentially out of political
conviction rather than affectional preference.

356. ALLEN, HILARY. "Political Lesbianism and Femin-
      ism--Space for a Sexual Politics?" **M/F** (London), 7
      (1982), 15-34.
Examines difficulties inherent in political lesbianism and
the consequences for feminist politics of sexuality.

357. BARRETT, MICHELE. **Women's Oppression Today:**
      Problems in Marxist Feminist Analysis. New
      York: Schocken, 1980. 269 pp.
Criticizes the semantic unclarity of three key terms:
patriarchy, ideology, and reproduction. See index for
"homosexuality" and "lesbianism."

358. BEAUVOIR, SIMONE DE. **The Second Sex.** Translated by
      H. M. Parshley. New York: Modern Library, 1968.
      732 pp.
A much admired and influential work, first published in
France in 1949 and prophetic of the "second wave" of
feminism, by an existentialist thinker and novelist. See
Chapter 15, "The Lesbian" (pp. 404-24).

359. CARTLEDGE, SUE, and JOANNA RYAN (eds.). **Sex and**
      Love: New Thoughts and Contradictions. London:
      Women's Press, 1983. 237 pp.
Fourteen original essays reflecting "the diversity of
women's experience--both within the categorizations
'lesbian' and 'heterosexual,' and across the whole
continuum--and the plurality of options this neces-
sitates."

360. CHODOROW, NANCY. "Feminism and Difference: Gender,
      Relation, and Difference in Psychoanalytic Perspec-
      tive," **Socialist Review**, 46 (1979), 51-69.
Examines problems with the project of degendering society
in order to eliminate male dominance.

361. COWARD, ROSALIND. **Patriarchal Precedents: Sexual-
      ity and Social Relations.** Boston: Routledge and
      Kegan Paul, 1983. 326 pp.
Critical examination of the history of the concept of
patriarchy in Marxist, psychoanalytic, and anthropological
theory. Contends that this multiple legacy, stemming
mainly from the 19th and early 20th centuries, has
contributed to our present misunderstanding of the
family, sexual relations, and sexual characteristics.

362. DALY, MARY. **Gyn/ecology: The Metaethics of Radical
      Feminism.** Boston: Beacon Press, 1978. 485 pp.
A theologian turned radical feminist theorist has created
a compendium of religio-historical speculation, together
with neologism-laden visions for a post-patriarchal
future. Daly defines the concept lesbian broadly, as
"woman-identified woman." See also her: **Pure Lust, Ele-
mental Feminist Philosophy** (Boston: Beacon, 1984; 471
pp.).

363. DEFRIES, ZIRA. "Political Lesbianism and Sexual
      Politics," **Journal of the American Academy of
      Psychoanalysis,** 6 (1978), 71-78.
Found that some women who had sought security in lesbianism experienced disenchantment as they discovered that the
interpersonal dynamics of female-female and male-female
relationships were similar.

364. DEMING, BARBARA. **We Are All Part of One Another: A
      Barbara Deming Reader.** Edited by Jane Meyerding,
      with a Forward by Barbara Smith. Philadelphia: New
      Society Publishers, 1984. 320 pp.
Representative collection spanning her work (1959-81) as
an activist for civil rights, feminism, and lesbianism.
See also her: **Remembering Who We Are** (Tallahassee: Naiad
Press, 1981; 240 pp.).

365. DONOVAN, JOSEPHINE. **Feminist Theory: The Intellec-
      tual Traditions of American Feminism.** New York:
      Frederick Ungar, 1985. 237 pp.
An expository synthesis, mapping the following traditions: enlightenment liberal feminism, cultural feminism,
Marxism, psychoanalysis, existential, radical feminism,
and the "new feminist moral vision." With considerable
attention to lesbian theory, this useful guide offers
numerous quotations and references.

366. EICHLER, MARGRIT. **The Double Standard: A Feminist
      Critique of the Social Sciences.** New York: St.
      Martin's Press, 1980. 151 pp.
In this broad-gauged critique, see esp. pp. 86, 130-31.

367. EVANS, SARAH. **Personal Politics: The Roots of
      Women's Liberation in the Civil Rights Movement and
      the New Left.** New York: Knopf, 1979. 274 pp.
Historical reconstruction which highlights some of the

contradictions prevalent during the 1960s. See "Lesbianism" (pp. 225-31).

368.   FADERMAN, LILLIAN. "The 'New Gay' Lesbians," JH,
        10:3-4 (1984), 85-95.
Presents the developmental process of women who have come
to lesbianism through the radical feminist movement of
the past fifteen years.

369.   FRIEDAN, BETTY. The Feminine Mystique. New
        York: Norton, 1963. 410 pp.
Catalytic statement for "second wave" feminism in North
America, helping to precipitate a general reexamination of
sex and gender roles, and thereby influencing the gay and
lesbian movement. In the text, however, Friedan claimed
that "the shallow unreality, immaturity, promiscuity, and
lack of lasting human satisfaction that characterize the
homosexual's sex life usually characterize all his life
and interests."

370.   Love Your Enemy? The Debate Between Heterosexual
        Feminism and Political Lesbianism. London: Only-
        women, 1981. 68 pp.
Theoretical letters and articles by British women.

371.   MCALLISTER, PAM (ed.). Reweaving the Web of Life:
        Feminism and Nonviolence. Philadelphia: New
        Society, 1982. 440 pp.
This feminist-pacifist anthology includes an interview
with Barbara Deming by Mab Segrest and an essay on Natalie
Barney by Karla Jay.

372.   MASSEY, MARILYN CHAPIN. Feminine Soul: The Fate of
        an Ideal. Boston: Beacon Press, 1985. 219 pp.
Reconstructs a Central European concept as embodied in
Romantic works of imagination by Johann Heinrich Pestaloz-
zi, Novalis, and Friedrich Froebel. The conclusion
points to parallels with such contemporary thinkers as
Mary Daly and Adrienne Rich.

373.   MYRON, NANCY, and CHARLOTTE BUNCH. Lesbianism and
        the Women's Movement. Baltimore: Diana Press,
        1975. 120 pp.
Collection of essays reprinted from The Furies discussing
aspects of lesbian-feminist politics: heterosexual
privilege, bisexuality, heterosexism, and lesbian separatism.

374.   PRESTON, JOHN. "Goodbye, Sally Gearhart: Gay Men
        and Feminists Have Reached a Fork in the Road,"
        Christopher Street, no. 58 (November 1981), 17-26.
Holds that the activities of antipornography women mandate
a reassessment of the relationship between gay men and
feminists, including lesbians. See also: Brian Mossop,
"Gay Men's Feminist Mistake," Body Politic, no. 67
(October 1980), 32.

375.   SNITOW, ANN, et al. (eds.). **The Politics of Sexual-
        ity.** New York: Monthly Review Press, 1983. 489 pp.
Collection of chiefly sex-positive papers and statements,
all by women scholars, except for two (by Allen Berube
and John D'Emilio).

376.   VANCE, CAROLE S. (ed.). **Pleasure and Danger: Ex-
        ploring Female Sexuality.** Boston: Routledge and
        Kegan Paul, 1984. 462 pp.
Papers from the controversial 1982 Barnard College conference. They are generally supportive of an exploratory,
libertarian approach and opposed to antipornographic
rigorism.

                    C. WOMEN'S STUDIES REFERENCE

With the acceptance of women's studies in many universities in North America and abroad, there has been an almost
explosive growth in scholarship. To survey the field
adequately would require a work several times the size of
the present one. The following citations will enable one
to find other references.

377.   DAVIS, NANETTE J., and JONE M. KEITH. **Women and
        Deviance: Issues in Social Conflict and Change: An
        Annotated Bibliography.** New York: Garland, 1984.
        236 pp.
Describes some 500 items (articles and books), in such
areas as criminal behavior, substance abuse, lesbianism,
and mental illness.

378.   EVANS, MARY, and DAVID MORGAN. **Work on Women: A
        Guide to the Literature.** New York: Methuen, 1980.
        83 pp.
Unannotated bibliography divided into nine subject-
specific chapters.

379.   GILBERT, V. F., and D. S. TATLA. **Women's
        Studies: A Bibliography of Dissertations 1870-1982.**
        Oxford: Basil Blackwell, 1986. 512 pp.
Lists over 12,000 unpublished dissertations completed in
Britain and North America in a range of disciplines.

380.   HABER, BARBARA. **Women in America: A Guide to
        Books.** Second ed. Urbana: University of Illinois
        Press, 1981. 262 pp.
Selected, annotated list of books arranged by subject
and covering the period 1963-79.

381.   HINDING, ANDREA (ed.). **Women's History Sources: A
        Guide to Archives and Manuscript Collections in the
        United States.** New York: R. R. Bowker, 1979. 2

vols.
Very comprehensive, but inadequately indexed for lesbianism. Permits access to much otherwise unretrievable
material.

382. JACOBS, SUE ELLEN. **Women in Perspective: A Guide
      for Cross-Cultural Studies.** Urbana: University of
      Illinois Press, 1974. 299 pp.
An anthropologist provides help in escaping Western
parochialism.

383. KRICHMAR, ALBERT. **The Women's Movement in the
      Seventies: An International English-Language
      Bibliography.** Metuchen, NJ: Scarecrow, 1977. 875
      pp.
Presents 8,637 citations, with one-line annotations.
Complements the author's **The Women's Rights Movement in
the United States, 1848-1970: A Bibliography and
Sourcebook** (Metuchen, NJ: Scarecrow, 1972; 436 pp.).

384. OAKES, ELIZABETH H., and KATHLEEN E. SHELDON. **Guide
      to Social Science Resources in Women's Studies.**
      Santa Barbara: ABC-Clio, 1978. 162 pp.
Selective, well-annotated bibliography aimed primarily at
"professors of introductory interdisciplinary women's
studies" and other teachers. Core lists in anthropology,
economics, history, psychology, sociology, and contemporary feminist thought, stressing contemporary book-
length contributions. Well indexed.

385. REINHARZ, SHULAMIT, et al. "Methodological Issues
      in Feminist Research: A Bibliography of Literature
      in Women's Studies, Sociology and Psychology,"
      Women's Studies International Forum, 6 (1983),
      437-54.
Presents material on such issues as institutional bases,
sex biases, feminist critiques, and cognitive style
differences between men and women.

386. SAHLI, NANCY. **Women and Sexuality in America: A
      Bibliography.** Boston: G. K. Hall, 1984. 404 pp.
Annotated, with material from the late 19th century on,
which is of value in tracing historical antecedents of
present positions. See "Lesbians" (pp. 281-303).

387. SEARING, SUSAN E. **Introduction to Library Research
      in Women's Studies.** Boulder, CO: Westview Press,
      1985. 257 pp.
"User friendly" guide to practical aspects of research,
offering selected annotated lists by subject. See
esp. pp. 123-24, 184, 218-19.

389. STINEMAN, ESTHER. **Women's Studies: A Recommended
      Core Bibliography.** Littleton, CO: Libraries
      Unlimited, 1979. 672 pp.
Selected list of 1,763 books and periodicals, grouped in

twenty-one subject areas, with thoughtful, detailed
annotations.

390.   TERRIS, VIRGINIA R. **Women in America: A Guide to
        Information Sources.** Detroit: Gale, 1980. 520 pp.
Ambitious research guide and bibliography, with author,
title, and subject indexes.

391.   WARREN, MARY. **The Nature of Women: An Encyclopedia
        and Guide to the Literature.** Inverness, CA: Edge-
        press, 1980. 701 pp.
This massive volume offers a collection of short essays on
topics and authors, arranged alphabetically. Each essay
presents first an objective summary, followed by the
author's judgments. Strong on philosophy and theory.

392.   WILLIAMSON, JANE. **New Feminist Scholarship: A
        Guide to Bibliographies.** Old Westbury, NY: Feminist
        Press, 1979. 139 pp.
Lists nearly 400 bibliographies under 30 subject headings: about half the items are annotated. See also: Patricia K. Ballou, **Women: A Bibliography of Bibliographies**
(Boston: G. K. Hall, 1980; 155 pp.--annotates material
from 1970 through 1979); and Maureen Ritchie, **Women's
Studies: A Checklist of Bibliographies** (London: Mansell,
1980; 107 pp.--unannotated list of about 500 items).

            D. COMPARISONS OF LESBIANS AND GAY MEN

The considerable differences between lesbian and male-
homosexual behavior have been relatively little discussed. Sometimes they are taken for granted as reflecting more general differences between men and women. Apart
from the fact that these differences are as yet poorly
understood, it cannot be excluded that just as male and
female homosexuals differ from their heterosexual counterparts, they will differ from each other in ways that are
not predictable from heterosexual-based studies of
male-female differences. Others seek to minimize
lesbian-gay male differences because of an allegiance to
a concept of human androgyny, which stresses the mallea-
bility of all gender conditioning. Finally, there are
those who hold that the political necessity of an alliance
between lesbians and gay men makes discussion of differences inexpedient.

393.   DE MONTEFLORES, CARMEN, and STEPHEN J. SCHULTZ.
        "Coming Out: Similarities and Differences for
        Lesbians and Gay Men," **Journal of Social Issues,** 34
        (1978), 59-72.
Differences in the coming-out experiences of men and
women are related to conformity to a violation of

sex-role expectations, as well as to political and legal issues.

394.   "DOB Questionnaire Reveals Some Comparisons between
        Male and Female Homosexuals," **Ladder,** 4:12 (1960),
        4-25.
Gay men did not show as great an income superiority as
expected, and they had experienced more frequent conflicts
with the law. Men had more frequent and earlier homosexual experiences, but fewer of them had had heterosexual
experiences.

395.   HENDERSON, ANN F. "Homosexuality in the College
        Years: Developmental Differences between Men and
        Women," **Journal of American College Health,** 32
        (1984), 216-19.
Contends that sexual orientation is established later for
women than for men, and is subjected to different psychological stresses.

396.   KARR, M. A. "Sally Gearhart: Wandering--and
        Wondering--on Future Ground," **Advocate,** no. 286
        (February 26, 1980), pp. 21-22.
Gearhart, a San Francisco lesbian activist and writer,
holds that women have a "unique capacity for collective
psychic power," which men lack. For this and other
reasons, an alliance between lesbians and gay men is
problematic.

397.   NYBERG, KENNETH L. "Sexual Aspirations and Sexual
        Behaviors among Homosexually Behaving Males and
        Females: The Impact of the Gay Community," **JH,** 2
        (1976), 29-38.
Interprets questionnaire results as indicating that differences between lesbians and gay men reflect not only
gender and general cultural differences determined by the
larger society, but also the differing reception of specific movements for social change among them.

398.   SAGHIR, MARCEL T., and ELI ROBINS. "Male and Fe-
        male Homosexuality: Natural History," **Comprehen-
        sive Psychiatry,** 12 (1971), 501-10.
Finds that the homosexual male begins his sexual involvement in early adolescence while the lesbian begins several
years later.

399.   SCHÄFER, SIEGRID. "Sociosexual Behavior in Male and
        Female Homosexuals: A Study in Sex Differences,"
        Archives of Sexual Behavior, 6 (1977), 355-64.
Interpretation of West German data indicates that being a
woman tends to influence the sociosexual behavior of lesbians more than being homosexual.

400.   WINCZE, JOHN P., and C. BRANDON QUAILS. "A Compar-
        ison of Structural Patterns of Sexual Arousal in
        Male and Female Homosexuals," **Archives of Sexual**

Behavior, 13 (1984), 361-70.
In a study of responses to films, it was found--not
surprisingly--that lesbians showed little response to
male erotic films and gay men were correspondingly
indifferent to lesbian erotic films.

III. HISTORY AND AREA STUDIES

A. GENERAL

Inasmuch as homosexual behavior is practiced by individuals, the biographical method has often proved appealing--
hence the "hall of fame" approach singling out homosexual
notables, who are often presented as moral exemplars
set apart from their historical context. (See "Biographies: Collective," III.T). A contrasting historiographic
trend seeks to determine context, and then to situate the
individuals within it. This approach, often associated
with the Social Construction research program, has its own
problems stemming from its tendency to reduce individuals
to the status of mere puppets of their social situation
and to obscure continuities linking experience from one
era to another. There is also a trend to broaden the
scope of inquiry to comprise **homosociality,** including
same-sex friendship, whether or not this be expressed
genitally (see "Friendship," XIV.K). Another area of
uncertainty is the parallelism that has often been
assumed--rather than demonstrated--between lesbian and
gay male experience. Historically, many cultures have not
regarded the two as homologous. This section cites
short methodological studies as well as larger works
attempting synthesis.

401. AGUIAR, ASDRÚBAL ANTÓNIO D'. "Evolução da Pederas-
      tia e do Lesbismo na Europa," **Arquivo da Univer-
      sidade do Lisboa,** 11 (1926), 336-620.
Survey of the history of male homosexuality and lesbianism
in Europe from classical antiquity to the present, citing
many texts. While much is understandably culled from
other sources, this major study is useful for Spain and
Portugal, and for statutory law (including that pertaining
to lesbianism).

402. ARIÈS, PHILIPPE, and ANDRÉ BÉJIN (eds.). **Western
      Sexuality: Practice and Precept in Past and
      Present.** Oxford: Basil Blackwell, 1985. 220 pp.
Collection of papers treating the history of sexuality
from ancient Greece onwards, several directly relevant.
Translated from **Communications** [Paris], no. 35 (1982).

403. BOSWELL, JOHN. "Revolutions, Universals and Sexual
      Categories," **Salmagundi,** no. 58-59 (1982-83), 89-
      113.
Methodological reflections which seek to clarify the
problem of continuity in sexual history by proposing a
threefold typology. Boswell proposes to apply the medieval conflict between nominalism and essentialism as a

71

model for understanding current controversies.

404. BULLOUGH, VERN. **Sex, Society and History.** New
      York: Science Society Publications, 1976. 186 pp.
Reprints fourteen scholarly papers ranging from ancient
Mesopotamia through the middle ages to nineteenth-
century America.

405. BULLOUGH, VERN. **Sexual Variance in Society and
      History.** New York: John Wiley, 1976. 715 pp.
An ambitious work of synthesis, correlating homosexuality
with other modes of sexual behavior, and showing the
overarching control of culture, including religion. The
contrast between sex-positive and sex-negative societies
is overly schematic. The notes offer much documentation.
See also his introductory work: **Homosexuality, A History:
From Ancient Greece to Gay Liberation** (New York: New
American Library, 1979; 196 pp.).

406. BULLOUGH, VERN, and BONNIE BULLOUGH. **Sin, Sickness
      and Sanity: A History of Sexual Attitudes.** New
      York: New American Library, 1977. 276 pp. (Merid-
      ian Books)
Stimulating but rapid survey of a vast domain; see pp.
3-4, pp. 3-4, 52-53, 84-85, 154-55, 201-10.

407. CHAMBERLAIN, J. EDWARD, and SANDER L. GILMAN
      (ed.). **Degeneration: The Dark Side of Progress.**
      New York: Columbia University Press, 1985. 303 pp.
Papers of varying quality on the permutations of the
concept in several fields, mainly in Europe in the 19th
and 20th centuries. Considerable indirect interest. For
an exhaustive study of a related problem, see: Alexander
Demandt, **Der Fall Roms: Die Auflösung des Römischen
Reiches im Urteil der Nachwelt** (Munich: C. H. Beck, 1984;
695 pp.), which lists 210 factors--including homosexual-
ity--which have been implicated in the fall of Rome.

408. CROMPTON, LOUIS. "Gay Genocide from Leviticus to
      Hitler," in: L. Crew (ed.), **The Gay Academic.**
      Palm Springs, CA: Etc., 1978, 67-91.
Surveys the persecution of male homosexuals through the
application of the death penalty, from Biblical times
through the Nazi era.

409. DALL'ORTO, GIOVANNI. "L'evoluzione del concetto
      di 'omosessualità' nei secoli," in: F. Castellano
      (ed.), **Essere omosessuale.** Cuneo: AGA, 1981, 39-
      62.
Outline of changing concepts of homosexual behavior
from the Greeks to the present.

410. DANIEL, MARC (pseud.). "Essai de méthodologie
      pour l'étude des aspects homosexuels de l'his-
      toire." **Arcadie,** no. 131 (November 1964), 497-505;
      no. 132 (December 1964), 559-65.

Criticizes methods of historical analysis applied by US
Movement scholars. A shortened version appeared in: **ONE
Quarterly** (Fall 1960).

411.   DYNES, WAYNE, and WARREN JOHANSSON. "Eros, Myth
       and Stigma: The Historical Semantics of Sexual
       Intolerance," **The Voice [San Francisco],** 3:2
       (January 14, 1981), 8.
Continues in successive issues of the newspaper until 3:10
(May 8, 1981), 34. Examines the historical role of such
concepts as the unnatural, decadence, and sexism.
Largely incorporated in: Dynes, **Homolexis** (New York: Gay
Academic Union, 1985; 177 pp.).

412.   EAUBONNE, FRANÇOISE D'. **Eros minoritaire.** Paris:
       Ballard, 1970. 326 pp.
Literary-historical survey of "minority" sexual behavior.

413.   EGLINTON, J. Z. (pseud.). **Greek Love.** New
       York: Oliver Layton Press, 1964. 504 pp.
The title notwithstanding, this book offers a comprehensive study of sexual and educational relationships
between men and boys with special reference to historical aspects over the centuries (not limited to Greece).
There is considerable emphasis on literary works and legal
sources.

414.   FLANDRIN, JEAN-LOUIS. **Le sexe et l'Occident.**
       Paris: Seuil, 1981. 376 pp.
Collection of essays by a French historian who has become
influential through his pioneering use of quantitative and
and analytical methods. Of general, rather than specifically homosexual interest.

415.   FOUCAULT, MICHEL. **The History of Sexuality: Vol.
       I: An Introduction.** Translated from French by
       R. Hurley. New York: Pantheon, 1978. 170 pp.
Stimulating, but sometimes opaque essay on the conceptual
foundations of modern sexuality, which has had a great
influence on the Social Construction school of homosexual
history. This programmatic text--published in Paris in
1976 as **La volonté de savoir**--was to be followed by five
more volumes offering supporting detail for recent centuries. Although this project was not realized, two
volumes dealing instead with classical antiquity did
appear just before his death in 1984.

416.   FRIELE, KAREN-CHRISTINE. **De vorsvant bare ...
       Fragmente av homofiles historie.** Oslo: Gyldendal
       Norsk Forlag, 1985. 200 pp.
A noted Norwegian lesbian activist and scholar presents
aspects of homosexual history from Old Testament times
to ca. 1950.

417.   GREENBERG, DAVID, and MARCIA BYSTRYN. "Capitalism,
       Bureaucracy, and Male Homosexuality," **Contemporary**

Crises, 8 (1984), 33-56.
Argues that the late 19th- and 20th-century stigmatization
of homosexual behavior is a consequence of competitive
capitalism and bureaucratic organization.

418.   HARDMAN, PAUL D. **Homoaffectionalism: The Civiliz-
       ing Factor.** Los Angeles: One Institute, 1985.
Reviews history from the Hittites through the Middle Ages
in a new theoretical perspective.

418A. HOFFMAN, RICHARD J. "Clio, Fallacies, and Homo-
       sexuality," **JH,** 10:3/4 (Winter 1984), 45-52.
Signals such methodological faults as the assertion of
assumptions as proven, monothematism, semantic distortion, ethnocentrism, anachronism, historicism, the
pathetic fallacy, and tunnel history.

419.   KEPNER, JIM. **Becoming a People ... A 4,000 Year
       Gay and Lesbian Chronology.** Los Angeles: National
       Gay Archives, 1983. 79 pp.
Persons and events from history marshalled chronologic-
ally, with introductory reflections on method. "Prepub-
lication Edition" containing some imperfections.

420.   Lesbian History Issue. **Frontiers: A Journal of
       Women's Studies,** 4:3 (Fall 1979). 88pp.
Collection of essays, many containing references, chiefly
on recent history. Note especially: Judith Schwartz,
"Questionnaire on Issues in Lesbian History," pp. 1-12.

421.   LICATA, SALVATORE, and ROBERT J. PETERSEN (eds.).
       Historical Perspectives on Homosexuality. New
       York: Stein and Day/Haworth Press, 1981. 224 pp.
Book publication of a special number of **JH** (6:1/2;
Fall-Winter 1980-81) containing twelve papers of excep-
tional quality (high Middle Ages to the 20th century).

422.   NOONAN, JOHN T. **Contraception: A History of Its
       Treatment by the Catholic Theologians and Canon-
       ists.** Cambridge, MA: The Belknap Press, 1966. 561
       pp.
Study of remarkable scope with considerable indirect
application to homosexuality.

423.   PADGUG, ROBERT. "Bibliography," **Committee on
       Lesbian and Gay History Newsletter** (Summer 1983),
       12-16.
Classified list of 119 items, many annotated. Contin-
ued in **Newsletter,** no. 8 (Summer 1984) [published in **IGLA
Bulletin,** no. 2], 38-42 (142 items).

424.   PADGUG, ROBERT. "Sexual Matters: On Conceptualiz-
       ing Sexuality in History," **Radical History Review,**
       20 (1979), 3-23.
A gay historian attempts to fuse the Social Construction approach to the history of the development of sex-

ual behavior with Marxist immanentism. See also Bert
Hansen, "Historical Construction of Homosexuality." ibid.,
66-73.

425. PARKER, WILLIAM. "Homosexuality in History: An
Annotated Bibliography," **JH**, 6:1/2 (Fall-Winter
1980-81), 191-210.
Classified selection of 123 items, all in the English
language.

426. SPRAGUE, GREGORY A. "Male Homosexuality in Western
Culture: The Dilemma of Identity and Subculture in
Historical Research." **JH**, 10:3/4 (Winter 1984),
29-43.
Reviews recent scholarship on the emergence of homosexual
identities and subcultures in Western societies.

427. STONE, LAWRENCE. "Sex in the West." **New Republic**
(July 8, 1985), 25-37.
A noted historian's thoughtful synthesis for the lay
reader of publications in the history of sexuality over
the last decade.

428. TAYLOR, GORDON RATTRAY. **Sex in History.** New
York: Vanguard, 1954. 336 pp.
Offers a dualistic scheme of history as a succession of
"matrist" and "patrist" eras. Only in the former, in
which women had high status, did homosexuality come to
flourish openly. Willful.

429. USSEL, JOSEF MARIA WILLEM VAN. **Sexualunterdrück-
ung.** Hamburg: Rowohlt, 1970. 248 pp.
A Belgian scholar interprets the sexual history of Europe
as a pattern of repression--a view that is probably
overstated. This work, translated from a Dutch original
(1968), derives from a thesis emphasizing the 18th century, which remains the most useful aspect of the book in
its several published versions.

B. ANCIENT NEAR EAST AND EGYPT

The civilizations of the ancient Near East, here embracing
an arc from Egypt to Iran, are difficult for the nonspec-
ialist to penetrate. Because of the hermetic complexities
of the written and archaeological evidence, progress in
our knowledge is of necessity in the hands of trained
specialists. In evaluating the citations listed below it
is well to bear in mind that some are relatively specialized
and technical, while others are addressed to the lay
reader. In addition to their intrinsic importance, the
civilizations of the ancient Near East are significant
as a foundation for ancient Greece (see III.C) and a major
influence on the Bible (see VII.B).

430. ALDRED, CYRIL. **Akhenaten, Pharaoh of Egypt: a New
      Study.** New York: McGraw-Hill, 1968. 272 pp.
See Chapter 8, "The Pathology of Akhenaten" (pp.
133-39), advancing a dubious medical explanation for the heretical
ruler's androgynous appearance, which has often been
remarked.

431. BIGGS, ROBERT D. **ŠA.ZI.GA: Ancient Mesopotamian
      Potency Incantations in Texts from Cuneiform
      Sources.** Locust Valley, NY: J. J. Augustin,
      1967. 86 pp.
Texts shedding light on the attitudes toward sexuality in
general, and about homosexuality, including anal intercourse. See also his: "Medicine in Ancient Mesopotamia,"
History of Science, 8 (1969), 94-105.

432. BOTTÉRO, JEAN, and H. PETSCHOW. "Homosexualität,"
      Reallexikon der Assyriologie, 4 [1975], 459-68.
Well-documented survey in French of ancient Mesopotamian
written and artistic evidence.

433. BULLOUGH, VERN. "Attitudes toward Deviant Sex in
      Ancient Mesopotamia," **Journal of Sex Research,** 7:3
      (1971), 184-203.
Argues that there were fewer prohibitions against sex in
these early societies than in our own time.

434. BULLOUGH, VERN. "Homosexuality as Submissive
      Behavior," **Journal of Sex Research,** 9:4 (1973),
      283-88.
Argues, chiefly from mythological evidence, that the
Egyptians used anal intercourse to symbolize dominance.
For a broader perspective on ancient Egypt, see the
author's **Sexual Variance in Society and History** (New
York: Wiley, 1976), 58-73.

435. DEAKIN, TERENCE J. "Evidence for Homosexuality in
      Ancient Egypt," **International Journal of Greek
      Love,** 1:1 (1966), 31-38.
A useful survey, critical and well referenced.

436. DORNSEIFF, FRANZ. "Ägyptische Liebeslieder,
      Hoheslied, Sappho, Theokrit," **Zeitschrift der
      Deutschen morgenländischen Gesellschaft,** 90 (1931),
      588-601.
Detects an Egyptian model for Sappho's poetry.

437. DUCHESNE-GUILLEMIN, JACQUES. **Symbols and Values in
      Zoroastrianism: Their Survival and Renewal.** New
      York: Harper and Row, 1966. 167 pp.
In Iran the procreative ethic of Zoroastrianism produced
sometimes virulent condemnations of homosexuality, though
Herodotus (1:135) mentions it as flourishing there (p. 149
ff.).

438. GOEDICKE, HANS. "Unrecognized Sportings," **Journal**

of the **American Research Center in Egypt**, 6 (1967),
97-102.
Maxim 32 of the Instructions to Ptahhotep (Papyrus Prisse
14.4-6) is interpreted (uncertainly) as an admonition to
refrain from pederastic assault after meeting objections
to advances.

439.   GRIFFITHS, JOHN GWYN. **The Conflict of Horus and
       Seth.** Chicago: Argonaut, 1969. 182 pp.
Interpretation of key Egyptian mythological texts with
salient homoerotic features. See also his: **The Origins
of Osiris and His Cult** (Leiden: E. J. Brill, 1980; 287
pp.), p. 15.

440.   HELD, GEORGE F. "Parallels between The Gilgamesh
       Epic and Plato's Symposium," **Journal of Near
       Eastern Studies**, 42 (1983), 133-41.
Close reading of the language of Gilgamesh's dream reveals
its homoerotic character. Translations of the epic tend
to be bowdlerized in this and other regards. Note also
an earlier article by Thorkild Jacobsen, "How Did Gilgameš
Oppress Uruk?" **Acta Orientalia**, 8 (1930), 70 ff.; as well
as Giuseppe Furlani, "L'epopea di Gilgameš come inno
all'amicizia," **Belfagor**, 1 (1946, 577-89. See also: A.
D. Kilmer; and B. Thorbjornsrud, below.

441.   HILLERS, DELBERT R. "The Bow of Aqhat: The Meaning
       of a Mythological Theme," in: Harry A. Hoffner, Jr.
       (ed.). **Orient and Occident.** Kevelaer: Verlag
       Butzon und Bercker, 1973, pp. 70-80.
Transvestism, eunuchism, and male cult prostitution in
the ancient Near East.

442.   HOFFMAN, RICHARD J. "Vices, Gods, and Virtues:
       Cosmology as a Mediating Factor in Attitudes toward
       Male Homosexuality," **JH**, 9:2/3 (1983-84), 27-44.
Using historical and anthropological evidence, argues a
contrast between monotheism and polytheism with regard
to male homosexuality. Speculative.

443.   HOFFNER, HARRY A., JR. "Incest, Sodomy and
       Bestiality in the Ancient Near East," in: Hoffner
       (ed.), **Orient and Occident.** Kevalaer: Verlag
       Butzon und Bercker, 1973, pp. 81-90.
Comparative study of texts from different regions of the
ancient Near East.

444.   KILMER, ANNE DRAFFKORN. "A Note on an Overlooked
       Word Play in the Akkadian Gilgamesh," in: G. Van
       Driel et al. (eds.), **Zikir Šumim: Assyriological
       Studies Presented to F. R. Kraus on the Occasion of
       His Seventieth Birthday.** Leiden: E. J. Brill,
       1982, pp. 128-32.
On homosexual puns in the Gilgamesh epic.

445.   LAMBERT, W. G. "Morals in Ancient Mesopotamia," **Ex**

oriente lux, 15 (1957-58), 184-96.
Reveals some striking contrasts with our own attitudes.

446.   LECLANT, JEAN. "Les textes de la Pyramide de Pépi
        I (Saqqara)," **Académie des Inscriptions et Belles
        Lettres, Comptes-Rendus**, 1977, pp. 269-290.
For an Old Kingdom text from Saqqara on the relation
between Osiris and Seth, see pp. 278-79.

447.   MANNICHE, LISE. "Some Aspects of Ancient Egyptian
        Sexual Life," **Acta Orientalia**, 38 (1977), 11-23.
See pp. 14-15 for brief comments on male homosexuality and
lesbianism.

448.   MONTET, PIERRE. "Le fruit défendu," **Kémi: Revue de
        Philologie et d'Archéologie Egyptiennes et Coptes**,
        11 (1950), 85-116.
Discusses problems of translating early Egyptian texts
that seem to forbid homosexuality.

449.   MORAN, W. L. "New Evidence from Mari on the
        History of Prophecy," **Biblica**, 50 (1969), 15-56.
Possible citations from Mesopotamian palace correspondence
to homosexual favorites of the king, and to homosexual
cult officials.

450.   MORET, ALEXANDRE. **Du caractère religieux de la
        royauté pharaonique**. Paris: Ernest Leroux, 1902.
        (Annales du Musée Guimet, Bibliothèque d'Etudes,
        15).
For symbolic divine homosexual embraces in the coronation
rites of Ramses II and II, see pp. 45-48, 100-01, 106-08.
See also his: **Le rituel du culte divin journalier en
Egypte**. (Paris: Ernest Leroux, 1902; Annales du Musée
Guimet, Bibliothèque d'Etudes, 14), pp. 22-24, 99-101.

451.   NIBLEY, HUGH. **The Message of the Joseph Smith
        Papyri: An Egyptian Endowment**. Salt Lake City:
        Deseret, 1976. 305 pp.
For description of the ritual coronation embraces of
the Egyptian king, see pp. 241-66.

452.   POSENER, GEORGES. "Le conte de Neferkaré et du
        général Sisiné," **Revue d'Egyptologie**, 11 (1957),
        119-37.
Text, translation and commentary and of Middle Kingdom
Egyptian story of King Pepy II's (2355-2261 B.C.) amorous trysts with his general. See also his: "Sur
l'emploi euphématique de hftj(w) 'ennemi(s),'" **Zeitschrift für ägyptische Sprache**, 96 (1969), 30-35.

453.   PRITCHARD, JAMES B. (ed.). **Ancient Near Eastern
        Texts Relating to the Old Testament**. Third ed.
        Princeton: Princeton University Press, 1969. 710
        pp.
In this standard collection of translations, see pp. 34-35

(Egyptian Protestation of Guiltlessness), p. 181 (Middle
Assyrian Laws), and p. 196 (Hittite Laws: father-son
incest is a capital offense).

454.   REEDER, GREG. "Journey to the Past: Egypt and
        a Gay Tomb?" **Advocate** (May 12, 1983), 25ff.
Finds homosexuality in an Old Kingdom tomb's frescos.
The tomb is published in Ahmed M. Moussa and Hartwig
Altenmuller, **Das Grab des Nianchnum und Chnumhotep.**
(Mainz: Von Zabern, 1977; 180 pp. Archäologische Ver-
öffentlichungen des Deutschen Archäologischen Instituts,
Abteilung Kairo, 21).

455.   RIEFSTAHL, ELIZABETH. "An Enigmatic Faience Fig-
        ure," in: **Miscellanea Wilbouriana** (Brooklyn
        Museum), vol. 1, p. 137ff.
An ithyphallic figurine found in a tomb at Lisht is cautiously interpreted as a catamite for the enjoyment of
the deceased.

456.   THORBJORNSRUD, BERIT. "What Can the Gilgamesh Myth
        Tell Us about Religion and the View of Humanity in
        Mesopotamia?" **Temenos,** 19 (1983), 112-37.
Interprets the relationship of Gilgamesh and Enkidu as a
homosexual friendship that entails the rejection of
Ishtar, the female principle. Much later, the Assyrians
prohibited male homosexuality and abolished the cult
prostitution connected with the shrines of Ishtar.

457.   VELDE, H. TE. **Seth, God of Confusion.** Leiden: E.
        J. Brill, 1967. 183 pp.
This standard work on the somewhat sinister Egyptian God
Seth includes discussion of his homoerotic relation with
Horus.

458.   WESTENDORF, WOLFHART. "Homosexualität," **Lexikon
        der Ägyptologie,** 2 (1977), cols. 1272-74.
Concise summary of current knowledge about ancient Egyptian homosexuality, with references.

                   C. GREECE AND ROME

Interest in Greek and Roman homosexuality as a subject
begins with the Renaissance, as part of the learned
enterprise of humanistic philology, which provided "cover"
for the exploration of pederastic themes. In the 18th
century, neoclassicism sparked a new wave of interest,
as seen in the career of J. J. Winckelmann, who is often
regarded as the first modern art historian. With new
critical methods and the beginnings of field archaeology,
the 19th century revolutionized the study of the ancient
past. Classical philology played an important part in the

formation of the ideas of such homosexual scholars as
J. A. Symonds and K. H. Ulrichs. Since about 1965 there
has been a fresh wave of classical scholarship throwing
light on (homo)sexuality by profiting from the removal of
taboos. See also Ancient Art (VI.B), for the important
subject of vase painting, a medium that also yields social
and historical data. For ancient medicine, see XXIII.D.
The classical sources themselves, which exist in many
editions, are not listed here as such; see the bibliographies in the monographs of K. J. Dover (491), F. Buffière (477), and S. Lilja (536), as well as the Personal
Names Index.

459.   AFRICA, THOMAS. "Homosexuals in Greek History,"
        Journal of Psychohistory, 9:4 (1982), 401-20.
Focusing largely on the relatively neglected Hellenistic
period, the author attempts a biographical approach,
which is marred by anachronistic psychoanalytic assumptions. For a critique, suggesting homophobia on Africa's
part, see Fernando Gonzalez-Reigosa and Angel Velez-Diaz,
ibid., 10:4 (1983), 511-19; followed by Africa's intemper-
ate response, ibid., 11:1 (1983), 129-32.

460.   ARBOIS DE JUBAINVILLE, HENRI D.' La famille cel-
        tique. Paris: Bouillon, 1905. 221 pp.
The appendix (pp. 187-199) treats the question: were the
ancient Celts homosexual?

461.   BABUT, DANIEL. "Les Stoiciens et l'amour," Revue
        des Etudes Grecques, 76 (1963), 55-63.
Refutes Flaceliere's claim that the later Stoic thinkers
condemned homosexual love. See also J. M. Rist, Stoic
Philosophy (Cambridge: Cambridge University Press, 1969),
pp. 56-69.

462.   BAIRD, LORRAYNE Y. "Priapus gallinaceus: The Role
        of the Cock in Fertility and Eroticism in Classical
        Antiquity and the Middle Ages," Studies in Iconog-
        raphy, 7-8 (1981-82), 81-111.
Extensively documented study on the erotic connotations of
the rooster. "In ancient Greece and surrounding areas,
the most common erotic association of the cock ... seems
to have been with homosexual affairs."

463.   BALSDON, J. P. V. D. Romans and Aliens. Chapel
        Hill: University of North Carolina Press, 1979.
        310 pp.
This encyclopedic work helps to situate Roman concepts
of pederasty in the framework of their attitudes toward
foreigners. See pp. 225-27.

464.   BERNAY, JÉRÔME. "Folies romaines: les homosexuels
        dans l'oeuvre de Juvénal," Arcadie, no. 259-60
        (July-August 1975), 356-64.
Characters in the poet's satires. See also his: "La

repression de l'homosexualité dans la Rome antique,"
ibid., no. 250 (October 1974), 443-55.

465.   BETHE, ERICH.   "Die dorische Knabenliebe: ihre
        Ethik und ihre Idee," **Rheinisches Museum**, 62
        (1907), 438-75.
This influential study by a noted philologist offers an
imaginative reconstruction of the dynamics of the relation
between the male lover and his beloved in ancient Greece.
Yet Bethe's attribution of the origins of the Greek institution of pederasty to the Dorian influx has been
weakened by recent criticisms by Sir Kenneth Dover. The
paper was reissued in 1983 in Berlin (Verlag Rosa Winkel)
as an independent brochure (48 pp.), with an introduction
by Wolfram Setz.

466.   BEYER, RUDOLF.   **Fabulae graecae quatenus quave
        aetate puerorum amore commutatae sint.** Weida,
        Thuringia: Thomas und Hubert, 1910. 77 pp.
This published dissertation in Latin is an important
source for Greek myths of affairs between gods and their
beloved boys.

467.   BLOCH, ROBERT.   **De Pseudo-Luciani amoribus: disser-
        tatio inauguralis.** Strasbourg: Truebner, 1907. 49
        pp.
Valuable philological analysis, in Latin, of the essay on
love mistakenly attributed to Lucian.

468.   BOWRA, CECIL MAURICE, SIR.   **Greek Lyric Poetry:
        from Alcman to Simonides.** Second, revised ed.
        Oxford: Clarendon Press, 1961. 444 pp.
Contains chapters on Sappho (pp. 176-240); Ibycus (pp.
241-67); and Anacreon (pp. 268-307, esp. pp. 277-84).

469.   BOWRA, CECIL MAURICE, SIR.   **Pindar.** Oxford: Clar-
        endon Press, 1964. 446 pp.
Standard account in English of the great Theban poet; see
esp. pp. 106-07, 166-70, 274, 362, 386-88.

470.   BRELICH, ANGELO.   **Paides e parthenoi.** Rome: Edi-
        zioni dell'Ateneo, 1969. 500 pp.
Greek rites of initiation, including pederasty, from
a comparative perspective.

471.   BREMMER, JAN.   "An Enigmatic Indo-European Rite:
        Paederasty," **Arethusa**, 13:2 (1980), 279-98.
Controversial cross-cultural analysis of parallels for
Greek initiatory homosexuality.

472.   BRIGHT, DAVID F.   **Haec mihi fingebam: Tibullus and
        His World.** Leiden: Brill, 1978. 275 pp.
Includes discussion of lyrics addressed to the boy
Marathus.

473.   BRISSON, LUC.   "Aspects politiques de la bisexual-

ité: l'histoire de Polycrite." In: M. B. De Boer
and T. A. Eldridge (eds.), **Hommages à Maarten
J. Vermaseren.** Leiden: Brill, 1978, vol. 1,
pp. 80-122.
On a legend found in Phlegon of Tralles and Proclus concerning the birth of an androgynous monster. See also
his: **Le mythe de Tirésias** (Leiden: Brill, 1976; 189 pp.).

474. BROUWER, PETRUS VAN LIMBURG. **Histoire de la
      civilisation morale et religieuse des Grecs.**
      Groningen: W. van Boekeren, 1833-42.
See volume 4 (of part 2), pp. 224-75, for a Dutch classicist's detailed and relatively objective account of
"l'amour des males," remarkable for its time.

475. BRUYN, E. B. DE. **Sex en eros bij Martialis.** Am-
      sterdam: Arbeiderspers, 1979. 225 pp.
Sex and love in the epigrams of Martial.

476. BUCKLER, JOHN. **The Theban Hegemony, 371-362 B.C.**
      Cambridge, MA: Harvard University Press, 1980. 339
      pp.
The period of the triumph of the Theban Band, whose
homosexual character is regrettably scanted by Buckler.

477. BUFFIÈRE, FÉLIX. **Eros adolescent: la péderastie
      dans la Grèce antique.** Paris: Les Belles Lettres,
      1980. 703 pp.
Monumental survey of Greek homosexuality, including its
prolongation into Hellenistic and Roman times, with
numerous textual analyses and translations. Sometimes
uncritical. Note esp. the full index of ancient authors
(pp. 660-71).

478. BURNETT, ANNE PIPPIN. "Desire and Memory (Sappho
      frag. 94).," **Classical Philology,** 74 (1979),
      16-27.
On the poet's poignant lyric of parting. In general, see
Jeffrey Duban, **Ancient and Modern Images of Sappho**
(Lanham, MD: Classical Association of the Atlantic
States/University Press of America, 1983; Classical World
Special Series, 2).

479. CALAME, CLAUDE. **Les choeurs de jeunes filles en
      Grèce archaïque.** Rome: Ateneo & Bizzarii, 1977. 2
      vols.
See vol. 2 esp. for evidence from Alcman's poems on lesbian aspects of girls' initation rites in early Greece.

480. CARTLEDGE, PAUL. "The Politics of Spartan Peder-
      asty," **Proceedings of the Cambridge Philological
      Society,** 207 (1981), 17-36.
Useful, but somewhat inconclusive review of the evidence.

481. CLARKE, W. M. "Achilles and Patroclus in Love,"
      Hermes, 106 (1978), 381-96.

From a review of textual evidence and ancient parallels,
the author concludes that Homer's heroes were indeed in
love. Contrast D. S. Barrett, "The Friendship of Achilles
and Patroclus," **Classical Bulletin,** 57 (1981), 87-93, who
(writing evidently in ignorance of Clarke's arguments) excludes homoeroticism. See also D. S. Sinos, **Achilles,**
Patroklos and the Meaning of 'Philos' (Innsbruck: 1980);
and W. Thomas MacCary, **Childlike Achilles: Ontogeny and**
Phylogeny in the Iliad (New York: Columbia University
Press, 1982).

482. CODY, JANE M. "The **senex amator** in Plautus'
      Casina," Hermes, 104 (1976), 453-76.
Useful study of the Roman playwright's most homosexual
work.

483. COLIN, JEAN. "Juvénal et le mariage mystique de
      Gracchus," **Atti della Accademia delle scienze di**
      Torino, 90:2 (1955-56), 114-216.
Detailed study of a kind of male-male marriage under re-
ligious auspices, citing not only Juvenal but many other
Latin authors.

484. COURTNEY, E. C. **A Commentary on the Satires of**
      Juvenal. London: Athlone Press, 1980. 662 pp.
The most detailed commentary on the Roman poet's text.
See satires 2 and 9; also 5:56-62; 6:33-37; 11:145-58;
and 15: 135-37. See also J. Gerard, **Juvenal et la**
realite contemporaine (Paris, 1956).

485. CROMPTON, LOUIS. "What Do You Say to Someone Who
      Claims that Homosexuality Caused the Fall of Greece
      and Rome?" **Christopher Street** (March 1978), 49-52.
Useful concise demolition of such myths.

486. DANIEL, MARC. **Des dieux et des garçons: étude sur**
      l'homosexualité dans la mythologie grecque. Paris:
      Arcadie, 1968. 38 pp.
Magico-religious elements in Greek pederasty.

487. DELCOURT, MARIE. **Hermaphrodite: Myths and Rites of**
      the Bisexual Figure in Classical Antiquity.
      Translated by Jennifer Nicholson. London: Studio
      Books, 1961. 109 pp.
A standard work on the varied aspects of the hermaphrodite
myth in Greco-Roman times. See also her complementary
work, stressing archaeology and art: **Hermaphroditéa:**
recherches sur l'être double promoteur de la fertilité
dans le monde classique (Brussels: Latomus/Revue d'Etudes
Latines, 1966; 76 pp.).

488. DELEPIERRE, JOSEPH OCTAVE. **Dissertation sur les**
      idées morales des Grecs et sur le danger de lire
      Platon. Rouen: J. Lemonnyer, 1879. 20 pp.
Curious period document introducing the term "philopede"

derived from Greek **philopais.**

489.   DELORME, JEAN, and WOLFGANG SPEYER. "Gymnasium,"
        Reallexikon für Antike und Christentum, 13 (1984),
        cols. 155-76.
Includes a concise account of pederasty in the gymnasia,
and of Christian objections thereto. See also Delorme's
book: **Gymnasion: Etude sur les monuments consacrés à
l'éducation en Grèce** (Paris: E. de Boccard, 1960; 530
pp.).

490.   DEVEREUX, GEORGE. "Greek Pseudo-homosexuality and
        the 'Greek Miracle.'" **Symbolae Osloenses,** 42
        (1967), 69-92.
Paradoxical psychoanalytic study treating Greek pederasty
as both an indispensable element of Greek high culture and
a symptom of immaturity. See also his: "The Nature of
Sappho's Seizure in fr 31 LP as Evidence of Her Inversion," **Classical Quarterly,** N.S., 20 (1970), 17-31; and
"Why Oedipus Killed Laius," **International Journal of Psychoanalysis,** 34 (1953), 132-41.

491.   DOVER, KENNETH J., SIR. **Greek Homosexuality.** Cam-
        bridge, MA: Harvard University Press, 1978. 244
        pp. 106 illustrations.
Penetrating study of literary sources for classical Greece
(largely excluding the Hellenistic and Roman sequels, for
which see esp. Buffiere, above). Beginning with a detailed analysis of Aeschines' "Contra Timarchum," the
analysis broadens to encompass a wide range of topics,
some of which are discussed brilliantly. The treatment
of the iconography of vase painting is less satisfactory
(compare, e.g., H. A. Shapiro, "Courtship Scenes in
Attic Vase Painting, **"American Journal of Archaeology,** 85,
1981, 133-43). For critical reflections on the book, see
John Ungaretti, "De-moralizing Morality: Where Dover's
Greek Homosexuality Leaves Us," JH 8 (1983), 1-17. See
also Dover: "Eros and Nomos," **Bulletin of the Institute
of Classical Studies** (London), 11 (1964), 31-42.

492.   DOVER, KENNETH J., SIR. **Greek Popular Morality in
        the Time of Plato and Aristotle.** Oxford: Basil
        Blackwell, 1975. 330 pp.
An attempt to correct the traditional overintellectualized
picture of Greek attitudes, including those pertaining to
sex, by retrieving the views of the man and woman in the
street.

493.   DUBOIS, PAGE. "Phallocentrism and Its Subversion
        in Plato's Phaedrus," **Arethusa,** 18 (1985), 91-103.
Revising an interpretation of Jacques Derrida, seeks to
show that Plato appropriated maternity to the male philosopher. See also: Dorothea Wender, "Plato: Misogyn-
ist, Paedophile, and Feminist," **Arethusa,** 6 (1973), 75-90.

494.   DUGAS, LUDOVIC. L'amitié antique d'après les

moeurs populaires et les theories des philosophes.
Paris: Felix Alcan, 1894. 654 pp.
Reprinted New York: Arno Press, 1976. In this comprehensive work concerning ancient ideas of friendship, see
esp. "L'amour grec" (pp. 84-104), on pederasty. A more
recent synthesis is Jean Fraisse, **Philia: la notion
d'amitié dans la philosophie antique** (Paris: J. Vrin,
1974; 504 pp.).

495. DUMÉZIL, GEORGES. **Romans de Scythie et d'alen-
      tour.** Paris: Payot, 1978. 380 pp.
A distinguished French scholar of comparative Indo-European institutions reflects on the noted passage in
Herodotus 4:67, concerning Scythian effeminacy in relation
to subarctic shamanism ("La maladie des Enarées," pp. 212-
18).

496. DYOR, EUGÈNE. "Dialogues sur l'amour," **Arcadie,**
      no. 67-68 (July-August 1959), 397-405.
On the work attributed to Plutarch. See also the edition
of this text, **Dialogues sur l'amour (Eroticos).** Text,
translation, and introduction by Robert Flacelière (Paris: Les Belles Lettres, 1952; 141 pp.; an enlarged edition
appreared in 1980).

497. EYBEN, EMIEL. **De jonge Romein volgens de literaire
      bronnen der periode ca. 200 v. Chr. tot ca. 500
      n. Chr.** Brussels: 1977. (Verhandelingen van de
      Koninklijke Academie voor Wetenschappen, Letteren
      en Schone Kunsten van België, Klasse der Letteren,
      39, 81). 691 pp.
Granting that in young Romans the expression of homosexual
impulses was stimulated by the school, the gymnasia and
the army, Eyben tends to overstate negative attitudes
(see esp. pp. 197, 475-79). There is a 29-page English
summary.

498. FERRI, SILVIO. "Sui vasi greci con epigrafi
      'acclamatorie,'" **Rendiconti della R. Accademia
      nazionale dei lincei; classe di scienze morali
      storiche e filologiche,** 6th ser., 14 (1938), 93-
      179.
Claims (unconvincingly) that the love names on Greek vases
are in honor of deceased youths; useful appendix of texts,
pp. 158-79.

499. FIGUEIRA, THOMAS J., and GREGORY NAGY (eds.).
      Theognis of Megara: Poetry and Polis (Baltimore:
      Johns Hopkins University Press, 1985. 346 pp.
Essays on the archaic Greek poet and the associated
corpus (the Theognidea). See esp. Daniel B. Levine,
"Symposium and the Polis (pp. 176-96), John M. Lewis,
"Eros and the Polis in Theognis Book II (197-222), and
Walter Donlan, "Pistos Philos Hetairos" (223-45).

500. FINLEY, MOSES I. **The World of Odysseus.** Second

ed. New York: Viking, 1978. 188 pp.
This influential analysis of Homeric culture, first published in 1954, highlights the intensity of male bonding
in contrast to the relative unimportance of marital relationships.

501.   FLACELIÈRE, ROBERT. **Love in Ancient Greece.** New
       York: Crown, 1962. 224 pp.
Translation of **L'amour en Grèce** (Paris: Hachette, 1960).
Although this book is by a classical scholar of repute,
the chapter on homosexuality (pp. 63-100) is tendentious
and sometimes inaccurate. See also: Paul Frischauer, **La
sexualité dans l'antiquite** (Paris: Stock, 1969); Jacques
Mazel, **Les métamorphoses d'Eros: L'amour dans la Grèce
antique** (Paris: Presses de la Renaissance, 1984); Frida
Wion, "L'amour grec," **Bulletin de l'Association Guillaume
Budé,** 4th ser., 2 (1970), 249-58.

502.   FORNARA, CHARLES W. "The Cult of Harmodius and
       Aristogeiton," **Philologus,** 114 (1970), 155-80.
On the Athenian custom of commemorating the tyrant
slayers, who were homosexual lovers.

503.   FOUCAULT, MICHEL. **L'usage des plaisirs.** Paris:
       Gallimard, 1984. 285 pp.
This posthumously published volume 2 of **Histoire de la
sexualité** (on a very different plan from that originally
envisaged) concentrates on ancient Greek texts bearing on
the economy of self-management, including pleasure and
sex. There is an English translation by Robert Hurley: **The
Use of Pleasure** (New York: Pantheon, 1985; 293 pp.). Followed by **Le souci de soi** (Paris: Gallimard, 1984; 284
pp.).

504.   FRANCIS, E. D. and M. VICKERS. "Leagros Kalos,"
       Proceedings of the Cambridge Philological Society,
       207 (1981), 97-136.
Major review of historical problems arising from one of
the most famous of the love names found on Greek vases.

505.   FRIEDRICH, PAUL. **The Meaning of Aphrodite.** Chica-
       go: University of Chicago Press, 1978. 243 pp.
Primarily a reconstruction of proto-Indo-European cosmol-
ogy, this monograph includes a discussion of Sappho and
female homosexuality on Lesbos (pp. 108-17).

506.   FUCHS, HERMANN. **Die Hylasgeschichte bei Apollonios
       Rhodios und Theokrit.** Würzburg: Universität,
       1969. 85 pp. (Inaugural-Dissertation)
The tragic story of Hercules' beloved Hylas, as rendered
by two leading Hellenistic writers.

507.   GARLAND, YVON, and O. MASSON. "Les acclamations
       pédérastiques de Kalami (Thasos)," **Bulletin de
       Correspondance Hellénique,** 106 (1982), 3-22.
Publishes a collection of explicit pederastic inscriptions

from the island of Thasos. See also Merle K. Landon,
"Hymettiana," **Hesperia**, 54 (1985), 257-70 (esp. p. 264ff.
on Attic kalos graffiti).

508. GARRIDO-HORY, MARGUERITE. "La vision du dépendant
chez Martial à travers les relations sexuelles,"
Index (Naples), 10 (1981), 298-315.
Structuralist analysis of evidence from Martial's Epigrams
for homosexual (and heterosexual) relations between masters and slaves. In the same issue, see: Jerzy Kolendo,
"L'esclavage et la vie sexuelle des hommes libres à Rome,"
288-97; and Claudine Leduc, "Le discours d'Aristophane
et de Ménandre sur la sexualité des maîtres et des
esclaves," 271-87; and in vol. 11 (1982), Maria Anton-
ietta Cervellera, "Omosessualità e ideologia schiavistica
in Petronio," 221-34.

509. GOLDEN, MARK. "Slavery and Homosexuality at Athens," **Phoenix**, 38 (1984), 308-24.
Holds that the influence of the institution of slavery
affected, sometimes negatively, even relations between
free-born males.

510. GONFROY, FRANÇOISE. "Homosexualité et idéologie
esclavagiste chez Cicéron," **Dialogues d'histoire
ancienne**, 4 (1978), 219-65. (Besancon, Université:
Annales littéraires, 225)
Exposes Cicero's exploitation of sexual invective for
political ends; note useful charts of terms, pp. 238-62.

511. GRANAROLO, JEAN. "L'heure de verité pour Tallus le
cinède (Catulle XXV)," **Revue des Etudes Anciennes**,
60 (1958), 290-306.
Observations on the meaning of **cinaedus** in Roman life.
See also his: **L'oeuvre de Catulle: aspects religieux,
éthiques et stylistiques** (Paris: Les Belles Lettres,
1967; 406 pp.), pp. 160-204.

512. GRIFFIN, JASPER. "Augustan Poetry and the Life of
Luxury," **Journal of Roman Studies**, 66 (1976), 87-
105.
Challenges the view that homosexual poems are of a different order of unreality from heterosexual ones (as maintained, e.g., by Gordon Williams, **Tradition and Originality in Roman Poetry**. London: Oxford University Press,
1968, p. 551). Insists that Augustan writers in both
homosexual and heterosexual poetry reflect "a mode of
life familiar to their reader." See also Griffin, **Latin
Poets and Roman Life** (London: Duckworth, 1986; 240 pp.).

513. GRIMAL, PIERRE. **L'amour à Rome**. Second ed. Paris: Les Belles Lettres, 1980. 346 pp.
While this monograph on Roman sexual life scants homosexual themes, it is useful for comparative purposes.

514. HERMANN, ALFRED. "Antinous infelix: Zur Typologie

des Heiligen-Unheiligen in der Spätantike," in:
Mullus: Festschrift für Theodor Klauser. Mün-
ster: Aschendorff, 1964, pp. 155-67.
Early Christian transformations of the image of Hadrian's
favorite Antinous into that of an "unsaint," a demonic
counter-figure to the Christian saint.

515.   HERTER, HANS.   "Effeminatus," **Reallexikon für
        Antike und Christentum,** 4 (1959), cols. 620-50.
Important learned article on effeminacy and androgyny in
Greco-Roman and early Christian civilization, and the
explicit condemnation of the effeminate "lifestyle" by the
Church.

516.   HOFFMAN, RICHARD J.   "Some Cultural Aspects of
        Greek Male Homosexuality," **JH,** 5:3 (1980), 217-26.
Stresses the centrality of the Greek family in relation to
the acceptance of homosexual behavior.

517.   HOWELL, PETER.   **A Commentary on Book One of the
        Epigrams of Martial.** London: Athlone Press, 1980.
        369 pp.
Provides detailed comment on the 20-odd sexually explicit
poems, including one lesbian example.   A dense treatment
of another book is N. M. Kay, **Martial: Book XI: A Commentary** (London: Duckworth, 1985; 304 pp.).   See also the
commentary of C. Citroni, accompanying his edition of **M.
Valerii Martialis Epigrammata** (Florence, 1975).

518.   HUBERT, CURT.   **De Plutarchi amatoria.**   Kirchhain:
        Max Schmersow, 1903.   98 pp.
Philological commentary on the essay on love attributed to
Plutarch.

519.   HUNGER, HERBERT.   **Lexikon der griechischen und
        römischen Mythologie.** Sixth ed. Vienna: Hollinek,
        1969.   444 pp.
Valuable concise lexicon of Greco-Roman mythology, providing not only the essentials of the myths and their
sources, but also lists of later works using them as
themes.   See entries for Ganymedes, Hyakinthos, Hylas,
etc.

520.   JEANMAIRE, HENRI.   **Couroi et courètes: essai sur
        l'éducation spartiate et sur les rites d'adoles-
        cence dans l'antiquité hellénique.** Lille: Biblio-
        thèque Universitaire, 1939.   638 pp.
Reprinted New York: Arno Press, 1975. See esp. pp. 456-60
on the pederastic graffiti of the island of Thera.

521.   JOCELYN, H. D.   "A Greek Indecency and Its Stu-
        dents: **laikazein,**" **Proceedings of the Cambridge
        Philological Society,** 206 (1980), 12-66.
On fellation from evidence in literary works and graffiti.

522.   KEULS, EVA C.   **The Reign of the Phallus: Sexual**

politics in **Ancient Greece.** New York: Harper and
Row, 1985. 452 pp.
Argues that there is a close bond between the Athenian
fixation on the phallus and the exploitative domination
of women and slaves, on the one hand, and ruthless imperial aggression, on the other. Overstated and sometimes
inaccurate, as when it claims that pederasty involved
prepubertal boys.

523. KIEFER, OTTO. **Sexual Life in Ancient Rome.** New
York Dutton, 1935. 379 pp.
A somewhat routine compilation, but occasionally quite
useful. Translated by Gilbert and Helen Highet from
Kiefer's **Kulturgeschichte Roms** (1933).

524. KISELBERG, STEFFEN. **De gamle graekere og den nye
mand.** Copenhagen: Museum Tusculanum Forlag, 1982.
93 pp. (Rudimenta Graecolatina, 4)
Seeks to relate the ancient Greeks to today's sociosexual movements.

525. KNIGHT, RICHARD PAYNE. **Sexual Symbolism; A History
of Phallic Worship.** New York: Julian Press, 1957.
217, 196 pp.
A pioneering investigation (1786), using archaeological
and literary evidence. In this edition Knight's work--
originally titled **A Discourse on the Worship of Priapus**--
is followed by Thomas Wright's **The Worship of the Gener-
ative Powers** (1866).

526. KRENKEL, WERNER A. "Pueri meritorii," **Wissen-
schaftliche Zeitschrift der Wilhelm Pieck Univer-
sität Rostock,** 28 (1979), 179-89.
Review of sources on male prostitution in ancient Greece
and Rome, arguing that the boundaries between ordinary
relations and prostitution are fluid. See also his:
"Fellatio und irrumatio," ibid., 29 (1980), 77-88; and
"Masturbation in der Antike," ibid., 28 (1979), 159-78.

527. KROLL, WILHELM. **Freundschaft und Knabenliebe.**
Munich: Ernst Heimeran, 1927. 39 pp. (Tusculum-
Schriften, 4)
Reprinted by September Verlag, Almendingen, 1983. Survey
of Greco-Roman pederasty by a noted classical scholar.
See also: H. Reynen, "Philosophie und Knabenliebe,"
Hermes, 95 (1967), 308-16).

528. LAMBERT, ROYSTON. **Beloved and God: The Story of
Hadrian and Antinous.** New York: Viking, 1984. 298
pp.
Sensitive retelling of the most famous homoerotic love
affair in antiquity. A more explicitly fictionalized
version is Marguerite Yourcenar's celebrated **Hadrian's
Memoirs** (New York: Farrar, Straus and Young, 1954; 313
pp.).

529.   LESKY, ALBIN. **Vom Eros der Hellenen.** Gottingen:
       Vandenhoeck und Ruprecht. 1976. 155 pp.
Somewhat rambling essay on ancient Greek Eros as god and
concept; for pederasty, see p. 78ff.

530.   LEWIS, THOMAS S. W. "Brothers of Ganymede," **Sal-
       magundi,** no. 58-59 (Fall 1983-Winter 1983), 147-
       65.
Seeks to downplay the physical side of Greek homoeroticism.

531.   LICHT, HANS (pseud. of Paul Brandt). **Beiträge zur
       antiken Erotik.** Dresden: P. Aretz, 1924. 230 pp.
Collected essays on (homo)eroticism by the greatest
scholar of the subject of his time (1875-1929).

532.   LICHT, HANS. "Homoerotik in den homerischen
       Gedichte," **Anthropophyteia,** 9 (1912), 291-300.
On homoerotic themes in the Homeric poems. See also: "Die
Erotik in den epischen Gedichten der Griechen mit be-
sonderer Berücksichtigung des Homoerotischen," **Zeitschrift für Sexualwissenschaft,** 9 (1922), 65-74; "Der
paidon eros in der griechischen Literatur: I. Die lyrische
und bukolische Dichtung," JfsZ, 8 (1906). 619-84; "Der
paidon eros in der griechischen Dichtung: II. Die Gedichte
der Anthologie," (by "P. Stephanus," pseud.), **JfsZ** 9
(1908), 213-312; and "Der **paidon eros** in der griechisch-
en Dichtung: III. Die attische Komödie," **Anthropophyteia,**
7 (1910), 128-78.

533.   LICHT, HANS. **Die Homoerotik in der griechischen
       Literatur: Lukianos von Samosata.** Bonn: A. Marcus
       & E. Weber, 1921. 78 pp. (Abhandlungen aus dem
       Gebiet der Sexualforschung, 3:3)
Homoerotic themes in the work of Lucian. See also: "Die
homoerotischen Briefe des Philostratos," **Anthropophyteia,**
8 (1911), 216-23; and "Sexuelles aus dem Geschichtswerk
des Herodot," **JfsZ,** 22:3/4 (1922), 65-71.

534.   LICHT, HANS. **Sappho: Lebensbild aus den Frühlings-
       tagen altgriechischer Dichtung.** Leipzig: Rott-
       barth, 1905. 144 pp.
Critical-biographical study of Sappho that utterly fails
to deal with the evidence for her lesbianism.

535.   LICHT, HANS. **Sexual Life in Ancient Greece.** Lon-
       don: London: Routledge and Kegan Paul, 1932. 555
       pp.
Several times reprinted, including New York: Barnes and
Noble, 1953. This encyclopedic work, a landmark in its
time, has not entirely been replaced by the recent contributions of K. Dover and F. Buffière. There are some
minor cuts from the original German text, whose sump-
tuous plate volume (now rare) was not retained: **Sittengeschichte Griechenlands** (Dresden, 1925-28, 3 vols., with
some 500 plates).

536. LIDA TARAN, SONYA. "Eisi triches: An Erotic Motif
      in the Greek Anthology," **Journal of Hellenic
      Studies,** 105 (1985), 90-107.
Discusses the theme of transitoriness in the pederastic
poems of Book XII, as exemplified by the motif fo the
growth of hair, which marks the end of the short span of
sexual attractiveness.

537. LILJA, SAARA. **Homosexuality in Republican and
      Augustan Rome.** Helsinki: Societas Scientiarum
      Fennica, 1983. 164 pp. (Commentationes Humanarum
      Litterarum, 74)
Judicious and penetrating study of the ancient sources,
including Plautus, Catullus, Vergil, Horace, and Cicero--
as well as graffiti and legal evidence. See also her: **The
Roman Elegists' Attitudes to Women** (New York: Garland,
1978), pp. 219-25.

538. LUCK, GEORG. **The Latin Love Lyric.** New York:
      Barnes and Noble, 1960. 182 pp.
See pp. 85-92 on Tibullus.

539. MACMULLEN, RAMSAY. "Roman Attitudes to Greek
      Love," **Historia,** 31 (1982), 484-502.
Reviews some negative attitudes toward homosexuality found
in Roman sources.

540. MARCOVICH, MIROSLAV. "Anacreon 358 PMG," **American
      Journal of Philology,** 104 (1983), 372-83.
Lesbianism in an early Greek lyric.

541. MARROU, HENRI-IRENEE. **A History of Education in
      Antiquity.** Translated by George Lamb. New York:
      New American Library, 1956. 600 pp.
In Chapter 3, "Pederasty in Classical Education" (pp.50-
62), the noted French scholar points out that Greek
homosexuality was associated not only with military
comradeship, but also with idealized pedagogy. The
English translation has been criticized, and it is
preferable to use the original: **Histoire de l'éducation
dans l'antiquité** (Paris: Le Seuil, 1948).

542. MAXWELL-STEWART, P. G. "Strato and the **musa
      puerilis," Hermes,** 100 (1972), 116-40.
Philological examination of the pederastic poems of the
Greek Anthology, stressing the deployment of wit.

543. MORGAN, M. GWYN. "Catullus 112: A Pathicus in
      Politics," **American Journal of Philology,** 100
      (1979), 377-80.
Critique of one of the Roman poet's more enigmatic and
sardonic lyrics.

544. MUECKE, FRANCES. "Portrait of the Artist as a
      Young Woman," **Classical Quarterly,** N.S., 32 (1982),
      41-55.

Lesbian insights.

545.   MURGATROYD, P.   "Tibullus and the puer delicatus,"
        Acta Classica: Proceedings of the Classical
        Association of South Africa, 20 (1977), 105-19.
Useful article on the Greek and Augustan background of the
Tibullus' poems to the boy Marathus.

546.   PACION, STANLEY.   "The Life of Nero: Sex and the
        Fall of the Roman Empire," **Medical Aspects of Human**
        Sexuality, 5 (March 1971), 171-85.
Journalistic repackaging of Suetonius, of interest only as
a specimen of the genre.

547.   PAGE, DENNIS L.   **Sappho and Alcaeus.**   Oxford: Ox-
        ford University Press, 1955. 340 pp.
Selected texts with extended commentary; useful for
lesbian themes in Sappho, which the writer, a distin-
guished English philologist, affirms. For a different
view, see: Judith P. Hallett, "Sappho and Her Social
Context: Sense and Sensuality," **Signs,** 4 (1979), 447-64.
See also Giuseppe Giangrande, "Sappho and the **olisbos,**"
Emerita, 48 (1980), 249-50.

548.   PATZER, HARALD.   **Die griechische Knabenliebe.**
        Wiesbaden: Franz Steiner Verlag, 1982. 131 pp.
        (Sitzungsberichte der Wissenschaftlichen Gesell-
        schaft an der Johann Wolfgang Goethe Universität
        Frankfurt am Main)
Rambling, sometimes obtuse reflections on some modern
works on Greek pederasty, concluding that there were two
successive types, the Dorian and the classic, and that
in each the sexual element was secondary. See critical
remarks by Detlev Fehling, **Gnomon,** 57 (1985), 116-20.

549.   PETERS, E. BROOKS.   "Freud's Blind Spot," **Christo-**
        pher Street, 7:5 (June 1983), 38-42.
On Oedipus' homosexual father Laius, and the occultation
of his character in Freud's theory. See also G. Devere-
eux, above.

550.   POGEY-CASTRIES, L. R. DE. (pseud. of Georges
        Herelle).   **Histoire de l'amour grec dans l'antiqu-**
        ité. Paris: Stendhal, 1930. 316 pp.
This book, which has been several times reprinted, is a
revised and enlarged version of a comprehensive German
article by M. H. E. Meier in **Allgemeine Encyclopädie der**
Wissenschaften und Künste, 9 (1837), 149-88. Though dated
and sometimes inaccurate, this book is still useful for
aspects not covered by other authors. The unpublished
papers of Herelle, which contain drafts for a supplementary volume, are preserved in the Bibliothèque Municipale,
Troyes.

551.   RICHARDSON, T. WADE.   "Homosexuality in the Satir-
        icon," **Classica et Mediaevalia,** 35 (1984), 104-27.

Despite a mild psychoanalytic bias, useful as a refutation of the common scholarly view that Petronius' masterwork is essentially a parody of the heterosexual love
romance tradition. See also Cecil Wooten, "Petronius and
'Camp,'" **Helios,** N.S., 11 (1984), 133-39.

552. RICHLIN, AMY. **The Garden of Priapus: Sexuality and
Aggression in Roman Humor.** New Haven: Yale University Press, 1983. 296 pp.
While the book's central theme is sexism in Roman society
and literature, it offers some material on male homosexuality. For a searching critique, see H. D. Jocelyn, **Echos
du Monde Classique/Classical Views,** 29 (1985), 1-30.

553. ROSENBAUM, JULIUS. **The Plague of Lust.** Paris:
Charles Carrington, 1898. 2 vols.
This work, an anonymous translation from the German **Geschichte der Lustseuche im Alterthume** (1839 and successive
editions), has been several times reprinted. The treatment of the "feminine disease" of the Scythians (vol 1,
pp. 143-256) is still worth consulting, as well as the
discussion of other aspects of Greek homosexuality.

554. SARTRE, MAURICE. "L'homosexualité dans la Grèce
ancienne," **L'Histoire,** no. 76 (March 1985), 10-17.
Upholds the initiatory character of Greek pederasty.

555. SERGENT, BERNARD. **Homosexuality in Greek Myth.**
Translated by Arthur Goldhammer. Boston: Beacon
Press, 1986. 288 pp.
Contrary to the findings of other scholars, this innovat-
ory monograph locates the roots of Greek homosexuality in
a postulated institutionalized pederasty of ancient Indo-
European culture. Sergent relates pederastic myths to the
foundation legends of Greek cities.

556. SHACKLETON-BAILEY, D. R. **Profile of Horace.** Cambridge, MA: Harvard University Press, 1982. 142
pp.
Refutes the claim of Gordon Williams and others that
the Roman poet's homoerotic references are a mere "literary exercise."

557. SKINNER, MARILYN B. "Pretty Lesbius," **Transactions of the American Philological Association,** 112
(1982), 197-208.
Homosexual innuendoes in Catullus' poem 79.

558. SLATER, PHILIP. **The Glory of Hera: Greek Mythology
and the Greek Family.** Boston: Beacon Press, 1968.
513 pp.
Psychoanalytically slanted approach to Greek male-female
relations, ostensibly seen through a mythological mirror.
For another approach to the matter, see Curtis Barnett,
God as Form: Essays in Greek Theology. (Albany: SUNY
Press, 1976).

559. STIGERS, EVA. "Sappho's Private World," **Women's Studies**, 8 (1981), 47-63.
Argues that Sappho's poetry is "fundamentally different from that of the male lyric poets."

560. SYMONDS, JOHN ADDINGTON. **A Problem in Greek Ethics.** London: n. p., 1901. 73 pp.
Only 100 copies of this first edition were printed for private circulation; the text has been several times reprinted, sometimes in truncated form. See now the anthology of Symonds's work edited by John Lauritsen, **Male Love** (New York: Pagan Press, 1983). The noted scholar's discrete but forceful defense of the ideals of Greek homosexuality is a landmark in the English-language discussion of the subject.

561. THESLEFF, HOLGER. "The Interrelation and Date of the Symposia of Plato and Xenophon," **Bulletin of the Institute of Classical Studies** [London], 25 (1978), 157-70.
For Plato's text, see the edition by K.J. Dover, Cambridge: Cambridge University Press, 1980.

562. TURCAN, ROBERT. **Héliogabale et le sacré du soleil.** Paris: Albin Michel, 10985. 285 pp.
Study of the outrageous 3rd-century emperor by a senior French academic, who emphasizes the Semitic religious background, neglecting the psychosexual aspects. Does not discuss the image of Heliogabalus in 20th-century creative literature.

563. TYRRELL, WILLIAM BLAKE. **Amazons: A Study in Athenian Mythmaking.** Baltimore: Johns Hopkins University Press, 1982. 192 pp.
Employs structuralist methodology to explore the myth within the context of the sharp male-female polarities of Athenian culture.

564. UNGARETTI, JOHN. "Pederasty, Heroism, and the Family in Classical Greece," **JH**, 3 (1978), 291-300.
Argues that the concept of the ideal warrior documented from Homer onwards is essential to the understanding of homosexual relations in Greece.

565. VERSTRAETE, BEERT C. **Homosexuality in Ancient Greek and Roman Civilization: A Critical Bibliography with Supplement.** Toronto: Canadian Gay Archives, 1982. 14 pp. (Publication no. 6)
Reprints the annotated bibliography of 38 items published in **JH** 3 (1979), 79-81, adding 13 new entries. Limited to secondary works. See the critical supplement by Wayne Dynes in **Gay Books Bulletin**, 8 (Fall-Winter 1982), 13-15.

566. VERSTRAETE, BEERT C. "Slavery and the Social Dynamics of Male Homosexual Relations in Ancient Rome," **JH** 5 (1980), 227-36.

Holds that more than any other institution, slavery places
its stamp on male homosexual relations in ancient Rome.

567. VEYNE, PAUL. "L'homosexualité à Rome," **Communica-
      tions,** no. 35 (1982), 26-33.
Brief synthesis by a noted French historian.

568. WILHELM, FRIEDRICH. "Zu Achilles Tatius," **Rhein-
      isches Museum,** N.S. 57 (1902), 55-75.
A still useful article on the sources of the Greek genre
of debating the worth of the two genders as sexual objects.

569. WILKENSON, L. P. "Classical Approaches. IV: Homo-
      sexuality," **Encounter,** 51:3 (September 1978),
      20-31.
A fairly traditional survey of Greece and Rome by an
English classical scholar.

570. WISEMAN, T. P. **Catullus and His World: A Reap-
      praisal.** Cambridge: Cambridge University Press,
      1985. 305 pp.
Although discussion of Catullus' homosexual poems forms
only a small portion of the text, this book is useful for
understanding Roman sexuality as a whole. See also: Brian
Arkins, **Sexuality in Catullus** (Hildesheim: Altertumswis-
senschaftliche Texte und Studien [8], 1982); and the commentary of John Ferguson, **Catullus** (Lawrence, KN: Coronado
Press, 1985).

D. MIDDLE AGES

Until recently the subject of homosexuality in this period
was neglected. Perceiving a parallel to the witch craze,
lay persons tended to view medieval homophobia as a vast,
but undifferentiated rage for persecution of homosexuals,
or simply as a subject about which little was known (the
"Dark Ages"). Recently, considerably more data have
become available, in large part funneled through the controversy surrounding John Boswell's book (578). These
studies emphasize the Mediterranean heritage to which most
of the evidence pertains, yet Scandinavian sources also
disclose an important but independent tradition. Homosexuality in Byzantium and the Slavic middle ages has scarcely begun to be explored. See also "Religion," VII.Bff.

571. ANSEN, JOHN. "The Female Transvestite in Early
      Monasticism: The Origin and Development of a
      Motif," **Viator,** 5 (1974), 1-32.
Interprets material from the lives of the saints.

572. BARBER, MALCOLM. **The Trial of the Templars.** Cam-

bridge: Cambridge University Press, 1978. 312 pp.
Concluding that the charges of sodomy made against the
Templar Order in 1308 are unproven, exposes the use of
antihomosexual prejudice in late-medieval politics.

573.   BERNARDINO OF SIENA, ST. **Le prediche volgari.**
Edited by Piero Bargellini. Milan: Rizzoli, 1936.
1173 pp.
In this collection of vernacular sermons by the fifteenth-
century monk, there are two vituperative ones against
sodomy: predica 35 (pp. 795-797) and predica 39 (pp. 893-
919). Other references occur in his Latin works (e.g.,
sermons 11 and 15, in: **Opera omnia,** Florence, 1950).

574.   BIELER, LUDWIG (ed.). **The Irish Penitentials.**
Dublin: Institute for Advanced Studies, 1963. 367
pp.
The early medieval penitentials, or confessional formular-
ies, are an important source for attitudes towards sodomy
and sexual variation in general. This edition tends
somewhat to obscure the matter; see P. J. Payer, below.

575.   BLEIBTREU-EHRENBERG, GISELA. **Tabu Homosexualität: die Geschichte eines Vorurteils.** Frankfurt am
Main: S. Fischer, 1978. 444 pp.
Traces the history of prejudice against homosexuals from
early German times, marshalling an abundance of documentary evidence. May overstate the Germanic contribution
to antihomosexual sentiment.

576.   BLOCH, IWAN. "Die Homosexualität in Köln am Ende
des 15. Jahrhunderts," **Jahrbuch für Sexualwissenschaft,** 1 (1908), 528-35.
Analyzes a Low German text showing the existence of a
sodomite subculture in late 15th-century Cologne.

577.   BOLOGNA, CORRADO (ed.). **Liber monstrorum de
diversis generibus: libro delle mirabili diffor-
mita.** Milan: Bompiani, 1979. 221 pp.
Example of a genre of medieval literature evoking marvels
and monsters; this specimen begins with a description of a
homosexual.

578.   BOSWELL, JOHN. **Christianity, Social Tolerance and
Homosexuality: Gay People in Western Europe from
the Beginning of the Christian Era to the Fourteenth Century.** Chicago: Chicago University Press,
1980. 424 pp.
An ambitious, erudite, and much-acclaimed treatment of:
the meaning and exegetical destiny of the main Biblical
proof-texts (controversial); the Roman heritage; the
sexual lore of the hare, the hyena, and the weasel;
continuity of themes of passionate friendship and boy-love
in Christian writers; the concept of Nature as sexual
norm; and the putative social causes of toleration and
repression of homosexual behavior. For criticism see

W. Johansson et al., below.

579.   BOSWELL, JOHN. **Rediscovering Gay History: Arche-
       types of Gay Love in Christian History.** London: Gay
       Christian Movement, 1982. 21 pp. (Michael Harding
       Memorial Address)
Offers some oblique answers to criticisms of the work
cited above, and unveils a "gay marriage" thesis.

580.   BULLOUGH, VERN. "Transvestites in the Middle
       Ages," **American Journal of Sociology,** 79 (1974),
       1381-94.
Analyzes material from the lives of the transvestitic
saints (Margaret-Pelagius, Marina, Athanasia, et al.). Reprinted with changes in the following collection.

581.   BULLOUGH, VERN, and JAMES BRUNDAGE (eds.). **Sexual
       Practices and the Medieval Church.** Buffalo: Prome-
       theus, 1982. 289 pp.
Eighteen papers, some reprinted with revisions from
earlier publications. Opens new institutional perspectives.

582.   BYNUM, CAROLINE WALKER. **Jesus as Mother: Studies
       in the Spirituality of the High Middle Ages.**
       Berkeley: University of California Press, 1982.
       282 pp.
See pp. 110-69 for "Jesus as Mother and Abbot as Mother:
Some Themes in Twelfth-Century Cistercian Writing."
Compare Rudolf Berliner, "God is Love," **Gazette des
Beaux-Arts,** ser. 6, 42 (1953), 9-26.

583.   CLEUGH, JAMES. **Love Locked Out: A Survey of Love,
       License, and Restriction in the Middle Ages.** Lon-
       don: Anthony Blond, 1963. 320 pp.
Dated, semipopular panorama covering a bit of everything,
including homosexuality.

584.   CROMPTON, LOUIS. "Sodomy and Civil Doom: The
       History of an Unchristian Tradition," **Vector**
       (November 1975), 23-27, 57-58.
Overview of Christian hostility to homosexual behavior.
The writer is preparing a book-length treatment of the
subject.

585.   CURTIUS, ERNST ROBERT. **European Literature and the
       Latin Middle Ages.** Translated by Willard R. Trask.
       New York: Pantheon, 1953. 662 pp.
In this major work by a great German humanistic scholar,
see "Sodomy" (p. 113ff.), which offers a succinct analysis
of some leading themes.

586.   DAMIAN, PETER, ST. **Book of Gomorrah.** Translated
       by Pierre J. Payer. Waterloo, Ont.: Wilfred
       Laurier University Press, 1982. 108 pp.
Diatribe by an 11th-century rigorist against "unnatural

vice" in the medieval church. An improved edition of the
Latin text appears in Kurt Reindel (ed.), **Die Briefe des
Petrus Damiani,** 1. (Munich: Monumenta Germaniae Histor-
ica, 1983; 509 pp.)

587.   DEMURGER, ALAIN. **Vie et mort de l'ordre du Temple.**
       Paris: Le Seuil, 1985. 336 pp.
Traces the whole history of the Templar Order, situating the sodomy charges brought against the Templars in
their contemporary political context.

588.   DRONKE, PETER. **Medieval Latin and the Rise of
       European Love-Lyric.** Second ed. Oxford: Clarendon
       Press, 1968. 2 vols. (603 pp.)
In this landmark work of philology, see vol. 1, pp. 195-
201, 218-19; vol. 2, 495.

589.   EVANS, ARTHUR. **Witchcraft and the Gay Countercul-
       ture.** Boston: Fag Rag Books, 1978. 180 pp.
This seemingly scholarly book paints a fantastic picture
of a benign Old Religion in which homosexuals and women
were honored. Counterculture utopian revery disguised
as research.

590.   GOODICH, MICHAEL. **The Unmentionable Vice: Homosex-
       uality in the Later Medieval Period.** Santa
       Barbara: Ross-Erikson, 1979. 164 pp.
Useful essays on attitudes toward homosexuality in Western
Europe from the eleventh through the fifteenth centuries.
Many references from legal and ecclesiastical sources;
literary and artistic evidence is scanted.

591.   GREENBERG, DAVID. F., and MARCIA H. BYSTRYN.
       "Christian Intolerance of Homosexuality," **American
       Journal of Sociology,** 88 (1982), 515-48.
Surveys evidence, mainly as conveyed by secondary sources,
concluding that intolerance was "variable."

592.   HERMAN, GERALD. "The 'Sin against Nature' and Its
       Echoes in Medieval French Literature," **Annuale
       mediaevale,** 17 (1976), 70-87.
Discusses a number of authors, including Gilles de Cor-
beil, John of Salisbury, Gautier de Coincy, and Marie
de France, who tend to be hostile to homosexual behavior.

593.   HORN, WALTER, and ERNEST BORN. **The Plan of
       St. Gall.** Berkeley: University of California
       Press, 1979. 3 vols.
This monumental commentary on the ninth-century monastic
plan includes a discussion of the Benedictine regulations designed to prevent sexual contacts with young
monks, and their architectural embodiment.

594.   IVO OF CHARTRES. **Decretum.** In: J.-P. Migne (ed.),
       Patrologia Latina, 161 (ca. 1860), cols. 47-1022.
See cols 681-82 for denunciations of sodomy and lesbian-

ism. The issuance of a number of ecclesiastic collections
of this type from ca. 850 onwards shows that opposition
to homosexuality was by no means stilled among clerical
authorities during this obscure period.

595. JENKINS, ROMILLY J. H. **Byzantium: The Imperial
      Centuries, A.D. 610-1071.** New York: Random House,
      1967. 400 pp.
As yet little research has been done on Byzantine homosexuality; see pp. 88, 165-66, 198-99, and 301 for some
suggestive aperçus. For the survival of Greek genres of
erotic writing, see Hans-Georg Beck, **Byzantinisches
Erotikon: Orthodoxie-Literatur-Gesellschaft.** Munich:
1984. 174 pp. (Bayerische Akademie der Wissenschaften,
Phil.-hist. Klasse, Sitzungsberichte, 1984, no. 3)

596. JOHANSSON, WARREN. "London's Medieval Sodomites,"
      Cabirion, 10 (1984), 6-7, 34.
Using a text of Richard of Devizes, Johansson uncovers a
homosexual subculture in late 12th-century London.

597. JOHANSSON, WARREN, et al. **Homosexuality, Intoler-
      ance and Christianity: A Critical Examination of
      John Boswell's Work.** New York: Scholarship Commit-
      tee, Gay Academic Union, 1981. 22 pp. (Gai Saber
      Monograph no. 1)
Contains: **"Ex parte Themis:** The Historical Guilt of the
Christian Church" by Warren Johansson; "Christianity and
the Politics of Sex" by Wayne Dynes; **"Culpa ecclesiae:**
Boswell's Dilemma" by John Lauritsen. The conclusions
of the essays are convergently negative towards the book.
An enlarged edition of this critique appeared in 1985,
with an annotated bibliography of responses to the Boswell
monograph.

598. KAY, RICHARD. **Dante's Swift and Strong: Essays in
      Inferno: Essays in Inferno XV.** Lawrence: Regent's
      Press of Kansas, 1978. 446 pp.
Argues that the "sodomy" depicted in Canto XV is meant in
a broader, spiritual sense, rather than in an exclusively
sexual one. See also his "The Sin of Brunetto Latini,"
Medieval Studies, 31 (1969), 262-86; as well as: Sally
Mussetter, "'Ritornare a lo suo principio': Dante and
the Sin of Brunetto Latini," **Philological Quarterly,** 63
(1984), 431-48; and A. Pézard, below.

599. KUSTER, HENDRIKUS JOHANNES. **Over homoseksualiteit
      in middeleeuws West-Europa (Some Observations on
      Homosexuality in Medieval Western Europe).**
      Utrecht: The author, 1977. 175 pp.
Doctoral dissertation offering an overview, but depending
too much on incompletely assimilated secondary sources.
See the critical review by A. H. Bredero, **Tijdschrift
voor Geschiedenis,** 91 (1978), 256-62.

600. LEA, HENRY CHARLES. **A History of the Inquisition**

of the Middle Ages. New York: Harper, 1887. 3
vols.
Dated and with a Protestant bias, but still worth consulting. See vol. 1, pp. 32-34, 85, 101; vol 2, pp. 150,
335, 408; vol. 3, p. 639.

601.   MCALPINE, MONICA. "The Pardoner's Homosexuality
        and How It Matters," Publications of the Modern
        Language Association, 95 (1980), 8-22.
Argues that the phrase "a mare"in Chaucer's portrait of
the Pardoner should be translated as "a homosexual."
See also Jill Mann, Chaucer and Medieval Estates Satire,
Cambridge: Cambridge University Press, 1973, pp. 145-52;
Beryl Rowland, "Chaucer's Idea of the Pardoner," Chaucer
Review, 14 (1979), 140-54 (holds that the Pardoner is a
"testicular pseudo-hermaphrodite of the feminine type");
and Melvin Storm, "The Pardoner's Invitation: Questor's
Bag or Beckett's Shrine," Publications of the Modern
Language Association, 97 (1982), 810-18 (emphasizes
sterility).

602.   MCCALL, ANDREW. The Medieval Underworld. London:
        Hamish Hamilton, 1979. 319 pp.
Chapter 7, "Homosexuality" (pp. 199-209), is a superficial
compilation from other sources. Nonetheless this book is
of some interest for the overall context.

603.   MCNEILL, JOHN THOMAS, and HELENA M. GAMER (eds.).
        Medieval Handbooks of Penance. New York: Columbia
        University Press, 1938. 476 pp.
The largest collection of these materials in English. For
analysis, see P. Payer, below.

604.   MARCHIELLO-NIZIA, CHRISTIANE. "Amour courtois,
        société masculine et figures de pouvoir," Annales
        ESC (November-December 1981), 969-82.
Courtly love as a disguised expression of homoeroticism.

605.   MARTÍNEZ PIZARRO, JOAQUÍN. "On Nid against Bish-
        ops," Medieval Scandinavia, 11 (1978-79), 149-53.
Cites texts that show four instances in which "[t]he
principles and models of behavior of the Christian
church clashed strongly with Germanic values of honor
and virility." See also T. L. Markey, "Nordic nidvisur:
An Instance of Ritual Inversion," ibid, 5 (1972), 7-19.

606.   MEULENGRACHT SORENSEN, PREBEN. Unmanly Men: Con-
        cepts of Sexual Defamation in Early Northern
        Society. Odense: Odense University Press, 1983.
        115 pp.
Thorough analysis of textual evidence in Old Norse for
homosexual behavior and defamatory accusations thereof.

607.   PARTNER, PETER. The Murdered Magicians: The
        Templars and Their Myth. London: Oxford University
        Press, 1982. 209 pp.

Suggests, in effect, that where there is smoke there is
fire; that is, that the charges of sodomy leading to the
arrest of the French Templars in 1307 were not entirely
baseless.

608.   PAYER, PIERRE J. **Sex and the Penitentials: The
       Development of a Sexual Code, 550-1150.** Toronto:
       Toronto University Press, 1984. 219 pp.
Careful study of the surviving body of documents compiled
to aid early medieval confessors in Western Europe. As
regards homosexuality, Payer reaches substantially more
negative conclusions than does Boswell; see esp. pp. 135-
39.

609.   PÉZARD, ANDRÉ. **Dante sous la pluie de feu (Enfer,
       chant XV).** Paris: J. Vrin, 1950. 468 pp. (Etudes
       de philosophie medievale, 40).
On the sodomites in Inferno 15, especially Brunetto
Latini. See also R. Kay, above.

610.   ROBY, DOUGLASS. "Early Medieval Attitudes toward
       Homosexuality." **Gai Saber,** 1 (1977), 67-79.
An introductory sketch, now dated.

611.   ROSELLÓ VAQUER, RAMÓN. **L'homosexualitat a Mallorca
       a la edat mitjana.** Barcelona: Olaneta, 1978.   32
       pp.
Discusses several cases of executions in the 15th century
on the island of Majorca.

612.   ROTH, NORMAN. "Deal Gently with the Young Men:
       Love of Boys in Medieval Poetry in Spain," **Spec-
       ulum,** 57 (1982), 20-51.
Comprehensive study of Hebrew pederastic poetry in Moorish
Spain citing many examples.

613.   ROUGEMONT, DENIS DE. **Love in the Western World.**
       Translated from the French by Montgomery Belgion.
       New York: Pantheon, 1956. 336 pp.
Influential argument that romantic love is unknown before
the rise of **amour courtois** in Western Europe in the 11th
century. Strongly criticized by Peter Dronke (see above)
and others.

614.   ROUSSELLE, ALINE. **Porneia: de la maîtrise du corps
       à la privation sensorielle--IIe-IVe siècles de
       l'ère chrétienne.** Paris: Presses Universitaires de
       France, 1983. 254 pp.
Seeks to trace the rise of ascetic and sex-negative attitudes in late antiquity through patristic, medical, and
other texts.

615.   SCHIRMANN, JEFIM. "The Ephebe in Medieval Hebrew
       Poetry," **Sefarad,** 15 (1955), 54-68.
An introduction to Hebrew pederastic poetry in Moorish
Spain inspired by Arabic models; treated more extensively

by N. Roth, above.

616.   SCHRÖTER, MICHAEL. "Staatsbildung und Triebkon-
        trolle: zur gesellschaftlichen Regulierung des
        Sexualverhaltens vom 13. bis 16. Jahrhundert,"
        Amsterdams Sociologisch Tijdschrift, 8 (May
        1981), 48-90.
On the intensification of state intervention to control
sexuality from the 13th to the 16th century.

617.   "Spuren von Kontrarsexualität bei den alten
        Skandinaviern: Mitteilungen eines norwegischen
        Gelehrten," **JfsZ,** 4 (1902), 244-63.
Pioneering article by an anonymous Norwegian scholar on
evidence for homosexuality in medieval Scandinavia.

618.   STEHLING, THOMAS (ed.). **Medieval Latin Poems of
        Love and Friendship.** New York: Garland Publishing,
        1984. 167 pp.
Comprehensive anthology of 127 items; English translations
with Latin **en face.** See also his "To Love a Medieval
Boy," **JH,** 8:3/4 (1983), 151-70, which analyzes poems by
Marbod of Rennes, Baudri of Bourgueil, and Hilary the
Englishman.

619.   STROM, FOLKE. **Nid, Ergi and Old Norse Moral
        Attitudes.** London: University College, 1974.   20
        pp. (Dorothea Coke Memorial Lecture)
Analyzes use of accusations of passive homosexuality as
insults. In addition to verbal attacks, "fighting words,"
small sculptures were carved for this purpose.

620.   VANGGAARD, THORKIL. **Phallos: A Symbol and Its
        History in the Male World.** New York: International
        Universities Press, 1973. 231 pp.
Arguing for the generalized existence of a "homosexual
radical" in men, the author of this semipopular work takes
much of his historical material from medieval Scandinavia.

621.   ZIOLKOWSKI, JAN. **Alan of Lille's Grammar of
        Sex: The Meaning of Grammar to a Twelfth-Century
        Intellectual.** Cambridge, MA: The Medieval Academy
        of America, 1985. 171 pp. (Speculum Anniversary
        Monographs, 10)
Includes discussion of the use of grammatical metaphors to
castigate sexual deviation, including homosexuality. See
also John A. Alford, "The Grammatical Metaphor: A Survey
of Its Use in the Middle Ages," **Speculum,** 57 (1982), 728-
60; and Richard Hamilton Green, "Alan of Lille's **De planc-
tu naturae,**" **Speculum,** 31 (1956), 649-74.

E. EARLY MODERN EUROPE

This period, broadly from the 15th through the 18th centuries, saw the spread of Renaissance ideals throughout
Europe. The revival of Greco-Roman culture, particularly
as evident in the philosophical doctrine known as Neo-
platonism, fostered a cautious exploration of the theme of
pederasty. The Reformation and Counterreformation caused
an intensification of religious zealotry, in which charges
of sodomy were hurled on both sides. The exploration of
the New World produced some findings, interpreted at the
outset in a totally hostile manner, on cross-cultural comparisons in regard to homosexual behavior (see Meso-Amer-
ican and South American Indians; IV.F). There is much
detailed evidence for legal prosecutions and executions of
male homosexuals (see also the following sections on individual countries; and "Law," XX).

622.   CROMPTON, LOUIS. "The Myth of Lesbian Impunity,"
       JH, 6 (1980-81), 11-26.
Shows that beginning in the 13th century some theologians assimilated lesbianism to male homosexuality as
worthy of death. However, only about ten executions are
known, chiefly of women who had made use of a dildo.

623.   DEJOB, CHARLES. **Marc-Antoine Muret: un professeur
       français en Italie dans la seconde moitié du XVIe
       siècle.** Paris: E. Thorin, 1881. 497 pp.
Reprinted by Slatkine, Geneva in 1970. See Chapter 3, pp.
46-61, on his imprisonment and condemnation for sodomy.

624.   FOUCAULT, MICHEL. **Madness and Civilization: His-
       tory of Insanity in the Age of Reason.** Translated
       by Richard Howard. New York: Pantheon, 1965. 299
       pp.
An influential study by the late French historian on the
link between the definition of madness and authoritarian
social control. Note that the English version derives
from an abridged French edition. For full references,
consult the revised full text: **Histoire de la folie à
l'âge classique** (Paris: Gallimard, 1972; 613 pp.)

625.   GERARD, KENT, and GERT HEKMA (eds.). **The Pursuit
       of Sodomy in Early Modern Europe: Male Homosex-
       uality from the Renaissance through the Enlighten-
       ment.** Special issue of **JH**, 12:4/13:4 (Winter
       1985/Spring 1986).
Papers covering virtually the whole of western Europe, but
with special attention to the Netherlands.

626.   GILBERT, ARTHUR N. "Conceptions of Homosexuality
       and Sodomy in Western History," **JH**, 6 (1980-81),
       57-68.

Contrasts the biographical approach with broader inquiries
of labeling and intolerance. In the latter, Gilbert argues
that irrational fears of anal intercourse may have
played a greater role than is usually allowed.

627. HAGSTRUM, JEAN H. **Sex and Sensibility: Ideal and
      Erotic Love from Milton to Mozart.** Chicago: Univer-
      sity of Chicago Press, 1980. 350 pp.
This sensitive study in cultural history has a general
bearing, as well as some specific discussion; see esp.
pp. 45-46, 82-83, 86, 102-04, 146, 189, 193, 202-03, 217,
22, 234, 269-70, 295, 305.

628. KARLSTADT, ANDREAS BODENSTEIN VON. **De coelibatu,
      monachatu et viduitate ...** Wittenberg: Melchior
      Lotter, 1521. 36 pp.
A characteristic Lutheran attack on monastic vices, esp.
sodomy and masturbation.

629. MONTER, E. WILLIAM. "Sodomy and Heresy in Early
      Modern Switzerland," **JH,** 6 (1980-81), 42-55.
Compares sodomy trials from Protestant Geneva with those
in Catholic Fribourg, showing also an urban vs. rural
contrast.

630. MURRAY, STEPHEN, and KENT GERARD. "Renaissance
      Sodomite Subcultures?" in: **Among Men, Among Women.**
      Amsterdam: Universiteit, 1983 [Congress preprints],
      183-96.
Surveys our present knowledge, chiefly from records of
trials and executions, with suggestions for further
research.

631. PRESCOTT, ANNE LAKE. "English Writers and Beza's
      Latin Epigrams," **Studies in the Renaissance,** 21
      (1974), 83-117.
Theodore de Beze, a major leader of Calvinism, was
subjected to considerable criticism for lechery and
homosexuality because of some early Latin poems. See
the edition of the poems by Alexandre Machard (Paris:
Liseux, 1879).

632. ROUSSEAU, G. S. "The Pursuit of Homosexuality in
      the Eighteenth Century: 'Utterly Confused Category'
      and/or Rich Repository?" **Eighteenth-Century Life,** 9
      (1985), 132-68.
Analyzes literary materials according to a six-category
schema, citing many little known texts.

633. RUIG, ROB DE. **In de schaduw van de grand seig-
      neur.** Utrecht: E.J. van Himbergen, 1984.
Class differences, esp. homosexuality as a feature of the
pleasure life of the nobility, in ancien regime Europe.

634. SCHOUTEN, H. J. "Die vermeintliche Päderastie des
      Reformators Jean Calvin," **JfsZ,** 7 (1905), 289-306.

Although the Reformer John Calvin was probably not homosexual, the efforts of Catholic polemicists to discredit
him by such accusations form an interesting chapter in
cultural history.

635. TRUMBACH, RANDOLPH. "Sodomite Subcultures, Sod-
      omitical Roles, and the Gender Revolution of the
      Eighteenth Century: The Recent Historiography,"
      Eighteenth-Century Life, 9 (1985), 109-21.
Analysis of assumptions and findings of a decade of study
of homosexual behavior in Western Europe.

                        F. BRITISH ISLES

Students of British history are beset by two opposing
temptations: to regard the islands as sui generis, at most
linking them to the English-speaking world (exceptionalism); or to regard them as offshore dependencies of the
European continent (Europeanism). Both trends may be
found in actual British attitudes toward homosexual
behavior. Exceptionalism is evident in a preference for
slow change, rather than abrupt breaks; a desire to preserve propriety and respectability, sometimes at the cost
of even forbidding discussion of sexual matters; and a
tendency to avoid theoretical approaches among intellectuals. On the other hand, the reception of Christian
hostility toward homosexuality, the Reformation inflection
of them, and in recent times the emergence of sexual
reform attest successive waves of influence from the European continent. Legal aspects are treated under XX.D;
the public school tradition under XI.A, and military
history under XII.A.

636. ACKERLEY, JOSEPH R. **My Father and Myself**. New
      York: Coward-McCann, 1968. 219 pp.
Autobiographical memoir in which the English writer-editor
(1896-1967) reconstructs his father's bisexual past, with
many revealing historical sidelights. See also: **The Ack-
erley Letters**. Edited by Neville Braybrooke (New York:
Harcourt Brace, 1975; 354 pp.) and **My Sister and Myself:
The Diaries of J. R. Ackerley**. Edited by Francis King
(London: Hutchinson, 1982; 217 pp.).

637. ACKLAND, VALENTINE. **For Sylvia: An Honest Ac-
      count**. New York: W. W. Norton, 1986. 135 pp.
Ackland (b. 1906) describes her relationship with the
writer Sylvia Townsend Warner, offering insights on the
situation of British lesbians in the first half of the
present century.

638. BARNARD (BERNARD), NICHOLAS. **The Penitent Death of
      ... John Atherton**. Dublin: Society of Stationers,

1641.
An account of the notable hanging of the Anglican Bishop
of Waterford and Lismore for buggery. Further editions
appeared in London in 1642 and 1651.

639.   BARRETT, CONNIE. "Wearing of the Gay," **Christopher
        Street**, no. 70 (November 1982), 32-38.
On gay life in today's Ireland.

640.   BINGHAM, CAROLINE. "Seventeenth Century Attitudes
        toward Deviant Sex," **Journal of Interdisciplinary
        History**, 1 (1971), 447-68.
Focuses on the trial and execution of the Earl of Castle-
haven (1631) for sodomy.

641.   BLOCH, IWAN. **Das Geschlechtsleben in England.** By
        Eugen Duhren (pseud.). Berlin: Barsdorf, 1901-03.
        3 vols.
This massive history is a quarry of information. Regrettably, the English version--**Sexual Life in England Past
and Present** (London: Aldor, 1938; also several other
printings)--is heavily abridged and should be avoided.

642.   BRAY, ALAN. **Homosexuality in Renaissance England.**
        London: Gay Men's Press, 1982. 149 pp.
Argues that a major shift developed in the course of the
seventeenth century from an older, quasimagical concept of
homosexual behavior to a stigmatized, subcultural form,
which foreshadows our own.

643.   BRISTOW, EDWARD J. **Vice and Vigilance: Purity
        Movements in Britain since 1700.** Totowa, NJ: Row-
        man and Littlefield, 1977. 274 pp.
A useful synthesis of outbreaks of antisexual attitudes
and their forms of social organization.

644.   BURFORD, E. J. **The Orrible Synne: A Look at London
        Lechery from Roman to Cromwellian Times.** London:
        Calder and Boyars, 1973. 256 pp.
In this popularized panorama, see pp. 19, 23, 47-48, 67,
75, 139, 144, 149, 167, 218, and 233.

645.   BURG, R. R. **Sodomy and the Perception of Evil:
        English Sea Rovers in the Seventeenth-Century
        Caribbean.** New York: New York University Press,
        1983. 215 pp.
Something of a shaggy dog story, inasmuch as little
evidence in this potentially fascinating area is offered.
See also his: "Ho Hum: Another Work of the Devil," **JH**, 6
(1981-82), 69-78.

646.   CALDER-MARSHALL, ARTHUR. "Havelock Ellis and Com-
        pany," **Encounter**, 37 (December 1971), 8-23.
On controversies about sexuality in the 1890s.

647. CROFT-COOKE, RUPERT. **Feasting with Panthers.** New
      York: Holt, Rinehart and Winston, 1967. 309 pp.
Depicts some late Victorian figures, including John
Addington Symonds and Oscar Wilde, as their lives inter-
sected with homosexuality.

648. CROMPTON, LOUIS. **Byron and Greek Love: Homophobia
      in 19th-Century England.** Berkeley: University of
      California Press, 1985. 419 pp.
Comprehensive study of George Gordon, Lord Byron's (1788-
1824) bisexuality, set against the English background of
the time--including the thought of Jeremy Bentham.

649. DANIEL, MARC (pseud.). "L'homosexualité en Angle-
      terre," **Arcadie,** no. 47 (November 1957), 5-10;
      no. 48 (December 1957), 12-17; no. 49 (January
      1958), 40-42; no. 51 (March 1958), 28-30.
Views of a French archivist and historian, who subsequently produced a major biography: Michel Duchein,
Jacques Ier Stuart: le roi et la paix, Paris: Presses de
la Renaissance, 1985. 429 pp.

650. ELTON, GEOFFREY R. **Policy and Politics: The En-
      forcement of the Reformation in the age of Thomas
      Cromwell.** Cambridge: Cambridge University Press,
      1972. 447 pp.
A distinguished English historian shows the complicated
permutations of Henry VIII's policies, which included the
first civil statute in England against buggery (1533).

651. FADERMAN, LILLIAN. **Scotch Verdict.** New York: Mor-
      row, 1983. 320 pp.
Subjective investigation of an Edinburgh controversy
(1811-19) involving lesbian allegations.

652. GILBERT, ARTHUR N. "Sexual Deviance and Disaster
      during the Napoleonic Wars." **Albion,** 9 (1977),
      98-113.
Shows how after a period of neglect, the persecution of
sodomites reached new heights in Britain in the early
19th century, culminating in 1810 with the exposure of
the Vere Street Coterie. Gilbert suggests scapegoating
as an explanation. See also his: "The Africaine Courts-
Martial: A Study of Buggery and the Royal Navy," **JH,** 1
(1974), 111-22; and "Buggery and the British Navy, 1700-
1861," **Journal of Social History,** 10 (1976-77), 72-98.

653. GORDON, MARY LOUISA. **The Chase of the Wild Goose.**
      London: Hogarth Press, 1936. 279 pp.
On the "ladies of Llangollen," Lady Eleanor Butler and
Sarah Ponsonby, who conducted a passionate relationship
in 18th-century Britain.

654. GRAHAM, JAMES. **The Homosexual Kings of England.**
      London: Universal Tandem Publishing, 1968. 92 pp.
Lackluster biographical sketches of William Rufus,

Richard the Lion-hearted, Edward II, Richard II, James
I, and William Rufus.

655.   GREEN, MARTIN BURGESS. **Children of the Sun: A
        Narrative of Decadence in England after 1918.** New
        York: Basic Books, 1976. 470 pp.
Sometimes tendentious account of English aesthetes in
the interwar period, esp. Brian Howard and Harold Acton.

656.   HALSBAND, ROBERT. **Lord Hervey: Eighteenth-Century
        Courtier.** London: Oxford University Press, 1979.
        380 pp.
Detailed and judicious social history and biography, show-
ing that the acerbic and epicene minister of George II had
an affair with the ambitious Stephen Fox. See also James
R. Dubro, "The Third Sex: Lord Hervey and His Coterie,"
Eighteenth-Century Life, 2:4 (June 1976), 89-95.

657.   HARRIS, JOHN. **The Destruction of Sodom: A Sermon
        Preached at a Public Fast, before the Honourable
        Assembly of the Commons House of Parliament.**
        London: G. Lathum, 1628.
An example of the graphic exploitation of the horrors of
Sodom's fate, as seen in many parts of Europe in the first
half of the 16th century. Attacks "[m]asculine bestiality: a sinne, none but a Divell, come out of Hell in the
likeness of a man, dares to comitt; a sinne, enough to
defile the tongue that talks of it." Exceedingly rare.

658.   HARVEY, A. D. "Prosecution for Sodomy in England
        at the Beginning of the Nineteenth Century,"
        Historical Journal, 21 (1978), 939-48.
On the last great wave of persecution in western Europe;
see also A. N. Gilbert, above.

659.   HEIMANS, H. E. **Het karakter van Willem III, ko-
        ning-stadhouder: proove eener psychografie.** Am-
        sterdam: 1925. 298 pp.
A study of the character of William III, king of England
(1689-1702), and stadholder of Holland.

660.   HYDE, H. MONTGOMERY. **The Cleveland Street Scan-
        dal.** New York: Coward, McCann and Geoghegan,
        1976. 266 pp.
Account of the discovery of a male brothel in London
(1889-90) and the three resulting trials. See also C.
Simpson et al., below.

661.   HYDE, H. MONTGOMERY. **The Love that Dared Not Speak
        Its Name: A Candid History of Homosexuality in
        Britain.** Boston: Little, Brown, 1970. 323 pp.
Standard survey of homosexual behavior in Britain from
William Rufus to the post-Wolfenden era.

662.   HYDE, H. MONTGOMERY (ed.). **The Three Trials of
        Oscar Wilde.** New York: University Books, 1956.

384 pp.
Transcript of the three trials in London in 1895, accompanied by useful introduction and appendices by Hyde.

663.   IVES, GEORGE CECIL. **Man Bites Man: The Scrapbook**
       of an Edwardian Eccentric. Edited by Paul Sieveking. London: Jay Landesman, 1980.
Selections from some 20,000 pages of the diary of a man
(1867-1950) who seemingly knew everyone, chosen from 122
volumes (now in the Library of the University of Texas,
Austin).

664.   JEFFREYS, SHEILA. **The Spinster and Her Enemies:**
       Feminism and Sexuality 1880-1930. London: Pandora
       Press, 1985.
Examines the later phases of the social purity movement in
England and the beginnings of serious sex research and
sexual reform. Documents some tenacious antilesbian attitudes.

665.   JENKYNS, RICHARD. **The Victorians and Ancient**
       Greece. Cambridge, MA: Harvard University Press,
       1980. 386 pp.
Presents relevant material on Walter Pater, J. A. Symonds,
and Oscar Wilde; unsympathetic.

666.   KNOWLES, DAVID. **Bare Ruined Choirs: The Dissolu-**
       tion of the English Monasteries. Cambridge: Cambridge University Press, 1976. 330 pp.
In this study by a major historian of British monasticism,
see pp. 177-78, 184-85, 188. Items 667-676 omitted.

677.   LIPSHITZ, SUSAN. **Sexual Politics in Britain: A**
       Bibliographical Guide with Historical Notes.
       Hassocks, England: Harvester Press, 1977. 41 pp.
Introduces an emerging field of study.

678.   LUTTRELL, NARCISSUS. **A Brief Historical Relation**
       of State Affairs. Oxford: Oxford University Press,
       1857. 6 vols.
Contains references to executions and persecutions between
1687 and 1707. See vol. 1, p. 395; vol. 2, pp. 596, 613,
615; vol. 3, pp. 317, 320; vol. 4, pp. 461-62; 543;
vol. 6, p. 219, 222-26.

679.   MARCUS, STEPHEN. **The Other Victorians.** New
       York: Basic Books, 1966. 292 pp.
This landmark study of several salient (heterosexual)
figures lifted the mask of Victorian respectability.

680.   MAVOR, ELIZABETH. **The Ladies of Llangollen.**
       London: Joseph, 1971. 238 pp.
The story of the 18th-century lesbian couple. See also
M. L. Gordon, above.

681.   **Miss Marianne Woods and Miss Jane Pirie against**

Dame Helen Cumming Gordon. New York: Arno Press, 1975.
Reprint of records of the Edinburgh lesbian trial, 1811-19; see also L. Faderman, above.

682.   O'NEILL, JOHN H.   "Sexuality, Deviance, and Moral Character in the Personal Satire of the Restoration," **Eighteenth-Century Life,** 2 (1975), 16-19.
William III accused of homosexuality.

683.   PAVIA, I. LEO.   "Die männliche Homosexualität in England mit besondere Berücksichtigung Londons," **JfsZ,** 10 (1909-10), 362-78; 11 (191-11), 18-51, 397-408; and 12 (1911-12), 32-49, 166-81, and 297-316.
A somewhat harsh account of attitudes toward homosexuality in England before World War I, concentrating on the concept of hypocrisy, which the author holds to have been pervasive. Offers some interesting sidelights on meeting places and customs.

684.   PEARCE, FRANK, and ANDREW ROBERTS.   "The Social Regulation of Sexual Behavior and the Development of Industrial Capitalism in Britain," in Roy Bailey and Jock Young (eds.), **Contemporary Social Problems in Britain.** Lexington, MA: Lexington Books, 1973, pp. 51-72.
Seeks to place changing social control of homosexuality in the context of capitalist industrialization and changing family structure.

685.   PEARSALL, RONALD.   **The Worm in the Bud: The World of Victorian Sexuality.** New York: Macmillan, 1969.   560 pp.
In this readable panorama, see esp. 448-96.   See also: Kellow Chesney, **The Anti-Society: An Account of the Victorian Underworld** (Boston: Gambit, 1970; 398 pp.), pp. 16, 96, 100, 327-29.

686.   PODHORETZ, NORMAN.   "The Culture of Appeasement," **Harper's,** 255 (October 1977), 25-32.
Insinuates that homosexuality was a major factor in the pacifism that flourished between the World Wars.

687.   ROLLISON, DAVID.   "Property, Ideology and Popular Culture in a Gloucestershire Village, 1660-1740," **Past and Present,** no. 93 (November 1981), 70-97.
Despite the author's failure to grasp the implications, this article is a vivid account of a charivari held as a symbolic exorcism of a sodomite relationship.

688.   SIMPSON, COLIN, LEWIS CHESTER, and DAVID LEITCH.   **The Cleveland Street Affair.** Boston: Little, Brown, 1976.   236 pp.
Account of the scandal that developed when a male brothel was discovered in London in 1889; see also H. M. Hyde,

above.

689.   **Sins of the Cities of the Plain; or the Recollec-
        tions of a Mary Anne, with Short Essays on Sodomy
        and Tribadism.** London: Leicester Square, 1881.   95
        pp.
On the Bolton-Park scandals and other contemporary
matters.

689A.   STAVES, SUSAN. "A Few Kind Words for the Fop,"
        SEL: Studies in English Literature 1500-1800, 22
        (1982), 413-28.
Presents evidence, drawn from plays, for the different
meanings of effeminacy in the 17th and 18th centuries.

690.   TELLEGEN, JAN-WILLEM. "'Some Unmanly Oddities':
        enige spekulaties over de konstruktie van manne-
        lijkheid en homoseksualiteit in victoriaans
        Engeland," **Psychologie en Maatschappij,** 8:4 (1984),
        457-78.
Reflections on the construction of male identity and
homosexuality in 19th-century England.

691.   THOMPSON, ROGER. **Unfit for Modest Ears: A Study
        of Pornographic, Obscene and Bawdy Works Written or
        Published in England in the Second Half of the Sev-
        enteenth Century.** London: Macmillan, 1979. 233 pp.
See pp. 10, 13, 32-33, 36, 41, 43-44, 51, 124-129, 137-39,
141, 149, 170, 172, 198. See also David Foxon, **Libertine
Literature in England, 1660-1745** (New Hyde Park, NY: University Books, 1965; 70 pp.); and Peter Naumann, **Keyhole
und Candle: John Clelands "Memoirs of a Woman of Pleasure"
und die Entstehung des pornographischen Romans in England**
(Heidelberg: Carl Winter, 1976; 468 pp.).

692.   TRUMBACH, RANDOLPH. "London's Sodomites: Homosexu-
        al Behavior in the Eighteenth Century," **Journal of
        Social History,** 11 (1977), 1-33.
Argues from a survey of the anthropological literature and
from the evidence of the raids on the London sodomite
sub-culture in the 1720s that Europeans were unique in not
tolerating homosexual behavior and that there had probably
been illicit sodomite subcultures in the cities of Europe
since the 12th century.

693.   TRUMBACH, RANDOLPH (ed.). **Sodomy Trials: Seven
        Documents.** New York: Garland Publishing, 1986.
        (Marriage, Sex, and the Family in England, 1660-
        1800, vol. 44)
Includes: **The Tryal and Condemnation of Mervin, Lord
Audley Earl of Castle-Haven ... 1631 (1699); The Woman-
Hater's Lamentation (1707); A Faithful Narrative of the
Late Affair between the Rev. Mr. John Swinton, and
Mr. George Baker (1739); The Whole Proceedings on the
Wicked Conspiracy ... (1751); The Trial of Samuel
Scrimshaw and John Ross (1759); The Trial of Richard**

Branson (1760); and **The Phoenix of Sodom, or the Vere Street Coterie** (1813). In this series of Garland reprints see also **Select Trials at the Sessions House in the Old Bailey** (4 vols. reprinted in 2), vol. 1, 105, 158-60, 280-82, 329-30; vol. 2, 362-72; vol. 3,36-40, 74-75.

694.   VICINUS, MARTHA. **Independent Women: Work and Community for Single Women, 1850-1920.** Chicago: Chicago University Press, 1985. 396 pp.
Kaleidoscopic picture of single women in Britain from High Victorianism through the Suffragette era. including discussion of schoolgirl crushes ("raves") and intense "spiritual friendships."

695.   WARD, EDWARD (NED). **A Compleat and Humorous Account of All the Remarkable Clubs and Societies in the Cities of London and Westminster.** London, 1756.
First edition 1709. Includes an account of the molly houses.

696.   WEEKS, JEFFREY. **Sex, Politics and Society: The Regulation of Sexuality Since 1800.** London: Longman, 1981. 306 pp.
Paints a broad canvas, including such themes as social control, male and female sex roles, prostitution, eugenics, and the sexual purity movement. For homosexuality, see esp. pp. 96-121. Sometimes marred by Franglais jargon and murky analysis. See also his: **Coming Out: Homosexual Politics in Britain from the Nineteenth Century to the Present** (New York: Horizon Press, 1977; 278 pp.); and "Inverts, Perverts and Mary-Annes: Male Prostitution and the Regulation of Homosexuality in England in the Nineteenth and Early Twentieth Centuries," JH, 6 (1980-81), 113-34.

697.   WILDEBLOOD, PETER. **Against the Law.** London: Weidenfeld and Nicolson, 1956. 189 pp.
An English journalist offers a first-hand account of his arrest, conviction and imprisonment through involvement in the Lord Montagu case (1954).

                            G. FRANCE

The evidence for homosexual behavior in France, especially from literary sources, is extensive. Perhaps for this reason, no satisfactory syntheses have been produced. It is evident, however, that just as the Revolution of 1789 constitutes the great divide of French history as a whole, so it also separates homosexual history into two phases. From the Middle Ages (see III.D), France had preserved the religious and legal prohibitions of same-sex behavior. But then, relying on conceptual foundations

laid by the Enlightenment thinkers, the Revolution decriminalized sodomy--the first accomplishment of this goal in
any European country. Social toleration was slower
in coming, however, and the 19th century provides much
evidence of continuing social disapproval and official
surveillance of homosexual behavior. The defeat of 1940
and the ensuing Vichy regime saw a deterioration of the
situation of homosexuals in France, which was not fully
overcome until the modernization process hit its stride in
the 1960s and 70s.

698. **Anandria, ou confessions de Mademoiselle Sapho;**
      contenant les détails de sa réception dans la Secte
      Anandrine sous la présidence de Mlle Raucourt et
      ses diverses aventures. Paris: "En Grèce," 1789.
      140 pp.
This text, first published in 1784, is one of several
purported accounts of initiation into the lesbian coterie
surrounding the actress Françoise Raucourt ("les anan-
drines," or menless women).

699. **Anecdotes pour servir à l'histoire des Ebugors.**
      Amsterdam: J. P. du Valis, 1733. 106 pp.
Fanciful account of a war between the Ebugors (bougres)
and the Cythereans (heterosexual women). The modern
edition prepared by Jean Hervez for the Bibliothèque des
Curieux, Paris, 1912, provides additional material,
including the "Statuts des Sodomites au XVIIe siecle."

700. AUBIGNÉ, THÉODORE AGRIPPA D'. **Oeuvres.** Edited by
      Henri Weber. Paris: Gallimard, 1969. 1594 pp.
In this collected edition of the works of the French
Protestant statesman and writer, see pp. 72, 73 (1. 827,
"androgame"), 74, 76 (1. 934, "un Bathille"), 79, 81, 84,
85, 339, 344, (1. 52, "bougrerie"), 585-89, 605, 606
("amour philosophique et sacrée"), 610 ("frères de la
Sacrée Société") 616, 626 ("bougre agent"; "bougre patient"), 647, 828.

701. BARBEDETTE, GILLES, and MICHEL CARASSOU. **Paris gay**
      1925. Paris: Les Presses de la Renaissance, 1981.
      312 pp.
Panorama of the homosexual scene in Paris in the 1920s,
featuring interviews with survivors and excerpts from the
pioneering magazine **Inversions** (1924-25). For a hostile
contemporary report, see: Georges Anquetil, **Satan conduit**
le bal (Paris: Georges-Anquetil, 1925; 536 pp.).

702. BAUDRY, ANDRÉ. **La condition des homosexuels.** Tou-
      louse: Privat, 1982.
Overview of the present situation by the director of Arcadie, the French homophile organization (1957-82).

703. BAUMANN, F. "Duelle homosexueller Frauen in
      Paris," **Die Zeitschrift** (Hamburg), 31 (1912), 54-

63.
Lesbian duels in Paris.

704.   BAYLE, PIERRE. **Dictionnaire historique et cri-
       tique.** Third ed. Rotterdam: M. Bohm, 1720. 4
       vols.
In this magnum opus by the noted rationalist critic (1647-
1706), see the following articles: Adonis, Anacreon, Antinous, Bathylle, de Bèze, Chrysippe, Dassouci, Ganymède,
Hadrien, Jules II, Sixte IV, Vayer, as well as the section
entitled "Eclaircissements sur les obscénités."

705.   BÉNÉDICTI, JEAN. **La somme des péchés et le remède
       d'iceux.** Paris: G. Chaudière, 1601. 827 pp.
In this influential manual for confessors, see "De
mollesse" and "De sodomie," pp. 152-62.

706.   BERNAY, JÉRÔME (pseud. of François Jacques).
       **Grand'peur et misère des homosexuels français: en-
       quête auprès des homophiles provinciaux.** Paris:
       Éditions Arcadie, 1977. 74 pp.
From interviews constructs a picture of the often lonely
lives of French homosexuals living in the provinces.

707.   BLOCH, IWAN. **Der Marquis de Sade und seine Zeit:
       ein Beitrag zur Kultur- und Sittengeschichte des
       18. Jahrhunderts, mit besonderer Beziehung auf die
       Lehre von der Psychopathia Sexualis.** By Eugen
       Dühren (pseud.). Berlin: Barsdorf, 1900. 502 pp.
A major study of the late 18th century with much information about French sexual "nonconformists." Unfortunately,
the English version is heavily abridged: **Marquis de Sade,
the Man and His Age** (Newark, NJ: Julian, 1931; 290 pp.;
various reprints).

708.   BON, MICHEL, and ANTOINE D'ARC. **Rapport sur
       l'homosexualité de l'homme.** Paris: Éditions
       Universitaires, 1974. 526 pp.
Based on a survey of members of Arcadie, presents a five-
part study of causation, sociology, sex behavior, couples,
and social settings. These findings are updated in Jean
Cavailhes et al., **Rapport gai: enquête sur les modes de
vie homosexuels en France** (Paris: Persona, 1984; 273 pp.).

709.   BONNET, MARIE-JO. **Un choix sans équivoque: re-
       cherches historiques sur les relations amoureuses
       entre les femmes, xvie-xxe siècle.** Paris: Denoël,
       1981. 295 pp.
Major study, well documented with literary and other references, on the understanding of lesbianism from the Renaissance to the present.

710.   BOUCHARD, JEAN-JACQUES. **Confessions.** Paris: Li-
       seux: 1881. 256 pp.
Offers some contemporary information on homosexual
behavior among schoolboys and in the Corsican galley

station (ca. 1630)

711.   BRANTÔME, PIERRE. **The Lives of Gallant Ladies.**
        Translated by Alec Brown. London: Elek, 1962.   537
        pp.
Translation of a work published posthumously in 1665.
This French classic contains a number of important
references to lesbian behavior in the time of the writer
(1535?-1614).

712.   BRASSAÏ (pseud. of Gyula Halasz). **The Secret Paris
        of the 30's.** Translated by Richard Miller. New
        York: Pantheon Books, 1976.   200 pp.
In this album of work and text by the noted photographer,
see the sections, "The Urinals of Paris" and "Sodom and
Gomorrah."

713.   BRÉCOURT-VILLARS, CLAUDINE. **Petit glossaire
        raisonné de l'erotisme saphique, 1880-1930.**
        Paris: J.-J. Pauvert, 1980.   123 pp.
Profusely illustrated book on lesbian eroticism during the
Third Republic.

714.   BRÉZOL, GEORGES. **Henri III et ses mignons.**
        Paris: Les Editions de Bibliophiles, 1911.   245 pp.
Account of France's 16th-century homosexual king and his
male favorites.

715.   CARLIER, FRANÇOIS. **Etudes de pathologie sociale:
        les deux prostitutions, 1860-1870.** Paris: Dentu,
        1887.   514 pp.
As chief of the the vice squad in Paris under the Second
Empire, Carlier drew upon personal knowledge and his
extensive files to produce a detailed picture of urban
prostitution and street life. See "Prostitution anti-
physique," pp. 275-473.

716.   COUROUVE, CLAUDE. **Les gens de la manchette.**
        Paris: The author, 1978.   24 pp.
Presents 18th-century archival documents documenting the
existence of a homosexual subculture in Paris. Much
useful information also appears in Courouve's major work
of historical semantics **Vocabulaire de l'homosexualité
masculine** (Paris: Payot, 1985; 248 pp.).

717.   COUROUVE, CLAUDE. "Sodomy Trials in France," **Gay
        Books Bulletin,** 1:1 (1979), 22-23, 26.
Annotated list of 53 known sodomy trials between 1317 and
1783.

718.   COWARD, D. A. "Attitudes to Homosexuality in
        Eighteenth-Century France," **Journal of European
        Studies,** 10:4 (December 1980), 231-55.
Well documented study of the sometimes elusive attitudes
toward sexual variation in the last century of the Ancien
Regime.

719.   DANIEL, MARC (pseud.). "A Study of Homosexuality
       in France during the Reigns of Louis XII and Louis
       XIV," **ONE Institute Quarterly,** no. 14 (Summer
       1961), 77-93; and no. 15 (Fall 1961), 125-36.
Translated by "Marcel Martin" (Ross Ingersoll) from
articles in **Arcadie** (December 1956-September 1957).
Informative survey based mainly on the lives of prominent
persons. See also his **Hommes du grand siècle** (Paris: Arcadie, 1957; 65 pp.).

720.   DELON, MICHEL. "The Priest, the Philosopher, and
       Homosexuality in Enlightenment France," **Eighteenth-
       Century Life,** 9 (1985), 122-131.
Citing a variety of evidence, including observations of
exotic peoples, Delon claims that "the Englightenment
helped to conceive a polymorphos **body of pleasure** which
replaced the **body of glory** of theology." Emphasis on
Diderot and Voltaire. See also: Jacob Stockinger,
"Homosexuality and the French Enlightenment," in: G. Stambolian and E. Marks (eds.), **Homosexualities and French
Literature.** Ithaca: Cornell University Press, 1978, pp.
161-85.

721.   DESMON, ANDRE CLAUDE (pseud. of A. Lafond).
       "L'homophilie dans la France d'aujourd'hui,"
       Arcadie, no. 202 (October 1970), 457-95.
Report on contemporary French conditions and public attitudes.

722.   DICKERMAN, EDMUND H. "Henry III's Devotions: A
       Study in Sex and Religion," **Journal of Psycho-
       history,** 5:3 (1978), 429-42.
Psychoanalytic study linking the king's religious mania to
his "feminine nature."

723.   DUBOIS-DESAULLE, GASTON. **Prêtres et moines non-
       conformistes en amour: Mémoires secrets de la
       Lieutenance Générale de Police.** Paris: Editions de
       la Raison, 1902. 344 pp.
Confidential police records as evidence of forbidden
sexual activities among the Ancien Regime clergy.

724.   DUPERRAY, MICHEL. **De l'état et da la capacité des
       ecclésiastiques pour les ordres et bénéfices.**
       Paris: P. Eméry et M. Brunet, 1703. 683 pp.
For sodomites among the clergy, see pp. 312-20 (III, 8).

725.   **Les enfans de Sodome a l'Assemblée Nationale, ou
       députation de l'Ordre de la Manchette.** Paris:
       "Chez le Marquis de Villette," 1790. ca. 35 pp.
A rare pamphlet of the French Revolution, naming some 160
purported homosexuals, male and female, and proffering the
bylaws of a secret society, l'Ordre de la Manchette. A
similar pamphlet, **Les petits bougres au manège** (Paris,
"Chez Pierre Pousse-Fort," 1790; 31 pp.) advocates a
kind of proto-gay rights position, under the cover of

facetiousness.

726.   ESTRÉES, PAUL D' (pseud. of Henri Quentin). **Les**
       infâmes sous l'ancien régime. Paris: Gugy, 1902.
Collects unpublished police documents from the Bibliothèque Nationale and the Bibliothèque de l'Arsenal, Paris.

727.   FLEISCHMANN, HECTOR. **L'enfer de la galanterie a la**
       fin de l'ancien régime: le cénacle libertin de Mlle
       Raucourt (de la Comédie Française). Paris: Biblio-
       thèque des Curieux, 1912. 329 pp.
Attempts to synthesize what is known about the actress
Francoise Raucourt, who ostensibly founded a lesbian
secret society during the reign of Louis XVI.

728.   FLEISCHMANN, HECTOR. **Histoire licencieuse: les**
       maîtresses de Marie Antoinette. Paris: Editions
       des Bibliophiles, 1910. 260 pp.
Historical gossip about the queen's supposed lesbian
liaisons. See also his: **Mme de Polignac et la cour**
galante de Marie Antoinette d'après les libelles obscènes
(Paris: Bibliothèque des Curieux, 1910. 255 pp.).

729.   FOURNIER-VERNEUIL, and H. DE MONTROUGE. **Paris:**
       tableau moral et philosophique. Paris: 1826. 632
       pp.
For pederastic cliques in Paris since the Revolution, see
pp. 313-14, 335-38, 367, and 397-98.

730.   GLATIGNY, ALBERT, et al. **La Sultane Rozréa,**
       Badinguette et autres chansons contemporaines.
       Strasbourg: Société des Bibliophiles Cosmopolites,
       1871. 84 pp.
See pp. 17-22 for the homosexual clique known as the
Société des Emiles, discovered by the French police in
1864, whose president was an Alsatian officer (later
senator of the Second Empire) who had killed the poet
Pushkin in a duel in 1837. Prints the songs "Lamentation
des filles" and "Les deux trous."

731.   HAHN, PIERRE (ed.). **Nos ancêtres les pervers: la**
       vie des homosexuels sous le second empire. Paris:
       Olivier Orban, 1971. 336 pp.
Selection of original texts offering a panorama of homosexual life in France (1852-1870), with lengthy introduction.

732.   HERNANDEZ, LUDOVICO (pseud.). **Les procès de sodo-**
       mie aux xvie, xviie et xviiie siècles. Paris: Bib-
       liothèque des Curieux, 1920.
Provides texts of court records of sodomy trials under
the Ancien Régime.

733.   HERVEZ, JEAN (pseud. of Raoul Vèze). **Les sociétés**
       d'amour au xviiie siècle. Paris: Daragon, 1906.
       358 pp.

On 18th century secret societies; see pp. 238-74.

734.   JARRIGE, PIERRE. **Les jesuites mis sur l'eschauf-
        faud.** Leiden: J. Nicolas, 1649.
In this polemical work by an ex-Jesuit converted to Calvinism, see Chapter 5, "Les impudicites des jesuites dans
leurs classes."

735.   JULLIAN, PHILIPPE. **Montmartre.** Translated by Anne
        Carter. New York: E. P. Dutton, 1977. 206 pp.
In this study of one of Paris's major modern literary and
artistic quarters, see pp. 88-95 ("Mount Lesbos") and pp.
178-85 ("The Boulevards of Sodom").

736.   JURIEU, PIERRE. **Préjugés légitimes contre le
        papisme.** Amsterdam: H. Desbordes, 1685.
Includes violent attacks on sodomy among the Catholic
clergy.

737.   LACHÈVRE, FRÉDÉRIC. **Le prince des libertins du
        xviie siècle: Jacques Vallée des Barreaux, sa vie
        et ses poésies (1599-1673).** Paris: H. Leclerc,
        1907. 264 pp.
During this period libertine primarily connoted free
thought, and only secondarily sexual licence. See,
however, pp. 44, 61, 184-87, 221, 228.

738.   LACHÈVRE, FRÉDÉRIC (ed.). **Le libertinage au xviie
        siècle.** Paris: H. Champion, 1909-11. 2 vols.
See vol. 2, pp. 85-86 (epigram by Denys Sanguin de Saint-
Pavin; 1595-1670); and pp. 287-91 (poems by Théophile de
Viau; 1590-1626).

739.   LEDUC, VIOLETTE. **Mad in Pursuit.** New York: Far-
        rar, Straus and Giroux, 1971. 351 pp.
In the period covered by this memoir (1945-49), Leduc entered the literary world, becoming acquainted with Simone
de Beauvoir, Jean Cocteau, and Jean Genet.

740.   LEVER, MAURICE. **Les bûchers de Sodome.** Paris:
        Fayard, 1985. 426 pp.
Social history chiefly concerning the 17th and 18th centuries in France; provides considerable information, but
in a largely anecdotal context.

741.   LORENZ, PAUL. **Sapho 1900: Renée Vivien.** Paris:
        Julliard, 1977. 184 pp.
Study of the noted Anglo-French lesbian writer and her
times.

742.   MACÉ, GUSTAVE. **Mes lundis en prison.** Paris: Char-
        pentier, 1889. 415 pp. (Police parisienne)
Account by the Chef de Service de la Sûreté of homosexual-
ity in the French capital during the early years of the
Third Republic, when the vice squad came into operation.

743.   MAGNE, EMILE. **Le plaisant abbé de Boisrobert,**
        fondateur de l'Académie Française, 1592-1662;
        documents inédits. Paris: Mercure de France,
        1909. 497 pp.
Publication of primary documents on the poet François de
Metel, sieur de Boisrobert, with commentary by Magne,
which somewhat slights his homosexuality; compare N. Praetorius, below.

744.   MARAIS, MATHIEU. **Journal et mémoires sous la**
        régence et le règne de Louis XV (1715-1737). Par-
        is: Firmin-Didot, 1863-68. 4 vols.
In this chronicle of the regency period and the first part
of the reign of Louis XV, see vol. 1, p. 278; vol. 2, pp.
319-22, 467; vol. 3, pp. 65, 114, 290-300, 308-09, 393-
94, 423, 462; vol. 4, pp. 3-4, 8, 226-17, 142, 146-47,
149-152, 155, 168, 305.

745.   MERCIER, LOUIS-SEBASTIEN. **Tableau de Paris.**
        Amsterdam: n. p., 1782-88. 4 vols. in 12.
In these social commentaries by the dramatist (1740-1814),
see vol. 1 p. 278 (the Greek taste revived); vol. 2,
p. 158 (the elegant replaces the petit-maitre); vol. 3,
pp. 130-32 (new vices a hundred years before)' vol. 4,
p. 239 (punishment of pederasts as a public scandal).

746.   MONNIER, ADRIENNE. **The Very Rich Hours of Adrienne**
        Monnier. Translated with additional material by
        Richard McDougall. New York: Scribner's, 1976.
Memoirs of the noted proprietor of a left-bank bookstore,
with reminiscences of many lesbian and gay luminaries in
the 1920s and 1930s.

747.   NOUVEAU, PIERRE. "Le péché philosophique ou de
        l'homosexualité du xviiie siècle," **Arcadie,**
        nos. 254-259/60 (February-October 1975),   77-82,
        134-41, 275-81, 334-39, 396-400, 556-62.
Various aspects of homosexuality in 18th-century France.

748.   ORLÉANS, DUCHESSE D'. **A Woman's Life in the Court**
        of the Sun King: Letters of Liselotte von der
        Pfalz, 1652-1722 (Elisabeth Charlotte, Duchesse
        d'Orleans). Translated from the German by Elborg
        Forster. Baltimore: Johns Hopkins University Press,
        1985. 287 pp.
Letters written by the second wife of Philippe, Duc d'Orleans, the homosexual brother of Louis XIV, which contain
acerbic comments on the homoerotic leanings of aristocrats
of several European countries. An annotated edition of
the material pertinent to homosexuality is in preparation by Claude Courouve and Roland Schaer.

749.   PEYREFITTE, ROGER. **Voltaire, sa jeunesse et son**
        temps. Paris: Albin Michel, 1985. 2 vols.
This leisurely life (by a prolific French homosexual
novelist) of Voltaire up to his thirty-second year shows

the role of nonconformity, including libertinism in his development--his Jesuit education notwithstanding. Reveals the role of the Société du Temple, a parasodomital group.

750. PEYRONNET, PIERRE. "Le péché philosophique." In: **Aimer en France, 1760-1860.** (Clermont-Ferrand: Association des publications de la Faculté des lettres et des sciences humaines, 2, 1980), 471-78.
Apercus mainly concerning lesbianism.

751. PORCHE, FRANÇOIS. **L'amour qui n'ose pas dire son nom.** Paris: Bernard Grasset, 1927.
An advanced and tolerant text for the period, written by a heterosexual.

752. PRAETORIUS, NUMA (pseud. of Eugen Wilhelm). "Der homosexuelle Abbé Boisrobert, der Gründer der Académie Française," **Zeitschrift für Sexualwissenschaft,** 9 (1922), 4-7, 33-43.
On Boisrobert (1592-1662), poet and one of the founders of the French Academy. Compare E. Magne, above.

753. PRAETORIUS, NUMA. "Das Liebesleben l. des Königs Heinrich III von Frankreich, 2. des Bruders von Ludwig XIV, Königs von Frankreich, Philipp d'Orléans, 3. des Königs Ludwig XVIII von Frankreich," **Zeitschrift für Sexualwissenschaft,** 18 (1932), 522-654.
Homosexual aspects of the lives of three leading French royals.

754. PRAETORIUS, NUMA. "Zwei französische Dichter des 17. Jahrhunderts (Théophile de Viau und Jacques Valle des Barreaux) und ihre Beziehungen zur Homosexualität," **Zeitschrift für Sexualwissenschaft,** 5 (1918), 95-108.
On two 17th-century poets; on another, see his "Ein homosexueller Dichter des 17. Jahrhunderts Saint-Pavin, der 'König von Sodom,'" ibid., 5:8 (1918-19), 261-71. See also F. Lachèvre, above.

755. RABUTIN, ROGER DE, COMTE DE BUSSY (ascribed to). **Histoire amoureuse de Gaules.** Paris: Grance, 1754. 5 vols.
See the chapter "La France devenue italienne" (which was not, however, written by Rabutin).

756. RAYNAUD, ERNEST. "Voltaire et les fiches de police," **Mercure de France,** 199 [no. 705] (November 1, 1927), 536-56.
Discusses the accusation that Voltaire was homosexual.

757. RELIQUET, PHILIPPE. **Gilles de Rais, maréchal, monstre et martyr.** Paris: Belfond, 1982. 282 pp.

Recent attempt to arrive at the truth about the 15th century mass-murderer of boys, sometimes identified with the
legendary Bluebeard. The secondary literature on Gilles de
Rais--much of it semifictional--is enormous; suffice it to
mention the names of M. Bataille (1965), E. Ferrero
(1975), J. Rouille (1978) and J. Bressler (1981).

758. REY, MICHEL. "Police et sodomie à Paris au xviiie
      siècle: du péché au désordre," **Revue d'histoire
      moderne et contemporaine**, 29 (1982), 113-24.
Based chiefly on the Archives of the Bastille, now kept in
the Bibliothèque de l'Arsenal, Paris. See the English
version "Parisian Homosexuals Create a Lifestyle, 1700-
1750: The Police Archives," **Eighteenth-Century Life**, 9
(1985), 179-91. See also his "L'art de 'raccrocher' au
xviiie siècle," **Masques**, 24 (Winter 1984-85), 92-99 (on
cruising in 18th-century Paris).

759. RÖMER, L. S. A. M. VON. "Die Homosexualität
      Heinrichs des Dritten, Königs von Frankreich und
      Polen," **JfsZ**, 4 (1902), 572-669.
Solid study of the homosexuality of Henry III and its
treatment in contemporary sources.

760. SHEHADI, PHILIP. "Action in a Socialist France,"
      Advocate, no. 330 (November 12, 1981), 14-15, 18,
      52.
On the favorable response of the newly elected Mitterand
government to the requests of homosexual spokespeople.

761. SOMAN, ALFRED. "The Parlement of Paris and the
      Great Witch-Hunt," **Sixteenth Century Journal**, 9
      (1978), 30-44.
Presents research into unpublished trial appeals showing
that 178 sodomy cases were judged by the Parlement of
Paris during the years 1565-1640, with 77 death sentences
confirmed.

762. TALLEMANT DES REAUX, GEDEON. **Historiettes**. Edited
      by A. Adam. Paris: Gallimard, 1960-61. 2 vols.
These texts offer many revealing apercus of the erotic
life of this time (1619-1692).

763. THOMAS, ARTUS, SIEUR D'EMBRY. **L'Isle des Hermaph-
      rodites**. Paris: 1605. 235 pp.
Satire on effeminates at the court of Henry III, inspired
by accounts of the berdaches in the New World. An
enlarged edition was published in Cologne in 1724.

764. TORCHE, ANTOINE. **La toilette galante de l'amour**.
      Paris: E. Loyson, 1670. 246 pp.
See pp. 106-26, "La mariage d'amitié entre deux belles,"
and following discussion. (Contemporary comment on
"lesbian marriage.")

765. VOLTAIRE. **Dictionnaire philosophique**. Edited by

Raymond Naves. Paris: Garnier, 1967. 632 pp.
See the article, "Amour nommé Socratique," pp. 18-21, the
best known of Voltaire's writings on homosexuality,
which first appeared in the edition of 1769. See also
the articles "Amitié," "Ange," "Genèse."

H. GERMANY AND AUSTRIA

Drawing upon secure foundations developed by philological
and scientific research, the scholarly study of homosexuality emerged in German-speaking countries in the 19th
century. It is a curious fact, however, that this re-
search--being conceived as a universalizing endeavor--
never brought forth a comprehensive picture of the history
of homosexual and lesbian behavior in Germany, Austria,
and German-speaking Switzerland. Moreover, there is a
break in continuity caused by the 1933-45 (Nazi) period--
which has in itself been the subject of a certain amount
of specialized research with regard to the situation of
homosexuals. For the homosexual rights movement in
Germany, see III.V.

766.   BLEUEL, HANS PETER. **Sex and Society in Nazi
        Germany.** Translated from the German by J. Maxwell
        Littlejohn. Philadelphia: Lippincott, 1973. 272
        pp.
In this popular account, see "Ernst Roehm, A Taste for
Men," pp. 95-101; and "Drowned in a Bog," pp. 217-25.

767.   **Documents of the Homosexual Rights Movement in
        Germany, 1836-1927.** New York: Arno Press, 1975.
Reprints ten texts, nine in German and one in French. A
comprehensive list of German-language nonfiction materials through 1975 appears in Manfred Herzer, **Bibliographie zur Homosexualität** (Berlin: Verlag Rosa Winkel,
1982). Only a small selection of these can be offered
here.

768.   EISSLER, W. U. **Arbeiterparteien und Homosexuellen-
        frage: zur Sexualpolitik von SPD und KPD in der
        Weimarer Republik.** Berlin: Verlag Rosa Winkel,
        1980. 142 pp.
Analysis of how the two major left parties, the Socialists
(SPD) and the Communists (KPD), dealt with the subject of
homosexuality in the 1920s. English summary.

769.   **Eldorado: Homosexuelle Frauen und Männer in Berlin
        1850-1950: Geschichte, Alltag und Kultur.** Berlin:
        Frolich & Kaufmann, 1984. 216 pp.
Collection of essays (derived from an exhibition in the
Berlin Museum) providing a remarkable conspectus of gay
male and lesbian life in Berlin over a century.

770.   ERIKSSON, BRIGITTE. "A Lesbian Execution in
       Germany, 1721: The Trial Records," **JH**, 6 (1980-81),
       27-40.
Translation of a record of a court proceeding that ended
in one woman's being condemned to death.

771.   GALLO, MAX. **Night of the Long Knives.** New York:
       Harper and Row, 1972. 310 pp.
A somewhat confusing narration of Hitler's 1934 massacre
of Ernst Rohm and his homosexual Brownshirt circle.

772.   GAUER, KARL. **Neudefinitionen abweichenden Sexual-
       verhaltens gegen Ende des 19. Jahrhunderts.**
       Constance: Universität, 1979. 112 pp. (disser-
       tation)
Attributes the major shift in conceptualizing sexual
deviance (late 19th century) to changing social conditions reaching back to the 18th century.

773.   GRAND-CARTERET, JOHN. **Derrière "Lui" (L'homosexu-
       alité en Allemagne).** Paris: E. Bernard, 1908.
       176 pp.
Contemporary comment on the scandals at the court of
Wilhelm II ("Lui"). Illustrated with 150 caricatures of
the period.

774.   HAEBERLE, ERWIN J. "Swastika, Pink Triangle and
       Yellow Star--the Destruction of Sexology and the
       Persecution of Homosexuals in Nazi Germany,"
       Journal of Sex Research, 17 (1981), 270-87.
Links the official policy of persecuting homosexuals to a
hostility toward sexology. For a different view, see M.
Herzer, below.

775.   HARTHAUSER, WOLFGANG (pseud. of Reimar Lenz). "Der
       Massenmord an Homosexuellen im Dritten Reich," In:
       Wilhart Schlegel (ed.), **Das grosse Tabu: Zeugnisse
       und Dokumente zum Problem der Homosexualität,**
       Munich: Rutten & Loening, 1967, pp. 7-37.
An early attempt to draw a comprehensive picture of the
persecution of homosexuals in the Third Reich.

776.   HEGER, HEINZ. **The Men with the Pink Triangle.**
       Translated, with an introduction by David Fern-
       bach. London: Gay Men's Press, 1980. 128 pp.
Moving account by an Austrian homosexual inmate of
Hitler's concentration camps, first published in German
in 1972. This book is one of the sources for Martin
Sherman's famous play, **Bent.**

777.   HENDERSON, SUSAN W. "Frederick the Great of
       Prussia: A Homophile Perspective," **Gai Saber**, 1:1
       (Spring 1977), 46-54.
Gathers literary evidence purveying innuendoes of the
king's (1712-86) homophile orientation, and that of
others of the period.

778.   HERZER, MANFRED. "Nazis, Psychiatrists, and Gays:
        Homophobia in the Sexual Science of the National
        Socialist Period," **Cabirion**, no. 12 (1985), 1-5.
Shows that sexual research did continue during the Nazi
era, and that Nazi attitudes regarding homosexuality were
more diverse than is usually allowed.

779.   HIRSCHFELD, MAGNUS. **Berlins drittes Geschlecht.**
        Berlin: Hermann Seemann, 1904. 77 pp.
The noted sexologist offers a kind of tour through Berlin's homosexual subculture at the turn of the century
cliques, gathering places, hustlers, etc. Reprinted in
Documents, above (767). Also appeared in a French
version: **Le troisième sexe: les homosexuels de Berlin**
(Paris: Rousset, 1908; 103 pp.).

780.   HOHMANN, JOACHIM S. **Keine Zeit für gute Freunde.**
        Frankfurt am Main: Foerster, 1982. 176 pp.
Reconstructs the situation of homosexuals in Germany after
World War II.

781.   HUGLANDER, F. (pseud. of Hugo Friedländer). "Aus
        dem homosexuellen Leben Alt-Berlins," **JfsZ**, 14
        (1914), 45-63.
Glimpses of homosexual life in Berlin, chiefly in the
first half of the 19th century, before the city became a
great imperial capital.

782.   IGRA, SAMUEL. **Germany's National Vice.** London:
        Quality Press, 1945. 102 pp.
Grotesque specimen of the "fascist perversion" myth,
linking the Nazis to homosexuality. Such smears were
common in the émigré literature, e.g.,Hans Erich Kaminski,
El nazismo como problema sexual (Buenos Aires: Iman, 1940;
186 pp.; see esp. pp. 13-15 and 41-65).

783.   ISHERWOOD, CHRISTOPHER. **Christopher and His Kind,
        1929-1939.** New York: Avon, 1977. 340 pp.
The real story of the writer's Berlin years.

784.   JANSEN, VOLKER (ed.). **Der Weg zu Freundschaft und
        Toleranz: männliche Homosexualität in den 50er
        Jahren.** Berlin: Verlag Rosa Winkel, 1985. ca. 96
        pp.
Exhibition catalogue with contributions by H. W. Bendt,
M. Herzer, and O. Stuben on homosexuals in West Germany
during the "Adenauer era."

785.   KOKULA, ILSE. **Weibliche Homosexualität um 1900 in
        zeitgenössischen Dokumenten.** Munich: Frauenoffen-
        sive, 1981. 288 pp.
Reprints documents on lesbianism and women's emancipation
from 1880 to 1912.

786.   KOLPA, RONALD et al. (eds.). **Fascisme en homosek-
        sualiteit.** The Hague: De Woelrat, 1985. 208 pp.

Articles in Dutch chiefly on Nazism and its affinities, with several seeking to discern contestable current parallels (i.e.,with S & M).

787. LAUTMANN, RÜDIGER. "The Pink Triangle: The Per-
      secution of the Homosexual Male in Nazi Germany,"
      JH, 6 (1980-81), 141-60.
In this shortened extract from the following work, Lautmann estimates the total number of pink-triangle inmates at about 10,000: Rüdiger Lautmann and others, **Seminar: Gesellschaft und Homosexualität.** (Frankfurt am Main: Suhrkamp, 1977; 570 pp.).

788. LEONHARDT, W. "Die Homosexualität der altesten
      deutschen Literatur," **JfsZ**, 12 (1911-12), 153-65.
Homosexual elements in medieval German literature.

789. **Lesbianism and Feminism in Germany, 1895-1910.** New
      York: Arno Press, 1975.
Eleven German-language texts. Some of this material, together with related items appears in translation in Lillian Faderman and Brigitte Eriksson (eds.), **Lesbian/ Feminism in Turn-of-the-Century Germany** (Weatherby Lake, MO: Naiad Press, 1980).

790. LINNHOFF, URSULA. **Weibliche Homosexualität
      zwischen Anpassung und Emanzipation.** Cologne: Kiep-
      enheuer & Witsch, 1976. 141 pp.
Examines lesbian progress in West Germany from several perspectives.

791. MARKUS, GEORG. **Der Fall Redl.** Vienna: Amalthea,
      1984. 286 pp.
On the Austrian double agent, who was blackmailed for his homosexuality by the Russians in the years before World War I. This book, which reflects new research, cites correspondence documenting Redl's affection for young men. Now obsolete is Robert B. Asprey, **The Panther's Feast** (New York: Putnam, 1959; 317 pp.).

792. MEYER, ADELE. **Lila Nächte: die Damenklubs der
      zwanziger Jahre.** Berlin: Zitronenpresse, 1981.
      172 pp.
The lesbian cabaret scene in Weimar Germany.

793. MILLS, RICHARD. "A Man of Youth: Wilhelm Jansen
      and the German Wandervogel Movement," **Gay Sunshine**,
      no. 44-45 (1980), 48-50.
Traces the career of a little-known figure in the German gay movement (1866-1943). See also Mills's previous article, "A Matter of Honor: Hans Blüher and Magnus Hirschfeld," ibid., no. 42-43 (Spring 1980), 21-25. For a general treatment, see J. Steakley, below.

794. MIRABEAU, HONORÉ GABRIEL RIQUETTI, COMTE DE. **The
      Secret History of the Court of Berlin.** London:

1789. 2 vols.
Translation of **Histoire secrète de la cour de Berlin**
(Paris: 1789). Contains gossip about the court of Frederick the Great, mentioning also the homosexuality of his
brother Prince Henry, a sometime candidate for the throne
of the United States. On Prince Henry, see also Numa
Praetorius, "Die Homosexualität des Prinzen Heinrich von
Preussen, des Bruders Friedrich des Grossen," **Zeitschrift
für Sexualwissenschaft**, 15 (1928-29), 465-76.

795.   MOSSE, GEORGE. **Nationalism and Sexuality: Respec-
       tability and Abnormal Sexuality in Modern Europe.**
       New York: Howard Fertig, 1985. 232 pp.
Somewhat diffuse series of studies dealing with such
themes as nudity, life-style reform, classicism, taste,
friendship, and homosexuality.

796.   PLANT, RICHARD. **The Pink Triangle: The Nazi War
       against Homosexuals.** New York: Holt, 1986. 259
       pp.
Clearly and eloquently written, this is the best account
in English of these terrible events.

797.   SCHILLING, HEINZ-DIETER. **Schwule und Faschismus.**
       Berlin: Elephanten-Presse, 1983. 174 pp.
Narrative of homosexual persecution in the Third Reich.

798.   SHEPHERD, NAOMI. **Wilfred Israel: German Jewry's
       Secret Ambassador.** London: Weidenfeld and Nicol-
       son, 1984. 297 pp.
Biography of courageous opponent of the Nazi regime (1899-
1944), who was also a closeted homosexual.

799.   STEAKLEY, JAMES D. "Gays under Socialism: Male
       Homosexuality in the German Democratic Republic,"
       Body Politic, 29 (December 1976-January 1977),
       15-18.
Paints a somewhat too rosy picture of conditions in East
Germany (with background from 1949). See also: Siegrid
Schäfer, "Sexuelle und soziale Probleme von Lesbierinnen
in der DDR," in: E. Schorsch and G. Schmidt (eds.), **Ergebnisse der Sexualforschung** (Cologne: Wissenschaft-Ver-
lag, 1975), pp. 299-325; as well as Steakley, "The Gay
Movement in Germany Today," **Body Politic**, 13 (May-June
1974), 14-15, 21, 23.

800.   STEAKLEY, JAMES D. **The Homosexual Emancipation
       Movement in Germany.** New York: Arno Press, 1975.
       121 pp.
Factual account of the efforts, centering largely on
Magnus Hirschfeld and his Scientific-humanitarian Com-
mittee, to abolish Article 175 of the penal code, and to
promote toleration for homosexuals in Wilhelmine and then
Weimar Germany. See also John Lauritsen and David
Thorstad, **The Early Homosexual Rights Movement (1864-
1935).** (New York: Times Change Press, 1974).

801.   STEAKLEY, JAMES D. "Iconography of a Scandal: Pol-
       itical Cartoons and the Eulenburg Affair," **Studies
       in Visual Communication,** 9:2 (1983), 20-51.
Judicious reconstruction of the scandals involving a
homosexual favorite of the Kaiser's from 1907 to 1909,
accompanied by 39 cartoons.

802.   STÜMKE, HANS-GEORG, and RUDI FINKLER. **Rosa Winkel,
       rosa Listen: Homosexuelle und "gesundes Volksem-
       pfinden" von Auschwitz bis heute.** Reinbek bei
       Hamburg: Rowohlt, 1981. 512 pp.
Detailed account with many quotations of persecution of
and discrimination against homosexuals in Germany in the
second third of the 20th century.

803.   WEINDEL. HENRI DE, and F. P. FISCHER. **L'homosexu-
       alité en Allemagne: étude documentaire et anec-
       dotique.** Paris: Félix Juven, 1908. 315 pp.
Inspired by the contemporary Harden-Eulenburg-von Moltke
scandals.

804.   WILDE, HARRY. **Das Schicksal der Verfemten: die
       Verfolgung der Homosexuellen im "Dritten Reich" und
       ihre Stellung in der heutigen Gesellschaft.**
       Tubingen: Katzmann, 1969. 154 pp.
Sympathetic account of the fate of homosexuals under the
Nazis and their uncertain status in the immediate postwar
period.

805.   WITTE, HEINRICH. **Der letzte Puller von Hohenburg:
       ein Beitrag zur politischen und Sittengeschichte
       des Elsasses und der Schweiz im 15. Jahrhundert
       sowie zur Genealogie des Geschlechts von Puller.**
       Strasbourg: Heitz und Mundel, 1893. (Beiträge zur
       Landes- und Volkskunde von Elsass-Lothringen, 16)
Traces the career of the noble Richard Puller von Hohenburg in Alsace and Switzerland, where he was repeatedly
arrested for sodomy and finally executed. For a review
of the relevant aspects, see Numa Praetorius, "Ein homosexueller Ritter des 15. Jahrhunderts," **JfsZ,** 12 (1911-
12), 207-29.

806.   YOUNG, IAN. **Gay Resistance.** Toronto: Stubblejumper
       Press, 1985. 23 pp.
Pamphlet offering an account of homosexuals (and possible
homosexuals) in the German resistance against Hitler.

                      I. LOW COUNTRIES

While the Netherlands was one of the main centers of the
homosexual rights movement in the first decades of the
present century, intensive scholarship on the history of
homosexuality in the Low Countries developed only from

about 1965 onwards. The number and quality of publications, of which only a selection is presented here, are
impressive. Continuing work can be monitored in the
bimonthly **Homologie** and in the annual **Homojaarboek** (both
published in Amsterdam).

807.   BOON, LEO J. "De grote sodomietenvervolging in het
       gewest Holland, 1730-1731," **Holland**, 8:3 (June
       1976), 140-52.
Account, with references to primary documents, of the
great persecution of sodomites in the Province of Holland,
1730-31. See also his article "Het jaar waarin elke
jongen een meisje nam: de sodomietenvervolgingen in
Holland in 1730," **Groniek**, 12:6 (January 1980), 14-17.

808.   "'Utrechtenaren': de sodomieprocessen in Utrecht,
       1730-1732," **Spiegel Historiael**, 17:11 (November
       1982), 553-58.
Sodomy trials in Utrecht, 1730-32. **Utrechtenaar** (someone
from Utrecht) is Dutch slang for a homosexual male, a
usage Boon derives from these trials.

809.   COHEN TERVAERT, G. M. **De Grietman Rudolf de
       Mepsche.** The Hague: 1921.
Monograph on the Groningen official who condemned 22 sodomites to death in 1731.

810.   DEBEUCKELAERE, GEERT. "Hoe meer zielen, hoe meer
       vreugde: homosubkultuur in Antwerpen 1781,"
       Homokrant, 9:2 (February 1983), 9-12.
On Antwerp's homosexual subculture in 1781. See also
his: "Mayken en Leene: een lesbische geschiedenis in
Brugge uit 1618," **Homokrant**, 9:9 (May 1983), 3-5; "'Ver-
keerd zijn' in beroerde tijden: de Gentse sodomieten
processen van 1578," **Homokrant**, 7:3 (March 1981), 3-6.

811.   EVERARD, MYRIAM. "Tribade of zielsvriendin,"
       Groniek, no. 77 (May 1982), 16-20.
Treats several cases of Dutch women charged with sodomy in
the late 18th century.

812.   **Groniek: Gronings Historische Tijdschrift**, no. 66
       (January 1980); no. 77 (May 1982).
These two theme numbers of the Groningen periodical are
devoted entirely to homosexual history, chiefly Dutch.

813.   HEKMA, GERT. "Profeten op papier, pioniers op
       pad," **Spiegel Historiael**, 17:11 (November 1982),
       566-71.
Discusses several aspects of male homosexual life in
Amsterdam in the 19th century, including Platonic friend-
ships, cliques, street life, and cafes.

814.   HEKMA, GERT. "De strijd om homoseksualiteit: de
       oprichting van een Janusbeeld," **Groniek**, no. 77

(May 1982), 7-15.
On changing concepts of homosexuality, mainly in the 19th
century. Some of this material is summarized in his
"Social Philosophies, Social Practices: Some Preludes to
the Homosexual," **Among Men, among Women**, Amsterdam: Uni-
versiteit, 1983, 258-67, 578. See also his "Homoseksualiteit: van zonde tot geaardheid," **Spiegel Historiael**,
15:9 (September 1980), 484-91.

815.   HUUSSEN, AREND H., JR. "Gerechtelijke vervolging
       van 'sodomie' gedurende de 18e eeuw in de Repub-
       liek, in het bijzonder in Friesland," **Groniek**,
       no. 66 (January 1980), 18-33.
Judicial prosecution of sodomy in the Dutch Republic in
the 18th century, especially in Friesland.

816.   HUUSSEN, AREND H., JR. "Strafrechtelijke vervolging
       van 'sodomie' in de Republiek," **Spiegel Historiael**,
       17:11 (November 1982), 547-52.
Criminal prosecution for sodomy in the Dutch Republic.
English version, "Sodomy in the Dutch Republic in the
Eighteenth Century," **Eighteenth-Century Life**, 9 (1985),
169-78.

817.   KOENDERS, PIETER. **Homoseksualiteit in bezet
       Nederland, verzweyen hoofstuk.** The Hague: De
       Woelrat, 1983. 173 pp.
Discusses various aspects of homosexual oppression and
persecution in the occupied Netherlands during World War
II.

818.   MEER, THEO VAN DER. "'Liefkozerijen en Vuylig-
       heden'" **Groniek**, no. 66 (January 1980), 34-37.
Discusses the sodomy trials of several Amsterdam women in
the late 18th century.

819.   MEER, THEO VAN DER. **De wesentlijke sonde van
       sodomie en andere vuyligheeden: Sodomietenvervol-
       gingen in Amsterdam 1730-1811.** Amsterdam: Tab-
       ula, 1984. 237 pp.
Major study treating the period from the onset of the
great persecution in 1730 to the decriminalization of
1811, as a result of the introduction of the Napoleonic
Penal Code upon annexation by France.

820.   MEIJER, MAAIKE. "Pious and Learned Female Bosom-
       Friends in Holland in the Eighteenth Century,"
       Among Men, among Women, Amsterdam: Universiteit,
       1983, 404-19, 573-76.
On circles of women and their publications.

821.   NIP, R. I. A. "Bengaert Say, een 15de eeuws
       ambtenaar," **Holland**, 15:2 (April 1983), 65-75.
Discusses the role of Say, prosecutor general of the
Estates of Holland in the 1448 trial and execution for
sodomy of Gooswijn de Wilde, president of the Estates of

Holland. See also Gerrit Kuijk and Renée Valens-Nip,
"Saeye Zonden," **Groniek**, no. 78 (July-August 1982),
17-21, which concerns the 1495 denunciation for sodomy
of Philips Say, son of Bengaert.

822. NOORDAM, DIRK JAAP. "Homosexual Relations in
      Leiden (1533-1811)," **Among Men, among Women**,
      Amsterdam: Universiteit, 1983, 218-23, 603.
See also his more detailed article: "Homosexualiteit en
sodomie in Leiden," 1533-1811, **Leids Jaarboekje**, no. 75
(1983), 72-105; as well as his "Homoseksuele relaties in
Holland in 1776," **Holland**, 16:1 (February 1984), 3-34.

823. OVEZALL, J. J. "Over het sociale aspect van de
      homosexualiteit in de 18e eeuw in Nederland,"
      **Nederlands Tijdschrift voor de Psychologie en haar
      grensgebieden**, N.S. 8 (1953), 305-49.
Social aspects of homosexuality in the 18th century
Netherlands, when economic decline was followed by
persecution.

824. RAMSAY, RONALD W., P. M. HERINGA, and I. BOORSMA.
      "A Case Study: Homosexuality in the Netherlands,"
      in J. A. Loraine (ed.), **Understanding Homosexual-
      ity: Its Biological and Psychological Bases**, New
      York: American Elsevier, 1974, pp. 121-59.
The recent situation viewed through the lens of a now
somewhat dated methodology. Note also the comparative
discussion of the Netherlands in Martin S. Weinberg and
Colin J. Williams, **Male Homosexuals: Their Problems and
Adaptations** (New York: Oxford University Press, 1974; 316
pp.).

825. RÖMER, L. S. A. M. VON. "Der Uranismus in den
      Niederländen bis zum 19. Jahrhundert, mit besonder-
      er Berücksichtingung der grossen Uranierverfolgung
      im Jahre 1730," **JfsZ**, 8 (1906), 365-512.
Extensive study, now obsolete in some details, of homosexuality in the Natherlands, with special emphasis on the
great persecution beginning in 1730.

826. SALDEN, MAARTEN J. M. "Van doodstraf tot straffe-
      loosheid," **Spiegel Historiael**, 17:11 (November
      1982), 559-65.
Historical-legal study of the evolution in the Netherlands
that finally led to the abrogation of the medieval laws
in 1811.

827. SCHUYF, JUDITH. "Homosocial Existence and Patriar-
      chy," **Among Men, among Women**, Amsterdam: Univer-
      siteit, 1983, 450-53, 597.
Discusses "passing women" and female friendship forms
in the early modern Netherlands.

828. **Spiegel Historiael**, 17:11 (November 1982).
Special number on the history of homosexuality in the

Netherlands.

829.   TANG, A. VAN DER. "De zaak Jillis Bruggeman,"
       Scyedam, 5:6 (1979), 4-13.
On the Bruggeman affair, a sodomy case from 1803.

830.   TIELMAN, ROB. **Homoseksualiteit in Nederland: stud-
       ie van een emancipatiebeweging.** Meppel: Boom,
       1982. 336 pp.
Comprehensive work on homosexuality in the Netherlands,
concentrating on the homophile movement from 1911 onwards.

831.   VANDEPITTE, G. "Van Hekse en de Boze, Sappho 1618,
       Mayken de Brauwere en Magdaleene van Steene," **Rond
       de Poldertorens**, 24 (1982), 127-35.
On a witchcraft case of 1618 with lesbian overtones.

832.   VLEER, W. T. **"Sterf Sodomieten!" Rudolf de
       Mepsche, de homofielenvervolging, het Faanse
       zedenproces, en de massamoord te Zuidhorn.**
       Norg: VEJA, 1972.
On the Groningen persecutor of sodomites, Rudolf de
Mepsche, the Faan morals trial, and the mass execution at
Zuidhorn.

                      J. IBERIA

The traditional Christian condemnation of homosexuality
took on particular ferocity in Spain and Portugal owing to
the Inquisition and the struggle with the Moors, who were
on occasion stereotyped as sodomites. In modern times the
continuing alliance of throne and altar has imposed a
pervasive censorship that made investigation of heretical
sexuality difficult. Only in the last few years then,
prompted by a vigorous trend towards intellectual modernization and the rise of homosexual rights movements,
especially in Catalonia, have some historical elements of
Iberian homosexual culture begun to emerge from obscurity.

833.   ALCALDE DE ISLA, JESÚS, and RICARDO JAVIER BARCELÓ.
       Celtiberia gay. Barcelona: Editorial Personas,
       1976. 174 pp.
Popular account. See also: Alberto García Valdes, **Historia y presente de la homosexualidad** (Madrid: Akal,
1981); and José Antonio Valverde, **El macho herido: retrato
sexual de los españoles** (Madrid: Quorum, 1986).

834.   ALONSO TEJADA, LUIS. **La represión sexual en la
       España de Franco.** Barcelona: Caralt, 1977. 261
       pp.
Post-1936 sexual repression in Spain and its gradual
recession; see esp. pp. 217-24.

835.   ALZIEU, PIERRE et al. (eds.). **Poesía erótica del
        siglo de oro.** Second ed. Barcelona: Editorial
        Critica, 1984. 361 pp.
In this anthology and commentary on 17th-century erotic
poetry, see pp. 46-47 (lesbian sonnet); and 238-40, 250-54
(satires on male homosexuals).

836.   ANABÁRBITE RIVAS, HÉCTOR, and RICARDO LORENZO
        SANZ. **Homosexualidad: el asunto está caliente.**
        Madrid: Queimada, 1979. 112 pp.
Historical account, with some data on Inquisition persecutions, followed by exposition of then-current gay liberation theory and politics.

837.   BAROJA, JULIO CARO. "Honour and the Devil," in
        J. G. Peristiany (ed.), **Honour and Shame: the
        Values of Mediterranean Society,** Chicago: Chicago
        University Press, 1970, pp. 79-137.
Discusses the social penalties imposed by southern Spanish
culture for gender-role deviation.

838.   BARRIOBERO Y HERRÁN, EDUARDO. **Los delitos sexuales
        en las viejas leyes españoles.** Madrid: Mundo La-
        tino, 1930. 206 pp.
Excerpts, with commentary, from older Spanish legal codes
on sexual crimes. See also: Victoriano Domingo Loren
(ed.), **Los homosexuales frente a la ley: los juristas
opinan** (Barcelona: Plaza y Janes, 1977; 315 pp.).

839.   BENNASSAR, BARTOLOMÉ. **The Spanish Character: At-
        titudes and Mentalities from the Sixteenth to the
        Nineteenth Century.** Translated from the French by
        Benjamin Keen. Berkeley: University of California
        Press, 1979. 325 pp.
In this stimulating work of cultural history, sodomy is
discussed in several contexts; see pp. 28-30, 59, 85,
207-10, 292-93.

840.   BERNALDO DE QUIRÓS, CONSTANCIO, and J. M. LLANAS
        AUGILANIEDO. **La mala vida en Madrid: estudio
        psico-sociológico.** Madrid: B. Rodriguez Serra,
        1901. 363 pp.
In this study of street life in fin-de-siècle Madrid, see
pp. 262-85 for effeminate homosexuals and hustlers.

841.   CABALLERO, OSCAR. **El sexo del franquismo.** Madrid:
        Editorial Cambio 16, 1977. 319 pp.
Journalistic account of sexual life in Spain under Franco;
see pp. 193-211.

842.   ENRÍQUEZ, JOSÉ RAMÓN (ed.). **El homosexual ante la
        sociedad enferma.** Barcelona: Tusquets, 1978. 227
        pp.
Articles by Spanish and Mexican authors attacking patterns
of social repression of homosexuality.

843. GARCÍA CÁRCEL, RICARDO. **Herejía y sociedad en el
      siglo XVI: la Inquisición en Valencia, 1530-1609.**
      Barcelona: Ediciones 62, 1980. 352 pp.
See "La sexualidad contranatura," pp. 288-94.

844. GARCÍA Y PEREZ, ALFONSO. **La rebelión de los
      homosexuales.** Madrid: Pecosa, 1977. 160 pp.
Journalistic presentation of mixed quality.

845. GIL DE BIEDMA, JAIME. "Homosexuality in the
      Spanish Generation of 1927: a Conversation with
      Jaime Gil de Biedma" (Interview conducted by Bruce
      Swansey and José Ramón Enríquez), **Gay Sunshine,**
      no. 42-43 (1980), 18-20, 14.
A contemporary Spanish writer speaks about Cernuda, Lorca,
and others.

846. GÓMES, JÚLIO. "Portugal" in his: **A Homossexualida-
      de no Mundo,** vol. 2, Lisbon: The author, 1983,
      pp. 175-270.
Discusses law, famous Portuguese homosexuals, hustling,
crime, and employment.

847. LEA, HENRY C. **A History of the Inquisition in
      Spain.** New York: 1922. 4 vols.
In this now dated study, see vol. 4, pp. 361-77, for
executions between 1497 and 1723. For a contemporary
approach to the general subject, see Henry Kamen, **Inquisition and Society in Spain in the Sixteenth and Seventeenth Centuries** (London: Weidenfeld and Nicolson, 1985;
312 pp.)

848. LÓPEZ Y LINAGE, JAVIER (ed.). **Grupos marginados y
      peligrosidad social.** Madrid: Campo Abierto,
      1977. 204 pp.
Analyzes the social effect of the Law of Social Dangerousness on several marginalized groups.

849. MCCASKELL, TIM. "Out in Basque Country," **Body
      Politic** (August 1980), 25-28.
Reports on the flourishing gay culture that has developed
in the Basque provinces of northern Spain.

850. MARAÑÓN, GREGORIO. **Ensayo biológico sobre Enrique
      IV de Castilla y su tiempo.** Madrid: Espasa Calpe,
      1956. 216 pp.
In this reprint of a work first published in 1930, the
writer claims that Henry IV of Castille (1425-1475)
suffered from eunuchism and acromegaly. On this book, see
Daniel Eisenberg, "Enrique IV and Gregorio Marañón,"
Renaissance Quarterly, 21 (1976), 21-30. See also
Townsend Miller, **Henry IV of Castile** (Philadelphia: Lip-
pincott, 1972).

851. MONTEIRO, ARLINDO CAMILO. "Il peccato nefando in
      Portugallo ed il Tribunale dell'Inquisizione,"

Rassegna di studi sessuali, 6 (1926), 161-76 and
265-80; 7 (1927), 1-28.
Somewhat labored study of sodomites caught in the Inquisition's net in Portugal. There is also a good deal of
information on Portugal in his magnum opus: **Amor sáfico
e socrático** (Lisbon: The author, 1922; 552 pp.).

852.   MONTOYA, BALDOMERO. **Los homosexuales.** Barcelona:
Dopesa, 1977. 128 pp.
A somewhat old-fashioned presentation of the forms of
homosexual behavior.

853.   PERRY, MARY ELIZABETH. **Crime and Society in Early
Modern Seville.** Hanover, NH: University Presses of
New England, 1980. 298 pp.
In 16th century Seville rapid urban growth was accompanied
by the spectacle of executing sodomites, generally from
the lower class. Perry's main source is a 1619 account of
309 persons attended by Pedro de León prior to their
execution, including 52 convicted of sodomy.

854.   SERRANO Y VICENS, RAMÓN. **La sexualidad de la
mujer.** Madrid: Jucar, 1975.
Surveys the sexual behavior of Spanish women, including
lesbianism.

K. ITALY

The homosexual history of Italy has left rich deposits in
literature, art, and historical records. Because of the
political fragmentation of the country (until 1870), this
history has been expressed in regional terms--Lombardy,
Venice, Florence, etc.--and an overall history has not yet
emerged. This task is the goal of a number of scholars
now working in Italy. For Renaissance and Baroque art,
see VI.C.

855.   BALDELLI, IGNAZIO. "Lingua e letteratura di un
centro trecentesco: Perugia," **Rassegna della
letteratura italiana,** 66 (1962), 3-21.
Treats a group of homoerotic poets active in Perugia in
the 14th century (pp. 4-9).

856.   BARTOLINI, ELIO. **L'assassinio di Winckelmann: gli
atti originali del processo criminale (1768).**
Milan: Longanesi, 1971.
Text of the trial of the murderer of the great archaeologist Winckelmann, which took place in Trieste 1768.

857.   BELGRANO, LUIGI. **Della vita privata dei Genovesi.**
Second ed. Genoa: Tipografia dell'Istituto
Sordomuti, 1875. 538 pp.

See pp. 427-29 on sodomy in Genoese history.

858.   BENVENUTI, MATTEO.   "Come facevasi guistizia nello
       stato di Milano dall'anno 1471 al 1763," **Archivio
       storico lombardo,** 9 (1882), 442-82.
See pp. 452-53 for a list of condemnations for sodomy pronounced between 1572 and 1615; see also p. 448.

859.   BERTOLOTTI, A.   "Gli studenti a Roma nel secolo
       XVI," **Giornale storico della letteratura italiana,**
       2 (1883), 141-48.
Reconstructs a scandal of 1555 provoked by carousing
students in Pavia who had read a carnevalesque "praise of
sodomy" in Latin.

860.   BONGI, SALVATORE.   **Bandi Lucchesi del secolo deci-
       moquarto tratti dai registri Archivio di stato
       in Lucca.** Bologna: Progresso, 1863.   434 pp.
See pp. 377-81 and 386 for medieval and Renaissance laws
in Lucca (Tuscany), including an account of the burning
of a sodomite in 1369.

861.   BROWN, JUDITH C.   **Immodest Acts: The Life of a
       Lesbian Nun in Renaissance Italy.** New York: Oxford
       University Press, 1985.   214 pp.
Reconstructs the life of Sister Benedetta Carlini of
Pescia (Tuscany) as disclosed by official records of an
inquiry in 1619-23.   Her sexuality was enveloped within an
elaborate religious imagery that allowed her erotic
licence inside the confines of a magical mental world.

862.   BRUCKER, GENE.   **The Society of Renaissance Flor-
       ence: A Documentary Study.** New York: Harper and
       Row, 1971.   262 pp.
For the operations of the special anti-sodomy magistracy
established in 1432, see pp. 201-06.

863.   CARINI, ISIDORO.   **La "difesa" di Pomponio Leto.**
       Bergamo: Flandinet, 1894.
Discusses the defense of the humanist Pomponio Leto,
accused of having sought to seduce two boys in Venice
(pp. 27-28, 35-37).

864.   CERUTTI, FRANCO.   "L'homosexualité dans les lettres
       italiennes contemporaines," **Arcadie,** no. 67-68
       (July-August 1959), 406-15.
Reflects 1950s attitudes. See also his "Ombres et lumières
en Italie," ibid., no. 78 (June 1960), 329-40.

865.   CHASTEL, ANDRÉ.   **Art et humanisme à Florence au
       temps de Laurent le Magnifique.** New ed.   Paris:
       Presses Universitaires de France, 1961.   580 pp.
This standard work on quattrocento culture in Florence
offers a short but interesting section on attitudes
toward "Socratic love" on pp. 289-98.

866.   CORRADI, A. "Nuovi documenti per la storia delle
        malattie veneree in Italia dalla fine del 1400 alla
        meta del 1500," **Annali universitari di medicina e
        chirurgia**, 269 (October 1884), 289-386.
Presents several documents relating to sodomy in the 16th
century (pp. 310-17, 366-82).

867.   DALL'ORTO, GIOVANNI. "Antonio Rocco and the
        Background of His 'L'Alcibiade Fanciullo a Scola'
        (1652)," in: **Among Men, among Women.** Amsterdam:
        University, 1983, pp. 224-32, 571-72.
Scholarly investigation of this milestone work in the
history of pederastic love.

868.   DALL'ORTO, GIOVANNI. "L'omosessualità nella poesia
        volgare italiana fino a Dante," **Sodoma,** 3 (1986),
        13-37.
Close study of evidence from early Italian poetry. See
also his: "Le parole per dirlo," ibid., 81-95; (with Carlo
Marcandalli), "Arsi finché morte ne segua," **Lotta Continua**
(April 10, 1982), 11-13; and "Peccati politici e peccati
capitali," ibid. (April 24, 1982), 19.

869.   DALL'ORTO, GIOVANNI. "Le ragioni di una persecu-
        zione." In: Martin Sherman, **Bent** (Ital. version).
        Turin: Edizioni Gruppo Abele, 1984, pp. 101-19.
The first general study of the treatment of homosexuals in
Fascist Italy, though several novels and films have explored the subject. More information appears in Dall'Orto, "Per il bene della razza al confino il pederasta,"
Babilonia (April 1986), 14-18 (continued in the following
issue). For references to Italian history and literature,
esp. of the 19th and 20th centuries, see the fundamental
bibliography of Dall'Orto, **Leggere omosessuale: bibliografia** (Turin: Edizioni Gruppo Abele, 1984; 108 pp.).

870.   DALL'ORTO, GIOVANNI. "An Unpublished Document from
        the Archivio di Stato, Venice (1717)," **Gay Books
        Bulletin,** no. 9 (Spring/Summer 1983), 24-25.
Translation and commentary of the minutes of a sodomy
trial, illustrating the 18th-century legal situation.

871.   DELFINO, GIOVANNI. "Dei martiri e delle pene: il
        caso Bonfadio," **Sodoma: rivista omosessuale di
        cultura,** 1 (Autumn-Winter 1984), 81-92.
Analyzes documents and texts on the execution of Jacopo
Bonfadio for sodomy in Genoa on July 19, 1550.

872.   FERRAI, L. "Dalla supposta calunnia del Vergerio
        contra il Duca di Castro," **Archivio storico per
        Trieste, l'Istria e il Trentino,** 1 (1882), 300-12.
On the purported intervention of the humanist Pier Paolo
Vergerio in the matter of Pier Luigi Farnese and the Bish-
op of Fano, and a similar affair concerning Marco Bracci.

873.   FRATI, LODOVICO. **La vita privata di Bologna dal**

secolo XIII al XVIII. Bologna: Zanichelli, 1900.
287 pp.
For sodomy trials in Bologna, see pp. 81-82.

874. FULIN, RINALDO. "Gli inquisitori dei Dieci,"
Archivio veneto, 1 (1871), 1-64, 298-318; 2,
(1871), 357-391.
Publishes some interesting material on deliberations
concerning sodomy by the Venetian Council of Ten (pp. 18-
19, 45-46, 306, 317, 368, 370-81).

875. FUSCO, DOMENICO. **L'Aretino sconosciuto e apocrifo,**
Turin: Berruto, 1953. 64 pp.
The chapter "Fu l'Aretino sodomita?" (pp. 34-39) discusses
accusations that the Venetian writer (1492-1556) was a
sodomite, concluding that they are probably calumnies.

876. GUERRI, DOMENICO. **La corrente popolare nel
Rinascimento: Berte burle e baie.** Florence: San-
soni, 1931. 174 pp.
An important text for the understanding of 14th and 15th
century burlesque literature touching homosexuality
(pp. 36, 44, 51-84, 121-71). See also his: "Dal 'gagno'
di Alighiero e fra' Timoteo," **La nuova Italia,** 2 (1931),
493-96; and "Ancora il 'gagno' d'Alighiero," ibid., 3
(1932), 458-67.

877. GUNDERSHEIMER, WERNER. "Crime and Punishment in
Ferrara," in: Lauro Martines (ed.), **Violence and
Civil Disorder in Italian Cities.** Berkeley: Uni-
versity of California Press, 1972.
Finds that 4% (of 200) capital punishments between 1440
and 1550 were for sodomy (p. 114).

878. INFESSURA, STEFANO. **Diario della città di Roma.**
Rome: Forzani (Istituto Storico Italiano), 1890.
334 pp.
See pp. 155-56, where the diarist (ca. 1440-1500) asserts
that Pope Sixtus IV (1414-84) made his barber a cardinal
because he was his son's lover.

879. LABALME, PATRICIA H. "Sodomy and Venetian Justice
in the Renaissance," **Tijdschrift voor Rechts-
geschiedenis/The Legal History Review,** 52:3
(1984), 217-54.
Survey, with many citations of primary documents, of
measures taken by the Venetian state against sodomy from
1407 to the end of the 16th century, covering magistrat-
ure, surveillance, court procedures, special treatment
of patricians and clergy, and punishments.

880. LABATE-CARIDI, VALENTINO. "Il cavaliere Marino
nella tradizione popolare," **Rivista abruzzese di
scienze, lettere et arti,** 12 (1897), 312-22.
Treats a series of pornographic writings attributed to
Giambattista Marino (1569-1625).

881. LANDUCCI, LUCA. **A Florentine Diary from 1450 to
      1516, Continued by an Anonymous Writer till 1542.**
      Translated by A. de Rosen Jervis. New York: Dut-
      ton, 1927. 308 pp.
In these witnesses of stormy times for Florence, see
pp. 77-78, 101, 124, 181, 201, 218, and 237.

882. LANZA, ANTONIO. **Polemiche e berte letterarie nella
      Firenze del primo Quattrocento.** Rome: Bulzoni,
      1972. 409 pp.
An important study of the polemic-jocose literature of the
first half of the 15th century in Florence. See esp. pp.
103-08, 136-71, 309-57, and 396-406. Se also his edition
of **Lirici toscani del Quattrocento** (Rome: Bulzoni, 1973;
2 vols.).

883. LORENZONI, PIERO. **Erotismo e pornografia nella
      letteratura italiana.** Milan: Il Formichiere, 1976.
      322 pp.
Although this book is strictly speaking an anthology of
erotic literary texts, it offers much material on the
history of homosexuality and homosexual writers, esp. during the Renaissance in Italy.

884. LUZIO, ALESSANDRO. **Pietro Aretino nei primi suoi
      anni a Venezia e la corte dei Gonzaga.** Turin: Loe-
      scher, 1888. 135 pp.
Cites two sonnets in which the Venetian writer confesses
himself to be a sodomite (pp, 23-24) and two relevant
letters of Federico Gonzaga of February 1528 (pp. 78-79).

885. MARIOTTI, ETTORE. "Giovanni della Casa," **Arcadie,**
      no. 79-80 (July-August 1960), 401-06.
On the prelate and writer (1503-57), founder of the Papal
Index, who had the ill-repute of being a self-confessed
sodomite because of his poem "Il Capitolo del forno."

886. MARTI, MARIO. **Cultura e stile nei poeti giocosi
      del tempo di Dante.** Pisa: Nitri-Lischi, 1953. 228
      pp.
Treats a number of homosexual poets of the 13th-14th
century, esp. in Tuscany. See also his: **Poeti giocosi del
tempo di Dante** (Milan: Rizzoli, 1959).

887. MASINI, MARIO, and GIUSEPPE PORTIGLIOTTI. "I
      famuli di Sisto IV," **Archivio di Antropologia
      Criminale,** 37 (1916), 462-81.
Useful study of homosexuality in 15th-century Italy, with
emphasis on the papal court of Sixtus IV. See also
their: "Attraverso il Rinascimento: Pier Luigi Farnese,"
Archivio di Psichiatria, 38 (1917), 177-92.

888. NOVATI, F. "Gli scolari romani nei secoli XIV e
      XV," **Giornale storico della letteratura italiana,** 2
      (1883), 129-40.
Account of Roman students' carnival pranks in the Renais-

sance, with discussion of the homosexuality of Porcellio.
Publishes a short satirical Latin poem on the subject.

889. OMBROSI, LUCA. **Vita dei Medici sodomiti.** Florence:
      Canesi, 1965. 171 pp.
Lives of the 18th-century grand dukes of Tuscany--Ferdin-
and II, Cosimo III, and Gian Gastone--as well as of Prince
Ferdinand and Cardinal Francesco Maria, written by a contemporary. This material was in part utilized in Jonathan
Drake, "The Florentine Medici," **Kalos,** no. 1 (Spring
1976), 9-15.

890. PAVAN, ELISABETH. "Police des moeurs, société et
      politique à Venise à la fin du Moyen Âge," **Revue
      Historique,** 264 (1981), 241-88.
In this study of mechanisms of social control in Venice at
the end of the middle ages, see esp. pp. 266-88.

891. PETRARCA, VALERIO. "L'osceno letterario nell
      lirica dialettale de Nicola Capasso," **Sociologia
      della letteratura,** no. 4-5 (1979), 191-203.
On a Neapolitan dialect poet of the 17th century and his
times.

892. RUGGIERO, GUIDO. **The Boundaries of Eros: Sex,
      Crime and Sexuality in Renaissance Venice.** New
      York: Oxford University Press, 1985. 223 pp.
See Chapter VI: "Sodom and Venice" (pp. 109-45), which
analyzes the rationale of Venetian measures against sodomy
and heterosexual buggery. Complements his earlier
studies, "Sexual Criminality in the Early Renaissance:
Venice, 1338-1358," **Journal of Social History,** 8 (1975),
18-37; and **Violence in Early Renaissance Venice** (New
Brunswick: Rutgers University Press, 1980; 235 pp.).

893. SCARABELLO, GIOVANNI. "Devianza ed interventi di
      giustizia a Venezia nella prima metà del XVI
      secolo," in: **Tiziano e Venezia.** Venice: Neri Pozza,
      1980, pp. 75-84.
The background of legal proceedings against deviants in
Venice in the age of Titian and Aretino.

894. SEMPRINI, GIOVANNI. "L'erotismo nel Rinascimento,"
      Rassegna di studi sessuali, 2 (1922), 272-77.
Discusses Benedetto Varchi, Pomponio Leto (Roman human-
ists), Antonio Loredano (Venetian ambassador at Rome),
Politian, Filelfo, Bracciolini, and others.

895. SHREVE, JACK. "Homosexuality in Renaissance
      Italy," **Gay Literature,** 2 (Spring 1975), 10-14.
Brief discussion of literary evidence.

896. SOLERTI, ANGELO. "Anche Torquato Tasso?" **Giornale
      storico dell letteratura italiana,** 9 (1887), 431-
      40.
Presents some letters of the great 16th century writer,

which seem to treat homoerotic love in a veiled fashion.

897.   TASSINI, GIUSEPPE. Il libertinaggio in Venezia.
       Venice: Filippi, 1968. 128 pp.
See pp. 27-32 which present a summary of the deliberations
of the Venetian Council of Ten on sodomy, with a discussion of two cases. See also his: Alcune delle piu clamo-
rose condanne capitali eseguite in Venezia sotto la
Repubblica (Venice: Filippi, 1970), pp. 91-94, 162-63;
and Curiosità veneziane (Venice: Filippi, 1970), pp. 41,
131, 307, 389, 456, 655, 732.

898.   VARCHI, BENEDETTO. "Sopra la pittura e scultura
       (1546)," in his: Scritti. Trieste: Lloyd Austri-
       aco, 1858-59, vol. 2, pp. 611-27.
Towards the end of this discussion the humanist turns
to two homoerotic sonnets of Michelangelo, which prompt
cautious statements about same-sex love.

899.   VOLPI, GUGLIELMO. Il bel giovine nella letteratura
       volgare del sec. XIV. Verona: Donato Tedeschi,
       1891. (reprinted from Biblioteca delle scuole
       italiane, 15)
Analyzes the stereoype of male beauty found in 14th-
century poetry, including references to some unpublished
homoerotic compositions.

900.   ZANETTE, EMILIO. Suor Arcangela, monaca del
       Seicento veneziano. Venice: Istituto per la
       Collaborazione Culturale, 1960.
See pp. 21-22 and 133-34 for discussion of lesbianism in
Venetian nunneries.

901.   ZAPPERI, ROBERTO. L'uomo incinto: la donna,
       l'uomo, il potere. Cosenza: Lerici, 1979.
In this interesting study of male pseudo-pregnancy, see
pp. 126-37, discussing some facetiae on sodomy in the
Renaissance.

                    L. EASTERN EUROPE

The sexual life of the pagan Eastern Slavs has scarcely
been investigated. The Greek Orthodox heritage of Kievan
and then Muscovite Russia gave the sexuality of the
"white" (parish) clergy a different cast from that of the
secular clergy in the Latin West. The extent to which the
early Soviet regime tolerated homosexuality remains a
topic of controversy among leftists and emigre scholars.
For the most part the history of homosexual behavior in
other eastern European countries is even more obscure than
that of Russia. The southern Balkans, where in modern
Greece and Albania remnants of once-flourishing homoerotic
subcultures survive, are something of an exception, though

more work is needed.

902.   BATKIS, GREGORIĬ A. **Die Sexualrevolution in
        Russland.** Berlin: E. Kater, 1925. 23 pp. (Beiträ-
        ge zum Sexualproblem, 4)
A Soviet functionary's explanation--for foreign consump-
tion--of the regime's purportedly liberal sexual policies
in the 1920s.

903.   DE JONG, BEN. "'An Intolerable Kind of Moral
        Degeneration': Homosexuality in the Soviet Union,"
        Review of Socialist Law (The Hague), 4 (1982),
        341-57.
Surveys opinion and law enforcement, chiefly in regard to
male homosexuality, since ca. 1960. "[T]he Soviet authorities' policy of giving incomplete and distorted information on the subject has the effect of reinforcing existing
prejudices among the population."

904.   DÉMIS (pseud.). "Chronique athénienne," **Arcadie,**
        no. 108 (December 1962), 651-54; no. 109 (January
        1963); no. 111 (March 1963), 151-55; no. 113 (May
        1963), 306-11; no. 118 (October 1963), 469-73.
A series of reports reflecting the situation in Greece
before the Colonels' coup.

905.   "G." "The Secret Life of Moscow," **Christopher
        Street,** (June 1980), 15-30.
American academic's candid account of his trip to the
Soviet capital in 1979. Compare the impressions of George
Schuvaloff: "Gay Life in Russia," **Christopher Street**
(September 1976), 14-23.

906.   GEL'MAN, IZRAIL' GRIGOR'EVICH. **Polovaia zhizn'
        sovremennoi molodiozhi.** Moscow: Gosudarstvennoe
        Izdatel'stvo, 1923.
In this work entitled "Sexual Life of Contemporary Youth,"
see pp. 117-21 ("Sexual Anomalies) for a pathological
interpretation of two lesbian cases. There is a Spanish
translation of this book: **La vida sexual de la juventud
contemporanea** (Madrid: M. Aguilar, 1932).

907.   HERBERSTEIN, SIGMUND, FREIHERR VON. **Description of
        Moscow and Muscovy, 1557.** Translated by J. B. C.
        Grundy. New York: Barnes and Noble, 1969. 105 pp.
In this translation of **Rerum Moscovitarum commentarii,** see
pp. 40, 52.

908.   HORNER, TOM. **Eros in Greece: A Sexual Inquiry.**
        New York: Aegean Books, 1978. 128 pp.
Contrasts in modern Greece between accepted views and
practice; see esp. pp. 54-74.

909.   HOSI WIEN, AUSLANDSGRUPPE. **Rosa Liebe unterm roten
        Stern: zur Lage der Lesben und Schwulen in Ost-**

europa. Hamburg: Fruhlings Erwachen, 1984. 142 pp.
Comprehensive work on social life, laws, culture, media
and gay movement stirrings in Eastern Europe. Compiled
by members of Homosexuelle Initiative, Vienna, which
also publishes reports in its periodical **Lambda Nachrichten** as a function of the Eastern Europe Information
Pool of the International Gay Association.

910. IAROSLAVSKIĬ, EMEL'IAN MIKHAĬLOVICH (pseud. of
      MINEĬ IZRAILEVICH GUBEL'MAN). **Bibliia dlia
      veruiushchikh i neveruiushchikh. Chast' II. Kniga
      Bytiia.** [The Bible for Believers and Unbelievers.
      Part II. The Book of Genesis]. Moscow and Lenin-
      grad: Gosudarstvennoe izdatel'stvo, 1925, pp. 34-
      39.
In this classic of Soviet antireligious literature, originally published as a series of articles in the journal
Bezbozhnik in 1922-25, the chapter entitled "Sodomitskie
greshniki i sodomitskie pravedniki" [The sinners of Sodom
and the righteous of Sodom] likens the sexual practices of
the Sodomites to Oriental and Greek pederasty and to the
vices that flourished in Christian monasteries. The book
continues to be reprinted and translated in the Soviet
Union as a mainstay of propaganda against religion.

911. KARLINSKY, SIMON. "Russia's Gay Literature and
      History (11th-20th centuries)," **Gay Sunshine,**
      nos. 29-30 (Summer-Fall 1976), 1-7.
Useful survey concentrating on the late 19th-early 20th
century flowering of Russian culture (including gay
culture). Attacks the facile view that things were rosy
under Lenin's regime. Enlarged Italian version: **Sodoma,** 3
(1986), 47-70. See also his: "Gay Life before the
Soviets: Revisionism Revised," **Advocate,** no. 339 (April 1,
1982), 31-34.

912. NÄCKE, PAUL. "On Homosexuality in Albania,"
      International Journal of Greek Love, 1:1 (1965),
      39-47.
On brotherhood pacts between men. Translated by Warren
Johansson from the German text in **JfsZ,** 9 (1908), 325-37.

913. ROZANOV, VASILIĬ VASIL'EVICH. **Four Faces of
      Rozanov: Christianity, Sex, Jews, and the Russian
      Revolution.** New York: Philosophical Library,
      1978. 310 pp.
Pp. 39-194 of this strange period document--the original
Russian text in question (**Liudi lunnogo sveta**) dates from
1913--offer an attack on the "moonlight men," i.e., sexual
deviates who are held responsible for the ascetic bias
of medieval Christianity. There is a short study of the
author by Renato Poggioli: **Rozanov** (New York: Hillary
House, 1962; 104 pp.).

914. SHARGORODSKIĬ, MIKHAIL DAVIDOVICH, and PAVEL
      PAVLOVICH OSIPOV. "Prestupleniia protiv lichnosti"

[Crimes against the person], in: A. A. Zhdanov
University (Leningrad), **Kurs sovetskogo ugolovnogo
prava** [A Course in Soviet Criminal Law], vol. 3,
Leningrad: Izdatel'stvo Leningradskogo universite-
ta, 1973, pp. 645-648.
On Article 121 of the Penal Code of the RSFSR (**muzhelozhstvo** = sodomy). The authors criticize the existing Soviet
law, saying that for some persons homosexuality is a
natural form of sexual gratification and that Soviet juridical literature has never furnished a satisfactory
scientific basis for making consensual sodomy a criminal
act. The trend in both capitalist and socialist countries
is toward repeal of the law.

915.   STERN, BERNHARD. **Geschichte der öffentlichen
        Sittlichkeit in Russland.** Berlin: Barsdorf, 1908.
        652 pp.
A general history of morals in Tsarist Russia, with some
relevant material in the second volume, including homoerotic poems from the reign of Nicholas I.

916.   STERN, MIKHAIL. **Sex in the USSR.** Edited and
        translated from the French by Mark Howson and Cary
        Ryan. New York: Times Books, 1980. 304 pp.
Composite picture drawn by an endocrinologist who emigrated in 1977; see esp. pp. 214-27.

917.   VONK, HANS. **Homoseksualiteit in staatssocialist-
        iese landen.** Amsterdam: Subfaculteit der Algemene
        Politieke en Sociale Wetenschappen, 1983.   59 pp.
        (Mededelingen, 36)
Seeks to assemble what is known of gay life and its restrictions in the countries of "actually existing socialism" (Eastern Europe, China, Cuba, and Nicaragua).

918.   WEISSENBERG, S. "Das Geschlechtsleben des russ-
        ischen Studententums der Revolutionszeit," **Zeit-
        schrift für Sexualwissenschaft,** 11 (1924), 209-216.
Evaluates questionnaires administered to Soviet students
on their sex life, with some conclusions on the incidence of homosexuality. See also the writer's article "Die
Verwahrlosung der Jugend in Sowjetrussland," ibid., 15
(1928), 225-53.

919.   WORTIS, JOSEPH. **Soviet Psychiatry.** Baltimore:
        Williams & Wilkins, 1950. 314 pp.
On pp. 213-15 the author, an American psychiatrist, introduces in a tone of cynical amusement the Stalinist laws of
1934, asserting that "deliberate efforts were made to
break up the sequestered coteries of sexual deviates...
by enacting more stringent legislation on certain abnormal
sex practices."

M. SCANDINAVIA

In the Nordic countries of Denmark, Finland, Norway, and
Sweden--commonly known as Scandinavia--lively homosexual
rights movements have stimulated scholarship since the end
of World War II. Important advances have also been
registered in the legal and social status of lesbians and
male homosexuals. For medieval Scandinavia, see III.D.

920.   BOHM, KRI. **Oppet brev om lesbisk karlek.** Stock-
        holm: Forum, 1977. 75 pp.
Advice from a Swedish lesbian on coping with society.

921.   CARLING, FINN. **De homofile: en skisse av en stengt
        tilvaerelse.** Oslo: Gyldendal Norsk Forlag, 1965.
        89 pp.
Difficulties of homosexual life in Norway in the 1960s
discussed by a sympathetic heterosexual.

922.   CHRISTENSEN, AKSEL. **Et seksuelt mindretal: en
        skitsemaessig beskrivelse af det homoseksuelle
        problem.** Copenhagen: Hans Reitzels Forlag, 1961.
        182 pp.
Evaluates the "homosexual problem" on the basis of 104
interviews. For presentation based on a slightly later
period, see Martin S. Weinberg and Colin J. Williams,
Male Homosexuals: Their Problems and Adaptations (New
York: Oxford University Press, 1974), esp. Chapter 6.

923.   ELLIOTT, NEIL. **Sexuality in Scandinavia.** New
        York: Weybright and Talley, 1970. 271 pp.
In this popular work, see Chapter 17, "Homosexuality"
(pp. 186-99); and Chapter 18, "Lesbians, pederasts and
boy prostitution" (pp. 200-07).

924.   FRIELE, KAREN-CHRISTINE. **Fra undertrykkelse til
        opprør.** Oslo: Gyldendal, 1975. 161 pp.
Outspoken book on the situation of male and female
homosexuals in Norway by a lesbian activist.

925.   HALLBECK, NILS. **Mannen och pojken.** Stockholm:
        Forfatteres Bokmaskin, 1980. 56 pp.
A somewhat rhapsodic defense of man-boy love.

926.   HANSSON, JOHAN (ed.). **Homosexella och omvarlden.**
        Stockholm: Liber, 1982. 250 pp.
Collection of articles on the situation of homosexuals in
society, including official and church attitudes.

927.   **Homosex: Om konsroller, samlevnad och sexuellt
        fortryckt.** Stockholm: Prisma, 1976. 144 pp.
Interviews with male homosexuals and lesbians in Sweden,
together with information on homosexual organizations.

928.   KOCH, MARTIN. **Guds Vackra Värld.** Stockholm: Bon-
        nier, 1916. 2 vols.

Hostile account of homosexuality in Sweden, which is
nonetheless useful for the information it gives on
street life, hustling, and meeting places.

929. MELIN, OLLE-PETTER. **Homosexualitet--en bibliografi.** Borås: Bibliotekshogskolan, 1975. 88 pp.
Extensive bibliographical compilation of relevant Swedish
material, concentrating on fiction and belles lettres,
but with some scholarly books and articles.

930. NYCANDER, GUNNAR. **En sjukdom som bestraffas: En
studie i homosexualitetens psykofysik.** Stockholm: Wahlstrom & Widstrand, 1933. 159 pp.
Although this book incorporated negative psychiatric
attitudes, it did advocate legal reform for homosexuals
which was then being debated in the Swedish parliament.
For the discussions, see: Vilhelm Lundstedt, **Otukt mot
naturen** (Stockholm: Bonnier, 1933; 111 pp.).

931. PALLESEN, HENNING. **De avvikande.** Stockholm: Bonnier, 1964. 180 pp.
A relatively positive text for the period, with a number
of case histories.

932. PARIKAS, DODO. **Frigorelse: Leva oppet som bog
eller lesbisk.** Stockholm: Liber, 1981. 182 pp.
Handbook on lesbian life and liberation in Sweden today.

933. REGMAN, CARL (pseud. of Carl Rademyr). **Konsten att
alska annorlunda: Den homosexuella erotiken.**
Norrkoping: AKRO, 1966. 163 pp.
Sociological study of life ways of Swedish male homosexuals.

934. SIEVERS, KAI, and OLLI STALSTROM (eds.). **Rakkauden
monet kasvot: homoseksuaalisesta rakkaudesta
ihmisoikeuksista ja vapautumisesta.** Espoo: Weilin &
Goos, 1984. 440 pp.
Articles by various authors on the homosexual situation in
Finland today.

935. SILVERSTOLPE, FREDERIK. "Upon the diversity of
Love: Pontus Wikner (1837-1888)," in: **Among Men,
among Women.** Amsterdam: University, 1983, pp. 268-
77, 577.
On a closeted Swedish philosopher and his times. See also
the biography by Lechard Hoannesson, **Pontus Wikner: Dag-
bokerna berätter** (Bodafors: Doxa, 1982; 139 pp.).

936. STOCKHOLM, NATIONALMUSEUM. **Christina, Queen of
Sweden--a Personality in European Civilization.**
Stockholm: Nationalmuseum, 1966. 622 pp. 96 illus.
Offers a many-sided picture of the famous bisexual queen
(1626-89) and her times. See also Sven Stolpe, **Christina
Queen of Sweden** (London, 1965), and Sophie Hochstetter,
"Christine von Schweden in ihre Jugend," **JfsZ**, 9 (1908),

168-96.

937.   THORSELL, ERIC. **En homosexuell arbetares memoar-
        er: järnbruksarbetaren Eric Thorsell berättar.**
        Edited by Frederik Silverstolpe. Stockholm:
        Barrikaden, 1981. 213 pp.
Autobiography of a Swedish iron and steel worker (1899-
1980).

N. NORTH AMERICA

For the most part attitudes toward homosexuality in colonial America were imported from England, though a good
deal of laxity prevailed with regard to the enforcement of
legal sanctions. In the second half of the 19th century,
urban subcultures of male homosexuals came to the attention of the authorities, leading to increased surveillance
and eventual repression. In North America homosexuality
did not assume a character distinct from that of Europe
until after World War II, when adaptation to the consumer
society, together with the rise of the American homosexual
rights movement (see III.U) made it paradigmatic for advanced Western industrial countries.

938.   ANDERSON, NELS. **The Hobo: the Sociology of the
        Homeless Man.** Chicago: University of Chicago,
        1961. 196 pp.
First published in 1923; see pp. 144-49. See also his
"The Juvenile and the Tramp," **Journal of Criminal Law,**
14 (1923), 290-312. See also Roger A. Bruns, **Knights of
the Road: A Hobo History.** (New York: Methuen, 1980; 214
pp.).

939.   BALL, JOHN. **Trip to Homoland.** Los Alamitos CA:
        Manifest Publications, 1968. 192 pp.
Typical example of a pseudo-sociological exploitation literature that flourished in the 1950s and 60s. Revealing
for its incarnation of now fortunately dated attitudes.

940.   BÉRUBÉ, ALAN. "Marching to a Different Drummer,"
        Advocate (October 15, 1981), 20-24.
Account of gay men and lesbians in the US armed forces in
World War II and, in many cases, their expulsion from the
service with dishonorable discharges (beginning in 1943).
For general background, see: John Costello, **Virtue under
Fire: How World War II Changed Our Social and Sexual
Attitudes** (Boston: Little, Brown, 1986; 309 pp.).

940.   BOX-CAR BERTHA. **Sister of the Road: the Autobiog-
        raphy of Box-car Bertha as Told to Dr. Ben L. Reit-
        man.** New York: Gold Label Books, 1937. 314 pp.
In this period document of hobo life, see pp. 62, 65-67,

69-70, 94, 149-50, 210, 228, 265, 283, 288.

942.   BULLOUGH, VERN, and BONNIE BULLOUGH. "Lesbianism
        in the 1920s and 1930s: A Newfound Study," **Signs**,
        2:4 (1977), 895-904.
Reviews contents of an unfinished manuscript describing
an informal group of 25 lesbians in a middle-sized
American city.

943.   BULLOUGH, VERN, and MARTHA VOGT. "Homosexuality
        and Its Confusion with the "Secret Sin" in Pre-
        Freudian America," **Journal of the History of
        Medicine and Allied Sciences**, 27:2 (April 1973),
        143-55.
The secret sin is masturbation.

944.   BURNS, ROBERT J. "'Queer Doings': Attitudes
        towards Homosexuality in 19th Century Canada," **Body
        Politic**, no. 29 (December 1976-January 1977), "Our
        Image" Section, pp. 4-7.
In 1838 George Markland, Inspector General of Upper
Canada, was forced to resign in the course of an inquiry
into his fraternizing with young men.

945.   CHAMBERS-SCHILLER, LEE VIRGINIA. **Liberty a Better
        Husband: Single Women in America: The Generation of
        1780-1840.** New Haven: Yale University Press,
        1984. 285 pp.
Based on writings of over 100 northeastern women. See
pp. 199, 204.

946.   DAVIS, MADELEINE, and ELIZABETH LAPOVSKY KENNEDY.
        "Oral History and the Study of Sexuality in the
        Lesbian Community: Buffalo, New York, 1940-1960,"
        Feminist Studies, 12 (1986), 7-26.
Shows that the butch-femme distinction was socially sanctioned in the lesbian community during this period.

947.   D'EMILIO, JOHN. "Gay Politics and Gay Community:
        the San Francisco Experience," **Socialist Review**,
        11:1 (January-February 1981), 77-104.
Account of changes in San Francisco since World War II.
The story is continued, from a different perspective, by
David Thomas, "The Gay Quest for Equality in San Francis-
co," in: J. K. Bowles (ed.), **The Egalitarian City.** (New
York: Praeger, 1986), pp. 27-41. See also D'Emilio's
book: **Sexual Politics, Sexual Communities.** (Chicago: Uni-
versity of Chicago Press, 1983).

948.   DUBERMAN, MARTIN. **About Time: Exploring the Gay
        Past.** New York: Seahorse Press, 1986. 425 pp.
Reprints documents, mainly from the 19th and first half of
the 20th century, some of them having first appeared
serially in the **New York Native** under the rubric "About
Time." Supplements the two volumes edited by Jonathan
Katz, cited below.

949.   DUBERMAN, MARTIN. "'I Am Not Contented': Female
        Masochism and Lesbianism in Early Twentieth-Century
        New England," **Signs**, 5 (1980), 825-41.
Psychiatric records from the second decade of the century.

950.   DUBERMAN, MARTIN. "'Writhing Bedfellows': 1826--
        Two Young Men from Antebellum South Carolina's
        Ruling Elite Share 'Extravagant Delight.'" **JH**, 6
        (Fall-Winter 1980-81), 85-102.
Two titillating letters written by the 22-year-old Thomas
Jefferson Withers to James H. Hammond.

951.   DUGGAN, LISA. "Lesbianism and American History: a
        Brief Source Review," **Frontiers**, 4:3 (Fall 1979),
        80-85.
Useful indications.

952.   ESCOFFIER, JEFFREY. "Sexual Revolution and the
        Politics of Gay Identity, **Socialist Review**, no.
        81-82 (July-October 1985), 119-53.
Interprets the development of sexual politics in the
United States since World War II in terms of three factors: the impact of Kinsey's **Reports**; "Keynsianism"
(postwar prosperity); and shifts in the sex/gender code.

953.   FLYNT, JOSIAH (pseud. of J. F. Willard). **Tramping
        with Tramps.** New York: The Century Company,
        1893. 398 pp.
An early classic of hobo life.

954.   FOSTER, MARION, and MURRAY KENT. **A Not So Gay
        World: Homosexuality in Canada.** Toronto: McClellan
        and Stewart, 1972. 240 pp.
Despite the title, a reasonably balanced picture for the
period, based on interviews with 50 persons. Contains a
list of organizations.

955.   GAY, PETER. **The Tender Passion.** New York: Oxford
        University Press, 1985. 490 pp. (The Bourgeois
        Experience: Victoria to Freud, 2)
Provides an idealized picture of 19th century marriage and
love in Europe and North America. On homosexuality, Gay
presents some new material from the diary of Yale student
Albert Dodd in the 1830s.

956.   GERASSI, JOHN. **The Boys of Boise: Furor, Vice and
        Folly in an American City.** New York: Macmillan,
        1966. 328 pp.
Ten years after it occurred, an investigative reporter
reconstructs the "homosexual scandal" of the Idaho capital, and the wrecked lives that resulted.

957.   GERBER, HENRY ("Parisex"). "In Defense of Homosex-
        uality," **The Modern Thinker** (June 1932), 286-97.
This article was written by Gerber, a pioneer in the campaign for civil rights for homosexuals, in response to a

hostile article by an Adlerian psychiatrist (W. Beran
Wolfe) in the April issue. It was reprinted in **A Homosexual Emancipation Miscellany.** (New York: Arno Press, 1975).

958.   GRUBE, JOHN. "Queens and Flaming Virgins: Towards
       a Sense of Gay Community," **Rites** (Toronto), 2:9
       (February 1986), 14-17.
Presents results of an interview project with 30 older
Toronto gay men that reveal the mentality and lifestyles
that prevailed before 1969.

959.   HAMILTON, WALLACE. **Christopher and Gay: a Partis-
       an's View of the Greenwich Village Homosexual
       Scene.** New York: Saturday Review Press, 1973.   215
       pp.
Personal narrative of the impact of Manhattan's street
people on a middle-aged writer.

960.   HARTLAND, CLAUDE. **The Story of a Life.** San
       Francisco: Grey Fox Press, 1985. 99 pp.
First published in 1901, this book is believed to be
the first autobiography written by an open homosexual in
America.

961.   INTERRANTE, JOSEPH. "From the Puritans to the
       Present: 350 Years of Gay History in Boston,"
       Alternate, 3:17 (January 1981), 23-29.
An example of a genre of local history that is developing
in many places in North America.

962.   JOHNSON, WILLIAM. "The Gay World." In: William
       Edward Mann (ed.), **The Underside of Toronto.**
       Toronto: McClellan & Stewart, 1970, pp. 322-33.
Reprinted from: W. E. Mann (ed.), **Deviant Behaviour in
Canada** (Toronto: Social Science, 1968, pp. 519-28).
Paints an unattractive picture.

963.   KATZ, JONATHAN. **Gay American History: Lesbians and
       Gay Men in the U.S.A.: a Documentary.** New York:
       Thomas W. Crowell, 1976. 690 pp.
Vast collection of 186 documents, many little known, covering the period from 1528 to the early seventies, accompanied by an at times controversial commentary. Unaccoun-
tably neglects religion; no continuous narrative. Many
references in the notes lead to other items. For a
detailed review of contents and underlying methodology,
see Jim Levin, **Reflections on the American Homosexual
Rights Movement.** (New York: Gay Academic Union, 1983),
pp. 57-67.

964.   KATZ, JONATHAN (NED). **Gay/Lesbian Almanac: a New
       Documentary.** New York: Harper and Row, 1983.   769
       pp.
Sequel to the preceding. The documents are selected from
the period 1607-1740 and 1880-1950. The gap apparently
signals Katz' conversion to the Social Construction

approach, which holds that the "modern homosexual" came
into existence only in the closing decades of the 19th
century. Like the other book, this one is furnished with
an abundance of references; as these volumes are readily
available most of them will not be repeated here.

965.   KENNEDY, HUBERT C. "The Case for James Mills
        Peirce," **JH**, 4 (Winter 1978), 179-84.
Proposes that Peirce (1834-1906), a mathematician and Dean
of Harvard's graduate school, wrote a defense of homosexuality that was published anonymously in 1897.

966.   MITZEL, JOHN. **The Boston Sex Scandal.** Boston:
        Glad Day Books, 1980. 148 pp.
Account of the persecution by Boston police and courts of
a group of homosexuals and pederasts, which was the pre-
lude to the formation of NAMBLA.

967.   OAKS, ROBERT F. "Things Fearful to Name: Sodomy
        and Buggery in Seventeenth-Century New England,"
        Journal of Social History, 12 (1978), 268-81.
Punishments became less common as religious zeal waned in
the latter part of the century. See also his "Perceptions of Homosexuality by Justices of the Peace in Colonial Virginia," **JH**, 5 (1979-80), 35-41.

968.   RUGOFF, MILTON. **Prudery and Passion: Sexuality in
        Victorian America.** New York: G. P. Putnam's Sons,
        1971. 413 pp.
Popular history beginning in colonial times and extending
to the end of the 19th century. See pp. 263-70 and 365-69.

969.   "S., H." "Gay Old New York," **Der Kreis**, 21:6 (June
        1953), 31-34.
Unusual glimpse of Greenwich Village in the immediate
postwar years.

970.   SCHWARTZ, JUDITH. **Radical Feminists of Hetero-
        doxy: Greenwich Village, 1912-1940.** Lebanon, NH:
        New Victoria Publishers, 1982. 110 pp.
Recreates a largely lesbian New York circle of women who
were outspoken and often militant.

971.   SÉGUIN, ROBERT-LIONEL. **La vie libertine en
        Nouvelle-France au dix-septième siècle.** Montreal:
        Leméac, 1972. 2 vols.
See vol. 1, p. 343ff.: "La sodomie et l'inceste."

972.   SMITH-ROSENBERG, CARROLL. **Disorderly Conduct: Vis-
        ions of Gender in Victorian America.** New York: Al-
        fred A. Knopf, 1985. 357 pp.
On women's changing roles in response to socio-economic
thinking, eventuating (at the turn of the century) in a
kind of androgynous or sexual-convergence ideal. Offers
some contestable observations on male homosexuality.

972.   SPRAGUE, GREGORY. "Chicago Past: A Rich Gay
        History," **Advocate**, no. 374 (August 18, 1983),
        28ff.
Gay life in the Second City during the 20th century.

973.   SYLVESTRE, PAUL-FRANÇOIS. **Bougrerie en Nouvelle
        France.** Hull, Quebec: Editions Asticou, 1983.
Various incidents in the French colony of Canada or New
France; bibliography, pp. 87-89.

974.   TAYLOR, CLARK. "Folk Taxonomies and Justice in
        Dade County," **ARGOH Newsletter**, 4:1 (1982), 9-16;
        4:2 (1982), 17-28; 4: 4 (1983), 13-22.
Account of a 1950s campaign against homosexuals in south
Florida.

                        O. LATIN AMERICA

The existence of flourishing homosexual subcultures in the
cities of Latin America has long been known to travelers,
but until recently it has not been regarded as a suitable
subject for scholarly investigation, except in Brazil,
which displays a different range of attitudes from those
found in the Hispanic Americas. The spread of gay liberation groups in Latin America and the attention of sympathetic foreign scholars has begun to alter and flesh
out our picture of a major aspect of world homosexuality.
For the indigenous (Amerindian) cultures of Mexico,
Central and South America, see IV.F.

975.   ARBOLEDA G. MANUEL. "Gay Life in Lima," **Gay
        Sunshine**, no. 42-43 (1980, 30.
Knowledgeable report on cruising and social patterns in
the Peruvian capital.

976.   ARCILA GONZÁLEZ, ANTONIO. **Les lesbianas.** Bogota:
        Ediciones Sexo y Cultura, 1969. 195 pp.
Negative, popularized presentation. See also his: **El
tercer sexo** (Medellín: Ediciones Sexo y Cultura, 1961;
186 pp.).

977.   ARGÜELLES, LOURDES, and B. RUBY RICH. "Homosexual-
        ity, Homophobia, and Revolution: Notes toward an
        Understanding of the Cuban Lesbian and Gay Male
        Experience: I," **Signs**, 9 (1984), 683-99.
Reports interviews among exiles in the U.S., Puerto Rico,
Mexico, and Spain. While ostensibly arguing for a "socialist countercritique" on behalf of homosexuality,
this article (concluded in the following issue) in fact
tends to excuse the homophobic policies of the Castro
regime.

978. BLAIR, DONIPHAN. "Gay Men in Nicaragua: Living on
      Both Sides of the Revolution," **Advocate**, no. 422
      (June 11, 1985), 48, 51.
Interviews with Nicaraguans of several political persua-
sions who reported that conditions for gay people were
deteriorating under the Sandinistas.

979. BOOGAARD, HENK VAN DEN. **Homoseksualiteit: Ideologie
      en politiek, Cuba.** Amsterdam: SUA, 1982. 120 pp.
While granting that homosexuals have a hard life in Cuba,
the author, active in the Cuban-Dutch friendship organiza-
tion, nonetheless perceives hopeful signs. See also:
Boogaard and Kathelijne van Kammen, "We Cannot Jump over
Our Own Shadow: On Cuban Actions against Homosexuals and
Against Antihomosexuality," in: **IGA Pink Book 1985.**
(Amsterdam: COC, 1985), pp. 29-41; and A. Young, below.

980. CAMINHA, ADOLFO. **Bom Crioulo (The Black Man and
      the Cabin Boy).** Translated from the Portuguese by
      E. A. Lacey. San Francisco: Gay Sunshine Press,
      1982. 141 pp.
A novel first published by a Brazilian writer (1867-97)
in 1895, this book affords a rare glimpse of male homosexual life and feelings in Rio de Janeiro. This English-
language edition includes notes on words and places.

981. CAPISTRANO DE ABREU, J. (ed.). **Primeira visitação
      do Santo Officio as partes do Brasil ...: Confissõ-
      es da Bahia, 1591-92.** Rio de Janeiro: Briguiet,
      1935. 195 pp.
Edited version of the official records of the inquisitors' clerk in the Bahia region at the end of the 16th
century. There are many confessions by sodomites and
lesbians. See also: R. Garcia, **Terceiro livro das
denunciaçoes de Pernambuco (1593-95)** (São Paulo, 1929).

982. CARRIER, JOSEPH M. "Mexican Male Homosexuality,"
      JH, 11 (1985), 75-85.
Analysis of material collected by the author over a
fifteen-year period suggests that bisexual behavior is
more easily accepted by Mexican males and is more widely
practiced than in the United States. See also his:
"Cultural Factors Affecting Urban Male Homosexual Behavior," **Archives of Sexual Behavior,** 5 (1976), 103-24;
"Family Attitudes and Mexican Male Homosexuality," **Urban
Life,** 5 (1976), 359-75; and "Unusual Cross-Gender Behavior
in Northwestern Mexico," **ARGOH Newsletter,** 3:3 (1981),
2-5.

983. CIONE, OTTO MIGUEL. **Luxuria: la vida nocturna de
      Buenos Aires.** Santiago de Chile: Editorial
      Ercilla, 1936. 328 pp.
See "Natura morta" (pp. 132-38) on homosexuals and lesbians in the night life of Buenos Aires in the 1930s.

984. DA GRIS, CARLOS A. **El homosexual en la Argentina.**

LATIN AMERICA   153

       Buenos Aires: Continental Service, 1965. 298 pp.
   Journalistic account of Argentine homosexual life, mainly
   in Buenos Aires, before the repression of the 1970s.
   Appendix on Japan. See now: Alejandro Jockl, **Ahora, los
   gay** (Buenos Aires: La Pluma, 1984).

985.   DOURADO, LUIZ ÁNGELO. **Homossexualismo (masculino e
       feminino) e Delinquência.** Second ed. Rio de
       Janeiro: Zahar, 1967. 245 pp.
   Psychiatrically oriented study based in part on projective
   tests administered to Brazilian homosexual subjects.

986.   ESPINOSA MOLINA, CLAUDIO. **Crimines sexuales en
       Chile.** Santiago: Neupert, 1965. 182 pp.
   Journalist's report on sex crimes in Chile; see esp. "El
   rey de los homosexuales" (pp. 93-101).

987.   FICHTE, HUBERT. **Xango: Die afroamerikanischen
       Religionen: Bahia, Haiti, Trinidad.** Frankfurt am
       Main: S. Fischer Verlag, 1976. 351 pp.
   Account by a gifted German gay writer (1935-1986) of his
   experiences with Afro-American religious cults. There
   is also a sequel: **Petersilie: Die afroamerikanischen
   Religionen Santo Domingo, Venezuela, Miama, Grenada**
   (Frankfurt am Main: S. Fischer Verlag, 1980; 401 pp.).

988.   FREYRE, GILBERTO. **The Masters and the Slaves.**
       Translated by Samuel Putnam. New York: Knopf,
       1956. 537 pp.
   In this noted study of colonial and imperial Brazil,
   see pp. 33, 117, 119, 121, 123, 149.

989.   FRY, PETER. "Male Homosexuality and Spirit
       Possession in Brazil," **JH,** 11:3-4 (1985), 137-53.
   On the relationship between male homosexual and the Afro-
   Brazilian possession cults in Belem do Para. Analyzes two
   categories, **bicha** and man, with discussions of advantages
   acquired by those who assume the former status. See also
   Peter Fry (ed.), **Para Inglês Ver: Identidade e Politica
   na Cultura Brasileira** (Rio de Janeiro: Zahar, 1982); and
   Fry and E. McRae, **O que é Homossexualidade** (São Paulo:
   Editorial Brasiliense, 1983).

990.   JAIME, JORGE. **Homossexualismo Masculino.** Rio de
       Janeiro: The author, 1947. 170 pp.
   Published version of a thesis for the Faculdade Nacional
   de Direito. Following a brief medico-legal account,
   Jaime reprints letters and a long diary by Brazilian
   homosexuals.

991.   KUTSCHE, PAUL. "Situational Homosexuality in Costa
       Rica," **ARGOH Newsletter,** 4:4 (1983), 8-13.
   Discusses lack of gay identity in three men interviewed.

992.   LACEY, E. A. "Latin America," **Gay Sunshine,** no. 40
       (1979), 22-31.

Overstates the absolute character of the **activo/passivo**
contrast in the self-consciousness and organization of
Latin American homosexuals, but does recognize differences caused by economic disparities.

993.   LANDES, RUTH. "A Cult Matriarchate and Male
        Homosexuality," **Journal of Abnormal and Social
        Psychology**, 35 (1940), 386-97.
Early description of Afro-Brazilian cults with prominent
male transvestism.

994.   LANE, ERSKINE. **Game Texts: A Guatemalan Journal.**
        San Francisco: Gay Sunshine Press, 1978. 156 pp.
Poetic travel reminiscences, including sexual encoun-
ters with adolescent **activos.** See also his: "Guatemalan
Diary," **Gay Sunshine**, no. 26-27 (Winter 1975-76), 13-15.

995.   LENNOX, DAVID R. "Gay Life in Macho Mexico,"
        Christopher Street (July 1977), 6-18; and (August
        1977), 34-42.
Points up contrasts with customs and habits in the U.S.

996.   LEYLAND, WINSTON (ed.). **My Deep Dark Pain Is
        Love: A Collection of Latin American Fiction.**
        Translated from the Spanish and Portuguese by E.
        A. Lacey. San Francisco: Gay Sunshine Press,
        1983. 383 pp.
Translations of fiction from a number of Latin American
countries offering insights into attitudes and the
texture of homosexual life there. There is a useful
Introduction and notes by the translator. See also the
earlier anthology edited by Leyland: **Now the Volcano: An
Anthology of Latin American Gay Literature** (San Francisco: Gay Sunshine Press, 1979; 287 pp.).

997.   LIMA, DÉLCIO MONTEIRO DE. **Comportamento Sexual do
        Brasileiro.** Third ed. Rio de Janeiro: F. Alves,
        1978. 220 pp.
Semipopular report on sexual behavior in contemporary
Brazil; see pp. 135-73.

998.   MCCASKELL, TIM. "Sex and Sandinismo: Gay Life in
        the New Nicaragua," **Body Politic**, no. 73 (May
        1981), 19-21.
Nicaraguan gay life remains profoundly affected by class
differences. The revolution has no concept of sexual
politics. See also his: "Gay Life in Colombia: Hiding,
Hustling, and Coming Together," ibid., no. 68 (December
1980-January 1981), 25-27.

999.   MOTT, LUIZ R. B. "Slavery and Homosexuality,"
        Quarterly (San Francisco), no. 24 (Winter 1985),
        10-25.
Evidence mainly from Brazil (16th-18th century), with some
reference to the African background.

1000. MURRAY, STEPHEN O. **Latino Homosexuality.** San
       Francisco: Social Networks, 1980. 14 pp.
Booklet with brief comments on various locales and discussion of social-structure obstacles to gay institutional
elaborations among Latinos.

1001. PARKER, RICHARD. "Masculinity, Femininity, and
       Homosexuality: On the Anthropological Interpreta-
       tion of Sexual Meanings in Brazil," **JH,** 11:3-4
       (1985), 155-63.
Reviewing recent research, contends that male homosexuality in Brazil can only be fully understood when situated
in the wider context of sexual meanings.

1002. PAZ, OCTAVIO. **The Labyrinth of Solitude: Life and
       Thought in Mexico.** New York: Grove, 1950. 212
       pp.
In this classic study of the Mexican national character
(including sexual aspects), note esp. p. 39.

1003. REICHEL-DOLMATOFF, GERARDO, and ALICIA REICHEL-
       DOLMATOFF. **The People of Aritama: The Cultural
       Personality of a Colombia Mestizo Valley.**
       Chicago: Chicago University Press, 1961. 483 pp.
In this study of a mestizo community, which was Indian
only a hundred years ago, see pp. 49-50, 105-06.

1004. SALAS, LUIS. **Social Control and Deviance in
       Cuba.** New York: Praeger, 1979. 399 pp.
Perceives a shift in Castro's Cuba from an "extreme
position...during the initial phase" to "a more moderate
reaction...in more recent times." See pp. 150-77.

1005. SANZIO, ALAIN et al. "Cuba: un goulag tropical,"
       Masques, no. 22 (Summer 1984), 87-101.
Reflections on the repression of homosexuals in Cuba and
the tendency to conceal this abroad promoted by the film
"Improper Conduct." Includes an interview with the
filmmaker Nestor Almendros and the texts of the repressive legislation.

1006. TAYLOR, CLARK. "Mexican Male Homosexual Interac-
       tion in Public Contexts," **JH,** 11:3-4 (1985),
       117-36.
Using game theory, shows the modus operandi and locales
for homosexual encounters in Mexico, which are quite
different from U.S. patterns. Based on the author's
Ph.D. dissertation (anthropology, University of Califor-
nia, Berkeley, 1978). See also his: "Ethnographic
Material on Mexican Male Homosexual Transvestites," **ARGOH
Newsletter,** 3:1 (1981), 3-6; and "Mexican Gay Life in
Historical Perspective," **Gay Sunshine,** no. 26-27 (Winter
1975), 1-4.

1007. TREVISAN, JOÃO. **Perverts in Paradise.** London:
       Gay Men's Press, 1986. 208 pp.

Pot-pourri of vibrant Brazilian gay life and culture from
the 16th century to the present, including voodoo priests,
prize-winning dramatists, papal inquisitors, and Guevarist
revolutionaries.

1008. VALDIOSERA, RAMÓN. **El lesbianismo en Mexico.**
Second ed. Mexico City: Editores Asociados M.,
1980. 157 pp.
Semipopular; includes case histories.

1009. WHITAM, FREDERICK L. "Entendidos de São Paulo,"
Gay Sunshine, 38 (1979), 16-17.
Profiles a "gay life" consisting mostly of friendship
cliques with a few commercial establishments.

1010. YOUNG, ALLEN. "Gay Gringo in Brazil," in: Len
Richmond and Gary Noguera (eds.). **The Gay Liberation Book.** San Francisco: Ramparts Press, 1973),
pp. 60-67.
Social and political reflections based on two year's
residence. See also: Dennis Altman, "Down Rio Way,"
Christopher Street, 4:8 (April 1980), 22-27.

1011. YOUNG, ALLEN. **Gays under the Cuban Revolution.**
San Francisco: Grey Fox Press, 1981. 112 pp.
In this incisive book a scholar and former New Left
journalist and scholar documents the homophobia of Cuba's
revolutionary regime, and the sufferings that it has
caused. He also criticizes the left, including the gay
left in the United States, for its crime of silence.

1012. ZAPATA, LUIS. **Adonis García: A Picaresque Novel.**
Translated by E. A. Lacey. San Francisco: Gay
Sunshine Press, 1981. 208 pp.
Although cast in the form of a novel, this work gives--
through the eyes of its hustler-narrator--vivid glimpses
of homosexual life in Mexico City today. First published in Spanish as: **Las aventuras, desventuras, y
sueños de Adonis García, el vampiro de la Colonia Roma**
(Mexico City: Editorial Grijalbo, 1979).

P. ISLAM

Although some homosexuals in Western countries tend to
idealize homosexual life in Islam, it is clear that that
civilization harbored a number of ambiguities toward it.
Social conditions often fostered same-sex relations, at
least for men, but these factors were counterbalanced by
traditional and religious currents of disapproval. Male-
male love, especially in its pederastic form, was often
celebrated in writings in Arabic, Persian, Turkish,
and Urdu. The abundance of literary evidence on the
subject makes this field a fruitful one for historical

research.

1013.   ABBOTT, NABIA. **Two Queens of Baghdad: Mother and Wife of Harun al-Rashid.** Chicago: University of Chicago Press, 1946. 277 pp.
Panorama of aristocratic life under the Abbasid caliphate. See pp. 210-12 for the homosexuality of Muhammad al-Amin, his infatuation with his eunuchs (whom he dressed as girls), and his favorite poet, the pederast Abu Nuwas.

1014.   ARNOLD, THOMAS WALKER, SIR. **Painting in Islam.** New York: Dover, 1965. 159 pp.
In this now somewhat dated work (first published in 1928), see pp. 89-90, 146.

1015.   BABINGER, FRANZ CARL HEINRICH. **Mehmed the Conquerer and His Time.** Translated from the German by Ralph Manheim. Princeton: Princeton University Press, 1978. 549 pp.
On the pederastic Turkish sultan Mehmed II (1430-81); see pp. 93, 96, 212, 334, 427, 450, 475.

1016.   BABUR (ZAHIR UD-DIN MUHAMMAD). **The Babur-nama in English.** Translated by Annette Susannah Beveridge. London: Luzac, 1922. 2 vols.
Autobiographical work of the founder of the Mughal dynasty of India (1483-1530), whose career began in Central Asia.

1017.   BADAYUNI, 'ABDUL QAIR. **Muntakhabu-'t-tawarikh.** Translated by George Ranking, W. H. Lowe, and Sir Wolseley Haig. Patna: Academica Asiatica, 1973. 3 vols.
For pederastic poets and rulers of Mughal India, see vol. 1, 611-12; vol. 2, 13-17; vol. 3, 243, 256-57, 265, 331, 333, 339.

1018.   BARBER, NOËL. **The Sultans.** New York: Simon and Schuster, 1973. 304 pp.
In this history of Turkey, see pp. 35-36, 45, 83, 102-03.

1019.   BLOUNT, HENRY. **A Voyage into the Levant.** London: Andrew Crooke, 1636. 126 pp.
For Turks see pp. 14, 79, 112.

1020.   **The Book of the Thousand Nights and a Night: the Arabian Nights Entertainments.** Translated by (Sir) Richard F. Burton. Benares: Kamashastra Society, 1885-88. 16 vols.
Apart from the notes to individual tales, see vol. 10, pp. 63-260, for the Terminal Essay, which contains important historical and comparative material on homosexuality in Islam.

1021.   BOSWORTH, C. E. et al. "Liwat" [Sodomy], in: **Encyclopedia of Islam.** New ed. Leiden: E. J.

Brill, vol. 5 (1986), 776-79.
Covers the ambivalent attitudes toward homosexuality in
Islamic society from the time of the Prophet to the end of
the Middle Ages.

1022. BOUHDIBA, ABDELWAHAB. **La sexualité en Islam.**
Paris: Presses Universitaires de France, 1975.   320
pp.
Study of Islamic sexual attitudes based on Arabic sources.
For a somewhat scanty and negative presentation of homosexuality, see pp. 44-45 on **liwat** (male homosexuality) and
musah'aqa (lesbianism), as well as pp. 203-07 on the
hammam (baths). For different view of the whole subject,
see Vern Bullough, **Sexual Variance in Society and History**
(New York: Wiley, 1976), 205-244.

1023. BRUNEL, RENÉ. **Le monachisme errant dans l'Islam:
Sidi Heddi et les Heddawa.** Paris: Librairie
Larose, 1955.   471 pp. (Publications de l'Institut
des Hautes Etudes Marocaines, 47)
Pederasty in a heterodox Moroccan Islamic order whose mem-
bers could not marry.

1024. CHÉNIER, LOUIS DE. **The Present State of the Empire
of Morocco.** Anonymous translation. London: G. and
J. Robinson, 1788. 2 vols. in 1.
In this translation of **Recherches historiques sur les
Maures,** vol. 3, see vol. 1, p. 73; vol. 2, pp. 250, 287,
pertaining to Sultan Abdallah V (ruled 1729-57).

1025. CHRISTOWE, STOYAN. **The Lion of Yannina.** New
York: Modern Age Books, 1941. 424 pp.
On the Albanian homosexual leader Ali Pasha (ca. 1744-
1822); see pp. 77, 141, 158, 191, 203, 276, 294, 327,
342-43.

1026. CLINE, WALTER. **Notes on the People of Siwah and El
Garah in the Libyan Desert.** Menasha, WI: George
Banta Publishing Co., 1936. 64 pp. (General
series on Anthropology, 4)
Asserts that in this oasis culture, "all men and boys
practiced sodomy," speaking freely of their experiences.
Confirmed by Robin Maugham, **Journey to Siwa** (New York:
Harcourt, Brace, 1950; 120 pp.)

1027. CONTINENTE FERRER, J. M. "Aproximación al estudio
del tema del amor en la poesía hispano-árabe en los
siglos XII y XIII," **Awraq** (Instituto Hispano-árabe
de Cultura), 1 (1978), 12-28.
Surveys the characteristic themes of pederastic love in
the Moorish poetry of Spain. Compare Norman Roth, "'Deal
Gently with the Young Man': Love of Boys in Medieval
Hebrew Poetry of Spain," **Speculum,** 57 (1982), 20-51.

1028. COON, CARLETON. **Tribes of the Rif.** Cambridge,
MA: Peabody Museum, 1931. 417 pp.

For boy slave markets in Morocco see pp. 110-11.

1029. DANIEL, MARC. "La civilisation arabe et l'amour
       masculine," **Arcadie,** no. 253 (January 1975), 8-19;
       no. 254 (February 1975), 83-93; no 255 (March
       1975), 142-50; no. 257 (May 1975), 269-74; and
       no. 258 (June 1975), 326-330.
A major study, with numerous references, emphasizing
poetry. An English translation by Winston Leyland
appeared in **Gay Sunshine,** no. 32 (Spring 1977), 1-11, 27.

1030. DANIEL, MARC. "L'Ayatolla et les pelotons de
       l'exécution," **Arcadie,** no. 305 (1979), 388-89.
On the pederastic poetry of Saadi and Omar Khayyam.

1031. DAVEY, RICHARD. **The Sultan and His Subjects.** New
       ed. London: Chatto and Windus, 1907. 507 pp.
Contains some material on harem catamites in Turkey.

1032. DE MARTINO, GIANNI, and ARNO SCHMITT. **Kleine
       Schriften zu zwischenmännlicher Sexualität und
       Erotik in der muslimischen Gesellschaft.** Berlin:
       Schmitt, 1985. 58 pp.
Essays on several aspects of homosexual life in Islam past
and present, including a critique of John Boswell's
treatment of Moorish Spain. English summary by Schmitt,
the principal author, "Some Reflections on Male-Male
Sexuality in Muslim Society" (pp. 54-58).

1033. ÐORÐEVIĆ (GJORGJEVIC), BARTOLOMEJ. **De Turcarum
       moribus epitome.** Lyon: Jean de Tournes, 1555. 184
       pp.
Account of the writer's capture and enslavement by the
Turks, with observations on pederastic practices. There
is a contemporary English version (London, 1560).

1034. DRAKE, JONATHAN (pseud. of Parker Rossman). "'Le
       Vice' in Turkey," **International Journal of Greek
       Love,** 1:2 (1966), 13-27.
Well-documented study of pederasty in the Turkish domains
(14th-20th cent.), including the slave trade.

1035. DUCHESNE, EDOUARD ADOLPHE. **De la prostitution dans
       la ville d'Alger depuis la conquête** [1830]. Paris:
       Bailliere, 1853. 231 pp.
Offers some information on hustling by Algerian youths.

1036. EDWARDES, ALLEN (pseud. of D. A. Kinsley). **The
       Jewel in the Lotus: A Historical Survey of the
       Sexual Culture of the East.** New York: Julian,
       1959. 293 pp.
Diverting anecdotal material, chiefly on the Arab world
and India. Derived mainly from 19th-century sources,
this book often relays their stereotypes uncritically,
and must be used with caution. See esp. pp. 199-263.

1037. FABRI, FÉLIX. **Le voyage en Egypte, 1483.** Translated into French by Jacques Masson. Cairo: Institut Français d'Archéologie Orientale du Caire,
1975. 3 vols. (1066 pp.)
A westerner's observations on the last days of Mamluk
rule; see vol. 2, pp. 704-07.

1038. FLAUBERT, GUSTAVE. **The Letters of Gustave Flaubert, 1830-1857.** Translated by Francis Steegmuller. Cambridge, MA: Harvard University Press,
1979. 267 pp.
See pp. 111 and 129 for baths in Cairo and male brothels
in Constantinople. For the original texts see: **Correspondence, I 1830-1851.** Edited by Jean Bruneau (Paris:
Gallimard, 1973; 1173 pp.), pp. 567-74, 638, 669.

1039. GIFFEN, LOIS ANITA. **Theory of Profane Love among
the Arabs: The Development of the Genre.** New
York: New York University Press, 1971. 167 pp.
While somewhat reticent on the subject of homosexuality,
this scholarly study focusing on twenty essays and
treatises throws light on the concepts of **'ishq** (passionate love) and **hawa** (desire, lust).

1040. GLAZER, MARK. "On Verbal Duelling among Turkish
Boys," **Journal of American Folklore,** 89 (1976),
88-91.
Challenges the interpretation of homosexual themes offered
by A. Dundes et al. ("The Strategy of Turkish Boys' Duelling Rhymes" in: J. Gumperz and D. Hynes, eds., **Directions in Sociolinguistics,** New York, 1972, pp. 130-60).

1041. GLUBB, JOHN B. **Soldiers of Fortune: The Story of
the Mamlukes.** New York: Stein and Day, 1973. 480
pp.
Court and military history of the dynasty that ruled Egypt
in pre-Ottoman times, detailing a number of homosexual
intrigues.

1042. GODARD, ERNEST. **Egypte et Palestine, observations
médicales et scientifiques.** Paris: V. Masson,
1867. 458 pp.
In this travel account, see pp. 104-06 and 111-12.

1043. GROTZFELD, HEINZ. **Das Bad im arabischen Mittel-
alter: eine kulturgeschichtliche Studie.** Wiesbad-
en: Harrassowitz, 1970. 159 pp.
On homosexual activity in the medieval Islamic sauna
(hammam), see pp. 89-91. For a somewhat negative analysis
of the modern hammam, see Abdelwahab Bouhdiba, "Le hammam:
contribution à une psychanalyse de l'Islam," **Revue Tuni-
sienne des Sciences Sociales,** 1 (September 1964), 7-14.

1044. HANSEN, WALDEMAR. **The Peacock Throne.** New
York: Holt, Rinehart and Winston, 1972. 560 pp.
For the career of Sarmad, a Persian Jewish homosexual

convert to Islam, see Chapter 24 (pp. 396-412).

1045. HELLER, BERNHARD, and GEORGES VAJDA. "Lut" [Lot],
      in: **Encyclopedia of Islam.** New ed. Leiden: E. J.
      Brill, vol. 5 (1986), pp. 832-833.
On the Koranic and later Islamic versions of the Biblical
legend of Lot in Sodom. It is remarkable that in Islam
the Sodomites have become the **ahl Lut** (people of Lot), and
so **luti** has acquired the sexual meaning of sodomite.

1046. HERBERT, THOMAS, SIR. **A Relation of Some Yeares
      Travaile into Afrique, Asia, Indies.** New York: Da
      Capo Press, 1971. 225 pp.
Facsimile of the 1634 edition. For Persia in the early
17th century, see pp. 63-64, 75, 87, 98-99.

1047. HERVÉ, GUY, and THIERRY KERREST. **Les enfants de
      Fez.** Paris: Editions Libres Hallier, 1979. 202
      pp.
Evidence taken from tape recordings of the life of young
people in the ancient Moroccan city, including hustling.

1048. HEYD, URIEL. **Studies in Old Ottoman Criminal Law.**
      Edited by V. L. Menage. Oxford: Clarendon Press,
      1973. 340 pp.
For legal provisions affecting pederasty, see pp. 30,
100-03, 136, 261, 265, 278.

1049. HOUEL, CHRISTIAN. **Maroc: marriage, adultère,
      prostitution: anthologie.** Paris: H. Daragon,
      1912. 202 pp.
"If there are many prostitutes in Morocco, there are even
more sodomites." See esp. pp. 139-42. See also P. Rem-
linger, "La prostitution en Maroc," **Annales d'Hygiène
Publique** (February 1913).

1050. IBN AL-NADIM, MUHAMMAD. **The Fihrist: a Tenth-cen-
      tury Survey of Muslim Culture.** Translated by
      Bayard Dodge. New York: Columbia University Press,
      1970. 2 vols.
In this encyclopedic work, see vol. 1, pp. 247-48, 333-36,
392, 503; vol. 2, pp. 737, 927.

1051. IBN DAWUD (MUHAMMAD IBN DAWUD AL-ISFAHANI). **Kitab
      al-zahra (The Book of the Flower).** Arabic text ed.
      by Richard Nykl. Chicago: Oriental Institute,
      1932. 406 pp.
This 9th-century compilation includes love poetry to boys
by several authors.

1052. IBN HAZM, ALI IBN AHMAD. **A Book Containing the
      Risala Known as the Dove's Neckring, about Love and
      Lovers.** Translated by Alois Nykl. Paris: Geuth-
      ner, 1931. 244 pp.
An erotic classic compiled by an 11th-century scholar
residing in Cordoba.

1053. IBN KHALDUN, ABD AL-RAHMAN. **The Muqaddimah: an
       Introduction to History.** Translated by Franz
       Rosenthal. New York: Pantheon, 1958. 3 vols.
In this work by the celebrated historical theorist, see
the poems in vol. 3, pp. 444-78.

1054. IBN KHALLIKAN. **Wafayat al-a'yan wa anba' abna'
       al-zaman.** Translated by Baron McGucklin de
       Slane. Ed. by S. Mopinul Haq. Karachi: Pakistan
       Historical Society, 1964-76.
This classic biographical dictionary (of which this is the
only unexpurgated version) contains numerous references
(e.g.,on Yahya ibn Aktham, vol. 6, pp. 230-34).

1055. IBN SASRA, MUHAMMAD. **A Chronicle of Damascus,
       1389-1397.** Translated by William M. Brinner.
       Berkeley: University of California, 1963. 2 vols.
In this Syrian source, see vol. 1, pp. 189, 217.

1056. IBN TAGHRIBIRDI, ABU AL-MAHASIN YUSUF. **History of
       Egypt, 1382-1469.** Translated by William Popper.
       Berkeley: University of California Press, 1954. 7
       vols.
For Mamluk sultans, see vol. 1, p. 43.

1057. INGRAMS, WILLIAM HAROLD. **Abu Nuwas in Life and
       Legend.** Port Louis, Mauritius: La Typographie
       Moderne, 1933. 95 pp.
Stories and poems by and about the famous Arab homosexual
poet (762-ca. 815).

1058. JAHIZ, AL-, 'AMR IBN BAHR. **The Life and Works of
       Jahiz.** Translated (from the French of Charles
       Pellat) by D. M. Hawke. Berkeley: University of
       California Press, 1969. 286 pp.
Regrettably this selection from the 9th-century writer's
work omits his debate on the merits of women and boys
(**Kitab Mufakharat al jawari wa-al-ghilman.** Ed. by Charles
Pellat. Beirut: Dar al Makshuf, 1958; 94 pp.). See, how-
ever, pp. 27, 269-71.

1059. JAMES, BEN. **The Secret Kingdom: an Afghan Journey.**
       New York: Reynal and Hitchcock, 1934. 295 pp.
For King Amanullah (1892-1960), see pp. 194-97, 215.

1060. KARSCH-HAACK, FERDINAND. "Die Rolle der Homoerotik
       im Arabertum," **JfsZ,** 23 (1923), pp. 100-170.
Survey of then-current historical knowledge on homosexuality among the Arabs.

1061. KOCHER, ADOLPHE. **De la criminalité chez les
       Arabes.** Paris: Baillière, 1884. 242 pp.
See pp. 169-77 for male and female homosexuality among
the Algerians.

1062. **The Koran Interpreted.** A translation by Arthur

J. Arberry. London: George Allen & Unwin, 1955. 2
vols. (350, 358 pp.)
Includes pejorative comment on the **ahl Lut** or "people of
Lot" (i.e.,Sodomites), which have been taken by some ex-
egetes (as in fundamentalist Iran) as authorizing the
death penalty for male homosexuals. See viii, 78-84
("you approach men lustfully instead of women"; vol. 1,
p. 181); xi, 74-84 ("we turned it [Sodom] uppermost
nethermost"; 1, pp. 248-49); xv, 57-77 (1, pp. 284-85);
xxvi, 160-74 (2, p. 72); and xxvii, 54-59 (2, p. 81).

1063. LINDHOLM, CHARLES. **Generosity and Jealousy: The
       Swat Pukhtun of Northern Pakistan.** New York: Col-
       umbia University Press, 1982. 321 pp.
For changing patterns in the role of the **bedagh** (catamite), see esp. pp. 224-27.

1064. MASSIGNON, LOUIS. **The Passion of al-Hallaj:
       Mystic and Martyr.** Translated by Herbert Mason.
       Princeton: Princeton University Press, 1982. 4
       vols.
Encyclopedic work on the poet who was killed in 922, with
considerable indirect interest.

1065. MAXWELL, GAVIN. **Lords of the Atlas.** London: Cen-
       tury, 1983. 312 pp.
Travel book first published in 1966. Deals with the
French satrap El Glaoui in southern Morocco.

1066. NÄCKE, PAUL. "Die Homosexualität im Orient,"
       **Archiv für Kriminal-Anthropologie und Kriminalist-
       ik,** 16 (1904), 353-55.
Followed by "Die Homosexualität in Konstantinopel,"
ibid., 26 (1906), 106-08. Both deal with homosexual
behavior in Istanbul.

1067. NAFZAWI (NEFZAOUI), SHAYKH. **Le Jardin parfumé du
       Cheikh Nefzaoui.** Paris: I. Liseux, 1886. 300 pp.
This text of the 15th-century Tunisian erotological
treatise seemingly contains the whole of Chapter 26 on
pederasty, which is usually truncated in the English
renderings.

1068. OLEGNA, R. "Il catechismo turco e l'omosessual-
       ità," **Rassegna di studi sessuali,** 2 (1922), 354-56.
On a Turkish Islamic catechism which does not consider
homosexuality as such as a sin. Brief further discussion
in ibid., 3 (1923), 115-18.

1069. PARET, RUDI. **Früharabische Liebesgeschichten: ein
       Beitrag zur vergleichenden Literaturgeschichte.**
       Bern: Haupt, 1927. 80 pp.
Noted Arabist studies the motifs of early Arabic love
narratives.

1070. PÉRÈS, HENRI. **La poésie andalouse en arabe**

classique au XIe siècle. Paris: Maisonneuve, 1953. 541 pp.
Reviews principal themes of Moorish love poetry, with some attention to pederastic elements.

1071.   PROTHRO, EDWIN TERRY. "Sexual Behavior of University Students in the Arab Near East," **Journal of Abnormal and Social Psychology,** 49 (1954), 63-64.
Survey research on attitudes and behavior.

1072.   REED, DAVID. "The Persian Boy Today: Sexual Politics in Teheran," **Christopher Street** (August 1978), 15-17.
Personal experiences from pre-Khomeini Iran revealing strong gender-role polarization among those engaging in homosexual acts. For the survival of the millennial Iranian pederastic tradition, even after the executions of 1981-82, see Hélène Kafi, "Téhéran: L'amour à jet de pierres," **Gai Pied,** no. 190 (October 19-25 1955), 44-47.

1073.   RITTER, HELLMUT. **Das Meer der Seele: Gott, Welt und Mensch in den Geschichten Fariduddin 'Attars.** Leiden: E. J. Brill, 1955. 777 pp.
Fundamental study of Sufi mystical imagery as refracted in the work of 'Attar, with considerable attention to infatuation with beloved youths. in particular the love of Sultan Mahmud of Ghazna for his slave boy Ayaz.

1074.   ROSENTHAL, FRANZ. "Ar-Razi on the Hidden Illness," **Bulletin of the History of Medicine,** 52 (1978), 45-60.
On a treatise by Abu Bahr ar-Razi (Rhazes; 865-925) on **ubnah** (passive male homosexuality). If the disease is prolonged it is incurable, but if it is ego-alien and the patient is ashamed of his urges, it can be treated by a regime of physical and medicinal therapy.

1075.   RYCAUT, PAUL. **The History of the Present State of the Ottoman Empire.** London: Cleve, 1701.
A French traveler's classic account of the sultan's rule, with some discussion of catamites.

1076.   SAYYID-MARSOT, AL-, AFAF LUTFI (ed.). **Society and the Sexes in Medieval Islam.** Malibu, CA: Undena Publications, 1979. 149 pp.
Seven papers. Note esp. James A. Bellamy, "Sex and Society in Islamic Popular Literature," pp. 23-42; cf. also pp. 47-48, 58-60, 111,, 130-33, 139.

1077.   SCHIMMEL, ANNEMARIE. **Mystical Dimensions of Islam.** Chapel Hill: University of North Carolina Press, 1975. 506 pp.
See pp. 287-343 for the Sufi poetical tradtion as a mingling of love for beloved youths with love of God.

1078.   SHALAQ, ALI. **La poésie érotique d'Abu Nuwas.**

Paris: 1952.
Thesis, published in Beirut in Arabic in 1954, on the
works of the noted homosexual poet (762-ca. 815).

1079. SONNINI DE MANONCOUR, CHARLES-NICOLAS-SIGISBERT.
       Travels in Upper and Lower Egypt. London: John
       Stockdale, 1799. 2 vols.
"The passion contrary to nature ... is generally diffused
over Egypt; the rich and the poor are equally infected
with it; contrary to the effect it produces in colder
countries, that of being exclusive, it is there associated
with the love of women." (vol.1, pp. 251-52).

1080. SOUTHGATE, MINOO S. "Men, Women and Boys: Love and
       Sex in the Works of Sa'di," **Iranian Studies,** 17
       (1984), 413-52.
Characteristic themes in the work of the great Persian
poet (d. 1291).

1081. STERN, BERNHARD. **Medizin, Aberglaube und Ge-**
       schlechtsleben in der Turkei. Berlin: H. Bars-
       dorf, 1903. 2 vols.
In this work on medical and sexual folklore in Turkey,
Chapter 42 discusses homosexuality.

1082. SURIEU, ROBERT. **Sarv-é Naz: an Essay on Love and**
       the Representation of Erotic Themes in Ancient
       Iran. Translated by James Hogarth. New York:
       Nagel, 1967. 185 pp.
Scants homosexual love, but useful for comparative material.

1083. TALBOT, SERGE. "Les tabous sexuels de l'Islam,"
       Arcadie, no. 118 (October 1963), 451-59.
The existence of sexual taboos shows that Islam is not as
"sex positive" as some have claimed.

1084. THESIGER, WILFRED. **The Marsh Arabs.** New York:
       Dutton, 1964. 242 pp.
See pp. 123-24 for male prostitution and transvestite
dancers in southern Iraq, where peer homosexuality is also
practiced discreetly by young men before marriage.

1085. WAGNER, EWALD. **Abu Nuwas: eine Studie zur arab-**
       ischen Literatur der frühen 'Abbasidenzeit. Wies-
       baden: F. Steiner, 1965. 532 pp.
Massive study by the leading contemporary authority on the
classical homosexual poet (762-ca. 815).

1086. WALTHER, WIEBKE. **Women of Islam.** Translated by
       C. S. U. Salt. Montclair, NJ: Abner Schram, 1981.
       204 pp.
A lavishly illustrated popular work that covers the
subject from the beginning of Islam to the present day.
See pp. 117-18.

1087. WELCH, STUART CARY. **Wonders of the Age: Master
       pieces of Early Safavid Painting, 1501-1576.** Cam-
       bridge, MA: Fogg Art Museum, 1979. 223 pp.
For miniatures of beloved youths, see pp. 180-81, 186-89,
192-97, 200-01, 212-18.

1088. WESTERMARCK, EDWARD. **Ritual and Belief in Morocco.**
       London: Macmillan, 1926. 2 vols.
See vol. 1 of this classic anthropological study for the
benefits of sexual intercourse with a saintly person, as
well as negative attitudes to boy prostitutes and passive
adult homosexuals. See also his "The Moorish Conception
of Holiness," **Finska Vetenskaps-Societetens Forhandling-
ar,** 58 [Afd. B, no. 1] (1915-16), p. 85ff.

1089. WESTPHALL-HELLBUSCH, SIGRID. "Transvestiten bei
       arabischen Stämmen," **Sociologus,** n. s. 6:2 (1956),
       126-37,
On South Arabian singers and dancers who are homosexual
transvestites.

1090. WIKAN, UNNI. "Man Becomes Woman: Transsexualism in
       Oman as a Key to Gender Roles," **Man,** N.S. 12
       (1977), 304-19.
Interprets anthropological field work among the **xanith,** or
male prostitutes in the town of Sohar (northeast Arabian
peninsula), who are in some respects classed socially as
women. Note also the occasionally caustic ensuing discussion, and replies by Wikan: ibid., 13 (1978), 133-34, 322-
23, 473-75; 15 (1980), 541-42. See also Wikan's book: **Behind the Veil in Arabia: Women in Oman** (Baltimore: Johns
Hopkins University Press, 1982; 314 pp.). For further
details on the **muxannath** and the **mutaraggala** (the woman
dressed in man's clothing), see Carlo de Landberg, **Etudes
sur les dialectes de l'Arabie méridionale. II. Datinah**
(Leiden: E.J. Brill, 1905), pp. 937-40.

1091. WORMHOUDT, ARTHUR. "Classic Arabic Poetry," **Gay
       Books Bulletin,** 4 (Fall 1980), 23-25.
Discusses verse by Abu Tammam, al-Tanisi, and others.

                  Q. CHINA, KOREA, AND CENTRAL ASIA

China can boast the longest continuous record of homosexual behavior of any civilization. Until the Ch'ing
Dynasty (1644-1912), male homosexuality seems to have been
discussed with considerable frankness. This rich vein of
material--manifested in novels, poetry, and works of art,
as well as documentary sources--is only now beginning to
be exploited.

1092. ALABASTER, ERNEST. **Notes and Commentaries on**

Chinese Criminal Law. London: Luzac, 1899. 677
    pp.
See "Unnatural Offenses" (pp. 368-69) on the Ch'ing
period. When treated as fornication, 100 strokes of
bamboo are imposed; when violence is involved, or a boy
under 12 years, it is regarded as rape. See also M. J.
Meijer, below.

1093. AOKI MASARU. **Chung-kuo chin-shih-hsi ch'u-shih**
       [The History of Modern Chinese Drama]. Hong
       Kong: Chung-hua shu-ch'u, 1975. 2 vols.
For homosexual practices among Ch'ing dynasty actors, see
pp. 446-53.

1094. BAO RUO-WANG (formerly Jean Pasqualini), with
       RUDOLPH CHELMINSKI. **Prisoner of Mao.** New York:
       Penguin, 1976. 326 pp.
Personal account of thought-reform in prison camps of the
People's Republic, including summary execution of homosex-
ual man (pp. 188-190).

1095. BARROW, JOHN, SIR. **Travels in China.** London: T.
       Cadell and W. Davies, 1804. 636 pp.
Includes references to male prostitution.

1096. BEURDELEY, MICHEL et al. **Chinese Erotic Art.** Rut-
       land, VT: Tuttle, 1969. 215 pp.
Offers some discussion of male homosexuality under the
rubric "cut sleeves," pp. 161-69. Illustrated.

1097. BODDE, DERK (translator). **Law in Imperial China:
       Exemplified by 190 Ch'ing Dynasty Cases.** Trans-
       lated from the Hsing-an hui-lan. Annotated by Derk
       Bodde and Clarence Morris. Cambridge, MA: Harvard
       University Press, 1967. 615 pp.
See pp. 383, 409, and 428 for cases of 1809 and 1819.

1098. BRACKMAN, ARNOLD C. **The Last Emperor.** New York:
       Scribner's Sons, 1975. 360 pp.
Frank account of the life of China's last Ch'ing (Manchu)
ruler, the homosexual "Henry" P'u Yi. See esp. pp. 121-
22. Reissued as **The Prisoner of Peking** (New York: Van
Nostrand Reinhold, 1980. 360 pp.).

1099. CHANG CHING-SHENG. **Sex Histories: China's First
       Modern Treatise on Sex Education.** Translated by
       Howard S. Levy. Yokohama: 1967. 117 pp.
Written in the 1920s (original title: **Hsing shih**). See
pp. 3, 54-56, 69, 90, 93.

1100. CHOU, ERIC. **The Dragon and the Phoenix.** New
       York: Bantam Books, 1972. 290 pp.
History of Chinese sexuality, based on sources in
Chinese, but not intended for scholars. Offers some
material on Manchu emperors. See pp.14-15, 90-93, 112-
16.

1101. CLARK, CHARLES ALLEN. **Religions of Old Korea.**
Seoul: Christian Literature Society of Korea,
1961. 295 pp.
See pp. 182-86 for cross-dressing shamans.

1102. COHEN, JEROME ALAN, et al. (eds.). **Essays on
China's Legal Tradition.** Princeton: Princeton
University Press, 1980. 438 pp.
See pp. 178-80.

1103. EBERHARD, WOLFRAM. **China und seine westlichen
Nachbarn: Beiträge zur mittelalterlichen und
neueren Geschichte Zentralasiens.** Darmstadt: Wis-
senschaftliche Buchgesellschaft, 1978. 343
pp.
A noted sinologist's collected essays on China's relations
with Central Asian peoples. See pp. 111-17, 186-246, 291-
98.

1104. FRIEND, ROBERT. "Homosexuality in China," **Eastern
Horizon** (July 1978), 36-37.
Offers a rather optimistic view of attitudes in the
People's Republic, which is said to practice tolerance--
though it is held that homosexuality is more prevalent
in disintegrating societies.

1105. GULIK, ROBERT HANS VAN. **Sexual Life in Ancient
China: A Preliminary Survey of Chinese Sex and
Society from ca. 1500 B. C. till 1644 A. D.**
Leiden: E. J. Brill, 1961. 392 pp.
Copiously documented study of evidence until the end of
the Ming dynasty; scants homophile aspects, but useful
for comparative purposes. There is also a French translation, **La vie sexuelle dans la Chine ancienne** (Paris: Gallimard, 1971; 466 pp.), with some additional notes by
Jacques Reclus. Gulik, a major scholar known to the
general public by his Judge Dee mystery novels, died in
1967.

1106. HENTHORN, WILLIAM E. **A History of Korea.** New
York: Free Press, 1971. 256 pp.
See pp. 44-45 for the hwarang, an elite military corps
selected partly for their physical charms (Silla period).

1107. HONG KONG, LAW REFORM COMMISSION. **Report on Laws
Governing Homosexual Conduct.** Hong Kong: Government
Printer, 1983. 374 pp.
Wide-ranging collection of material, including history,
laws in Asia, oral and written testimony, newspaper
articles, and recommendations for reform. (Available
from Alternative Distribution, PO Box 29627, Philadelphia, PA 19144.)

1108. KARSCH-HAACK, FERDINAND. **Das gleichgeschlechtliche
Leben der Kulturvölker: I: Das gleichgeschlecht-**

liche Leben der Ostasiaten: Chinesen, Japaner, Koreer. Munich: Seitz und Schauer, 1906. 134 pp. (Forschungen über gleichgeschlechtliche Liebe) A noteworthy attempt to sum up what was known at the time of writing of homosexual life among the Chinese, Koreans, and Japanese; with many bibliographical references to older works. Rare. (The planned series on homosexuality in the high cultures was not continued.) For a more recent attempt at synthesis for China, see Vern Bullough, **Sexual Variance in Society and History** (New York: Wylie, 1976), 281-314.

1109. KAYE, BARRINGTON. **Upper Nankin Street, Singapore: A Sociological Study of Chinese Households.** Singapore: University of Malaya Press, 1960. 439 pp.
See pp. 232-33 in relation to lesbianism.

1110. KIM, YOUNG JA. "The Korean Namsadang," **Drama Review**, 15 (1981), 9-16.
On an indigenous touring troupe of the early 20th century.

1111. KLEINMAN, ARTHUR, and TSUNG-YI LIN (eds.). **Normal and Abnormal Behaviour in Chinese Culture.** Dordrecht: Reidel, 1981. 436 pp.
The essay by James McGough contains some material on same-sex unions.

1112. LANGLOIS, JOHN D. (ed.). **China under Mongol Rule.** Princeton: Princeton University Press, 1981. 487 pp.
See esp. Morris Rossabi "The Muslims in the Early Yuan Dynasty," (pp.257-95); also pp. 212-54, 304, 318-19, 434-65.

1113. LAUFER, BERTHOLD. "Homosexuelle Bilder aus China," **Anthropophyteia**, 6 (1909), 162-66.
Brief commentary on Chinese homosexual art.

1114. LETHBRIDGE, H. L. "The Quare Fellow: Homosexuality and the Law in Hong Kong," **Hong Kong Law Journal**, 6 (1976), 292-326.
In keeping with the present illegality, homosexuals are generally discreet in Hong Kong. There are three patterns: impersonal sex; domestic (dyadic); and male prostitution. See also his: "Pandora's Box: The Inspector MacLennan Enigma," ibid., 12 (1982), 4ff.

1115. LEVY, HOWARD SEYMOUR. **Chinese Footbinding: The History of a Curious Erotic Custom.** New York: W. Rawls, 1966. 352 pp.
See pp. 125, 131-32, 194-95, 318.

1116. LEVY, HOWARD SEYMOUR. **Chinese Sex Jokes in Traditional Times.** Taipei: Orient Cultural Service, 1974. 361 pp.

Includes a collection of jokes from classical texts
which deal with homosexual themes (pp. 252-65).

1117. LIEH-MAK, F., K. M. O'HOY, and S. L. LUK. "Les-
        bianism in the Chinese of Hong Kong," **Archives of
        Sexual Behavior**, 12 (1983), 21-30.
Following a short review of the background of lesbianism in China, the authors present findings derived from
15 Chinese lesbian subjects.

1118. LIU MAO TSAI. **Die chinesischen Nachrichten zur
        Geschichte der Ost-Türken (T'u-kue).** Wiesbaden:
        Otto Harrassowitz, 1958. 2 vols. (831 pp.)
Analyzes Chinese reports of the Eastern Turks of Central
Asia.

1119. LI YÜ. **Wu sheng hsi** [Dramas without Sound]. Ed.
        by Helmut Martin. Taipei: Chin-hsueh shu-chu, 1969.
The story "Nan-Meng-mu fang-he san-ch'ian" ("A Male Mother
Named Meng Is Forced to Change Residence Three Times,"
pp. 5381-5452) describes the tribulations of a man and his
boy lover. The work begins with a short apologia of
homosexuality.

1120. MACKERRAS, COLIN P. **The Rise of the Peking Opera,
        1770-1870: Social Aspects of the Theatre in Manchu
        China.** Oxford: Clarendon Press, 1972. 316 pp.
Throughout this work the author describes homosexual
relations between famous male actors and their literati
patrons.

1121. MACLENNAN, JOHN RICHARD. "Scandal in Hong Kong:
        Hugh Johnson," **Medico-legal Journal**, 51:2 (1983),
        70-84.
One of a flurry of articles occasioned by the suicide of a
homosexual policeman. See also Linda Jawin, "Homosexuality, Controversy in Hong Kong," **Asiaweek** (March 8, 1982),
20-21; and Mary Lee, "Homosexuality and the Police in
Hong Kong," **Far Eastern Economic Review**, 109 (July 18,
1980), 18-20; 112 (June 26, 1981), 18-19; and 114 (October
9, 1981), 46-47.

1122. MAO, NATHAN KWOK-KUEN. **Li Yu's Twelve Towers, Re-
        told by Nathan Mao.** Hong Kong: Chinese University
        of Hong Kong, 1975. 137 pp.
Pages 52-62 contain a translation of "Ts'ui-ya lou" ("The
Elegant Eunuch"), a 17th-century short story of homosexual
desire which ends in castration and retribution.

1123. MATIGNON, JEAN-JACQUES. "Deux mots sur la péder-
        astie en Chine," **Archives d'anthropologie crimi-
        nelle**, 14 (1899), 38-53.
Affirms that homosexuality is widely tolerated and
practiced in (imperial) China, but there is a reluctance
to discuss the matter openly. See also his book: **La Chine
hermétique: superstition, crime et misère.** New ed.

Paris: Librairie Orientaliste Paul Geuthner, 1936; 397
pp.; "Deux mots ...," pp. 263-81, and "Les eunuques,"
201-222).

1124. MEIJER, M. J. "Homosexual Offenses in Ch'ing Law,"
        T'oung Pao, 71 (1985), 109-33.
Study of the **Ta Ch'ing Lü Li** (1679ff.), apparently the
first Chinese law code to introduce provisions against
homosexual relations. The cases examined, mainly from the
19th century, show that it was applied mainly when there
was violence or some other complication. Distinctions of
age and class were also important. Homosexuality between
consenting adults seems to have engaged the attention of
the authorities very rarely.

1125. MICHAEL, JAY (pseud.). "Gays in China," **Advocate,**
        no. 423 (June 25, 1985), 28-29, 32-33.
Claims that gay street life flourishes in the People's
Republic today. See also" John Cabral, "Gay Life in
Mainland China," **Christopher Street,** no. 62 (March 1982),
27-34.

1126. MITAMURA TAISUKE. **Chinese Eunuchs.** Translated by
        Charles A. Pomeroy. Rutland, VT: Tuttle, 1970. 176
        pp.
Of considerable cognate interest.

1127. PAI HSIEN-YUNG. **Wandering in the Garden, Waking
        from a Dream: Tales of Taipei Characters.** Blooming-
        ton: Indiana University Press, 1982. 199 pp.
The story "A Sky Full of Bright, Twinkling Stars" (pp.
138-44), presents a view of homosexual life in modern
Taiwan by one of China's leading authors.

1128. PAN KWONG-TAN. **Psychology of Sex.** Shanghai: The
        Commercial Press, 1947.
See "Cases of Homosexuality in the Chinese Documents and
Literature" (pp. 380-408), discussing evidence from the
Shang dynasty onwards.

1129. RIASANOVSKY, V. A. **Customary Law of the Mongol
        Tribes (Mongols, Buriats, Kalmucks).** Harbin: Ar-
        tistic Printing House, 1929. 306 pp.
A fragment of the great Yassa, a law code introduced by
Genghis Khan, provides death for sodomy. The early 19th-
century Laws of Mongol and Kalmuk peoples provided a
fine of one animal and fifty strokes with a whip for
pederasty--less than for rape.

1130. RUTT, RICHARD. "The Flower Boys of Silla (Hwa-
        rang): Notes on the Sources," **Transactions of the
        Korean Branch of the Royal Asiatic Society,** 38
        (1961), 1-66.
Historical evolution of Korean female impersonators/boy
dancers; pederasty during the Yi dynasty.

1131. SAMSHASHA (Xiaomingxiang). **Zhongguo tongxingai
       shilu** [History of Homosexuality in China]. Hong
       Kong: Pink Triangle Press, 1985. 378 pp.
Illustrated overview in Chinese by a gay scholar, concentrating on historical and literary figures. Detailed
table of contents in English.

1132. SANKAR, ANDREA. "Sisters and Brothers, Lovers and
       Enemies: Marriage Resistance in Southern Kwang-
       tung," **JH**, 11:3-4 (1985), 69-82.
Examines the structure and content of relationships among
members of a sisterhood in Hong Kong. This institution
has roots in the Pearl River Delta surrounding Canton
from ca. 1865 onwards.

1133. SCHLEGEL, GUSTAAF. "Iets over de prostitutie in
       China," **Verhandelingen van het Bataviaasch genoot-
       schap van kunsten en wetenschap** [Batavia: Lange],
       32:3 (1866). 25 pp.
See pp. 21-25 for notes on male prostitutes and the relevant terminology in China. Apparently Schlegel's **Histoire de la prostitution en Chine** (Rouen: J. Lemonnyer,
1880; 47 pp.) is an enlarged version of this monograph.

1134. SPENCE, JONATHAN D. **Emperor of China: Self-por-
       trait of K'ang-hsi.** New York: Vintage Books,
       1975. 218 pp.
Account of the Chinese contemporary of Louis XIV (reigned
1661-1722) in his own words. See pp. xxi, 125-27, and
129 for his disapproval of the apparent homosexual behavior of his son Yin-jeng.

1135. SPENCE, JONATHAN D. **The Memory Palace of Matteo
       Ricci.** New York: Viking Press, 1984. 350 pp.
Reconstruction from diaries and letters of the background
of the Jesuit savant's life (d. 1610) in China, with considerable material contrasting Catholic and Asian attitudes toward homosexual behavior.

1136. TREVOR-ROPER, HUGH. **Hermit of Peking: The Hidden
       Life of Sir Edmund Backhouse.** New York: Penguin
       Books, 1978. 391 pp.
Account of the shady life of an English baronet and
sinologist who lived most of his life (1873-1944) in
Peking, based on his unpublished memoirs, which--despite
their unreliability--offer fascinating glimpses of late
Ch'ing China. Trevor-Roper has been criticized for his
facile assumption of the "decadent" character of the
homosexual Backhouse.

1137. **Tuan hsiu pien** [Record of the Cut Sleeve]. in:
       Hsiang yen tsung shu, chi 9, chuan 2. Shanghai:
       Kuo-hsueh fu-lun-she, 1909-11.
A 17th-century anonymous compilation of biographies and
short accounts of famous homosexuals.

1138. WANG CH'UNG. **Lun-heng: Philosophical and Miscel-
       laneous Essays.** Second ed. New York: Paragon Book
       Gallery, 1962. 577 and 536 pp.
Reprint of 1907-11 edition. See vol. 1, p. 309; vol. 2,
p. 34.

1139. WANG SHU-NU. **Chung-kuo ch'ang-chi shih** [The
       History of Chinese Prostitution]. Shanghai: Sheng-
       huo shu-tien, 1935. 358 pp.
Pp. 46-49 discuss ancient Chinese homosexuals. Pp. 62-66
treat homosexuals of the Wei and Chin dynasties. Pp. 225-
30 deal with Ming dynasty homosexuals. Pp. 317-28 discuss
Ch'ing dynasty homosexuality. Consists mainly of short
quotations from classical Chinese sources, with minimal
commentary and interpretation.

1140. WEI-HSING-SHIH-KUAN-CH'I-CHU. **Chung-kuo t'ung-
       hsing-luan-mi-shih** [The Secret History of Chinese
       Homosexual Practices]. Hong Kong: Chai-you
       chu-pan-she, 1964. 2 vols.
This compilation of classical sources by an anonymous
association of scholars is the only extensive modern
treatment of Chinese homosexuality.

1141. WU SHAN SHENG. **Erotologie de la Chine.** Paris:
       Jean-Jacques Pauvert, 1963.
For male homoerotic art and homosexuality among palace
eunuchs, see pp. 89, 157-58.

                          R. JAPAN

A broad range of homosexual behavior has been presented
in scholarly and popular works in Japanese, of which only
some aspects are reflected in works in European languages.
Historically homosexual life in Japan has been organized
around a number of foci, some of them essentially indigenous (the Samurai tradition) and others linked to developments abroad (Buddhist monasticism, the theatre, the
Western influenced bar culture of today).

1142. AKIYAMA MASAMI. **Homo tekkunikku.** Tokyo: 1968.
       238 pp.
Illustrated popular work on "homosexual technique."

1142. BOWERS, FAUBION. **Japanese Theatre.** New York: Her-
       mitage House, 1952. 294 pp.
For the female impersonation tradition, see pp. 45-49.

1143. BOXER, CHARLES RALPH. **The Christian Century in
       Japan, 1549-1650.** Berkeley: University of Califor-
       nia Press, 1967. 535 pp.

For sexual aspects of the culture clash, see pp. 35, 66, 69, 459.

1144. BURUMA, IAN. **Behind the Mask: On Sexual Demons, Sacred Mothers, Transvestites, Gangsters, Drifters and Other Japanese Cultural Heroes.** New York: Pantheon, 1984. 242 pp.
British observer's account of some striking aspects of Japanese popular culture today, a book which has been criticized by some as purveying stereotypes. See esp. pp. 15 and 127-31.

1145. CARON, FRANÇOIS. **A True Description of the Mighty Kingdoms of Japan and Siam.** Edited by C. R. Boxer. London: Argonaut Press, 1935. 197 pp.
In this edition of the 1663 translation of a Dutch work, see pp. 23-24 and 43. (The material on Siam is by Joost Schouten.)

1146. CHILDS, MARGARET. "Chigo monogatari: Love Stories or Buddhist sermons?" **Monumenta Nipponica,** 35 (1980), 127-51.
Concerning stories about monks' loves for boys aged 7 to 14, chiefly from the Muromachi period. Includes translated specimen (ca. 1372).

1147. CHILDS, MARGARET. "Japan's Homosexual Heritage," **Gai Saber,** 1 (1977), 41-45.
Presents some historical and literary evidence for nanshoku (male homosexuality).

1148. DANIEL, MARC (pseud.). "Les amants du soleil levant," **Arcadie,** no. 66 (June 1959), 346-51.
Manly love among the samurai compared with ancient Greek paiderasteia. Note the earlier exploration of the parallel by Edward Carpenter, **Intermediate Types among Primitive Folk** (London: Allen and Unwin, 1919), pp. 137-60.

1149. **Danshokumonoshu.** 37 (1978), 192 pp.
This volume is devoted to anecdotes, facetiae, and satire concerning homosexuality in Japanese literature.

1150. DE VOS, GEORGE et al. **Socialization for Achievement: Essays on the Cultural Psychology of the Japanese.** Berkeley: University of California Press, 1973. 597 pp.
See pp. 237 and 269-70.

1151. DOI TAKEO. **The Anatomy of Dependence.** Translated by John Bester. Tokyo: Kodansha, 1973. 170 pp.
On the national character of the Japanese, emphasizing amae (dependence), and arguing that the desire for passive love among socially intimate males is "the essence of homosexual feelings." (p. 118).

1152. DOMOTO MASAKI. **Danshoku engeki shi.** New ed.
      Tokyo: Bara Jujisha, 1976. 293 pp.
Homosexuality in Japanese literature and drama.

1153. DOWNSBOROUGH, NIGEL. **Paedomorphs I: The Story of a
      Young Boy in Pre-War Japan.** Taipei: Kinyado
      Publishing Co., 1979.
Purports to be the first part of the autobiography of the
late Karl Kliest, covering his teenage loves in Japan,
edited by his attorney.

1154. FITZPATRICK, WILLIAM. **Tokyo after Dark.** New
      York: MacFadden, 1955. 128 pp.
Popular paperback with two chapters on male prostitution.

1155. HACHIMONJIYA JISHO. **The Actors' Analects (Yakusha
      rongo).** Edited and translated by Charles J. Dunn
      and Bunzo Torigoe. New York: Columbia University
      Press, 1969. 306 pp.
In this 18th-century compilation, see pp. 5, 9, 41-43,
51, 58-60, 92-93, 172, 194.

1156. HIRANO TOSHIZO. **Doseiai no sekai.** Tokyo: 1968.
      254 pp.
Popular work on "the world of homosexuality."

1157. HIRATSUKA RYOSEN. **Nihon ni okeru nanshoku no
      kenkyu.** Tokyo: Ningen no Kagakusha Shuppan
      Jigyabu, 1983.
"A Study of Male Homosexuality in Japan."

1158. IHARA SAIKAKU. **Tales of the Samurai.** Tokyo:
      Tuttle, 1972. 135 pp.
This prolific author of the Tokugawa era wrote several
collections of stories on the homosexual loves of the
Samurai. This one dates from 1682. See also the collec-
tion translated by Caryl Ann Callahan: **Tales of Samurai
Honor** (Tokyo: Monumenta Nipponica, 1982; 156 pp.).

1159. INAGAKI TARAHO. **Shonen'ai no bigaku.** Tokyo:
      1968. 245 pp.
"Aesthetics of Boy Love."

1160. IWATA JUN'ICHI. **Honcho nanshoku ko.** Tokyo: 1973.
      340 pp.
Historical survey of pederasty and homosexuality in Japan.

1161. IWATA JUN'ICHI. **Nanshoku bunken shoshi.** Tokyo:
      1973. 371 pp.
Bibliography of homosexuality in Japan.

1162. IWAYA SUYEWO. "Nan sho k': Die Päderastie in
      Japan," **JfsZ**, 4 (1902), 263-71.
Some aspects of pederasty in newly modernizing Japan,
with a look backward at the heritage of the Tokugawa
era. Perhaps the first article on the subject in a

Western language.

1163. KEENE, DONALD. **World without Walls: Japanese
      Literature of the Pre-Modern Era, 1600-1867.** New
      York: Holt, Rinehart and Winston, 1976. 605 pp.
In this standard English-language work, see Chapter 8 on
Ihara Saikaku (1642-1693), pp. 167-215 (esp. p. 188ff.).

1164. KIRKUP, JAMES. **These Horned Islands.** New York:
      Macmillan, 1962. 447 pp.
Autobiographical response of a homosexual British poet to
residence in Japan.

1165. KRAUSS, FRIEDRICH SALOMO. **Das Geschlechtsleben in
      Glauben, Sitte, Brauch und Gewohnheit der Japaner.**
      Second ed. Leipzig: Ethnologischer Verlag, 1911.
      314 pp.
This general monograph on Japanese sexual life contains a
contribution by "Doriphorus" on the prevalence of pederasty in modern Japan.

1166. KYOOKA SUMIKO. **Onna to onna.** Tokyo: 1968. 174
      pp.
Popular work on lesbianism ("Woman to Woman"); illustrated.

1167. LEVY, HOWARD S. **Sex, Love and the Japanese.** Wash-
      ington, DC: Warm-Soft Village Press, 1971. 91
      leaves.
See esp. leaf 10.

1168. LOHR, STEVE. "The New Face of Kabuki," **New York
      Times Magazine** (May 30, 1982), 13-17.
Gay Japanese are among the followers of Kabuki, with its
traditional art of male impersonation.

1169. LOUIS, FRÉDÉRIC (pseud.). **Daily Life in Japan at
      the Time of the Samurai, 1185-1603.** Translated by
      Eileen M. Lowe. New York: Praeger, 1972. 256 pp.
See pp. 37-38.

1170. MONTANUS, ARNOLDUS. **Atlas Iappanensis.** Translated
      by John Ogilby. London: T. Johnson, 1670. 488 pp.
Translation of a 1669 Dutch work by an official of the
Netherlands East India Company, with observations on
homosexual conduct in Japan. See also Bernardus Varenius,
Descriptio regni Iaponiae (Amsterdam: Elzevier, 1649; 2
vols.).

1171. NARABAYASHI YASUSHI. **Rezubian rabu.** Tokyo: 1967.
      235 pp.
Popular work on lesbianism ("Lesbian Love").

1172. OKIHERA SHUNJI. **Onnagata.** Tokyo: Tamasaburo
      Bando, 1983.
Lavish color photo book on the traditional female imper-

sonators of the Kabuki theater.

1173. PINKERTON, JOHN. **A General Collection of the Best and Most Interesting Voyages and Travels in All Parts of the World.** London: Longman, 1811. For homosexuality among Japanese priests and nobility in the early 17th century, see vol. 7, pp. 629-31.

1174. SCOTT-STOKES, HENRY. **The Life and Death of Yukio Mishima.** New York: Farrar, Straus and Giroux, 1974. 344 pp. Sympathetic account of the life of this major bisexual author (1925-70), whose novels **Confessions of a Mask** and **Forbidden Colors** provide a remarkable conspectus of gay life in Japan. See also John Nathan, **Mishima: A Biography** (Boston: Little, Brown, 1974; 300 pp.); and Marguerite Yourcenar, **Mishima, ou la vision du vide** (Paris: Gallimard, 1980; 124 pp.).

1175. TYTHERIDGE, A. C. "Beobachtungen über Homosexualität in Japan," **JfsZ**, 22 (1922), 23-36. Observations on homosexuality in Japan.

S. SOUTH AND SOUTHEAST ASIA

Apart from East Asia and Islamic West Asia, homosexual behavior has been relatively little studied in Asia. On the whole Hinduism has not favored it, with the significant exception of the **hijras.** Thailand, the Philippines, and Indonesia seem to be significant areas. With rapid modernization, much evidence seems to be disappearing.

1176. AMIR, MOHAMMED. "Il Travestismo in Batavia," **Archivio di antropologia criminale,** 54 (1934), 896-906. Cross-dressing in Java under Dutch rule.

1177. BAIÃO, ANTONIO. **A Inquisição de Goa: Correspondência dos Inquisidores da Índia.** Coimbra: Imprensa da Universidade, 1930. Reports from the Portuguese colony of Goa in India, and instructions to it, some concerning the repression of sodomy.

1178. BERCKMANN, JEAN-NOËL. **La sexualité à travers le monde: étude sur la péninsule Indochinoise.** Paris: Le Trèfle d'Or, 1966. 170 pp. For male prostitution in Vietnam, see pp. 78-80, 85.

1179. BLATT, EMILY. "Wadam and Bisu: Male Transsexualism and Homosexuality in Indonesia," **Gay Community News** (Australia), 4:6 (July 1982), 26-27.

Account of a visit to a **wadam** show in Java, with some
examination of the background as known from the 17th
century onwards.

1180. CARSTAIRS, G. MORRIS. **The Twice-born: A Study of a
        Community of High Caste Hindus.** Bloomington: In-
        diana University Press, 1967. 343 pp.
Includes information on the **hijara (hijra)**, cross-gender
behaving males of northern India. Carstairs' interpretations were harshly reviewed by Morris E. Opler, **American
Anthropologist**, 61 (1957), 140-41; and ibid. 62 (1960),
505-12. See also: A. M. Shah, "A Note on the Hijadas of
Gujarat," ibid., 63 (1961), 1325-30; and S. Nanda, below.

1181. CIPRIANI, LIDIO. **The Andaman Islanders.** Trans-
        lated by D. Taylor Cox. New York: Praeger, 1966.
        159 pp.
See pp. 22-23.

1182. COLE, FAYE-COOPER. **The Tinguian: Social, Re-
        ligious, and Economic Life of a Philippine Tribe.**
        Chicago: Field Museum, 1922. 493 pp.
See pp. 360-01 and plate 36.

1183. DE LEEUW, HENDRIK. **Crossroads of the Java Sea.**
        New York: Cape and Smith, 1931. 350 pp.
In this work on the customs of the Dutch East Indies,
now Indonesia, see pp. 47, 104-05, 231, and 288-90.

1184. DEVI, SHAKUNTALA. **The World of Homosexuals.** New
        Delhi: Vikas Publishing House, 1977. 160 pp.
Positive account, partly general and partly explicitly
concerned with India.

1185. EDWARDES. ALLEN (pseud. of D. A. Kingsley). **The
        Rape of India: A Biography of Robert Clive and a
        Sexual Conquest of Hindustan.** New York: Julian
        Press, 1966. 350 pp.
Racy account of the sexual exploits of the soldier (1725-
1774) who founded the British empire in India, based on
manuscript and other materials. See also the anonymous
contemporary **Intrigues of a Nabob ... or, Bengall the
Fittest Soil for the Growth of Lust** (1773).

1186. FRANCO, GUIDO ("G. F."). **Desert patrol (une aven-
        ture sous les tropiques).** Paris: Editions de
        la Jungle, 1980. 185 pp.
Text and photos presenting an unflattering image of
Caucasian boy-lover tourists in Southeast Asia. Similar
is his: **Prières pour des paradis meilleurs** (Paris: Editions de la Jungle, 1984).

1187. FREEMAN, JAMES M. **Untouchable: An Indian Life
        History.** Stanford: Stanford University Press,
        1979. 421 pp.
Offers material on the **hijras** (pp. 16, 24-25, 61, 250,

SOUTH AND SOUTHEAST ASIA   179

256, 294-315).

1188. **Gays in Indonesia: Selected Articles from Print
       Media.** Fitzroy, Australia: Sybylla Press, 1984.
       61 pp.
Articles chosen and translated by the Gays in Indonesia
Translation Group, PO Box 108, North Carlton, Victoria
3054, Australia.

1189. GEERTZ, CLIFFORD. **The Religion of Java.** Glencoe,
       IL: Free Press, 1960. 392 pp.
Pages 289-300 deal with various forms of popular enter-
tainment--dramatic presentations and parties--in which
male homosexual and transvestite dancers play a considerable role. The dances and street shows contain explicitly
homosexual elements, and the town of Ponorogo, where the
art of the wandering troupes is said to be at its strongest, is noted for male homosexuality.

1190. HAMILTON, ALEXANDER. **A New Account of the East
       Indies ... from the Year 1688 to 1723.** Edinburgh:
       J. Mosman, 1727. 2 vols.
Provides several references, including one to Sultan Mahmud I of Johore (ruled 1683-99).

1191. HARRIS, MAX. "A Hell for Homosexuals," **Spectator,**
       239 (November 12, 1977), 16-17.
Despite evidence to the contrary, claims that homosexuality is unknown on the island of Bali because of an absence of dependency needs.

1192. HART, DONN V. "Homosexuality and Transvestism in
       the Philippines," **Behavioral Science Notes,** 3
       (1968), 211-48.
Reports on the complex social organization of a town on
Cebu which focuses around a drag "beauty contest." The
tolerance of homosexuality in Filipino society may reflect
the view that it is natural and inborn.

1193. HEIDE, AB VAN DE. **De zaak tegen Mr. L. A. Ries,
       thesaurier-generaal bij het Departement van
       Financiën: eenige beschouwingen en kritische
       opmerkingen.** The Hague: Leopold, 1936. 74 pp.
Commentary on a morals scandal that rocked the Dutch
administration in the East Indies (now Indonesia). See
also B. T. de Jongh, **Wat de Indische zedenmisdrijven ons
te zeggen hebben** (Amsterdam: De Ploeger, 1939; 24 pp.).

1194. HEIMANN, ELLIOTT, and CAO VAN LE. "Transvestism in
       Vietnam," **Archives of Sexual Behavior,** 4 (1975),
       89-96.
Confusingly conflates urban homosexual prostitutes and
village cross-gender shamans.

1195. HURGRONJE, CHRISTIAAN SNOUCK. **The Achehnese.**
       Translated by A. W. S. O'Sullivan. Leiden: Brill,

1906. 2 vols.
In this monograph on a Sumatran tribe, see vol. 1, p. 361.

1196. JACOBS, JULIUS. **Het familie- en kampongleven op groot-Atjeh, eene bijdrage tot de ethnographie van noord-Sumatra.** Leiden: Brill, 1894. 2 vols.
In this study of family and village life in great Atjeh (north Sumatra), see vol. 1, p. 80ff.

1197. JUNGHUHN, FRANZ. **Die Battalander auf Sumatra.** Berlin: Reimer, 1847. 2 vols.
On the Bataks of Sumatra; see vol. 1, p. 157.

1198. KIEFER, THOMAS M. "A Note on Cross-dressing Identification among Musicians," **Ethnomusicology,** 12 (1968), 107-08.
"Professional musician" (**mangangalang**) is a niche for sensitive men (**bantut**) in the Islamic Taosug warrior culture of the Sulu archipelago. See also Kiefer, **The Tausug** (New York: Holt, 1972; 145 pp.--p. 36).

1199. KOCH, OSKAR. **Der indianischer Eros.** Berlin: Continent-Verlag, 1925. 122 pp.
In this popular work on love in India, see pp. 61-65.

1200. KROEF, JUSTUS M. VAN DER. "Transvestism and the Religious Hermaphrodites in Indonesia," **University of Manila Journal of East Asiatic Studies,** 3 (1954), 257-65.
"Transvestism is .. the consequence of the religious adjustment of two cultures, in one of which the women traditionally had a pre-eminent place as the chief socio-economic unit ..., while in the other the male had or attained a similar place."

1201. LEVIN, THOMAS HERBST. **Wild Races of South-Eastern India.** London: W. H. Allen, 1870. 352 pp.
Contains some information on transvestites among tribal peoples.

1202. MARION, A.-P. "L'homme nu," **Arcadie,** no. 69 (September 1959), 478-87.
Report on travel to Laos and Vietnam. See also his: "Voyage à Kandy (Ceylon)," **Arcadie,** no. 58 (October 1958), 14-20.

1203. MARK, MARY ELLEN. **Falkland Road: Prostitutes of Bombay.** New York: Knopf, 1981. 17 pp.; 66 plates.
Photodocumentary; includes some transvestite males (**hijra**).

1204. MARNAIS, PHILIP. **Saigon after Dark.** New York: MacFadden-Bartell, 1967. 127 pp.
Contains a section on gay life in the South Vietnamese capital during the civil war and American intervention.

1205. MARSDEN, WILLIAM. **History of Sumatra.** London: J.
       McCreery, 1811.
See p. 261ff.

1206. MEYER, JOHANN JACOB. **Sexual Life in Ancient India:
       A Study of the Comparative History of Indian Cul-
       ture.** New York: Dutton, 1930. 2 vols.
Focuses on an analysis of the sexual practices in the
Ramayana and Mahabharata, and in consequence is largely
tangential to our subject.

1207. NANDA, SERENA. "The Hijras of India: Cultural and
       Individual Dimensions of an Institutionalized Third
       Gender Role," **JH,** 11:3-4 (1985), 35-54.
The most informative field study of this group (whose members include Hindus and Muslims), showing that they do engage in homosexual relations. See also her: "The Hijras
of India: A Preliminary Report," **Medicine and Law,** 3
(1984), 59-75.

1208. NERY, LAMBERTO C. "The Covert Subculture of Male
       Homosexual Prostitutes in Metro Manila," **Philippine
       Journal of Psychology,** 12 (1979), 27-32.
Conclusions derived from interviewing six 18-22-year-old
call boys at a brothel/gay bar. Although money is important, they made statements indicating enjoyment of their
work.

1209. NIMMO, H. ARLO. "The Relativity of Sexual Devi-
       ance: A Sulu Example," **Papers in Anthropology,** 19
       (1980), 91-97.
Contrasts acceptance of prostitution and homosexuality in
two cultures in the Sulu archipelago. One, Islamic, shows
elaborated homosexuality.

1210. OBEYESEKERE, GANANATH. **The Cult of the Goddess
       Pattini.** Chicago: University of Chicago Press,
       1984. 629 pp.
Male homosexuality is common in Sri Lanka before marriage,
though a taboo on anality restricts contact to interfemor-
al. The book contains material on transvestism among
priests of the goddess, whose cult, the author holds,
was introduced in late antiquity by Syrian merchants.

1211. O'FLAHERTY, WENDY DONIGER. **Women, Androgynes and
       Other Mythical Beasts.** Chicago: Chicago University
       Press, 1980. 382 pp.
This book, by a noted contemporary Indologist, discusses
sexual metaphors and animal imagery in over 3000 years of
Indian mythological development.

1212. SALETORE, RAJARAN NARAYAN. **Sex Life under Indian
       Rulers.** Delhi: Hind, 1974. 251 pp.
Popular account including information on homosexuality
under Moghul and Hindu rule.

1213. SCHNEEBAUM, TOBIAS. **Wild Man.** New York: Viking
       Press, 1979. 243 pp.
New York artist's low-key memoir of travels, chiefly in
India, Indonesia, and New Guinea, where he sought to
avail himself of male sexual encounters.

1214. STAVORINUS, JOHAN SPLINTER. **Voyages to the East-
       Indies.** Translated by S. H. Wilocke. London: G.
       G. Robinson, 1798.
See pp. 455-57 for male and female homosexuality and
bestiality in Moghul Bengal.

1215. SUTLIVE, VINSON, H., JR. "The Iban Manang: An
       Alternate Route to Normality," in: G. N. Appell,
       Studies in Borneo Societies. DeKalb: Northern
       Illinois University Press, 1976, 64-71. (Center for
       Southeast Asian Studies, Northern Illinois Univers-
       ity, Special Report, 12)
For those unable to fulfill societal prescriptions for
masculine achievement, the status of **manang** (shaman)
provides "emotional supports" and "collective solutions
to the basic problems of existence."

1216. THIEULOY, JACK. **La passion indonésienne.** Paris:
       Presses de la Renaissance, 1984. 400 pp.
Enthusiastic account of sexual adventures in today's Indonesia.

1217. WALKER, BENJAMIN. **The Hindu World.** New York:
       Praeger, 1968. 2 vols.
An encyclopedic survey of Hindu thought and civilization;
see e.g. "Androgyny," 1, 43-45; "Gender," 1, 388-89.

                   T. BIOGRAPHIES: COLLECTIVE

The impulse to draw up extensive biographical lists of
notable homosexuals of the past began with 19th-century
homosexual scholars in German-speaking countries. Parallel tendencies occur with scholars representing other
minority groups, where such lists seem to function to
provide historical witness of the collective worth of an
ostracized group. This "hall of fame" approach has
recently been criticized as skewing homosexual and lesbian
history towards an unrepresentative elite, effacing
historical variety and class differences. The search for
famous homosexuals also provokes a largely fruitless
series of disputes over whether figures of the past, such
as Socrates or Caesar, were truly homosexual. A more
recent trend is toward collective biographies of living
individuals, with the aim of producing a representative
cross-section rather than a roster of notables.

1218.   ADAIR, NANCY, and CASEY ADAIR (eds). **Word Is
        Out: Stories of Some of Our Lives.** New York: Dell,
        1978. 320 pp.
Experiential accounts of the lives of gay men and lesbians
from college students to senior citizens. The text cor-
responds, in large part, to the film of the same name.

1219.   BUUREN, HANNEKE VAN, and PAUL DE VILDER (eds).
        **Als je me de bek openbreekt: homofielen over zich
        self.** Amsterdam: Wetenschappelijke Uitgeverij,
        1974. 136 pp.
Personal testimonies of Dutch gay men and lesbians.

1220.   CASSIDY, JULES, and ANGELA STEWART-PARK (eds).
        We're Here: Conversations with Lesbian Women.
        London: Quartet, 1976. 150 pp.
Interviews and photographs of British lesbians from
various walks of life.

1221.   CRUIKSHANK, MARGARET (ed). **The Lesbian Path: 37
        Lesbian Writers Share Their Personal Experiences,
        Viewpoints, Traumas, and Joys.** Monterey, CA: Angel
        Press, 1980. 248 pp.
Short autobiographies by contemporaries. See also: Ruth
Baetz (ed.), **Lesbian Crossroads: Personal Stories of
Lesbian Struggles and Triumphs** (New York: Morrow, 1980;
273 pp.); Laurel Galana and Gina Covina, **The New Les-
bians: Interviews with Women Across the U.S. and Canada**
(Berkeley, CA: Moon, 224 pp.); and Susan J. Wolfe and
Julia Penelope Stanley, **The Coming Out Stories** (Waterton,
MA: Persephone Press, 1980; 251 pp.).

1222.   DUROC, PIERRE. **Homosexuels et lesbiennes il-
        lustres: dictionnaire anecdotique.** Brussels: Les
        Auteurs Réunis, 1983. 505 pp.
Alphabetical listing of some 1000 famous homosexuals (or
persons claimed as such), including mythological figures,
with spare documentation. Emphasis on Greco-Roman and
French figures.

1223.   EBERT, ALAN. **The Homosexuals.** New York: Macmil-
        lan, 1977. 332 pp.
Depressing collection of interviews with seventeen
ostensibly representative homosexual men. Similar is:
David Gottlieb, **The Gay Tapes: A Candid Discussion
about Male Homosexuality** (New York: Stein and Day, 1977;
178 pp.).

1224.   GREIF, MARTIN. **The Gay Book of Days.** Secaucus,
        NJ: Lyle Stuart, 1982. 224 pp.
Described as an "illustrated Who's Who of who is, was,
may have been, probably was, and almost certainly seems
to have been gay during the past 5,000 years," this volume offers amusing profiles of gay men and a few lesbians. Evidence is rarely given for the anecdotes: the
book is entertainment rather than scholarship. Index of

almost 1000 names.

1225. GARDE, NOEL I. (pseud.). **Jonathan to Gide: The Homosexual in History.** New York: Vantage Press, 1964. 751 pp.
Biographies of some 300 men alleged in other sources to be homosexual. Based on secondary sources, this book must be used with caution. There is no doubt, however, that it belongs to a venerable tradition of "ancestor hunting" that has served as a stimulus to research. See also W. H. Kayy (pseud.), **The Gay Geniuses: Psychiatric and Literary Studies of Famous Homosexuals** (Glendale, CA: Marvin Miller, 1965; 223 pp.).

1226. GRIER, BARBARA, and COLETTA REID (eds.). **Lesbian Lives: Biographies of Women from The Ladder.** Oakland, CA: Diana Press, 1976. 432 pp.
Biographical sketches of some sixty women in history who were or may have been lesbians: famous couples, adventurers, novelists, queens and their consorts, poets, artists, writers, and pathbreakers. See also: Charlotte Bunch and Nancy Myron (eds.), **Women Remembered** (Baltimore: Diana Press, 1974; 92 pp.).

1227. HENNEFELD, PAUL. **Gay and Lesbian History on Stamps: Achilles to Zeus.** Upper Montclair, NJ: The author, n.d. (ca. 1982). about 60 pp.
Alphabetical listing by personality, with Scott Catalog numbers. Some illustrations. There is also an **Addendum** (6 pp.), ca. 1983.

1228. LÉONETTI, PAUL-FRANÇOIS. **Je suis un homo ... comme ils disent.** Paris: Alain Lefeure, 1980. 300 pp.
Contemporary testimonies of French male homosexuals.

1229. LEYLAND, WINSTON (ed.). **Gay Sunshine Interviews.** San Francisco: Gay Sunshine Press, 1978. 328 pp.
Interviews with such writers as William Burroughs, Charles Henry Ford, Jean Genet, Allen Ginsberg, as well as with the composer Lou Harrison. See also: **Gay Sunshine Interviews, Volume Two** (San Francisco: Gay Sunshine Press, 1983; 288 pp.

1230. PERRIN, ELULA. **So Long as There Are Women.** Translated by H. Salemson. New York: Morrow, 1978. 216 pp.
Lives of nine lesbians as told by the owner of a Paris cabaret for women, Kathmandu.

1231. RIESS, CURT. **Auch Du, Cäsar ... Homosexualität als Schicksal.** Munich: Universitas, 1981. 447 pp.
Thirty-one short biographies of male homosexuals in history--writers, artists, athletes, and political figures.

1232. ROWSE, ALFRED L. **Homosexuals in History: Ambisexuals in Society, Literature, and the Arts.** New

York: Macmillan, 1977. 346 pp.
A British academic and popularizer offers opinionated
anecdotal sketches of homosexual men from the time of
Richard Lion Heart to the present (Englishmen, Frenchmen,
Italians, Germans, Russians, and a few Americans).

1233. SONENSCHEIN, DAVID. **Some Homosexual Men: Inter-
       views from 1967.** Austin, TX: The author, 1983.
       217 pp.
Transcriptions of tapes made with street contacts when
he was conducting work under the auspices of the [Kinsey]
Institute for Sex Research.

1234. STAMBOLIAN, GEORGE. **Male Fantasies/Gay Realities.**
       New York: Sea Horse Press, 1984. 167 pp.
Interviews with ten east-coast gay men, emphasizing
sexuality and identity.

U. THE HOMOSEXUAL MOVEMENT: UNITED STATES

After an abortive attempt initiated by Henry Gerber in
Chicago in 1924-25, the contemporary American homosexual
rights movement commenced in Southern California at the
end of the 1940s, spreading to a number of other cities in
the following decade. This movement began largely in
ignorance of European precedents and parallels, though
relations were quickly established with groups in Europe.
Historians have articulated the relatively short history
of the American movement into several periods, of which
one may best perhaps retain three: the "homophile phase,"
concentrating on a largely integrationist civil-rights
approach (1950-1969); the high radical phase, ushered in by
the Stonewall Rebellion (1969-73); and the post-radical
era, which tended to synthesize the two previous approaches.

1235. ALTMAN, DENNIS. **Homosexual: Oppression and
       Liberation.** New York: Outerbridge and Dienstfrey,
       1971. 242 pp.
An "instant interpetation" by a gay Australian journalist
and politics professor of the goals and theory of U.S.
homosexual liberation, with New Left overtones. Perceiving a need for a complete transformation of society--in
the utopian vein of the period--Altman stressed the analogies with the aims and tactics of the black and women's
liberation movements. See also his essay collection: **Coming Out in the Seventies** (Sydney: Wild and Woolley, 1979;
312 pp.); and his: **The Homosexualization of America, the
Americanization of the Homosexual** (New York: St. Martin's
Press, 1982; 242 pp.).

1236. BELL, ARTHUR. **Dancing the Gay Lib Blues: A Year in**

the **Homosexual Liberation Movement.** New York:
Simon and Schuster, 1971. 189 pp.
Gay journalist's memoir of the gay liberation movement in
New York City immediately after the Stonewall Rebellion,
focusing on the Gay Activists Alliance. See also: Arnie
Kantrowitz, **Under the Rainbow: Growing Up Gay** (New York:
Morrow, 1977; 255 pp.).

1237. BENENSON, ROBERT. "Gay Politics," **Editorial Re-
      search Reports,** 1:24 (June 29, 1984), 471-88.
Contrasts the political activities of the gay movement
with the religious condemnation of homosexual conduct
and the refusal of the churches to approve the "gay
lifestyle."

1238. BLAKE, ROGER. **The Homosexual Explosion.** North
      Hollywood, CA: Brandon House, 1966. 188 pp.
Sensationalistic expose of "the sexual revolution that is
sweeping the world." A pulp document of the period.

1239. COLE, ROB. "Collision in San Francisco," **Advocate,**
      no. 43 (September 30-October 13, 1970), 1-2, 6-7,
      12, 23; no. 44 (October 24-27, 1970), 8, 11.
Report of the four-day convention (August 25-28) in San
Francisco of the North American Conference of Homophile
Organizations (NACHO), which led to the demise of this
sole attempt to organize the diverse movement groups
into a single, national body.

1240. CORZINE, JAY et al. "The Gay Movement and Social
      Change," **Heuristics,** 7 (1977), 44-57.
Contends that the gay movement is developing "new men" who
embody a homoerotic consciousness fully grounded in eros
and constituting an alternative to the heteroerotic consciousness grounded in logos--and hence in domination,
role inequality, and other aspects of non-sensuous materialism.

1241. CUTTLER, MARVIN (pseud. of W. Dorr Legg/William
      Lambert). **Homosexuals Today: A Handbook of
      Organizations and Publications.** Los Angeles: ONE,
      Inc., 1956. 188 pp.
Surveying the homophile movement in the United States and
abroad (France, Germany, The Netherlands, Italy, Scandinavia, and Switzerland) a decade after the end of World War
II, this book is a valuable record of the outlook and expectations prevailing at that time. Lists of organizations and publications.

1242. D'EMILIO, JOHN. **Sexual Politics, Sexual Commu-
      nities: The Making of a Homosexual Minority in the
      United States, 1940-1970.** Chicago: Chicago Univer-
      sity Press, 1983. 257 pp.
An account of the gay and lesbian movement in the United
States showing the 1940s background out of which it arose
in Southern California, early growth pains, the "homo-

phile" phase, and incipient radicalization following the
Stonewall Rebellion (1969). Despite a few factual errors
and mistaken emphases, this book is generally recognized
as the standard account of the history of the U.S. movement. See also his: "Gay Politics, Gay Community: San
Francisco's Experience," **Socialist Review,** no. 55 (1981),
77-104.

1243. DENNENY, MICHAEL. "Sixteen Propositions for the
      Eighties," **Gay News** (London), no. 213 (April 1981),
      15-17.
A strongly worded manifesto, first published in **Christopher Street** (January 1981), and reflecting a major strand
of contemporary gay opinion on the eve of the AIDS crisis. See response by Ian Harvey, "Sixteen Questionable
Propositions Questioned," ibid., no.216 (May-June 1981,
31. See also: Pat Califia, "What is 'Gay Liberation'?"
Advocate, no. 320 (June   25, 1981), 30, 36-37, 58.

1244. DEVALL, WILLIAM. "Gay Liberation: An Overview,"
      Journal of Voluntary Action Research, 2 (1973),
      24-35.
Sociologist's review of the literature covering precipit-
ating factors, organization, ideology, and impact.

1245. ELSHTAIN, JEAN BETHGE. "Homosexual Politics: The
      Paradox of Gay Liberation," **Salmagundi,** no. 58-59
      (1982-83), 252-80.
Unsympathetic critique, chiding gay-liberation politics
with seeking to collapse the distinction between private
and public spheres, and for seeking validation through
enactment of symbolic legislation. Contends that "maximal
liberationists" practice a "politics of self-delusion and
narcissistic insulation."

1246. FABER, CHARLES. "30 and Going Strong," **Advocate,**
      no. 349 (August 19, 1982), 32-35.
Account of ONE, Inc., of Los Angeles, which celebrated its
thirtieth anniversary under the guidance of W. Dorr
Legg, making it the oldest continuous gay organization
in the country.

1247. GERBER, HENRY. "The Society for Human Rights--
      1925," **One Magazine,** 10:9 (September 1962), 5-11.
Autobiographical account of Gerber's (1896-1972) founding
of a gay rights organization in Chicago, the first that
is known in this country.

1248. GREENBERG, JERROLD S. "The Effects of a Homophile
      Organization on the Self-Esteem of Its Members,"
      JH, 1 (1976), 313-17.
In a study of members of one group, it was found that at
first self-esteem remained unaffected while alienation
levels decreased, but started rising again after one year
of participation.

1249. GUNNISON, FOSTER. "The Homophile Movement in
       America," in: Ralph W. Weltge (ed.), **The Same
       Sex: An Appraisal of Homosexuality.** Philadelphia:
       United Church Press, 1969, pp. 113-28.
A short history of the homophile movement in the United
States with special emphasis on the 1960s, when the author
(now director of the Institute of Social Ethics in Hartford, CT) played a key role in a number of organizations.

1250. HAEBERLE, ERWIN J. "A Movement of Inverts: An
       Early Plan for a Homosexual Organization in the
       United States," **JH,** 10 (1984), 127-33.
Presents letters documenting a 1930 plan of Ernest F. Elm-
hurst to form an organization, apparently in ignorance of
Henry Gerber's efforts a few years previously in Chicago.

1251. HARDING, CARL B. (pseud. of Elver A. Barker). **Edu-
       cation Handbook: Individual and Group Projects and
       Organizational Techniques.** San Francisco: Mat-
       tachine Society, 1959. 63 pp.
Guide produced by the leading homosexual rights group of
the period to foster the progress of individuals "toward
self-understanding and acceptance," as well as to promote
the education of the general public.

1252. HAY, HARRY. "Preliminary Concepts" by Eann Mac-
       Donald (pseud.), in: **A Homosexual Emancipation
       Miscellany, ca. 1835-1952.** New York: Arno Press,
       1975, 6 pp.
Reproduction from typescript of the prospectus (1950) for
what became the Mattachine Society in Los Angeles, by the
first theoretician of the American movement.

1253. HUMPHREYS, LAUD. **Out of the Closets: The Sociology
       of Homosexual Liberation.** Englewood Cliffs, NJ:
       Prentice-Hall, 1972. 176 pp.
A sociologist and participant-observer traces of the American homosexual rights movement--its evolution, aspirations, tactics and radicalization--over the course of the
previous three decades. Contains a case study of a
particular group, Mandrake of St. Louis (pp. 79-100).

1254. JOHNSTON, GORDON. **Which Way Out of the Men's
       Room: Options for the Male Homosexual.** Cranbury,
       NJ: A. S. Barnes,1980. 330 pp.
Somewhat ponderous critique of late-70s attitudes and
lifestyles of gay men.

1255. KEPNER, JIM. **A Brief History on Gay Movement
       History and Goals.** Hollywood: International Gay
       and Lesbian Archives, 1985. 32 pp.
Reflections by a senior statesman of the Southern Cal-
ifornia homosexual movement, founder and curator of the
International Gay and Lesbian Archives. The brochure is
subtitled: "Why Can't We All Get Together? and: What Do
We Have in Common After All?"

1256. KIRK, MARSHALL K., and ERASTES PILL (pseuds.).
       "Waging Peace," **Christopher Street**, no. 95 (1985),
       33-41.
Analyzes the heterosexuals' aversion to gays (which
"purple Polyannas" underestimate) as manifestations of
the unknown, the alien, the loathsome, and the contrary. Proposes an aggressive strategy to combat this
negativism.

1257. LEITSCH, DICK. "A New Frontier for Freedom,"
       Social Action, 34 (1967), 21-29.
Brief historical review and optimistic forecast by the
sometime leader of the Mattachine Society of New York.

1258. LEVIN, JIM. **Reflections on the American Homosexual
       Rights Movement.** New York: Gay Academic Union,
       1983. 67 pp.
After outlining the conditions that made the emergence of
the movement possible after World War II, argues that the
"radicalized" period after 1969 was a deflection ("tempor-
arily off course"). The book contains an "Afterword" by
Wayne Dynes, as well as Levin's essay-review of Jonathan
Katz' **Gay American History** (New York: Crowell, 1976).

1259. LICATA, SAL. "The Homosexual Rights Movement in
       the United States: A Traditionally Overlooked Area
       of American History," **JH**, 6 (1980-91), 161-89.
Presents the movement as developing in eight stages: (1)
sporadic individual attempts, 1908-45; (2) the dawning of
minority consciousness, 1945-50; (3) search for identity, 1950-52; (4) righteous indignation, 1952-53; (5)
information and education, 1953-60; (6) civil rights
activism, 1961-69; (7) gay liberation, 1969-73; and (8)
institutional responses, 1973-79.

1260. MCCAFFREY, JOSEPH A. (ed.). **The Homosexual Dial-
       ectic.** Englewood Cliffs, NJ: Prentice-Hall, 1972.
       218 pp.
Collection of articles and manifestos, most of them reprints, reflecting the radical ferment of the time (though
including also some negative material by Irving Bieber and
others). Makes accessible a widely noticed text of the
time: Carl Wittman, "Refugees from Amerika: A Gay Manifesto" (pp. 157-71).

1261. MAROTTA, TOBY. **The Politics of Homosexuality: How
       Lesbians and Gay Men Have Made Themselves a Polit-
       ical and Social Force in Modern America.** Boston:
       Houghton Mifflin, 1981. 369 pp.
After some background on Southern California, Marotta
concentrates narrowly on New York City, chiefly during the
period 1969-73.

1262. MASTERS, ROBERT E. L. **The Homosexual Revolution: A
       Challenging Expose of the Social and Political
       Directions of a Minority Group.** New York: Julian

Press, 1962. 230 pp.
A typical "would you believe this" document of the period.
Contains some information on the Mattachine Society, ONE,
Inc., and the Daughters of Bilitis, showing how Masters
thought they should be perceived by the general public.

1263. MILLER, MERLE. **On Being Different: What It Means
      to Be a Homosexual.** New York: Random House, 1971.
      65 pp.
An expanded version of an article first published in the
New York Times Magazine (January 1971), this autobiographical sketch caught the attention of mainstream America
because of the author's status as a respected novelist and
broadcaster who was coming out of the closet.

1264. MURPHY, JOHN. **Homosexual Liberation: A Personal
      View.** New York: Praeger, 1971. 182 pp.
Although some historical material is included, this book
is valuable chiefly as a record of one individual's experiences in the post-Stonewall New York movement, esp.
with the Gay Liberation Front. See also: Peter Fisher,
The Gay Mystique (New York: Stein and Day, 1972; 258 pp.).

1265. NORTH AMERICAN MAN BOY LOVE ASSOCIATION. **A
      Witchhunt Foiled: The FBI vs. NAMBLA.** New York:
      NAMBLA, 1985. 93 pp.
Claims that in December 1982 the FBI launched a "crusade"
against NAMBLA, which the organization thwarted. While
there is no doubt that the repressive campaign demonstrated hysteria and misinformation, NAMBLA's self-serving
presentation of its role as that of a David slaying
Goliath reflects a grandiosity that erodes credibility.

1266. ONGE, JACK. **The Gay Liberation Movement.** Chicago:
      Alliance Press, 1971. 90 pp.
Brief journalistic account of the homophile movement in
the 1950s and 1960s, with some use of movement source
materials.

1267. PRAUNHEIM, ROSA VON (pseud. of Holger Mischwitzky).
      Army of Lovers. London: Gay Men's Press, 1980.
      207 pp.
A German gay filmmaker and activist records his encounters
with gay leaders in the U.S. and elsewhere.

1268. ROGERS, MARTIN. "Critical Incidents in the
      Evolution of a Gay Liberation Group," **Homosexual
      Counseling Journal**, 2 (1975), 18-25.
A faculty member at California State University, Sacramento, reports on the attitudinal, behavioral, and self-concept changes which took place during the growth of the
group.

1269. RUSSO, ANTHONY J. **Power and Influence in the
      Homosexual Community: A Study of Three California
      Cities.** Claremont: Claremont Graduate School,

1982. 186 pp. (unpublished Ph. D. dissertation,
      psychology and sociology)
Based on a 17-page schedule of inquiry submitted to
leaders in Los Angeles, San Diego, and San Francisco,
Russo found that the power was "expert, referent, and
conjunctive."

1270. SAGARIN, EDWARD. **Structure and Ideology in an
       Association of Deviants.** New York: Arno Press,
       1975. 446 pp.
A reprint of Sagarin's 1966 dissertation (New York University), this sociological study stems from the writer's
participant-observation (as "Donald Webster Cory") in
the Mattachine Society of New York. As an organization,
MSNY was found to be strongly instrumental on the manifest
level, while latently almost entirely expressive. The
somewhat negative picture of factionalism and confusion
that the author gives would appear to reflect in part his
own frustrations in being rejected in his candidacy for
president. See also his: **Odd Man Out: Societies of Deviants in America** (Chicago: Quadrangle, 1969).

1271. STEIN, THEODORE J. "Gay Service Organizations: A
       Survey," **Homosexual Counseling Journal,** 3 (1976),
       84-97.
Presents data from questionnaires returned by 38 organizations.

1272. SWEET, ROXANNA. **Political and Social Action in
       Homophile Organizations.** New York: Arno Press,
       1975. 252 pp.
Reporting on San Francisco organizations, finds important
similarities to the early labor movement, and the women's
and black civil rights movement. Argues that homophile
organizations must be seen in the context of American
values and institutions. The book is a reprint of her
Ph.D. dissertation in criminology, University of California, Berkeley.

1273. TEAL, DONN. **The Gay Militants.** New York: Stein
       and Day, 1971. 355 pp.
This detailed study of New York City from June 1969 to
June 1970, with particular attention to the Gay Liberation Front and the Gay Activists Alliance, incorporates
much primary material from periodicals and leaflets.

1274. TOBIN, KAY, and RANDY WICKER. **The Gay Crusaders.**
       New York: Paperback Library, 1972. 238 pp.
Autobiographical sketches of eleven male and four female
leaders prominent in the American gay movement at the
time.

1275. YEARWOOD, LENNOX, and THOMAS S. WEINBERG. "Black
       Organizations, Gay Organizations: Sociological
       Parallels," in: Martin P. Levine (ed.), **Gay
       Men: The Sociology of Male Homosexuality** (New

York: Harper and Row, 1979, pp. 301-16.
Based on a literature review, the authors find a number of
significant parallels in ideology, tactics, structure, and
goals.

V. THE HOMOSEXUAL MOVEMENT: ABROAD

Although several earlier theorists had conceived of the
idea in some form--and indeed its spiritual roots are
situated in the 18th-century Enlightenment--the homosexual
rights movement began with the founding of the Scientific-
humanitarian Committee in Berlin in 1897. From the beginning the German movement operated on two fronts: the
legal-legislative and the scholarly. It was recognized
that unless an enlightened intelligentsia could be formed
that would be prepared to discard inherited stereotypes in
favor of solid scientific and scholarly information, no
lasting reforms could be achieved or maintained. Although
the movement spread into neighboring countries of northern
Europe, Germany remained dominant until 1933, when Hitler's suppression of all homosexual groups combined with
the Great Depression to end two generations of fruitful
work. In a tentative fashion, gay rights movements
revived in a number of European countries after World
War II (a tenuous continuity had been maintained in
Switzerland and Sweden). In the 1970s these groups, then
well established, received a vigorous infusion of American
activist concepts and lifestyle elements. Despite some
stirrings in the Third World, which the International Gay
Association (founded in England in 1978) has sought to
foster, the gay and lesbian movement has remained largely
restricted to the industrialized countries of the Western
world. Regarding homosexuality itself as a mark of capitalist decadence, Marxist regimes do not permit any independent organized homosexual groups.

1276. ADAM, BARRY D. "A Social History of Gay Politics,"
       in: Martin P. Levine, **Gay Men: The Sociology of
       Male Homosexuality.** New York: Harper and Row,
       1979, pp. 285-300.
From a Marxian perspective, a Canadian scholar argues that
capitalism generated the social conditions which produced
the gay subculture and the homosexual rights movements.
(Adam does not explain why Germany, the last of the major
capitalist powers to emerge, should have been the first to
develop a homosexual rights movement.)

1277. AXGIL, AXEL, and HJELMER FOGEDGAARD. **Homofile
       kampar: Bøsseler gjennom tiderne.** Ridkøbing: For-
       laget Grafolio, 1985. 216 pp.
Account of the founding and growth of the Danish gay-
rights group Forbundet af 1948 and of the periodical

Vennen, which Fogedgaard edited.

1278. BANENS, MAKS. "De eerste jaren van het COC,"
Homojaarboek (Amsterdam), 1 (1981), 133-60.
Account of the first five years (1946-51) of the leading
Dutch homosexual social and rights organization Cultuur
en Ontspannings Centrum (COC; now NVIH/COC). This volume
contains other articles on homosexual rights work in the
Netherlands by Judith Schuyf, Maurice van Lieshout, and
Rob Tielman. The major synthesis of the matter is: Rob
Tielman, **Homoseksualiteit in Nederland** (Amsterdam: Boom
Meppel, 1982; 336 pp.).

1279. BAUDRY, ANDRÉ, et al. **Le regard des autres.**
Paris: Arcadie, 1979. 260 pp.
Proceedings of the international homosexual congress held
in Paris in May 1979 to celebrate the 25th anniversary of
the French Arcadie organization. This was to prove the
last such congress conducted by Arcadie before its dissolution in 1982. See also the earlier proceedings,
**L'homophilie à visage découvert: actes du colloque inter-
national organisé par Arcadie, Paris, 1, 2 et 3 Novembre
1973** (Paris: Arcadie, 1973; 138 pp.). For the origins
of the group, see: Baudry, "La naissance d'Arcadie,"
Arcadie, no. 100 (April 1962), 204-09.

1280. BOUCHARD, ALAIN. **Nouvelle approche à l'homosexualité: style de vie.** Montreal: Homeureux, 1977. 129
pp.
Asserts that the construction of a positive lifestyle is
the homosexual's first task. See also his: **Le complexe
des dupes** (Montreal: Homeureux, 1980); as well as Jean Le
Derff, **Homolibre** (Montreal: René Ferron, 1974); and **Homosexuelle? Et pourquoi pas!** (Montreal: René Ferron, 1973).

1281. COHEN, ALFREDO, et al. **La politica del corpo.**
Rome: Savelli, 1976. 208 pp.
Collection of texts published in the Turin gay liberation
periodical **FUORI! (1971-75).**

1282. DÉMERON, PIERRE. **Lettre ouverte aux hétérosex-
uels.** Paris: Albin Michel, 1969. 144 pp.
(Collection Lettre ouverte)
Good-humored prohomosexual statement.

1283. DIECKMANN, BERNHARD, and FRANCOIS PESCATORE.
**Elemente einer homosexuellen Kritik: französische
Texte 1969-77.** Berlin: Verlag Rosa Winkel, 1979.
239 pp.
Translations of French articles and manifestos, mainly
stemming from left sources, such as the Front Homosexuel
d'Action Révolutionnaire, and from the post-structuralist
trend. See also their (ed.): **Drei Milliarden Perverse**
(Berlin: Verlag Rosa Winkel, 1980; 185 pp.).

1284. **Documents of the Homosexual Rights Movement in**

Germany, 1836-1927. New York: Arno Press, 1975.
Reprints nine texts by German activists and scholars
(Edwin Bab, Adolf Brand, Magnus Hirschfeld, Ferdinand
Karsch-Haack, and Karl Heinrich Ulrichs), together with
a hostile French critique by Ambroise Got.

1285.   FINDLAY, DENNIS, et al. **The Operation Socrates
        Handbook.** Waterloo, Ont.: Operation Socrates,
        Federation of Students, University of Waterloo,
        1973. 39 pp.
Provides information on Canadian gay movement groups and
resources at the time of writing.

1286.   FRIELE, KAREN-CHRISTINE. **Homofili.** Oslo: Det
        Norske Forbundet av 1948, 1972. 28 pp.
Statement by a lesbian spokesperson for the chief Norwegian homosexual rights group.

1287.   FRIELING, WILLI (ed.). **Schwule Regungen--schwule
        Bewegungen.** Berlin: Verlag Rosa Winkel, 1985. 205
        pp.
Essays, reports, and conversations on the German gay movement by a group of German men, most of whom became active
in the radical phase after 1968, and who now reflect on
the changes that have ensued since. Includes chronology, 1969-83 (pp. 183-200).

1288.   FRONT D'ALLIBERAMENT GAI DE CATALUNYA. **Manifest.**
        Barcelona: FAGC, 1977. 47 pp.
Manifesto of the most important gay liberation group in
Catalonia.

1289.   FRONT HOMOSEXUEL D'ACTION RÉVOLUTIONNAIRE. **Rapport
        contre la normalité.** Paris: Champ Libre, 1971. 125
        pp.
Manifesto of the French radical group (FHAR) stemming from
the events of May 1968.

1290.   GIRARD, JACQUES. **Le mouvement homosexuel en France
        1945-1980.** Paris: Syros, 1981. 206 pp.
Although though this book is presented as a history of the
homosexual movement in France, the presentation is selective and skewed towards radical groups, such as FHAR.
Marred by minor factual mistakes and typographical errors.

1291.   HOCQUENGHEM, GUY, and JEAN-LOUIS BORY. **Comment
        nous appelez-vous déjà? ces hommes que l'on dit
        homosexuels.** Paris: Calmann-Levy, 1977. 237 pp.
Subjective memoirs by two French writers and activists.

1292.   HOFFMÜLLER, UDO, and STEPHAN NEUER. **Unfähig zur
        Emanzipation? Homosexuelle zwischen Getto und Be-
        freiung: Eine Untersuchung zur Stagnation der
        Homosexuellenbewegung.** Giessen: Focus Verlag,
        1977. 316 pp.
Leftist, jargon-laden presentation of factors that are

considered to be retarding the progress of the homosexual
emancipation movement in the German Federal Republic.

1293. INTERNATIONAL COMMITTEE FOR SEXUAL EQUALITY.
      Rapport du troisième congrès international.
      Amsterdam: I.C.S.E., 1953. 93 pp.
Report of the Third International Congress of the Comité
International pour l'Egalité Sexuelle (ICSE), Amsterdam,
September 12-24, 1953. ICSE arose after World War II to
continue the international work of sexual reform that had
been interrupted by the Depression and the rise of Hitler
fifteen years before.

1294. JOUHANDEAU, MARCEL. **Ces messieurs: Corydon résumé
      et augmenté.** Paris: Lilac, 1951. 104 pp.
A portion of this book by a noted French writer is a
reworking of Gide's ideas as expressed in **Corydon**.

1295. KUCKUK, INA (pseud.; ed.). **Der Kampf gegen Unter-
      drückung: Materialien aus der deutschen Lesbier-
      innenbewegung.** Munich: Verlag Frauenoffensive,
      1975. 143 pp.
Documents from the German lesbian movement.

1296. KYPER, JOHN. "Organizing in Mexico," **Gay Community
      News**, 7:8 (September 15, 1979), 10-11.
On the Frente Homosexual de Acción Revolucionaria, formed
in Mexico City in April 1978.

1297. LAURITSEN, JOHN, and DAVID THORSTAD. **The Early
      Homosexual Rights Movement (1864-1935).** New
      York: Times Change Press, 1974. 93 pp.
Offers a clear account of scholarly and political activity, mainly in Germany, but also in England, with biographical sketches of key figures (including Karl Heinrich
Ulrichs, Magnus Hirschfeld, and Edward Carpenter). The
later sections overstate the case for the socialist-com-
munist contribution in Germany, and the book has been used
to buttress the uncertain case that there is a special
affinity between homosexual emancipation and the revolutionary left. There are German, Italian, and Spanish
translations. See also: James Steakley, **The Homosexual
Emancipation Movement in Germany** (New York: Arno Press,
1975; 121 pp.).

1298. LEE, JOHN. "Remembering Stonewall: The Relevance
      of Stonewall to Australian Homosexuality," **Gay
      Changes** (Australia), 2:4 (1979), 4-5, 10.
Treats the emergence of CAMP, Inc., in 1970 and Sydney Gay
Liberation in 1971, the latter ostensibly more radical.

1299. MENARD, GUY. **L'homosexualité demystifiée: questions
      et réponses.** Montreal: Leméac, 1980. 188 pp.
Seeks to destroy myths with straightforward answers to
questions.

1300. MIELI, MARIO. **Homosexuality and Liberation: Elements of a Gay Critique.** Translated by David
Fernbach. London: Gay Men's Press, 1980. 247 pp.
This book, which appeared in Italy in 1977, is the chief
Italian contribution to the theory of homosexual liberation. Mieli considers that the chief problem is the repression of homosexuality latent in heterosexuals. The
text is sometimes overambitious and confusingly paradoxical.

1301. MODUGNO, ELIO. **La mistificazione eterosessuale.**
Milan: Gammalibri, 1977. 276 pp.
A gay Marxist criticizes psychoanalytic trends which
"mystify" homosexuality.

1302. OKITA, HIRO (pseud.). **Homossexualismo: da Opressão
a Libertação.** São Paulo: Proposta, 1980. 74 pp.
A brief history of the earlier movements from a Marxist
point of view serves as a prologue to an account (pp. 44-
75) of recent developments in the Brazilian gay movement.

1303. SPOLATO, MARIA SILVIA. **I movimenti omosessuali di
liberazione.** Rome: Samona e Savelli, 1972. 159
pp.
An objective work surveying the origins of the gay liberation movement in Italy and abroad.

1304. SYLVESTRE, PAUL-FRANÇOIS. **Les homosexuels s'orga-
nisent au Québec et ailleurs.** Montreal: Homeureux,
1979. 166 pp.
An examination of the legal status of homosexuality in
Canada and of the gay liberation movement, esp. in Quebec,
since 1969. See also his: **Propos pour une liberation
homosexuelle** (Montreal: Editions de l'Aurore, 1976; 154
pp.).

1305. **Tuntenstreit: Theoriediskussion der Homosexuellen
Aktion Westberlin.** Berlin: Verlag Rosa Winkel,
1977.
Reprints texts from 1974-75 on the question of whether the
homosexual movement should be autonomous or integrated
into the labor movement.

1306. WALTER, AUBREY (ed.). **Come Together: The Years of
Gay Liberation, 1970-73.** London: Gay Men's Press,
1980. 218 pp.
Texts, documents, and photographs from the formative years
of the English gay movement, with special attention to
feminist theory and the relationship between lesbians and
gay men.

1307. **Was soll das Volk vom Dritten Geschlecht wissen?**
Leipzig: Spohr, 1901. 26 pp.
An explanation of homosexuality for the lay public prepared by the Berlin Scientific-Humanitarian Committee
under the direction of Magnus Hirschfeld. This pamphlet,

which was often reprinted, is the prototype of educational brochures created by homosexuals throughout the world in an effort to reach the public directly and refute myths and slanders.

1308. WEEKS, JEFFREY. **Coming Out: Homosexual Politics in Britain from the Nineteenth Century to the Present.** London: Quartet Books, 1977. 278 pp.
In the late 19th century, according to Weeks, capitalist society sought to control homosexual behavior by defining it in increasingly hostile terms. This repression led, by way of reaction, to the creation of a homosexual subculture, and eventually to efforts toward reform. Weeks offers considerable attention to individual reformers (Havelock Ellis, John Addington Symonds, Edward Carpenter) and to developments before and after World War II, leading to the Wolfenden Report and the implementation of its recommendations in 1967. See also: Sheila Rowbotham and Jeffrey Weeks, **Socialism and the New Life: The Personal and Sexual Politics of Edward Carpenter and Havelock Ellis** (New York: Pluto Press, 1980; 200 pp.).

1309. WRIGHT, LES. "The RFSL and Gay Liberation in Sweden," **Gay Books Bulletin**, no. 5 (1981), pp. 25-27.
Brief account of the Swedish homosexual rights group, RFSL (National Union for Sexual Equality), which separated from its Danish parent, Forbundet av 1948, in 1950.

IV. ANTHROPOLOGY

A. CROSS-CULTURAL APPROACHES

Although Europeans had become familiar with homosexual
behavior in other cultures through medieval contact with
Islam and Renaissance conquests in Asia and the Americas,
an attempt to present some image of the world-wide diffusion of "strange sexual practices" began only in the
19th century with such globetrotters as Sir Richard Burton, Paolo Mantegazza, and "Jacobus X." The approach
has lingered in pulp publications--some of them approx-
imating adult-bookstore fare. Beginning with the large
armchair synthesis of the German scholar Karsch-Haack
(1333), professional anthropologists attempted more
factual balance sheets. Despite the recording of substantial quantities of information, the still-tentative character of these summations demonstrates that more ethnol-
ogies (and more accurate and revealing ones) are needed
from many parts of the world before we can attempt a great
map, so to speak, of world homosexuality that will accur-
ately mirror both the genuine typological affinities and
the profound differences in cultural form that define
homosexual behavior in various societies.

1310. BAUMANN, E. D. "Vervrouwelijking bij de primi-
       tieven," **Mensch en Maatschappij**, 10 (1934), 118-33.
Surveys ancient literature and anthroplogical accounts for
evidence of "change of sex," ranging from mere cultic
transvestism to the homosexual aspect of the berdache.
Stresses the universality of the phenomenon of feminiz-
ation.

1311. BAUMANN, HERMANN. **Das doppelte Geschlecht: ethno-
       logische Studien zur Bisexualität in Ritus und
       Mythus.** Berlin: Reimer, 1955. 420 pp.
Despite questionable Jungian assumptions, this major
study collects much tribal material on "bisexuality,"
that is to say androgynous concepts of the divine and
gender-mixing behavior. Africa is specially emphasized.
His "Der kultische Geschlechtswandel bei Naturvölkern,"
Zeitschrift für Sexualforschung, 1:1 (1950), 97-114;
1:3-4 (1950), 259-97, was largely incorporated in this
book.

1312. BENEDICT, RUTH. **Patterns of Culture.** Boston:
       Houghton Mifflin, 1934. 290 pp.
In this influential statement of cultural relativism by
a closeted lesbian anthropologist (1887-1948), see pp.
262-65. See also her: "Anthropology and the Abnormal,"
Journal of General Psychology, 10 (1934), 59-82.

1313. BLACKWOOD, EVELYN (ed.). **Anthropology and Homosex-
       ual Behavior.** Binghamton, NY: Haworth Press,
       1986. 217 pp.
Thirteen new scholarly papers, generally on non-Western
cultures. This collection provides a useful conspectus of
much of what has been accomplished, suggesting also future
avenues of research. Many references; index. Originally
published as **JH**, 11:3-4 (1985).

1314. BLEIBTREU-EHRENBERG, GISELA. **Der Weibmann: kult-
       ische Geschlechtswandel im Schamanism: eine Studie
       zur Transvestition und Transsexualität bei Natur-
       völkern.** Frankfurt am Main: Fischer, 1984. 200
       pp.
Comparative study of transvestism and transsexualism in
Eurasian shamanism, with some information on other cultural spheres. The author posits a linear developmental
process linking these "archaic" magico-sexual phenomena.

1315. BLOCH, IWAN. **Beiträge zur Aetiologie der Psycho-
       pathia sexualis.** Desden: H. R. Dohrn, 1902-03. 2
       vols.
Vol. 1 was translated (by Keith Wallace) as **Anthropological Studies in the Strange Sexual Practices of All Races
in All Ages, Ancient and Modern, Oriental and Occidental,
Primitive and Civilized** (New York: Anthropological Press,
1933; 246 pp.); vol. 2 (by Ernst Vogel) as **Anthropological
and Ethnological Studies in the Strangest Sex Acts in
Modes of Love of All Races Illustrated, Oriental, Occidental, Savage, Civilized** (New York: Falstaff Press, 1935).
Although Bloch was a distinguished Berlin historian of
sexual behavior, these early works do not rank among his
best productions.

1316. BROUDE, GWEN J., and SARAH J. GREENE. "Cross-Cul-
       tural Codes on Twenty Sexual Attitudes and Prac-
       tices," **Ethnology**, 15 (1976), 409-29.
Tabulates data on homosexuality in 37 of 200 societies
surveyed. Schematic and of uncertain value. Similar is
L. Minturn et al., "Cultural Patterning of Sexual Beliefs
and Behavior," ibid., 8 (1969), 301-18.

1317. BROWN, JULIA S. "A Comparative Study of Deviations
       of Sexual Mores," **American Sociological Review,** 17
       (1952), 135-46.
Correlates data on 110 societies from the Human Relations
Area File (HRAF). Male homosexuality was found to be
punished by 68% of the 44 societies in which it was reported. Note that this conclusion differs from that of
C. S. Ford and F. A. Beach, below, and that the reliability of HRAF in detail has been questioned.

1318. CALLENDER, CHARLES, and LEE M. KOCHEMS. "Men and
       Not-Men: Gender-Mixing Statuses and Homosexuality,"
       JH, 11:3-4 (1985), 165-78.
The writers contend that in cultures exhibiting a ber-

dache-type institution, observers' frequent equation of
gender-mixing statuses with homosexuality is a misunderstanding: in these contexts sex with men is a secondary
and derivative characteristic.

1319. CARDÍN, ALBERTO. **Guerreros, chamanes y travestis:-
indicios de homosexualidad entre los exóticos.**
Barcelona: Tusquets, 1984.
Semipopular study of warrior and shamanic homosexuality in
tribal societies.

1320. CARPENTER, EDWARD. **Intermediate Types among Primitive Folk.** Second ed. London: George Allen and
Unwin, 1911. 185 pp.
Presents cross-cultural evidence first for the the wizard
type, often "hermaphroditic" (gender-mixing), and then for
its polar opposite, the warrior homosexual, of which
the samurai is the quintessential embodiment.

1321. CARRIER, JOSEPH M. "Homosexual Behavior in Cross-
Cultural Perspective," in: Judd Marmor (ed.), **Homosexual Behavior: A Modern Reappraisal.** New York:
Basic Books, 1980, pp. 100-22.
An anthropologist seeks to convey the multifariousness of
our knowledge by presenting examples of accomodating and
disapproving societies, societies with ritualized masculinity, and the availability of sexual partners. See
also his: "Sex-Role Preference as an Explanatory Variable
in Homosexual Behavior," **Archives of Sexual Behavior,** 6
(1977), 53-65.

1322. CARSTAIRS, G. MORRIS. "Cultural Differences in
Sexual Deviation," in Ismond Rosen (ed.), **The
Pathology and Treatment of Sexual Deviation: A
Methodological Approach.** London: Oxford University
Press, 1964, pp. 419-34.
Reviewing the diversity of patterns in societies where
such behavior is known, concludes that the evidence
"supports the contention that all human beings are
capable of learning to respond in homosexual relationships; this potentiality is realized in all the members
of some societies, but in only a few members of others."

1323. DAVENPORT, WILLIAM. "Sex in Cross-Cultural Perspective," in: Frank A. Beach (ed.), **Human Sexuality in Four Perspectives.** New York: Wiley, 1977,
pp. 115-63.
Seeks to balance the conflicting claims of the biological
and the cultural approaches. See esp. pp. 153-57.

1324. DAVIS, NIGEL. **The Rampant God: Eros Throughout the
World.** New York: William Morrow, 1984. 300 pp.
Popular cross-cultural survey, with many references to
homosexuality. The bibliography (pp. 285-91) suggests
that the writer's research has been less than exhaustive.

1325. EDWARDES, ALLEN, and R. E. L. MASTERS. **The Cradle
       of Erotica.** New York: Julian Press, 1963. 362 pp.
Potpourri of sexual practices in African and Asian soc-
ieties. Uncritical in its use of sources, this book
nonetheless offers some suggestive material. See also:
Edwardes, **The Jewel in the Lotus** (New York: Julian Press,
1959; 293 pp.); Masters, **Forbidden Sexual Behavior and
Morality: An Objective Re-examination of Perverse Sex
Practices in Different Cultures** (New York: Julian Press,
1962; 431 pp.); and George Allgrove, **Love in the East**
(London: A. Gibbs and Phillips, 1962; 159 pp.).

1326. ELIADE, MIRCEA. **Shamanism: Archaic Techniques of
       Ecstasy.** Translated from the French by Willard
       R. Trask. Princeton: Princeton University Press,
       1964. 610 pp.
This major work by a leading scholar in the field of comparative religion is somewhat disappointing on transvestism and the berdache-like aspects of shamanism; see
however pp. 168, 258, 351-53, 395, and 461.

1327. FEHLING, DETLEV. **Ethnologische Ueberlegungen auf
       dem Gebiet der Altertumskunde: Phallische Demon-
       stration, Fernsicht, die Steinigung.** Munich: Beck,
       1974. 107 pp. (Zetemata, 61)
Presents cross-cultural (and cross-species) material on
phallic presentation.

1328. FITZGERALD, THOMAS K. "A Critique of Anthropolog-
       ical Research on Homosexuality," **JH**, 2 (1977),
       385-97.
Examines some methodological presuppositions underlying
current endeavors. Bibliography, pp. 395-97.

1329. FORD, CLELLAN STEARNS, and FRANK A. BEACH. **Pat-
       terns of Sexual Behavior.** New York: Harper, 1951.
       307 pp.
Scholarly survey by an anthropologist (Ford) and a psychologist (Beach). In Chapter 7 (pp. 125-42) it is indicated
that of 77 societies for which records were available to
the authors, 49 (64%) tolerated or encouraged homosexual
behavior. Also occurring in subhuman primates and lower
animals, it must be considered natural.

1330. GOODLAND, ROGER. **A Bibliography of Sex Rites and
       Customs: An Annotated Record of Books, Articles,
       and Illustrations in All Languages.** London: Rout-
       ledge, 1931. 752 pp.
Inasmuch as this major bibliography scants homosexual
behavior, it can only serve comparative purposes.

1331. GREGERSEN, EDGAR. **Sexual Practices: The Story of
       Human Sexuality.** London: M. Beazley, 1982. 320
       pp.
Semipopular survey by an anthropologist, stressing the
variety of sexual customs.

1332. KARDINER, ABRAM. **The Individual and His So-**
       ciety. New York: Columbia University Press, 1939.
       503 pp.
Psychoanalytic approach drawing on some ethnological
material from the Marquesas Islands, Madagascar, etc.

1333. KARSCH-HAACK, FERDINAND. **Das gleichgeschlechtliche**
       Leben der Naturvölker. Munich: Ernst Reinhardt,
       1911. 668 pp.
Intended as a grand synthesis in the 19th-century manner,
this massive survey of male homosexuality and lesbianism
among tribal peoples in Africa, the Americas, the Pacific
regions, and Siberia does distill much information, providing copious bibliographical references and quotations.
Some methodological assumptions are dated, so that the
work must be used with care. (Reprinted by Arno Press, New
York, 1975).

1334. LABARRE, WESTON. **The Human Animal.** Chicago:
       Chicago University Press, 1954. 371 pp.
A speculative anthropologist attempts to discredit religion by claiming that patriarchal monotheism is a
product of the male homosexual imagination of the Greeks
(pp. 267-302).

1335. LEWANDOWSKI, HERBERT, and HARRY BENJAMIN (ed.).
       Ferne Länder—fremde Sitten: Einführung in die
       Vergleichende Sexualethnologie. Stuttgart: H. E.
       Gunther, 1958. 337 pp.
Anthology of papers on comparative sexual ethnology. Bibliography, pp. 319-29.

1336. MANTEGAZZA, PAOLO. **Anthropological Studies of**
       Sexual Relations of Mankind. Translated by James
       Bruce. New York: Anthropology Press, 1932. 258
       pp.
First published in Italian in 1886, this early "best-sell-
er" of popular anthropology set the pattern for the
"strange customs of distant peoples" genre. It does
contain some material on homosexual behavior, presented
in a relatively objective fashion.

1337. MARSHALL, DONALD S., and ROBERT C. SUGGS (eds.).
       Human Sexual Behavior: Variations in the Ethno-
       graphic Spectrum: Studies in Sex and Society. New
       York: Basic Books, 1971. 302 pp.
Collection of nine papers with some material on homosexual
conduct.

1338. MEAD, MARGARET. **Male and Female: A Study of the**
       Sexes in a Changing World. New York: William
       Morrow, 1949. 477 pp.
Influential statement of cultural relativism by an anthropologist whose accomplishments have recently become the
focus of controversy. Mead contends that in some cultures, as the American Plains Indians, homosexuality and

transvestism may result from failure to meet pressures and
demands for masculinity. In other cultures, homosexual
behavior may be accepted, in some circumstances at least,
as unproblematic. This book, its flaws notwithstanding,
presents a more balanced picture than her widely cited
(and vulnerable) study: **Sex and Temperament in Three
Primitive Societies** (New York: William Morrow, 1935; 335
pp.). On Mead's own bisexuality—including her relationship with Ruth Benedict (see 1312)—see the biography
by her daughter, Mary Catherine Bateson, **With a Daughter's Eye: A Memoir of Margaret Mead and Gregory Bateson**
(New York: Morrow, 1984; 242 pp.).

1339.   MUNROE, ROBERT L., and RUTH H. MUNROE. "Male
        Transvestism and Subsistence Economy," **Journal of
        Social Psychology**, 103 (1977), 307-08.
Finds that a society is likely to institutionalize a male
transvestite role if high subsistence requirements exist
for the men or if differentiation between male and female
roles is relatively small. See also Robert L. Munroe,
"Male Transvestism and the Couvade: A Psycho-Cultural
Analysis," **Ethos**, 8 (1980), 49-59; and Robert Munroe et
al., "Institutionalized Male Transvestism and Sex Distinctions," **American Anthropologist**, 71 (1969), 87-91.

1340.   MURRAY, STEPHEN O. "Fuzzy Sets and Abominations,"
        Man, 18 (1983), 396-99.
Difficulties with categories do not necessarily result
in a sense of danger which leads to the tabooing of the
unclassifiable (as the theory associated with Mary Douglas
would suggest). It is in societies where gender is not
the most salient criterion of social organization and
without a rigid sexual division of labor that homosexual
behavior has been targeted for extirpation.

1341.   OPLER, MARVIN K. "Anthropological and Cross-Cul-
        tural Aspects of Homosexuality," in: Judd Marmor
        (ed.), **Sexual Inversion: The Multiple Roots of
        Homosexuality**. New York: Basic Books, 1965, pp.
        108-23.
Suggests that the extreme diversity of sexual customs
disclosed by anthropological investigation falsifies
linear Freudian notions of normal sexual development.

1342.   SELIGMAN, CHARLES GABRIEL. "Sexual Inversion among
        Primitive Races," **Alienist and Neurologist**, 23
        (1902), 580-83.
This early article by a leading British social anthropologist (1873-1940) documents various cases of homosexuality, pederasty, pseudo-hermaphroditism, and marked inversion of the secondary sexual characters among primitive
peoples of the New World and of (British) New Guinea.

1343.   SONENSCHEIN, DAVID. "Homosexuality as a Subject of
        Anthropological Inquiry," **Anthropological Quarter-
        ly**, 39 (1966), 73-82.

Holds that anthropologists can advance the knowledge of
homosexuality through their field work among tribal
peoples, as well as through the study of homosexuality
as a subculture in more advanced societies.

1344. WERNER, DENNIS. "A Cross-Cultural Perspective on
       Theory and Research on Male Homosexuality," **JH**, 4
       (1979), 345-62.
Favors a "cultural materialist theory," which views homosexuality as adaptive under conditions of population
pressure. See also: "Erratum," ibid., 5 (1980), 333-34.

1345. WINTHUIS, JOSEF. **Das Zweigeschlechterwesen bei den
       Zentralaustraliern und anderen Völkern.** Leipzig:
       Hirschfeld, 1928. 297 pp.
Universalizing perspective on androgyny (with special
emphasis on Australia) by a Catholic priest.

1345A. X, JACOBUS (pseud.). **The Erogenous Zones of the
       World: Description of the Intra-Sexual Manners and
       Customs of the Semi-Civilized Peoples of Africa,
       Asia, America, and Oceania.** New York: Book Awards,
       1964. 448 pp.
An example of the "strange customs" genre. Impressions
gathered by a French army surgeon beginning in the 1860s.

                     B. AFRICA, SUB-SAHARAN

A belief traceable to the 18th century holds that homosexual behavior is unknown in sub-Saharan Africa, a notion
that sometimes resurfaces even today. As the entries that
follow indicate, this concept of African exceptionalism
cannot be sustained. In keeping with the great variety of
African social organizations, there are many types of male
homosexual and lesbian behavior, and further field work
will be necessary to elucidate the full picture. For
North Africa, see III.P.

1346. AMBROGETTI, P. **La vita sessuale nell'Eritrea.**
       Rome: Capaccini, 1900. 19 pp.
See pp. 15-19 for native lesbianism, and pederasty involving Italian colonial troops.

1347. BESMER, FREMONT E. **Horses, Musicians, & Gods: The
       Hausa Cult of Possession-Trance.** South Hadley, MA:
       Bergin & Garvey, 1983. 304 pp.
For cult transvestism and homosexuality in this West
African people, see pp. 18-21, 27-28, and 122-23.

1348. BIEBER, FRIEDRICH J. "Brieflicher Bericht über
       Erhebungen unter äthiopischen Völkerschaften,"
       Anthropophyteia, 6 (1909), 402-05.

Letter on pederasty and lesbianism among Ethiopian
tribes. Continued in his: "Neue Forschungen über das
Geschlechtsleben in Äthiopien," **ibid.**, 7 (1910), 227-32; 8
(1911), 184-93.

1349. BRINCKER, H. "Character, Sitten und Gebräuche
        speciell der Bantu Deutsch-Südwestafrikas,"
        **Mitteilungen des Seminars für orientalische
        Sprachen an der K. Friedrich-Wilhelms-Universität
        zu Berlin**, 3 (1900) [Abteilung 3: Afrikanische
        Studien], 66-99.
On the Bantu of Namibia (former German Southwest Africa).

1350. BRYK, FELIX. **Voodoo-eros: Ethnological Studies in
        the Sex-life of the African Aborigines.** Translated
        by Mayne F. Sexton. New York: United Book Guild,
        1964. 251 pp.
In this popular work, which first appeared in German as
Neger-Eros (1925), see pp. 226-30.

1351. BUXTON, JEAN. "Mandari Witchcraft," in: John
        Middleton and W. H. Winter (eds.), **Witchcraft and
        Society in East Africa.** New York: Praeger, 1963,
        pp. 99-121.
The Mandari of Equatoria Province, Sudan, tend to link
witchcraft and homosexuality. See also her **Religion and
Healing in Mandari** (London, 1973), p. 209.

1352. COLSON, ELIZABETH. **Marriage and the Family among
        the Plateau Tonga of Northern Rhodesia.** Manchest-
        er: Manchester University Press, 1958. 379 pp.
In this ethnography see pp. 139-40.

1353. DYNES, WAYNE. "Homosexuality in Sub-Saharan Af-
        rica: An Unnecessary Controversy," **Gay Books
        Bulletin**, 9 (Spring-Summer 1983), 20-21.
List of 84 items in several languages, refuting the notion
that homosexuality is unknown in Black Africa. For the
older literature, see Ferdinand Karsch-Haack, **Das gleichgeschlechtliche Leben der Naturvölker** (Munich: Ernst
Reinhardt, 1911), pp. 116-80 (male homosexuality) and
471-84 (lesbianism), as well as the relevant notes.

1354. EVANS-PRITCHARD, EDWARD EVAN. "Sexual Inversion
        among the Azande," **American Anthropologist**, 72
        (1970), 1428-34.
The study of Sudanese groups was virtually the life work
of the influential British social anthropologist. Here he
presents data and observations omitted from his better
known books.

1355. FALK, KURT. "Gleichgeschlechtliches Leben bei
        einigen Negerstämmen Angolas," **Archiv für Anthro-
        pologie**, N.S. 20 (1920), 42-45.
Homosexual behavior among the Wawike, Ovivangella, and
Ngine (Angola), as reported by a long-time resident.

1356. FALK, KURT. "Homosexualität bei den Eingeborenen
       in Südwest-Afrika," **Archiv für Menschenkunde** 1
       (1925-26), 202-14.
Account of homosexuality among the indigenous peoples of
Namibia (Southwest Africa).

1357. FAUPEL, J. F. **African Holocaust: The Story of the
       Uganda Martyrs.** New York: P. J. Kennedy, 1962.
       242 pp.
King Mwanga's 1886 persecution of the Christian pages was
largely motivated by their rejection of his homosexual
advances (pp. 9-10, 68, 82-83).

1358. GAY, JUDITH. "'Mummies and Babies' and Friends and
       Lovers in Lesotho," **JH**, 11:3-4 (1985), 97-106.
Examines a pattern of institutionalized friendship among
adolescent girls and young women in a southern African
society, where a large proportion of the men are away
performing migrant labor.

1359. HABERLANDT, M. "Conträre Sexualerscheinungen bei
       der Negerbevölkerung Sansibars," **Verhandlungen der
       Berliner Anthropologischen Gesellschaft,** 31 (1899),
       668ff.
Sexual inversion among the Negro people of the island of
Zanzibar.

1360. HALLPIKE, C. R. **The Konso of Ethiopia: A Study of
       the Values of a Cushite People.** Oxford: Oxford
       University Press, 1972. 342 pp.
In this ethnography see pp. 13-37, 150-51, 279.

1361. HAMMER, WILHELM. "Liebesleben und -Leiden in
       West-Mittelafrika," **Geschlecht und Gesellschaft,**
       4 (1909), 193-201.
Homosexuality among the Kru of Liberia and other groups.

1362. HANRY, PIERRE. **Erotisme africain: le comportement
       sexuel des adolescents guinéens.** Paris: Payot,
       1970. 201 pp.
Contains information on the incidence of homosexual behavior among high school students in Guinea (West Africa).

1363. HERSKOVITS, MELVILLE JEAN. **Dahomey: An Ancient
       West African Kingdom.** Evanston: Northwestern
       University Press, 1967. 2 vols.
In this classic ethnography (first edition 1938), see vol.
1, pp. 239-42, 288-89. See also his "A Note on 'Woman
Marriage' in Dahomey, **Africa,** 10 (1937), 335-41.

1364. JUNOD, HENRI ALEXANDRE. **The Life of a South
       African Tribe.** Neuchatel: Attinger Freres, 1912.
       2 vols.
For "unnatural vice in the Johannesburg compounds," see
vol. 1, pp. 492-95.

1365. KRIGE, M. J. "Woman-marriage with special refer-
      ence to the Lovedu," **Africa**, 44 (1974), 11-36.
Suggests, not altogether convincingly, that the marriages
are without a sexual component.

1366. LA FONTAINE, JEAN SYBIL. **The Gisu of Uganda.** Lon-
      don: International Africa Institute, 1959. 68 pp.
In this ethnography see pp. 34, 60-61.

1367. LASNET, ALEXANDRE. "Notes d'ethnologie et de méde-
      cine sur les Sakalaves du Nord-Ouest," **Annales
      d'hygiène et de médecine coloniale**, 2 (October-De-
      cember 1899), 471-97.
Report on pederasty and berdaches among a Madagascar
group.

1368. LAUBSCHER, BAREND J. F. **Sex, Custom and Psycho-
      pathology: A Study of South African Pagan Natives.**
      New York: Humanities Press, 1952. 347 pp.
See pp. 23, 25, 31, 257-59, 283-84.

1369. LAURENT, EMILE. "Les Ahimbavy de Madagascar,"
      Archives d'Anthropologie Criminelle, 26 (1911),
      241-48.
Describes a highly feminized Hova group, claiming that
they rarely engage in homosexual acts.

1370. MARTIN, MAURICE. **Au coeur de l'Afrique équatoriale
      (journal d'un officier).** Lille: Lefebure-Ducrocq,
      1912. 215 pp.
In this account by a French officer of service in central
Africa, see pp. 139-60, 164, 187-88.

1371. MERRIAM, ALAN P. "Aspects of Sexual Behavior among
      the Bala (Basongye)," in: D. Marshall and R. Suggs
      (eds.), **Human Sexual Behavior.** New York: Basic
      Books, 1971, 71-102.
Discusses the **kitesha**, a gender-crossing role among the
Bala people in Kasai Oriental Province, Democratic Re-
public of the Congo. See also his: **An African World: The
Basongye Village of Lupupa Ngye.** (Bloomington: Indiana
University Press, 1974; 347 pp.), pp. 319-21.

1372. MORRIS, DONALD R. **The Washing of the Spears: A
      History of the Rise of the Zulu Nation under Shaka
      and Its Fall in the Zulu War of 1879.** New York:
      Simon and Shuster, 1965. 655 pp.
In this massive narrative see pp. 35-36, 46, 51-52, 54,
66, 107-08, 117, 279-81, 287-88, 587. See also Brian
Roberts, **The Zulu Kings** (New York, 1975), pp. 86-87.

1373. NADEL, S. F. "Two Nuba Religions: An Essay in
      Comparison," **American Anthropologist**, 57 (1955),
      661-79.
While among the Heiban male homosexuals are regarded as
abnormal, among the Otoro they are "allocated a special

role, allowed to dress as females and to live in most
respects a woman's life" (p. 677).

1374. OBOLER, R. S. "Is the Female Husband a Man?
       Woman/Woman Marriage among the Nandi of Kenya,"
       Ethnology, 19 (1980), 69-88.
The erotic dimensions of such union are a matter of controversy.

1375. PARIN, PAUL, FRITZ MORGENTALER, AND GOLDY PARIN-
       MATTHEY. **Fear Thy Neighbor as Thyself: Psycho-
       alysis and Society among the Anyi of West Africa.**
       Chicago: University of Chicago Press, 1980. 408
       pp.
This somewhat opaque text indicates pederastic preferences
for some Anyi (pp. 204-10).

1376. RACHEWILTZ, BORIS DE. **Black Eros: Sexual Customs
       of Africa from Prehistory to the Present Day.**
       Translated by Peter Whigham. New York: L. Stuart,
       1968. 329 pp.
In this popular account by an Italian Egyptologist, see
pp. 191, 280, 282.

1377. ROUX, J. "Note sur un cas d'inversion sexuelle
       chez une Comorienne," **Bulletin de la Société
       d'Anthropologie,** 6 (1905), 218-19.
Lesbian case in the Comoro Islands (near Madagascar).

1378. SELIGMAN, CHARLES GABRIEL, AND BRENDA Z. SELIGMAN.
       Pagan Tribes of the Nilotic Sudan. London: Rout-
       ledge, 1932. 565 pp.
In this major ethnological work on the peoples of the
upper Nile, see pp. 506-07, 515.

1379. SIGNORINI, ITALO. "Agonwole agyale: il matrimonio
       tra individui dello stesso sesso negli Nzema de
       Ghana sud-occidentale," **Rassegna Italiana di
       Sociologia,** 12 (1971), 529-45.
While informants deny that there is an overt sexual element these marriages between older and younger same-sex
persons, sexual objectification is certainly present.

1380. TEGNAEUS, HARRY. **Blood-brothers: An Ethno-socio-
       logical Study of the Institution with Special
       Reference to Africa.** New York: Philosophical
       Library, 1952. 181 pp.
Includes also comparative material and perspective for
other areas.

1381. TESSMANN, GUENTHER. "Die Homosexualität bei den
       Negern Kameruns," **JfsZ,** 21 (1921), 121-38.
Report from the former German colony of Cameroun.

1382. WEEKS, JOHN H. "Anthropological Notes on the
       Bangala of the Upper Congo River," **Journal of the**

Anthropological Institute of Great Britain and
Ireland, 39 (1909), 97-136, 416-59 (esp. pp.
448-49).
Solitary and mutual masturbation, as well as sodomy, are
"very common."

1383. WILSON, MONICA. **Good Company: A Study of the
Nayakusu Age-Villages.** London: Oxford University
Press, 1951. 278 pp.
Homosexuality among adolescent males is accepted practice
(pp. 87-88, 196-97).

C. PACIFIC SOCIETIES

For Europeans of the 18th century, the South Seas loomed
as a kind of hedonistic dreamland in which sexual pleasures (heterosexual) were freely available. Such dreams
of a sensual utopia still color our view of Hawaii and
Tahiti. Only in the 20th century, however, did anthropologists begin to investigate the homosexual aspects of
Pacific cultures. It was found that the **mahu** phenomena of
relatively advanced Polynesia were different from the
ritual initiatory homosexuality of Melanesia, and that
the Stone Age aborigines of Australia formed a third
sphere. Recently, Melanesian New Guinea has emerged as an
area of particular richness for evidence of homosexuality;
see the thorough bibliographical review in G. H. Herdt
(1400).

1384. BAAL, JAN VAN. **Dema: Description and Analysis of
Merindanim Culture (New Guinea).** The Hague: Martinus Nijhoff, 1966. 988 pp.
In this comprehensive ethnology of a Melanesian group, the
Dutch scholar presents adolescent boys "subjected to homosexual intercourse" as part of an initiation ritual (pp.
479-80). See also his: "The Dialectics of Sex in Merindanim Culture," in Gilbert H. Herdt (ed.), **Ritualized Homosexuality in Melanesia.** (Berkeley: University of California Press, 1984), pp. 167-210.

1385. BERNDT, RONALD M., and CATHERINE H. BERNDT. **Sexual
Behavior in Western Arnhem Land.** New York: Viking
Fund, 1951. 247 pp. (Publications, 16)
In this monograph on Australian aborigine behavior, "Sexual Abnormality" (pp. 66-68) mentions mutual masturbation
and homosexual experiments among single boys who sleep in
a collective camp.

1386. BLEIBTREU-EHRENBURG, GISELA. **Mannbarkeitsriten:
zur institutionellen Päderastie bei Papuas und
Melanesiern.** Berlin: Ullstein, 1980. 175 pp.
Reviews the ethnological literature on homosexual initia-

tion rites in New Guinea and other parts of the world
where analogous customs occur. See also G. H. Herdt
(ed.), below.

1387. BOUGE, J. L. "Un aspect du rôle rituel du "mahu"
       dans l'ancien Tahiti," **Journal de la Société des
       Océanistes**, 11 (1955), 147-49.
Ritual functions of the **mahu** in pre-acculturation Tahiti.

1388. COOK, JAMES. **The Journals of Captain James Cook on
       His Voyages of Discovery.** Edited by J. C. Beagle-
       hole. Cambridge: Cambridge University Press,
       1955-68. 4 vols.
For Hawaii in 1779, see vol. 3, part 1, pp. 509, 596, 624;
part 2, pp. 1171-72, 1184.

1389. CREED, GERALD W. "Sexual Subordination: Institu-
       tionalized Homosexuality and Social Control in
       Melanesia," **Ethnology**, 23 (1984), 157-76.
"Ritualized institutionalized homosexuality in New Guinea
[is] a mechanism of social control that operates to
perpetuate a system of inequality based on sex and age."

1390. DANIELSSON, BENGT, et al. "Polynesia's Third Sex:
       The Gay Life Starts in the Kitchen," **Pacific
       Islands Monthly** (August 1978), 10-13.
On the **mahu** (French polynesia), **fafalieti** (Tonga), and
fa'a fafine (Samoas). See also the issues of October
1978, pp.8-9, and February 1983, pp. 11-12.

1391. DAVENPORT, WILLIAM. "Sexual Patterns and Their
       Regulation in a Society of the Southwest Pacific,"
       in: Frank A. Beach (ed.), **Sex and Behavior.** New
       York: Wiley, 1965, 164-207.
In an unnamed Melanesian group (in the Santa Cruz Islands,
east of New Guinea), male homosexuality is engaged in extensively by nearly every male. There are two types: that
between young single males of similar age and that between
older men and boys.

1392. DEACON, A. B. **Malekula: A Vanishing People in the
       New Hebrides.** London: Routledge, 1934.
See pp. 260-62 and 267 for ritualized homosexuality among
the Big Nambas, a Melanesian group.

1393. DU TOIT, BRIAN M. **Akuna: A New Guinea Village
       Community.** Rotterdam: Balkema, 1975. 386 pp.
Homosexual play among boys and girls continues until the
participants are sixteen or seventeen, dispite disapproval
voiced by adults (pp. 219-20). Enforced abstinence during
pregnancy may result in homosexuality in both sexes (p.
269).

1394. GLUCKMAN, LAURIE K. "Transcultural Considerations
       of Homosexuality with Special Reference to the New
       Zealand Maori," **Australian and New Zealand Journal**

of **Psychiatry,** 8 (1974), 121-25.
Claims that homosexuality in both sexes was unknown in New
Zealand before European contact--an ex-silentio argument
based on mere lack of indigenous terms in missionary dictionaries and translations of the Bible. See the critique
by Manuel Arboleda G. and Stephen O. Murray, "The Dangers
of Lexical Inference with Special Reference to Maori Homosexuality," **JH,** 12 (1986), 129-34. See also Gluckman,
"Lesbianism in the Maori: A Series of Three Interconnected
Clinical Studies," **Australian and New Zealand Journal of
Psychiatry,** 1 (1967), 98-103.

1395. GODELIER, MAURICE. "Le sexe comme fondement ultime
       de l'ordre social et cosmique chez les Baruya de
       Nouvelle-Guinée," in A. Verdiglione, **Sexualité et
       pouvoir.** Paris: Payot, 1976, pp. 268-306.
Provides a symbolic contextualization of homoerotic activities in a Buruya New Guinea tribe.

1396. GRAY, J. PATRICK. "Growing Yams and Men: An Aspect
       of Kiman Male Ritualized Behavior," **JH,** 11:3-4
       (1985), 55-68.
Explores the meaning of ritualized homosexual behavior
involving the transfer of sperm from older males in a
society of Kokpom Island near Irian Jaya (eastern New
Guinea), Indonesia.

1397. HAGE, PER. "On Male Initiation and Dual Organiza-
       tion in New Guinea," **Man,** 16 (1981), 268-75.
Contends that ritual homosexuality in New Guinea stems
from an underlying structure of "sexual symmetry," which
is also reflected in dual organizations, initiation rites,
and a "big man complex." See also Ann S. Meigs, "Male
Pregnancy and the Reduction of Sexual Opposition in a New
Guinea Highlands Society," **Ethnology,** 15 (1976), 393-407;
and Harriet Whitehead, "The Varieties of Fertility Cultism
in New Guinea," **American Ethnologist,** 13 (1986), 80-99.

1398. HARDMAN, EDWARD T. "Notes on Some Habits and
       Customs of the Natives of the Kimberley District,
       Western Australia," **Proceedings of the Royal Irish
       Academy,** 17 (1888), 70-75.
The boy at five years of age is usually given as boy-wife
to one of the young men. There is no doubt that the two
have sexual connection, but the natives "repudiate with
horror and disgust the idea of Sodomy."

1399. HERDT, GILBERT. **Guardians of the Flutes: Idioms of
       Masculinity.** New York: McGraw-Hill, 1981. 382 pp.
In-depth documentation and analysis of a secret male cult
practicing ritualized fellatio in a remote tribe in the
New Guinea highlands (the "Sambia"). While this study is
of great value as ethnology, some have questioned the
introjection of psychoanalytic concepts based in part on
the ideas of Robert Stoller. See also his: "Fetish and
Fantasy in Sambia Initiation," in: Herdt (ed.), **Rituals of**

Manhood (Berkeley: University of California Press, 1982),
pp. 44-98; and "Semen Depletion and the Sense of Male-
ness," **Ethnopsychiatrica**, 3 (1980), 79-116.

1400. HERDT, GILBERT H. (ed.), **Ritualized Homosexuality
      in Melanesia.** Berkeley: University of California
      Press, 1984. 409 pp.
This major work is a collective contribution to our knowledge of tribal homosexual behavior. The first essay, by
Herdt (pp. 1-82), is a comprehensive review of the scholarly literature from 1862 to 1983 that must be consulted
by anyone concerned with the subject. The other eight
contributors both summarize and reconsider their own earlier work and evaluate the contributions of others. It
has been remarked that a number of the contributors reflect the concerns of the "culture and personality"
approach in anthropology, with its psychoanalytic
affinities. Also, as the title indicates, the book
concerns only the major phenomenon of ritual homosexuality
in Melanesia, without considering non-ritual or secular
same-sex behavior.

1401. HOGBIN, HERBERT IAN. "Puberty to Marriage: A Study
      of the Sexual Life of the Natives of Wogeo [New
      Guinea]," **Oceania,** 16 (1946), pp. 185-209.
Discusses homosexual behavior among migrant workers (pp.
205-06). See also his: **Transformation Scene: The Changing
Culture of a New Guinea Village** (London: Routledge and
Kegan Paul, 1951; 326 pp.), pp. 190-93, 269.

1402. KABERRY, PHYLLIS M. **Aboriginal Woman, Sacred and
      Profane.** London: George Routledge and Sons, 1939.
      294 pp.
Finds acceptance of close relationships between women
in Australian aborigines.

1403. KELLY, RAYMOND. **Etoro Social Structure.** Ann
      Arbor: University of Michigan Press, 1980.
Provides a contrast of three neighboring tribes' use of
oral, anal, and masturbatory homosexuality in initiation
rites with the ethnography of the Etoro (p. 80).

1404. LAYARD, JOHN. "Homo-eroticism in a Primitive
      Society as a Function of the Self," **Journal of
      Analytical Psychology,** 4 (1959), 101-15.
Argues that in Australia and Oceania homosexual behavior
functions as an incest substitute.

1405. LEVY, ROBERT ISAAC. **Tahitians: Mind and Experience
      in the Society Islands.** Chicago: University of
      Chicago Press, 1973. 547 pp.
Offers information on village **mahu** transvestites and theri
role, also noting an incipient "gay" role (**raerae**). See
pp. 38, 72-73, 116, 127, 130-41, 235-36, 239, 420, 471-73,
486. See also his: "The Community Function of Tahitian
Male Transvestites: A Hypothesis," **Anthropological Quar-**

terly, 44 (1971), 12-21.

1406. MACFARLANE, D. F. "Transsexual Prostitution in New
       Zealand: Predominance of Persons of Maori Extrac-
       tion," **Archives of Sexual Behavior,** 13 (1984),
       301-09.
Based on 27 subjects, concludes that 90% of the transsexual prostitute population of Wellington is Maori (where
they constitute only 9% of the total population).

1407. MATHEWS, R. H. "Native Tribes of Western Austra-
       lia," **Proceedings of the American Philosophical
       Society,** 39 (1900), 123-25.
After undergoing circumcision and subincision, the man is
assigned a boy who has not undergone the operations and
is a brother of the woman whom the man is entitled to
claim as his wife. The boy is used for pederastic purposes. See also his: "Phallic Rites and Initiation
Ceremonies of the South Australian Aborigines," ibid.,
pp. 622-38; and "The Bora," **Journal of the Royal Anthropological Institute,** 25 (1896), 318-39.

1408. MEAD, MARGARET. **Growing Up in New Guinea.** New
       York: William Morrow, 1930. 215 pp.
See pp. 193-99 for homosexual behavior among migrant
workers.

1409. MÉTRAUX, ALFRED. **Ethnology of Easter Island.**
       Honolulu: Bishop Museum, 1940. 432 pp.
Reports that "abnormal sexual relations between women
[were] tolerated and accepted" (p. 108).

1410. OLIVER, DOUGLAS L. **A Solomon Island Society.** Cam-
       bridge, MA: Harvard University Press, 1955. 535
       pp.
Claims that sodomy was introduced by outside natives, who
learned the practice from white sailors (pp. 498-99

1411. PURCELL, BRABAZON H. "Rites and Customs of Austra-
       lian Aborigines," **Verhandlungen der Berliner
       Gesellschaft für Anthropologie, Ethnologie, und
       Urgeschichte,** 25 (1893), 286-89.
Reports pedophilia in the Kimberley District: sexual
contact between "every useless member of the tribe" and
a boy about 5-7 years old (p. 287), as well as a ceremony
in which the youth is made to drink semen.

1412. RAVENSCROFT, A. G. B. "Some Habits and Customs of
       the Chingalee Tribe, Northern Territory, S. A.,"
       **Transactions of the Royal Society of South Austra-
       lia,** 15 (1892), 21-22.
Old men are often accompanied by one or two boys whom they
jealously guard and with whom they "indulge in the vice."

1413. ROHEIM, GÉZA. "Psychoanalysis of Primitive Types,"
       International Journal of Psycho-analysis, 13

(1932), 1-224.
Roheim, a Freudian specializing in Australian ethnology,
often referred to homosexual behavior in his publications. Here he notes that the "boy wife" precedes his
sister among the Nambutji of Australia and is later given
a sister of the older man. See also his: **Children of the
Desert: The Western Tribes of Central Australia.** Ed. by
Werner Muensterberger (New York: Basic Books, 1974; 262
pp.), pp.183, 243-44, 247-48, 251.

1414. SCHIEFFELIN, EDWARD L. **The Sorrow of the Lonely
       and the Burning of the Dancers.** New York: St. Mar-
       tin's Press, 1976. 243 pp.
Includes an ethnological reconstruction of anal homosexual
initiation rites among the Kaluli of New Guinea.

1415. SPENCER, BALDWIN, and F. J. GILLEN. **The Arunta.**
       London: Macmillan, 1927. 2 vols.
In a primitive Australian desert culture, boys were used
to fulfil a family's obligation to provide a wife.

1416. SUGGS, ROBERT C. **Marquesan Sexual Behavior.** New
       York: Harcourt Brace, 1966. 251 pp.
This study of the behavior of an Austronesian group re-
vises an earlier interpretation put forward by Ralph
Linton.

1417. THOMPSON, DENISE. **Flaws in the Social Fabric:
       Homosexuals and Society in Sydney.** Sydney: Allen
       and Unwin (Australia), 1985. 220 pp.
Sociological account of the social management of homosexuality in the Australian city since the 19th century.

1418. WILLIAMS, F. E. **Papuans of the Trans-Fly.** Oxford:
       Clarendon Press, 1936. 450 pp.
Although this study was preceded by other more concise
accounts, it was the first to draw widespread attention
to the importance of homosexual initiation in New Guinea.
See pp. 182, 199, 200-04.

                      SUBARCTIC CULTURES

Towards the end of the 19th century, travelers began to
report that the shamanistic religious practices of some
tribes, especially in Siberia, involved ritual transvestism and homosexuality. This phenomenon is related
typologically--and possibly historically--to the Amerindian berdache (see IV.E).

1419. BILLINGS, JOSEPH. **An Account of a Geographical and
       Astronomical Expedition to the Northern Parts of
       Russia ... in the Year 1785 ... to 1794.** London:

Cadell and Davies, 1802. 332, 58 pp.
Prepared for publication by Martin Sauer. See pp. 160,
175 on Siberian tribes and the Eskimo.

1420. BLEIBTREU-EHRENBERG, GISELA. "Homosexualität und
       Transvestition in Schamanismus," **Anthropos**, 65
       (1970), 189-228.
Overview of research on Eurasian shamanism in relation
to homosexuality and cross-dressing; brief English
summary. See now her book **Der Weibmann: Kultischer Geschlechtswandel im Schamanismus** (Frankfurt am Main:
Fischer, 1984; 200 pp.).

1421. BOGORAS, WALDEMAR (VLADIMIR BOGORAZ). **The Chuk-
       chee.** New York: American Museum of Natural His-
       tory, 1904-09. 3 parts (733 pp.) (Jessup Exped-
       ition Report, 7)
Landmark account of Siberian tribal people, including
discussion of homosexual shamanism (pp. 37, 44, 98-99,
415-16, 448-57). See also Bogoras' articles in **American
Anthropologist**, 3 (1901), 80-108; and 4 (1902), 577-683.

1422. CZAPLICKA, MARIE ANTOINETTE. **Aboriginal Siberia: A
       Study in Social Anthropology.** Oxford: Clarendon
       Press, 1914. 374 pp.
A pioneering anthropological investigation which discusses
the link between homosexuality and transvestism in
shamanism (pp. 243-53).

1423. OHLMARKS, ÅKE. **Studien zum Problem des Schamanis-
       mus.** Lund: C. W. K. Gleerup, 1939. 396 pp.
On shamanism as a phenomenon of sub-Arctic culture. Pp.
293-301 deal with change of sex and ritual transvestism as
traits of the shaman. The bibliography includes both
Scandinavian and Russian sources.

E. NORTH AMERICAN INDIANS

In what is now the United States, homosexual behavior
attracted the attention of Europeans in the 18th century,
when the distinctiveness of the berdache (originally
spelled bardache, a French word derived from Persian)
phenomenon was noted. Affinities to the berdache--essen-
tially a cross-dressing priest-like figure who may or may
not engage in homosexual behavior--have been found outside
North America, but the nature of the phenomenon is still
being debated. Still little known is non-berdache homosexuality among American Indians, as well as acculturation types resulting from the reception of the gay lifestyle.

1424. ALLEN, PAULA GUNN. "Lesbians in American Indian

Cultures," **Conditions**, 7 (1981), 67-87.
Subjective approach. A somewhat shortened version
appears in: T. Darty and S. Potter (eds.), **Women-identified Women** (Palo Alto, CA: Mayfield, 1984), pp. 83-96.

1425. ANGELINO, HARRY, and CHARLES SHEDD. "A Note on
      Berdache," **American Anthropologist**, 57 (1955),
      121-25.
Discusses some conceptual problems in the research on the
subject, including the term itself. For the latter, see
now Claude Courouve, "The Word 'Berdache,'" **Gay Books
Bulletin**, no. 8 (1982), 18-19.

1426. BLACKWOOD, EVELYN. "Sexuality and Gender in
      Certain Native American Tribes: The Case of
      Cross-gender Females," **Signs**, 10:4 (Autumn 1984),
      27-42.
From evidence from thirty-three tribes concludes that
their position was not symmetrical with that of the male
berdache.

1427. BROCH, HARALD B. "A Note on Berdache among the
      Hare Indians of Northwestern Canada," **Western
      Canadian Journal of Anthropology**, 7 (1977), 95-101.
Shows berdache adaptations to acculturation, including
acquisition of new trades.

1428. CALLENDER, CHARLES, and LEE M. KOCHEMS. "The North
      American Berdache," **Current Anthropology**, 24:4
      (August-October 1983), 443-70.
Thorough review and analysis of the literature on the
berdache phenomenon in 113 tribal groups, with comments
by other scholars and extensive bibliography. See also
the earlier bibliography compiled by Stephen Wayne Foster,
included in J. Katz (ed.), **Gay American History** (New
York: Crowell, 1976), pp. 619-27.

1429. CATLIN, GEORGE. **Letters and Notes on the Manners,
      Customs and Conditions of the North American
      Indians, Written During Eight Years' Travel
      (1832-1839)**. New York: Dover, 1973. 2 vols.
Reprint of the London 1844 edition, with numerous additional reproductions of the paintings. See vol. 1, pp.
96, 111-14; and (for the berdache dance), vol. 2, pp. 214-
15.

1430. CROWE, K. J. **A History of the Original Peoples of
      Northern Canada**. Montreal: McGill University
      Press, 1974. 226 pp.
See pp. 72-90 for "strong women" among Athapascan tribes.

1431. DEVEREUX, GEORGE. "Institutionalized Homosexuality
      of the Mojave Indians," **Human Biology**, 9 (1937),
      498-527.
Identifies two types: the **alyha** (men who dress as women
and assume the female role) and **hwame** (women who take male

roles). Describes the ceremonies of initiation, physiological and psychological patterns, courtship, and social
aspects of their role. An often-cited article by a
Freudian anthropologist.

1432. FORGEY, DONALD G. "The Institution of the Berdache
       among the North American Plains Indians," **Journal
       of Sex Research,** 11 (1975), 1-15.
Attempts a synthetic treatment.

1433. FRANKLIN, JOHN, SIR. **Narrative of a Second
       Expedition to the Shores of the Polar Sea, in the
       Years 1825, 1826, and 1827.** London: J. Murray,
       1828. 320 & clvii pp.
See pp. 305-06 for a rare early reference to lesbianism
among Amerinds.

1434. GREENBERG, DAVID F. "Why Was the Berdache Ridi-
       culed?" **JH,** 12:3-4 (1985), 179-189.
Finds that since apparent ridicule of berdaches occurs
during traditional joking activity, it need not be interpreted as evidence that the Indians held negative views of
homosexuality.

1435. HAMMOND, WILLIAM A. "The Disease of the Scythians
       (morbus feminarum) and Certain Analogous Con-
       ditions," **American Journal of Neurology and
       Psychiatry,** 1:3 (1882), 339-55.
An early attempt to understand the berdache, in part
through Herodotus. See also Henry Hay, "The Hammond
Report," **ONE Institute Quarterly,** 6 (1963), 1-21, 65-67.

1436. HENNEPIN, LOUIS. **Nouvelle découverte d'un très
       grand pays situé dans l'Amérique entre le Nouveau
       Mexique et la Mer Glaciale.** Utrecht: G. Broedelet,
       1697. 506 pp.
See Chapter 33 (p. 217 ff.) on the "unnatural sins" of the
Illinois Indians.

1437. HILL, WILLARD WILLIAMS. "The Status of the Her-
       maphrodite and Transvestite in Navaho Culture,"
       American Anthropologist, 37 (1935), 273-79.
Illustrates the fading of the formerly honorific status
of the berdache in this culture. See also his "Notes on
the Pima Berdache," ibid., 40 (1938), 338-40 (they lead
a covert existence).

1438. HOLDER, A. B. "The Bote: Description of a Peculiar
       Perversion Found among North American Indians," **New
       York Medical Journal,** 1 (1889), 623-25.
"The word bo-te' ... is used by the Absaroke Indians of
Montana, and literally means 'not man, not women.'" See
also William J. Robinson, "The Bote," **Journal of Sexology
and Psychoanalysis,** 1 (1923), 544-46.

1439. JACOBS, SUE ELLEN. "Berdache: A Brief Review of

the Literature," **Colorado Anthropologist**, 1 (1968),
25–40.
Seeks to pull together the scattered literature on the
subject.

1440. KROEBER, ALFRED. **Handbook of the Indians of
       California.** Washington, DC: Government Printing
       Office, 1925. 995 pp. (Bureau of Ethnology,
       Smithsonian Institution, Bulletin 78)
A classic work of synthesis in Anthropology; see pp. 46,
180, 497, 500, 647, 748, 803. See also his article "Psychosis or Social Sanction," **Character and Personality**, 8
(1940), 204–15, esp. pp. 209–10.

1441. LABARRE, WESTON. **The Ghost Dance: Origins of
       Religion.** New York: Dell, 1972. 677 pp.
This ambitious and controversial work contains a good
deal on the berdache institution.

1442. LAFITAU, JOSEPH FRANÇOIS. **Customs of the North
       American Indians Compared with the Customs of
       Primitive Times.** Edited and translated by William
       N. Fenton and Elizabeth L. Moore. Toronto: Champlain Society, 1974. 2 vols.
Translation of **Moeurs des sauvages amériquains** (Paris:
1724). The French Jesuit was one of the first to address
the berdache question on a comparative basis.

1443. LANDES, RUTH. **The Mystic Lake Sioux: Sociology of
       the Mdewakantonwan Santee.** Madison: Wisconsin
       University Press, 1968. 224 pp.
For Santee youths forced to wear dresses at social dances,
see pp. 206–07; see also pp. 29, 31–32, 57, 66, 112–13,
127–28, 153, 193.

1444. LANDES, RUTH. **Ojibwa Sociology.** New York: Columbia University Press, 1937. 144 pp.
A basic source for the female berdache.

1445. LANTIS, MARGARET. "The Aleut Social System, 1750
       to 1810." In M. Lantis (ed.), **Ethnohistory in
       Southwestern Alaska and the Southern Yukon.** Lexington: University of Kentucky Press, 1970,
       pp. 139–301.
See pp. 205–14 for open acceptance of transvestites who
did women's work.

1446. LURIE, NANCY O. "Winnebago Berdache," **American
       Anthropologist**, 55 (1953), 708–12.
"Most informants felt that the berdache was at one time
a highly honored and respected person, but that the
Winnebago had become ashamed of the custom because white
people thought that it was amusing or evil."

1447. MCMURTRIE, DOUGLAS C. "A Legend of Lesbian Love
       among the North American Indians," **Urologic and**

Cutaneous Review (April 1914), 192-93.
A rare source for this period.

1448. MILLER, JAY. "People, Berdaches, and Left-handed
     Bears: Human Variations in Native America," **Journal
     of Anthropological Research**, 38 (1982), 274-87.
Attempts a structuralist approach, regarded by some as
eccentric.

1449. OSGOOD, CORNELIUS. **Ingalik Social Culture.** New
     Haven: Yale University Press, 1958. (Publications
     in Anthropology, 53). 289 pp.
See pp. 222-23 for discussion of homosexual activity.

1450. SIGNORINI, ITALO. "Transvestism and Institution-
     alized Homosexuality in North America." In: **Atti
     del XL Congresso Internazionale degli America-
     nisti.** Genoa: Tilgher, 1972, vol. 2, 153-63.
Discussing a number of neglected European sources,
Signorini stresses the uniting of male and female, serving
to attain "totality" and acquire power. The sexual ambiguity of the berdache commanded respect because it represented access to socially needed qualities.

1451. STEWART, OMER C. "Homosexuality among the American
     Indians and Other Native Peoples of the World,"
     Mattachine Review, 6 (January 1960), 9-15, and
     (February 1960), 13-19.
Broad survey of the berdache and seemingly kindred
phenomena on other continents.

1452. STOLLER, ROBERT J. "Two Feminized Male American
     Indians," **Archives of Sexual Behavior**, 5 (1976),
     529-38.
Two young adult American Indians who wished to change
sex.

1453. WHITEHEAD, HARRIET. "The Bow and the Burden
     Strap," in: Sherry S. Ortner and Harriet Whitehead
     (eds.), **Sexual Meaning: The Cultural Construction
     of Gender.** New York: Cambridge University Press,
     1981, pp. 80-115.
Emphasizing occupations and prestige, regards the chief
defining feature of the berdache role as "doing women's
work."

1454. WILLIAMS, WALTER L. **The Spirit and the Flesh: Sex-
     ual Diversity in American Indian Culture.** Boston:-
     Beacon, 1986. 312 pp.
A comprehensive work, synthesizing the existing literature
with the author's fieldwork. Shows the positive role of
the berdache in tribal cultures and the survival of the
institution into today's world. See also his: "Persistence and Change in the Berdache Tradition among Contemporary Lakota Indians," **JH**, 11:3-4 (1985), 191-200.

F. MESO-AMERICAN AND SOUTH AMERICAN INDIANS

The Spanish conquistador writers produced a certain
quantity of hostile information on homosexual practices,
which were vigorously suppressed. In addition to European
written records, there is also a small quantity of surviving artistic evidence from pre-Columbian societies.
Indigenous homosexuality survived in areas untouched by
European conquest or was transformed into new forms
adapted to the mestizo culture of the cities (see "Latin
America," III.O). Only recently have a few anthropologists begun to collect data on contemporary homosexual
practices among indigenous peoples of the remote areas of
South America.

1455.   ANGHIERA, PIETRO MARTIRE D'. **The Decades of the
        New World or West India.** Translated by Richard
        Eden. London: William Powell, 1555.
For a description of Balboa's vicious destruction of some
forty effeminate Indians, members of a male harem of the
king of Quarequa, by sicking dogs on them, see fol. 89b-
90. Anghiera's **De rebus oceanicis et orbe novo decades
tres** (Basel, 1533) was one of the first histories of the
discovery of America.

1456.   ARBOLEDA G., MANUEL. "Representaciones artisticos
        de actividades homoéroticos en la cerámica Moche,"
        Boletín de Lima, 16 (1981), 98-107.
Archaeological considerations on pottery depicting homo-
sexual acts from Moche, a pre-Inca kingdom of northern
Peru.

1457.   BANCROFT, HUBERT HOWE. **The Works.** San Francis-
        co: Bancroft, 1883-90. 39 vols.
Vols. 1-5 are a reprint of **The Native Races of the Pacific States of North America** (1875-76), which includes a
discussion of Mexico and Central America. See vol. 1,
pp. 58, 81-82, 92, 415, 515, 585-86, 773-74; vol. 2,
pp. 467-69, 664, 677-78; vol. 5, p. 198.

1458.   BEALS, CARLETON. "Latin America, Sex Life in,"
        in: Albert Ellis and Albert Abarbanel (eds.), **The
        Encyclopedia of Sexual Behavior.** New York: Haw-
        thorn, 1967, pp. 599-613.
In this general survey, see esp. p. 605.

1459.   BEALS, RALPH L. "The Contemporary Culture of the
        Cahita Indians," **Bureau of American Ethnology
        Bulletin,** 142 (1945). 244 pp.
Yaqui and Nayo have reputations for homosexuality, but
themselves insist that only mestizos practice it, except
for one Mayo woman who reported lesbianism as well as
male homosexuality (p. 82). See also Beals: **Cheran: A**

Sierra Tarascan Village (Washington, DC: Government
Printing Office, 1946), p. 177; and The Comparative
Ethnology of Northern Mexico before 1750 (Berkeley: Uni-
versity of California Press, 1932), p. 205.

1460. BLAFFER, SARAH C. The Black Man of Zinacantan.
Austin, University of Texas Press, 1972. 194 pp.
In this ethnographic study of a group in southern Mexico,
see p. 8.

1461. BRICKER, VICTORIA REIFLER. Ritual Humor in
Highland Chiapas. Austin: University of Texas
Press, 1973. 257 pp.
For female impersonators and sexual badinage in southeast-
ern Mexico, see pp. 148-49, 185-87, 212.

1462. CALANCHA, ANTONIO DE LA. Cronica moralizada del
Orden de San Augustin en el Peru, con suceso
egenplares en esta monarquia. Barcelona: 1638.
968 pp.
For the Jesuit's denunciation of sodomy in the New
World, see pp. 571-79.

1463. CASTAÑEDA DE NÁGERA, PEDRO DE. Relation du voyage
de Cibola, entrepris en 1540. Paris: A. Bertrand,
1838. 392 pp.
For sodomy among the Indians of northern Mexico, see pp.
150, 152, 155-56.

1464. CHAGNON, NAPOLEON A. Yanomamo. New York: Holt,
1977. 174 pp.
In this Amazonian tribe "some of the teen-age males
have homosexual affairs with each other" (p. 76).

1465. CHINAS, BEVERLY. "Isthmus Zapotec 'Berdache,'"
ARGOH Newsletter, 7:2 (1980), 1-4.
In a society in which women have a prominent economic
role, ira' muxe, a third sex, is accepted more readily
than lesbian couples.

1466. CIEZA DE LEÓN, PEDRO DE. The Travels of Pedro
Cieza de León, A. D. 1532-50, Contained in the
First Part of his Chronicle of Peru. Translated by
C. R. Markham. London: Hakluyt Society, 1864. 438
pp.
In this first part of his relation, Cieza detects sodomy
in every province, esp. in what is now Ecuador. He
claims, however, that the Incas prohibited it. See
also his: The Incas. Translated by Harriet de Onis.
(Norman: University of Oklahoma Press, 1959; 397 pp.),
pp. 93, 113, 178-81, 293, 313-15.

1467. CLASTRES, PIERRE. Chronique des Indiens Guayaki.
Paris: Plon, 1972. 366 pp.
On the Ache nomads of Paraguay, see pp. 273-308.

1468. CLAVÍGERO, FRANCISCO JAVIER. **Storia antica del Messico**. Cesena: Gregorio Biasini, 1780-81. 4 vols.
In this "potent idealization of Mexican society" (B. Keen), Clavigero combats Cornelis De Pauw's claims that toleration of sodomy weakened the Indians. See vol. 4, pp. 195, 199-200. A somewhat unreliable English version was published in London in 1787; the Spanish original did not appear until 1945.

1469. FERNÁNDEZ DE PIEDRAHITA, LUCAS. **La historia general de las conquistas del Nuevo Reino de Granada**. Bogota: Imprensa de la Editorial ABC, 1942. 4 vols.
In what is now Colombia, among the Laches, the sixth son was brought up as a girl (**cusmo**); see vol. 1, pp. 25-26, 86.

1470. FOSTER, STEPHEN WAYNE. "A Bibliography of Homosexuality among Latin-American Indians," **Cabirion and Gay Books Bulletin**, no. 12 (1985), pp. 17-19.
Lists about 110 items in five languages.

1471. FRIEDERICI, GEORG. **Die Amazonen Amerikas**. Leipzig: Verlag von Simmel & Co., 1910. 25 pp.
The author, a distinguished Americanist of the first half of the century, mentions (pp. 7, 11-13, 19-20) accounts of lesbianism among the native women of Brazil and New Granada as one source of the Amazon legend in the New World.

1472. FRIEDERICI, GEORG. **Der Charakter der Entdeckung und Eroberung Amerikas durch die Europäer: Einleitung zur Geschichte der Besiedlung Amerikas durch die Völker der alten Welt**. Stuttgart: Verlag Friederich Andreas Perthes, 1925. 3 vols.
See vol. 1, pp. 259-63 for the Spanish conquistadors' rationale that the sodomy of the Indians justified their subjection and enslavement.

1473. GARCILASO DE LA VEGA. **The Inca: The Royal Commentaries of the Inca**. Translated by Maria Jolas; notes by Alain Gheerbrandt. New York: Avon, 1964. 447 pp.
The author (1539-1616), a scion of the Inca nobility on his mother's side, wrote this account to record the glorious traditions of his ancestors for a Spanish audience. For this reason, perhaps, one need not take altogether at face value his insistence that the Incas abhorred sodomy (pp. 103, 201, 216, 326-28).

1474. GOSSEN, GARY H. **Chamulas in the World of the Sun: Time and Space in a Maya Oral Tradition**. Cambridge, MA: Harvard University Press, 1974. 382 pp.
For a typical exchange of sexual badinage, see pp. 99-105.

1475. GREGOR, THOMAS. **Anxious Pleasures: The Sexual
       Lives of an Amazonian People.** Chicago: University
       of Chicago Press, 1985. 223 pp.
Although Mehinaku men disdain homosexual contacts, they
sometimes practice them with white men. However, "myths
and rituals suggest that there is a feminine core to the
male personality that is in normal times shouted down."
See pp. 59-61. See also Gregor's earlier ethnography
(which this book complements), **Mehinaku: The Drama of
Daily Life in a Brazilian Indian Village** (Chicago: University of Chicago, 1977; 382 pp.).

1476. GRIFFEN, WILLIAM B. **Notes on Seri Indian Culture,
       Sonora, Mexico.** Gainesville, FL: University of
       Florida Press, 1959. 54 pp. (Latin American
       Monographs, 10)
In former times a man who took a woman's duties and lived
like a member of the opposite sex was thought to be very
intelligent. Inverse behavior on the part of women in-
curs disapproval (p. 33).

1477. GUERRA, FRANCISCO. **The Pre-Columbian Mind: A Study
       into the Aberrant Nature of Sexual Drives, Drugs
       Affecting Behaviour, and the Attitude towards Life
       and Death, with a Survey of Psychotherapy in Pre-
       Columbian America.** London: Seminar Press, 1971.
       335 pp.
Quoting extensively from post-Conquest sources, this
work documents the attitudes of the Spaniards as well as
their (often harshly disapproving) records of sodomy
among the Indians. See esp. pp. 26-27, 34, 45, 222-29.

1478. HELFRICH, KLAUS. "Sexualität und Repression in der
       Kultur der Maya," **Baessler-Archiv,** N.S., 20 (1972),
       139-71.
Includes discusssion of Maya bisexual gods, as well as
a fieldwork report of sexual practices among the Chol
today, who ridicule homosexual behavior among mestizos.

1479. HIDALGO, MARIANA. **La vida amorosa en el México
       antiguo.** Mexico City: Diana, 1979. 118 pp.
In this popular work, see "Homosexualidad y sodomía"
(pp. 69-81).

1480. HUGH-JONES, STEPHEN. **The Palm and the Pleiades:
       Initiation and Cosmology in Northwest Amazonia.**
       Cambridge: Cambridge University Press, 1979. 332
       pp.
Claims that homosexual behavior amounts only to joking
play, which "does not entail sexual satisfaction." See
also: Christine Hugh-Jones, **From the Milk River: Spatial
and Temporal Processes in Northwest Amazonia** (Cambridge:
Cambridge University Press, 1979), pp. 160-61.

1481. **Handbook of the South American Indians.** New
       York: Cooper Square, 1963. 7 vols.

In this standard reference work, see vol. 1, pp. 160,
324; vol. 2, pp. 187, 400, 544, 710, 750, 805; vol. 3,
pp. 304, 337, 366; vol. 4, pp. 363, 379, 453, 467, 478,
486, 531; vol. 5, pp. 588-89, 723, 757.

1482. KAUFMANN-DOIG, FEDERICO. **Sexual Behaviour in
      Ancient Peru.** Lima: Kompaktos, 1979. 181 pp.
General study by an archaeologist of the evidence from
ceramics (see esp. pp. 46-51, 90-91, 140-41). See
also: Paul H. Gebhard, "Sexual Motifs in Prehistoric
Peruvian Ceramics," in: Theodore Bowie et al., **Studies in
Erotic Art** (New York: Basic Books, 1970), pp. 109-69.

1483. KEEN, BENJAMIN. **The Aztec Image in Western
      Thought.** New Brunswick, NJ: Rutgers University
      Press, 1971. 668 pp.
European writers tended to ascribe sodomy stereotypically
to Amerindians, without regard to nuances. A few tribes
seem to have been homophobic. See pp. 61-63, 83, 85,
87, 101, 111, 140, 149, 153, 171-72, 222.

1484. KRACKE, WAUD H. **Force and Persuasion: Leadership
      in an Amazonian Society.** Chicago: University of
      Chicago Press, 1978. 322 pp.
This study of the Kagwahu tribe (Tupi speaking) of the
Amazon River discusses homoerotic dreams; homosexual tales
about others; the fantasy that the passive partner is
magically turned into a woman; irrational jealousy and
sadism as ways of coping with homosexual feelings; the
homoerotic component of male bonding; homosexual attraction to the men dominated by the leader; and a psychoanalytic interpretation of the role of the bisexual in
personality integration and conflict. See pp. 212-13,
221-25, 230-31, 241, 264-65.

1485. LABARRE, WESTON. **The Aymara Indians of the Lake
      Titicaca Plateau.** Menasha, WI: American Anthropo-
      logical Society Memoirs, 1948. (no. 68). 250 pp.
Records the former existence of male and female gender-
crossing homosexuality as attested by an 18th-century
Jesuit dictionary. Provides no ethnographic report of
homosexual behavior today. See pp. 133-35.

1486. LATCHAM, R. E. "Ethnology of the Araucanos,"
      **Journal of the Royal Anthropological Institute of
      Great Britain and Ireland,** 39 (1909), 334-70.
"Pederasty was common among the **machis** (medicine men)
an still is to a great extent, though not so much as
formerly. Those who exercise the office are called
hueye." (p. 353).

1487. LÉVI-STRAUSS, CLAUDE. **Tristes tropiques.** Trans-
      lated by John Weightman and Doreen Weightman. New
      York: Atheneum, 1974. 425 pp.
This anthropological classic by a French scholar mingles
personal experience with observations in Brazil. See pp.

313-34, 356-57. See also his: "The Social Use of Kinship Terms among Brazilian Indians," **American Anthropologist,** 45 (1943), 395-401, esp. p. 400; and "La vie familiale et sociale des Indiens Nambikwara," **Journal de la Société des Américanistes de Paris,** 37 (1948), 75-76.

1488. LÓPEZ DE GOMARA, FRANCISCO. "Hispania victrix: primera y segunda parte de la Historia general de las Indias," **Biblioteca de autores españoles,** 22 (1852), 155-455.
See chapters 46, 47 and 224 on sodomy among the Indians.

1489. LUCENA SALMORAL, MANUEL. "Bardaje en una tribu Guahibo del Tomo," **Revista Colombiana de Antropología,** 14 (1966), 263-66.
Reports interview with a 25-year-old man who dressed and worked as a women, and had been married to his "sister's son." Compare the 1736 report of Juan Rivero on Guahibo polygamy (**Historia de la misiones de los llanos de Casanare y los ríos Orinoco y Meta,** Bogota).

1490. MAGALHÃES DE GANDAVO, PERO DE. **The Histories of Brazil.** Translated by John B. Stetson, Jr. New York: Cortes Society, 1922. 2 vols.
For females who follow all the pursuits of men and have a female companion as wife, see vol. 2, pp. 89-90, 173.

1491. MONTESINOS, FERNANDO. **Memorias antiguas, historiales y políticas del Perú.** Madrid: Ginesta, 1882. 259 pp.
A 17th-century writer reports on Inda sodomy legends; see pp. 54, 85, 88-92, 102-04, 106, 115-16, 199-200.

1492. PARSONS, ELSIE CLEWS. **Mitla, Town of the Souls and Other Zapoteec-Speaking Pueblos of Oaxaca, Mexico.** Chicago: University of Chicago Press, 1936. 590 pp.
See p. 437 (description of an **efeminado**) and p. 506 (one man, a Spaniard, reputed to be a "hermaphrodite").

1493. REQUENA, ANTONIO. "Noticias y consideraciones sobre las anormalidades sexuales de los aborigenes americanos: sodomia," **Acta Venezolana,** 1:1 (1945), 1-32.
Useful survey of information by tribe and source of homosexual practices among Amerinds. See the English version: "Sodomy among Native American Peoples," **Gay Sunshine,** no. 38-39 (Winter 1279), 37-39.

1494. REICHEL-DOLMATOFF, GERARDO. **Amazonian Cosmos: The Sexual and Religious Symbolism of the Tukano Indians.** Chicago: University of Chicago Press, 1971. 290 pp.
The Desana of Colombia "operate cultural mechanisms that produce a very marked sexual repression." Their world view focuses on intense struggle between the sexes. They

also have a high incidence of homosexuality. See pp. 19-20, 68, 244.

1495. ROMOLI, KATHLEEN. **Balboa of Darien.** Garden City,
       NY: Doubleday, 1953. 431 pp.
For the conquistador's murderous reaction to indigenous
homosexuality, see pp. 55, 157, 217.

1496. SCHNEEBAUM, TOBIAS. **Keep the River on Your
       Right.** New York: Grove, 1969. 184 pp.
This book purports to give an account of a New Yorker's
stay among a wholly homosexual tribe in the upper Amazon.
Doubts have been expressed about the authenticity of this
report.

1497. SORENSON, ARTHUR P. "Linguistic Exogamy and
       Personal Choice in the Northwest Amazon," **Illinois
       Studies in Anthropology,** 14 (1984), 180-93.
Occasional sex is regarded as behavior to be expected
among male friends.

1498. THOMPSON, JOHN ERIC S. **Maya History and Religion.**
       Norman: University of Oklahoma Press, 1970. 415
       pp.
Records a wooden sculptural group representing two men
engaged in sodomy (p.21). See also pp. 46, 286.

1499. VALDIZÁN, HERMILIO, and ÁNGEL MALDONADO. **La
       medicina popular peruana: contribución al folklore
       médico del Perú.** Lima: Torres Aguirre, 1922. 3
       vols.
For sexual folklore, see pp. 310-30, esp. the list of
terms on p. 314.

1500. VILLAVICENCIO, VÍCTOR, LUCIO. **La vida sexual del
       indígeno peruano.** New ed. Lima: 1966. 110 pp.
Holds that in old Peru sodomy generally had a religious
character (pp. 73-77).

1501. WAGLEY, CHARLES. **Welcome of Tears.** New York: Ox-
       ford University Press, 1977. 328 pp.
Study of a southern Amazonian tribe, the Tupirape, where
until recently men had engaged in anal intercourse (p.
160).

1502. WILBERT, JOHANNES. **Survivors of Eldorado: Four
       Indian Cultures of South America.** New York: Prae-
       ger, 1972. 212 pp.
Among the Yanoama homosexuality occurs between women, but
is considered repulsive (p. 55). Among the Warao references to homosexual acts appear in oral literature. Male
transvestites occur; the trait is supposed to run in families. The transvestites are not persecuted.

1503. WILBERT, JOHANNES, and KARIN SIMONEAU (eds.). **Folk
       Literature of the Ge Indians.** Los Angeles: UCLA

Latin American Center, 1984. Vol. 2. 684 pp.
From "The Origin of Women": In the beginning there were
only men who practiced homosexual intercourse. One of
them became pregnant, but was unable to give birth and
died. The supernatural origin of women ensued.

V. TRAVEL

A. TRAVELERS

Although the link has never been adequately studied, it seems that there is an affinity between homosexuality and travel. Often dissatisfied with opportunities in his own country or region, the male homosexual yields to the "grass is greener" syndrome. Having been accustomed at home to combine surface conformity with a covert quest of the unconventional, he may find it easier to "fit in" abroad than does the ordinary tourist. There too he may discover, at least on a short visit, sexual opportunities harder to find in his own country. The outsider's ignorance of the rules serves as an excuse for violating them--a violation that the natives affect to find quaint rather than offensive. A related phenomenon is the prominence of homosexual contacts during wartime, which brings its own suspension of peacetime norms. The travel literature pertinent to homosexuality begins in the 16th century. Only a few representative examples are cited here; others appear in the sections concerned with the countries and regions visited (e.g.,Islamic Countries, III.P; China, III.Q; Japan, III.R.; South and Southeast Asia, III.S; Africa, IV, B; Pacific Societies, IV, C; Meso-America and South America, IV, F).

1504. CAMUS, RENAUD. **Notes sur les manières du temps.** Paris: P. O. L., 1985. 412 pp.
Modern moral reflections based on the novelist's travels in a number of countries.

1505. CHURCHILL, AWNSHAM, and JOHN CHURCHILL (eds.). **A Collection of Voyages and Travels ...** London: Walthoe, 1732. 6 vols.
In this massive anthology, see vol. 1, pp. 68, 231; vol. 2, p. 235; vol. 3, p. 522; vol. 5, pp. 689, 703; vol. 6, p. 685.

1506. DE TERRA, HELMUT. **Humboldt: The Life and Times of Alexander von Humboldt, 1769-1859.** New York:- Knopf, 1955. 386 pp.
Life of the polymath German scientist, explorer, statesman, and homophile.

1507. FARIA E SOUSA, MANUEL DE. **Ásia Portuguesa.** Porto: Livraria Civilização, 1945-47. 6 vols.
A collection of Portuguese travel narratives from the 16th and 17th centuries. See vols. 2 and 3 on sodomy in Pegu (Burma), Japan, and Celebes (Indonesia).

1508. GEMELLI CARRERI, GIOVANNI FRANCESCO. **Giro del**
       mondo. Naples: 1699-1700. 6 vols.
Account of travels around the world, including Turkey,
Persia, India, China, the Philippines, and New Spain.

1509. GÓMES VIANA, ANTÓNIO JÚLIO. **A homossexualidade no**
       mundo. Lisbon: The author, n. d. [1979-81?]. 2
       vols.
Observations by the author, a world traveler, arranged by
country and supplemented by secondary sources.

1510. HOCQUENGHEM, GUY. **Le gay voyage: guide et regard**
       homophile sur les grands métropoles. Paris: Albin
       Michel, 1980. 238 pp.
A French novelist and homosexual theorist's impressions of
Berlin, Amsterdam, New York, Rome, and Rio de Janeiro.

1511. HOUGH, RICHARD A. **The Bounty.** New York: Penguin,
       1984. 293 pp.
For observations on the emotional relationship between
Captain William Bligh and Fletcher Christian (culminating
in the mutiny of 1789), see pp. 34-35, 42, 55, 90, 273-
78. This is a new edition of a book first published in
1972.

1512. HUNTFORD, ROLAND. **Scott and Amundsen: The Race to**
       the South Pole. New York: Putnam, 1980.
Includes discussion of the homosexuality of Sir Clements
Markham, president of the Royal Geographical Society.

1513. LE GOLIF, LOUIS ADHEMAR TIMOTHEE. **The Memoirs of a**
       Buccaneer. Translated and edited by Malcolm
       Barnes. London: Allen and Unwin, 1954. 235 pp.
Rare account of homosexual behavior among 17th-century
pirates in the West Indies.

1514. LITHGOW, WILLIAM. **The Totall Discourse of the Rare**
       Adventures and Painful Peregrinations. Glasgow: P.
       MacLehouse, 1906. 448 pp.
A Scotsman reports on sodomy in Italy and the Turkish Empire during travels, 1609-22.

1515. PSALMANAZAR, GEORGE. **Memoirs of **** commonly**
       known by the Name of George Palmanazar, a Reputed
       Native of Formosa. London: R. Davis, 1714. 364.
Purports to be the memoirs of a convert to Christianity,
with observations on homosexual behavior on the island
of Formosa (Taiwan) and other countries visited.

1516. RAYFIELD, DONALD. **The Dream of Lhasa: The Life of**
       Nikolay Przhevalsky, Explorer of Central Asia.
       Columbus: Ohio University Press, 1977. 221 pp.
Life of the Russo-Polish soldier-explorer Przewalski
(1839-88), who was homosexual.

1517. WHITE, EDMUND. **States of Desire: Travels in Gay**

America. New York: E. P. Dutton, 1980. 336 pp.
A noted homosexual novelist, then residing in Manhattan,
reports on his observations of gay life in a number of
American cities. While his comments are sometimes penetrating, White's stay in most of the places mentioned
was too short for him to permit him to draw a convincing
profile.

B. GUÍDES

The 18th century saw the appearance of a minor genre of
expose literature treating the "naughty" side of life
in the great cities of Europe, especially London and
Paris. As late as the first half of the 20th century,
however, this literature included only incidental or
ambiguous mention of homosexual places and pleasures. At
some point, which is now impossible to determine, gay
people began to make their own summary lists, a kind of
samizdat multiplied only in carbon copies or through the
mimeograph, and sold--if at all--only surreptitiously.
This clandestinity helped to protect the establishments
themselves, which would suffer police harassment if their
character were too widely advertised. In any event, after
World War II such lists began to make their way into
print--eventually blossoming (in tandem with the growth of
gay entrepreneurship itself) into thick tomes of hundred
of pages. Subject to social and legal pressures, as well
as rapid changes of fashion, the life cycle of most gay
and lesbian meeting places is short. In historical retrospect, the guides help to reconstruct the "homo-geo-
graphy" of former times. See also XIV.L on the so-called
gay ghettos.

1518. **The Advocate Gay Visitors Guide to Los Angeles.**
        San Mateo, CA: Liberation Publications, 1982. 157
        pp.
Organized by topic, this pocket-sized paperback includes
general information and addresses for the visitor, as well
as ones of specific interest to gay men and lesbians in
the greater Los Angeles area. Also covers Palm Springs.

1520. **The Advocate Gay Visitors Guide to San Francisco.**
        San Mateo, CA: Liberation Publications, 1982. 155
        pp.
Similar to the preceding. Provides a chapter on gay
history in the city. Also covers Russian River and side
trips.

1521. BABILONIA. **Italia gay 1984.** Milan: Edizioni
        Moderne, 1984. 252 pp.
Listings by city for Italy prepared by the editors of the
country's leading gay monthly. In addition, provides data

for metropolitan centers in other European nations.

1522. BARD, BRICE (BRUCE). **Le guide gris (The Grey
       Guide).** Ninth edition. San Francisco: Mattachine
       Society, 1972. 249 pp.
World-wide guide (excluding the United States) of gay entertainment spots and meeting places. First issued in
1958.

1523. BAXANDALL, LEE. **World Guide to Nude Beaches and
       Recreation.** New York: Harmony House, 1983. 220
       pp.
Up-to-date guide to these sometimes hard-to-find beaches,
with reports on gay status where appropriate.

1524. **Berlin von hinten.** Berlin: Bruno Gmünder Verlag,
       1981. 256 pp.
Offers well-informed articles on gay history in Berlin by
Manfred Herzer, Peter Schult, and others, as well as
directory listings by category.

1525. **Best Guide to Great Britain 1987.** Amsterdam: Aco-
       lyte Press, 1986. 228 pp.
The most comprehensive guide to gay Britain, reflecting
extensive visits and research.

1526. **Bob Damron's Address Book 1985.** San Francisco: Bob
       Damron Enterprises, 1985. 460 pp.
Pocket guide emphasizing places of sexual contact (commer-
cial establishments and cruising spots) for gay men in the
U.S. and Canada.

1526A. BOUCHARD, ALAIN. **Le guide gay du Québec.** Third
       ed. Montreal: Editions Homeureux, 1983. 130 pp.
About two-thirds of the contents of this guide, written by
an established French-Canadian author, pertain to Montreal
and environs.

1527. BURNS, RICHARD and others. **Gay Jubilee: A Guide to
       Gay Boston--Its History and Resources.** Boston:
       Lesbian and Gay Task Force, 1980. 64 pp.
Includes historical notes as well as contemporary listings.

1528. COX, CHRISTOPHER. **A Key West Companion.** New
       York: St. Martin's Press, 1983. 214 pp.
A literate narrative history and guide to the Florida
resort.

1529. **Eurogay 86: Pocket Guide to Gay Europe.** Halbaek,
       Denmark: Coq International, 1986. 229 pp.
Concise listings on a country-by-country basis.

1530. FOERSTER, K.-J. **Gay Guide 1981: Reiseführer fur
       die Bundesrepublik Deutschland, Schweiz und
       Oesterreich.** Berlin: Foerster, 1980. 320 pp.

Lists hotels, bars, bathhouses, and other places of accomodation and entertainment in West Germany, Switzerland, and Austria.

1531. **Frankfurt/Offenbach/Main/Wiesbaden von hinten.**
       Berlin: Bruno Gmünder Verlag, 1984. 224 pp.
Addresses, with some historical notes, for these West German cities.

1532. **GaYellow Pages.** Fourteenth ed. New York: Renaissance House, 1985. 252 pp.
Carefully edited directory of service organizations and commercial establishments for gay men and lesbians in the United States and Canada. A standard work because of its thorough and reliable coverage by state and city with brief annotations. Includes national and local periodical publications and newsletters. Also published in regional editions.

1533. GAI PIED HEBDO. **Guide Gai pied 85.** Paris: Gai Pied, 1985. 290 pp.
Prepared by the staff of the leading French gay weekly, this is the fullest gay guide to France (with some additional material on Switzerland and Belgium). First issued in 1983 as **Guide France.** Although primarily directed at gay men, the present edition includes some women's addresses.

1534. **Gay German Guide 1986.** Hamburg: Pink Rose Press, 1985. 412 pp.
Listings for Germany, mainly of places of entertainment, by postal code (pp. 33-241); the remainder of the book is a somewhat patchy "Gay Guide International."

1535. **Gay Scandinavia 1983.** Holbaeck, Denmark: COQ International, 1983. 128 pp.
Text in Danish, English and German. Covers Denmark, Finland, Iceland, Norway, and Sweden.

1536. GLENCROSS, PETER (ed.). **Best Guide to Amsterdam 1986.** Amsterdam: Eden Cross, 1985. 224 pp.
Easygoing, but informative guide to Amsterdam for foreign gay male visitors.

1537. **Guild Guide 1964.** Washington, DC: Guild Press, 1964. 93 pp.
State-by-state listing of gay meeting places in the United States issued by a well-known porno publisher of the period.

1538. **Hamburg von hinten.** Berlin: Bruno Gmünder Verlag, 1982. 256 pp.
In addition to directory chapters, contains valuable information on gay history in the Hanseatic city.

1539. HEYSLIN, PHILIPPE, and MARC BERARD. **Paris gay**

province. Paris: Henri Veyrier, 1983. 157 pp.
Three-fifths of this guide concern Paris, the rest covers
France selectively by provinces.

1540. HOMOSEXUAL INFORMATION CENTER. **Directory of
Homosexual Organizations and Publications.** Sixth
ed. Hollywood, CA: HIC, 1982. 62 pp.
About 1000 entries for the United States and Canada, with
useful category index.

1541. HORN, SANDY. **Gaia's Guide International.** Twelfth
ed. New York: Gaia's Guide, 1986. 300 pp.
Comprehensive guide to places to go for women in North
America, Europe, Australia, New Zealand and some Latin
American countries.

1542. HUNTER, JOHN FRANCIS (pseud. of John Paul Hudson).
The Gay Insider USA. New York: Stonehill, 1972.
629 pp.
Heroic one-man job, of interest for the author's opinions
which reflect the gay liberation/counter-culture mood of
the period. See also his: **The Gay Insider: A Hunter's
Guide to New York and a Thesaurus of Phallic Lore** (New
York: Traveller's Companion, 1971; 300 pp.).

1543. **Incognito guide: Europe, Mediterranée.** Paris:
A.S.L., 1965. 48 pp.
With comments in English, this guide to gay meeting places
was much used by American and British travelers in the
period. An enlarged ed. (71 pp.) appeared in 1966.

1544. KENT, KIM (ed). **Eos-Guide 69.** Fourth ed. Copenhagen: Eos, 1968. 259 pp.
Alphabetical listings, by city, of gay meeting places
throughout the world, prepared by a Danish gay leader and
entrepreneur. The first ed. appeared in 1966.

1545. **Köln von hinten.** Berlin: Bruno Gmünder Verlag,
1983. 256 pp.
Includes articles on gay history in Cologne, as well as
a directory arranged by category.

1546. **Lesbische Informatie Boekje '85/'86.** Amsterdam:
COC-Magazijn, 1985. 74 pp.
Comprehensive listing of groups, meeting places, and
cultural facilities for lesbians and women generally in
the Netherlands.

1547. **Man to Man: Gay/Lesbian Gyuide to Holland 1986/87.**
Amsterdam: City Map Produkties, 1986. 104 pp.
Comprehensive listing of Dutch cities with annotations in
English. English and French. There is an appended Belgian
section, mainly covering the Flemish part of the country.

1548. MARCUS, ERIK, and PAUL VERSTRETEN. **Amsterdam in je
kontzak: een homo-stadsgids.** Amsterdam: Stichting

JIF, 1984. 288 pp.
Comprehensive listings of businesses, places of entertainment, cultural centers and organizations, etc., preceded
by historical and interpretive articles on the Dutch
city. Male emphasis.

1549. **München von hinten.** Berlin: Bruno Gmünder Verlag,
    1983. 224 pp.
Offers essays as well as listings by category for the
Bavarian capital and environs.

1550. NERF, SWASARNT, PETER ASTI, and DAPHNE DILLDOCK
    (pseuds.). **The Gay Girl's Guide: A Primer for
    Novices: A Review for Roues.** [New York?:]
    Phallus, 1949. 69 pp.
Campy mimeographed guide for gay men, with sections on
vocabulary and technique. The main part, a directory of
"where to make contacts" begins on p. 46 (bars, bathhouses, and public places). There were at least two
subsequent eds., in 1950 and in the mid-1950s.

1551. **New England Community Guide for Gay Males and
    Lesbians, 1983.** Boston: The Community Guide,
    1983. 96 pp.
Contains short articles, as well as listings of places of
entertainment, businesses, and service organizations.

1552. **Odysseus 85: An Accommodations Guide for Gay
    Men.** Flushing, NY: Odysseus Enterprises, 1985.
    273 pp.
Lists and describes some 450 places to stay, especially
guest houses, small hotels, and ranches, mainly in North
America.

1553. **Party Guía Gay de España.** Barcelona: Ediciones
    Amaika, 1984. 130 pp.
Annotated guide to bars, clubs, bathhouses, restaurants,
cinemas, and outdoor cruising places in major Spanish
cities and resort areas.

1554. **Places of Interest 1984: Gay Guide with Maps, USA
    and Canada.** Phoenix: Ferrari Publications, 1984.
    238 pp.
Maps make this guide esp. useful for the motorist.

1555. **Places of Interest to Women.** Fourth ed. Phoenix:
    Ferrari Publications, 1985. 145 pp.
Covers about 700 cities in the U.S., Canada, and the Car-
ibbean.

1556. RAND, BILL, and BO SIEWART. **Barfly.** Los Angeles:
    Advocate, 1972. 2 vestpocket vols.
Guide to "more than 1000" gay bars in the U.S. (also some
Canadian and Mexican listings) divided into an eastern
and western half.

1557. STAMFORD, JOHN A. (ed.). **Spartacus Guide for Gay
       Men.** Amsterdam: Spartacus, 1984. 784 pp.
This hefty tome--virtually the standard work--covers bars,
clubs, discos, saunas, beaches, cruising places, hotels,
restaurants, cafes, and gay stores throughout the world
(except for the U.S. section, which is quite brief).
Useful for Third World countries not covered elsewhere,
though some complaints have been made that the information is not always complete or up-to-date. Texts in
English, German, French, and Spanish.

1558. TAYLOR, JEFF. **Gay Guide for the Pacific Northwest.**
       Bellevue, WA: The author, 1975. 32 pp.
Covers Seattle, Portland, and Vancouver, BC.

1559. VOIGT, WOLFGANG, and KLAUS HEINRICH. **Hamburg ahoi!**
       Berlin: Verlag Rosa Winkel, 1982. 300 pp.
Contains articles on the history of gay life in Hamburg
since the 18th century, together with illustrations and
listings.

VI. HUMANITIES

A. ART: GENERAL

Researchers in the field of homosexuality in art have
tended to concentrate on a few broad cultual areas: classical antiquity, the Renaissance, modern Europe and north
America (see the following sections), and Islam (see
III.P). While certain themes from classical mythology and
history are homosexual in content, and many individual
artists have been homosexual or lesbian, attempts to
define a distinctive homosexual sensibility in the fine
arts have proved elusive.

1560. AYMAR, BRANDT. **The Young Male Figure in Paintings,
      Sculptures, and Drawings from Ancient Egypt to the
      Present.** New York: Crown, 1970. 247 pp.
Collection of 275 reproductions, chiefly of mainstream
works, arranged historically (separate section on Asia).
No overt eroticism.

1561. BECKER, RAYMOND DE. **The Other Face of Love.**
      Translated by Margaret Crosland and Alan Daventry.
      New York: Grove Press, 1969. 209 pp.
Although this book, originally published in Paris as
L'érotisme d'en face in 1964, seems intended as a general
history of same-sex love, it is valuable mainly for its
varied complement of illustrations.

1562. BEURDELEY, CECILE (ed.). **L'Amour bleu.** New York:
      Rizzoli, 1978. 304 pp.
Lavishly produced volume offering 290 illustrations of
works of art from the Greeks to the present, interspersed with apt selections from literary classics. Male
interest.

1563. **Bilderlexikon der Erotik.** Vienna: Verlag für
      Kulturforschung, 1928-31. 4 vols.
Apart from the definitions, this pictorial lexicon presents a wide-ranging repertory of visual material for
the whole field of erotic imagery. The work was reissued
in Hamburg, 1961, in 8 volumes, with two supplementary
volumes prepared by Armand Mergen.

1564. DYNES, WAYNE. "Gay Art Research: A Bibliographical
      Review," **Cabirion and Gay Books Bulletin,** no. 11
      (Fall-Winter 1984), 8-9.
Selective presentation with running commentary.

1565. KIEFER, OTTO. **Der schöne Jungling in der bildenden
      Kunst aller Zeiten.** Berlin: Adolf Brand/Der

236

Eigene, 1922. 68 pp.
Compilation of art works depicting beautiful youths.

1566. LUCIE-SMITH, EDWARD. **Eroticism in Western Art.**
New York: Praeger, 1972. 273 pp.
Fluent survey of major aspects of European high art,
marred by some glib Freudian assertions. See pp. 84-87,
130-33, 180-81, 202-07, 234-36, 264-65, 272.

1567. RAWSON, PHILIP. **Erotic Art of the East: The Sexual
Theme in Oriental Painting and Sculpture.** New
York: G. P. Putnam's Sons, 1968. 380 pp.
Offers nearly 300 illustrations (interspersed with classic
texts) from the major art traditions of Asia. Like most
such works, this volume scants homoerotic aspects.

1568. SASLOW, JAMES. "Closets in the Museum: Homophobia
and Art History," in: Karla Jay and Allen Young
(eds.), **Lavender Culture.** New York: Jove, 1978,
215-27.
On the obscuring of homosexual themes and lives in art by
art historians seeking to preserve their own respectability.

1569. WALTERS, MARGARET. **The Nude Male: A New Perspective.** New York: Paddington Press, 1978. 352 pp.
Feminist study of the nude from the Greeks to the present,
complementing Lord Kenneth Clark's resolutely asexual
The Nude, while proffering some questionable views as to
how homosexual men view erotic art. A similar perspective appears in: Sarah Kent, "The Erotic Male Nude," in:
S. Kent and J. Morreau (eds.), **Women's Images of Men**
(London: Writers and Readers, 1985), pp. 75-105. For
bibliography on the larger problem, see Andreas Kuntz,
**Der blosse Leib: Bibliographie zur Nacktheit und Körper-
lichkeit** (Frankfurt: Europäische Hochschulschriften,
1985; 260 pp.).

B. ART: ANCIENT AND MEDIEVAL

The prominence of homoerotic elements in Greek civilization as a whole has assured the salience of such themes in
art, especially in vase painting. In other media, however, such as sculpture, the professional reticence of
classical scholars has hindered the foregrounding of
relevant themes and aspects.

1570. BEAZLEY, JOHN DAVIDSON, SIR. "Some Vases in the
Cyprus Museum," **Proceedings of the British Academy,**
33 (1947), 197-244.
Under this innocuous title is hidden a discussion and
classification of Greek vases showing male-male court-

ship scenes. Beazley's list is supplemented by Kurt
Schauenberg, "Erastes und Eromenos auf einer Schale des
Sokles," **Archäologischer Anzeiger** (1965), 845-67.

1571. BOARDMAN, JOHN, and EUGENIO LA ROCCA. **Eros in
Greece.** New York: Erotic Art Book Society, 1977.
175 pp.
Picture book offering some male-male examples from ancient
Greek art (chiefly vase paintings).

1572. BONGHI JOVINO, MARIA. "Una tabella Capuana con
ratto di Ganimede," in: **Hommages à Marcel Renard.**
Brussels: Collection Latomus, 1969, vol. 3,
pp. 66-78.
On a newly discovered representation of Zeus abducting
Ganymede.

1573. BRENDEL, OTTO J. "The Scope and Temperament of
Erotic Art in the Greco-Roman World," in: Theodore
Bowie (ed.), **Studies in Erotic Art.** New York:
Basic Books, 1970, pp. 3-107.
Well-documented account by an archaeologist of the state
of the question, somewhat slighting the homosexual elem-
ent.

1574. BRUNEAU, PHILIPPE. "Ganymède et l'aigle: images,
caricatures et parodies animales du rapt," **Bulletin
de Correspondance Hellénique,** 86 (1962), 193-228.
Account of caricatures of Zeus' abduction of Ganymede in
later Greek art; complements H. Sichtermann, below.

1575. BRUNNSAKE, STURE. **The Tyrant-slayers of Kritios
and Nesiotes.** Second ed. Stockholm: Svenska
Institutet i Athen, 1971. 189 pp.
Art historical account of the important group created in
477 B.C. to commemorate the heroic Athenian male couple
Harmodios and Aristogeiton. See also Burkhard Fehr, **Die
Tyrannentöter, oder, kann man der Demokratie ein Denkmal
setzen?** (Frankfurt am Main: Fischer, 1984; 82 pp.).

1576. CLAIRMONT, CHRISTOPH. W. **Die Bildnisse des Antinous: ein Beitrag zur Porträtplastik unter Kaiser
Hadrian.** Rome: Schweizerisches Institut, 1966. 62
pp.
Standard work on the surviving corpus of sculptural portraits of Hadrian's favorite, who died tragically in
A.D. 130.

1577. DAVIES, MARK I. "The Tickle and Sneeze of Love,"
American Journal of Archaeology, 86 (1982), 115-18.
On a painted, inscribed vase by Duris in the Louvre.

1578. DELCOURT, MARIE. **Hermaphroditéa: Recherches sur
l'être double promoteur de la fertilité dans le
monde classique.** Brussels, 1966. 76 pp.
Provides a typology of the Hermaphrodite. This monograph

complements her **Hermaphrodite: Myths and Rites of the Bisexual Figure in Antiquity** (London: Studio Books, 1961;
109 pp.).

1579. DYNES, WAYNE. "Orpheus without Eurydice," **Gai
      Saber**, 1:3/4 (1978), 267-73.
Overview, with references, of the homoerotic Orpheus in
Greece, Rome, and Renaissance Europe.

1580. FORSYTH, ILENE H. "The Ganymede Capital at Veze-
      lay," **Gesta**, 15 (1976), 241-46.
Analyzes a 12th-century Romanesque carved capital depicting the Abduction of Ganymede, interpreting it as
referring to monastic oblates.

1581. GRANT, MICHAEL. **Eros in Pompeii: The Secret Rooms
      of the National Museum in Naples.** New York: Mor-
      row, 1975. 170 pp.
Presents 160 color plates made from photographs taken by
Antonia Mulas of explicit works of painting and sculpture,
a few of them homoerotic.

1582. IMMERWAHR, H. R. "A Lekythos in Toronto and the
      Golden Youth of Athens," **Studies in Attic Epig-
      raphy, History and Topography Presented to Eugene
      Vanderpool (Hesperia** Supplement, 19, 1982), 59-65.
A painted vase and its connections.

1582A. JOHNS, CATHERINE. **Sex or Symbol: Erotic Images of
      Greece and Rome.** Austin: University of Texas
      Press, 1982. 160 pp.
Fluent, but somewhat superficial illustrated account of
ancient erotic art. Homosexuality is treated, oddly, in
the chapter "Men and Beasts" (pp. 97-114).

1583. KAEMPF-DIMITRIADOU, SOPHIA. **Die Liebe der Götter
      in der attischen Kunst des 5. Jahrhunderts v. Chr.**
      Basel: Antike Kunst, 1979. 125 pp.
See pp. 7-21 and 76-92 for representations in vase
painting of boys beloved of the gods, with catalogue of
works. See also her article: "Zeus und Ganymed auf
einer Pelike des Hermonax," **Antike Kunst**, 22 (1979),
49-54.

1584. KOCH-HARNACK, GUNDEL. **Knabenliebe und Tierge-
      schenke.** Berlin: Mann, 1983. 288 pp.
Analysis of scenes in vase paintings showing gifts
(rabbits, roosters, foxes, etc.) presented by the older
wooer to the desired boy, with cross-cultural reflections. Some related material appears in Dietrich von
Bothmer, **The Amasis Painter and His World** (New York:
Thames and Hudson, 1985).

1585. KUNZE, EMIL. "Zeus und Ganymedes: eine Terrakotta-
      gruppe," in: **Hundertstes Winckelmanns-Programm der
      Archaeologischen Gesellschaft zu Berlin.** Berlin:

1940, pp. 25-50.
Account of the discovery and formal properties of a major
sculpture found at Olympia.

1586. LEGG, W. DORR. "The Sodomy Rite," **ONE Institute
      Quarterly,** 1:3 (1958), 98-101.
Detects homosexual implications in the Altamira and other
cave paintings.

1587. MARCADE, JEAN. **Eros kalos: Essay on Erotic Ele-
      ments in Greek Art.** New York: Nagel, 1962. 167 pp.
Lavishly illustrated coffee-table book with some relevant
material. See also the companion volume: **Roma amor: Essay
on Erotic Elements in Etruscan and Roman Art** (New York:
Nagel, 1961; 129 pp.).

1588. MILLER, STELLA G. "Eros and the Arms of Achilles,"
      American Journal of Archaeology, 90 (1986), 159-70.
Beginning with a late-5th-century vase from Olynthus,
reconstructs and iconographical scheme in which the figure
of Eros represents the love-friendship of Achilles and
Patroclus.

1589. MOON, WARREN G. (ed.). **Ancient Greek Art and
      Iconography.** Madison: University of Wisconsin
      Press, 1983. 346 pp.
See pp. 147-51 (by Jiri Frel) and 226 (by Eva C. Keuls).

1590. NAPOLI, MARIO. **La Tomba del Tuffatore: La scoperta
      della grande pittura greca.** Bari: De Donato,
      1970. 213 pp.
Documents the discovery of Greek frescoes in a tomb at
Paestum in Campania, including one showing male lovers
banquetting. See esp. 124-28.

1591. PINNEY, G. FERRARI. "For the Heroes Are at Hand,"
      Journal of Hellenic Studies, 104 (1984), 181-83.
Interprets an Attic red-figured vase in Hamburg (ca. 480
B.C.) as showing a comic homosexual encounter.

1592. RICHTER, GISELA. **Kouroi: Archaic Greek Youths.**
      Third ed. London: Phaidon, 1970. 365 pp.
Standard corpus of plates and catalogue of the monumental
male nude sculpture of the archaic period. Sedulously
avoids placing the figures against their historical background, a task that needs to be addressed.

1593. ROBINSON, DAVID M., and EDWARD J. FLUCK. **A Study
      of the Greek Love-Names, including a Discussion of
      Paederasty and Prosopographia.** Baltimore: Johns
      Hopkins Press, 1937. 204 pp.
Comprehensive study of the **kalos** names (invocations of
admired youths) on the vases.

1594. SCHEFOLD, KARL. **Die Göttersage in der klassischen
      und hellenistischen Kunst.** Munich: Hirmer, 1981.

391 pp.
In this comprehensive work on the legends of the gods in
classical and Hellenistic art, see pp. 192-93 (Eros),
211-18 (Zeus and Ganymede), 248-49 (Poseidon and Pelops),
298-99 (Hermes), 300-01 (Pan), 304-05 (Hermaphroditos)
307-18 (Eos pursuing Tithonos and Kephalos), 324-27
(Zephyros and Hyakinthos).

1595. SHAPIRO, H. ALAN. "Courtship Scenes in Attic Vase
       Painting," **American Journal of Archaeology**, 85
       (1981), 133-43.
Useful survey collecting previous literature; somewhat
controversial on the sociopolitical background. See also
his related articles: "Epilikos and Skythes," ibid., 86
(1982), 285; "Hippokrates Son of Anxileos," **Hesperia**, 49
(1980), 289-93; and "Kallias Kration Alopethen," ibid., 51
(1982), 69-73.

1596. SICHTERMANN, HELLMUT. **Ganymed: Mythos und Gestalt
       in der antiken Kunst.** Berlin: Mann, 1953. 125 pp.
Standard work on the iconography of Zeus' favorite in
Greco-Roman art.

1597. VERMEULE, EMILY. "Some Erotica in Boston," **Antike
       Kunst**, 12 (1969), 9-15.
Publication (with 9 pp. of plates) of vases, painted
chiefly by Athenian artists, ca. 540-470 B.C., most of
them given to the Museum of Fine Arts in the early years
of the century by the homophile writer and collector Edward Perry Warren.

          C. ART: THE RENAISSANCE TRADITION

In the Italian Renaissance the custom of using teenage
garzoni as models and shop assistants seems to have
fostered homosexuality and bisexuality among artists. At
first tolerated, this tradition was largely driven underground as a result of the spread of the Counter-Reformation in the second half of the 16th century. The
revival of classical subject matter led to the cultivation
of a certain number of subjects, such as Ganymede and
Orpheus, that were congenial to homoerotic interpretation.

1598. BOUSQUET, JACQUES. **Mannerism: The Painting and
       Style of the Late Renaissance.** Translated by Simon
       Watson Taylor. New York: Braziller, 1964. 347 pp.
In this lavishly illustrated monograph of the "stylish
style" of the 16th century, see pp. 196-202, 295, 323.

1599. CLEMENTS, ROBERT L. **The Poetry of Michelangelo.**
       New York: New York University Press, 1965. 368 pp.
In this study by a noted Romance philologist, see Chapter

6 ("The Fifty Poems for the Truffle, Turtle and Trout,"
pp. 134-53), illustrating themes of homosexual longing, as
well as pp. 205-16. Clements' conclusion that Michelangelo's sexual feelings for his **garzoni** were actualized, is
contradicted (probably mistakenly) by Robert S. Liebert,
**Michelangelo: A Psychoanalytic Study of His Life and
Images** (New Haven: Yale University Press, 1983. 447 pp.).

1600. EEKHOUD, GEORGES. "Saint Sébastien dans la pein-
       ture," **Akademos**, 1 (February 15, 1909), 171-75.
The Belgian novelist, writing at the end of the fin-de-
siecle era, was the first to try to put into perspective
the modern fascination of homosexuals with the figure of
St. Sebastian.

1601. EEKHOUD, GEORGES. "Un illustre uraniste du XVIIe
       siècle: Jérôme Duquesnoy," **JfsZ**, 2 (1900), 277-87.
First study of the Belgian sculptor's homosexuality, which
was disclosed by his condemnation and execution for sodomy
with two boys in Ghent (1654). See also: Lydie Hadermann-
Misguich, **Les Duquesnoy** (Gembloux, 1970); and Geert Debeuckelaere, "'Omme dieswille dat Gij, Hieronymus Duquesnoy ...," **Tijdskrift voor Homo-Geschiedenis**, 1:1 (February
1984), 5-22.

1602. FERNANDEZ, DOMINIQUE. **Signor Giovanni.** Paris:
       Balland, 1981. 99 pp.
Review of evidence concerning the murder of J. J. Winckelmann in Trieste in 1768, arguing that the great archaeologist was sexually repressed almost until the end, when he
embarked on a fatal fling. See also W. Leppmann, and
T. Pelzel, below.

1603. FROMMEL, CHRISTOPH LUDWIG. **Michelangelo und
       Tommaso dei Cavalieri.** Amsterdam: Castrum Per-
       egrini, 1979. 129 pp.
Account of Michelangelo's Platonic love for the nobleman
Cavalieri, and the anguished drawings he produced to ex-
press his feelings.

1604. FUMAGALLI, GIUSEPPINA. **Eros di Leonardo.** New ed.
       Florence: Sansoni, 1971. 242 pp.
A standard (though reticent) work on Leonardo's sexuality,
criticizing earlier approaches, including the Freudian.

1605. GRECI, LUIGI. "Benvenuto Cellini nei delitti e nei
       processi fiorentini, riconstruiti attraverso le
       leggi del tempo," **Archivio di antropologia crimi-
       nale**, 50 (1930), 342-85 and 509-42.
Surveys the documentary evidence for the artist's (1500-
1571) homosexual behavior, and the legal steps taken to
punish him.

1606. HIBBARD, HOWARD. **Caravaggio.** New York: Harper and
       Row, 1983. 404 pp.
This book is recognized as the best general monograph on

the Italian artist (1571-1610). For interesting, but
incomplete observations on his sexuality, see pp. 87-88,
151-60, 247, 258, 306. See also D. Posner, below.

1607. JANSON, HORST W. **The Sculpture of Donatello.**
       Princeton, NJ: Princeton University Press, 1957. 2
       vols.
This monograph, which ranks as one of the finest studies
ever produced on a major Renaissance artist, also opened
the way to an interpretation of the homosexuality of
Donatello (1386-1466). See the discussion of two sculptures, David and St. George, the latter serving as a
focus for the homosexual fantasies of others. Recently,
Janson's interpretation has been subjected to a harsh,
unmerited attack by John Pope-Hennessy, "Donatello's
Bronze David," in: Mauro Natale (ed.), **Scritti di storia
dell'arte in onore di Federico Zeri** (Milan: 1984),
pp. 122-27.

1608. KEMPTER, GERDA. **Ganymed: Studien zur Typologie,
       Ikonographie und Ikonologie.** Cologne: Bohlau
       Verlag, 1980. 231 pp.
Able, well-illustrated survey of the fortunes of the
Ganymede image in European art. See also J. Saslow,
below.

1609. KUPPFER, ELISAR VON. "Giovan Antonio--il Sodoma,
       der Maler der Schönheit," **JfsZ,** 9 (1908), 71-167.
A sensitive, subjective interpretation of the Sienese
painter (1477-1549), by a German homophile artist and
poet, which has been neglected by recent scholarship
(e.g.,Andree Hayum, **Giovanni Antonio Bazzi--"Il Sodoma."** New York: Garland, 1976; 335 pp., which ignores
the psychosexual aspects).

1610. LANGEARD, PAUL. **L'intersexualité dans l'art: psy-
       chologie intersexuelle en général et chez Michel-
       Ange en particulier.** Montpellier: Imprimerie de la
       Presse, 1936. 186 pp.
Published version of medical dissertation.

1611. LEPPMANN, WOLFGANG. **Winckelmann.** New York: Knopf,
       1970. 324 pp.
Somewhat prosaic account of the life and times of the
founder of modern archaeology (1717-1768), who linked the
cult of ancient works of art to homoerotic sensitivity.
See pp. 11, 32, 49-52, 158, 161, 165, 172-73, 209, 251-
54. For Winckelmann in relation to his milieu, see the
classic biography of Karl Justi, **Winckelmann: sein Leben,
seine Werke und seine Zeitgenossen** (Leipzig: F. C. W.
Vogel, 1866-1872. 3 vols.).

1612. LE TARGAT, FRANÇOIS. **Saint-Sébastien dans l'his-
       toire de l'art depuis le XVe siècle.** Paris: Paul
       Vermont, 1977. 204 pp.
Reproductions of paintings and other works of art depic-

ting the Christian figure who has been hailed as the "gay saint," though this reputation is apparently not older than the late 19th century. See also **Saint Sébastien: Adonis et martyr** (Paris: Éditions Persona, 1983; 128 pp.); and J. Saslow, below.

1613. LISE, GIORGIO. **L'altro Michelangelo.** Milan: Cordani, 1981. 145 pp.
A knowledgeable work which seeks honestly to link Michelangelo's work with his psychosexual character, without necessarily commanding the assent of other scholars in all respects. Compare with R. J. Clements, above.

1614. MARONE, SILVIO. "Homosexuality and Art," **International Journal of Sexology,** 7:4 (1954), 175-90.
Psychoanalytic approach employed with particular reference to major Renaissance artists.

1615. MASINI, MARIO. "Gli immorali nell'arte: Giovanni Antonio Bazzi detto il Sodoma," **Archivio di antropologia criminale,** 36 (1915), 129-51 and 257-77.
An important documentary study of the Sienese painter's sexuality.

1616. PEDRETTI, CARLO. **Leonardo da Vinci: A Study in Chronology and Style.** Berkeley: University of California Press, 1973. 192 pp.
A leading Leonardo scholar, in the course of a general study, offers some views on new information bearing on the artist's sexuality (p. 140ff.). Compare Stanley J. Pacion, "Leonardo da Vinci: A Psychosexual Enigma," **Medical Aspects of Human Sexuality,** 5:12 (December 1971), 34-41.

1617. PELZEL, THOMAS. "Winckelmann, Mengs and Casanova: A Reappraisal of a Famous Eighteenth Century Forgery," **Art Bulletin,** 14 (1972), 301-15.
Discusses "Jupiter and Ganymede," a forgery created to appeal to Winckelmann. See also Elio Bartolini and Cesare Pagnini, **L'assassinio di Winckelmann: gli atti del processo criminale** (Milan: Longanesi, 1971; 306 pp.)

1618. PERRIG, ALEXANDER. "Bemerkungen zur Freundschaft zwischen Michelangelo und Tommaso de' Cavalieri," in: **Stil und Überlieferung in der Kunst des Abendlandes,** Berlin: Mann, 1967, vol. 2, pp. 164-71.
Remarks on Michelangelo's passionate friendship with a young Roman nobleman as clarified by the drawings. See also Judith Anne Testa, "The Iconography of the Archers: A Study of Self-Concealment and Self-Revelation in Michelangelo's Presentation Drawings," **Studies in Iconography,** 5 (1979), 44-72.

1619. POPE-HENNESSY, JOHN, SIR. **Cellini.** New York: Abbe-

ville, 1985. 324 pp.
Lavishly produced biography concentrating on the major
works of the artist (1500-71), and treating his sexuality on pp. 11, 28-29, 31, 172, 178, 228, 231, 253-55. See
also **The Life of Benvenuto Cellini**, translated by John
Addington Symonds (first published, London, 1887, and
often reprinted).

1620. POSNER, DONALD. "Caravaggio's Early Homo-erotic
       Works," **Art Quarterly**, 24 (1971), 301-26.
Shows that the painter's early Roman works were created in
the ambit of his homosexual patron, Cardinal del Monte.
See also Christoph Liutpold Frommel, "Caravaggios Frühwerk
und der Kardinal Francesco Maria del Monte," **Storia dell'
arte** (1971), 5-52.

1621. SASLOW, JAMES M. **Ganymede in the Renaissance: Ho-
       mosexuality in Art and Society.** New Haven: Yale
       University Press, 1986. 265 pp.
Thoughtful discussion of the Ganymede theme with special
reference to the homoerotic aspects. The author focuses
on portrayals of the Phrygian youth by Michelangelo,
Correggio, Giulio Romano, and Cellini, showing how the
Counter-Reformation altered the intellectual climate in
which such images flourished. See also Anette Kruszyn-
ski, **Der Ganymed-Mythos in Emblematik und mythograph-
ischer Literatur des 16. Jahrhunderts** (Worms: Wernersche
Verlagsgesellschaft, 1985).

1622. SASLOW, JAMES M. "The Tenderest Lover: Saint
       Sebastian in Renaissance Painting: A Proposed
       Iconology for North Italian Art, 1450-1550," **Gai
       Saber** 1:1 (Spring 1977), 58-66.
Attempts to anchor homoerotic sentiment in choice of
subject matter with particular reference to the controversial question of St. Sebastian. See reply by Wayne Dynes,
ibid., 1:2 (Summer 1977), 150-51.

1623. SCHENK, J. "Homoseksualiteit in de Nederlandse
       beeldende kunst voor 1800," **Speculum Historiaele,**
       17:11 (November 1982), 576-83.
Treats homosexual themes in Netherlandish art up to 1800
in several categories, including mythology and scenes of
execution.

1624. SCHNEIDER, LAURIE. "Donatello and Caravaggio: The
       Iconography of Decapitation," **American Imago**, 33
       (1976), 76-91.
Applies psychoanalytic concepts derived from Freud and
Ferenczi to Donatello's bronze "David" and Carvaggio's
paintings "David with the Head of Goliath" and "Medusa's
Head." Criticized by John W. Dixon, "The Drama of
Donatello's David: Re-examination of an Enigma," **Gazette
des Beaux-Arts,** 93 (January 1979), 6-12; to which Schneid-
er replied, ibid., 94 (July-August 1979), 48.

1625. SCHUSTER, PETER-KLAUS. "Zu Dürer's Zeichnung 'Der
       Tod des Orpheus' und verwandter Darstellungen,"
       Hamburger Kunstsammlungen, 23 (1978), 7-24.
Compares Albrecht Dürer's drawing of Orpheus as a homosexual with the artist's "Hercules."

1626. STEINBERG, LEO. **The Sexuality of Christ in
       Renaissance Art and in Modern Oblivion.** New
       York: Pantheon, 1984. 222 pp.
While not about homosexuality, this book provides an
invaluable paradigm for the investigation of the web
linking art, genitality, and religion.

1627. WITTKOWER, RUDOLF, and MARGOT WITTKOWER. **Born
       under Saturn.** New York: W. W. Norton, 1963. 344
       pp.
In this study of the characterology of Renaissance artists, see esp. pp. 169-75.

                        D. ART: MODERN

The history of art in the 19th and 20th centuries discloses a number of significant figures who led closeted
lives--and more recently openly gay and lesbian artists.
Investigations designed to find distinctive styles or
traits applicable collectively to the work of gay and/or
lesbian artists have not as yet produced plausible results. Apart from their work as artists, homosexuals
and lesbians have sometimes excelled as taste-makers--
critics, collectors, dealers, and aestheticians. Taste
formation is a field in which much relevant information
probably remains to be discovered, and only when this is
done will an adequate synthesis be possible.

1628. ALPATOV, MIKHAIL VLADIMIROVICH. **Aleksandr Andre-
       evich Ivanov: zhizn' i tvorchestvo.** Moscow: Iskus-
       stvo, 1956. 2 vols.
The prominent Russian academic-romantic painter Ivanov
(1806-1858) combined mystical Christian subject matter
with a pronounced appreciation for the young male form.

1629. BATE, NEEL ("BLADE"). **The Barn, 1948; and More
       Dirty Pictures by Blade.** New York: Stompers; and
       Leslie-Lohman Galleries, 1980. 32 pp.
Reissue of an explicit album that originally appeared in
an edition limited to 12 copies; with additional material.
Of slight interest as art, this collection reveals something of the taste of ordinary gay men during the period.

1630. BOIME, ALBERT. "The Case of Rosa Bonheur: Why
       Should A Woman Want to Be Like a Man?" **Art History**,
       4 (1981), 384-409.

Examines her defiance of gender role expectations, female
friendships, and her art as an animal painter as related
phenomena. See also Dore Ashton and Denise Brown Hare,
Rosa Bonheur: A Life and a Legend (New York: Studio/Vi-
king, 1981; 206 pp.).

1631. BOIME, ALBERT. **Thomas Couture and the Eclectic
        Vision.** New Haven: Yale University Press, 1980.
        683 pp.
Not stressed by Boime and probably impossible to show
definitively, pederastic motives are implied by Couture's (1815-79) paintings of adolescents. See pp. 90-
93, 106-14, 335-42.

1632. BRION, MARCEL. **Léonor Fini et son oeuvre.** Paris:
        Jean-Jacques Pauvert, 1955. unpaged
Illustrated monograph on the surrealist painter whose
works explore androgyny, lesbianism, and matriarchy.

1633. BURK, CAROLYN. "Gertrude Stein, the Cone Sisters
        and the Puzzle of Female Friendship," **Critical
        Inquiry,** 8 (1982), 543-64.
Stein played a major role in the diffusion of the taste
for modernist painting in the English-speaking world, in
part through her attachment to the art-collecting Cone
sisters. See also: Brenda Richardson: **Dr. Claribel and
Miss Etta** (Baltimore: Museum of Art, 1986; 202 pp.).

1634. CALLOWAY, STEPHEN. **Charles Ricketts: Subtle and
        Fantastic Decorator.** New York: Thames and Hudson,
        1979. 100 pp.
Although the author conceals Ricketts' (1866-1931) homosexuality (including his "marriage" to Charles Shannon),
the illustrations tell their own story.

1635. CAMERON, DAN. **Extended Sensibilities.** New
        York: New Museum, 1981. (exhibition catalogue)
The exhibition of gay male and lesbian artists was organized around Cameron's detection of a neo-Mannerist
tendency. See also Nicolas A. Mouffarege, "Lavender: On
Homosexuality and Art," **Arts Magazine,** 57:2 (October
1981), 78-87.

1636. CLAY, JEAN. **Romanticism.** Secaucus, NJ: Chart-
        well, 1981. 320 pp.
In this lavishly produced survey, see pp. 122-28.

1637. CLIFF, MICHELE. "Object into Subject: Some
        Thoughts on the Work of Black Women Artists,"
        Heresies, no. 15 (1982), 34-40.
Subjective reflections by a Black lesbian writer.

1638. COOPER, EMMANUEL. **The Sexual Perspective: Homosex-
        uality and Art in the Last 100 Years in the West.**
        London: Routledge and Kegan Paul, 1986. 320 pp.
Attempts a summing up, stressing major living figures.

1639. CORINNE, TEE A. **Labiaflowers.** Tallahassee: Naiad
       Press, 1981. 40 pp.
Drawings of labia adapted from photographs. (Revised ed.
of the **Cunt Coloring Book.**)

1640. CRAWFORD, ALAN. **C. R. Ashbee: Architect, Design-
       er, and Romantic Socialist.** New Haven: Yale
       University Press, 1985. 499 pp.
Detailed biography of the life, times, and work of Charles
Robert Ashbee (1863-1942), a disciple of Edward Carpenter
and an influential figure in the arts and crafts movement.

1641. DE ANTONIO, EMILE, and MITCH TUCHMAN. **Painters
       Painting: A Candid History of the Modern Art Scene,
       1940-70.** New York: Abbeville, 1984. 192 pp.
Purveys some intimate details about Andy Warhol, Henry
Geldzahler, and others in the New York art scene.

1642. DE PISIS, FILIPPO. **Il marchesino pittore.** Milan:
       Bompiani, 1969.
Includes frank reminiscences by the painter (1869-1956)
about his homosexual life in Paris. See also his **Poesie**
(Milan: Vallecchi, 1942), which has a dozen poems about
boys. The artist's oeuvre includes about 200 male nudes,
of which only a few were shown at the 1983 retrospective
of his work.

1643. DETROIT INSTITUTE OF ARTS. **French Painting,
       1774-1830: The Age of Revolution.** Detroit Insti-
       tute of Arts, 1975. 712 pp. (exhibition catalogue)
See pp. 54, 360-61 ("Funeral of Patroclus," by Jacques-
Louis David); 180, 339-41 ("Death of Hyacinth," by Jean
Broc); and 264, 404-05 ("Apollo and Cyparissus," by
Claude-Marie Dubufe).

1644. DUBSKY, MARIO. **Tom Pilgrim's Progress among the
       Consequences of Christianity and Other Drawings.**
       Introduction by Edward Lucie-Smith. London: Gay
       Men's Press, 1981. 84 pp.
Reproduces some fifty drawings by the English gay artist,
chiefly male nudes.

1645. EGGUM, ARNE. "Munch's Self-portraits," in: Robert
       Rosenblum et al., **Edvard Munch: Symbols and
       Images.** Washington, DC: National Gallery of Art,
       1978, pp. 11-31.
Contains brief discussion of the Norwegian artist's (1863-
1944) enigmatic homoerotic masterwork of 1904, "Bathing
Boys" (Oslo, Munch-Museet), pp. 20-22.

1646. ELIASOPH, PHILIP. **Paul Cadmus: Yesterday and
       Today.** Oxford, OH: Miami University Art Museum,
       1981. 128 pp.
This monograph on the American realist painter, which
also served as an exhibition catalogue, presents the
fruit of a scholars' serious study of the artist, but is

insufficient on the homoerotic aspects of the iconography. See review by Jim Wickliff, **Cabirion & Gay Books Bulletin**, no. 10 (Winter-Spring 1984), 25-27.

1647. ELLIOT, MARGUERITE TUPPER. "Lesbian Art and the Community," **Heresies**, no 3 (Fall 1977), 106-07.
Discusses the lesbian-feminist art community in Los Angeles during the mid 1970s. This issue contains other relevant items.

1648. ENDICOTT-ROSS, MICHAEL, et al. [Gay Art Issue.] **Alternate**, 2:12 (1980), 8-42.
Presents the then-growing phenomenon of galleries specializing in male imagery, followed by brief profiles of a dozen artists.

1649. FALKON, FELIX LANCE (pseud. of George Scithers). **A Historic Collection of Gay Art**. San Diego: Greenleaf, 1972. 225 pp.
Chiefly commercial and exploitation material.

1650. FARNHAM, EMILY. **Charles Demuth: Behind a Laughing Mask**. Norman: University of Oklahoma Press, 1971. 238 pp.
Somewhat conventional biography of the American homophile painter (1883-1934), but reproducing several revealing works. A Demuth catalogue raisonne is in preparation by Alford L. Eiseman.

1651. HAMMOND, HARMONY. **Wrappings: Essays in Feminism, Art and the Martial Arts**. New York: T.S.L. Press, 1984. 112 pp.
Essays by an outspoken New York lesbian artist and critic.

1652. HARDISON, SAM. "The Art and Politics of the Male Image: A Conversation between Sam Hardison and George Stambolian," **Christopher Street**, 4:7 (March 1980), 14-22.
Sam Hardison was director of the Robert Samuel Gallery (New York City), specializing in male-image art.

1653. HASKELL, BARBARA. **Marsden Hartley**. New York: New York University Press, 1980. 224 pp.
Based on a the comprehensive exhibition at the Whitney Museum, this is the first adequate account of the American artist's (1877-1943) life and imagery. Bibliography and list of exhibitions.

1654. HENDRICKS, GORDON. **The Life and Work of Thomas Eakins**. New York: Grossman, 1974. 367 pp.
Although concrete evidence of practice is still lacking, elements of homoerotic sensibility have been detected in the work of Eakins (1844-1916), one of America's greatest painters. See also Hendricks: **The Photographs of Thomas Eakins** (New York: Grossman, 1972. 214 pp.); includes a number of nude photographs of men and boys.

1655. HERRERA, HAYDEN. **Frida: A Biography of Frida
      Kahlo.** New York: Harper and Rowe, 1983. 256 pp.
Biography of the tempestuous life of the bisexual Mexican
painter.

1656. HIERONYMUS, EKKEHARD. **Elisar von Kupffer (1872–
      1942).** Basel: Kunsthalle, 1979. 20 pp.
Account of the artist-poet's life and neo-gnostic philosophy (Klarismus), together with his villa at Minusio in
Switzerland, the Sanctuarium Artis Elisarion, which became
the physical embodiment of his vision.

1657. HOCKNEY, DAVID. **David Hockney by David Hockney.**
      Edited by Nikos Stangos; introduction by Henry
      Geldzahler. New York: Abrams, 1976. 312 pp.
Candid autobiography, enriched with 414 illustrations, of
the chic English artist, including his affair with Peter
Schlesinger. For a more conventional art-historical
account of his development as a painter, see Marco Liv-
ingstone, **David Hockney** (New York: Holt, Rinehart and
Winston, 1981; 250 pp.).

1658. JULLIAN, PHILIPPE. **Dreamers of Decadence: Symbolist
      Painters of the 1890s.** Translated by Robert
      Baldick. New York: Praeger, 1971. 272 pp.
Remarkable conspectus of typical themes of late 19th-cen-
tury Symbolism, including some homosexual artists and
writers (pp. 47-48, 1121-13, 164, 183, 193).

1659. KIRSTEIN, LINCOLN. **Paul Cadmus.** New York: Imago,
      1984. 144 pp.
Handsomely produced book with 100 illustrations of paintings, drawings, and etchings. The text, by a long-time
associate of Cadmus, is regrettably opaque.

1660. LAMBOURNE, LIONEL, et al. **Solomon: A Family of
      Painters.** London: Geffrye Museum, 1985. 88 pp.
Exhibition catalogue of the work of the siblings Abraham,
Rebecca, and Simeon Solomon, of whom the last, a pre-Raph-
aelite with fin-de-siecle connections, was convicted
for buggery in 1873.

1661. LEONARD, MICHAEL. **Changing.** London: Gay Men's
      Press, 1983. 112 pp.
Sensitive drawings of chaste male striptease by a younger
English gay artist.

1662. LLOYD, PHOEBE. "Washington Allston: American Mar-
      tyr," **Art in America,** 72:3 (March 1984), 145-55,
      177-79.
Includes a sensitive exploration of the possible homosexuality of one of the "founding fathers" of American
painting.

1663. LUCIE-SMITH, EDWARD. **The Male Nude.** New York:
      Rizzoli, 1985. 176 pp.

The images derive from a 1983 London exhibition curated by François de Louville. Works by 49 artists, many English, and most executed in the 1970s and 80s.

1664. NEDRA, PIERRE. "Géricault et ses amis," **Arcadie**, no. 35 (November 1956), 31-40.
Argues that the French pioneer of romanticism (1791-1824) was homosexual based on his friendships. The argument has been accepted by Lord Kenneth Clark, but is rejected by Lorenz Eitner, a leading Géricault scholar.

1665. PAYNE, ELIZABETH ROGERS. "Anne Whitney, Sculptor," **Art Quarterly**, 25 (Autumn 1962), 244-61.
Whitney (1821-1915), an abolitionist and suffragist, lived with Adeline Manning, who devoted her life to her.

1666. PINCUS-WITTEN, ROBERT, et al. **Keith Haring.** New York: Tony Shafrazi Gallery, 1982. about 130 pp. (exhibition catalogue)
Documents the work (occasionally sexually explicit) of the New York wunderkind. For his subway graffiti, see Henry Geldzahler, **Art in Transit: Subway Drawing by Keith Haring.** (New York: Harmony Books, 1984; about 80 pp.).

1667. PLAGENS, PETER. "Gilbert and George: How English Is It?" **Art in America**, 72 (October 1982), 178-83.
On the art of the London-based duo, which incorporates sardonic camp elements.

1668. PORCELLA, ANTONIO (ed.). **Renzo Vespignani.** Venice, 1982. 82 pp.
Retrospective of a contemporary Italian artist.

1669. RADER, DOTSON. **Harold Stevenson.** New York: Alexander Iolas Gallery, 1973. (exhibition catalogue)
The work of a muralist active in Idabel, OK.

1670. RAVEN, ARLENE, and RUTH ISKIN. "Through the Peephole: Towards a Lesbian Sensibility in Art," **Chrysalis: A Magazine of Women's Culture,**no. 4 (1977), 19-31.
Begins an effort to define a lesbian aesthetic.

1671. REED, DAVID. "Repression and Exaggeration: The Art of Tom of Finland," **Christopher Street,** 4:8 (April 1980), 16-21.
The cartoon-like figures of this Finnish artist, each seemingly more macho than the last, have attained the status of minor gay-male icons.

1672. RESTREPO PELÁEZ, PEDRO. **El homosexualismo en el arte actual.** Bogota: Ediciones Tercer Mundo, 1969. 126 pp.
Echoing the ideas of the New York psychoanalyst Edmund Bergler, Restrepo holds that homosexuals are manipulating the art market and public taste to create transitory

fads. Abstract art is a product of this "feminizing tendency."

1673. RIVERS, LARRY. **Drawings and Digressions.** With
      Carol Brightman. New York: Clarkson N. Potter,
      1979. 164 pp.
This primarily heterosexual painter's recollections of his
love affair with poet Frank O'Hara casts valuable light
on the "bisexual" side of the New York School.

1674. ROCHE, PAUL. **With Duncan Grant in Southern Turkey.**
      London: Honeyglen, 1982. 134 pp.
The English artist Grant intersperses contemporary comment in his old age with reminiscences of the Bloomsbury
scene.

1675. RUSSELL, JOHN. **Francis Bacon.** Revised ed. New
      York: Oxford University Press, 1979. 192 pp.
Perceptive analysis of the imagery, which is sometimes
searingly homoerotic, of the leading British artist.
Bacon himself supervised the choice of the 241 illus-
trations making up Michel Leiris, **Francis Bacon** (New
York: 1984).

1676. SASLOW, JAMES. "Ars Gratia Erotica: The Laidback
      Leslie-Lohman Gallery Is Home for Homoerotic Art,"
      Advocate, no. 252 (October 18, 1978), 38-39.
On the unfortunately brief boomlet in gay-image galleries;
see also Saslow et al., "Gay Art and the Galleries,"
Advocate, no. 263 (March 22, 1979), 20-23. Saslow, an
Advocate editor, wrote many articles for the publication
on gay art in the the 1970s and early 80s.

1677. SECREST, MERYL. **Between Me and Life.** Garden City,
      NY: Doubleday, 1974. 432 pp.
Full-scale biography of the American artist Germaine
Brooks, a major figure in the Parisian expatriate scene.
In 1975 Arno Press of New York reprinted Brooks' **Por-
traits, Tableaux, Dessins,** which first appeared in Paris
in 1952.

1678. SOKOLOWSKI, THOMAS W. **The Sailor 1930-45: The
      Image of an American Demigod.** Norfolk, VA: Chrys-
      ler Museum, 1983. 116 pp. (exhibition catalogue)
Paintings, drawings, prints, photographs and advertisements of the American "gob," where--in many instances--a
homosexual subtext is evident.

1678A. STANLEY, NICK (ed.). **Out in Art.** London: Gay
       Men's Press, 1986. 96 pp.
Documents the work of five artists in their twenties--
Christopher Brown, Christopher Corr, Norman, Richard
Royle, and Graham Ward--exploring such themes as the
masculine stereotype, pornography, the fragility of relationships, the celebration of the male body, and the
need for tenderness.

1679. STILLMAN, AMY. [Bibliography of Lesbian Art and
       Artists], **Heresies**, no. 3 (Fall 1977), 115-17.
Records over 100 items, published and unpublished.

1680. TAVEL, HANS CHRISTOPH VON, et al. **Otto Meyer-Am-
       den: Begegnungen.** Bern: Kunstmuseum, 1985. 208 pp.
Exhibition catalogue, with supporting documentation, of
the work of the reclusive Swiss artist (1885-1933), who
often depicted young boys.

1681. TOMKINS, CALVIN. **Off the Wall: Robert Rauschenberg
       and the Art World of Our Time.** Garden City, NY:
       Doubleday, 1980. 324 pp.
Treats (with some discretion) the American artist's (b.
1925) liaisons with Jasper Johns, Steve Paxton, and Robert Peterson. (See p. 260 for the curious notion of a
"homintern" in the arts.)

1682. TYLER, PARKER. **The Divine Comedy of Pavel Tcheli-
       tchew.** New York: Fleet, 1967. 504 pp.
A pioneering effort to capture the sensibility of the
Russian-American surrealist painter.

E. PHOTOGRAPHY

Only in the early 20th century did such figures as Fred
Holland Day and Wilhelm von Gloeden open paths for exploring themes such as the male nude which had long been
of interest to homosexual artists. The 1970s saw a surge
of interest in erotic photography, making possible the
establishment of new reputations as well as the exploration of forgotten earlier figures.

1683. BARNES, LAWRENCE (ed.). **The Male Nude in Photog-
       raphy.** Waitsfield, VT: Vermont Crossroads Press,
       1980. 96 pp.
Representative selection based on an exhibition.

1684. BIREN, JOAN E. (pseud.: JEB). **Eye to Eye: Por-
       traits of Lesbians.** Washington, DC: Glad Hag
       Books, 1979.
Forty photographs, with introductory essay on the history
of lesbian photography by Judith Schwarz. See also: JEB,
"Lesbian Photography--Seeing through our Own Eyes,"
Studies in Visual Communication, 9 (Spring 1983), 81-95.

1685. BLANK, JOANI (ed.). **I Am My Lover.** Burlington,
       CA: Down There Press, 1978.
Photographs by Honey Lee Cottrell and Tee Corinne of women
masturbating.

1686. BLOK, DIANA, and MARLO BROEKMANS. **Invisible**

Forces. Amsterdam: Uitgeverij Bert Bakker, 1983.
Somewhat surreal imagery exploring women-women relationships.

1687. CORINNE, TEE. **Yantras of Woman Love.** Tallahassee,
       FL: Naiad Press, 1982. 64 pp.
The artist photographed women being sensual, and then sol-
arized and processed her images to create kaleidoscopic
patterns. See also her: **Labia Flowers** (Tallahassee, FL:
Naiad Press, 1981; 36 pp.).

1688. DOAN, WILLIAM, and CRAIG DIETZ. **Photoflexion: A
       History of Bodybuilding Photography.** New York:
       St. Martins Press, 1984. 127 pp.
One-hundred fifteen black-and-white photos originally
gathered for an exhibition. The text, while usefully surveying the history of this popular art form its
turn-of-the-century origins to the present, underplays
the homoerotic component.

1689. EMORY, MICHAEL (ed.). **The Gay Picture Book.**
       Chicago: Contemporary Books, 1978. 125 pp.
Images from 35 gay and lesbian photographers, assembled to
create a kind of community scrapbook, a blend of street
photography, photojournalism, and art.

1690. FALZONE BARBARO, MICHELE, MARINA MIRAGLIA, and
       ITALO MUSSA. **Le fotografie di Von Gloeden.**
       Milan: Longanesi, 1980. 128 pp.
Picture book on the noted German photographer of boys
(1856-1931), who resided in Sicily; with biographical
data. See also C. Leslie, below.

1691. FISCHER, HAL. **18th near Castro St x 24.** San
       Francisco: NFS Press, 1979. 56 pp.
Photographs taken over a 24-hour period at the corner of
18th and Castro streets in San Francisco.

1692. HOLABIRD, KATHERINE (ed.). **Women on Women.** Arber,
       NY: A & W Publishers, 1979.
Black-and-white and color photographs by twelve women
photographers. Holabird's introduction relates the
sensual character of the photos to women's need to
define their own sexuality.

1693. JUAN-CARLOS, RICARDO. **Photographing the Male.** New
       York: Crescent, 1983. 159 pp.
Phil Flasche's stunning photographs of men in every sort
of revealing pose make this book more an album than a how-
to guide.

1694. JUSSIM, ESTELLE. **Slave to Beauty.** Boston: David
       R. Godine, 1981. 310 pp.
Illustrated biography of the long-neglected, but historically important Boston art photographer F. Holland Day
(1864-1933), who among other things discovered the poet

Kahlil Gibran.

1695. KÖHLER, MICHAEL, and GISELA BARCHE. **Das Aktfoto:**
       Ansichten vom Körper im fotografischen Zeitalter:
       Aesthetik, Geschichte, Ideologie. Munich: Bucher,
       1985. 391 pp.
Attempts an encyclopedic survey of 150 years of nude
photography, both male and female, with many references
and index.

1696. LESLIE, CHARLES. **Wilhelm von Gloeden: Photograph-**
       er. New York: Soho Photographic Publishers,
       1977. 143 pp.
Documents the work of the German photographer (1856-1931),
who developed a romantic genre idealizing Sicilian youths
in pseudo-classical poses.

1697. LEYLAND, WINSTON (ed.). **Physique: A Pictorial**
       History of the Athletic Model Guild. San Francis-
       co: Gay Sunshine Press, 1983.
Presents the work of the Los Angeles firm that set an
exotic style which proved to be in tune with the tastes
of gay men from the 1940s to the 60s.

1698. LYNES, GEORGE PLATT. **George Platt Lynes Photo-**
       graphs, 1931-1955. Pasadena, CA: Twelvetrees
       Press, 1981. 156 pp.
Representative selection of 85 works of Lynes (1931-55),
who created a distinctive style by fusing elegance of pose
with expressive contrasts of light and shadow. While
influencing women's high fashion photography, at the same
time he was publishing many of his homophile photos in the
Swiss gay monthly **Der Kreis/Le Cercle** (under the pseudonym
of "Rolf").

1699. MAPPLETHORPE, ROBERT. **Robert Mapplethorpe.**
       Frankfurt am Main: Frankfurter Kunstverein, 1981.
       136 pp.
Catalogue of a retrospective exhibition of the contemporary American photographer, who specializes in transgressive themes.

1700. MARCUSE PFEIFFER GALLERY. **The Male Nude: A Survey**
       of Photography. New York: Marcuse Pfeiffer Gallery
       1978.
Catalogue for an exhibition, June 13-July 28, 1978. Introduction by Shelley Rice.

1701. MAROT, GÉRARD. **Les p'tits mecs.** Poissy: Editions
       Imagine, 1983. 62 pp.
Photographs of boys. See also his **Transparence** (Paris: G.
Tautin, 1977; 32 pp.)

1702. MICHALS, DUANE. **Homage to Cavafy.** New York: Addi-
       son, 1979.
Interpretive photographs by Michals to accompany ten poems

by Constantine Cavafy.

1703. PHILLIPS, DONNA-LEE, and LEW THOMAS (eds.). **Eros
       and Photography: An Exploration of Sexual Imagery
       and Photographic Practice.** San Francisco: Camera-
       work/NFS Press, 1977. 119 pp.
Essays and photographs.

1704. PUIG, HERMAN. **Akadémia: le nu académique français.**
       Paris: Puig, 1982.
Selection of historic academic photographs of the male
nude; one of several such collections gathered by this
author.

1705. RUSSELL, BRUCE. "Wilhelm von Pluschow and Wilhelm
       von Gloeden: Two Photo Essays," **Studies in Visual
       Communication,** 9:2 (1983), 57-80.
Affords a glimpse of the work and career of von Pluschow,
cousin of the better known von Gloeden.

1706. SECORD, FREDERICK. **Twelve: A Day in the Life of a
       Boy.** New York: Book Adventures, 1966. 156 pp.
Romantic photographs of a boy. A characteristic "soft-
core" publication of the period. Edited by Georges
St. Martin (pseud. of Martin W. Swithinbank).

1707. STEWART, STEPHEN. **Positive Image: A Portrait of
       Gay America.** New York: William Morrow, 1985. 191
       pp.
Photodocumentary recording many gay and lesbian leaders of
note assembled from extensive cross-country travel.

1708. TRESS, ARTHUR. **Facing Up.** New York: St. Martins
       Press, 1980. 79 pp.
Photographs of men in setting suggestive of the New York
City pier scene, now vanished. Introduction by Yves
Navarre.

1709. VICKERS, HUGO. **Cecil Beaton: A Biography.** Boston:
       Little, Brown, 1986. 656 pp.
Frank biography of the English society photographer, who
was an ultra-snob and "homosexualist" (his term), using
material expurgated from the published version of his
Diaries.

1710. WAUGH, TOM. "Photography, Passion and Power," **Body
       Politic** (March 1984), 29-33.
Describes a remarkable collection of historical gay photographs preserved in the Kinsey Institute, Indiana University.

1711. WEBER, BRUCE. **Photographs.** Pasadena,CA: Twelve-
       trees Press, 1983.
Weber's work created a new definition of male beauty in
the advertising world. Ninety gravure plates.

F. FILM

There were several exceptional films on homosexual themes
in the silent era. In the 1930s homosexuality went
largely underground, represented, up to a point, by sissy
parts and occasional "drag" performances. With the relaxation of formerly stringent U. S. censorship in the
1960s (see I.L), more overt depictions became possible
even in the mainstream cinema. At the same time a genre
of gay pornographic films appeared, becoming gradually
more explicit and finding a home in a series of "adult
theatres" in major cities. A special topic is the
existence of homosexual and lesbian performers, whose
orientation tends to be carefully concealed but sometimes
emerges, at least after their death. Only recently
have openly gay directors appeared, most of them European.

1712. ALLEN, NICK (pseud.). **Dynasty of Decadence.** North
        Hollywood, CA: Brandon House, 1966. 176 pp.
Anecdotes purporting to show that a "homosexual clique"
dominates the film and television industry in Hollywood.

1713. ANGER, KENNETH. **Hollywood Babylon II.** New York:
        Dutton, 1984. 332 pp.
This second helping of raunchy gossip offers some relevant
tidbits, unlike its predecessor **Hollywood Babylon** (Phoenix: Associated Professional Services, Inc. 1965; 271
pp.). Regrettably, neither book reflects the filmic
brilliance of the creator of **Fireworks** and **Scorpio Rising.**

1714. ARCE, HECTOR. **The Secret Life of Tyrone Power.**
        New York: William Morrow, 1979. 317 pp.
Notes a number of the bisexual actor's (1913-58) homosexual affairs with (usually unnamed) actors.

1715. ATWELL, LEE. "'Word Is Out' and 'Gay USA,'" **Film
        Quarterly,** 32 (Winter 1978-79), 50-57.
Sympathetic presentation of two film documentaries. Atwell is also author of a two-part article: "Homosexual
Themes in the Cinema," **Tangents,** 1:6 (March 1966), 4-10;
and 1:7 (April 1966), 4-9.

1716. AUSTIN, BRUCE A. "Portrait of a Cult Film Audi-
        ence: The Rocky Horror Picture Show," **Journal of
        Communication,** 31 (1981), 43-54.
The leading "midnight movie" cult, involving spectacular
participation rituals, which have attracted many young
gay people.

1717. BACHSTEIN, HEIM. "Anders als die Anderen: Homo-
        sexualität in Film," **Retro** (Munich), 16 (July-Au-
        gust 1982), 5-12.
Brief survey of homosexuality in the cinema.

1718. BATTCOCK, GREGORY (ed.)   **The New American Cinema:**
       A Critical Anthology. New York: Dutton, 1967.   256
       pp.
Twenty-nine essays reflecting the heyday of the so-called
Underground Cinema, which was strongly tinged with gay
sensibility, while rarely displaying overt homosexual
content.

1719. BECKER, EDITH et al.   "Lesbians and Film," **Jump**
       Cut, nos. 25-26 (1981), 17-21.
Argues that while feminist criticism has developed new
theoretical tools with which to examine cinematic images,
structures, and themes, nevertheless there has been a
failure to confront lesbian issues. This article introduces a valuable special section of the issue on lesbians
and film (with filmo graphy).

1720. BECKER, RAYMOND DE.   "Notes sur un cinéma homo-
       phile," **Arcadie,** no. 74 (February 1960), 97-100.
Perhaps the first article on the subject.

1721. BELL-METEREAU, REBECCA.   **Hollywood Androgyny.** New
       York: Columbia University Press, 1985.   260 pp.
Subjective examination of American films involving
cross-dressing and sex-role reversals from Charlie
Chaplin's "The Masquerader" (1914) to the present.

1722. BOSWORTH, PATRICIA.   **Montgomery Clift: A Biography.**
       New York: Harcourt Brace Jovanovich, 1978.   438 pp.
An honest and sympathetic account of the homosexual actor's tormented life.   See also Robert LaGuardia, **Monty: A**
Biography of Montgomery Clift (New York: Arbor House,
1977;   304 pp.).

1723. BRIAN, DENNIS.   **Tallulah, Darling: A Biography of**
       Tallulah Bankhead. New York: Macmillan, 1980.   292
       pp.
Somewhat more forthcoming than the other biographies of
the much gossipped-about actress (see pp. 2, 48, 66, 240-
41, 283).

1724. CODY, BART.   "How Movies Got Gay ... and Gayer
       .. and Gayer," **Advocate,** 2 (August 1968), 16-19.
First report in the Los Angeles magazine.

1725. COMMISSION ON GAY/LESBIAN ISSUES IN SOCIAL WORK
       EDUCATION.   **Annotated Filmography of Selected Films**
       with Lesbian/Gay Content. New York: Council on
       Social Work Education, 1984.   25 pp.
Part I is a comprehensive list of about 70 "educational
films;" Part II a selection of 25 feature-length films.
Appendix provides a list of distributors.

1726. CONNOR, EDWARD.   "Film in Drag: Transvestism on the
       Screen," **Films in Review,** 32 (1981), 398-405.
Short survey of the material documented more fully by

H. Dickens, below.

1727. DAVIDSON, SARAH. **Rock Hudson: His Own Life.** New
        York: William Morrow, 1986. 311 pp.
Authorized biography made with the actor's assistance
before he died of AIDS on October 2, 1985. See also Mark
Bego, **Rock Hudson: Public and Private.** (New York: New
American Library, 1986: 189 pp.); and J. Oppenheimer and
J. Vitek, **Idol** (New York: Villard Books, 1986; 224 pp.).

1728. DAWSON, BONNIE. **Women's Films in Print: An
        Annotated Guide to 800 Titles of 16mm Films by
        Women.** San Francisco: Bootlegger, 1975. 165 pp.
Complements the historical list prepared by K. Sullivan,
below.

1729. DICKENS, HOMER. **What a Drag: Men as Women and
        Women as Men in the Movies.** New York: Quill,
        1984. 266 pp.
A picture book of stills with index of performers that
reveals a surprising amount of material.

1730. DURGNIAT, RAYMOND. **Sexual Alienation in the
        Cinema: The Dynamics of Sexual Freedom.** London:
        Studio Vista, 1973. 319 pp.
Concentrating on the period 1966-73, offers some material
on Kenneth Anger and Andy Warhol.

1731. DYER, RICHARD. "Pasolini and Homosexuality"
        in: Paul Willemen (ed.), **Pier Paolo Pasolini.**
        London: British Film Institute, 1977, pp. 56-63.
Argues that the representation of the male figure in
Pasolini's work is embedded in a tradition of self-
oppressive rhetoric, which "reiterates heterosexual
norms." See also his: "Don't Look Now--The Male Pin-up,"
Screen, 23:3/4 (1982).

1732. DYER, RICHARD. "Victim: Hermeneutic Project," **Film
        Form,** 1 (1977), 3-22.
Analysis of the landmark 1961 British film featuring Dirk
Bogarde.

1733. DYER, RICHARD (ed.). **Gays and Film.** Enlarged ed.
        New York: New York Zoetrope, 1984. 110 pp.
The original core of the 1977 edition (London: British
Film Institute) comprised three essays: "Lesbians and
Film--Some Thoughts: by Caroline Sheldon (pp. 5-26);
"Stereotyping" by Richard Dyer (pp. 27-39); and "Camp
and Gay Sensibility" by Jack Babuscio (pp. 40-57). While
employing different political perspectives, all reflect
the gay-liberation approach characteristic of the period.
The enlarged edition contains a new essay, "Notes on
Recent Gay Film Criticism" Andy Medhurst (pp. 58-64), and
important new filmography (pp. 69-107), and additional
bibliography.

1734. EDWARDS, DOUGLAS et al. "Gays and the Art of
      Motion Picture Making," **Advocate,** no. 285 (Febru-
      ary 7, 1980), 28-32+.
Inside scrutiny of gays in Hollywood and recent trends
in film.

1735. EISNER, LOTTE. **Murnau.** Revised ed. Berkeley:
      University of California Press, 1973. 287 pp.
Somewhat reticent account of life and works of the noted
homophile German-American director, who died mysteriously
in 1931.

1736. FASSBINDER, EGON et al. (eds.). **Film.** Berlin: Ro-
      sa Winkel Verlag, 1986. 96 pp. (Klappentexte, 6)
A mixed bag of interviews and essays by German gay film
makers and critics.

1737. FORBES, DENNIS. "Creating Peter Berlin," **After
      Dark,** 7 (February 1975), 44-51.
Peter Berlin (a.k.a. Peter Burian), a German actor working
in the United States, fashioned his own image as a porn
star.

1738. GARS, JEAN-FRANÇOIS. **Cinémas homosexuels.** Paris:
      1983. 165 pp.
Originally published as **CinémAction,** no. 15 (1981). A
mixed bag: short, sometimes superficial pieces, many
translated from English-language sources; filmography of
200 items (pp. 160-65).

1739. GIDAL, PETER. **Andy Warhol: Films and Paintings.**
      London: Studio Vista, 1971. 160 pp.
Survey of the American pop artist at the height of his
film-making phase.

1740. GUTHMAN, EDWARD. "Gay Film Festivals," **Advocate,**
      no 345 (June 24, 1982), 59-63.
On a annual institution emerging in a number of North
American and European cities.

1741. HAYMAN, RONALD. **Fassbinder: Film Maker.** London:
      Weidenfeld and Nicolson, 1984.
Factual, but shallow biography of the late German director, asserting that "Fassbinder's importance as a film
maker depends on his ability to translate his neurosis
into cinematic fiction." There is an extensive and
growing literature in German, some of which has contributed, inadvertently or intentionally, to the myth of the
doomed gay director--a German counterpart to the Pasolini
image.

1742. HEPWORTH, JOHN. "Hitchcock's Homophobia," **Chris-
      topher Street,** no. 64 (May 1982), 42-49.
While this article on the noted director received a mixed
review, it raises a kind of question that needs to
be asked.

1743. HETZE, STEFANIE. **Happy-end für wen? Kino und
      lesbischen Frauen.** Frankfurt am Main: Tende,
      1986. 190 pp.
Attempts a comprehensive view of lesbianism in film
(including such stereotypes as the old maid, trousers
roles, and vampires) from a lesbian-feminist standpoint.
Filmography with short descriptive comments.

1744. HIGHAM, CHARLES. **Charles Laughton: An Intimate
      Biography.** Garden City, NY: Doubleday, 1976. 239
      pp.
Frank life of the English actor (1889-1962), with sympathetic Introduction by his wife, Elsa Lanchester.

1745. HIGHAM, CHARLES. **Errol Flynn: The Untold Story.**
      New York: Doubleday, 1979. 370 pp
Controversial, possibly unreliable account of the Austra-
lian-born film actor (1909-59) as bisexual and spy.

1746. HINXMAN, MARGARET, and SUSAN D'ARCY. **The Cinema of
      Dirk Bogarde.** South Brunswick, NJ: A. S. Barnes,
      1974. 200 pp.
Survey of the work of one of the few major film stars to
"come out" as a homosexual. Recently, Bogarde has written
several novels and memoirs of relevance.

1747. HIRSCHFELD, MAGNUS, and HERMANN BECK. **Gesetze der
      Liebe: aus der Mappe eines Sexualforschers.** Ber-
      lin: Neue Gesellschaft, 1927. 64 pp.
Summary of the German silent film made to propagate
Hirschfeld's ideas, with stills.

1748. HOBERMAN, JAMES, and JONATHAN ROSENBAUM. **Midnight
      Movies.** New York: Harper and Row, 1983. 338 pp.
Well-informed account of the popular-culture phenomenon,
including the (largely gay) cult that has grown up
around "The Rocky Horror Picture Show"; and the John
Waters films (featuring Divine).

1749. HOCQUENGHEM, GUY. **Race d'ep: un siècle d'images de
      l'homosexualité.** Paris: Editions Libres/Hallier,
      1977. 192 pp.
Glimpses from 100 years of male homosexuality, closely
following the film of the same title, sometimes known in
English-speaking countries as "The Homosexual Century."
Many illustrations.

1750. HUGHES, JEREMY. "Professional Innovator," **In
      Touch,** 19 (August-September 1975), 54-57.
About Pat Rocco, Los Angeles film-maker and gay community
leader.

1751. JACOBSON, WOLFGANG et al. **Rosa von Praunheim.**
      Munich: Hansen, 1984. 280 pp.
Essays on the controversial German gay film-maker (a.k.a.
Holger Mischwitzky), with filmography.

1752. JARMAN, DEREK. **Derek Jarman's Caravaggio.** London:
Thames and Hudson, 1986. 132 pp.
Illustrated text of the film liberally interpreting the
life of the Italian artist, which won a Silver Bear award
at the 1986 Berlin film festival. On the British director's work, see the special issue, "Derek Jarman ... Of
Angels and Apocalypse," **Afterimage,** no. 12 (1986); 89 pp.

1753. JESTER, KLAUS. "Die 'Normalen' ihre eigene
Betroffenheit bewusst machen," **Cinema** (Switzerland), 3 [no. 77], (1980), 20-32.
On gay films as political instruments for "consciousness raising."

1754. KANE, B. M. "Thomas Mann and Visconti," **Modern
Languages,** 53 (June 1972), 74-79.
On the translation of Mann's novella "Death in Venice"
to the screen.

1755. KEPNER, JIM. "The Posthumous Trial of Ramon
Novarro," **Advocate,** 3:9 (October 1969), 5, 20-21,
23; 3:10 (November 1969), 1, 3, 8; 3:11 (December
1969), 5, 36-37; 4:1 (January 1970), 5-6, 9.
Careful coverage of the trial of Thomas and Paul Ferguson
for the murder of silent film star Novarro (1905-1968).

1756. KLEINHANS, CHUCK et al. [Special Section:] "Gays
and Film," **Jump Cut,** no. 16 (November 1977), 13-33.
Stimulating pieces, generally from a "cultural-left"
perspective. See also Ray Olson, "Gay Film Work: Affecting but Too Evasive," **Jump Cut,** no. 20 (May 1979),
9-12.

1757. KNIGHT, ARTHUR, and HOLLIS ALPERT. **Playboy's Sex
in Cinema.** Chicago: Playboy Press, 1971. 144 pp.
Includes some material on homosexuality, esp. in the
experimental cinema.

1758. KUREISHI, HANIF. **My Beautiful Laundrette and The
Rainbow Sign.** London: Faber, 1986. 111 pp.
Script of the 1984 British film, which concerns a love
affair between an Anglo-Pakistani youth and his punk
Wasp assistant, followed by an astringent, partly autobio-
graphical essay by Kureishi.

1759. LANCINI, FIORENZO, and PAOLO SANGALLI. **La gaia
musa.** Milan: Gammalibri, 1981. 133 pp.
Somewhat impressionistic account of the international
"gay film" (as seen in and from Italy). Index of "Filmi
citati," pp. 129-32.

1760. LAVALLEY, AL. "The Great Escape," **American Film,**
10 (April 1985), 29-34, 70-71.
During the years of absence of any real representation of
themselves on screen, gay audiences created their own
canons for straight films, yielding an aesthetic that

was part projection and part exposure of strands of gay
sensibility brought to celluloid by homosexual set de-
signers, makeup men, costumers, writers, actors, and
directors.

1761. LAVALLEY, AL, et al. "Out of the Closet and on to
       the Screen," **American Film**, 7:10 (September 1982),
       57-64, 81.
Symposium of nine gay film critics exploring positive
aspects of recent Hollywood films, esp. "Making Love."

1762. LENNE, GERARD. **Sex on the Screen: Eroticism in
       Film.** New York: St. Martin's Press, 1985. 352 pp.
Popular survey, with 300 photographs, including some
discussion of gay men and lesbians, as well as S & M and
fetishism.

1763. LEOPOLD, ALLAN. "Actor Calvin Culver," **In Touch**
       (July 1979), 16-23.
Profile of the New York actor who (as "Casey Donovan")
projected a wholesome-sexy image in "The Boys in the Band"
and succeeding porno films.

1764. **Liebe der Nacht: Homosexuelle in Film.** Basel:
       HABS, 1982. 54 pp.
Listing and description of homosexual-theme films, with
filmography, bibliography, addresses, and stills.

1765. LIMBACHER, J. L. **Sexuality in World Cinema.**
       Metuchen, NJ: Scarecrow, 1983. 2 vols. (1511 pp.)
This reference work includes sections on lesbians and
gay men in film.

1766. MCDONALD, BOYD. **Cruising the Movies: A Sexual
       Guide to "Oldies" on TV.** New York: Gay Presses of
       New York, 1985. 175 pp.
Sassy animadversions on popular entertainment figures,
gay and straight, as seen on TV, by the founding editor
of **Straight to Hell** magazine.

1767. MELLEN, JOAN. **Women and Their Sexuality in the New
       Film.** New York: Horizon Press, 1973. 255 pp.
In this feminist study, see "Lesbianism in the Movies"
(pp. 74-105), "Visconti's Death in Venice" (pp. 203-15),
and "Outfoxing Lawrence" (pp. 216-28).

1768. PERRY, GEORGE. **Life of Python: And Now for Some-
       thing Completely Different.** Boston: Little, Brown,
       1983. 192 pp.
Popular illustrated account of the British satire group
Monty Python, first on television and more recently in
films. Apart from the high camp character of the troupe,
many of its principals have been gay.

1769. PETERSON, WOLFGANG, and ULRICH GREIWE. **Die
       Resonanz: Briefe und Dokumente zum Film "Die**

Konsequenz." Frankfurt am Main: Fischer, 1981.
Articles and letters responding to the pro-homosexual
film made from the novel by Alexander Ziegler.

1770. PEVNIK, STEFAN. "Gay Filmmakers Confront Media
Homophobia in the US," **Advocate,** no 331 (November
26, 1981), 37-38.
The National Association of Lesbian and Gay Filmmakers
is addressing the need to crate a market for gay media.
It seeks to provide a support network, offers financial
consultation and funding leads, pursues job markets, and
has supported demonstrations against homophobic films.

1771. PHILBERT, BERTRAND. **L'homosexualité a l'écran.**
Paris: H. Veyrier, 1984. 180 pp.
Lavishly illustrated survey. See also: Armand Jammot,
Les homosexuels aux dossiers de l'écran. (Paris: Robert
Laffont, 1975; 93 pp.).

1772. PHILIPS, GENE D. "The Boys on the Bandwagon: Homosexuality and the Movies," in: Thomas R. Atkins
(ed.), **Sexuality in the Movies.** Bloomington: Indiana University Press, 1975, pp. 157-71.
Hollywood began coming to grips with homosexuality in
the late 1960s, still trailing behind Britain and the
U.S. Underground.

1773. PRAUNHEIM, ROSA VON (pseud. of Holger Mischwitzky).
Sex und Karriere. Reinbek bei Hamburg: Rowohlt,
1978. 349 pp.
Provocative memoir by the Berlin film-maker and activist;
with filmography to date.

1774. PURDON, NOEL. "Gay Cinema," **Cinema Papers,** no. 10
(September-October 1976), 115-19.
Notes by an English film critic.

1775. RAYNS, TONY (ed.). **Fassbinder.** Second ed. London: British Film Institute, 1980. 121 pp.
Essays covering various aspects of the late German director's career.

1776. ROWE, CAREL. **The Baudelairean Cinema: A Trend
within the American Avant-Garde.** Ann Arbor, MI:
UMI Research Press, 1982. 172 pp.
Argues that a trend in American avant-garde ("under-
ground") cinema, esp. as seen in the work of Jack Smith,
Kenneth Anger, and Andy Warhol, continues the 19th-century
decadent/symbolist aesthetic rooted in the work of the
French poet Charles Baudelaire.

1777. RUSSO, VITO. **The Celluloid Closet: Homosexuality
in the Movies.** New York: Harper and Row, 1981.
256 pp.
Restores visibility by unearthing neglected and repressed
moments of film history. Includes an important essay on

the "sissy" type. Informed by 1970s gay-liberation politics, sometimes overstated in terms of righteous indignation. See the thoughtful essay-review by Richard Dyer,
in: **Studies in Visual Communication**, 9:2 (Spring 1982),
52-56.

1778. SANZIO, ALAIN, and PAUL-LOUIS THIRARD. **Luchino
      Visconti cinéaste.** Paris: Persona, 1984. 174 pp.
Seductively illustrated survey of the films of the Italian
director (1906-76).

1779. SCHEUGL, HANS. **Sexualität und Neurose im Film:
      Kinomythen von Griffith bis Warhol.** Munich: Han-
      ser, 1974. 433 pp.
This survey of "neurosis" in film includes considerable
discussion of homosexuality.

1780. SCHIDOR, DIETER. **Querelle: The Film Book.** New
      York: 1983. 180 pp.
Script and stills from Rainer Werner Fassbinder's last,
controversial film, derived from Jean Genet's novel.

1781. SCHUMACH, MURRAY. **The Face on the Cutting Room
      Floor: The Story of Movie and Television Censor-
      ship.** New York: William Morrow, 1964. 305 pp.
Comprehensive and temperate account of the 40-year blight
of censorship in Hollywood, which goes far to explain the
stunted history of gay representation in the medium.

1782. SERVADIO, GAIA. **Luchino Visconti.** New York: Frank-
      lin Watts, 1983. 262 pp.
Life of the great Italian director (1906-76), showing his
shift to homosexuality in Paris during the 1930s and subsequent relationships.

1783. SHOELL, WILLIAM. **Stay Out of the Shower: 25 Years
      of Shocker Films Beginning with "Psycho."** New
      York: Dembner Books, 1985. 184 pp.
Popular illustrated survey, including "snuff" and "splat-
ter" films. See esp. pp. 57-66.

1784. SICILIANO, ENZO. **Pasolini: A Biography.** Trans-
      lated by John Shepley. New York: Random House,
      1982. 435 pp.
Stresses political aspects of the director-writer's life.
See also **Pasolini on Pasolini: Interviews with Oswald
Stack** (Bloomington: Indiana University Press, 1969; 176
pp.).

1785. SIEBENAND, PAUL ALCUIN. **The Beginnings of Gay
      Cinema in Los Angeles: The Industry and the
      Audience.** Los Angeles: University of Southern
      California, 1975. 213 pp. (unpublished disser-
      tation, Department of Communications and Cinema)
Careful study of the subject, created with the help of
ONE Institute and the filmmakers themselves.

1786. SIKOV, ED. "Homosexuals, Bandits, and Gangsters:
      Gay Images in La Cage aux folles," **Cineaste**, 2:4
      (1982), 30-35.
Holds that this "comic froufrou" demands camp recognition,
but ultimately disfigures camp humor by appealing to re-
actionary stereotypes.

1787. SITNEY, P. ADAMS. **Visionary Film: The American
      Avant-Garde, 1943-1978.** Second ed. New York: Ox-
      ford University Press, 1979. 463 pp.
First in-depth study of the so-called "cinema Under-
ground," including the work of Kenneth Anger, James
Broughton, Gregory Markopoulos, Ron Rice, and Jack Smith.

1788. STORA, JEAN-PIERRE. **Jean Marais.** Paris: Pac
      Editions, 1984.
Album of photographs of the actor, a protege of Jean
Cocteau, some of whose unpublished writings on Marais
are included here, as well as interview material by
Stora.

1789. STREFF, JEAN. **Le masochisme au cinéma, dans l'art
      et la littérature.** Paris: Veyrier, 1978. 272 pp.
A study of masochism in the arts, with some relevance to
our subject.

1790. SULLIVAN, KAYE. **Films for, by and about Women.**
      Metuchen, NJ: Scarecrow, 1980. 552 pp.
See index under "homosexuality" and "lesbianism."

1791. TUCHMAN, MITCH. "Journals: L.A.," **Film Comment**,
      13 (May-June 1977), 4-5.
Interview with Bill Dakota, publisher of the **Hollywood
Star**, a raunchy gay scandal sheet.

1791A. TUCKER, SCOTT. "Sex, Death and Free Speech: The
       Fight to Stop Friedkin's Cruising," in Elliott
       Shore et al. (eds.), **Alternative Papers: Selections
       from the Alternative Press, 1979-1980** (Philadel-
       phia: Temple University Press, 1982), pp. 322-29.
Thoughtful essay on the implications of the street effort
to stop the/filming. Reprinted from **Body Politic** (Novem-
ber 1979), 23-27; and followed by a note by Leo Case and
Gary Kinsman, pp. 329-30. See also Scottie Ferguson, "The
Film as Film: A Different Critical View," **Advocate**, no.
290 (April 17, 1980), 15, 20; Tom Ryan, "Cruising 1,"
Cinema Papers, no. 29 (October-November 1980), 322-24; and
Louis Tjetje and Gary Schuler, "Setting 'Cruising'
Straight," **Union Seminary Quarterly Review**, 35 (Spring-
Summer 1980), 211-16.

1792. TURAN, KENNETH, and STEPHEN F. ZITO. **Sinema: Amer-
      ican Pornographic Films and the People Who Make
      Them.** New York: New American Library, 1974. 273
      pp.
Comprehensive popular study with interviews of filmakers

and stars; see esp. pp. 120-27 (on Pat Rocco) and pp. 209-
19 (the homosexual blue movie).

1793. TYLER, PARKER. **Screening the Sexes: Homosexuality
       in the Movies.** New York: Holt, Rinehart and
       Winston, 1972. 367 pp.
Landmark work by the veteran American homophile writer
and critic, now somewhat dated because of reliance on
inappropriate psychoanalytic concepts.

1793A. VERSTRAETEN, PAUL. "Homoseksualiteit in de film:
        weg bij de pisbak," **VPRO-Cinema**, 2 (January-April
        1985), 14-18.
Discusses a number of old and new films. This issue of
the Dutch periodical contains several other relevant
short articles.

1794. VOGEL, AMOS. **Film as a Subversive Art.** New
       York: Random House, 1974. 336 pp.
In this study by a New York critic active in the Under-
ground Cinema, see the chapter, "The Breaking of Sexual
Taboos: Homosexuality and Other Variants."

1795. WATNEY, SIMON. "Hollywood's Homosexual World,"
       Screen, 23:3/4 (September-October 1982), 107-21.
Includes discussion of the "Cruising" controversy.

1796. WAUGH, TOM. "Men's Pornography: Gay and Straight,"
       Jump Cut, no. 30 (March 1985), 30-35.
Presents a series of charts comparing the two film genres
as to production, consumption, iconography (sexual acts
presented), and political context.

1796A. WAUGH, TOM (THOMAS). "Murnau: The Films Behind the
        Man," **Body Politic**, no. 51 (March-April 1979),
        31-34.
Seeks to show how the art of the director Friedrich Wilhelm Murnau (1888-1931) was shaped by his place in the
heterosexist society of the day.

1797. WERNER, GÖSTA. **Mauritz Stiller och hans filmer
       1912-1916.** Stockholm: Norstet & Soners, 1969.
       380 pp.
Contains the text of Stiller's 1916 film "The Wings,"
based on Herman Bang's novel **Mikael.** This is said to be
the "first gay film" by Mark Finch, **Body Politic**, no 107
(October 1984), 32.

1798. WOOD, ROBIN. "Responsibilities of a Gay Film
       Critic," **Film Comment**, 14 (January-February 1978),
       12-17.
Reflections of a respected British critic, who is now
Professor of Film Studies, York University, Ontario.
See also his essay collection: **Hollywood from Vietnam to
Reagan** (New York: Columbia University Press, 1986; 328
pp.).

1799. WRANGLER, JACK (pseud. of Jack Stillman), and CARL
      JOHNES. **The Jack Wrangler Story: What's a Nice Boy
      Like You Doing in a Business Like This?** New York:
      St. Martins Press, 1984. 256 pp.
Sympathetic, but not altogether candid account of the gay
porno star's extensive career, concluding in a heterosexual relationship with singer Margaret Whiting.

1800. YACOWAR, MAURICE. **Tennessee Williams and Film.**
      New York: Frederick Ungar, 1977. 168 pp.
Fifteen chapters on the major films made from his writings, from "The Glass Menagerie" (1950) onwards.

1801. ZIMMERMAN, BONNIE. "Daughters of Darkness: Lesbian
      Vampires," **Jump Cut**, no. 24-25 (1981), 23-24.
Pre-1970 examples express a nostalgia for death and a
subtle "juxtaposition of erotic and macabre imagery";
after 1970 film-makers began to explore the links between
sex and violence not only in a heterosexual context, but
in a lesbian one as well.

                    G. THEATER AND DANCE

Homosexual themes occurred as a matter of course in
ancient Greek tragedy and comedy (see III.C). This
tradition was interrupted in late Roman times, and the
Renaissance theater represents a new start (though it was
influenced, especially in Italy, by classical prototypes). The employment of boy actors in women's roles led
to a certain undercurrent of same-sex feeling, as seen
particularly in the Elizabethan theater. Analogous
phenomena are found in the dramas of China (III.Q) and
Japan (III.R). The prominence of homosexual and lesbian
players (and their counterparts in the dance) in the 19th
and 20th century is well known, but has been little
studied as such.

1802. ACKROYD, PETER. **Dressing Up: Transvestism and
      Drag: The History of an Obsession.** New York: Simon
      and Schuster, 1979. 160 pp.
Broad-gauged survey of historical and cross-cultural
aspects. See esp. "Transvestism as Performance" (pp. 89-
140). 146 illustrations.

1803. ARMSTRONG, JAMES. "Interview: Charles Pierce,
      Female Impersonator," **Advocate**, no. 190 (May 19,
      1976), 19-21.
Pierce's career reflects a considerable tradition in
American gay-male entertainment. For an anthropological
approach to the broader context, see Esther Newton, **Mother
Camp: Female Impersonators in America** (Englewood Cliffs,
NJ: Prentice-Hall, 1972; 136 pp.).

1804. BAKER, ROGER. **Drag: A History of Female Imperson-
       ation on the Stage.** London: Triton Books, 1968.
       256 pp.
Performance transvestism culminating in "intentional
glamor" in the 20th century.

1805. BARISH, JONAS A. **The Antitheatrical Prejudice.**
       Berkeley: University of California Press, 1981.
       499 pp.
In this substantial history of a persistent tradition,
gender crossing emerges as one source of the prejudice;
see pp. 44, 287, 321-22.

1806. BINNS, J. W. "Women or Transvestites on the
       Elizabethan Stage: An Oxford Controversy," **Six-
       teenth Century Journal,** 5 (October 1974), 95-120.
Reviews the controversy among Gager, Gentili, and Rain-
olds, with its reflexes on both the academic and popular
stages.

1807. BOWERS, FAUBION. **Theatre in the East: A Survey of
       Asian Dance and Drama.** New York: T. Nelson, 1956.
       374 pp.
In this somewhat uneven survey, see pp. 140, 158, 189,
198-99, 228-31, 260-61.

1808. BOYETTE, PURVIS E. "Wanton Humor and Wanton
       poets: Homosexuality in Marlowe's Edward II,"
       Tulane Studies in English, 22 (1977), 33-50.
A study of themes and imagery.

1809. BRADBURY, GAIL. "Irregular Sexuality in the
       Spanish Comedia," **Modern Language Review,** 76 (July
       1981), 566-80.
Spanish gender-disguise plays of the **siglo de oro** and
their roots in Italian Renaissance comedy.

1810. BRAVO VILLASANTE, CARMEN. **La mujer vestida de
       hombre en el teatro Español, siglos XVI-XVII.**
       Madrid: Revista de Occidente, 1955. 238 pp.
In this study of women dressed as men on the classic
Spanish stage, see pp. 196-98 on Catalina Erauso, the
female ensign.

1811. BRECHT, STEFAN. **Queer Theatre.** Frankfurt am
       Main: Suhrkamp, 1978. 178 pp.
Occasional essays on the experimental theater in New York
City from 1965 on, esp. in the work of Charles Ludlam,
Jack Smith, Ronald Tavel, and Andy Warhol.

1812. BUCKLE, RICHARD. **Diaghilev.** New York: Athenaeum,
       1979. 616 pp.
Standard biography of the great Russian ballet impresario
(1872-1929), with candid discussion of his sexual liaisons. See also Buckle: **Nijinsky.** (New York: Simon and
Schuster, 1971; 482 pp.). See also S. Karlinsky, below.

1813. CANALES, LUIS. "O Homossexualismo como Tema no
       Moderno Teatro Brasileiro," **Luso-Brazilian Review**,
       18 (1981), 173-81.
Analyzes some recent plays as evidence that Brazilian
society is freeing itself of taboos about homosexuality.

1814. CARLSEN, JAMES W. "Images of the Gay Male in
       Contemporary Drama," in: James W. Chesebro (ed.),
       Gayspeak. New York: Pilgrim Press, 1981, pp. 163--
       74.
Assesses recent plays, using Mart Crowley's "Boys in
the Band"(1968) as the watershed.

1815. CHESLEY, ROBERT. "A Perfect Relationship with Gay
       Theatre: Playwright Doric Wilson," **Advocate**, no.
       264 (April 5, 1579), 33-34.
Profile of a key figure in NYC's gay theater movement.

1816. CURTIN, KAIER. "We Can Always Call Them Bulgar-
       ians," **New York Native** (August 1-14, 1983), 39-41.
Lesbianism in American theater from the late 19th century
onwards.

1817. DAVIES, W. ROBERTSON. **Shakespeare's Boy Actors**.
       London: 1939. 217 pp.
Standard, but reticent work on this important aspect of
Elizabethan theater practice.

1818. DEATS, SARA MUNSON. "Myth and Metamorphosis in
       Marlowe's Edward II," **Texas Studies in Literature
       and Language**, 22 (Fall 1980), pp. 304-32.
Shows the playwright's use of mythological allusion, particularly as illustrative of the relationship between the
king and his favorite Gaveston.

1819. **Drag Show**. Woollhara, Australia: Currency Press,
       1977. 144 pp.
Includes Reg Livermore on Sydney's transvestites, Rose
Jackson on drag queens, Holly Brown on being on stage,
members of the Seashore Club talking about transvestism,
and the texts of two drag plays (by Peter Kenna and Steve
J. Spear).

1820. DYNES, WAYNE. "Bibliographical Essay: Homosexual-
       ity and Theater," **Cabirion and Gay Books Bulletin**,
       no. 12 (Spring-Summer 1985), 20-22.
Historically arranged survey of secondary literature.

1821. EMDE BOAS, COENRAAD VAN. **Shakespeare's sonnetten
       en hun verband met de travesti-double spelen: een
       medisch-psychologische studie**. Amsterdam: Wereld-
       Bibliothek, 1952. 528 pp.
Studies the Sonnets in comparison with Shakespeare's
double-disguise plays ("As You Like It," "Cymbeline,"
"Twelfth Night," and "Two Gentlemen of Verona"); with
extensive citations and bibliography. Short summaries in

English are his: "The Connection between Shakespeare's
Sonnets and his 'Travesti-double' Plays," **International
Journal of Sexology**, 4 (1950), 67-72; and "The Boy Actor
and the 'Double Disguise' in Shakespeare's Works," **International Journal of Greek Love**, 1:1 (1965), 18-23.

1822. FRANK, LEAH D. "Torch Song Lights Up Broadway:
       First Gay Play to Go Legit, **Advocate**, no.347 (July
       22, 1982), 41-43.
On the phenomenal success of Harvey Fierstein's trilogy.
See also Anna Mayo, "Harvey Fierstein and 'Torch Song
Trilogy' on Broadway," **Village Voice** (October 12, 1982),
43-47.

1823. FREEBURG, VICTOR OSCAR. **Disguise Plots in Elizabe-
       than Drama: A Study in Stage Tradition.** New York:
       Columbia University Press, 1915. 241 pp.
See "The Boy Bride," pp. 61-120.

1824. FROW, GERALD. **"Oh, Yes It Is!" A History of Pan-
       tomime.** London: British Broadcasting Corporation,
       1985. 192 pp.
Well-researched history of the British pantomime tradition—which has incorporated both male and female cross--
dressing perfomances—from its origins in the **commedia
dell'arte** to the present.

1825. FUCHS, HANNS. "Die Homosexualität in Dramen der
       Gegenwart und Zukunft," **Die Kritik des öffentlichen
       Lebens**, 17 [no. 215] (August 1902), 512-18.
Homosexuality in the plays of the present and the future.
Probably the first article on the subject.

1826. GELLERT, BRUCE. "A Survey of the Treatment of the
       Homosexual in Some Plays," **Mattachine Review**, 7:3
       (March 1961), 11-21.
Pioneering American article.

1827. HALL, RICHARD. **Three Plays for a Gay Theater and
       Three Essays.** San Francisco: Grey Fox Press,
       1983. 179 pp.
The Essays (pp. 147-77) offer thoughtful reflections by a
writer who is both a playwright and a critic.

1828. HELBING, TERRY. "Gay Plays, Gay Theatre, Gay
       Performance," **Drama Review**, 25 (1981), 35-46.
Assigns the plays written in the 1970s to several categories, including relationships, the old-young theme, coming
out, and the old-college-friend type. Notes the growth
of gay theater companies. See also Helbing: "Boom Time
for Theatre," **Advocate**, no. 335 (January 21, 1982), 43,
51-55.

1829. HELBING, TERRY. **Gay Theatre Alliance Dirctory of
       Gay Plays.** New York: JH Press, 1980. 180 pp.
Invaluable alphabetical roster of some 400 plays, many

unpublished, with plot and character summaries, as well
as information on rights.

1830. HOFFMAN, WILLIAM M. (ed.) **Gay Plays: The First
     Collection.** New York: Avon, 1979. 493 pp.
Editor's Introduction offers considerable historical
information. There is also an extensive bibliography
(pp. 475-87).

1831. HOWE, FREDERICK. "Homosexuality in English Drama"
     and "Homosexuality in American Drama," **Advocate,** no
     210 (February 23, 1977), 43-45; and no 211 (March
     9, 1977), 41-43.
Journalistic surveys. See also his: "Gay Theater USA,"
Advocate, no. 234 (Feburary 8, 1978), 29-30.

1832. JACKSON, GRAHAM. "The Theatre of Implication:
     Homosexuality in Drama," in: Ian Young (ed.), **The
     Male Homosexual in Literature: A Bibliography.**
     Second ed. Metuchen, NJ: Scarecrow Press, 1982,
     pp. 246-58.
Sensitive observations by a Canadian critic.

1833. JACKSON, GRAHAM. "Toeing the Line: In Search of
     the Gay Male Image in Contemporary Classical
     Ballet," in: Karla Jay and Allen Young (eds.),
     Lavender Culture. New York: Jove, 1978, pp. 157-
     70.
Discusses stereotyped responses to male love in ballet.

1834. KARLINSKY, SIMON. "Diaghilev: Public and Private,"
     Christopher Street, 4:7 (March 1980), 48-54.
The ballet impresario's relationships with Dima Filosofov,
Vaslav Nijinsky, Leonide Massine, Anton Dolin, Serge
Lifar, and Igor Markevich. See also R. Buckle, above.

1835. KIRK, KRIS. and ED HEATH. **Men in Frocks.** London:
     Gay Men's Press, 1984. 160 pp.
Numerous photographs, with commentary on the English panto
and drag scene since World War II.

1836. KURIYAMA, CONSTANCE BROWN. **Hammer or Anvil: Psy-
     chological Patterns in Christopher Marlowe's Plays.**
     New Brunswick, NJ: Rutgers University Press, 1980.
     288 pp.
Some assumptions of this psychocritical study have been
questioned (discussion of "repressed homosexual themes").

1837. LAHR, JOHN. **Coward the Playwright.** New York: Avon,
     1983. 179 pp.
Study of Noel Coward's sensibility as a comedy writer.

1838. LAHR, JOHN. **Prick up Your Ears: The Biography of
     Joe Orton.** New York: Knopf, 1978. 302 pp.
Incorporating diary materials, probably the most explicit
account of the homosexual life of a contemporary play-

wright.

1839. LEAVITT, DINAH LUISE. **Feminist Theatre Groups.**
       McFarland and Co., 1980. 154 pp.
Account of four Minneapolis groups, including the Lavender
Cellar Theatre.

1840. LIEBERMAN, JOSEPH ALPHONSUS. **The Emergence of**
       Lesbians and Gay Men as Characters in Plays Pro-
       duced on the American Stage from 1922 to 1954. New
       York: City University, 1981. 592 pp. (unpublished
       dissertation)
Surveys over a hundred works, including some not previously noticed, showing the stifling effects of censorship as
well as the ultimately successful efforts to overcome it.

1841. LOEFFLER, DONALD L. **An Analysis of the Treatment**
       of the Homosexual Character in Dramas Produced in
       the New York Theater from 1950 to 1968. New
       York: Arno Press, 1975. 201 pp.
Useful as a narrative history, but Loeffler is somewhat
uncritical about stereotypes and changing standards of
permissiveness. (This book is a slightly enlarged version of a dissertation submitted at Bowling Green State
University in 1969.)

1842. "DIE MAINTOCHTER." **Die Wildnis der Doris Gay: Be-**
       schreibung eines schwulen Projects. Berlin: Verlag
       Rosa Winkel, 1979. 125 pp.
Text and discussion of a provocative West German gay-liberation theater event.

1843. NELSON, IDA. **La sottie sans souci: essai d'inter-**
       prétation homosexuelle. Paris: H. Champion, 1977.
       276 pp. (Bibliotheque du XVe siecle, 39)
Detects homosexual wordplay in texts of a genre of late
medieval satirical drama, the **sottie.**

1844. PATRICK, ROBERT. "Gay Analysis," **Drama Review,** 22
       (Summer 1978), 67-72.
Reflections of the iconoclastic playrwright, who for sev-
eral years wrote a column in the gay paper, **The New York**
City News.

1845. PERCIVAL, JOHN. **Theatre in My Blood: A Biography**
       of John Cranko. New York: Franklin Watts, 1984.
Cranko, who died in 1973, was mainly active as choreog-
rapher of the Stuttgart Ballet, where he developed innovative concepts that have spread everywhere.

1846. PORZGEN, HERMANN. **Theater ohne Frau: Das Bühnen-**
       leben kriegsgefangenen Deutschen 1914-1920.
       Königsberg: Ost-Europa Verlag, 1933. 221 pp.
On plays and dramatic skits in prisoner-of-war camps
during the First World War.

1847. ROSE, MARY BETH. "Women in Men's Clothing: Apparel
       and Social Status in The Roaring Queen," **English
       Literary History**, 14:1 (Autumn 1984), 367-91.
Reflections on the character of Moll Frith in the play of
Middleton and Decker (ca. 1608-11), seen against contemporary discussions of women in men's clothing (the "man-
woman").

1848. S., W. "Vom Weibmann auf der Bühne," **ZfsZ**, 3
       (1901), 313-25.
An anonymous physician reports on his acquaintance with
eight theatrical female impersonators.

1849. SANCHEZ MARÍN, CRISTOBAL. **Los homosexuales en la
       danza**. Madrid: Napint, 1979. 84 pp.
Popular account of homosexuals in ballet and dance.

1850. SCHÄFER, MARGARETE. "Theater, Theater!" in
       **Eldorado: Homosexuelle Frauen und Männer in Berlin
       1850-1950**. Berlin: Frölich und Kaufmann, 1984,
       pp. 180-86.
Well-informed account of lesbian themes in German theater
under the Weimar Republic.

1851. SCHAUER, JOHN. "Arpino: Dance and the Male Mys-
       tique," **Advocate**, no. 237 (March 22, 1978), 32-33.
On an influential figure in contemporary dance, Gerald
Arpino. See also Schauer, "The Tiptoeing Trockadero,"
ibid., no. 203 (November 17, 1976), 24-26+ (on the New
York cross-dressing ballet company).

1852. SENELICK, LAURENCE. "The Evolution of the Male
       Impersonator in the Nineteenth Century Stage,"
       Essays in Theatre (Guelph, Ont.), 1 (1982), 31-44.
Reconstructs the lives and careers of several actresses
taking male parts on the English and American stage, ca.
1850-1914; with useful reference notes on this underre-
searched topic.

1853. SHAPIRO, STEPHEN RICHARD. **The Theme of Homosexual-
       ity in Selected Theatrical Events Produced in the
       United States between 1969 and 1974**. Santa Bar-
       bara: University of California, 1976. 234 pp. (un-
       published dissertation)
Discusses 28 plays, concluding that the stage continues to
propagate the idea of homosexuals as "a troubled, unstable, unhappy group of human beings."

1854. SHAWN, TED, and GRAY POOLE. **One Thousand and
       One Night Stands**. Garden City, NY: Doubleday,
       1960. 288 pp.
Reminiscences of Shawn (1891-1972) who, though a closeted
homosexual, managed to convince the American public that
modern dance was a manly activity; his association with
Ruth St. Denis and the founding of Jacob's Pillow. See
also: Walter Terry, **Ted Shawn, Father of American Dance: A**

Biography. (New York: Dial, 1976; 186 pp.), which is frank about Shawn's problems in handling knowledge of his homosexuality.

1855. SISLEY, EMILY L. "Notes on Lesbian Theatre," **Drama Review**, 25 (1981), 47-56.
While the definition of lesbian theatre is contested, it is clear that it is tied to the great surge of feminism in the 1960s and 1970s. Women's theatre groups that have specifically identified themselves as lesbian are few.

1856. SOLOMON, ALISA. "The WOW Cafe," **The Drama Review**, 29:1 (1985), 92-101.
Account of a woman's performance space and its companies in New York's East Village. This issue contains several other short articles on current happenings in the off-off-Broadway scene.

1857. STEWART, PAMELA D. "A Play on Doubles: **La Calandria**," **Modern Language Studies**, 14 (1984), 23-32.
On the 1513 work of Bernardo Dovizi da Bibbiena, the prototype of the titillating Renaissance gender confusion comedy, in which a male (or female) character is disguised as a female (or male), attracts the amorous attentions of a person of the "wrong" sex, but ultimately reveals himself (herself), so that heterosexual normality is restored.

1858. SUMMERS, MONTAGUE. **The Playhouse of Pepys.** London: Routledge, 1935. 485 pp.
Provides considerable information on homosexuality in the Restoration stage. Summers goes so far as to speak of "the prevalence of uranianism in the theatre" during this period (p. 295).

1859. TAUBMAN, HOWARD. "The Subtle Persuasion in the American Theater," **Cosmopolitan**, 155 (November 1963), 88-91.
A characteristic specimen of homophobia in the theater criticism of the period. Taubman claims that "homosexuality is nearly everywhere," and "it often poisons what you see and hear." This insidious critical trend was effectively anatomized by Benjamin DeMott, "But He's a Homosexual...," in Irving Buchen (ed.), **The Perverse Imagination** (New York: New York University Press, 1970), pp. 147-64.

1860. TOUCHET, GENE RAY. **American Drama and the Emergence of Social Homophilia.** Tallahassee: University of Florida, 1974. 213 pp.
Detects a surprisingly sunny pattern in the 20 plays examined.

1861. WANDOR, MICHELENE. **Understudies: Theatre and Sexual Politics.** New York: Methuen, 1981. 80 pp.
The author, who has worked with feminist and gay theater companies in Britain, provides an account of this activity

in the 1970s.

1862. WEINER, BERNARD. "The Romans in Britain Controver-
      sy," **Drama Review**, 25 (1981), 57-68.
On the brouhaha occasioned by the London staging (with a
simulated act of sodomy) of Howard Brenton's play.

1863. WILLIAMS, GWYN. **Person and Persons in Shake-
      speare.** Cardiff: University of Wales Press, 1981.
      141 pp.
Contains an essay "The Loneliness of the Homosexual in
Shakespeare." It may be noted that despite the enormous
production of scholarship on the greatest playwright in
English, the homosexual aspects of his work have been
surprisingly obscured. See, however, Seymour Kleinberg,
"The Merchant of Venice: The Homosexual as Antisemite in
Nascent Capitalism," **JH** 9:3/4 (Spring-Summer 1983), 113-
26); Philip J. Traci, "As You Like It: Homosexuality
in Shakespeare's Play," **CLA Journal**, 25 (September 1981),
91-105; and C. van Emde Boas (1821), above. A strong case
for the bard's personal bisexuality is made in: Joseph
Pequigney, **Such Is My Love: A Study of Shakespeare's
Sonnets** (Chicago: University of Chicago Press, 1985).

                H. LITERARY STUDIES: GENERAL

Although countless literary figures are now known to have
been homosexual, in many instances their orientation is
not emphasized in the work; indeed, to the ordinary reader
it may be imperceptible, occasioning astonishment and
disbelief when well-known writers of the past are revealed
to be homosexual or lesbian. At a higher level of gener-
ality, it has proved difficult to define a specific "aesthetic" or sensibility of either gay male or lesbian
writing. However this may be, our growing knowledge
of these figures guarantees that, rightly or wrongly, they
will be taken as representative of key aspects of the
homosexual experience. In keeping with the character of
the present **Guide**, primary works of fiction and poetry are
not listed in this and the following two sections, though
the items cited, especially bibliographies, may be used to
locate them.

1864. BEACH, SYLVIA. **Shakespeare and Company: The Story
      of an American Bookshop in Paris.** New York: Har-
      court, Brace, 1959. 248 pp.
Beach recalls her days as proprietor of the famous bookshop in Paris where expatriate American and British
writers met--many of them gay or lesbian. Noel Riley
Fitch, **Sylvia Beach and the Lost Generation: A History
of Literary Paris in the 20s and 30s** (New York: Norton,
1983; 417 pp.).

1865. BITHELL, JETHRO. **Modern German Literature, 1880–
       1950.** Third ed. London: Methuen, 1959. 548 pp.
In this general survey, see pp. 56, 117, 140-41, 184,
216, 229, 272, 307, 312, 374, 386, 471, 476.

1866. BOLD, ALAN (ed.). **The Sexual Dimension in Liter-
       ature.** Totowa, NJ: Barnes and Noble, 1982. 224
       pp.
Essays by various hands, including some discussions of the
literary underground.

1867. BOSWELL, JEANETTA. **Past Ruined Ilion: A Bibliog-
       raphy of English and American Literature Based on
       Greco-Roman Mythology.** Metuchen, NJ: Scarecrow,
       1982. 321 pp.
Listing arranged by author, with annotations describing
the nature of the treatment of the myth. See index for
such figures as Antinous, Ganymede, Hylas, etc. Replaces
Helen Law, **Bibliography of Greek Myth in English Poetry.**
Revised ed. (Folcraft: Folcraft Press, 1955; 39 pp.).

1868. BUSST, A. J. L. "The Image of the Androgyne in the
       Nineteenth Century," in: Ian Fletcher (ed.), **Roman-
       tic Mythologies.** London: Routledge and Kegan Paul,
       1967, pp. 1-96.
Comprehensive survey of concepts of the androgyne in 19th-
century French literature and social thought. See also:
Jean Molino, "Le Mythe de l'androgyne," in: P. Viallaneix
and J. Ehrard, **Aimer en France, 1760-1760.** Clermont-Ferrand: Faculté des Lettres, 1980, pp. 401-11.

1869. CARTER, ALFRED EDWARD. **The Idea of Decadence in
       French Literature.** Toronto: Toronto University
       Press, 1958. 154 pp.
This topic has considerable generic significance (see
pp. 23, 39-42, and 89-122). See also: Koenraad Swart,
The Sense of Decadence in Nineteenth-century France (The
Hague: Martinus Nijhoff, 1964); and John P. Reed, **Decadent
Style** (Athens: Ohio Universities Press, 1985; 234 pp.).

1870. CHARNEY, MAURICE. **Sexual Fiction.** New York: Meth-
       uen, 1981. 180 pp.
Examines issues posed by leading works of (chiefly heterosexual) erotic fiction, from Sade to Erica Jong (but
see pp. 74, 91, 96-98, 164).

1871. COCKSHUT, A. O. J. **Man and Woman: A Study of Love
       and the Novel, 1740-1940.** New York: Oxford Univer-
       sity Press, 1978. 221 pp.
The title notwithstanding, this book does discuss same-sex
relations in English fiction: "The Male Homosexual" (pp.
161-85) and "The Lesbian Theme" (pp. 186-208).

1872. CREW, LOUIE, and RICTOR NORTON (eds.) "The
       Homosexual Imagination," **College English,** 36:3
       (November 1974), 174-404.

Special issue of 14 articles, mainly by gay and lesbian teachers reflecting on their pedagogical experiences and expectations.

1873. CUCCO, ENZO (ed.). **Orgoglio e pregiudizio: l'eros lesbico e omosessuale nella letteratura del Novecento.** Turin: Fondazione Sandro Penna, 1984. 137 pp.
Contributions by several gay and lesbian scholars on such writers as Comisso, Lezama Lima, Pasolini, Penna, Testori, and Woolf--as well as on American literature from Whitman to Ginsberg.

1874. DUFFY, MAUREEN. **The Erotic World of Faery.** London: Hodder and Stoughton, 1972. 352 pp.
Wide-ranging survey of considerable indirect relevance, from the middle ages to the present, of the hidden world of meaning in fantasy--marred by occasional Freudian over-interpretation.

1875. EDEL, LEON. **Bloomsbury: A House of Lions.** New York: Avon, 1980. 333 pp.
Readable and well-informed account of the celebrated group of British intellectuals and aesthetes--including Duncan Grant, John Maynard Keynes, Lytton Strachey, Virginia Woolf, and others. The secondary literature on the Bloomsbury group is very extensive; it is perhaps best approached through critical works on the individual figures.

1876. EICKHORST, WILLIAM. **Decadence in German Fiction.** Denver: Swallow, 1953. 179 pp.
See esp. pp. 125-30 on Friedrich Huch. Bibliography, pp. 165-77.

1877. FASSLER, BARBARA. "Theories of Homosexuality as Sources of Bloomsbury's Androgyny," **Signs**, 5:3 (Winter 1979), 237-51.
Influence of the turn-of-the-century theorists, chiefly on V. Sackville-West and Lytton Strachey.

1878. FLETCHER, IAN (ed.). **Decadence and the 1890s.** London: Edward Arnold, 1979. 216 pp. (Stratford-on--Avon Studies, 17).
Eight papers, chiefly on British literature, including discussions of Walter Pater and Oscar Wilde.

1879. FORD, HUGH. **Published in Paris: American and British Writers, Printers, and Publishers in Paris, 1920-1939.** New York: Macmillan, 1975. 454 pp.
In this standard work on the (often nonconformist) ex-patriates, see Chapter 21 (Robert McAlmon, pp. 34-94); Chapter 6 (Gertrude Stein, pp. 231-52); and references in index to Djuna Barnes, Charles Henri Ford, Radclyffe Hall, and others.

1880. GATLAND, JAN OLAV. "Homofile tema: norsk littera-
       tur," **Samtiden**, 92)2 (1983), 74-79.
Homosexual motifs in Norwegian literature.

1881. GAUTHIER, XAVIÈRE. **Surréalisme et sexualité.**
       Paris: Gallimard, 1971. 381 pp.
In this monograph on the role of sexuality in surrealist
imagery, see esp. pp. 230-45.

1882. GIESE, FRITZ. **Der romantische Charakter, 1. Band:
       Die Entwicklung des Androgynenproblems in der
       Früh-Romantik.** Langensalza: Wendt und Klawell,
       1919. 466 pp.
Study of the development of the androgyne theme in the
literature of early romanticism.

1883. GOODMAN, JAN. "Out of the Closet, But Paying the
       Price: Lesbian and Gay Characters in Children's
       Literature," **Interracial Books for Children
       Bulletin**, 14: 3/4 (1982), 13-14.
Critical of some current trends in this genre.

1884. HARDY, ROBIN. "Gunsels and Gumshoes," **Advocate**,
       no. 353 (October 14, 1982), 63-65, 73.
Writers of the hardboiled detective genre have included
homosexuals as part of their vision of the modern city
as dominated by corruption and alienation. See also:
Vern Bullough, "'Deviant Sex' and the Detective Story,"
Mystery and Detection Annual, 2 (1973), 326-30; and Jim
Levin, "Pervo Killers and Gay Dicks: Gays in American
Mystery Novels," **New York Native** (May 10, 1982), 26-27+

1885. KELLOGG, STUART (ed.). **Essays on Gay Literature.**
       New York: Harrington Park Press, 1985. 174 pp.
Twelve essays, mainly on Anglo-American literature. In
the Introduction (pp. 1-12) the editor explores the variety of uses of homosexuality in literature. This book is
a reissue of **JH**, 8:3/4 (Spring-Summer 1983), which also
appeared in 1983 as **Literary Visions of Homosexualty.**

1886. LEGMAN, GERSHON. **Love and Death.** New York: Hacker
       Art Books, 1963. 95 pp.
Reprint of 1949 Freudian diatribe on literary manifestations of American sexual malaise, including homosexuality
as a symptom of immaturity.

1887. LEWANDOWSKI, HERBERT. **Das Sexualproblem in der
       modernen Literatur und Kunst.** Dresden: Paul Aretz,
       1927. 362 pp.
A pioneering survey of sexuality in literature and the
arts.

1888. LIESHOUT, MAURICE VAN. "Homo's tussen fiktie en
       werkeligheid: uitgangspunten voor literaire-his-
       torisch onderzoek naar homoseksualiteit," **Homol-
       ogie**, 7:1 (January-February 1984), 33-37.

Advances criteria for the evaluative discussion of homosexuality in literature.

1889. MAYER, HANS. **Outsiders: A Study in Life and
        Letters.** Translated by Denis Sweet. Cambridge,
        MA: MIT Press, 1982. 434 pp.
A threefold study by a German Marxist critic of the
literary image of women, Jews, and homosexuals. The
treatment of the latter has been criticized as external
and incomplete.

1890. NICOLSON, NIGEL. **Portrait of a Marriage.** New
        York: Athenaeum, 1973.
A frank account by their son of an unusual English literary couple: the lesbian Vita Sackville-West and the
homosexual Harold Nicolson. See esp. pp. 135-85.

1891. OTT, VOLKER. **Homotropie und die Figur des
        Homotropen in der Literatur des zwanzigsten
        Jahrhunderts.** Frankfurt: Peter D. Lang, 1979. 452
        pp.
Somewhat ponderous study (originating in a doctoral
dissertation) of selected works of fiction and drama in
German, English, and French.

1892. PAGLIA, CAMILLE. "The Apollonian Androgyne and the
        Faerie Queene," **English Literary Renaissance,** 9
        (1979), 42-63.
Sensitive essay on three of Edmund Spenser's Amazons.

1893. PRAZ, MARIO. **The Romantic Agony.** Translated by
        Angus Davidson. Second ed. London: Oxford
        University Press, 1951. 502 pp.
A classic work on the origins and vogue for decadence
in European fiction; see esp. the Chapter 5, "Byzantium," pp. 287-411.

1894. RUITENBEEK, HENDRIK M. (ed.). **Homosexuality and
        Creative Genius.** New York: Astor-Honor, 1967.
        330.
Essays, sometimes dated but still worth consulting, on
Oscar Wilde, John Addington Symonds, Walt Whitman,
Radclyffe Hall, Denis de Saint-Pavin, Arthur Rimbaud,
Andre Gide, Marcel Proust, Percy Bysshe Shelley, and
Emile Zola.

1895. SINFIELD, ALAN (ed.). **Society and Literature
        1945-1970.** London: Methuen, 1985. 266 pp.
Collection of essays (note esp. Jonathan Dollimore,
"The Challenge of Sexuality") with considerable discussion of literary homophobia (e.g., in the Angry Young Men
writers of the 1950s).

1896. STAMBOLIAN, GEORGE, and ELAINE MARKS. **Homosexual-
        ities and French Literature: Cultural Contexts,
        Critical Texts.** Ithaca, NY: Cornell University

Press, 1979. 387 pp.
Essays and interviews on 19th-century and 20th-century
French writing. An uneven collection, some items being of
ephemeral significance, others marred by fashionable, but
opaque jargon.

1897. STOCKINGER, JACOB. "Homotextuality: A Proposal,"
      in: Louie Crew (ed.), **The Gay Academic.** Palm
      Springs, CA: ETC, 1978, pp. 135-51.
Proposes critical strategies for recovering and evaluating
"homotextual space." See also his "Toward a Gay Criticism," **College English,** 36 (1974), 303-10.

I. LITERARY STUDIES: MALE

Homosexuality in literature has been the occasion of much
evasiveness and hypocrisy on the part of both authors and
critics. The former employed the "language of Aesop" to
sneak their writings past the informal but pervasive censorship of publishers and to escape the disapproval of
a heterosexual reading public, while the latter often
chose to ignore or conceal the homoerotic elements which
they perceived beneath the surface of the works they were
analyzing. This was particularly true in critical writings destined for college courses in which such a corrupting theme as same-sex relations would have been
intolerable. So it is only in recent decades that the
truth about many homosexual or bisexual authors has been
frankly treated in biographical or critical studies. The
insightful analysis of prose and poetry with homoerotic
themes enables us to appreciate aspects of the homosexual sensibility of periods in which such feelings had to
be carefully hidden from the vindictive scrutiny of an
intolerant heterosexual society.

1898. ADAMS, STEPHEN. **The Homosexual as Hero.** Totowa,
      NJ: Barnes and Noble, 1980. 208 pp.
Straightforward, but somewhat lackluster studies of the
work of Gore Vidal, James Baldwin, James Purdy, John
Rechy, E. M. Forster, Christopher Isherwood, Angus Wil-
son, Jean Genet, and others. See also Adams, **James Purdy**
(London: Vision Press, 1966; 166 pp.).

1899. AUSTEN, ROGER. **Playing the Game: The Homosexual
      Novel in America.** Indianapolis: Bobbs-Merrill,
      1977. 240 pp.
Sure-footed selective account, which is highly readable,
charting the constraints and conventions of the American
gay novel as the genre developed until ca. 1965. See
also J. Levin, below.

1900. BERRY, FAITH. **Langston Hughes: Before and After**

Harlem. Westport,CT: Lawrence Hill and Co., 1983.
376 pp.
Although the author of the this critical biography of the
noted Black poet (1902-67) was denied access to some documents, the homophile (though perhaps necessarily highly
closeted) sensibility of Hughes is evident.

1901. BERTHIER, PHILIPPE. "Balzac du coté de Sodome,"
L'Année balzacienne (1979), 147-77.
Comprehensive account of homosexual characters and themes
in the work of the most encyclopedic of all French novelists. See also his, "Portrait de Stendhal en Evêque de
Clogher," **Stendhal Club,** no. 98 (January 15, 1983), 244-
54.

1902. BINDING, PAUL. **Lorca: The Gay Imagination.** Lon-
don: Gay Men's Press, 1985. 238 pp.
Somewhat inconclusive study of the work of Federico Garcia
Lorca, centered on **Poeta en Nueva York.** See also: Ian
Gibson, **The Assassination of Federico Garcia Lorca** (New
York: Penguin, 1983); and Richard L. Predmore, **Lorca's New
York Poetry: Social Injustice, Dark Love, Lost Faith**
(Durham, NC: Duke University Press, 1980; 116 pp.), pp.
65-88.

1903. BLANCH, LESLIE. **Pierre Loti: The Legendary Romantic.** New York: Carrol and Graf, 1983. 336 pp.
Biography of the fin-de-siècle writer and adventurer
(1850-1923), whose sometimes exotic works conjured up
ambivalent images.

1904. BOONE, BRUCE. "Gay Language as Political Praxis:
The Poetry of Frank O'Hara," **Sociotext,** no. 1
(Winter 1979), 59-92.
Attempts to create a Marxist methodology for a realm
lying on the border between sociolinguistics and literary
criticism.

1905. CARPENTER, EDWARD (ed.). **Ioläus: An Anthology of
Friendship.** London: Sonnenschein, 1902. 190 pp.
A collection of writings on male same-sex friendship from
classic times through the 19th century, interspersed with
comment by Carpenter. This collection was inspired by
what appears to be the first example of the genre, Elisar
von Kupffer, **Lieblingsminne und Freundesliebe in der Welt-
literatur** (Berlin: Adolf Brand, 1900; 220 pp.). The 1917
edition of Carpenter's work was reprinted by Pagan Press,
New York, 1982. An offshoot, unacknowledged as such, of
Carpenter's anthology is Byrne Fone (ed.), **Hidden Heritage: History and the Gay Imagination** (New York: Avoca-
tion, 1980; 323 pp.).

1906. CARPENTER, HUMPHREY. **W. H. Auden: A Biography.**
Boston: Houghton Mifflin, 1981. 496 pp.
In the burgeoning secondary literature on the poet (1907-
1973), this biography is outstanding: detailed, well-bal-

anced, and frank. On Auden's thirty-year relationship with Chester Kallman, see the anecdotal acccount of Dorothy J. Farman, **Auden in Love: The Intimate Story of A Lifelong Affair** (New York: New American Library, 1985; 253 pp.). An indispensable work of criticism is Edward Mendelson, **Early Auden** (New York: Viking, 1981; 407 pp.). See also Barry Cambray Bloomfield and Edward Mendelson, **W. H. Auden: A Bibliography, 1924-1969**. Second ed. (Charlottesville: Bibliographical Society of the University of Virginia, 1972; 420 pp.), and Martin E. Gingerich, **W. H. Auden: A Reference Guide** (Boston: G. K. Hall, 1977; 145 pp.).

1907. CHEEVER, SUSAN. **Home before Dark**. Boston: Houghton, Mifflin, 1984. 243 pp.
Reveals the bisexuality of her father, novelist John Cheever, including his attraction to his elder brother, Fred.

1908. CLAY, JAMES WILLIAM. "Self and Roles in Relation to the Process of Writing in Jean Genet's Journal du voleur and John Rechy's City of Night," **Gai Saber**, 1:2 (Summer 1977), 112-31.
A somewhat turgid, but useful comparative study focusing on the concept of role.

1909. COE, RICHARD N. **The Vision of Jean Genet**. New York: Grove, 1968. 343 pp.
Thematic study examining the works seriatim. The critical approach is strongly influenced by the existentialism of Jean-Paul Sartre, **Saint Genet: Actor and Martyr**. Translated by Bernard Frechtman (New York: Braziller, 1963; 625 pp.). See also: Marion Luckow, **Die Homosexualität in der literarischen Tradition: Studien zu den Romanen von Jean Genet**. (Stuttgart: Enke, 1962; 149 pp.); and Philip Thody, **Jean Genet: A Study of His Novels and Plays** (New York: Stein and Day, 1968; 261 pp.); as well as J. W. Clay, above; and esp. R.C. and S. A. Webb, below.

1910. CRAFT, CHRISTOPHER. "'Kiss Me with Those Red Lips': Gender and Inversion in Bram Stoker's **Dracula**," **Representations**, no. 8 (1984), 107-33.
Finds occult or displaced homoeroticism in Harker's passivity and in the mingling of male blood in Lucy's transfusions.

1911. DE-LA-NOY, MICHAEL. **Denton Welch: The Making of a Writer**. New York: Viking, 1984. 303 pp.
A frank, but somewhat uncritical biography of the late English novelist. See also Welch, **The Journals**. Edited by Michael De-La-Noy (New York: Dutton, 1984; 378 pp.), which replaces the heavily cut version issued in 1952.

1912. DELAY, JEAN. **The Youth of André Gide**. Abridged and translated from the French by June Guicharnaud. Chicago: University of Chicago Press, 1963.

498 pp.
Shortened version of a major, though contestable study
of the formation of Gide's personality in terms of
"angelism." The French version, in two volumes, was
published by Gallimard, Paris, in 1956-57. See also:
C. D. E. Tolton, **André Gide and the Art of Autobiography**
(Toronto: Macmillan of Canada, 1975; 122 pp.); Eric Marty,
L'ecriture du jour: le Journal d'Andre Gide (Paris: Seuil,
1985; 272 pp.) and, for the political aspect, Rudolf
Maurer, **André Gide et l'URSS** (Bern: Tillier, 1983; 252
pp.); as well as R. Fernandez, below.

1913. DELLAMORA, RICHARD. "An Essay in Sexual Libera-
       tion, Victorian Style: Walter Pater's 'Two Early
       French Stories,'" **JH**, 8 (1983), 139-50.
From two medieval stories by the English writer Dellamora
concludes that Pater was an important originator of homosexual criticism. See also Michael Levey, **The Case of
Walter Pater**. (London: Thames and Hudson, 1978; 255 pp.).

1914. DE MOTT, BENJAMIN. "But He's a Homosexual ...,"
       in: Irving Buchen (ed.), **The Perverse Imagination**.
       New York: New York University Press, 1970, pp. 147-
       64.
Incisive critique of then-prevalent manipulative techniques of critics decrying the influence of homosexuals in the arts.

1915. DOWDEN, GEORGE. **A Bibliography of Works by Allen
       Ginsberg**. San Francisco: City Lights, 1971. 343
       pp.
Helps to trace the poet's fugitive publications (1943-
1967). Supplemented by Michelle Kraus, **Allen Ginsberg:
An Annotated Bibliography, 1969-1979** (Metuchen, NJ: Scarecrow Press, 1980; 362 pp.).

1916. EDEL, LEON. **Henry James: The Master, 1901-1916**.
       Philadelphia: Lippincott, 1972. 591 pp.
This final volume of Edel's magisterial biography contains
some reflections on the novelist's sexuality and material
on his male acolytes. For a theory that James was in love
with his brother William, see Richard Hall, "An Obscure
Hurt: The Sexuality of Henry James," **New Republic**,
180:16 (April 28, 1979) and 180:18 (May 5, 1979).

1917. EDWARDS, A. S. G. "The Authorship of **Sodom**,"
       Papers of the Bibliographical Society of America,
       71 (1977), 208-12.
On the "closet drama" attributed, probably falsely, to
Rochester. See also: Richard Elias, "Political Satire in
Sodom," **Studies in English Literature**, 18 (1978), 423-38.

1918. EDWINSON, EDMUND (pseud. of Edward Mark Slocum).
       Men and Boys: An Anthology. Second ed. New
       York: Coltsfoot Press, 1978. 54, 83 pp.
This reprint of a 1924 anthology of pederastic verse

contains a lengthy scholarly introduction by Donald
H. Mader, providing biographical material on the poets
included.

1919. ELLMANN, RICHARD, and JOHN ESPEY. **Oscar Wilde: Two
       Approaches: Papers Read at a Clark Library Seminar,
       April 17, 1976.** Los Angeles: William Andrews Clark
       Library, 1977. 56 pp.
Ellmann's paper ("A Late Victorian Love Affair," pp.
3-21) "traces the destructive course of Wilde's affair with
Lord Alfred Douglas and explores the literary manifestations of the homosexual theme in the works of Wilde and
others." See also Ellmann's book, **Golden Codgers: Biographical Speculations** (New York: Oxford University Press,
1973; 192 pp.), which offers penetrating observations on
literary relations between Pater and Wilde, and between
Wilde and Gide.

1920. ERKKILA, BETSY. **Walt Whitman among the French:
       Poet and Myth.** Princeton: Princeton University
       Press, 1980. 296 pp.
Model study of the American poet's influence in one
country; of especial interest is the link with Andre
Gide.

1921. FAAS, EKBERT. **Young Robert Duncan: Portrait of
       the Poet as Homosexual in Society.** Santa Bar-
       bara: Black Sparrow Press, 1983. 361 pp.
Biographical and critical study of the formative years
of the influential Bay Area poet (b. 1919). See also
Duncan's collected essays: **Fictive Certainties** (New
York: New Directions, 1986; 320 pp.). Primary works are
logged in Robert Berthoff, **Robert Duncan: A Descriptive
Bibliography** (Santa Barbara: Black Sparrow Press, 1984;
500 pp.).

1922. FERNANDEZ, RAMON. **Gide ou le courage de s'enga-
       ger.** Preface by Pierre Masson. Paris: Klinck-
       sieck, 1985. 143 pp.
Reissue (with supplementary materials) of a perceptive
critical study first published in 1931 by an associate,
who was an influential figure in his own right (see esp.
pp. 62-79 on **Corydon**).

1923. FIEDLER, LESLIE. **An End to Innocence: Essays in
       Culture and Politics.** Boston: Beacon, 1955. 214
       pp.
The famous essay, "Come Back to the Raft Ag'in Honey"
(pp. 142-51), links the Negro and the homosexual as an
"archetypal complex" informing some of America's greatest
fiction (an idea said to have been purloined from Gershon
Legman). Subsequently Fiedler presented the concept more
diffusely and negatively in his book: **Love and Death in
the American Novel.** (New York: Criterion Books, 1960; 603
pp.).

1924. FINNEY, BRIAN. **Christopher Isherwood: A Critical
       Biography.** New York: Oxford University Press,
       1979. 336 pp.
This careful work is the essential vademecum for the study
of the Anglo-American novelist (1904-1986). See also,
however, Claude J. Summers, **Christopher Isherwood** (New
York: Frederick J. Ungar, 1980; 182 pp.), as well as
Isherwood's own autobiographical works.

1925. FONE, BYRNE R. "This Other Eden: Arcadia and the
       Homosexual Imagination," **JH** 8:3/4 (1983), 13-34.
Varied functions of the Arcadian ideal in the homosexual literary tradition--as redoubt, context, and metaphor.

1926. FORREY, ROBERT. "Male and Female in London's The
       Sea Wolf," **Literature and Psychology,** 24 (1974),
       135-43.
Interprets Jack London's novel as an unconscious attempt
to resolve the author's homosexual components.

1927. FOSTER, STEPHEN WAYNE. "Beauty's Purple Flame:
       Some Minor American Gay Poets, 1786-1936," **Gay
       Books Bulletin,** 7 (Spring 1982), 15-17.
Forgotten poets retrieved through their imagery and subject matter.

1928. FOSTER, STEPHEN WAYNE. "Latin American Studies,"
       Cabirion and Gay Books Bulletin, no. 11 (1984),
       2-7, 29.
On Central American and Chilean novelists.

1929. FOSTER, STEPHEN WAYNE. "Sandro Penna's Lyrical
       Realism," no. 5 (1981), 27-29.
Presentation of the noted Italian poet (1906-1977), with
bibliography to date. See now also: Maria Grazia
Boccolini, **Sandro Penna: il cosmo, il fanciullo, il kouros
e il cinema dell'Eros** (Rome: Il Ventaglio, 1985); Cesare
Garboli, **Penna Papers** (Milan: Garzanti, 1984; 99 pp.); and
Elio Pecora, **Sandro Penna: una chieta follia** (Milan: Fras-
sinelli, 1984; 238 pp.).

1930. FREEDMAN, SANFORD. **Roland Barthes: A Bibliograph-
       ical Reader's Guide.** New York: Garland, 1983. 409
       pp.
Comprehensive guide to primary texts, with detailed summaries; selective annotated bibliography of secondary
writing on Barthes. Since the French critic (1915-1980)
led a closeted life, details of his homosexuality remain
somewhat sparse. See, however, Richard Sennett: "An
Evening of Barthes," **Christopher Street,** 7:4 [no. 76]
(1983), 22-28.

1931. FURBANK, PHILIP N. **E. M. Forster: A Life.** New
       York: Harcourt Brace Jovanovich, 1978. 359 pp.
Full biography of the English novelist, including his
homosexual relationships. Since Forster's death in 1970,

increasing awareness of the importance of his sexual
orientation to his work has generated a considerable, but
scattered secondary literature, of which only a few
examples can be cited here: Judith S. Herz, "The Double
Nature of Forster's Fiction: A Room with a View and The
Longest Journey," **English Literature in Transition,** 21
(1978), 254-65; Dixie King, "The Influence of Forster's
Maurice on Lady Chatterley's Lover," **Contemporary Literature,** 23 (1982), 65-82; Robert K. Martin, "Edward Carpenter and the Double Structure of Maurice," **JH,** 8:3/4
(1983), 35-46; Barbara Rosecrance," Forster's Comrades,"
Partisan Review, 47 (1980),591-603; Wilfred Stone,
"Overleaping Class: Forster's Problem in Connection,"
Modern Language Quarterly, 39 (1978), 386-404; and Anne
M. Wyatt Brown, "Buried Life: E. M. Forster's Struggle
with Creativity," **Journal of Modern Literature,** 10
(March 1983), 109-24. See also C. J. Summers, below.

1932. FUSSELL, PAUL. **The Great War and Modern Memory.**
       New York: Oxford University Press, 1975. 364 pp.
Chapter 8 ("Soldier Boys," pp. 270-308) of this well
regarded study on the impact of World War I on British
writing includes the following topics: Mars and Eros;
the British Homoerotic Tradition; the Homoerotic Sensuousness of Wilfred Owen; and Soldiers Bathing. See also:
John Lehmann, **The English Poets of the First World War**
(London: Thames and Hudson, 1981; 144 pp.).

1933. GARDE, NOEL I. (pseud.). **The Homosexual in Litera-
       ture: A Chronological Bibliography circa 700
       B.C.-1958.** New York: Village Press, 1959. 32 pp.
"A chronological listing of ... books in the English
language, in the general field of fiction, concerned with
male homosexuality, or having homosexual characters."
Theme and author indices. Reprinted in **A Gay Bibliography**
(New York: Arno Press, 1975).

1934. GIANTVALLEY, SCOTT. "Recent Whitman Studies and
       Homosexuality," **Cabirion and Gay Books Bulletin,**
       no. 12 (1985), 14-16.
Knowledgeable review of work since 1968. Supplements
Giantvalley's major work, **Walt Whitman, 1838-1939: A
Reference Guide** (Boston: G. K. Hall, 1981; 465 pp.); and
R. Martin, below.

1935. GNERRE, FRANCESCO. "The Homosexual Novel in It-
       aly," **Gay Books Bulletin,** no. 9 (1983), 22-23, 26.
Supplements his **L'eroe negato** (1946) by discussing some
novels of the late 1970s and early '80s. A somewhat
shortened version of this article appeared as "'Ecco': The
New Gay Literature in Italy," **Advocate,** no. 367 (May 12
1983), 33, 36-37.

1936. GNERRE, FRANCESCO. **L'eroe negato: il personaggio
       omosessuale nella narrativa italiana contempor-
       anea.** Milan: Gammalibri, 1981. 164 pp.

Systematic presentation of the Italian gay novel since
World War II, evaluating strengths and weaknesses. Bibliography, pp. 159-61.

1937. GRAVES, RICHARD. **A. E. Housman: The Scholar Poet.**
New York: Scribner's, 1980. 304 pp.
Sensitive and frank account of the somewhat melancholy
life of the English classicist and lyric poet (1859-
1936). Some additional material is supplied by: Norman
Page, **A. E. Housman: A Critical Biography** (London: Macmillan, 1984; 236 pp.).

1938. HAFKAMP, HANS. "Homosexualiteit in de Nederlandse
literatuur," **Spiegel Historiael,** 17:11 (1982),
548-93.
Account of homosexual themes and writers in Dutch literature.

1939. HAGSTRUM, JEAN. "Gray' Sensibility," in: J. Downey
and B. Jones (eds.), **Fearful Joy: Papers from the
Thomas Gray Bicentenary Conference at Carleton
University.** Montreal: McGillQueen's University,
1974, pp. 6-19.
On the homoerotic sensibility of the English poet (1716-
1771), esp. as reflected in his attachment to Charles
Victor de Bonstetten.

1940. HARRISON, GILBERT A. **The Enthusiast: A Life of
Thornton Wilder.** New Haven: Ticknor and Fields,
1983. 403 pp.
This biography, the fullest available, includes a meagre
discussion of Wilder's homosexuality, whose secret the
writer so carefully tried to conceal.

1941. HATFIELD, HENRY CARAWAY. **Aesthetic Paganism in
German Literature: From Winckelmann to the Death of
Goethe.** Cambridge, MA: Harvard University Press,
1964. 283 pp.
Chapter 1 ("Winckelmann and the Myth of Greece," 1-23)
shows the power of the homosexual archaeologist's influence on the emerging German **Klassik.**

1942. HELMS, ALAN. "Whitman Revised," **Etudes anglaises,**
37:3 (July-September 1984), 259-71.
Addresses the question: how can the knowledge of Whitman's
homosexuality help us read his poetry more clearly? See
also: Joseph Cady, "Homosexuality and the Calamus Poems,"
American Studies, 19 (1978), 5-22; and S. Giantvalley,
above.

1943. HODGES, ROBERT R. "Deep Fellowship: Homosexuality
and Male Bonding in the Life and Fiction of Joseph
Conrad," **JH** 4:4 (1979), 379-93.
Methodologically interesting, in that Hodges shows how
the homoerotic strands have been ignored because Conrad
is viewed as a "male writer."

1944. HOLLAND, NORMAN NORWOOD. **Psychoanalysis and
       Shakespeare.** New York: McGraw-Hill, 1966. 412 pp.
This book has been influential in its (perhaps contestable) genre. See pp. 83-88, 93-94, 99, 108, 119,139, 156,
182-83, 194, 209, 238-39, 249-51, 280-81, 330-31, 342,
366.

1945. HOLROYD, MICHAEL. **Lytton Strachey: A Critical
       Biography.** New York: Holt, Rinehart and Winston,
       1967-68. 2 vols. (1233 pp.)
This massive, but engaging biography broke new ground
in treating the homosexual life of the English critic
and historian (1880-1932) fully and fairly, while helping
to revive Strachey's reputation and contributing to the
vogue of Bloomsbury.

1946. HOWES, ROBERT W. "Fernando Pessoa, Poet, Publish-
       er, and Translator, **British Library Journal**, 9:2
       (1983), 161-70.
Factual account of the works of Portugal's greatest
20th-century poet (1888-1935), including homoerotic poems
written in English. The criticism of Pessoa in Portuguese is enormous; see José Blanco, **Fernando Pessoa: esbo-
ço de uma bibliografia** (Lisbon: Imprensa Nacional/Casa da
Moeda, 1983; 482 pp.).

1947. HOYT, EDWIN P. **Horatio's Boys: The Life and work
       of Horatio Alger, Jr.** Radnor, PA: Chilton Books,
       1974. 263 pp.
Offers a frank discussion of the pederastic scandal that
ended Alger's schoolteaching career, and indirectly
launched him on the path of becoming one of America's
most influential novelists. There are some additional
insights in Gary Scharnhorst, **Horatio Alger, Jr.** (Boston:
Twayne, 1980).

1948. HYDE, H. MONTGOMERY. **Oscar Wilde: A Biography.** New
       York: Farrar, Straus and Giroux, 1975. 410 pp.
The most detailed and accurate life. However, Oscar
Wilde's own letters, as edited by Rupert Hart-Davis, con-
vey a much more lively picture. See also Mark Nicholls,
**The Importance of Being Oscar: The Life and Wit of Oscar
Wilde** (New York: St. Martin's, 1980; 238 pp.); Rodney
Shewan, **Oscar Wilde: Art and Egotism** (New York: Barnes and
Noble, 1978; 239 pp.); and R. Ellmann, above.

1949. HYDE, LEWIS (ed.). **On the Poetry of Allen Gins-
       berg.** Ann Arbor, MI: University of Michigan Press,
       1984. 462 pp.
Intended as a comprehensive anthology of critical re-
sponses to the poet's work from 1952 to 1982, this book
scants homoerotic analysis. See also Paul Portuges, **The
Visionary Poetics of Allen Ginsberg** (Santa Barbara: Ross-
Erickson, 1978).

1950. HYNES, SAMUEL. **The Auden Generation: Literature**

and **Politics in England in the 1930s.** New York:
Viking Press, 1977. 429 pp.
Useful critical overview of a period in English letters
when many of the leading writers were homosexual (though
Hynes does not stress the sexual aspect).

1951. KARLINSKY, SIMON. **The Sexual Labyrinth of Nikolai
Gogol.** Cambridge, MA: Harvard Unviersity Press,
1976. 334 pp.
A closely argued study, concluding that the key to the
writer's (1809-52) complex personality lies in repressed
homosexual longing. See also Alex Alexander, "Two Ivan's
Sexual Underpinnings," **Slavic and East European Journal,**
25 (1981), 24-37.

1952. KARLINSKY, SIMON. "The Soviet Union vs. Gennady
Trifonov," **Advocate,** no. 453 (August 10), 1986),
43-49.
Trials and triumphs of the only openly gay poet living in
the U.S.S.R.

1953. KEILSON-LAURITZ, MARITA. **Von der Liebe die Freundschaft heisst ...? Relevanz und Aussagestrategien
der Homoerotik im Werk Stefan Georges.** Amsterdam:
University, 1986. 138 pp. (Ph. D. dissertation
issued in a limited edition by Vrolijk bookshop)
Careful analysis of elusive but important homoerotic
elements in the work of Germany's greatest 20th-century
poet.

1954. KIKEL, RUDY. "After Whitman and Auden: Gay Male
Sensibility in Poetry Since 1945," **Gay Sunshine,**
no. 44/45 (1980), 34-39.
Reflects the critical attitude of the post-Stonewall
years.

1955. KNIGHT, GEORGE WILSON. **Lord Byron's Marriage: The
Evidence of Asterisks.** London: Routledge and
Kegan Paul, 1957. 398 pp.
Provided the first exposure of the Don Leon poems and of
Byron's pederastic tendencies. See now Louis Crompton,
Byron and Greek Love (Berkeley: University of California
Press, 1985).

1956. KRIEG, JOANN P. (ed.). **Walt Whitman: Here and
Now.** Westport, CT: Greenwood Press, 1985. 248 pp.
Proceedings of a Conference held at Hofstra University in
1980, with relevant papers by Harold Aspiz, Joseph Cady,
Alan Helms, and M. J. Killingsworth

1957. KRÖHNKE, FRIEDRICH. **Jungen in schlechter Gesellschaft: Zum Bild des Jugendlichen in der deutschen
Literatur von 1900-1933.** Bonn: Bouvier, 1980. 213
pp.
Study of youth in German literature in the first third of
the century, with special attention to the works of P. M.

Lampel. Also discusses Bronnen, George, Schonsted, Vogel, and Wedekind.

1958. KUZMIN, MIKHAIL ALEKSEEVICH. **Sobranie stikhov.**
Edited by John E. Malmstad and V. Markov. Munich: Wilhelm Fink Verlag, 1977-78. 3 vols.
Volume 3 of this collected edition of the works of the brilliant Russian homosexual writer (1872-1936) contains a biography in English by Malmstad.

1959. LANGGUTH, A. J. **Saki: A Life of Hector Munro.** New York: Simon and Schuster, 1981. 366 pp.
Documents the homosexuality of the English writer (1870-1916), best known for the sardonic wit of his short stories.

1960. LEHMANN, DAVID, and CHARLES BERGER. **James Merrill: Essays in Criticism.** Ithaca: Cornell University Press, 1983. 329 pp.
Eleven essays, generally reticent, exploring aspects of the contemporary American poet's work. To be supplemented by Edmund White, "The Inverted Type: Homosexuality as a Theme in James Merrill's Prophetic Books," **JH**, 8:3/4 (1983), 47-52.

1961. LEVIN, JAMES. **The Gay Novel: The Male Homosexual Image in America.** New York: Irvington Press, 1983. 404 pp.
Enlarges the purview of Austen's **Playing the Game** (see above), examining the novels as evidence of social changes and shifts in sexual-personal self-consciousness, as well as bringing the story to the early 1980s. See review by Leon Clavius, **Cabirion and Gay Books Bulletin**, no. 12 (1985), 24-27.

1962. LIDDELL, ROBERT. **Cavafy: A Critical Biography.** London: Duckworth, 1974. 222 pp.
Frank biography of the Alexandrian Greek poet (1874-1935). For the poetry, consult Edmund Keeley, **Cavafy's Alexandria: A Study of Myth in Progress** (Cambridge, MA: Harvard University Press, 1976; 196 pp.); Carmen Capri-Karka, **Love and the Symbolic Journey in the Poetry of Cavafy, Eliot, and Seferis** (New York: 1982); and J. L. Pinchin, below.

1963. MCCANN, JOHN S. **The Critical Reputation of Tennessee Williams: A Reference Guide.** Boston: G. K. Hall, 1983. 430 pp.
Annotated list of secondary literature, with detailed index.

1964. MARTIN, ROBERT BERNARD. **Tennyson: The Unquiet Heart.** New York: Oxford University Press, 1980. 643 pp.
Shows the lifelong importance of the poet's (1809-1892) intense feeling for Arthur Henry Hallam, who occasioned

his greatest poem, "In Memoriam."

1965. MARTIN, ROBERT K. **Hero, Captain, and Stranger:**
      Male Friendship, Social Critique, and Literary Form
      in the Sea Novels of Herman Melville. Chapel
      Hill: University of North Carolina Press, 1986.
      144 pp.
Contends that the novelist's fundamental orientation was a
homosexual one, but that he could not realize that desire
at home. Only in the world of the ship and the "primitive" cultures of the South Sea could he envisage an honorable place for male-male affection.

1966. MARTIN, ROBERT K. **The Homosexual Tradition in**
      American Poetry. Austin: University of Texas
      Press, 1980. 259 pp.
Concentrates on forerunners (Fitz-Greene Halleck and
Bayard Taylor) and followers (Hart Crane, Richard Howard,
et al.) of Walt Whitman, for whose own poetry Martin
offers challenging close readings.

1967. MEYERS, JEFFREY. **Homosexuality and Literature**
      1890-1930. Montreal: McGill-Queens University
      Press, 1977. 183 pp.
Essays on mainstream writers based on the premise that
repression offers a positive stimulus to literary subtlety.

1968. MILLER, JAMES E., JR. **T.S. Eliot's Personal**
      Wasteland: Exorcism of the Demons. University
      Park: Pennsylvania State University Press, 1977.
      176 pp.
Argues that Eliot's masterpiece reflects in part his
love for a young Frenchman, Jean Verdenal. While this
thesis has been received with scepticism by Eliot scholars, the larger question of Eliot's sexual quandary
abides. John Soldo is preparing a new study. This
subject was first broached in an article by John Peters,
"A New Interpretation of The Waste Land," **Essays in**
Criticism, 2 (July 1952), 242-66, which Eliot tried to
suppress; it was reprinted in ibid., 19 (April 1969),
with a "Postscript," 165-66.

1969. MITZEL, JOHN. **John Horne Burns: An Appreciative**
      Biography. Dorchester, MA: Manifest Destiny,
      1976. 135 pp.
Subjective reflections on a neglected American novelist.

1970. MORGAN, TED. **Maugham.** New York: Simon and Schus-
      ter, 1980. 711 pp.
Treats Maugham's (1874-1965) homosexuality (including
his long partnership with Gerald Haxton) honestly,
showing that the novelist's obsessive concern with concealment stunted his life--and perhaps his art as well.

1971. MORRISON, KRISTIN. "Lawrence, Beardsley, Wilde:
        The White Peacock and Sexual Ambiguity," **Western
        Humanities Review**, 30 (1976), 241-48.
Turn-of-the-century links in British culture.

1972. MOTTRAM, ERIC. **William Burroughs: The Algebra of
        Need**. London: Marion Boyars, 1977. 282 pp.
Sometimes volcanic effort at a summation by a sympathetic
English critic, who stresses Burroughs' interest in
contemporary morality and his concern over technolog-
ical and bureacratic erosion of individual choice. A
more conventional study is: Jenie Skerl, **William S. Burroughs** (Boston: Twayne, 1985; 127 pp.).

1973. NELSON, EMMANUEL S. "James Baldwin, John Rechy and
        the American Double Minority Literature," **Journal
        of American Culture** (Summer 1983), 70-74.
Brief exploration of an understudied question.

1974. NIN FRÍAS, ALBERTO. **Homosexualismo creador**.
        Madrid: Javier Morata, 1933. 383 pp.
An early exploration of homosexuality in Spanish and
European fiction by a little known critic and novelist
(1882-1937). Bibliography, pp. 369-76. See also his:
Alexis o el significado de temperamento urano (Madrid:
Javier Morata, 1932; 195 pp.).

1975. NORSE, HAROLD. "Cutting Up at the Beat Hotel,"
        Advocate, no. 377 (September 29, 1983), 38-41.
Gay poet's memoir of William Burroughs and other proto-
Beats in Paris in the 1950s. Chapter from a projected
autobiography.

1976. NORTON, RICTOR C. **The Homosexual Literary
        Tradition: An Interpretation**. New York: Revision-
        ist Press, 1974. 399 pp.
Stimulating, but unconvincing exploration of purported
archetypal patterns in Greco-Roman and Elizabethan literature.

1977. O'BRIEN, JUSTIN. "Albertine the Ambiguous: Note on
        Proust's Transposition of Sexes," **PMLA**, 64 (Decem-
        ber 1949), 933-52.
Pioneering exploration of Proust's disguise of a male
lover as a woman in his masterwork, sometimes termed the
"Albertine complex."

1978. PEQUIGNEY, JOSEPH. **Such Is My Love: A Study of
        Shakespeare's Sonnets**. Chicago: University of
        Chicago Press, 1985. 264 pp.
Subjecting previous scholarship of the Sonnets to wither-
ing criticism, offers a close reading of selected texts
to argue that the poems are "the grand masterpiece of
homoerotic poetry." See also: Judith Kegan Gardiner,
"The Marriage of Male Minds in Shakespeare's Sonnets,"
Journal of English and Germanic Philology, 84 (1985),

328-47.

1979. PERKINS, MICHAEL. **The Secret Record: Modern Erotic
        Literature.** New York: William Morrow, 1977.
In this selective critical study, see "Homosexual Erotic
Fiction" (pp. 168-86), which chiefly concerns pulp novels.

1980. PERLOFF, MARJORIE. **Frank O'Hara: Poet among
        Painters.** New York: George Braziller, 1977.   234
        pp.
This book is primarily a critical study, seeking to situate the New York poet in the context of American modernist poetry and his relation to painting. However, there
is some discussion of his love affairs, e. g.,with Vincent
Warren. See also: Bill Berkson and Joe LeSeuer (eds.),
Homage to Frank O'Hara (Berkeley: Creative Arts, 1982; 224
pp.).

1981. PETERS, ROBERT. **The Great American Poetry Bake-
        off.** Metuchen, NJ: Scarecrow Press, 1979.   274 pp.
Critical essays by a poet on Walt Whitman, Allen Ginsberg,
Harold Norse, Frank O'Hara, Gerard Malanga, and others. A
second series was issued by the same publisher in 1982;
409 pp.

1982. PINCHIN, JANE LAGOURDIS. **Alexandria Still: For-
        ster, Durrell, and Cavafy.** Princeton: Princeton
        University Press, 1976.   256 pp.
Evaluates the influence of the genius loci of the Egyptian
city and its tutelary spirit, the poet Cavafy, on two
English writers, one homosexual, the other including
major homosexual characters in his work.

1983. RADER, DOTSON. **Tennessee: Cry of the Heart.**
        Garden City, NY: Doubleday, 1985.   348 pp.
A boon companion's gossipy, but probably largly authentic
account of Williams' later years, emphasizing his homosexuality. More comprehensive and factual, though somewhat
lackluster is Donald Spoto, **The Kindness of Strangers: The
Life of Tennessee Williams** (Boston: Little, Brown, 1985;
409 pp.). See also: Williams, **Memoirs** (Garden City, NY:
Doubleday, 1975; 264 pp.); and J. S. McCann, above.

1984. READ, BRIAN (ed.). **Sexual Heretics: Male Homosex-
        uality in English Literature from 1850 to 1900.**
        London: Routledge and Kegan Paul, 1970.   459 pp.
Anthology reprinting 89 original texts in prose and
poetry, here cited for the Introduction (pp. 1-56), which
provides considerable bibliographical and other information.

1985. REINHARDT, KARL J., et al. "The Image of Gays in
        Chicano Prose Fiction," **Explorations in Ethnic
        Studies** (July 1981), 41-55.
Panel discussion.

1986. RIVERS, JULIUS E. **Proust and the Art of Love: The Aesthetics of Sexuality in the Life, Times and Art of Marcel Proust.** New York: Columbia University Press, 1980. 440 pp.
In this important monograph Rivers' performs a recuperative analysis, whereby the negative stereotypes are transformed, by placing them against the evolving character of contemporary thinking about homosexuality, into positive insights. See also: Henri Bonnet, **Les amours et la sexualité de Marcel Proust** (Paris: Nizet, 1985; 103 pp.); and David R. Ellison, "Comedy and Significance in Proust's **Recherche**: Freud and the Baron de Charlus," **Modern Language Notes**, 98 (1983), 657-74.

1987. SAROTTE, GEORGES-MICHEL. **Like a Brother, Like a Lover.** New York: Anchor Press/Doubleday, 1978. 339 pp.
This French critic's study of homosexuality in major authors of American fiction and drama is regarded by some as hampered by dated critical concepts.

1988. SCHLOSSER, RUDOLF. **August Graf von Platen.** Munich: Piper, 1930. 2 vols.
Comprehensive study of the German homosexual poet (1796--1835), using the diaries. Much of the subsequent extensive Platen literature is listed in Fritz Redenbacher, **Platen-Bibliographie.** Second ed. (Hildesheim: Georg Olms, 1972). For an account of his life in English, see Xavier Mayne (pseud.), **The Intersexes** (Naples: The author, 1908), pp. 563-620.

1989. SCHMIDT, E. A. "Künstler und Knabenliebe: Eine vergleichende Skizze zu Thomas Manns Tod in Venedig und Vergils 2. Ekloge," **Euphorion**, 68 (1974), 437-46.
Mann's novella compared to a Latin analogue.

1990. SCHNEIDER, LUIS MARIO. "El tema homosexual en la nueva narrativa mexicana," **Casa del tiempo,** 5 [no. 49-50] (February-March 1985), 82-86.
Homosexual themes in Mexican fiction, esp. after 1960.

1991. SCHWARTZ, JOSEPH. **Hart Crane: A Reference Guide.** Boston: G. K. Hall, 1983. 251 pp.
Chiefly an annotated list of writings about the poet, 1919-80. A large, somewhat uncritical and evasive compendium is: John Unterecker, **Voyager: The Life of Hart Crane** (New York: Farrar, Straus and Giroux, 1969; 787 pp.).

1992. SCHWARTZ, KESSEL. "Homosexuality as a Theme in Representative Contemporary Spanish American Novels," **Kentucky Romance Studies,** 32 (1975), 247-57.
Although it mentions some earlier writers, this article concentrates on works of the 1960s, by such authors as

Jose Donoso, Jose Lezama Lima, Renato Pellegrini, and
Oswaldo Reynoso.

1993. SCHWENTGER, PETER. **Phallic Critiques: Masculinity
        and Twentieth Century Literature.** London: Routledge
        and Kegan Paul, 1984. 172 pp.
Explores "ambivalence" of masculine assertion in such
writers as Ernest Hemingway, Norman Mailer, Aloberto
Moravia, and Yukio Mishima.   See also Kate Millett, **Sexual Politics** (Garden City, NY: Doubleday, 1970).

1994. SEDGWICK, EVE KOSOFSKY. **Between Men: English
        Literature and Male Homosocial Desire.** New
        York: Columbia University Press, 1985. 244 pp.
Structuralist-feminist essays concerning such authors as
Shakespeare, Sterne, Wicherley, Tennyson, and Dickens.
Often opaque in style and thought; possibly innovative.

1995. SIMES, GARY. "Gai Saber: Homosexuality and the
        Poetic Imagination," **Gay Information** (Sydney),
        no. 14-15 (1984), 21-33.
Explorations of subtlety and indirection, mainly in
examples of the 19th and 20th century.

1996. SIPRIOT, PIERRE. **Montherlant sans masque: tome
        I: L'enfant prodigue, 1895-1923.** Paris: Robert
        Laffont, 1982. 504 pp.
Reveals the homosexuality of the French novelist and
playwright, who remained closeted throughout his life
(1895-1932).   A revealing, even scandalous light on his
later years is cast by Henry de Montherlant/Roger Peyrefitte, **Correspondence** (Paris: Robert Laffont, 1983; 321
pp.).

1997. SMITH, TIMOTHY D'ARCH. **Love in Earnest: Some Notes
        on the Lives and Writings of English Uranian Poets
        from 1889 to 1930.** London: Routledge and Kegan
        Paul, 1970. 280 pp.
An invaluable study of the lives, work and themes of
the often obscure "Calamite" poets of the late 19th and
early 20th century who wrote on the love of adolescent
boys.   See also: Brian Taylor, "Motives for Guilt-free
Pederasty: Some Literary Considerations," **Sociological
Review,** N.S. 24 (1976), 97-114.

1998. STARKIE, ENID. **Flaubert: The Making of the
        Master.** London: Penguin Books, 1971. 461 pp.
This biography first explored the homosexual strand in the
character of the great French novelist (1821-80).   See
pp. xiii-xiv, 40, 169, 299. For some of the evidence, see
Flaubert, **The Letters.** Translated by Francis Steegmuller
(Cambridge, MA: Harvard University Press, 1980), pp. 105,
107, 110-12, 125, 129, 148.   See also the diffuse magnum
opus of Jean-Paul Sartre, **L'idiot de la famille** (3 vols.
Paris: Gallimard, 1971-72).

1999. STEEGMULLER, FRANCIS. **Cocteau: A Biography.**
      Boston: Little, Brown, 1970. 582 pp.
Straightforward account of the life, loves and friendships
of the many-sided French homosexual writer Jean Cocteau
(1889-1963). See also: **Jean Cocteau and the French
Scene** (New York: Abbeville Press, 1984; 239 pp.), which
is an illustrated composite account with contributions
by Dore Ashton, Neal Oxenhandler, Ned Rorem, Francis
Steegmuller, and others.

2000. STEWARD, SAMUEL M. "The Life and Hard Times of
      the Legendary Porn Writer Phil Andros," **Advocate,**
      no. 307 (December 11, 1980), 23-27.
Reminiscences showing the writer's cautious progress
towards sexual explicitness--in Steward's case through
the Phil Andros stories he began to publish in European
homophile magazines in the 1960s. See also his: **Chapters from an Autobiography** (San Francisco: Grey Fox Press,
1981; 147 pp.).

2001. SUMMERS, CLAUDE J. **E. M. Forster.** New York:
      Frederick Ungar, 1983. 416 pp.
Sensitive book-by-book survey integrating the novelist's
sexuality into the critical perspective. See also P. N.
Furbank, above.

2002. SYLVANDER, CAROLYN WEDIN. **James Baldwin.** New
      York: Frederick Ungar, 1980. 181 pp.
Thoughtful and well-documented account of the Black novelist's work to date, not scanting sexual themes. See also
Fred L. Standley, **James Baldwin: A Reference Guide** (Boston: G. K. Hall, 1980; 310 pp.).

2003. TYTELL, JOHN. **Naked Angels: The Lives and Liter-
      ature of the Beat Generation.** New York: McGraw-
      Hill, 1976. 274 pp.
Perhaps the best synthetic critical study of the lives and
works of William Burroughs, Jack Kerouac, and Allen Gins-
berg. Much new information is disclosed in Gerald
Nicosia, **Memory Babe: A Critical Biography of Jack Kerouac**
(New York: Grove Press, 1983; 787 pp.).

2004. VENEMA, ADRIAAN. **Homoseksualiteit in de Neder-
      landse literatuur.** Amsterdam: Manteau, 1972. 205
      pp.
Survey of homosexuality in Dutch literature; regarded by
some Dutch critics as offering a somewhat arbitrary selection of authors. See also H. Hafkamp, above.

2005. WEBB, RICHARD C., and SUZANNE A. WEBB. **Jean Genet
      and His Critics: An Annotated Bibliography, 1943-
      1980.** Metuchen, NJ: Scarecrow, 1982. 600 pp.
Provides full documentation of analyses of Genet (1910-86)
and his work in French and English, with extensive coverage of reviews and newspaper articles, including those of
productions of plays, permitting one to chart the impact

of his work. 1790 items.

2006. WHITE, PATRICK. **Flaws in the Glass: A Self-Por-
        trait.** London: Cape, 1981. 260 pp.
The novelist, a Nobel laureate, describes his long-term
relationship with Manoly Lascaris and his extended process
of coming to terms with himself as an Australian and a
homosexual.

2007. WINSTON, RICHARD. **Thomas Mann: The Making of an
        Artist.** New York: Knopf, 1981. 352 pp.
Although this biography is incomplete, it does include
discussion of the novelist's (1875-1955) self-recognition
as an "urning."

2008. YOUNG, IAN. **The Male Homosexual in Literature.**
        Second ed. Metuchen, NJ: Scarecrow Press, 1982.
        360 pp.
Much enlarged edition of an indispensable reference book
(first published 1975), now comprising 4282 items arranged
alphabetically by author (fiction, plays, poetry). Anal-
ytics are provided for anthologies; index of titles;
additional prose essays. Limited to works published in
English (including translations). Some reservations
have been expressed about a few inclusions, and about
the system of starring items according to importance.

2009. ZWEIG, PAUL. **Walt Whitman: The Making of the
        Poet.** New York: Basic Books, 1984. 372 pp.
Seeks to show how Whitman's personal life and his creative
energies intersected in the 1850s to transform him into
a bardic figure. Includes some discussion of the role
that his male attachments played in this change. See
also Harold Aspiz, **Walt Whitman and the Body Beautiful**
(Urbana: University of Illinois Press, 1980; 290 pp.);
and Justin Kaplan, **Walt Whitman: A Life** (New York: Simon
and Schuster, 1980; 432 pp.). Whitman's own diaries and
autobiographical writings are being published in monumental editions by New York University Press.

2010. ZYNDA, STEFAN. **Sexualität bei Klaus Mann.** Bonn:
        Bouvier, 1986. 157 pp.
Traces the evolving nature of Klaus Mann's sexual self-
awareness in relation to his works.

                    J. LITERARY STUDIES: LESBIAN

The attention accorded women writers in the past often
overlooked the lesbian strain, even when the overall merit
of the work gained it national or international acclaim.
More recent critics and biographers have sought to redress
this omission, and to place the creations of lesbian
writers within the larger context of women's literature.

Likewise, feminist critics have called attention to the distinctive character of this literature and its contribution to the women's movement for equality in a male-dominated society. The specific consciousness of women not psychologically dependent upon men is a notable quality of lesbian writing and one of its major inputs into the feminist movement.

2011. AUERBACH, NINA. **Communities of Women: An Idea in Fiction.** Cambridge, MA: Harvard University Press, 1978. 222 pp.
Traces the history of the idea of separation in literature, from the Graie and Amazons through 19th and early 20th century authors to the present.

2012. BARCLAY, GLEN ST. JOHN. **Anatomy of Horror: The Masters of Occult Fiction.** New York: St. Martin's Press, 1979. 144 pp.
For lesbianism in the novels of Dickens, Le Fanu, and Meredith, see pp. 25, 27, 33-38, 129-30.

2013. BARR, MARLENE S. (ed.). **Future Females: A Critical Anthology.** Bowling Green, OH: Bowling Green State University Popular Press, 1981.
Includes discussions of Ursula LeGuin, Marge Piercy, Joanna Russ, and others. See also Betty King: **Women of the Future: The Female Main Character in Science Fiction.** (Metuchen, NJ: Scarecrow, 1984).

2014. BELL, QUENTIN. **Virginia Woolf.** New York: Harcourt Brace Jovanovich, 1972. 2 vols. in 1
The standard biography of the noted bisexual novelist (1882-1941), by a younger member of the Bloomsbury circle who had direct access to the milieu. See also Lyndall Gordon, **Virginia Woolf: A Writer's Life** (London: Oxford University Press, 1984; 341 pp.); and S. M. Squier, **Virginia Woolf and London: The Sexual Politics of the City** (Durham: North Carolina University Press, 1985; 220 pp.).

2015. BLOUIN, LENORA P. **May Sarton: A Bibliography.** Metuchen, NJ: Scarecrow Press, 1978. 236 pp.
Standard bibliography of the novelist.

2016. BRADY, MAUREEN, and JUDITH MCDANIEL. "Lesbians in the Mainstream: Images of Lesbians in Recent Commercial Fiction," **Conditions: Six** (Summer 1980), 82-105.
Monitoring the changing image.

2017. BRIDGMAN, RICHARD. **Gertrude Stein in Pieces.** New York: Oxford University Press, 1970. 411 pp.
Critical study which makes a useful contribution to the interpretation of lesbian elements in her work.

2018. BRIGHT, JOYCE. "A Decade of Tending the Well-

spring: Barbara Grier and the Naiad Press," **Advocate**, no. 382 (December 8, 1938), 38+
On the contribution of the Naiad Press to lesbian literature (and of Grier--"Gene Damon"--whose work goes back to the 1950s).

2019. BRITTAIN, VERA MARY. **Radclyffe Hall: A Case of Obscenity?** London: Femina, 1968. 185 pp.
Account of the court trials and attempt to suppress her novel **Well of Loneliness** (1925). See also: Michael Baker, **Our Three Selves: A Life of Radclyffe Hall** (London: Hamilton, 1985; 380 pp.); Inez Martinez, "The Lesbian Hero Bound: Radclyffe Hall's Portrait of Sapphic Daughters and Their Mothers," **JH**, 8:3/4 (1983), 127-37; and Esther Newton, "The Myth of the Mannish Lesbian: Radclyffe Hall and the New Woman," **Signs**, 9:4 (1984), 557-75.

2020. BROWN, LINDA. "Dark Horse: A View of Writing and Publishing by Dark Lesbians," **Sinister Wisdom**, 13 (Spring 1980), 42-50.
Surveys the emergence of writing and publishing by lesbians of color (1975ff.); with contact lists.

2021. BROWNE, F. W. STELLA. "Der weibliche Typus inversus in der neueren Literatur: Renée Vivien, Colette Willy, Mary MacLane," **Die neue Generation**, 18 (1922), 90-96.
Early study of lesbian fiction--from a clinical standpoint.

2022. BULKIN, ELLY. "An Interchange on Feminist Criticism on 'Dancing through the Minefield,'" **Feminist Studies**, 8 (Fall 1982), 635-54.
Concerning homophobia and racism in feminist literary criticism. See also her: "Heterosexism and Women's Studies," **Radical Teacher**, 17 (Winter 1981), 25-31; and "Racism and Writing: Some Implications for White Lesbian Critics," **Sinister Wisdom**, 13 (1980), 3-22.

2023. BULKIN, ELLY. "'A Whole New Poetry Beginning Here': Teaching Lesbian Poetry," **College English**, 40 (1979), 874-88.
Distills experiences in practical criticism through teaching.

2024. CADOGAN, MARY, and PATRICIA CRAIG. **You're a Brick Angela: The Girls' Story 1839-1945.** New ed. London: Gollancz, 1986. 405 pp.
Study of British children's literature emphasizing the "girls at school" genre, including the novels of the ever-popular Angela Brazil. A postscript discusses the 1980s.

2025. CARR, VIRGINIA SPENCER. **The Lonely Hunter: A Biography of Carson McCullers.** Garden City, NY:

Doubleday, 1975. 600 pp.
Candid and detailed account of the bisexual Southern
writer (1917-67), including her friendships with Tennessee
Williams, Truman Capote, and W. H. Auden.

2026. CARRUTHERS, MARY J. "Re-vision of the Muse:
        Adrienne Rich, Audre Lorde, Judy Grahn, Olga
        Broumas," **Hudson Review**, 36 (1983), 293-322.
Comparison of four proudly lesbian contemporary poets.

2027. CHENEY, ANNE. **Millay in Greenwich Village.**
        Tuscaloosa: University of Alabama Press, 1975. 160
        pp.
Makes the lesbianism of the poet Edna St. Vincent Millay
(1892-1950) quite evident.

2028. CLARKE, CHERYL et al. "Black Women on Black
        Women: Conversations and Questions," **Conditions:
        Nine** (1983), 88-137.
Dialogue among Clarke, Jewelle Gomez, Bonnie Johnson, and
Linda Powell.

2029. COOK, BLANCHE WIESEN. "'Women Alone Stir My
        Imagination': Lesbianism and the Cultural Tradi-
        tion," **Signs**, 4 (1979), 718-39.
Literary evidence of the emergence of modern lesbian
consciousness in the first part of the 20th century.

2030. COOPER, JANET. "Female Crushes, Affections, and
        Friendships in Children's Literature," **Gai Saber**,
        1:2 (1977), 83-88.
Such themes flourished in American children's literature
up to the 1920s, when they were gradually extinguished.

2031. CROWDER, DIANE GRIFFIN. "Amazons and Mothers?
        Monique Wittig, Hélène Cixous and Theories of
        Women's Writing," **Contemporary Literature**, 24:2
        (1983), 117-44.
Contrasts the political views of the two French writers,
seeking to show how these differences mold differences of
style.

2032. CRUIKSHANK, MARGARET. "Notes on Recent Lesbian
        Autobiographical Writing," **JH**, 8:1 (1982), 19-26.
Emphasizes work produced in the late 1970s and early 80s,
arguing that in the strict sense little true lesbian
autobiography existed before then, owing to reticence and
self-censorship. A number of literary topics are covered
in Margaret Cruikshank (ed.), **Lesbian Studies: Present and
Future** (Old Westbury, NY, Feminist Press, 1982; 286 pp.).

2033. DEEGAN, DOROTHY. **The Stereotype of the Single
        Woman in American Novels.** New York: King's Crown
        Press, 1951. 252 pp.
With the wisdom of hindsight, one can perceive that some
of these women characters were "variant," or ambiguously

lesbian.

2034. EMPLAINCOURT, MARILYN. **La Femme Damnée: A Study of the Lesbian in French Literature from Diderot to Proust.** Tuscaloosa: University of Alabama, 1977. 445 pp. (unpublished dissertation)
From the appearance of **La Religieuse** at the end of the 18th century onwards, discerns several phases of development keeping pace with general literary fashion.

2035. EVERARD, MYRIAM. "Galerij der vrouwenliefde: 'Sex Variant Women' in de Nederlandse literatuur, 1880-1940," in: Mattias Duyves (ed.), **Homojaarboek 2.** Amsterdam: Van Gennep, 1983, 80-112.
Traces a number of themes in Dutch lesbian literature up to World War II: classical antiquity, schoolgirl romances, decadence, inversion, the woman as man, prostitution, free love, and the women's movement.

2036. FADERMAN, LILLIAN. "Lesbian Magazine Fiction in the Early Twentieth Century," **Journal of Popular Culture,** 11 (1978), 800-17.
Commercial outlets were more hospitable at this period than later.

2037. FADERMAN, LILLIAN. **Surpassing the Love of Men: Romantic Friendship and Love between Women from the Renaissance to the Present.** New York: William Morrow, 1981. 496 pp.
This major study, of theoretical as well as historical importance, presents literary evidence from both Europe and North America to trace a broad pattern of homosocial behavior among women (rather than necessarily lesbianism). Copious references in the notes.

2038. FIELD, ANDREW. **Djuna: The Life and Times of Djuna Barnes.** New York: G. P. Putnam's Sons, 1983. 287 pp.
Readable, but superficial account of the life of the innovative American writer (1892-1982) in Greenwich Village and Paris, which tends to downplay her lesbianism. See also Mary Lynn Broe (ed.), **Silence and Power: A Reevaluation of Djuna Barnes** (Carbondale: Southern Illinois University Press, 1986; 186 pp.); Louis F. Kannenstine, **The Art of Djuna Barnes: Duality and Damnation** (New York: New York University Press, 1977); and James B. Scott, **Djuna Barnes** (Boston: Twayne, 1976).

2039. FOSTER, JEANNETTE H. **Sex Variant Women in Literature: A Historical and Quantitative Survey.** New York: Vantage Press, 1956. 412 pp.
This still-standard work covers literature in English, French, and German, with discussion of themes and characters of works and bibliographical data. The reissues of 1975 (Baltimore: Diana Press) and 1985 (Tallahassee: Naiad Press) contain some supplementary bibliography.

2040. FRIEDMAN, SUSAN STANFORD. "'I Go Where I Love': An
Intertextual Study of HD and Adrienne Rich,"
Signs, 4:2 (1983), 228-45.
Comparison of the two poets; followed by Rich's comment
(pp. 733-38) and Friedman's reply (738-40).

2041. GLENDINNING, VICTORIA. **Vita.** New York: Knopf,
1983. 464 pp.
Life of the English bisexual writer Victoria Sackville-
West (1892-1962), who had an affair with Virginia Woolf
and was married to Harold Nicolson. See also: Sackville-West, **Letters to Virginia Woolf.** Edited by L. De
Salvo and M. Leaska (London: Hutchinson, 1984; 473 pp.).

2042. GRAHN, JUDY. **The Highest Apple: Sappho and the
Lesbian Poetic Tradition.** San Francisco: Spin-
sters' Ink, 1985. 159 pp.
Subjective essays on Sappho, Emily Dickinson, Amy Lowell,
Gertrude Stein, Adrienne Rich, Paula Gunn Allen, Audre
Lorde, Olga Broumas, and Judy Grahn.

2043. GRIER, BARBARA. **Lesbiana: Book Reviews from the
Ladder, 1966-1972.** Weatherby Lake, MO: Naiad
Press, 1976. 309 pp.
Chronicle of reviews from the monthly column of **The
Ladder** (as by "Gene Damon"), with index, pp. 293-309.

2044. GRIER, BARBARA. **The Lesbian in Literature.** Third
ed. Tallahassee: Naiad Press, 1981. 168 pp.
This standard work contains about 2100 entries, including
many rare and out-of-the-way items, twice the number of
the second (1975) edition. Entries are coded for relevance and quality. While the emphasis is mainly creative
work (novels, short stories, drama, and poetry), biographies and some critical works also appear. The first
edition (1967), reprinted in 1975 in **A Gay Bibliography**
(New York: Arno Press), preserves references to a quantity
of "lesbian trash" items that were subsequently jet-
tisoned. For a supplement covering 1981-83, see Margaret
Cruikshank, **New Lesbian Writing: An Anthology** (San
Francisco: Grey Fox Press, 1984; 200 pp.), pp. 184-200.

2045. GUBAR, SUSAN. "Blessings in Disguise: Cross-dressing as Redressing for Female Modernists," **Massachusetts Review** 22 (1981), 477-508.
Speculative observations on the theme in Virginia Woolf
and others.

2046. GUBAR, SUSAN. "Sapphistries," **Signs**, 10 (1984),
43-62.
The influence of the Greek poet on such writers as Renee
Vivien, H. D., Amy Lowell, and Marguerite Yourcenar.

2047. GUEST, BARBARA. **Herself Defined: The Poet H. D. and
Her World.** Garden City, NY: Doubleday, 1984. 384
pp.

Although awkwardly written, this book affords the fireal
understanding of the link between H. D. (Hilda Doo-
little) and Bryher (Annie Winifred Ellerman), whose
relationship spanned three countries and four decades.

2048. HACKER, HANNA. "Eigensinn und Doppelsinn in
       frauenbezogenen und lesbischen literarischen Texten
       österreichischer Autorinnen, 1900-1938," **Kultur-
       jahrbuch: Wiener Beiträge zu Kulturwissenschaft und
       Kulturpolitik**, 2 (1983), 264-81.
Woman-identified and lesbian themes in Austrian women
authors from the turn of the century to the Anschluss.

2049. HEILBRUN, CAROLYN G. **Toward a Recognition of
       Androgyny**. New York: Knopf, 1973. 189 pp.
Examines works by Virginia Woolf and the Bloomsbury
circle, finding in them a plea for reducing the distance
between the genders.

2050. HENNEGAN, ALISON. "Lesbians in Literature," **Gay
       Left**, no. 9 (1979), 20-25.
Reflections on the complexities of discovering or deciding
who lesbians were and what lesbianism is from literary
evidence.

2051. HODGES, BETH (ed.). **Lesbian Feminist Writing and
       Publishing**. Special Issue of **Margins: A Review of
       Little Magazines and Small Press Books** (August
       1975). 72 pp.
Useful overview, by several hands, of what was being
accomplished in the first half of the 1970s.

2052. JACQUEMIN, GEORGES. **Marguerite Yourcenar**. Lyon:
       La Manufacture, 1985. 250 pp.
Biographical study of the noted French novelist, the first
woman to be a member of the French Academy.

2053. KARLINSKY, SIMON. **Marina Tsvetaeva: The Woman, Her
       World, and Her Poetry**. Cambridge: Cambridge
       University Press, 1986. 289 pp.
Critical and biographical study of a major Russian
poetess of the 20th century, who was famous for the
violent crushes she conceived for persons of both sexes.

2054. KAYE, MELANIE. "Culture-making: Lesbian Classics
       in the Year 2000?" **Sinister Wisdom**, no. 13 (Spring
       1980), 23-34.
On canon formation in relation to lesbian writing.

2055. KENNARD, JEAN E. "Ourself behind Ourself: A Theory
       for Lesbian Readers," **Signs**, 9 (1984), 647-62.
Proposes a theory of polar reading, permitting the
participation of the lesbian reader in any text, thus
opening the possibility of wide literary experience
without involving the reader's denial of her sexual
identity and self.

2056. KLAICH, DOLORES. **Woman + Woman: Attitudes toward Lesbianism.** New York: Simon and Schuster, 1974. 287 pp.
Includes sensitive critical interpretation of such literary figures as Sappho, Renee Vivien, Colette, Radclyffe Hall, and Virginia Woolf.

2057. LANGER, ELINOR. **Josephine Herbst.** Boston: Little, Brown, 1984. 384 pp.
Sympathetic study of East Coast literary radical (1892-1969), who loved both men and women.

2058. LIBERTIN, MARY. "Female Friendship in Women's Verse: Towards a New Theory of Female Poetics," **Women's Studies,** 9 (1982), 291-308.
Poetry as a vehicle for women's homosocial perceptions.

2059. MACLEAN, JUDY. "New Writing by Lesbians of Color," **Advocate,** no. 382 (December 8, 1983), 38-39.
Review essay on recent (and some not-so-recent) literature by minority lesbians.

2060. MAY, GEORGES CLAUDE. **Diderot et "La Religieuse": Etude historique et litteraire.** New Haven: Yale University Press, 1954. 245 pp.
Study of Denis Diderot's lesbian novel.

2061. MELLOW, JAMES R. **Charmed Circle: Gertrude Stein and Company.** New York: Praeger, 1974. 528 pp.
The fullest account of the fascinating circle around the American writer in Paris. See also Linda Simon, **The Biography of Alice B. Toklas** (New York: Avon, 1977. 407 pp.); Samuel Steward (ed.), **Dear Sammy: Letters from Gertrude Stein and Alice B. Toklas** (Boston: Houghton-Mifflin, 1977).

2062. O'BRIEN, SHARON. "'The Thing Not Named': Willa Cather as a Lesbian Writer," **Signs** (1984), 576-99.
Thoughtful examination of the appropriateness of the concept to the work of the American novelist (1873-1947). See also Phyllis C. Robinson, **Willa: The Life of Willa Cather** (New York: Holt, Rinehart and Winston, 1984); and Deborah Lambert, "The Defeat of a Hero: Autonomy and Sexuality in **My Antonia,**" **American Literature** 53 (1982), 676-90.

2063. PATAI, DAPHNE. "When Women Rule: Defamiliarization in the Sex Role Reversal Utopia," **Extrapolation,** 23 (1982), 56-69.
Discusses a number of science fiction and fantasy novels portraying societies in which women dominate or there is no distinction between the sexes.

2064. PATTERSON, REBECCA. **The Riddle of Emily Dickinson's Imagery.** Boston: Houghton-Mifflin, 1951. 434 pp.

Pioneering, but still controversial work arguing Dickinson's lesbianism from internal evidence found in the poems. See also Richard B. Sewall, **The Life of Emily Dickinson** (New York: Farrar, Straus and Giroux, 1974).

2065. PHELPS, ROBERT. **Belles saisons: A Colette Scrapbook.** New York: Farrar, Straus and Giroux, 1978. 302 pp.
Illustrated biography of the French novelist (1873-1954). See also: Genevieve Dormann, **Amoureuse Colette** (Paris; Herscher, 1984; 319 pp.).

2066. RULE, JANE. **Lesbian Images.** Garden City, NY: Doubleday, 1975. 246 pp.
Canadian novelist offers interpretations of the lives and writings of Radclyffe Hall, Gertrude Stein, Willa Cather, Vita Sackville-West, Ivy Compton-Burnett, Elizabeth Bowen, Colette, Violette Leduc, Margaret Anderson, Dorothy Baker, May Sarton, and Maureen Duffy.

2067. RUSS, JOANNA. **How to Suppress Women's Writing.** Austin: University of Texas Press, 1983. 159 pp.
Passionate defense of the qualities of women's writing, and the dangers she perceives to its existence. See also her **Magic Mommas, Trembling Sisters, Puritans and Perverts.** (Trumansburg, NY: Crossing Press, 1985).

2068. SAHLI, NANCY. "Smashing: Women's Relationships before the Fall," **Chrysalis,** no. 8 (1979), 17-27.
Argues that after 1875 same-sex crushes became suspect.

2069. SCHOPPMANN, CLAUDIA. **"Der Skorpion": Frauenliebe in der Weimarer Republik.** Hamburg: Fruhlings Erwachen, 1985. 81 pp.
Study of Anna Elisabet Weirauch (1887-1970), and her novel **Der Skorpion,** against the background of lesbian life in Germany, 1918-33.

2070. SEGREST, MAB. "Lines I Dare to Write: Lesbian Writing in the South," **Southern Experience,** 9 (1981), 53-55 and 57-62.
Poet and editor reflects on her sisters in Dixie.

2071. SHAKTINI, NAMASCAR. "Displacing the Phallic Subject: Wittig's Lesbian Writing," **Signs,** 8 (1982), 19-44.
Philological and mythological aspects of the transformations effected by the French writer.

2072. SHAW, NANETTE. "Jocelyn François: An Introduction," **Thirteenth Moon,** 7 (1984), 39-49.
Includes excerpts by, and interview with the French novelist.

2073. SHOCKLEY, ANN ALLEN. "The Black Lesbian in American Literature: An Overview," in: Trudy Darty and

Sandee Potter (eds.), **Women-identified Women.** Palo Alto, CA: Mayfield (1974), 267-75.
Reasons for the neglect of this literature and discussions of work by Maya Angelou, Ann Shockley, Rosa Guy, Gayl Jones, Pat Parker, and others.

2074. STIMPSON, CATHARINE. "Zero Degree Deviancy: The Lesbian Novel in English," **Critical Inquiry,** 8 (1981), 363-79.
Thoughtful essay treating a few selected examples, including **The Well of Loneliness** and **Lover.**

2075. TUBACH, SALLY P. **Female Homoeroticism in German Literature and Culture.** Berkeley: University of California, 1980. 582 pp. (unpublished dissertation)
Explores reasons for late emergence in German literature; Bettina von Arnim, effects of psychiatric theories; 20th-century authors (including Ingeborg Bachmann and Verena Stefan).

2076. WELLEK, RENE. "Vernon Lee, Bernard Berenson and Aesthetics," in: Vittorio Gabrieli (ed.), **Friendship's Garland: Essays Presented to Mario Praz on His Seventieth Birthday.** Rome: Edizioni di Storia e Letteratura, 1966, pp. 529-47.
On the English writer Vernon Lee and her circle in Florence.

2077. WHITE, RAY LEWIS. **Gertrude Stein and Alice B. Toklas: A Reference Guide.** Boston: G. K. Hall, 1984. 282 pp.
Chiefly an annotated list of writings about the famous couple (1909-81). See also: Maureen R. Liston, **Gertrude Stein: Annotated Critical Bibliography** (Kent, OH: Kent State University Press, 1979; 230 pp.).

2078. ZIMMERMAN, BONNIE. "Is 'Chloe Liked Olivia' a Lesbian Plot?" **Women's Studies International Forum,** 6 (1983), 169-75.
Author calls for all women to destroy patriarchal myths about lesbians; recover the works of lesbians, and proclaim the word "lesbian" forcefully. See also her "The Politics of Transliteration: Lesbian Personal Narratives," **Signs,** 9 (1984), 663-82; and "What Has Never Been: An Overview of Lesbian Feminist Criticism," **Feminist Studies,** 7 (1981), 451-75.

K. MUSIC

In its essence abstract, music would seem to be unrelated to sexual orientation. However, closer inspection reveals a number of interesting facets: the historical vogue of

castrati, individual homosexual and lesbian composers and
performers, and homosexual elements in lyrics and lib-
rettos of musical works. An unsolved problem in the
sociology of taste is why certain types of music (opera,
musical comedy, organ music) seem to hold great attraction
for homosexual audiences and others not. See also
"Theater and Dance," VI.G.

2079. ALBERTSON, CHRIS. **Bessie.** New York: Stein and
       Day, 1972. 243 pp.
In this life of the great Black blues singer Bessie Smith
(1874-1937), see pp. 14, 116-20 for lesbian aspects. In
general see: Derrick Stewart-Baxter, **Ma Rainey and the
Classic Blues Singers** (New York: Stein and Day, 1970;
112 pp.).

2080. AVICOLLI, TOMMI. "Images of Gays in Rock Music,"
       in: Karla Jay and Allen Young, **Lavender Culture.**
       New York: Jove, 1978, pp. 182-94.
"Bisexual chic" and gay/lesbian themes in rock music.

2081. BARRICELLI, JEAN-PIERRE, and LEO WEINSTEIN.
       Ernest Chausson: The Composer's Life and Works.
       Norman: University of Oklahoma Press, 1955. 241
       pp.
For Chausson's attachment to Claude Debussy, see pp. 37,
59-70.

2082. BENTLEY, GLADYS. "I Am a Woman Again," **Ebony,** 7
       (August 1952), 92-98.
A Black songwriter, pianist, and male impersonator writes
with some reticence about her past.

2083. BOWERS, FAUBION. **The New Scriabin: Enigma and
       Answers.** New York: St. Martin's Press, 1973.
       210 pp.
A study that mentions the feminine elements in the personality of the 19th-century Russian composer.

2084. BROWN, DAVID. **Tchaikovsky: The Early Years,
       1840-1874.** New York: Norton, 1978. 348 pp.
For the Russian composer's homosexuality, see pp. 50,
248-49. Continued in two subsequent vols. See also
Brown: "Tchaikovsky, Pyotr Il'yich," **New Grove Dictionary
of Music and Musicians,** 18 (1980), pp. 606-36 (on pp. 626-
28 Brown endorses the controversial theory of the composer's death: see A. Orlovska, below).

2085. BROWN, PETER, and STEVEN GAINES. **The Love You
       Make: An Insider's Story of the Beatles.** London:
       Macmillan, 1983. 401 pp.
Franker on manager Brian Epstein's homosexuality than
earlier accounts.

2086. CASERTA, PEGGY, and DAN KNAPP. **Going Down with**

Janis. New York: Dell, 1974. 367 pp.
Account of life with the tormented rock singer Janis
Joplin (1943-1970), by her lesbian lover.

2087. DEVOE, JOHN. "Pop Music: What's Gay About It,"
      Advocate, no. 187 (April 7, 1976), 24-25.
Beginning of a special section (pp. 24-40) on the pop
music world.

2088. DOBKIN, ALIX. **Alix Dobkin's Adventures in Women's
      Music.** Preston Hollow, NY: Tomato Publications,
      1979. 70 pp.
Compositions of the popular lesbian performer, with commentary, photos, drawings, and an autobiographical
essay.

2089. EWEN, DAVID. **American Composers: A Biographical
      Dictionary.** New York: G. Putnam's Sons,1982. 742
      pp.
See pp. 147-51 on Henry Cowell, mentioning his morals
charge, incarceration in San Quentin, and subsequent loss
of friendship with Charles Ives, a vehement homophobe.

2090. FABER, NANCY. "Never in the Closet or on the
      Charts: Holly Near Sings Uncompromisingly of Gay
      Love," **People Weekly,** 16 (July 13, 1981), 103-04.
Noted lesbian singer keeps her principles and distinctive
style.

2091. FUCHS, HANNS. **Richard Wagner und die Homosexual-
      ität; unter besonderer Berücksichtigung der
      sexuellen Anomalien seiner Gestalten.** Berlin:
      Barsdorf, 1903. 278 pp.
Period study of Wagner (1813-1883) and homosexuality, with
special reference to the sexual anomalies of his characters.

2092. GRECO, STEPHEN, et al. "Merry Musicmakers,"
      Advocate, no 312 (March 5, 1981), T7-10.
On gay men's choruses in New York City, Los Angeles,
Chicago, and San Francisco.

2093. GRILLO, RUDY. "Gay Moments in Straight Music," **Gay
      Books Bulletin,** no 8 (Fall-Winter 1982), 22-26.
Perceptive analysis of lyrics and other aspects of American popular music, chiefly in the first half of the
20th century.

2094. GRUEN, JOHN. **Menotti: A Biography.** New York: Mac-
      millan, 1978. 245 pp.
Covers the American composer's (1911-) long-term relationship with the late Samuel Barber, and with young
proteges.

2095. GUTMAN, ROBERT W. **Richard Wagner: The Man, His Mind
      and His Music.** London: Penguin, 1971. 693 pp.

Chapter 10 (pp. 329-69) shows the German composer's man-
ipulation of the homoerotic longing of his patron, King
Ludwig II, and his use of a homosexual motif in **Tristan
und Isolde.**

2096.   HARRISON, LOU. [Interview], in: Winston Leyland
        (ed.), **Gay Sunshine Interviews.** San Francisco: Gay
        Sunshine Press, 1978, pp. 163-89.
The innovative contemporary composer speaks frankly of his
music and gay relationships.

2097.   HENZE, HANS WERNER. **Music and Politics: Collected
        Writings, 1953-81.** Translated by Peter Labanyi.
        Ithaca, NY: Cornell University Press, 1982. 286
        pp.
Mixture of music and ingenuous leftism by the contemporary
German composer (b. 1926), who moved to Italy in 1953 to
escape homophobia in his own country.

2098.   HERBERT, DAVID (ed.). **The Operas of Benjamin
        Britten.** New York: Columbia Unversity Press,
        1979. 400 pp.
The British homosexual composer's (1913-76) articles and
libretti, some of which contain homophile themes.

2099.   HERIOT, ANGUS. **The Castrati in Opera.** London:
        Secker and Warburg, 1956. 243 pp.
Traces the history of the fashion for castrati down
through the 19th century, with biographical sketches of
celebrated performers.

2100.   HOWE, FREDERICK. "The American Musical: Grand,
        Gaudy, and Guardedly Gay," **Advocate,** no 213 (April
        6, 1977), 17-19.
Historically the Broadway musical, so beloved of gay men,
has by and large sought to present a seemingly straight
facade to the middle-class audience.

2101.   JENNINGS, BRIAN (pseud. of William Jennings
        Bryan). "Music: The Hermaphroditic Art," **ONE
        Institute Quarterly,** 7:1-2 (Winter-Spring 1964),
        20-24.
A Los Angeles gay pianist reflects on music.

2102.   JIOZEMGA, CHRIS. "Tom Robinson 'Comes Out' with a
        New Album," **After Dark,** 11 (May 1978), 78-80.
Britain's first openly gay rock musician gives an overview
of the gay influence in contemporary rock and punk. See
also Adam Block's interview with Robinson, **Advocate,**
no. 420 (May 14, 1985), 31-32.

2103.   KIRK, KRIS. **The Vinyl Closet.** London: Gay Men's
        Press, 1986. 160 pp.
Multifaceted survey of the gay side of the pop music
scene, including interviews and photos. Comprehensive
gay discography.

2104. KOPKIND, ANDREW. "Gay Rock: The Boys in the Band,"
      Ramparts, 11 (March 1973), 49-51.
Extravagances of the counterculture era.

2105. KUPPER, WILLIAM H. "Immortal Beethoven: A Re-
      pressed Homosexual?" **ONE Magazine**, 15 (February
      1967), 4-6.
Homoerotic components of Beethoven's personality have long
been suspected, but remain elusive. See, e.g., Editha
and Richard Sterba, **Ludwig van Beethoven und sein Neffe**
(Munich: Szczesny, 1964; 350 pp.).

2106. MAISEL, EDWARD. **Charles T. Griffes: The Life of an
      American Composer.** New York: Knopf, 1984. 336 pp.
Enlarged reissue of the 1943 original, which was (for the
period) surprisingly frank about Griffes' (1884-1920)
homosexual liaisons, notably with a married New York City
Police officer. Many important documents were destroyed
by his homophobic family. This new edition adds reference
notes.

2107. MITCHELL, DONALD. **Britten and Auden in the
      Thirties: The Year 1936.** London: Faber, 1981. 176
      pp.
Intersection of the careers of England's two leading
homosexual creative figures of the time.

2108. ORLOVA, ALEXANDRA. "Tchaikovsky: The Last Chap-
      ter," **Music and Letters**, 62 (April 1981), 125-45.
Orlova's macabre reconstruction of the circumstances of
the composer's death has been criticized as inadequately
documented.

2109. PLASKIN, GLENN. **Horowitz: A Biography of Vladimir
      Horowitz.** New York: William Morrow, 1983. 607 pp.
The noted pianist is said to have remarked: "There are
three kinds of pianists: Jewish ones, homosexual ones,
and bad ones." This frank and detailed biography covers
his sexual orientation--as well as his marriage to Wanda
Toscanini.

2110. RIMMER, DAVE. **Like Punk Never Happened: Culture
      Club and the New Pop.** London: Faber, 1985. 195
      pp.
Journalist for **Smash Hits** speaks his mind on Boy George,
Frankie Goes to Hollywood, and other androgynous/gay
phenomena of the 1980s British pop scene. See also
Chris Cutler, **File under Popular** (London: November Books,
1985).

2111. ROREM, NED. **The Paris Diary of Ned Rorem.** New
      York: Braziller, 1966. 240 pp.
The American composer recounts frankly his exploitation
of his good looks and homosexual affairs as an expatriate,
1951-55. He continues the story in **The New York Diary**
(New York: Braziller, 1967; 218 pp.) and **The Final**

Diary, 1961-72 (Holt, Rinehart and Winston, 1974; 439 pp.).

2112.   SALES, GROVER. "The Strange Case of Charles Ives or, Why is Jazz Not Gay Music," **Gene Lee's Jazzletter,** 4:5 (December 1984), 1-8.
Argues that jazz musicians are hardly ever homosexual (without noting the exceptions of Bix Beiderbecke and Bunny Berrigan). Despite overstatement of the case, an interesting discussion of musical taste and sexual orientation.

2113.   SCHWARTZ, CHARLES. **Cole Porter.** New York: Dial Press, 1978. 365 pp.
Life of the noted popular music figure (1893-1964), whose sophisticated lyrics are one of the defining instances of High Camp.

2114.   SHILTS, RANDY. "Pop Music: Strictly between the Lines," **Advocate,** no 187 (April 7, 1976), 25-27.
Commercial constraints make "coming out" hard in the music business.

2115.   SIMELS, STEVEN. **Gender Chameleons: Androgyny in Rock and Roll.** New York: Arbor House, 1985. 112 pp.
Illustrated journalistic book: from fifties origins to Boy George and Michael Jackson.

2116.   SMITH, A. E. "Peter Ilyich Tschaikovsky: His Life and Loves Re-examined," **ONE Institute Quarterly,** no 12 (1961), 20-36.
Argues that the Russian composer was a vigorous and creative homosexual, as well adjusted as the circumstances of his time would allow. His life was not the tragedy that some have claimed.

2117.   THORSON, SCOTT. "Liberace Bombshell--Boyfriend Tells All about Their Six Year Romance," **National Enquirer** (November 2, 1982), 48-51.
Less a bombshell perhaps than a confirmation of what had long been evident to the discerning regarding one of America's most popular entertainers.

2118.   TILCHEN, MAIDA. "Lesbians and Women's Music," in: Trudy Darty and Sandee Potter (eds.), **Women Identified Women,** Palo Alto, CA: Mayfield, 1984, pp. 287-303.
Fifteen years of women's (separatist) music from tentative beginnings to growing recognition and institutional forms.

2119.   WEAVER, NEAL. "In Search of Gay Heroes: Singers Michael Cohen and Steven Grossman," **In Touch** (October 1974), 22-27, 75-76.
On two upfront gay vocalists of the counterculture era.

2120. WHITCOMB, IAN. **Rock Odyssey.** Garden City, NY:
      Doubleday, 1983.
Memoirs of British singer/rock impresario in Hollywood
during the late sixties and seventies.

2121. WHITE, ERIC WALTER. **Benjamin Britten: His Life and
      Operas.** Second ed. Berkeley: University of
      California Press, 1984. 320 pp.
The new edition brings the account up to date, by incorporating the last six years of the composer's life (1913-
1976).

2122. YOUNG, IRENE. **For the Record.** Oakland, CA:
      Olivia, 1982. 58 pp.
Photographic portraits of performers in the women's music
scene.

2123. ZIEGLER, MARION. "The Great Gay Composers," in:
      Dennis Sanders (ed.), **Gay Source.** New York: Berke-
      ley, 1977, pp. 83-95.
Notes on the lives of Handel, Beethoven, Schubert, Tchaikovsky, and others. While present evidence in some cases
may be thin, this article offers many leads which later
researchers should follow up.

VII. PHILOSOPHY AND RELIGION

A. PHILOSOPHY AND ETHICS

The exploration of philosophical issues related to homosexuality, particularly as regards the metaphysic of
love, began in ancient Greece, when most leading thinkers
were either bisexual or homosexual (see III.C). In the
many renascences of Greek thought, however, this aspect
has been occulted or neglected altogether. In the 20th
century, philosophy--especially in English speaking
countries--adopted an austere credo known as the analytic
philosophy, which discouraged the exploration of social
and ethical questions. Recently, however, philosophers
have begun to concern themselves with "mortal issues"
affecting people's lives, such as abortion, the handicapped, and sexuality. The women's movement has also made
an appreciable impact; for this, see also "Lesbian-Feminist Theory," II.B. Some ethical aspects are discussed
in the following sections on "Religion," VII.Bff. Moreover, as in every other field of human endeavor, there
is the question of which philosophers were homosexual, and
how their orientation may have affected their thought.

2124. ARAGONA, TULLIA. **Della infinità d'amore.** Ed.
        by Alessandro Zilioti. Milan: G. Daellei, 1864.   93
        pp.
See pp. 64-74 for Renaissance discussion (1547) in dialogue form of the tradition of Greek love according
to Plato and Ficino.

2125. BAKER, ROBERT, and FREDERICK ELLISTON (eds.).
        Philosophy and Sex. Second enlarged ed. Buffalo:
        Prometheus Books, 1984. 521 pp.
Includes papers specifically addressing homosexuality by
Jeremy Bentham, Frederick Elliston, Michael Ruse, Frederick Suppe, and Joyce Trebilcot--together with much other
indirectly relevant material. A useful bibliography, compiled by William Vitek, appears on pp. 471-521. The first
edition of this book (1975) contains some papers omitted
from the new edition.

2126. BARTHES, ROLAND. **A Lover's Discourse: Fragments.**
        Translated by Richard Howard. New York: Hill and
        Wang, 1978. 234 pp.
Somewhat cryptic but suggestive comments on the nature
of love, in which the homosexuality of the writer, an influential French literary critic and structuralist (1915-
1980), emerges between the lines. See Richard Sennett,
"An Evening of Barthes," **Christopher Street,** no. 76
(1983), 22-28.

2127. BARTLEY, WILLIAM WARREN, III. **Wittgenstein.**
Philadelphia: Lippincott, 1973. 192 pp.
Presents the first gathering of evidence, since fully
confirmed, that the Austro-British philosopher (1889-
1951) was homosexual. The new edition (La Salle, IL: Open
Court, 1985) contains an Afterword, "On Wittgenstein and
Homosexuality," reflecting on the controversy that developed when the Wittgenstein establishment tried to suppress
the information, the text of which is substantially the
same as the author's article in **Salmagundi**, no. 58-59
(1982), 166-96.

2128. BENSON, R. O. D. **In Defense of Homosexuality, Male
and Female: A Rational Evaluation of Social
Prejudice.** New York: Julian Press, 1965. 239 pp.
A critical examination of the arguments against homosexuality, concluding that homosexual behavior is as ethically defensible as heterosexual behavior. Reprinted as:
What Every Homosexual Knows (New York: Ace Books, 1965).

2129. BENTHAM, JEREMY. "Offenses against One's Self:
Paederasty," **JH**, 3 (1978), 389-405; 4 (1978),
91-107.
First publication, edited by Louis Crompton, of an essay
written by the utilitarian philosopher about 1785. Arguing that homosexual acts do not "weaken" men or threaten
population or marriage, he offers the first known argument
for homosexual law reform in England. A later essay on
the subject (1814-16), "Offenses against Taste," was
published by C. K. Ogden in his edition of Bentham, **The
Theory of Legislation** (London: Kegan Paul, 1931), 476-97.
For the historical background, see Louis Crompton, **Byron
and Greek Love** (Berkeley: University of California Press,
1985).

2130. BRÈS, YVON. **La psychologie de Platon.** Paris:
Presses Universitaires de France, 1968. 438 pp.
An ambitious, but flawed attempt to combine psychoanalysis and classical philology to show links between Plato's
life and his thought. See the critical remarks by Luc
Brisson, **Revue des Etudes Grecques**, 86 (1973), 224-31.
Compare Hans Kelsen, "Platonic Love," **American Imago**, 3
(1949), 1-70 (translation of a German article that
appeared in 1933).

2131. CANGEMI, JOSEPH P. et al. "The Philosophy of
Existentialism and a Psychology of Irreversible
Homosexuality," **College Student Journal Monograph,**
8:3, part 2 (September-October 1974). 12 pp.
Stresses that the essence of man is his existence, and
the individual's richest existence is to be what he can
become.

2132. DESMON, ANDRE-CLAUDE (pseud. of A. Lafond). "A la
recherche d'une éthique: méditations spinozistes,"
Arcadie, no. 73 (January 1960), 9-17; no. 74 (Feb-

ruary 1960), 80-87.
Advocates a version of Spinoza's philosophy.

2133. DIDEROT, DENIS. **Oeuvres.** Paris: Gallimard, 1951.
       1480 pp.
In this selection of the works of the Enlightenment poly-
math (1713-84), see "Suite de l'Entretien" (pp. 939-42);
"Supplément au Voyage de Bougainville" (pp. 999-1001); and
"Essai sur la peinture" (pp. 1143-44).

2134. DOVER, KENNETH J., SIR. "Aristophanes' Speech in
       Plato's Symposium," **Journal of Hellenic Studies,** 86
       (1966), 41-50.
Close reading of this celebrated disquisition on the
origins of same-sex attraction. See also Dover, "Eros
and Nomos," **Bulletin of the Institute of Classical Studies**
(London), 11 (1964), 31-42; and the notes to his edition
of the Greek text of the **Symposium** (Cambridge: Cambridge
University Press, 1980; 185 pp.).

2135. FOUCAULT, MICHEL. **The Foucault Reader.** Ed. by
       Paul Rabinow. New York: Pantheon, 1984. 390 pp.
Even before his death in Paris in 1984, Foucault had
emerged as a figure of vast and ramifying influence.
This book is a selection from a number of his works,
emphasizing the theoretical dimension and focusing in
part on his overarching concept of power as it manifests
itself in schools, hospitals, factories, and sexual
arrangements. Indispensible for a thorough study of
Foucault's work is: Michael Clark, **Michel Foucault: An
Annotated Bibliography** (New York: Garland, 1983; 608
pp.). See also: John Rajchman, **Foucault: The Freedom of
Philosophy** (New York: Columbia University Press, 1985;
131 pp.).

2136. FOUCAULT, MICHEL. **Power/Knowledge: Selected Inter-
       views and Other Writings, 1972-1977.** Ed. by
       Colin Gordon. New York: Pantheon, 1980. 270 pp.
Occasional pieces focusing upon Foucault's concern with
the mechanisms whereby power "reaches into the very grain
of individuals, touches their bodies and inserts itself
into their actions and their discourses, learning processes and everyday lives."

2137. FRAISSE, JEAN-CLAUDE. **Philia: la notion d'amitié
       dans la philosophie antique.** Paris: J. Vrin,
       1974. 504 pp.
Encyclopedic work on the ideas of friendship put forth by
the philosophers of Greco-Roman antiquity. See also Ludovic Dugas, **L'amitié antique d'après les moeurs populaires
et les théories des philosophes** (Paris: Félix Alcan, 1894;
454 pp.).

2138. FRYE, MARILYN. **The Politics of Reality: Essays in
       Feminist Theory.** Trumansburg: Crossing Press,
       1983. 150 pp.

Papers by a lesbian philosopher treating such issues as abortion, women's oppression, separatism, race, and homophobia.

2139. GOLDBERG, STEVEN. "Is Homosexuality Normal?" **Policy Review** no. 21 (1982), 119-38.
Tendentious effort to restore the judgmental efficacy of the concept of abnormality. Discussion in no. 23 (1983), 3-9. Compare M. Levin, below.

2140. GRAVES, JOHN. "Philosophy and Sexuality," **Gai Saber,** 1:1 (Spring 1977), 23-26.
Attempts a general theory of the categories of sex.

2141. HELLMANN, RODERICH. **Ueber Geschlechtsfreiheit: ein philosophischer Versuch zur Erhöhung des menschlichen Glücks.** Berlin: Staude, 1878. 287 pp.
A pioneering exploration of sexual libertarianism. See, e.g., p. 179 for a description of the taste of semen.

2142. HILLER, KURT. "Ethische Aufgabe der Homosexuellen," **Der Kreis,** 28:4 (1960), 2-6.
The German homosexual activist reflects on the ethical task of the homosexual.

2143. HIRSCHFELD, MAGNUS. "Ueber den Begriff der "Widernatürlichkeit," **JfsZ** 12 (1911-12), 282-96.
An early critique of the pseudo-scientific (and religious) concept of the unnatural. See now Wayne Dynes, **Homolexis** (New York: GAU-NY, 1985), pp. 100-01.

2144. HUME, DAVID. **An Inquiry Concering the Principles of Morals; with a Supplement: A Dialogue.** Indianapolis: Bobbs-Merrill, 1957. 158 pp.
The Dialogue (1751) concerns a Utopia where pederasty is respected (see pp. 142, 145-46).

2145. INGRAM, KENNETH. **Sex-Morality Tomorrow.** London: Allen and Unwin, 1940. 175 pp.
Quasi-visionary reflections by a closeted man. See "Homosexuality" pp. 99-130.

2146. JURTH, MAX. "Confucius, ou une religion accessible aux homophiles," **Arcadie,** no. 85 (January 1961), 26-35.
Confucianism as an ethical guide for homosexuals.

2147. KANT, IMMANUEL. **Lectures on Ethics.** Translated by L. Infield. New York: Harper and Row, 1963.
Classroom lectures (1775-80) as taken down by students. Kant defends the idea that sex is only permissible within the boundaries of a monogamous heterosexual relationship. He condemns homosexual behavior as "contrary to the ends of humanity," whereby "the self is degraded below the level of the animals." (p. 170).

2148. KOERTGE, NORETTA (ed.). **Philosophy and Homosexual-**
ity. New York: Harrington Park Press, 1985. 98 pp.
Four papers, by Michael Ruse, Lynda I. A. Birke, John P.
De Cecco, and Frederick Suppe, which chiefly concern sociobiological issues, rather than strictly philosophical
ones. Originally published as JH 6:4 (Summer 1981).

2149. KRISTELLER, PAUL OSKAR. **The Philosophy of Marsilio**
Ficino. Translated by Virginia Conant. Glouce-
ster: P. Smith, 1964. 441 pp.
In this overview of the thought of the Florentine neo-Pla-
tonist, see pp. 277-88.

2150. LAGERBORG, ROLF HERIBERT HJALMAR. **Die Platonische**
Liebe. Leipzig: Felix Meiner, 1926. 295 pp.
According to B. C. Verstraete, "Although very much dated
..., this remains a sensitive and often penetrating study
of the idealized homoerotic love advocated by Plato. Lagerborg dwells at great length on the close link between
repressed sexuality and religious and philosophical mys-
ticism." (Translated from the Swedish: **Den platoniska**
kärleken.)

2151. LA METTRIE, JULIEN OFFRAY DE. "L'art de jouir,"
in his: **Oeuvres philosophiques.** Berlin: 1791,
vol. 3.
The Enlightenment thinker (1709-51) explores "that realm
of love which knows no limits save those of pleasure."

2152. LA MOTHE LE VAYER, FRANÇOIS DE. **Cincq dialogues**
faits à l'imitation des anciens. Mons: P. de la
Flèche, 1671. 332 pp.
In this work by the French sceptic, see the "Banquet
sceptique" [1630] (pp. 129-131).

2153. LEVIN, MICHAEL. "Why Homosexuality is Abnormal,"
The Monist, 67 (1984), 251-83.
Attempts, with spurious logic, to revive a teleological
theory to the effect that homosexual acts are "a misuse
of bodily parts"; consequently the homosexual lifestyle
inevitably leads to unhappiness.

2154. LEVY, DONALD. "The Definition of Love in Plato's
Symposium," **Journal of the History of Ideas,** 40
(1979), 285-90.
Close reading of the argument.

2155. LEVY, DONALD. "Perversion and the Unnatural as
Moral Categories," **Ethics,** 90 (1980), 191-202.
Seeks to clarify and rehabilitate the natural/unnatural
dichotomy, purging it of homophobic content.

2156. LEVY, PAUL. **Moore: G. E. Moore and the Cambridge**
Apostles. New York: Holt, Rinehart and Winston,
1980. 335 pp.
The philosopher's influence on Goldsworthy Lowes Dickin-

son, John Maynard Keynes, Lytton Strachey, Ludwig Wittgenstein, and others, ca. 1895-1914.

2157. MASON, H. A. "Plato's Comic Masterpiece? A Dis-
cussion of the Scope and Function of Plato's
'Drinking Party,'" **Cambridge Quarterly**, 9 (1980),
114-42.
Reexamines the narrative strategy and arguments of Plato's
Symposium.

2158. MERRITT, THOMAS M. "Homophile Ethics," **ONE
Institute Quarterly**, 3:4 (Fall 1960), 262-67).
Advocates an approach he terms "personalistic or dynamic
idealism." See also his "Philosophy for the Homophile,"
ibid., 2:3 (Summer 1959), 77-82.

2159. MONTAIGNE, MICHEL DE. **The Complete Essays of
Montaigne**. Translated by Donald M. Frame. Stanford, CA: Stanford University Press, 1958. 883
pp.
In this celebrated work by the French Renaissance thinker
(1533-92), see esp. I, 28 ("Of Friendship"), II, 12
("Apology for Raymond Sebond"), and III, 5 ("On Some
Verses of Virgil"). A start has been made towards analysis of Montaigne's significance in this field by William
John Beck, "Montaigne face à l'homosexualité," **Bulletin de
la Société des amis de Montaigne**, no. 9/10 (1982), 41-50.

2160. NAGEL, THOMAS. "Sexual Perversion," **Journal of
Philosophy**, 66 (1969), 1-17.
This often-cited paper argues that perversion is a psychological state rather than a physiological act; perversions
are "truncated or incomplete versions of the complete fig-
uration" (e. g., bestiality, where there is lack of
reciprocity).

2161. NIETZSCHE, FRIEDRICH. **Menschliches allzu Menschliches**. New ed. Leipzig: Fritsch, 1882. 377 pp.
This work by the German thinker (1844-1900)--several times
translated as "Human, All-Too Human"--contains a number of
pertinent remarks. Some of Nietzsche's comments were collected by L. S. A. M. von Römer, "Stellen aus Friedrich
Nietzsche's Werke über Uranismus," **Zeitschrift für Sexualwissenschaft**, 1 (1908), 39-46.

2162. OBERHOLZER, W. DWIGHT (ed.). **Is Gay Good?: Ethics,
Theology and Homosexuality**. Philadelphia: Westminster, 1971. 287 pp.
A collection of essays refelcting the climate of the late
1960s--"balanced" in that some are favorable, others
unfavorable.

2163. ROSAN, LAURENCE J. "Philosophies of Homophobia and
Homophilia," in: Louie Crew (ed.), **The Gay Academic**. Palm Springs, CA: ETC Publications, 1978, pp.
255-81.

Valuable overview of the bearing of major philosophical
traditions on homosexuality (materialism, idealism, sol-
ipsism, dualism).

2164. RUSE, MICHAEL. **Is Science Sexist? and Other Prob-
        lems in the Biomedical Sciences.** Boston: D. Reid-
        el, 1981. 299 pp.
Well-referenced paper by a philosopher of science, chiefly
on evolutionary theory, genetics, and sociobiology. Note
esp. no. 1: "Are Homosexuals Sick" (pp. 245-76), which
sets firm limits on the way in which such a claim could be
meaningfully advanced.

2165. SADE, DONATIEN A. F. DE, MARQUIS. **La philosophie
        dans le boudoir.** Paris: Union Générale d'Editions,
        1972. 313 pp.
Exposition, in dialogue form, of his libertine concepts of
sex; first published in 1795. The character Dolmance is a
homosexual spokesman. There are several English versions.

2166. SCHOPENHAUER, ARTHUR. **The World as Will and Repre-
        sentation.** Translated by E. F. J. Payne. New
        York: Dover, 1966. 2 vols.
Schopenhauer (1788-1860) thought that, in the male, homosexual relations are appealing before puberty and in old
age, when generation is not possible (vol. 2, pp. 541,
560-69). His relatively favorable views of homosexuality (pederasty) have sometimes been linked to his misog-
yny.

2167. SCRUTON, ROGER. **Sexual Desire.** London: Weidenfeld
        and Nicolson, 1985. 428 pp.
A florid, but sometimes stimulating book by a conservative
English philosopher. Scruton concedes that homosexual-
ity is not a perversion, but still finds it problematic.

2168. SOBLE, ALAN (ed.). **Philosophy of Sex: Contem-
        porary Readings.** Totowa, NJ: Littlefield and Adams,
        1980. 412 pp.
Includes articles by Thomas Nagel, Robert Gray, and Donald
Levy, attempting to clarify the nature of perversion.

2169. VANNOY, RUSSELL. **Sex without Love: A Philosopher's
        Exploration.** Buffalo: Prometheus, 1980. 226 pp.
Examines and rejects the traditionalist approach that sex
should occur only between two people who are in love.

2170. VEST, D. B. (pseud. of Gerald Heard). "The Phyl-
        ogeny of Homo Crescens," **ONE Institute Quarterly,**
        3:4 (Fall 1960), 252-57.
Syncretistic presentation, combining evolutionary biology
with Eastern thought. The British writer Gerald Heard
(1889-1971) was active in Southern California, where he
attracted a circle of devotees. See also his: "The Iso-
phyl as a Biological Variant: An Enquiry into the Racial
and Civilic Value of the Human Intergrade," ibid., 1:2

(Summer 1958), 43-47.

B. RELIGION: GENERAL

The traditional condemnation of homosexuality in Christian
moral theology--as the heritage of Hellenistic Judaism--
has been the starting point for efforts to mitigate the
harshness of the prohibition and to find a modus vivendi
for the homosexual in Christian society. These have taken
the form of confrontations with the older theological
views and appeals for a humanistic approach to the plight
of the homosexual seeking to live a Christian existence,
though the ascetic principles of Christian thought make
it difficult to convince those who feel a profound moral
commitment to the time-honored beliefs. For Christianity
and history, see also "Middle Ages," III.C. For Judaism,
see VII.C, VII.H. The great religious traditions of the
East are best examined in an area-studies context; see
"Islam," III.P; "China, Korea, and Central Asia," III.Q;
and "Japan," III.R.

2171. AERWYN, TOM. "Law, Morality and Religion in a
        Christian Society," **Religious Studies,** 20 (March
        1984), 79-98.
Post-Wolfenden perspectives.

2172. ALEXANDER, JOHN F., et al. (eds.). [Special
        Issue.] **The Other Side: A Magazine of Christian
        Discipleship,** no. 81 (June 1978).
Issue devoted, somewhat patronizingly, to "the gay person's lonely search for answers."

2173. ANDERSEN, W. E., and B. V. HILL (eds.). "Homosex-
        uality and the Education of Persons," **Journal of
        Christian Education,** 59 (September 1977), 3-82.
Articles of some length devoted to Christian education and
sexuality.

2174. ATKINSON, D. J. **Homosexuals in Christian Fellow-
        ship.** Grand Rapids, MI: Eerdmans, 1979. 128 pp.
An English scholar grounds his conservative approach in a
knowledgeable scrutiny of Biblical texts.

2175. BAILEY, DERRICK SHERWIN, CANON. **Homosexuality and
        the Western Christian Tradition.** London: Longmans,
        Green, 1955. 181 pp.
Pioneering examination of Biblical, historical, and legal
topics--now dated. Bailey interprets the Sodom story as
condemning the sin of inhospitality (rather than intended
homosexual rape). Surveys Roman law, medieval canon law
and Church practice, and recent social attitudes and law
(in England). Permeated by an overall bias towards excul-

pation of the Christian church from responsibility for the
intolerance of homosexuality in Western civilization.

2176. BATCHELOR, EDWARD (ed.). **Homosexuality and
        Ethics.** New York: Pilgrim Press, 1980. 261 pp.
Reprints papers and selections from books reflecting a
spectrum of Protestant, Catholic and Jewish views--from
homosexuality as "intrinsically evil" to "naturally
good." Authors range from Thomas Aquinas to Robert
Gordis, Norman Pittenger, and Rosemary Ruether. There is
a useful appendix of official statements adopted by
Christian denominations.

2177. BLÜHER, HANS. **Die Aristie des Jesus von Nazareth:
        Philosophische Grundlegung der Lehre und Erschein-
        ung Christi.** Prien: Kampmann und Schnabel, 1921.
        325 pp.
Curious blend of German homosexual movement ideas, psychoanalysis, male bonding theories, and Christianity.

2178. CAHILL, LISA SOWLE. "Sexual Issues in Christian
        Theological Ethics: A Review of Recent Studies,"
        Religious Studies Review, 4 (1978), 1-14.
Critical overview of 1970s publications.

2179. CARPENTER, EDWARD. "On the Connection between
        Homosexuality and Divination and the Importance of
        the Intermediate Sexes Generally in Early Civiliza-
        tions," **American Journal of Religious Psychology
        and Education,** 4 (1911), 210-43.
Based in part on ethnological evidence of the berdache and
shaman types, holds that homosexuals have special religious qualifications. Reprinted as the first four chapters of his **Intermediate Types among Primitive Folk** (London: Allen and Unwin, 1918).

2180. CHARLIE, ROBERT. **La chasteté cléricale.** Brus-
        sels: Librairie Socialiste de Henri Kistemaeckers,
        1878. 208 pp.
Attack on the vices of the clergy in France and Belgium,
including purported sexual attacks on boys. A specimen
of a type of writing fairly common in the heyday of the
anticlerical movement in Europe.

2181. COLEMAN, JOHN. "Révolution homosexuelle et
        herméneutique," **Concilium,** no. 193 (June 1984),
        95-110.
Canvases some ideas of psychiatric origin, and offers a
critique of the United States gay movement.

2182. COLEMAN, PETER. **Christian Attitudes to Homosexual-
        ity.** London: S.P.C.K., 1980. 376 pp.
Following surveys of the Biblical texts and the development of attitudes in history, Coleman discusses the recent
shift in Christian ethical judgment from hostility to tolerance and towards acceptance.

2183. COURT, J. H. "Homosexuality: A Scientific and
       Christian Perspective," **Interchange**, no. 13 (1973),
       24-40.
An Australian view.

2184. "David und der heilige Augustin, zwei Bisexuelle,"
       JfsZ, 2 (1900), 288-94.
Early attempt to compare David and St. Augustine as bisexuals revered by the Church.

2185. FARRAKHAN, LOUIS. "Breaking Your Agreement with
       Hell," **Final Call**, 1:6 (1981), 2-5, 8-9, 18.
Black Muslim leader's antihomosexual statement.

2186. FERM, DEAN W. **Alternative Lifestyles Confront
       the Church.** New York: Seabury, 1983. 144 pp.
What many churches are (and are not) doing to meet the
need of congregants who are not part of traditional family
units--including homosexuals.

2187. FRANKLIN, PATRICK. "Religion: Bond or Bondage for
       Gays," **Advocate**, no. 306 (1980), 21-23.
Argues that gay people should avoid committing themselves
to any group within the Judeo-Christian tradition, because
of the record of intolerance and persecution.

2188. **Geloof, kerk en homoseksualiteit.** Amsterdam:
       N.V.I.H.-C.O.C., 1984. 22 pp.
Bibliography of mainly positive Dutch religious books and
articles. See also Franz-Joseph Hirs, "Homoseksualiteit
en theologie: een overzicht over de afgelopen tien jaar,"
Tijdschrift voor theologie, 22 (1982), 178-98.

2189. GREENBERG, DAVID, and MARCIA H. BYSTRYN. "Christian
       Intolerance of Homosexuality," **American Journal of
       Sociology**, 88 (1982), 515-48.
Links Early Christian intolerance to ascetic movements in
late antique society. After a period of occultation in
the earlier Middle Ages, Christian sexual intolerance revived after A.D. 1000 because of the Gregorian reforms,
coupled with social and economic changes. Bibliography,
pp. 544-48. The presentation is more even-handed than
that of John Boswell, **Christianity, Social Tolerance,
and Homosexuality** (Chicago: University of Chicago Press,
1980; 424 pp.).

2190. GUINDON, ANDRÉ. **The Sexual Language: An Essay in
       Moral Theology.** Ottawa: University of Ottawa
       Press, 1976.
See "Homosexuality," pp. 299-377.

2191. HORNER, TOM. **Homosexuality and the Judaeo-Chris-
       tian Tradition: An Annotated Bibliography.**
       Metuchen, NJ: Scarecrow Press, 1981. 131 pp.
Judicious selection and annotation--459 entries--by an
authority in the field. Restricted to English-language

material: books, pamphlets, and articles. Subject and
author indices. Additional references, esp. for older
and foreign material, appear in Vern Bullough et al.
(eds.), **An Annotated Bibliography of Homosexuality** (New
York: Garland, 1976), vol. 1, pp. 331-62.

2192. JONES, CLINTON. **Understanding Gay Relatives and
Friends.** New York: Seabury Press, 1978. 133 pp.
Sympathetic guide for the lay reader by the canon at the
Hartford (CT) Episcopal Cathedral.

2193. JONES, E. KIMBALL. **Towards a Christian Understanding of the Homosexual.** New York: Association
Press, 1966. 160 pp.
Holds that the "true homosexual" can only achieve self-realization in an encounter with a person of the same sex.

2194. LAURITSEN, JOHN. **Religious Roots of the Taboo on
Homosexuality: A Materialist View.** New York: The
author, 1974. 26 pp.
An indictment, from an atheist and materialist standpoint,
of the Christian church as the prime source of antihomosexual prejudice in Western civilization.

2195. MALLOY, EDWARD A. **Homosexuality and the Christian
Way of Life.** Washington, DC: University Press of
America, 1981. 382 pp.
"Moderately conservative" response by University of Notre
Dame professor to the increasing visibility of gays in
the Church. Opposed to homosexuality, but not rabidly so.

2196. MILETICH, LEO N. "Now I Lay Me Down to Sleep,"
Humanist, 44 (1984), 28-31.
Humanist critique of religion.

2197. STINE, ESTHER C. (ed.). "Homophobia: The Overlooked Sin," **Church and Society,** 73 (November-December 1982), 3-71.
Articles on antihomosexual attitudes in the churches, and
steps that are being taken to reduce them.

2198. THEVENOT, XAVIER. **Homosexualité masculine et
morale chrétienne.** Paris: Le Cerf, 1985. 326 pp.
A somewhat jargon-ridden essay in moral theology heavily
dependent on the psychoanalytic concepts of Jacques
Lacan. This book is a revised version of a dissertation
for the doctorate in theology at the Institut Catholique
in Paris (1980). See André Guindon, "Homosexualités et
méthodologie éthique: à propos d'un livre de Xavier
Thevenot," **Eglises et Theologie,** 17 (1986), 57-84.

2199. TWISS, HAROLD (ed.). **Homosexuality and the Christian Faith: A Symposium.** Valley Forge, PA: Judson,
1978. 110 pp.
Essays representing a variety of views, both pro- and
antihomosexual.

2200. WILLENBECHER, THOM. "Gay Atheists Come Out," **Ad-
       vocate,** no. 284 (January 10, 1980), 19-21.
Presents views of some leading gay atheists—which can be
examined in greater detail in their periodical **GALA,** published by the San Francisco chapter of the Gay Atheists
League of America.

2201. WOGGON, HARRY A. "A Biblical and Historical Study
       of Homosexuality," **Journal of Religious Health,** 20
       (1981), 156-73.
Argues that for responsible persons, sexual orientation
and behavior as such should not be a barrier to church
membership.

2202. WOOD, ROBERT W. **Christ and the Homosexual.** New
       York: Vantage Press, 1960. 221 pp.
This sympathetic, though perhaps now dated work was a
milestone: an early admonition to the churches that their
traditional attitudes must be reexamined.

                  C. BIBLICAL STUDIES

A few significant passages in both the Old and the New
Testament have served as reference points for the continuing Jewish and Christian condemnation of homosexuality.
Subsequent discussion has focused on the elucidation of
these texts, as well as attempting a broader theological
interpretation of the place of sexuality and homosexuality. For the Near Eastern background to the Old
Testament, see III.B.

2203. ASTOUR, MICHAEL. "Tamar the Hierodule," **Journal of
       Biblical Literature,** 85 (1966), 185-96.
Presents evidence from Ugarit and Sumeria suggesting that
the **qédéshim** of the Old Testament were indeed male cult
prostitutes.

2204. BARTLETT, DAVID L. "A Biblical Perspective on
       Homosexuality," **Foundations: Baptist Journal of
       History and Theology,** 20 (1977), 133-47.
Holds that the biblical references to homosexuality are
condemnatory. Yet God's grace is stronger than any
condemnation; hence acceptance is indicated.

2205. BROOTEN, BERNADETTE. "Paul's Vision of the Nature
       of Women and Female Homosexuality," in: Clarissa
       W. Atkinson et al., **Immaculate and Powerful.** Bos-
       ton: Beacon Press, 1985, pp. 66-87.
Although this paper makes the questionable assumption that
Romans 1:26-27 condemns female homosexuality, it does review a number of pieces of evidence for lesbianism in the
ancient world.

2206. COLE, WILLIAM GRAHAM. **Sex and Love in the Bible.**
       New York: Julian Press, 1956. 448 pp.
Chapter 10, "Homosexuality in the Bible" (pp. 342-72),
finds the major Scriptural passages to be condemnatory,
but with his vulgar psychoanalytic bias Cole asserts
that "the homosexual is sick and knows he is sick."

2207. DEVOR, RICHARD C. "Homosexuality and St. Paul,"
       Pastoral Psychology, 23 [no. 224] (May 1972),
       50-58.
Argues that Paul's list in I Corinthians 6:9-10 reflects
the Jewish view of the Gentile world as swarming with
those guilty of various perversions.

2208. DOUGHTY, DARRELL J. "Homosexuality and Obedience
       to the Gospel," **Church and Society,** 67:5 (May-June
       1977), 12-23.
Holds that we cannot appeal to the letter of the New
Testament to be justified, for this itself would be contrary to the spirit of the gospel, which requires theological, rather than historical or legalistic answers.

2209. ENGLAND, MICHAEL. **The Bible and Homosexuality.**
       San Francisco: Metropolitan Community Church (MCC),
       1980. 44 pp.
England, pastor of a gay church (MCC), examines eight
major passages in the Old Testament and the New Testament, concluding that their antihomosexual content is
time-bound or otherwise minimal.

2210. FURNISH, VICTOR PAUL. **The Moral Teaching of
       Paul: Selected Issues.** Nashville: Abingdon, 1979.
Finds that Paul knew only the exploitative type of homosexuality, and it is only to this type that his condemnation applies (pp. 52-83).

2211. GANGEL, KENNETH. **The Gospel and the Gay.** Nash-
       ville: Nelson, 1978. 202 pp.
Despite the title, mainly concerned with the Old Testament; regards homosexuality as a "tragic involvement."

2212. HAY, HENRY. "The Moral Climate of Canaan at the
       Time of the Judges," **ONE Institute Quarterly,** no. 1
       (Spring 1958), 8-16; and no. 2 (Summer 1958),
       50-59.
Somewhat subjective reflections by one of the founders
of the American gay movement.

2213. "Homosexualität und Bibel; von einem katholischen
       Geistlichen," **JfsZ,** 4 (1902), 199-243.
Pioneering examination, by an anonymous Catholic religious, of several key biblical proof texts, suggesting that
they are less antihomosexual than the received interpretation holds--thus foreshadowing the ideas of Canon
Bailey and Father McNeill.

2214. HORNER, TOM. **Jonathan Loved David: Homosexuality
      in Biblical Times.** Philadelphia: Westminster,
      1978. 161 pp.
Treating both the Old Testament and the New Testament,
this careful, comprehensive study makes sensible criticisms of previous work. As was perhaps inevitable in
an ambitious work of synthesis such as this, disagree-
ments have been registered in some areas (e.g.,the reconstruction of the Canaanite background and the lesbian
interpretation of the Ruth and Naomi story).

2215. HORNER, TOM. **Sex in the Bible.** Rutland, VT:
      Tuttle, 1974. 188 pp.
Ranges the material under twenty-four headings. See
Prostitution, pp. 65-73; Eunuchs and Transvestites,
pp. 76-80; and Homosexuality, pp. 81-92.

2216. JEREMIAS, JOACHIM. "Zu Rm I 22-32," **Zeitschrift
      für die neutestamentliche Wissenschaft,** 45 (1954),
      119-21.
Offers careful analysis of the argument of Romans I:22-32,
which stigmatizes homosexual conduct as "unnatural."

2217. JOHANSSON, WARREN. "**Ex parte** Themis: The Histor-
      ical Guilt of the Christian Church," in: **Homosexu-
      ality, Intolerance, and Christianity: A Critical
      Examination of John Boswell's Work.** Second ed.
      New York: Scholarship Committee (GAU), 1985, pp.
      1-7.
A searching philological inquiry into the meaning of
the two key terms in I Cor. 6:9, **malakós** and **arsenokoítes,**
showing that they are unmistakeably antihomosexual.

2218. JOHANSSON, WARREN. "Whoever Shall Say to His
      Brother, **Racha** (Matthew 5:22)," **Cabirion and Gay
      Books Bulletin,** no. 10 (1984), 2-4.
Closely argued philological study of the term **rachâ,**
concluding that it is a Hellenistic loanword from the
Hebrew **rakh** "passive-effeminate homosexual."

2219. KAHLER, ELSE. "Exegese zweier neutestamentlicher
      Stellen," in: Theodor Bovet (ed.), **Probleme der
      Homophilie in medizinischer, theologischer und
      juristischer Sicht.** Bern: Haupt, 1965, pp. 12-43.
Interprets the New Testament texts, Romans 1:18-32 and
I Corinthians 6:9-11.

2220. KRAUSS, SAMUEL. **Das Leben Jesu nach jüdischen
      Quellen.** Berlin: S. Calvary, 1902. 309 pp.
Mentions Hebrew, Judeo-German and Latin sources for a
version of the combat in the air between Judas Iscariot
and Jesus in the **Toledoth Jeshu,** in which Judas sodomizes
his adversary to break the magic spell that envelops him
(pp. 8, 268).

2221. MCNEILL, JOHN J. **The Church and the Homosexual.**

Kansas City, KN: Sheed, Andrews and McMeel, 1976.
211 pp.
This work by a Jesuit theologian maintains that the Bible
does not forbid homosexuality as we understand it, but
only perverse forms of it. His exegesis of the Sodom
story in Genesis 19 as a condemnation of inhospitality
follows Canon D. S. Bailey.

2222. MARTIN, A. DAMIEN. "The Perennial Canaanites: The
       Sin of Homosexuality," **Etc**, 41 (1984), 340-61.
Citing passages in Genesis, Leviticus, and the New Testament, questions the fundamentalist Christian use of
the scriptures as infallible evidence of the sinfulnesss
of homosexuality.

2223. MOUNT, ERIC, and JOHANNE W. H. BOS. "Scriptures on
       Sexuality: Shifting Authority," **Journal of Presbyt-
       erian History**, 59 (Summer 1981), 219-42.
Seeks to place changing interpretations in context.

2224. NIDITCH, SUSAN. "The 'Sodomite' Theme in Judges
       19-20: Family, Community, and Social Disintegra-
       tion," **Catholic Biblical Quarterly**, 44 (1982),
       365-78.
Shows important parallels with the Sodom legend proper
(Gen. 19:1-11).

2225. PATAI, RAPHAEL. **Sex and the Family in the Bible
       and the Middle East.** Garden City, NY: Doubleday,
       1959.
Assuming an essential continuity in Middle Eastern folkways, uses modern travelers' reports and anthropological
data to interpret the Old Testament. See esp. pp. 168-
76.

2226. PHILLIPS, ANTHONY. "Uncovering Father's Skirt,"
       Vetus Testamentum, 30 (1980), 38-43.
Interprets Deuteronomy 23:16, Leviticus 18:7 and Genesis
9:20ff. (Ham's uncovering his father's nakedness) as prohibitions, prompted by anti-Canaanite sentiment, of sons
seducing their fathers. On the Ham incident, see also
H. Hirsch Cohen, **The Drunkenness of Noah** (University:
University of Alabama Press, 1974), p. 13ff. (where,
however, Ham's act is interpreted as a visual violation).

2227. RIDDERBOS, SIMON JAN. "Bibel und Homosexualität,"
       in: **Der homosexuelle Nächste.** Hamburg: Fusche
       Verlag, 1963, pp. 50-73.
Perspective by a Dutch scholar, sympathetic for its time.

2228. ROTH, WOLFGANG. "What of Sodom and Gomorrah? Homo-
       sexual Acts in the Old Testament," **Explor**, 1:2
       (Fall 1975), 7-14.
Holds that the men of Sodom and Gomorrah are condemned
chiefly because they break covenant between host and
guest. In discussing the Leviticus passages, employs the

ideas of the anthropologist Mary Douglas (**Purity and Danger.** London: Routledge and Kegan Paul, 1966).

2229. SCHOEPS, HANS-JOACHIM. "Homosexualität und Bibel," **Zeitschrift für evangelische Ethik,** 6 (1962), 369-74.
Observations by one of the pioneers in the study of the subject, now chiefly of historical interest.

2230. SCROGGS, ROBIN. **The New Testament and Homosexuality.** Philadelphia: Fortress Press, 1983. 158 pp.
Argues that New Testament references to homosexuality deal not with same-sex preferences in general, but with specific forms prevalent at the time of the composition of the texts. Hence they cannot provide a basis for Christian condemnation of homosexuality today. Offers some discussion of Greek evidence on pederasty (a familiar phenomenon to the New Testament writers), Jewish sources, and patristic texts.

2231. SHEPPARD, GERARD T. "The Use of Scripture within the Christian Ethical Debate Concerning Same-Sex Oriented Persons," **Union Theological Seminary Quarterly Review,** 40 (1985), 13-35.
Seeks to set forth hermeneutic foundations for the interpretation of homosexual behavior which will both "affirm the authority of scripture" and "explicate the Gospel as a message of human liberation."

2232. SMITH, MORTON. **Clement of Alexandria and a Secret Gospel of Mark.** Cambridge, MA: Harvard University Press, 1973. 453 pp.
Complex learned investigation seeking to authenticate a purported Gospel fragment describing Jesus' nocturnal initiation of a young man. See also Smith's more popular presentation: **The Secret Gospel: The Discovery and Interpretation of the Secret Gospel of Mark** (New York: Harper and Row, 1973); and his review of the matter (which remains controversial): "Clement of Alexandria and Secret Mark: The Score at the End of the First Decade," **Harvard Theological Review,** 75 (1982), 449-61.

2233. STRECKER, GEORG. "Homosexualität in biblischer Sicht," **Kerygma und Dogma,** 28 (1982), 127-41.
Homosexuality, though forbidden in the Old Testament and attacked in the New, must be evaluated today not legalistically, but in the context of God's judgment and grace.

2234. TARACHOW, SIDNEY. "St. Paul and Early Christianity: A Psychoanalytic and Historical Study," in: W. Muensterberger (ed.), **Psychoanalysis and the Social Sciences.** New York: International Universities Press, 1955, vol. 4, pp. 223-81.
Holds that Paul had a need for male companionship, not women. "His ethics, his life and this theology bear a strong, latent passive homosexuality."

2235. UKLEJA, P. MICHAEL. "Homosexuality and the Old
      Testament," **Bibliotheca sacra**, 104 (1983), 259-66.
Rejecting the arguments of homophile scholars, supports
the traditional (rigorist) interpretation. See also
the companion article: "Homosexuality in the New Testament," ibid., 104 (1983), 350-58 (affirms the antihomosexual character of Rom 1:26-27; 1 Cor. 6:9; and 1 Tim.
1:10).

2236. WEBER, JOSEPH C. "Does the Bible Condemn Homosexu-
      al Acts?" **Engage/Social Action**, 3:5 (May 1975),
      28-31, 34-35.
Offers an original interpretation of the Pauline texts.

2237. WHITE, ANDREW DICKSON. **A History of the Warfare of
      Science with Theology in Christendom.** New York: D.
      Appleton and Co., 1890. 2 vols.
In this work by a closeted university president and diplomat, Chapter 18 (pp. 209-63 of vol. 2) deals with the
legend of Sodom, "From the Dead Sea Legends to Comparative Mythology," showing that the account in Genesis 19
is without historical foundation, but is a geographical
legend inspired by the barrenness and salinization of
the region around the shores of the Dead Sea.

2238. WINK, WALTER. "Biblical Perspectives on Homosexual-
      ity," **Christian Century**, 96:36 (November 7, 1979),
      1082-86.
After reviewing a number of texts, Wink concludes that the
Bible has not a sexual ethic, but "only a love ethic."
See readers' responses, ibid. (January 2-9, 1980), 20-25.

2239. WOOD, ROBERT W. "Homosexual Behavior in the
      Bible," **ONE Institute Quarterly**, 5:1 (1962), 10-19.
Regards both the David-Jonathan story and the Ruth-Naomi
one as probably homosexual.

2240. WRIGHT, DAVID F. "Homosexuals or Prostitutes? The
      Meaning of Arsenokoitai (1 Cor. 6:9, 1 Tim.
      1:10)," **Vigiliae Christianae**, 38 (1984), 125-53.
Painstaking and probably definitive philological demonstration that the koine Greek word cannot be assigned the
meaning "prostitute" as John Boswell maintains. See
also W. Johansson, above.

2241. ZAAS, PETER. "Was Homosexuality Condoned in the
      Corinthian Church?" in: P.J. Achtemeier (ed.),
      **Society of Biblical Literature 1979 Seminar
      Papers.** Missoula: SBL, 1979, vol. 2, pp. 205-
      12.
In providing a negative answer, Zaas offers some interesting comparative material from ancient moral and astrological texts.

D. MAIN CHRISTIAN DENOMINATIONS

The recent social visibility of homosexuality, as well as the concerns of homosexual persons within the churches, have stimulated a reexamination of the issues by church bodies. The resulting studies represent a wide range of opinion, from a relatively high degree of toleration to a harsh reaffirmation of traditional positions.

2242. ARCHDIOCESE OF SAN FRANCISCO, COMMISSION ON SOCIAL JUSTICE. **Homosexuality and Social Justice: Report of the Task Force on Gay/Lesbian Issues.** San Francisco: Commission on Social Justice, 1982. 155 pp.
In the view of the Commission's Chairperson, "In this report we have the most systematic, comprehensive, and theologically articulate presentation on homosexuality and Roman Catholicism yet available." The report--not approved by the diocesan hierarchy--deals with such issues as violence, intercommunity relations, the family, and spiritual considerations in the lives of gay men and lesbians.

2243. BARNHOORN, J. A. J., et al. **Het vraagstuk der homosexualiteit.** Roermond: Romen, 1941. 192 pp.
Papers from a Dutch Roman Catholic conference held just before the outbreak of World War II, when attitudes remained largely negative. For the enormous strides made subsequently, see Willem Berger and Jacques Janssen, [The Catholics and Their Psychology], **Tijdschrift voor Psychologie en haar Grensgebieden,** 35 (1980), 451-65.

2244. BARTH, KARL. **Church Dogmatics.** Edinburgh: T. and T. Clark, 1949-65. 4 vols. in 12
In vol. 3, part 4, the noted Protestant Swiss theologian sets forth his negative views about homosexuality, which he regards as both a sin (disobedience) and unnatural (a perversion of the created order).

2245. BAUM, WILLIAM, CARDINAL, et al. **Educational Guidance in Human Love.** Vatican City: Sacred Congregation for Catholic Education, 1983. 36 pp.
Holds that homosexuality, along with extramarital relations and masturbation, is a moral disorder. Homosexuals should be helped to overcome their "social maladaptation." See also: Franjo Cardinal Seper, **Declaration on Certain Questions Concerning Sexual Ethics** (Rome: Sacred Congregation for the Doctrine of the Faith, 1975).

2246. BERRY, C. MARKHAM. "The Christian Homosexual," **Journal of Psychiatry and Christianity,** 1 (1982), 33-38.
The homosexual who is a Christian can find his condition a gift rather than a curse. The church has much to gain

from accepting these brethren openheartedly.

2247. BLAMIRES, DAVID. **Homosexuality from the Inside.**
       London: Social Responsibility Council of the
       Religious Society of Friends, 1973. 45 pp.
       Positive English Quaker statement.

2248. BROWNING, DON S. "Homosexuality, Theology, the
       Social Sciences and the Church," **Encounter** 40
       (1979), 223-43.
Evaluates denominational studies of homosexuality by the
Disciples of Christ, The United Church of Christ, and
Roman Catholics.

2249. BRUSSARD, A. J. A., et al. **Een mens hoeft niet
       alleen te bleven: een evangelische visie op
       homofilie.** Baarn: Ten Have, 1977. 179 pp.
       Dutch evangelical views.

2250. BUCKLEY, MICHAEL J. **Morality and the Homosexual: A
       Catholic Approach to a Moral Problem.** Westminster,
       MD: Newman Press 1960. 214 pp.
Manual for Roman Catholic priests, purporting to offer a
deeper understanding of the nature of homosexuals' "psychosexual disorder." Also, defends the traditional interpretation of the Sodom legend in a vehement critique of
Canon Bailey's work with texts from the Church fathers as
the main evidence.

2251. CATHOLIC COUNCIL FOR CHURCH AND SOCIETY (THE
       NETHERLANDS). **Homosexual People in Society: A
       Contribution to the Dialogue within the Faith
       Community.** Translated by Bernard A. Nachbar.
       Mt. Rainier, MD: New Ways Ministry, 1980. 21 pp.
A pioneering document advocating a new approach and
showing sympathy for homosexual people.

2252. CAVANAUGH, JOHN R., and JOHN F. HARVEY. **Counseling
       the Homosexual.** Huntington, IN: Our Sunday
       Visitor, 1977. 352 pp.
Revision of a work first published in 1965, retaining its
traditional negative stance.

2253. CHURCH OF ENGLAND, GENERAL SYNOD BOARD FOR SOCIAL
       RESPONSIBILITY. **Homosexual Relationships: A Con-
       tribution to Discussion.** London: CIO Publishing,
       1979. 94 pp.
Concludes that "there are circumstances in which individ-
uals may justifiably choose to enter into a homosexual
relationship." See Basil Mitchell, "The Homosexuality
Report," **Theology,** 83 (1980), 184-90; and the conservat-
ive attack on it: Michael Greene et al., **The Church and
Homosexuality: A Positive Answer to Current Questions**
(London: Hodder and Stoughton).

2254. CHURCH OF ENGLAND IN AUSTRALIA AND TASMANIA,

DIOCESE OF SYDNEY, ETHICS AND SOCIAL QUESTIONS
COMMITTEE. **Report on Homosexuality.** Sydney: Church
of England, Diocese of Sydney, 1973. 60 pp.
The muted Australian reception of the Anglican trend
towards reform.

2255. COLEMAN, GERALD D. **Homosexuality—An Appraisal.**
Chicago: Franciscan Herald, 1978. 88 pp.
Favors civil rights for gays, but clings to the official
Catholic position that homosexuality is a moral disorder.
See also Conrad Baars, **The Homosexual's Search for
Happiness** (Chicago: Franciscan Herald, 1977; 34 pp.); and
George Anthony Kelly, **The Political Struggle of Active
Homosexuals to Gain Social Acceptance** (Chicago: Franciscan
Herald, 1975; 104 pp.).

2256. "A Colloquy on Homosexuality and the Church," **The
Circuit Rider,** 4:3 (March 1980), 3-13.
Six articles in the magazine of the United Methodist
clergy. See also: "Homosexuality: A Re-examination: E/SA
Forum 60," **Engage/Social Action,** 8:3 (March 1980), 9-56.

2257. DOUMA, JOCHEN. **Homophilie.** Fifth ed. Kampen:
Uitgeverij van den Berg, 1984. 117 pp.
Moderate views of a theologian of the Dutch Reformed
(Calvinist) Church, with considerable emphasis on Biblical
passages. Opposes discrimination.

2258. DRAKEFORD, JOHN W. **A Christian View of Homosexual-
ity.** Nashville: Broadman, 1977. 140 pp.
A conservative, yet not entirely condemnatory approach
by a faculty member of the Southwest Baptist Theological
Seminary, who favors modifying behavior through "Integrity
Therapy,"

2259. DURAND, GUY. **La sexualité et la foi: synthèse de
théologie morale.** Montreal: Fides, 1983. 426 pp.
In this French-Canadian Roman Catholic work, see Chapter
10, "L'homosexualité" (pp. 235-81).

2260. EARLY, TRACY. "The Struggle in the Denominations:
Shall Gays Be Ordained?" **Christianity and Crisis,**
37:9/10 (May 30-June 13, 1977), 118-22.
Surveys how mainline Protestant churches have approached
the issue.

2261. EICHRODT, WALTHER, et al. **Homosexualität in
evangelischer Sicht.** Wuppertal: Aussaat-Bucherei,
1965. 103 pp.
Four papers from a German Evangelical point of view.

2262. **Fede cristiana ed omosessualità.** Prali, Italy:
Edizioni Centro Ecumenico di Agape, 1981.
Acts of a conference held in 1980 to evaluate links
between Christianity and homosexuality from various
standpoints—Protestant, Roman Catholic, and atheist.

2263. FISHER, DAVID H. "The Homosexual Debate: A
       Critique of Some Recent Critics," **St. Luke's
       Journal of Theology**, 22 (1979), 176-84.
Anglican statement arguing in essence: wait and see.

2264. FULIGA, HOSE B. "Christian Moral Theological
       Reflections on the Ethical Issue of Homosexuality,"
       South East Asia Journal of Theology, 16:2 (1975),
       40-44.
A Third World perspective.

2265. GALLAGHER, JOHN (ed.). **Homosexuality and the
       Magisterium.** Mount Rainier, MD: New Ways Ministry,
       1985.
Anthology of twenty complete or excerpted official Catholic statements, pastoral letters, plans for ministry and
other documents from Roman congregations, the U.S. National Conference of Catholic Bishops, individual cardinals,
archbishops, and bishops as well as individual diocesan
organizations.

2266. GEARHART, SALLY, and WILLIAM R. JOHNSON (eds.).
       **Loving Women/Loving Men: Gay Liberation and the
       Church.** San Francisco: Glide, 1974. 165 pp.
Positive essays issued under the auspices of a pro-gay
church.

2267. GOTTSCHALK, JOHANNES. "Pastorale Betrachtungen und
       moraltheologische Ueberlegungen zur Frage der
       Homosexualität," in: W. S. Schlegel (ed.), **Das
       grosse Tabu.** Munich: Rütten und Loening, 1967,
       pp. 120-46.
Relatively positive German considerations.

2268. HAAS, HAROLD L. "Homosexuality," **Currents in
       Theology and Mission**, 5:2 (April 1978), 82-104.
Scholarly Lutheran essay concluding that the churches
should be accepting of ethically structured, stable relationships.

2269. HARVEY, JOHN F. "Reflections on a Retreat for
       Clerics with Homosexual Tendencies," **Linacre
       Quarterly**, 46 (May 1979), 6-40.
Recent article by a prolific Roman Catholic author, who
has not essentially revised his conservative viewpoint
since he first presented it in 1955.

2270. HILLIARD, DAVID. "'Unenglish and Unmanly': Anglo-
       Catholicism and Homosexuality," **Victorian Studies**,
       25 (1982), 181-210.
The Oxford Movement fostered intense and demonstrative
male friendships, the practice of celibacy, and the consequent foundation of religious brotherhoods. These
trends laid the foundations for an enduring tradition of
affinity between homosexual aesthetes and Anglo-Cathol-
icism.

2271. JAEKEL, HANS GEORG. **Ins Ghetto gedrängt--Homosex-
       uelle berichten.** Hamburg: Lutherisches Verlags-
       haus, 1978. 180 pp.
German Lutheran presentation, including ten personal
accounts by gay men and lesbians.

2272. JONES, JOE R. "Christian Sensibility with Respect
       to Homosexuality," **Encounter,** 40 (1979), 209-221.
Although "the homosexual does not stand under any special
condemnation from God," the author thinks that it is an
option that should not be exercised.

2273. KEYSOR, CHARLES W. (ed.). **What You Should Know
       about Homosexuality.** Grand Rapids, MI: Zondervan,
       1979. 254 pp.
Six papers, chiefly from a conservative Methodist viewpoint, that tend to present homosexuality as intrinsically
wrong.

2274. KOSNIK, ANTHONY (ed.). **Human Sexuality: New Direc-
       tions in American Catholic Thought.** New York:
       Paulist Press, 1977. 322 pp.
A very progressive, unofficial Roman Catholic inquiry. A
positive discussion of homosexuality appears on pp. 186-
218. A counterstatement is: Dennis Doherty (ed.), **Dimensions of Human Sexuality** (Garden City, NY: Doubleday,
1979; 249 pp.).

2275. KUHN, DONALD. **The Church and the Homosexual: A
       Report on a Consultation.** San Francisco: Glide
       Urban Center, 1965.
This brochure is an early positive statement.

2276. LINDSELL, HAROLD. "Homosexuals and the Church,"
       Christianity Today, 17:25 (September 1973), 8-12.
Negative: the church cannot admit, he says, those whom God
excludes.

2277. LOOSER, GABRIEL. **Homosexualität: menschlich--
       christlich-moralisch.** Frankfurt: P. Lang, 1984.
       385 pp.
Dissertation of a Roman Catholic theologian on the moral
status of homosexuality within the framework of normative
ethics.

2278. MARTIN, ENOS D., and RUTH K. MARTIN. "Developmen-
       tal and Ethic Issues in Homosexuality: Pastoral
       Implications," **Journal of Psychology and Theology,**
       9 (1981), 58-68.
Authors seek to show how homosexual orientation can be
approached within a supportive Christian ministry, while
adhering to the church's traditional values.

2279. METHODIST CHURCH (ENGLAND). DIVISION OF SOCIAL
       RESPONSIBILITY. **A Christian Understanding of Human
       Sexuality: A Report of a Working Party for the**

**National Conference of the Methodist Church, June
1979.** London: Division of Social Responsibility of
the Methodist Church, 1979. 13 pp.
Section C10 states that homosexual relationships should be
judged by the same criteria as heterosexual ones.

2280. MOORE, PAUL, JR. **Take a Bishop like Me.** San
Francisco: Harper and Row, 1979. 200 pp.
The Episcopal bishop of New York discloses his compassionate view toward homosexuality, discussing also his
ordination of Rev. Ellen Barrett, first avowed lesbian
priest. Subsequently, Bishop Moore has taken a prominent
role in the fight against AIDS discrimination.

2281. NELSON, JAMES B. **Embodiment: An Approach to
Sexuality and Christian Theology.** Minneapolis:
Augsburg, 1978.
In the view of the author, a United Church of Christ
ethics professor, the flesh does not oppose the spirit
but embodies it. He contends that most forms of the
sexual outlet, including homosexuality, are good and
should be accepted (see pp. 180-210). See also his article "Homosexuality and the Church: Towards a Sexual
Ethics of Love," **Christianity and Crisis,** 37:5 (April 4,
1977), 63-69 (discussion in issue 9-10, May 30-June 13,
1977, pp. 116-18).

2282. ODENWALD, ROBERT P. **The Disappearing Sexes.** New
York: Random House, 1965. 175 pp.
Views of a Roman Catholic psychiatrist.

2283. ORAISON, MARC. **The Homosexual Question: An Attempt
to Understand an Issue of Increasing Urgency within
a Christian Perspective.** Translated by Jane Z.
Flynn. New York: Harper and Row, 1977. 132 pp.
A French Roman Catholic priest and psychiatrist presents
relatively liberal views.

2284. PHILPOTT, KENT. **The Gay Theology.** Plainfield, NJ:
Logos International, 1977. 194 pp.
Presents testimonies of homosexuals who were reputedly
able to change their orientation through "the power of
Christ."

2285. **Principles to Guide Confessors in Question of Homo-
sexuality.** Washington, DC: National Council of
Catholic Bishops, 1973.
Pamphlet reaffirming traditional attitudes.

2286. RAMM, BERNARD L. **The Right, the Good and the
Happy.** Waco, TX: Word Books, 1971. 188 pp.
An Evangelical teacher adopts surprisingly liberal at-
titudes.

2287. SAMUEL, K. MATTHEW. "A Judeo-Christian Attitude to
Homosexuality: An Historical View," **AME Zion**

Quarterly Review, 93 (April 1981), 24-31.
Views of a Black clergyman and scholar.

2288. SCANZONI, LETHA, and VIRGINIA RAMEY MOLLENKOTT. **Is the Homosexual My Neighbor? Another Christian View.** San Francisco: Harper and Row, 1978. 176 pp.
Pro-gay book by two Evangelical feminists, who challenge their coreligionists to abandon bigoted attitudes.

2289. SIMS, BENNETT J. "Sex and Homosexuality: A Pastoral Statement," **Christianity Today,** 22:10 (February 24, 1978), 23-30.
The Episcopal bishop of Atlanta gives voice to his anti-homosexual views.

2290. SMITH, HERBERT F., and JOSEPH A. DILENNO. **Sexual Inversion: The Questions with Catholic Answers.** Boston: Daughters of St. Paul, 1979. 177 pp.
Negative.

2291. SPIJKER, ANTONIUS VAN DE. **Die gleichgeschlechtliche Zuneigung: Homotropie--Homosexualität, Homoerotik, Homophilie-und die katholische Moraltheologie.** Olten: Walter, 1968. 321 pp.
Learned and (for the time) liberal views of a Dutch Catholic priest. Useful for its many references.

2292. THIELICKE, HELMUT. **The Ethics of Sex.** Translated by John Doberstein. New York: Harper and Row, 1964. 338 pp.
The German Protestant theologian regards homosexuality as in fact a perversion in the perspective of God's creation, but recognizes the dilemma for those so inclined. For them he recommends celibacy, though some ethically responsible relationships may be allowed. At the time, even these views were often found to be too liberal; see Klaus Bockmühl, "Homosexuality in Biblical Perspective--An Interview," **Christianity Today,** 17 (February 16, 1973), 12-18; and Walter Eichrodt, "Homosexualität: Andersartigkeit oder Perversion," **Reformatio** (Zurich), 12 (1963), 67-82.

2293. **Towards a Quaker View of Sex: An Essay by a Group of Friends.** Ed. by Alastair Heron. London: Friends Home Service Committee, 1963. 84 pp.
A pioneering Quaker statement, which distinguishes between acts (possibly wrong) and the homosexual condition itself. Rejects the notion that homosexual feelings are "unnatural" per se.

2294. TRIMBOS, CORNELIS J. B. J. (ed.). **Pastorale zorg -voor homofielen.** Utrecht: Spectrum, 1968. 58 pp.
Papers on pastoral care for homosexuals from a Dutch conference held under joint Protestant and Roman Catholic auspices.

2295. UNITED CHURCH OF CHRIST. **Human Sexuality: A Pre-
       liminary Study.** New York: United Church, 1977.
       258 pp.
Study commissioned in 1975 by the denomination's General
Synod, which reached relatively pro-homosexual conclu-
sions.

2296. UNITED PRESBYTERIAN CHURCH IN THE U.S.A., AD-
       VISORY COUNCIL. **Report on the Work of the Task
       Force to Study Homosexuality.** New York: Advisory
       Council on Church and Society (UPCUSA), 1978. 201
       pp.
The majority report recommended that the ordination of
self-acknowledged practicing homosexuals would not
necessarily threaten the unity of the Church. However,
the Church's Assembly, which had commissioned the Report,
did not accept this recommendation.

2297. VALENTE, MICHAEL. **Sex: The Radical View of a Cath-
       olic Theologian.** Milwaukee: Bruce, 1970. 158 pp.
Strongly libertarian views of a professor of religion, who
subsequently left the church.

2298. WAGENAAR, THEODORE C., and PATRICIA E. BARTOS. "Or-
       thodoxy and Attitudes of Clergymen towards Homosex-
       uality and Abortion," **Review of Religious Research,**
       18:2 (Winter 1977), 114-25.
Clergy who do not have a unidimensional view of life, and
who distinguish their own religious sense of what is
right from the standpoint of civil society, are more
accepting.

2299. WIEDEMANN, HANS-GEORG. **Homosexuelle Liebe: Für
       eine Neuorientierung in der christlichen Ethik.**
       Stuttgart: Kreuz Verlag, 1982. 220 pp.
Sympathetic views of a parish priest in Dusseldorf, who
denies that homosexual behavior is sick. Ethical and
theological condemnations are to be rejected.

2300. WIGNEY, TREVOR J. "Mates and Lovers: Theological
       Perspectives on Gay Relationships in Australia,"
       St. Mark Review, no. 106 (June 1981), 24-35.
Argues that the churches in Australia have, in effect,
colluded with popular attitudes of bigotry, which are un-
Christian. The churches should take positive steps to
improve the situation of homosexuals (including open
acceptance in the church and ordination).

2301. WOODS, RICHARD. **Another Kind of Love: Homosexual-
       ity and Spirituality.** Revised ed. Garden City,
       NY: Doubleday, 1978. 155 pp.
A Dominican priest makes cautious recommendations for
acceptance, with advice to the ministry.

2302. WRIGHT, ELLIOTT. "The Church and Gay Liberation,"
       Christian Century, 88:9 (March 3, 1971), 281-85.

Shows the first effects on the churches of the post-Stonewall era.

E. GAY CHURCHES, ORGANIZATIONS, AND OBSERVERS

A visible homosexual presence in certain Anglican church
congregations, especially those emphasizing elaborate
liturgy and vestments, became evident in the late 19th
century. However, the formation of gay churches as
independent and self-declared organizations begins only in
the 1960s. A period of rapid growth which then set in saw
the development of gay and lesbian organizations corresponding to virtually every significant Christian denomination.

2303. AFFIRMATION, GAY AND LESBIAN MORMONS. **After
      Marriage What?** Los Angeles: Affirmation, 1980. 39
      pp.
Self-help advice with some personal testimonies.

2304. ANDERSON, SCOTT. "Gay Religious Groups Call for
      Acceptance," **Advocate**, no. 288 (March 20, 1980),
      22-23, 47.
Overview of gay religious organizations that emerged in
the 1970s.

2305. ARTHUR, L. ROBERT. **Homosexuality and the Conser-
      vative Christian.** Los Angeles: Universal Fellow-
      ship Press (SEC Publications), 1982. 56 pp.
Homosexuality in the light of Biblical language and culture; an evangelical approach sanctioned by the Metropolitan Community Church, the leading gay church.

2306. BAUER, PAUL F. "Homosexual Subculture at Worship:
      A Participant Observation Study," **Pastoral Psychol-
      ogy,** 25 (Winter 1976), 115-27.
Short "ethnographic" study of a gay church.

2307. BIRCHARD, ROY. "Metropolitan Community Church: Its
      Development and Significance," **Foundations: Baptist
      Journal of History and Theology,** 20:2 (April-June
      1977), 127-32.
Brief history of the predominantly gay church (MCC), from
its foundation by the Reverend Troy Perry to the date of
writing.

2308. BLAIR, RALPH. **Homophobia in the Church.** New
      York: The author, 1979. 25 pp.
Evangelical homosexual urges Christians who fear and
loathe homosexuals overcome their negative feelings
through return to a sound Christian ethic. See also
his: **An Evangelical Look at Christianity.** (New York: The

author, 1972; 12 pp.); and **Holier-than-Thou Hocus Pocus and Homosexuality.** (New York; The author, 1977; 48 pp.).

2309. BLAIR, RALPH. **Wesleyan Praxis & Homosexual Practice.** New York: The author, 1983. 36 pp. Presents sympathetic elements in the Methodist tradition.

2310. BLAIR, RALPH (ed.). **Homosexuality and Religion.** New York: National Task Force on Student Personnel Services and Homosexuality, 1972. 21 pp. Four papers by gay religionists (Christian Science; Roman Catholic; liberal Protestant; and Evangelical).

2311. CREW, LOUIE. "At St. Luke's Parish: The Peace of Christ Is Not for Gays," **Christianity and Crisis,** 37:9-10 (May 30-June 13, 1977), 140-44. A professor of English at a state college in Georgia-- and a founder of Integrity, the Episcopal gay group-- recounts the harassment he and his Black male spouse endured at their local church.

2312. EDWARDS, GEORGE R. **Gay Lesbian Liberation: A Biblical Perspective.** New York: Pilgrim Press, 1984. 153 pp. While the main part of this book consists of a somewhat routine review of the Bailey-McNeill et al. arguments for mitigating the chief biblical proof texts, the book's main contribution lies in its attempt to apply Latin American liberation theology to the situation of homosexuals.

2313. ENROTH, RONALD M., and GERALD E. JOHNSON. **The Gay Church.** Grand Rapids, MI: Eerdmans, 1974. 144 pp. An early attempt to come to grips with the gay church movement. Written from a fundamentalist perspective, the book has negative conclusions.

2314. FORTUNATO, JOHN. **Embracing the Exile: Healing Journeys of Gay Christians.** New York: Seabury Press, 1982. 137 pp Fortunato writes of his experiences in several Christian denominations, gay and mainstream, recounting the stages of his spiritual odyssey and self-analysis.

2315. GEYER, MARCIA LEE. **Human Rights or Homophobia? The Rising Tide.** Los Angeles: Universal Fellowship, 1977. Advice from a Metropolitan Community Church minister on coping with homophobia through "a Christ-like program of loving action."

2316. GINDER, RICHARD. **Binding with Briars: Sex and Sin in the Catholic Church.** Englewood Cliffs, NJ: Prentice-Hall, 1975. 251 pp. A radical critique by a respected Catholic writer of the Church's sexual ethic, endorsing masturbation and homosexuality. The book caused a scandal, leading its author to come out as gay.

2317. GRAMMICK, JEANNINE (ed.). **Homosexuality and the Catholic Church.** Chicago: Thomas Moore Press, 1983. 176 pp.
Nine articles on "Sociological Perspectives" and "Ecclesiastical Perspectives" by Catholic laity and religious; based on presentations given at the First National Symposium on Homosexuality and the Catholic Church, Washington, DC, November 1981.

2318. GROS, JEFFREY. "Gay Church in the NCC?" **Christianity and Crisis,** 43 (May 2, 1983), 167-71.
On the controversial application of the Universal Fellowship of the Metropolitan Community Church to join the National Council of Churches. For other comment, see **Christian Century,** 99 (April 14,1982), 461-62; (December 1, 1982),1222-23; 100 (April 6, 1983), 299-300; (June 1, 1983), 539-40.

2319. HALLORAN, JOE. **Understanding Homosexual Persons.** Hicksville, NY: Exposition Press, 1979. 81 pp.
The writer, a Roman Catholic priest, reports on a year's work with Dignity, the Catholic gay group, in the Bay Area.

2320. IRLE, ROGER D. "Minority Ministry: A Definition of Territory," **International Review of Modern Sociology,** 9 (1979), 193-209.
Sets forth a typology of four kind of organizations: 1) the independent gay church; (2) gay caucuses within denominations; (3) interdenominational groups; (4) ex-gay groups.

2321. ITKIN, MIKHAIL. **The Radical Jesus and Gay Consciousness.** Second ed. Long Beach, CA: Communiversity West, 1972. 64 pp.
One of a number of documents, which are now rare, by a counterculture priest (Syrian Orthodox) and theoretician, who resides in San Francisco.

2322. JOHNSTON, MAURY. **Gays under Grace: A Gay Christian's Response to the Moral Majority.** Nashville, TN: Winston-Derek, 1983. 225 pp.
Seeks to ground rebuttal to Moral Majority positions in Scripture.

2323. KRODY, NANCY E. "An Open Lesbian Looks at the Church," **Foundations: Baptist Journal of History and Theology,** 20:2 (April-June 1977), 148-62.
Krody expresses the ambivalence felt by some lesbians in continuing in seminaries and congregations.

2324. LUCAS, DONALD S. (ed.). **The Homosexual and the Church.** San Francisco: Mattachine Society,

1966. 50 pp.
A compilation of the responses of forty gay men to a
questionnaire about their attitudes toward religion.

2325. MCNAUGHT, BRIAN. **A Disturbed Peace: Selected
       Writings of an Irish Catholic Homosexual.** Washing-
       ton, DC: Dignity, 1981. 125 pp.
Eloquent, brief pieces reflecting on the writer's personal
difficulties with the Catholic establishment in Detroit
and Boston, and the predicament of gay Catholics more
generally.

2326. MACOURT, MALCOLM (ed.). **Towards a Theology of Gay
       Liberation.** London: SCM, 1977. 113 pp.
Essays on homosexuality and scripture and male homosexual relationships and lifestyles reflecting gay Christian
experience in England.

2327. MENARD, GUY. **De Sodome à l'Exode: Jalons pour une
       théologie de la libération gaie.** Montreal: Uni-
       vers, 1980. 268 pp.
A French-Canadian theologian examines the sources of the
traditional condemnation, which he finds to be of cultural
rather than divine origin.

2328. MICHAEL, GARY. **Jesus Christ Homosexual.** Denver:
       Church of World Peace, 1984. 64 pp.
Subjective reflections on passages from the Gospels.
Conclusion: "If it is even possible that Jesus was homosexually inclined, Christians should pause before condemning homosexuality on religious grounds."

2329. MICKLEY, RICHARD R. **Christian Sexuality: A Re-
       flection on Being Christian and Sexual.** Second ed.
       Los Angeles: Universal Fellowship, 1976.
Manual intended for local church study groups of the
Metropolitan Community Church.

2330. NUGENT, ROBERT. **A Challenge to Love: Gay and
       Lesbian Catholics in the Church.** New York: Cross-
       road, 1983. 290 pp.
Thoughtful essays by various writers, some with extensive
references.

2331. PENNINGTON, SYLVIA. **But Lord, They're Gay.**
       Hawthorne, CA: Lambda Christian Fellowship, 1981.
       171 pp.
Minister writes of her progress from a mission to "save"
gays to being pastor of a predominately gay congregation.

2332. PERRY, TROY, with CHARLES LUCAS. **The Lord is My
       Shepherd and He Knows I'm Gay.** Los Angeles: Nash
       Publishing Co., 1972. 232 pp.
The story of the founder of the Metropolitan Community
Church, the personal and organizational obstacles he had
to overcome, and his commitment to forceful action for

gay civil rights.

2333. PITTENGER, NORMAN. **Time for Consent.** London: SCM,
      1967. 124 pp.
Work by a noted Anglican theologian presenting homosexuality as an accepted part of the created order. Regarded
by many at the time as an important breakthrough. Third,
enlarged ed., 1976. See also his: **Making Sexuality Human**
(New York: United Church, 1970); and **Gay Lifestyles: A
Christian Interpretation of Homosexuality and the Homosexual** (Los Angeles: Universal Fellowship, 1977).

2334. PRESTON, D. **The Gay Bible.** Revised ed. New
      York: The author, 1978. 36 pp.
A gay layperson offers homespun advice for grappling with
the stumbling blocks offered by Bible passages

2335. **Prologue: An Examination of the Mormon Attitude
      towards Homosexuality.** Salt Lake City: Prometheus
      Enterprises, 1979. 58 pp.
Difficulties of being gay in a church that has remained
steadfastly negative.

2336. SWICEGOOD, TOM. **Our God Too.** New York: Pyramid,
      1974. 379 pp.
Account of the founding of the Metropolitan Community
Church by Reverend Troy Perry and its remarkable growth up
to the time of writing.

2337. THOMPSON, MARK. "Getting in the Habit to 'Give Up
      Guilt,'" **Advocate,** no. 311 (February 19, 1981),
      T11-13.
On the Sisters of Perpetual Indulgence, an order of "gay
male nuns" based chiefly in San Francisco. In the eyes of
some a scandal, the sisters have earned the plaudits of
others as offering a useful sendup of the pomposities and
contradictions of organized religion.

2338. WICKLIFF, JAMES (ed.). **In Celebration.** Oak Park,
      IL: Integrity, 1975. 91 pp.
Papers and addresses from the first national convention of
Integrity, the gay Episcopalian society. The first half
of the book is the keynote speech of Norman Pittenger (see
above).

2339. WOODS, RICHARD, et al. "Toward a Gay Christian
      Ethic," **Insight: A Quarterly of Lesbian/Gay
      Catholic Opinion,** 3:2 (Spring-Summer 1979), 5-12.
The writers address the topic of ways of conducting
oneself as an ethical person and a homosexual.

                         F. GAY CLERGY

Evidence exists from the Middle Ages (see III.D) of the
attraction of homosexuals and lesbians to the sex-seg-
regated institutions of the Catholic church. During the
Reformation their presence attracted the polemical scorn
of Protestant writers, and this critique was later taken
up by secularist and atheist writers seeking to discredit
the church. Only in the second half of the 20th century
have significant numbers of homosexual and lesbian
religious, from various denominations, come forward to
tell their own stories.

2340. BERRIGAN, DANIEL. "The Leveling of John McNeill,"
      Commonweal, 104 (1977), 778-83.
On the Church's silencing the Jesuit scholar for the outspoken views embodied in his: **The Church and the Homosexual** (Kansas City, KN: Sheed, Andrews and McMeel, 1976).

2341. BOYD, MALCOLM. **Take Off the Masks.** Garden City,
      NY: Doubleday, 1978. 160 pp.
In this, one of a number of autobiographical books, the
religious activist speaks for the first time with full
frankness about his homosexuality. He is now an Anglican
priest in Santa Monica, CA.

2342. BREWSTER, RALPH HENRY. **The 6000 Beards of Athos.**
      London: L. and V. Woolf, 1935. 219 pp.
Discreet account of the all-male monastic enclave in northern Greece.

2343. CURB, ROSEMARY, and NANCY MANAHAN (eds.). **Lesbian
      Nuns: Breaking the Silence.** Tallahassee, FL: Naiad
      Press, 1985. 383 pp.
Personal recollections of some 50 former and present
religious women on "particular friendships" and self-
discovery.

2344. **Defensa de los religiosos de Convento de la Merced
      contra el proyecto de ley sobre supresión de las
      comunidades en el Perú.** Lima: 1886.
Defense of a monastery that was slated for dissolution because of "unnatural practices."

2345. DE MARIA-KUIPER, JOHANNES W. **Hot under the Col-
      lar: Self-Portrait of a Gay Pastor.** Columbia, MO:
      Mercury Press, 1983. 177 pp.
A former minister of the Reformed Dutch Protestant Church
tells how he was forced to leave that denomination and
join the Metropolitan Community Church, where he could
pursue a career as a gay activist.

2346. DE STEFANO, GEORGE. "Gay under the Collar: The
      Hypocrisy of the Catholic Church," **Advocate,** no.
      439 (February 4, 1986), 43-48.
How gay priests, nuns, and brothers, estimated at 30% to
60% of the total number of religious, are coping with

the Church's rigid attitudes.

2347. DLUGOS, TIM. "A Cruel God: The Gay Challenge to
      the Catholic Church," **Christopher Street**, 4:9
      (September 1979), 20-39.
From interviews and personal experience, postulates that
much homosexual behavior is occurring behind cloister and
parish walls.

2348. FISKE, ADELE M. **Friends and Friendship in the
      Monastic Tradition.** Cuernavaca, Mexico: Centro
      Internacional de Documentacion, 1970.
Facsimiles of articles written by a nun on same-sex
friendships in the Middle Ages.

2349. GUIRDHAM, ARTHUR. **Christ and Freud: A Study in
      Religious Experience and Observance.** London: Allen
      and Unwin, 1959. 193 pp.
See "Homosexuality in Clericalism" (pp. 122-28).

2350. GRIFFIN, DAVID R. "Ordination for Homosexuals?
      Yes," **Encounter**, 40 (1979), 265-72.
Makes a brief case in a controversy that continues to
simmer. For a differing view, see: Ronald E. Osborn,
"Ordination for Homosexuals: A Negative Answer Qualified
by Some Reflections," ibid., 245-63.

2351. HEYWARD, CARTER. "Coming Out: Journey without
      Maps," **Christianity and Crisis**, 39:10 (June 22,
      1979), 153-56.
Professor at the Episcopal Divinity School, Cambridge, MA,
speaks of her decision to acknowledge her lesbianism
publicly.

2352. HONEFFER, AUGUST. **Der Priester, seine Vergangen-
      heit und seine Zukunft.** Jena: Eugen Diederichs,
      1912. 2 vols.
Homosexuality among priests is discussed in vol. 2.

2353. HOOYDONK, JAN VAN (ed.). **Homo en pastor.** Amers-
      foort: De Horstink, 1983. 142 pp.
Analysis of questionnaires filled out by some 350 priests
in the Utrecht diocese.

2354. JOHNSON, WILLIAM R. "The Saga of Bill Johnson,"
      Trends, 5 (July-August 1973), 3-9.
Johnson was the first open homosexual ordained as a
minister by a major denomination (United Church of
Christ). See also his essay: "Protestantism and Gay
Freedom," in: Betty Berzon and Robert Leighton (eds.),
Positively Gay (Millbrae, CA: Celestial Arts, 1979),
65-78.

2355. KRAFT, WILLIAM F. "Homosexuality and Religious
      Life," **Review for Religious**, 40 (1981), 370-81.
See also his: "Homogenitalism," in: **Sexual Dimensions**

of the Celibate Life (Kansas City, KN: Sheed, Andrews and McMeel, 1979), 151-62.

2356. KRATT, MARY. "Church 'Always Resistant to
       Change,'" **Christian Century,** 97 (1980), 237-38.
Lesbian priest vistis her hometown church in North
Carolina.

2357. RABINOWITZ, SEYMOUR. "Developmental Problems in
       Catholic Seminarians," **Psychiatry,** 32 (1969),
       107-17.
Working with 25 Roman Catholic seminarians,claims to
have found "three types of psychopathology": homosexuality, psychophysiology, and related responses and depression.

2358. SCOTT, DAVID A. "Ordaining a Homosexual Person: A
       Policy Proposal," **St. Luke's Journal of Theology,**
       212:3 (June 1979), 185-96.
Holds that ordination should be conditional on the candidate's not promoting, by example or teaching, genital
homosexual relations as a normative alternative; in other
words, one must remain in the closet.

2359. WAGNER, RICHARD, O. M. I. **Gay Catholic Priests: A
       Study of Cognitive and Affective Dissonance.** San
       Francisco: Institute for Advanced Study of Human
       Sexuality, 1980. (dissertation)
Reflects interviews with fifty Roman Catholic priests,
one quarter of whom had a current lover.

2360. WARD, W. RALPH. "United Methodists Won't Ordain
       Homosexuals," **United Methodists Today,** 2:6 (June
       1975), 77-83.
The bishop of the New York area of the United Methodist
Church rejects homosexual ordination.

2361. WOODS, RICHARD. "Gay Candidates, the Religious Life
       and the Priesthood," **Call to Growth/Ministry,** 4:4
       (Summer 1979), 24-43.
Argues in favor of admitting gay and lesbian candidates
to the religious life.

G. RELIGIOUS BACKLASH

The rise of the contemporary homosexual movement since
1950, and the increasing visibility of homosexuals within
the church, has provoked a new literature attacking these
developments. In large measure this backlash material
simply recycles older traditionalist condemnations, with
minor variations according nominal recognition to changed
conditions. In a few instances, however, there is a more
sustained effort to grapple with the new situation.

2362. ARMSTRONG, HERBERT. **The Missing Dimension in Sex.**
Pasadena: Ambassador College Press, 1971. 236 pp.
Displays the antihomosexual views of the founder of the
World Wide Church of God.

2363. BAHNSEN, GREG L. **Homosexuality: A Biblical View.**
Grand Rapids, MI: Baker, 1978. 152 pp.
Professor at the Reformed Theological Seminary, Jackson,
MS, says that homosexuality is not only a sin, but a crime
which must be prohibited by law. He advocates discrimina-
tion in housing and employment.

2364. BARNHOUSE, RUTH TIFFANY. **Homosexuality: A Symbolic**
Confusion. New York: Seabury Press, 1976. 190 pp.
Mingling religious exhortation, myth, and trickle-down
psychiatry, this book is aptly titled.

2365. BRADFORD, BRICK, et al. **Healing for the Homosex-**
ual. Oklahoma City: Presbyterian Charismatic
Commununion, 1978. 64 pp.
Essays, with case histories, arguing the homosexuality can
and should be overcome.

2366. BRYANT, ANITA. **The Anita Bryant Story: The Sur-**
vival of Our Nation's Families and the Threat of
Militant Homosexuality. Old Tappan, NJ: Revell,
1977. 156 pp.
Chronicles her vocal opposition to gay rights in Dade
County, FL, culminating in the referendum held there in
June 1977. Following her apparent triumph, Bryant
quickly faded from view; see Cliff Jahr, "Anita Bryant's
Startling Reversal," **Ladies Home Journal**, 97 (December
1980), 60-68.

2367. CAMERON, PAUL and KENNETH P. ROSS. "Social
Psychological Aspects of the Judeo-Christian Stance
toward Homosexuality," **Journal of Psychology and**
Theology, 9 (1981), 40-57.
Argues that the Judeo-Christian position is that homosexuality, and toleration of it, tend toward lethality (evil)
and away from social cohesion and respect for human life.
Cameron, cynically exploiting the AIDS crisis, has since
emerged as one of the most determined opponents of
homosexual rights.

2368. DU MAS, FRANK M. **Gay Is Not Good.** Nashville:
Thomas Nelson, 1979. 332 pp.
Revealing farrago of backlash arguments against homosexual
visibility by a provincial psychologist seeking to
generate a militant heterosexual response. Advocates
sections of "heterosexual books" in public libraries.

2369. FALWELL, JERRY. **Listen America!** Garden City, NY:
Doubleday, 1980. 269 pp.
Mr. Moral Majority's call for a return to rigid tradition-
al morality; see pp. 181-86. Other publications of Fal-

well's group teem with antihomosexual exhortation and
exposes.

2370. JOHNSON, BARBARA F. **Where Does a Mother Go To
      Resign?** Minneapolis: Bethany Fellowship, 1979. 154
      pp.
Hostile statement of a parent.

2371. KIRK, JERRY. **The Homosexual Crisis in the Mainline
      Church: A Presbyterian Minister Speaks Out.**
      Nashville: Nelson, 1978. 191 pp.
Written by a Cincinnati pastor to oppose liberalization
in his Church. The only hope for homosexuals, he holds,
lies in repentance.

2372. LA HAYE, TIM. **The Unhappy Gays: What Everyone
      Should Know about Homosexuality.** Wheaton, IL: Tyn-
      dale House, 1978. 207 pp.
Presents an eighteen-point program for overcoming homosexuality. See also: Paul Morris, **Shadow of Sodom: Facing
the Facts of Homosexuality** (Wheaton, IL: Tyndale House,
1978; 164 pp.).

2373. LOVELACE, RICHARD F. **Homosexuality and the
      Church.** Old Tappan, NJ: Revell, 1978. 158 pp.
Evangelical theologican argues that the church should not
alter its traditional attitude of disapproval of homosexuality.

2374. RODGERS, WILLIAM D. **The Gay Invasion: A Christian
      Look at the Spreading Homosexual Myth.** Denver:
      Accept Books, 1977. 160 pp.
Naively antihomosexual book concocted by a fundamentalist
layman (an advertising executive).

2375. ROSE, TERENCE B. "Emerging Social Problems in
      Jamaica and Their Pastoral Implications," **Caribbean
      Journal of Religious Studies,** 6 (1985), 29-45.
Complains of increasing toleration of homosexuality in
Jamaica, fostered by growing acceptance in U. S. churches.

2376. RUEDA, ENRIQUE F. **The Homosexual Network: Private
      Lives and Public Policy.** Old Greenwich, CT: Devin
      Adair, 1982. 680 pp.
By far the largest (though padded) assemblage of antihomosexual arguments, authored in this case by a Cuban Roman
Catholic priest. As a scare tactic, Rueda vastly exagger-
ates the size and power of the gay movement. A main selection of the Conservative Book Club.

2377. SCANZONI, LETHA. "Conservative Christians and Gay
      Civil Rights," **Christian Century,** 93:32 (October
      13, 1976), 857-62.
Article by a progay author documenting the 1975 controversy in Bloomington, Indiana, over a gay rights ordinance.

2378. WHITE, JOHN. **Eros Defiled.** Downers Grove,IL: In-
        ter-Varsity, 1977. 172 pp.
The author regrets the homosexual experiences of his youth
(pp. 105-39).

2379. WILLIAMS, DON. **The Bond That Breaks: Will Homosex-
        uality Split the Church?** Los Angeles, CA: BIM
        Publishing Co., 1978. 176 pp.
Replies to several writers who, in his view, have made
unwarranted defenses of homosexuality. Relies on European
theologians, together with some Bible interpretation.

2380. YOUNG, PERRY DEAN. **God's Bullies: Native Reflec-
        tions on Preachers and Politics.** New York: Holt,
        Rinehart and Winston, 1982.
Gay journalist exposes chicanery employed by the religious
right in an effort to impose its values on America. See
pp. 36-54, 132-52.

                        H. JUDAISM

The subject of attitudes to homosexuality in normative
Judaism (from approximately the third century of our era
to the present) has not yet been studied adequately. For
Biblical precedents, see VII.C; see also "Middle Ages,"
III.D. Recent increases in societal awareness have
prompted a reexamination of the problem in ethical terms
on the part of several sections of Jewish opinion.
Paralleling the rise of the gay churches is the founding
of gay synagogues.

2381. AMADO LÉVY-VALENSI, ELIANE. **Le grand désarroi: aux
        racines de l'énigme homosexuelle.** Paris: Editions
        Universitaires, 1973. 177 pp.
Speculative and eclectic essay, using Biblical quotations
to weave an antihomosexual argument.

2382. BECK, EVELYN T. (ed.). **Nice Jewish Girls: A Les-
        bian Anthology.** Watertown, MA: Persephone Press,
        1982. 286 pp.
Essays from a variety of standpoints: personal, religious,
and historical.

2383. BLUE, LIONEL. **Back Door to Heaven.** London: Dar-
        ton, Longman and Todd, 1977.
Memoirs of a gay rabbi.

2384. BRICK, BARRETT L. "Judaism in the Gay Community,"
        in: Betty Berzon and Robert Leighton (eds.), **Pos-
        itively Gay.** Millbrae, CA: Celestial Arts, 1979,
        pp. 79-87.
Emphasizes the Jewish tradition of opposition to oppres-

sion and discrimination, and charts the growth of the
gay synagogue movement.

2385.   EDWARDES, ALLEN (pseud. of D. A. Kinsley).   **Erotica**
        Judaica: A Sexual History of the Jews.   New
        York: Julian Press, 1967.   238 pp.
Fascinating collection of historical data and folklore
about erotic aspects of Jewish life from the Old Testament
onwards.   Not always reliable.

2386.   FEINBERG, ABRAHAM L.   **Sex and the Pulpit.**   Toronto:
        Methuen, 1981.
See "Homosexuality: Salute to a Gay Friend" (pp. 230-66).
A leftist heterosexual rabbi's response to the gay
movement and to the formation of gay Jewish groups and
synagogues.   Concludes with a plea for toleration of
homosexual expression.

2387.   GENGLE, DEAN.   "Beth Chayim Chadashim: Gay Jewish
        Temple in Los Angeles," **Advocate,** no. 197 (August
        25, 1976), 16-17.
Early report on one of the most successful of the gay
synagogues.

2388.   GORDIS, ROBERT.   **Love and Sex: A Modern Jewish**
        Perspective.   New York: Farrar, Straus and Giroux,
        1978.   290 pp.
See Chapter 10, "Homosexuality and the Homosexual" (pp.
149-61), where the theologian declares that homosexuality
is an illness, nonetheless "homosexuals deserve the same
inalienable rights as do all their fellow human beings."

2389.   GORDIS, ROBERT (ed.).   "Homosexuals and Homosexual-
        ity: Psychiatrists, Religious Leaders and Laymen
        Compare Notes," **Judaism,** 32 (Fall 1983), 390-443.
Symposium reflecting various mainstream views, tending
toward the moderately conservative.

2390.   GREENGROSS, WENDY.   **Jewish and Homosexual.**   Lon-
        don: Reform Synagogues of Great Britain, 1982.   50
        pp.
Sympathetic overview for the lay public.

2391.   HERMAN, ERWIN.   "A Synagogue for the Jewish Homo-
        sexual," **Central Conference of American Rabbis**
        Journal (Summer 1973), 33-40.
Observes that "[t]he congregation consists, in the main,
of men and women homosexuals who represent a variety of
Jewish backgrounds, socially, economically, and intel-
lectually."

2392.   JACOBOVITS, IMMANUEL.   "Homosexuality," **Encyclopedia**
        Judaica, 8 (1971), 961-62.
An overview of historical data in the post-Biblical literature.   Claims, implausibly, that the relative paucity of
references (as now known), reflects the rarity of homosex-

ual practice among Jews.

2393. LAMM, MAURICE. **The Jewish Way in Love and Mar-riage.** San Francisco: Harper and Row, 1980. 288 pp.
Traditional viewpoint (see pp. 65-70).

2394. LAMM, NORMAN. "Judaism and the Modern Attitude to Homosexuality," in: **Encyclopedia Judaica Yearbook 1973.** Jerusalem: Encyclopedia Judaica, 1974, pp. 194-205.
"Judaism allows no compromise in its abhorrence of sodomy, but encourages both compassion and efforts at rehabilitation."

2395. MARKS, NEIL A. "New York Gaycult: The Jewish Question and Me," **Christopher Street,** no. 58 (November 1981), 8-21.
Reflections of a secular Jew and gay activist writer.

2396. MATT, HERSCHEL J. "Sin, Crime, Sickness, or Alternative Life Style? A Jewish Approach to Homosexuality," **Judaism: A Quarterly of Jewish Life and Thought,** 27 (Winter 1978), 13-24.
Because of the centrality of the family to its tradition, homosexuality poses a problem for Judaism. Nonetheless, Matt urges compassion.

2397. MEHLER, BARRY ALAN. "Gay Jews: One Man's Journey from Closet to Community," **Moment** (January 1977), 22-24, 55-56.
"I am a homosexual, and it was in 1972 that I 'came out' .... And it was then that my life came unglued."

2398. MILLER, JUDEA. "Exclusive Rites?" **Moment** (December 1982), 62-63.
Jewish community group has problem in sharing holocaust memories with homosexuals.

2399. ROSSO UBIGLI, LILIANIA. "Alcuni aspetti della concezione della 'porneia' nel tardo-giudaismo," **Henoch,** 1 (1979), 201-45.
On the sexual material in the pseudepigraphical Testaments of the Twelve Patriarchs, which strongly influenced the New Testament and the nascent Christian Church.

2400. ROTH, NORMAN. "'My Love Is Like a Gazelle': Imagery of the Beloved Boy in Religious Hebrew Poetry," **Hebrew Annual Review** (Ohio State University), 8 (1984), 143-65.
Discusses the allegorical use of the "beloved boy" motif in the religious poetry of medieval Spain. See also his: "'Deal Gently with the Young Man': Love of Boys in Medieval Hebrew Poetry of Spain," **Speculum,** 57 (1982), 20-51; "The Lyric Tradition in Hebrew Secular Poetry of Medieval Spain," **Hispanic Journal,** 2:2 (1981), 7-26;

"'Sacred' and 'Secular'" in the Poetry of Ibn Gabirol,"
Hebrew Studies, 20-21 (1979-80), 75-79; and "Satire and
Debate in Two Famous Medieval Hebrew Poems from Al-Anda-
lus: Love of Boys vs. Girls, the Pen and Other Themes,"
Maghreb Review, 4 (1979), 105-13.

2401. SCHINDLER, RUBEN. "Homosexuality, the Halacha, and
        the Helping Professions," **Journal of Religion and
        Health**, 18 (April 1979), 132-38.
Orthodox Jewish social-work perspective.

2402. SCHWARTZ, BARRY DOV. **The Jewish Tradition and Homo-
        sexuality.** New York: Jewish Theological Seminary
        of American, 1979. 173 pp. (unpublished disserta-
        tion)
Traces the Jewish view historically and legally in the
context of the overall view of sexuality. Discusses pro-
hibitions in Leviticus and Deuteronomy, as well as
Rabbinic and post-Rabbinic comments. See also his:
"Homosexuality: A Jewish Perspective," **United Synagogue
Review**, 30 (1977), 4-5, 23, 25-27.

2403. SPERO, MOSHE H. "Homosexuality: Clinical and
        Ethical Challenge," **Tradition** (September 1979),
        17-53.
Adheres to the Orthodox viewpoint regarding homosexuality: "Judaism cannot admit this sexual orientation into
its continuum of sanctified behavior." Nonetheless,
"Homosexuals are bona fide members of the Jewish community."

2404. YOUNGMAN, BARRY. "Gay Life in Israel," **Advocate**,
        no. 272 (July 26, 1979), 20-22.
Despite religiously motivated restrictions, gay life
flourishes there.

                  J. "NEW AGE" SPIRITUALITY

From time to time homosexuals and lesbians, having
concluded that Christianity and Judaism have little to
offer, have sought religious affirmation in other traditions. In the late 19th century, Theosophy began to
attract some homosexuals. (Helena Blavatsky, the founder
of the sect, is considered by some to have been a Lesbian). The Theosophical affinity foreshadowed the
counterculture enthusiasm for Eastern religions in the
1960s. This decade also saw the rise of neopagan forms
of worship, some of them finding positive values in witchcraft and others seeking to establish anew a putative
faith in the Great Goddess of archaic human history.
Goddess worship has appealed particularly, though not
exclusively, to women involved in what is known as
cultural (rather than political) lesbianism.

2405. ADLER, MARGOT. **Drawing Down the Moon: Witches,
       Druids, Goddess-worshippers, and Other Pagans in
       America Today.** New York: Viking Press, 1979. 455
       pp.
This book, which relates to a number of trends among
women, has also had some impact on the (male) "fairy
spirituality" movement. [For an attempt to give a myth-
historical foundation to the latter, see Arthur Evans,
Witchcraft and the Gay Counterculture (Boston: Fag Rag
Books, 1978)]. See pp. 123, 147, 177, 179, 183, and
220.

2406. CARSON, ANNE. **Feminist Spirituality and the
       Feminine Divine: An Annotated Bibliography.**
       Trumansburg, NY: Crossing Press, 1986. 140 pp.
Alphabetical list by author of 739 items; subject index.

2407. DONNELLY, DODY H. **Radical Love: An Approach to
       Sexual Spirituality.** Minneapolis: Wilson Press,
       1984. 135 pp.
Holding that alienating dichotomies should be overcome,
the author affirms sexual pluralism. She condemns the
idolatry of using heterosexual intercourse as the norm.

2408. FREIMARK, HANS. "Helena Petrovna Blavatzky: ein
       weiblicher Ahasver," **JfsZ** (1906), 525-64.
Argues that the founder of Theosophy had a "mannweibliche"
(androgynous) disposition.

2409. ISHERWOOD, CHRISTOPHER. **My Guru and His Disciple.**
       New York: Farrar, Straus and Giroux, 1980. 338 pp.
The novelist's account of his encounter with Vedanta in
Los Angeles in the 1940s.

2410. JOHNSON, EDWIN CLARK. **In Search of God in the
       Sexual Underworld.** New York: Quill, 1983. 238 pp.
Combines an account of the writer's experiences as a
researcher among hustlers and marginal types of San
Francisco's Tenderloin with somewhat jejune religious
effusions, mingling Jung, J. D. Salinger, and Theosophy.

2411. LARKIN, PURUSHA. **The Divine Androgyne.** San
       Diego: Sanctuary Publications, 1982. 200 pp.
Lavishly illustrated presentation of a personalized neo-
Hinduism.

2412. LAWTON, GEORGE. "The Psychology of Spiritualist
       Mediums," **Psychoanalytic Review,** 19 (1932), 418-45.
Mentions frequency of homosexual orientation among
mediums.

2413. LUTYENS, MARY. **Krishnamurti: The Years of Awaken-
       ing.** New York: Farrar, Straus and Giroux, 1975.
       325 pp.
The religious thinker was discovered as a boy in India by
the Liberal Catholic bishop C. W. Leadbeater, a pederast,

causing a great controversy (see G. Tillett, below). See
pp. 15-16, 42, 61-62, 64, 66, 68-70, 78, 142-44, and 146.

2414. PILLION, NUMA. **Numa: A Life Reading: A Metaphys-
       ical Autobiography.** Great Neck, NY: Todd and
       Honeywell, 1984. 278 pp.
Autobiography of a gay quasidrifter and spiritualist (born
1927), who has been influenced by Edgar Cayce.

2415. RUMAKER, MICHAEL. **My First Saturnalia.** Bolinas,
       CA: Grey Fox Press, 1978. 180 pp.
Somewhat star-struck account of a visit to a fairy-spir-
ituality gathering in New York City.

2416. SPRETNAK, CHARLENE (ed.). **The Politics of Women's
       Spirituality: Essays on the Rise of Spiritual Power
       within the Feminist Movement.** Garden City, NY:
       Anchor Press/Doubleday, 1982. 591 pp.
A set of essays denouncing patriarchal religion and
calling for a return of the worship of feminine deities.

2417. STARHAWK. **The Spiral Dance: A Rebirth of the
       Ancient Religion of the Great Goddess.** San
       Francisco: Harper and Row, 1979. 214 pp.
Poetic overview of the older history and modern reemer-
gence of witchcraft as a religion with special relevance
to the women's movement.

2418. STONE, MERLIN. **When God Was a Woman.** New York:
       Harcourt, Brace Jovanovich, 1978. 265 pp.
Attempts to reconstruct the primordial religion of the
Goddess, and to show how this worship was suppressed in
the Judeo-Christian tradition. This and other books of
Merlin Stone, have been influential in the development
of "new age" spirituality.

2419. TILLETT, GREGORY. **The Elder Brother: A Biography
       of Charles Webster Leadbeater.** Boston: Routledge
       and Kegan Paul, 1982. 338 pp.
Life of the eccentric English clergyman, theosophist and
pederast, who founded the first gay church (Australia
1916).

2420. WALKER, MITCH. **Visionary Love: A Spirit Book of
       Gay Mythology and Transmutational Faerie.** San
       Francisco: Treeroot Press, 1980. 102 pp.
This book, inspiring or vapid according to taste, helped
to launch the radical fairy movement.

2420A. WRIGHT, EZEKIEL, and DANIEL INESSE. **God is Gay: An
       Evolutionary Spiritual Work.** San Francisco: Tayu,
       1979. 100 pp.
Account of personal experiences in spiritual expression in
the San Francisco Bay area.

A. LANGUAGE STUDIES

Apart from the intrinsic interest of all words, and especially those concerned with sexual behavior, the study
of language offers a number of valuable perspectives for
the understanding of homosexuality. The structure of
vocabulary employed by the larger society to describe
homosexuality, whether the terms be of learned or slang
origin, belongs broadly to the apparatus of social control, and stands over against the body of words created,
adopted, and adapted by homosexuals themselves, which
reflect, however incompletely, a tendency of resistance to
control. Moreover, the meaning of words alters over
time, and these semantic changes can be used--with all due
caution--to monitor shifting patterns of conceptualizing
and stereotyping. The existence of homosexual vocabular-
ies in the various languages offers considerable vistas
for cross-cultural comparison--though at present only the
classical and modern European languages have been examined
in this light. Much work of all sorts--lexical, semantic,
and sociolinguistic--remains to be done among the languages not influenced by the classical tongues of Europe.

2421. ADAMS, J. N. **The Latin Sexual Vocabulary.** London:
       Duckworth, 1982. 272 pp.
A major contribution to the study of Latin semantics,
metaphor, and the definition of words. Treats the semantic fields of penis, female genitalia, sexual acts,
and (concisely) anus/rectum. For more detail on the last
topic, see his "'Culus,' 'Clunes' and Their Synonyms in
Latin," **Glotta,** 59 (1981), 231-64.

2422. ARANGO, ARIEL C. **Las malas palabras.** Buenos
       Aires: Legasa, 1983. 223 pp.
Psychoanalytically oriented study of taboo words; international rather than purely Hispanic emphasis.

2423. ASHLEY, LEONARD R. N. "Kinks and Queens: Linguist-
       ic and Cultural Aspects of the Terminology for
       Gays," **Maledicta,** 3:2 (Winter 1979), 215-56.
Witty, but somewhat impressionistic collage of character-
istic expressions in American and British slang. See also
his: "Lovely, Blooming, Fresh and Gay: The Onomastics of
Camp," ibid., 4:2 (1980), 223-48; and "Dike Dictum: The
Language of Lesbians," ibid., 6 (1982), 123-62.

2423A. BARON, DENNIS. **Grammar and Gender.** New Haven:
       Yale University Press, 1986. 249 pp.
Historical notes on such questions as the search for a

gender-neutral third person singular pronoun, the origin
of Ms., and changes in occupational names prompted by
feminism.

2424. CHAUTARD, EMILE. **La vie étrange de l'argot.** Par-
       is: Denoël et Steele, 1931. 720 pp.
"Comment ils aiment" (pp. 155-393) contains an extensive
vocabulary of sexual expressions from the slang of the
French criminal underworld. Still other terms are
scattered throughout the volume. An "Index alphabé-
tique" appears on pp. 685-720.

2425. CORY, DONALD WEBSTER (pseud. of Edward Sagarin).
       "The Language of the Homosexual," **Sexology**, 32:3
       (1965), 163-65.
Comments on the use of the sublanguage as a device for
reinforcing social solidarity among its users, with a
short glossary. A longer lexicon--about 80 items--
appears in his (with John P. Leroy): **The Homosexual and
His Society** (New York: Citadel, 1963), 161-66. See also
Sagarin, **The Anatomy of Dirty Words** (New York: L. Stuart,
1962), pp. 109-12.

2426. COUROUVE, CLAUDE. **Vocabulaire de l'homosexualité
       masculine.** Paris: Payot, 1985. 248 pp.
Precise and richly documented essays on 74 key words in
the French language for male homosexuality, with many
insights on French history and literature. About 1000
source citations are included. Appendices of texts; bibliography; index. See also his "Aspects of Male Love in
the French Language," **Gay Books Bulletin,** no. 7 (1982),
13-14; and "The Word 'Bardache,'" ibid., no. 8 (1982),
17-19.

2427. DAHLSTEDT, KARE-HAMPUS. "Spraksituationen i
       Norden," **Nordisk utredningsserie,** 32 (1975), 19-30.
On minority speech, including gay speech, in Scandinavia.

2428. DYNES, WAYNE. **Homolexis: A Historical and Cultural
       Lexicon of Homosexuality.** New York: Scholarship
       Committee, Gay Academic Union, 1985. 177 pp.
A series of essays on historical semantics intended
chiefly as a contribution to the history of ideas (and
of ideology), though information is given on more than
600 words, including their sources in other languages.
Annotated bibliography; index of words.

2429. FÉRAY, JEAN-CLAUDE. "Une histoire critique du mot
       homosexualité," **Arcadie,** no. 325 (January 1981),
       11-21; no. 326 (February 1981), 1150-24; no. 327
       (March 1981), 171-81; and no. 328 (April 1981),
       246-58.
Traces the German origins and diffusion of the term "homo-
sexual(ity)," with useful references.

2430. FISCHER, EDITH. **Amor und Eros: eine Untersuchung**

des Wortfeldes "Liebe" im Lateinischen und Griechischen. Hildesheim: Gerstenberg, 1973. 83 pp.
Philological study of Greek and Latin words for "love."

2431. GALLI DE' PARATESI, NORA. Le brutte parole: se-
       mantica dell'eufemismo. Milan: Mondadori, 1969.
       221 pp.
Study of linguistic substitution and censorship, particularly in the sexual sphere (see esp. pp. 132-36). Bibliography; index of expressions.

2432. GRAHN, JUDY. Another Mother Tongue: Gay Words, Gay
       Worlds. Boston: Beacon, 1984. 325 pp.
While the personal narrative of this popular book is
lively and sometimes moving, as a contribution to philology and historical semantics it is fanciful and unreliable (as seen in the absurd derivation of the word "dyke"
from Queen Boudicca).

2433. GUIRAUD, PIERRE. Le jargon de Villon, ou le gai
       savoir de la coquille. Paris: Gallimard, 1968. 326
       pp.
Advances a controversial argument interpreting the obscure
language of Francois Villon's (b. 1431) six Ballades as
being written (at one level) in homosexual argot. For
another speculative contribution to this period, see: Ida
Nelson, La sottie sans souci: essai d'interprétation
homosexuelle (Paris: Champion, 1977).

2434. HENDERSON, JEFFREY. The Maculate Muse: Obscene
       Language in Attic Comedy. New Haven: Yale Univer-
       sity Press, 1975. 251 pp.
Of limited value: scants homoerotic material and is sometimes unreliable for what it does contain.

2435. HILLER, KURT. "Zur Frage der Bezeichnung," Der
       Kreis, 14:8 (1946), 2-6.
Proposes the terms Androtrope and Gynäkotrope for the male
and female homosexual respectively.

2435A. HOLZINGER, HERBERT. Beschimpfung im heutigen
       Französisch: Pragmatische, syntaktische und sem-
       antische Aspekte. Salzburg: Universitat, 1984.
       292 pp. (dissertation)
Contemporary French insults as found in novels and
cartoons; includes the semantic field pede.

2436. JOHANSSON, WARREN. "The Etymology of the Word
       'Faggot,'" Gay Books Bulletin, no. 6 (1981), 16-18,
       33.
Definitive study of this controversial term, showing that
it is an American slang use of the British dialectal word
faggot, a contemptuous term for a fat, slovenly woman, and
has nothing to do with the supposed burning of sodomites
at the stake in medieval England.

2437. KAHANE, HENRY, and RENEE KAHANE. "Romano-Aegypti-
       aca: I. The Stone **peridot**," **Romance Philology,** 14
       (1961), 287-89.
Peridot, at present a designation of the chrysolite and
olivine, derives from the Greek **paideros,** "boy love."

2438. KRAMARAE, CHERIS, and PAULA A. TREICHLER. **A
       Feminist Dictionary.** Boston: Pandora, 1985. 588
       pp.
A resolutely engage work, mingling exhortation and
feminist assertion with fact. Some will question the
assumption that there are two entirely different genres
of dictionaries, one for men and the other for women, as
implying a cognitive dichotomy of all human experience.
Useful for the numerous quotations.

2439. MEÏLAKH, MIKHAIL. "L'argot de la subculture homo-
       sexuelle en Russie," **Spirales,** no. 12 (February
       1982), 10-11.
Soviet scholar's summary of his research on Russian homosexual slang in the USSR, which may never be published in
full because of his arrest.

2440. NEVIS, JOEL A. **"Gai, Gei, Homo,** and **Homoseksuali** in
       Finnish," **Maledicta** 8 (1984-85), 158-60.
Difficulties of integrating the international vocabulary
into Finnish.

2441. OPELT, ILONA. **Die lateinische Schimpfwörter und
       verwandte sprachliche Erscheinungen.** Heidelberg:
       Winter, 1965. 283 pp.
In this study on terms of abuse in Latin, see pp. 122,
155, 174-75, 228, 260, 264.

2442. RICHLIN, AMY. "The Meaning of **irrumare** in Catullus
       and Martial," **Classical Philology,** 76 (1981), 40-
       46.
On the Latin expression for active buccal thrusts during
fellation. See also her book: **Garden of Priapus.** (New
Haven: Yale University Press, 1983).

2443. ROBERTS, J. R. "In America They Call Us Dykes: -
       Notes on the Etymology and Use of 'Dyke,'" **Sinister
       Wisdom,** no. 9 (Spring 1979), 3-11.
Offers a plausible explanation, based on conventions of
dress. Reprinted in E. Shore (ed.) **Alternative Papers**
(Philadelphia: Temple University Press, 1982), pp. 313-
17. See also R. A. Spears, below.

2443A. SPEARS, RICHARD A. "On the Etymology of **Dike,**"
       American Speech 60:4 (1985), 318-27.
Canvases a broader range of possibilities than J. Roberts
(above), suggesting that the word may be a clipped form of
"bulldike" and its variants.

2444. STONE, CHARLES. "The Semantics of Gay," **Advocate,**

no. 325 (September 3, 1981), 20-22.
Suggests that the outrage expressed by pop grammarians at
the purported "kidnapping" of the word **gay** (in contrast
to their silence vis-a-vis **pansy, fruit,** and **fairy**) reflects their discomfort in seeing homosexuals manifest
their own power. See also: Scott Tucker, "The Power of
Naming," **Christopher Street,** no. 58 (1982), 60-63.

B. DICTIONARIES AND GLOSSARIES

Dictionaries and word lists that are useful in studying
homosexual words are of two kinds: general and specialized
(erotic). While older dictionaries tend to restrict
coverage of sexual words, there are exceptions, and
in any case it is often necessary to examine the older
works in order to trace the development of current terms.

2445. ALMEIDA, HORÁCIO DE. **Dicionário de Termos Eróticos
        e Afins.** Second ed. Rio de Janeiro: Civilização
        Brasileira, 1981. 285 pp.
Brazilian-Portuguese sexual vocabulary, including some
local Brazilian dialect terms; occasional source citations
from other dictionaries and novels.

2446. BARDIS, PANOS D. "A Glossary of Homosexuality,"
        Maledicta, 4:1 (1980), 59-64.
Modest roster of 46 terms, ostensibly chosen because of
their rarity.

2447. BLONDEAU, NICOLAS. **Dictionnaire érotique latin-
        français.** Paris: Liseux, 1885. 152 pp.
Blondeau's manuscript, which was completed in the 17th
century, contains much material of value in deciphering
Renaissance erotic poetry.

2448. BORNEMAN, ERNEST. **Sex im Volksmund: der obszöne
        Wortschatz der Deutschen.** Reinbek bei Hamburg:
        Rowohlt, 1974. 2 vols.
Dictionary of contemporary German sexual slang, particularly rich in the language of prostitutes. Vol. 1
presents the words in alphabetical order; vol. 2 offers
a thematic classification in the manner of Roget's Thesaurus.

2449. BOSWORTH, JOSEPH, and T. NORTHCOTE TOLLER. **An
        Anglo-Saxon Dictionary.** London: Oxford University
        Press, 1898. 1302 pp.
See pp. 65 (**baeddel, baedling**); and 1156 (**waepen-
wifestre**) all defined as "hermaphrodite." According to
most authorities, the first two are the origin of the
modern English word "bad." See also the 1921 **Supplement**
to the work, where (p. 61), **baedling** is defined as "an

effeminate person."

2450. BURNADZ, JULIAN M. **Die Gaunersprache der Wiener
       Galerie.** Lubeck: Verlag für polizeiliches Fach-
       schrifttum Georg Schmidt-Romhild, 1966. 124 pp.
A lexicon of the argot of the Viennese criminal underworld. Unlike many previous glossaries in this field, it
is rich in terms for male and female homosexuality,
since "in the underworld everything in the last analysis
turns around easily acquired money and (much of the time
perverted) sexuality." Compare: Max Pollak, "Wiener
Gaunersprache," **Archiv für Kriminal-Anthropologie und
Kriminalistik,** 15 (1904), 171-237.

2451. CANTAGALLI, RENZO. **Con rispetto parlando: seman-
       tica del doppiamento.** Milan: Sugar, 1972. 239 pp.
Dictionary of common Italian double-entendre terms (see
e.g.,the entries for **bagascia, bardascia, checca, finoc-
chio, frocione, zia).**

2452. CARADEC, FRANCOIS. **Dictionnaire du français
       argotique et populaire.** Paris: Larousse, 1977.
       251 pp.
Practical and up-to-date lexicon of French vernacular,
essential for contemporary French studies. See also:
Rene James Herail and Edward Lovatt, **Dictionary of
Modern Colloquial French** (Boston: Routledge and Kegan
Paul, 1984; 327 pp.); and Emile Chautard, **La vie étrange
de l'argot** (Paris: Denoël et Steele, 1931: 720 pp.).

2453. DELVAU, ALFRED. **Dictionnaire érotique moderne, par
       un professeur de langue verte.** Brussels ["Free-
       town"]: Gay, 1864. 320 pp.
This pioneering dictionary of taboo words, several times
enlarged and reprinted, is with its quotations from
the erotic classics an archetypal work in the genre.

2454. DE MAURO, TULLIO. "Lessico dell'omosessualità,"
       in: Riccardo Reim et al., **Pratiche innominabili.**
       Milan: Mazzotta, 1979, pp. 98-112.
Despite De Mauro's established reputation, this word list
is insufficient and unreliable; it will be replaced by a
major work by Giovanni Dall'Orto in preparation.

2454A. ENDT, ENNO, and LIENEKE FRERICHS. **Bargoens
       woordenboek.** Revised ed. Amsterdam: Bakker,
       1986. 193 pp.
Glossary of current Dutch urban slang with many entries
for homosexuals and lesbians.

2455. FARMER, JOHN STEPHEN. **Vocabula amatoria: A
       French-English Glossary.** New York University
       Books, 1966. 268 pp.
Reprint of the 1903 edition, when it appeared as vol. 8
of Farmer and W. E. Henley's classic **Dictionary of Slang
and Its Analogues, Past and Present.** This vol., assembled

by compiling several French-language dictionaries, gives
English definitions, together with brief source citations.

2455A. FERRERO, ERNESTO. **I gerghi della mala vita del
       cinquecento a oggi.** Milan: Mondadori, 1972. 383
       pp.
Dictionary of Italian argot and low-life terms; see index
under "omosessuale."

2456. FORBERG, FRIEDRICH KARL. **Manual of Classical
       Erotology (De figuris veneris).** New York: Grove
       Press, 1966. 2 vols. in 1.
Reprint of the 1884 edition (including misprints). Originally written as a learned appendix to Forberg's 1824
edition of Panormita's **Hermaphroditus,** this landmark of
erudition quotes some 500 passages from about 150 Greek
and Latin authors. Index of terms (vol. 2, pp. 211-35).

2457. GALLO, CRISTINO. **Language of the Puerto Rican
       Street: A Slang Dictionary with English Cross-Ref-
       erence.** Santurce, PR: Book Service of Puerto Rico,
       1980. 214 pp.
Contains a fair number of terms for popular terms for
homosexuality--many of which are known, of course, among
Spanish speakers of the eastern continental United
States.

2458. **Guild Dictionary of Homosexual Terms.** Washington,
       DC: Guild Press, 1965. 51 pp.
Brochure containing about 700 terms (some are proper
names--homosexual historical figures).

2459. GUIRAUD, PIERRE. **Dictionnaire érotique.** Paris:
       Payot, 1978. 639 pp.
This large work by a noted philologist subsumes, somewhat
uncritically, the gleanings of a long series of glossaries
of **la langue verte.** For Guiraud's exploration of the
issues involved, see his: **Sémiologie de la sexualité**
(Paris: Payot, 1978; 247 pp.); and **Les gros mots** (Paris:
Presses Universitaires de France, 1975; 127 pp.).

2460. HENKE, JAMES T. **Courtesans and Cuckolds: A
       Glossary of Renaissance Dramatic Bawdy (Exclusive
       of Shakespeare).** New York: Garland, 1979. 329 pp.
Cites some relevant material from the works of Dekker,
Jonson, Marlowe, Marston etc. See also E. A. M. Colman,
The Dramatic Use of Bawdy in Shakespeare (London: Long-
man, 1974; 230 pp.), which has a glossary, pp. 182-224.

2461. IRWIN, GODFREY. **American Tramp and Underworld
       Slang.** New York: Sears, 1931. 264 pp.
Despite the reference to homosexuals as "degenerates,"
this book offers a number of early citations; see pp. 19,
39, 43, 70, 77, 88, 110, 117-19, 124, 127, 131, 151-53,
174, 176, 195-96, 201. See also Noel Ersine, **Underworld
and Prison Slang** (Upland, IN: Freese, 1933; 80 pp.

2462. KUPPER, HEINZ. **Illustriertes Lexikon der deutsch-
       en Umgangssprache.** Stuttgart: Klett, 1982. 8
       vols.
Lavishly illustrated popular dictionary of contemporary
German slang. Numerous entries, but without source
citations.

2463. LEGMAN, GERSHON. "The Language of Homosexuality: An
       American Glossary," in: George W. Henry, **Sex Var-
       iants** (New York: P. B. Hoeber, 1941), pp. 1147-78.
The first such list published in the United States, with
329 terms (omitted in the second edition of Henry's book).

2464. PETROPOULOS, ELIAS. **Kaliardá.** Fourth ed. Athens:
       Nepheli, 1980. 262 pp.
Glossary of specialized contemporary Greek gay argot. This
edition contains commentary on press and other responses
to previous editions. For description and analysis, see
John Taylor, **Gay Books Bulletin,** 9 (1983), 14-19, and
Cabirion, no. 11 (1984), 10-11; as well as Steve A. Dema-
kopoulos, "The Greek Gays Have a Word for It," **Maledicta,**
2 (1978), 33-39.

2465. PIERRUGUES, PIERRE. **Glossarium eroticum linguae
       latinae.** Paris: Dondey-Duprey, 1826. 518 pp.
A learned Latin dictionary, in Latin; still useful.

2466. RODGERS, BRUCE. **The Queens' Vernacular: A Gay
       Lexicon.** San Francisco: Straight Arrow Books,
       1972. 254 pp.
Campy, uncritical lexicon of over 12,000 items, including
many (evidently) nonce expressions invented ad hoc by
teasing queens. Reissued without change as **Gay Talk**
(New York: Putnam's, 1979).

2467. RODRÍGUEZ CASTELO, HERNÁN. **Lexicón sexual ecuator-
       iano y latino-americano.** Quito: Libri Mundi,
       1979. 401 pp.
Thoughtful, scholarly work on Spanish-American sexual
language; see pp. 321-49.

2468. SOUTO MAIOR, MÁRIO. **Dicionário do Palavrão e
       Termos Afins.** Third ed. Recife: Guararapes,
       1980. 166 pp.
Brazilian-Portuguese dictionary of erotic language, with
many source citations.

2469. VORBERG, GASTON. **Glossarium eroticum.** Stuttgart:
       Puttmann, 1932. 768 pp.
Ambitious illustrated dictionary of Greek and Latin erotic
terms with explanations in German; not always reliable.

                      C. SOCIOLINGUISTICS

Sociolinguistics, which is concerned with the use of
language in human encounter situations, is a recent
development in the ensemble of linguistic fields. While
the discipline holds considerable promise in view of the
social anchoring of homosexual behavior, as yet the
results have been somewhat limited.

2470. ALLEN, IRVING LEWIS. **The Language of Ethnic Con-
      flict: Social Organization and Lexical Culture.**
      New York: Columbia University Press, 1983. 162 pp.
Presents results of an analysis of more than a thousand
terms of abuse which have been used for and by 53 different groups of ethnic Americans. Shows correlations between the number of slurs, the size of a group, and a
group's contact and conflict with other groups. The
perspectives disclosed by this book should be extended
to gay men and lesbians.

2471. CHESEBRO, JAMES W. "Paradoxical Views of 'Homosex-
      uality' in the Rhetoric of Social Scientists: A
      Fantasy Theme Analysis," **Quarterly Journal of
      Speech,** 66 (1980), 127-39.
Using a method created by E. G. Bormann, identifies three
themes: the homosexual as degenerate, mainstreaming the
homosexual, and cultural compatibility of the heterosexual and homosexual cultural systems.

2472. CHESEBRO, JAMES W. (ed.). **Gayspeak: Gay Male and
      Lesbian Communication.** New York: Pilgrim Press
      1981. 367 pp.
Twenty-five papers of varying quality on communications
and sociolinguistics arranged under six topics: the
social meanings of the words homosexual, gay, and lesbian;
inside the gay community; homophobia; institutional forces
shaping the public images of gay males and lesbians; gay
liberation as a rhetorical movement; and gay rights and
the political campaign.

2473. FARRELL, R. A. "The Argot of the Homosexual Subcul-
      ture," **Anthropological Linguistics,** 14:3 (1972),
      97-109.
Analyzes the responses to a questionnaire, concluding that
homosexual slang expresses the preoccupations of the gay
subculture.

2474. GOLDHABER, GERALD M. "Gay Talk: Communication
      Behavior of Male Homosexuals," **Gai Saber,** 1:2
      (1977), 136-49.
Combines anecdotal and statistical evidence to suggest
patterns of communication, verbal and nonverbal.

2475. HAYES, JOSEPH. "Gayspeak," **Quarterly Journal of
      Speech,** 62 (1976), 256-66.
Examines three major aspects of homosexual language--
secret, social, and radical activist--reviewing current

research problems.

2476. HAYES, JOSEPH. "Language and Language Behavior of
       Lesbian Women and Gay Men: A Selected Bibliog-
       raphy," **JH**, 4:2 (Winter 1978), 201-212; and 4:3
       (Spring 1979), 299-309.
A remarkably comprehensive roundup, which may be used to
supplement the items listed here. However, as Hayes'
astute annotations demonstrate, much of the material
published up to the time of his writing was methodologically immature.

2477. KEY, MARY RITCHIE. **Male-female Language; with a
       Comprehensive Bibliography.** Metuchen, NJ: Scare-
       crow, 1975. 200 pp.
Surveys the problem of gender-marked differences in vocabulary and usage.

2478. LERMAN, J. W., and P. H. DANUTE. "Voice Pitch of
       Homosexuals," **Folia Phoniatrica**, 21 (1969), 340-46.
A start on the study of a neglected topic.

2479. LUMBY, MALCOLM E. "Code Switching and Sexual
       Orientation: A Test of Bernstein's Sociolinguistic
       Theory," **JH** 1:4 (Summer 1976), 383-99.
Concludes that the ideas of the British sociologist cannot
be accepted without modification for stigmatized groups.

2480. MURRAY, STEPHEN O. "Lexical and Institutional
       Elaboration: The 'Species Homosexual' in Guate-
       mala," **Anthropological Linguistics**, 22 (1980),
       177-85.
Analyzes the social elements characterizing the use of
words by local informants.

2481. MURRAY, STEPHEN O., and ROBERT C. POOLMAN, JR.
       "Labels and Labeling: Folk Models of 'Gay Com-
       munity'." **Working Papers of the Language Behavior
       Research Laboratory**, 52 (1982). 34 pp.
Sexual and social notions of who is included in San
Francisco gay men's understanding of "gay community."

2482. PONSE, BARBARA. "Secrecy in the Lesbian World,"
       Urban Life, 3 (1976), 313-38.
Analyzes lesbian techniques for minimizing self-revelation, including nonverbal communication.

2483. SAGARIN, EDWARD (Donald Webster Cory). "Language
       of the Homosexual Subculture," **Medical Aspects of
       Human Sexuality**, 4:4 (April 1970), 37, 39-41.
Anecdotal evidence. This article is a condensation of a
chapter in Cory, **The Homosexual in America** (New York:
Greenberg, 1951.)

2484. SONENSCHEIN, DAVID. "The Homosexual's Language,"
       Journal of Sex Research, 5 (1969), 281-91.

Presents the results of a participant-observation study in
a southwestern U. S. city, showing how at that time gay
men's argot effeminized nouns and pronouns, from which
Sonenschein draws conclusions about their social role.

2485. STANLEY, JULIA PENELOPE. "Homosexual Slang,"
       American Speech, 45 (1970), 45-59.
Interprets questionnaires to conclude that gay men posses
a more extensive "marginal vocabulary" than either heterosexual men or lesbians. See also her: "When We Say
'Out of the Closets'," **College English,** 36 (November
1974), 385-92.

2486. TAUB, DIANE, and ROBERT G. LEGER. "Argot and the
       Creation of Social Types in a Young Gay Community,"
       Human Relations, 37 (1984), 181-89.
Gay terms and expressions collected were grouped in a
method similar to factor analysis to locate specific
dimensions of behavior in a community of college-age
persons. Special attention was given to the presence of
binary oppositions. See also: Aaron Bruce W. Ostrom, "A
Study of Lexical Items in the Gay Subculture," in: J. A.
Edmondson (ed.), **Research Papers of the Texas SIL: Pilot
Studies in Sociolinguistics** (Dallas: Summer Institute
of Linguistics, 1983), 72-87.

2487. THORNE, BARRIE, CHERIS KRAMARAE, and NANCY HENLEY.
       Language, Gender and Society. Rowley, MA: Newbury
       House, 1983. 342 pp.
Ten papers seeking to display progress made in the field
since 1975, followed by a noteworthy annotated bibliography (pp.151-331). See esp. pp. 125-37 and 327.

2488. VETTERLING-BRAGGIN, MARY (ed.). **Sexist Language: A
       Modern Philosophical Analysis.** Totowa, NJ: Little-
       field, Adams and Co., 1981. 329 pp.
Papers seeking to state the rationale and implications of
the feminist-sponsored language reform. Although most
of the contributors in the anthology tend to take the
feminist critique of language too much for granted, a
number of secondary issues are usefully canvased. Bibliography, pp. 319-23.

                        D. GRAFFITI

Although surviving graffiti from Greece and Rome (including some that bear on homosexuality; see III.C) have been
studied for linguistic and social attitudes, in subsequent
centuries the practice has been neglected. Contemporary
graffiti have, however, attracted the attention of folk-
lorists and amateurs since the beginning of the century.

2489. ALEXANDER, BOB. "Male and Female Restroom Graf-
       fiti," **Maledicta**, 2 (1978), 42-59.
Finds that homosexual graffiti in male restrooms tend
to be aggressive, while graffiti in female restrooms
have "an element of what might be called tenderness."
See also Wendy Reich et al., "Notes on Women's Graffiti," **Journal of American Folklore**, 90 (April 1977),
188-91.

2490. **Il cesso degli angeli.** Milan: Gammalibri, 1979.
       122 pp.
Anonymous illustrated work treating graffiti as indices
of the male mentality; see pp. 47-66.

2491. EIGELTINGER, WILFRIED. **Graffiti für Vespasian: Die
       Kunst im Pissoir.** Berlin: Verlag Rosa Winkel,
       1981. 94 pp.
Attempts to place graffiti in historical context so as
to evaluate them as a "continuing cultural achievement of
humanity."

2492. ERNEST, ERNEST (pseud.). **Sexe et graffiti.**
       Paris: Alain Moreau, 1979. 349 pp.
Texts selected from several thousand graffiti collected
by the author over fifteen years in Paris, the French
provinces, and several neighboring countries. See pp.
85-315 for homosexual examples.

2493. PRAETORIUS, NUMA (pseud. of Eugen Wilhelm).
       "Homosexuelle Pissoir-Inschriften aus Paris,"
       Anthropophyteia, 8 (1911), 410-22, 425-26.
Report on homosexual graffiti observed in Parisian toi-
lets.

2494. SECHREST, LEE, and LUIS FLORES. "Homosexuality in
       the Philippines and the United States: The Hand-
       writing on the Wall," **Journal of Social Psychology,**
       79 (1969), 3-12.
Comparing samples from the two countries it was found
that the American ones were more likely to be humorous,
political, and philosophical, while the Philippine ones
had a higher amount of hostile content and disapproval
of sexual ideation. See also Lee Sechrest and A. K. Olson, "Graffiti in Four Types of Institutions of Higher
Education," **Journal of Sex Research**, 7 (1971), 62-71.

                         E. FOLKLORE

Until recently folklorists--with the exception of a few
Freudians--have tended to avoid dealing explicitly with
sexual matters. The study of homosexuality in folklore
has not yet achieved defined parameters. Accordingly, the
entries listed below offer only a few glimpses of the

broader panorama that may one day be unfolded.

2495. DUNDES, ALAN, JERRY LEACH, and BORA ÖZKÖK. "The
       Strategy of Turkish Boys' Verbal Dueling," in: J.
       Gumpertz and D. Hymes (eds.) **Directions in Socio-
       linguistics: The Ethnography of Communication.** New
       York: Holt, 1972, pp. 130-60.
Accusations of passive homosexuality as insults. Note
the modification proposed by M. Glazer, "On Verbal Dueling
Among Turkish Boys," **Journal of American Folklore,** 89
(1976), 87-89.

2496. FLYNN, CHARLES P. "Sexuality and Insult Behavior,"
       Journal of Sex Research, 12 (1976), 1-13.
Insults indicate the boundaries of acceptable sexual
behavior in a given culture. The frequency of homosexual insults in American culture contrasts with their
apparent absence from many tribal cultures.

2497. GOODWIN, JOSEPH PAUL. **More Man Than You'll Ever
       Be: Gay Folklore and Acculturation.** Bloomington:
       Indiana University, 1984. 386 pp. (unpublished
       dissertation)
Seeks to determine the socio-cultural meaning of gay
argot, jokes, female impersonation, and the like--in-
cluding their role in maintaining social cohesion and in
coping with conflict.

2498. GREENBERG, H. R., et al. "The Jelly Baby," **Psychi-
       atric Quarterly,** 42 (1968), 211-16.
A folk practice occurring among certain menstruating
lesbians, and the fantasies associated with it.

2499. HOFFMAN, FRANK. **Analytical Survey of Anglo-Amer-
       ican Traditional Erotica.** Bowling Green, OH: Bow-
       ling Green University Popular Press, 1973. 309 pp.
Emphasizes literature and film.

2500. KOUKOULES, MARY. **Loose-Tongued Greeks: A Miscel-
       lany of Neo-Hellenic Erotic Folklore.** Translated
       by John Taylor. Paris: Digamma, 1983. 181 pp.
Erotic sayings and rhymes collected in modern Greece
(bilingual); a few examples refer to homosexuality. An
appendix is "A Glossary of Modern Greek Erotic Speech."

2501. LEGMAN, GERSHON. **The Horn Book: Studies in Erotic
       Folklore and Bibliography.** New Hyde Park, NY: Uni-
       versity Books, 1964. 565 pp.
Includes a study of "Pisanus Fraxi" (Henry Spencer Ashbee); great collectors of erotica; and a series of papers
on problems of erotic literature.

2502. MURRAY, STEPHEN O. "The Art of Gay Insulting,"
       Anthropological Linguistics, 21 (1979), 211-23.
Parallels and contrasts with the better-known art of in-

sults among blacks. See also his: "Ritual Insults in Stigmatized Subcultures--Gay--Black--Jew," **Maledicta**, 7 (1983), 189-211.

2503. MONEY, JOHN, and GEOFFREY HOSTA. "Negro Folklore of Male Pregnancy," **Journal of Sex Research**, 4 (1968), 34-50.
Seeks to link the folk belief (documented from nine black homosexuals) in the "blood baby" to the mother-centered Black culture of the United States.

2504. WESTERMEIER, CLIFFORD P. "The Cowboy and Sex," in: Charles W. Harris and Buck Rainey (eds.), **The Cowboy: Six Shooters, Songs and Sex**. Norman: University of Oklahoma Press, 1976, pp. 98-105.
Throws a little light on a still very obscure subject.

F. HUMOR AND CAMP

As a general rule, minority groups tend to create distinctive forms of humor as a defensive device and for ironic self-reflection. Among male homosexuals this "ethnic" humor has tended to take the form of camp, an ironic self-parody which also functions as social criticism. Lesbian humor, which has been falsely claimed to be nonexistent, has not yet been sufficiently studied to afford generalizations. Cross-cultural studies are entirely lacking. Needless to say, there exists a substantial body of jokes told by heterosexuals, which convey hostile stereotypes; this form of humor offers some insight into popular attitudes, including response to changing events (e.g.,the 1980s vogue of AIDS jokes).

2505. BALLIET, BEV, and PATTI PATTON. **Graphic Details**. Phoenix: Star Publications, 1980. 44 pp.
Lesbian erotica and humor in prose, poetry, and photography.

2506. BOOTH, MARK. **Camp**. London: Quartet, 1983. 189 pp.
Attempts to define the phenomenon and plot its history and characteristics. Holds that camp is not the same as gay, though there is a large overlap. Offers almost 200 illustrations, from Carpaccio to David Bowie.

2507. BROWN, HUDSON. **The First Official Gay Handbook: Manual for Quiche Eaters**. New York: Printed Matter, 1983. 160 pp.
Exploits the brief vogue of the "quiche eater" satire, supposedly the favorite food of certified wimps.

2508. CORE, PHILIP. **Camp: The Lie That Tells the**

Truth. New York: Delilah Books, 1984. 192 pp.
An illustrated biographical dictionary of campy persons
and those who have been the objects of camp veneration.
The choice of entries--including Alexander the Great,
Fran Lebowitz, and Cardinal Newman--is sophisticated,
but sometimes debatable.

2509. DE MOSS, VIRGINIA. "The Joke's on Us: The Fag Joke
      Phenomenon," **Advocate**, no. 289 (April 3, 1980),
      26-30.
Antihomosexual jokes in the media, especially television,
trivialize a whole range of experience, and the gay community seems unable or unwilling to combat the practice.

2510. EDWARDS, VAL. "Robin Tyler: Comic in Contradic-
      tion: A Profile," **Body Politic**, no. 56 (September
      1979), 21-23.
Situates the popular lesbian comic in the context of the
new women's humor which gave women the opportunity to
make not themselves the brunt of the jokes, but the
society that oppresses them. See also M. A. Karr,
Advocate, no. 268 (May 31, 1979), 26+.

2511. GITECK, LENNY. "Gay Humor: Comedy Comes Out of the
      Closet," **Advocate**, no. 300 (September 4, 1980),
      23-26.
On some gay and lesbian performers.

2512. HENLEY, CLARK. **The Butch Manual.** New York: Sea
      Horse Press, 1982. 111 pp.
Send up of gay mimicry of macho styles, with numerous
photographs.

2513. HOHMANN, JOACHIM S. (ed.). **"Hoffentlich sind die
      Jungs auch pünklich."** Berlin: Rosa Winkel Verlag,
      1976. 92 pp.
Male homosexual jokes and wit.

2514. LEGMAN, GERSHON (ed.). **The Limerick: 1700 Ex-
      amples, with Notes, Variants and Index.** New York:
      Bell, 1974. 508 pp.
All more or less erotic. See Chapter 5, "Buggery" (pp.92-
108); and Chapter 6 "Abuses of the Clergy" (pp. 109-17).
See also the sequel: **The New Limerick: 2750 Unpublished
Examples, American and British** (New York: Crown, 1977;
729 pp.).

2515. LEGMAN, GERSHON. [**No Laughing Matter.**] **Rationale
      of the Dirty Joke: An Analysis of Sexual Humor:
      Second Series.** New York: Breaking Point, 1975.
      992 pp.
Sequel to his 1968 volume. Although much interesting
material is included, the analysis is largely vitiated by
heavy-handed and homophobic Freudian interpretations. See
"Homosexuality" (pp. 55-183).

2516. LYNCH, MICHAEL, and MARIANA VALVERDE. "Pat Bond:
       (Role) Playing Stein," **Body Politic**, no. 59 (Decem-
       ber 1979-January 1980), 21-24.
Interview with comedian Pat Bond who states: "Gertrude
Stein is important to lesbians today because she's a
role model for us." See also M. A. Karr, **Advocate**, no.
256 (December 13, 1978), 27-28.

2517. ORTLEB, CHARLES, and RICHARD FIALA. **Le Gai
       Ghetto: Gay Cartoons from** Christopher Street. New
       York: St. Martin's Press, 1980. about 50 pp.
Sophisticated cartoons in the mould of **New Yorker** maga-
zine. Other collections of the work of gay cartoonists
include Joe Johnson, ... **And So,This Is Your Life, Miss
Thing** (Los Angeles: Funny Bone Press, 1973); Nazario,
Anarcoma (New York: Catalan Communications, 1983; 69 pp.);
Hippolyte Romain, **Les Cheries** (Paris: Leroy, 1984; 46
pp.); and Stefan, **Der Schwuchtelpeter** (Berlin: Verlag Rosa
Winkel, 1980; 32 pp.). Under the editorship of Harold
Cruse, five issues of **Gay Comics** magazine have appeared.

2518. PAINTER, DOROTHY S. "Lesbian Humor as a Normal-
       ization Device," in: Virginia A. Erman and Cynthia
       L. Berryman (eds.), **Communication, Language and
       Sex: Proceedings from the First Annual Conference.**
       Rowley, MA: Newbury, 1980, 132-48.
Derived from her doctoral dissertation: **A Communicative
Study of Humor in a Lesbian Speech Community: Becoming a
Member** (Columbus: Ohio State University, 1978; 237 pp.)

2519. SCHMIDT, CASPER G. "AIDS Jokes: Or, **Schadenfreude**
       around an Epidemic," **Maledicta**, 8 (1984-85), 69-75.
A first approach to this repellent genre of contemporary
folklore. More examples appear on page 214-16 of this
issue; see also ibid., 7 (1983), 280, 290-93.

2520. SONTAG, SUSAN. "Notes Toward a Definition of
       Camp," **Partisan Review**, 31 (1964), 515-30.
Widely-read essay that put camp "on the map" among the
intelligentsia. See also Jim Hunter, "On Camp: The
Sensibility of Innocent Frivolity," **Journal of the West
Virginia Philosophical Society**, 9 (Fall 1975), 28-30;
Vito Russo, "Camp," in: Martin Levine (ed.), **Gay Men: The
Sociology of Male Homosexuality** (New York: Harper and
Row, 1979), pp. 205-10; as well as M. Booth, and P. Core,
above.

2521. STANLEY, JULIA P., and SUSAN W. ROBBINS. "Lesbian
       Humor," **Women**, 5 (1980), 26-29.
Hypothesizes that humor serves a bonding function for
lesbians, in somewhat the same manner as the special
vocabulary of gay men (which lesbians largely lack).
See also idem, "Mother Wit: Tongue in Cheek," in: Karla
Jay and Allen Young (eds.), **Lavender Culture** (New York:
Jove, 1979), 299-307.

2522. SUMMERBELL, RICHARD. **Abnormally Happy: A Gay
       Dictionary.** Vancouver: New Star Books, 1985. 66
       pp.
A gentle Devil's Dictionary, with illustrations by Paul
Aboud.

2523. TURNER, GLENN. **Fairy Tales: A Treasure of Gay
       Jokes.** New York: Pinnacle Books, 1985. 119 pp.
Pulp collection of longer jokes and quickies told by or
ridiculing homosexuals. Some were originally straight
jokes, transformed into gay ones.

2524. WATSON, LARRY. **The Homosexual Joke Book.** New
       York: Gay Presses of New York, 1985. 63 pp.
Mostly one-liners, some quite amusing.

IX. LIFESTYLES

A. SOCIAL SEMIOTICS AND LIFESTYLE TRENDS

In this section, the term semiotics is not used in the usual sense of a science of signs and symbols, but refers to repertoires of nonverbal tokens of communication. As the homosexual subculture has become less clandestine, the character of such tokens and gestural patterns has shifted from that of the carefully guarded possession of an insider culture to that of a more open and accessible repertoire (as seen, for example, in the lambda symbol, which is often worn to **elicit** comment). With the advancing social pluralism of Western industrial societies, it was perhaps inevitable that subcultural groups be more and more identified with distinctive and visible lifestyles. The increasing salience of male homosexuals and lesbians has become part and parcel of this development.

2525. ALFRED, RANDY. "Will the Real Clone Please Stand Up?" **Advocate**, no. 338 (March 18, 1982), 22-23.
Views the clone consciousness as one of passive consumerism. See also: Phillip Carswell, "Clones," **Gay Community News** (Melbourne), 2:9 (November 1980), 24-26.

2526. ALTMAN, DENNIS. **The Homosexualization of America, the Americanization of the Homosexual.** New York: St. Martin's Press, 1982. 242 pp.
Ambitious but impressionistic attempt to characterize the leading trends of the current situation in the United States and their interaction with the rest of the non-Communist world. Contains many references to stories in the gay and mainstream press.

2526A. ANDERSON, TIMOTHY. "Psychosexual Symbolism in the Handwriting of Male Homosexuals," **Psychological Reports,** 58 (1986), 75-81.
Claims to find differences between male homosexuals and male heterosexuals in the formation of the letter "I" (but not for other letters).

2527. BERGLER, EDMUND. **Fashion and the Unconscious.** New York: Brunner, 1953. 305 pp.
The antihomosexual psychoanalyst claims that women's fashions are a "masculine invention secondarily thrust upon women to alleviate man's unconscious masochistic fear of the female body," and that women's fashions are designed by male homosexuals, "their bitterest enemies." See also: Michael M. Miller et al., "Viewpoints: Why Are the Women's Fashion and Hair-styling Industries Dominated by Homosexual Males?" **Medical Aspects of Human Sexuality,**

5 (May 1971), 60-67.

2528. BOIGEY, MAURICE. "Les détenus tatoués," **Archives d'anthropologie criminelle**, 25 (1910), 439-57.
On tattooing among convicts, a subject of great interest to criminologists at the turn of the century as a criminal (and homosexual) subcultural trait.

2529. BOURGEOIS, M., and A. CAMPAGNE, "Tatouage et psychiatrie," **Annales médico-psychologiques**, 129/2 (October 1971), 391-413.
Presents a historical overview of the relation between tattooing and psychopathological states, supplemented by clinical data. Claims that "latent or overt homosexual elements are easily identified."

2530. BROWN, GABRIELLE. **The New Celibacy: Why More Men and Women Are Abstaining from Sex--and Enjoying It.** New York: McGraw-Hill, 1980. 200 pp.
Popular work on the vogue of sex sabbaticals (not life-long abstinence) among the upwardly mobile.

2531. BURKE, TOM. "The New Homosexuality," **Esquire**, 73 (December 1969), 178, 304-18.
Article bringing to the attention of the mass audience the new salience of non-stereotypical ("masculine") homosexuals.

2532. CORY, DONALD WEBSTER (pseud. of Edward Sagarin). "Can Homosexuals Be Recognized?" **ONE Magazine**, 1:9 (1953), 7-11.
Although only about five to ten percent of homosexuals are recognizable to the general public through their effeminate or other mannerisms, the author claims that most homosexuals are recognizable to other homosexuals by means of more subtle signs (dress, hair style, tonal modulation in speech, gait, eye contact, etc.).

2533. DEVALL, WILLIAM. "Leisure and Lifestyles among Gay Men: An Exploratory Essay," **International Review of Modern Sociology**, 9 (1979), 166-86.
Postulates that the leisure activities of gay men, as for example tourist travel, may prefigure patterns of post-modern leisure in other segments of the population.

2534. EISLER, BENITA. **Class Act: America's Last Dirty Secret.** New York: Franklin Watts, 1983. 352 pp.
Chapter 9, "Coming Out and Moving Up" (pp. 197-225), presents observations (otherwise rare in the recent spate of popular books on class) on upward mobility among gay men and downward mobility among lesbians.

2535. ENGEL, PETER. "Androgynous Zones," **Harvard Magazine** (January-February 1983), 24-32.
Spots a trend in 1980s fashion and popular culture.

2536. FARREN, MIKE. **The Black Leather Jacket.** New
       York: Abbeville, 1985. 96 pp.
Fashion and lifestyle survey from World War II through the
'fifties and S & M to punk; 150 photographs.

2537. FISCHER, HAL. **Gay Semiotics: A Photographic Study
       of Visual Coding among Homosexual Men.** San
       Francisco: NFS Press, 1977. 56 pp.
Stimulating but brief study of handkerchief and other visual codes among gay men.

2538. FRINGS, MATTHIAS, and ELMAR KRAUSHAAR (eds.).
       **Männer-Liebe: Ein Handbuch fur Schwule und alle,
       die es werden wollen.** Reinbek bei Hamburg: Ro-
       wohlt, 1982. 382 pp.
Sometimes playful collage of words and pictures on facets
of gay-male culture in West Germany today (coming out,
bars and entertainment, social circles, the gay movement).

2539. HARRIS, MAZ. **Bikers: Birth of a Modern-day Out-
       law.** London: Faber, 1985. 128 pp.
Illustrated account of a lifestyle that has shown affinities with both macho homophobia and the gay leather
subculture.

2540. HUMPHREYS, LAUD. "New Styles in Homosexual Manli-
       ness," **Trans-action** (March-April 1979), 38-46,
       64-66.
Spotlighting trends towards virilization and subcultural
diversity, Humphreys discusses five major classes of
homosexuals--trade, ambisexuals, closet queens, gays,
and hustlers.

2541. MCDONALD, SHARON. "My Body or My Politics,"
       Advocate, no. 357 (December 9, 1982), 33-35.
Identifies a new openness among lesbians occasioned by
the popularity of punk styles and a willingness to discard restrictivist taboos--whether ordained by feminists
or by parents.

2542. MARSAULT R., RALF. "Pascal, t'as tout tatoué," **Gai
       pied**, no. 202 (11-17 January 1986), 52-55.
Interview with a tattooed French gay man, showing the
melding of attitudes with those of tattooed straight men.

2543. MARSHALL, JOHN. "The Macho Debate," **Gay News**
       (London), no. 242 (June 10-23 1982), 28-29.
Argues that macho images can be employed for a wide range
of reasons, "not all of which are personally or politically dubious." See also: Peter York, "Machomania," **Harpers and Queen** (February 1979), 58-61.

2544. PARRY, ALBERT. **Tattoo: Secrets of a Strange Art as
       Practiced among the Natives of the United States.**
       New York: Simon and Schuster, 1933. 171 pp.
Useful period document.

2545. RICHIE, DONALD, and IAN BURUMA. **The Japanese
       Tattoo.** Tokyo: Weatherhill, 1980. 116 pp.
Attempts a history of tattooing in Japan from early times
to the present, treating also iconography, sociosexual
significance, and traditional techniques. Numerous
photographs.

2546. THOMPSON, MARK. "To the Limits and Beyond: Folsom
       Street," **Advocate** no. 346 (July 8, 1982), 28-31,
       57.
If the clone uniform of the 1970s announced a kind of
adolescent camaraderie, it is the stoic and more highly
charged semiology of black leather, Thompson claims, that
will define many men's quest for maturity in the 1980s.

2547. VINING, DONALD. "Signs and Shibboleths," **Advocate**,
       no. 338 (March 18, 1982), 24-27.
Reminiscences of one man's acculturation to the gay semiotics of the 1940s and 50s (rings, silver identification
bracelets, jacket worn over the shoulder, etc.).

                    B. POPULAR CULTURE

The term popular culture lacks sharp definition. It may
apply to entertainments diffused by the mass media, especially radio and television, or simply to diversions
preferred by the masses--in contradistinction to high
culture. Some popular culture elements, such as astrology
are many centuries old. Apart from the efforts of a few
interested individuals, the prejudices of the educated
have hindered the investigation of popular culture. Lack
of study is especially evident for popular culture variants common among homosexuals, which require far more
study than they have hitherto received.

2548. AUSTEN, HOWARD, and BEVERLY PEPPER. **The Myra
       Breckinridge Cookbook.** Boston: Little, Brown,
       1970. 344 pp.
Typical of a number of campy cookbooks intended for the
gay-male reader. Includes recipes for "Flaming Faggot
Trout," "Cod Pieces," and "Cumin Covered Cook." See also
(e.g.): Rick Leed, **Dinner for Two: A Gay Sunshine Cookbook**
(San Francisco: Gay Sunshine Books, 1981).

2549. BRONSKI, MICHAEL. **Culture Clash: The Making of Gay
       Sensibility.** Boston: South End Press, 1984. 249
       pp.
Gay-male popular culture and its interaction with the
mainstream--including such topics as the gay movement,
Hollywood, publishing, and advertising--analyzed from a
moderate left point of view.

2550. CALIFIA, PAT. "The Sex Industry and Its Workers,"
       Advocate, no. 378 (October 13, 1983), 41-44.
Protests against reductivist critiques of the sex industry
as mere exploitation. Advocates deregulation and the
legalization of brothels.

2551. CARTNAL, ALAN. **California Crazy.** Boston: Houghton
       Mifflin, 1981. 204 pp.
New-journalist account of the intersecting worlds of rock,
pop, and film in Southern California.

2552. DAM, WIM VAN. **Astrology and Homosexuality.** York
       Beach, ME: Samuel Weiser, 1985. 93 pp.
First published in Dutch in 1983, this book draws on the
Hindu navamsa tradition, concluding that astrology does
not distinguish between male and female homosexuality.

2553. DYER, RICHARD. "In Defense of Disco," **Gay Left,**
       no. 8 (1979), 20-23.
Argues that disco is more than a form of music, it is a
sensibility.

2554. EMERSON, KEN. "The Village People: America's Male
       Ideal?" **Rolling Stone,** no. 275 (October 5, 1978),
       26-27.
On the (brief) mainstream success of a musical group that
mimicked macho. See also: David Rensin, "Can't Stop the
Muse," **Playboy,** 27 (July 1982), 106-07.

2555. FRASER, BRAD. "Coming Out in the Comics," **Body
       Politic,** no. 105 (July-August 1984), 31-34.
Recalls gay subtexts detectable in the comic strips of his
youth.

2556. HEIMSOTH, KARL-GUENTHER. **Character-Konstellation:
       mit besonderer Berücksichtigung der Gleichge-
       schlechtlichkeit.** Munich: Barth Verlag, 1928. 200
       pp.
Astrological approach, apparently the first in modern
times, but in fact reviving an old, suppressed tradition
stemming from Teucer of Babylon, Ptolemy, Girolamo Car-
dano, and others.

2557. JAY, KARLA, and ALLEN YOUNG (eds.). **Lavender
       Culture.** New York: Jove (Harcourt Brace Jovano-
       vich), 1978. 491 pp.
Reprints a broad selection of 43 articles on gay culture
in the narrower sense (art, music, drama, and literature),
together with others on sociology and the state of the
movement.

2558. JAY, MICHAEL. **Gay Love Signs.** New York: Ballan-
       tine, 1980. 416 pp.
Popular astrology for homosexual men, modeled on Linda
Goodman's **Sun Signs.** See also Vivian E. Robson, **An
Astrology Guide to Your Sex Life** (New York: Arc Books,

1963), pp. 47-51; and John Savage, **The Gay Astrologer**
(Port Washington, NY: Ashley Books, 1982; 119 pp.).

2559. LEMAY, HELEN. "The Stars and Human Sexuality,"
        Isis, 71 (1980), 127-37.
Shows the origins and development in medieval Islam of a
hermetic tradition of astrological determination of
sexual orientation.

2560. PERKINS, K. B. "Gay Pornography and Sex Parapher-
        nalia Shops: An Ethnography of Expressive Work
        Settings," **Deviant Behavior**, 2 (1981), 305-12.
Makes a beginning on studying the sites of the commerce,
rather than just the goods that are sold, which have
been the main focus up to now.

2561. PETERSON, DAVID M., and PAULA DRESSEL. "Equal Time
        For Women: Social Notes on the Male Stripper,"
        Urban Life, no. 11 (1982), 185-208.
About the homosocial environment and sexual objectification of masculinity for performers, some of whom are gay.

2562. RIDDIOUGH, CHRISTINE. "Culture and Politics," in:
        **Working Papers on Gay/Lesbian Liberation and
        Socialism**. Chicago: New American Movement, 1979,
        pp. 12-28.
Gay culture includes such institutions as bars, centers,
and newspapers, as well as the language, humor and ideas
of gay people. Despite the charge of complicity with capitalism, this culture has a basically subversive nature.

2563. WERTHAM, FREDERIC. **The Seduction of the Innocent**.
        New York: Rinehart, 1954. 397 pp.
A typical pop-psychiatric diatribe of the period, con-
juring up all sorts of horrors in the comics, including
homosexuality as implicit in male bonding.

                        C. SPORTS

The stereotypical concept of the male homosexual as a mere
milktoast precluded any understanding of gays in sports--a
blindspot that has been erased by individual revelations
as well as the Gay Games which are held in San Francisco.
While lesbian participation was somewhat more visible, the
discussion of it was considered taboo--but this rule too
has been broken. What has not yet been investigated is
whether there are particular concentrations of gay men and
lesbians in particular sports and, if so, what dynamic may
lie behind this pattern of attraction.

2564. CASAS, SIMON, and PIERRE CARPENTIER. **Tous Toreros**.
        Paris: Denoel, 1985. 96 pp.
Casas, director of the arenas at Nimes and Valencia, holds

that homosexuality is constant, though in a latent form, in all aspects of bull-fighting, including the bond between the torero and the audience. With photographs by Roland Cros.

2565. COBHAN, LINN NI. "Lesbians in Physical Education and Sport," in: Margaret Cruikshank (ed.), **Lesbian Studies**. Old Westbury, NY: Feminist Press, 1982, pp. 179-86.
From observations in the physical education department of a large university, concludes that while there are many lesbians in sports and physical education, they seem to find their core identity more as athletes than as lesbians.

2566. DEFORD, FRANK. **Big Bill Tilden: The Triumphs and the Tragedy.** New York: Simon and Schuster, 1976. 286 pp.
Life of America's greatest tennis star (1893-1953), who was persecuted and humiliated for his homosexuality.

2567. DUNDES, ALAN. "Into the Endzone for a Touchdown: A Psychoanalytic Consideration of American Football," **Western Folklore,** 37 (1978), 75-88.
Quasi-Freudian speculations (perhaps not entirely serious) on homosexual ritual behavior in football, using mainly linguistic evidence.

2568. GARNER, BRIAN, and RICHARD W. SMITH. "Are There Really Any Gay Male Athletes? An Empirical Survey," **Journal of Sex Research,** 13 (1977), 22-34.
Questionnaires answered by male college athletes on three California university teams indicate that a substantial minority had engaged in gay activity.

2569. **Gay Athletic Games I: Summer 1982.** San Francisco: Gay Athletic Games, 1982. 64 pp.
Brochure produced to accompany this historic international event, originally to be called the Gay Olympic Games. See also: Paul Trefziger, "The Gay Olympic Games," **Advocate,** no. 348 (August 5, 1982), 18-19; and Stephen Kulieke and Pat Califia, "In the True 'Olympic' Tradition: The Gay Games," **Advocate,** no. 353 (October 14, 1982), 29-34.

2570. HICKS, BETTY. "Lesbian Athletes," **Christopher Street,** 4:3 (October-November 1979), 42-50.
A major portion of lesbian athletes' energies must be directed toward maintaining straight facades. See also Hicks: "The Billie Jean King Affair," ibid. (July 1981), 13-17.

2571. KING, BILLIE JEAN, and FRANK DEFORD. **Billie Jean.** New York: Viking, 1982. 128 pp.
A somewhat evasive account of the career and recent troubles of the tennis ace whose lesbianism was revealed by her ex-lover Marilyn Barnett's lawsuit. The revel-

ation received much attention in the mainstream media
during 1981.

2572. KOPAY, DAVID, and PERRY D. YOUNG. **The David Kopay
      Story: An Extraordinary Self-Revelation.** New
      York: Arbor House, 1977. 247 pp.
Kopay describes his Catholic childhood, his career as a
professional football player, his unsuccessful marriage,
his acceptance of his homosexuality, and the consequences
of his public coming out.

2573. LIEBER, JILL, and JERRY KIRSHENBAUM. "Stormy
      Weather at South Carolina," **Sports Illustrated,** 56
      (February 8, 1982), 30-37.
A former basketball coach is dragged out of the closet.

2574. LORGE, BARRY. "...Women's Tennis and the Feminine
      Mystique," **World Tennis** (January 1982), 43-48, 73.
Broader aspects of the role of women in tennis brought to
light by the attention bestowed on the Billie Jean King
revelations.

2575. MITZEL, JOHN. **Sports and the Macho Male.** Boston:
      Fag Rag Books, 1976. 31 pp.
Sharp attack on the cult of sports in contemporary America: "Competitive team athletics are used by macho
straight men to concentrate, stereotype, and enforce their
superficial heterosexuality."

2576. NAVRATILOVA, MARTINA, and GEORGE VECSEY. **Martina.**
      New York: Knopf, 1985.
The star speaks frankly about the emergence of her lesbian
feelings in Czechoslovakia and her recent partnerships.

2577. SMITH, MICHAEL J. "The Double Life of a Gay
      Dodger," **Inside Sports** (October 1982), 57-63.
Sympathetic account of a black California athlete, who
lived two lives for six years, one as a professional
ballplayer, the other as a homosexual.

2578. SUÁREZ-OROZCO, MARCELO. "A Study of Argentine
      Soccer: The Dynamics of Its Fans and Their Folk-
      lore," **Journal of Psychoanalytic Anthropology,** 5
      (1982), 7-28.
Suggests that the popularity of soccer among Argentine men
is owing to their need for a therapeutic outlet for taboo
thoughts and fears of homosexuality and emasculation.

2579. THOMPSON, MARK et al. "The Western Range,"
      Advocate, no. 315 (April 16, 1981), T11-14.
On gay cowboys and rodeos.

D. ETIQUETTE AND SELF-HELP

In keeping with the older stereotype of homosexual men as
aping feminine manners, they were thought to be particularly concerned with the cultivation of refinements of
etiquette--a notion that has been exploited by Quentin
Crisp, among others. Apart from this older notion of
special sensitivity, it has recently become clear that
differences in lifestyle may require alterations or
special inflections of social prescriptions. Moreover,
the dispensing of useful advice regarding behavior to
homosexuals cannot escape dealing with the consequences of
internalized self-contempt. The newer manuals therefore
deal not solely with interpersonal concerns, but with
the cultivation of a respectful self-image.

2580.   CLARK, DON. **Loving Someone Gay.** New York: New
        American Library, 1978. 274 pp.
California clinical psychologist seeks to show "how gays
can give support to one another, shed guilt, form meaningful relationships, gain self-respect, and grow stronger."
The book also "helps families, friends, and caring non-
gays to confront their own fears and prejudices." See
also his: **Living Gay** (Millbrae,CA: Celestial Arts,
1979; 192 pp.).

2581.   CRISP, QUENTIN. **How to Have a Lifestyle.** New
        York: Methuen, 1979. 178 pp.
A series of aphorisms and amusing anecdotes, rather than
strictly a guide. One of several short books by the
English eccentric extending material from his stage
presentations.

2582.   CURZON, DANIEL. **The Joyful Blue Book of Gracious
        Gay Etiquette.** San Francisco: D. Brown Books,
        1980. 115 pp.
Campy and serious reflections by the noted gay novelist.
See also: Kevin Michaels, **The Gay Book of Etiquette** (New
York: MLP Enterprises, 1982; 72 pp.).

2583.   D'ARCANGELO, ANGELO (pseud. of Joseph Busch). **The
        Homosexual Handbook.** New York: Ophelia Press,
        1968. 281 pp.
Offered as "a clearly written guide to homosexual pleasure
and practice, full of 'helpful hints,' advice and diagram-
matic explanation." An amusingly outrageous work now
redolent of the atmosphere of the incipient post-Stonewall era.

2584.   GITECK, LENNY. **Cruising to Win: A Guide for Gay
        Men.** San Francisco: Pnatera Press, 1982. 250 pp.
An **Advocate** editor's breezy guide to making out and
afterwards; a kind of hard sell of the "you deserve to
give yourself these pleasures" genre. Some will find the

mood of carefree enjoyment unsuited to the AIDS era.

2585. GOODSTEIN, DAVID. **Superliving: You Can Have the
       Life You Want!** Englewood Cliffs, NJ: Prentice-
       Hall, 1983. 202 pp.
Advice, esp. on financial independence, by the late tycoon
and **Advocate** owner, with biographical asides.

2586. LOOVIS, DAVID. **Gay Spirit: A Guide to Becoming a
       Sensuous Homosexual.** New York: Strawberry Hill/
       Grove Press, 1974. 171 pp.
Generally sensible advice about becoming more sensuous,
as well as dressing, cruising, sexual techniques, and
keeping a lover. Although the period flavor is there,
this book has held up surprisingly well.

2589. MARSAN, HUGO. **Un homme, un homme.** Paris: Autre-
       ment, 1983. 192 pp.
Readable, somewhat lightweight exposition of the middle-
of-the-road approach to gay life supported by the **Gai pied**
editorial group.

2590. MUCHMORE, WES, and WILLIAM HANSON. **Coming Out
       Right: A Handbook for the Gay Male.** Boston: Aly-
       son, 1982. 200 pp.
A basic and usable work for the truly inexperienced:
how to get up your courage to enter a gay bar, how to
converse, turn someone down tactfully, etc. See also the
sequel: **Coming Along Fine: Today's Gay Man and His World**
(Boston: Alyson, 1986; 149 pp.).

2591. SIEMS, MARTIN. **Coming Out: Hilfen zur homosexuel-
       len Emanzipation.** Reinbek bei Hamburg: Rowohlt,
       1980. 237 pp.
Advice by a homosexual therapist on self-acceptance,
recommending yoga exercises and encounter groups.

            E. SEXUAL TECHNIQUES: MALE

In late Victorian times, as it came to be recognized that
the mass of the population was woefully ignorant of sexual
techniques--including contraceptive methods--the first
cautious manuals began to appear. In the 1920s these
works became more explicit and more freely available, but
they did not address the needs of homosexuals. To do so
would have been regarded as patently pornographic, and in
fact the first attempts (not recorded here) were illustrated exploitation brochures sold, as often as not, under
the counter. There is now a considerable range of genuine
works in this field. Also included here are some studies
on the symbolism and physiology of the penis, of particular (though not exclusive) interest to gay men. For
medical problems that may be associated with male homosex-

ual behavior, see XXII.A-C.

2592. BARTON-JAY, DAVID. **The Enema as an Erotic Art and
        Its History.** Second ed. New York: The author,
        1984. 329 pp.
Illustrated omnium gatherum compiled by an enthusiast.

2593. BERKELEY, BUD, and JOE TIFFENBACH. **Foreskin: Its
        Past, Its Present & ... Its Future?** San Francisco:
        Bud Berkeley, 1983. 208 pp.
Illustrated survey, including personal testimonies, intended for those with an erotic or other preference for
the uncut. For a strong condemnation of the practice,
with many individual testimonies, see Rosemary Romberg,
Circumcision: The Painful Dilemma (South Hadley, MA:
Bergin and Garvey, 1985; 435 pp.).

2594. DEMARTINO, MANFRED F. **Human Autoerotic Practices.**
        New York: Human Sciences Press, 1979. 378 pp.
Reprints 21 papers on masturbation in both men and women,
by such writers as Alex Comfort, Havelock Ellis, Helen
Singer Kaplan, and Masters and Johnson, with concluding
comment by the editor. In contrast to earlier scares,
these papers are generally approving of the practice.
Bibliography, pp. 361-66. See also Robert E. L. Masters
(ed.), **Sexual Self-Stimulation** (Los Angeles: Sherbourne,
1967; 352 pp.); and Irving Sarnoff and Suzanne Sarnoff,
Masturbation and Adult Sexuality (New York: Evans, 1985;
336 pp.).

2595. FOURNIER, R. A. **The Intelligent Man's Guide to
        Handball (The Sexual Sport).** New York: The author,
        1983. 69 pp.
Advocacy pamphlet on anal penetration with the fist--now
recognized to be a very dangerous practice. See also
Angus MacKenzie, "Lust with a Very Proper Stranger," **Body
Politic,** no. 82 (April 1982), 50-51; and J. Morin, below.

2596. FREEDMAN, MARK, and HARVEY MAYES. **Loving Man: A
        Photographic Guide to Gay Male Lovemaking.** New
        York: Hark Publishing Co., 1976. 132 pp.
Clear and comprehensive account of positions and pleasures, illustrated with photographs by Edd Dundas.

2597. LEGMAN, GERSHON. **Oragenitalism.** New York: Julian
        Press, 1969. 320 pp.
Chapter 2, "Fellatio" (pp. 169-245), purports to incorporate a "practical treatise" translated from a French manuscript, as the author claims that his aversion to the
subject prevented direct treatment. As with all of Legman's work, there is some psychoanalytic overinterpreta-
tion.

2598. MORIN, JACK. **Anal Pleasure and Health: Guide for
        Men and Women.** Burlingame, CA: Down There Press,

1981. 241 pp.
A well-balanced manual which stresses both the development
of positive feelings (escaping from inherited taboos) and
safeguarding health. See also Jeremy Agnew, "Some Anatomical and Physiological Aspects of Anal Sexual Practices,"
JH, 12 (1986), 75-96.

2599. MORIN, JACK. **Men Loving Themselves: Images of Male
Self-sexuality.** Burlingame, CA: Down There Press,
1980. 104 pp.
Self-oriented sensuousness as a mark of healthy self-
acceptance.

2600. RABOCH, JAN. "Penis Size: An Important New Study,"
Sexology (June 1970), 16-18.
Summarizes the results of a study of more than 20,000
European males, finding that homosexuals exceed hetero-
sexuals by 10% in penis length and by 8% in breadth.

2601. RANCOUR-LEFERRIERE, DANIEL. "Some Semiotic Aspects
of the Human Penis," **VS: Quaderni di studi semio-
tici**, no. 24 (September-December 1979), 37-82.
Includes cross-cultural and visual material. The analysis
shows the impact of feminist discussions. See also his
book: **Signs of the Flesh: An Essay on the Evolution of
Hominid Sexuality** (Berlin: Mouton/de Gruyter, 1985; 460
pp.). On a more popular level, see: Mark Strage, **The
Durable Fig Leaf: A Historical, Cultural, Medical, Social,
Literary, and Iconographic Account of Man's Relations with
his Penis** (New York: Morrow, 1980); and Kit Schwartz, **The
Male Member** (New York: St. Martin's Press, 1985).

2602. SILVERSTEIN, CHARLES, and EDMUND WHITE. **The Joy of
Gay Sex: An Intimate Guide for Gay Men to the
Pleasures of a Gay Lifestyle.** New York: Crown,
1977. 239 pp.
Based on the model established by the popular Alex Comfort
books, this work offers a positive and detailed account,
illustrated with line drawings.

2603. WALKER, MITCHELL. **Men Loving Men: A Gay Sex Guide
and Consciousness Book.** San Francisco: Gay
Sunshine Press, 1981. 160 pp.
Intended to develop positive feelings, this book offers
historical and psychological asides, as well as the
essential "how to" information. Illustrated with photographs and drawings.

F. SEXUAL TECHNIQUES: FEMALE

Lesbian sexual behavior has been a source of some curiosity on the part of men and nonlesbian women--much more so
than gay-male behavior, which can apparently be conceptua-

lized by analogy with heterosexual copulation. With the
exception of the first two works (2604-05), the items
listed below are entirely written by lesbians and for
lesbians. Although perceptions of the use of dildos have
been much exaggerated, there does seem to be a certain
popularity of vibrators among lesbians and single women.

2604. BLANK, JOANI. **Good Vibrations: The Complete Guide
to Vibrators.** Burlingame, CA: Down There Press,
1983. 52 pp.
Guide to selection of vibrators and related appliances,
as well as the sexual enhancement they afford.

2605. BOSTON WOMEN'S HEALTH COLLECTIVE. **The New Our
Bodies Ourselves.** New York: Simon and Schuster,
1984. 647 pp.
In this encyclopedic work on women's bodies, health, and
social concerns, see esp. pp. 141-61.

2606. CALIFIA, PAT. **Sapphistry: The Book of Lesbian
Sexuality.** Weatherby Lake, MO: Naiad Press, 1980.
195 pp.
Frank and explicit textbook on lesbian sexual behavior,
with illustrations by Tee Corinne.

2607. CEDAR and NELLY (eds.). **A Woman's Touch: An
Anthology of Lesbian Eroticism and Sensuality for
Women Only.** Eugene, OR: Womanshare Books, 1979.
158 pp.
Covers a variety of experience, including S & M.

2608. LOULAN, JOANN. **Lesbian Sex.** San Francisco: Spinsters Ink, 1985. 309 pp.
Perhaps the most far-reaching book in this category. In
addition to the basic "how to" information, offers
affirmative discussion of such topics as sexual addiction, levels of desire, orgasmic problems, fantasies, aids
to improved communication, alcoholism and sobriety, aging,
and youth.

2609. NOMADIC SISTERS. **Loving Women.** Second ed. Son-
ora, CA: Nomadic Sisters, 1976. 55 pp.
A brief, evocative guide.

2610. SISLEY, EMILY, and BERTHA HARRIS. **The Joy of
Lesbian Sex.** New York: Simon and Schuster, 1977.
223 pp.
Ranges beyond sex to such topics as consciousness raising
and the upbringing of children. Sometimes speculative.

G. S & M

The association of sex and pain in the form of master-
slave domination has been found in many historical cultures (e.g.,ancient Rome and imperial China). However,
sadomasochism in the sense of consensual play activity
between two persons seems to have been known only in
Western countries for roughly the last two centuries. The
interpretation of the behavior remains controversial: some
hold that by dramatizing power relationships it has an
emancipatory effect, while others insist that it rein-
forces existing patterns of domination. The physiological mechanisms that lie behind sadomasochistic experiences are as yet imperfectly understood.

2611. BUHRICH, NEIL. "The Association of Erotic Piercing
       with Homosexuality, Sadomasochism, Bondage, Fetish-
       ism, and Tattoos," **Archives of Sexual Behavior,** 12
       (1983), 167-71.
Content analysis of the "dalliance columns" of a genital
piercing magazine (6 females and 154 males).

2612. CALIFIA, PAT. "Beyond Leather: Expanding the Realm
       of the Senses to Latex," **Advocate,** no. 395 (May 29,
       1984), 26-28, 52.
Fantasy affinities of rubber in relation to bondage.

2613. CALIFIA, PAT. "Unraveling the Sexual Fringe: A
       Secret Side of Lesbian Sexuality," **Advocate,** no.
       283 (December 27, 1979), 19-23.
Holds that in a S & M context the uniforms and roles and
dialogue become a parody of authority, a challenge to
it, and a recognition of its secret sexual nature. See
also her: "Feminism and Sadomasochism," **Heresies,** no. 12
(1981), 30-34.

2614. ELLIS, H. HAVELOCK. "Love and Pain," in his:
       Studies in the Psychology of Sex, vol. 3. Phila-
       delphia: F. A. Davis, 1920, pp. 66-188.
Perceiving a base in violent courtship among some animals,
the noted sex researcher presents cross-cultural data on
love bites, flagellation, genital appliances, and strangu-
lation.

2615. GIBSON, IAN. **The English Vice: Beating, Sex and
       Shame in Victorian England and After.** London:
       Duckworth, 1978. 364 pp.
A detailed and in some respects standard work, reticent
on homosexuality (but see sections on schools and the
Navy).

2616. GOSSELIN, CHRIS, and GLENN WILSON. **Sexual Varia-
       tions: Fetishism, Sadomasochism, Transvestism.** New
       York: Simon and Schuster, 1980. 191 pp.
Popular effort at a comparative approach.

2617. GREENE, GERALD, and CAROLINE GREENE. **S/M: The Last
       Taboo.** New York: Grove, 1974. 345 pp.

Popular account with relatively little direct treatment
of homosexuality.

2618. GRUMLEY, MICHAEL. **Hard Corps: Studies in Leather
       and Sadomasochism.** Photographs by Ed Gallucci.
       New York: E. P. Dutton, 1977. 88 pp.
Provocative photographs of both homosexual and heterosexual sadomasochists, accompanied by brief text.

2619. HALBERSTADT-FREUD, H. **Het sadomasochisme: Proust
       en Freud.** Amsterdam: Arbeiderpers, 1977. 370 pp.
Psychoanalytic approach using literary materials.

2620. KAMEL, G. W. LEVI. "Leathersex: Meaningful Aspects
       of Gay Sadomasochism," **Deviant Behavior,** 1 (1980),
       171-91.
Outlines a six-stage "career" model of S & M: disenchantment, depression, curiosity, attraction, drifting, and
limiting.

2621. LEE, JOHN A. "The Social Organization of Sexual
       Risk," **Alternative Lifestyles,** 2 (1979), 69-100.
Comprehensive examination of problems of entrusting one's
body to the control of others.

2622. LÉLY, GILBERT. **The Marquis de Sade: A Biography.**
       Translated by Alec Brown. New York: Grove, 1970.
       464 pp.
Includes reliable accounts of the bisexual French writer's
(1740-1814) own somewhat limited experiments in pain and
sex.

2623. LINDEN, ROBIN RUTH (ed.). **Against Sadomasochism: A
       Radical Feminist Analysis.** East Palo Alto, CA:
       Frog in the Well, 1982. 208 pp.
Various papers, some subjective responses, others seeking
to set forth an ideological rationale for opposition to S
& M.

2624. MAINS, GEOFF. **Urban Originals: A Celebration of
       Leather Sexuality.** San Francisco: Gay Sunshine
       Press, 1984. 187 pp.
Mingles advocacy, graphic scenes (San Francisco), and some
new speculations about biological release mechanisms.

2625. RUBIN, GAYLE. "The Leather Menace," **Body Politic,**
       no. 82 (April 1982), 33-35.
Cautions against restrictivist "good girl" feminism,
asserting that there is much to be learned from sexual
outlaws.

2626. SAMOIS COLLECTIVE. **Coming to Power: Writings and
       Graphics on Lesbian S/M.** Boston: Alyson, 1981.
       240 pp.
Collection of many short pieces, the longest being Pat
Califia's account of the creation of a lesbian S and M

community in the San Francisco Bay area, over strong
objections from "politically correct" feminists.

2627. SCHAD-SOMERS, SUZANNE P. **Sadomasochism.** New
      York: Human Sciences Press, 1982. 300 pp.
Holds that S and M is "an adaptive response to the sadism
of the parent." Psychoanalytically prescriptive point
of view.

2628. SCHRIM, JANICE. "S/M for Feminists," **Gay Community
      News,** 8:41 (May 9, 1981), 8-9, 13.
Holds that the anti-S & M campaign is at least in part an
attempt to keep the women's movement "respectable." Anti-S
& M feminists endanger the very existence of the women's
movement through their lack of regard for the principles
of civil liberties: they covertly cherish censorship.

2629. SCOVILLE, JOHN W. **Sexual Domination Today.** New
      York: Irvington Press, 1985. 243 pp.
Overview, from a social-science point of view, of S & M,
mainly gay male.

2630. SPENGLER, ANDREAS. "Manifest Sadomasochism of
      Males: Results of an Empirical Study," **Archives of
      Sexual Behavior,** 6 (1977), 441-56.
Comparative study based on responses from 245 West German
men, presenting conclusions with respect to the invisibility of the deviant behavior, seeking of partners, participation in the subculture, realization of desires, self--
acceptance, preferences for S & M roles and practices,
masturbation, and coming out. See also his book: **Sado-
masochisten und ihre Subkulturen.** (Frankfurt am Main: Campus Verlag, 1979).

2631. STEKEL, WILHELM. **Sadism and Sadomasochism: The
      Psychology of Hatred and Cruelty.** Translated by
      Louise Brink. New York: Livewright, 1955. 2 vols.
Popular presentation by one of Freud's more simplistic
followers, with many case histories in the venerable
Krafft-Ebing manner.

2632. TOWNSEND, LARRY. **The Leatherman's Handbook II.**
      New York: Modernismo Publications, 1983. 333 pp.
Like the original work (**The Leatherman's Handbook.** New
York: The Other Traveler, 1972; 319 pp.)--of which this is
both a sequel and a revision--this book offers information
and personal comment (generally sound), interspersed with
titillating vignettes of the various "scenes."

2633. WEINBERG, THOMAS S. "Sadism and Masochism: Socio-
      logical Perspectives," **Bulletin of the American
      Academy of Psychiatry and the Law,** 6 (1978),
      284-95.
Attempts to apply Irving Goffman's frame analysis to the
phenomenon. See also Weinberg and Gerhard Falk, "The
Social Organization of Sadism and Masochism," **Deviant**

Behavior, 1 (1980), 379-93.

2634.   WEINBERG, THOMAS S., and G. W. LEVI KAMEL (eds.).
        S and M: Studies in Sadomasochism. Buffalo: Pro-
        metheus Books, 1983.   211 pp.
Some early views (Krafft-Ebing, Havelock Ellis, etc.),
followed by recent work in a "social dramaturgy" vein.
Includes some heterosexual material, though the bulk of
the work is directly relevant.

A. ECONOMICS, BUSINESS, AND LABOR

Conditions in business firms, whether large or small, are
not as a rule conducive to "coming out" on the part of
gays and lesbians. The stereotypical images of the gay
hairdresser or lesbian truckdriver serve to mask the fact
that homosexuals are found in every profession. Although
data are lacking, it seems likely that homosexuals are
nonetheless more strongly represented in some job areas
than in others. A different phenomenon is the appearance
of businesses which are not sexually related, but which
cater to gays and lesbians (banks, legitimate bookstores,
guesthouses, etc.). These are listed in various director-
ies, including specialized telephone books. See also
"Travel," V.A-B, "Lifestyles," IX.A-B, and "Discrimination," XII.C.

2635. APRIL, WAYNE. "Business Boom of Gay Savings and
        Loan," **New York Native** (December 6, 1982), 24-25.
On a trend in banking in New York City and San Francisco.
See also George Heymont, "There's Nothing Queer about a $3
Bill: The Gay Business Community Flexes Its Muscle," **New
York Native** (March 1, 1982), 11-13.

2636. CARRIGAN, TIM, and JOHN LEE. "Male Homosexuals and
        the Capitalist Market," **Gay Changes** (Australia),
        2:4 (1979), 39-42.
Male homosexual subculture is now a multimillion-dollar
industry affecting not only the social lives of many
male homosexuals but also their politics.

2637. ESCOFFIER, JEFFREY. "Stigmas, Work Environment,
        and Economic Discrimination against Homosexuals,"
        Homosexual Counseling Journal, 2 (1975), 8-17.
Workplace problems occasioned by overt and covert discrimination.

2638. ESKOW, JOHN. "Mirage on the Mountain," **New Times**,
        10 (March 6, 1978), 44-46.
On a motel for homosexuals.

2639. FAIN, NATHAN, and BRANDON JUDELL. "The Gay Market:
        A Sign of Progress?" **Advocate**, no. 352 (October 14,
        1982), 37-42.
Assesses recent developments.

2640. FIELDS, STEVE. "Gay Business Groups Are Growing,"
        Advocate, no. 236 (March 8, 1978), 17-18.
The trend toward forming business associations.

2641. FLOWER, JOE. "Gays in Business: The Prejudice and
       the Power," **San Francisco Magazine,** 22:9 (Septem-
       ber 1980), 41-45.
The view from San Francisco, where matters are less rosy
than they might seem.

2642. "Fundraising for the Gay Community," **Advocate,**
       no. 346 (July 8, 1982), 21-23.
Excerpts from a report prepared and published by San
Francisco Gay Care. Of 55 nonprofit gay organizations
in San Francisco, the 1981 identifiable expenditure
easily exceeds $2,000,000. The organizations are much
stronger, have larger programs, better publicity and
more volunteer workers.

2643. HOLLEY, STEVE. "Gay and Lesbian Lifestyles Expo: A
       Different Kind of Trade Show," **Advocate,** no. 308
       (December 1980), 14-25, 30.
Expo (December 12-14, 1980) was organized to provide the
business community direct sales contact with the Los
Angeles gay population amid such attractions as live
entertainment, dancing, fashion shows, physical fitness
exhibitions, cooking and craft demonstrations, contests,
and prize drawings.

2644. "The Homosexual Economy," **Economist** (January 23,
       1982), 73-74.
On surveys of gay lifestyles by **Gay News** (UK) and **The
Advocate** (US). This periodical has published a number of
short articles on the gay and lesbian market.

2645. JACOBS, BRUCE A. "Homosexuals in Management,"
       Industry Week, 202 (July 23, 1979), 52-59.
A hidden phenomenon attracts attention in the mainstream
media.

2646. MCCAGHY, CHARLES H., and JAMES K. SKIPPER, JR.
       "Lesbian Behavior as an Adaptation to the Occupa-
       tion of Stripping," **Social Problems,** 17 (1969),
       262-70.
In stripping the adaptation appears to be related to the
following conditions: (a) isolation from affective
social relationships; (b) stunted relationships with
men; (c) an opportunity structure allowing for a wide
range of sexual behavior.

2647. MILLER, ALAN V. **Homosexuality and Employment: A
       Selected Bibliography.** Toronto: Ontario Ministry
       of Labour, 1978. 111 pp.
A wide-ranging list, unannotated.

2648. RUSSO, VITO. "When It Comes to Gay Money Gay Lib
       Takes Care of the Pennies; Will Big Business Take
       Care of the Pounds?" **Gay News,** no. 212 (April
       1981), 16-17.
An independent study has shown that gays control more than

19% of the spendable income in the United States. Yet gay
businesses seem unable to tap more than a small portion
of this.

2649. SCHNEIDER, BETH. "Peril and Promise: Lesbians'
       Workplace Participation," in: Trudy Darty and
       Sandee Potter (eds.), **Women-Identified Women.**
       Palo Alto, CA: Mayfield, 1984, pp. 211-30.
Analyzes a study of 228 lesbian workers with respect to
making friends; finding a partner; coming out; and being
harassed. See also her: "Consciousness about Sexual Harassment among Heterosexual and Lesbian Women Workers,"
Journal of Social Issues, 38 (December 1982), 75-97.

2650. SCHROEDEL, JEAN REITH. **Alone in the Crowd: Women
       in the Trades Tell Their Story.** Philadelphia: Tem-
       ple University Press, 1985.
Personal accounts of 25 women. They indicate that lesbians in nontraditional jobs can experience a degree of
isolation, alienation, and loneliness not felt by their
heterosexual co-workers.

2651. SIMONOT, PHILIPPE. **Le sexe et l'économie, ou la
       monnaie des sentiments.** Paris: Jean-Claude Lattes,
       1985. 249 pp.
Somewhat impressionistic exploration of the connections
between sex and economy--including the venerable idea
that sperm is a kind of capital.

2652. SKIDELSKY, ROBERT. **John Maynard Keynes: I. Hopes
       Betrayed, 1883-1920.** New York: Viking, 1986. 447
       pp.
In this first volume of the major biography of the most
influential economist of the 20th century, his early
homosexual affairs are frankly discussed. The author
avoids making simplistic connections between his sexuality
and his innovative theories. See also Charles H. Hession,
John Maynard Keynes: A Personal Biography (New York: Macmillan, 1984; 400 pp.).

2653. STABINER, KAREN. "Tapping the Homosexual Market,"
       New York Times Magazine (May 2, 1982), 34, 36, 74,
       78, 80-82, 84-85.
"For the first time, advertisers are vying for homosexuals' buying power, though they worry about offending
mainstream consumers. ... The homosexual community asks
if economic acceptance is true acceptance."

2654. WEINSTEIN, JESS. "Four Lies about Gay Male
       Fashion: Hit 'Em with Your Pocketbook, Stanley,"
       Village Voice (April 8-14, 1981), 70-74.
Illusions and realities of fashion marketing.

2655. WESTON, KATHLEEN M., and LISS B. ROFEL. "Sexuality,
       Class and Conflict in a Lesbian Workplace," **Signs,**
       9 (1984), 623-46.

Issues involved in a workers' strike at a lesbian auto-
repair shop that employed ten self-identified lesbians,
including the two owners. This study shows flaws in a
number of concepts: lesbian-feminist assumptions of solidarity, liberal analysis downplaying social-structure
strains, and the heterosexual bias of socialist and soci-
alist-feminist approaches.

2656. WHITAM, FREDERICK L., and MARY JO DIZON. "Occupa-
       tional Choice and Sexual Orientation," **Internation-
       al Review of Modern Sociology,** 9 (1979), 137-49.
Comparison of occupational choices of male homosexuals in
the United States and Brazil shows a strong interest in
entertainment in both societies. This congruence calls
into question prevailing notions of the shaping of occupational choice by labeling and description.

XI. EDUCATION

A. GENERAL

The once-dominant pattern of segregation of pupils by
gender, particularly in early adolescence, inevitably
produced a tendency to same-sex eroticization, which
perhaps reached its height in the English public school
tradition. In the--now typical--coeducational schools,
the emergence of sexual feelings during the school years
has stimulated interest in sex education, though such
programs remain controversial in some quarters, and the
attention accorded homosexual behavior within them is
slight. In the late 1960s gay student organizations
emerged on North American college campuses and have since
spread elsewhere, chiefly in the English-speaking world.
On the opinions of college students in general regarding
sexual behavior, see I.J.

2657. BLAINE, GRAHAM B., and CHARLES C. MCARTHUR.
       Emotional Problems of Students. Second ed. New
       York: Appleton-Century-Crofts, 1971. 388 pp.
Traditional approach; see Chapter 6, "Basic Character
Disorders and Homosexuality" (pp. 94-108).

2658. BLAIR, RALPH. **Student Personnel Services and
       Homosexuality: A National Review of Provisions and
       Opinions of Deans of Students, Directors of Coun-
       seling, and Homosexual College Students.** New York:
       National Task Force on Student Personnel Services
       and Homosexuality, 1972. 7 pp.
This brochure, incorporating material from Blair's dissertation (Ed.D., Pennsylvania State University, 1971),
is no. 2 of the Otherwise Monograph Series (edited by
Blair), which contains several items of educational
interest, as does the **Homosexual Counseling Journal,**
also edited by Blair.

2659. BRAATEN, LEIF JOHAN, and C. DOUGLAS DARLING.
       "Overt and Covert Homosexual Problems among Male
       College Students," **Genetic Psychology Monographs,**
       71:2 (1965), 269-310.
Presents some methodologically dubious procedures for
detecting homosexual students. Their "problems" are
assessed only in the perspective of departure from the
heterosexual norm.

2660. CHANDOS, JOHN. **Boys Together: English Public
       Schools, 1800-1864.** New Haven: Yale University
       Press, 1984. 412 pp.
Using journals, letters, and autobiographies of the time,

the author reconstructs life in the English elite boarding schools in the period before the reform of 1862-64. See Chapter 14, "A Dream Hovering" (pp. 284-319).

2661. CHANG, CHWEE LYE. "Adolescent Homosexual Behavior and the Health Educator," **Journal of School Health,** 50 (1980), 517-21.
Reflects perspectives of high school professionals and bureaucrats.

2662. CORBETT, SHERRY L., et al. "Tolerance as a Correlate of Experience with Stigma: The Case of the Homosexual," **JH,** 3 (1977), 3-13.
Findings suggest that although gay students expressed a significantly higher amount of tolerance for other unconventional groups, they appeared to have reservations in terms of total personal acceptance.

2663. CREW, LOUIE. "Before Emancipation: Gay Persons as Viewed by Chairpersons of English," in: Crew (ed.), **The Gay Academic.** Palm Springs, CA: ETC, 1978, 3-48.
Evaluation of a questionnaire mailed to 893 Chairpersons showed the persistence of much antihomosexual sentiment. See also: Crew and Karen Keener, "Homophobia in the Academy: A Report of the Committee on Gay/Lesbian Concerns," **College English,** 43 (1981), 77-84.

2664. CULLINAN, ROBERT G. "'Gay' Identity Emerges on Campus Amidst a Sea of Prejudice," **National Association of Student Personnel Administrators Journal,** 10 (1973), 344-77.
An early report reflecting the new visibility of gay groups on campus.

2665. DUBERMAN, MARTIN. **Black Mountain: An Exploration in Community.** New York: Dutton, 1972. 578 pp.
This detailed study of the history of Black Mountain College in North Carolina shows that, despite the school's image as a progressive, proto-counterculture institution, authorities there could be as homophobic as anywhere else, and were perhaps more than most.

2666. EIGUER, ALBERT. "Falstaff et le prince Henry ou l'homosexualité initiatique," **Etudes psychothérapeutiques,** 13 (1982), 281-89.
On the latent homosexual component in student-teacher and student-prince relationships.

2667. GATHORNE-HARDY, JONATHAN. **The Old School Tie: The Phenomenon of the English Public School.** New York: Viking, 1978. 480 pp.
Anecdotal, but serious study of the English elite schools from their Tudor beginnings to the present. See pp. 38, 45, 80-82, 159-80, 214-15, 301, 363-64, 406.

2668. GIBBS, ANNETTE. "Colleges and Gay Student Organ-
       izations: An Update," **NASPA Journal,** 22 (Summer
       1984), 38-41.
After fifteen sometimes turbulent years, they seem to be
here to stay.

2669. GREENBERG, JEROLD S. "A Study of Personality
       Change Associated with the Conduction of a High
       School Unit on Homosexuality," **Journal of School
       Health,** 45 (1975), 394-98.
Comparison of students who took a homosexuality unit with
a control group who did not suggests that the former had
become somewhat more accepting, though this was hard to
measure.

2670. HONEY, JOHN RAYMOND DE SYMONS. **Tom Brown's
       Universe: The Development of the English Public
       School in the Nineteenth Century.** New York:
       Quadrangle, 1977. 416 pp.
While this book offers a good picture of the setting in
which homosexuality developed in the schools in their
heyday, it does little to explore the underlying psychology; see pp. 24, 178-94, 201-02, 209, 378-81.

2671. KENDALL, ELAINE. **Peculiar Institutions: An In-
       formal History of the Seven Sisters Colleges.** New
       York: Putnam's, 1976. 272 pp.
In this account of the Northeast's elite women's colleges,
see Chapter 13, "Strong Characters."

2672. KIRKENDALL, LESTER ALLEN. **Sex Education as Human
       Relations.** New York: Inor, 1950. 351 pp.
This study by a pioneer in the promotion of more enlightened attitudes to sexuality in education contains a
number of references to homosexuality.

2673. KLESZCZ, ANNETTE, and HOLGER NEUHAUS. **Wie anti-
       homosexuell sind unsere Sexualkundebücher? Die
       Darstellung des Themas "Homosexualität" in Schrift-
       en zur Sexualerziehung 1969-1979.** Münster in
       Westfalen: Universität Münster Kopiedruck, 1980.
       122 pp.
Study of the treatment of homosexuality in German sex
education textbooks, showing transmission of negative
attitudes.

2674. KRIEGMAN, GEORGE. "Homosexuality and the Educa-
       tor," **Journal of School Health,** 39 (1969), 305-11.
Traditional approach: regards the educator's role as one
of prevention and cure.

2675. LEHMANN, J. LEE (ed.). **Gays on Campus.** Washing-
       ton, DC: National Students Association, 1975. 88
       pp.
Anthology reflecting the rapid growth of gay student
groups and sense of identity, with list of organizations

and gay-studies syllabi.

2676. LÉVY, J. M. **Maîtres et élèves: essai de psycho-
      pédagogie affective.** Paris: Vrin, 1935.
In this study of the bonds between teachers and students,
see "Facteurs érotiques" (pp. 156-69). See also: René
Félix Allendy and H. Lobstein, **Le problème sexuel à
l'école.** (Paris: Fernand Aubier, 1938; 253 pp.).

2677. MCDANIEL, JUDITH, et al. "We Were Fired: Lesbian
      Experiences in Academe," **Sinister Wisdom,** 20
      (Spring 1982), 30-43.
Accounts of a fate that was all too common among those
who came out in the heady days of gay/lesbian liberation.

2678. MANFORD, MORTY. "Gay Columbia: Yesterday and
      Today: A Study of Institutional Alienation," **Gai
      Saber,** 1:3/4 (Summer 1978), 263-67.
Reflections by a gay activist on student days (early
1970s) in the Ivy League, emphasizing institutional
insensitivity.

2679. MARTIN, ROBERT. "The Student Homophile League:
      Founder's Retrospect," **Gay Books Bulletin,** 9
      (1983), 30-33.
Recollections of the formation of the first gay student
group in the United States--at Columbia University
in New York in April 1967.

2680. MELIKIAN, LEVON H., and E. TERRY PROTHRO. "Sexual
      Behavior of University Students in the Arab Near
      East," **Journal of Abnormal and Social Psychology,**
      49 (1954), 59-64.
Study of 113 Beirut students showed that more Arab than
American students had positive histories of both homosex-
ual and heterosexual intercourse. See also Melikian,
"Social Change and Sexual Behavior of Arab University
Students," **Journal of Social Psychology,** 73 (1967),
169-75.

2681. MORIN, STEPHEN F. "Educational Programs as a Means
      of Changing Attitudes toward Gay People," **Homosex-
      ual Counseling Journal,** 1 (1974), 160-65.
Improved attitudes were found in a group of advanced
college students after exposure to gay speakers.

2682. NAVA, MICA. "Everybody's Views Were Just Broad-
      ened: A Girls' Project and Some Responses to
      Lesbianism," **Feminist Review,** 10 (Spring 1982),
      37-60.
Reports on a project with some thirty teenage girls.

2683. NEWTON, DAVID E. "Representations of Homosexuality
      in Health Science Textbooks," **JH,** 4 (1979), 247-54.
A careful analysis of strengths and weaknesses. See also
his: "A Note on the Treatment of Homosexuality in Sex

Education Classes in the Secondary Schools, **JH**, 8 (1982),
97-99.

2684. NEWTON, DAVID E., and STEPHEN J. RISCH. "Homosex-
uality and Education: A Review of the Issue," **High
School Journal**, 64 (1981), 191-202.
A clear account, refuting some false perceptions.

2685. NUEHRING, ELANE M., et al. "The Gay College Student: Perspectives for Mental Health Professionals," **Counseling Psychologist**, 4:4 (1974), 64-72.
Asserts that the "illness" model is not appropriate in
dealing with gay clients. Their primary problem is that
of any other minority: discrimination.

2686. SEGAL, JAY. **The Sex Lives of College Students.**
New York: Dell, 1984.
Popular presentation claiming to distill some 24,000
"sexual autobiographies."

2687. SERDAHELY, WILLIAM, and GEORGIA Z. ZIEMBA. "Changing Homophobic Attitudes through College Sexuality
Education," **JH**, 10 (1984), 109-16.
Results of a controlled experiment show some improvement
in attitudes.

2688. SHIVELY, MICHAEL, and JOHN P. DE CECCO. "Sexual
Orientation Survey of Students on the San Francisco
State University Campus," **JH**, 4 (1978), 29-39.
Analysis of questionnaires of 1039 students showed that
significantly more homosexual students majored in subjects
emphasizing "divergent" thinking.

2689. SNYDER, SUSAN UNTENER, and SOL GORDON. **Parents as
Sexuality Educators: An Annotated Print and
Audiovisual Bibliography for Professionals and
Parents (1970-1984).** Phoenix: Oryx Press, 1984.
212 pp.
Lists 2531 items, including periodicals, audiovisual
materials, reading lists and Spanish-language books.
See Subject Index: "Homosexuality" and "Lesbianism."

2690. THOMPSON, GEORGE H., and WILLIAM R. FISHBURN.
"Attitudes toward Homosexuality Among Graduate
Counseling Students," **Counselor Education and
Supervision**, 17 (1977), 121-30.
Finds that student counselors feel ill-prepared to deal
with homosexual clients.

2691. VICINUS, MARTHA. "Distance and Desire: English
Boarding-School Friendships," **Signs**, 9 (1984),
600-22.
Uses literary sources to try to reconstruct "raves"
(crushes) in boarding schools, ca. 1870-1930, when women
were being prepared to enter public life.

2692. VISSER, R. S. "De 16PF-scores van een groep
       homofiele studenten," **Nederlands Tijdschrift voor
       de Psychologie en haar Grensgebieden**, 26 (1971),
       159-68.
In this study of male university and high school students,
the homosexuals (n = 41) exceeded the controls in self-
confidence, fickleness, independence, impatience, indo-
lence, nonconformity, eccentricity, introversion, sensitivity, and emotionality.

2693. WEITZ, ROSE. "From the Closet to the Classroom:
       Homosexuality in Abnormal Psychology and Sociology
       of Deviance Textbooks," **Deviant Behavior**, 3
       (1982), 385-98.
In an analysis of 22 texts, the sociology books that discuss homosexuality tend to be more accurate. Psychology
texts published since 1974 are more accurate and sympathetic than the older ones.

2694. WYNEKEN, GUSTAV ADOLPH. **Eros.** Lauenberg: Saal,
       1921. 72 pp.
Programmatic statement by a controversial German educator
on the role of homerotic attraction in teaching. On
Wyneken see: Erich Ebermayer, **Gustav Wyneken: Chronik
einer grossen Freundschaft.** (Frankfurt am Main: Dipa-Ver-
lag, 1969; 146 pp.).

                           B. TEACHERS

The ancient Greeks held that homosexual feelings, far from
being a defect, could be an asset to a teacher in foster-
ing a special sensitivity to students' needs. However
this may be, modern associations of gay and lesbian
teachers have essentially the character of trade unions,
designed to protect the interests of members from discrimination. For legal aspects of employment, see XX.J.

2695. DRESSLER, JOSHUA. "Gay Teachers: A Disesteemed
       Minority in an Overly Esteemed Profession,"
       Rutgers/Camden Law Journal, 9 (1978), 399-345
A spirited defense. See also his: "Study of Law Student
Attitudes regarding the Rights of Gay People to Be
Teachers," **JH**, 4 (1979), 315-29.

2696. HECHINGER, GRACE, and FRED M. HECHINGER. "Should
       Homosexuals Be Allowed to Teach?" **McCall's** (March
       1978), 100, 160, 162-64.
"No rational obstacle should stand in the way of letting
homosexuals become and remain teachers, subject to those
controls and standards of behavior that the profession
applies to all teachers." See also Steven W. Hendryx,
"In Defense of the Homosexual Teacher," **Viewpoints in**

Teaching and Learning, 56 (Fall 1980), 74-84.

2697. KANTROWITZ, ARNIE. **Under the Rainbow: Growing Up
       Gay.** New York: William Morrow, 1977. 255 pp.
Autobiographical account of English professor at Staten
Island College (CUNY), stressing his gay activism. See
also his: "Teachers: The Human Cost of Coming Out,"
Advocate, no. 277 (October 4, 1979), 22-23.

2698. NATIONAL COUNCIL FOR CIVIL LIBERTIES. **Homosexuality
       and the Teaching Profession.** London: NCCL, 1975.
Presents the replies of forty-seven local education authorities canvased in England and Wales. Two-thirds
were classified as "unbigoted," though some hedged.

2699. ROBINSON, PAUL. "In the First Person--Dear
       Paul: An Exchange between Teacher and Student,"
       Salmagundi, no. 58/59 (1982), 25-41.
Subjective account of the mutual self-revelation of a
California university professor and his student.

2700. ROFES, ERIC. **Socrates, Plato and Guys Like
       Me: Confessions of a Gay Schoolteacher.** Boston:
       Alyson, 1985. 163 pp.
Candid account of the entry-level experiences of an
openly gay teacher in suburban Massachusetts, September
1976-June 1978.

2701. RUBIN, MARC. "Gay Teachers Association--New York
       City," **Gai Saber,** 1 (1977), 89-92.
Founder's account of the formation of the Gay Teachers
Association as a result of a struggle with the United
Federation of Teachers (1974).

2702. WARBURTON, JOHN. **Open and Positive.** London: Gay
       Teachers Group, 1978.
London teacher dismissed because he refused to sign a
document saying that he would not discuss homosexuality
with pupils.

2703. WARD, MICHAEL, and MARK FREEMAN. "Defending Gay
       Rights: The Campaign against the Briggs Amendment,"
       Radical America, 13:4 (1979), 11-26.
On the successful campaign in November 1978 against the
Briggs Amendment, which would have barred homosexual
teachers from employment.

2703A. WELLS, ANNA M. **Miss Marks and Miss Woolley.** Bos-
        ton: Houghton Mifflin, 1978. 268 pp.
Account of the life-long love of Mary Woolley, president
of Mount Holyoke College, and Jeanette Marks, a professor
there.

C. GAY AND LESBIAN STUDIES

In Germany the early homosexual-rights movement recognized
the need for primary research into the history and nature
of homosexual behavior and its situation in the larger
society (see I.B). For the most part this work, which
often produced impressive results, was conducted by private scholars, unsupported by academic appointments and
largely ignored by the tenants of professorial chairs.
In contrast to the institutional good fortune of women's
studies, efforts to establish gay studies in universities
have borne little fruit thus far (except in the Netherlands). Faute de mieux, it appears that the tradition of
the private scholar is destined to remain dominant.

2704. ALTMAN, DENNIS. "Gay Studies and the Quest for
      Academic Legitimacy," **Advocate**, no. 378 (October
      13, 1983), 32-34.
Contrasts the merits of separate courses on gay studies
vs. integrating the material into "mainstream" courses.

2705. BROGAN, JAMES E. "Teaching Gay Literature in San
      Francisco," in: Louie Crew (ed.), **The Gay Academ-
      ic.** Palm Springs, Ca; ETC, 1978, pp. 152-63.
Recounts personal experiences in teaching courses in gay,
lesbian, and bisexual literature at San Francisco State
College over a number of years. See also Brogan's
memoir: **Jack and Jim: A Personal Journal of the '70s.** (Bolinas, CA: Equanimity Press, 1982; 174 pp.).

2706. FOLLETT, RICHARD J. "Censors in Our Midst,"
      College English, 43 (1981), 690-93.
Informed comment on problems of teaching gay literature.
See also his: "Is It Dishonest of English Teachers to
Ignore the Homosexuality of Literary Figures Whose Works
They Teach?" **English Journal,** 71 (April 1982), 18-21.

2707. GAY ACADEMIC UNION. **The Universities and the Gay
      Experience: Proceedings of the Conference Sponsored
      by the Women and Men of the Gay Academic Union,
      November 23 and 24, 1973.** New York: Gay Academic
      Union, 1974. 105 pp.
Texts from some of the papers and addresses at the historic first GAU Conference, held at John Jay College
of Criminal Justice (CUNY), New York City. Although a
variety of points of view are represented, many contributions preserve a strong period flavor of the counterculture.

2708. GOMEZ, JOSÉ. **Demystifying Homosexuality: A
      Teaching Guide.** New York: Irvington, 1984. 175
      pp.
Compilation sponsored by the Human Rights Foundation,
affiliated with the National Gay Task Force. Includes

lesson plans and reading lists.

2709. GORDON, LENORE (ed). "Homophobia and Education,"
      Interracial Books for Children, 14:3/4 (1983). 40
      pp. (special issue)
Offers a variety of short articles, with recommended
readings.

2710. MOHR, RICHARD C. "Gay Studies in the Big Ten: A
      Survivor's Manual," **Teaching Philosophy**, 7:2
      (1984), 97-108.
Lively, revealing account of experiences in getting a
philosophy course off the ground at the University of
Illinois, Urbana.

2711. NORTON, RICTOR. "Homosexual Literary Tradition:
      Course Outline and Objectives," **College English**, 35
      (1974), 674-78.
Detailed outline broken up into course units, which occasioned some controversy. See critique by Thomas K. Gordon, ibid., 36 (1974), 503-04.

2712. **Radical Teacher**, no. 24 (Fall 1983). [Gay Studies
      issue.] Includes reflections by Dan Allen, Mar-
      garet Cruikshank, and others.

2713. SCHREIBER, RON. "Giving a Gay Course," **College
      English**, 36 (1974), 316-23.
Personal report by a poet and literary scholar.

2714. SMITH, BARBARA (ed.). "Sample Syllabi for Courses
      on Lesbianism," in: Margaret Cruikshank (ed.),
      Lesbian Studies. Old Westbury, NY: Feminist Press,
      1982, pp. 217-35.
Syllabi by nine scholars, which can be used as models for
courses. This volume contains much other relevant material, including personal experiences and a detailed
bibliography, pp. 239-73. Other syllabi, including gay-
male ones, appear in J. Lee Lehman (ed.), **Gays on Campus**
(Washington, DC: National Students Association, 1975),
pp. 59-66.

XII. POLITICS

A. GENERAL

Until recently societal sanctions have dictated that most
homosexuals live in a state of clandestinity and invisibility ("the closet"). The perceived need for concealment
has deprived them of the opportunity of intervening openly
in politics on their own behalf. A few courageous heterosexuals have spoken out for them. A different aspect
of politics is reflected by individual homosexuals in the
diplomatic corps and in espionage and kindred areas of the
intelligence community.

2715. ASPREY, ROBERT B. **The Panther's Feast.** New
        York: Putnam, 1959. 317 pp.
Lightly fictionalized biography of Alfred Redl, the
Austrian intelligence officer who was a double agent and
a homosexual in the years before World War I. For new
data on the Redl affair, see Georg Markus, **Der Fall Redl:
Mit unveröffentlichten Geheimdokumenten zur folgenschwer-
sten Spionage-Affaire des Jahrhundterts** (Vienna: Amalthea,
1984; 286 pp.).

2716. BAMFORD, JAMES. **The Puzzle Palace: A Report on
        America's Most Secret Agency.** Boston: Houghton
        Mifflin, 1982. 465 pp.
Account of the U.S. National Security Agency, including
queer-baiting episodes in 1960 and 1980.

2717. BAUMAN, ROBERT. **The Gentleman from Maryland: The
        Conscience of a Gay Conservative.** New York: Arbor
        House, 1986. 276 pp.
The ex-Republican congressman retraces his years in the
as a closet gay and a closet alcoholic, culminating in his
public exposure. More briefly, he recounts his frustrations in seeking help after his being "forced out" (rather
than coming out).

2718. BEBEL, AUGUST. "The Man Who Spoke Out: 80th
        Anniversary of a Landmark in Gay Rights," **Gay News**
        (London), no. 136 (February 1978), 18.
Translated excerpts--with commentary by John Lauritsen--of
a speech by the Social Democratic leader (1840-1913) in
the German Parliament, January 13, 1898. For the original
text, see: **JfsZ** 1 (1899), 272-80.

2719. BERNSTEIN, EDUARD. **Bernstein on Homosexuality: Ar-
        ticles from "Die neue Zeit," 1895 and 1898.** Trans-
        lated by Angela Clifford. Belfast: Athol Books,
        1977. 40 pp.

The German Social Democrat's (1850-1932) reflections on
the situation of homosexuals, occasioned by the trials of
Oscar Wilde.

2720. BOYLE, ANDREW. **The Fourth Man: The Definitive
Account of Kim Philby, Guy Burgess, and Donald
Maclean, and Who Recruted Them to Spy for Russia.**
New York: Dial Press, 1979. 504 pp.
Detailed account of a group of double agents, three of
whom were homosexual. The book explores the participa-
tion of art historian (Sir) Anthony Blunt. (Published
in Britain as: **The Climate of Treason: Five Who Spied
for Russia.**) See also: Bruce Page et al., **The Philby
Conspiracy** (New York; Ballantine Books, 1981; 295 pp.);
Andrew Sinclair, **The Red and the Blue: Intelligence,Trea-
son, and the Universities** (London: Weidenfeld and Nicolson, 1986; 175 pp.); and Douglas Sutherland, **The Great
Betrayal** (New York: Penguin, 1980; 174).

2721. BRANCH, TAYLOR. "Closets of Power," **Harpers**, 265
[no. 1589] (October 1982), 34-50.
Profile of Dan Bradley, former head of the Legal Services
Corporation in Washington, combining his personal story
with observations on homosexuals in politics.

2722. BUCKLEY, WILLIAM F., JR. **Right Reason.** New York:
Doubleday, 1985. 454 pp.
Selections of newspaper columns by the Tory writer and
publisher of the **National Review,** including some diatribes
against homosexuals.

2723. BUSH, LARRY. "The Anatomy of a Scandal: Who Created
It: For What Purpose?" **Advocate,** no. 353 (October
14, 1982), 21-25.
On the bizarre case of a Congressional page who first
claimed to have had sex with several Congressmen, and then
admitted that he had been lying.

2724. BUSH, LARRY. "Has the FBI Been in Your Closet? Investigation of Gay People Confirmed," **Advocate,**
no. 346 (July 8, 1982), 16-20.
Information about 1970s surveillance obtained through the
Freedom of Information Act. See also: Sasha Gregory-Lewis, "Secret Investigation of Gay People: A Gay Bugaboo or
a Reality?" **Advocate,** no. 199 (September 23, 1976), 6-9;
as well as ibid., no. 210 (February 23, 1977), 12-15; no.
211 (March 9, 1977), 13-16+; no. 215 (May 4, 1977), 7-9;
and no. 22 (August 24, 1977), 36-38.

2725. BUSH, LARRY. "Homosexuality and the New Right,"
Village Voice (April 20, 1982), 1, 16, 18.
Conservative leader Terry Dolan, rumored to be gay,
opposes verbal attacks and discrimination against homosexuals by his allies. See also Bush: "New Right Leader
Terry Dolan," **Advocate,** no. 340 (April 15, 1982), 15-17;
and "Naming Gay Names: Larry Bush on the Ethics of Dis-

closure," **Village Voice** (April 27, 1982), 22, 24-25.

2726. BUSH, LARRY, and RICHARD GOLDSTEIN. "Where Have
       All the Liberals Gone?" **Advocate,** no. 321 (July 9,
       1981), 17-19.
Warns against anti-gay coalition building by the New
Right. Liberals and moderates should be made to realize
that faggots are being used to fuel a fire that may en-
gulf them as well. (Reprint of an article, "The Anti-Gay
Backlash," published in **The Village Voice,** April 8-14,
1981).

2727. CARPENTER, TERESA. "From Heroism to Madness: The
       Odyssey of the Man Who Shot Al Lowenstein," **Village
       Voice** (May 13-19, 1981), 3, 20-24.
This Pulitzer Prize winning story hints that the assassin
of the former New York congressman had been entangled in
a homosexual affair with his victim. Subsequently, Lowenstein's closeted homosexual side has been much dis-
cussed--e.g.,in David Harris, **Dreams That Die Hard: Three
Men's Journey through the Sixties** (New York: St. Martin's,
1982; 341 pp; and Richard Cummings' controversial **The
Pied Piper: Allard K. Lowenstein and the Liberal Dream**
(New York: Grove Press, 1985).

2728. CHESTER, LEWIS, MAGNUS LINKLATER, and DAVID MAY.
       Jeremy Thorpe: A Secret Life. London: Fontana,
       1979. 384 pp.
Well-documented account of the scandalous 1979 London
trial of the former leader of the Liberal Party on
charges of conspiring to murder his former lover, Norman
Scott. See also: Peter Bessell, **Cover Up: The Jeremy
Thorpe Affair** (Oceanside, CA: Simons Books, 1981; 574
pp.); Peter Chippendale and David Leigh, **The Thorpe
Committal** (London: Arrow, 1980; 189 pp.); and Auberon
Waugh, **The Last Word: An Eyewitness Account of the Trial
of Jeremy Thorpe** (Boston: Little, Brown, 1980; 240 pp.).

2729. COLQUHOUN, MAUREEN. **A Woman in the House.** Lon-
       don: Scan Books, 1980.
Memoirs of an openly lesbian member (Labour Party) of the
British House of Parliament (1974-79).

2730. COOK, BLANCHE WIESEN. "Female Support Networks an
       Political Activism: Lillian Wald, Crystal Eastman,
       Emma Goldman," **Chrysalis,** no. 3 (1977), 43-61.
Explores the relationship between female homosociality and
political activism in the early decades of the present
century.

2731. **Does Support For Gay Rights Spell Political Sui-
       cide? A Close Look at Some Long-held Myths.** New
       ed. Washington: Gay Rights National Lobby/National
       Gay Task Force, 1980. 42 pp.
Documents successes of openly gay political figures, and
gay interventions in politics.

2732. ELSHTAIN, JEAN BETHKE. "Homosexual Politics: The
       Paradox of Gay Liberation," **Salmagundi**, no. 58/59
       (1982-83), 252-80.
Negative critique, sometimes thoughtful, but based on a
straw-man concept--a reconstruction of homosexual aims
that is not generally held.

2733. FRIEDMAN, NANCY. "Gay Power: From Closet to Voting
       Booth," **California Journal** (October 1975), 341-44.
Shows results of gay organizing in the nation's most
populous state.

2734. GALLOWAY, BRUCE (ed.). **Grass Roots: A Campaign
       Manual for Gay People.** London: Grass Roots Group/
       Campaign for Homosexual Equality, 1982.
Pamphlet on practical political work in Britain.

2735. GALLOWAY, BRUCE, and BERNARD GREAVES. **Out from
       the Closet: A Liberal Focus on Gay Rights.** Hebden
       Bridge, West Yorks: Association of Liberal Coun-
       cillors, 1983. 23 pp.
Covers discrimination against gay people, changing law and
public opinion, and "the Liberal commitment."

2736. GOLDSTEIN, RICHARD. "Sex on Parole: The Future of
       Gay Liberation," **Village Voice** (August 20-26,
       1980), 1, 20-23.
Asserting that most people are aware of a gap between what
the movement hopes to gain from civil rights and what they
want out of life, urges preservation of the Stonewall
spirit.

2737. GREGORY-LEWIS, SASHA. "Anti-gay Crusade," **Advo-
       cate**, no. 223 (September 7, 1977), 6-7.
Key article in a series by this writer exploring New Right
coalitions and networking.

2738. GREGORY-LEWIS, SASHA. "A Fresh Look at the GOP,"
       Advocate, no. 200 (October 7, 1976), 7-8, 10.
An early look at Republican potential, prior to the more
recent growth of gay Republican groups.

2739. HAMILL, PETE, and DENNIS HAMILL. "The Rise and
       Fall of Fred Richmond," **New York Magazine** (November
       22, 1982), 36-44.
Tragic history of New York's disgraced gay congressman.

2740. HUMM, ANDREW. "Personal Politics of Lesbian and Gay
       Liberation," **Social Policy**, 11 (Summer 1980),
       40-45.
Reflections of a New York City gay political leader.

2741. KENNEDY, HUBERT. "J. B. von Schweitzer, the Faggot
       Marx Loved to Hate," **Fag Rag**, no. 19 (Spring 1977),
       6-8.
A well-documented study of the now obscure German polit-

ician Jean-Baptiste von Schweitzer, who became the butt of a homophobic tirade on the part of Karl Marx.

2742. KNIGHTLEY, PHILIP, and COLIN SIMPSON. **The Secret Lives of Lawrence of Arabia.** New York: McGraw-Hill, 1969. 333 pp.
Makes use of new materials to explore the tormented life of the British archaeologist, military leader, and writer (1888-1935), whose political activities in the Middle East are obscurely linked to his sexuality. See also: Desmond Stewart, **T. E. Lawrence: A New Biography** (New York: Harper and Row, 1977; 352 pp.).

2743. LACHMAN, LINDA. "Electoral Politics: Interview with Elaine Noble," in: Ginny Vida (ed), **Our Right to Love.** Englewood Cliffs, NJ: Prentice-Hall, 1976, 128-32.
Outspoken views of the openly lesbian Massachusetts legislator. See also: Judith Nies, "Elaine Noble Not Just Another Legislator," **Ms. Magazine** (August 1975), 58-61, 79, 108.

2744. LAIT, JACK, and LEE MORTIMER. **Washington Confidential.** New York: Crown, 1951. 310 pp.
This expose, a characteristic example of prurient gossip during the McCarthy period, offers some description of the "homosexual underground" in the nation's capital.

2745. LANSDOWN, ANDREW. "Homosexuals on the Offensive," **Quadrant** (Australia), no. 154 (June 1980), 26-31.
Misgivings of a heterosexual regarding purported excesses of the gay movement in Australia.

2746. LASSWELL, HAROLD DWIGHT. **Psychopathology in Politics.** New ed. New York: Viking, 1960. 319 pp.
This political-science study (first edition, 1930) was one of the first to give attention to homosexuality; see pp. 99, 109-11, 123, 125-26, 178-79.

2747. LERNER, MAX. **The Unfinished Country: A Book of American Symbols.** New York: Simon and Schuster, 1959. 733 pp.
The then-liberal columnist reprints (pp. 311-19) newspaper articles on the McCarthyite persecution of homosexuals.

2748. MCCRACKEN, SAMUEL. "Are Homosexuals Gay?" **Commentary**, 67 (January 1979), 19-29.
An antihomosexual academic attempts to grapple with some recent serious books on the subject. Note also the many sharp responses, ibid. (April 1979), pp. 12-31.

2749. MILLIGAN, DON. **The Politics of Homosexuality.** London: Pluto Press, 1973. 19 pp.
An attempt to articulate a gay British perspective from the Gay Liberation Front days.

2750. MITZEL, JOHN. **The Boston Sex Scandal.** Boston: Glad Day, 1980. 149 pp.
Hard-hitting expose of a government campaign against boy lovers in Massachusetts, with broader implications.

2751. PORTLAND TOWN COUNCIL. **A Legislative Guide to Gay Rights.** Portland: Portland Town Council, 1977.
Comprehensive brochure prepared by the leading Oregon gay rights group, giving background and practical advice for effecting change, much of which remains valid.

2752. PRESSMAN, STEVEN. "The Gay Community Struggles to Fashion an Effective Lobby," **National Journal**, 16 (August 4, 1984), 1470-72.
Growing pains of gay political intervention.

2753. REAL, JERE. "Gay Rights and Conservative Politics. I. Minority Report: Mad about the Boys," **National Review** (March 17, 1978), 342-45.
Gay conservatives and how some Republicans are alienating them.

2754. REEVES, THOMAS C. **The Life and Times of Joe McCarthy.** New York: Stein and Day, 1982. 819 pp.
The Wisconsin Senator (1908-57) made homosexuality a secondary target in his anti-Communist witchhunt. This exhaustive biography also discusses the rumors, which apparently cannot be substantiated, that the Senator was himself a closeted homosexual.

2755. REID, B. L. **The Lives of Roger Casement.** New Haven: Yale University Press, 1976. 532 pp.
Full life of the Irish humanitarian and patriot (1864-1916), assessing his homosexuality in relation to the evidence of the diaries which the British used to discredit him. See also: Brian Inglis: **Roger Casement** (New York: Harcourt Brace, 1973; 448 pp.); and Roger Sawyer, **Casement: The Flawed Hero** (Boston: Routledge and Kegan Paul, 1984; 199 pp.).

2756. SEDGWICK, DEREK. "Out of Hiding: The Comradeship of Daniel Guerin," **Salmagundi**, no. 58-59 (1982-83), 197-220.
Explores the complexities of the life of a French bisexual political writer, showing how his gay experiences meshed (and did not mesh) with his radical politics.

2757. SHILTS, RANDY. **The Mayor of Castro Street: The Life and Times of Harvey Milk.** New York: St. Martin's Press, 1982. 388 pp.
Full account of the noted gay politician, from his childhood on Long Island, through his struggles and triumphs in San Francisco, and his murder by Dan White in 1978. See also: Warren Hickle, **Gayslayer!** (Virginia City, NV: Silver Dollar, 1985; 100 pp.).

2758. SNODGRASS, TOM (ed.). **For Men against Sexism.** New
       York: Times Change Press, 1977.
Collection of articles on sex, power, sexism, the male
movement, homosexuality and racism--generally enunciating
an utopian male-effeminist point of view.

2759. "Studds Comes Out," **Nation,** 237 (August 20-27,
       1983), 132.
One of a number of articles in the mainstream press mark-
ing the courage of Massachusetts Rep. Gerry E. Studds,
who frankly discussed his homosexuality on the floor of
the House of Representatives. (He was subsequently re-
elected in 1984.)

2760. VASSALL, JOHN. **Vassall: The Autobiography of a
       Spy.** London: Sidgwick and Jackson, 1975. 200 pp.
Account of a British spy, less well known than Burgess and
Maclean (see A. Boyle, above).

2761. VIDAL, GORE. "Neo-Con Homophobia: 'Some Jews' and
       'the' Gays," **Nation,** 233 (November 14, 1981), 489,
       509-17.
Controversial article attacking the homophobia of the
Commentary group of writers. See responses in ibid., 234
(1982), 2+.

2762. ZELIGS, MEYER A. **Friendship and Fratricide: An
       Analysis of Whittaker Chambers and Alger Hiss.** New
       York: Viking Press, 1967. 476 pp.
Zeligs' revelation of ex-Communist Chambers' homosexuality, though perhaps politically motivated, was subsequently confirmed through release of FBI records.

                        B. POLITICAL THEORY

Several of the pioneers of homosexual studies, including
Edward Carpenter and Kurt Hiller, were socialists of one
sort or another, while others, such as Hans Bluher and
Benedikt Friedlaender, advocated conservative theories
(see I.B). Owing in part to the conjunction of the rise
of gay liberation (1969ff.) with the counterculture, much
recent political theorizing has been influenced by New
Left and radical feminist ideas. As the utopian hopes of
the 1970s have faded and homosexuals and lesbians have
concomitantly become less alienated from existing society,
centrist opinions have become more prominent.

2763. BRADLEY, IAN. **The Strange Rebirth of Liberal
       Britain.** London: Chatto and Windus, 1985. 259 pp.
Extended political manifesto and prognosis, seeing homosexuals as playing a role in the revival of centrist politics in Britain.

2764. DAWSON, KIPP. **Gay Liberation.** New York: Path-
       finder, 1975. 127 pp.
Marxist perspective of the Socialist Workers Party
(Trotskyist).

2765. DYNES, WAYNE. "Homophobia--Liberal and Illiberal,"
       Gay Books Bulletin, no. 3 (1980), 2, 28.
Identifies a trend toward resistance to homosexual rights
among some mainstream liberals in the 1970s.

2766. ENGELS, FRIEDRICH. **The Origin of the Family,
       Private Property and the State; in the Light of the
       Researches of Lewis H. Morgan.** Translated by Alec
       West (revised). Introduction and notes by Eleanor
       Burke Leacock. New York: International Publish-
       ers, 1972. 285 pp.
In this work of speculative history, first published in
German in 1884 and recently fashionable in some circles,
Marx's collaborator denounces the "abominable practice
of sodomy" among the Greeks (p. 128). See also pp. 129,
140. See also **Marx-Engels Werke** (Berlin: Dietz, 1953ff.),
vol. 32, p. 122 (on Karl Boruttau) and pp. 324-25 (attacks
on K. H. Ulrichs and J. B. von Schweitzer).

2767. FERNBACH, DAVID. **The Spiral Path: A Gay Contribu-
       tion to Human Survival.** Boston: Alyson, 1981. 240
       pp.
Seeks to integrate perspectives of gay liberation, feminism, socialism, and ecology. Eccentric, stimulating, and
occasionally bizarre. See also his: "Toward a Marxist
Theory of Gay Oppression," **Socialist Revolution,** 6:2
(1976), 29-41.

2768. FOURIER, FRANÇOIS MARIE CHARLES. **Vers la liberté
       en amour.** Edited, with an introduction by Daniel
       Guérin. Paris: Gallimard, 1975. 256 pp.
Collection of texts advocating sexual liberty by the
French radical prophet (1772-1837). There are several
English-language selections from Fourier's work, but none
focuses closely on his visionary sexual ideas--including
same-sex relations.

2769. GAY LEFT COLLECTIVE (London). **Homosexuality: Power
       and Politics.** London: Allison and Busby, 1980.
       224 pp.
Seventeen essays reflecting the viewpoint of the review
Gay Left, from which some of them were reprinted.

2770. GIOVANNINI, FABIO. **Comunisti e diversi: il PCI e
       la questione omosessuale.** Bari: Dedalo, 1980. 206
       pp.
Traces the halting efforts, mainly in the 1970s, of the
Italian Communist Party to attain a better comprehension
of homosexuality. For an indication of further progress,
see Nichi Vendola, "L'omosessualità esce del ghetto,"
Democrazia e diritto (September-October 1984).

2771. GOODMAN, GERRE, et al. **No Turning Back: Lesbian
       and Gay Liberation for the '80s.** Philadelphia: New
       Society Publishers, 1983. 153 pp.
Attempting to bring up-to-date the New Left perspectives
of the 1970s, presents a five-stage program for moving
towards a liberated society, illustrating each stage with
examples from the gay and other struggles.

2772. GOTTLIEB, RHONDA. "The Political Economy of
       Sexuality," **Review of Radical Political Economy,** 16
       (Spring 1984), 143-65.
Presents heterosexual and homosexual relations in a
"manner analogous to Marx's labor theory of value."

2773. GOUGH, JAMIE, and MIKE MACNAIR. **Gay Liberation in
       the Eighties.** London: Pluto Press, 1985. 131 pp.
British primer attempting to refurbish gay Marxism; the
product seems more nostalgic than contemporary.

2774. GRAF, THORSTEN, and MIMI STEGLITZ. "Homosexuel-
       lenunterdrückung in der bürgerlichen Gesellschaft,"
       Probleme der Klassenkampf, no. 4 (1974), 17-50.
Marxist analysis of the oppression of homosexuals in
bourgeois society.

2775. GUÉRIN, DANIEL. **Proudon oui et non.** Paris: Gal-
       limard, 1978. 245 pp.
See pp. 195-230 on the repressed sexuality of the socialist thinker Pierre-Joseph Proudhon (1805-1865).

2776. GUÉRIN, DANIEL. **Homosexualité et révolution.**
       Saint-Denis: Les Cahiers du Vent du Ch'min, 1984.
       70 pp.
Somewhat schematic summary of his ideas (which partake
of both socialism and anarchism), with quotations from
earlier writings.

2777. KATZ, JONATHAN. "Gay Men, Lesbians and Socialism: A
       Bibliography of Some Relevant Books, Pamphlets,
       Essays, Peridicals, and News Items," **Gay Insur-
       gent,** no. 4-5 (Spring 1979), 51-56.
A knowledgeable and useful compilation.

2778. LENIN, VLADIMIR IL'ICH. **The Emancipation of Women.**
       New York: International Publishers, ca. 1969. 136
       pp.
The remarks recorded by Clara Zetkin in the fall of 1920
(pp. 97-132) show Lenin's (1870-1924) vehement opposition
to the bourgeois obsession with "decadence" and "perversion," which he saw as distracting the communist movement
from the urgent tasks of the revolution. See also the
fuller text in Clara Zetkin, **Reminiscences of Lenin** (New
York: International Publishers, 1934).

2779. LOS ANGELES RESEARCH GROUP. **Toward a Scientific
       Analysis of the Gay Question.** Cudahy, CA: Los

Angeles Research Group, 1975. 40 pp.
Left-sectarian position paper by a Marxist group seeking
to "refute the incorrect analyses that are dominant today
in the communist movement," especially the "anti-gay
line" which excludes homosexuals from Communist organizations oriented toward Moscow or Peking.

2780. MCCUBBIN, BOB. **The Gay Question: A Marxist
      Approach.** New York: World View, 1976. 83 pp.
A simplistic Marxist catechism of history from pre-
historic times to the present by a member of the Workers
World Party.

2781. MITCHELL, PAM (ed.). **Pink Triangles: Radical
      Perspectives on Gay Liberation.** Boston: Alyson,
      1980. 187 pp.
Fourteen essays generally from a New Left point of view on
political theory, culture, pornography, pedophilia, etc.

2782. MOVEMENT FOR A NEW SOCIETY, GAY THEORY WORK GROUP.
      **Gay Oppression and Liberation, or: Homophobia: Its
      Causes and Cure.** Philadelphia: Movement for a New
      Society, 1977. 134 pp.
Somewhat utopian sociopolitical critique from a New Left
and feminist perspective.

2783. RAICO, RALPH. **Gay Rights: A Libertarian Approach.**
      Washington, DC: McBride for President Committee,
      ca. 1976.
Well-reasoned pamphlet, presenting the extension of state
power as the principal obstacle to sexual liberation, and
comparing the Libertarian view with that of other parties.

2784. RAIMONDO, JUSTIN. **In Praise of Outlaws: Rebuilding
      Gay Liberation.** San Francisco: Students for a
      Libertarian Society, 1979. 47 pp.
Vigorous manifesto from a Libertarian-Anarchist point of
view; San Francisco emphasis.

2785. REICHE, REIMUT. **Sexuality and the Class Struggle.**
      New York: Praeger, 1971. 175 pp.
German Marxist discussion, with some material on homosexuality (see pp. 115-20).

2786. THORSTAD, DAVID (ed.). **Gay Liberation and Social-
      ism: Documents from the Discussion on Gay Libera-
      tion Inside the Socialist Workers Party (1970-
      1973.** New York: The author, 1976. 142 pp.
Preserves verbatim the often turgid debates within this
Trotskyist group. The material is supplemented by: Steve
Forgione and Kurt T. Hill (eds.), **No Apologies: The Unau-
thorized Publication of Internal Discussion Documents of
the Socialist Workers Party (SWP) concerning Lesbian/Gay
Male Liberation** [Part II: 1975-1979] (New York: Privately
printed, 1981; 149 pp.).

2787. YOUNG, ALLEN. "Silence on the American Left,"
      Advocate, no. 330 (November 12, 1981), 14-17.
Indicts straight left periodicals for their failure to
criticize or even discuss discrimination against gays in
Castro's Cuba, an inquiry that deserves to be broadened.
This article is an excerpt from the author's book, **Gays
Under the Cuban Revolution** (San Francisco: Grey Fox
Press, 1981).

C. DISCRIMINATION

Inasmuch as most homosexuals and lesbians remain "in the
closet," it has been hard to document discrimination
against them and to devise legal remedies. The popular
mind supports prejudice and discrimination by various
myths and canards, which are not unlike those that linger
regarding racial and ethnic minorities.

2788. BEER, CHRIS, et al. **Gay Workers: Trade Unions and
      the Law.** London: National Council for Civil
      Liberties, 1981.
Overview of employers' discrimination against gay and
lesbian workers, showing how the discrimination is rein-
forced by the power of the state.

2789. DE CECCO, JOHN P., and MARY C. FIGLIUOLO. "Method-
      ology for Studying Discrimination Based on Sexual
      Orientation and Social Sex-role Stereotypes," **JH**, 3
      (1978), 235-41.
Seeks to determine how departures in sexual orientation
and social sex-role serve as pretexts for the abridgment
of civil liberties. See also, Marcy R. Adelman, "Sexual
Orienatation and Violations of Civil Liberties," **JH**, 2
(1977), 327-30: John De Cecco, "Studying Violations of
Civil Liberties of Homosexual Men and Women," **JH**, 2
(1977), 315-22; Mary C. Figliuolo et al., "The Relationship of Departures in Social Sex-role to the Abridgment of
Civil Liberties," **JH**, 3 (1978), 249-55; Petra Liljestrand
et al., "The Relationship of Assumption and Knowledge of
the Homosexual Orientation to the Abridgment of Civil Liberties," **JH**, 3 (1978), 243-48; and Michael G. Shively
and Marny A. Hall, "Departures from Sex-Role Stereotypes
of Appearance and Violations of Civil Liberties," **JH**, 2
(1977), 331-35.

2790. GALLOWAY, BRUCE (ed.). **Prejudice and Pride: Dis-
      crimination against Gay People in Modern Britain.**
      Boston: Routledge and Kegan Paul, 1983. 246 pp.
Eleven well-prepared essays by Campaign for Homosexual
Equality members on discrimination against gay men and
lesbians at home, at school, at work, on the streets, and
in prison. Indicates the inadequacies of the 1967 law

reform, which meant that homosexuality was merely tolerated when hidden.

2791.   HODGES, ANDREW, and DAVID HUTTER. **With Downcast
        Gays--Aspects of Homosexual Oppression.** Toronto:
        Pink Triangle, 1974. 42 pp.
This deservedly widely read pamphlet analyzes some aspects
of the way in which homosexuals have internalized contempt
for their own kind stemming from the host society, thereby
collaborating in the perpetuation of their own oppression.

2792.   LEVINE, MARTIN P. "Employment Discrimination
        Against Gay Men," **International Journal of Modern
        Sociology.** 9 (1979), 150-62.
Reviews the literature on job discrimination, detailing
discriminatory practices and extent of discrimination.
See also Jeffrey Escoffier, "Stigmas, Work Environment,
and Economic Discrimination against Homosexuals," **Homosexual Counseling Journal,** 2 (1975), 8-17.

2793.   LEVINE, MARTIN P., and ROBIN LEONARD. "Discrimina-
        tion against Lesbians in the Work Force," **Signs,** 9
        (1984), 700-10.
Reviews the existing literature, and presents new evidence
from 203 lesbian women in a metropolitan area, serving to
confirm the fact that employment discrimination is a
serious problem.

2794.   THOMPSON, DENISE. **Discrimination and Homosexual-
        ity.** Sydney: New South Wales Anti-discrimination
        Board, 1982.
A major study of the problem in Australia.

                    D. GOVERNMENT DOCUMENTS

Because of the notion that homosexual behavior merits
social control, gay people have been the repeated object
of official investigation in English-speaking countries.
Some other items of this kind are listed in the appropriate subject categories, especially those pertaining to
law (see XX.A ff.).

2795.   CALIFORNIA. LEGISLATURE, ASSEMBLY. **Preliminary
        Report of the Subcommittee on Sex Crimes of the
        Assembly Interim Committee on Judicial System and
        Judicial Process.** Sacramento: Assembly, 1950. 269
        pp.
The first of three negative reports from this body; the
others appeared in 1951 and 1952. The enquiry did engender a more enlightend document prepared by the Department
of Mental Hygiene and the Langley Porter Clinic, headed by
Karl M. Bowman, **Final Report on California Sexual Devia-**

tion Research (Sacramento: Assembly, 1954; 164 pp.).

2796. CANADA. ROYAL COMMISSION ON THE CRIMINAL LAW
       RELATING TO CRIMINAL SEXUAL PSYCHOPATHS. **Report.**
       Ottawa: Queen's Printer, 1958. 130 pp.
Also known as the McRuer Commission Report. Needless to
say, it is unsympathetic to homosexuality.

2797. CHICAGO. VICE COMMISSION. **The Social Evil in
       Chicago: A Study of Existing Conditions by the
       Vice Commission of Chicago.** Chicago: Gunthorp-
       Warren, 1911. 399 pp.
In this characteristic document of the confluence of the
social-purity trend with muckraking reform, see pp. 295-98
for a brief, but revealing glimpse of the gay subculture
in Chicago.

2798. **Government versus Homosexuals.** New York: Arno
       Press, 1975.
A reprint collection of three government documents. Contains: (1) **Alleged Immoral Conditions at Newport** [Rhode
Island] **Training Station** (Washington, DC: U. S. Senate,
Committee on Naval Affairs, 1921)--a scandal involving
vice squad investigators who entrapped homosexuals; (2)
**Employment of Homosexuals and Other Sex Perverts in Gov-
ernment** (Washington, DC: U.S. Senate, Subcomittee on
Expenditures in the Executive Departments, 1950)--in
which the committee appointed in the wake of charges made
by Senator McCarthy determined that homosexuals are unfit
for federal employment because they are security risks,
criminals and social outcasts; and (3) **Homosexuality and
Citizenship in Florida: A Report** (Tallahassee; Florida
Legislative Investigation Committee, 1964)--a sometimes
laughable, but also deadly serious document, which con-
templated severe restrictions on the civil rights of
homosexuals.

2799. GREAT BRITAIN. HOME OFFICE. **Report of the Working
       Party on Vagrancy and Street Offenses.** London: Her
       Majesty's Stationery Office, 1976. 30 pp.
One of a number of official British reports (which properly belong under the category of law) following the Wolfenden Report of 1957 and the legal reform of 1967. See
pp. 22-23, 26.

2800. MYERS, VICTORIA. **A Sexual Preference Study.** Tul-
       sa, OK: City of Tulsa, 1976. 93 pp.
After a brief summary of the literature on homosexuality,
presents sumaries of resolutions, policies and ordinances
passed by national organizations and cities dealing with
discrimination based on sexual orientation, as well as the
results of surveys of attitudes among business people,
employers, landlords, and the general public in Tulsa.

2801. SULLIVAN, GERARD. "A Bibliographic Guide to Gov-
       ernment Hearings and Reports, Legislative Action,

and Speeches Made in the House and Senate of the
United States Congress on the Subject of Homosexuality," **JH**, 10 (1984), 135-89.
An invaluable, annotated guide to this material, which is
sometimes difficult to trace. Except for one entry--for
1921--all are from 1948 to 1983.

XIII. MILITARY

A. GENERAL

The citizen armies of ancient Greece were directly linked,
in many cases, with the institution of pederasty (see
III.C). In Europe, from the 18th century onwards, there
are documented cases of homosexual generals and military
officers. Wartime experiences seem to foster the emergence of homosexual patterns of behavior. On the other
hand, since the late 19th century there has been a
controversy over the fitness of homosexuals for military
service, which still continues in the United States armed
forces (see XX.M).

2802. ANDERSON, CHARLES. "On Certain Conscious and
        Unconscious Homosexual Responses to Warfare,"
        British Journal of Medical Psychology, 20 (1944),
        161-74.
Of 5000 patients admitted to a World War II neurosis
center, 4% were conscious homosexuals and another 4% were
"latent homosexuals." Anderson claims that combat experience can lead to the reactivation of homosexual sado-
masochistic trends.

2803. AUSTEN, ROGER. "But for Fate and Ban: Homosexual
        Villains and Victims in the Military," **College
        English,** 36 (1974), 352-59.
A literary critic examines judgments of homosexuality
implicit in the works of several modern writers dealing
with the officer-subordinate relationship.

2804. BERUBE, ALAN. "Coming Out under Fire," **Mother
        Jones,** 8:11 (February-March 1983), 23-29, 45.
Trials and triumphs of gay and lesbian servicemen in World
War II. This article is part of a larger study the author
is undertaking on the official decision, in the middle of
World War II, to identify homosexuals in the service and
discharge them--and the malign effects of the decision
in American society generally after the war. See also
his: "Lesbian and Gay GIs in World War II: Marching to a
Different Drummer," **Advocate,** no. 328 (October 15, 1981),
20-24.

2805. BERUBE, ALAN, and JOHN D'EMILIO. "The Military and
        Lesbians during the McCarthy Years," **Signs,** 9
        (1984), 759-75.
Includes transcripts of official documents and letters
pertaining to the policy of expelling lesbians from the
service.

2806. BLEY, WULF. "Spionage und anormale Veranlagung,"
       in: **Die Weltkriegsspionage.** Munich: Moser, 1931,
       pp. 378-83.
Espionage and "abnormality" in World War I.

2807. BOONE, JOEL T. "The Sexual Aspects of Military
       Personnel," **Journal of Social Hygiene,** 27:3 (1941),
       113-24.
Claims that homosexuality is regarded with loathing and
contempt by most men in the U. S. Navy, who report deviates so that they may be sent to naval psychiatric
institutions for treatment.

2808. BOTCHAREVA, MARIA LEONTIEVNA. **Yashka: My Life as
       Peasant, Officer and Exile.** New York: Stokes,
       1919. 340 pp.
In these reminiscences of a leader of "Kerensky's Amazons," recorded by Isaac Don Levine, see pp. 82, 106, 121.

2809. BRAUBACH, MAX. **Prince Eugen von Savoyen.** Vienna:
       Oldenbourg, 1963-65. 5 vols.
Standard life of the great homophile general and statesman
(1662-1736) in the service of the Habsburgs.

2810. BRICKENSTEIN, RUDOLF. "Homosexualität und Wehr-
       dienst," **Wehrmedizin,** 4:9-10 (1966), 193-97.
Argues that homosexuals are unsuited for military service. One of a series of articles by this author, re-
suming an argument that was much canvased in Wilhelmine
Germany.

2811. BULLINGA, MARCEL. **Het leger maakt een man van je.**
       Amsterdam: SUA, 1984. 192 pp.
Interviews with some 50 present and former Dutch servicemen about attitudes to gender and sex in the military.

2812. BÜRGER-PRINZ, HANS, et al. **Beurteilung der Wehr-
       diensttauglichkeit und Dienstfähigkeit Homosexuell-
       er.** Beuel: Sanitätsamt des Bundeswehr, 1966. 102
       pp. (Beiträge zur Wehrpsychiatrie, 2)
Papers discussing the fitness of homosexuals for military
service from several points of view on the eve of the 1969
West German decriminalization.

2813. CHAVIGNY, PAUL. "L'homosexualité dans l'armée,"
       Revue de l'hypnotisme, 23 (1908), 39-40.
Only violations of public decency, abuse of authority, or
forceful acts were punishable as homosexual offenses in
the French army. In regiments composed of natives of
the French colonies, homosexual activity was so widespread that it was virtually disregarded save in circumstances that would have merited criminal proceedings in
civilian life.

2814. CHILES, JOHN A. "Homosexuality in the United
       States Air Force," **Comprehensive Psychiatry,** 13

(1972), 529-32.
Brands current U.S. Air Force treatment of homosexuals as
needlessly punitive and confusing because regulations do
not provide clear answers as to what homosexuality is and
how to deal with it. Questions the assumption that all
homosexuals should be excluded from the service.

2815. DAUTHEVILLE, LOUIS. "Le cafard ou psychose des
       pays chauds," **Archives d'anthropologie criminelle,**
       26 (1911), 5-27.
See esp. pp. 13-14 for homosexuality, ostensibly induced
by climate, among French troops in North Africa. See
also: R. Jude, **Les dégénerés dans les bataillons d'Afrique**
(Vannes: Le Beau, 1907), 33-39.

2816. DRUSS, RICHARD G. "Cases of Suspected Homosexual-
       ity Seen at an Army Mental Hygiene Consultation
       Service," **Psychiatric Quarterly,** 41 (1967), 62-70.
Discusses anomalies in the Army's handling of homosexuals,
recommending that they be discharged, but with no punitive
measures.

2817. DUBERMAN, MARTIN. "Case of the Gay Sergeant," **New
       York Times Magazine** (November 9, 1975), 16-17, 58.
On the sensational affair of Air Force Sergeant Leonard
Matlovich, who refused to be discharged quietly. See also
Time, 105 (June 9, 1975), 18-19.

2818. "Frauen als Soldaten im Weltkrieg," **JfsZ,** 15
       (1915), 36-47, 95-97, 120-47; 16 (1916), 66-87; 17
       (1917), 37-47, 102-14, 170-81.
A series of contemporary reports on women soldiers on both
sides in World War I, ascribing their success to "masculine" qualities which Hirschfeld assimilated to lesbianism.

2819. FROMAGET, GEORGES. **Les mesures de protection a
       l'égard des pervers qui s'engagent dans l'armée.**
       Lyon: Bosc, 1935. 99 pp.
"Prophylactic" measures to be taken against perverts in
the French army of the interwar period.

2820. "Gay People and the Military: Advocate Special
       Report," **Advocate,** no. 167 (July 2, 1975), 19-29.
Articles by Arnie Kantrowitz and others, including one
on the Leonard Matlovich case.

2821. GIBSON, E. LAWRENCE. **Get Off My Ship: Ensign Berg
       v. the U. S. Navy.** New York: Avon, 1978. 385 pp.
Detailed account of the ordeal of Ensign Vernon E. Berg
III, who challenged the Navy's policy towards homosexual
personnel, written by Berg's lover.

2822. GILBERD, KATHLEEN, and JOSEPH SCHUMAN (eds.).
       Fighting Back: Lesbian and Gay Draft, Military, and

Veterans' Issues. Chicago: Midwest Committee for Military Counseling, 1985. 142 pp.
Manual for activist lawyers and counselors including analysis of pertinent regulations for the military, selective service, and Veteran's Administration, as well as step-by-step guidance for draft, military, and veterans' cases.

2823. GILBERT, ARTHUR N. "The 'Africaine' Courts Martial: A Study of Buggery in the Royal Navy," **JH,** 1 (1974), 111-22.
Reconstructs the investigation and trial that led the British Navy (1815-16) to hang four members of the ship's crew.

2824. GILBERT, ARTHUR N. "Buggery and the British Navy, 1700-1861," **Journal of Social History,** 10 (1977), 72-98.
Shows that sanctions against homosexual conduct--when detected--were quite severe in this period, esp. during the wars with revolutionary and then imperial France. In some instances it was possible, however, to escape by a type of plea bargaining. See also Gilbert, "Sexual Deviance and Disaster during the Napoleonic Wars," **Albion,** 9 (1977), 98-113.

2825. HARRY, JOSEPH. "Homosexual Men and Women Who Served Their Country," **JH,** 10 (1984), 117-25.
Reports interview data on 1456 respondents collected in 1969 and 1970.

2826. HIRSCHFELD, MAGNUS, and ANDREAS GASPAR. **Sittengeschichte des Weltkrieges.** Leipzig: Verlag für Sexualwissenschaft Schneider, 1930. 2 vols. (Sittengeschichte der jungsten Zeit, 2-3)
Lavishly produced compilation on sex life in World War I that naturally reflects Hirschfeld's concern with homosexuality. A 40 pp. supplementary fascicle appeared in 1931. An abridged English version, **Sexual History of the World War** (New York: Panurge) appeared in 1934, and was several times reissued.

2827. KERIEN, ANDRÉ. "L'homosexuel face au service militaire," **Arcadie,** no. 219 (March 1972), 109-15; 220 (April 1972), 194-98.
A French perspective reflecting the immediate post-De Gaulle years.

2828. KERRUEL, YVES. **Des pavois et des fers.** Paris: Julliard, 1971. 252 pp.
Account of French naval officer dismissed for homosexuality. See also his: **Le soldat nu** (Paris: Julliard, 1974; 224 pp.).

2829. LATTES, LEONE. **Gli omosessuali nell'esercito.** Rome: Voghera, 1917. 14 pp.

Homosexuals in the Italian military in World War I.

2830. LEEXOW, KARL FRANZ (pseud.). **Armee und Homosexual-
      itat: Schadet Homosexualität die militarische
      Tüchtigkeit der Rasse?** Leipzig: Max Spohr, 1909.
      112 pp.
Disputes the notion that homosexuality undermines military
fitness. See also: Benedict Friedlaender, "Schadet die
Freigabe des homosexuellen Verkehrs die kriegersiche
Tüchtigkeit der Rasse?" **JfsZ,** 7 (1905-06), 463-70, 614.

2831. LEVY, CHARLES J. **Spoils of War.** Boston: Houghton
      Mifflin, 1974. 172 pp.
For homophobia among the American troops in Vietnam, see
pp. 51-72. See also his: "ARVN as Faggots: Inverted Warfare in Vietnam," **TransAction,** 8 (October 1971), 18-27.

2832. LOESER, LEWIS H. "The Sexual Psychopath in the
      Military Service: A Study of 270 Cases," **American
      Journal of Psychiatry,** 102 (1945), 92-101.
Period document offering generalizations from 270 unrepresentative cases.

2833. MCCRARY, JEREL, and LEWIS GUTIEREZ. "The Homosex-
      ual Person in Military and in National Security
      Employment," **JH,** 5 (1979), 115-46.
A maze of regulations exists to promote government exclusionary policies, but their implementation can often be
successfully fought on a case-by-case basis.

2834. MURPHY, JOHN. "Cleaning Up Newport: The U.S.
      Navy's Persecution of Homosexuals after World War
      I," **Journal of American Culture,** 7 (1984), 57-64.
Reconstructs an official effort to eliminate homosexuals
from the Navy at Newport, RI, spearheaded by Franklin D.
Roosevelt. See also: George Chauncey, Jr., "Christian
Brotherhood or Sexual Perversion? Homosexual Identities
and the Construction of Sexual Boundaries in the World War
One Era," **Journal of Social History,** 19 (1985), 198-211.

2835. PFEIFFER, GEORG PHILIPP. **Männerheldentum und
      Kameradenliebe im Krieg.** Berlin: Brand/Der Eigene,
      1924. 24 pp.
Interprets letters and other documents of male comradeship in World War I.

2836. PORCH, DOUGLAS. **The Conquest of Morocco.** New
      York: Alfred A. Knopf, 1983. 335 pp.
Includes discussion of the homosexuality of Marshall
Louis Hubert Gonzalve Lyautey (1854-1934), who organized
the French conquest.

2837. RICHARDSON, FRANK M. **Mars without Venus: A Study
      of Some Homosexual Generals.** Edinburgh; William
      Blackwood, 1981. 188 pp.
From Prince Eugene to Lawrence of Arabia. Offers some

useful biographical information, but set in a naive psychiatric framework derived from Alfred Adler. Richardson
is also the author of **Napoleon: Bisexual Emperor** (New
York: Horizon Press, 1972; 255 pp.), a book which has met
a poor reception from Napoleon scholars.

2838. ROYLE, TREVOR. **Death before Dishonor: The True
      Story of Fighting Mac.** Edinburgh: Mainstream,
      1982. 176 pp.
Biography of British Major-General Sir Hector MacDonald,
who committed suicide in Paris in 1903 when faced with a
homosexual scandal. At the end, the book is marred by
some unlikely speculation.

2839. SCHWALM, GEORG. "Die Streichung des Grundtatbe-
      standes homosexueller Handlungen und ihre Aus-
      wirkung auf das Disziplinarrecht," **Neue Zeitschrift
      für Wehrrecht,** 12:3 (1970), 81-98.
Discusses effects of decriminalization on military discipline in the army of the German Federal Republic.

2840. SCHWELING, OTTO PETER. **Die deutsche Militarjustiz
      in der Zeit des Nazionalsozialismus.** Edited by
      Erich Schwinge. Marburg: N. G. Elwert, 1977. 396
      pp.
See pp. 286-90 for German military prosecutions for homosexuality under Articles 175 and 175a during the Nazi
era. As a residue of Hirschfeld's campaign for the constitutional etiology of homosexuality, the practice of
German military justice was less sweeping than the American one.

2841. SNYDER, WILLIAM P., and KENNETH L. NYBERG. "Gays
      and the Military: An Emerging Policy Issue,"
      Journal of Political and Military Sociology, 8
      (1980), 71-84.
In recent years the military, though still attempting
to exclude homosexuals, has mitigated its policies by
tending to give honorable discharges. The article considers the potential effects of possible further liberalization.

2842. SOCIETY FOR INDIVIDUAL RIGHTS. **The Armed Servies
      and Homosexuality.** San Francisco: SIR, 1968. 12
      pp.
One of a number of brochures published by homosexual
groups in a period when the Vietnam war was creating
ambivalence about the draft and military service.

2843. WARREN, CAROL A., and JOANN S. DE LORA. "Student
      Protest in the 1970s: The Gay Student Union and the
      Military," **Urban Life,** 7 (1978), 67-90.
Case study of the effectiveness of a protest against the
campus ROTC unit by the gay student organization of a
small Western university.

2844. WATKINS, JOHN. **The Respectful Memorial of John
      Watkins, Late a Major in the Fifth Regiment of
      Light Cavalry, Madras Establishment.** London: 1835.
      20 pp.
Account of a scandal provoked by a British army officer's
unsuccessful pursuit of an Indian subject.

2845. WEINBERG, MARTIN S., and COLIN J. WILLIAMS. **Homo-
      sexuals and the Military: A Study of Less Than
      Honorable Discharge.** New York: Harper and Row,
      1971. 221 pp.
Using an interview sample obtained through homosexual
organizations, evaluates the effect of official labeling. Undesirable discharges generate employment discrimination and psychological trauma sometimes leading to
suicide. Moreover, separation procedures violate basic
civil rights.

2846. WEISS, ISIDORE I. "Homosexuality with Special
      Reference to Military Prisoners," **Psychiatric
      Quarterly,** 20 (1946), 485-523.
Claims that in an armed forces rehabilitation center a
small number of homosexuals induce others to engage in
homosexual acts.

2847. WEST, LOUIS JOLYON, et al. "An Approach to the
      Problem of Homosexuality in Military Services,"
      American Journal of Psychiatry, 115 (1958),
      392-401.
Asserts that methods then in use failed to distinguish
the "true" from the "incidental" homosexual, thus losing
valuable personnel. Suggests that safeguards for accused
individuals are insufficient, and that punitive attitudes of the command should be modified.

2848. WILLIAMS, COLIN J., and MARTIN S. WEINBERG. "Being
      Discovered: A Study of Homosexuals in the Mil-
      itary," **Social Problems,** 18 (1970), 217-27.
The most common type of discovery entailed being turned
in by another person; the second, voluntary admission
with the hope of receiving a discharge; the last, being
caught engaging in homosexual relations. The study also
compares the backgrounds of individuals who received
honorable discharges with those of personnel receiving
dishonorable discharges.

XIV. SOCIOLOGY

A. SOCIAL THEORY

Inasmuch as homosexual behavior by definition involves the
interaction of two or more persons, it would seem to be a
prime case for social science investigation. Yet the
founders of modern sociology, both in Europe and in North
America, tended to ignore homosexuality, and it is only in
recent years that social theory has attempted to come to
grips with it. This new seriousness is linked to the fact
that an increasing number of trained scholars are openly
homosexual, and can combine experiential with theoretical
perspectives. Current bibliography may be monitored in
Social Sciences Index (1974-) and **Sociological Abstracts**
(1952-).

2849. ADAM, BARRY D. "Inferiorization and 'Self-Es-
      teem,'" **Sociometry**, 41 (1978), 47-53.
Critique of the social-psychological tendency to conflate
the consequences of discrimination with the internal
formation of self-images.

2850. ADAM, BARRY D. "Structural Foundations of the Gay
      World," **Comparative Studies of Society and History**,
      27 (1985), 658-71.
Following in part a Marxist-feminist approach, "puts forth
some structural linkages which set homosexuality within
the context of the larger histories of gender, family,
and production." Argues that Western industrial capitalism has given birth to the new configuration of the gay
world, i.e. modern homosexuality as we know it.

2851. ADAM, BARRY D. **The Survival of Domination: Inferi-
      orization and Everyday Life.** New York: Elsevier,
      1978. 179 pp.
Comparative study of the social psychology of oppression, presenting Jews, blacks, and gay people as salient
instances in our society. Using a neo-Marxist methodology, Adam examines the process whereby such groups are
inferiorized, the countertactics evolved to cope with
inferiorization, and how such responses coalesce with
structures of domination.

2852. ASHWORTH, A. E., and W. M. WALKER. "Social
      Structure and Homosexuality: A Theoretical Apprais-
      al," **British Journal of Sociology**, 23 (1972),
      146-58.
Emphasizes situations in which social structure restricts
accesss by members of one sex to the other, as in unisex
communities (boarding schools and prisons) and in certain

occupational and ethnic groups. In these circumstances
homosexuality may be functional.

2853. BACH, GERARD. **Homosexualités: Expression/repres-**
       sion. Paris: Le Sycomore, 1982. 120 pp.
Social-psychological study based on present-day conditions
in France, offering linguistic and historical background
as well as future vistas. On a factual plane, see Jean
Cavailhes, Pierre Dutrey, and Gérard Bach-Ignasse, **Rap-**
port gai: enquête sur les modes de vie homosexuels (Paris:
Persona, 1984; 275 pp.).

2854. BELL, ALAN P., and MARTIN S. WEINBERG. **Homosexual-**
       ities: A Study of Diversity among Men and Women.
       New York: Simon and Schuster, 1978. 505 pp.
Sets forth conclusions derived from in-depth interviews
of 979 San Francisco Bay area residents, conducted under
the auspices of the Kinsey Institute of Indiana University, mainly in 1969. Offers a five-fold typology of
homosexuals: close-coupled, open-coupled, functional,
dysfunctional, and asexual. This typology has been criticized as not strictly following from the data (as
claimed), and as serving to bolster the book's underlying message--its ideology, so to speak--that is to say,
the integrationist notion that in terms of sociosexual adjustment homosexuals are much like everyone else.
Compare M. S. Weinberg and C. J. Williams, below--to which
this book is to some extent a sequel.

2855. DANK, BARRY M. "The Social Construction and
       Destruction of the Homosexual," **Humanity and**
       Society, 4 (1980), 133-47.
Social science has often acted to transform persons into
objects and things. Through acceptance of the dehumanized
concept of a homosexual problem, social science allows
itself to be transformed into a means of social control.

2856. DANNECKER, MARTIN. **Theories of Homosexuality.**
       Translated by David Fernbach. London: Gay Men's
       Press, 1981. 123 pp.
Concise observations--sometimes shrewd, sometimes truis-
tic--on current sociological and psychiatric approaches.
See also his: "Towards a Theory of Homosexuality: Socio-
Historical Perspectives," JH, 9:4 (Summer 1984), 1-8.

2857. DANNECKER, MARTIN, and REIMUT REICHE. **Der gewöhn-**
       liche Homosexuelle: eine soziologische Untersuchung
       uber männliche Homosexuelle in der Bundesrepublik.
       Frankfurt am Main: Fischer, 1974. 430 pp.
Using questionnaires and interviews (summarized in
statistical tables), attempts a full-scale description of
the individual and social development of male homosexuals
in West Germany. Deals with coming out, friendship, sexuality, employment, the homosexual subculture, and psychological maladjustment. For an English summary of some
of the findings, see: Reimut Reiche and Martin Dannecker,

"Male Homosexuality in West Germany: A Sociological Investigation," **Journal of Sex Research,** 13 (1977), 35-53.

2858. DAVIES, CHRISTIE. "Sexual Taboos and Social
      Boundaries," **American Journal of Sociology,** 87
      (1982), 1032-63.
Argues that historically certain closely knit groups
(e.g.,Old Testament Israelites, Parsees, and modern
armies) have sought to maintain a strong sense of social
boundaries, using such deviations as homosexuality, bestiality, and transvestism as markers of exclusion from the
group. This approach was anticipated by Fritz Wittels,
"Collective Defense Mechanisms against Homosexuality,"
Psychoanalytic Review, 31 (1944), 19-33.

2859. DUYVES, MATTIAS. "Bij de meerderjarigheid van
      homostudies: Nederlandse sociologen over homosek-
      sualiteit 1965-1985," **Sociologische Gids,** 32
      (1985), 332-351.
Until the end of the 1970s Dutch sociological investigation of homosexuality was concerned with the interplay
of social discrimination and individual deviance. In
the 1980s departments of gay studies were established in
some Dutch universities (Amsterdam, Utrecht), while
research approaches came under the influence of the
"constructionist" trend.

2860. FITZGERALD, THOMAS K. "A Theoretical Typology of
      Homosexuality in the U. S.," **Corrective Psychiatry
      and Social Therapy,** 9 (1963), 28-35.
Classification of homosexual types according to the degree
that they have internalized the values of the environing
society.

2861. GAGNON, JOHN H. and WILLIAM SIMON. **Sexual Con-
      duct: The Social Sources of Human Sexuality.**
      Chicago: Aldine, 1973. 316 pp.
In keeping with symbolic interactionism, holds that sexual
behavior is learned through social scripts which vary
cross-culturally and historically. Sets forth a model of
psychosexual development, articulated into various phases
of the life cycle. See pp. 129-216, 235-59.

2862. GOFFMAN, ERVING. **Stigma: Notes on the Management
      of Spoiled Identity.** Englewood Cliffs, NJ: Pren-
      tice-Hall, 1963. 147 pp.
Not concerned primarily with homosexuality, this influential work deals in part with "passing" and the problems
that arise from the creation of the self under the constraints that require such a strategem.

2863. GUÉRIN, DANIEL. **Shakespeare et Gide en correction-
      nel: essais.** Paris: Scorpion, 1959. 127 pp.
A French anarcho-socialist thinker's observations on the
social and cultural determination of the situation of
homosexuals.

2864. HARRY, JOSEPH, and MAN SINGH DAS. **Homosexuality in**
       International Perspective. New Delhi: Vikas,
       1980. 134 pp.
Nine essays of high quality on such topics as occupational
choice, employment discrimination, leisure, religion,
public opinion, male prostitution, and schools. This
book is a reissue of a special number of **International**
Review of Modern Sociology, 9:2 (1979).

2865. HART, JOHN, and DIANE RICHARDSON. **The Theory and**
       Practice of Homosexuality. Boston: Routledge and
       Kegan Paul, 1981. 206 pp.
Collection of twelve papers written from a social construction viewpoint, stressing divergent processes of
socialization within present constraints of gender
identity. The writers tend to regard homosexuality as
something that is chosen and maintained, rather than
constitutionally or biologically given. They also emphasize everyday problems, which theory must confront.

2866. HAUSER, RICHARD. **The Homosexual Society.** London:
       The Bodley Head, 1962. 167 pp.
Discerns a number of types in the English homosexual community: the bisexual, the married man, the self-isolated
homosexual, the "fully sublimated" homosexual, prostitutes
(with five subtypes), "sugar daddies," prison "queers,"
pub and club types, pedophiles, psychopaths, voyeurs,
and transvestites.

2867. HOCQUENGHEM, GUY. **Homosexual Desire.** Translated
       by Dangoor Daniella. New York: Schocken, 1980.
       144 pp.
A somewhat opaque French New Left essay, which grounds the
social fear of homosexuality in the replication of the
Oedipal family under capitalist conditions and finds
the transgressive essence of the homosexual challenge in
anality.

2868. HOFFMAN, MARTIN. **The Gay World: Male Homosexuality**
       and the Social Construction of Evil. New York:
       Basic Books, 1968. 212 pp.
A pioneering ethnographic account of gay life in San
Francisco, written by a then-closeted gay psychiatrist
(1935-1981). Now somewhat dated and judgmental.

2869. HOOKER, EVELYN. "Male Homosexuals and Their
       'Worlds,'" in: Judd Marmor (ed.), **Sexual Inver-**
       sion: The Multiple Roots of Homosexuality. New
       York: Basic Books, 1965, 83-107.
Based on Los Angeles observations, describes homosexual
public meeting places; patterns of public encounter and
interaction; and communication and socialization.
Stresses the gay bar as a key institution. Dr. Hooker was
perhaps the first important American social scientist to
adopt the working hypothesis that homosexuals were not
per se neurotic or maladjusted, an idea one can see

emerging in her early paper, "A Preliminary Analysis of Group Behavior of Homosexuals," **Journal of Psychology,** 42 (1956), 217-25.

2870.   HUMPHREYS, LAUD. **Out of the Closets: The Sociology of Homosexual Liberation.** Englewood Cliffs, NJ: Prentice-Hall, 1972. 176 pp.
Attempts, perhaps prematurely, a typological placement of gay liberation as a social movement. Characterizes the reality of the oppression of homosexuals, which is conceived as having three facets: legal-physical, occupational, and ego-destructive. See also his: "Exodus and Identity: The Emerging Gay Culture," in: Martin Levine (ed.), **Gay Men: The Sociology of Male Homosexuality.** New York: Harper and Row, 1979, pp. 134-47.

2871.   KING, DAVE. "Condition, Orientation, Role or False Consciousness? Models of Homosexuality and Transsexualism," **Sociological Review,** 32 (1984), 38-56.
Posits four models, two regarding the deviant behavior as acceptable (orientation; role) and two as unacceptable (condition; false consciousness).

2872.   LAUTMANN, RÜDIGER (ed). **Seminar: Gesellschaft und Homosexualität.** Frankfurt am Main: Suhrkamp, 1977. 570 pp.
In this group endeavor, coordinated and largely written by Professor Lautmann, the chief emphasis is on the many facets of discrimination against homosexuals (law, medicine, church, media, etc.). There is also a major section on the response and resistance on the part of homosexuals themselves.

2873.   LEVINE, MARTIN P. "The Sociology of Male Homosexuality and Lesbianism: An Introductory Bibliography," **JH,** 5 (1980), 249-75.
An exemplary annotated bibliography, the items included being chosen for their impact in terms of being widely read, cited, or discussed. Contains about 140 entries, grouped into three general sections: theoretical perspectives, methodological assessments, and social world.

2874.   LEVINE, MARTIN P. (ed.). **Gay Men: The Sociology of Male Homosexuality.** New York: Harper and Row, 1979. 346 pp.
Organized around a minority-group framework, this collection of 21 papers (many of them reprints) describes many aspects of gay men's place in society. There are two main sections: Oppression (negative public opinion; legal sanctions; therapeutic abuse); and Social World (identity formation; lifestyles; gathering places; political movements).

2875.   LINDNER, ROBERT. **Must You Conform?** New York: Rinehart, 1956. 210 pp.

Psychoanalytic approach to the problem of conformity,
which was much discussed in the Eisenhower years. Perceives homosexuality as a response of nonconformity or
rebellion; since the conformance pressure in society
is becoming more intense, so is homosexuality.

2876. MARMOR, JUDD (ed.). **Homosexual Behavior: A Modern
       Reappraisal.** New York: Basic Books, 1980. 416 pp.
Collection of twenty-three essays, a few retained from the
Marmor-edited **Sexual Inversion: The Multiple Roots of
Homosexuality** (New York: Basic Books, 1965; 358 pp.). (A
comparison of what has been retained and what omitted
offers an interesting commentary on changing fashions in
social science.) While some of the essays, particularly
in the biological and general social science areas, are
useful surveys of current knowledge, others are trivial
and inadequate.

2877. MILESKI, MAUREEN, and DONALD J. BLACK. "The Social
       Organization of Homosexuality," **Urban Life and
       Culture,** 1 (1972), 187-202.
Employing participant-observation data, attempts to deal
with social mechanisms that facilitate homosexual behavior.

2878. MURRAY, STEPHEN. **Social Theory, Homosexual Real-
       ity.** New York: Scholarship Committee, Gay Academic
       Union, 1984. 83 pp. (Gai Saber Monographs, 3)
Concise but searching review of leading theories--Move-
ment, symbolic interactionist, functionalist, psychoan-
alytic--as they bear on sociology and anthropology. This
pithy and challenging monograph is an essential guide to
the strengths and weaknesses of the social theory of
same-sex behavior.

2879. PAUL, WILLIAM, et al (eds.). **Homosexuality: Soci-
       al, Psychological and Biological Issues.** Beverly
       Hills, CA: Sage, 1982. 416 pp.
A collective work, conceived under the sponsorship of the
Society for the Psychological Study of Social Issues, with
the aim of providing a fair, comprehensive, and positive
synthesis of the achievements of the social and biological sciences. Unfortunately, the individual essays--
which are often valuable in themselves--are not organized
into a coherent whole.

2880. PLUMMER, KENNETH. **Sexual Stigma: An Interactionist
       Account.** Boston: Routledge and Kegan Paul, 1975.
       258 pp.
Applying symbolic interactionism, Plummer concentrates on
such questions as stigma, career construction, subcultural development, and interactional problems--with
special emphasis on homosexuality. Although it ranks as
an important contribution, this book originated as a doctoral dissertation, and is not exempt from the **longueurs**
that afflict the species.

2881. PLUMMER, KENNETH (ed). **The Making of the Modern Homosexual.** Totowa, NJ: Barnes and Noble, 1981. 280 pp.
A collection of eight essays, some new and others reprinted, by English academics who are generally adherents of the social construction approach. Influenced by Michel Foucault, they hold that, although same-sex behavior may have existed throughout human history, the concept of the "homosexual" is a particularly modern idea which has structured recent patterns of experience. Culture, rather than nature, is the decisive shaping force.

2882. SAGHIR, MARCEL T., and ELI ROBBINS. **Male and Female Homosexuality: A Comprehensive Investigation.** Baltimore: Williams and Wilkens, 1973. 341 pp.
Interpreting interviews with 89 gay men and 57 lesbians in Chicago and San Francisco, seeks to determine developmental attributes, sexual behavior, romantic attachments, psychopathology, family background, and demographic characteristics.

2883. SCHOFIELD, MICHAEL GEORGE. **Sociological Aspects of Homosexuality: A Comparative Study of Three Types of Homosexuals.** Boston: Little, Brown, 1965. 244 pp.
In this British study, 150 male homosexuals were considered in three groups of 50: those in prison, those currently under treatment, and those who had never been in prison or under treatment. These were matched with several control groups. Concludes that male homosexuals differ from male heterosexuals mainly in the choice of sex object. See also his previous monograph, published under the name of "Gordon Westwood," **A Minority: A Report on the Life of the Male Homosexual in Great Britain** (London: Longmans, Green, 1960).

2884. WARREN, CAROL A. **Identity and Community in the Gay World.** New York: John Wiley, 1974. 191 pp.
Explores ways in which members of an upper-class gay community relate to each other and to the environing straight world. Discusses the gay concepts of space and time; rituals, interactions, and relationships; vocabulary, literature, and ideology; and secrecy, stigma, and existential identity.

2885. WEEKS, JEFFREY. **Sexuality and Its Discontents: Meanings, Myths and Modern Sexuality.** London: Routledge and Kegan Paul, 1985. 324 pp.
Oscillating between present concerns and 19th and 20th century foundations, Weeks attempts to unravel the web of historical, theoretical, and political forces that have produced the contemporary "crisis of sexual meanings and values." Includes discussion of the New Right, the pornography conflict, Freud, and the sexological tradition (which the author holds has ascribed an inflated impor-

tance to sexuality). See also his: "The Development of
Sexual Theory and Sexual Politics," in: Mike Brake (ed.),
**Human Sexual Relations: Towards a Redefinition of Sexual
Politics** (New York: Penguin, 1982), 293-309.

2886. WEINBERG, MARTIN S., and COLIN J. WILLIAMS. **Male
        Homosexuals: Their Problems and Adaptations.** New
        York: Oxford University Press, 1974. 316 pp.
Working under the auspices of the Kinsey Institute
(compare A. Bell and M. Weinberg, above), the authors
collected data on ca. 2400 homosexuals in the United
States, the Netherlands, and Denmark. The book attempts
a comparative ethnographic sketch of gay life in each of
the three countries, and provides data on passing, self-
esteem, social skills, social isolation, employment, and
problems of adjustment.

B. METHODOLOGICAL PROBLEMS

The clandestinity in which the majority of homosexuals
continue to exist poses problems of sampling, inasmuch as
a truly random sample is usually impossible to attain.
Despite every precaution, there remains the possibility
that data are skewed toward the more overt, easily
accessible types. This danger is particularly evident in
the so-called "convenience sample," whereby responses are
collected from self-selected volunteers. Conversely,
publication of some which have been obtained by surrep-
titious means may violate "closet rights."

2887. BEAUCHAMP, TOM L., et al (eds.). **Ethical Issues in
        Social Science Research.** Baltimore: Johns Hopkins
        University Press, 1982.
For the controversy centering on Laud Humphreys' monograph
Tearoom Trade, see pp. 11-16, 22, 24, 28, 32, 34, 35, 60,
61, 85, 105, 106, 108, 110, 118, 154, 168, 169, 211, 212,
241, 250, 251, 258, 259. See also: Myron Glazer, **The
Research Adventure: Promise and Problems of Field Work**
(New York: Random House, 1972), pp. 107-24.

2888. BELL, ALAN P. "Research in Homosexuality: Back to
        the Drawing Board," **Archives of Sexual Behavior, 4**
        (1975), 421-31.
Calls for more sophisticated methodology, permitting the
disclosure of the multifariousness of ways in which individuals are homosexual, and for awareness of the propensity of theoretical bias to cloud our comprehension of
the quality of real experience.

2889. BULLOUGH, VERN. "Challenges to Societal Attitudes
        toward Homosexuality in the Late Nineteenth and
        Early Twentieth Centuries," **Social Science**

Quarterly, 58 (June 1977), 29-44.
"Changes in attitudes of the scientists involved are dependent not only upon internal developments within a field but [upon] basic changes within society itself."

2890. BURDICK, J. ALAN, and STEWART D. YVETTE. "Differences between 'Show' and 'No Show' Volunteers in a Homosexual Population," **Journal of Social Psychology,** 92 (1974), 159-60.
Results indicate that homosexuals who voluntarily participate as research subjects may be more neurotic and extraverted than the total population of homosexuals.

2891. DE CECCO, JOHN, and MICHAEL G. SHIVELY. "From Sexual Identity to Sexual Relationships: A Contextual Shift," **JH,** 9:2-3 (1983-84), 1-26.
Pointing out various sorts of problems that have arisen in existing work, urges redirection of research on sexual identity so that the focus is on sexual relationships.

2892. KAYAL, PHILIP. "Homophobia in Sociology," **Gai Saber,** 1:2 (1977), 95-98.
The sociological profession lacks a humanistic and comprenhensible base from which to operate; if something cannot be quantified, it is not studied. In addition, present procedures tend to enshrine the parochial views of heterosexual males as eternal verities.

2893. KOERTGE, NORETTA. "The Fallacy of Misplaced Precision," **JH,** 10:3-4 (1984), 15-21.
Complaints about confusing and inappropriate terminology in research on homosexuality may be invalid, inasmuch as it has been established that other disciplines often make use of cluster concepts and fuzzy sets to grasp reality.

2894. KOWALSKI, STAN (pseud.). "A Problem in Greek Ethics and Methodology," **Sociologists' Gay Caucus Newsletter,** no. 22 (1980), 5-7.
Weighs bias in samples of one's sexual partners against increased confidence (validity) in behavior participation rather than relying on self-reports.

2895. LEZNOFF, MAURICE. "Interviewing Homosexuals," **American Journal of Sociology,** 62 (1956), 202-04.
Overt homosexuals try to draw the interviewer into inter-clique quarrels, while closeted ones are reluctant to participate. The researcher's unfamiliarity with gay argot may lead to misunderstandings.

2896. MACDONALD, A. P., JR. "Reactions to Issuues Concerning Sexual Orientations, Identities, Preferences, and Choices," **JH,** 10:3-4 (1984), 23-27.
Cautions against monothematic explanations, which focus on single causes to the exclusion of other contributory factors, and against rigid dichotomies.

2897. RICHARDSON, DIANE. "The Dilemma of Essentiality in
       Homosexual Theory," **JH**, 9:2-3 (1983-84), 79-90.
Homosexuality has been viewed as a general state of being,
as a state of desire, as a form of behavior, and as a
personal identification. These conflicting views reflect
difficulties with the essentialist approach, which should
be discarded.

2898. ROSS, MICHAEL W. "Retrospective Distortion in
       Homosexual Research," **Archives of Sexual Behavior**,
       9 (1980), 523-31.
Concludes that sex-role rigidity and attitudes toward
homosexuality may play an important part in differences
between a Swedish and an Australian group that completed
questionnaires.

2899. SAGARIN, EDWARD. "Ideology as a Factor in the
       Consideration of Deviance," **Journal of Sex Re-
       search**, 4:2 (1968), 84-94.
Contends that behavioral scientists have allowed their
own values to color their attitudes toward deviants; out
of sympathy for the plight of the deviant they have
attempted to picture him as normal and unable to change.

2900. SIMON, WILLIAM, and JOHN H. GAGNON. "Homosexual-
       ity: The Formulation of a Sociological Perspec-
       tive," **Journal of Health and Social Behavior**, 8:3
       (1967), 177-85.
Calls for abandonment of monothematic emphases on single
factors such as etiology in favor of a flexible approach
recognizing the variety of individual development within
the maturational process.

2901. SUPPE, FREDRICK. "In Defense of a Multidimensional
       Approach to Sexual Identity," **JH**, 10:3-4 (1984),
       7-14.
Argues that current conceptions need to be examined in the
context of the **Verstehen** controversies in the philosophy
of science. In this light, some current notions are revealed as unidimensional.

2902. TROIDEN, RICHARD R. "Self, Self-Concept, Identity,
       and Homosexual Identity: Constructs in Need of
       Definition and Differentiation," **JH**, 10:3-4
       (1984), 97-109.
Uses symbolic interactionist theory to clarify the terms
self, self-concept, identity, and **homosexual identity.**

2903. WARREN, CAROL A. "Fieldwork in the Gay World:
       Issues in Phenomenological Research," **Journal of
       Social Issues**, 33:4 (1977), 93-107.
Field research in the gay world is shaped by two factors:
the secrecy of many gay groups and the stigmatization both
of gays and of researchers who study them. While entry
into public gay settings is often easy, entry into more
private arenas depends upon the establishment of interper-

sonal relationships. See also her: "Observing the Gay
Community," in: Jack D. Douglas (ed.), **Research on De-
viance** (New York: Random House, 1972), 139-63; and Carol
A. Warren and Paul K. Rasmussen, "Sex and Gender in Field
Research," **Urban Life,** 6 (1977), 349-69.

2904. WEINBERG, MARTIN A. "Homosexual Samples: Differ-
      ences and Similarities," **Journal of Sex Research,** 6
      (1970), 312-25.
While the clandestinity of much homosexual life precludes
representative sampling, the researcher can approach this
desideratum by pooling samples derived from gay bars,
homosexual clubs, and mail organizations, each involving a
different type of subject.

2905. WESTWOOD, GORDON (pseud. of Michael Schofield).
      "Problems of Research into Sexual Deviations," **Man
      and Society,** 1 (1961), 29-32.
Discusses bureaucratic obstacles, problematic cooperation
with other individuals and agencies, sampling, questionnaire construction, level of information elicited, interviewer bias, and interpretation of the data.

                          C. AGING

The emergence of gerontology as a serious body of knowledge is rather recent. In the case of gay men and lesbians it has disclosed one important counterintuitive
finding: homosexual individuals do not become more unhappy
as they grow older, but in many instances adjust well to
the aging process. Social work intervention has also
developed in this sphere, though only in an incipient
stage.

2906. ALMVIG, CHRIS. **The Invisible Minority: Aging and
      Lesbianism.** Utica, NY: Syracuse University Press,
      n. d. (ca. 1983). 198 pp.
After a review of the literature, presents results of
questionnaire administered in 1977 and 1978 to 74 lesbians
over 50. Almost half had been married at one time, little
religious belief was held, most had adequate income, and
few reported serious psychological problems.

2907. BARACKS, BARBARA, and KENT JARRATT (eds.). New
      York: Teachers and Writers Collaborative, 1980.
      115 pp.
Anthology of journals, poetry, fiction, and other literature by four women and four men, produced in the writing
workshop of Senior Action in a Gay Environment (SAGE).

2908. BAUDRY, ANDRE. "Le vieillard homophile," **Arcadie,**
      no. 141 (September 1965), 367-72.

Observations on homosexual aging by the founder of the
Arcadie group.

2909. BENNETT, KEITH C., and NORMAN L. THOMPSON. "Social
       and Psychological Functioning of the Ageing Male
       Homosexual," **British Journal of Psychiatry**, 137
       (1980), 361-70.
Findings from 478 Australian male homosexuals do not
support the stereotype of the older male homosexual
(i.e., disengagement from the homosexual world, loneliness, rejection, depression, and unhappiness).

2910. BERGER, RAYMOND M. **Gay and Gray: The Older Homosex-
       ual Man.** Urbana: University of Illinois Press,
       1982. 233 pp.
Interpretive sociological study, followed by in-depth
profiles of six men. Concludes that the stereotypes of
the life of the older gay man as lonely and hopeless are
wide of the mark. See also his: "Psychological Adaptation of the Older Homosexual Male," **JH**, 5 (1980), 161-75;
"Realities of Gay and Lesbian Aging," **Social Work**, 29
(1984), 57-62; and "The Unseen Minority: Older Gays and
Lesbians," **Social Work**, 27 (1982), 236-42.

2911. BRECHER, EDWARD M., et al. **Love, Sex and Aging.**
       By Edward M. Brecher and the Editors of **Consumer
       Reports.** Boston: Little, Brown, 1984. 384 pp.
Reports findings of a 1978-79 study, conducted with 4,246
volunteer respondents, aged 50 to 93.

2912. CALLEJA, M. A. "Homosexual Behavior in Older Men,"
       Sexology, 34 (1967), 46-48.
Personal interviews with 1,737 older men, mostly in Spain,
show that homosexuality is more common among them than is
usually supposed. For some, homosexual activity began
only after 60 years of age.

2913. CATALANO, DONALD, SHARON RAPHAEL, and MINA K. ROB-
       INSON. **Bibliography: Lesbian and Gay Aging.** San
       Francisco: National Association of Lesbian and Gay
       Gerontologists, [1982]. 10 pp.
Mimeographed list recording books (including a few novels), articles, theses, and papers.

2914. FRANCHER, J. SCOTT, and JANET HENKIN. "The Meno-
       pausal Queen: Adjustment to Aging and the Male
       Homosexual," **American Journal of Orthopsychiatry**,
       43 (1973), 670-74.
Extensive interviews with ten over-50 male homosexuals,
suggest that they commonly experience a "life crisis"
early in their development and are therefore less affected
by the trauma of role loss that occurs for most men in
later life.

2915. FRIEND, RICHARD A. "GAYging: Adjustment and the
       Older Gay Male," **Alternative Lifestyles,** 3

(1980), 231-48.
Reports on interviews with 43 self-identified older gay
men in relation to coming out, support systems, and sex-
role flexibility.

2916. GWENWALD, MORGAN. "The SAGE Model for Serving Older
        Lesbians and Gay Men," **Journal of Social Work and
        Human Sexuality**, 2:2-3 (1983-84), 53-61.
Gives the history and character of New York's Senior Action in a Gay Environment (SAGE), which was founded in
1977. A small number of paid staff work with a large
group of volunteers to provide a monthly social event,
publicity and outreach programs, discussion and writing
groups, financial planning, and intake and matching of
new volunteers.

2917. HADER, MARVIN. "Homosexuality as Part of Our Aging
        Process," **Psychiatric Quarterly**, 40 (1966), 515-24.
Interviews with 23 Jewish males, 73 to 94 years old,
suggest that homosexual interests increase in old age
among men.

2918. HARRY, JOSEPH, and WILLIAM DEVALL. "Age and Sexual
        Culture among Homosexually Oriented Males,"
        Archives of Sexual Behavior, 7 (1978), 199-209.
Utilizing data from 243 males from the Detroit area, finda
that the thesis that gay men are heavily youth-oriented
has been exaggerated. Preference for younger partners
varies according to social status, lifestyle, and other
factors.

2919. KANTROWITZ, ARNIE. "Gay and Gray," **Advocate**,
        no. 192 (June 16, 1976), 21, 29.
First of several articles in this issue on gay seniors.
See also: Judy MacLean, "National Conference on Lesbian
and Gay Aging," **Advocate**, no. 334 (January 7, 1982),
15-17.

2920. KELLY, JAMES. "The Aging Male Homosexual: Myth and
        Reality," **Gerontologist**, 17 (1977), 328-32.
A study of 241 gay men found little evidence to suggest
that being homosexual itself causes problems in old age,
but that societal stigma does.

2921. KIMMEL, DOUGLAS. "Adult Development and Aging: A
        Gay Perspective," **Journal of Social Issues**, 34
        (1970, 113-30.
Studies older homosexual men using D. J. Levinson's con-
cept of developmental periods. Finds that stereotypes are
not valid for the majority. See also his: "Life-History
Interviews of Aging Gay Men," **International Journal of
Aging and Human Development**, 10 (1980), 239-48; and "Psy-
chotherapy and the Older Gay Man," **Psychotherapy: Theory,
Research and Practice**, 15 (1978), 386-402.

2922. LANER, MARY R. "Growing Older Female: Heterosexual

and Homosexual," **JH,** 4 (1979), 219-35, 267-75.
Analyzed the age-related content of personals advertisements placed by heterosexual and homosexual women. Contrary to popular notions, lesbians were not found to be
seeking young partners. See also her: "Growing Older
Male: Heterosexual and Homosexual," **Gerontologist,** 18
(1978), 496-501, showing a similar method and results.

2923. LEVY, NORMAN J. "The Middle-aged Male Homosexual,"
       Journal of the American Academy of Psychoanalysis,
       7 (1970), 405-18.
Discussion from the point of view of depth psychoanalysis.

2924. MINNIGERODE, FRED A. "Age Status Labeling in
       Homosexual Men," **JH** 1 (1976), 273-76.
Asked 95 gay men between 25 and 68 years of age to clas-
sify themselves as young, middle-age, or old. The popular suggestion of accelerated aging in homosexual men was
not supported.

2925. MINNEGERODE, FRED A., and MARCY R. ADELMAN. "El-
       derly Homosexual Women and Men: Report on a Pilot
       Study," **Family Coordinator,** 27 (1978), 451-56.
Reports on in-depth interviews with eleven 60-77-year-old
homosexual women and men, examining physical change and
physical health; work, retirement, and leisure time; social behavior; psychological functioning; sexual behavior;
and personal perspective on the life course.

2926. RAPHAEL, SHARON, and MINA K. ROBINSON. "The Older
       Lesbian: Love Relationships and Friendship Pat-
       terns," **Alternative Lifestyles,** 3 (1980), 207-29.
Concentrates on support and intimacy as fostered by love
relationships and friendship patterns. Based on a sample
of twenty California women over 50.

2927. VACHA, KEITH (ed.). **Quiet Fire: Memories of Older
       Gay Men.** Trumansburg, NY: Crossing Press, 1985.
       219 pp.
From over 100 interviews, Vacha has selected 17 to show a
range of experiences and attitudes.

2928. VINING, DONALD. "The Advantages of Age," **Advocate,**
       no. 313 (March 19, 1981), 22-23.
Subjective observations by the diarist and playwright, now
retired from his office job.

2929. WEG, RUTH B. (ed.). **Sexuality in the Later Years:
       Roles and Behavior.** New York: Academic Press,
       1983. 299 pp.
Although there is no single paper concerned with gay and
lesbian aging in this collection, the subject is frequently discussed in context. See index.

2930. WEINBERG, MARTIN S. "The Male Homosexual: Age-Re-
      lated Variations in Social and Psychological Char-
      acteristics," **Social Problems**, 17 (1970), 527-37.
A sample recruited in San Francisco and New York refutes
negative views of older gay men, who are found in fact
to be better adjusted psychologically than younger gay
men, though they are more likely to be withdrawn from
the gay world.

D. BARS

The tendency of homosexual men ("sodomites") to gather in
taverns, where they encountered other socially marginal
elements, seems to begin in 15th-century Europe, though
these locales did not come into their own until the 19th
century. The modern gay bar seems to be a distinctively
northern European and North American institution. In much
of North America, the bars are, apart from the gay
churches, the only homosexual gathering places. Regulation of alcohol consumption has repeatedly brought homosexual bar patrons into conflict with the police and,
in the wake of Prohibition, also the underworld (see
XXI.A).

2931. ACHILLES, NANCY. "The Development of the Homosexual
      Bar as an Institution," in: John H. Gagnon and Wil-
      liam Simon (eds.), **Sexual Deviance**. New York: Har-
      per and Row, 1967, pp. 228-44.
In large cities different kinds of bars can specialize so
as to serve more specific functions. Facing the difficulties of underworld control and police corruption, the community and the bar owners find cohesion in their reaction
to police hostility. Decor and personnel are important in
establishing the individual character of a bar. (Reflects
her 1964 M.A. thesis, University of Chicago).

2932. BEARCHELL, CHRIS. "Bar-Hopping," **Body Politic**,
      no. 77 (October 1981), 15-27.
Traces changing patterns in Toronto lesbian bars over
two decades. Unlike the city's gay men's bars, the lesbian bars remain a combination of straight-owned and
"underground" membership clubs. Compare Nancy L. Lisagor,
Lesbian Identity in the Subculture of Women's Bars
(unpublished Ph.D. dissertation, Sociology, University
of Pennsylvania, 1980; 244 pp.).

2933. BRANSON, HELEN P. **Gay Bar.** San Francisco: Pan-
      Graphic Press, 1957. 89 pp.
The owner of a Los Angeles establishment with a homosexual
(mostly male) clientele describes her bar, comments on the
problems of her customers, and characterizes the types of
people she meets.

2934. CARSWELL, PHILLIP. "Life behind Bars," **Gay Commun-**

ity News (Melbourne), 2:4 (May 1980), 30-33.
While it is easy to conclude that the sole purpose of bars
is for cruising, bars can serve other purposes, and indeed
have real potential for change.

2935. CAVAN, SHERRI. **Liquor Licence: An Ethnography of
        Bar Behavior.** Chicago: Aldine, 1966. 246 pp.
Characterizes the nature of gay bars in terms of the
acceptability of displays of affection, milling, pickups,
and erotic behavior. Frequent comparisons with heterosexual bars are offered. See also her "Interaction in
Home Territories," **Berkeley Journal of Sociology,** 8
(1963), 17-32.

2936. DALLAS, MICHAEL, et al. **De leerscene--een onder-
        zoek naar de ontwikkeling van mannelijkheid.** Am-
        sterdam: University, Sociologisch Instituut, 1985.
        105 pp.
Theoretical and empirical considerations by a team of
Amsterdam graduate students on the leather scene, esp. as
observed in the city's bars.

2937. HARRY, JOSEPH. "Urbanization and the Gay Life,"
        Journal of Sex Research, 10 (1974), 238-47.
With increasing size of cities there is increasing
specialization of gay bars. In metropolitan cities bars
cater to different age groups and different lifestyles,
and this diversity encourages migration of small town gays
to urban areas.

2938. HIGHLAND, JIM. "Raid!" **Tangents,** 2:4 (January
        1967), 4-7.
Account of the Black Cat raid by the Los Angeles police,
which triggered a street confrontation two years before
the Stonewall riot that involved several hundred people.

2939. HOOKER, EVELYN. "The Homosexual Community," in:
        John H. Gagnon and William Simon (eds.), **Sexual
        Deviance.** New York: Harper and Row, 1967, pp. 176-
        94.
In the gay community, bars serve as sexual marketplaces;
they are centers of communication and social activity;
and they function as induction, training and integration
centers for new members of the community.

2940. JACKMAN, JIM. "Missing the Ports of Call," in:
        Karla Jay and Allen Young (eds.), **Lavender Cul-
        ture.** New York: Jove, 1978, pp. 150-54.
Recollections of a gay bar in Worcester, MA. See also
John Kelsey, "The Cleveland Bar Scene in the Forties,"
ibid., 146-49; and Thomas J. Noel, "Gay Bars and the
Emergence of the Denver Homosexual Community," **Social
Science Journal,** 15 (April 1978), 59-74.

2941. MYRICK, FRED L. "Homosexual Types: An Empirical
        Investigation," **Journal of Sex Research,** 10 (1974),

226-37.
Analyzing the attitudes of gay bar patrons, finds that
homosexuality exists on a continuum from complete concealment to complete disclosure.

2942. POULIQUEN, JEAN-PAUL. "La Tournée des bars," **Gai
        pied**, no. 103 (January 21-27, 1984), 24-27, 58.
Problems of gay bars in Paris, including high costs and
police intimidation.

2943. READ, KENNETH E. **Other Voices: The Style of a Male
        Homosexual Tavern.** Novato, CA: Chandler and Sharp,
        1980. 212 pp.
Closeted anthropologist's ostensibly reflexive ethnography
of a Seattle Tenderloin bar.

2944. REITZES, DONALD C., and JULIETTE K. DIVER. "Gay
        Bars as Deviant Community Organizations: The
        Management of Interactions with Outsiders," **Deviant
        Behavior**, 4 (1982), 1-18.
Interprets data collected in 10 Atlanta area bars to show
the processes used by the bars to define the role of outsiders and manage interaction through the use of location,
announcement, screening and interior design. Four outsider roles were identified: antagonist, guest, compet-
itor, and customer.

2945. SHILTS, RANDY. "Big Business: Gay Bars and Baths
        Come Out of the Bush Leagues," **Advocate**, no. 191
        (June 2, 1976), 37-38+.
Gay liberation has meant increasing prosperity and visibility for once clandestine gay meeting places.

2946. WEIGHTMAN, BARBARA A. "Gay Bars as Private
        Places," **Landscape** (Berkeley), 24 (1980), 9-16.
Physical aspects of the bars as home territories.

                    E. BATHHOUSES AND BEACHES

In ancient Rome and in Islamic civilization public baths
were frequently patronized by those in search of homosexual contact, though few seem to have been exclusively
devoted to such traffic. The emergence of the distinctively gay sauna (popular known as "the baths") seems to
be essentially a product of the last hundred years or so:
as the need for public baths among the general population
decreased, the few remaining ones tended, in many instances, to acquire an exclusively homosexual character. Outdoor homosexual bathing areas may have their origin in the
traditional "old swimming holes" where men and boys bathed
in the nude and therefore without female companionship.

2947. BERUBE, ALAN. "The History of the Gay Bathhouse,"
      Coming Up! (San Francisco), 6:3 (December 1984),
      15-19.
Includes information on the Baker Steet Club Raid (1918)
and Jack's Baths in the 1930s and '40s, both in San
Francisco.

2948. BOYD, JERRY T. **The "P" Street Beach Handbook: The
      Art of Gay Sunbathing in the Nation's Capital.**
      Washington,DC: PSBH Associates, 1985. 130 pp.
Campy tidbits revolving around "our national gay park."

2949. BROWN, RITA MAE. "Queen for a Day: A Stranger in
      Paradise," in: Karla Jay and Allen Young (eds.),
      Lavender Culture. New York: Jove, 1978, 69-76.
Lesbian writer visits New York gay sauna clandestinely and
emerges with a positive impression. In this volume, see
also: Arthur Bell, "The Gay Bath Life Gets Respectability," pp. 77-84.

2950. CANAVAN, PETER. "The Gay Community at Jacob Riis
      Park," in Vernon Boggs et al. (eds.), **The Apple
      Sliced.** South Hadley, MA: Berger and Garvey, 1984,
      pp. 67-82.
Reports 1974 interviews with gay men regarding nude
bathing and pickups at a popular New York City beach.

2951. COSSOLO, FELIX, and IVAN TEOBALDELLI. **Cercando il
      paradiso perduto.** Milan: Gammalibri, 1981. 113
      pp.
Photographs, interviews, poetry, and articles from the
"gay summer camps" at the beach in Greece and Southern
Italy, 1978-80.

2952. DECTER, MIDGE. "The Boys at the Beach," **Commen-
      tary,** 70:3 (September 1980), 36-48.
Hostile account of gay lifestyle on Fire Island, NY, prior
to 1970, attempting to discredit gay liberation by associ-
ating it with "drugs, S-M, and suicide."

2953. DOUGLAS, JACK D., and PAUL K. RASMUSSEN. **The
      Nude Beach.** Beverly Hills, CA: Sage, 1977. 244
      pp.
All the big nude beaches have "gay scenes," and both heterosexuals and homosexual greatly prefer sexual segregation (pp. 184-90). See also: Lee Baxandall, **World Guide
to Nude Beaches and Recreation** (New York: Harmony House,
1983; 220 pp.).

2954. FLEMING, THOMAS. "Criminalizing a Marginal Commu-
      nity: The Bawdy House Raids," in: Thomas Fleming
      and L. A. Visano (eds.), **Deviant Designations:
      Crime, Law and Deviance in Canada.** Toronto: But-
      terworth, 1983, pp. 37-60.
A case study of the 1979-81 Toronto raids of gay bathhouses demonstrates that the pursuit of deviant groups,

and the selection of previously tolerated behaviors for
criminalization, carry significant costs for society, the
criminalized, and the police. See also Gerald Hannon,
"Rage, Raids and Bawdyhouses," in: Ed Jackson and Stan
Persky (eds.), **Flaunting It!** (Vancouver: New Star, 1982),
pp. 273-94.

2955. KEPNER, JIM. "Gay Beach" [by "Frank Golovitz,
      pseud.], **ONE Magazine**, 6:7 (July 1958), 5-10.
Captures something of what it was like at a popular late
1950s beach in Southern California.

2956. NESTLE, JOAN. "Lesbian Memories 1: Riis Park, New
      York City, ca. 1960," **Common Lives/Lesbian Lives**
      (Summer 1983), 14-16.
Recollections of Riis Park when it was **the** beach for gay
men as well as many lesbians of New York.

2957. NICHOLS, JACK. **Welcome to Fire Island.** New York:
      St. Martin's Press, 1976. 148 pp.
A noted gay journalist offers appropriately breezy comment
on the noted Long Island resort.

2958. RUMAKER, MICHAEL. **A Day and Night at the Baths.**
      Bolinas, CA: Grey Fox Press, 1978. 81 pp.
Perhaps the best subjective account of the pre-AIDS exper-
ience of visiting a gay baths (NYC). See also: Richard
Goldstein, "A Night at the Continental Baths," **New York**, 6
(January 8, 1973), 51-55.

2959. STYLES, JOSEPH. "Outsider/Insider: Researching Gay
      Baths," **Urban Life**, 8 (1979), 135-52.
A young sociologist becomes a participant-observer at a
bathhouse. Presents an eight-step typology of relationship escalation, from sexual encounter **tout court** to long-
term relationship.

2960. WEINBERG, MARTIN S., and COLIN J. WILLIAMS. "Gay
      Baths and the Social Organization of Impersonal
      Sex," **Social Problems**, 23 (1975), 124-36.
Conditions described by patrons as ideal include: protection; ample, accessible opportunities; a known, shared,
and organized reality; bounding of the experience; con-
geniality; and a comfortable physical setting.

F. BISEXUALITY

The term bisexuality has an uncertain conceptual status,
in that while there are heterosexual and homosexual acts,
there is no such thing as a bisexual act. Determination
of who is a bisexual may then be attempted either on the
basis of comparative frequency of the two types of acts or
inner psychic attunement. The controversial concept of

universal bisexuality stems from psychoanalytic speculation (see XVII.B-C).

2961. ALTSHULER, KENNETH Z. "On the Question of Bisexual-
       ity," **American Journal of Psychotherapy,** 38
       (1984), 484-93.
Contends that sexual choice is dichotomous, rather than
continuous, and inferences based on a continuum are un-
tenable. Self-labeling of oneself as bisexual is held
to be a matter of face-saving, status, and denial of
conflict.

2962. BISHOP, GEORGE. **The Bisexuals.** Los Angeles: Cen-
       tury, 1964. 154 pp.
Pulp account displaying then-current popular attitudes.
See also: D. Wise, **Understanding Bisexuality** (Los Angeles: Centurion Press, 1971; and D. Wise and J. Jar-
dine, **The Bisexual Male** (Los Angeles: Centurion Press,
1971).

2963. BLUMSTEIN, PHILIP, and PEPPER SCHWARTZ. "Bisexual-
       ity in Men," **Urban Life,** 5 (1976), 339-58.
Data from 75 men shows that they commonly exhibit sexual
behavior inconsistent with self-identity. The authors
suggest that the term "ambisexuality" should replace "bisexuality," since equal attraction to men and women is
virtually nonexistent; instead one finds varying degrees
of eroticization of both genders. See also their: "Bisexuality: Some Social Psychological Issues," **Journal of
Social Issues,** 33 (1977), 30-45.

2964. BLUMSTEIN, PHILIP, and PEPPER SCHWARTZ. "Lesbian-
       ism and Bisexuality," in: Erich Goode and Richard
       R. Troiden (eds.), **Sexual Deviance and Sexual
       Deviants.** New York: William R. Morrow, 1975,
       pp. 278-95.
As in the parallel study with men, data from 75 women show
discordance between sexual identity and sexual behavior.
In the case of women there is the complication that lesbian activists discourage bisexual behavior, while sexual
libertarians welcome it.

2965. BODE, JANET. **View from Another Closet: Exploring
       Bisexuality in Women.** New York: Hawthorn Books,
       1976. 252 pp.
Semipopular, anecdotal treatment.

2966. BREITNER, BURCHARD. **Das Problem der Bisexuali-
       tät.** Vienna: M. Maudrich, 1951. 77 pp.
Theoretical considerations from a medical-psychiatric
standpoint.

2967. DOUGLAS, JASON. **Bisexuality.** London: Canova,
       1970. 191 pp.
Popular but informed presentation covering a broad range

of subjects: the nature of bisexuality,the naking of a
bisexual, the all-round lover, the bisexual woman and
man, the nymphomaniac and the satyr, the bisexual in
literature, and the future of bisexuality.

2968. FAST, JULIUS, and HAL WELLS. **Bisexual Living.** New
York: M. Evans, 1975. 240 pp.
Popular account for the titillation of the curious. See
also: Bernhardt J. Hurwood, **The Bisexuals** (Greenwich, CT:
Fawcett, 1974; 208 pp.).

2969. HERDT, GILBERT. "A Comment on Cultural Attributes
and Fluidity of Bisexuality," **JH**, 10:3-4 (1984),
53-61.
Presents examples from Melanesia as cross-cultural evidence in relation to current debates.

2970. KAPLAN, GISELA T., and LESLEY J. ROGERS. "Breaking
Out of the Dominant Paradigm: A New Look at Sexual
Attraction," **JH**, 10:3-4 (1984), 71-75.
Contends that genital organs are not the prime focus of
sexual attraction. Careful studies may reveal that sexual
arousal is based on criteria that transcend genital
categories.

2971. KLEIN, FRED. **The Bisexual Option: A Concept of One
Hundred Percent Intimacy.** New York: Arbor House,
1978. 222 pp.
Popular account proselytizing for bisexuality as the best
of three worlds, with discussions of literary treatments
and list of "famous bisexuals."

2972. KLEIN, FRITZ, and TIMOTHY J. WOLF (eds.). **Two
Lives to Lead: Bisexuality in Men and Women.** New
York: Harrington Park Press, 1958. 255 pp.
Collection of papers treating theoretical issues; psychological aspects of bisexuality; cross-cultural perspectives; women in marriages; men in marriages; bisexual organizations; and bibliography. Claims to the contrary
notwithstanding, many of the authors seem to accept the
concept of bisexuality as unproblematic, avoiding the
thornier problems. This volume is a reprint of **JH**, 11:1-2
(Spring 1985).

2973. KOHN, BARRY, and ALICE MATUSOW. **Barry and Alice: -
Portrait of a Bisexual Marriage.** Englewood Cliffs,
NJ: Prentice-Hall, 1980. 217 pp.
Lightweight joint autobiography of two people, a Philadel-
phia couple, who regard themselves as bisexual, though
their modalities are clearly different.

2974. MCINNESS, COLIN. **Loving Them Both: A Study of
Bisexuality and Bisexuals.** London: Martin Brian
and O'Keefe, 1973. 55 pp.
Semisubjective study by an Anglo-Australian novelist, himself bisexual, whose fictional writings show many insights

into the sexual diversity found in contemporary London.

2975.   PAUL, JAY P.   "The Bisexual Identity: An Idea
        without Social Recognition," **JH**, 9:2-3 (1983-84),
        45-63.
Asserts that the disadvantage self-identified bisexuals
now face, that of being marginal to the other groups, can
be turned into an asset, in that they are more able to
adopt a broader and more integrated perspective on sexuality and human relationships.

2976.   ROSS, MICHAEL W.   "Beyond the Biological Model: New
        Directions in Bisexual and Homosexual Research,"
        JH, 10:3-4 (1984), 63-70.
Questions two assumptions: (1) that gender is the critical
determinant of a sexual relationship; and (2) that sexual
orientation is an essential condition.

2977.   SPIERS, DUANE E.   "The No-Man's Land of the Bisex-
        ual," **Corrective and Social Psychiatry and Journal
        of Behavior Technology, Methods and Therapy,** 22
        (1976), 6-11.
The bisexual person must struggle to find a livable lifestyle and an adequate reference group for socialization.
The bisexual person cannot easily be located on Kinsey's
7-point scale.   Clinicians working with bisexuals should
be careful not to "dichotomize" them.

2978.   STEIR, CHARLES.   "A Bibliography on Bisexuality,"
        JH, 11:1-2 (1985), 235-48.
About 375 entries, mainly English-language, with occasional annotations.   This list, which spreads a broad net,
should be consulted to extend the selection included in
the present work.

2979.   STEKEL, WILHELM.   **Bi-Sexual Love.**   Translated from
        the German by James S. Van Teslaar.   Brooklyn:
        Physicians and Surgeons Book Co., 1934.   359 pp.
Popularization of Stekel's psychoanalytic ideas, including
the claim that "All persons are bisexual." (p. 27).   This
view was to be rejected by many analysts in North America,
beginning with Sandor Rado.   Stekel provides many case
histories and dream analyses.

2979A. WOLFF, CHARLOTTE.   **Bisexuality: A Study.**   London:
        Quartet Books, 1977.   245 pp.
Psychoanalytically oriented observations, chiefly on
women, by a British-based therapist, with roots in the
Central European tradition of sexology.

                          G.   BLACKMAIL

A much-discussed problem in the 19th and first half of the

20th century was the blackmailing of homosexuals, either
by professionals or by opportunistic amateurs. A related
peril was **entolage**, the theft of valuable items from homosexuals in the assurance that the victims would not dare
report the loss to the police. The emphasis on blackmail
in the propaganda of the early homophile movement boomer-
anged in the late 1940s and after, when the fear that
homosexuals could be the object of pressure by Communist
intelligence services made them "security risks" in
the eyes of counterintelligence. With more tolerant
social attitudes, accompanied by easing of legal sanctions, these problems have fortunately become rare in
Western countries, even if the discriminatory regulations
remain. Travelers to Third World nations sometimes
experience these difficulties.

2980. BURCHARD, ERNST. **Erpresser-Prostitution.** Ber-
        lin: Kampf-Verlag, 1905. 14 pp.
Short study on blackmail as practiced by male prostitutes,
one of the most serious problems faced by homosexuals in
Wilhelmine Germany. See also Ludwig Frey, "Zur Character-
isierung des Rupfertums," **JfsZ,** 1 (1899), 71-96; and
Magnus Hirschfeld, "Aus der Erpresserpraxis," **JfsZ,** 13
(1912-13), 288-315.

2981. CANLER, LOUIS. **Mémoires de Canler, ancien chef du
        Service de sureté.** Edited by Jacques Brenner. Par-
        is: Mercure de France, 1968. 551 pp.
See Chapter 33, "Les antiphysiques et les chanteurs."
While homosexuality as such was not criminal in France,
those practicing it, esp. foreign visitors from countries
where it remained illegal, were often victimized. These
memoirs of the French security chief (1797-1865) were
first published in 1862 in a censored version, which was
immediately banned. An English translation also appeared:
Autobiography of a French Detective from 1818 to 1858
(London: Ward and Lock, 1862; 315 pp.).

2982. HENTIG, HANS VON. **Die Erpressung.** Tubingen: Mohr,
        1959. 318 pp.
Discussion of blackmail in postwar Germany, with particular emphasis on the sexual aspects.

2983. KINBERG, OLOF. "On the So-Called Vagrancy: Medico-
        Sociological Study," **Journal of the American In-
        stitute of Criminal Law and Criminology,** 24 (1933),
        409-27, 552-83.
See pp. 418-20, 553-55 on prostitutes, including the practice of **entolage** (theft from clients).

2984. LEGG, W. DORR. "Blackmailing the Homosexual,"
        Sexology, 33 (1967), 554-56.
Discussing the situation at that period, from his observations at ONE, Inc., Legg comments that then-existing legal
codes and social mores provided a screen behind which the

blackmailer could operate with impunity, threatening not
only the confirmed homosexual but also those who had
casual or unique experiences with their own sex. See
also: Dane Mohler, "Homosexual Blackmail," **Tangents**, 2
(December 1966), 4-8.

2985. REINHOLD, JOSEPH. **Die Chantage: ein Beitrag zur
        Reform der Strafgesetzgebung.** Berlin: Guttertag,
        1909. 118 pp.
Urges legal reform to prevent blackmail.

2986. SCHIMA, KONRAD. **Erpressung und Nötigung: eine
        kriminologische Studie.** Vienna: Springer, 1973.
        264 pp.
See pp. 121-26 (homosexuality as basis for blackmail) and
178-80 (hustlers as blackmailers).

2987. TARDIEU, AMBROISE. **Etude médico-légale sur les
        attentats aux moeurs.** 7th edition. Paris: Bail-
        lière, 1878. 296 pp.
This study by an influential French specialist in forensic
medicine (first ed. 1857) has a section (pp. 194-294)
entitled "De la pédérastie et de la sodomie." The auth-
or's first-hand observations of the homosexual underworld of the Paris of 1845-75 are supplemented by material
drawn from foreign authors, in particular the French
translation of Johann Ludwig Casper, **Traité pratique de
médecine légale** (Paris: Baillière, 1862; 2 vols.). Much
of the book is concerned with the question of determining
the physical traces of sodomitical practices in suspects.
Of the 302 subjects examined by the author 101 had
"habitudes à la fois actives et passives," that is to say
they were "modern" homosexuals well before the advent
of the homophile movement and the psychiatric notion of
sexual inversion. The book establishes beyond a doubt
that a vast homosexual subculture flourished in mid-19th
century Paris despite the depredations of professional
blackmailers and occasional harassment by the police.

2988. TRESCKOW, HANS VON. "Erpressung auf sexueller
        Grundlage," in: **Zur Reform des Sexualstrafrechts.**
        Berlin: Bircher, 1926, pp. 177-86.
Informed comment on blackmail of homosexuals, written by
the Chief of the Berlin Police, together with his suggestions for reform. Tresckow also published **Von Fürsten und
anderen Sterblichen. Erinnerungen eines Kriminalkommissars**
(Berlin: Fontane, 1922; 240 pp.), which deals with the
background of the homosexual scandals that rocked the
German capital in the first decade of the 20th century,
and in particular the Harden-Eulenburg affair, the heroes
of which had figured in the dossier kept by the Berlin
vice squad. His personal experience with the problem of
blackmail led him to support Hirschfeld's efforts to
obtain repeal of Paragraph 175.

H. COUPLES

The tendency of adult homosexuals and lesbians to form
dyadic pairs can be studied beginning in the 18th century,
when homosocial forms, necessarily clandestine, began to
be influenced by new notions of companionate (heterosexual) marriage. It was only in the second half of the 20th
century, when large numbers of unmarried heterosexual
pairs began to be visible, that the study of "the couple"
--whether straight or gay--became a fashionable theme of
social science. Conceptually, the fading of strong
moralizing condemnation has fostered the abandonment of
the earlier sharp contrast between the positively charged
married pair and the negatively charged fornicating/adul-
terous pair (including homosexuals); now there is a
neutral, tripartite division: married heterosexuals;
unmarried, cohabiting heterosexuals; and cohabiting
homosexuals--all ranged under the umbrella category of
couples. (For the controversial, perhaps even quixotic
concept of homosexual marriage, see XX.L).

2989. ALAIN (pseud.). "Du couple homophile," **Arcadie,**
       no. 100 (April 1962), 210-24.
Essay on male homosexual couples in France. See also: Antoine D'Arc, "Essai socio-psychologique sur le couple
homosexuel," **Arcadie,** no. 196 (April 1970), 178-82; no.
197 (May 1970), 234-42; no. 198 (June 1970), 287-95.

2990. BABUSCIO, JACK. "Splitting Up," **Gay News** (Lon-
       don), no. 220 (July 23-August 5, 1981), 22-23; no.
       221 (August 6-19, 1981), 24-25.
The fact that many gays and lesbians do, contrary to popular stereotypes, form at least one deep dyadic relationship in their lives is attested by the intensity and complexity of the feelings that accompany and last beyond the
experience of breaking up.

2991. BLUMSTEIN, PHILIP, and PEPPER SCHWARTZ. **American
       Couples: Money, Work, Sex.** New York: William
       Morrow, 1983. 656 pp.
Reflects data collected from over 4000 heterosexual
couples, nearly 1000 male couples, and 788 female couples.
The book is divided into five major sections: how couples
handle finances; how they balance work and relationship
commitments; their sexual behavior; a follow-up study;
and vignettes of twenty couples.

2992. BOYDEN, TOM, et al. "Similarity and Attraction in
       Homosexual Males: The Effects of Age and Masculin-
       ity-Femininity," **Sex Roles,** 10 (1984), 939-48.
Interpretation of a questionnaire completed by 110 gay men
suggests that long-term partner preference among homosexual males is determined by the same principles that guide
heterosexual selection.

2993. CARDELL, MONA. "Sex-Role Identity, Sex-Role Be-
       havior, and Satisfaction in Heterosexual, Lesbian,
       and Gay Male Couples," **Psychology of Women Quarter-
       ly**, 5 (1981), 488-94.
Satisfaction was related to the amount and type of sex-
role behavior, but unrelated to gender, background characteristics, BSRI score, or couple type.

2994. CLARKE, LIGE, and JACK NICHOLS. **Roommates Can't
       Always Be Lovers: An Intimate Guide to Male-Male
       Relationships.** New York: St. Martin's Press,
       1974. 194 pp.
Light essays on male-male relationships alternating with
letters to and from Clarke and Nichols when they were
editors of **Gay,** a now-defunct New York City periodical.

2995. DAILEY, DENNIS M. "Adjustment of Heterosexual and
       Homosexual Couples in Pairing Relationships: An
       Exploratory Study," **Journal of Sex Research,** 15
       (1979), 143-57.
In a limited sample, homosexual couples showed significantly lower levels of success than did married couples.
Lesbians had lower scores on self-esteem and generalized
contentment, suggesting that being lesbian and a woman may
be a twofold problem. See also his: "Legitimacy and Per-
manence in the Gay Relationship: Some Intervention Alternatives," **Journal of Social Welfare,** 4:2-3 (1977), 81-88.

2996. DE CECCO, JOHN P., and MICHAEL G. SHIVELY. "A
       Study of Perceptions of Rights and Needs in
       Interpersonal Conflicts in Homosexual Relation-
       ships," **JH,** 3 (1978), 205-16.
Interviews with 91 men and 34 women indicated that the
right most frequently perceived as important was participation in decision making, and the need most frequently
perceived was power.

2997. DENNENY, MICHAEL. **Decent Passions: Real Stories
       about Love.** Boston: Alyson, 1984. 223 pp.
Interviews with a a gay couple, a lesbian couple, and an
interracial heterosexual couple emphasizing love and
passion. See also his: **Lovers: The Story of Two Men.**
Interviews with Philip Gefter and Neil Alan Marks (New
York: Avon, 1979; 159 pp.).

2998. FALBO, TONI, and LETITIA A. PEPLAU. "Power
       Strategies in Intimate Relationships," **Journal of
       Personality and Social Psychology,** 38 (1980),
       618-28.
Presents a model of power strategies, which is of uncertain value inasmuch as no differences were disclosed in
this dimension between homosexuals and heterosexuals.

2999. "Gay Couple Counseling," **Homosexual Counseling
       Journal,** 1:3 (1974), 88-139.
Condensed proceedings of a conference sponsored by the

Homosexual Community Counseling Center in May 1974.

3000. HARRY, JOSEPH. "Decision Making and Age Differ-
      ences among Gay Male Couples," **JH**, 8:2 (1982) 9-21.
In an exploration of patterning of attractions among 1,556
gay men, age was found to be the major criterion defining
pools of potential erotic and romantic partners. Moreover, age defined the dominance structure in a relationship.

3001. HARRY, JOSEPH. **Gay Couples.** New York: Praeger,
      1984. 152 pp.
Based on a study of over 1000 Chicago men, the author
finds support for the "resource theory" of family dynamics; the homogamous selection hypothesis; and predominant
nonexclusiveness (which is not necesarily a negative
factor). Also treats cohabitation; gender-role playing;
intimacy; and masculinity/femininity. See also: Joseph
Harry and Robert Lovely, "Gay Marriages and Communities
of Sexual Orientation," **Alternative Lifestyles,** 2 (1979),
177-200; and Joseph Harry, "Gay Male and Lesbian Relationships," in: Eleanor D. Macklin and Roger H. Rubin (eds.),
Contemporary Families and Alternative Lifestyles (Beverly
Hills, Ca: Sage, 1983), 216-34.

3002. IHARA, TONI, and RALPH WARNER. "Gay Couples,"
      in: **The Living Together Kit.** Second ed. Occiden-
      tal, CA: Nolo Press, 1979, pp. 184-200.
Practical advice in the context of today's joint living
arrangements.

3003. JENSI, MEHRI S. "Role Differentiation in Female
      Homosexual Quasi-Marital Unions," **Journal of
      Marriage and the Family,** 36 (1974), 360-67.
Interviews with 34 lesbians record adherence to butch/
femme role-differentiation pattern.

3004. JONES, RANDALL W., and JOHN E. BATES. "Satisfaction
      in Male Homosexual Couples," **JH,** 3 (1978), 217-24.
Records the development of a Gay Relationship Questionnaire.

3005. LANER, MARY R. "Permanent Partner Priorities: Gay
      and Straight," **JH,** 3 (1977), 21-39.
In a survey of two groups of students it was found that
heterosexuals and homosexuals look for the same qualities in partners, but misperceive the priorities of
others.

3006. LEWIS, ROBERT A., et al. "Commitment in Same-Sex
      Love Relationships," **Alternative Lifestyles,** 4
      (1981), 22-42.
In a questionnaire study of 32 lesbians and 50 gay men
who had lived in coupled relationships for at least six
months, lesbians scored higher than gay men on three
separate indices of commitment, but on the whole there

were surprisingly few differences between the two groups.

3007. MCWHIRTER, DAVID P., and ANDREW M. MATTISON. **The Male Couple: How Relationships Develop.** Englewood Cliffs, NJ: Prentice-Hall, 1984. 341 pp.
Based on a five-year program of interviews with 156 male couples living in Southern California. The study outlines a sequence of six stages in which the couples are claimed to pass over many years.

3008. MENDOLA, MARY. **The Mendola Report: A New Look At Gay Couples.** New York: Crown, 1980. 269 pp.
Journalistic presentation of gay male and lesbian life-styles, based on some 400 couples.

3009. MORRIS, VICKI. "Helping Lesbian Couples Cope with Their Jealousy," **Women and Therapy,** 1:4 (1982), 27-34.
Explores special factors that may engender jealousy in a lesbian relationship, and offers a speculative treatment model (declaring feelings, clarifying misinformation, consciousness raising, negotiation of needs and rights, and individual therapy as needed).

3010. NANDA, SERENA, and J. SCOTT FRANCHER. "Culture and Homosexuality: A Comparison of Long Term Gay Male and Lesbian Relationships," **Eastern Anthropologist,** 33 (1980), 139-52.
In a study of 20 male and 20 female homosexuals of New York City, who have been in committed same-sex relationships for at least ten years, it was found that the men came out earlier than the lesbians, had much less hetero-sexual experience, and far more frequently engaged in casual sex encounters.

3011. NESTLE, JOAN. "Butch-Fem Relationships: Sexual Courage in the 1950s," **Heresies,** no. 12 (1981), 21-24.
Based on personal experience, Nestle argues that butch-fem relationships among lesbians were complex erotic state-ments, not mere mimicry of heterosexual dyads.

3012. NICHOLS, MARGARET. "The Treatment of Inhibited Sexual Desire (ISD) in Lesbian Couples," **Women and Therapy,** 1:4 (1982), 49-66.
Even in a loving, considerate relationship ISD may occur. The author recommends H. S. Kaplan's technique of sensate focus exercises as therapy.

3013. PENDERGRASS, VIRGINIA E. "Marriage Counseling with Lesbian Couples," **Psychotherapy: Theory, Research and Practice,** 12 (1975), 93-96.
Highlights fears of dependence and role conflict; the acceptance of a particular dominant or submissive role is not necessarily consonant with acceptance of a correspond-ing sex identity.

3014. PEPLAU, LETITIA ANN. "What Homosexuals Want in
       Relationships," **Psychology Today**, 15 (March 1981),
       28-34, 37-38.
"Whatever their sexual preferences, people in intimate
relationships today struggle to reconcile a longing for
closeness with a desire for independence and self-realization." See also Peplau et al., "Loving Women: Attachment and Autonomy in Lesbian Relationships," **Journal of
Social Issues**, 34:2 (1978), 71-27.

3015. PEPLAU, LETITIA ANN. "Research on Homosexual
       Couples: An Overview," **JH**, 8 (1982), 3-8.
Reviews current literature on gay male and lesbian
couples, which is presented as moving in accord with the
trend in sociology away from the deviance perspective to
one studying "alternate lifestyles."

3016. PINGEL, ROLF, and WOLFGANG TRAUTVETTER. **Homosex-
       uelle Partnerschaften: Eine empirische Untersuch-
       ung.** Berlin: Verlag Rosa Winkel, 1986. 112 pp.
Investigates the functioning of dyadic relationships of
gay men in West Germany.

3017. REECE, REX, and ALLEN E. SEGRIST. "The Association
       of Selected 'Masculine' Sex-Role Variables with
       Length of Relationship in Gay Male Couples," **JH**, 7
       (1981), 33-47.
Separated respondents to a self-report battery scored
lower on cooperation than members of ongoing relationships and were more likely to be androgynous. See also
Reece: "Coping with Couplehood," in: Martin P. Levine
(ed.), **Gay Men** (New York: Harper and Row, 1979), 211-21.

3018. SCHULLO, STEPHEN A., and BURTON L. ALPERSON.
       "Interpersonal Phenomenology as a Function of
       Sexual Orientation, Sex, Sentiment, and Trait
       Categories in Long-Term Dyadic Relationships,"
       Journal of Personality and Social Psychology, 47
       (1984), 983-1002.
Applied the Extended Personal Attributes Questionnaire
(modified) to 20 gay male, 20 lesbian, and 40 heterosexual
couples.

3019. SILVERSTEIN, CHARLES. **Man to Man: Gay Couples in
       America.** New York: Quill, 1981. 347 pp.
Providing extended profiles of individual gay couples,
explores their problems and satisfactions.

3020. SONENSCHEIN, DAVID. "The Ethnography of Male
       Homosexuals' Relationships," **Journal of Field
       Research**, 4:2 (1968), 69-83.
An associate of the Kinsey Institute offers a typology of
gay-male relationships based on field work in a Southwest city.

3021. STARN, JACK. "Homosexual Couple: Jack Baker and

Michael McConnell," **Look**, 35 (January 26, 1971),
69-71.
Journalist's profile of a Minnesota pair who attempted
(unsuccessfully, but with much publicity) to obtain a
legal marriage.

3022. TANNER, DONNA M. **The Lesbian Couple.** Lexington,
MA: Lexington Books, 1978. 142 pp.
From in-depth interviews with 24 lesbian couples in
Chicago, explores how homosexual women form and maintain
dyadic relationships. Indicates how they define household
tasks, financial arrangements, and sexual patterns.

3023. THERRIAULT, JACQUES. **Homosexualité et vie à deux.**
Montreal: Leméac, 1981. 239 pp.
A kind of "letter" on the life of homosexual couples ad-
dressed to heterosexuals.

3024. TULLER, NEIL R. "Couples: The Hidden Segment of
the Gay World," **JH**, 3 (1978), 331-43.
Of 15 couples interviewed, found that the partners met in
social as contrasted to sexual settings, that relationships were more common for females than for males, that
females required sexual fidelity more than males, that
males desired children more than females, and that butch-
femme role playing was absent.

3025. UHRIG, LARRY. **The Two of Us.** Boston: Alyson,
1984. 140 pp.
Commonsense guide for couples concerning "affirming,
celebrating and symbolizing gay and lesbian relationships" in what are sometimes termed holy unions. Author
is pastor of the Metropolitan Community Church, Washington, DC.

I. DEVIANCE

Sociologists and criminologists have taken deviance to
refer to behavior that is prohibited, censured, stigmatized, or penalized. The boundaries of the concept, and
its appropriateness for homosexuality, have not been
settled; it originated in the wish for a neutral term that
would not imply approval or disapproval of the activity,
whatever the attitude of the environing society might be.
Critics of the approach assert that it offers little more
than a jumble of "nuts, sluts, and perverts." For the
study of homosexuality, however, its value may lie in the
fact that it does make one think of analogies and differences between homosexuals and other groups. Compare the
discussion of the minority concept, XIV.S.

3026. BEST, JOEL, and DAVID F. LUCKENBILL. "The Social

Organization of Deviance," **Deviant Behavior,** 2
(1982), 231-58.
Distinguishes three forms: individual deviance, deviant
exchange, and deviant exploitation.

3027. BRYANT, CLIFTON (ed.). **Sexual Deviancy in Social
        Context.** New York: New Viewpoints, 1977. 292 pp.
Reprints 21 papers, generally of current interest in
spheres of popular culture and street life. Two are of
direct interest, by Alan J. Davis (on jailhouse rape)
and Kenneth N. Ginsburg (on hustling).

3028. CLINARD, MARSHALL B., and ROBERT F. MEIER. **Soci-
        ology of Deviant Behavior.** Fifth ed. New York:
        Holt, Rinehart and Winston, 1979. 613 pp.
In this updated edition of a popularly used textbook,
homosexuality is presented as a form of social deviance.

3029. COCHRANE, RAYMOND. "Values as Correlates of Devi-
        ancy," **British Journal of Social and Clinical
        Psychology,** 13 (1974), 257-67.
Arguing that value systems are potentially the most profitable variable to study in the etiology of deviance,
examines four groups: prisoners, delinquents, drug users,
and homosexuals.

3030. DURBIN, STEVE C. "The Moral Continuum of Deviancy
        Research," **Urban Life,** 12 (1983), 75-94.
Discussion of the Chicago school of sociology approach
to taxi-dance halls, including Saul Alinsky's observations on a homosexual one.

3031. FARRELL, RONALD A., and JAMES F. NELSON. "A Causal
        Model of Secondary Deviance: The Case of Homosex-
        uality," **Sociological Quarterly,** 17 (1976), 109-20.
Self-definition among homosexuals is shown not to be related to secondary deviance, but affected by perceived
rejection. Implications for the labeling, anomie, and
social and cultural support theories are discussed. See
also: Ronald A. Farrell and Clay W. Hardin, "Legal Stigma
and Homosexual Career Deviance," in: M. Riedel and T. P.
Thornberry (eds.), **Crime and Delinquency: Dimensions of
Deviance** (New York: Praeger, 1974), 128-40; and Farrell,
"Deviance Imputations, Early Recollections and the Reconstruction of Self," **International Journal of Social Psychiatry,** 30 (1984), 189-99.

3032. GOODE, ERICH, and RICHARD TROIDEN. **Sexual Deviance
        and Sexual Deviants.** New York: William Morrow,
        1975. 409 pp.
In this anthology prepared by two academic sociologists
with a special interest in the theme, see "Coming Out
among Lesbians" by Denise M. Cronin (pp. 268-77); "Femininity in the Lesbian Community" by William Simon and John
H. Gagnon (pp. 256-67); "The Homosexual" by Barry M. Dank
(pp. 174-210); "Lesbianism" by Goode and Troiden (pp. 229-

37); "Lesbianism and Bisexuality" by Philip W. Blumstein
and Pepper Schwartz (pp. 278-95); and "Male Homosexuality" by Goode and Troiden (pp. 149-60).

3033. JACOBS, JERRY (ed.). **Deviance: Field Studies and
        Self-Disclosures.** Palo Alto, CA: National Press,
        1974. 190 pp.
A series of readings on deviant behaviors--prostitution,
drug addiction, homosexuality, etc.--and the way in which
they are handled by courts and other bureaucratic agencies.

3034. KELLY, DELOS H. **Deviant Behavior: Readings in the
        Sociology of Deviance.** New York: St. Martin's
        Press, 1979. 769 pp.
Reprints articles by Robert Emerson, Charles McCaughy and
James Skipper, Jay Corzine and Richard Kirby, and Albert
Reiss (pp. 334-44, 478-88, 574-628).

3035. SCHUR, EDWIN M. **The Politics of Deviance: Stigma
        Contests and the Uses of Power.** Englewood Cliffs,
        NJ: Prentice-Hall, 1980. 241 pp.
An influential sociologist deals with such topics as control through commitment, the role of the state and the
power elite, stigma contests, stereotypes and propaganda,
and deviant protest movements. Homosexuality is discussed
throughout (see esp. pp. 212-27). With its broad range
and many references, this volume is useful for orientation.

3036. SIMMONS, JERRY L. **Deviants.** Berkeley: Glendessary
        Press, 1969. 134 pp.
A study of stereotyping of homosexuals and other social
deviants on the part of students. The study was replicated on the East Coast by Russell Ward, "Typification
of Homosexuals," **Sociological Quarterly,** 20 (1979),
411-23.

3037. WINSLOW, ROBERT W., and VIRGINIA WINSLOW. **Deviant
        Reality: Alternative World Views.** Boston: Allyn
        and Bacon, 1974. 335 pp.
Intended as an introduction to psychological and sociological theories of deviance, presents thirteen types of
deviant behavior (including homosexuality) through transcripts of interviews and discussions with individuals involved.

                       J. DISABILITY

Study of the problems of the handicapped as persons is
quite recent. Handicapped homosexuals face two special
problems: double discrimination; and difficulties in
achieving sexual contact. With regard to nonhandicapped

persons, there has been little academic study of the
erotic interest in crippled and physically defective
partners.

3038. BARTHELL, CHARLES N. "Deaf and Gay: Where is My
       Community?" **Readings in Deafness,** no. 9 (1983),
       147-57.
Attitudes of the hearing and deaf population toward
deaf sexuality and gay deaf persons, the incidence of
homosexuality in the deaf community, the attitude toward
homosexuals as reflected in American Sign language and
patterns of support among the deaf/gay population.

3039. BROWNE, SUSAN E., et al. (eds.). **With the Power of
       Each Breath: A Disabled Women's Anthology.** Pitts-
       burgh: Cleis, 1985. 360 pp.
Personal testimonies from over 50 contributors affirming
self-worth and women's solidarity. See also: Jo Campling
(ed.), **Images of Ourselves: Women with Disabilities Talking.** (Boston: Routledge and Kegan Paul, 1981.)

3040. CHESLEY, ROBERT, and DAVID GLASBERG. "See Me! Hear
       Me!" **Advocate,** no. 274 (August 23, 1979), 17-20.
The gay blind and deaf ask to be heard. See also: Neal
Twyford, "The Double Closet: Disabled Gays Who Cope with
Coming Out--Twice," ibid., no. 336 (February 18, 1982),
18-21.

3041. DANNENBERG, J. "Jugendliches Stottern und Homosex-
       ualität," **Jahrbuch der Psychoanalyse: Beiträge aur
       Theorie und Praxis,** 1 (1960), 253-74.
The problems of young stutterers in relation to homosexuality.

3042. DE LA CRUZ, FELIX F., and GERALD D. LAVECK (eds.).
       Human Sexuality and the Mentally Retarded. New
       York: Brunner/Mazel, 1973. 347 pp.
This volume represents the proceedings of a conference
sponsored by the National Institute of Child Health and
Human Development, U. S. Department of Health, Education
and Welfare. See index for references to homosexuality.

3043. DIXON, DWIGHT. "An Erotic Attraction to Amputees,"
       Sexuality and Disability, 6 (1983), 3-19.
Reviews data from a study conducted in 1976 by an enterprise selling amputee fantasy materials. Those who returned the questionnaire were typically married white
males of above-average educational and occupational
achievement.

3044. FRECHETTE, DAVE. "Fat and Gay," **Advocate,** no. 419
       (April 30, 1985), 29-31.
One man's story of life in the "fat lane," along with a
look at some of the organizations for gay heavyweights.

3045. HANNON, GERALD. "No Sorrow, No Pity: The Gay

Disabled," in: Ed Jackson and Stan Persky (eds.),
Flaunting It! Vancouver: New Star, 1982, pp.64-71.
Hard-hitting profiles of gay disabled, esp. blind persons.

3046.   HESLINGA, K. **Wij zijn niet van steen: seksuele
        problematiek van de gehandicapte mens.** Leiden:
        Stafleu, 1972. 212 pp.
Sexual problems of the handicapped, who are "not made of
stone."

3047.   MILAM, LORENZO WILSON. **The Cripple Liberation
        Front Marching Band Blues.** San Diego: Mho and Mho
        Works, 1984. 219 pp.
Searing memoirs of an adolescent polio victim who, after
much anguish, reconstructed his life as a productive gay
man.

3048.   RIVLIN, MARK. "The Disabled Gay: An Appraisal,"
        Sexuality and Disability, 3 (1980), 221-22.
Discusses the effects of attitudinal prejudice on disabled
homosexual clients, the activities of two British organizations for them, and the problems created by grouping
disabled homosexuals with disabled heterosexuals.

3049.   ZAKAREWSKY, GEORGE. "Patterns of Support among Gay
        and Lesbian Deaf Persons," **Sexuality and Disabil-
        ity,** 2 (1979), 178-91.
For deaf gay men and lesbians, assimilation into the
homosexual subculture can be as difficult as assimilation into the hearing world because the same prejudices
permeate both.

                        K. FRIENDSHIP

The subject of friendship clearly parallels that of
homosexuality, though experientially the two are usually
found to be distinct. Some favor a new term, **homosociality,** to include both same-sex friendship and homosexual
attraction. The subject was extensively canvased in
ancient Greece and Rome, where sex segregation meant that
most significant friendships were between two people of
the same sex (see also III.C). In the middle ages (see
III.D) "special friendships" developed in monasteries and
nunneries; their homosexual character is uncertain, and
clearly varied from case to case. See also the discussion
of gay clergy, VII.F.

3050.   ADAMS, MARGARET. **Single Blessedness: Observations
        on the Single Status in Married Society.** New
        York: Penguin, 1978. 264 pp.
Social worker's report on in-depth interviews with 27
unmarried men and women in Boston, New York, and Phila-

delphia, including the male-female and homosexual friendships.

3051. AELRED OF RIEVAULX. **Spiritual Friendship.** Trans-
        lated by M. E. Laker. Introduction by Douglass
        Roby. Kalamazoo, MI: Cistercian Publications,
        1974. 144 pp.
This study by an Anglo-French Cistercian (1110-1167) is
justly regarded as a landmark in the "special friendship" tradition--though it is problematic whether it can
be annexed without anachronism to a "gay" sensibility.
See, e.g., Kenneth C. Russell, "Aelred, the Gay Abbot of
Rievaulx," **Studia Mystica,** 5:4 (Winter 1982), 51-64.

3052. ALGER, WILLIAM ROUNSEVILLE. **The Friendships of
        Women.** Boston: Roberts Brothers, 1875. 416 pp.
See "Friendships of Woman with Woman" and "Pairs of
Female Friends" (pp. 266-363). This remarkably rich
source on passionate friendships between women was first
published in 1867.

3053. ARIES, ELIZABETH J., and FERN L. JOHNSON. "Close
        Friendship in Adulthood: Conversational Content
        between Same-Sex Friends," **Sex Roles,** 9 (1983),
        1183-96.
Results of a questionnaire completed by 62 male and 74
middle-aged adults support sex-stereotypical assumptions
about the nature of male-male and female-female conversations (i.e.,the former being about business, sports
and other "objective" concerns; the latter being more
intimate and personal).

3054. ARISTOTLE. **Nicomachean Ethics.** Translated by
        H. Rackham. Cambridge, MA: Harvard University
        Press, 1975 [1934]. 650 pp.
Books 8 and 9 (pp. 450-575) offer a clasic statment on
the mutuality of friendship, based on equality, which
time is required to solidify. Concentrates on close,
deep friendships.

3055. AVRILLON, JEAN-BAPTISTE-ELIE, FATHER. **Traités de
        l'amour de Dieu à l'égard des hommes, et de l'amour
        du prochain.** Paris: Pierres, 1740. 430 pp.
Discusses "particular friendships" on pp. 347-92.

3056. BAB, EDWIN. **Die gleichgeschlechtliche Liebe
        (Lieblingminne): ein Wort über ihr Wesen und ihre
        Bedeutung.** Berlin: Schildeberger, 1903. 79 pp.
Defends a concept of **Lieblingminne** (a neo-medieval expression, sometimes rendered "chivalric love"), rejecting
earlier medical theories. See also his: **Frauenbewegung
und Freundesliebe: Versuch einer Lösung des geschlecht-
lichen Problems** (Berlin: Brand, 1904; 24 pp.); reprinted
in **Lesbianism and Feminism in Germany, 1895-1910** (New
York: Arno Press, 1975).

3057. BARKAS, JANET L. **Friendship: A Selected, Annotated Bibliography.** New York: Garland, 1985. 135 pp.
List of 670 English-language items, many annotated. Not strong on homosexuality, but useful for comparative study.

3058. BELL, ROBERT R. **Worlds of Friendship.** Beverly Hills, CA: Sage, 1981. 216 pp.
Holds that friendship has become more important in modern American society "because of the weakening of many kinship ties."

3059. BERNIKOW, LOUISE. **Among Women.** New York: Harmony Books, 1980. 196 pp.
On intimate friendships, chiefly among writers. See pp. 155-92, 281-85.

3060. BLUEHER. HANS. **Die Rolle der Erotik in der männlichen Gesellschaft: eine Theorie der menschlichen Staatsbildung nach Wesen und Wert.** Jena: Eugen Diederichs, 1917-19. 2 vols.
Influential, though sometimes murky work of a significant German homosexual theorist. Stresses the importance of male bonding in the genesis of the state as opposed to the family, which is grounded in heterosexual relations with reproduction as its aim.

3061. BRAIN, ROBERT. **Friends and Lovers.** New York: Basic Books, 1976. 287 pp.
Includes cross-cultural discussion of ritual friendship. The author, an Australian, is not well disposed to homosexual behavior.

3062. BRY, ADELAIDE. **Friendship: How to Have a Friend and How to Be a Friend.** New York: Grosset and Dunlap, 1979. 193 pp.
In this popular work, see pp. 42, 68-69, 78, 81, 89, 161-62.

3063. CHARLIER, YVONNE. **Erasmus et l'amitié d'après sa correspondance.** Paris: Les Belles Lettres, 1977. 358 pp.
Friendship in Erasmus of Rotterdam (ca. 1466-1536) as revealed by his correspondence (in which homoerotic subtexts have sometimes been detected).

3064. CICERO. "On Friendship," in: **De senectute, De amicitia, De divinatione.** Translated by William Armistead Falconer. Cambridge, MA: Harvard University Press, 1971 [1923], pp. 108-224.
Following Aristotle, Cicero--writing in 44 B.C.--stresses that self-sufficiency is essential for friendship, which requires respect, virtue, and honesty. For an anonymous translator-commentator's relevant glosses, see **Cicero's Laelius: with a Dialogue Preferring Friendship above Love, Written by the Translator** (London: William Crooke, 1691).

3065. COTT, NANCY. **The Bonds of Womanhood.** New Haven:
       Yale University Press, 1977. 225 pp.
Concentrating on middle-class Protestant New Englanders,
charts the emergence in 19th-century America of a "newly
self-conscious and idealized concept of female friendship." More recently, this matter has been extensively
treated by Lillian Faderman, **Surpassing the Love of Men:
Romantic Friendship and Love between Women from the
Renaissance to the Present.** (New York: William Morrow,
1981; 496 pp.).

3066. CRONT, GHEORGHE. **Instituţii medievale romăneşti:
       Infrăţivea de moşie; Jurătorii.** Bucharest: Editura
       Academiei Republicii Socialiste România, 1969. 244
       pp. (Biblioteca istorică, 18).
Account of Romanian blood-brotherhood rites and their role
in feudal society. See also: Harry Tegnaeus, **Blood-Brothers: An Ethno-Sociological Study of the Institution** (New
York: Philosophical Library, 1952; 181 pp.).

3067. DAVIDSON, LYNNE R., and LUCILE DUBERMAN. "Friend-
       ship, Communication, and Interactional Patterns in
       Same-Sex Dyads," **Sex Roles,** 8 (1982), 809-22.
Specifies three levels of communication--topical, rela-
tional, and personal--concluding that women relate on all
three levels, while men relate primarily on the topical
level.

3068. DIETRICH, HANS (pseud. of Hans Dietrich Hellbach).
       Die Freundesliebe in Literatur. Leipzig: Hellbach,
       1931. 192 pp.
Close friendships in German literature. (Originally the
author's thesis, University of Leipzig, 1930.) See also:
Wolfdietrich Rasch, **Freundschaftskult und Freundschafts-
dichtung im deutschen Schrifttum des 18. Jahrhunderts vom
Ausgang des Barock bis zu Klopstock** (Halle: Niemeyer,
1936); and Eva Thaer, **Die Freundschaft im deutschen Roman
des 18. Jahrhunderts** (Hamburg: Berngruber, 1917; 125 pp.).

3069. DUCK, STEVE. **Friends for Life: The Psychology of
       Close Relationships.** New York: St. Martin's
       Press, 1983. 200 pp.
Psychologist's delineation of the stages through which
friendship evolves.

3070. EISENSTADT, S. N. "Ritualized Personal Relations:-
       Blood Brotherhood, Best Friends, Comrades, etc.:
       Some Comparative Hypotheses and Suggestions," **Man,**
       96 (1956), 90-96.
Concludes that all these relationships share the fact that
they are "particularistic, personal, voluntary, and fully
institutionalized (usually in ritual terms)." Contrast
Yehudi A. Cohen, "Patterns of Friendship," in his (ed.):
Social Structures and Personality (New York: Holt, Rinehart and Winston, 1961), pp. 351-86.

3071. HINDY, CARL G. "Children's Friendship Concepts and
      the Perceived Cohesiveness of Same-Sex Friendship
      Dyads," **Psychological Reports,** 47 (1980), 191-203.
A study of 149 girls and 129 boys in grades 1-8 provides
support for a three-stage model: 91) the unilateral physicalistic; (2) the reciprocal physicalistic; and (3) the
reciprocal emotional.

3072. KLEINBERG, SEYMOUR. "Alienated Affections: Friend-
      ships between Gay Men and Straight Women," **Chris-
      topher Street,** 4:3 (October-November 1979), 26-40.
Finds strongly positive qualities in close friendships
between gay men and heterosexual women. Both find it a
relationship purged of sexual tension, and the men are
able vicariously to explore aspects of the feminine that
intrigue them. See also, in the same issue, Roberta
Pliner, "Tea and Empathy: Friendships between Straight
Women and Gay Men--Fag Hags, Friends or Fellow Travelers?" ibid., pp. 15-25; and J. W. Malone, below.

3073. HIRSCHFELD, MAGNUS. "Bündnissformen homosexueller
      Männer und Frauen," **Geschlecht und Gesellschaft,** 9
      (1913), 465-80.
On types of bonding between homosexual men and women.

3074. LANKHEIT, KLAUS. **Das Freundschaftsbild der Roman-
      tik.** Heidelberg: Winter, 1952. 200 pp.
On the custom of German intellectuals to commission dual
portraits in token of spiritual friendship (late 18th-19th
century).

3075. LEPP, IGNACE. **The Ways of Friendship: A Psycholog-
      ical Exploration of Man's Most Valuable Relation-
      ship.** New York: Macmillan, 1966. 127 pp.
Views of a European Christian therapist, who considers
homosexuality resulting from sexual experiences with
adolescent friends to be a "deplorable aberration" and
"a rare exception."

3076. LEWIS, ROBERT A. "Emotional Intimacy among Men,"
      Journal of Social Issues, 34 (1978), 108-21.
Although men report more same-sex friendships than women
do, most of these are not close, intimate, or characterized by self-disclosure. Homophobia may play a part in
these limitations.

3077. MALONE, JOHN W. **Straight Women/Gay Men: A Special
      Relationship.** New York: Dial Press, 1980. 207 pp.
Perhaps the best of a series of popular publications on
this type of dyad, involving a gay man and a so-called
"fag hag." See also: Camilla Decarnin, "Interviews
with Five Faghagging Women," **Heresies,** no. 12 (1981),
10-14; S. Kleinberg, above; Rebecca Nahas and Myra Tur-
ley, **The New Couple: Women and Gay Men** (New York: Seaview
Books, 1979; 291 pp.); and Laurie Stone, "Women Who Live
with Gay Men," **Ms.** (October 1981), 103-04, 106, 108.

3078. MICHAELIS, DAVID. **The Best of Friends: Profiles of
       Extraordinary Friendships.** New York: William
       Morrow, 1983. 318 pp.
Journalistic account of the role of friendship in the
lives of fourteen men, most of them upper-class Americans.

3079. MILLER, STUART. **Men and Friendship.** Boston:
       Houghton Mifflin, 1983. 206 pp.
Fear of homosexuality inhibits the formation of close
bonds among men.

3080. MILLS, LAURENS J. **One Soul in Bodies Twain:
       Friendship in Tudor Literature and Stuart Drama.**
       Bloomington, In: Principia Press, 1937. 470 pp.
Standard, conventional work on this theme in English
literature. See also: Hans Kliem, **Sentimentale Freundschaft in der Shakespeare-Epoche** (Jena: Vopelius, 1915; 62
pp.; Ph.D. dissertation).

3081. MONTAIGNE, MICHEL DE. "Of Friendship," in: **The
       Complete Essays of Montaigne.** Translated by Donald
       M. Frame. Stanford: Stanford University Press,
       1958, pp. 135-44.
Following Aristotle and Cicero, Montaigne (1533-92) insists that friendship requires equality. Affection for
women cannot be characterized as friendship. See: Maurice Riveline, **Montaigne et l'amitié** (Paris: F. Alcan,
1939; 268 pp.).

3082. NESTOR, PAULINE. **Female Friendships and Communit-
       ies: Charlotte Bronte, George Eliot, Elizabeth
       Gaskell.** Oxford: Clarendon Press, 1985.
Explores the attitudes to, and representations of female
friendships and communities in the lives and works of
three major 19th-century British women writers, set
against the contemporary controversy over single "super-
abundant" women and the public debate about women's relationships with women.

3083. PEBWORTH, TED-LARRY. "Cowley's **Davideis** and the
       Exaltation of Friendship," in: Raymond-Jean Fron-
       tain and Jan Wojcik (eds.), **The David Myth in
       Western Literature.** West Lafayette, IN: Purdue
       University Press, 1980, pp. 97-200.
The David and Jonathan relationship as portrayed in a
Biblical epic of 1656.

3084. PLATO. "Lysis," in: **Lysis, Sumposium, Gorgias.**
       Translated by W. R. M. Lamb. Cambridge, MA: Har-
       vard University Press, 1975 [1925], pp. 1-71.
Through the friendship of two boys, Lysis and Menaxenus,
Plato explores the concept of friendship. See: David
Bolotin, **Plato's Dialogue on Friendship: An Interpreta-
tion of the Lysis, with a New Translation** (Ithaca, NY:
Cornell University Press, 1979; 227 pp.). See also

passages in such other works of Plato as the Symposium,
Phaedrus, Timaeus, Republic, Statesman, and Laws.

3085. RAYMOND, JANICE G. **A Passion for Friends: Toward**
      a Philosophy of Female Affection. Boston: Beacon
      Press, 1986. 275 pp.
A radical feminist proposes a new theory of friendship--
individual and communitarian--based in part on historical
evidence.

3086. SAHLI, NANCY. "Smashing: Women's Relationships
      before the Fall," **Chrysalis,** no. 8 (1979), 17-27.
Discusses a network of intimate supportive relationships
among American women during much of the 18th and 19th
centuries, which was subjected to increasing stress after
ca. 1875.

3087. SIMMEL, GEORG. **The Sociology of Georg Simmel.**
      Translated by Kurt H. Wolff. New York: Free Press,
      1950. 445 pp.
The writings of the German sociologist Georg Simmel (1858-
1918) on the dyad and the triad have been widely influential. He also dealt with the "stranger" as social type,
as well as the social psychology of secrecy, subordination, and urbanism.

3088. STEINBERGER, JOSEPH. **Begriff und Wesen der**
      Freundschaft bei Aristoteles und Cicero. Erlang-
      en: 1955. 175 pp.
German dissertation analyzing the writings of the two most
influential writers on friendship from classical antiquity.

3089. TALBOT, SERGE. "La Fraternité du sang, " **Arcadie,**
      no. 194 (February 1970), 76-82.
On homosexual aspects of blood brotherhood in a number of
cultures.

3090. TAMASSIA, GIOVANNI. **L'affratellamento (adelpho-**
      poiia): studio storico-giuridico. Turin: Fratelli
      Bocca, 1886. 77 pp.
A comparative study of blood brotherhood in the context of
Mediterranean high cultures, emphasizing legal aspects.

3091. TAWHIDI, ABU HAIYAN 'ALI IBN MUHAMMAD AL-. **Epitre**
      as-Sadaqa wa s-sadiq (L'ami et l'amitié). Edited
      and annotated by Ibrahim Kailani. Damascus: Dar
      al-Fikr, 1964. 540 pp.
Arabic text of a treatise on friendship, by an author
who died in A. D. 1023.

3092. TENNOV, DOROTHY. **Love and Limerance: The Exper-**
      ience of Being in Love. New York: Stein and Day,
      1979. 336 pp.
This much-noticed popular work launched a brief vogue of
the neologism "limerance" (in effect, romantic love),

which differs from both lust and simple friendship.

3093. TIGER, LIONEL. **Men in Groups.** New York: Random
       House, 1969. 254 pp.
An anthropologist's semisensationalized approach to male
bonding, which was treated as of major importance by the
popular press when it appeared, but which has proved to
have little lasting resonance.

3094. TODD, JANET. **Women's Friendships in Literature.**
       New York: Columbia University Press, 1980. 434 pp.
A solid work of literary criticism, emphasizing British
and American literature.

3095. WARREN, CAROL A. "Women among Men: Females in the
       Male Homosexual Community," **Archives of Sexual
       Behavior,** 5 (1976), 157-69.
Employed participant observation and interviewing to
examine the types of interaction and relationship among
male homosexuals and lesbians and female heterosexuals.
Women gave four reasons for this involvement: greater
sociability of gay men compared to lesbians, a liking
for traditionally "feminine" women (whom they would meet
in the cliques), the safety factor, and functional reasons.

3096. WELTER, ERNST GÜNTHER. **Bibliographie Freund-
       schaftseros einschliesslich Homoerotik, Homosexual-
       ität und die verwandte und vergleichende Gebiete.**
       Frankfurt am Main: Dipa Verlag, 1964. 145 pp.
Wide-ranging, but somewhat personal bibliography on
friendship stressing the homoerotic aspects but sharply
distinguishing it from overt "modern" homosexuality. In
addition to print materials, mostly German, has information on films, photography, and statues.

3097. WITTELS, FRITZ. "Collective Defense Mechanisms
       against Homosexuality," **Psychoanalytic Review,** 31
       (1944), 19-33.
Asserts that covenants of men--religious, military, and
small groups--operate as a defense against homosexuality
by sublimating or desexualizing it. If the bonds of the
group are weakened, overt homosexuality can break through
strongly, since the energy of the drive was fed in the
group.

                        L. GHETTO, GAY

In recent years the term ghetto has undergone a perhaps
excessive expansion from its original definition as a
quarter of late medieval cities where Jews were required
to live. Through journalistic usage, the expression "gay
ghetto" has gained a certain currency. Under this cat-

egory are included various studies of the spatial organization of urban homosexuals--whether or not these living and socializing arrangements constitute ghettos in
any strict sense of the term.

3098. BURKS, JOHN. "The Gay Mecca; But San Francisco is
      Still No Utopia for Homosexuals," **San Francisco**
      (April 1970), 30-34, 42-45.
Profile of the city just prior to the changes symbolized
by the rise of Castro Street.

3099. CASTELLS, MANUEL, and KAREN MURPHY. "Cultural
      Identity and Urban Structure: The Spatial Organ-
      ization of San Francisco's Gay Community," in: Nor-
      man Fainstein and Susan Fainstein (eds.). **Urban
      Policy under Capitalism.** Beverly Hills, CA: Sage,
      1982.
Offers a neo-Marxist approach. See also Castells, **The
City and the Grassroots: A Cross-Cultural Theory of Urban Social Movements** (Berkeley: University of California Press, 1983; 450 pp.).

3100. EIGHNER, LARS. "The Ghetto and the Gay Ghetto,"
      Cabirion and Gay Books Bulletin, 12 (1985), 6-8.
Sketch of historical and sociological conceptualizations
of the idea. Finds the first (metaphorical) use of the
term "homosexual ghetto" in Alfred A. Gross, **Strangers
in Our Midst** (Washington: Public Affairs Press, 1962),
pp. 131-33.

3101. FISCHER, CLAUDE S. **To Dwell among Friends: Person-
      al Networks in Town and City.** Chicago: University
      of Chicago Press, 1982. 451 pp.
Influential contrast of personal networks in the San Francisco Bay area. See esp. pp. 63-74, 237-40 on gay and
black cultures in the city.

3102. GITECK, LENNY. "How Gay Are the Ghettos?" **Advocate,**
      no. 275 (September 6, 1979), 15-18.
Report on the current scene by a San Francisco journalist.
See also: Gordon Johnston, "Keys to the Ghetto," **Christo-
pher Street** (January 1980), 21-32.

3103. HANSEN, EDWARD, et al. **The Tenderloin Ghetto: The
      Young Reject in Our Society.** San Francisco: Coun-
      cil on Religion and the Homosexual, 1966. 29 pp.
Pioneering study of conditions in San Francisco's inner
city, its dweller (including many young gay males), and
the availability of social services.

3104. HARRY, JOSEPH, and WILLIAM B. DEVALL. **The Social
      Organization of Gay Males.** New York: Praeger,
      1978. 223 pp.
Integrates existing knowledge with data obtained from 243
Detroit gay males and field work elsewhere. In addition

to material on gay ghettos, offers information on stereotypes, age preferences, and job discrimination. Shows
that differentiation of specialty bars is a predictable
function of population size. See also Joseph Harry, "Urbanization and Gay Life," **Journal of Sexual Research**,
10 (1974), 238-47.

3105. HELMER, W. J. "New York's Middle-Class Homosexu-
       als," **Harper's**, no. 226 (March 1963), 85-92.
The public is becoming aware of "pansy patches" and "fairy
flats" in the large cities.

3106. KOPKIND, ANDREW. "Gay City on the Hill: Once Upon
       a Time in the West," **Nation** (June 1, 1985), 672-67.
The factors that produced the first incorporated municip-
ality with a gay majority on the city council (West Hollywood, CA).

3107. LEE, JOHN ALAN. "The Gay Connection," **Urban Life**,
       8:2 (July 1979), 175-98.
Essays a theoretical overview, including boundaries,
population, territory, time, and niches.

3108. LEVINE, MARTIN P. "Gay Ghetto," **JH**, 4 (1979),
       363-77.
Spotmaps and fieldwork in five American cities (Boston,
Chicago, Los Angeles, New York, and San Francisco) doc-
ument the existence of (chiefly male) gay enclaves.
Applies Wirth and Park's conceptualization to them.

3109. LEZNOFF, MAURICE, and W. A. WERTLEY. "The Homosex-
       ual Community," **Social Problems**, 2 (1956), 257-63.
Through 60 in-depth interviews and participant observation, charts the social structure of Montreal homosexuals. Cliques provide social support.

3110. MCNEE, BOB. "If You Are Squeamish," **East Lakes
       Geographer**, 19 (1984), 16-27..
A gay professional geographer's account of Denver's East
Colfax strip. See also his "It Takes One to Know One,"
**Transitions: Quarterly Journal of the Socially and
Ecologically Responsible Geographers**, 14:3 (Fall 1983,
12-15 (reflections on thirty-five years of observation of
the urban gay "turf").

3111. MURRAY, STEPHEN O. "Institutional Elaboration of a
       Quasi-Ethnic Community," **International Review of
       Modern Sociology**, 9 (1979), 165-78.
Discussion of the applicability of "community" in its
technical meaning with data on the residential and
recreational ecology of Toronto.

3112. VAN DYNE, LARRY. "Is DC Becoming the Gay Capital
       of America?" **Washington**, 15 (September 1980),
       96-101, 133, 141.
Reflects the enhanced visibility of the gay and lesbian

community in the nation's capital, as well as the significance of the black contribution.

3113. VOJIR, DAN. **The Sunny Side of Castro Street: A
        Diary of Sorts.** San Francisco: Strawberry Hill
        Press, 1982. 144 pp.
Lightweight personal memoir, contrasting growing up in a
lower middle-class Chicago suburb with initiation into San
Francisco's premier gay ghetto.

3114. WARE, CAROLINE. **Greenwich Village 1920-1930: A
        Comment on American Civilization in the Post-War
        Years.** New York: Harper and Row, 1965. 496 pp.
An early mention of residential concentration of homosexuals, as part of "Bohemia." (pp. 238, 252). This book was
first published in 1935 (Boston: Houghton Mifflin).

3115. WEIGHTMAN, BARBARA. "Commentary: Towards a Geog-
        raphy of the Gay Community," **Journal of Cultural
        Geography,** 1 (1981), 106-112.
Offers a territorial approach.

3116. WILLENBECHER, THOM. "Gentrification: Has the Gay
        Role in Urban Restoration Built Up a Backlash?"
        Advocate, no. 298 (August 7, 1980), 17-19.
The straight press, relying on a number of misconceptions,
tends to portray the housing problem in a number of inner
city areas as a struggle between poor minorities and
decadent well-healed gays. See also: Allen Young,
"Gentrification," **Fag Rag,** no. 26 (1979), 14-15, 30.

                    M. IDENTITY FORMATION

The idea of identity has both an individual dimension, the
self-concept that is rooted in the human capacity for re-
flexivity and self-awareness, and a social dimension, in
which identity is shaped and reshaped in interaction with
others. Apart from investigations by sociologists and
social psychologists, homosexuals themselves have evolved
a way of speaking and thinking about the process of identity formation, which they term "coming out." The question remains complex and hard to clarify, probably because it involves both contested areas of social theory
and the variable life adjustments of individuals in a
society that continues to stigmatize them.

3117. CASS, VIVIENNE C. "Homosexual Identity: A Concept
        in Need of Definition," **JH,** 9:2-3 (1983-84), 105-
        26.
In a sphere where previous attempts have been characterized by confusion, disarray, and ambiguity, it is necessary to undertake a serious multidisciplinary approach.

See also her: "Homosexual Identity Formation: A Theoretical Model," **JH,** 4 (1979), 219-35, which outlines a six-stage model and has proven influential; and "Homosexual Identity Formation: Testing a Theoretical Model," **Journal of Sex Research,** 20 (1984), 143-67.

3118. DANK, BARRY M. "Coming Out in the Gay World," **Psychiatry,** 34 (1971), 180-97.
Questionnaire results suggest that at this point homosexuals were beginning to come out at an earlier age, and their assimilation into the gay community was less fraught with alienating effects. A salient finding is the gap between recognizing homosexual desire and coming out.

3119. FARRELL, RONALD A., and JAMES F. NELSON. "A Causal Model of Secondary Deviance: The Case of Secondary Deviance," **Sociological Quarterly,** 17 (1976), 109-20.
Association with gay groups, stemming from perceived social rejection, appears to be the major cause of career homosexuality.

3120. FEIN, SARA BECK, and ELANE M. NUEHRING. "Intrapsychic Effects of Stigma: A Process of Breakdown and Reconstruction of Social Reality," **JH,** 7 (1981), 3-13.
Posits that in both breakdown and reconstruction stigma has a master status, deriving from the stereotypes associated with the stigma and the actual and imagined responses of others.

3121. GERSHMAN, HARRY. "The Stress of Coming Out," **American Journal of Psychoanalysis,** 43 (1983), 129-38.
Stress varies in intensity according to the individual's degree of integration and the support given by friends and family.

3122. HARRY, JOSEPH. "Sexual Orientation as Destiny," **JH,** 10:3-4 (1984), 111-24.
Sexual orientation, defined as erotic attraction rather than sexual behavior, is established at an early age and largely immutable in adulthood.

3123. HELLMAN, RONALD E., et al. "Childhood Sexual Identity, Childhood Religiosity, and 'Homophobia' as Influences in the Development of Transsexualism, Homosexuality, and Heterosexuality," **Archives of General Psychiatry,** 38 (1981), 910-915.
Data support the hypothesis that early developmental aspects of sexual identity, and later concerns over homosexuality that are partly of a religious derivation, may contribute to a transsexual outcome.

3124. HENCKEN, JOEL D. "Conceptualizations of Homosexual Behavior which Preclude Homosexual Self-Labeling," **JH,** 9:4 (1984), 53-63.

Identifies a variety of common coneptualizations of "homosexual behavior" which permit the indiviaul to avoid the
stigma of homosexual self-labeling ("intricate psychological footwork"). See also: Joel D. Hencken and William
O'Dowd, "Coming Out as an Aspect of Identity Formation,"
Gai Saber, 1 (1977), 18-22.

3125. HUMPHREYS, LAUD, and BRIAN MILLER. "Identities in
       the Emerging Gay Culture," in: Judd Marmor (ed.),
       Homosexual Behavior: A Modern Reappraisal. New
       York: Basic Books, 1980, 142-56.
Presents the salient features of identity theory; a typology of cultural units (gay scenes, subcultures, and
satellite units); the emergence of a gay culture in the
1970s; and the phylogeny of gay culture as disclosed by
the authors' research with gay fathers.

3126. JACOBS, JOHN A., and WILLIAM H. TEDFORD. "Factors
       Affecting the Self-Esteem of the Homosexual
       Individual," **JH,** 5 (1980), 373-82.
Finds that the factors of alienation and openness are
the most important in predicting self-esteem.

3127. LARSON, PAUL C. "Sexual Identity and Self-Con-
       cept," **JH,** 7 (1981), 15-32.
Investigated the relationship among gender, social sex
roles, and sexual orientation as components of sexual
identity--finding that each component was individually
important in the relationship of sexual identity to
self-concept.

3128. LEE, JOHN A. "Going Public: A Study in the Sociol-
       ogy of Homosexual Liberation," **JH,** 3 (1977), 49-78.
The process of resolving and announcing one's sexual
orientation as "homosexual" is classified into three
stages: signification, coming out, and going public. Not
everyone passes through every step. (Critics have said
that one reaches the third stage only by becoming a
celebrity.)

3129. MCCONAGHY, N., and M. S. ARMSTRONG. "Sexual
       Orientation and Consistency of Sexual Identity,"
       Archives of Sexual Behavior, 12 (1983), 317-27.
Claims that sexual identity is different in "normals"
from that found in the sexually deviant, on whom our
conceptualization of sexual identity has been frequently
based.

3130. MALYON, ALAN K. "Biphasic Aspects of Homosexual
       Identity Formation," **Psychotherapy: Theory,
       Research and Practice,** 19 (1982), 335-40.
Contends that because of conflicts in the establishment
of homosexual identity in adolescence, unfinished tasks
of psychic integration are postponed, to be taken up in
the third decade or later.

3131. MILLER, BRIAN. "Adult Sexual Resocialization: Ad-
        justment toward a Stigmatized Identity," **Alterna-
        tive Lifestyles,** 1 (1978), 207-34.
Employing a social construction of reality perspective,
explores the lifestyles of gay husbands (coping strategies, coming out patterns, and gay identity development).

3132. MINTON, HARRY, and GARY J. MCDONALD. "Homosexual
        Identity Formation as a Developmental Process," **JH,**
        9:2-3 (1983-84), 91-104.
Using J. Habermas' theory of ego development, conceptual-
izes homosexual identity as a life-spanning development
process in three stages (egocentric, norm-acquisitive,
and post-conventional).

3133. MONTEFLORES, C., and S. J. SCHULTZ. "Coming Out:
        Similarities and Differences for Lesbians and Gay
        Men," **Journal of Social Issues,** 34 (1978), 59-72.
Apart from significant similarities, differences between
lesbians and gay men in coming out are ascribed to gender
role socialization and political and legal concerns.

3134. MOSES, ALICE. **Identity Management in Lesbian
        Women.** New York: Praeger, 1978. 120 pp.
Social work report which explores the effect of labeling,
exploring new concepts in the sphere of deviance.

3135. PONSE, BARBARA. **Identities in the Lesbian World:
        The Social Construction of Self.** Westport, CT:
        Greenwood Press,   228 pp.
Within a symbolic interactionist framework, the author
sets forth the process whereby lesbians develop a sexual
identity, noting the difference between identity and
sexual behavior and bringing out the importance of reference groups. See also her "Secrecy in the Lesbian
World," **Urban Life,** 5 (1976), pp. 313-38.

3136. TROIDEN, RICHARD R. "Becoming Homosexual: A Model
        of Gay Identity Acquisition," **Psychiatry,** 42
        (1979), 362-73.
Proposes the following sequence: sensitization; dissocia-
tion and signification; coming out as self-definition;
commitment. See also: Richard R. Troiden and Erich
Goode, "Variables Related to the Acquisition of a Gay
Identity," **JH,** 5 (1980), 383-392.

3137. WEINBERG, THOMAS S. **Gay Men, Gay Selves: The
        Social Construction of Homosexual Identities.** New
        York: Irvington Press, 1983. 329 pp.
Using interview material, Weinberg presents sex activity
as almost always preceding identity, which--once it has
been constructed--is not a static artifact but must be
maintained over one's career. Symbolic interactionist
approach. See also his: "On Doing and Being Gay: Sexual
Behavior and Homosexual Self-Identity," **JH** 4 (1978),

143-56.

N. IMPERSONAL SEX

Often dismissed as "promiscuity," impersonal sex contacts
have long been significant for gay men, for whom they can
be documented as early as the 12th century in Europe. In
20th-century North America, impersonal or anonymous sex
encounters have undergone significant modifications
through the universalization of the car culture--a nexus
aptly conveyed by the term "pick up." Uncommon among
lesbians, impersonal sex patterns among homosexual men are
generally associated with high numbers of partners.

3138. CORZINE, JAY, and RICHARD KIRBY. "Cruising the
      Truckers: Sexual Encounters in a Highway Rest
      Area," **Urban Life,** 6 (1977), 171-92.
Ethnographic study of encounters beween gay male "cruis-
ers" and truckers in the vicinity of St. Louis.

3139. DELPH, EDWARD W. **The Silent Community: Public
      Homosexual Encounters.** Beverly Hills, CA: Sage,
      1978. 188 pp.
Field study of modes of communication in anonymous sexual encounters in New York City (sex clubs, bathhouses,
subway restrooms, backrooms, and parks).

3140. GOODE, ERICH, and RICHARD R. TROIDEN. "Correlates
      and Accompaniments of Anonymous Sex among Male
      Homosexuals," **Psychiatry,** 43 (1980), 51-59.
From interviews with individuals from the New York City
and Minneapolis areas, an attempt is made to differentiate them according to degree of promiscuity and dangers
incurred (e.g. assault, venereal disease, arrest).

3141. HUMPHREYS, LAUD. **Tearoom Trade: Impersonal Sex in
      Public Places.** Chicago: Aldine, 1970. 180 pp.
Field study of anonymous sex acts in public restrooms
(near St. Louis, IL), showing the modus operandi of the
participants, cautions observed, and their background.
Owing to its controversial methodology, this monograph
has gained a certain notoriety. In the expanded 1975
edition (New York: Hawthorne), Humphreys prints some
critics' comments with his reply.

3142. LEE, JOHN A. **Getting Sex: A New Approach, More
      Fun, Less Guilt.** Don Mills, Ont.: Musson Book Co.,
      1978. 318 pp.
Ethnography of mid-1970s Toronto area bars, bathouses, and
bushes.

3143. PONTE, MEREDITH R. "Life in a Parking Lot: An

Ethnography of a Homosexual Drive-In," in: Jerry
Jacobs (ed.), **Deviance: Field Studies and Self-Dis-
closures.** Palo Alto, CA: National Press Books,
1974, pp. 7-29.
Car-engineered encounters (also restroom) at a Los Angeles
Beach.

3144. RECHY, JOHN. **The Sexual Outlaw: A Documentary.**
New York: Grove Press, 1978. 307 pp.
Lightly fictionalized account of a series of impersonal
sex encounters in Los Angeles.

3145. SURZUR, ROLAND. "Les autoroutes de l'amour," **Gai
pied**, no. 189 (October 12-18, 1985), 23-25.
Sex at reststops on French superhighways; with two maps.

3146. TROIDEN, RICHARD R., and ERICH GOODE. "Homosexual
Encounters in a Highway Reststop," in: Goode and
Troiden (eds.), **Sexual Deviance and Sexual Devi-
ants.** New York: William Morrow, 1975, pp. 211-28.
Field study of participants--some gay-identified, some
straight-identified--at a rest area in the Northeast.
Treats techniques of solicitation, sexual practices, and
reasons for participation.

3147. VASSI, MARCO. **The Metasex Manifesto.** New York:
Bantam, 1976. 213 pp.
Experiential discussion of impersonal sex at the trucks
(pp.121-130) and the baths (pp. 145-65) in New York City.

O. INCEST

Definitions of incest vary not only cross-culturally but
also over the course of Western civilization, an element
of variability that has been obscured by the current sensationalizing of the problem. While serving to foster
unreasoning dread and even hysteria in the popular mind,
the current association of sexual relations within the
family with child abuse and rape has had the by-product
of focusing attention on neglected aspects, including
homosexual incest.

3148. BIXLER, RAY. "Homosexual Twin Incest Avoidance,"
Journal of Sex Research, 19 (1983), 296-302.
Reviews literature, tentatively concluding that homosexuals orient sexually toward same-sex siblings much as do
heterosexuals toward opposite-sex siblings. The actual
dynamics of the avoidance remain to be explained.

3149. CABANIS, DETLEF, and EHRARD PHILLIP. "Der pado-
phil-homosexuelle "Inzest" vor Gericht," **Deutsche
Zeitschrift für die gesamte gerichtliche Medizin,**

66 (1969), 47-47.
Legal sanctions against "pedophile-homosexual incest" in
the German Federal Republic.

3150. DE YOUNG, MARY. **Incest: An Annotated Bibliog-
        raphy.** Jefferson, NC: McFarland, 1985. 161 pp.
Classified list of 410 items with descriptive annotations
arranged by categories. Author and subject indexes.

3151. HAMILTON, GILBERT VAN TASSEL. "Homosexuality,
        Defensive," in: Victor Robinson (ed.), **Encyclo-
        pedia Sexualis.** New York: Dingwall-Rock, 1936,
        pp. 334-42.
Claiming that "fear of incest is the most important of the
factors involved in the overdelopment of the homsexual
tendency," Hamilton suggests that overt homosexuality in
both males and females is a defensive "flight from incest," though female homosexuality has a more complex
determination.

3152. JUSTICE, BLAIR, and RITA JUSTICE. **The Broken
        Taboo: Sex in the Family.** New York: Human Sciences
        Press, 1979. 304 pp.
In this semipopular work, see pp. 74, 89, 128, 196-97,
291.

3153. LANGSLEY, DONALD G., et al. "Father-Son Incest,"
        Comprehensive Psychiatry, 9 (1968), 218-26.
Profiles a case of father-son incest through investigations of both parents, the son and the family group as a
unit.

3154. MYERS, MICHAEL F. "Homosexuality, Sexual Dysfunc-
        tion, and Incest in Male Identical Twins," **Canadian
        Journal of Psychiatry,** 27 (1982), 144-47.
Describes a set of adult male monozygotic twins (aged 27
years) who were living together in a "highly ambivalent
incestual relationship." Therapy induced separation.

3155. RUBIN, RICK, and GREG BYERLY. **Incest: The Last
        Taboo: An Annotated Bibliography.** New York: Gar-
        land, 1983. 169 pp.
Presents 419 items (about fifteen directly relevant).
Periodical, author, and subject indexes.

3156. SIMARI, C. GEORGIA, and DAVID BASKIN. "Incestuous
        Experiences within Homosexual Populations: A Pre-
        liminary Study," **Archives of Sexual Behavior,** 11
        (1982), 329-44.
Retrospectively examines the incidence, frequency rates,
and effects of both homosexual and heterosexual incestuous experiences within lesbian and male homosexual
populations (29 women and 54 men). Essentially the same
article appears in **Child Psychiatry Quarterly,** 17 (1984),
21-40.

P. INCIDENCE

In earlier centuries impressionistic notions of the rarity
of homosexual contacts went hand in hand with their conceptualization as abnormal or unusual pathology. Although
some European studies had questioned the conventional
wisdom of low incidence, it was the massive data that was
accumulated by Alfred Kinsey and his associates at Indiana
University that first revealed how widespread homosexual
activity was, thus compelling a rethinking of the problem
and its relation to the purported "unnaturalness" of
same-sex behavior.

3157. DAVIS, KATHERINE B., and MARIO E. KOPP. **Factors in
       the Sex Life of Twenty-two Hundred Women.** New
       York: Harper, 1929. 430 pp.
In this report on 1,000 married and 1,200 single women
(mostly college educated, from the Northeast U.S.), about
40% disclosed that they had had an "intense emotional
relationship with other women." Some 14% of the married
and 19% of the unmarried reported some overt lesbian contact.

3158. FRIEDEBERG, L. VON. **Zum Umfrage in der Intim-
       sphare.** Stuttgart: F. Enke, 1953.
About 23% of West German males surveyed reported homosexual experiences.

3159. GEBHARD, PAUL H. "Incidence of Overt Homosexuality
       in the United States and Western Europe," in: John
       M. Livingood (ed.), **Final Report and Background
       Papers, National Institute of Mental Health Task
       Force on Homosexuality.** Washington, DC: Govenment
       Printing Office, 1972, pp. 22-29.
Surveys the existing literature on incidence in Europe and
the United States, indicating the need for a more consistent definition of homosexual behavior so that results can
be compared. Much existing work shows a bias towards
upper-middle and upper class respondents, including students. Because of overrepresentation of prisoners, the
1948 Kinsey male data are distorted--though independent
evidence suggests that the famous figure of 37% for overt
male homosexual experience is not much exaggerated.
(Nonetheless it is essential to consult the 1948 and 1953
Reports of Alfred Kinsey et al.).

3160. GIESE, HANS, and GUNTER SCHMIDT. **Studenten-Sexual-
       ität: Verhalten und Einstellung.** Reinbek bei
       Hamburg: Rohwohlt, 1968. 415 pp.
Results of a questionnaire returned by West German university students show that 15% of the males and 3% of the
females reported homosexual experience, mainly in adolescence.

3161. HIRSCHFELD, MAGNUS. "Ergebnisse und statistische
Untersuchungen über den Prozentsatz der Homosexuellen," **JfsZ**, 6 (1904), 109-75.
From questionnaires sent to students and to metalworkers,
estimates the homosexual population of the German Empire
as about 2.3%, with 3.4% bisexual. See also the supplementary remarks in **Vierteljarhresbericht des Wissenschaft-
lich-humanitären Komites** (1913), 14-22, 166-74.

3162. RÖMER, L. S. A. M. VON. **Die uranische Familie:
Untersuchungen über die Aszendenz der Uranier.**
Amsterdam: Maas & Suchtelen, 1906. 107 pp.
Of 308 Dutch male university students responding, 1.9%
reported that they were homosexual and 3.9 said they were
bisexual.

3163. SPENCER, S. J. G. "Homosexuality among Oxford
Undergraduates," **Journal of Mental Science,** 105
(1959), 394-405.
Of 200 students, half of them psychiatric patients, 13%
reported recent homosexual activity.

Q. INTERNATIONAL COMPARISONS

Cross-cultural comparisons, even among Western societies,
are still uncommon in homosexual studies. This neglect
may be attributed to a variety of causes: the need to
record local manifestations which in many spheres are only
just emerging from clandestinity; lack of research funds;
and an unanalyzed notion that homosexuality is the same
everywhere. It is just the latter question that the
neglect of this kind of research begs. Also needed, of
course, is more work on non-Western societies (see
IV.A-F).

3164. ALTMAN, DENNIS. "The Ockerism of Gay Sydney," **Mean-
jin** (June 1983), 215-19.
Holds that the gay world in Australia is marked by
working-class culture, while that of the U. S. reflects
the hegemony of middle-class values.

3165. BATSELIER, STEVEN DE, and H. LAURENCE ROSS (eds.).
**Les minorités homosexuelles: une approche compar-
ative: Allemagne, Pays-Bas, Etats-Unis.** Gembloux:
Duculot, 1973. 294 pp.
Offers separate, but to some extent coordinated presentations on Germany (by Johannes Werres, pp. 81-150), The
Netherlands (by Cees Straver, pp. 151-208), and the United
States (by Edward Sagarin, pp. 208-66). Comparative material on Denmark, The Netherlands, and the U. S. appears
in Martin S. Weinberg, and Colin J. Williams, **Male Homosexuals: Their Problems and Adaptations** (New York: Oxford

University Press, 1974; 316 pp.).

3166. BROWN, MARVIN, and DONALD M. AMOROSO. "Attitudes
       toward Homosexuality among West Indian Male and
       Female College Students," **Journal of Social
       Psychology**, 97 (1975), 163-68.
Complementing the measures of attitudes toward homosexuality, sexual liberalism vs. conservatism, and sex guilt,
previously given by J. Dunbar et al. (see below) to Canadian and Brazilian students, tests were administered to
69 male and 51 female West Indian students. The males
scored more anti-homosexual than the Canadians, but less
so than the Brazilians.

3167. BUHRICH, N., et al. "Bisexual Feelings and Oppo-
       site Sex Behavior in Male Malaysian Medical Stu-
       dents," **Archives of Sexual Behavior**, 11 (1982),
       387-93.
Of 65 Malaysian medical students (21-26 years old), 40%
were aware of homosexual feelings before age 15, and 17%
were currently aware of such feelings. Results are discussed in the light of a similar investigation with
Australian medical students.

3168. DUNBAR, JOHN, et al. "Attitudes toward Homosexual-
       ity among Brazilian and Canadian College Students,"
       Journal of Scoial Psychology, 90 (1973), 173-83.
Compared with Canadians, Brazilian antihomosexual subjects
were more disapproving of variant sexual practices and
reported greater sex guilt than pro-homosexual subjects.
They were also more inclined to classmate homosexuals as
"feminine."

3169. GODBILL, BONNIE M. "Power Relations, Homosexuality
       and the Family: A Review of the Literature, Includ-
       ing Cross-Cultural Studies (Homosexuality and the
       Family in the Mohave, Chinese and Iraqi Cultures),"
       Journal of Comparative Family Studies, 14 (1983),
       315-331.
Finds that the Mohave culture is accepting of alternative
sex-roles for either sex. In China, an occultation
process occurs, but when homosexuality does appear, it
tends to be somaticized. In Iraq, homosexuality was
traditionally practiced as a normal phase in masculine
development.

3170. GRANERO, MIRTA. "Diferencias entre homosexuales y
       heterosexuales (varones y mujeres) en temores,
       asertividad y autosuficiencia," **Revista latinoame-
       ricana de psicologia**, 16 (1984), 39-52.
In this Argentine report, it was found that homosexuals
had more fears than heterosexuals, and women had more
fears than men; there were typical homosexual fears and
typical female fears. The differences were explained
in terms of early learning.

3171. GRAY, J. PATRICK, and JANE E. ELLINGTON. "Institu-
       tionalized Male Transvestism, the Couvade, and
       Homosexual Behavior," **Ethos**, 12 (1984), 54-63.
Hypothesized that there was a negative association between the presence of a couvade in a society and the frequency of male homosexual behavior. Comparisons are
offered between tribal societies and contemporary Western
ones.

3172. JANSSENS, MARIE-JOSE, and WILHELMINA VAN WETERING.
       "Mati en lesbiennes: homoseksualiteit en etnische
       identiteit bij Creools Surinaamse vrouwen en Neder-
       land," **Sociologische Gids**, 32 (1985), 394-415.
Shows that among creole Suriname women who emigrate to
the Netherlands, the indigenous **mati** pattern of female
homosociality persists, without assimilating to the
metropolitan lesbian model.

3173. MORSE, STANLEY. "Requirements for Love and Friend-
       ship in Australia and Brazil," **Australian Journal
       of Psychology**, 35 (1983), 469-76.
Females and Brazilians expect somewhat more from friendship than males and Australians.

3174. OYHENART-PERERA, M. F. "La iniciacion sexual de
       varones androtropicos," **Revista de psiquiatria y
       psicologia medica**, 16 (1984), 469-90.
Examined the characteristics of the sexual initiation
of 118 Uruguayan and 100 Spanish male homosexuals.

3175. ROSS, MICHAEL W. "Femininity, Masculinity and
       Sexual Orientation: Some Cross-Cultural Compari-
       sons," **JH**, 9 (1983), 27-36.
Administering the Bem Sex-Role Inventory to males from
Australia, Sweden, and Finland suggests that while there
is no relationship between femininity and degree of homosexuality, masculinity is inversely related depending on
the degree of sex-role stereotyping and anti-homosexual
attitudes of the society the subjects live in. See also
his: "Societal Relationships and Gender Role in Homosexuals: A Cross-Cultural Comparison," **Journal of Sex Research**, 19 (1983), 273-88; and "Actual and Anticipated
Societal Reaction to Homosexuality and Adjustment in Two
Societies [Australia and Sweden]," **Journal of Sex Research**, 21 (1985), 40-55.

3176. WHITAM, FREDERICK L. "Culturally Invariable
       Properties of Male Homosexuality: Tentative
       Conclusions from Cross-Cultural Research," **Archives
       of Sexual Behavior**, 12 (1983), 207-26.
Based on field work in homosexual communities in the
U.S., Guatemala, and the Philippines, Whitam offers six
tentative conclusions about cultural invariability: (1)
homosexual persons appear in all societies; (2) the percentage of homosexuals seems to be about the same; (3)
social norms neither impede or facilitate the emergence of

homosexual orientation; (4) given sufficient aggregates of
people, homosexual subcultures appear in all societies;
(5) homosexuals in different societies tend to resemble
one another; (6) all societies produce similar continua,
from overtly masculine to overtly feminine homosexuals.
These findings are elaborated in Whitam and Robin M.
Mathy, **Male Homosexuality in Four Societies: Brazil,
Guatemala, the Philippines, and the United States** (New
York: Praeger, 1986; 240 pp.). For criticism, see Joseph
M. Carrier, "Childhood Cross-gender Behavior and Adult
Homosexuality," **Archives of Sexual Behavior**, 15 (1986),
87-91.

R. LABELING

The sociological concept of labeling, which posits that
behavioral patterns of individual deviants are shaped
by the epithets and classifications that society attaches
to them, remains controversial, though it seems clear that
it has some explanatory power. The term stigma emphasizes
the negative consequences of labeling.

3177. BOBYS, RICHARDS. and MARY R. LANER. "On the
       Stability of Stigmatization: The Case of Ex-Homo-
       sexual Males," **Archives of Sexual Behavior**, 8
       (1979), 247-61.
Analysis of data obtained by questionaire from 281 respondents (17-75 years old) showed that the variable
most strongly related to stigmatization of ex-homosex-
uals was degree of "dangerousness" attributed to them.

3178. HENCKEN, JOEL D. "Conceptualizations of Homosexual
       Behavior Which Preclude Homosexual Self-Labeling,"
       JH, 9 (1984), 53-63.
Because of the pervasiveness of the stigma, those who
would engage in homosexual acts, yet avoid self-labeling
must engage in intricate psychological footwork.

3179. KARR, RODNEY G. "Homosexual Labeling and the Male
       Role," **Journal of Social Issues**, 34 (1978), 73-84.
In comparisons with control groups, men were perceived as
being less masculine and less preferred as a fellow participant when they were labeled homosexual.

3180. KITSUSE, JOHN I. "Societal Reactions to Deviant
       Behavior: Problems of Theory and Method," **Social
       Problems**, 9 (1963), 247-56.
While not directly pertinent, this article has been influential, and is in fact regarded as a locus classicus of
labeling theory.

3181. POLLACK, STEPHEN et al. "The Dimensions of

Stigma: The Social Situation of the Mentially Ill
Person and the Male Homosexual," **Journal of
Abnormal Psychology,** 85 (1976), 105-12.
Reports two studies designed to test the assumptions that
stigmatizing labels not only lead observers to perceive
more deviance but also lead the labeled individual to behave more deviantly.

3182. SCHUR, EDWIN M. **Labeling Deviant Behavior: The
        Sociological Implications.** New York: Harper and
        Row, 1971. 177 pp.
Introduction to the concept of labeling with some references to homosexuality, by an influential, humanistically
oriented sociologist.

3183. SCHUR, EDWIN M. **Labeling Women Deviant: Gender,
        Stigma and Social Control.** Philadelphia: Temple
        University Press, 1984. 286 pp.
Examines the ways in which societal definitions of behavior deemed problematic have a negative impact on
women, including lesbians. A well referenced work,
affording many vistas.

                    S. MINORITY CONCEPT

Originally a political term, referring to nongoverning
groups in a parliamentary organization, the term minority
came to be widely applied to ethnic groups constituting
permanent minorities in a parliamentary multi-national
state such as Austria-Hungary or Switzerland in the
aftermath of the discussion of President Wilson's Fourteen
Points at the close of World War I. With the increasing
attention to ethnic and racial minorities in recent
decades, especially in the United States, the concept began to appeal to homosexual researchers and political figures. To be sure, prejudice and discrimination
(see XII.C) directed toward gay men and lesbians are not
unlike those employed against racial and religious minority members. Yet homosexuality has failed to gain acceptance in the field of minority studies, and many homosexuals feel little affinity for the idea.

3184. ADAM, BARRY D. "Some Continuities in Out-Group
        Stereotypes," **Gai Saber,** 1 (1977), 72-77.
Posits commonalities in the stereotypes of Jews, blacks,
and homosexuals. The argument of this article was pursued
in greater detail in his: **The Survival of Domination: Inferiorization and Everyday Life** (New York: Elsevier, 1978;
180 pp.).

3185. ALLEN, FREDERICK H. "Homosexuality in Relation to
        the Problem of Human Differences," **American Journal**

of **Orthopsychiatry**, 10 (1940), 129-35.
Contends that there is a parallel between nationalism and
homosexuality, both phenomena springing from a feeling of
insecurity.

3186. BETH, HANNO. "Minorität und Majorität: das Bei-
        spiel Homosexualität," **Liberal**, 11 (1969), 198-210.
Political science approach to the minority-majority
contrast, using homosexuality as the focus.

3187. BUSH, LARRY. "The Challenge of Community," **Advo-
        cate**, no. 370 (June 23, 1983), 42-45, 80.
Problems connected with the national groups that claim
to speak for gays and lesbians.

3188. CORY, DONALD WEBSTER (pseud. of Edward Sagarin).
        The Homosexual in America: A Subjective Approach.
        New York: Greenberg, 1951. 326 pp.
In its time probably the most widely read work on the
subject, this book is organized around the minority concept, which is deployed not only as a means of understanding the folkways of (mainly) male homosexuals, but also
as a political argument for greater tolerance. Sagarin
offers useful ethnographic observations for the period,
including bars, cruising, and couples. Some psychoanalytic concepts are uncritically relayed. A second edition,
with some additional material but also with omissions,
was published in 1960 (New York: Castle; 334 pp.); the
1975 edition (New York: Arno Press) combines the material
from both editions. See also: Edward Sagarin, **Odd Man
In: Societies of Deviants in America** (Chicago: Quadrangle,
1969; 287 pp.).

3189. HACKER, HELEN M. "Homosexuals: Deviant or Minority
        Group," in: Edward Sagarin (ed.), **The Other Minor-
        ities.** Waltham, MA: Ginn and Co., 1971, pp. 000.
Contends that homosexuals meet the requisite for classification as a minority group, and that this concept should
be preferred to that of deviance. Yet they differ from
other minority groups in that their status is acquired and
not merely ascribed, and that their minority status is
contested. Twenty years earlier Hacker wrote a prescient
article on "Women as a Minority." **Social Forces**, 30
(1951), 60-69.

3190. HUMPHREYS, LAUD. "Exodus and Identity: The Emerging
        Gay Culture," in Martin P. Levine (ed.), **Gay Men:
        The Sociology of Male Homosexuality.** New York:
        Harper and Row, 1979, pp. 134-47.
Traces how gay liberation transformed the gay world from a
frightened, clandestine existence to an open, vital community, thus helping to repair damaged feelings of self-
worth.

3191. ITALIAANDER, ROLF. "Die Homophilen," in: Bernhard
        Doerdelmann (ed.), **Minderheiten in der Bundesrepub-**

lik. Munich: Delp, 1969, pp. 131-57.
Chapter by a pioneering German gay-rights champion in an
anthology on minorites in the German Federal Republic.

3192. MARTIN, A. DAMIEN. "The Minority Question," **Etc.**,
       39 (1982), 22-42.
The evaluation of whether "any hated group deserves minority ... status" does not depend upon its numbers or
upon the existence of negative social attitudes. The
proof rests upon the adequacy of the rationale for the
fear and hatred. If the negative attitude--however
rationalized--can be shown to be erroneous and based on
overgeneralization, then the prejudice is a manifesta-
tion of bigotry.

3193. MILLER, WAYNE CHARLES. **A Comprehensive Bibliog-
       raphy for the Study of American Minorities.** New
       York: New York University Press, 1976. 2 vols.
       (1380 pp.).
Contains 29,300 entries on major and minor European
groups, American Indians, blacks, Asian settlers, Middle
Eastern and Spanish immigrants. Does not deal with sexual minorities, and hence is useful chiefly for comparative purposes.

3194. PARKER, WILLIAM. "The Emerging Homosexual Minor-
       ity," **Civil Liberties Review,** 2 (1975), 136-44.
Civil rights perspective.

3195. POPERT, KEN. "Dangers of the Minority Game," **Body
       Politic,** no. 63 (May 1980), 3-7.
If we view ourselves simply as a minority group we risk
dead-ending ourselves into a political strategy which
neglects the large number of so-called heterosexuals who
have a stake in gay liberation. Ethnic minorities are
accidents of history; gay people are part of the working
out of history.

3196. SCHLACHTER, GAIL A. **Minorities and Women: A Guide
       to Reference Literature in the Social Sciences.** Los
       Angeles: Reference Service Press, 1977. 349 pp.
Substantially annotated lists covering American Indians,
Asian Americans, black Americans, Spanish Americans, and
women. Indirect relevance.

3197. ULLERSTAM, LARS. **The Erotic Minorities.** New York:
       Grove, 1966. 172 pp.
Popular discussion, treating homosexuality alongside the
paraphilias (fetishism, s/m, etc.).

                    T. PROSTITUTION, MALE

Male prostitutes serving male clients are known (inter
alia) from ancient Mesopotamia, Biblical Israel, ancient
Greece, and China (see the appropriate historical sections). In recent decades these individuals, often
described by the street term **hustlers**, have been recorded
by journalists and sociologists. No female equivalent--
that is women performing sexual services for other
women--is known. Thus both categories of prostitutes,
female and male, have men as their customers.

3198. ACKERMARK, LARS-ERIK. "44 prostituerade pojkar: ett
stickprobe pa den homosexelle prostitutione i
Stockholm," **Popular tidskrift for psykologi och
sexualkunskap**, 6 (1955), 13-18.
Study of 44 boy prostitutes in Stockholm.

3199. ADAM, CORINNA. "A Special House in Hamburg," **New
Statesman**, 85 (April 13, 1973), 521-22.
On a male brothel in West Germany, where they were then
legally permitted.

3200. ALLEN, DONALD M. "Young Male Prostitutes: A Psychosocial Study," **Archives of Sexual Behavior**, 9
(1980), 399-426.
From a three-year study of 98 male prostitutes, separated
them into four groups: full-time street and bar hustlers;
full-time call boys or kept boys; part-time hustlers; and
peer delinquents, who used the activity as an extension of
other deliquent acts.

3201. BELOUSOV, V. A. "Sluchaĭ gomoseksuala--muzhskoĭ
prostitutki," **Prestupnik i prestupnost'. Sbornik**
[Moscow, Kabinet i klinika po izucheniiu lichnosti
prestupnika i prestupnosti], 2 (1927), 309-17.
Case history of a male prostitute arrested for theft in
Moscow in 1927. The subject was 32, a native of Smolensk
gubernia, and had been a homosexual prostitute since the
age of 15.

3202. BENJAMIN, HARRY, and R. E. L. MASTERS. "Homosexual
Prostitution," in their: **Prostitution and Morality**.
New York: Julian Press, 1964, pp. 286-337.
Reviews the history of prostitution from ancient civiliz-
ations until the 1950s. Includes a report by Hall Call
on male prostitution on the U. S. west coast.

3203. BLOCH, IWAN. **Die Prostitution**. Berlin: L. Marcus,
1911-25. (Handbuch der gesamten Sexualwissenschaft
in Einzeldarstellungen, Bd 1 & Bd. 2, Halfte 1)
A major work of synthesis on prostitution, with many
erudite references to the history of the subject. Male
homosexual prostitution is dicussed in vol. 1, esp. pp.
387-427.

3204. BOYER, DEBRA K., and JENNIFER JAMES. "Prostitutes

as Victims," in: Donal E. MacNamara and Andrew
Karmen (eds.), **Deviants: Victims or Victimizers?**
Beverly Hills, CA: Sage, 1983, pp. 109-46.
An exploration of the hazards of the prostitute's trade,
male and female.

3205. BRULE, CHRISTIAN. **Nom: toxicomane; sexe: masculin;
profession: prostitué; specialité: hommes.** Ver-
sailles: Association d'aide aux jeunes en difficul-
te, 1984. 140 pp.
Unsympathetic presentation of drug problems among French
hustlers.

3206. BULLINGA, MARCEL, et al. **Van de liefde kun je niet
leven: Interviews met hoeren en hoerenjongens.**
Nijmegen: SOF, 1982.
Interviews with Dutch female and male prostitutes, as well
as an analysis of the social world of homosexual prostitution.

3207. BULLOUGH, VERN, et al. **A Bibliography of Prostitution.** New York: Garland, 1977. 419 pp.
Vast, but uncritical and misprint-ridden repertoire of
some 5500 citations, with relatively restricted coverage
of homosexual prostitution (pp. 239-243--occasional references elsewhere).

3208. BUTTS, WILLIAM MARLIN. "Boy Prostitutes of the
Metropolis," **Journal of Clinical Psychopathology,** 8
(1947), 637-81.
In-depth interviews with 26 boys allow a presentation of
their backgrounds, living arrangements, and charactero
logy.

3209. CAUKINS, SIVAN E., and NEIL R. COOMBS. "The
Psychodynamics of Male Prostitution," **American
Journal of Psychotherapy,** 30 (1976), 782-89.
Evaluates research with 33 youths in Los Angeles, clas-
sifying them among the following subtypes: street hus-
tlers, bar hustlers, call boys, and kept boys.

3210. COOMBS, NEIL R. "Male Prostitution: A Psychosocial
View of Behavior," **American Journal of Orthopsychiatry,** 44 (1974), 782-89.
Study based on 41 hustlers in Los Angeles, ages 12 to 28.
Finds that the majority exhibited constellations of negative traits, concluding that "[t]his group appeared to
contain men for whom competition has proved too much,
losers in the game of economic survival."

3211. CRAFT, MICHAEL. "Boy Prostitutes and Their Fate,"
British Journal of Psychiatry, 112 (1966), 111-14.
Observations from the life histories of 33 "apprehended
and treated" British hustlers, many of whom transacted
business in movie houses.

3212. DECKER, JOHN F. **Prostitution: Regulation and Control.** Litteleton, CO: Fred B. Rothman, 1979. 572
pp.
In this massive legal and criminological study, see esp.
pp. 207-14.

3213. DEISHER, ROBERT W., et al. "The Adolescent Female
and Male Prostitute," **Pediatric Annals,** 11 (1982),
819-25.
Offers a comparative perspective.

3214. DEISHER, ROBERT W., et al. "The Young Male Prostitute," **Pediatrics,** 43 (1967), 936-41.
Research with 63 hustlers in San Francisco and Seattle.

3215. DESPINE, PROSPER. **Psychologie naturelle: étude sur
les facultés intellectuelles et morales dans leur
état normal et dans leur manifestations anormales
chez les aliénés et chez les criminels.** Paris: F.
Savy, 1868. 3 vols.
Provides some discussion in vol. 3 of male prostitution.
For this period in France, see also esp. François Carlier,
Etude de pathologie sociale: les deux prostitutions (Paris: Dentu, 1887), pp. 275-473.

3216. DIETZ, PARK ELLIOTT. "Medical Criminology Notes
#5: Male Homosexual Prostitution," **Bulletin of the
American Academy of Psychiatry and the Law,** 6
(1978), 468-71.
Concise evaluation of the existing literature.

3217. DUARTE, ANTONIO, and HERMINIO CLEMENTE. **Prostituç-
ão masculino em Lisboa.** Lisbon: Contra-regra,
1982. 177 pp.
Two journalists on the life of hustlers in Lisbon, with
interviews and photographs.

3218. DUNNE, GARY. "The Male Street-Walker: A Sydney
Report," **Forum: The Australian Journal of Interper-
sonal Relations,** 7 (1979), 7-12.
Australian conditions follow essentially the European-
North American pattern.

3219. FIDANZA, DENISE. **Etude sur les prostitués homosexuels travestis.** Paris: AGEMP, 1966. 157 pp.
On cross-dressing hustlers in France (study presented as a
medical thesis).

3220. GANDY, PATRICK, and ROBERT W. DEISHER. "Young Male
Prostitutes: The Physician's Role in Social Rehabilitation," **JAMA: Journal of the American Medical
Association,** 212 (1970), 1661-66.
Reports on a fifteen-month intervention program for vocational retraining. Prospects for success are poor with
(1) psychopathic personalities, and (2) very successful
hustlers.

3221. "FLAME." **Flame: A Life on the Game.** London: Gay
       Men's Press, 1984. 159 pp.
Reminiscences of working-class Liverpool youth who became
a hustler in London

3222. GINSBURG, KENNETH N. "The 'Meat-Rack': A Study of
       the Male Homosexual Prostitute," **American Journal
       of Psychotherapy,** 21 (1967), 170-85.
Sets forth the theory that the hustler's family constel-
lation engenders a pathologic state characterized by an
unstable self-identity, an inadequate self-evaluation, and
little learned interaction potential or alternatives for
action.

3223. GIZA, JERZY S. "Prostitucja homoseksualna w
       swietle badań terenowych," **Państwo i prawo,** 18
       (1963), 889-97.
A study of male and female prostitutes in Poland, with
statistics on age at which the subjects began their
careers, social origins, and number of convictions.
Also legal recommendations. See also his: "Wielko-
miejskie srodowisko homoseksualne--studium kryminologicz-
ne," **Sluzba MO,** 6 (1969), 729-44; and "Zur Problematik
der homosexuellen Prostitution in Polen," **Archiv für
Kriminologie,** 133 (1964), 146-56.

3224. HARLAN, SPARKY, et al. **Male and Female Adolescent
       Prostitution: Huckleberry House Sexual Minority
       Youth Services Project.** Washington, DC: Youth
       Development Bureau, U. S. Department of Health and
       Human Services, 1981.
Study based primarily on runaways. See also: Jennifer
James, **Entrance into Juvenile Male Prostitution** (Wash-
ington, DC: National Institute of Mental Health, 1982).

3225. HARRIS, MERVYN. **The Dillyboys: The Game of Male
       Prostitution in Piccadilly.** Rockville, MD: New
       Perspectives, 1973. 126 pp.
Tolerant and well informed field study presenting an
ethnographic account of English teenage male prostitution.

3226. HENNIG, JEAN-LUC. **Les garçons de passe: enquête
       sur la prostitution masculine.** Paris: Hallier,
       1978. 374 pp.
Gifted French journalist's assemblage of interview materials on present-day hustling in the Paris region, including ethnic aspects.

3227. HOFFMAN, MARTIN. "The Male Prostitute," **Sexual
       Behavior,** 2 (1972), 16-21.
Discusses two groups: one of teenagers who sold their
bodies but did not regard themselves as hustlers; another
slightly older one consisting of men who did regard themselves as hustlers but not homosexuals. Concludes that,
"protective coloration" aside, there are some hustlers who
are homosexual and some who are not.

3228. JANUS, MARK-DAVID, et al. "Youth Prostitution,"
     in: A. W. Burgess (ed.), **Child Pornography and Sex
     Rings.** Lexington, MA: Lexington Books, 1984, pp.
     127-46.
From a study in metropolitan Boston, describes the various
types of hustlers. Also discusses backgrounds, involvement in pornography, and sadomasochism.

3229. KEARNS, MICHAEL. **The Happy Hustler: My Own Story.**
     By Grant Tracy Saxon [pseud.]. New York: Warner
     Paperback Library, 1975. 189 pp.
Frivolous, but occasionally insightful "autobiography" of
a bisexual male prostitute, meant in part as a satire on
Xaviera Hollander's **The Happy Hooker.** The author is a
successful Hollywood starlet.

3230. KLEMENS, KLAUS ULRICH. **Die kriminelle Belastung
     der männlichen Prostituierten: zugleich ein Beitrag
     zur Rückfallsprognose.** Berlin: Duncker und Hum-
     blot, 1967. 123 pp. (Berliner jurischer Abhand-
     lungen, 15)
Criminality of male prostitutes, together with a consideration of the prognosis for recidivism.

3231. LASERSTEIN, BOTHO. **Strichjunge Karl: ein inter-
     nationaler kriminalistischer Tatsachenbericht aus
     dem Land der Liebe, die ihren Namen nicht nennt.**
     Hamburg: Hansen Schmidt, 1954. 78 pp.
Profile of a typical West German street hustler, with
international comparisons.

3232. LLOYD, ROBIN. **For Money or Love: Boy Prostitution
     in America.** New York: Vanguard Press, 1976.
     326 pp.
Superficial, sensationalist presentation in the guise of
tough investigative journalism. Attempts to offer some
historical background (pp. 63-77).

3233. LUCKENBILL, DAVID F. "Entering Male Prostitution,"
     Urban Life, 14 (1985), 131-53.
Uses Chicago interview data to demonstrate two paths of
initial involvement: defensive (in which boys turn to hustling to solve desperate living and financial problems)
and adventurous (in which youths seek extra money or
"kicks," sometimes including sexual pleasure). The first
group advances quickly into regular involvement, the second only months or years after the initial experiment.

3234. MACKAY, JOHN HENRY. **The Hustler.** Translated by
     Hubert Kennedy. Boston: Alyson, 1985. 299 pp.
Novel, first published in German as **Der Puppenjunge** in
1926, which serves to document not only the milieu of
teenage hustlers in Berlin of the Weimar era, but also
the psychology of an idealistic client. A similar work
from this period is Friedrich Radszuweit, **Männer zu ver-
kaufen: Wirklichkeitsroman aus der Welt der männlichen**

Erpresser und Prostituierten (Leipzig: Lipsia, 1932; 125 pp.).

3235. MARKHAM, FRED. "Fred's Piece," **Fag Rag**, no. 30 (1982), 4-8.
Memoirs of a 1950s hustler in Seattle.

3236. MARLOWE, KENNETH. **Mr. Madam: Confessions of a Male Madam.** Los Angeles: Sherbourne Press, 1964. 246 pp.
A Hollywood transvestite describes the origins of his own career and the operations of a call-boy service, which he managed. Some skepticism is in order regarding details.

3237. NICOSIA, GERALD, and RICHARD ROFE. **Bughouse Blues: An Intimate Portrait of Gay Hustling.** New York: Vantage Press, 1977. 166 pp.
Composite derived from interviews with male prostitutes in Chicago's "Bughouse Square" (officially Washington Square).

3238. O'DAY, JOHN. **Confessions of a Male Prostitute.** As told to John O'Day, with psychological evaluations by Leonard A. Lowag. Los Angeles: Sherbourne Press, 1964. 136 pp.
Purports to be the reminiscences of a male prostitute who services both men and women. Like other pulp exposes of the period, this book is of some interest for contemporary attitudes.

3239. PARENT-DUCHÂTELET, ALEXANDRE J. B. **De la prostitution dans la ville de Paris.** Paris: Baillière, 1836. 2 vols.
This pioneering sociological-criminological study of prostitution in Paris concentrates on women, but has a few references to male homosexual prostitution as well.

3240. PIEPER, RICHARD. "Identity Management in Adolescent Male Prostitution in West Germany," **International Review of Modern Sociology,** 9 (1979), 239-59.
Combines reports in the literature with field work in Hamburg (West Germany) to describe the phenomenon, esp. with respect to the inherent strains. Presents a typology of the participants and a model of the process of development and stabilization of the role.

3241. PITTMAN, DAVID J. "The Male House of Prostitution," **TransAction,** 8:5-6 (1971), 21-27.
Field study recording the modus operandi of a male brothel.

3242. RAVEN, SIMON. "Boys Will Be Boys: The Male Prostitute in London," in: Hendrik M. Ruitenbeek (ed.), **The Problem of Homosexuality in Modern Society.** New York: E. P. Dutton, 1963, pp. 279-90.

Journalist finds five categories of male prostitutes in
London: servicemen; men who wish to improve their incomes;
men of low intelligence and background; men who are
accustomed to shady enterprises; and the full-time professional prostitute, with no other source of income.

3243. RECHY, JOHN. **City of Night**. New York: Grove
Press, 1963. 410 pp.
Written in the form of a novel, this is the account of a
hustler's life in New York City, California, and New
Orleans. In the introduction to the 1985 reissue of the
book Rechy explains how he came to write it and something
of the degree of correspondence to his real life.

3244. REDHARDT, REINHARDT. "Zur gleichgeschlechtlichen
männlichen Prostitution," in: **Studien zur männlich-
en Homosexualität**. Stuttgart: Enke, 1954, pp. 22-
72 (Beitrage zur Sexualforschung, 5)
Criminological study attributing a role to endocrinology,
as well as psychological problems connected with puberty.

3245. REIM, RICCARDO. **Una questione diversa**. Cosenza:
1978.
Includes a series of interviews with Italian hustlers.

3246. REISS, A. J., JR. "The Social Integration of
Queers and Peers," **Social Problems**, 9:2 (1961),
102-20.
An often-cited study revealing the dissonance between
sexual identity and behavior in lower-class boys in
Nashville, and showing how potential image problems are
regulated in transactions with clients.

3247. ROSS, H. LAURENCE. "The 'Hustler' in Chicago,"
Journal of Student Research, 1 (1959), 13-19.
Interviews with one client and seven male hustlers serve
as the basis for generalizations about types and motivations.

3248. RUSSELL, DONALD H. "On the Psychopathology of Boy
Prostitutes," **International Journal of Offender
Therapy**, 15 (1971), 49-52.
Claims that early maternal deprivation is at the root of
many boy prostitute's choice of career.

3249. SALVARESI, ELISABETH. **Travelo**. Paris: Les Presses
de la Renaissance, 1982. 184 pp.
Inquiry concerning French cross-dressing prostitutes, with
personal narratives.

3250. SCHICKEDANZ, HANS-JOACHIM. **Homosexuelle Prostitution: eine empirische Untersuchung über sozial-des-
kriminiertes Verhalten bei Strichjungen und Call-
boys**. Frankfurt am Main: Campus Verlag, 1979. 252
pp.
West German empirical study of street hustlers and call

boys.

3251. SCHMIDT-RELENBERG, NORBERT, et al. **Strichjungen-
       Gespräche: Zur Soziologie jugendlicher homosexu-
       ellen Prostitution.** Darmstadt: Luchterhand, 1975.
       254 pp.
Combines interviews with young West German hustlers, presented in their own words, and sociological analysis.

3252. SERENY, GITTA. **The Invisible Children: Child
       Prostitution in America, West Germany and Great
       Britain.** New York: Knopf, 1985. 254 pp.
This collection of interviews with prostitutes includes
two with hustlers, "Ruprecht" (West Germany) and "Alan"
(Britain).

3253. SHEARER, JOHNNY. **The Male Hustler.** Cleveland:
       Century Books, 1966. 190 pp.
"Soft-core" pulp presentation, typical of the period.

3254. STIEBER, WILHELM JOHANN CARL EDUARD. **Die Prostitu-
       tion in Berlin und ihre Opfer.** Berlin: Hofmann,
       1846. 210 pp.
An early criminological study (published anonymously),
which chiefly concerns female prostitution, but with
some references to male homosexual prostitution.

3255. URBAN AND RURAL SYSTEMS ASSOCIATES (URSA). **An
       Annotated Bibliography on Adolescent Male and
       Female Prostitution and Related Topics.** Washing-
       ton, DC: Youth Development Buireau, U. S. Depart-
       ment of Health and Human Services, 1981.
One of a number of official publications, reflecting
growing public concern. See also: URSA, **Juvenile Prostitution: A Resource Manual** (Washington, DC: U. S. Department of Health and Human Serives, 1982).

3256. VIGNOLI, GIULIO. **Contributo ad una indagine sulla
       prostituzione maschile.** Savona: 1973. 35 pp.
Theoretical and practical considerations on male prostitution in Italy.

3257. WEISBERG, D. KELLY. **Children of the Night: A Study
       of Adolescent Prostitution.** Lexington, MA: Lexing-
       ton Books, 1985. 298 pp.
Concentrates on etiology, the young prostitutes' lifestyle, and involvement with the juvenile justice and
social service delivery systems. Ethnographic research
was conducted in San Francisco and New York City. For
hustlers, see pp. 19-83, and for comparison of female
and male adolescent prostitution, pp. 153-88.

3258. WEISS, JOEL. **Arraché au trottoir: le drame de la
       prostitution masculine.** Paris: Garancière, 1985.
       191 pp.
Account focused largely on one male prostitute, whom the

author helped to leave his profession.

3259. WINICK, CHARLES, and PAUL M. KINSIE. "Male Homo-
       sexual Prostitution," in: The Lively Commerce:
       Prostitution in the United States. Chicago:
       Quadrangle, 1971, pp. 89-96.
A brief but comprehensive description of hustlers, their
modus operandi, sociological profile, psychology, and
rehabilitation programs aimed at their resocialization.

U. RACE AND ETHNICITY

In view of the attention that has rightly been bestowed on
the questions of race, race relations, and ethnicity in
the United States over the last few decades, it is surprising how little these matters have been considered
in relation to sexual orientation. This neglect is now
yielding to enquiries on a number of fronts.

3260. BASS-HASS, RITA. "The Lesbian Dyad," Journal of
       Sex Research, 4 (1968), 108-26.
Interpreting interviews with 370 women, compares white and
black lesbians with respect to class and demography, sociosexual relationships, and domestic arrangements.

3261. BEAME, THOM. "From a Black Perspective: Racism (A
       Conversation)," Advocate, no. 339 (April 1, 1982),
       23-25.
Transcript of a discussion among three black gays regarding race and class bias in the gay community in San Francisco. See also: "Mike Smith (An Interview with the
Founder of Black and White Men Together)," ibid., (December 23, 1982), 21-23.

3262. BULKIN, ELLY, MINNIE BRUCE PRATT, and BARBARA
       SMITH. Yours in Struggle: Three Feminist Perspec-
       tives on Anti-Semitism and Racism. Brooklyn: Long
       Hall Press, 1984. 233 pp.
Frank comments by three women of different identities and
backgrounds--white Southerner, Afro-American, Ashkenazi
Jewish.

3263. BUTTS, JUNE. "Is Homosexuality a Threat to the
       Black Family?" Ebony (April 1981), 138-40, 142-44.
After reviewing evidence from Africa and the U. S., concludes that "homosexuality is not a threat either to the
stability or the future of the Black family."

3264. CLIFF, MICHELLE. Claiming an Identity They Taught
       Me to Despise. Watertown, MA: Persephone Press,
       1980. 64 pp.
A Jamaica-born women's autobiographical prose-poetry

recording her journey toward self-definition.

3265. CORNELL, MICHIYO. "Invisible among the Invisible,"
      Azalea, no. 4 (1981), 6-8.
Reflections of a Japanese-American woman writer.

3266. CORNWALL, ANITA. **Black Lesbian in White America.**
      Tallahassee: Naiad Press, 1983. 160 pp.
Fiction, essays, and interviews by an established writer.

3267. DANIELS, MATTHEW. "Breaking the Color Barrier,"
      Advocate, no. 331 (November 26, 1981), 17-18.
On the success of Black and White Men Together, an interracial group formed in San Francisco in March 1980.

3268. DAY, BETH. **Sexual Life between Blacks and Whites:**
      The Roots of Racism. New York: World, 1972. 376
      pp.
Contends that the incidence of homosexuality is low in
Africa, and that whites imposed it on American blacks—a
myth that has often been echoed. For refutation, see:
Wayne Dynes, "Homosexuality in Sub-Saharan Africa," **Gay**
Books Bulletin, no. 9 (1983), 20-21.

3269. GARBER, ERIC. "Tain't Nobody's Business: Homosex-
      uality in Harlem in the 1920s," **Advocate,** no. 342
      (May 13, 1982), pp. 39-43+.
Fascinating glimpses of famous literary figures and others
of the Harlem Renaissance. For a full exposition of the
milieu, see David Levering Lewis, **When Harlem Was in Vogue**
(New York: Knopf, 1981; 381 pp.).

3270. GITECK, LENNY. "Gays from Other Ghettos," **Advo-**
      cate, no. 265 (April 19, 1979), 12-13, 15.
Journalist's notes on homosexuals of color in the United
States.

3271. HACKER, HELEN MAYER. "The Ishmael Complex," **Amer-**
      ican Journal of Psychotherapy, 6 (1952), 494-512.
Explores themes in American literature (e.g. **Moby Dick,**
Huckleberry Finn) of an "isolated aim-inhibited, homosexual relationship between a declassed American lad and a
colored outcast." This article apparently represents a
variant of the better-known thesis of the literary critic Leslie Fiedler (as seen, e.g., in his 1952 collection,
An End to Innocence.)

3272. HIDALGO, HILDA A., and ELIA H. CHRISTENSEN. "The
      Puerto Rican Lesbian and the Puerto Rican Com-
      munity," **JH,** 2 (1976-77), 109-21.
From interviews and questionnaires with Puerto Rican
persons living in the United States, concluded that
increasing numbers of Puerto Rican lesbians are coming
out, but that their horizons are restricted by the
group's Hispanic culture, which stigmatizes lesbians as
mannish and repulsive. See also Hidalgo, "The Puerto

Rican Lesbian in the United States," in: Trudy Darty and Sandee Potter (eds.), **Women-Identified Women** (Palo Alto, Ca: Mayfield, 1984), pp. 105-15.

3273. HUGHES, CHARLES W. "An Organization of Colored Erotopaths," **Alienist and Neurologist,** 14 (1893), 731-32.
Censorious account of a black drag ball in Washington, D. C. See also his: "Homosexual Complexion Perverts in St. Louis," ibid., 28 (1907), 487-88.

3274. LORDE, AUDRE. **Zami: A New Spelling of My Name.** Trumansburg, NY: Crossing Press, 1983. 256 pp.
A "biomythography" by a noted black poet, recalling her growing up "fat, Black, nearly blind, and ambidextrous in a West Indian household" in Harlem in the 1930s and '40s, and her coming of age as a lesbian in the 1950s.

3275. MALLON, GERALD L. (ed.). **Resisting Racism: An Active Guide.** Lafaytette Mill, PA: International Black and White Men Together, 1984. 114 pp.
Chiefly reprints, including the bibliography of Harry Wiemhoff (see below).

3276. MARKS, JIM. "From Politics to Poetry: Black Gay Life in the Nation's Capital Presents a Strong Point," **Advocate,** no. 440 (February 18, 1986), 36-39.
Black activists, social clubs, religious groups, poetry and art in Washington, DC.

3277. MAYS, VICKIE M. "I Hear Voices But See No Faces: Reflections on Racism and Women-Identified Relationships of Afro-American Women," **Heresies,** no.12 (1981), 74-76.
Contends that the climate created by the Euro-American world with its capitalism, racism and patriarchy has kept the Afro-American lesbian invisible.

3278. MORAGA, CHERRIE, and GLORIA ANZALDUA (eds.). **This Bridge Called My Back: Writings by Radical Women of Color.** Watertown, MA: Persephone Press, 1981. 261 pp.
Poetry, essays, personal narrative, and fiction by black, Latin and Asian-American women, reflecting their passionate demand for an end to invisibility. See also: Cherrie Moraga, **Lo que nunca paso por sus labios: Loving in the War Years** (Boston: South End Press, 1983; 150 pp.--poems, stories, essays).

3279. PARIN, PAUL. "'The Mark of Oppression': Ethnopsychoanalytische Studie über Juden und Homosexuelle in einer relativ permissiven Kultur," **Psyche: Zeitschrift für Psychoanalyse und ihre Anwendungen,** 39 (1985), 193-219.
An ethnopsychiatric study of Jews and homosexuals revealed

similarities between the two groups related to oppression. This common experience results in similarities in the psychic constitution of the two groups that are independent of early childhood development. Compare Barry D. Adam, **The Survival of Domination: Inferiorization and Everyday Life** (New York: Elzevier, 1978; 179 pp.).

3280. RICH, ADRIENNE. "'Disloyal to Civilization': Feminism, Racism, and Gynephobia," **Chrysalis**, no. 7 (1979), 9-27.
Holds that much feminist thinking and writing labors under a burden of false guilt. Real transcendence of the past demands difficult work, for which lesbian-feminism is particularly suited.

3281. ROBERTS, J. R. **Black Lesbians: An Annotated Bibliography.** Tallahassee, FL: Naiad Press, 1981. 93 pp.
An exemplary bibliography and handbook, collecting a remarkable range of information on life-ways, oppression and resistance, literature, music, and the military.

3282. ROSCOE, WILL. "Gay Americn Indians: Creating an Identity from Past Traditions," **Advocate**, no. 432 (October 29, 1985), 45-48.
Profiles of Indian activists in San Francisco and elsewhere.

3283. SMITH, MICHAEL J. (ed.). **Black Men/White Men: A Gay Anthology.** San Francisco, CA: Gay Sunshine Press, 1983. 240 pp.
Well-selected and edited collection of short stories personal accounts, biographical profiles, and research.

3284. SMITH, MICHAEL J. (ed.). **Colorful People and Places.** San Francisco: Quarterly, 1983. 123 pp.
"A resource guide for Third World Lesbians and Gay men" and for white people who share their interests. Entries arranged by state and city, with some historical notes; also some data on foreign countries.

3285. TSUI, KITTY. **The Words of a Woman Who Breathes Fire.** San Francisco: Spinsters Ink, 1983. 84 pp.
Vivid and sensitive account of the life of a Chinese-American woman in poems and stories.

3286. VASQUEZ, E. "Homosexuality in the Context of the Mexican-American Culture," in: D. Kuhnel (ed.), **Sexual Issues in Social Work: Emerging Concerns in Education and Practice.** Honolulu: University of Hawaii School of Social Work, 1979, pp. 131-47.
Problems vary depending on whether the person is still living in a strongly Mexican culture with its polarized gender role behavior or has become detached from it.

3287. VERNON, RON. "Growing Up in Chicago Black and Gay,"

Gay Sunshine, no. 6 (March 1971), 14-17.
Autobiographical recollections from the Second City's
ghetto.

3288. WIEMHOFF, HENRY. **Race, Racism and the Gay Male: A
        Preliminary Bibliography and Resource Guide.** New
        York: Black and White Men Together, n. d. [ca.
        1982]. 7 pp.
Fiction and nonfiction, including some general works on
racism and race relations.

3289. WOODEN, WAYNE S., HARVEY KAWASAKI, and RAYMOND '
        MAYEDA. "Identity Maintenance of Japanese-American
        Gays," **Alternative Lifestyles,** 6 (1983), 236-43.
Evaluates questionnaire results from Los Angeles and San
Francisco concerning family roles and conflicting demands
of gay "master identity."

                        V. ROLE

The sociological term "role" has been defined as "the
expected behavior associated with a social position."
Although the concept is protean and sometimes confusing,
it does not seem possible to dispense with it. Derived
terms are "role model" (reflecting the notion that young
people tend to imitate admired persons) and "role playing," which is sometimes used to critize ostensibly
stereotyped behavior, especially of the kind entailed by
traditional male/female oppositions.

3290. COTTON, WAYNE L. "Role-Playing Substitutions among
        Homosexuals," **Journal of Sex Research,** 8 (1972),
        310-23.
Studied 36 male homosexuals living in New York City, concluding that (1) sexual partners are seldom considered
part of the close circle of friends; (2) close friends
do not have sexual contacts with each other; and (3) a
means of making status distinctions is absent.

3291. COTTON, WAYNE L. "Social and Sexual Relationships
        of Lesbians," **Journal of Sex Research,** 11 (1975),
        139-48.
A field study of New York City lesbians discloses major
differences between them and male homosexuals. The
women tend to be coupled with partners of the same socio-
economic status, and couples are integrated into each
partner's friendship network.

3292. GOODE, ERICH. "Comments on the Homosexual Role,"
        Journal of Sex Research, 17 (1981), 54-65.
Disagrees with critics of the concept of the homosexual
role who assert that it has no validity, arguing that

their views reflect an "essentialistic" misunderstanding
both of the nature of homosexuality and of the sociological concept of role. See also F. L. Whitam, below.

3293. HARRY, JOSEPH. "On the Validity of Typologies of
      Gay Males," **JH**, 2 (1976-77), 143-52.
Analysis of data from 243 gay men did not validate the
popular stereotype of a dichotomy between inserter and
insertee. The most popular set of sexual preferences was
for all roles combined, both active and passive, anal and
oral.

3294. MCINTOSH, MARY. "The Homosexual Role," **Social
      Problems**, 16 (1968), 182-92.
Argues that homosexuality should not be conceptualized as
a condition but rather as a social role; however, not all
those engaging in same-sex relations are playing the
role. Often cited as an illuminating breakthrough, this
article now seems truistic. Another pioneering article
was Albert J. Reiss, "The Social Integration of Queers
and Peers," **Social Problems**, 9 (1961), 102-20.

3295. RIDDLE, DOROTHY I. "Relating to Children: Gays as
      Role Models," **Journal of Social Issues**, 34 (1978),
      38-58.
A review of the literature on role modeling leads to the
conclusions that children internalize particular traits
from a variety of models and that gays are more likely
to serve as nontraditional sex-role models than as de-
terminers of same-sex sexual preference.

3296. SCHÄFER, SIEGRID. "Sociosexual Behavior in Male
      and Female Homosexuals: A Study in Sex Differ-
      ences," **Archives of Sexual Behavior**, 6 (1977),
      355-64.
Comparison of two West German studies on male and female
homosexuals respectively reveals major differences in
coming out, heterosexual experience, and sexual behavior. The author suggests that gay men adhere to societal
prescriptions for the male gender role, and lesbians to
those for the female gender role.

3297. WHITAM, FREDERICK L. "The Homosexual Role: A Re-
      consideration," **Journal of Sex Research**, 13 (1977),
      1-11.
Contends that to treat homosexuality as a social role
violates the definition of a role. Roles require anticip-
atory socialization and structural prescriptions, and
homosexuality, lacking both, should be classified as a
sexual orientation. This paper occasioned a considerable controversy: Richard C. Omark, "A Comment on the
Homosexual Role," ibid., 14 (1978), 273-74; Frederick
L. Whitam, "Rejoinder to Omark's Comment on the Homosexual
Role," ibid, 14 (1978), 274-75; Frederick L. Whitam, "A
Reply to Goode on 'The Homosexual Role,'"ibid., 17 (1981),
66-72; and Richard C. Omark, "Further Comment on the

Homosexual Role: A Reply to Goode," ibid., 17 (1981),
73-75; Erich Goode, "The Homosexual Role: Rejoinder to
Omark and Whitam," ibid., 17 (1981), 76-83. See also E.
L. Goode, above.

W. SUBSTANCE ABUSE: ALCOHOL

The problem of alcoholism has been widely recognized in
Western society since the 18th century, when the availability of cheap distilled spirits made it possible for
the large number of the poor and other disadvantaged persons to "drown their sorrows" in liquor. The role that
alcohol may play in the relaxation of sexual inhibitions
has been known for an even longer period. It remains
curious that in the early decades of the century, when
psychiatrists and others were inclined to charge homosexuals with every kind of deficiency, the problem of alcoholism was little recognized. That it has now been singled
out is largely the work of concerned homosexuals and lesbians themselves.

3298. BEATON, STEPHEN, and NAOME GUILD. "Treatment for
       Gay Problem Drinkers," **Social Casework,** 57 (1976),
       302-08.
Describes treatment of gay men and lesbians in a group
with straight therapists.

3299. CHRISTENSON, SUSAN, et al. **Lesbians, Gay Men and
       Their Alcohol and Other Drug Use Resources.** Mad-
       ison, WI: Clearinghouse for Alcohol and Other Drug
       Use Information, 1980. 17 pp.
Practical information from a social-work perspective.

3300. COLLA, I. E. "Drei Fälle von homosexuellen
       Handlungen im Rauschzuständen," **Vierteljahres-
       schrift für gerichtliche-medizinisches und öffent-
       liches Sanitätswesen,** ser. 3, vol. 31 (1905), 50-
       61.
Alcohol intoxication as a facilitator of homosexual behavior: three cases.

3301. DIAMOND, DEBORAH, and SHARON C. WILSNACK. "Al-
       cohol Abuse among Lesbians: A Descriptive Study,"
       JH, 4 (1978), 123-42.
Interviews with ten lesbian alcoholics indicate that lesbians with this problem need therapists who will accept
their sexual orientation and treatment that will help them
increase their sense of power and self-esteem without
alcohol. See also James L. Hawkins, "Lesbians and Alcoholism," in M. A. Greenblatt and M. A. Schlacht (eds.),
Alcohol Problems in Women and Children (New York: 1976),
137-53; and Brenda Weathers, "Alcoholism and the Lesbian

Community," in: Naomi Gottlieb, **Alternative Social Ser-**
vices for Women (New York: Columbia University Press,
1980), pp. 158-68.

3302. FINEGAN, DANA G., and DAVID COOK. "Special Issues
       Affecting the Treatment of Male and Lesbian Alco-
       holics," **Alcoholism Treatment Quarterly**, 1:3
       (1984), 85-98.
Counselors who treat gay alcoholics should examine their
own attitudes, become acquainted with healthy gay men
and lesbians to dispel stereotypes, learn to tolerate
clients' defensive reactions, and be willing to discuss
sober sex and the question of gay bars.

3303. FORREST, GARY G. **Alcoholism and Human Sexuality.**
       Springfield, IL: Charles C. Thomas, 1983. 395 pp.
Judgmental therapeutic approach strongly influenced by
psychoanalysis. Chapter 5, "Alcoholism and Homosexuality" (pp.181-215), is followed by discussions of child
molestation, incest, rape, etc. Holds that clinicians
should treat alcoholism first, then homosexuality: "The
total person must recover."

3304. GAY COUNCIL ON DRINKING BEHAVIOR. **The Way Back:**
       The Stories of Gay and Lesbian Alcoholics. Wash-
       ington, DC: Whitman Walker Clinic, 1981. 90 pp.
Personal accounts of ten persons who have recovered from
alcoholism with the help of Alcoholics Anonymous.

3305. HIRSCHFELD, MAGNUS. **Der Einfluss des Alkohols auf**
       das Geschlechtsleben. Berlin: Michaelis, 1906. 16
       pp.
The affect of alcohol on sex life. Lecture given by the
noted sexologist--himself a teetotaller--before a workers' temperance group.

3306. ISRAELSTAM, S., and SILVIA LAMBERT. "Homosexuality
       as a Cause of Alcoholism: A Historical Review,"
       International Journal of the Addictions, 18 (1983),
       1085-1107.
Critical examination of the psychoanalytic theory that
linked alcoholism causally with homosexuality. The development of the humanistic model in the 1960s and 70s, the
emergence of labeling theory, and the work of better-in-
formed social scientists and clinicians laid much of the
old theory to rest by the 1970s.

3307. LEWIS, COLLINS E., et al. "Drinking Patterns in
       Homosexual and Heterosexual Women," **Journal of**
       Clinical Psychiatry, 43: 7 (1982), 277-79.
Heavy drinking was more common in a sample of 57 lesbians
as compared to a control group of 43 heterosexual women.

3308. LOHRENZ, LEANDER J., et al. "Alcohol Problems in
       Several Midwestern Homosexual Communites," **Journal**
       of Studies on Alcohol, 39 (1978), 1959-63.

In 42 gay male alcoholics, drinking was perceived as a
solution to problems, and related to urban living, education, current sexual preference, and reliance on pre-
scription drugs.

3309. MICHAEL, JOHN. **The Gay Drinking Problem ... There
       is a Solution.** Minneapolis, MN: CompCare Publica-
       tions, 1976. 15 pp.
Approach stemming from Alcoholics Anonymous. See also
his: **Sober, Clean and Gay** (Minneapolis, MN: Compcare,
Publications, 1978; 19 pp.).

3310. NARDI, PETER. "Alcohol Treatment and the Non-trad-
       itional 'Family' Structures of Gays and Lesbians,"
       Journal of Alcohol and Drug Education, 27:2 (1982),
       83-89.
Sociological perspective showing that friendship networks
and dyads function otherwise in this context than they
do for heterosexuals. See also his: "Alcohol and Homosexuality: A Theoretical Perspective," JH, 7 (1981-82), 9-25.

3311. O'FARRELL, TIMOTHY J., CAROLYN A. WEYLAND, and
       DIANE LOGAN. **Alcohol and Sexuality: An Annotated
       Bibliography on Alcohol Use, Alcoholism, and Human
       Sexual Behavior.** Phoenix: Oryx Press, 1983. 131
       pp.
Provides 542 citations of materials published from 1900 to
1982. See Chapter 3, Section C. See also: **N.A.G.A.P.
Bibliography: Resources on Alcoholism and Lesbians/Gay
Men** (Oakland, NJ: National Association of Gay Alcoholism
Professionals, 1980).

3312. SAUNDERS, F. J. "Homosexual Recovering Alcohol-
       ics: A Descriptive Study," **Alcoholic Health and
       Research World,** 8 (1983-84), 18-22.
Interviews with 28 male homosexuals and one lesbian highlighted the role of bars as places for meeting and
socializing.

3313. SHILTS, RANDY. "Alcoholism: A Look in Depth at How
       a National Menace is Affecting the Gay Community,"
       Advocate, no. 184 (February 25, 1976), 16-25.
A somewhat alarmist view of the incidence of what is con-
cededly a grave problem among gay men and lesbians.

3314. SMALL, EDWARD J., and BARY LEACH. "Counseling
       Homosexual Alcoholics," **Journal of Studies on Al-
       cohol,** 38 (1977), 2077-86.
Since homosexuality and alcoholism are independent states,
homosexuality need not be an obstacle to treatment for
alcoholism.

3315. SWALLOW, JEAN (ed.). **Out from Under: Sober Dykes
       and Our Friends.** San Francisco: Spinsters Ink,
       1983. 275 pp.
Anthology of personal accounts of lesbian alcoholism and

recovery. Replication of parental alcoholism patterns
is found to be significant.

3316. ZEHNER, MARTA A., and JOYCE LEWIS. "Homosexuality
       and Alcoholism: Social and Developmental Perspec-
       tives," **Journal of Social Work and Human Sexuality**,
       2 (1983-84), 75-89.
Inherent stresses, issues, and patterns engender an
alcoholism rate in the homosexual community that is two to
three times that of the general population. Regrettably,
even the process of formation of a positive gay identity
can create stress situations that put one at risk for
alcoholism.

3317. ZIEBOLD, THOMAS O., and JOHN E. MONGEON (eds.).
       Alcoholism and Homosexuality. New York: Haworth
       Press, 1982. 128 pp.
Ten papers offering theoretical, counseling, social-work,
and therapeutic perspectives by William E. Bittle, Ronnie
W. Colcher, Rosanne Driscoll, Emily B. McNally and Dana
G. Finnegan, Mongeon and Ziebold, Peter Nardi, Tom Mills
Smith, Scott Whitney, and Tricia A. Zigrang. A key an-
thology for the study of the subject. Reprint of **JH**,
7:4 (1982). See also Ziebold and Mongeon, **Ways to Gay
Sobriety** (Washington, DC: Whitman-Walker Clinic, 1980;
15 pp.); and Ziebold, "Ethical Issues in Substance-Abuse
Problems Relevant to Sexual Minorities," **Contemporary
Drug Problems**, 8 (1980), 413-18.

                    X. SUBSTANCE ABUSE: DRUGS

The potential for drug addiction in Western society has
been fostered by a number of factors, including the spread
of previously exotic substances through international
trade patterns, the chemical synthesis of new stimulants,
and the growth of a youth culture which tends to prefer
drugs to alcohol. The spread of drug use in the gay community was undoubtedly aided by the 1960s symbiosis with
the counterculture. The formerly widespread use of amyl
nitrites ("poppers") among gay men became a matter of
concern because of an alleged link with AIDS.

3318. ABEL, ERNEST L. **Drugs and Sex: A Bibliography.**
       Westport, CT: Greenwood Press, 1983. 129 pp.
Provides 1432 annotated items arranged under headings: alcohol, amphetamines, antidepressants, antipsychotics,
barbiturates, benzidiazepines, caffeine, cocaine, LSD,
marihuana, methaqualone, narcotics, nitrites, PCP,
tobacco, and general.

3319. AMENDT, GUNTER. **Haschisch und Sexualität: eine
       empirische Untersuchung über die Sexualität Jugend-**

licher in der Drogensubkultur. Stuttgart: Enke, 1974. 124 pp.
Inquiry into drugs and sex among West German youth.

3320. FREUDENBERGER, HERBERT J. "The Gay Addict in A Drug and Alcohol Therapeutic Community," **Homosexual Counseling Journal,** 3 (1976), 34-45.
On special problems encountered by gay members of drug abuse treatment communities.

3321. GAY, GEORGE, et al. "The Sensuous Hippie: 1. Drug/ Sex Practice in the Haight-Ashbury," **Drug Forum,** 6 (1977-78), 27-47.
Examined individual subjective experiences regarding the effects of a variety of drugs on sexual habits--aggressiveness; changes in libido; pleasure derived; and general experience, practice, beliefs and attitudes. See also: "Love and Haight: The Sensuous Hippie Revisited: Drug/Sex Practices in San Francisco," **Journal of Psychoactive Drugs,** 14 (1982), 111-23.

3322. GONZALEZ, R. M. "Hallucinogenic Dependency During Adolescence as a Defense against Homosexual Fantasies: A Reenactment of the First Separation-Individuaion Phase in the Course of Treatment," **Journal of Youth and Adolescence,** 8 (1979), 63-71.
Psychoanalytic interpretation presenting a single case history.

3323. GOODE, ERICH, and RICHARD R. TROIDEN. "Amyl Nitrite Use among Homosexual Men," **American Journal of Psychiatry,** 136 (1979), 1067-69.
Interviews with 150 homosexual men suggest that use of amyl nitrite (poppers) is strongly related to a number of unconventional practices and to certain medically related problems. See also: Stephen Israelstam et al., "Use of Isobutyl Nitrite as a Recreational Drug," **British Journal of Addiction,** 73 (1978), 319-20; and Thomas P. Lowry, "Psychosexual Aspects of the Volatile Nitrites," **Journal of Psychoactive Drugs,** 14 (1982), 77-79.

3324. LAURITSEN, JOHN, and HANK WILSON. **Death Rush: Poppers and AIDS: With Annotated Bibliography.** New York: Pagan Press, 1986. 64 pp.
A contentious, sometimes eccentric statement of the case against amyl nitrites. While extensive, the bibliography is selected and annotated to make the case against poppers more alarming than it is. The brochure concludes with some unlikely speculations about AIDS.

3325. MILLS, BRONWYN G., and MARIAH B. NELSON. "Perspectives on Treatment of Drug Dependent Lesbians," **N.I.D.A.-Treatment Research Monograph Series: Treatment Services for Drug Dependent Women,** 2 (1982) [ADM82-1219], 443-76.
Key issues that counselors need to address are--apart from

their own attitudes--the "coming out" process, self-acceptance, and relationship issues.

3326. NEWMEYER, JOHN A. "The Sensuous Hippie: II. Gay/
        Straight Differences in Regard to Drugs and Sex-
        uality," **Drug Forum**, 6 (1977-78), 49-55.
Among other findings, gay men were found to have active,
but separate enjoyment of drugs and sex, while lesbians
tended to combine the two.

3327. SCHOENER, GARY. "The Heterosexual Norm in Chemical
        Dependency Treatment Programs: Some Personal Obser-
        vations," **Stash Capsules,** 8 (1976), 1-4.
On the need for greater sensitivity in therapeutic personnel.

3328. WELLISCH, DAVID K., et al. "A Study of Therapy of
        Homosexual Adolescent Drug Users in a Residential
        Treatment Setting," **Adolescence,** 16 (1981),
        689-700.
Finds that individual therapy is more helpful than group
therapy in the residential treatment of homosexual drug
users.

                        Y. YOUTH

While claims by some historians that earlier centuries did
not recognize childhood as a separate stage of human development are unconvincing, it is probably true that the
conceptualization of **adolescence** as a stage between childhood and adulthood is relatively recent. The rise of
a "youth culture" with its special preferences in the consumer society has become possible only through the spread
of prosperity in Western industrial countries. Focus on
this stage of life has caused particular problems for
young gay and lesbian people, inasmuch as the youth culture is highly conformist and sometimes punitively antihomosexual. For their part, heterosexual adults and
parents tend to decry homosexual activity and identity in
the teen years as fixing supposedly labile personalities
in a state of permanent deviance. Serving as a counter-
weight to these restrictive tendencies is an increasing
awareness that young people, at least those past the stage
of puberty, are autonomous personalities who should be
permitted to develop according to their own nature.

3329. ALYSON, SASHA (ed.). **Young, Gay and Proud.** Boston:
        Alyson, 1980. 94 pp.
Young peoples' guide to the joys and hazards of coming
out, an adaptation of a publication of the same title
prepared by the Gay Teachers and Students Group of
Melbourne, Australia.

3330. AMSTERDAMSE JONGEN AKTIE GROEPEN. **Homoseksual-
       iteit: jongen-jongen/meisje-meisje.** The Hague:
       NVSH, 1971. 96 pp.
Sympathetic presentation of the situation of male and
female homosexual youth in the Netherlands.

3331. BLÜHER, HANS. **Die deutsche Wandervogelbewegung als
       erotisches Phänomenon: Ein Beitrag zur sexuellen
       Inversion.** Berlin: Weise, 1912. 160 pp.
This exploration of the homoerotic substratum of the great
German youth movement, the Wandervogelbewegung, stirred
up a storm of controversy when it was first published. An
enlarged edition appeared in 1914. For a somewhat one-
sided interpretation of Blüher's significance in this
sphere, see Gunther Schloz, "Wandervogel, Volk, und
Führer: Männergesellschaft und Antisemitismus bei Hans
Blüher," in: **Propheten des Nationalismus** (Munich: List,
1969), pp. 211-27, 279-80, 303-04. For general background, see Walter Laqueur, **Young Germany: A History of
the Youth Movement** (London: Routledge & Kegan Paul, 1962).

3332. CAMPBELL, PATRICIA. **Sex Education Books for Young
       Adults, 1892-1979.** New York: R. R. Bowker, 1979.
       169 pp.
In this narrative study, see index ("Homosexuality,"
"Lesbianism") for numerous references.

3333. COLES, ROBERT, and GEOFFREY STOKES. **Sex and the
       American Teenager.** New York: Harper and Row,
       1985. 238 pp.
Sometimes cloudy interpretation of results of a survey of
1067 respondents (commissioned by **Rolling Stone** magazine). See pp. 135-44, 190-93 for peer pressures on
attitudes toward homosexual behavior.

3334. DAHER, DOUGLAS. "Identity Confusion in Late
       Adolescence: Therapy and Values," **Psychotherapy:
       Theory, Research and Practice,** 14 (1977), 12-17.
Questions the current practice of trying to explain homosexual interests to adolescent clients as "sexual identity
confusion."

3335. GADPAILLE, WARREN J. "Homosexuality in Adolescent
       Males," **Journal of the American Academy of Psycho-
       analysis,** 3 (1975), 361-71.
Attempts to discriminate three "treatment types": (a)
adolescents involved in experimental homoerotic activity; (b) "pseudohomosexuals"; and (c) true, erotically
motivated homosexuals.

3336. GLASSER, MERVIN. "Homosexuality in Adolescence,"
       British Journal of Medical Psychology, 50 (1977),
       217-25.
Contends that different types of homosexuality emerge
during adolescence according to different psychodynamic
conditions that occur in different stages.

3337. HANCKEL, FRANCES, and JOHN CUNNINGHAM. **A Way of
Love, a Way of Life: A Young Person's Introduction
to What it Means to Be Gay.** New York: Lothrop, Lee
and Shepard, 1979. 192 pp.
Down-to-earth, positive approach to self-understanding,
family relationships and friendships, as well as legal
and medical aspects. Includes personal testimonies, "a
dozen gay lives."

3338. HEROLD, EDWARD S. **Sexual Behavior of Canadian
Young People.** Markham, Ont.: Fitzhenry and
Whiteside, 1984. 183 pp.
Offers a synthesis of predominately Canadian research,
including government statistics. The chapter on homosexuality acknowledges preference, behavior, and identity as
variables of sexual orientation.

3339. HERON, ANN (ed.). **One Teenager in Ten: Writings by
Gay and Lesbian Youth.** Boston: Alyson, 1983. 120
pp.
Twenty-eight young people between 15 and 24 tell their
own stories of how their homosexual feelings took shape.
See also: Michael Burbidge and Jonathan Walters (eds.),
Breaking the Silence: Gay Teenagers Speak for Themselves
(London: Joint Council for Gay Teenagers, 1981).

3340. HERTOFT, PREBEN. **Undersogelser over unge maends
seksuelle adfaerd, viden og holdning.** Copenhagen:
Akademisk Forlag, 1968. 2 vols.
Sexologist's report on research on the sexual behavior,
knowledge, and attitudes of young people; see pp. 246-86.

3341. HETTLINGER, RICHARD F. **Sex Isn't That Simple: The
New Sexuality on Campus.** New York: Seabury Press,
1974. 250 pp.
See Chapter 5, "Gay Can Be Good" (pp. 138-54).

3342. HUNT, MORTON. **Gay: What You Should Know about
Homosexuality.** New York: Farrar, Straus and
Giroux, 1977. 210 pp.
A somewhat fuzzy book, in which the author attempts to
explain to young people matters about which he himself
is not always clear.

3343. JENKINS, CHRISTINE, and JULIE MORRIS. **A Look at
Gayness: An Annotated Bibliography of Gay Materials
for Young People.** Second ed. Ann Arbor, MI: Kindred Spirit Press, 1982. 19 pp.
Excellent selection of fiction, nonfiction, comics, and
records. See also: Stephen McDonald, "Young, Gay and
the Problem of Self-Identity: An Annotated Bibliography," **Emergency Librarian** (September-October 1980),
8-11; and E. Paolella, below.

3344. JONES, GERALD P. "Using Early Assessment of
Prehomosexual Boys as a Counseling Tool: An Ex-

ploratory Study," **Journal of Adolescence,** 4 (1981),
231-48.
Early assessment of the beginnings of lifelong homosexual
adaptation is presented as a valuable tool for the
counselor or therapist to help the client adapt to a
sometimes hostile world.

3345. LE SHAN, EDA. **Sex and Your Teenager: A Guide for
Parents.** New York: David McKay, 1969. 239 pp.
Perhaps the first mainstream guide for parents to sound a
positive note on homosexuality, which is regarded as
natural.

3346. MARTIN, A. DAMIEN. "Learning to Hide: The Socialization of the Gay Adolescent," **Adolescent Psychiatry,** 10 (1982), 52-65.
In contrast with the present situation, young people
should have access to accurate information on homosexuality and to the possibility of maintaining personal,
social, ethical, and professional integrity with a homosexual orientation.

3347. MCCLEARY, ROLAND D. "Patterns of Homosexuality in
Boys: Observations from Illinois," **International
Journal of Offender Therapy and Comparative Criminology,** 16 (1972), 139-42.
Suggests that the neglected children of the rich and of
the ghetto tend to accept all types of sexuality in a
matter-of-fact manner, while those from more closely-knit
middle-class families have intense guilt feelings and tend
to project blame.

3348. MORIN, STEPHEN F., and STEPHEN J. SCHULTZ. "The
Gay Movement and the Rights of Children," **Journal
of Social Issues,** 34 (1978), 137-48.
Based on the premise that a gay identity and lifestyle is
a positive option to which all adults have a right, the
developmental requirements for the acquisition of a positive gay identity are explored.

3349. **Ook zo? Informatie voor jongeren over homoseksualiteit.** Amsterdam: NVIH-COC/Schorenstichting,
1981. 63 pp.
Illustrated handbook prepared by leading Dutch gay organizations for gay youth, covering such topics as school,
parents and siblings, venereal disease, and useful
addresses.

3350. PAOLELLA, EDWARD. "Resources for and about Lesbian
and Gay Youth: An Annotated Survey," **Reference
Services Review,** 12:2 (1984), 72-94.
One hundred items are chosen and annotated with additional
readings suggested. Categories include biography, reference, counseling, history, literature, minorities, parents, religion, and sex education. Author and title indexes. See also: C. Jenkins and J. Morris, above.

3351.   ROESLER, THOMAS, and ROBERT W. DEISHER.   "Youthful
        Male Homosexuality: Homosexual Experience and the
        Process of Developing Homosexual Identity in Males
        Aged 16 to 22 Years," **JAMA: Journal of the American
        Medical Association,** 219 (1972), 1018-23.
From interviews with 60 young men, attempts to discern
significant events that preceded the subject's self-des-
ignation, "I am a Homosexual."

3352.   SORENSON, ROBERT C. **Adolescent Sexuality in Con-
        temporary America.** New York: World, 1973. 549 pp.
In this attempt at synthesis, see pp. 283-329 (Chapter # 11).

3353.   SPRING, MARJORIE P. "A Contribution to the Study
        of Homosexuality in Adolescence," in: M. Harley
        (ed.), **The Analyst and the Adolescent at Work.** New
        York: Quadrangle, 1974, pp. 68-109.
Psychoanalytic perspective.

3354.   SULLIVAN, TERRENCE. "Adolescent Homosexuality: -
        Social Constructions and Developmental Realities,"
        Journal of Child Care, 1 (1984), 11-27.
Suggests that for a number of prehomosexual youngsters
strong homosexual feelings lead them to identify themselves as different from their peers, leading to a step-
by-step consolidation of a homosexual identity.

3355.   TRENCHARD, LORRAINE, and HUGH WARREN. **Something to
        Tell You ... The Experiences and Needs of Young
        Lesbians and Gay Men in London.** London: London Gay
        Teenagers Group, 1984. 165 pp.
Report of the findings of a research project undertaken in
1983 using a questionnaire completed by 416 persons.
Treats income and social class, coming out to family,
schooling, unemployment, making contacts, going out, law,
and police.

3356.   WHITAM, FREDERICK L. "Childhood Indicators of Male
        Homosexuality," **Archives of Sexual Behavior,** 6
        (1977), 89-96.
Arguing that there are behavioral aspects related to one's
sexual orientation which may begin to emerge early in
childhood, notes six significant factors: interest in
dolls, cross-dressing, preference for the company of
girls, preference for the company of older women, sissi-
hood, and sexual interest in boys. See also his book
(with Robin M. Mathy), **Male Homosexuality in Four Societies** (New York: Praeger, 1986; 240 pp.).

XV. SOCIAL WORK

A. COUNSELING AND SOCIAL SERVICES

The social work approach to human problems first appeared
in Victorian England, but it quickly spread to the United
States, where its activist and pragmatic spirit had great
appeal. Counseling services have become established
features of many state-supported schools and other institutions. Private persons and organizations, including
professedly gay and lesbian ones, also provide counseling. The need for such separate institutions suggests a
limitation in the counseling/social work ethos. To the
extent that the counselor clings to unexamined societal
prejudices communication will be hindered. In fairness,
it must be noted that many heterosexual counselors are
aware of this problem, and have sought to make themselves
more sensitive to the needs of gay and lesbian clients.
There is no doubt that counseling and social work has done
much good. This is especially true in the mental field,
where large numbers of people, particularly those who are
young, cannot afford psychotherapy--which may in fact be
less effective.

3357. ATKINSON, DONALD R., et al. "Sexual Preference
      Similarity, Attitude Similarity, and Perceived
      Counselor Credibility and Attractiveness," **Journal
      of Counseling Psychology**, 28 (1981), 504-09.
In a study of 84 homosexual men, the counselor advising a
male client on matters of sexual preference was rated more
expert, trustworthy and attractive, when he expressed a
positive sexual preference for men.

3358. BABUSCIO, JACK. **We Speak for Ourselves: Expe-
      riences in Homosexual Counseling.** Philadelphia:
      Fortress Press, 1977. 146 pp.
Case studies and sympathetic practical advice by an American activist based in England. Intended for both lay and
religious counselors.

3359. BEANE, JEFFREY. "'I'd Rather Be Dead Than Gay':
      Counseling Gay Men Who Are Coming Out," **Personnel
      and Guidance Journal**, 60:4 (1981), 222-26.
Focusing on the initial phase of counseling male clients
who have a negative gay identity which they wish to
change, the article presents some basic concepts in
Gestalt therapy.

3360. BERGER, RAYMOND M. "An Advocate Model for Inter-
      vention with Homosexuals," **Social Work**, 22 (1977),
      280-83.

Proposes a model for social work intervention that is based on the premise that homosexuality is a legitimate lifestyle option.

3361.   BERGSTROM, SAGE, and LAWRENCE CRUZ (eds.). **Counseling Lesbians and Gay Male Youth: Their Special Lives/Special Needs.** Washington, DC: National Network of Runaway and Youth Services, 1983. 85 pp.
Focuses on the growing problem of young people, many of them working class and minority, who have been pushed out of their home situation because of their lifestyle.

3361A. BERNSTEIN, BARTON E. "Legal and Social Interface in Counseling Homosexual Clients," **Social Casework**, 58 (1977), 36-40.
Although biological offspring are not involved, almost every other problem facing a married couple must be considered by a homosexual couple (e.g.,the homestead, personal property, insurance, wills, and child custody).

3362.   BLAIR, RALPH EDWARD. **Vocational Guidance and Gay Liberation.** New York: National Task Force on Student Personnel Services and Homosexuality, 1972. (Otherwise Monograph Series, 19)
Reflections by a pioneer in counseling services to the gay and lesbian community. Blair, who is based in New York City, edited the **Homosexual Counseling Journal**, which contains much relevant material.

3363.   BOWLES, JAMES K. "Dealing with Homosexuality: A Survey of Staff Training Needs," **College Student Personnel**, 22 (1981), 276-77.
In 1979 the Department of Residence Halls at the University of Tennessee, Knoxville, conducted a survey on the need for floor counselors to be trained in dealing with homosexuality. A large number of the men revealed hostility or aversion with respect to the subject.

3364.   BRITTON, JEFF, and SCOTT ANDERSON. "A Tale of Two Community Centers," **Advocate**, no. 309 (January 8, 1981), 24-27.
On the gay and lesbian service centers in Philadelphia (since closed) and Los Angeles. See also: Linda M. Poverny, **The Organizational Life Cycle and the Process of Adaptation: A Case Study of the Los Angeles Gay and Lesbian Community Services Center** (Ph. D. dissertation; Los Angeles, University of Southern California, 1983).

3365.   CARNES, PATRICK. **The Sexual Addiction.** Minneapolis: CompCare, 1983. 185 pp.
Self-help and group procedures for sexual compulsives, heterosexual and homosexual, based on the twelve steps of Alcoholic Anonymous.

3366.   CORNELL, CARLTON W., and ROSS A. HUDSON. "Social

Work Practice, Homosexuality, and the Psychoanalytic Approach," **Journal of Social Work and Human
Sexuality,** 3 (1984), 39-50.
Contends that the acceptance of psychoanalytic thought in
the helping professions has made them complicitous in the
derogation of homosexuals that has been pervasive in
American society.

3367. DECKER, BEVERLY. "Counseling Gay and Lesbian
        Couples," **Journal of Social Work and Human Sexual-
        ity,** 2:2-3 (1983-84), 39-52.
When dyadic fusion occurs, the partners form a single
unit, closing themselves off to outsiders, possibly
leading to problems of loss of ego boundaries, dissolution of the self, and suppression of all aggressive and
sexual drives.

3368. DULANEY, DIANA D., and JAMES KELLY. "Improving
        Services to Gay and Lesbian Clients," **Social Work,**
        27 (1982), 178-83.
Among practitioners of the mental health professions,
homophobia has been found most prevalent among social
workers, who need to confront their own attitudes.

3369. ENRIGHT, MICHAEL A., and BRUCE V. PARSONS. "Train-
        ing Crisis Intervention Specialists and Peer Group
        Counselors as Therapeutic Agents in the Gay
        Community," **Community Mental Health Journal,** 12
        (1976), 383-91.
Describes the development of a training program, utilizing
gay nonprofessionals.

3370. FERRIS, DAVE. **Homosexuality and the Social Ser-
        vices: The Report of an NCCL Survey of Local Au-
        thority Social Service Committees.** London: Nation-
        al Council for Civil Liberties, 1977. 89 pp.
Reports a mixed pattern of accomplishment in Britain.

3371. GAIR, CINDI, et al. **Gay Peer Counseling at Mich-
        igan.** New York: National Task Force on Student
        Personnel Services and Homosexuality, 1972. 9
        pp. (Otherwise Monograph Series, 9)
Evaluates the pioneering work of part-time assistants
funded by the University of Michigan, Ann Arbor.

3372. GAMBRILL, EILEEN D., et al. "Social Services Use
        and Need among Gay/Lesbian Residents of the San
        Francisco Bay Area," **Journal of Social Work and
        Human Sexuality,** 3 (1984), 51-69.
Greatest needs reported were employment counseling, help
in locating housing and services, community mental health
clinics, assistance in meeting people, counseling for
personal growth, and treatment for depression.

3373. GOCHROS, HARVEY, et al. **Helping the Sexually
        Oppressed.** Englewood Cliffs, NJ: Prentice-Hall,

1986. 282 pp.
Twenty chapters by various writers. Part 1 offers an
overview on human sexuality and oppression. Part 2
discusses specific groups, including gay men (Raymond
M. Berger) and lesbians (Janne Dooley).

3374. GOULDEN, T. "The Gays Counseling Service of
       N.S.W.," **Australian Social Work**, 38 (1985), 38-41.
A volunteer organization in Sydney that operates a telephone Gayline, and offers counseling of various types,
including work with AIDS patients.

3375. GRAHAM, DEE L., et al. "Therapists' Needs for
       Training in Counseling Lesbians and Gay Men,"
       Professional Psychology Research and Practice, 15
       (1984), 482-96.
Therapists' major concerns in counseling gay clients were
the maintenance of objectivity, countertransference, and
lack of knowledge of homosexuality.

3376. GRAMICK, JEANNINE. "Homophobia: A New Challenge,"
       Social Work, 28 (1983), 137-41.
Contends that if social workers are to be effective in
helping their clients, they must deal with the irrational
fear of homosexuality.

3377. HART, JOHN. "Counseling Problems Arising from the
       Social Categorization of Homosexuals," **Bulletin of
       the British Psychological Society**, 35 (1982), 198-
       200.
Discusses the therapeutic/counseling implications of a
sociological challenge to the notion of sexual orientation difference as being an essential characteristic of
certain people.

3378. HAYNES, ALPHONSO W. "The Challenge of Counseling
       the Homosexual Client," **Personnel and Guidance
       Journal**, 56 (1977), 243-46.
Counseling the homosexual client must be fully contractual and consensual, and conducted with the awareness
that some individuals may have good reason to fear disclosure of their homosexuality.

3379. HIDALGO, HILDA, TRAVIS L. PETERSON, and NATALIE
       JANE WOODMAN (eds.). **Lesbian and Gay Issues: A
       Resource Manual for Social Workers**. Silver Spring,
       MD: National Association of Welfare Workers, 1985.
       220 pp.
Part 1 deals with specific subgroups (adolescents,
couples, lesbian mothers, the disabled, rural gays,
etc.). Part 2 concerns institutional intervention.
Part 3 scrutinizes agency politics which negatively
affect gays and lesbians as employees, offering suggestions for change.

3380. JONES, CLINTON R. **Homosexuality and Counseling.**

Philadelphia: Fortress Press, 1974. 132 pp.
The writer, Canon at Hartford Episcopal Cathedral, offers
humanistic and religious advice on how to help homosexuals "out of pain and toward fulfillment" as self-accep-
ting persons. Includes case studies.

3381. JONES, GERALD P. "Counseling Gay Adolescents,"
       Counselor Education and Supervision, 18 (1978),
       144-52.
Counselors who would help adolescent homosexuals toward
self-acceptance and in confronting their educational and
career problems must expect to encounter some miscompre-
hension on the part of the public.

3382. MACOURT, MALCOLM. **Can We Help You?** London: Gay
       Men's Press, 1986. 112 pp.
With ten years of experience in gay counseling in Britain,
the author evaluates gay helplines, designed for both the
counseling community and the lay public.

3383. MILLER, RHODA. "Counseling the Young Adult Les-
       bian," **Journal of the National Association for
       Women Deans, Administrators, and Counselors**, 43:3
       (1980), 44-48.
The author suggests that the counselor (1) encourage the
client to unburden herself of her thoughts and feelings;
(2) guide her in coming out; (3) explain the legal situation to her; (4) facilitate socializing with other lesbians; and (5) publicly promote gay rights.

3384. MOSES, A. ELFIN, and ROBERT O. HAWKINS. **Counseling
       Lesbian Women and Gay Men: A Life-Issues Approach.**
       St. Louis: C. V. Mosby, 1982. 263 pp.
Background and recommendations for positive intervention
with gay clients, covering: how the world views gay
people; the gay experience; and special issues in counseling gay clients--Third World persons, rural gays, confidentiality, gay college students, aging, and gay parents.
Bibliography, pp. 231-52.

3385. MYERS, MICHAEL F. "Counseling the Parents of Young
       Homosexual Male Patients," **JH**, 7:2-3 (1981-82),
       131-43.
Describes the author's practice of interviewing the parents of young homosexual men in therapy, specifically
parents traumatized by the discovery of their son's homosexuality.

3386. NEEDHAM, RUSSELL. "Casework Intervention with a
       Homosexual Adolescent," **Social Casework**, 58 (1977),
       387-94.
Mental health professionals need to see the gay client as
a non-pathological subject who most often needs supportive
case work in adjusting to a commonly hostile, prejudicial
environment.

3387. NORTON, JOSEPH L. "The Homosexual and Counseling,"
       Personnel and Guidance Journal, 54 (1976), 374-77.
The task of the counselor today is to help gay clients to
learn that they can lead happy, productive, fulfilled
lives. The standard fears and anxieties are discussed
together with the professional dilemma of coming out as
a gay counselor. See also his: "Integrating Gay Issues
into Counselor Education," **Counselor Education and Supervision,** 21 (1982), 208-12.

3388. POTTER, SANDRA J., and TRUDY E. DARTY. "Social
       Work and the Invisible Minority: An Exploration of
       Lesbianism," **Social Work,** 26 (1981), 187-92.
Experiencing the "double jeopardy" of belonging to two
minority groups, lesbians are the object of many myths and
false beliefs. Social workers must become knowledgeable
and comfortable with lesbianism as a sexual preference
and a lifestyle.

3389. ROSS-REYNOLDS, GARY, and BARBARA HARDY. "Crisis
       Counseling for Disparate Adolescent Sexual Dil-
       emmas: Pregnancy and Homosexuality," **School Psy-
       chology Review,** 14 (1985), 300-12.
Holds that the school counselor must be accepting of
adolescents confronting these crises and create an environment in which they feel safe to discuss their feeling
and concerns.

3390. RUSSELL, A., and R. WINKLER. "Evaluation of Asser-
       tive Training and Homosexual Guidance Service
       Groups Designed to Improve Homosexual Functioning,"
       Journal of Consulting and Clinical Psychology, 45
       (1977), 1-13.
Reports a study with 27 Australian men that seems to
validate the approach.

3391. RUTLEDGE, AARON L. "Treatment of Male Homosexuality
       through Marriage Counseling: A Case Presentation,"
       Journal of Marriage and Family Counseling, 1
       (1975), 51-62.
Examines several theoretical issues, including mixed
sexual and dominance-submission dynamics, a transference
family concept, and the "economy" of the homosexual
syndrome.

3392. SANG, BARBARA E. "Psychotherapy with Lesbians:
       Some Observations and Tentative Generalizations,"
       in: Edna I. Rawlings and Dianne R. Carter (eds.),
       **Psychotherapy for Women: Treatment toward Equal-
       ity.** Springfield, IL: Charles C. Thomas, 1977,
       pp. 266-75.
A major obstacle to satisfactory counseling and therapy is
professionals' lack of practical knowledge about homosexuality and homosexual lifestyles. Also, women entering a
lesbian relationship in mid-life have feelings of inadequacy and incompetence because society has denied them

early experience.

3393. SCHEPP, KAY FRANCES. **Sexuality Counseling: A
        Training Program.** Muncie, IN: Accelerated Develop-
        ment, 1986. 510 pp.
A comprehensive survey with emphasis on psychological
aspects, organized in terms of 51 learning experiences.
Presents numerous cases and reading lists. See esp. pp.
72-78, 296-303.

3394. SCHOENBERG, ROBERT, et al (eds.). **Homosexuality
        and Social Work.** New York: Haworth Press, 1984.
        156 pp.
Nine papers on (1) life stages and statuses; (2) life
problems; and (3) professional issues. Reprinted from
Journal of Social Work and Human Sexuality, 2:2-3 (1983-
84).

3395. SIEGAL, RIVA L., and DAVID D. HOEFER. "Bereavement
        Counseling for Gay Individuals," **American Journal
        of Psychotherapy,** 35 (1981), 517-25.
Discusses the lack of societal mechanisms, sanctions, and
resources to aid in the bereavement process.

3396. SILVERBERG, ROBERT A. "Being Gay: Helping Clients
        Cope," **Journal of Psychosocial Nursing and Mental
        Health Services,** 22 (1984), 19-25.
The therapist should focus on helping the client establish
his/her own values in a nonjudgmental atmosphere, avoiding
premature labeling, in case the client is just beginning
to explore sexuality.

3396. SITTES, M. CYNARA. "Mental Health Services for Gay
        Students: Gay-Straight Rap," **Journal of American
        College Health,** 32 (1983), 86-87.
Describes a drop-in discussion group which considers such
topics as discovering one's homosexuality, overcoming
one's negative stereotypes, deciding how "out" to be,
handling dormitory roommates, and coping with harassment.

3397. SOPHIE, JOAN. "Counseling Lesbians," **Personnel
        and Guidance Journal,** 60 (1982), 341-45.
This group is highly diverse with respect to sexual/affec-
tional history, lifestyle, and personal identity. The
counselor should help the client explore her feelings
without premature self-labeling, challenge the client's
assumptions about sex roles, become familiar with community resources, and prepare clients for coming out to
significant people.

3399. TARTAGNI, DONNA. "Counseling Gays in a School
        Setting," **School Counselor,** 26 (1978), 26-32.
Many high school counselors put their heads in the sand
whenever homosexuality becomes a public issue. The result
is that "the loneliest person in the country is the homosexual adolescent in the typical high school of today."

3400. TULLY, CAROL, and JOYCE C. ALBRO. "Homosexual-
      ity: A Social Worker's Imbroglio," **Journal of
      Sociology and Social Welfare,** 6 (1979), 154-67.
Acceptance of the client by the social worker, specialized
counseling, an awareness of the homosexual subculture
within one's community and referral to competent legal
professionals are desiderata in providing services to
homosexual clients.

3401. TURNER, RICHARD. "Byzantine Maneuverings Shake
      Community Services Centre," **Campaign** (Australia),
      no. 68 (August 1981), 16-17.
Turmoil at the Sydney Gay Community Centre because of
conflicting institutional interests and fears of a leftist take-over.

3402. VERGARA, TACIE L. "Meeting the Needs of Minority
      Youth: One Program's Response," **Journal of Social
      Work and Human Sexuality,** 2:2-3 (1983-84), 19-38.
Describes the development of services to meet the needs of
sexual minority youth at the Eromin Center in Philadelphia, since closed.

3403. WAY, PEGGY. "Homosexual Counseling as a Learning
      Ministry," **Christianity and Crisis,** 37 (1977),
      123-31.
Contends that women in ministry are more open to discussion of homosexuality than are men, because the latter
have been emotionally scarred by homosexual advances in
their youth.

3404. WESTEFELD, JOHN S., and WINKELPLECK, JUDY M.
      "University Counseling Service Groups for Gay
      Students," **Group Behavior,** 14 (1983), 121-28.
Describes a group counseling program, the Student Counseling Service, for gay students at Iowa State University,
which uses a semistructured approach.

3405. WOODMAN, NATALIE JANE, and HARRY R. LENNA. **Coun-
      seling with Gay Men and Women: A Guide for Facilit-
      ating Positive Life-Styles.** San Francisco: Jossey-
      Bass, 1980. 144 pp.
The book covers a whole range of problems confronting the
counselor. Topics include social and clinical responses
to homosexuality, basic concepts and counseling procedures, sexual identity, promoting a positive self-image,
dilemmas of social acceptance, special problems of youth,
enhancing interpersonal relationships, and building com-
munity-based support systems. Annotated bibliography and
list of references.

XVI. PSYCHOLOGY

A. GENERAL

Unlike psychoanalysis (XVII.C), modern psychology generally eschews grand theories of sexual orientation and
behavior, preferring to concentrate of testable assertions
regarding specific aspects. For this reason there is
little in the way of synthesis to guide the neophyte. In
compensation for this lack, the control of current
progress in research is facilitated through the monthly
issues of **Psychological Abstracts** (1927-), in which each
paper cited is accompanied by a resume. (In addition to
thorough coverage of English-language work, **PA** offers some
material on research in other languages.)

3406. AKERS, RONALD L. **Deviant Behavior: A Social
Learning Approach.** Belmont, CA: Wadsworth, 1985.
421 pp.
See pp. 192-203 for a learning-theory analysis of homosexual careers and subcultures.

3407. BERNARD, LARRY C. "Sex-Role Factor Identification
and Sexual Preference of Men," **Journal of Personality Assessment,** 46 (1982), 292-99.
Compared with heterosexual subjects, homosexual subjects
appeared to be more open, to engage in more domestic activity, to be less concerned with practical and recreational activities, and to be less conservative.

3408. COURT, JOHN H., and RAYMOND O. JOHNSTON. "Psycho-
sexuality: A Three-Dimensional Model," **Journal of
Psychology and Theology,** 6 (1978), 90-97.
The proposed model includes morality and "the spiritual
aspects of humans."

3409. GONSIOREK, JOHN. **Psychological Adjustment and
Homosexuality.** Washington, DC: American Psychological Association, 1977. 49 pp. (MS 1478)
Selective evaluation of the literature organized according
to various models, including the cross-species, cross-cultural, demographic, biological, psychoanalytic, psychometric, and sociological. Limited to English-language material, chiefly recent. Bibliography, pp. 40-47.

3410. GONSIOREK, JOHN (ed.). "Homosexuality: The End of
the Illusion," **American Behavioral Scientist,** 25
(March-April 1982), 367-496.
Symposium of nine papers dealing with such issues as psychological testing, ethics, therapy, psychoanalysis, and
coming out. Substantially the same contents as Part 2

511

(pp. 57-161) of William Paul et al. (eds.), **Homosexuality: Social, Psychological and Biological Issues** (Beverly
Hills, CA: Sage, 1982).

3411. GREENBERG, JERROLD. "A Study of Male Homosexuals
        (Predominantly College Students)," **Journal of the
        American College Health Association,** 22 (1973),
        56-60.
Results of a questionnaire taken by 86 students on sexual
behavior, family background, religious attitudes, drug
usage, and demography.

3412. HARRY, JOSEPH. **Gay Children Grown Up.** New York:
        Praeger, 1982. 269 pp.
A major study using survey data from Chicago and the region (122 Illinois students and 1461 gay non-students)
to focus on childhood effeminate interests.

3413. HAYNES, STEPHEN N., and L. JEROME OZIEL. "Homosex-
        uality: Behaviors and Attitudes," **Archives of Sex-
        ual Behavior,** 5 (1976), 283-89.
Of 4,251 university students, the rate of homosexual experiences was appreciably lower than that commonly reported
in the literature and was not significantly related to
race, religion, or region of residence.

3414. HOWELLS, KEVIN (ed.). **The Psychology of Sexual
        Diversity.** Oxford: Basil Blackwell, 1984.   270 pp.
Papers covering gender identity, homosexuality, harmless
and harmful sexual disorders, and sexual inadequacy in
men and animals--including roles played by genetic, endo-
crinologic, neurologic, and postnatal factors in regard to
sexual development.

3415. MACDONALD, A. C., JR. **An Annotated Subject-indexed
        Bibliography of Research on Bisexuality, Lesbianism
        and Male Homosexuality (1975-78).** Washington,
        DC: American Psychological Association, 1981.   38
        pp. (MS 2206)
Summarizes "major findings" of 115 English-language
studies referenced in **Psychological Abstracts** in the
four-year period. Intended as a continuation of S. F.
Morin (3418), below. Subject index, pp. 35-37.

3416. MALLEN, C. ANNE. "Sex-Role Stereotypes, Gender
        Identity and Parental Relationships in Male Homo-
        sexuals and Heterosexuals," **JH,** 9 (1983), 55-74.
Data show a tendency of homosexuals and heterosexuals to
converge, that is, similarities are greater than differences.

3417. MONEY, JOHN. "Sexual Dimorphism and Homosexual
        Gender Identity," **Psychological Bulletin,** 74
        (1970), 425-40.
Arguing that the classification of homosexuality as
hereditary or constitutional vs. acquired is outmoded,

suggests that the differentiation should be between
chronic, obligative, or essential vs. transient, facul-
tative, or optional.

3418. MORIN, STEPHEN F. **Annotated Bibliography of Re-
       search on Lesbianism and Male Homosexuality (1967-
       1974).** Washington, DC: American Psychological
       Association, 1976. 57pp. (MS 1191)
Outlines "major findings" of 139 studies published in
English-language journals referenced in **Psychological
Abstracts** during the eight-year period. Continued by
A. P. MacDonald (3415), above.

3419. MORIN, STEPHEN F. "Heterosexual Bias in Psycholog-
       ical Research on Lesbianism and Male Homosexual-
       ity," **American Psychologist,** 32 (1977), 629-37.
Argues that the reconceptualization of homosexuality as a
valid option for an adult lifestyle would suggest changes
in the questions formulated, the data collected, and the
interpretations made in research. Reply by G. A. Rekers,
ibid., 33 (1978), 510-12. See also: Morin, "Psychology
and the Gay Community: An Overview," **Journal of Social
Issues,** 34:3 (1978), 1-6 (introduces a special issue on
homosexuality).

3420. NUNGESSER, LON G. **Homosexual Acts, Actions and
       Identities.** New York: Praeger, 1983. 215 pp.
Accessible presentation of components of sexual identity;
beliefs and systems of belief (including stereotypes);
prejudice; and fears and phobias.

3421. SOBEL, HARRY J. "Adolescent Attitudes toward Homo-
       sexuality in Relation to Self Concept and Body
       Satisfaction," **Adolescence,** 11 (1976), 443-53.
Findings of tests suggest that an adolescent with high
self-concept and body image has a propensity for rigidity,
and these individuals may project fears of losing social
reinforcement and status onto minorities such as homosexuals.

3422. STOLLER, ROBERT J. "Problems with the Term 'Homo-
       sexuality,'" **Hillside Journal of Clinical Psychi-
       atry,** 2 (1980), 3-25.
Holds that the word has been used in so many ways that,
unless one clearly states how it is employed at a given
moment, the surplus meanings stifle understanding.

3423. STRINGER, PETER, and TADEUSZ GRYGIER. "Male Homo-
       sexuality, Psychiatric Patient Status, and Psycho-
       logical Masculinity and Femininity," **Archives of
       Sexual Behavior,** 5 (1976), 15-27.
Results of the Dynamic Personality Inventory administered
to both psychiatric patients and others in Britain show
that homosexuality can be characterized independent of
clinical status.

3424. TEMPLER, DONALD I., et al. "The Death Anxiety of
       Gays," **Omega: Journal of Death and Dying,** 14
       (1983-84), 211-14.
Administration of the Death Anxiety Scale to 260 male and
female homosexuals show scores similar to those obtained
for predominantly heterosexual populations. Abnormality
of gays is not supported by their DAS scores.

3425. VAN WYK, PAUL H., and CHRISANN S. GEIST. "Psycho-
       social Development of Heterosexual, Bisexual, and
       Homosexual Behavior," **Archives of Sexual Behavior,**
       13 (1984), 505-44.
Results of a study of 7,669 adults indicate that intense
sexual experiences and feelings of arousal, pleasure or
discomfort were the strongest precursors of adult sexual
orientation, followed by gender-related factors and family
influences.

                        B. CREATIVITY

The popular mind tends to regard creativity as the product
of suffering. To the extent that homosexuals are considered unhappy, they are conceived as being sensitive and
creative as a consequence. This stereotype is complemented by a tendency among homosexuals themselves (in common
with members of other minorities) to conceive of themselves as possessing special sensitivity and intelligence. Unfortunately, it has not proved possible to obtain any solid evidence in support of these assumptions.
It may be, however, that "creativity" is itself significantly unmeasurable and unverifiable, so that this matter
is destined to remain in the sphere of intuition.

3426. CORY, DONALD WEBSTER, and JOHN P. LEROY. "Are
       Homosexuals Creative?" **Sexology,** 29 (1962), 162-65.
Cautioning against inferences from clinical populations,
argues that since the homosexual stands outside the mainstream of life, he sees humanity differently, originally,
and hence "stands closer to the wellsprings from which
true creativity flows."

3427. DEMARTINO, MANFRED F. **Sex and the Intelligent
       Woman.** New York: Springer, 1974. 308 pp.
The first work to deal specifically and seriously with the
sexual attitudes, desires, experiences, and practices of
women of high intelligence as measured by the IQ test.
Pages 171-77 discuss homosexual activity, which was not
widespread in the group; only 21% said that they had ever
had any lesbian experience.

3428. DOMINO, GEORGE P. "Homosexuality and Creativity,"
       JH, 2 (1977), 261-67.

Administering a battery of nine creativity measures to
four separate groups of homosexuals and controls yielded
no support for the contention that homosexuals are more
creative.

3429. HODGES, ANDREW. **Alan Turing: The Enigma.** New
York: Simon and Schuster, 1983. 587 pp.
Definitive biography of the great British scientist (1912-
1954), who committed suicide after official persecution.
Because of the detailed investigation of his personality,
this monograph offers vistas for the study of other
homosexual scientists and their relation to society.

3430. KAYY, W. H. (pseud. of William Howard Kupper). **The
Gay Geniuses: Psychiatric and Literary Studies of
Famous Homosexuals.** Glendale, CA: Marvin Miller,
1965. 223 pp.
Contending that homosexuality, overt and latent, is
associated with genius, this popular work presents the
personal histories of more than 70 famous historical
figures--intellectuals, artists and musicians, military
men, rulers, and religious leaders.

3431. RABOCH, JAN, and I. ŠIPOVÁ. "Intelligence in Homosexuals, Transsexuals and Hypogonadal Eunuchoids,"
Journal of Sex Research, 10 (1974), 156-61.
With respect to several groups that exhibited an IQ above
average, it is hypothesized that disorders in the supply
of steroid hormone during the formation period of hypo-
thalamus disturb the sexual development and also have a
tendency to increase the mental level. See also the
article (in Czech) of I. Šipová, **Československá Psychiatrie,** 71 (1975), 131-36.

3431A. TERMAN, LEWIS M., and MELITA H. ODEN. **The Gifted
Child Grows Up.** Stanford: University Press, 1947.
448 pp. (Genetic Studies of Genius, 4)
For 11 homosexual men and 6 women, see pp. 120-22. See
also the fifth volume in the series, **The Gifted Group at
Mid-Life** (Stanford: Stanford University Press, 1959),
pp. 21, 46-51. On Terman's work, see May Violet Seagoe,
Terman and the Gifted (Los Altos, CA: W. Kaufmann, 1975),
pp. 82-84 and 142-44.

3432. WEINRICH, JAMES D. "Nonreproduction, Homosexuality, Transsexualism, and Intelligence: I. A Systematic Literature Search," **JH,** 3 (1978), 275-89.
Most studies surveyed found the more homosexual subject
groups' scores to be higher than those of the more heterosexual controls, and all exceptions to this trend are concentrated in one subgroup: prisoners.

3433. WILMOTT, MARTIN, and HARRY BRIERLY. "Cognitive
Characteristics and Homosexuality," **Archives of
Sexual Behavior,** 13 (1984), 311-19.
No differences were found in IQ between 20 homosexual

males, 20 heterosexual males, and 20 females, but "social
differences in verbal and nonverbal ability were marked."

C. EFFEMINACY AND SISSINESS

The notion of inversion, which lingers in the popular
mind, suggests that male homosexual are effeminate, while
lesbians are mannish. There is some support for the
assertion that at some stage of development, at least, a
significant number of male homosexuals exhibit some
effeminate traits--though this may simply be a product
of the internalization of societal attributions.

3434. BLANCHARD, ROY, et al. "Measuring Physical Aggres-
        siveness in Heterosexual, Homosexual, and Transsex-
        ual Males," **Archives of Sexual Behavior,** 12 (1983),
        511-24.
Results of a self-report measure of boyhood aggressiveness used with adult males suggest that whatever underlying factor relates male homosexuality to feminine gender
identity in childhood relates this erotic preference to
anomalously low levels of physical aggressiveness in
childhood as well.

3435. FREUND, KURT, et al. "Measuring Feminine Gender
        Identity in Homosexual Males," **Archives of Sexual
        Behavior,** 3 (1974), 249-60.
Questions the appropriateness of measuring "femininity" in
homosexual males by means of the usual masculinity-fem-
ininity tests, but holds that an appropriate scale can
be devised. See also: Freund et al., "Femininity and
Preferred Partner Age in Homosexual and Heterosexual
Males," **British Journal of Psychiatry,** 125 (1974), 442-46.

3436. FRIEDMAN, RICHARD C., and LENORE O. STERN. "Juven-
        ile Aggressivity and Sissiness in Homosexual and
        Heterosexual Males," **Journal of the American
        Academy of Psychoanalysis,** 8 (1980), 427-40.
A study of 34 adult males suggests that male-male peer
aggressiveness competency learned after the juvenile
period will not alter homosexual orientation. Contrast
Marcel T. Saghir and Eli Robins, **Male and Female Homosexuality: A Comprehensive Investigation** (Baltimore: Williams
and Wilkins, 1973; 341 pp.).

3437. GREEN, RICHARD. "One-Hundred Ten Feminine and
        Masculine Boys: Behavioral Contrasts and Demograph-
        ic Similarities," **Archives of Sexual Behavior,** 5
        (1976), 425-46.
Characterizes a group of 60 feminine boys as against a
matched control group of 50. See also: "Diagnosis and
Treatment of Gender Identity Disorders during Childhood,"

Archives of Sexual Behavior, 1 (1971), 167-73; and "Childhood Cross-Gender Behavior and Subsequent Sexual Preference," **American Journal of Psychiatry,** 136 (1979), 106-08.

3438. GRELLERT, EDWARD A. "Childhood Play Behavior of
        Homosexual and Heterosexual Men," **Psychological
        Reports,** 51 (1982), 607-10.
Differences were found on 11 activities: drawing, hiding, bicycling, baseball, basketball, football, parties, hopscotch, kickball, marbles, and talking. Homosexuals also named more girl playmates than did the comparison group. See also his: "Childhood Play Activities of Male and Female Homosexuals and Heterosexuals," **Archives of Sexual Behavior,** 11 (1982), 451-78.

3439. HARRY, JOSEPH. "Defeminization and Social Class,"
        Archives of Sexual Behavior, 14 (1985), 1-11.
From interviews with 686 homosexual men concludes that gay men who become effeminate tend to come from blue-collar backgrounds. See also his: **Gay Children Grown Up** (New York: Praeger, 1982; 269 pp.).

3440. LEBOVITZ, PHIL S. "Feminine Behavior in Boys: Aspects of Its Outcome," **American Journal of Psychiatry,** 128 (1972), 1283-89.
Of 16 subjects who had exhibited feminine behavior as young boys, there appeared to be two peaks for the age of onset of symptoms: before age 6 and after age 10.

3441. LUTZ, DAVID J., et al. "Feminine Gender Identity and Psychological Adjustment of Male Transsexuals and Male Homosexuals," **Journal of Sex Research,** 20 (1984), 350-62.
Since the age of six transsexuals reported preferring female activities and desiring to be female significantly more than did homosexuals.

3442. REKERS, GEORGE A., et al. "Sex-Role Stereotypy and Professional Intervention for Childhood Gender Disturbance," **Professional Psychology,** 9 (1978), 127-36.
Contends that the psychological profession should promote greater social tolerance for individuals with deviant sex roles and individual tolerance in children for androgyny in their own sex role.

3443. SCHATZBERG, ALAN F., et al. "Effeminacy: I. A Quantitative Rating Scale," **Archives of Sexual Behavior,** 4 (1975), 31-41.
Knowledge of subject's effeminacy rating is of little predictive value in determining his sexual orientation.

3444. STOLLER, ROBERT C. "Boyhood Gender Aberrations: Treatment Issues," **Journal of the American Psychoanalytic Association,** 26 (1978), 541-58.
Once an evaluation has revealed that femininity is in-

tense, treatment should quickly begin and should, when
possible, include both mother and father.

3445. WESTFALL, MICHAEL P. "Effeminacy: II. Variation
       with Social Context," **Archives of Sexual Behavior**,
       4 (1975), 43-51.
Videotapes of 19 subjects in encounter groups showed large
variations in expressivity of effeminacy.

3446. WHITAM, FREDERICK L., and MICHAEL ZENT. "A Cross-
       Cultural Assessment of Early Cross-Gender Behavior
       and Familial Factors in Male Homosexuality," **Ar-
       chives of Sexual Behavior**, 13 (1984), 427-39.
From studies in the U. S., Guatemala, Brazil, and the
Philippines, concludes that (1) early cross-gender behavior is an intrinsic characteristic of male homosexuals,
wherever they may be found, and (2) familial factors frequently regarded as conducive to homosexuality are probably not causative but rather are culturally variable
reactions to emerging homosexuality. See also: Whitam
and Robin M. Mathy, **Male Homosexuality in Four Societies**
(New York: Praeger, 1986; 240 pp.).

3447. ZUGER, BERNARD. "Effeminate Behavior Present in
       Boys from Childhood: Ten Additional Years of
       Follow-up," **Comprehensive Psychiatry**, 19 (1978),
       363-69.
Reports a ten-year follow-up of 16 boys with early effeminate behavior, of whom 12 developed some form of deviant
behavior (homosexuality in 10, transvestism in 1, transsexualism in 1). The original article is: "Effeminate
Behavior Present in Boys from Early Childhood," **Pediatrics**, 69 (1966), 1089-1107.

                  D. FAMILY BACKGROUNDS

Once persuaded to reject traditional constitutional and
genetic theories of the etiology of homosexuality, the
popular mind focuses on the family as the incubator of
homosexual identity. Hence the self-lacerating complaint
of parents: "What did we do wrong?" More specifically,
some American psychoanalysts tend to attribute male
homosexuality to the "close-binding mother" (see XVII.C).
Apart from proving or disproving particular theories,
there is a need to study in a descriptive and unbiased way
the family backgrounds of gay men and lesbians (in this
regard, see the testimonies of parents of gays, XVIII.F).

3447. BIEBER, IRVING. "A Discussion of 'Homosexuality:
       The Ethical Challenge,'" **Journal of Consulting and
       Clinical Psychology**, 44 (1976), 163-66.
In keeping with his earlier position, the psychoanalyst

argues that homosexuality is pathological, being the out-
come of adverse experiences with both parents. See
Bieber et al., **Homosexuality: A Psychoanalytic Study**
(New York: Basic, 1962; 358 pp.); and John R. Snortum et
al., "Family Dynamics and Homosexuality," **Psychological
Reports**, 24 (1969), 763-70.

3448. BENE, EVA. "On the Genesis of Male Homosexual-
       ity: An Attempt at Clarifying the Role of Parents,"
       British Journal of Psychiatry, 111 (1965), 803-13.
From administering a questionnaire to 85 male homosexuals and 84 married men concludes that, compared to heterosexual men, homosexual men more often have poor relationships with their fathers, whom they tend to consider
ineffectual and unsuitable as role models.

3449. BLOCH, DOROTHY. "The Threat of Infanticide and
       Homosexual Identity," **Psychoanalytic Review**, 62
       (1975-76), 579-99.
Based on four patients, contends that a defense against
the fear of infanticide leads, inter alia, to the acted-
out fantasy of a sexual reversal.

3450. BUHRICH, NEIL, and NATHANIEL MCCONAGHY. "Parental
       Relationships during Childhood in Homosexuality,
       Transvestism and Transsexualism," **Australian and
       New Zealand Journal of Psychiatry**, 12 (1978),
       103-08.
While all three groups reported that, during childhood,
their fathers lacked interest in them or were absent from
home, there was little evidence to support the view that
homosexual, transvestite, or transsexual subjects had
pathological relationships with their mothers.

3451. DEVINE, JACK L. "A Systemic Inspection of Affec-
       tional Preference Orientation and the Family of
       Origin," **Journal of Social Work and Human Sexual-
       ity**, 2:2-3 (1983-84), 9-17.
Presents a five-stage developmental model reflecting
systematic changes undergone by a family in which a child
has a same-gender affectional preference.

3452. FREUND, KURT, and RAY BLANCHARD. "Is the Distant
       Relationship of Fathers and Homosexual Sons Related
       to the Sons' Erotic Preference for Male Partners,
       or to the Sons' Atypical Gender Identity, or
       Both?" **JH**, 9 (1983), 7-25.
From three studies, the authors conclude that the relationship is chiefly in terms of atypical childhood gender
identity.

3453. GUNDLACH, RALPH H. "Sibship Size, Sibsex, and
       Homosexuality among Females," **Transnational Mental
       Health Research Newsletter**, 19 (1977), 1, 3-7.
Concludes that birth order and family atmosphere together
influence lesbianism.

3454. IBRAHIM, AZMY. "The Home Situation and the Homo-
      sexual," **Journal of Sex Research**, 12 (1976), 263-
      82.
From interviews with 31 subjects, contends that a positive
relationship exists between the incidence of homosexuality and the unhappy childhood of the homosexual.

3455. LANG, THEO. "Studies on the Genetic Determination
      of Homosexuality," **Journal of Nervous and Mental
      Disease**, 92 (1940), 55-64.
Based on police records in Munich and Hamburg, Germany,
finds that the families of male homosexuals have a
higher proportion of male to female siblings than would
be expected. See also: K. Jensch, "Zur Genealogie der
Homosexualitat," **Archiv für Psychiatrie und Nervenkrankheiten**, 112 (1941), 527-40, 679-96; and William H. James,
"Sex Ratios of Half-Sibs of Male Homosexuals," **British
Journal of Psychiatry**, 118 (1971), 93-94.

3456. LONEY, JAN. "Family Dynamics in Homosexual Women,"
      Archives of Sexual Behavior, 2 (1973), 343-50.
With eleven healthy lesbian subjects, finds that overall
scores on the Family Adjustment Test confirm the prediction that lesbians would show more evidence of adverse
factors in their upbringing than controls.

3457. MANOSEVITZ, MARTIN. "Early Sexual Behavior in
      Adult Homosexual and Heterosexual Males," **Journal
      of Abnormal Psychology**, 3 [76:1] (1970), 396-402.
Comparison of 28 homosexual with 22 heterosexual men indicates that the developmental sequence of sexual activity
for homosexuals and heterosexuals follows orderly, though
different progressions. The prehomosexual child seems to
become sexually active earlier than the preheterosexual.
See also his: "The Development of Male Homosexuality,"
Journal of Sex Research, 8 (1972), 31-40.

3458. MILLER, JUDITH A,. et al. "Comparison of Family
      Relationships: Homosexual versus Heterosexual
      Women," **Psychological Reports,** 46 (1980). 1127-32.
Statistically significant differences indicate that lesbians experienced less positive nuclear family relationships.

3459. PERKINS, MURIEL W. "On Birth Order among Les-
      bians," **Psychological Reports**, 43 (1978), 814.
From a study of 212 lesbians, it was concluded that there
is no significant relationship between being an only child
and the etiology of lesbianism.

3460. PILLARD, RICHARD C., et al. "A Family Study of
      Sexual Orientation," **Archives of Sexual Behavior**,
      11 (1982), 511-20.
Fifty homosexual subjects reported a significant excess of
homosexual brothers and more distant male relatives, but
not of lesbian sisters or female relatives. About 25% of

brothers of homosexual men were reported to be homosexual.

3461.   SCHUBERT, HERMAN J., et al. "Sibship Size, Sibsex,
        Sibgap, and Homosexuality among Male Outpatients,"
        Transnational Mental Health Research Newsletter,
        18:4 (1976), 1, 3-8.
It was found that as outpatient family size increased, so
did the percentage of homosexuals. The percentage of outpatient homosexuals who had a younger sister or who were
later-borns in all-male sibling groups was higher than
for contrasting sibling combinations.

3462.   SHAVELSON, EILEEN, et al. "Lesbian Women's Percep-
        tions of Their Parent-Child Relationships," **JH,** 5
        (1980), 205-15.
In a comparison of 26 lesbians with a group of 26 heterosexual women, no significant family background variable or
parental sex-role adherence variable was found that correlated with sexual orientation.

3463.   SIEGELMAN, MARVIN. "Birth Order and Family Size of
        Homosexual Men and Women," **Journal of Consulting
        and Clinical Psychology,** 41 (1973), 164.
Finds that neither birth order nor family size represent
distinct or meaningful contrasts between male or female
homosexuals or heterosexuals.

3464.   SIEGELMAN, MARVIN. "Parental Background of Male
        Homosexuals and Heterosexuals," **Archives of Sexual
        Behavior,** 3 (1974), 3-18.
In a study involving 307 male homosexuals and 138 heterosexuals, results question the assumption that negative
parental behavior, esp. of mothers, plays a critical
role in differentiating the backgrounds of homosexuals
and heterosexuals. See also his: "Parental Background
of Homosexual and Heterosexual Women," **British Journal
of Psychiatry,** 124 (1974), 14-21; "Parental Backgrounds
of Homosexual and Heterosexual Women: A Cross-National
Replication," **Archives of Sexual Behavior,** 10 (1981),
371-78; and "Parental Backgrounds of Homosexual Men: A
Cross-National Replication," ibid., pp. 505-513.

3465.   ŠIPOVÁ, IVA, and ANTONIN BRŽEK. "Parental and
        Interpersonal Relationships of Transsexual and
        Masculine and Feminine Homosexual Men," **JH,** 9
        (1983), 75-85.
Finds that the fathers of homosexuals and transsexuals
were more hostile and less dominant than fathers of
controls.

3466.   SLATER, ELIOT. "Birth Order and Maternal Age of
        Homosexuals," **Lancet,** 1 (1962), 69-71.
In a study of 401 British male homosexuals, seen clinically, it was found that they were generally born later
in sibship and their mothers were older. See also: E.
H. Hare and P. A. Moran, "Parental Age and Birth Order

in Homosexual Parents: A Replication of Slater's Study,"
British Journal of Psychiatry, 134 (1979), 178-82.

3467. THOMPSON, NORMAN L., et al. "Parent-Child Relation-
       ships and Sexual Identity in Male and Female Homo-
       sexuals and Heterosexuals," **Journal of Consulting
       and Clinical Psychology,** 41 (1973), 120-27.
In two studies lesbians were more distant from both
parents, while male homosexuals reported more close-
binding, intimate mothers and hostile, detached fathers
than the heterosexual controls.

                        E. FANTASIES

Fantasies, sometimes dismissively termed "daydreaming,"
have only recently engaged the interest of psychologists,
though they have long been of central interest to psychoanalysis. The "sexual revolution" of the 1960s has also
generated a good deal of interest in erotic fantasies, and
the relation between such imagings and the enacted scripts
of sexual encounter.

3468. FRIDAY, NANCY. **Men in Love: Men's Sexual Fanta-
       sies: The Triumph of Love over Rage.** New York:
       Delacorte, 1980. 527 pp.
Personal accounts with the author's pop psychological
commentary. See "Straight Men, Gay Fantasies" (pp. 345-
60), "Bisexuals" (pp. 361-82), "Homosexuals" (pp. 383-
404), and "Transvestites" (pp. 405-22).

3469. FRIDAY, NANCY. **My Secret Garden: Women's Sexual
       Fantasies.** New York: Trident, 1973. 361 pp.
This first popular volume contains some lesbian material.

3470. LEHNE, GREGORY K. "Gay Male Fantasies and Real-
       ities," **Journal of Social Issues,** 34 (1978), 28-37.
In 47 gay men, fantasies occurring around age twelve
preceded interpersonal sexual experience by an average
of four years. They functioned as a source of self-
knowledge about subjects' affectional preference and
influenced early homosexual experiences.

3471. SCHIMEL, JOHN L. "Homosexual Fantasies in Hetero-
       sexual Males," **Medical Aspects of Human Sexuality,**
       6 (1972), 138-51.
Although such fantasies are deemed worthy of investigation, they need not be construed as an embodiment of the
subject's real life problems.

3472. STORMS, MICHAEL D. "Theories of Sexual Orienta-
       tion," **Journal of Personality and Social Psychol-
       ogy,** 38 (1980), 783-92.

Tests administered to 185 heterosexual, bisexual, and
homosexual undergraduates yielded strong support for the
hypothesis that sexual orientation relates primarily to
erotic fantasy orientation. The results support a two-dim-
ensional model of sexual orientation in which homosexuality and heterosexuality are treated as separate, independent factors. See also his: "A Theory of Erotic Orientation Development," **Psychological Review,** 88 (1981),
340-53.

F. FUNCTIONING AND ADJUSTMENT

In its various forms, the disease model of homosexuality
suggests that homosexuals function less well in society
than heterosexuals. Inasmuch as for many decades most
data gathered about homosexuals came from clinical
patients and prisoners, this assumption seemed to have
been confirmed. Following Evelyn Hooker's pioneering
investigations in the 1950s with unbiased samples, the
notion that homosexuals were, by virtue of their orientation alone, less well equipped to cope with society than
heterosexuals has been overturned. More work is now
needed on **how** gay men and lesbians adjust, despite the
social disapproval that they still face.

3473. ARON, HENRY. "The Homosexual," **Journal of Human
       Relations,** 17 (1969), 58-70.
Holds that homosexuality is "not a problem, not a danger,
not an illness, not immaturity." The so-called "gay
world" is in almost all measures indistinguishable from
the "non-gay world."

3474. CARLSON, HELENA M., and LESLIE A. BAXTER. "Androg-
       yny, Depression, and Self-Esteem in Irish Homosex-
       ual and Heterosexual Males and Females," **Sex Roles,**
       10 (1984), 457-67.
While Irish homosexuals were classified as androgynous
more frequently than heterosexuals, they did not differ
from heterosexuals in self-esteem or depression scores.

3475. CATTELL, RAYMOND B., and JOHN H. MORONY. "The Use
       of the 16 PF in Distinguishing Homosexuals, Normals
       and General Criminals," **Journal of Consulting
       Psychology,** 26 (1962), 531-40.
In an application of the Sixteen Personality Factor
Questionnaire, it was found that the profile of homosex-
uals--all of them imprisoned felons--was similar to the
profile of neurotics.

3476. CLARK, THOMAS R. "Homosexuality and Psychopathol-
       ogy in Nonpatient Males," **American Journal of
       Psychoanalysis,** 35 (1975), 163-68.

In a comparison of seven groups based on the Kinsey scale,
no significant differences were found in terms of self-
criticism, defensiveness, self-concept, general emotional
maladjustment, neurosis personality-character disorder,
and overall personality integration. Homosexuality is
not a criterion predictor of psychopathology.

3477. EVANS, RAY B. "Adjective Check List Scores of
      Homosexual Men," **Journal of Personality Assessment,**
      35 (1971), 344-49.
Analysis of the scores suggests that the homosexuals had
more problems in self-acceptance and in relating to
others, but that only a small minority differed from the
heterosexuals sufficiently to be considered neurotic.

3478. FREEDMAN, MARK. **Homosexuality and Psychological
      Function.** Belmont, CA: Brooks/Cole, 1971. 124 pp.
Stresses positive aspects, based in large measure on
studies done with women for his Ph.D. degree at Case Western University (1967). In comparisons between homosexual
and heterosexual women he found significant differences
between the two groups in three areas: the lesbians had
more independence and inner direction, had greater acceptance of aggression, and found greater satisfaction in
work than the control group. See also his: "Homosexuals
May Be Healthier Than Straights," **Psychology Today** (March
1975), 28-32.

3479. GREENBERG, JERROLD. "A Study of Self-Esteem and
      Alienation of Male Homosexuals," **Journal of Psy-
      chology,** 83 (1973), 137-43.
The study indicated that homosexuals had greater alienation than heterosexual men but similar self-esteem
levels.

3480. HAMMERSMITH, SUE K., and MARTIN S. WEINBERG.
      "Homosexual Identity: Commitment, Adjustment, and
      Significant Others," **Sociometry,** 36 (1973), 56-79.
Data from 2497 male homosexuals in the U.S., the Netherlands, and Denmark indicate that commitment to a homosexual identity is positively correlated with (a) psychological adjustment, and (b) support of significant others.

3481. HART, MAUREEN, et al. "Psychological Adjustment of
      Nonpatient Homosexuals: Critical Review of the
      Research Literature," **Journal of Clinical Psychi-
      atry,** 39 (1978), 604-08.
Concludes that findings to date have not demonstrated
that homosexuals are any less psychologically adjusted
than heterosexuals.

3482. HOFFMAN, MARTIN. "Homosexual," **Psychology Today,**
      3:2 (July 1969), 43-45, 70.
While male homosexuals are not necessarily ill, societal
hostility tends to engender disorders related to reaction
formation, incorporative wishes toward the male, and the

shallowness of the relationship.

3483. HOOKER, EVELYN. "The Adjustment of the Male Overt
      Homosexual," **Journal of Projective Techniques**, 21
      (1957), 18-31.
Reports on a pioneering study with nonclinical homosexuals, concluding that homosexuality is not a single
clinical entity; that it is a deviation in sexual pattern
which is still within the normal range psychologically;
and that there is no necessary relation between sexual
orientation and other aspects of a person's intrapsychic
or interpersonal functioning.

3484. LIDDICOAT, RENEE. "A Study of Non-Institutional-
      ized Homosexuals," **Journal of the National Insti-
      tute of Personnel Research**, 8 (1961), 217-49.
In a study of 100 male and female homosexuals in South
Africa, no evidence of psychopathology was discovered.

3485. MYRICK, FRED. "Attitudinal Differences between
      Heterosexually and Homosexually Oriented Males and
      between Covert and Overt Male Homosexuals," **Journal
      of Abnormal Psychology**, 83 (1974), 81-86.
From questionnaires completed by patrons of bars in Texas,
the author claims to be able to discriminate between heterosexuals and homosexuals.

3486. NURIUS, PAULA S. "Mental Health Implications of
      Sexual Orientation," **Journal of Sex Research**, 19
      (1983), 119-36.
Using four measures of clinical psychopathology (depression, self-esteem, marital discord, sexual discord), found
significant mean differences among sexual orientation
groups, but the prediction of clinical psychopathology
based on these differences proved to be limited.

3487. OBERSTONE, ANDREA K., and HARRIET SUKONECK. "Psy-
      chological Adjustment and Life Style of Single
      Lesbians and Single Heterosexual Women," **Psychology
      of Women Quarterly**, 1 (1976), 172-88.
Differences between lesbians and heterosexual women were
found only on items directly related to sexual orientation.

3488. OHLSON, E. LAMONTE. "A Preliminary Investigation
      into the Self-Disclosing Ability of Male Homosexu-
      als," **Psychology**, 11 (1974), 21-25.
In this study of undergraduates, negative findings were
not confirmed, suggesting that homosexuality should be
viewed as a nonpsychopathological phenomenon.

3489. ROSS, MICHAEL W. "The Relationship of Perceived
      Societal Hostility, Conformity, and Psychological
      Adjustment in Homosexual Males," **JH**, 4 (1978),
      157-68.
Interpretation of a three-group sample indicated that

putative societal reaction was a critical variable producing conformity and psychological maladjustment in
homosexual males.

3490. SAGHIR, MARCEL, et al. "Homosexuality: III. Psy-
        chiatric Disorders and Disability in the Male
        Homosexual," **American Journal of Psychiatry**, 126
        (1970), 1079-86.
In a group of 35 unmarried men little difference was
demonstrated in the prevalence of psychopathology.

3491. SCHMITT, J. PATRICK, and LAWRENCE A. KURDEK.
        "Correlates of Social Anxiety in College Students
        and Homosexuals," **Journal of Personality Assess-
        ment**, 48 (1984), 403-09.
Correlational patterns were remarkably similar in both
samples, homosexual and general, and sensitization
emerged as the best single predictor in both samples.

3492. SIEGELMAN, MARVIN. "Adjustment of Homosexual and
        Heterosexual Women," **British Journal of Psychiatry**,
        120 (1972), 477-81.
In a battery of tests, homosexual women were found to
be as well adjusted as the heterosexuals. See also his:
"Adjustment of Male Homosexuals and Heterosexuals," **Archives of Sexual Behavior**, 1 (1972), 9-25; "Adjustment
of Homosexual and Heterosexual Women: A Cross-National
Replication," ibid., 8 (1979), 121-25; and "Psychological Adjustment of Homosexual and Heterosexual Men," ibid.,
7 (1978), 1-11.

3493. SKRAPEC, CANDICE, and K. R. MACKENZIE. "Psycholog-
        ical Self-Perception in Male Transsexuals, Homosex-
        uals, and Heterosexuals," **Archives of Sexual
        Behavior**, 10 (1981), 357-70.
Of the three groups, transsexuals reflected lowest self-
esteem. Homosexuals reported the highest self-esteem and
saw themselves the most similar to males and the most dissimilar to females.

3494. STOKES, KIRK, et al. "Sexual Orientation and Sex
        Role Conformity," **Archives of Sexual Behavior**, 12
        (1983), 427-33.
Admininistering the Bem Sex-Role Inventory to 186 subjects
showed no significant support for prevailing stereotypes
of effeminate male homosexuals and butch lesbians.

3495. THOMPSON, NORMAN L. "Personal Adjustment of Male
        and Female Homosexual and Heterosexuals," **Journal
        of Abnormal Psychology**, 78 (1971), 237-40.
Homosexuals did not differ in important ways from heterosexuals in defensiveness, personal adjustment, or self-
confidence as measured by the Adjective Check List; or
in self-evaluation as measured by semantic differential.
Compared with heterosexuals, male homosexuals were less
defensive and less self-confident, while lesbians were

more self-confident.

3496. TOWNES, BRENDA D., et al. "Differences in Psychological Sex, Adjustment, and Familial Influences
among Homosexual and Nonhomosexual Populations,"
JH, 1 (1976), 261-72.
Findings from a battery of tests suggest that variations
in sexual lifestyle can be understood as manifestations
of different combinations of the components of psychological sex and that a nurturant father is important in the
development of a heterosexual lifestyle.

3497. WILLMOTT, MARTIN, and HARRY BRIERLEY. "Cognitive
Characteristics and Homosexuality," **Archives of
Sexual Behavior,** 13 (1984), 311-19.
A battery of tests administered in England to 20 homosexual men, 20 heterosexual men, and 20 women revealed few
differences among the groups. In the male groups, however, verbal ability appeared to be strongly characteristic of a homosexual identity.

3498. WILSON, M. LEE. "Neuroticism and Extraversion of
Female Homosexuals," **Psychological Reports,** 51
(1982), 559-62.
In the Eysenck Personality Inventory, heterosexuals scored
higher on the neuroticism scale than did homosexuals.

3499. WILSON, MARILYN M., and ROGER L. GREENE. "Personality Characteristics of Female Homosexuals," **Psychological Reports,** 28 (1971), 407-12.
In a battery of tests, there was only a slight personality
pattern difference between the lesbians and neither group
showed a pathological personality pattern.

3500. ZUCKERMAN, MARVIN, and PATRICIA L. MYERS. "Sensation Seeking in Homosexual and Heterosexual Males,"
Archives of Sexual Behavior, 12 (1983), 347-56.
Concludes that male homosexuals, as a general group, do
not differ from heterosexuals on the sensation-seeking
trait, though the trait might be related to variety of
homosexual behavior and partners, just as it is to variety of heterosexual experience.

G. GROUP DYNAMICS

The emphasis on collective activity that developed in
1960s social change movements, as well as in social work,
has prompted study of the social psychological-dynamics of
such groups. The vogue of "consciousness raising" seems
to have begun with leftist-feminist groups, and then
spread to gay and lesbian ones.

3501. BAKER, ANDREA J. "The Problem of Authority in
       Radical Movement Groups: A Case Study of Lesbian-
       Feminist Organization," **Journal of Applied Behavior
       Science,** 18 (1982), 323-41.
A case study of four stages of organization in a lesbian-
feminist community shows how adherence to principles of
radical feminism hindered the maintenance of a bureaucratic structure.

3502. CHESEBRO, JAMES W., et al. "Consciousness-Raising
       among Gay Males," in: Chesebro (ed.), **Gayspeak.**
       New York: Pilgrim Press, 1981, pp. 211-23.
Study of small-group practice common in the early 1970s,
based on the expectation that face-to-face interaction
will serve to reshape personality, honing its "revolutionary" edge.

3503. FEIN, SARA B., and ELANE M. NUEHRING. "Perspec-
       tives on the Gender-Integrated Gay Community: Its
       Formal Structure and Social Function," **Homosexual
       Counseling Journal,** 2 (1975), 150-63.
Utilizing quasi-participant observation and interviewing,
studied a community of about 30 homosexuals who were
present for almost all social functions and a peripheral
membership of about 100.

3504. FITZGERALD, THOMAS K. "Suicide Prevention and Gay
       Self-Help Groups in Sweden and Finland," **Crisis:
       International Journal of Suicide Studies,** 2 (1981),
       58-68.
Study of crisis handling in Scandinavia as compared to the
United States.

3505. MASTERSON, JILL. "Lesbian Consciousness-Raising
       Discussion Groups," **Journal for Specialists in
       Group Work,** 8 (1983), 24-30.
Results of three discussion groups in which 28 lesbian
participants were led by a facilitator in a structured,
topic-oriented format. Concludes that the structured
format helped to lower the high anxiety level sometimes
engendered by group therapy.

3506. MORSON, TOM, and ROBERT MCINNESS. "Sexual Identity
       Issues in Group Work: Gender, Social Sex Role, and
       Sexual Orientation Conditions," **Social Work with
       Groups,** 6 (1983), 67-77.
Asserting that polarized thinking about gender, social sex
roles, and sexual orientation has resulted in sexual identity confusion, presents group interventions for work with
this confusions.

3507. STERN, RICHARD. "A Peer Self-Help Group of Homo-
       sexuals on the North Side of Chicago," **Psychother-
       apy: Theory, Research and Practice,** 12 (1975),
       418-24.
The success of the Loyola Gay Students group is attributed

to its flexibility, its lack of formal structure and its
avoidance of financial complications by finding a free
place to meet.

3508. TWENTY-FIVE TO SIX BAKING AND TRUCKING CO. **Great
       Gay in the Morning: One Group's Approach to Com-
       munal Living and Sexual Politics.** Washington, NJ:
       Times Change Press, 1972. 95 pp.
Experiential account of the values and practices of a
rural countercultural group, typical of the early 1970s.

H. HOMOPHOBIA AND STEREOTYPING

Aversion to homosexuality was first studied in the context
of prejudice and intolerance. This approach brought out
similarities between dislike of homosexuals and negative
attitudes toward ethnic groups. And, as in ethnic groups,
negativism towards ones group may be internalized, as in
the self-hating homosexual. Concentration on the prejudice perspective may have served, however, to hinder
recognition of specific features characterizing aversion
to homosexual behavior, which evokes deep-rooted irrational fears that differ fundamentally from those involved in
racial prejudice. The term "homophobia," which will
probably survive because it is convenient, is nonetheless
misleading since phobic reactions are only one aspect of
dislike of homosexuality. Some prefer the term "homonegativism." For extreme aspects of acting out of hatred of
homosexuals, expressed as violence and "fag bashing," see
XX.A.

3509. ADORNO, THEODOR WIESENGRUND, et al. **The Author-
       itarian Personality.** New York: Harper and Row,
       1950. 990 pp.
Although this massive study treats homosexuality only
in passing, it fostered a kind of "unified field" concept
of prejudice to which some recent studies of homophobia
are implicitly indebted. The study's political subtext
(it grew out of the Marxist assumptions of the Frankfurt
School) and its statistical procedures have attracted some
criticism.

3510. AGUERRO, JOSEPH A., et al. "The Relationship among
       Sexual Beliefs, Attitudes, Experience, and Homo-
       phobia," **JH,** 10 (1984), 95-107.
Finds that the greatest dislike of homosexuals appears in
subjects with negative affect and belief that homosexuality was a learned orientation.

3511. BANENS, MAKS. **De homo-aversie: een analyse van de
       maatschappelijke onderdrukking van homoseksual-
       iteit.** Groningen: Historische Uitgeverij, 1981.

A historical overview of aversion to homosexuality, together with analysis of theories that attempt to explain
it.

3512. BLACK, KATHRYN N., and MICHAEL R. STEVENSON. "The
       Relationship of Self-Reported Sex-Role Characteris-
       tics and Attitudes Towards Homosexuality," **JH**, 10
       (1984), 83-93.
Seeks to measure links between concepts of sex role and
homonegativism.

3513. CERNY, JEROME, and JAMES POLYSON. "Changing
       Homonegative Attitudes," **Journal of Social and
       Clinical Psychology**, 2 (1984), 366-71.
In a college human-sexuality course on homonegative attitudes, subjects showed significant decreases in negative
views at the end of the semester as compared with a control group--suggesting that education can be effective in
changing such prejudice.

3514. CUENOT, RANDALL G., and STEPHEN S. FUGITA. "Per-
       ceived Homosexuality: Measuring Heterosexual
       Attitudinal and Nonverbal Reactions," **Personality
       and Social Psychology Bulletin**, 8 (1982), 100-06.
Investigation of the reactions of 80 undergraduate heterosexuals to a perceived homosexual or nonhomosexual
inteviewer during an ongoing interaction.

3515. DAHME, G., et al. ["Identity as a Man and Attitude
       toward Male Homosexuals: An Empirical Study of 104
       Vocational and High School Students,"] **Psychologie
       und Praxis**, 25 (1981), 69-80.
Interaction with homosexuals threatened the male identity
of heterosexuals. A positive correlation was found
between the strength of subjects' self concepts and their
discrimination against homosexuals.

3516. DE CECCO, JOHN P. (ed.). **Bashers, Baiters, and
       Bigots: Homophobia in American Society**. New
       York: Harrington Park Press, 1984. 202 pp.
Collection of eleven papers in psychology and sociology,
dealing directly and indirectly with prejudice against
homosexuals. In contrast with the impression that the
title might suggest, does not deal with criminological
aspects (i.e.,the violent acting out of homonegativism).
Reprinted from **JH**, 10:1-2 (1984).

3517. DE CRESCENZO, TERESA A. "Homophobia: A Study of
       the Attitudes of Mental Health Professionals toward
       Homosexuality," **Journal of Social Work and Human
       Sexuality**, 2 (1983-84), 115-36.
In a questionnaire administered to 140 mental health
professionals, social workers achieved the highest homophobia scores, psychologists the lowest.

3518. DEW, MARY A. "The Effect of Attitudes on Infer-

ences of Homosexuality and Perceived Physical
Attractiveness in Women," **Sex Roles**, 12 (1985),
143-55.
A study of 50 male and female undergraduates supported
the hypothesis that inferences of homosexuality would be
made more frequently about women perceived to be less
physically attractive than about women perceived to be
more attractive.

3519. DUNBAR, JOHN, et al. "Some Correlates of Attitudes
        toward Homosexuality," **Journal of Social Psychol-
        ogy**, 89 (1973), 271-79.
In tests given to 126 male undergraduates, the anti-homosexual subjects were more intolerant of a variety of
heterosexual behaviors and reported more personal sex
guilt and higher repression of their own sexual impulses
than did pro-homosexual subjects. Findings confirm those
of W. Churchill, **Homosexual Behavior among Males** (New
York: Hawthorn, 1967).

3520. FARRELL, RONALD A., and THOMAS J. MORRIONE. "So-
        cial Interaction and Stereotypic Responses to
        Homosexuals," **Archives of Sexual Behavior**, 3
        (1974), 425-42.
Interprets survey data from a midwestern sample to
ascertain in which settings gay men are most likely to
encounter homophobic responses and which types of gay
men are most likely to evoke them.

3521. FYFE, BILL. "'Homophobia' or Homosexual Bias
        Reconsidered," **Archives of Sexual Behavior**, 12
        (1983), 549-54.
Argues that broad usage of the concept of homophobia
threatens to restrict understanding of negative reaction
to homosexuals. Recommends that the concept be abandoned in favor of another concept such as homosexual
bias--except in rare cases where anxiety arousal leads
to overt phobic avoidance. For an incisive critique of
the concept of homophobia, see: Lon G. Nungesser, **Homosexual Acts, Actors and Identities** (New York: Praeger, 1983),
pp. 133-63.

3522. GURWITZ, SHARON B., and MELINDA MARCUS. "Effects
        of Anticipated Interaction, Sex, and Homosexual
        Stereotypes on First Impressions," **Journal of
        Applied Social Psychology**, 8 (1978), 47-56.
A simulation test yielded the conclusion that both males
and females liked the stimulus person less and attributed
stereotypic traits to him more when he was homosexual
than when he was not.

3523. HANSEN, GARY L. "Androgyny, Sex-Role Orientation,
        and Homosexism," **Journal of Psychology**, 112 (1982),
        39-45.
In tests administered to college students, "homosexism"
(dislike of homosexuals) was significantly related to

sex-role orientation among males and to both androgyny
and sex-role orientation among females. See also his:
"Measuring Prejudice against Homosexuality (Homosexism)
among College Students: A New Scale," **Journal of Social
Psychology,** 117 (1982), 233-36.

3524. HEINEMANN, WOLFGANG, et al. "Meeting a Deviant
        Person: Subjective Norms and Affective Reactions,"
        European Journal of Social Psychology, 11 (1981),
        1-25.
Studied differences in nonverbal and physiological responses during a confrontation with a male confederate
role-playing either a physically handicapped, homosexual,
or unmarked individual. Results supported a distinction
between intended (action-type) and unintended (reaction-
type) components of behavior.

3525. HEREK, GREGORY M. "Beyond 'Homophobia': A Social
        Psychological Perspective on Attitudes Toward
        Lesbians and Gay Men," **JH,** 10 (1984), 1-21.
Proposes as tripartite model of attitudes: experiential
(reflecting past experiences with homosexual persons);
defensive; and symbolic (expressing abstract ideological
concepts). Concludes by stressing the importance of distinguishing attitudes toward lesbians from those focused
on gay men. See also his: "Attitudes toward Lesbians and
Gay Men: A Factor-Analytical Study," **JH,** 10 (1984),39-51;
and "On Heterosexual Masculinity: Some Psychical Consequences of the Social Construction of Gender and Sexuality," **American Behavioral Scientist,** 29 (1986), 563-77.

3526. HUDSON, WALTER W., and WENDELL A. RICKETTS. "A
        Strategy for the Measurement of Homophobia," **JH,** 5
        (1980), 357-72.
Homophobia is regarded as but one facet of the larger
phenomenon of homo-negativism. A new measure of homophobia, the Index of Homophobia, is presented.

3527. ISTVAN, JOSEPH. "Effects of Sexual Orientation on
        Interpersonal Judgment," **Journal of Sex Research,**
        19 (1983), 173-91.
Study of undergraduates testing the hypotheses that homosexuals are regarded by heterosexuals as being obsessed
with sex and that the derogation of homosexuals extends to
minor aspects of their personality.

3528. KEPNER, JIM. "Homophobia is Not Just a Straight
        Disease," **In Touch,** 1:5 (February 1973), 22-23,
        60-62.
A senior gay activist's reflections on the internalization
of oppressive stereotypes. See also Andrew Hodges and
David Hutter, **With Downcast Gays.** (London: Pomegranate
Press, 1974; 42 pp.); and, in a broader context, Barry
D. Adam, **The Survival of Domination** (New York: Elzevier,
1978; 179 pp.).

3529. KITE, MARY E. "Sex Differences in Attitudes
        toward Homosexuals: A Meta-Analytic Review," **JH**, 10
        (1984), 69-81.
Males tend somewhat more to negative attitudes than
females.

3530. KITSUSE, JOHN I. "Societal Reaction to Deviant
        Behavior: Problems of Theory and Method," **Social
        Problems**, 9 (1962), 247-56.
Interviews with college students disclosing wide variation
in response to homosexuals, reflecting subjects' interpretation of what constitutes homosexuality and their relation with persons thought to be homosexual.

3531. KRULEWITZ, JUDITH E., and JANET E. NASH. "Effects
        of Sex Role Attitudes and Similarity on Men's
        Rejection of Male Homosexuals," **Journal of Person-
        ality and Social Psychology**, 38 (1980), 67-74.
Using a standard attraction paradigm design, subjects
rated a bogus "partner," who was represented as having
attitudes either similar or dissimilar to theirs.

3532. LARSEN, KNUD S., et al. "Anti-Black Attitudes,
        Religious Orthodoxy, Permissiveness, and Sexual
        Information: A Study of the Attitudes of Heterosex-
        uals toward Homosexuality," **Journal of Sex Re-
        search**, 19 (1983), 105-18.
Results show significant differences suggesting that
sexual behavior still reflects a double standard in U.S.
society. See also Larsen et al., "Attitudes of Heterosexuals toward Homosexuality: A Likert-Type Scale and Con-
struct Validity," **Journal of Sex Research**, 16 (1980),
245-57.

3533. LAUTMANN, RÜDIGER. "Stigma Homosexualität: Fälsch-
        er Ansatz der Forschung verstarkt Vorurteil," **Sex-
        ualmedizin**, 3 (1974), 443-46.
Research misconceptions as promoters of prejudice. For a
fuller statement of his views, see: Lautmann (ed.), **Seminar: Gesellschaft und Homosexualität** (Frankfurt: Suhrkamp, 1977; 570 pp.).

3534. LEHNE, GREGORY K. "Homophobia among Men," in: D.
        S. David and R. Brannon (eds.), **The Forty-Nine
        Percent Majority**. Reading, MA: Addison-Wesley,
        1976, pp. 66-88.
Contends that homophobia functions as an underlying motivation in maintaining traditional gender roles. It
is not an isolated trait, but tends to appear in individuals who are generally sexist, conservative, and authoritarian.

3535. LEITENBERG, HAROLD, and LESLEY SLAVIN. "Comparison
        of Attitudes toward Transsexuality and Homosexual-
        ity," **Archives of Sexual Behavior**, 12 (1983), 337-
        46.

Of 318 undergraduates, more subjects felt that homosexuality was "wrong" than felt transsexualism was "wrong." Hence homosexual denial and "homophobia" in some transsexuals may reflect society's greater condemnation of homosexuality.

3536. LEITNER, L. M., and SUZANA CADO. "Personal Constructs and Homosexual Stress," **Journal of Personality and Social Psychology,** 43 (1982), 869-72.
Evaluates a personal-construct approach to the assessment of the potential for homosexual threat (homosexual stress).

3537. MCDONALD, A. P. "Homophobia: Its Roots and Meanings," **Homosexual Counseling Journal,** 3 (1976), 23-33.
Evaluates a number of explanations which have been put forward for anxiety about homosexuality. See also his: "The Importance of Sex-Role to Gay Liberation," ibid., 1 (1974), 169-80; and McDonald and Richard G. Games, "Some Characterstics of Those Who Hold Positive and Negative Attitudes toward Homosexuals," JH, 1 (1974), 9-27.

3538. MARET, STEPHEN M. "Attitudes of Fundamentalists toward Homosexuality," **Psychological Reports,** 55 (1984), 205-06.
While few fundamentalists would advocate capital punishment for homosexuals, findings suggest a continuing condemnation of homosexuality, as is consistent with biblical precepts.

3539. MARTIN, CLYDE V. "Treatment of Homophobia: I." **Corrective and Social Psychiatry and Journal of Behavior Technology, Methods and Therapy,** 29 (1983), 70-73.
Findings indicate that negative attitutds toward homosexuals persist even after attempts to explain homosexuality and to remove myths associated with it.

3540. MILLHAM, JIM, and LINDA E. WEINBERGER. "Sexual Preference, Sex Role Appropriateness, and Restriction of Social Access," JH, 2 (1977), 343-57.
Data from undergraduates show that a significant proportion of aversion toward homosexuals resulted from the belief that their behavior is incongruent with their anatomical sex. See also: Weinberger and Millham, "Attitudinal Homophobia and Support of Traditional Sex Roles," ibid., 4 (1978-79), 237-46.

3541. MORIN, STEPHEN F., and ELLEN M. GARFINKLE. "Male Homophobia," **Journal of Social Issues,** 34 (1978), 29-47.
Explores the literature on the irrational fear of gay men, as well as the pervasiveness, manifestations, and correlates of homophobia, which the authors hold serves to keep men within the boundaries of traditionally defined roles.

See also Morin and Lonnie Nungesser, "Can Homophobia Be
Cured?" in: Robert A. Lewis (ed.), **Men in Difficult Times:**
Masculinity Today and Tomorrow (Englewood Cliffs, NJ:
Prentice-Hall, 1981), pp. 264-74.

3542. NEVID, JEFFREY. "Exposure to Homoerotic Stimuli:
        Effects on Attitudes and Affects of Heterosexual
        Viewers," **Journal of Social Psychology,** 119 (1983),
        249-55.
Results show higher levels of negative effects, such as
anxiety and hostility, among subjects immediately following the film presentation compared to subjects who had
not yet been exposed to the film.

3543. PLASEK, JOHN WAYNE, and JANICEMARIE ALLARD.
        "Misconceptions of Homophobia," JH, 10 (1984),
        23-37.
Questions overly general approaches, including the
assumption of homosexuality itself as a "master status
trait."

3544. SAN MIGUEL, CHRISTOPHER I., and JIM MILLHAM. "The
        Role of Cognitive and Situational Variables in
        Aggression toward Homosexuals," JH, 2 (1976),
        11-27.
Reports on a test intended to give information on the
"personal threat" and "scapegoating" hypotheses of
aggression toward homosexuals.

3545. SCHMIDT, GUNTER. "Homosexualität und Vorurteil,"
        Studium generale, 19 (1966), 346-55.
Reflections on homosexuality and prejudice. See also
Schmidt and Volkmar Sigusch, **Zur Frage des Vorurteils**
gegenüber sexuell devianten Gruppen (Stuttgart: Enke,
1967; 52 pp.; Beiträge zur Sexualforschung, 40).

3546. SMITH, KENNETH T. "Homophobia: A Tentative Per-
        sonality Profile," **Psychological Reports,** 29
        (1971), 1091-94.
A tentative profile suggests that individuals with a
negative attitude toward homosexuality may be status
conscious, authoritarian, and sexually rigid.

3547. STAATS, GREGORY R. "Stereotype Content and Social
        Distance: Changing Views of Homosexuality," **JH,** 4
        (1978), 15-27.
From administering an adjective checklist and the Bogardus
Social Distance Scale to undergraduates, concludes that
stereotypes about homosexuals are changing in a more
positive direction.

3548. STORMS, MICHAEL D. "Attitudes toward Homosexuality
        and Femininity in Men," **JH,** 3 (1978), 257-63.
Contrary to expectation, it was found that homosexual men
who do not conform to the feminine stereotype are disliked
even more than those who do.

3549. TAYLOR, ALAN. "Conceptions of Masculinity and
       Femininity as a Basis for Stereotypes of Male and
       Female Homosexuals," **JH**, 9 (1983), 37-53.
Literature review and results of questionnaires administered to residents of Aberdeen, Scotland. A majority of
the subjects believed that most homosexuals behave like
the opposite sex.

3550. TILLY, PENELOPE, and RUDOLF KALIN. "Effects of Sex
       Role Deviance in Disturbed Male Adlolescents on the
       Perception of Psychopathology," **Canadian Journal of
       Behavioural Science**, 11 (1979), 45-52.
Gender stereotyping correlated significantly with bias,
while sex-role ideology was not significantly correlated.

3551. WEISSBACH, THEODORE, and GARY ZAGON. "The Effect
       of Deviant Group Membership upon Impressions of
       Personality," **Journal of Social Psychology**, 95
       (1975), 263-66.
In a videotape presentation the person identified as
homosexual was judged more feminine, emotional, submissive, unconventional and weaker than when not so identified, but equally likeable.

3552. WOLFGANG, AARON, and JOAN WOLFGANG. "Exploration
       of Attitudes via Physical Interpersonal Distance
       toward Obese, Drug Users, Homosexuals, Police and
       Other Marginal Figures," **Journal of Clinical
       Psychology**, 27 (1971), 510-12.
Results of a stick figure test given to college male and
military personnel.

3553. WRIGHT, REX A., and MICHAEL D. STORMS. "Male
       Sexual Schemata and Responses to Male Homosexual-
       ity," **Personality and Social Psychology Bulletin**, 7
       (1981), 444-50.
College students were tested on their responses to
schemata that emphasized either the "heterosexual" or
"carnal" nature of male homosexuality.

3554. YARBER, WILLIAM L., and BERNADETTE YEE. "Hetero-
       sexuals' Attitudes toward Lesbianism and Male
       Homosexuality: Their Affective Orientation toward
       Sexuality and Sex Guilt," **Journal of American
       College Health**, 31:5 (1983), 203-08.
Sex guilt was related to both sexes' attitudes toward
lesbianism and male homosexuality; affective orientation
was related to attitudes toward lesbianism found in both
sexes, and related to attitudes toward male homosexuality in female subjects only.

                         I. PANIC, HOMOSEXUAL

Homosexual panic, sometimes known as Kempf's Syndrome, is the irrational and stressful reaction to the fear that one is, or is becoming homosexual. The intensity of the reaction, which was first observed in the second decade of the present century, probably reflects the extreme taboo placed on homosexuality during the first half of the 20th century. With the easing of the taboo, homosexual panic is probably becoming less common.

3555.   BIEBER, IRVING, AND TOBY BIEBER. "Heterosexuals Who Are Preoccupied with Homosexual Thoughts," **Medical Aspects of Human Sexuality**, 9:4 (April 1975), 152-68.
Reflections by psychiatrists who believe that homosexual acts display pathology; homosexual thoughts in heterosexuals, evidently, do not.

3556.   DANNELS, JOANNE C. "Homosexual Panic," **Perspectives in Psychiatric Care**, 10 (1972), 106-111.
Discusses the disruptive effect of an assertive lesbian in a hospital psychiatric unit, where the other patients exhibited anxiety, apprehension, uneasiness, and a sense of going to pieces.

3557.   GLICK, BURTON S. "Homosexual Panic: Clinical and Theoretical Considerations," **Journal of Nervous and Mental Disease**, 129 (1959), 20-28.
Defines acute homosexual panic as an acute schizophrenic reaction, usually temporary and "based on the patient's fear of loss of control of unconscious wishes to offer himself as a homosexual object which he feels will result in the most dire consequences."

3558.   GOLDBERG, RICHARD L. "Heterosexual Panic," **American Journal of Psychoanalysis**, 44 (1984), 209-11.
Discusses the bizarre case of a 29-year-old male homosexual who experienced feelings of doom, palpitations, diaphoresis, and lightheadedness--"heterosexual panic"--because of the commencement of feelings of sexual attraction toward women. After treatment the attacks abated, and he began a new homosexual relationship.

3559.   KEMPF, EDWARD JOHN. **Psychopathology.** St. Louis: C. V. Mosby, 1920. 762 pp.
As a result of Kempf's work with disturbed soldiers and sailors in World War I, he introduced the concept of homosexual panic, which is consequently sometimes known as "Kempf's syndrome." See Chapter 10, "The Psychology of the Acute Homosexual Panic" (pp. 477-515).

3560.   LEGRAND DU SAULLE, HENRI. **Le délire des persécutions.** Paris: H. Plon, 1871. 524 pp.
See pp. 461-64 on morbid fear of being taken for a "sodomite." Legrand du Saulle (1830-1886) was a French alienist who founded the Société de Médecine Légale.

3561. MOSHER, DONALD L., and KEVIN E. O'GRADY.
       "Homosex-
       ual Threat, Negative Attitudes toward Masturbation,
       Sex Guilt, and Males' Sexual and Affective Response
       to Explicit Sex Films," **Journal of Consulting and
       Clinical Psychology,** 47 (1979), 860-73.
From evaluation of responses to films, differentiates the
concept of homosexual threat from the concepts of fear
of homosexuals, homosexual panic, and homosexual prejudice.

3562. RAKIĆ, ZORAN. "Homoseksualna panika," **Psihijatrija
       Danas,** 16 (1984), 93-99.
The author, a Belgrade physician, regards homosexual panic
as an acute delusion episode that is not followed by a
process of psychotic development.

3563. SOLOFF, PAUL H. "Pseudohomosexual Psychosis in
       Basic Military Training," **Archives of Sexual
       Behavior,** 7 (1978), 503-10.
Viewing the military setting as a culturally specific
stress site generating pseudohomosexual anxieties in
predisposed individuals, presents three case studies
illustrating the power and dependency conflicts, sexual
symbolization, projective defenses, and restitutional
violence which characterize these patients.

                   J. PSYCHOMETRIC ASSESSMENT

With the increasing acceptance in the beginning decades of
the 20th century that male and female are a spectrum
rather than an absolute contrast, interest began to be
felt in measuring the presence of male and female characteristics in each individual. Initially these inquiries
were accompanied by an unconscious bias that too much
admixture was undesirable and abnormal--in fact an indication of male homosexuality or lesbianism. In the 1960s,
however, the very androgyny which had been dispised or at
any rate not positively valued, came to be looked upon by
some researchers--notably Sandra L. Bem and her associ-
ates--as an asset. Thus, despite the seemingly scientific
character of the psychometric protocols, this field has
been much bedeviled by ideological expectations about sex
roles, and many of the apparent findings should be treated
with a healthy dose of scepticism.

3564. ALTHOF, STANLEY E., et al. "An MMPI Subscale
       (**Gd**): To Identify Males with Gender Identity
       Conflicts," **Journal of Personality Assessment,** 47
       (1983), 42-49.
Reports on the development and cross-validation of a
31-item MMPI Gender Dysphoria (**Gd**) subscale intended to
discriminate between gender identity patients and matched

controls.

3565.   BEM, SANDRA L. "The Measurement of Psychological
        Androgyny," **Journal of Counseling and Clinical
        Psychology,** 42 (1974), 155-67.
One of several influential papers by this investigator
promoting a new paradigm of androgyny designed to replace
the overly dichotomous presentation of masculinity vs.
femininity. The Bem paradigm has come to mingle objective
investigation of androgynous traits with advocacy, in
the sense that the androgynous individual, male or female,
is regarded as superior in psychological functioning. See
A. G. Kaplan; and P. B. Zeldow, below.

3566.   BERNARD, LARRY C., and DAVID J. EPSTEIN. "Androg-
        yny Scores of Matched Homosexual and Heterosexual
        Males," **JH,** 4 (1978), 1698-78.
Using the Bem Sex-Role Inventory, a homosexual sample was
found to be "androgynous" and a heterosexual sample was
"highly masculine sex-typed."

3567.   BLAIR, RALPH. **Homosexuality and Psychometric
        Assessment.** New York: National Task Force on
        Student Personnel Services and Homosexuality,
        1972. 9 pp. (Otherwise Monograph Series, 15)
Reviews the literature on psychiatric tests (e.g.,MMPI,
TAT, and the Rorschach) as indicators of sexual orientation. No real support for theories which assume homosexuality to be an indicator of psychopathology was found;
when seeming support occurs subjects are generally from
psychiatric wards or prisons.

3568.   CARLSON, HELENA M., and JOANNE STEUER. "Age,
        Sex-Role Categorization, and Psychological Health
        in American Homosexual and Heterosexual Men and
        Women," **Journal of Social Psychology,** 125 (1984),
        203-11.
A study of 569 subjects showed that in all four categories
self-esteem increased as the masculinity scores increased.

3569.   CUBITT, G. H., and PAUL GENDREAU. "Assessing the
        Diagnostic Utility of MMPI and 16PF Indexes of
        Homosexuality in a Prison Sample," **Journal of
        Consulting and Clinical Psychology,** 39 (1972),
        342.
A series of tests of uncertain value leading to inconclu-
sive results. For other prison-based studies, see: David
M. Pierce, "MMPI HSX Scale Differences between Active and
Situational Homosexuality," **Journal of Forensic Psychol-
ogy,** 4 (1972), 31-38; and "Test and Nontest Correlates of
Active and Situational Homosexuality," **Psychology,** 10:4
(1973), 23-26.

3570.   CUNNINGHAM, JOHN D., and JOHN K. ANTILL. "A Com-
        parison among Five Masculinity-Femininity-Androgyny
        Instruments and Two Methods of Scoring Androgyny,"

Australian Psychologist, 15 (1980), 437-48.
Despite moderate to high correlations among androgyny
scores derived by different instruments in this Australian
study, there was at most only 65% agreement between any
two instruments in classifying subjects into the five Bem
or Four Spence et al. sex-role categories.

3571. HOOBERMAN, ROBERT L. "Psychological Androgyny,
        Feminine Gender Identity and Self-Esteem in
        Homosexual and Heterosexual Males," **Journal of Sex
        Research**, 15 (1979), 306-15.
Homosexuals scored higher on feminine gender identity,
femininity, and psychological androgyny. However, a
fairly high number of homosexual subjects scored as low as
did heterosexual subjects in feminine gender identity.

3572. HORSTMAN, WILLIAM R. "MMPI Responses of Homosexual
        and Hetersoexual College Students," **Homosexual
        Counseling Journal**, 2 (1975), 68-76.
Although homosexual subjects scored higher on the **Mf** and
Hsx scales than the heterosexuals, the cutting score data
demonstrate that neither functioned adequately in classifying homosexuals.

3573. KAPLAN, ALEXANDRA G. "Clarifying the Concept of
        Androgyny," **Psychology of Women Quarterly**, 3
        (1979), 223-30.
Discusses logical inconsistencies between S. Bem's theoretical and empirical definitions of androgyny, pointing
out that one can be high in both masculine and feminine
traits but that these can be expressed in inappropriate,
inflexible and dysfunctional ways.

3574. LANGEVIN, RON, et al. "Personality Characteristics
        and Sexual Anomalies in Males," **Canadian Journal of
        Behavioural Science**, 10 (1978), 222-38.
An examination of groups in terms of psychometric profiles
showed that exhibitionists appear to be relatively normal,
while pedophiles and multiple deviants showed considerable
emotional disturbance.

3575. LEE, ALDORA G., and VERNENE L. SCHEURER. "Psychol-
        ogical Androgyny and Aspects of Self-Image in Women
        and Men," **Sex Roles**, 9 (1983), 289-306.
The analyses indicated that the predominance of masculine
traits accounted more often than a combination of masculine and feminine traits for the more adaptive socres
for both women and men. Only for expectations of affilia-
tion success among women was there clear support for psychological androgyny theory.

3576. LEWIN, MIRIAM. "Psychology Measures Femininity and
        Masculinity, 2: From '13 Gay Men' to the Instru-
        mental-Expressive Distinction," in: Lewin (ed.), **In
        the Shadow of the Past: Psychology Portrays the
        Sexes** (New York: Columbia University Press, 1984),

179-204.
Shows how the definition of femininity in the Minnesota
Multiphasic Personality Inventory (MMPI), which is still
widely used, was deeply flawed at the start by its confusion of sexual inversion with gender identity (gay men
were used to create the feminine scale). Concludes: "Sixty years of MF testing have primarily demonstrated what
femininity and masculinity are not: they are not two sets
of matched traits." This book contains much else of direct and indirect interest.

3577. LONEY, JAN. "Background Factors, Sexual Experi-
        ences, and Attitudes toward Treatment in Two
        "Normal" Homosexual Samples," **Journal of Consulting
        and Clinical Psychology**, 38 (1972), 57-65.
In the MMPI and Family Adjustment Test administered to 60
male and 11 female homosexuals, differences between males
and females were found in the proportion of homosexual
marriages, the number of homosexual partners, and expressed satisfaction with the homosexual role. See also:
Loney, "An MMPI Measure of Maladjustment in a Sample of
"Normal" Homosexual Men," **Journal of Clinical Psychology**, 27 (1971), 486-88.

3578. MCCAULEY, ELIZABETH A., and ANKE A. EHRHARDT.
        "Role Expectations and Definitions: A Comparison of
        Female Transsexuals and Lesbians," **JH**, 3 (1977),
        137-47.
In a battery of tests, the female transsexual group reflected a more rigid gender role stereotype, while the
lesbians saw their options as more androgynous.

3579. MANOSEVITZ, MARTIN. "Item Analyses of the MMPI Mf
        Scale Using Homosexual and Heterosexual Males,"
        Journal of Consulting and Clinical Psychology, 35
        (1970), 395-99.
The analyis of individual items with total scores showed
the 31 items were significantly associated in both
groups. See also his: "Education and MMPI Mf Scores
in Homosexual and Heterosexual Males," ibid., 36 (1971),
395-99.

3580. OHLSON, E., et al. "Differentiating Female Homo-
        sexuals from Female Heterosexuals by Use of the
        MMPI," **Journal of Sex Research**, 10 (1974), 308-15.
Concludes that a personality scale could be developed
using items from the MMPI to detect lesbianism.

3581. OLDS, DEBRA E., and PHILLIP SHAVER. "Masculinity,
        Femininity, Academic Performance, and Health: Fur-
        ther Evidence Concerning the Androgyny Contro-
        versy," **Journal of Personality**, 48 (1980), 323-41.
Masculinity emerges as beneficial for both sexes, correlating negatively with achievement conflicts and stress
symptoms but positively with mastery and work.

3582. SINGER, MICHAEL I. "Comparison of Indicators of
       Homosexuality on the MMPI," **Journal of Consulting
       and Clinical Psychology**, 34 (1970), 15-18.
A study of 97 male psychiatric outpatients found that the
MF-scale related measures differentiated subjects who
admit to and are worried about homosexuality from subjects
who are neither overt homosexuals nor worried about it.

3583. WILLIAMS, STEPHEN G. "Male Homosexual Responses to
       the MMPI Combined Subscales MF_1 and MF_2," **Psychol-
       ogical Reports**, 49 (1981), 606.
Contends that the $Mf_{1.2}$ scale is useful for the study of
personality variables in male homosexuality independent of
traditional male-female stereotypes.

3584. WONG, MARTIN R. "MMPI Scale Five: Its Meaning, or
       Lack Thereof," **Personality Assessment**, 48 (1984),
       279-84.
A review of the literature indicates that the **Mf** scale
fails in its intended purpose of measuring homosexuality
and of measuring characteristics that reliably divide
males and females. The concept of sex differences is
inappropriately defined and establishes artificial
boundaries.

3585. ZELDOW, PETER B. "The Androgynous Vision: A
       Critical Examination," **Bulletin of the Menninger
       Clinic**, 46 (1982), 401-13.
Challenges S. Bem's contention that sex-typed individuals are limited in their behavioral repertoire and that
persons with androgynous personality traits enjoy better
mental health than sex-typed individuals.

          K. RORSCHACH AND OTHER PROJECTIVE TESTS

The Swiss psychiatrist Hermann Rorschach began his
experiments with inkblots in 1911. Although they enjoyed
a great vogue in the middle decades of the century, the
blots have been shown to be largely vitiated by subjectiv-
ism. In any event, these and similar projective tests
have no predictive value in determining sexual orientation
(though they may be of some use as an adjunct in some
therapeutic situations). The episode remains as an
instructive chapter in intellectual history.

3586. ADRADOS, ISABEL. "Rorschach: revisión crítica de
       los contenidos predictivos de homosexualidad,"
       Arquivos Brasileiros de Psicologia, 36 (1984),
       99-107.
Suggests that today's permissive sexual atmosphere may be
responsible for the fact that heterosexual subjects sometimes show homosexual tendencies on their Rorschachs.

3587. ANDERSEN, DENNIS O., and FRANK C. SEITZ. "Rorschach
       Diagnosis of Homosexuality: Schafer's Content
       Analysis," **Journal of Projective Techniques and
       Personality Assessment**, 33 (1969), 406-08.
Contends that the signs successfully discriminated three
groups: heterosexual, sex-role disturbed, and homosexual.
See also Seitz, Andersen, and George N. Braucht, "A Com-
parative Analysis of Rorschach Signs of Homosexuality,"
Psychological Reports, 35 (1974), 1163-69.

3588. ARMON, VIRGINIA. "Some Personality Variables in
       Overt Female Homosexuality," **Journal of Projective
       Techniques**, 24 (1960), 292-309.
From a study of 30 lesbians and 30 heterosexual women
who took the Rorschach and Figure-Drawing Tests, Armon
concluded that projective techniques were of no use in
differentiating between homosexually oriented and heterosexually oriented women.

3589. GOLDFRIED, MARVIN R. "Homosexual Signs," in:
       Goldfried et al. (eds.), **Rorschach Handbook of
       Clinical and Research Applications**. Englewood
       Cliffs, NJ: Prentice-Hall, 1971, pp. 188-216.
Standard exposition of the case for the value of the
signs.

3590. HENDLIN, STEPHEN J. "Homosexuality in the Ror-
       schach: A New Look at the Old Signs," **JH**, 1 (1976),
       303-12.
In comparing 30 homosexuals with 30 heterosexuals, concludes that the traditional index is not valid and that it
should not be used in a clinical setting as a measure to
assess homosexuality.

3591. HOOKER, EVELYN. "Male Homosexuality in the Ror-
       schach," **Journal of Projective Techniques**, 22
       (1958), 33-54.
Some kinds of homosexual records (anal orientation and
feminine emphasis) could be distinguished, but most could
not. Without other substantiating evidence the Rorschach
failed in a large number of instances.

3592. HOPKINS, JUNE H. "Lesbian Signs on the Rorschach,"
       **British Journal of Projective Psychology and Per-
       sonality Study**, 15 (1970), 7-14.
Not surprisingly, male homosexual signs were judged to
be inadequate for lesbians.

3593. JANZEN, WILLIAM R., and WILLIAM C. COE. "Clinical
       and Sign Prediction: The Draw-a-Person and Female
       Homosexuality," **Journal of Clinical Psychology**, 31
       (1975), 757-65.
Compared the validity of predicting lesbianism from empirical signs from the Draw-a-Person Test with the validity of psychologist's "blind" predictions from the same
DAP protocols.

3594. KUETHE, JAMES L. "Children's Schemata of Man and
       Woman: A Comparison with the Schemata of Heterosex-
       ual and Homosexual Populations," **Journal of Psy-
       chology**, 90 (1975), 249-58.
The schemata employed by the children in their figure
arrangements were significantly different from those of
adult heterosexuals and resembled those of adult homosexuals.

3595. LASZLO, KARL. **Die Homosexualität des Mannes im
       Szondi-Test: Ein Beitrag zur Erforschung der
       Homosexualität und zur Kritik der Szondi-Methode.**
       Stuttgart: F. Enke, 1956. 108 (Beitrage zur
       Sexualforschung, 8)
Criticism of the use of Szondi test, which consists of 48
cards bearing pictures of mental patients, some of them
homosexual.

3596. PASSI TOGNAZZO, D., and G. BARATELLA. "I contenuti
       umani alle tavole III e IV del Rorschach in un
       gruppo di omosessuali maschi dell'Italia Setten-
       trionale," **Psichiatria generale e dell'età evolu-
       tiva**, 19 (1981), 1-8.
From tests with northern Italian men, the authors find no
support for the claim that Rorschach responses are useful
in diagnosing homosexuality.

3597. RAYCHAUDHURI, MANAS, and KAMAL MUKERJI. "Rorschach
       Differentials of Homosexuality in Male Convicts: An
       Examination of Wheeler and Schafer Signs," **Journal
       of Personality Assessment**, 35 (1970), 22-26.
Reports mixed results from use of the signs with male convicts of a Calcutta jail.

3598. ROBACK, HOWARD B. et al. "Sex of Free Choice
       Figure Drawings by Homosexual and Heterosexual
       Subjects," **Journal of Personality Assessment**, 38
       (1974), 154-55.
Concludes that the first figure drawn on the Draw-a-Person
Test is not a useful measure of sexual inversion or gender
identity.

3599. STONE, NORMAN M., and ROBERT E. SCHNEIDER. "Con-
       current Validity of the Wheeler Signs of Homosex-
       uality in the Rorschach: P (Ci/Rj)," **Journal of
       Personality Assessment**, 39 (1975), 573-79.
Both homosexual and sex-role disturbed groups displayed
significantly more Wheeler signs than normals. For rebuttal, see Elizabeth A. Anderson, "The Elusive Homosexual," ibid., 39 (1975), 580-82.

3600. WHEELER, WILLIAM MARSHALL. "An Analysis of Ror-
       schach Indices of Male Homosexuality," **Rorschach
       Research Exchange and Journal of Projective
       Techniques**, 13 (1949), 97-126.
Reports on the use of twenty signs of the Rorschach,

the "Wheeler content signs test." Contends that there
is a need to develop objective Rorschach signs, inasmuch
as therapists' clinical judgments tend to be unreliable.
See also: Jay S. Kwawer, "Male Homosexual Psychodynamics
and the Rorschach Test," **Journal of Personality Assessment,** 41 (1977), 10-18.

L. SOCIAL SEX ROLE

Recent research, prompted in part by changing social
conditions, has sought to distinguish gender from sex
role, emphasizing the culturally contingent nature of the
latter. It was of course a commonplace of older stereotypes of homosexuality that "inverts" were characterized
by their compulsive adoption of traits of the other sex.
A more nuanced approach has made obsolete this notion,
though some have questioned whether--in view of the biological bedrock on which every human organism rests--we
can so confidently make an absolute separation between
gender and social sex role (see "Biology," XXIV.A). In an
area of research that is to some extent in flux, some have
argued that in American society, the traditional male sex
role is rigid, constricting, and not conducive to psychological health, others (and sometimes the same individuals) have urged that women incorporate these same
qualities, so as to more "androgynous" and effective at
work and at home.

3601. ARCHER, JOHN, and BARBARA LLOYD. **Sex and Gender.**
      Revised ed. New York: Cambridge University Press,
      1985. 355 pp.
Critical review for the lay reader of the accumulating
body of research on the extent to which men and women
differ, the origins and implications of the differences
in physical development, sexual experience, emotional
expression, mental health, aggression, power, family,
life, work, and achievement. The authors tend to favor
sociocultural and environmental explanations, downplaying biological approaches. For an opposing synthesis,
see Jo Durden-Smith and Diane Desimone, **Sex and the Brain**
(New York: Arbor House, 1983; 298 pp.).

3602. BERNARD, LARRY C., and DAVID J. EPSTEIN. "Sex Role
      Conformity in Homosexual and Heterosexual Males,"
      Journal of Personality Assessment, 42 (1978),
      505-11.
A battery of tests yielded nine principal components.

3603. BLANCHARD, RAY, and KURT FREUND. "Measuring
      Masculine Gender Identity in Females," **Journal of
      Consulting and Clinical Psychology,** 51 (1983),
      205-14.

Attempted to validate a psychometric instrument intended
to measure varying degrees of "masculine gender identity" in women.

3604. BRAKE, MIKE. "I May Be Queer, But at Least I Am a
       Man: Male Hegemony and Ascribed Versus Achieved
       Gender," in: Diana Leonard Barker and Sheila Allen
       (ed.), **Sexual Divisions and Society: Process and
       Change.** London: Tavistock, 1976, pp. 174-198.
From a gay liberation and feminist standpoint, uses ethnological and other data to argue that gender categories are
socially conditioned rather than natural.

3605. BROWN, DANIEL G. "The Development of Sex-Role
       Inversion and Homosexuality," **Journal of Pedi-
       atrics**, 50 (1957), 613-19.
Contends that while certain forms of homosexuality
(passive male and active female) are expressions of
personality inversion, other forms of homosexuality have
nothing to do with inversion.

3606. CARRIGAN, TIM, et al. "Towards a New Sociology of
       Masculinity," **Theory and Society**, 14 (1985),
       551-604.
Invaluble review of the literature since the 1950s on
the "male role," with special attention to empirical
discoveries, political assumptions and implications, and
theoretical framework.

3607. CLINGMAN, JOY, and MARGUERITE G. FOWLER. "Gender
       Roles and Human Sexuality," **Journal of Personality
       Assessment**, 40 (1976), 276-84.
Suggests that homosexuality may be appropriately conceived
as an alternate lifestyle rather than a nosological
entity, and that gender role may, in some instances, be
more important than biological sex with respect to an
individual's self-perceived personality characteristics.

3608. DITTES, JAMES E. **The Male Predicament.** New York:
       Harper and Row, 1985. 223 pp.
The author, a psychologist and theologican at Yale
Divinity School, holds that the problems of distorted
masculinity are essentially caused by males and must be
resolved by them.

3609. FRANKLIN, CLYDE W. **The Changing Definition of
       Masculinity.** New York: Plenum Press, 1984. 234
       pp.
Questioning the heterosexual-homosexual dichotomy, argues
that sexuality is more socialization than innate biology.

3610. GRADY, KATHLEEN, ROBERT BRANNON, and JOSEPH H.
       PLECK. **The Male Sex Role: A Selected and Annotated
       Bibliography.** Rockville, MD: National Institute of
       Mental Health, 1979. 196 pp.
Provides detailed abstracts on ca. 400 items; note esp.

section VIII: "Relations with Men" (pp. 116-2).

3611. HOOKER, EVELYN. "An Empirical Study of Some
      Relations between Sexual Patterns and Gender
      Identity in Male Homosexuals," in: John Money
      (ed.), **Sex Research: New Developments**. New
      York: Holt, Rinehart and Winston, 1965, pp. 24-52.
Urges that the masculine-feminine dichotomy for male
homosexuals be abandoned. Role and gender practices are
found to be highly variable.

3612. JONES, RANDALL W., and JOHN P. DE CECCO. "The
      Femininity and Masculinity of Partners in Hetero-
      sexual and Homosexual Relationships," **JH**, 8 (1982),
      37-44.
Examined whether (1) partners in homosexual relationships
perceived themselves as less stereotypically masculine or
feminine than heterosexual partners; (2) partners complement or match each other in their self-perceived femininity and masculinity; and (3) partner's femininity and
masculinity correlate with their views on attachment and
autonomy.

3613. KAPLAN, ALEXANDRA G., and JOAN P. BEAN. **Beyond
      Sex-Role Stereotypes: Readings toward a Psychology
      of Androgyny**. Boston: Little, Brown, 1976. 392 pp.
Reprints papers chosen for their support of a model of
well-being that draws from the valued characteristics of
both men and women. This anthology reflects a major
strand of feminist research that emerged in the 1970s.

3614. KESSLER, SUZANNE J., and WENDY MCKENNA. **Gender: An
      Ethnomethodological Approach**. New York: John
      Wiley, 1978. 233 pp.
Employing cross-cultural evidence, seeks to show that
gender is not an "irreducible fact" but a social construction, assumed by investigators rather than demonstrated.
Concentrates on the "gender attribution process," whereby
one classifies another as female or male.

3615. KRIEGEL, LEONARD. **On Men and Manhood**. New York:
      Hawthorn, 1979. 206 pp.
Popular tilt at the windmills of the masculine myth in its
demotic forms. See esp. Chapter 7, "The Homosexual as
Other" (pp. 157-72).

3616. LANGEVIN, RON (ed.). **Erotic Preference, Gender
      Identity, and Aggression in Men: New Research
      Studies**. Hillsdale, NJ: Lawrence Erlbaum Associ-
      ates, 1985. 375 pp.
Twelve papers emphasizing results of controlled research,
including material on homosexuality, pedophilia, and
cross-dressing.

3617. MACCOBY, ELEANOR E. (ed.). **The Development of Sex
      Differences**. Stanford: Stanford University Press,

1966. 351 pp.
Six papers on biological, cognitive, sociological and
psychological aspects. Note esp. "Annotated Bibliography" by Roberta M. Oetzel (pp. 223-321). This work is
complemented by Maccoby and Carol Nagy Jacklin, **The Psychology of Sex Differences** (Stanford: Stanford University
Press, 1974; 634 pp.), with "Annotated Bibliography," pp.
395-627.

3618. MACDONALD, GARY J., and ROBERT J. MOORE. "Sex-Role
      Self-Concepts of Homosexual Men and Their Attitudes
      toward Both Women and Male Homosexuality," **JH**, 4
      (1978), 3-14.
In terms of socially valued masculine and feminine characteristics, the majority of 88 gay men tested viewed themselves as predominately androgynous.

3619. MCGILL, MICHAEL E. **The McGill Report on Male
      Intimacy.** New York: Holt, Rinehart and Winston,
      1985. 300 pp.
Based on a decade of work with some 500 men and women,
aged 18-73, concludes that "[t]here is no intimacy in
most male friendships and none of what intimacy offers:
solace and support."

3620. MARECEK, JEANNE, et al. "Gender Roles in the Rela-
      tionships of Lesbians and Gay Men," **JH**, 8 (1982),
      45-49.
Recent research on gay male and lesbian couples suggests
that traditional gender role-playing sometimes occurs in
their relationships, though it is less common than in
heterosexual relationships.

3621. MONEY, JOHN, and ANTHONY J. RUSSO. "Homosexual
      Outcome of Discordant Gender Identity/Role in
      Childhood: Longitudinal Follow-Up," **Annual Progress
      in Child Psychiatry and Child Development** (1980),
      203-14.
Nine of eleven males with prepubertal discordance of gender identity/role have been maintained in the follow-up
until young adulthood. All are known to be homosexual
or predominantly so. See also: Money, "Sexual Dimorphism and Homosexual Gender Identity," **Psychological Bulletin**, 74 (1970), 425-40; as well as other papers by this
author.

3622. PLECK, JOSEPH H., and JACK SAWYER (eds.). **Men and
      Masculinity.** Englewood Cliffs, NJ: Prentice-Hall,
      1974. 184 pp.
Collection of essays generally maintaining that traditional concepts of masculinity are constricting and stressful,
and advocating their attenuation in keeping with a major
strand of the "men's liberation" trend.

3623. ROBINSON, BRYAN E., et al. "Sex Role Endorsement
      among Homosexual Men across the Life Span," **Ar-**

chives of Sexual Behavior, 11 (1982), 355-59.
A pattern of diverse sex-role endorsement was found from
adolescence to maturity in which subjects were equally
androgynous, masculine, feminine, and undifferentiated at
each age level.

3624. ROSS, MICHAEL W. "Homosexuality and Social Sex
        Roles: A Re-evaluation," JH, 9 (1983), 1-6.
Introduction to a special number of JH on social sex
roles, which has also been separately published as a
book: Homosexuality and Social Sex Roles (New York: Haworth Press,1983; 107 pp.). See also: Ross et al.,
"Stigma, Sex, and Society: A New Look at Gender Differentiation and Sexual Variation," JH 3 (1978), 315-30.

3625. ROSS, MICHAEL W. "Relationship between Sex Role
        and Sex Orientation in Homosexual Men," New Zealand
        Psychologist, 4 (1975), 25-29.
Concludes that sex role has no necessary correlation with
sex orientation and that high femininity scores on the
MMPI and CPI should not be taken as evidence of male
homosexuality.

3626. SHIVELY, MICHAEL G., et al. "The Identification of
        the Social Sex-Role Stereotypes," JH, 3 (1978),
        225-34.
Results of a test of 300 subjects support the hypothesis
that stereotypes for femininity and masculinity are
dimorphous.

3627. SMITH, SIDNEY GREER. "A Comparison among Three
        Measures of Social Sex Role," JH, 9 (1983), 99-107.
Results of comparison of De Cecco-Shively Social Sex-Role
Inventory (DSI) with the Bem Sex-Role Inventory (BSRI) and
the Personal Attributes Questionnaire (PAQ).

3628. STORMS, MICHAEL D. "Theories of Sexual Orienta-
        tion," Journal of Personality and Social Psychol-
        ogy, 38 (1980), 783-92.
Argues that homosexuality and heterosexuality may be
separate, orthogonal erotic dimensions rather than
opposite extremes of a single bipolar dimension. See
also his: "Sex-Role Identity and Its Relationship to
Sex-Role Attributes and Sex-Role Stereotypes," ibid., 37
(1979), 1779-89; and "A Theory of Erotic Orientation
Development," Psychological Review, 88 (1981), 340-53.

3629. TYSON, PHYLLIS. "A Developmental Line of Gender
        Identity, Gender Role, and Choice of Love Object,"
        Journal of the American Psychoanalytic Association,
        30 (1982), 61-86.
Attempts to merge today's more complex concepts of gender
role with the traditional psychoanalytic sequence of oral,
anal, phallic, latency, and adolescent phases.

3630. VETTERLING-BRAGGIN, MARY (ed.). "Femininity,"

"Masculinity," and "Androgyny": A Modern Philosophical Discussion. Totowa, NJ: Littlefield, Adams, 1982. 326 pp.
Collection of essays questioning straightforward identification of sex and gender and canvasing the viability of the androgyny concept.

M. STIMULUS-RESPONSE TESTS

Stimulus-response techniques are associated with behavioristic psychology, where they are central to the model of human behavior. Here a more specific application is meant. In studying sexual orientation special devices have been created to measure penile and vaginal response, as well as eye movements and pupil changes that are regarded as significant. In some instances, as with work with incarcerated pedophiles, there are serious ethical problems in the use of these techniques. Devices of this kind are sometimes used in behavior therapy (sometimes known as aversion therapy; see XVII.H).

3631. BARR, RON, and ALEX BLACZYNSKI. "Autonomic Responses of Transsexual and Homosexual Males to Erotic Film Sequences," **Archives of Sexual Behavior,** 5 (1976), 211-22.
Transsexual patients differ significantly from homosexual patients in autonomic response as measured by penile volume and GSRs. See also: Barr, "Responses to Erotic Stimuli of Transsexual and Homosexual Males," **British Journal of Psychiatry,** 123 (1973), 579-85; and Barr and N. McConaghy, "Penile Volume Responses to Appetitive and Aversive Stimuli in Relation to Sexual Orientation and Conditioning Performance," **British Journal of Psychiatry,** 119 (1971), 377-83.

3632. BURDICK, J. ALAN, et al. "Cardiac Activity and Verbal Report of Homosexuals and Heterosexuals," **Journal of Psychosomatic Research,** 18 (1974), 377-85.
Tonic heart rate increases were higher in both groups for slides of homosexual content.

3633. FREUND, KURT. "A Laboratory Method for Diagnosing Predominance of Homo- or Hetero-erotic Interests in the Male," **Behaviour Research and Therapy,** 1 (1963), 85-93.
Report of a study at a psychiatric hospital in Prague conducted to show that penile volume changes while the subject viewed erotic subjects served to detect sexual deviations. Subsequently, Freund became identified with this technique, sometimes termed "penile plethysmography." See also his: "Diagnosing Homo- or Heterosexuality and Erotic

Age-Preference by Means of a Psychophysiological Test,"
ibid., 5 (1967), 209-28; as well as Freund et al., "Heterosexual Aversion in Homosexual Males," **British Journal
of Psychiatry**, 122 (1973), 163-69; "Heterosexual Aversion
in Homosexual Males: A Second Experiment," ibid., 125
(1974), 177-80; "The Phobic Theory of Male Homosexuality,"
Archives of General Psychiatry, 31 (1974), 495-99; and
"Phallometric Diagnosis with 'Nonadmitters,'" **Behavior
Research and Therapy**, 17 (1979), 451-57.

3634.   GILSON, MARK, et al. "Sexual Orientation as
        Measured by Perceptual Dominance in Binocular
        Activity," **Personality and Social Psychology**
        8 (1982), 494-500.
Subjects reported what fit best with their sexual preference when vital components were missing from their binoc-
ular vision.

3635.   HESS, ECKHARD H. "Pupil Response of Hetero- and
        Homo-sexual Males to Pictures of Men and Women: A
        Pilot Study," **Journal of Abnormal and Social
        Psychology**, 70 (1965), 165-68.
Measurement of changes in pupil size in response to
pictorial stimuli--slides of nude figures--permitted
clear-cut discrimination between the two groups; see the
comments by Nicholas F. Skinner, **Perceptual and Motor
Skills**, 51 (1980), 844 and 897-98; and response by Hess
and Slobodan B. Petrovich, ibid., 51 (1980), 845-46.

3636.   LEE-EVANS, M. et al. "Penile Plethysmography
        Assessment of Sexual Orientation," **European Journal
        of Behavioural Analysis and Modification**, 1 (1975),
        20-26.
The influence of longer stimulus exposure times on the
amplitude and acceleration rate of penile colume change.
See comment by Kurt Freund, pp. 27-28; and reply by Lee-
Evans et al., p. 29.

3637.   MCCONAGHY, NATHANIEL. "Penile Volume Change to
        Moving Pictures of Male and Female Nudes in
        Heterosexual and Homosexual Males," **Behaviour
        Research and Therapy**, 5 (1967), 43-48.
Confirms Freund's experiments in penile volume changes as
a measure of sexual orientation. Unlike Freund, however,
McConaghy has sought to use the technique to change homosexual behavior to heterosexual. Among other papers, see
his: "Subjective and Penile Plethmysmograph Responses Following Aversion-Relief and Apomorphine Aversion Therapy
for Homosexual Impulses," **British Journal of Psychiatry**,
115 (1969), 723-30; "Penile Response Conditioning and
Its Relationship to Aversion Therapy in Homosexuals,"
Behavior Therapy, 1 (1970), 213-21; and "Measurements of
Change in Penile Dimensions," **Archives of Sexual Behavior**,
3 (1974), 381-88; "Heterosexual Experience, Marital
Status, and Orientation of Homosexual Males," ibid. 7
(1978), 575-81.

3638. O'NEIL, MICHAEL T., and JOHN W. HINTON. "Pupillographic Assessment of Sexual Interest and Sexual Arousal," **Perceptual and Motor Skills,** 44 (1977), 1278.
Correlation analysis compared pupil diameter increases with degree of sexual arousal (penis diameter) in thirteen male prisoners.

3639. PAPATHEOPHILOU, R., et al. "Electroencephalographic Findings in Treatment-Seeking Homosexuals: A Controlled Study," **British Journal of Psychiatry,** 127 (1975), 63-66.
Found that slow activity in the EEG in response to hyperventilation occurred in a significantly greater number of homosexuals as compared with heterosexual controls.

3640. SCHNELLE, JOHN F. "Pupillary Response as Indication of Sexual Preference in a Juvenile Correctional Institution," **Journal of Clinical Psychology,** 30 (1974), 146-50.
Three months after a first exposure, a group of 20 female inmates was retested with slides; a significant increase in interest in female figures was found.

3640A. SCOTT, THOMAS R., et al. "Pupillary Response and Sexual Interest Reexamined," **Journal of Clinical Psychiatry,** 23 (1967), 433-38.
In contrast to E. H. Hess et al., the researchers failed to find any difference in pupillary response for males and females, or between heterosexuals and homosexuals.

A. GENERAL

Modern psychiatry emerged as an independent medical
speciality in Europe in the 19th century (where, however,
it had been preceded by forensic medicine). See "Pioneers," I.B; and "Medical Archaeology," XXIII.D. The
medical origins, which set it apart from psychology (XVI.
A-M), have fostered a disease model of homosexuality.
This tendency rears its head in the countless discussions
of "etiology," which assume that the phenomenon of
same-sex behavior is intrinsically abnormal and undesirable, and hence must have a specific (and remediable)
cause. More recently, however, many psychiatrists have
come to accept homosexual orientation as lying within the
normal range of human experience, seeking only to alleviate other problems that are complicating life for the
patient. See "Psychotherapy," XVII.F.

3641. ACOSTA, FRANK X. "Etiology and Treatment of
       Homosexuality: A Review," **Archives of Sexual
       Behavior**, 4 (1975), 9-29.
While the author concedes that no existing body of
theory--biological, psychoanalytic, learning, or social
learning--provides a convincing etiology for homosexuality, he continues to favor prevention through the early
identification and treatment of the potential homosexual
child.

3642. AIKEN, B. A. "The Stroke Economy and Gay People,"
       Transactional Analysis Journal, 6 (1976), 21-27.
In keeping with the pop-psychiatric concepts of Eric
Berne, holds that "stroke deprivation" has led to an
emotional stunting of homosexuals.

3643. ALLEN, CLIFFORD. **Homosexuality: Its Nature,
       Causation and Treatment.** London: Staples Press,
       1958. 143 pp.
While this is a relatively liberal work for its time, the
author holds that homosexuality is a psychological disorder, stemming from hostility toward the mother or
father, excessive affection for the mother, or affection for an inadequately heterosexual father. Its
treatment and cure are possible. See also: Charles Berg
and Clifford Allen, **The Problem of Homosexuality** (New
York: Citadel Press, 1958; 221 pp.).

3644. AMERICAN PSYCHIATRIC ASSOCIATION, COMMISSION ON
       PSYCHOTHERAPIES. **Psychotherapy Research: Methodo-
       logical and Efficacy Issues.** Washington, DC: APA,

1982. 261 pp.
Attempts to respond to the criticisms of H. J. Eysenck
and others that outcomes of psychotherapeutic intervention
are no better that what is to be expected by providing
no treatment at all. Concludes cautiously, "[a]lthough
research in psychotherapy is still plagued by many problems connected with assignment of patients, use of statistics, outcome measures, and experimental designs, the
data have shown empirically that psychotherapy is effective with some populations and some problems." The report does not deal specifically with its effectiveness
with homosexuals.

3645.   BLAIR, RALPH. **Etiological and Treatment Literature
        on Homosexuality.** New York: Homosexual Community
        Counseling Center, 1972. 49 pp. (Otherwise
        Monograph Series, 5)
Reviews the literature on the physical, psychological, and
environmental factors in the etiology of homosexuality and
on various treatment goals, patient population, and kinds
of therapy. Concludes that until the medical and psychiatric professions acknowledge that homosexuality is not a
pathological sexual orientation, little can be reliably
said about its causes.

3646.   BRADY, JOHN, and H. KEITH H. BRODIE (eds.). **Psy-
        chiatry at the Crossroads.** Philadelphia: Saunders
        Press, 1980. 243 pp.
This somewhat miscellaneous collection includes "Should
Homosexuals Adopt Children" by Richard Green (pp. 132-49)
and "When (If Ever) Should Sex Change Operations Be Performed" by John Money and Richard Ambinder (pp. 150-64).

3647.   CAPRIO, FRANK. **Female Homosexuality: A Psychody-
        namic Study of Lesbianism.** New York: Citadel
        Press, 1954. 334 pp.
Characteristically unsympathetic study of the period,
covering historical and literary matters, theories of
causation, case history, and therapy. Caprio's reliance on the invented stories found in "true confessions"
pulp magazines undermines credibility.

3648.   CLECKLEY, HERVEY MILTON. **The Caricature of Love: A
        Discussion of Social, Psychiatric, and Literary
        Manifestations of Pathologic Sexuality.** New
        York: Ronald Press, 1957. 319 pp.
Opposing liberal trends then underway, combats the idea
that homosexuals can be fulfilled and happy if only they
are left alone, insisting that homosexuality is a psychiatric disorder that causes misery.

3649.   CORRAZE, JACQUES. **Les dimensions de l'homosexual-
        ité.** Toulouse: E. Privat, 1968. 253 pp.
A Sorbonne professor attempts a synthesis with particular
stress on psychoanalysis and then-current American work.

3650. EYSENCK, HANS J. **Fact and Fiction in Psychology.**
Harmondsworth: Penguin, 1965. 300 pp.
Eysenck, a London-based psychologist and prolific writer,
was one of the first to bring the therapeutic claims of
psychiatry into question. (Nonetheless, he has advocated a
version of behavior therapy.) See esp. pp. 179, 192,
214, 280.

3651. FRANK, K. PORTLAND. **The Anti-Psychiatry Bibliography and Resource Guide.** Second ed. Vancouver:
Press Gang, 1979. 160 pp.
Includes chapters on the mental patient experience; the
British antipsychiatry school; psychiatry and the law;
institutions; women and third world people; and the mental
patients liberation movement. See esp. pp. 100-04.

3652. GONSIOREK, JOHN C. **Homosexuality and Psychotherapy: A Practitioner's Handbook of Affirmative
Models.** New York: Haworth Press, 1982. 212 pp.
Sixteen papers on many topics, but all committed to
helping gay men and lesbians live more productive and
fulfilling lives without attempting to "cure" them. Many
references. Reprinted from **JH**, 7:2-3 (1981-82). See also
Gonsiorek (ed.), "Homosexuality: The End of the Illusion,"
American Behavioral Scientist, 25 (March-April 1982),
367-496 (symposium).

3653. GREEN, RICHARD. "Homosexuality as a Mental Illness," **International Journal of Psychiatry**, 10
(1972), 77-98.
Raises a number of questions, including potential biological and hormonal determinants, the appropriateness
of treatment, and the disease model of homosexuality.
Followed by commentary by Alan P. Bell (pp. 99-102),
Lawrence J. Hatterer (pp. 103-04), Martin Hoffman (pp.
105-07), and Arno Karlen (pp. 108-13).

3654. HENRY, GEORGE W. **Sex Variants: A Study of Homosexual Patterns.** New York: Hoeber, 1941. 2 vols.
A New York psychiatrist presents the results of his study
of male and female homosexuality through the analysis of
80 explicit case histories. Henry regards sex variance as
the consequence of the pressures of civilization, together with an overmasculinized or overfeminized family
background (resulting in lesbianism and male homosexuality
respectively). See also his: **All the Sexes: A Study of
Masculinity and Femininity** (New York: Rinehart, 1955; 599
pp.).

3655. IMIELIŃSKI, KAZIMIERZ. **Die Sexualperversionen.**
Vienna: W. Maudrich, 1967. 146 pp.
A Polish psychiatrist attempts to generate a unified-
field theory of sexual perversion by compiling data from
earlier publications. See also his: **Milieubedingte Entstehung der Homo- und Bisexualität** (Munich: Ernst Reinhardt, 1970; 79 pp.); and "Homosexuality in Males with

Particular Reference to Marriage," **Psychotherapy and Psychosomatics,** 17 (1969), 126-32.

3656.   KAMENY, FRANKLIN E. "Gay Liberation and Psychiatry," **Psychiatric Opinion,** 8 (February 1971), 18-27.
Acerbic remarks of a militant gay activist, who led the public campaign to induce psychiatrist's to retreat from their dogmatic claims that homosexuality is a mental disease.

3657.   KARPMAN, BENJAMIN. **The Sexual Offender and His Offenses: Etiology, Pathology, Psychodynamics and Treatment.** New York: Julian Press, 1954. 744 pp.
Part 1 offers a review of the literature from 1912-51. Homosexuality, classified as a biological paraphilia and a sign of "retarded emotional development," is discussed in Chapter 10. The etiology and treatment literature cited in this work can be supplemented (for the period 1940-68) by: Martin S. Weinberg and Alan P. Bell (eds.), **Homosexuality: An Annotated Bibliography** (New York: Harper and Row, 1972; 550 pp.).

3658.   KITTRIE, NICHOLAS N. **The Right to Be Different: Deviance and Enforced Therapy.** Baltimore: Penguin, 1973. 443 pp.
Comprehensive examination of assumptions and practices of enforced therapy for those classified as deviants: the mentally ill, delinquent youth, (sexual) psychopaths (including homosexuals, pp. 193-99), drug addicts, and alcoholics. The final two chapters consider the evils of unchecked power under the "therapeutic state" and the outlook for reducing the dominance of the savers.

3659.   LIVINGOOD, JOHN M. (ed.). **National Institute of Mental Health Task Force on Homosexuality: Final Report and Background Papers.** Rockville, MD: National Institute of Mental Health, 1972. 79 pp.
The Final Report, approved October 10, 1969, is printed, followed by Working Papers by Evelyn Hooker, Paul H. Gebhard, Edwin M. Schur, John Money, Judd Marmor, Robert L. Katz, and Jerome D. Frank. The papers are generally enlightened and well informed, making this brochure a landmark in the official discussion of the subject.

3660.   LOWENSTEIN, L. F., and K. B. LOWENSTEIN. "Homosexuality: A Review of the Research between 1978-1983," **British Journal of Projective Psychology and Personality Study,** 29 (1984), 21-24.
The main shift has been to abandon the emphasis on "curing" homosexuality and instead to adopt therapeutic goals and strategies designed to improve the quality of life of homosexual clients.

3661.   MOBERLY, ELIZABETH. "Homosexuality: Restating the Conservative Case," **Salmagundi,** 58-59 (1980-81),

281-99.
Contends that homosexuality results from non-fulfill-
ment of "legitimate homo-emotional developmental needs."
This paper is a sophisticated updating of traditional
views, maintaining that homosexuals should be cured.

3662. OLLENDORFF, ROBERT H. V. **The Juvenile Homosexual
       Experience and Its Effect on Adult Sexuality.** New
       York: Julian Press, 1966. 245 pp.
Holds that homosexuality is generated by "sex-negative"
societies, but not by sex-permissive ones. "Vegetother-
apy" is recommended--a technique combining self-expres-
sion and character analysis with examination of the mus-
cular system, facial expression, breathing, digestion,
and the sexual functions.

3663. ROSEN, ISMOND (ed.). **The Pathology and Treatment
       of Sexual Deviation: A Methodological Approach.**
       London: Oxford University Press, 1964. 510 pp.
A collection of articles intended to summarize for both
professional and lay readers then-current thinking on
the understanding and treatment of sexual deviation.
Sections on biology, general psychiatry, psychopathology, psychology, and sociology are included.

3664. ROSENFELS, PAUL. **Homosexuality: The Psychology of
       the Creative Process.** New York: Libra Publishers,
       1971. 169 pp.
Highly abstract presentation, adhering to no known school
of thought, by an openly gay New York psychiatrist.

3665. SZASZ, THOMAS STEPHEN. **The Myth of Mental Illness:
       Foundations of a Theory of Personal Conduct.** New
       York: Hoeber/Harper, 1961. 337 pp.
The first in a series of "emperor's new clothes" critiques
by this author, who denies both the theoretical cogency of
psychotherapy and its practical efficacy. A revised and
shortened paperback edition appeared in 1974 (New York:
Perennial Library). See also Chapter 10, "The Product
Conversion--From Heresy to Illness" (pp. 160-79) in his:
The Manufacture of Madness (New York: Harper and Row,
1970).

3666. WIDOM, CATHY SPATZ (ed.). **Sex Roles and Psycho-
       pathology.** New York: Plenum Press, 1984. 387 pp.
Most authors in this collection begin with the premise
that the problem stems from overly rigid gender role expectations against which individuals are judged.

3667. WILLIS, STANLEY E. **Understanding and Counseling
       the Male Homosexual.** Boston: Little, Brown, 1967.
       225 pp.
Argues that efforts at treatment have largely failed up
to now owing to an unwillingness to recognize that homosexuality is a complex, dynamic phenomenon rather than a
single static condition.

3668. WORLD HEALTH ORGANIZATION. **Manual of the International Statistical Classification of Diseases.**
Ninth ed. Geneva: WHO, 1977. 2 vols.
Unlike the the third edition of the **Diagnostic and Statistical Manual** of the American Psychiatric Association, which modified its treatment of homosexuality as pathology (see XVII.G), this work--in use throughout much of the world--still regards homosexuality as a disease.

B. FREUDIAN CONCEPTS

The concepts of Sigmund Freud (1856-1939), which have achieved an extraordinary diffusion throughout the Western world, are commonly thought to have introduced a central concern with sex into psychiatry. In fact sexology began somewhat earlier (see "Pioneers," I.B), and much of Freud's thinking is not directly involved with sex. The biographical and intellectual setting in which Freud fashioned his theories is currently undergoing detailed review. When this reexamination is completed, his image is likely to emerge substantially different.

3669. BERNHEIMER, CHARLES, and CLARE KAHANE (eds.). **In Dora's Case.** New York: Columbia University Press, 1985. 291 pp.
This book comprises an Introduction by the editors and 12 papers on this famous case. There is considerable discussion of the "gynecophilic friendships" of the eponymous Dora (Ida Bauer).

3670. CARROLL, MICHAEL P. "Freud on Homosexuality and the Super-Ego: Some Cross-Cultural Tests," **Behavioral Science Research,** 13 (1978), 255-71.
Claims that data from 51 societies support Freudian hypotheses concerning the etiological role of attentuated father-son contact.

3671. ELLENBERGER, HENRI F. **The Discovery of the Unconscious: The History and Evolution of Dynamic Psychiatry.** New York: Basic Books, 1970. 932 pp.
Fundamental reexamination of sources of the ideas of Pierre Janet, Sigmund Freud, Alfred Adler, and Carl Gustav Jung. Many useful references for the reconstruction of the thought universe out of which modern depth psychiatry arose.

3672. EYSENCK, HANS J., and GLENN D. WILSON. **The Experimental Study of Freudian Theories.** London: Methuen, 1973. 405 pp.
Reprints 21 papers which, in the opinion of the editors, constitute the most serious efforts to find evidence in support of Freudian psychoanalysis. In the editors' view,

such evidence is not forthcoming. See pp. 126-39, 297-316.

3673. FISHER, SEYMOUR, and ROGER P. GREENBERG. **The Scientific Credibility of Freud's Theories and Therapy.** New York: Basic Books, 1977. 502 pp.
Seemingly a thorough and balanced study, this large work in fact tends toward apologia for Freudian concepts. Chapters 5 and 6, for example, reaffirm the link between homosexuality and paranoia, providing a more favorable view of the present viability of this hypothesis than most would now grant (compare XVII.E). See also: Fisher and Greenberg (eds.), **The Scientific Evaluation of Freud's Theories and Therapy: A Book of Readings** (New York: Basic Books, 1978; 446 pp.), pp. 248-87.

3674. FREUD, SIGMUND. **Leonardo da Vinci, and a Memory of His Childhood.** Translated by Alan Tyson; introduction by Brian Farrell. Harmondsworth: Penguin, 1963. 192 pp.
An attempt to clarify the intrapsychic development of a great homosexual artist, first published in 1910 and then enlarged. (**Standard Edition**, 11, pp. 59-137). In the introduction (pp. 11-88) Farrell grapples with the various orders of difficulty posed by this essay in psychocultural hermeneutics. Some damaging flaws were isolated by Meyer Schapiro, "Leonardo and Freud: An Art-Historical Study," **Journal of the History of Ideas,** 17 (1956), 147-78.

3675. FREUD, SIGMUND. "Letter to an American Mother," in: Hendrik M. Ruitenbeek (ed.), **The Problem of Homosexuality in Modern Society.** New York: E. P. Dutton, 1963, pp. 1-2.
In this often-reprinted letter sent in 1935 to a woman who had written him concerning her son's homosexuality, Freud explains that the condition is not a vice, illness, or a degradation. No promise of a "cure" can be made. For earlier supportive statements by Freud, see Herb Spiers et al., "The Gay Rights Freud," **Body Politic** (May 1977), pp. 8-9 (where, however, the interview quoted from the newspaper **Die Zeit** is from 1905, not 1903 as claimed).

3676. FREUD, SIGMUND. **The Standard Edition of the Complete Psychological Works of Sigmund Freud.** Translated under the general editorship of John Strachey. London: Hogarth Press, 1953-64. 24 vols.
This stately edition, prepared with the collaboration of Freud's daughter Anna, is now the normative source for the study of Freud's work in English. Ideally it should be used in tandem with the German texts; while these are generally less fully annotated, the accepted English renderings for some Freudian technical terms are misleading, as Bruno Bettelheim and others have pointed out. See the indices for other papers on male homosexuality and lesbianism not cited here. Also useful is: Carrie Lee Rothgeb (ed.), **Abstracts of the Standard Edition of the**

Complete Psychological Works of Sigmund Freud (New York: International Universities Press, 1973; 572 + 189 pp.).

3677. FREUD, SIGMUND. **Three Essays on the Theory of Sexuality.** Translated by James Strachey. London: Imago, 1949. 126 pp.
First published in German in 1905 and subsequently enlarged. A basic work for Freud's problematic views on bisexuality and homosexuality. As the references acknowledge, it builds upon research conducted by others over the previous twenty years. (**Standard Edition**, 7, pp. 125-243).

3678. GRÜNBAUM, ADOLF. **The Foundations of Psychoanalysis: A Philosophical Critique.** Berkeley: University of California Press, 1984. 310 pp.
Often penetrating but poorly organized probings of the scientific status of Freudian psychoanalysis. The notes and bibliography are useful for other contributions to the ongoing debate. See also: Marshall Edelson, **Hypothesis and Evidence in Psychoanalysis** (Chicago: Chicago University Press, 1984; 179 pp.); and H. J. Eysenck and G. D. Wilson (eds.), above.

3679. HELLER, PETER. "A Quarrel over Bisexuality," in: Gerald Chapple and Hans H. Schulte (eds.), **The Turn of the Century: German Literature and Art, 1890-1915.** Bonn: Bouvier, 1981, 87-115.
Deals with Fliess's claim of priority for the concept of bisexuality against Otto Weininger and Hermann Swoboda. Heller supports Ernst Kris in assigning Freud the priority on the basis of a letter of December 6, 1896. See also J. M. Masson (ed.), below.

3680. KEYMEULEN, PETER VAN. **Homoseksualiteit: een kritische synthese uit het werk van Sigmund Freud.** Louvain: University, 1972. 354 pp. (unpublished doctoral dissertation in psychology)
Critical synthesis of Freud's views on homosexuality. Summarized in Steven De Batselier (ed)., **Les minorites homosexuelles** (Gembloux: Duculot, 1973), pp. 25-44. See also the dissertation of Jose Sanchez, **L'homosexualite feminine chez Freud** (Louvain: University, 1971; 172 pp.).

3681. KLINE, PAUL. **Fact and Fantasy in Freudian Theory.** Second ed. New York: Methuen, 1981. 510 pp.
In this generally pro-psychoanalytic study, see pp. 343-53 for a presentation of the mixed results of attempts to provide empirical evidence for Freudian ideas about homosexuality.

3682. MASSON, JEFFREY MOUSSAIEFF (ed.). **The Complete Letters of Sigmund Freud to Wilhelm Fliess, 1887-1904.** Cambridge, MA: Harvard University Press, 1985. 505 pp.
This long-delayed publication of Freud's complete cor-

respondence with an eccentric Berlin physician throws
light on the psychoanalytic concept of bisexuality, which
Freud developed in part through the stimulus of his
relationship with Fliess.

3683. MURPHY, TIMOTHY F. "Freud Reconsidered: Bisexual-
       ity, Homosexuality, and Moral Judgment," **JH**, 9:2-3
       (1983-84), 65-77.
Without ethically justifying his procedure, Freud transformed the course of psychosexual development as determined by psychoanalysis into a moral imperative against
which homosexuality is judged a fixated and immature
state.

3684. STANNARD, DAVID E. **Shrinking History: On Freud and
       the Failure of Psychohistory.** New York: Oxford
       University Press, 1980. 187 pp.
A sharp attack by an American historian, not only on
the current vogue of psychohistory, but also on its
shaky Viennese foundations. See pp. 5-9, 14-16, 87, 109-
14, 160-61. For an opposing view, see Peter Gay, **Freud
for Historians** (New York: Oxford University Press, 1985;
252 pp.).

3685. SULLOWAY, FRANK J. **Freud, Biologist of the Mind:
       Beyond the Psychoanalytic Legend.** New York: Ba-
       sic Books, 1979. 612 pp.
Reconstructing the intellectual climate in which Freud
developed his theories, shows how the originally biologis-
tic program yielded to a psychodynamic one. Sulloway
also unmasks the fabrication--by Ernest Jones and others--
of heroic legends (26 in all), designed to assure good
fortune for Freud and psychoanalysis. Numerous references
to homosexuality.

                    C. PSYCHOANALYSIS

Psychoanalysis is the body of theory and therapeutic
practice that grew out of the teaching of Sigmund Freud.
Although no alternative theoretical focus has appeared,
many concepts of the creator of psychoanalysis have been,
at various times and places, tacitly or explicitly revised. A salient example is the concept of universal
bisexuality, which has been largely abandoned by psychoanalysts as a result of Sandor Rado's critique (3711; compare XIV.F). Many latter-day psychoanalysis have adopted
a harshly negative view of homosexuality, contrasting with
the founder's more humane practice (though these homonegative psychiatrists would doubtless argue that the premises for their opinions are deeply embedded in psychoanalysis itself). Outside of psychoanalysis--and sometimes
within it--a debate rages as to the logical status of the
discipline: does it truly deserve the name of science, or

is it rather a mythological or even literary system? The
therapeutic efficacy of psychoanalysis--its capacity to
improve the mental health of analysands--has also been
brought into serious question.

3686. AARDWEG, GERARD J. VAN DEN. "A Grief Theory of
        Homosexuality," **American Journal of Psychotherapy,**
        26 (1972), 52-68.
Contends that male homosexuality is best correlated with
the concept "inferior-pitiable." Recommends a technique
based on the curative value of humor and laughter, which
destroy complaining and may "restore" heterosexual impulses. See also his: **On the Origins and Treatment of
Homosexuality** (New York: Praeger, 1986).

3687. BARGUES, JEAN-FRANÇOIS. "Sodome: Aspects cli-
        niques, mythologiques et métapsychologiques de
        l'homosexualité," **Annales médico-psychologiques,**
        132/2 (1974), 711-31.
Discusses Freudian contributions on male homosexuality,
linking them to themes derived from mythology and to
illustrative clinical examples.

3688. BERGLER, EDMUND. **Homosexuality: Disease or Way of
        Life?** New York: Hill and Wang, 1956. 302 pp.
Homosexuality is held to be a pathological disorder which
stems from the homosexual's longing for defeat, humiliation, and rejection. The homosexual is an "injustice
collector," who courts and cherishes disaster. Among the
embittered diatribes of this neo-Freudian pundit (1899-
1962), probably the most widely circulated were: **Coun-
terfeit Sex: Homosexuality, Impotence, Frigidity.** Second
ed. (New York: Grove Press, 1961; 380 pp.), and **One Thousand Homosexuals: Conspiracy of Silence, or Curing and
Deglamorizing Homosexuals?** (Paterson, NJ: Pageant Books,
1959; 249 pp.).

3689. BIEBER, IRVING (et al). **Homosexuality: A Psycho-
        analytic Study.** New York: Basic Books, 1962. 358
        pp.
This study by a ten-member Research Committee of the
Society of Medical Psychoanalysts based its conclusions
on 106 male homosexuals and 100 heterosexuals in clinical
treatment. It is a major source of the "close-binding
mother" thesis of the etiology of male homosexuality.
Critics allege that defects in methodology and research
design mask an antihomosexual bias, and that the conclusions are essentially an artifact of the design, and
therefore scientifically valueless. See Fritz A. Fluck-
iger, "Research, through a Glass, Darkly: An Evaluation of
the Bieber Study on Homosexuality," **Ladder,** 10:10 (July
1966), 16-26; 10:11 (August 1966), 18-26; and 10:12
(September 1966), 22-26; and Richard C. Friedman, "Psychodynamics and Sexual Object Choice: III. A Rereply to Drs.
I. Bieber and C. W. Socarides," **Contemporary Psychoanal-**

ysis, 12 (1976), 379-85. Finally, see Irving Bieber and
Toby B. Bieber, "Male Homosexuality," **Canadian Journal
of Psychiatry,** 24 (1979), 409-21.

3690. BYCHOWSKI, GUSTAV. "The Structure of Homosexual
Acting Out," **Psychoanalytic Quarterly,** 23 (1954),
48-61.
Contends that homosexual acting out stems from a weak
ego structure based upon a narcissistic and prenarcis-
sistic disposition.

3691. CALEF, VICTOR, and WEINSHEL, EDWARD M. "Anxiety
and the Restitutional Function of Homosexual
Cruising," **International Journal of Psycho-anal-
ysis,** 65 (1984), 45-53.
Suggests that homosexual cruising is an act of restitu-
tion, an effort to resurrect the father and to contra-
dict the ambivalent wishes to rob and murder him, and an
attempt to idealize the father, rendering him into an object of love.

3692. CAPPON, DANIEL. **Toward an Understanding of Homosexuality.** Englewood Cliffs, NJ: Prentice-Hall,
1965. 302 pp.
Views homosexuality as a product of "faulty development
and adaptation"--"a painful and destructive disorder, but
one which can be relieved and even cured."

3693. EISENBUD, RUTH-JEAN. "Early and Later Determinants
of Lesbian Choice," **Psychoanalytic Review,** 69
(1982), 85-109.
Holds that primary lesbian erotic love originates in a
precocious turn-on of erotic desire mandated by the ego
and that it is progresive, not regressive.

3694. ENDLEMAN, ROBERT. **Psyche and Society: Explorations
in Psychoanalytic Sociology.** New York: Columbia
University Press, 1981. 466 pp.
In this wide-ranging study, see Part 4, "Homosexuality:
Gay Liberation Confronts Psychoanalysis and the Social
Sciences" (pp. 235-337).

3695. EYSENCK, HANS J. **Decline and Fall of the Freudian
Empire.** New York: Viking, 1986. 224 pp.
Ambitious critique of psychoanalysis, seeking to expose
the paradoxes, limitations, and errors the author, a
London-based psychologist, believes to underlie Freudian
theory and practice.

3696. FELDMAN, SANDOR S. "On Homosexuality," in: Sandor
Lorand and Michael Balint (eds.), **Perversions: Psychodynamics and Therapy.** New York: Random House,
1956, 71-96.
Holds that homosexuals of both sexes began as heterosexuals, but that some traumatic situation shifted their heterosexual orientation toward homosexuality.

3697. FENICHEL, OTTO. **The Psychoanalytic Theory.** New
       York: W. W. Norton, 1945. 703 pp.
In a synthesis of psychoanalytic doctrines, male and
female homosexuality is discussed in relation to perver-
sions and impulse neuroses, as well as castration anxiety,
regression to a state of father fixation, and the Oedipal/
Electra complexes. Compare his "Outline of Clinical
Psychoanalysis: The Sexual Perversions," **Psychoanalytic
Quarterly,** 2 (1933), 260-308, esp. 270-90.

3698. FERENCZI, SÁNDOR. "Zur Nosologie der männlichen
       Homosexualität," **Zeitschrift für ärztliche Psycho-
       analyse,** 2 (1914), 131-42.
An influential statement by a member of Freud's circle,
who subsequently became estranged. Using his dichotomy
between "subject" (active) and "object" (passive) homosexuals, Ferenczi sought in effect to explain away homosexuality by assimilating it to heterosexual norms. For English version, see his: **Contributions to Psychoanalysis**
(New York: Brunner, 1950), pp. 296-318.

3699. GERSHMAN, HARRY. "Psychology of Compulsive Homo-
       sexuality," **American Journal of Psychoanalysis,**
       17 (1957), 58-77.
Seeks to distinguish between "homosexual behavior" and
"compulsive homosexuality." The latter, which reflects a
personality distortion originating in early childhood,
is not normal. See also his: "Reflections on the Nature
of Homosexuality," **American Journal of Psychoanalysis,** 26
(1966), 46-59; and "The Role of Core Gender Identity
in the Genesis of Perversions," **American Journal of
Psychoanalysis,** 30 (1970), 58-67.

3700. GONEN, JAY. Y. "Negative Identity in Homosexuals,"
       Psychoanalytic Review, 58 (1971), 345-52.
Utilizing ideas of Erik Erikson, contends that the concept of negative identity can be fruitfully applied to an
understanding of various social phenomena, including homosexuality.

3701. HASSELGREEN, HELGE. ["Searching for the Homococ-
       cus"], **Nordisk Psykiatrisk Tidsskrift,** 28 (1974),
       605-11.
Criticizing the psychiatric view that homosexuality is
pathological (as found in the works of I. Bieber and
E. Kringlen), argues that this assumption is without
foundation, being simply a residue of Judeo-Christian
belief systems.

3702. HENDIN, HERBERT. **The Age of Sensation: A Psycho-
       analytic Exploration.** New York: W. W. Norton,
       1974. 354 pp.
Study of college youth in New York City, portraying them
as victims of drugs, anomie, and sexual confusion, including homosexuality (esp. pp. 104-18). Catering to
popular fears about adolescents, this work is undermined

by statistical anomalies and preconceived formulations.
See also his: "Homosexuality: The Psychosocial Dimension,"
Journal of the American Academy of Psychoanalysis, 6
(1978), 479-96.

3703. HOROWITZ, GAD. **Repression: Basic and Surplus
      Repression in Psychoanalytic Theory: Freud, Reich,
      and Marcuse.** Toronto: University of Toronto Press,
      1977. 227 pp.
Expository study, emphasizing Marcuse's critic of surplus
repression, holding that while his argument is flawed, it
can be strengthened and made viable. See esp. pp. 82-86.

3704. JACKMAN, A. J. **The Paranoid Homosexual Basis of
      Anti-Semitism and Kindred Hatred.** New York: Van-
      tage, 1979. 191 pp.
An amateurish and subjective work, in some respects recal-
ling Samuel Igra, **Germany's National Vice** (London: Quality
Press, 1945), which was a product of wartime hatred.
Despite their polemical character, it may be that such
works raise issues deserving more serious consideration.

3705. KARDINER, ABRAHAM. **Sex and Morality.** Indianap-
      olis: Bobbs-Merrill, 1954. 266 pp.
In "Flight from Masculinity" (pp. 160-92), he contends
that in our culture homosexuality is a social disease
brought on by the pressures of western civilization.

3706. KWAWER, JAY S. "Transference and Countertransfer-
      ence in Homosexuality: Changing Psychoanalytic
      Views," **American Journal of Psychotherapy,** 34
      (1980), 72-80.
Identifies shifts in the dynamic understanding of transference phenomena, from an early emphasis on Oedipal
issues to the contemporary focus on early maternal relations and how disturbances in these are recapitulated in
homosexual transference.

3707. MARCUSE, HERBERT. **Eros and Civilization.** Boston:
      Beacon Press, 1955. 277 pp.
An attempt by a once-influential figure of the "Freudian
left" to posit a nonrepressive civilization. On Marcuse,
see G. Horowitz, above, and P. A. Robinson, below.

3708. MORGENTHALER, FRITZ. **Homosexualität Heterosexual-
      ität Perversion.** Frankfurt am Main: Qumran, 1984.
      192 pp.
Revised texts of speeches and papers of an independent
Swiss psychiatrist (1961-83), who evolved a nonpatho-
logical concept of homosexuality.

3709. OVESEY, LIONEL, and ETHEL PERSON. "Gender Identity
      and Sexual Psychopathology in Men: A Psychodynamic
      Analysis of Homosexuality, Transsexualism, and
      Transvestism," **Journal of the American Academy of
      Psychoanalysis,** 1 (1973), 53-72.

For each "disorder" a psychodynamic analysis of the symptoms is offered, as well as a hypothesis for developmental
origins.

3710. PERETTI, PETER O., et al. "Self-Image and Emotion-
       al Stability of Oedipal and Non-Oedipal Male Homo-
       sexuals," **Acta Psychiatrica Belgica**, 76 (1976),
       46-55.
In a study of 168 "oedipal" and "non-oedipal" male homosexuals, the former were found to be more negative, and to
have less self-worth, self-confidence, and self-acceptance
than the latter.

3711. RADO, SANDOR. "A Critical Examination of the Con-
       cept of Bisexuality," in: Judd Marmor (ed.), **Sexual
       Inversion: The Multiple Roots of Homosexuality.**
       New York: Basic Books, 1965, pp. 175-89.
In a widely read essay, first published in 1940, Rado
questions the earlier assumption of the universality of
bisexuality by Freud and others, maintaining that if the
term is used in a biologically limited sense, "there is
no such thing as bisexuality either in man or in any other
of the higher vertebrates."

3712. REICH, WILHELM. **Sex-Pol: Essays 1929-1934.** Edited
       by Lee Baxandall. New York: Vintage Books, 1972.
       378 pp.
The early Reich, some of whose writings are translated
here from the original German publications, has been influential in his attempt to fuse Freudian psychoanalysis
with Marxism, relating both to sexual enlightenment. Even
at this period, however, he disliked homosexuality, as-
sociating it with the right and the rise of Nazism (p.
297). For a contextualization of the Sex-Pol milieu, see
Hans-Peter Gente (ed.), **Marxismus, Psychoanalyse, Sex-Pol**
(Frankfurt: Fischer, 1976; 2 vols.).

3713. REICH, WILHELM. **The Sexual Revolution: Towards a
       Self-Governing Character.** Translated by Theodore
       W. Wolfe. Revised ed. New York: Farrar, Straus
       and Giroux, 1969. 273 pp.
The final state of this book incorporates many changes
since the publication of the original core in Vienna in
1930. A careful study of Reich's thought would have to
distinguish its various strata; as it is, too much of the
writing about him is uncritical advocacy. This book does
contain some discussion of the repression of homosexuality in Stalin's Soviet Union (pp. 153-57, 208-11).

3714. ROAZEN, PAUL. **Helene Deutsch.** New York: Anchor
       Press/Doubleday, 1985. 371 pp.
Biography of Freud's leading woman disciple, using documentary sources--including some that suggest a link
between her experiences with close associates and her
negative concepts of homosexuality. Some discussion of
lesbianism appears in Deutsch's major work, **The Psychology**

of Women (New York: Grune and Stratton, 1944-45; 2 vols.).

3715. ROBBINS, BERNARD S. "Psychological Implications of the Male Homosexual Marriage," **Psychoanalytic Review**, 30 (1943), 428-37.
Claims on the basis of the psychoanalysis of two men that the homosexual's dominant neurotic drive is sadism.

3716. ROBINSON, PAUL A. **The Freudian Left.** New York: Harper and Row, 1969.
Wilhelm Reich, Geza Roheim, and Herbert Marcuse seen through somewhat rose-colored glasses. See also: Richard King, **The Party of Eros: Radical Social Thought and the Realm of Freedom** (Chapel Hill: University of North Carolina Press, 1972; 227 pp.).

3717. RUSE, MICHAEL. "Are Homosexuals Sick?" in A. Caplan et al (eds.), **Current Concepts of Health and Disease.** Boston: Addison-Wesley, 1980, pp. 693-723.
Chiefly on the Freudian and other schools of clinical psychology.

3718. SADGER, ISIDOR. "Fragmente der Psychoanalyse eines Homosexuellen," **JfsZ**, 9 (1908), 339-424.
Sadger was the first member of Freud's circle to give concentrated attention to homosexuality. Among his contributions is the notion that homosexuality is caused by an impulse to eat the father's testicles. See also his: "Ist die konträre Sexualempfindung heilbar?" **Zeitschrift für Sexualwissenschaft**, 1 (1908), 712-20; and **Neue Forschungen zur Homosexualität** (Berlin: Fischer, 1915; 32 pp.).

3719. SALZMAN, LEON. "'Latent' Homosexuality," in: Judd Marmor (ed.), **Sexual Inversion: The Multiple Roots of Homosexuality.** New York: Basic Books, 1965, pp. 234-47.
The term "latent homosexuality" has been loosely used and abused by professionals as well as by laymen. Since it carries derogatory connotations, its validity should be demonstrated or else the term should be abandoned. See also his: "The Concept of Latent Homosexuality," **American Journal of Psychoanalysis**, 17 (1957), 161-69.

3720. SIEGEL, ELAINE V. "Severe Body Image Distortions in Some Female Homosexuals," **Dynamic Psychotherapy**, 2 (1984), 18-28.
Attempts to apply the theories of Charles Socarides (see below) to lesbians. See the discussion following by Bernard F. Riess, ibid., 29-30.

3721. SILVA, JORGE G. "Two Cases of Female Homosexuality: A Critical Study of Sigmund Freud and Helene Deutsch," **Contemporary Psychoanalysis**, 11 (1975), 357-87.

Criticizes their ideas on lesbianism, including Deutsch's
claim that the libido is never feminine.

3722. SOCARIDES, CHARLES W. **The Overt Homosexual.** New
       York: Grune and Stratton, 1968. 245 pp.
Resumes of earlier literature and clinical reports by a
neo-Freudian who remains obdurately attached to the sickness theory. Together with other contributions, the
material of this book is recycled in his omnium gatherum,
Homosexuality (New York: Jason Aronson, 1978; 642 pp.).

3723. STEKEL, WILHELM. **The Homosexual Neurosis.** Trans-
       lated by James Van Teslaar. Brooklyn: Physicians
       and Surgeons Book Co., 1922. 322 pp.
Popularization of Freudian ideas with case histories. See
also "Is Homosexuality Curable?" **Psychoanalytic Review,** 17
(1930), 443-52.

3724. STOLLER, ROBERT. **Observing the Erotic Imagina-
       tion.** New Haven: Yale University Press, 1985. 228
       pp.
Censorious and sex-negative studies on pornography, fantasies, and interpersonal rituals as "perversions" and
evidence of the hostility he believes pervades our
intimate relationships. See the other publications of
this prolific author, including: **Splitting: A Case of
Female Masculinity** (New York: Quadrangle, 1975); **Perversion: The Erotic Form of Hatred** (New York: Pantheon,
1977); **Sexual Excitement** (New York: Pantheon, 1979); and
Presentations of Gender (New Haven: Yale University Press,
1985).

3725. STREAN, HERBERT S. "Homosexuality: A Life-Style, A
       Civil Rights Issue or a Psycho-Social Problem?"
       Current Issues in Psychoanalytic Practice, 1
       (1984), 35-47.
With regard to the homosexual client, who has frequently
been scapegoated as a child by his/her parents and discriminated against as an adult, practitioners have to
respect and accept his/her lifestyle, behave in a way
that guarantees his/her civil rights, and maintain an
objective eye and an empathetic ear.

D. OTHER DEPTH PSYCHIATRY SCHOOLS

Two of Freud's rivals (originally his associates) reflect
the attitude of many non-Freudian depth psychologists
towards homosexuality: Adler hated it with an almost
unreasoning passion, while Jung tended to ignore it.
Hence the brevity of this section.

3726. ADLER, ALFRED. **Cooperation between the Sexes: Wri-**

tings on Women, Love and Marriage, Sexuality and
Its Disorders. Edited and translated by Henz
L. and Romena R. Ansbacher. Garden City, NY: Anchor Books, 1978. 468 pp.
For a time a close associate of Freud in Vienna, Adler
(1870-1937) seceded to form his own school of Individual
Psychology. He classed homosexuals among the "failures of
life," together with prostitutes and criminals. The
present collection includes two grimly anti-homosexual
papers (145-70, 205-47), which incorporate material from
several German texts (1917ff.).

3727. BOSS, MEDARD. Meaning and Content of Sexual
      Perversions: A Daseinanalytic Approach to the
      Psychopathology of the Phenomenon of Love. Trans-
      lated by Liese Lewis Abell. Second ed. New
      York: Grune and Stratton, 1949. 153 pp.
An existentialist approach, based in part on the ideas of
the philosopher Martin Heidegger.

3728. CHAPMAN, A. H. Harry Stack Sullivan: His Life and
      His Work. New York: Putnam, 1976. 280 pp.
Sympathetic account of the only major psychoanalyst (1892-
1949) known certainly to have been homosexual, suggesting
that the need to conceal this fact probably stunted both
his life and his career. His influence was largely exercised through personal contact during his life, and
his writings, which are rambling and often unfocused, do
not seem to deal explicitly with homosexuality.

3729. DONALD, PAUL. "Can the Homosexual Be Helped?" Mod-
      ern Psychologist, 1 (1933), 203-66.
Negative article in an Adlerian vein, chiefly interesting
for its adumbration of the concept of injustice collecting, later exploited to the hilt by the neo-Freudian
Edmund Bergler.

3730, ELLIS, ALBERT. Homosexuality: Its Causes and
      Cure. New York: Lyle Stuart, 1965. 288 pp.
Ellis, who achieved considerable notice during this period
as a kind of proto-pop psychiatrist, regarded exclusive
homosexuality as the result of emotional disturbance. He
recommended his own technique of "rational-emotive psychotherapy." Ellis gained the adherence of some homophile
figures at the time, notably Edward Sagarin (Donald
Webster Cory), who contributed an appendix to this book
on the mystique of the gigantic penis. For a strong
contemporary critique, see Jim Kepner, "An Examination
of the Sex Theories of Albert Ellis, Ph.D." ONE Institute Quarterly, 2:2 (Spring 1959), 40-51.

3731. FRIEDBERG, RONALD L. "Early Recollections of
      Homosexuals as Indicators of Their Life Styles,"
      Journal of Individual Psychology, 31 (1975),
      197-204.
An Adlerian study, finding only partial support for

Adler's assertion that the homosexual's most salient
character traits are inordinate ambition and pronounced
caution and fear of life.

3732. JUNG, CARL GUSTAV. **Collected Works.** Edited by
      Herbert Read et al. New York: Pantheon; and
      Princeton: Princeton University Press, 1953-79. 20
      vols. in 21.
The writings of Jung (1875-1961) generally avoid any
direct discussion of homosexuality and lesbianism. Some
have found the Jungian concept of the archetype to be
useful in rethinking gender-role categories. The final
of volume of the **Works** is a general index; see entries:
androgyny, bisexuality, hermaphrodite.

3733. KIVEL, CAROL I. "Male Homosexuals in a Changing
      Society," **Individual Psychology: Journal of Ad-
      lerian Theory, Research and Practice,** 39 (1983),
      218-21.
Contends that societal changes require modification of
Adler's negative view of homosexuality, which should no
longer be regarded as calling for mandatory therapy. See
comment by Harold H. Mosak, ibid., 222-36.

3734. KRAUSZ, ERWIN O. "Homosexuality as Neurosis,"
      International Journal of Individual Psychology, 1
      (1935), 30-39.
A negative article translated from the German to feature
in the first volume of Adler's English-language organ.

3735. LÓPEZ-PEDRAZA, RAFAEL. "The Tale of Dryops and the
      Birth of Pan: An Archetypal and Therapeutic
      Approach to Eros Between Men," **Spring** (1976),
      176-90.
Venezuelan psychiatrist, influenced by C. Rogers, who
holds that invocation of the Pan factor could be of
therapeutic value in relation to homosexuality.

3736. MANASTER, GUY J., and MARC KING. "Early Recollec-
      tions of Male Homosexuals," **Journal of Individual
      Psychology,** 29 (1973), 26-33.
Adlerian interpretation of five cases, all of which show a
recollection of conflict with a woman.

3737. RISTER, ESTHER S. "The Male Homosexual Style of
      Life: Contemporary Adlerian Interpretation,"
      Journal of Individual Psychology, 37 (1981), 86-94.
Applies Adlerian theory to explain the seemingly great
increase in male homosexuality in the second half of the
20th century. Unable to meet the challenge of women's
equality, they retreat into an immature life style that
revolves around avoidance.

Freud hypothesized that paranoia originated in a desperate effort on the part of the paranoid individual to repress homosexual desires. This controversy is presented here in some detail as it is paradigmatic of the fate of many Freudian theories: extensive and resourceful research has failed to find confirmation for Freud's claim.

3738. CHALUS, GARY ANTON. "An Evaluation of the Validity of the Freudian Theory of Paranoia." **JH,** 3 (1977), 171-88.
In essence the theory states that delusional thinking arises as a result of the reaction-formation and projection of threatening unconscious homosexual wishes. Chalus suggests a more parsimonious explanation. Extensive references.

3739. DASTON, PAUL G. "Perception of Homosexual Words in Paranoid Schizophrenia," **Perceptual and Motor Skills,** 6 (1956), 45-55.
Claims that selective responses to words provide support for the psychoanalytic interpretation. However, "[w]hether homosexuality was a major area of concern for paranoid individuals was not determined."

3740. DEB, SUBIMAL. "Repressed Homosexuality and Symptom Formation Like Paranoid Jealousy and Erotomania," **Samiksa,** 30 (1976), 41-46.
Contends that for the male paranoid jealousy begins with the choice of the father as the homosexual partner; this wish is then repressed, leading to erotomania.

3741. FERENCZI, SÁNDOR. "Uber die Rolle der Homosexualität in der Pathogenese der Paranoia," **Jahrbuch für psychoanalytische und psychopathologische Forschungen,** 3 (1911), 101-19.
Early statement of the purported link between homosexuality and the origins of paranoia, by a member of Freud's inner circle.

3742. FREUD, SIGMUND. "Psychoanalytic Notes on an Autobiographical Account of a Case of Paranoia (Dementia paranoides) [1911]," **Standard Edition** (London: Hogarth Press), 12 (1958), 12-84.
Analysis of the case of Judge Daniel Schreber, the locus classicus for the posited link. Holds that the type-situation is represented by the proposition: "I (a man) love him (a man)." On the single case on which Freud based his ambitious theory, see William Niederman, **The Schreber Case: Psychoanalytic Profile of a Paranoid Personality** (New York: Quadrangle, 1974; 172 pp.).

3743. HIGDON, JOHN F. "Paranoia: Power Conflict or

Homosexual Projection?" **Journal of Operational Psychiatry,** 7 (1976), 32-45.
A review of studies highlights the confusion of power conflicts with homosexual dynamics, showing that past research studies have not adequately distinguished between the two.

3744. KLAF, FRANLIN S. "Female Homosexuality and Paranoid Schizophrenia: A Survey of 75 Cases and Controls," **Archives of General Psychiatry,** 4 (1961), 84-86.
With reference to Freud's hypothesis, found no significant difference between the schizophrenics and the controls in the degree of their preoccupation with homosexuality.

3745. KLAF, FRANKLIN S., and CHARLES A. DAVIS. "Homosexuality and Paranoid Schizophrenia: A Survey of 150 Cases and Controls," **American Journal of Psychiatry,** 116 (1960), 1070-75.
Although Freud's theory appears to have been substantiated, more studies are needed. The two trends, paranoia and homosexuality, may exist together and yet not necessarily be related.

3746. LACAN, JACQUES. **De la psychose paranoiaque dans ses rapports avec la personnalité.** Paris: Editions du Seuil, 1975. 361 pp.
In his 1932 M. D. thesis, now republished, the influential French psychoanalyst discusses the Freudian theory of paranoia, stressing the value of his approach for the understanding of "thèmes délirants à signification homosexuelle."

3747. LESTER, DAVID. "The Relationship Between Paranoid Delusions and Homosexuality," **Archives of Sexual Behavior,** 4 (1975), 285-94.
A review of the literature on Freud's theory that paranoid delusions are motivated by unconscious homosexual impulses does not support the prediction.

3748. LIND, LIS. "Homosexuality and Paranoia," **Scandinavian Psychoanalytic Review,** 5 (1982), 5-30.
Uses case material to explore why the paranoiac and the manifestly homosexual male react so differently to their homosexual libido.

3749. MCCAWLEY, AUSTIN. "Paranoia and Homosexuality: Schreber Reconsidered," **New York State Journal of Medicine,** 71 (1971), 1506-13.
Contends that, whether one subscribes to Freud's specific interpretation or not, there seems to be a relationship between homosexuality and paranoia.

3750. ROSSI, R., et al. "The Problem of the Relationship between Homosexuality and Schizophrenia," **Archives of Sexual Behavior,** 1 (1971), 357-62.

Questioning the appropriateness of generating a theory
from a single case (that of Schreber), concludes that "the
data, examined from a clinical-statistical point of view,
do not support the analytical theory. ... The frequency
of homosexual elements does not appear to be high in
paranoid syndromes compared with other forms of schizophrenia."

3751. WOLOWITZ, HOWARD M. "The Validity of the Psycho-
       analytic Theory of Paranoid Dynamics: Evaluated
       from the Available Experimental Evidence," **Psychi-**
       atry [Washington, DC], 34 (1971), 358-77.
Reviews the relevant experimental research pertaining to
homosexual actions, fantasies, and defenses, finding
that males are more likely to fit the theory than females.

3752. ZAMANSKY, HAROLD S. "An Investigation of the
       Psychoanalytic Theory of Paranoid Delusions,"
       Journal of Personality, 26 (1958), 410-25.
Finds that the homosexuality of the male paranoid appears
as an intermediary process in the development of his de-
lusions, rather than being the primary etiological agent.
For critical comment, see Hans J. Eysenck and Glenn D.
Wilson, **The Experimental Study of Freudian Theories** (Lon-
don: Methuen, 1973), pp. 312-15. See also: Charles G.
Watson, "A Test of the Relationship between Repressed
Homosexuality and Paranoid Mechanisms," **Journal of Clin-**
ical Psychology, 21 (1965), 380-84.

                    F. PSYCHOTHERAPY: GENERAL

The older model of psychotherapy with homosexuals was
to replace the deviant orientation with a heterosexual one
acceptable to society. The term "cure" encapsulates this
attitude. In contrast, many therapists now stress that
they accept a homosexual orientation as normal and
healthy, and need not be changed. Their intervention is
based on their claim to be able help the patient remove
obstacles to happy adjustment within it. See also
"Counseling and Social Services," XV.A.

3753. AGEL, JEROME (ed.). **The Radical Therapist.** New
       York: Ballantyne, 1971. 291 pp.
Collection of short pieces by psychiatric dissidents
gathered under the rubric "therapy means change not adjustment." Many reflect the viewpoint of the journal
The Radical Therapist.

3754. ATKINS, MERRILEE, et al. "Brief Treatment of
       Homosexual Patients, **Comprehensive Psychiatry,** 17
       (1976), 115-24.
A crisis-oriented center must deal with challenges to

therapists' value systems and speedy identification of
patients' priorities.

3755. BENDA, CLEMENS E. "Existential Psychotherapy of
      Homosexuality," **Review of Existential Psychology
      and Psychiatry,** 3 (1963), 133-52.
Existential therapy seeks to enable the homosexual to form
loving, "normal" sexual attachments, and to correct his
"distorted view of existence" by providing strong emotional experiences.

3756. BERG-CROSS, LINDA. "Existential Issues in the
      Treatment of Lesbian Clients," **Women and Therapy,** 1
      (1982), 67-83.
The existential approach recommended is prolesbian without
minimizing the "contributing pathologies" afflicting many
lesbians who seek help in leading happier and more
productive lives.

3757. BERILLON, EDGAR. "Le traitement psychologique de
      l'homosexualité basé sur la rééducation sensori-
      elle," **Revue de l'hypnotisme,** 23 (1908), 44-46.
An early psychotherapeutic technique based on the premise
that "in the evocation of images capable of arousing his
sexual appetite, the male is olfactory and gustatory,
while the female, on the contrary, is in her sexual orientation visual and tactile."

3758. BLACKRIDGGE, PERSIMMON, and SHEILA GILHOOLY. **Still
      Sane.** Vancouver: Press Gang, 1985. 101 pp.
Account of Gilhooly's three-year struggle with compulsory psychiatric incarceration, in which shock treatments
and drugs were employed in an attempt to "cure" her lesbianism.

3759. BRADFORD, JOHN M. W. "Organic Treatments for the
      Male Sexual Offender," **Behavior Sciences and the
      Law,** 3 (1985), 355-75.
Discusses three treatments: antiandrogen or other hormonal
agents; surgical castration; and stereotaxic neurosurgery.
Extensive references. See also: Linda S. Gross, "Research
Directions in the Evaluation and Treatment of Sex Offenders: An Analysis," ibid., 421-40; and R. M. Wettstein,
below.

3760. BROOKS, VIRGINIA R. "Sex and Sexual Orientation as
      Variables in Therapists' Biases and Therapy Out-
      comes," **Clinical Social Work Journal,** 9 (1981),
      198-210.
In responses of 675 lesbians, female therapists--hetero-
sexual or lesbian--were assessed as more beneficial than
male therapists. The sex-role ideology of therapists may
be even more important.

3761. BROWN, LAURA S. "The Lesbian Feminist Therapist in
      Private Practice and Her Community," **Psychotherapy**

in Practice, 2:4 (Winter 1984), 9-16.
Suggests that the lesbian therapist's relationship to her community should be likened to living in a small town, where many overlapping relationships occur. See also Josette Escamilla-Mondanaro, "Lesbians and Therapy," in: Edna Rawlings and Dianne Carter, **Psychotherapy for Women** (Springfield, IL: Charles C. Thomas, 1977), pp. 256-65.

3762. CLIPPINGER, JOHN A. "Homosexuality Can Be Cured," **Corrective and Social Psychiatry and Journal of Behavior Technology, Methods and Therapy,** 20 (1974), 15-28.
Claims that cure rates are on the increase and, for the majority of homosexuals, it is a matter of choice if they desire to be changed.

3763. COLEMAN, ELI. "Toward a New Model of Treatment of Homosexuality: A Review," **JH,** 3 (1978), 345-59.
Challenging the illness or maladaptive presupposition, a new model is emerging to assist homosexuals to recognize, accept and value their sexual identity.

3764. DAILEY, DENNIS M. "Family Therapy with the Homosexual: A Search," **Homosexual Counseling Journal,** 1 (1974), 7-15.
Discusses the applicability of concepts derived from family therapy to work with homosexual couples.

3765. DAVISON, GERALD C. "Homosexuality: The Ethical Challenge," **Journal of Consulting and Clinical Psychology,** 44 (1976), 157-62.
It is probable that the very existence of change-of-orientation programs strengthens societal prejudices against homosexuality and contributes to the self-contempt and embarrassment that are determinants of the "voluntary" decision by some homosexuals to become heterosexual. See discussion by Seymour L. Halleck, ibid., 167-70; and Ellie T. Sturgis and Henry E. Adams, ibid., 46 (1978), 165-69. Davison replied to the latter critique, ibid., 170-72. Davison's paper was reprinted in **JH,** 2:3 (1977), 195-204, where it is followed by another discussion.

3766. DI BELLA, GEOFFREY A. "Family Psychotherapy with the Homosexual Family: A Community Psychiatry Approach to Homosexuality," **Community Mental Health Journal,** 15 (1979), 41-46.
Points out that homosexual families are not being treated by family psychotherapy despite an obvious need, and seeks to uncover the reasons for the neglect.

3767. DUEHN, WAYNE D., and NASNEEN S. MAYADAS. "The Use of Stimulus/Modeling Videotapes in Assertive Training for Homosexuals," **JH,** 1 (1976), 373-81.
The approach combines the use of stimulus-modeling videotapes with behavioral rehearsals, videotape feedback, and home assignments.

3768. FREUND, KURT. "Should Homosexuality Arouse Ther-
       apeutic Concern?" **JH,** 2 (1977), 235-40.
Holds that attempts to change homosexual's sexual orientation should not continue because social changes may be
sufficient to reduce distress in these persons and because
there is as yet no real "cure."

3769. GERSHMAN, HARRY. "The Use of the Dream in the
       Therapy of Homosexuality," **American Journal of
       Psychoanalysis,** 31 (1971), 80-94.
Advocates the use of the dream as a diagnostic, prognos-
tic, therapeutic, and curative index.

3770. GILBERT, S. F. "Homosexuality and Hypnotherapy,"
       British Journal of Medical Hypnotism, 5:3 (1954),
       2-7.
Discusses the therapeutic potential of hypnosis with
several types of homosexuals. See also R. G. Roden,
"Threatening Homosexuality: A Case Treated by Hypnosis,"
Medical Hypnoanalysis, 4 (1983), 166-69.

3771. GOTLIND, ERIK. **Basic Mechanisms of Psychothera-
       peutic Significance: Three Examples of One Kind of
       Analysis.** Stockholm: Almqvist & Wiksell, 1974.   90
       pp.
"Some Mechanisms Involved in Homosexuality" (pp. 9-44)
offers recommendations for psychotherapy: if the resolution of the emotional problem with the parent of the same
sex is achieved, the homosexual inclination will subside.

3772. GROVES, PATRICIA A., and VENTURA, LOIS A. "The
       Lesbian Coming Out Process: Therapeutic Considera-
       tions," **Personnel and Guidance Journal,** 62 (1983),
       146-49.
Problems and therapeutic needs of women in the process of
identifying themselves as lesbian--including denial
rationales.

3773. GUILMOT, P. H. ["New Perspectives in Medico-psy-
       chological Help for Homosexuals"], **Acta Psychi-
       atrica Belgica,** 72 (1972), 265-315.
Homosexuality is not connected with any typical psychiatric disorder, and final acceptance is the goal of
therapy.

3774. HALL, MARNY. **The Lavender Couch: A Consumer's
       Guide to Psychotherapy for Lesbians and Gay Men.**
       Boston: Alyson, 1985. 178 pp.
Offers an overview of the "therapy marketplace" together
with strategies for engaging a therapist and continuing
the relationship. A veritable zoo of over 250 therapies
is presented by Richie Herink (ed.), **The Psychotherapy
Handbook** (New York: New American Library, 1980; 724
pp.). See also: Otto Ehrenberg and Miriam Ehrenberg,
**The Psychotherapy Maze: A Consumer's Guide to the Ins and
Outs of Therapy** (New York: Holt, 1977; 192 pp.).

3775. HART, JOHN. "Therapeutic Implications of Viewing
      Sexual Identity in Terms of Essentialist and Con-
      structionist Theories," JH, 9:4 (1984), 39-51.
Constructionist theory, while it holds promise, has not
taken into account clinical evidence that clients may
adhere to "essentialist" beliefs.

3776. HATTERER, LAWRENCE. Changing Homosexuality in the
      Male: Treatment for Men Troubled by Homosexuality.
      New York: McGraw-Hill, 1970. 492 pp.
Dispensing with sophisticated psychotherapeutic theories,
Hatterer retreats to an old-fashioned reliance on will
power and moral conformity. Unlike other clinicians who
have made similar claims, he gives a clear, often dis-
quieting picture of what occurs in his therapy sessions.

3777. HERRON, WILLIAM G., et al. "New Psychoanalytic
      Perspectives on the Treatment of a Homosexual
      Male," JH, 5 (1980), 393-403.
Emphasizes the value of a psychoanalytic model in helping
people to attain their desired sexual identities.

3778. HETRICK, EMERY, and TERRY STEIN (eds.). Innova-
      tions in Psychotherapy with Homosexuals. Washing-
      ton, DC: American Psychiatric Press, 1984. 131 pp.
Six papers addressing the question of how the therapeutic
process can aid in resolving the problems that result
from negative attitudes about gay and lesbian people.

3779. HINRICHSEN, JAMES J., and KATAHN, MARTIN. "Recent
      Trends and New Developments in the Treatment of
      Homosexuality," Current Theory, Research and
      Practice, 12 (1975), 83-92.
Treats psychoanalysis, hypnosis, brain surgery, aversive
conditioning, covert sensitization, and combined treat-
ments--generally from the standpoint of changing orientation. See the reply by Eugene May, ibid., 14 (1977), 18-
20.

3780. JANOV, ARTHUR. The Primal Revolution: Towards a
      Real World. New York: Simon and Schuster, 1970.
      447
In this account by its founder of one of the leading pop
psychiatric fashions of the 1970s, see pp. 83-97. See
also his The Primal Scream: Primal Therapy--The Case
for Neurosis (New York: Putnam's Sons, 1970), pp. 281--
321; and [anon.], "Can Primal Therapy Cure Homosexuality?" Journal of Primal Therapy, 3 (1976), 226-29.

3781. KAUFMAN, P., et al. "Distancing for Intimacy in
      Lesbian Relationships," American Journal of
      Psychiatry, 141 (1984), 530-33.
Describes a collaborative treatment approach for lesbian
couples who are experiencing problems within their rela-
tionships--especially those too closely merged.

3782. KRONEMEYER, ROBERT. **Overcoming Homosexuality.** New
      York: Macmillan, 1980. 220 pp.
Advocates his own "Syntonic Therapy," an eclectic mixture
of Reich, Perls, and Reik.

3783. LANGEVIN, RON, and REUBEN A. LANG. "Psychological
      Treatment of Pedophiles," **Behavioral Sciences and
      the Law,** 3 (1985), 403-19.
Group therapy and image therapy have been found useful in
overcoming such difficulties as the egocentric, egosynton-
ic, and erotically gratifying nature of pedophilia to
the patient, his unwillingness to give up his behavior,
his tendency to rationalize his acts, and to see the
child as consenting. Many references.

3784. LEGO, SUZANNE M. "Beginning Resolution of the
      Oedipal Conflict in a Lesbian about to Become a
      'Parent' to a Son," **Perspectives in Psychiatric
      Care,** 19 (1981), 107-11.
The article presents a series of dreams of a lesbian
patient, who was contemplating having a child by artificial insemination.

3785. MARSHALL, W. L. "The Modification of Sexual
      Fantasies: A Combined Treatment Approach to the
      Reduction of Deviant Sexual Behavior," **Behavior
      Research and Therapy,** 11 (1973), 557-64.
Contends that direct modification of fantasies will provide an effective treatment method, reporting on results
with homosexuals, fetishists, rapists, and pedophiles.

3786. MARTIN, APRIL. "Some Issues in the Treatment of
      Gay and Lesbian Patients," **Psychotherapy: Theory,
      Research and Practice,** 19 (1982), 341-48.
Homophobic attitudes are the major problem. The therapist
may inadvertently reinforce the patient's homophobia or
inquiry into the causes of the patient's homosexuality or
into his/her failure to function heterosexually.

3787. MEREDITH, R. L., and ROBERT W. RIESTER. "Psycho-
      therapy, Responsibility, and Homosexuality: Clin-
      ical Examination of Socially Deviant Behavior,"
      Professional Psychology, 11 (1980), 174-93.
Focuses on professional and ethical issues, adopting an
intermediate position on the question of homosexual
functioning.

3788. MILLER, PETER M., et al. "Review of Homosexuality
      Research (1960-1966) and Some Implications for
      Treatment," **Psychotherapy: Theory, Research and
      Practice,** 5 (1968), 3-6.
Finds two schools: One focuses upon the replacement of
homosexual behavior with heterosexual behavior; the other
has as its goal the elimination of anxiety and discomfort
in the homosexual, but not of his homosexual behavior per
se.

3789. MITCHELL, STEPHEN A. "The Psychoanalytic Treatment
       of Homosexuality: Some Technical Considerations,"
       International Review of Psycho-analysis, 8 (1981),
       63-80.
Holds that the directive-suggestive approach that has
dominated the treatment of homosexuality rests on unproven
presuppositions, a conceptual unclarity concerning the
nature of activity and passivity, and an overvaluing of
behavioral alterations at the expense of internal con-
structive factors.

3790. MORRISON, ELIZABETH G. "Lesbians in Therapy,"
       **Journal of Psychosocial Nursing and Mental Health
       Services,** 22:8 (1984), 18-22.
On the dynamics of lesbian dyads where there is intense
fusion and the devices that may be used to achieve
distancing.

3791. MORRISON, JAMES K. "Homosexual Fantasies and the
       Reconstructive Use of Imagery," **Journal of Mental
       Imagery,** 4 (1980), 165-68.
Claims that "imagery therapy" not only reduced unwanted
homosexual fantasies but other sumptoms as well.

3792. MURRAY, ROSANNA. "Lesbians in Therapy: An Examina-
       tion of Some Issues in Theory and Practice," **Com-
       prehensive Psychotherapy,** 3 (1981), 141-56.
Examines various theoretical frameworks--developmental,
experiential, and feminist--and their impact on lesbians.

3793. PHILIPS, DEBORA, et al. "Alternative Behavioral
       Approaches to the Treatment of Homosexuality,"
       Archives of Sexual Behavior, 5 (1976), 223-28.
The traditional mandatory attempt to eradicate homosexual
behavior has been expanded into three options: (a) modification of homosexual in favor of heterosexual behavior;
(b) enhancement of homosexual behavior; and (c) ignoring
homosexual behavior if it is functionally unrelated
to the presenting symptoms.

3794. RIDDLE, DOROTHY, and BARBARA SANG. "Psychotherapy
       with Lesbians," **Journal of Social Issues,** 34
       (1978), 84-100.
Traces three aspects of women's socialization--self-con-
cept, feminine sex-role behavior, and sexuality--that
have particular relevance for lesbians.

3795. ROBINSON, LILLIAN H. "Adolescent Homosexual
       Patterns: Psychodynamics and Therapy," **Adolescent
       Psychiatry,** 8 (1980), 422-36.
Examines the issue of whether to treat or not treat adolescents with sexual identity problems.

3796. ROTHBERG, BARBARA, and VIVIAN UBELL. "The Co-ex-
       istence of System: Theory and Feminism in Working

with Heterosexual and Lesbian Couples," **Women and Therapy**, 4 (1985), 19-36.
As feminists enter the field of couple and family therapy, they are faced with the issue of how to integrate feminism and family systems therapy. Offers some suggestions for achieving this.

3797. SHERNOFF, MICHAEL J. "Family Therapy for Lesbian and Gay Clients," **Social Work**, 29 (1984), 393-96.
Discusses self-disclosure to other family members such as parents or children, including possible legal complications. Also describes the use of "family sculpting" to clarify perceptions. See also Scott Wirth, "Coming Out Close to Home: Principles for Psychotherapy with Families of Lesbians and Gay Men," **Catalyst: A Socialist Journal of the Social Services**, 1 (1979), 6-23.

3798. SILVERSTEIN, CHARLES. "Homosexuality and the Ethics of Behavioral Intervention: Paper 2," **JH**, 2 (1977), 205-11.
Discusses the reasons why attempts to change sexual orientation are doomed to fail and what an appropriate treatment would be. See reply by Nathaniel McConaghy, ibid., 221-27. (For "Paper 1," see G. C. Davison, above).

3799. SOLOMON, KENNETH, and NORMAN B. LEVY (eds.). **Men in Transition: Theory and Therapy**. New York: Irvington, 1982. 515 pp.
Collection of papers concerned with contemporary male roles and their relationship to the practice of psychotherapy. Topics discussed include: male inexpressiveness; the older man; men's groups; and the effect of changing sex roles on male homosexuals.

3800. STERLING, DAVID LYN. **Sex in the Basic Personality**. Wichita, KN: Hubbard Dianetic Foundation, 1952. 180 pp.
In Dianetics [i.e. Scientology], homosexuality is thought to endanger "potential survival through the family unit." The hope of cure is offered through dianetic processing.

3801. SYMONDS, MARTIN. "Homosexuality in Adolescence," **Pennsylvania Psychiatric Quarterly**, 9 (1969), 15-24.
Therapy is to be directed primarily at reducing depression and feelings of isolation. (Nonetheless, the writer makes an implicit comparison with tuberculosis.)

3802. WETTSTEIN, ROBERT M. "A Pharmacological Approach to Sexually Deviant Behavior in the Community," **International Journal of Sociology of the Family**, 12:2 (1982), 155-62.
Advocates control of paraphilias (including fetishism, transvestism, pedophilia, s & m) through hormonal alteration of sexual arousal with antiandrogens. See also J. M. W. Bardford, above.

3803. WILLS, SUE. "The Psychologist and the Lesbian,"
       Refractory Girl, 9 (1975), 41-45.
While most lesbians have never sought treatment from a
psychiatrist, most have suffered because of them through
the ripple effect of the sickness theory.

                    G. DSM CONTROVERSY

A prolonged controversy, described in the entries below,
led the American Psychiatric Association to abandon its
earlier definitions of homosexuality as an illness, while
retaining the curious diagnostic category of "ego-dystonic
homosexuality." Apart from the outcome, the history of
the dispute is revealing for its indication of the major,
in some instances perhaps decisive role that political
considerations may play in the resolution of what the lay
public regards as purely scientific issues.

3804. AMERICAN PSYCHIATRIC ASSOCIATION [APA]. **Diagnostic
       and Statistical Manual of Mental Disorders** [DSM].
       Second ed. Washington, DC: American Psychiatric
       Association, 1968. 134 pp.
This version of the APA's standard manual, like the first
edition of 1952, incorporated the classification of homosexuality as a mental disorder (p. 44). After intense
discussion and prodding by gay activists, on December 15,
1973, the APA Board of Trustees voted to remove homosexuality per se from the manual, substituting "sexual orientation disturbance" for those individuals "who are
bothered by, in conflict with, or wish to change their
sexual orientation." When the third edition, often referred to as "DSM-III," appeared (Washington, DC: APA,
1980; 494 pp.), it was found to include controversial new
material defining "Ego-Dystonic Homosexuality" [302.00],
pp. 281-83. Hence the continuing debate among those who
(1) insist that homosexuality is still "sick" and the
definition of DSM-II should not have been changed; (2)
defenders of the DSM-III compromise; and (3) those who
feel that further liberalization should take place,
striking both "ego-dystonic homosexuality" and the paraphilias from the DSM.

3805. BAYER, RONALD. **Homosexuality and American Psychi-
       atry: The Politics of Diagnosis.** New York: Basic
       Books, 1981. 216 pp.
This excellent book is noteworthy not only for its clear
and balanced reconstruction of the discussions that lay
behind the APA's 1973 decision, but also for its presentation of the larger issue of psychiatry's saturation with
moral and political concerns. See also: Bayer and Robert
L. Spitzer, "Edited Correspondence on the Status of Homosexuality in DSM-III," **Journal of the History of the Be-**

havioral Sciences, 18 (1982), 32-52.

3806. FERLEMANN, MIMI. "Homosexuality," **Menninger Perspective,** 5 (1974), 24-27.
The APA classification has spurred much dialogue, which may eventually lead to a clearer understanding of homosexuality.

3807. FRIEDMAN, RICHARD F., et al. "Reassessment of Homosexuality and Transsexualism," **Annual Review of Medicine,** 27 (1976), 57-62.
Reviews changes in the DSM during the past quarter century reflecting alterations in views about the relationship between sexual orientation and psychopathology.

3808. HADDEN, SAMUEL B. "Homosexuality: Its Questioned Classification," **Psychiatric Annals,** 6 (1976), 165-69.
Disapproves of the APA's efforts to eliminate the definition of homosexuality as a disease.

3809. SILVERSTEIN, CHARLES. "The Ethical and Moral Implications of Sexual Classification: A Commentary," **JH,** 9:4 (1984), 29-38.
Offers two hypotheses to account for the APA's change in DSM-III: (1) homosexuality is now viable as a lifestyle and therefore has become socially regulated; and (2) the normal is the intractible. Further argues that there is no reason to keep the paraphilias in DSM. See also his: "Even Psychiatry Can Profit from Its Past Mistakes," **JH,** 2 (1976-77), 153-57.

3810. SMITH, JAIME. "Ego-Dystonic Homosexuality," **Comprehensive Psychiatry,** 21 (1980), 119-27.
An attempt to define the developmental stages and character of the purported syndrome. See also his: "Treatment of Ego-Dystonic Homosexuality: Individual and Group Psychotherapies," **Journal of the American Academy of Psychoanalysis,** 13 (1985), 399-412.

3811. SOCARIDES, CHARLES W. "The Sexual Deviations and the Diagnostic Manual," **American Journal of Psychotherapy,** 32 (1978), 414-26.
Argues that the "normalizing" of homosexuality and the consequent revision of DSM reflecting this position will slow scientific progress, produce despair in those with a sexual deviation, and diminish efforts at prophylaxis.

3812. SPITZER, ROBERT L. "The Diagnostic Status of Homosexuality in DSM-III: A Reformulation of the Issues," **American Journal of Psychiatry,** 138 (1981), 210-15.
Describes the controversy surrounding the creation of the DSM-III category of Ego-Dystonic Homosexuality, arguing that the major issue involves a value judgment about heterosexuality rather than a factual dispute about

homosexuality.

3813. STOLLER, ROBERT J., et al. "A Symposium: Should
       Homosexuality Be in the APA Nomenclature," **Amer-
       ican Journal of Psychiatry**, 130 (1973), 1207-16.
Summarizes papers on criteria for psychiatric diagnosis,
homosexuality as an adaptive disorder, homosexuality and
cultural value systems, the gay activist position, findings from fifteen years of clinical research, the question
of including heterosexuality in the APA nomenclature,
homosexuality as an irregular form of sexual behavior,
and sexual orientation disturbance as a psychiatric
disorder.

3814. SUPPE, FREDERICK. "Classifying Sexual Disord-
       ers: The Diagnostic and Statistical Manual of the
       American Psychiatric Association," **JH,** 9:4 (1984),
       9-28.
Argues that that same criteria that led to the removal of
homosexuality per se as a mental disorder require the removal of the paraphilias per se, and that while there is
legitimacy for a generalized ego-dystonic category, such
ego dystonias are only incidentally sexual. Suggests that
the recent classification of sexual disorders is merely
the codification of social mores.

                  H. BEHAVIOR THERAPY

This mode has sought to apply conditioning techniques in
order to rid the individual of presumably unwanted homosexual impulses. Although behavior therapy has had some
success with peripheral problems, such as phobias, it does
not seem well suited to effect such a profound change as
the altering of sexual orientation. A more appropriate
use, employed by a few behavior therapists, would be to
adapt the technique to help homosexual persons achieve a
better adjustment to their orientation.

3815. ADAMS, HENRY E., and ELLIE T. STURGIS. "Status of
       Behavorial Reorientation Techniques in the Modif-
       ication of Homosexuality: A Review," **Psychological
       Bulletin,** 84 (1977), 1171-88.
Attempts to summarize the critical components of the reorientation programs developed since 1963, examine their
outcomes, and discuss possible shortcomings of the procedures currently used.

3816. CALLAHAN, EDWARD J., and HAROLD LEITENBERG.
       "Aversion Therapy for Sexual Deviation: Contingent
       Shock and Covert Sensitization, **Journal of Abnormal
       Psychology,** 81 (1973), 60-73.
Covert sensitization, which provides an imagined aversive

event following imagined sexual behavior, appears to be
more effective than contingent shock, which provides a
physical aversive event following erection to slides depicting sexually deviant material.

3817. COLSON, CHARLES E. "Olfactory Aversion Therapy for
        Homosexual Behavior," **Journal of Behavior Therapy
        and Experimental Psychiatry,** 3 (1972), 185-87.
Describes the use of noxious olfactory stimuli--in particular, ampules of aromatic ammonia--as a relatively
simple method for inducing controlled physical aversion.

3818. CONRAD, STANLEY R., and JOHN P. WINCZE. "Orgasmic
        Reconditioning: A Controlled Study of Its Effects
        upon the Sexual Arousal and Behavior of Adult Male
        Homosexuals," **Behavior Therapy,** 7 (1976), 155-66.
Study does not support previous case reports of success
with the technique. Aversion therapy produced no change
in arousal by deviant stimuli and only slight increases
in arousal by heterosexual stimuli.

3819. EARLS, CHRISTOPHER M., and VERNON L. QUINSEY.
        "What is To Be Done? Future Research on the
        Assessment and Behavioral Treatment of Sex
        Offenders," **Behavioral Sciences and the Law,**
        3 (1985), 377-90.
With regard to the problem of aggressive men, recommends
three directions: the extension and refinement of assessment methods, the further development of treatment techniques, and long-term follow-ups.

3820. FAUSTMAN, WILLIAM O. "Aversive Control of Maladap-
        tive Sexual Behavior: Past Developments and Future
        Trends," **Psychology,** 13 (1976), 53-60.
Traces the evolution and present status of the application
of aversion therapy to homosexuality, fetishism, and
transvestism, noting the generally poor outcomes obtained
with homosexuals.

3821. FELDMAN, M. P. "The Treatment of Homosexuality by
        Aversion Therapy," in: Hugh Freeman (ed.), **Progress
        in Behaviour Therapy: Proceedings of a Symposium.**
        Bristol: John Wright, 1968, pp. 59-72.
In this early report of the method, Feldman claims that
of the 43 patients treated, 25 were rated as "improved"
one year later. He concedes that a pretreatment history
of heterosexual interest is critical. See also (among
other contributions), Feldman and Malcolm J. MacCulloch,
Homosexual Behaviour: Therapy and Assessment (Oxford: Pergamon, 1971; 288 pp.); as well as Tomi S. MacDonough,
"A Critique of the First Feldman and MacCulloch Avoidance Conditioning Treatment for Homosexuals," **Behavior
Therapy,** 3 (1972), 104-11; and Sheelah James, "Treatment of Homosexuality," **Behavior Therapy,** 8 (1977),
840-48; 9 (1978), 28-36.

3822. GIJS, LUK. "Accepterende gedragstherapie, homosek-
       suele orientatie en uitbouw van een homoseksuele
       identiteit," **Gedragstherapie** (Netherlands), 16
       (1983), 87-103.
Reviews current viewpoints of behavior therapists on
conversion therapies for homosexuality and strategies for
improving homosexual functioning, discussing self-acceptance, coming out, and homosexual identity formation.

3823. HERMAN, STEVEN H., et al. "An Experimental
       Analysis of Classical Conditioning as a Method of
       Increasing Heterosexual Arousal in Homosexuals,"
       Behavior Therapy, 5 (1974), 33-47.
Studies the use of classical conditioning of sexual
response to female stimuli, using slides and films.

3824. MCCONAGHY, NATHANIEL, et al. "Controlled Compar-
       ison of Aversive Therapy and Covert Sensitization
       in Compulsive Homosexuality," **Behavior Research and
       Therapy,** 19 (1981), 425-34.
Attempted to evaluate behavior therapy for homosexuals in
response to ethical objections for such treatment. See
also: McConaghy, "Aversive Therapy of Homosexuality: Measures of Efficacy," **American Journal of Psychiatry,** 127
(1971), 1221-24; "Is a Homosexual Orientation Irreversible?" **British Journal of Psychiatry,** 129 (1976), 556-
63; and "Subjective and Penile Plethysmograph Responses
to Aversion Therapy for Homosexuality: A Follow-up
Study," ibid., 117 (1970), 555-60--among other studies by
this prolific Australian advocate of changing homosexual
behavior.

3825. MANDEL, K. H. "Probleme und Ansätze der Verhalt-
       enstherapie bei männlichen Homosexuellen," **Zeit-
       schrift für Psychotherapie und medizinische Psy-
       chologie,** 20 (1970), 115-25.
Recommends covert sensitization of male homosexuals with
the goal of establishing a stable heterosexual partnership.

3826. PRADHAN, P. V. "Homosexuality: Treatment by
       Behavior Modification," **Indian Journal of Psychi-
       atry,** 24 (1982), 80-83.
A marriageable age and indirect social pressures were
positively correlated with "improvement" in conjunction
with chemical, verbal and electrical aversive stimuli.

3827. ROSS, MICHAEL W. "Paradigm Lost or Paradigm
       Regained? Behaviour Therapy and Homosexuality," **New
       Zealand Psychologist,** 6 (1977), 42-51.
Critical examination of some ethical, ideological, and
practical problems posed by attempts to change sexual
orientation through behavior modification methods.

3828. WATSON, G. TERENCE, and GERALD C. DAVISON. "Beha-
       vior Therapy and Homosexuality: A Critical Perspec-

tive," **Behavior Therapy,** 5 (1974), 16-28.
Examines the rationale for the use of aversive techniques
in behavior therapy of homosexuality, suggesting an
expanded therapeutic regimen derived from learning theory.

I. GROUP THERAPY

Group therapy emerged in the 1960s as part of the trend
toward innovative therapies, and also as a way of reducing
the high costs entailed by individual therapy. The tendency also drew on the psychodrama model, which had been
pioneered in institutional settings.

3829.   BIEBER, TOBY. "Group and Individual Therapy with
        Male Homosexuals," **Journal of the American Academy
        of Psychoanalysis,** 2 (1974), 255-60.
After an initial period of individual therapy, group work
is recommended in order to effect shifts to heterosexuality.

3830.   BIRK, LEE. "Group Therapy for Men Who Are Homosex-
        ual," **Journal of Sex and Marital Therapy,** 1 (1974),
        29-52.
Contends that male-female group psychotherapy can foster
models, support, and reinforcement for new behavior: heterosexual interest and activity, increased assertiveness,
identification with the male therapist, and the emotional
experience of simultaneous rapport with the man and the
woman.

3831.   BROMBERG, WALTER, and GIRARD H. FRANKLIN. "The
        Treatment of Sexual Deviates with Group Psycho-
        drama," **Group Psychotherapy,** 4 (1952), 274-89.
Reports on work with men committed to Mendocino State
Hospital under California's sex psychopath law.

3832.   GERSHMAN, HARRY. "The Effect of Group Therapy on
        Compulsive Homosexuality in Men and Women," **Amer-
        ican Journal of Psychoanalysis,** 35 (1975), 303-12.
Seeks not to convert the patient to heterosexuality, but
to promote personal growth and self-acceptance through
confrontation, clarification, interpretation, and working
through his own feelings.

3833.   HADDEN, SAMUEL B. "Group Psychotherapy of Male
        Homosexuals," **Current Psychiatric Therapies,** 6
        (1966), 177-86.
In order to change orientation prefers groups consisting
solely of homosexuals to mixed groups (homosexuals and
heterosexuals). See also: Hindy Nobler, "Group Therapy
with Male Homosexuals," **Comparative Group Studies,** 3
(1972), 161-78; and Frank S. Pittman and Carol D. De

Young, "The Treatment of Homosexuals in Heterogeneous Groups," **International Journal of Group Psychotherapy,** 21 (1971), 62-73.

3834. JOHNSGARD, KEITH W., and RAY M. SCHUMACHER. "The Experience of Intimacy in Group Psychotherapy with Male Homosexuals," **Psychotherapy: Theory, Research and Practice,** 7 (1970), 173-76.
In working with college students to assist them in adjusting to their own homosexuality, it was found that "growth occurs in a therapeutic environment where more than one therpaist is involved and where emphasis is placed on increased therapist and client transparency in immediate emotional confrontation."

3835. ROGERS, CARL, et al. "Group Therapy with Homosexuals: A Review," **International Journal of Group Therapy,** 26 (1976), 3-27.
In a comprehensive review of the clinical literature, a "favorable outcome" was found in almost all cases whether the goal was one of achieving a change in sexual orientation or a reduction in the associated problems.

3836. SCOTT, JAMES M. and KENNETH N. ANCHOR. "Male Homosexual Behavior and Ego Function Strategies in the Group Encounter," **Journal of Clinical Psychology,** 33 (1977), 1079-84.
Analyzes characteristic patterns of interaction in a group treatment context according to both psychodynamic and behavioral criteria.

3837. TRUAX, RICHARD, and GARFIELD TOURNEY. "Male Homosexuals in Group Psychotherapy: A Controlled Study," **Diseases of the Nervous System,** 32 (1971), 707-11.
Contends that group work is efficacious in overcoming the homosexual's defense mechanisms of isolation, rationalization, and denial.

3838. WALKER, CAROLYN B. "Psychodrama: An Experiential Study of Its Effectiveness within the Homosexual Society," **Group Psychotherapy and Psychodrama,** 27 (1974), 83-97.
As an instrument of personal growth, psychodrama permits the homosexual to be his private, real self and to face roles and situations to which a successful adjustment has not been made.

J.   RELIGIOUS AND RELATED "CURES"

From the first appearance of psychotherapy as an organized discipline in North America, a certain affinity with established religion was evident. Both fields take upon

themselves the "care of souls." In recent years some
religionists, many of them fundamentalists, have claimed
the capacity to effect lasting sexual reorientation. However, the validity of these claims has been sharply
questioned as a result of follow-up studies.

3839. AARON, WILLIAM (pseud.). **Straight: A Heterosexual
       Talks about His Homosexual Past.** Garden City,
       NY: Doubleday, 1972. 217 pp.
In this popular autobiographical work the writer perceives
his past as empty and futile.

3840. BLAIR, RALPH. **Ex-gay.** New York: Homosexual
       Community Counseling Center, 1982. 50 pp.
A vigorous and well-informed critique of ostensible
"cures" achieved by the Christian right, and the manipula-
tion of reports of them for ideological purposes.

3841. EYRICH, HOWARD A. "Help for the Homosexual: The
       Case for Nouthetic Help," **Journal of Pastoral
       Practice**, 1:2 (1977), 19-33.
Contends that as a learned behavior, homosexuality can
be overcome through sympathetic "nouthetic counseling."

3842. GIL, V. E. "Homosexuality: A Reparative View,"
       Social Work and Christianity, 11:2 (1984), 10-28.
Rejecting the idea that a homosexual orientation is
"unchangeable," the author presents a reparative model to
point the individual to Jesus as the definitive answer to
external anxiety.

3843. KRANZ, SHELDON. **The H Persuasion: How Persons Have
       Permanently Changed from Homosexuality through the
       Study of Aesthetic Realism.** New York: Definition
       Press, 1971. 136 pp.
Personal testimonies of individuals who claim to have
achieved permanent reorientation through techniques
evolved within a metaphysical system (regarded by some
as a personality cult) founded by Eli Siegel.

3844. PATTISON, E. MANSELL and MYRNA L. PATTISON.
       "Ex-gays: Religiously Mediated Change in Homosexu-
       als," **American Journal of Psychiatry**, 137 (1980),
       1553-62.
Discusses eleven men purported to have changed sexual
orientation from exclusive homosexuality through participation in a pentacostal church fellowship. The claims
were sharply criticized in the subsequent discussion,
ibid., 138 (1980), 852-53.

3845. PERON, JIM. **Homosexuality and the Miracle Makers.**
       Glen Ellyn, IL: The author, 1978. 20 pp.
Seeks to show that the "cures" promised by various religious groups are not lasting or significant.

3846.   PHILPOTT, KENT. **The Third Sex? Six Homosexuals
        Tell Their Story.** Plainfield, NJ: Logos Inter-
        national, 1975. 208 pp.
Testimonies of changed lives, biblical passages concerning
homosexuality, and guidelines for counseling homosexuals
"toward freedom in Christ." See also his: **The Gay Theology** (Plainfield: Logos, 1977; 194 pp.).

3847.   POWELL, JOHN R. "Understanding Male Homosexual-
        ity: Developmental Recapitulation in a Christian
        Perspective," **Psychology and Theology,** 2:3 (1974),
        163-73.
Recommends the concept of developmental recapitulation,
linked to biblical teachings, as a means of guiding
therapy.

3848.   STRONG, STANLEY R. "Christian Counseling with
        Homosexuals," **Psychology and Theology,** 8 (1980),
        279-87.
Presents a theological rationale and a therapeutic method
for helping homosexuals change orientation through "trust-
ing in the power of the Holy Spirit."

                    K. SEX THERAPY

The increased understanding of the mechanisms of coitus
achieved by Masters and Johnson encouraged many therapists
to address the problem of sexual dysfunction. Most of
this work concerns heterosexual couples, though a few
therapists have addressed themselves wholly or partly to
homosexuals.

3849.   EVERAERD, WALTER, et al. "Treatment of Homosexual
        and Heterosexual Sexual Dysfunction in Male-Only
        Groups of Mixed Sexual Orientation," **Archives of
        Sexual Behavior,** 11 (1982), 1-10.
Reports considerable success with subjects who were regarded as hard to treat, having had a sexual dysfunction
averaging six years.

3850.   GUTSTADT, JOSEPH P. "Male Pseudoheterosexuality
        and Minimal Sexual Dysfunction," **Journal of Sex and
        Marital Therapy,** 2 (1976), 297-302.
When the patient can be helped to a comfortable acceptance
of his homosexual feelings, very often the dysfunction is
relieved, and there is a marked change in the ability of
the individual to achieve gratification in genuine heterosexuality.

3851.   KAPLAN, HELEN SINGER. **The Evaluation of Sexual
        Disorders: Psychological and Medical Aspects.** New
        York: Brunner/Mazel, 1983. 352 pp.
A comprehensive work divided into three major sections.

The first section, on psychological aspects, emphasizes
that it is important clearly to separate organic and
psychogenic causes. Section Two analyzes the medical
elements involved in sexual disorders. Section Three
offers a combined, integrative approach. See also her:
**Disorders of Sexual Desire; and Other New Concepts and
Techniques in Sex Therapy** (New York: Simon and Schuster,
1979; 238 pp.).

3852. McWHIRTER, DAVID P., and ANDREW M. MATTISON. "The
       Treatment of Sexual Dysfunction in Gay Male
       Couples," **Journal of Sex and Marital Therapy**, 4
       (1978), 213-18.
Reports encouraging results in a two-year experience in
treating sexual dysfunction in 22 gay male couples. See
also their: "Treatment of Sexual Dysfunction in Homosexual Male Couples," in: S. R. Leiblum and L. A. Pervin
(eds.), **Principles and Practice of Sex Therapy** (New York:
Guilford Press, 1980), pp. 321-45.

3853. MASTERS, WILLIAM H., and VIRGINIA E. JOHNSON.
       Homosexuality in Perspective. Boston: Little,
       Brown, 1979. 450 pp.
After their two major studies of heterosexuals, the noted
sex researchers undertook a laboratory study of the sexual
functioning of male and female homosexuals. It was found
that homosexual couples tend to understand each other's
sexual needs better than heterosexual ones. There was no
difference in sexual response between the two groups. The
book presents a therapeutic program for treating homosexual dysfunction and dissatisfaction. Some doubts have
been raised about claims for reorienting homosexuals to
heterosexuality, though in fairness it must be noted that
this was not the study's main purpose.

XVIII. FAMILY

A. HOMOSEXUALITY AND (HETEROSEXUAL) MARRIAGE

Until recently it was common for some therapists and
ministers to advise male homosexuals and lesbians to marry
in order to be "cured." In many instances unhappiness and
even tragedy ensued for both parties. Perhaps more common, especially for the female partner, is the situation
whereby pre-lesbian (or pre-homosexual) individuals marry
before they have achieved an understanding of their orientation. A third type is one in which a marriage is
contracted, for friendship or convenience, or even to
deceive straight society, with the clear understanding
that one or both parties will remain homosexual. See also
"Couples," XIV.H.

3854. BOZETT, FREDERICK W. "Heterogeneous Couples in
       Heterosexual Marriages: Gay Men and Straight
       Women," **Journal of Marital and Family Therapy,** 8
       (1982), 81-89.
Discusses the nature of the spousal relationships and the
almost inevitable marital disruption that occurs when a
husband discloses his homosexuality to his wife.

3855. DANK, BARRY M. "Why Homosexuals Marry Women,"
       Medical Aspects of Human Sexuality, 6:8 (1972),
       14-23.
Lacking any clear alternative at the age of marital
eligibility, many homosexuals follow the socially acceptable heterosexual marriage path, sometimes later con-
structing a gay identity.

3856. HATTERER, MYRA S. "The Problems of Women Married
       to Homosexual Men," **American Journal of Psychiatry,**
       131 (1974), 275-78.
Contends that in a therapeutic situation the wife's need
to maintain the "neurotic contract" of the marriage undermines her husband's treatment.

3857. HIRSCHFELD, MAGNUS. "Sind sexuelle Zwischenstufen
       zur Ehe geeignet?" **JfsZ,** 3 (1901), 39-71.
An early canvasing by the noted sexologist of the suitability of "sexual intermediates" for marriage.

3858. IMIELIŃSKI, KAZIMIERZ. "Homosexuality in Males
       with Particular Reference to Marriage," **Psychother-**
       apy and Psychosomatics, 17 (1969), 126-32.
A Polish researcher suggests that marriage may be appropriate for those who are (or who have attained through
therapy) the Kinsey 1 and 2 classes. For the 3-6 groups

it is not recommended.

3859. LATHAM, J. DAVID, and GEOFFREY D. WHITE. "Coping
       with Homosexual Expression within Heterosexual
       Marriages: Five Case Studies," **Journal of Sex and
       Marital Therapy,** 4 (1978), 198-212.
Presents five case studies of marriages where the homosexual partner's disclosure to the spouse was evident, examining the coping mechanisms involved when such marriages
do not end in divorce.

3860. MACKLIN, ELEANOR D. "Nontraditional Family
       Forms: A Decade of Research," **Journal of Marriage
       and the Family,** 42 (1980), 905-22.
Reviews research in several areas of alternatives to
the traditional nuclear family (including voluntary
childlessness, the binuclear family, and intimate same-sex
relationships)--with many references.

3861. MADDOX, BRENDA. **Married and Gay.** New York: Har-
       court Brace Jovanovich, 1982. 220 pp.
"[J]ust as there are happy homosexual couples, there are
some ... homo-heterosexual marriages that are good by
anybody's standards. ... [T]here may be a compatibility
and congruence in the man-woman relationship that trans-
cends sex."

3862. NUGENT, ROBERT. "Married Homosexuals," **Journal of
       Pastoral Care,** 37 (1983), 243-51.
Discusses the issues of homosexuality in heterosexual
marriage with regard to motivations for marriage, church
ministry with married homosexuals, solutions to married
homosexual dilemmas, and preventive approaches.

3863. ROSS, H. LAURENCE. "Modes of Adjustment of Married
       Homosexuals," **Social Problems,** 18 (1971), 385-93.
From interviews with eleven Belgian couples draws a profile of reasons for marriage and the nature of the ongoing relationship (platonic marriage, double-standard
marriage, and innovative marriage). See also his: "Odd
Couples: Homosexuals in Heterosexual Marriages," **Sexual
Behavior,** 2:7 (1972), 42-49.

3864. ROSS, MICHAEL W. **The Married Homosexual Man: A
       Psychological Study.** Boston: Routledge and Kegan
       Paul, 1983. 184 pp.
With regard to heterosexually married men, discusses the
reasons for marriage, internal problems, outside societal
pressures, and comparisons with other homosexuals (who are
either married and separated or never married) and bisexuals. Although the author works chiefly in Australia,
he provides international comparisons, together with a
review of the literature.

B. LESBIAN MOTHERS

According to older stereotypes, lesbians and male homosexuals do not, with a very few exceptions, have children.
We now know that there are many lesbian mothers who are
bringing up their children either singly, or with a female
"significant other." The disapproval that these arrangements sometimes incur unleashes custody battles; see
XVIII.D. Another issue is artificial insemination, an
option chosen by some lesbians who wish to have a child
without having sexual relations with a man.

3865. ABBITT, DIANE, and BOBBIE BENNETT. "Being a
        Lesbian Mother," in: Betty Berzon and Robert
        Leighton (eds.), **Positively Gay.** Millbrae, CA:
        Celestial Arts, 1979, 123-29.
Experiences of two lesbian mothers who are raising two
boys and two girls; they stress candor and basic parenting
skills.

3866. AGBAYEWA, M. OLUWAFEMI. "Fathers in the Newer
        Family Forms: Male or Female?" **Canadian Journal of
        Psychiatry,** 29 (1984), 402-06.
Suggests that women may function as fathers in the newer
family forms.

3867. BLACKMON, MARY K. **In the Best Interests of the
        Children.** Binghamton, NY: Iris, 1977. 21 pp.
Resource pamphlet for lesbian mothers by the maker of
the film of the same title.

3868. EBERT, ALLEN. "Lea Hopkins: Just Different,"
        Essence, 10:12 (April 1980), 88-89, 122, 124, 127,
        128, 130, 134.
Black lesbian mother living in the Midwest speaks of her
relations with her parents, her white lover, and her
son.

3869. GIBSON, CLIFFORD G., and MARY JO RISHER. **By Her
        Own Admission: A Lesbian Mother's Fight to Keep Her
        Son.** Garden City, NY: Doubleday, 1977. 276 pp.
Sympathetic account of a much-publicized Texas case in
which the divorced heterosexual father used economic
pressure and the courts to alienate a son's affection
from his mother.

3870. GOODMAN, BERNICE. "The Lesbian Mother," **American
        Journal of Orthopsychiatry,** 43 (1973), 283-84.
In a two-year study of heterosexual and lesbian mothers,
found that similarities far exceeded differences. Lesbian
mothers did need, however, to work through their sense of
guilt.

3871. HALL, MARNY. "Lesbian Families: Cultural and

Clinical Issues," **Social Work,** 23:5 (1978), 380-85.
Showing that the feminist and gay movement have fostered
greater openness among lesbian mothers and their companions, Hall urges social workers and other professionals
to be supportive so as to promote self-esteem.

3872. HANSCOMBE, GILLIAN E., and JACKIE FOSTER. **Rocking
      the Cradle: Lesbian Mothers: A Challenge in Family
      Living.** Boston: Alyson, 1982. 153 pp.
Based chiefly on English experience,offers considerable
attention to artificial insemination (AID) and the con-
troversy this procedure has aroused. See also: Roger
Higgs et al., "Lesbian Couples: Should Help Extend to
AID?" **Journal of Medical Ethics,** 4 (1978), 91-95; and
Donna Hitchens, **Lesbians Choosing Motherhood: The Implica-
tions of Donor Insemination.** (San Francisco: Lesbian
Rights Project, 1984); and D. G. Wolf, below.

3873. HITCHENS, DONNA J., and ANN G. THOMAS (eds.),
      **Lesbian Mothers and Their Children: An Annotated
      Bibliography of Legal and Psychological Materials.**
      Second ed. San Francisco: Lesbian Rights Project,
      1983. 67 pp.
Useful handbook covering legal aspects (including case
reports and law review articles) and social science aspects (functioning and adjustment of lesbians, mothering
among lesbians, mental health, and children). Annotations are detailed and critical; some sections preceded
by "Introduction and Summary."

3874. JULLION, JEANNE. **Long Way Home: The Odyssey of a
      Lesbian Mother and Her Children.** Pittsburgh: Cleis
      Press, 1985. 272 pp.
Personal account of the international campaign of a California lesbian to recover custody of her two boys.

3875. KLEIN, CAROLE. **The Single Parent Experience.** New
      York: Walker, 1973. 241 pp.
"Homosexual Parents" (pp. 77-90) argues that American
society is growing more receptive to alternative concepts
of sex role and sexual identity, which tends to make them
more accepting of lesbians and male homosexuals as parents.

3876. LEICK, NINI, and JOHN NIELSEN. **Om lesbiske fam-
      ilier.** Copenhagen: Studenterradet ved Kobenhavns
      Universitet, 1973. 162 pp.
A study of Danish lesbian families undertaken in the
psychology department of Copenhagen University.

3877. LEWIN, ELLEN, and TERRIE A. LYONS. "Everything in
      Its Place: The Coexistence of Lesbianism and
      Motherhood," in: William Paul et al. (eds.), **Homo-
      sexuality: Social, Psychological and Biological
      Issues.** Beverly Hills, CA: Sage, 1982, pp. 249-73.
Reports on a four-year study in the San Francisco Bay area

of adaptive strategies employed by lesbian and heterosexual single mothers, which disclosed substantial similarities between the two groups (salience of motherhood,
support from kin, role of friendship ties, intimate
relationships, relations with ex-husbands, and threats
to child custody). See also: Lewin, "Lesbianism and
Motherhood: Implications for Child Custody," **Human Organization**, 40 (1981), 6-14.

3878. LYONS, TERRIE. "Lesbian Mothers' Custody Fears,"
        Women and Therapy, 2 (1983), 231-40.
Comparison of lesbian and heterosexual mothers showed
remarkable congruence, with one exception: the lesbians
were disturbed by persistent custody fears. Court-awarded
custody is never final and can be challenged from a number
of sources.

3879. MUCKLOW, BONNIE M., and GALDYS K. PHELAN. "Lesbian
        and Traditional Mothers' Responses to Adult Re-
        sponse to Child Behavior and Self-Concept," **Psy-
        chological Reports**, 44 (1979), 880-82.
Analyses showed no difference in response to children's
behavior or in self-concept of lesbian and traditional
mothers.

3880. OSMAN, SHELOMO. "My Stepfather is a She," **Family
        Process**, 11 (1972), 209-18.
In this case presentation of a lesbian couple and their
two sons in treatment, the therapist holds that unre-
solved conflict about sexual preference may produce
therapeutic problems both for the adults and the children.

3881. PAGELOW, MILDRED D. "Heterosexual and Lesbian
        Single Mothers: A Comparison of Problems, Coping,
        and Solutions," **JH,** 5 (1980), 189-204.
While both groups reported oppression in the areas of
freedom of association, employment, housing, and child
custody, the degree of perceived oppression was greater
for lesbian mothers.

3882. SAPHIRA, MIRIAM. **Amazon Mothers**. Ponsonby, New
        Zealand: Papers, Inc., 1984. 86 pp.
Presents results of four years of research of lesbian
motherhood, based on a questionnaire filled out by
lesbians who have children, together with interview.

3883. SCHLESINGER, BENJAMIN. **The One-Parent Family in
        the 1980s: Perspectives and Annotated Bibliog-
        raphy.** Toronto: University of Toronto Press,
        1986. 284 pp.
Five essays review the literature from a variety of
perspectives, and a comprehensive bibliography includes
some 500 annotations of materials published between 1978
and 1984.

3884. SHAVELSON, EILEEN, et al. "Lesbian Women's Percep-

tions of Their Parent-Child Relationships," **JH**, 5
(1979-80), 205-15.
In a comparison with heterosexual mothers, differences
were found concerning sex-role adherence, with lesbian
women being more masculinely sex-role typed and more
satisfied in their sex lives.

3885. SOMERVILLE, MARGARET A. "Birth Technology, Parenting and 'Deviance,'" **International Journal of Law
and Psychiatry**, 5 (1982), 123-53.
Discusses the nature of the right to reproduce; birth
technology and homosexual, lesbian, transsexual, single,
and unmarried parents; the mentally retarded as parents;
and custody of and access to children.

3886. SUTTON, STUART. "Lesbian Family: Rights in
Conflict under the California Uniform Parentage
Act," **Golden Gate University Law Review**, 10 (1980),
1007-41.
On legal problems which may arise for lesbians who choose
to have children through artificial insemination or sexual
intercourse. Reviews both the U. S. Supreme Court cases
concerning parental rights and the provisions of California's Uniform Parentage Act.

3887. WOLF, DEBORAH GOLEMAN. "Lesbian Mothers and Artificial Insemination: A Wave of the Future," in:
Margarita Artschwager Kay (ed.), **Anthropology of
Human Birth**. Philadelphia: F. A. Davis, 1982, pp.
321-39.
The number of lesbians who are choosing to have children
through artificial insemination is small but growing. The
situation gives rise to two needs to which the health care
profession should respond; 1) a much greater flexibility
with hospital routine so that the mother's psychic needs
are considered; and 2) a health model of birth.

                         C. GAY FATHERS

Gay fathers are less likely than lesbian mothers to seek
full custody of their children, but they do generally
aspire to visiting rights. In many cities of North
America support groups of gay fathers have come into
existence, providing practical and emotional self-help for
these men.

3888. BOZETT, FREDERICK W. "Gay Fathers: Evolution of
the Gay-Father Identity," **American Journal of
Orthopsychiatry**, 51 (1981), 55259.
Interview data indicate that identity congruence evolves
over time as the men participate in both the world of
fathers and the world of gays. See also his "Gay Fath-

ers: How and Why They Disclose Their Homosexuality to
Their Children," **Family Relations,** 29 (1980), 173-79;
and "Gay Fathers: Identity Conflict Resolution through
Integrative Sanctioning," **Alternate Lifestyles,** 4 (1981),
90-107.

3889. FADIMAN, ANNE. "The Double Closet: How Two Gay
        Fathers Deal with Their Children and Ex-Wives,"
        Life Magazine, 6:5 (May 1983), 76-100.
Presents the life of a gay male couple, including relations with the men's former wives and the children of
the broken marriages.

3890. **Gay Fathers: Some of Their Stories, Experience and
        Advice.** Toronto: Gay Fathers of Toronto, 1981. 74
        pp.
Experiential account from one of the most successful of
the gay fathers' groups that have sprung up in North
America. See also: Michael Lynch, "Forgotten Fathers,"
in: Stan Persky and Ed Jackson (eds.), **Flaunting It!**
(Vancouver: New Star, 1982), pp. 54-63.

3891. MILLER, BRIAN. "Unpromised Paternity: Life-Styles
        of Gay Fathers," in: Martin P. Levine (ed.), **Gay
        Men: The Sociology of Male Homosexuality.** New
        York: Harper and Row, 1979, pp. 239-52.
Interviews with forty homosexual fathers disclose four
distinct life styles and the importance of relationships
with spouse and children. See also his: "Gay Fathers
and Their Children," **Family Coordinator,** 28 (1979),
544-52; as well as Bruce Voeller and James Walters, "Gay
Fathers," ibid., 27 (1978), 149-57.

3892. ROBINSON, BRYAN E., and PATSY SKEEN. "Sex-Role
        Orientation of Gay Fathers Versus Gay Nonfathers,"
        Perceptual and Motor Skills, 55 (1982), 1055-59.
Bem Sex-Role Inventory results show that gay fathers were
no more masculine than gay nonfathers.

3893. SKEEN, PATSY, and BRYAN E. ROBINSON. "Gay Fathers'
        and Gay Nonfathers' Relationship with Their
        Parents," **Journal of Sex Research,** 21 (1985), 86-
        91.
Results of a study of 60 men (30 + 30) found no difference
between the father's and nonfathers' perceptions of their
parents' acceptance of them. This finding supports the
growing body of research that questions the Freudian-
based concept of a causal relationship between early
familial relationship patterns and sexual orientation.

                        D. CUSTODY

The increasing visibility of lesbian mothers (and a few

gay fathers) who seek to bring up their children after
separation from the heterosexual parent has focused
attention on custody problems. The legal literature on
this subject is presented here, rather than in the Law
sections below.

3894. ARMANNO, BENNA F. "The Lesbian Mother: Her Right
        to Child Custody," **Golden Gate Law Review**, 4
        (1973), 1-18.
Summarizes California law on the child custody issue and
the precedents existing at the time of writing.

3895. BROWNSTONE, HARVEY. "Homosexual Parent in Custody
        Disputes," **Queen's Law Journal** (1980), 199-240.
Surveys both Canadian and U.S. cases, comparing treatment
of "immoral" heterosexuals with that of homosexuals.

3896. CAMPBELL, ROSE W. "Child Custody When One Parent
        is a Homosexual," **Judges Journal**, 17 (1978), 38-41;
        51-52.
A judge's reservations stemming from two lesbian mother
cases she has tried.

3897. CARDWELL, GARY L. "Doe vs. Doe: Destroying the
        Presumption that Homosexual Parents Are Unfit--The
        New Burden of Proof," **University of Richmond Law
        Review**, 16 (1982), 851-66.
The precedent set in Doe v. Doe instructs Virginia courts
to adhere to some more precise burden of proof as to the
homosexual factor in adoption, and probably, custody proceedings.

3898. CHESSLER, PHYLLIS. **Mothers on Trial: The Battle
        for Children and Custody.** New York: McGraw-Hill,
        1985. 651 pp.
Based on interviews with 60 women who were challenged
for custody in 1960-81, this radical feminist statement
of the case is marred by some contestable statistics.

3899. EVANS, MARIE WESTON. "M. J. P. v. J. G. P.: An
        Analysis of the Relevance of Parental Homosexuality
        in Child Custody Determinations," **Oklahoma Law
        Review**, 35 (1982), 633-58.
In child custody determinations, the best interests of
the child are served by continuing placement with the
psychological parent.

3900. GOODMAN, ELLEN. "Homosexuality of a Parent: A New
        Issue in Custody Disputes," **Monash Law Review**, 5
        (1978-79), 305-15.
Summary of Australian court decisions in child custody
issues involving lesbian mothers. While homosexuality
per se has been held not to render a parent unfit, some
Australian courts have found children to be adversely
affected by their mother's orientation. See also: Kate

Harrison, "Child Custody and Parental Sexuality: Just
Another Factor?" **Refractory Girl,** no. 20-21 (October
1980), 7-14; and Robyn Plaister, **Lesbian Mothers,** Campaign, no. 42 (April 1979), 13-14.

3901. HARRIS, BARBARA S. "Lesbian Mother Child Custody:
      Legal and Psychiatric Aspects," **Bulletin of the
      American Academy of Psychiatry and Law,** 5 (1977),
      75-89.
Summarizes the major reported cases, discussing misconceptions and how they can be dispelled by scientific research
findings.

3902. HITCHENS, DONNA. "Social Attitudes, Legal Stan-
      dards, and Personal Trauma in Child Custody Cases,"
      JH, 5 (1979-80), 89-95.
Lesbian mother cases and gay father visitation cases are
increasingly successful in the courts. The main hurdle
continues to be the lack of objective legal standards that
could make the outcome of these cases predictable.

3903. HITCHENS, DONNA, and BARBARA PRICE. "Trial Strat-
      egy in Lesbian Mother Cases: The Use of Expert
      Testimony," **Golden Gate University Law Review,** 9
      (1978-79), 451-79.
On the value of expert testimony in rebutting commonly
held misconceptions about the conseqences of raising
children in a lesbian household.

3904. HUNTER, NAN D., and NANCY D.POLIKOFF. "Custody
      Rights of Lesbian Mothers: Legal Theory and
      Litigation Strategy," **Buffalo Law Review,** 25
      (1976), 691-733.
Summarizing current law, argues that advocates should work
toward establishing a requirement that a specific logical
nexus be shown between a mother's lesbianism and her
ostensible unfitness as a parent before she can be denied
custody based on her homosexuality.

3905. LEITCH, PATRICIA. "Custody: Lesbian Mothers in the
      Courts," **Gonzaga Law Review,** 16 (1980), 147-70.
Focusing on Washington State, surveys lesbian mother
cases, esp. Schuster v. Schuster.

3906. MILLER, SUZANNE. "Rights of Homosexual Parents,"
      Journal of Juvenile Law, 7 (1985), 155-59.
Even though societal tolerance for alternative lifestyles
seems to be growing, the courts still tend to feel
justified in restricting the amount of exposure a child
may have to an overt homosexual relationship on the part
of the mother.

3907. PAYNE, ANNE T. "Law and the Problem Parent: Cus-
      tody and Parental Rights of Homosexual, Mentally
      Ill, Mentally Retarded, and Incarcerated Parents,"
      Journal of Family Law, 16 (1978), 797-818.

Offers a comparative analysis, including elements of sub-
jectivity and bias that often enter into legal proceedings and decisions in these spheres.

3908. RILEY, MARILYN. "Avowed Lesbian Mothers and Her
      Right to Child Custody: A Constitutional Challenge
      That Can No Longer Be Denied," **San Diego Law
      Review**, 12 (1974-75), 799-864.
Provides a detailed exposition of the constitutional
arguments against allowing a mother's lesbianism to
influence custody cases when no specific nexus of harm
can be demonstrated. Reviews professional literature
on sexual orientation as it serves to buttress the argument.

3909. SMART, BARBARA. "Bezio v. Patenauda: The "Coming
      Out" Custody Controversy of Lesbian Mothers in
      Court," **New England Law Journal**, 16 (1980-81),
      331-65.
Discusses a Massachusetts case in which a lesbian mother
sought to regain custody of her two children from a female
friend. The mother was successful on appeal in a decision
that set limits on the trial judge's discretion.

3910. SUSOEFF, STEVE. "Assessing Children's Best
      Interests When a Parent Is Gay or Lesbian: Toward a
      Rational Custody Standard," **UCLA Law Review**, 32
      (1985), 852-903.
Gay and lesbian parents seeking custody of their children
have met with increasing success in American courts since
the California Court of Appeal instructed a trial court
that it could not rule that a mother's homosexual orientation made her unfit to have custody of her child. See
also: Catherine Rand et al., "Psychological Health and
Factors Court Seeks to Control in Lesbian Mother Trials,"
JH, 8 (1982-83), 27-39.

3911. WHITTLIN, WILLIAM A. "Homosexuality and Child
      Custody: A Psychiatric Viewpoint," **Conciliation
      Courts Review**, 21 (1983), 77-79.
Although a specific incident will often trigger a legal
battle, its course may be determined by societal attitudes
(including homophobia) and the kind of research evidence
that is brought to bear.

E.   CHILDREN OF LESBIANS AND GAY MEN

The increasing visibility of households headed by lesbian
and homosexual single or coupled parents has evoked fears
that the children's psychological health might be adversely affected. Little if any support has been found for
this assumption of environmental determinism.

3912. GANTZ, JOE. **Whose Child Cries: Children of Gay Parents Talk about Their Lives.** Rolling Hills Estates, CA: Jalmar Press, 1983. 245 pp.
Concerns five American families raising children in openly gay homes. "Written from the perspective of the children, who range in age from seven to seventeen."

3913. GOLOMBOK, SUSAN, et al. "Children in Lesbian and Single-Parent Households: Psychological and Psychiatric Appraisal," **Journal of Child Psychology and Psychiatry and Allied Disciplines,** 24 (1983), 551-72.
Concludes that rearing in a lesbian household per se does not lead to atypical psychosexual development or constitute a psychiatric risk factor.

3914. GREEN, RICHARD. "The Best Interests of the Child with a Lesbian Mother," **Bulletin of the American Academy of Psychiatry and the Law,** 10 (1982), 7-15.
Concludes that difficulties experienced by children in lesbian mother households stem from reaction to divorce and not from the mother's lesbianism. See also his: "Sexual Identity of 37 Children Raised by Homosexual or Transsexual Parents," **American Journal of Psychiatry,** 135 (1978), 692-97.

3915. HOEFFER, BEVERLY. "Children's Acquisition of Sex Role Behavior in Lesbian-Mother Families," **American Journal of Orthopsychiatry,** 51 (1981), 536-44.
Using Block's Toy Preference Test no differences were found between children of lesbian and single heterosexual mothers. The writer suggests that children's peers have the greatest influence on their development.

3916. HOTVEDT, MARY E., and JANE BARCLAY MANDEL. "Children of Lesbian Mothers," in: William Paul et al. (eds.), **Homosexuality: Social, Psychological and Biological Issues.** Beverly Hills, CA: Sage, 1982, pp. 275-91.
Examines several areas of research, including impact of divorce, father absence, and children's adjustment.

3917. KIRKPATRICK, MARTHA, et al. "Lesbian Mothers and Their Children: A Comparative Survey," **American Journal of Orthopsychiatry,** 51 (1981), 545-51.
In this study of 40 children raised by lesbian and single parent mothers, no significant differences were found in sexual or gender identity between the groups. The lesbian mothers were more concerned with providing male figures for their children than were the heterosexual mothers.

3918. KWESKIN, SALLY L., and ALICIA S. COOK. "Heterosexual and Homosexual Mothers' Self-Described Sex-role Behavior and Idea Sex-Role Behavior in Children," **Sex Roles,** 8 (1982), 967-75.
Similarities in sex-role behavior and attitudes of hetero-

sexual and homosexual mothers far outweigh the present
subjects differences when determined by self-description
and attitudes toward ideal child behavior.

3919. LEWIS, KAREN GAIL. "Children of Lesbians: Their
       Point of View," **Social Work,** 25 (1980), 198-203.
Interviews with 21 children in the Greater Boston area
brought out several major problems. Early family discord
and the mother's lesbianism generated severe ambivalence,
yet the children generally desired to accept the mother's
new lifestyle.

3920. MAYADAS, NAZNEEN S., and WAYNE D. DUEHN. "Children
       in Gay Families: An Investigation of Services,"
       Homosexual Counseling Journal, 3 (1976), 70-83.
Argues that social service agencies and clinicians should
reexamine their value premises.

3921. MILLER, JUDITH ANN, et al. "The Child's Home En-
       vironment for Lesbian vs. Heterosexual Mothers: A
       Neglected Area of Research," **JH,**7 (1981), 49-56.
Children of lesbian mothers tend to live in a less afflu-
ent socioeconomic setting. A strong child-development
orientation was found among lesbian mothers, undermining
the stereotype of lesbians as aloof from children.

3922. NUNGESSER, LONNIE G. "Theoretical Bases for
       Research on the Acquisition of Social Sex-Roles by
       Children of Lesbian Mothers," **JH,** 5:3 (1980),
       177-87.
Theories from developmental, behavioral, and social psychology are applied in order to distinguish between the
acquisition of sex-typed behaviors and the actual performance of those behaviors.

          F. PARENTS OF GAYS AND LESBIANS

The increasing number of gay men and lesbians who have
"come out" to their parents, has led to the formation in
many cities of North American of support groups for these
parents. The literature being produced by these groups
enables one to understand the psychic process of resistance and acceptance that these mothers and fathers
undergo in confronting the child's orientation.

3923. BACK, GLORIA. **Are You Still My Mother? Are You
       Still My Family?** New York: Warner Books, 1985.
       236 pp.
Advice to parents of gay men and lesbians with an account
of the sex-session workshops which the author conducted
before her death in 1985.

3924. BORHEK, MARY V. **My Son Eric.** New York: Pilgrim, 1979. 160 pp.
Autobiographical account of a mother, recently divorced from her clergyman husband, who discovers that her son is homosexual. The book records her struggle towards acceptance, which was also a journey in self-discovery.

3925. FAIRCHILD, BETTY, and NANCY HOWARD. **Now That You Know: What Every Parent Should Know about Homosexuality.** New York: Harcourt Brace Jovanovich, 1979. 227 pp.
Compassionate and practical advice by two women active in the national organization Parents of Gays.

3926. GRIFFIN, CAROL WELCH, MARIAN J. WIRTH, and ARTHUR G. WIRTH. **Beyond Acceptance: Parents of Lesbians and Gays Talk about Their Experiences.** Englewood Cliffs, NJ: Prentice-Hall, 1986. 193 pp.
Reports of real-life experience of parents, disclosing a sequence of emotional stages--from the initial shock of the revelation that their offspring is gay, through anger and denial, to acceptance and often beyond. If this process is traversed to its logical completion, family relationships will be transformed and deepened.

3927. GROSSMANN, THOMAS. **Eine Liebe wie jede andere: Mit homosexuellen Jugendlichen leben und umgehen.** Reinbek bei Hamburg, 1984. 141 pp.
Advice and information to assist parents in becoming comfortable with their child's homosexuality.

3928. SEABROOK, JEREMY. **Mother and Son.** New York: Pantheon, 1980. 189 pp.
Sensitive autobiographical account of an English gay man's relationship with his working-class mother.

3929. SILVERSTEIN, CHARLES. **A Family Matter: A Parent's Guide to Homosexuality.** New York: McGraw-Hill, 1978. 214 pp.
A gay New York psychiatrist (not himself a parent) offers explanations and seeks to clear away myths.

3930. SWITZER, DAVID K., and SHIRLEY A. SWITZER. **Parents of the Homosexual.** Philadelphia: Westminster, 1980. 118 pp.
Although this book is written from a Christian religious point of view, it remains sympathetic.

3931. WYDEN, PETER, and BARBARA WYDEN. **Growing Up Straight: What Every Thoughtful Parent Should Know about Homosexuality.** New York: Stein and Day, 1968. 256 pp.
A somewhat dated book, offering psychiatrically biased etiological theories and focusing on "the means of prevention." Rearing children in a "sexually sound" home is the most effective prophylaxis.
Items 3932-3938 are omitted.

XIX. BOUNDARY CROSSING

A. INTERGENERATIONAL SEX

The term intergenerational sex has been recently introduced to describe relations between adults, on the one
hand, and (a) adolescents and (b) children, on the other.
Properly speaking, these two forms should be distinguished
as pederasty and pedophilia, respectively, but current
usage is often imprecise, owing to the emotional charge
such relations often evoke. (Logically, the concept of
intergenerational sex should also include gerontophilia,
sexual interest in old people, but this form of attraction
has been little studied; cf. "Aging," XIV.C.) In some
civilizations of the past, such as ancient Greece and
Islam (see III.C and III.P), pederasty has been the ideal,
dominant, even socially recognized form of homosexuality.
This pederastic mode also prevails in many tribal cultures
(see IV.A-F). Recently, support groups for pederasts and
pedophiles, such as the North American Man/Boy Love Association and the (British) Paedophile Information Exchange,
have emerged in a number of Western countries; these
groups remain small and controversial, isolated from the
larger movement, and often subjected to official surveillance and harassment.

3939. ABEL, GENE G., et al. "Complications, Consent, and
        Cognitions in Sex Between Children and Adults," In-
        ternational Journal of Law and Psychiatry, 7
        (1984), 89-103.
The authors hold that it is extremely difficult for a
child to give informed consent. The adult who is attracted to children changes his inner world by developing
cognitions and beliefs that support his behavior, but
these are markedly at variance with those of the culture
in which he lives.

3940. BANIS, VICTOR J. Men and Their Boys: The Homosex-
        ual Relationship between Adult and Adolescent. Los
        Angeles: Medco Books, 1966. 144 pp.
One of a series of "soft-core" popularizations of the boy
love theme, in this instance closely dependent on the
scholarly work of J. Z. Eglinton, cited below. See also:
Victor Dodson, Pederasty: Sex between Men and Boys (North
Hollywood, CA: Barclay House, 1968; 192 pp.).

3941. BERNARD, FRITS. Paedophilia: A Factual Report.
        Rotterdam: Enclave Press, 1985. 101 pp.
Concise version of a book first published in Dutch in
1975, then in a fuller form in German in 1979 and 1982.
Includes long-term effects on the child; description of a

pedophile group; age limits; normality of pedophiles; and
the social question. On pp. 87-98 there is a complete
bibliography of his writings on pedophilia and pederasty
between 1947 and 1985. Some of the early ones (e.g., **Ver-
volgde minderheid,** 1960) appeared under the pseudonym
Victor Servatius.

3942. BLEIBTREU-EHRENBERG, GISELA. "Der pädophile
       Impuls, **Der Monat,** N.S. no. 294 (1985), 175-92.
Places pedophilia within the range of normality as an
attempt to reactivate the world of childhood. Treatment
of pedophiles as criminals reflects a lingering theological concept.

3943. BRANT, R., and V. B. TISZA. "The Sexually Misused
       Child," **American Journal of Orthopsychiatry,** 47
       (1977), 80-90.
Attempts to distinguish between sexual abuse and nonabuse.

3944. BRONGERSMA, EDWARD. "The Meaning of 'Indecency'
       with Respect to Moral Offences Involving Children.
       With a Commentary by D. J. West," **British Journal
       Of Criminology,** 20 (1980), 20-34.
With reference to Dutch experience, which he has carefully
monitored, Brongersma contends that criminal prosecution
of consensual acts always does more harm than good. See
also his: "Aggression against Pedophiles," **International
Journal of Law and Psychiatry,** 7 (1984), 79-87. The
author has also used the pseudonym O. Brunoz.

3945. BRONGERSMA, EDWARD. **Das verfemte Geschlecht.**
       Munich: Lichtenberg, 1970. 267 pp.
A scholarly advocate's major study of boy love with extensive bibliography. An enlarged English edition is in
preparation.

3946. BROWNE, ANGELA, and DAVID FINKELHOR. "Impact of
       Child Sexual Abuse: A Review of the Research,"
       Psychological Bulletin, 99 (1986), 66-77.
Reviews the literature on short-term and long-term
effects of child sexual abuse. Discusses also the controversy over the impact of the phenomenon, suggesting
directions for future research efforts.

3947. CALIFIA, PAT. "The Age of Consent: An Issue and
       Its Effects on the Gay Movement," **Advocate,** no.303
       (October 16, 1980), 19-23, 45; no. 304 (October 30,
       1980), 17-23, 45.
Contends that the "Great Kiddy Porn Panic" of 1977 was
engineered by the right in order to disrupt the sexual
freedom movement.

3948. CAMERON, PAUL. "Homosexual Molestation of Chil-
       dren/Sexual Interaction of Teacher and Pupil,"
       Psychological Reports, 57 (1985), 1227-36.
The author, an antihomosexual researcher, claims that

one-third of reported child molestations involve homosexual acts, while girls account for about two-thirds of
children victimized. Contrast D. Newton, below.

3949. CAMPAIGN AGAINST PUBLIC MORALS. **Paedophilia and
      Public Morals.** London: CAMP, 1980. 58 pp.
Argues that the liberation of children and pedophiles
should be supported by the adult sexual political movement.

3950. CONSTANTINE, LARRY L., and FLOYD M. MARTINSON
      (eds.). **Children and Sex: New Findings, New Per-
      spectives.** Boston: Little, Brown, 1981. 288 pp.
Papers by professional researchers representing a range of
views treating sex, heterosexual and homosexual, with and
between children.

3951. COOK, MARK, and KEVIN HOWELLS (eds). **Adult Sexual
      Interest in Children.** New York: Academic Press,
      1981. 275 pp.
Nine papers generally written from a prevention and
social-control perspective, though there is also some
descriptive material.

3952. DANET, JEAN, et al. **Fous d'enfance.** Paris: Revue
      du Cerfi, 1979. 217 pp. (Recherches, 37)
Collection of essays and interviews by Michel Foucault,
Jean-Luc Hennig, René Schérer, and others on sexual re-
lations between adults and minors.

3953. DAVIDSON, MICHAEL. **Some Boys.** Kingston, NY: Ol-
      iver Layton Press, 1971. 251 pp.
Frank reminiscences by an English journalist and world
traveler. Unlike the British edition (London: Bruce and
Watson, 1969), this issue is unexpurgated. See also
Davidson's earlier memoir: **The World, The Flesh, and
Myself.** (London: Arthur Barker, 1962; 354 pp.).

3954. DUVERT, TONY. **Le bon sexe illustré.** Paris: Edi-
      tions de Minuit, 1974. 156 pp.
Critique of sexual taboos, notably in regard to pedophilia, by a French novelist. See also his **L'enfant au
masculin** (Paris: Editions de Minuit, 1980; 184 pp.).

3955. EGLINTON, J. Z. (pseud.). **Greek Love.** New
      York: Oliver Layton Press, 1964. 504 pp.
Comprehensive historical study of pederasty and pedophilia, emphasizing not only the origins of the Western
tradition in Greece but the subsequent development, which
is presented as flowing from Hellenic practices and
ideals--in sharp contrast with modern androphile homosexuality. Despite the sometimes overapologetic tone, this
book is a remarkable and well-documented conspectus,
providing analyses of many literary works.

3956. ENNEW, JUDITH. **The Sexual Exploitation of Chil-**

dren. London: Polity Press, 1986. 200 pp.
Examines recent cross-cultural evidence, and argues that
the sexual exploitation of children by adults is not an
abnormal occurrence, but rather an overdeveloped expression of normal attitudes to sexuality, women, and children.

3957. FISHER, GARY, and LEISLA M. HOWELL. "Psychological
       Needs of Homosexual Pedophiliacs," **Diseases of the
       Nervous System,** 31 (1970), 623-25.
Finds that subjects had need structures similar to those
of heterosexual pedophiles but different from those of
normal adult males; were low in achievement orientation,
inner direction, and assertiveness; and were guilt-ridden.

3958. FRASER, MORRIS. **The Death of Narcissus.** London:
       Secker and Warburg, 1976. 244 pp.
Urbane, moderately judgmental study of pedophilia--mainly
heterosexual--as expressed in 19th-century literary
sources, by a psychiatrist.

3959. FREUND, KURT. "Bisexuality in Homosexual Pedophil-
       ia," **Archives of Sexual Behavior,** 5 (1976), 415-23.
The author, a Czech who emigrated to Canada in 1968, found
that bisexual pedophilic males responded more than an
androphile (adult-oriented homosexual) group to 6-8 year
old female children, but less than them to adult females.
See also his "Erotic Preference in Pedophilia," **Behaviour
Research and Therapy,** 5 (1967), 339-48.

3960. FREUND, KURT, et al. "Pedophilia and Heterosexual-
       ity vs. Homosexuality," **Journal of Sex and Marital
       therapy,** 10 (1984), 193-200.
Finds that the development of erotically preferred partner
sex and of partner age are not independent of each other.
See also: Freund et al., "Experimental Analysis of Pedophilia," **Behaviour Research and Therapy,** 20 (1982), 105-
12.

3961. GEISER, ROBERT L. **Hidden Victims: The Sexual Abuse
       of Children.** Boston: Beacon Press, 1979. 191 pp.
Treats mainly heterosexual abuse (rape and incest), with
discussion also of pederasty, "male sex rings," gay kiddie
porn, and teenage hustlings. Despite this seemingly sensational range of topics, this book is low-keyed and relatively liberal.

3962. GROTH, A. NICHOLAS, and H. JEAN BIRNBAUM. "Adult
       Sexual Orientation and Attraction to Underage
       Persons," **Archives of Sexual Behavior,** 7 (1978),
       175-81.
Suggests that homosexuality and homosexual pedophilia may
be mutually exclusive and that the adult heterosexual
male constitutes a greater risk to the underage child
than does the adult homosexual male.

3963. HILLMAN, JAMES, et al. **The Puer Papers.** Irving,
      TX: Spring Publications, 1979. 245 pp.
Nine essays, several strongly Jungian, treating the boy as
an archetypal figure.

3964. HOCQUENGHEM, GUY, and RENÉ SCHÉRER. **Co-ire: album
      systématique de l'enfance.** Fontenay-sous-Bois: Re-
      cherches, 1976. 146 pp.
A sometimes opaque essay attempting to demythologize child
sexuality. See also: Schérer, **Une érotique puérile**
(Paris: Galilee, 1978; 188 pp.).

3965. HOHMANN, JOACHIM S. (ed.). **Pädophilie heute.**
      Frankfurt am Main: Foerster, 1980. 200 pp.
Positive essays by Hohmann, Edward Brongersma, Helmut
Bendt, Peter Schult, Hans-Peter Reichelt, Wolfgang
Selitsch, Gerd Talis, Hans-Dieter Horning and others.

3966. IVES, GEORGE. **The Graeco-Roman View of Youth.**
      London: Cayme Press, 1926. 90 pp.
An Edwardian eccentric and diarist uses the cover of the
values of ancient civilization to advance a cautious
defense of erotic interest in youth.

3967. JERSILD, JENS. **The Normal Homosexual Male versus
      the Boy Molester.** Translated by Eva Nissen. Copen-
      hagen: Arnold Busck, 1967. 112 pp.
A statistical study by the head of the vice squad in
Copenhagen, based on Danish police records and files,
which contrasts normal homosexual males with pedophil-
iacs.

3968. JONES, GERALD P. "The Social Study of Pederasty:
      In Search of a Literature Base: An Annotated Bib-
      liography of Sources in English," **JH,** 8 (1982),
      61-95.
Offers fair-minded and often detailed annotations of
items included. As the author recognizes, the list
could be extended. See also: "A Select Bibliography on
Paedophilia," **Gay Information** (Australia), no.7 (1981),
38-40; no. 14-15 (1984), 67; and **Literatuurlijst** (Antwerp:
Studiegroep Pedofilie, 1978; 38 pp.).

3969. KRAEMER, WILLIAM (ed.). **The Normal and Abnormal
      Love of Children.** London: Sheldon Press, 1976.
      150 pp.
Four papers largely reflecting Jungian perspectives.

3970. LINEDECKER, CLIFFORD L. **Children in Chains.** New
      York: Everest House, 1981. 334 pp.
Journalistic, somewhat sensationalized account. See also
Robin Lloyd, **Boy Prostitution in America** (New York: Vanguard Press, 1976; 236 pp.); and Gitta Sereny, **The Invisible Children: Child Prostitution in America, West Germany
and Great Britain** (New York: Knopf, 1985; 254 pp.).

3971. **Loving Boys.** New York: Semiotext(e), 1980.
Special number in tabloid format of **Semiotext(e)** magazine,
comprising interviews with David Thorstad, Mark Moffett
(both of NAMBLA), Kate Millett, together with a transcript
of an April 1979 radio broadcast by Michel Foucault.

3972. MARIOTTI, ETTORE. **La neofilia: contributo agli
studi di psicopatologia sessuale.** Rome: Mediter-
ranea, 1952. 212 pp.
A pioneering work of the early postwar period that cost
the author a prison sentence.

3973. MATZNEFF, GABRIEL. **Les moins de seize ans.**
Paris: Julliard, 1974. 116 pp.
Holds that young people under 16 constitute a single sex
apart, and that the choice of them as one's sexual orientation is of special significance.

3974. MOLLER, MONIQUE. **Pedofiele relaties.** Deventer:
Van Loghum Slaterus, 1983. 113 pp.
Based on interviews in the Netherlands, presents two
possible approaches to relations between children and
adults.

3975. MOODY, ROGER. **Indecent Assault.** London: Word is
Out/Peace News, 1980. 64 pp.
Pedophile advocacy with autobiographical elements.

3976. NEDOMA, KAREL. "Sexuální chovani a jeho vývoj u
pedofilních mužů," **Československá Psychiatrie,** 65
(1969), 92–98.
Pedophilic delinquents were oriented more towards a
specific age than toward the sex of the partner. See
related articles, ibid., 155–58, 366–70.

3977. NELSON, BARBARA. **Making an Issue of Child Abuse:
Political Agenda Setting for Social Problems.**
Chicago: Chicago University Press, 1984. 176 pp.
Traces the shift from a small private-sector charity concern into a multi-million dollar social welfare issue. The
matter has become a platform for social-policy directives
rather than an area of compassion and humanistic concern.

3978. NEWTON, DAVID E. "Homosexual Behavior and Child
Molestation: A Review of the Evidence," **Adolescence,** 13 (1978), 29–43.
Existing studies provide no reason to believe that
anything other than a random connection exists between
homosexual behavior and child molestation. The typical
offender is a heterosexual man.

3979. NICHOLS, DENNISON W. **Toward a Perspective for Boy
Lovers.** Lansing, MI: Editorial Creative Projects,
1976. 99 pp.
Subjective approach by a rural boy lover who seeks to
convey the mystique, as it were, which characterizes the

pederastic sensibility and to formulate a code of ethics.

3980. O'CARROLL, TOM. **Paedophilia: The Radical Case.**
       Boston: Alyson, 1982. 284 pp.
Reasoned argument, by a British member of the Paedophile
Information Exchange, for tolerance of the practice.
Asserting the natural sexuality of children and their
right to expression, he rejects the historical idealization embodied in the Greek Love arguments of J. Z. Eglinton and others. Asserts that police and parents frequently cause great harm to children in their traumatic efforts
at intervention.

3981. PINARD-LEGRY, J. L., and B. LAPOUGE. **L'enfant et
       le pédéraste.** Paris: Editions du Seuil, 1980. 128
       pp.
Adopts a critical stance toward pederasty and pedophilia.

3982. POTRYKUS, DAGMAR, and MANFRED WÖBCKE. **Sexualität
       zwischen Kindern und Erwachsenen.** Munich: Gold-
       mann, 1974. 112 pp.
Comprehensive examination of the question of sexual relations between adults and children, pointing out that
punitive societal reactions tend to be emotionally
charged and disproportionate to the objective consequences of the behavior.

3983. QUINSEY, VERNON L. "The Assessment and Treatment
       of Child Molesters: A Review," **Canadian Psycholog-
       ical Review,** 18 (1977), 204-220.
Compared to heterosexual child molesters, homosexual
offenders choose older (pubescent) partners, are more
likely to be recidivists, and are less numerous. Incestuous child molesters are almost always heterosexual.

3984. RAILE, ARTHUR LYON (pseud. of Edward Perry War-
       ren). **A Defense of Uranian Love.** London: Cayme
       Press, 1928-30. 3 vols.
A neo-Hellenic apologia by a Boston aesthete who lived
much of his life in England. The three volumes are
entitled: (1) The Boy Lover; (2) The Uranian Eros; and
(3) The Heavenly Wisdom and Conclusion.

3985. ROGERS, CARL M., and TREMAINE TERRY. "Clinical
       Intervention with Boy Victims of Sexual Abuse,"
       in: Irving R. Stuart and Joanne G. Greer (eds.),
       Victims of Sexual Aggression. New York: Van
       Nostrand Reinhold, 1984, pp. 91-104.
Psychotherapeutic perspective.

3986. ROSSMAN, PARKER. **Sexual Experience between Men and
       Boys: Exploring the Pederast Underground.** New
       York: Association Press, 1976. 247 pp.
A well-balanced study by an author sympathetic to pederasty, offering an international perspective. Notes, index,
and bibliography. See also: Dennis Drew and Jonathan

Drake (ps'eud. of Parker Rossman), **Boys for Sale: A Sociological Study of Boy Prostitution** (New York: Brown, 1969;
223 pp.).

3987. RUSH, FLORENCE. **The Best Kept Secret: Sexual Abuse
of Children.** Englewood Cliffs, NJ: Prentice-Hall,
1980. 226 pp.
A well-meaning work which reveals both the genuine concern and the confusions underlying the current campaign
against child sexuality. Fails adequately to distinguish
between sexual contact and physical harm.

3988. SANDFORT, THEO. **The Sexual Aspect of Paedophile
Relations: The Experience of Twenty-five Boys.**
Amsterdam: Pan/Spartacus, 1982. 136 pp.
Presents results of a study conducted under the auspices
of the Dutch government. The interviews, portions of
which are reproduced in translation, tend to show stable
relationships in which the boys take a positive attitude
toward sexual liaisons. See also his: "Pedophile Relationships in the Netherands: Alternative Lifestyle for
Children?" **Alternative Lifestyles,** 5 (1983), 164-83.

3989. SCHLESINGER, BENJAMIN. **Sexual Abuse of Children: A
Resource Guide and Annotated Bibliography.** Toronto: University of Toronto Press, 1982. 202 pp.
In this useful reference work, see pp. 142-45, 152-53,
174-77.

3990. SERBER, MICHAEL, and CLAUDIA G. KEITH. "Atascadero
Project: Model of a Sexual Retraining Program for
Incarcerated Homosexual Pedophiles," **JH,** 1 (1974),
87-97.
Describes the sexual retraining program at a maximum
security prison hospital that houses primarily pedophiles.

3991. TAYLOR, BRIAN. **Perspectives on Paedophilia.**
London: Batsford, 1981. 148 pp.
Eight papers representing a range of viewpoints, from
negative and punitive to liberal and descriptive.

3992. TINDALL, RALPH H. "The Male Adolescent Involved
with a Pederast becomes an Adult," **JH,** 3 (1978),
373-82.
Reports a longitudinal study of nine cases; the outcomes
are generally heterosexual.

3993. TSANG, DANIEL. **The Age Taboo: Gay Male Sexuality ,
Power and Consent.** Boston: Alyson, 1980. 178 pp.
Papers generally from a leftist standpoint, rejecting the
idealization of Greek love in Eglinton's work, but some
defending intergenerational sex as liberating, others reflecting a feminist argument to the effect that boy-love
is a destructive abuse of phallic power.

3994. UNITED STATES. HOUSE OF REPRESENTATIVES. **Sexual**

Exploitation of Children: A Problem of Unknown Magnitude. Washington, DC: U. S. Government Printing Office, 1983. 63 pp.
Report to the Chairman of the Subcommittee of Select Education, House Committee on Education and Labor, by the United States General Accounting Office, April 20, 1982. One of a number of such reports, which generally feature copious testimony by opponents of sexual freedom and others who seem to be seeking to manipulate the issue for political gain.

3995. VOGEL, WOLF. **Verbotene Liebe: Pädophilie und strafende Gesellschaft.** Regensburg: Roderer, 1984. 130 pp.
Pedosexuality and its legal repression.

3996. WILSON, GLENN, and DAVID N. COX. **The Child Lovers: A Study of Paedophiles in Society.** London: Peter Owen, 1983. 132 pp.
A moderately negative presentation, of some sociological interest.

3997. WILSON, PAUL. **The Man They Called a Monster: Sexual Experiences between Men and Boys.** Melbourne: Cassell, 1981. 150 pp.
In-depth, sympathetic study of a Queensland boy lover, a kind of sexual Stakhanovite, who kept detailed records on his several thousand partners before committing suicide.

B. CROSS DRESSING

While cross dressing has appealed to a certain number homosexuals, it also has its adherents among heterosexuals. The subject thus belongs only partly to the study of homosexuality; it deserves to be examined as an independent cultural phenomenon. For cross dressing in the theatre, see VI.G.

3998. ALPERT, GEORGE. **The Queens.** New York: Da Capo/ Plenum Press, 1975. 90 pp.
Photographic study of men who enjoy dressing as a woman or living as a women part or all of the time. See also: C. L. Gondanoff, **Mesdames "messieurs"** (Brussels: Paul Legrain, 1979); Kris Kirk and Ed Heath, **Men in Frocks** (London: Gay Men's Press, 1984; 120 pp.); and Mike Phillips and Barry Shapiro, **Forbidden Fantasies: Men Who Dare to Dress in Drag** (New York: Macmillan, 1980; 121 pp.).

3999. AMMANN, JEAN-CHRISTOPHE, and MARIANNE EIGENHEES (eds.). **Transformer: Aspekte der Travestie.** Lucerne: Kunstmuseum, 1974. 181 pp.
Text to accompany an exhibition on transvestism in photo-

graphy and art.

4000. BRIERLEY, HARRY. **Transvestism: A Handbook with Case Studies for Psychologists, Psychiatrists, and Counsellors.** New York: Pergamon, 1979. 259 pp.
Somewhat diffuse account for a professional audience of major facets of the question.

4001. BUHRICH, NEIL, and NATHANIEL MCCONAGHY. "Clinical Comparison of Transvestism and Transssexualism: An Overview," **Australian and New Zealand Journal of Psychiatry,** 11 (1977), 83-86.
Compared 35 members of a club for heterosexual transvestites with 29 male psychiatric patients seeking a full sex-change operation. See also their: "The Clinical Syndromes of Femmifilic Behavior," **Archives of Sexual Behavior,** 6 (1977), 397-412; "Tests of Gender Feelings and Behavior in Homosexuality, Transvestism and Transsexualism," **Journal of Clinical Psychology,** 35 (1979), 187-91; and "Three Clinically Discrete Categories of Fetishistic Transvestism," **Archives of Sexual Behavior,** 8 (1979), 151-57.

4002. BULLIET, CLARENCE JOSEPH. **Venus Castina: Famous Female Impersonators, Celestial and Human.** New York: Covici, Friede, 1928. 308 pp.
Popular work on men cross-dressing as women over the centuries. See also: Peter Ackroyd, **Dressing Up: Transvestism and Drag: The History of an Obsession** (New York: Simon and Schuster, 1979; 160 pp.).

4003. BULLOUGH, VERN, et al. "A Comparative Study of Male Transvestites, Male to Female Transsexuals, and Male Homosexuals," **Journal of Sex Research,** 19 (1983), 238-57.
Current sexual orientation and lifestyles suggest a dominant pattern for each group, but there were still enough subjects with variant patterns to suggest that most generalizations still need to be tentative.

4004. CHESHIRE, DAVID. "Male Impersonator," **Saturday Book,** 29 (1969), 245-52.
Women in men's attire. See also: Laurence Senelick, "The Evolution of the Male Impersonator in the Nineteenth Century Stage," **Essays in Theatre,** 1 (1982), 31-44.

4005. ELLIS, HAVELOCK. **Eonism and Other Supplementary Studies.** Philadelphia: Davis, 1928. 539 pp.
A historical and cultural survey by the noted English sexologist, who promoted the term "Eonism" (from the Chevalier d'Eon) for cross-dressing.

4006. FEINBLOOM, DEBORAH HELLER. **Transvestism and Transsexuals: Mixed Views.** New York: Delacorte Press, 1976. 303 pp.
Sociologist's data and conclusions drawn from interviews,

observations, and correspondence. The book deflates a
number of stereotypes. An appendix treats ethical problems that may be raised by research of this kind.

4007. FRANKEL, HIERONIMUS. "Homo mollis," **Medizinische
       Zeitung, Verein für Heilkunde in Preussen,** 22
       (1853), 102-03.
Early case study of a German-Jewish homosexual and transvestite.

4008. FREUND, KURT, et al. "Two Types of Cross-Gender
       Identity," **Archives of Sexual Behavior,** 11 (1982),
       49-63.
Contends that transvestism, and closely related conditions
of cross-gender identity, occur almost exclusively in heterosexuals.

4009. GILBERT, OSCAR PAUL. **Men in Women's Guise: Some
       Historical Instances of Female Impersonation.**
       Translated by Robert B. Douglas. New York: Bren-
       tano's, 1926. 234 pp.
Biographical approach. See also his: **Women in Men'
Guise.** (London: John Lane, 1932; 224 pp.).

4010. GILBERT, SANDRA M. "Costumes of the Mind: Trans-
       vestism as Metaphor in Modern Literature," **Critical
       Inquiry,** 7 (1980), 391-417.
Coercive and voluntary cross-dressing in Joyce, Lawrence,
Eliot, Woolf, Carpenter and others. See also: Susan
Gubar, "Blessings in Disguise: Cross-Dressing as Redres-
sing for Female Modernists," **Massachusetts Review,** 22
(1981), 477-508.

4011. HIRSCHFELD, MAGNUS. **Die Transvestiten: Eine
       Untersuchung über den erotischen Verkleidungstrieb
       mit umfangreichem casuistischen und historischen
       Material.** Berlin: Pulvermacher, 1910. 562 pp.
This major work of synthesis by the noted German sexologist introduced the word "transvestite." Hirschfeld
identified the phenomenon in only a few cases out of the
7000 homosexuals he had interviewed and examined by that
time.

4012. HOWE, FREDERICK. "An Exploration of the History of
       Female Impersonators," **Advocate,** no. 224 (September
       21, 1977), 26-29; and no. 225 (October 5, 1977),
       28-29.
Popular account emphasizing performance aspects.

4013. KING, DAVE. "Gender Confusions: Psychological and
       Psychiatric Conceptions of Transvestism and Trans-
       sexualism," in: Kenneth Plummer (ed.), **The Making
       of the Modern Homosexual.** Totowa, NJ: Barnes and
       Noble, 1981, pp. 155-83.
Critique of some widely held views.

4014. KUJATH, GERHARD. "Transvestitische Verhaltens-
       weisen im Kindesalter," **Praxis der Kinderpsycho-
       logie und Kinderpsychiatrie**, 20 (1971), 117-25.
Regards defects in rearing by mothers as releasing factors
in transvestism in childhood.

4015. LUKIANIEWICZ, NARCYZ. "Survey of Various Aspects
       of Transvestism in the Light of our Present
       Knowledge," **Journal of Nervous and Mental Disease**,
       128 (1959), 36-64.
Literature review with 104 citations. For others, see
Vern Bullough et al., **An Annotated Bibliography of Homo-
sexuality**. (New York: Garland, 1976), vol. 2, pp. 351-84.

4016. MINETTE (pseud.). **Recollections of a Part-Time
       Lady**. Edited by Steven Watson. New York: Flower-
       beneath-the-Foot Press, 1979.
Campy reminiscences.

4017. MONEY, JOHN, and ANTHONY J. RUSSO. "Homosexual
       vs. Transvestite or Transsexual Gender-Identity/
       Role: Outcome Studies in Boys," **International
       Journal of Family Psychiatry**, 2 (1981), 139-45.
Offers introspective data on males aged 23-29 years
who, as children, had overtly stated the wish to be a
girl and had acted out this wish through dress and play
activities.

4018. MUNROE, ROBERT. "Male Transvestism and the
       Couvade: A Psycho-Cultural Analysis," **Ethos**, 8
       (1980), 49-59.
A comparative ethnological approach. See also Robert
Munroe and Ruth Munroe, "Male Transvestism and Subsistence Economy," **Journal of Social Psychology**, 103 (1977),
307-08; and Robert Munroe et al., "Institutionalized Male
Transvestism and Sex Distinctions," **American Anthropologist**, 71 (1969), 87-91.

4019. NEWTON, ESTHER. **Mother Camp: Female Impersonators
       in America**. Englewood Cliffs, NJ: Prentice-Hall,
       1972. 136 pp.
Social scientist's participation-observation study of
homosexual transvestites who perform in drag shows. Analyzes professional aspects, the work situation, and the
effects of camp humor.

4020. PERKINS, ROBERTA. **Drag Queen Scene: Transsexuals
       in Kings Cross**. North Sydney, NSW: Allen and Un-
       win, 1983. 176 pp.
Attempts a composite picture of cross-dressers and transsexuals in Sydney's bohemian quarter.

4021. PERSON, ETHEL, and LIONEL OVESEY. "Transvestism:
       New Perspectives," **Journal of the American Academy
       of Psychoanalysis**, 6 (1978), 301-23.
Reappraises transvestism in the light of new concepts in

psychoanalytic theory, which are purportedly applicable
to the analysis of other "perversions." See also their:
"Homosexual Cross-Dressing," ibid., 12 (1984), 167-84.

4022. PRINCE, VIRGINIA. **The Transvestite and His Wife.**
       Los Angeles: Argyle Books, 1967. 143 pp.
One of a number of writings by this author, who has tire-
lessly propagandized for the cause, publishing an occasional journal **Transvestia.**

4023. ROBACK, HOWARD B., et al. "Self-Concept and Psy-
       chological Adjustment Differences between Self-
       Identified Male Transsexuals and Male Homosex-
       uals," **JH,** 3 (1977), 15-20.
Findings indicate that the homosexual group had a better
self-image and was better adjusted than the sex-change
group.

4024. TALAMINI, JOHN T. **Boys Will Be Girls: The Hidden
       World of the Heterosexual Male Transvestite.** Wash-
       ington, DC: University Presses of America, 1982.
       89 pp.
Seeking to distinguish the transvestite subculture from
others such as homosexuality and bisexuality, female
impersonation, transsexuality, argues that it qualifies
as a genuine minority. Discusses cross-cultural comparisons, the transvestites cumulative construction of his
female self, motives for cross-dressing, wives' attitudes,
and parent child-relationships. Bibliography, pp. 73-87.

4025. UNDERWOOD, PETER. **Life's a Drag: Danny LaRue and
       the Drag Scene.** London: Leslie Frewin, 1974. 192
       pp.
Journalistic account of the emergence of Britain's premier
female impersonator, star of stage and screen.

4026. WAAL, MIEKE VAN. **Vriendinnen onder elkaar, trav-
       estien en transsexuelen in Nederland.** Amsterdam:
       Arbeiderpers, 1983.
Ethnographic account of transvestites and transsexuals in
the Netherlands today.

4027. WISE, THOMAS N., and JON K. MEYER. "Transvestism:
       Previous Findings and New Areas for Inquiry," **Jour-
       nal of Sex and Marital Therapy,** 6 (1980), 116-28.
Reviews the literature and notes that the phenomenology of
the "disorder" reveals individuals to be heterosexual
males who have usually married and fathered children.
See also Wise et al., "Partners of Distressed Transvestites," **American Journal of Psychology,** 138 (1981), 1221-
24.

                C. TRANSSEXUALISM AND SEX REASSIGNMENT

Adopting the popular stereotype that a male homosexual is
really "a female soul trapped in a male body," and a
lesbian the reverse, some individuals have concluded that
they would be better off changing their sex. (For psychological reasons, most transsexuals deny that they are
or have ever been homosexual.) Although an experiment
was reported as early as 1904, the real trend toward
male-to-female operations emerged in Central Europe in the
1930s; the more difficult female-to-male operations were
developed later. Follow-up studies have shown that many
postoperative transsexuals exist in a state of almost
continual depression, and for this reason the operation is
now performed less often.

4028. BENJAMIN, HARRY. **The Transsexual Phenomenon.** New
       York: Julian Press, 1966. 286 pp.
An analysis by an American pioneer in the study of the
subject of persons desiring to change their sex; with case
histories of transsexuals.

4029. BENTLER, PETER M. "A Typology of Transsexualism:
       Gender Identity Theory and Data," **Archives of
       Sexual Behavior,** 5 (1976), 567-84.
An analysis of postoperative data obtained from 42 male-
to-female transsexuals showed them to fall into three
distinct categories: homosexual transsexuals, asexual
transsexuals, and heterosexual transsexuals.

4030. BILLINGS, DWIGHT B. and THOMAS URBAN. "The Socio-
       medical Construction of Transsexualism: An Inter-
       pretation and Critique," **Social Problems,** 29
       (1982), 266-82.
Contends that transsexualism is a socially constructed
reality that exists only in and through medical practice, which reflects and extends late-capitalist logics
of reification and commodification, while simultaenously
reaffirming traditional male and female gender roles.

4031. BINDER, HANS. "Verlangung nach Geschlechtsumwand-
       lung," **Zeitschrift für die gesamte Psychiatrie und
       Neurologie,** 143 (1932), 84-174.
On the desire for a sex change (then in practice not
surgically possible).

4032. CLARK, JOANNA M. **Legal Aspects of Transsexualism.**
       Second ed. Mission Viejo, CA: Renaissance Gender
       Identity Services, 1979.
Manual treating such aspects as military service, civil
rights, criminal law, family law, health benefits identity
and identification, and social security.

4032 A. COLE, WAYNE S. "Transsexuals in Search of Legal
       Acceptance: The Constitutionality of the Chromosome
       Test," **San Diego Law Review,** 15 (1978), 331-55.
Inasmuch as chromosomes cannot be changed through surgical

intervention, the acceptance of a chromosome test constitutes a barrier to the achievement of legal status by
transsexuals. See also: Douglas K. Browell, "M. T. v.
J. T.: An Enlightened Perspective on Transsexualism,"
Capital University Law Review, 6 (1977), 403-27.

4033. DE SAVITSCH, EUGENE. **Homosexuality, Transvestism
       and Change of Sex.** London: Heinemann Medical
       Books, 1958. 120 pp.
Attempts to separate the three phenomena, presenting in
detail the history of one individual who underwent a sex
change.

4034. EDLBACHER, OSKAR. "Transsexualität im Zivil- und
       im Personenstandsrecht," **Österreichische Juristen-
       Zeitung,** 36 (1981), 173-81.
Problems arising in Austrian public and private law. See
also: Arnulf Eberle, "Ausfüllung einer Gesetzlücke bei
Transsexualismus durch progressive Rechtsfindung oder
gesetzliche Fiktion?" **Neue juristische Wochenschrift,** 24
(1971), 220-24.

4035. EHRHARDT, ANKE A., et al. "Female-to-Male Trans-
       sexuals Compared to Lesbians: Behavioural Patterns
       of Childhood and Adolescent Development," **Archives
       of Sexual Behavior,** 8 (1979), 481-90.
The two groups differed significantly regarding childhood
cross-dressing, gender identity confusion in adolescence
(absent in lesbians), and negative reaction to breast
development and menarche. See also: Elizabeth A. Mc-
Cauley and Anke A. Ehrhardt, "Sexual Behavior in Female
Transsexuals and Lesbians," **Journal of Sex Research,** 16
(1980), 202-11.

4036. FREUND, KURT, et al. "The Trans-Sexual Syndrome in
       Homosexual Males," **Journal of Nervous and Mental
       Disease,** 158 (1974), 145-53.
There was no evidence that the gross deviations of nar-
cissism or masochism, or aversion to their own penis,
played a part in the syndrome. See also: Freund et al.,
"Parent-Child Relations in Transsexual and Non-Transsex-
ual Homosexual Males," **British Journal of Psychiatry,** 124
(1974), 22-23.

4037. GREEN, DAVID. "Legal Aspects of Transsexualism,"
       Archives of Sexual Behavior, 1 (1971), 145-51.
The author's experiences in acting as legal counsel to
transsexuals and the types of legal questions transsexuals in England are faced with, e.g. changing one's name
and birth certificate, marriage, and divorce.

4038. GREEN, RICHARD, and JOHN MONEY (eds.). **Transsexu-
       alism and Sex Reassignment.** Baltimore: Johns Hop-
       kins, 1969. 512 pp.
Encyclopedic synthesis with contributions from more than
thirty authors in the U. S. and Europe.

4039. HOYER, NIELS. **Man into Woman: An Authentic Record
       of a Change of Sex.** Translated from the German by
       J. J. Stanning. New York: Dutton, 1933. 288 pp.
Concerns the first widely publicized sex-change operation,
which was performed on Andreas Sparre, a Danish painter.

4040. JORGENSON, CHRISTINE. **Christine Jorgenson: A
       Personal Autobiography.** New York: Paul S. Eriks-
       son, 1967. 332 pp.
Jorgenson's sex change in Denmark received wide publicity,
sensationalizing the matter in the United States, and
probably contributing to a marked increase in the number
of applicants for the operation.

4041. KANDO, THOMAS. **Sex Change: The Achievement of
       Gender Identity among Feminized Transsexuals.**
       Springfield, IL: Charles C. Thomas, 1973. 159 pp.
Sociological study of identity formation among post-
operative male-to-female homosexuals. See also his:
"Males, Females, and Transsexuals," **JH,** 1 (1974), 64-69.

4042. LEVINE, EDWARD M., et al. "Behavioral Differences
       and Emotional Conflict among Male-to-Female Trans-
       sexuals," **Archives of Sexual Behavior,** 5 (1976),
       81-86.
Used interview data to study aspects of transsexualism
and homosexuality, prostitution and employment, affect-
lessness, need for reassurance, and deprecation of others
in eighteen transsexuals. See also: Ron Langevin et al.,
"The Clinical Profile of Male Transsexuals Living as
Females vs. Those Living as Males," ibid., 6 (1977),
143-54; and Edward M. Levine, "Male Homosexuals in the
Homosexual Subculture," **American Journal of Psychiatry,**
133 (1976), 1318-21.

4043. LOTHSTEIN, LESLIE MARTIN. **Female-to-Male Transsex-
       ualism: Historical, Clinical and Theoretical
       Issues.** Boston: Routledge and Kegan Paul, 1983.
       336 pp.
Following an approach derived from psychoanalysis, asserts
that female transsexualism is "not a normal variation of
sexuality or an alternative life style, but a profound
psychological disorder" that originates in intergenerational family dynamics in the second year of a girl's
life.

4044. MACKENZIE, K. ROY. "Gender Dysphoria Syndrome: To-
       wards Standardized Diagnostic Criteria," **Archives
       of Sexual Behavior,** 7 (1978), 251-62.
Notes that gender dysphoria syndrome has demonstrated a
propensity for creating self-fulfilling, self-validating
and reinforcing cycles on a number of levels.

4045. MONEY, JOHN. "Prefatory Remarks on Outcome of Sex
       Reassignment in 24 Cases of Transsexualism," **Ar-
       chives of Sexual Behavior,** 1 (1971), 163-65.

Reports a pattern of satisfaction (which subsequent
studies do not seem to have confirmed, leading to the
cessation of the operations at Johns Hopkins, Money's
institution). See also: Money and George Wolff, "Sex
Reassignment: Male to Female to Male," ibid., 2 (1973),
245-50; Money, "Two Names, Two Wardrobes, Two Personalities," **JH,** 1 (1974), 65-70; and Money and John G. Bren-
nan, "Heterosexual vs. Homosexual Attitudes: Male Partner's Perception of the Feminine Image of Male Transsexuals," **Journal of Sex Research,** 6 (1970), 193-209.

4046.   NELSON, C., et al. "Medicolegal Aspects of Trans-
        sexualism," **Canadian Psychiatric Association
        Journal,** 21 (1976), 557-64.
Contends that because there is no legal definition of
gender, the transsexual person faces serious risks and
disabilities in attempting to live as a member of the
gender into which he was not born.

4047.   PAULY, IRA B. "Female Transsexualism," **Archives of
        Sexual Behavior,** 3 (1974), 487-507, 509-26.
From a general study of the literature, concludes that
transsexualism would be far better prevented than treated.

4048.   PAULY, IRA B., and MILTON T. EDGERTON. "The Gender
        Identity Movement: A Growing Surgical-Psychiatric
        Liaison," **Archives of Sexual Behavior,** 15 (1986),
        315-29.
Discusses the origins of sex reassignment surgery and
present practice (about which the authors tend to be
positive), including follow-up studies. Extensive bibliography.

4049.   RAYMOND, JANICE. **The Transsexual Empire: The
        Making of the She-Male.** Boston: Beacon Press,
        1979. 220 pp.
Impassioned radical-feminist critique of male-to-female
operations, situating their rationale in a kind of hyper-
trophy of patriarchal domination: the creation of an
artificial female as a demonstration to biological females that they are, or might be, superfluous.

4050.   ROBERTO, L. G. "Issues in Diagnosis and Treatment
        of Transsexualism," **Archives of Sexual Behavior,** 12
        (1983), 445-73.
Criticizing previous approaches, author argues that we
should return to a very conservative use of sex-reassignment surgery.

4051.   SCHERRER, P. "Transexuels ou faux transexuels?"
        Annales médico-psychologiques, 143 (1985), 549-60.
Transsexualism is an iatrogenic illness created by the
advances in surgery and endocrinology and the diffusion
among the general public of an illusory solution to the
dilemma posed by K. H. Ulrichs' celebrated formula "a
female soul trapped in a male body."

4052.   STEINER, BETTY W. (ed.). **Gender Dysphoria: Devel-
        opment, Research, Management.** New York: Plenum
        Press, 1985. 430 pp.
Fifteen papers on clinical, medical-legal, and cultural
issues. See also: Erwin K. Koranyi, **Transsexualism in
the Male: The Spectrum of Gender Dysphoria.** (Springfield,
IL: Thomas, 1980; 198 pp.).

4053.   STOLLER, ROBERT J. "The Transsexual's Denial of
        Homosexuality," in his: **Sex and Gender: On the
        Development of Masculinity and Femininity.** New
        York: Science House, 1968, pp. 141-53.
The answer to why transsexuals and many transvestites
insist that they are not homosexual may lie in an understanding of the formation of, and the later struggle to
maintain, a gender identity. See also his: "The Bisexual
Identity of Transsexuals: Two Case Examples," **Archives
of Sexual Behavior,** 1 (1971), 17-28.

4054.   YUDKIN, MARCIA. "Transsexualism and Women: A
        Critical Perspective," **Feminist Studies,** 4 (1978),
        97-106.
Regards transsexuals as victims of culture's confusion
about gender identity and stress on sex role in identity, and of society's insistence that outward appear-
ances correlate with biological and social identity.

                    D. HERMAPHRODITISM

The fascination with hermaphrodites (sometimes also termed
androgynes), which began in classical antiquity (see
II.C), has enjoyed a long history. Hermaphroditism is
sometimes confused with homosexuality itself--either
literally or quasimetaphorically ("psychic hermaphroditism"). Medically, true hermaphrodites are very rare,
perhaps even nonexistent. For current concern with
androgyny as a dimension of personality, see XVI.L.

4055.   BAYER, HEINRICH. "Wahres und scheinbares Zwitter-
        tum," **Beiträge zur Geburtshilfe und Gynaekologie,**
        13 (1908), 180-97.
On true and pseudo-hermaphrodites.

4056.   FOUCAULT, MICHEL (ed.). **Herculine Barbin.** Trans-
        lated by Richard McDougall. New York: Pantheon,
        1980. 200 pp.
Memoirs of a French hermaphrodite who lived as a woman
until mid-teens, then was classified as a man and forced
to live as such. Accompanied by medical records and a
romance, "Ein skandaloser Fall," by Oscar Panizza, which
is based on the case.

4057. JONES, HOWARD WILBUR, and W. W. SCOTT. **Hermaphroditism, Genital Anomalies and Related Disorders.**
Second ed. Baltimore: Williams and Wilkins, 1971.
564 pp.
Medical text; first edition published in 1958.

4058. MONEY, JOHN. "Matched Pairs of Hermaphrodites:
Behavioral Biology of Sexual Differentiation from
Chromosomes to Gender Identity," **Engineering and
Science,** 33 (1970), 34-39.
A modern explanation by a professor of medical psychology (Johns Hopkins Medical Institutes). See also his: **Sex
Errors of the Body: Dilemmas, Education, Counseling** (Baltimore: Johns Hopkins Press, 1968; 145 pp.).

4059. NEUGEBAUER, FRANZ LUDWIG VON. "Zusammenstellung
der Literatur über Hermaphroditismus beim Menschen," **JfsZ,** 7 (1905), 471-670.
This ambitious bibliography by a Warsaw physician in
Hirschfeld's circle covers not only the intense investigation of his own day, but also includes many curiosa of
the older medical literature (16th-18th centuries). See
also his magnum opus: **Hermaphroditismus beim Menschen**
(Leipzig: Klinkhardt, 1908; 748 pp.).

4060. RÖMER, L. S. A. M. VON. "Ueber die androgynische
Idee des Lebens," **JfsZ,** 5 (1903), 707-940.
Encyclopedic survey of mythological themes of androgyny
in the literature and art of the European and Asian high
cultures.

4061. ZAPPERI, ROBERTO. **L'homme enceinte: l'homme, la
femme et le pouvoir.** Paris: Presses Universitaires
de France, 1983.
Study of the myth of male pregnancy and its connections
with the idea of androgyny. Translated from an Italian
original.

4062. ZOLLA, ELEMIRE. **The Androgyne.** London: Thames and
Hudson, 1979. 96 pp.
Useful collection of images of the hermetic tradition
of the androgyne/hermaphrodite. The text should be used
with caution.

A. GENERAL

The adoption of Christianity as the state religion of the
late Roman empire introduced a pattern of criminalizing
male homosexuality that persisted until the 18th century.
Even today the effects of centuries of legal stigmatization remain difficult to eradicate. While criminal
sanctions for adult homosexual conduct have disappeared
from the law codes of most advanced industrial countries
(though this is the case in only half of the American
states), they linger in some Marxist nations and are even
spreading in the Third World. In the light of this mixed
picture, a careful study of the premises of sexual law and
law reform is necessary.

4063.   BARNETT, WALTER. **Sexual Freedom and the Constitu-
        tion: An Inquiry into the Constitutionality of Re-
        pressive Sex Laws.** Albuquerque: University of New
        Mexico Press, 1973. 333 pp.
A valuable, if somewhat longwinded study of the history of
homosexual criminalization (chiefly in English-speaking
countries), stressing the case for reform. The extensive
notes are useful for bibliographical references; for
others, see Vern Bullough et al., **An Annotated Bibliography of Homosexuality.** (New York: Garland, 1976), vol.
1, pp. 278-316.

4064.   BECCARIA, CESARE BONESANA, MARQUIS. **Dei delitti e
        delle pene.** Edited by Franco Venturi, with a
        collection of related letters and documents. Tur-
        in: Einaudi, 1965. 680 pp.
This scholarly edition of Beccaria's epochal contribution
(1764) to Enlightenment reform of the criminal law is recommended because of the complementary material, showing
the impact of his ideas throughout Europe. See chapter 31
(36 in some editions) discussing **l'attica venere** (Greek
love). Several English translations exist.

4065.   BENTHAM, JEREMY. "Offenses against One's Self:
        Paederasty," **JH,** 3:4 (Summer 1978), 389-405; 4:1
        (Fall 1978), 91-107.
This is the first publication, edited by Louis Crompton,
of the arguments for law reform developed by the English
utilitarian thinker, ca. 1785. See also Bentham, **The
Theory of Legislation.** Edited by C. K. Ogden. (London:
Kegan Paul, 1931), pp. 476-97 (essay "Offenses against
Taste," 1814-16). Like the material published in 1978,
this essay drew extensively on continental thinkers of the
Enlightenment.

4066. BLACKBURN, CATHERINE E. "Human Rights in International Context: Recognizing the Right of Intimate
Association," **Ohio State Law Journal**, 43 (1982),
143-63.
Assesses recent progress of the right of privacy both
within the United States and internationally (the latter
with particular reference to article 8 of the European
Convention on Human Rights).

4067. DEVLIN, PATRICK, LORD. **The Enforcement of Morals.**
London: Oxford University Press, 1965. 25 pp.
British jurist's critique of the Wolfenden Committee
proposals for law reform; advocates continuing repression of homosexual conduct in obeisance to "sound public
sentiment." See esp. H. L. A. Hart's rebuttal, below.

4068. DWORKIN, RONALD. **Taking Rights Seriously.** Second
ed. Cambridge, MA: Harvard University Press,
1978. 371 pp.
Chapter 10, "Liberty and Moralism" (pp. 240-58) offers a
sharp critique of Devlin's restrictivist arguments.

4069. DYNES, WAYNE. "Privacy, Sexual Orientation and the
Self-Sovereignty of the Individual: Continental
Theories, 1762-1908," **Gay Books Bulletin**, 6 (Fall
1981), 20-23.
Traces the development of the Enlightenment tradition of
control over one's body from Beccaria to Hiller.

4070. FILANGIERI, GAETANO. **The Science of Legislation.**
Translated from the Italian by Richard Clayton.
London: T. Ostell, 1806. 2 vols.
This work, regarded as a classic of jurisprudential theory, is unfortunately obsessed with the pronatalist notion
that celibacy is opposed to the "progress of population"
(cf. e.g.,vol. 2, p. 4).

4071. GREY, THOMAS C. **The Legal Enforcement of Morality.** New York: Knopf, 1983. 212 pp.
Textbook with many short quotations from legal opinions
and articles. See "Sexual Freedom and the Constitution,"
pp. 37-102.

4072. HARRIS, ROBERT N. "Private Consensual Adult Behavior: The Requirement of Harm to Others in the
Enforcement of Morality," **UCLA Law Review**, 14
(1966-67), 581-603.
Society is seen as dominated by a "condemn or condone"
syndrome with regard to sexual law reform. Argues that
there is no criminal harm in homosexual behavior in private between consenting adults, as long as there is no
underlying need to increase the population.

4073. HART, HERBERT LIONEL ADOLPHUS. **Law, Liberty and
Morality.** Stanford: Stanford University Press,
1963. 88 pp.

Concurring with the ideas of J. S. Mill and the Wolfenden
Report, Hart (a major English legal philosopher) refutes
Lord Devlin's arguments for enforcing morality through
legal sanctions. On Hart see: Neil MacCormick, **H. L. A.**
Hart (Stanford: Stanford University Press, 1981; 184 pp.;
esp. pp. 150-53); and the bibliographical surveys of
C. F. Cranor, **Criminal Justice and Ethics,** 2 (1983),
59ff., and Stephen W. Ball, ibid. (1984), 68ff.

4074. HEASMAN, D.J. "Sexuality and Civil Liberties,"
       Political Quarterly, 48 (1977), 313-37.
Opposes gay rights on campus, questioning the value of
"legally coerced acceptance." See reply by Rodney Barker,
ibid., 49 (1978), 99-102.

4075. HILLER, KURT. **Das Recht über sich selbst: eine**
       strafrechtsphilosophische Studie. Heidelberg: Carl
       Winter, 1908. 114 pp.
In this pathfinding work (the author's doctoral dissertation), the concept of the right to control one's body is
examined with reference to suicide, abortion, incest,
duelling, homosexuality, and bestiality. See "Homosex-
ualverkehr," pp. 67-89.

4076. INTERNATIONAL GAY ASSOCIATION. **IGA Pink Book**
       1985. Amsterdam: COC, 1985. 192 pp.
This collective volume offers a series of essays on the
legal situation for homosexuals and lesbians in several
European countries, followed by a world survey of laws.

4077. KLARE, RUDOLF. **Homosexualität und Strafrecht.**
       Hamburg: Hanseatisches Verlags-Anstalt, 1937. 172
       pp.
This monograph by a Nazi legal scholar defends the repressive legislation of the "Nordic tradition" as progressive. Despite much offensive, and fortunately dated
material, this book does offer a world survey of relevant
laws, updating the tables found in Magnus Hirschfeld, **Die**
Homosexualität des Mannes und des Weibes. Second ed.
(Berlin: Louis Marcus, 1920), pp. 841-69, which display
the situation as of January 1, 1913.

4078. MACFARLANE, L. J. **The Theory and Practice of**
       Human Rights. London: Temple Smith, 1985. 193 pp.
This book contains much information on human rights
practices and violations. The author also provides a
number of personal opinions, including the assertion
that the state may ban the promotion of a homosexual
lifestyle on grounds of morality.

4079. MILL, JOHN STUART. **On Liberty.** London: J. W. Par-
       ker and Son, 1859. 207 pp.
Although this fundamental essay by the English thinker
does not deal directly with sexual expression, its
powerful and lucid advocacy of individual liberty has
exercized a continuing and beneficial influence. There

are several modern editions with useful commentary.

4080. MONTESQUIEU, CHARLES LOUIS DE SECONDAT, BARON
       DE. **De l'esprit des loix.** Geneva: Barillot,
       1748. 2 vols.
In this many-sided and perennially influential Enlightenment work on the foundations of law, see IV, 4; VI, 13;
VII, 9; VIII, 12; XII, 4, 6, and 21; XXXIII, 17; XXIV,
15; and XXVI, 3. There have been many subsequent editions
and several English translations.

4081. PRAETORIUS, NUMA (pseud. of Eugen Wilhelm). "Die
       strafrechtlichen Bestimmungen gegen die gleichge-
       schlechtliche Verkehr historisch und kritisch
       dargestellt," **JfsZ**, 1 (1899), 97-158.
Though uneven, this article is the earliest historical
survey of antihomosexual legislation from ancient times
to the time of writing. See also F. Wachenfeld, below.

4082. RICHARDS, DAVID A. J. **The Moral Criticism of Law.**
       Encino, CA: Dickenson, 1977. 278 pp.
See "Deviant Sexual Conduct and the Right of Privacy"
(pp. 77-134), which discusses the problem of the unnatural; the constitutional right of privacy; love as a
primary good; and the constitutionality of prohibiting
sexual deviation.

4083. RICHARDS, DAVID A. J. **Sex, Drugs, Death and the
       Law: An Essay on Human Rights and Overcriminaliza-
       tion.** Totowa, NJ: Rowan and Littlefield, 1982.
       316 pp.
Applies interdisciplinary perspectives to the problem
of overcriminalization, suggesting a new approach grounded
in a basic respect of the rights of persons and the
foundations of American constitutional law. An impressive
plea for decriminalization and legislative reform.

4084. RUBINSTEIN, AMNON. "The Enforcement of Morals in a
       Secular Society," **Israel Yearbook on Human Rights,**
       2 (1972), 57-98.
On the Wolfenden Report, the Hart-Devlin controversy, and
related matters.

4085. **Sexual Behaviour and Attitudes and Their Implica-
       tions for Criminal Law: Reports Presented to the
       Fifteenth Criminological Research Conference
       (1982).** Strasbourg: Council of Europe, 1984. 207
       pp. (Collected Studies in Criminological Research,
       21)
Six papers by Western European scholars treating national
differences, changes in public opinion and scientific
knowledge, "pressure groups" (including homosexuals), the
age of consent, etc.

4086. SZASZ, THOMAS S. **Law, Liberty and Psychiatry.** New
       York: Macmillan, 1963. 281 pp.

One of a number of polemical libertarian works by this
prolific author, who argues against the alliance of law
and psychiatry to regulate personal conduct.

4087. WACHENFELD, FRIEDRICH. **Homosexualität und Straf-
gesetz: Ein Beitrag zur Untersuchung der Reform-
bedürftigkeit des 175 St.G.B.** Leipzig: Weicher,
1901. 148 pp.
German jurist's examination of the background of criminalization of homosexuality in canon, Roman and Germanic
law. See the detailed review and critique by Numa Praetorius in: **JfsZ**, 4 (1902), 670-775.

B. ANCIENT, CIVIL, AND CANON LAW

Roman law, as codified at the behest of the Emperor Justinian in the 6th century, is the source of the civil law
tradition which came to prevail on the European continent
and, ultimately, through much of the world (with the major
exception of the English-speaking countries; see XX.D-M).
Canon law is the legal tradition of the Roman Catholic
church, which came--in the sexual sphere as in others--to
have a symbiotic relationship with the medieval civil law
tradition.

4088. BIENER, FRIEDRICH AUGUST. **Geschichte der Novellen
Justinian's.** Berlin: Ferdinand Dummler, 1824.
621 pp.
On Justinian's Novellae 77 and 141 and his persecution of
sodomites in Byzantium, see pp. 23, 27, 44-46, 455-56,
470-71, 518, 526, 583-84.

4088A. CARPZOV [CARPZOVIUS], BENEDICT. **Practica nova
imperialis Saxonica rerum criminalium.** Wittenberg
and Leipzig, 1652.
The influential leader (1595-1666) of the German Practical
School of legal scholars held that sodomites incur divine
vengeance in the form of famines, plagues, wars, earth-
quakes, floods and "other general scourges of this kind"
(Pars 11, Quaestio LXXVI, 5).

4089. CHRIST, JOHANNES FRIEDRICH. **Historia legis
Scatiniae.** Halle: Johannes Christoph Krebsius,
1727. 27 pp.
To date the only comprehensive treatise (in Latin) on the
obscure law of the Roman republic, the Lex Sca(n)tinia.
See now, however, Saara Lilja, **Homosexuality in Repub-
lican and Augustan Rome** (Helsinki: Societas Scientiarum
Fennica, 1983), 112-21.

4090. DAMHOUDER, JOOS DE. **Praxis rerum criminalium.**
Antwerp: Beller, 1601.

One of several editions of a treatise first issued in 1554
in Louvain. See pp. 390-97 (chapter 98), where the
learned author (1507-81) extends the boundaries of
sodomy to include bestiality, demonism, necrophilia, and
relations with heretics.

4091. D'AVACK, PIETRO AGOSTINO. "L'omosessualità nel
diritto canonico," **Ulisse**, 3:18 (1953), 680-97.
Well-documented study by a canonist on the history of
church law.

4092. FLORENCE. REPUBLIC. **Statuti della Repubblica
Fiorentina.** Edited by Romolo Caggese. Florence:
Comune, 1910-21. 2 vols.
See Chapter LIV (2, pp. 218-19), for a law of 1325 which
prescribes castration for active sodomites and a fine for
passive ones (if under age). An unusual provision in this
otherwise typical Italian law of the period is the prohibition on composing or singing sodomite songs.

4093. GAUTHIER, ALBERT. "La sodomie dans le droit
canonique médiéval," in: Bruno Rey (ed.), **L'érotisme au moyen âge.** Montreal: Aurore, 1977, pp.
111-22.
Brief account of the canon law tradition; inferior to
P. A. D'Avack, above.

4094. GOODICH, MICHAEL. "Sodomy in Medieval Secular
Law," **JH**, 1 (1976), 295-302.
Shows that in 13th and 14th century Europe kings and
lawmakers strove to make secular law conform with Christian moral theology.

4095. LOBINGIER, CHARLES SUMNER. "Lex Christiana: The
Connecting Link Between Ancient and Modern Law,"
Georgetown Law Journal, 20 (1931-32), 1-43, 160-95.
Places in context the process whereby "the whole province
of sex crimes was annexed by the church courts" (pp. 6,
160, 181).

4096. ORBACH, WILLIAM. "Homosexuality and Jewish Law,"
Journal of Family Law, 14 (1975), 353-81.
On the whole an uncritical traditionalist compilation
of Jewish law in relation to homosexuality from the Bible
to contemporary responsa, but useful for the many references to traditional and modern sources.

4097. SABELLUS, MARCUS ANTONIUS (MARCO ANTONIO SAVELLI).
Summa diversorum tractatum. New ed. Venice: Paulus Balleonium, 1707. 6 vols.
The crime of sodomy is discussed with many learned
references (4, pp. 128-32).

4098. SCHURIG, MARTIN. **Gynaecologia historico-medica,
hoc est congressus muliebris: Consideratio
physico-medico-forensis qua utriusque sexus**

**salacitas et castitas ... necnon coitus ... item
nefandus et sodomiticus raris observationibus et
aliquot casibus medico-forensibus exhibentur.**
Dresden and Leipzig: 1730.
Chapter VII (pp. 368-413) deals with the crime of sodomy
in all its forms: with members of the same sex, with
animals, intercourse with the opposite sex **per os et per
anum**, with corpses, and with inanimate objects. There are
extensive references to ancient and contemporary authors
in Latin and in German, including accounts of many little
known cases. All in all, a compendium of what was thought
on the subject on the eve of the Enlightenment campaign
for reform. See also Schurig's earlier treatise: **Spermat-
ologia historico-medica ...** (Frankfurt am Main, 1720).

4099.   SINISTRARI D'AMENO, LUIGI MARIO. **De delictis et
        poenis.** Venice: Hieronymus Albiriccius, 1700.
In this work written for the use of priests in the
confessional, see Section X, "Mollities" (pp. 250-68),
for the crime against nature. This section of Sinistrari's treatise has been several times republished in Latin,
French, and English. The English version first appeared
as **Peccatum mutum** (Paris: I. Liseux, 1893; 76 pp.).

4100.   **The Theodosian Code.** Edited and Translated by
        Clyde Pharr. Princeton: Princeton University
        Press, 1952. 643 pp.
See pp. 231-32 (IX.vii.3) for the antihomosexual law of
342, and pp. 232 (IX.vii.6) for the shorter text of the
390 law.

4101.   VOET, JOHANNES. **The Selective Voet: Being the
        Commentary on the Pandects (Paris Edition of 1829)
        by Johannes Voet (1647-1713) and the Supplement to
        That Work by Johannes van der Linden (1756-1835).**
        Translated with explanatory notes by Percival Gane.
        Durban: Butterworth Africa, 1955-58. 9 vols.
See vol. 7, Book XLVIII, Title 5, Section 24, where Voet
lists a dozen legal authorities of the 16th and 17th
centuries.

4102.   WOLFART, JOANNES HENRICUS. **Tractatio juridica de
        sodomia vera et spuria hermaphroditi; Von achter
        und unachter Sodomiterey eines Zwittern.** Frankfurt
        am Main: 1742. 32 pp.
Part I deals with sodomy committed by hermaphrodites of
either sex with each other, or with ordinary men and
women. Part II gives an account of a lesbian scandal of
1740.

                        C. EUROPEAN LAW

The French Revolution marks a decisive turning point in

the civil law tradition. With respect to homosexuality,
the French National Assembly decriminalized sodomy in
1791, and this omission was replicated in the body of law
known as the Code Napoleon, created in the first decade of
the 19th century. The decriminalization was imitated in
many countries under French influence, chiefly in southern
Europe and in Latin America. Change in the sodomy laws of
northern Europe was a slower process, but it was essentially achieved in the period after World War II.

4103. ANCEL, MARC (ed.). La réforme pénale soviétique.
        Paris: Centre Français de Droit Comparé, 1962.
        lxix, 248 pp.
See p. 51 (Art. 121 of the Penal Code of the RSFSR: buggery = muzhelozhstvo); p. 118 (Art. 126 of the Code of
Criminal Procedure: obligatory character of preliminary investigation).

4104. ANDENAES, JOHS. "Recent Trends in the Criminal Law
        and Penal System in Norway: I. Criminal Law," Brit-
        ish Journal of Delinquency, 5 (1954), 21-26.
Describes the prereform situation in Norway. Since
this time a remarkable improvement has occurred; see,
e.g., Lia Pedersen, "Norway: The Antidiscrimination
Law: The Experience So Far," IGA Pink Book (Amsterdam:
COC, 1985), 117-19.

4105. ANOSSOW, J. J. (I. I. ANOSOV). "Die Homosexualität
        im sowietischen Recht," Monatsschrift für Kriminal-
        psychologie und Strafrechtsreform, 23 (1932),
        583-86.
The penal codes of the union republics of the USSR with a
predominately Moslem population (Uzbekistan, Tadjikistan,
Turkmenistan) already had prescriptions against pederasty,
which was regarded as an aspect of the "old way of life."

4106. AUGSTEIN-THALACKER, RENATE. "Argumente für eine
        ersatzlose Streichung von Paragraph 175 StGB,"
        Liberal, 23 (1981), 931-40.
Arguments for the complete abolition of Article 175. Concerning this article of the German penal code, enacted in
its original form in 1871, there is an enormous literature, most of which is listed in Manfred Herzer, Bibliographie zur Homosexualität (Berlin: Verlag Rosa Winkel,
1982).

4107. BASLER, WALTER. Homosexualität im Strafrecht.
        Zurich: The author, 1941. 239 pp.
Legal dissertation with particular application to the new
liberalized Swiss code.

4108. BAUER, FRITZ, HANS BÜRGER-PRINZ, HANS GIESE, and
        HERBERT JÄGER. Sexualität und Verbrechen: Beiträge
        zur Strafrechtsreform. Frankfurt: Fischer, 1963.
        438 pp.

Twenty-two essays on various aspects of sex and the law
assembled during a period of intense discussion of law
reform in West Germany. Of particular interest are those
by Helmut Thielicke (Protestant theology and homosexuality in relation to the law) and Heinrich Ackermann (on the
question of punishing homosexual conduct: supports reform).

4109. BAUMANN, JÜRGEN. **Paragraph 175: über die Möglich-
        keit, die einfache, nichtjugendgefährdende und
        nichtöffentliche Homosexualität unter Erwachsenen
        straffrei zu lassen.** Berlin-Neuwied: Luchterhand,
        1968. 204 pp.
An argument for the reform of Article 175 of the (West)
German penal code, a step which was taken the following
year.

4110. BERGMANS, ALBERT, and J. DEBOIS. **Verslag en advies
        met betrekking tot art. 372bis Belgisch Strafwet-
        boek.** Antwerp: Federatie Werkgroepen Homofilie,
        1973. 39 pp.
On the antihomosexual article 372bis of the Belgian penal
code.

4111. BIEDERICH, PAUL HUGO. **Die gleichgeschlechtliche
        Unzucht in kriminal-politischer Sicht: eine stat-
        istische-taxonomische Untersuchung.** Hamburg:
        Arbeitsgemeinschaft zur Pflege der Humanität,
        1953. 39 pp.
A statistical and taxonomic inquiry concerning homosexual indecency in criminal-political perspective.

4112. BIEDERICH, PAUL HUGO. **Paragraph 175: die Homosexu-
        alität.** Regensburg: Verlag für Sexualliteratur,
        1950. 71 pp.
In addition to Biederich's essay on Article 175, contains
"Die lesbische Liebe im Spiegel der Gesetze" by Thea
Booss-Rosenthal, and "Zwischen Mann und Weib: Zwitter-
bildung beim Menschen" by K. Koeniger.

4113. BONDY, HUGO. "Ueber die Sexualparagraphen im
        tschechoslowakischen Entwurf des Strafgesetz-
        buches," in: International Congress of Sex Re-
        search, **Verhandlungen** [Berlin], 1926, 1-29.
On the sexual articles in the draft of the Czechoslovak
penal code, which was unfortunately not adopted during
the First Republic.

4114. BOUCHAL, M., and D. BARTOVÁ. "The Attitude of
        Homosexuals after the Change in the Criminal Code,"
        Activitas Nervosa Superior, 6 (1964), 100-01.
Evaluates changes in attitudes among homosexuals following
the 1962 law reform.

4115. BROCHER, TOBIAS and others. **Plädoyer für die
        Abschaffung des Paragraph 175.** Frankfurt am

Main: Suhrkamp Verlag, 1966. 146 pp.
Four essays by academic authorities (Tobias Brocher,
Armand Mengen, Hans Bolewski, and Herbert Ernst Müller)
arguing in favor of discarding Article 175.

4116. CHARLES, R. "Propos sur l'article 372bis du code
        pénal (article 87 de la loi du 8 avril sur la
        protection de la jeunesse)," **Revue de droit pénal
        et de criminologie**, 62 (November 1982), 809-35.
Complications of current Belgian law.

4117. COUROUVE, CLAUDE. **Contre nature? Etude sur l'in-
        crimination pénale de l'homosexualité.** Paris: The
        author, 1981. 16 pp.
Historical review of problems in French law concerning
homosexuality, esp. those stemming from the Vichy government's 1942 change of article 334 of the penal code, which
set the age of consent at 21.

4118. COUROUVE, CLAUDE. "1791 Law Reform in France,"
        Cabirion, 12 (1985), 9-10.
Sets forth some elements in Enlightenment thought that
made possible the decriminalization effected by the
National Assembly during the Revolution.

4119. DAMASKA, MIRJAM. "Les infractions contre la moral-
        ité sexuelle en droit yougoslave," **Revue interna-
        tionale de droit pénal**, 35 (1964), 1011-33.
Seriatim discussion of sexual law provisions in the Yugo-
slav penal code. Pp. 1022-27 contain some historical
material on the crime against nature.

4120. DANET, JEAN. **Discours juridique et perversions
        sexuelles.** Nantes: Faculté de Droit et des
        Sciences Politiques, 1977. 111 pp.
Changes in French legal attitudes toward sexual deviation
in the 19th and 20th centuries.

4121. DIECKHOFF, ALBRECHT DIEDRICH. **Zur Rechtslage im
        derzeitigen Sittenstrafrecht.** Hamburg: Kriminalis-
        tik, 1958. 112 pp.
Consideration of the German situation in the period
leading to reform, with extensive reference to the
Griffin Report and the Wolfenden Report (UK).

4122. DOMINGO LORÉN, VICTORIANO. **Los homosexuales frente
        a la ley.** Second ed. Barcelona: Editorial Plaza y
        Janes, 1978. 320 pp.
Somewhat prolix interviews with Spanish judges and legal
authorities.

4123. EUROPEAN COURT OF HUMAN RIGHTS. "Dudgeon Case,"
        Publications of the European Court of Human Rights
        [Strasbourg], Series A, vol. 45, 1982. 48 pp.
The existing statute in Northern Ireland was held to
violate Article 8 of the European Human Rights Conven-

tion ("right to privacy").

4124. FONTÁN BALESTRA, CARLOS. **Delitos sexuales, estudio jurídico, medico-legal y criminológico.** Buenos Aires: Depalma, 1945. 344 pp.
See p. 138ff. for brief discussion of "corruption" (homosexuality in its relation to sexual offenses).

4125. FRIEDRICHS, KARL AUGUST. **Homosexualität und Strafvollzug: Probleme der Straf- und Strafvollzugszwecke.** Munich: Goldmann, 1971. 234 pp.
Problems of the aims and methods of applying criminal penalties to homosexuals; revision of author's doctoral dissertation.

4126. FRITZSCHE, HANS. **Gerichtsverfassung, Strafgesetzbuch und Strafprozessordnung der RSFSR.** Berlin: VEB Deutscher Zentralverlag, 1962.
See p. 84 (Art. 121 of the criminal code of the Russian Soviet Federative Socialist Republic concerning **muzhelozhstvo,** "buggery"), and p. 195 (Art. 126 of the Code of Criminal Procedure: preliminary investigation obligatory).

4127. GALLETTO, T. "Identità di sesso e rifiuto delle pubblicazioni per la celebrazione del matrimonio," **Giurisprudenza Italiana** (February 1982), 169-73.
Well-informed article focussing on the attempt of two men to marry in Rome in 1980.

4128. GLASSL, KARL. "Zur Frage der Strafbarkeit der Homosexualität," **Kriminalistik,** 26 (1972), 47-51.
On the criminalization of homosexuality in Austria.

4129. GOLLNER, GUENTHER. **Homosexualität: Ideologiekritik und Entmythologisierung einer Gesetzgebung.** Berlin: Duncker und Humblot, 1972. 264 pp.
Attempts to exfoliate preconceptions conditioning penalization of homosexuality, and in particular rationalizations utilized by defenders of the existing law in Germany from 1897 to the time of writing.

4130. GOLLNER, GUENTHER. "Homosexualität--Tradition gegen Recht?" **Zeitschrift für Rechtspolitik,** 8 (1975), 231-34.
Discusses practical difficulties, esp. among the military, hindering the full effect of the West German legal reform of 1969.

4131. GONZÁLEZ DE LA VEGA, FRANCISCO. **Derecho penal mexicano: los delitos.** Seventh ed. Mexico City: Porrua, 1964. 463 pp.
In this standard commentary on Mexican penal law, the author defends the Latin pattern of exclusion of homosexuality from the penal code, for "the law should not invade the territory proper to conscience and individual morality" (pp. 323-25).

4132. GURY, CHRISTIAN. **L'homosexuel et la loi.** Lau-
        sanne: Editions de l'Aire, 1981. 380 pp.
Ambitious, but sometimes capricious effort to treat the
law of homosexuality in Europe: civil, criminal, and
institutional. Extensive, but not always adequate references.

4133. GUSMÃO, CHRYSOLITO DE. **Dos crimes sexuais: estup-
        ros ao pudor, defloramento e corrupção de menores.**
        Third ed. Rio de Janeiro: Freitas Bastos, 1945.
        418 pp.
Discussion of sexual crimes from a positivist standpoint,
treating medical background, Brazilian law, and comparative law (includes offences against decency and corruption
of minors).

4134. HAFTER, ERNST. "Homosexualität und Strafgesetz-
        geber," **Schweizerische Zeitschrift für Strafrecht,**
        43 (1929), 37-71.
Favors reform of Art. 169 of the draft of a penal code
for the Swiss confederation.

4135. HAMMELMANN, H. A. "Homosexuality and the Law in
        Other Countries," in: J. T. Rees and H. V. Usill
        (eds.), **They Stand Apart: A Critical Survey of the
        Problems of Homosexuality.** London: William Heine-
        mann, 1955, pp. 143-83.
Summary of the state of the law in Western European countries at the time of writing.

4136. HENTIG, HANS VON. **Die Kriminalität des homophilen
        Mannes.** Stuttgart: F. Enke, 1960. 182 pp.
Criminalistic study of the homosexual man conducted before
the 1969 law reform in West Germany.

4137. HENTIG, HANS VON. **Die Kriminalität der lesbischen
        Frau.** Second ed. Stuttgart: F. Enke, 1965. 107
        pp.
After a discussion of the lesbian social situation, deals
with aberrations such as murder, crimes against property,
and offenses against public morals.

4138. HIRSCHFELD, MAGNUS. **Paragraph 175 des Reichsstraf-
        gesetzbuchs: Die homosexuelle Frage im Urteile der
        Zeitgenossen.** Leipzig: Spohr, 1898. 71 pp.
One of scores of critiques of the antihomosexual Article
175 in the Imperial German Penal Code which appeared in
the period 1880-1933. For the most recent developments,
see R. Augstein-Thalacker, above.

4139. **Homosexualität oder Politik mit Paragraph 175.**
        With a forward by Hans Giese. Reinbek: Rowohlt,
        1967. 180 pp.
Political aspects of impending law reform in West Germany.

4140. JOUBERT, DIAN D. **Tot dieselfde geslag: Debat oor**

homoseksualiteit in 1968. Capetown: Tafelberg, 1975. 95 pp.
Analysis of discussions in South Africa in 1968 regarding legal reform, with coverage of the negative position of Roman-Dutch law as influenced by the Calvinist religious tradition.

4141. KIEL, PETER. "Paragraph 175 StGB: Relikt eines autoritären Sexualstrafrechts? Ein Beitrag zur Sexualpolitik der SPD," **Demokratie und Recht** 11 (1983), 428-37.
On the attitude of the West German Social Democratic Party to Article 175.

4142. LADAME, P. L. "L'homosexualité dans l'avant-projet du Code pénal suisse," **Schweizerische Zeitschrift für Strafrecht,** 27 (1914), 279-95.
Psychiatrist comments on the ongoing discussions concerning changes in the Swiss penal code, arguing for reform.

4143. MARTÍNEZ, JOSÉ AUGUSTÍN. **El homosexualismo y su tratamiento.** Mexico City: Ediciones Botas, 1947. 150 pp.
Three lectures delivered before the Tribunal Supremo of Cuba; hostile.

4144. MAURACH, REINHART. "Die Einführung der Strafbarkeit der Päderastie in der Sowetunion," **Zeitschrift für osteuropäisches Recht,** N.S. 1 (1934), 93-97.
Account of the Soviet recriminalization of sodomy. There is a reply by Sergeĭ Iakovlevich Bulatov in **Sovetskoe gosudarstvo,** 1-2 (1935), 159-61.

4145. NABOKOFF, VLADIMIR. "Die Homosexualität im Russischen Strafgesetzbuch," **JfsZ** (1903), 1159-71.
Russian jurist's account of Tsarist law before the Revolution of 1905.

4146. NORSKE FORBUNDET AV 1948. **Kommentar til Straffelovradets instilling om saerlig straffererenslig vern for homofilie.** Oslo: Forbundet, 1980. 95 pp.
Commentary on the current Norwegian situation by the leading Norwegian homosexual rights association.

4147. RADDATZ, THOMAS F. "Quid leges sine moribus? Gedenken zur aktuellen Menschenrechtpolitik des Europarates," **Liberal,** 24 (1983), 4-13.
Human rights, including those of homosexual persons, in the context of the Council of Europe.

4148. SCHMUTZ, MARCEL, and PETER THOMMEN. **Die Unzuchtsparagraphen 191 und 194 im Schweiz. Strafgesetzbuch.** Basel: Arcados, 1980. 57 pp.
Current Swiss law sets the age of consent for heterosexual acts at 16 and for homosexual acts at 20. It is proposed to make the latter conform to the former.

4149. SCHWULE INITIATIVE GEGEN DEN PARAGRAPHENSUMPF.
       Rechtschwul: Rechtsratgeber für Schwule. Berlin:
       Verlag Rosa Winkel. 288 pp.
A legal guide put together by gay German law students
and lawyers offering comprehensive coverage from simple
civil procedures to felonies. The guide also provides
advice for homosexuals in the civil service, the church,
and the army, as well as information about cohabitation
and inheritance rights.

4150. SEELBACH, SIEGFRIED. **Die Beratungen der Grossen
       Strafrechtskomission über das Problem der Bestraf-
       ung gleichgeschlechtlicher Unzucht zwischen
       Mannern.** Cologne: The author, 1965. 315 pp. (Doc-
       toral dissertation)
Account of West German parliamentary and other official
discussions preceding the reform of 1969 stimulated by
the English Wolfenden Report. Reissued as a book with a
somewhat different title by Enke in Stuttgart in 1966.

4151. STOKVIS, B. J. "Frage der Homosexualität im
       Hollandischen Strafrecht," **Monatsschrift für
       Kriminalpychologie,** 24 (1933), 740-46.
The Dutch law as amended in 1911.

4152. STURUP, GEORG K. "Sex Offenses: The Scandinavian
       Experience," **Law and Contemporary Problems,** 25
       (1960), 361-75.
Reports decriminalization of homosexual behavior between
persons 18 years of age and over.

4153. SZABÓ, A., and G. POLLNER. "Appreciation de
       l'homosexualité à la base du nouveau Code Pénal
       Hongrois," **Acta Medicinae Legalis et Socialis,** 19
       (1966), 325-26.
Discusses the exclusion of homosexual acts between men
from the Hungarian penal code of 1962. The age of consent is 20.

4154. TISSOT, OLIVIER DE. **La liberté sexuelle et la
       loi.** Paris: Ballard, 1984. 380 pp.
Theoretical considerations on sexual liberty with particular reference to French experience.

4155. VINCINEAU, MICHEL. **La débauche en droit, le droit
       à la débauche.** Brussels: Université Libre, 1985.
Reflections on the law by a Belgian professor, who is
also part owner of a gay sauna that has been harassed by
the authorities.

4156. VINCINEAU, MICHEL. "Homosexuels devant la Commis-
       sion européenne des droits de l'homme," **Revue de
       Droit Criminel et de Pénologie,** 59 (1979), 83-106.
Reviews some cases brought before the European Commission
on Human Rights.

4157. VIVAS MARZAL, LUIS. **Contemplación jurídico-penal de la homosexualidad.** Valencia: Academia Valenciana de Jurisprudencia y Legislación, 1963. 49 pp.
Inaugural lecture reflecting older Spanish attitudes.

D. BRITAIN

Britain's historic law tradition, known as the common law, stands apart from the civil law tradition of the European continent. This British legal tradition has been bequeathed to the other English-speaking countries, including (with the major modification of the principle of constitutional review) the United States. Accordingly, Henry VIII's law of 1533 against buggery is a landmark not only for England, but for all jurisdictions in this legal tradition. As far as modern research can determine, prosecutions were relatively uncommon. However, the English-speaking countries have inherited a body of commentary, as seen in the writings of Coke and Blackstone, that is harshly antihomosexual. This hostile strand of our tradition accounts in part for the fact that sodomy law reform has been slow to come to the English-speaking world. The publication of the Wolfenden Report in Britain in 1956 nonetheless marked an important turning point on the road to reform.

4157. ANDREWS, JOHN. "Homosexual Relationships in Northern Ireland," **European Law Review,** 7 (April 1982), 141-44.
On the Dudgeon decision, which brought about decriminalization in Northern Ireland, and virtually establishes the right of adult males, in those states which are parties to the European Convention on Human Rights, to engage in homosexual acts in private.

4158. AYER, ALFRED JULES, SIR. "Homosexuals and the Law," **Mattachine Review,** 5:6 (1959), 5-11.
A noted English philosopher urges adoption of the Wolfenden Committee proposals.

4159. BERG, CHARLES. **Fear, Punishment, Anxiety and the Wolfenden Report.** London: George Allen & Unwin, 1959.
In "The Wolfenden Report on Homosexual Offenses" (pp. 11-50), Berg argues that the Committee did not go far enough in separating the realm of law from the realm of private morality.

4160. BLACKSTONE, WILLIAM, SIR. **Commentaries on fhe Laws of England: A Facsimile of the First Edition of 1765-1769.** Chicago: University of Chicago Press,

1979. 4 vols.
In this most famous of all English law commentaries, see
vol., pp. 215-16, on "the infamous crime against nature
... a crime not fit to be named."

4161. BLOM-COOPER, LOUIS. "A Miscarriage of Justice—
English Style," **Medico-Legal Journal,** 49:3 (1981),
98-117.
On the murder of Maxwell Contait, a homosexual transvestite, followed by the conviction of three delinquent
boys, whose main activty was setting fire to buildings.

4162. BRETON, JOHN LE, SIR. **Britton.** Edited and translated by F. M. Nichols. Oxford: Clarendon Press,
1865. 2 vols.
This 14th-century treatise prescribes burning for arson-
ists, sorcerers, renegades, sodomites, and heretics
publicly convicted (vol. 1, pp. 41-42).

4163. BRITISH MEDICAL ASSOCIATION. **Homosexuality and
Prostitution: A Memorandum of Evidence Prepared by
a Special Committtee of the British Medical Association ...** London: BMA, 1955. 94 pp.
Although this report straddles the legal issue, it
suggests that "essential" homosexuality should be treated
differently from "acquired" homosexuality.

4164. CHESSER, EUSTACE. **Love and Let Live: The Moral of
the Wolfenden Report.** London: William Heinemann,
1958. 125 pp.
Affirms that the private behavior of consenting adults is
not the concern of the state.

4165. COHEN, STEVE, et al. **The Law and Sexuality: How
to Cope with the Law If You're Not 100% Convention-
ally Heterosexual.** Manchester: Law Centre (Grass
Roots Books), 1979. 176 pp.
Practical advice for homosexuals and other sexual minorities.

4166. COKE, EDWARD, SIR. **The Third Part of the Institutes of the Laws of England.** London: W. Lee and
D. Pakeman, 1644. 243 pp.
This influential treatise is harshly negative, prescribing
death by hanging or drowning. "Buggery is a detestable,
and abominable sin, amongst Christians not to be named,
committed by carnall knowledge against the ordinance of
the Creator, and order of nature, by mankind with mankind,
or with brute beast, or by womankind with brute beast."
(pp. 58-59). See also: **The Twelfth Part of the Reports
...** (London: Twyfford and Bassett, 1656), pp. 36-37.
(These texts are renderings from the original texts in
Law French.)

4167. COULTER, CAROL. "No Earthquake in Dublin," **New
Statesman,** 100 (1980), 34-35.

On the trial of homosexual activists challenging Ireland's gross indecency statute.

4168. CRANE, PAUL. **Gays and the Law.** London: Pluto
        Press, 1982. 244 pp.
A comprehensive work covering both criminal and civil law, as well as such topics as young homosexuals, pedophilia, obscenity, employment, housing, immigration, and child custody. The book concludes that further political action is needed to achieve complete reform.

4169. EDDY, J.P. "The Law and Homosexuality," **Criminal
        Law Review** (1956), 22-25.
Arguing that punitive laws should be retained as a goad to homosexuals to seek treatment, the author held that "a penal institution of a special kind" was needed where homosexuals could be given appropriate psychiatric attention.

4170. FAIRBURNE, NICHOLAS H. "Homosexuality and the
        Law," in: J.A. Loraine (ed.). **Understanding
        Homosexuality: Its Biological and Psychological
        Bases.** New York: American Elsevier, 1974, pp. 159-
        64.
Makes the significant but hitherto unmentioned point that "there is no case recorded in Scotland of a prosecution of consenting adults in private ... in the last 100 years." Thus Scottish practice has long **preceded** English statutory law reform. Concludes, however, that homosexual rights are best exercised in private, lest the community be offended. In this volume see also the pro-reform paper of Antony Grey, "Homosexuality: Some Social and Legal Aspects" (pp. 143-149).

4171. GORDON, GERALD H. **The Criminal Law of Scotland.**
        Edinburgh: W. Green & Son, 1967. lxxiii, 1104 pp.
On sodomy, attempted sodomy, gross indecency, rape ("a male person cannot be raped"), and indecent practices with children. The rule enunciated in a 1934 case is: All shamelessly indecent conduct is criminal. (Pp. 31-32, 120, 156-57, 773-74, 825, 836, 847, 849-52.)

4172. GREAT BRITAIN, CRIMINAL LAW REVISION COMMITTEE.
        Working Paper on Sexual Offenses, October 1980.
        London: H.M.S.O., 1980. 63 pp.
See esp. pp. 28-29, 33-34, 47-53. Seeks to reevaluate the Wolfenden recommendations on both private and public homosexual behavior.

4173. GREAT BRITAIN, POLICY COMMITTEE ON SEXUAL OFFEN-
        SES. **Working Paper on the Age of Consent in
        Relation to Sexual Offenses.** London: H.M.S.O.,
        1979.
Among other matters, considers whether the age of consent for homosexual acts should be assimilated to that stipulated for heterosexual acts.

4174. GREENLAND, CYRIL. "Sex Law Reform in an Interna-
       tional Perspective: England and Wales and Canada,"
       **Bulletin of the American Academy of Psychiatry and
       the Law**, 11:4 (1983), 309-30.
Supports reform of the law, including protection of the
civil rights of homosexuals, but concedes that public
opinion presents a formidable obstacle, as astute politicians avoid being associated with attempts to liberal-
ize the law out of fear of being attacked by religious
groups and right-wing opponents.

4175. HAILSHAM, QUINTIN HOGG, 2ND VISCOUNT. "Homosexual-
       ity and Society," in: J. T. Rees and H. V. Usill
       (eds.). **They Stand Apart: A Critical Survey of
       the Problems of Homosexuality**, London: William
       Heinemann, 1955, pp. 21-35.
Favors continued legal sanctions against homosexuality,
arguing that homosexual behavior is in the last analysis
moral failure. Note also in this volume: John Tudor
Rees, "Homosexuality and the Law," pp. 3-20 (a muddled,
conservative approach).

4176. "Homosexuality, Prostitution, and the Law; and
       Report of the Roman Catholic Advisory Committee on
       Prostitution and Homosexual Offenses and the
       Existing Law," **Dublin Review**, 230 (Summer 1956),
       57-65.
The Committee called for amendment of the criminal law
so as to exclude consensual acts in private by adult
males, but retain penalties for offenses against minors,
public indecency, and criminal vice.

4177. HONORÉ, TONY. **Sex Law in England**. Hamden, CT:
       Archon Books, 1978. 200 pp.
Scholarly, but accessible treatment by a major British
legal historian presenting a moderately conservative
position with regard to homosexual behavior (see pp. 41,
84-110, 124, 130-31, 149, 151, 165-67).

4178. JAMES, T. E. "Law and the Sexual Offender," in:
       Ismond Rosen (ed.), **Pathology and Treatment of
       Sexual Deviation: A Methodological Approach**.
       London: Oxford University Press, 1964, pp. 461-92.
General review naming three basic homosexual offenses:
sodomy, indecent assault, and gross indecency.

4179. JOHNSON, H. A. "Homosexual Propensity and Corrob-
       oration," **New Law Journal**, 125 (February 20 and 27,
       1974), 189-91 and 203-04.
Problems of corroboration after the 1967 reform as seen in
recent English cases.

4180. LAWTON, FREDERICK. "Sexual Offenses: Lord Justice
       Lawton," **Medico-Legal Journal**, 50 (1982), 19-31.
On the problem of the age of consent and the inconsistency
and hypocrisy of the law. The author accepts the view

that sexual orientation is fixed by the age of 16, but
maintains that the age of consent for homosexual activity
should be 18 to protect "the immature young man, who takes
a little longer to fix his sexual orientation."

4181. LYNCH, A. C. E. "Counseling and Assisting Homosex-
      uals," **Criminal Law Review** (1979), 630-44.
On the legal status of a hypothetical Homosexual Advice
Centre: would it be guilty of corrupting public morals?
Where the aim is to reduce the psychic distress and isolation of homosexuals, the activity is lawful. Where
the furtherance of overt sexual activity by homosexuals is
involved, statutory--and possibly common law--liability
exists.

4182. PANNICK, DAVID. "Homosexuals, Transexuals and the
      Sex Discrimination Act," **Public Law** (1983), 279-
      302.
The degree of protection afforded by the 1975 Sex Discrimination Act to homosexuals and transsexuals will depend
upon the judicial construction of the opaque language of
the legislation, the actual decisions will reflect the
willingness of the courts to protect weak and oppressed
minorities.

4183. ST. JOHN-STEVAS, NORMAN. **Life, Death and the
      Law: Law and Christian Morals in England and the
      U. S.** Bloomington: Indiana University Press, 1961.
      375 pp.
A moralistic approach with comparative perspectives. See
pp. 198-231 and esp. 310-35 ("Laws Concerning Homosexual
Offences").

4184. SMITH, F. B. "Labouchere's Amendment to the
      Criminal Law Amendment Bill," **Historical Studies**
      (Melbourne), 17 (1976), 165-75.
Provides background on the still somewhat obscure circumstances under which gross indecency between males was
appended to the 1885 Act, a provision that remained in
force until the reform of 1967.

4185. STURGESS, BOB. **No Offence: The Case for Homosexual
      Equality.** Manchester: Campaign for Homosexual
      Equality, 1975.
Statement representing the views of Britain's leading gay
rights organization.

4186. WALMSLEY, ROY. "Indecency between Males and the
      Criminal Offenses Act 1967," **Criminal Law Review**
      (1978), 400-07.
Retrospect: ten years after decriminalization in England
and Wales.

4187. WALMSLEY, ROY, and KAREN WHITE. **Sexual Offenses,
      Consent and Sentencing.** London: H.M.S.O., 1979.
      77 pp. (Home Office Research Study, 54)

Attempt to assess the results of recent changes in the law
on prosecutions for buggery, attempted buggery, and indecency between males (see pp. 26-28, 38-48).

4188. WOLFENDEN, JOHN, SIR, et al. **Report of the Com-
        mittee on Homosexual Offenses and Prostitution.**
        London: H.M.S.O., 1957. 155 pp.
This pivotal work, generally known as the Wolfenden
Report, laid the foundation for the English reform of
1957. The Report represented not only an idea whose time
had come, but persuaded with trenchant logic and remarkable clarity of exposition. In the English-speaking world
its beneficent effect has probably been second only to
that of the two Kinsey Reports. For some of the circumstances surrounding its creation, see Lord Wolfenden's
memoirs, **Turning Points** (London: Bodley Head, 1976),
pp. 129-46.

                    E. AUSTRALIA AND NEW ZEALAND

Australia, which became self-governing in 1901, inherited
the British legal system, with the exception of the fact
that it has a federal structure resembling that of the
United States. Accordingly, it has been necessary to
proceed to homosexual law reform in each of the state
jurisdictions individually. New Zealand, where reform
has been slow in coming, has a unitary system.

4189. BARTHOLOMEW, ALLEN A., et al. "Homosexual Necro-
        philia," **Medicine, Science, and the Law,** 18 (1978),
        29-35.
Based on two cases of homosexual necrophilia, argues that
defense based on the abnormal state of the accused should
be excluded.

4190. CHAPPELL, DUNCAN, and PAUL R. WILSON. "Changing
        Attitudes towards Homosexual Law Reform," **Austra-
        lian Law Journal,** 46 (1972), 22-29.
Public opinion on the subject of homosexuality is changing, but a wide disparity still exists between urban
and rural attitudes.

4191. GARDINER, JAMIE, et al. **A Proposal for Reform of
        the Law Relating to Homosexual Offenses.** Second
        ed. Fitzroy, Victoria: Homosexual Law Reform
        Coalition, 1979. 28 pp.
Includes legislation.

4192. GRAHAM, CARBERY. "Conditioned Legal Responses to
        Homosexuality," **Gay Changes,** 2:4 (1979), 23-28.
Shows how in practice Australian lawyers and judiciary
are influenced by antihomosexual prejudices.

4193. MCCLINTOCK, IAN, and JOHN ANDREWS. "Homosexual Law Reform in New South Wales--Who Is Satisfied," **Legal Service Bulletin** (Clayton, Victoria), 9 (1984), 138-41.
Compromises and maneuvres which led to (qualified) decriminalization in that state: buggery and indecent assault on males are abolished where both parties are over 18.

4194. MACKENZIE, D. F. "Homosexuality and the Justice Department," **New Zealand Medical Journal**, 66 (1967), 745-48.
Homosexual acts by males are punishable in New Zealand by imprisonment for up to 10 years if the partner is under 16, and up to 5 years if the partner is over 16. Women over 21 who participate in homosexual acts with girls under 16 are liable to imprisonment for a term up to six years; consenting adult women cannot be prosecuted for homosexuality.

4195. NEW SOUTH WALES. DEPARTMENT OF THE ATTORNEY GENERAL AND OF JUSTICE, **Homosexual Offenses.**
Sydney: New South Wales Bureau of Crime Statistics and Research, 1977. 43 pp.
Official statistics from one Australian state.

F. CANADA

Canada has inherited the English common law tradition to which it has largely adhered. Since Canada has a unitary system of law, sodomy has been decriminalized throughout the country--though the legal age of consent is 21. In addition, Quebec's Civil Rights Code includes "sexual orientation."

4196. ADAM, BARRY D. "Stigma and Employability: Discrimination by Sex and Sexual Orientation in the Ontario Legal Profession," **Canadian Review of Sociology and Anthropology**, 18 (1981), 293-98.
In matched personal resumes sent to law firms, employers' responses were less likely to be favorable to gays and women.

4197. ADAM, BARRY D., and KATHLEEN A. LAHEY. "Legal Oppression: A Survey of the Ontario Legal Profession," **Canadian Bar Review**, 59 (December 1981), 674-86.
In a questionnaire sent to the entire 1974 graduating class of Ontario law schools, 1.5% of the respondents indicated that they were homosexual or bisexual.

4198. ADELMAN, HOWARD. "Publicizing Pedophilia: Legal and Psychiatric Discourse," **International Journal of Law and Psychiatry**, 4 (1981), 311-25.

Discusses the legal definition of pedophilia, the credibility and objectivity of witnesses, and trial evidence as
illustrative of legal-psychiatric discourse.

4199. CARON, MADELEINE. "Les lois applicables au Québec
       concernant les homosexuels," **Revue Québecoise de
       Sexologie,** 2 (1981), 31-36.
The legal situation of homosexuals in Quebec.

4200. COHL, K. A. **Sexuality and the Law.** Toronto: I.P.
       I. Publishing Division, 1978.
In this popular survey, see pp. 67-76.

4201. DELEURY, EDITH. "L'union homosexuelle et le droit
       de la famille," **Cahiers du Droit** (Laval University,
       Quebec), (December 1984), 751-75.
One of a series of articles in this issue on homosexuality and the law, including Robert Demers, "De la Lex
scantinia aux recents amendements du Code criminel" (pp.
777-800); Nicole Duple, "Homosexualité et droits à
l'égalité dans les chartes canadienne et québecoise"
(pp. 801-42); and Richard A. Goreham, "Le droit à la vie
privée des personnes homosexuelles" (pp. 843-72).

4202. GIGEROFF, ALEX K. **Sexual Deviations in the Crim-
       inal Law: Homosexual, Exhibitionistic, and Pedo-
       philic Offenses in Canada.** Toronto: University of
       Toronto Press, 1968. 218 pp.
See esp. pp. 39-50, 82-95, 100-24, 159-68. On the crimes
of buggery, indecent assault, gross indecency, and the
like. One legislator is quoted as saying that there are
"fifty kinds of gross indecency."

4203. GOREHAM, RICHARD A. "Human Rights Code of British
       Columbia--Reasonable Cause for Discrimination--Dis-
       crimination against Homosexuals--Freedom of the
       Press," **Canadian Bar Review,** 59 (1981), 165-79.
In the case of Gay Alliance Toward Equality v. The Vancouver Sun, the Supreme Court of Canada invoked the
principle of freedom of the press to diminish the scope of
human rights legislation prohibiting discriminatory practices. See also: W. W. Black, "Gay Alliance Toward
Equality v. Vancouver Sun (1979) (2 N R 117)," **Osgoode
Hall Law Journal,** 17 (1979), 649-75; Harry Kopyto, "The
Gay Alliance Case Reconsidered," loc. cit., 18 (1980),
639-52; and Jeff Richstone and J. Stuart Russell,
"Shutting the Gate: Gay Civil Rights in the Supreme Court
of Canada," **McGill Law Journal,** 27 (1981), 92-117.

4204. RODGERS, RAYMOND SPENCER. **Sex and Law in Canada:
       Text, Cases and Comment.** Ottawa: Policy Press,
       1962. 62 pp.
On "Deviate behaviour not dangerous" which covers the
offenses of buggery and gross indecency under Canadian
law (pp. 67-74).

4205. RUSSELL, J. STUART. "The Offense of Keeping a
      Common Bawdy House in Canadian Criminal Law,"
      Ottawa Law Review, 14 (1982), 270-313.
On the ambiguity of the term "acts of indecency" in the
Canadian and British Criminal Codes, and the question
whether homosexual baths and bars constitute "common
baudy houses" because they existed "for no other reason
but to provide sexual gratification in the homosexual
sense."

4206. RUZOVSKY, L. E. and F. A. **Legal Sex.** Toronto:
      Doubleday Canada, 1982.
Popular account.

G. US LAW: GENERAL

Although the United States has inherited the British common law tradition, it has modified it in two significant
respects. 1) According to the principle of constitutional
review, no enactment of positive law can stand if it is in
conflict with the Constitution of the United States. In
addition, state laws must not violate state constitutions. This principle opens the door to challenges of
sodomy laws on constitutional grounds. 2) In keeping with
the federal system, each of the fifty states has its own
penal code. In practice this federalism has meant that
legal reform--in the absence of a general decision on the
part of the United States Supreme court on the unconstitu-
tionality of sodomy laws--must be achieved on a state-by-
state basis. The continuing production of law review
articles may be monitored in **Index to Legal Periodicals**
(1909-).

4207. ACHTENBERG, ROBERTA (ed.). **Sexual Orientation and
      the Law.** New York: Clark Boardman, 1985. ca. 600
      pp. (loose leaf)
Intended for legal practitioners and scholars, the work
organizes a diverse body of material (with many case
citations) under three major categories: Family and
Property; Civil Rights and Discrimination; and Criminal
Issues. Some users have felt that the volume has an
overemphasis on California.

4208. AMERICAN CIVIL LIBERTIES UNION OF SOUTHERN CALIFOR-
      NIA. "Statement of Policy Regarding Sexual Beha-
      vior," **One Magazine,** 14 (January 1966), 6-8.
After some years of sidestepping the issue, this was the
first positive ACLU statement, becoming a model for
national policy.

4209. AMERICAN LAW INSTITUTE. **Model Penal Code: Proposed
      Official Draft.** Philadelphia: American Law Insti-

tute, 1962. 346 pp.
Sections 213.0, 213.2, 213.2 and 213.6 refer to "deviate
sexual intercourse"; sections 251.1, 251.2, and 251.3
refer to open lewdness, prostitution, and loitering.
Various tentative and proposed drafts of the code were
published in the ten-year period prior to 1962, when
this version was finally adopted. The Institute draft
codified and modernized law for the use of legislators
and commissions considering new codes or reforms of
existing portion of codes in the separate states.

4210. APASU-GBOTSU, YAO, et al. (eds). "Survey on the
        Constitutional Right to Privacy in the Context of
        Homosexual Activity," **University of Miami Law
        Review**, 40 (1986), 521-657.
Comprehensive review of the historical background of privacy, including purported state interest in the prohibition of sodomy. This valuable survey was prepared by the
editors of the **Review** in connection with the consideration
of the (Georgia) Bowers v. Hardwick case, which the U.S.
Supreme Court resolved in June 1986, restoring the state
law. See also: "Elisa L. Fuller, "Hardwick v. Bowers: An
Attempt to Pull the Meaning of Doe v. Commonwealth's
Attorney out of the Closet," ibid., 39 (1985), 973-95.

4211. BAER, JUDITH A. **Equality under the Constitution.**
        Ithaca: Cornell University Press, 1983. 308 pp.
This scholarly work on the philosophy of Constitutional
law contains a relevant chapter.

4212. BLAIR, JERRY D. "Sex Offender Registration for
     · Section 647 Disorderly Conduct Conviction is Cruel
        and Unusual Punishment," **San Diego Law Review**, 13
        (1976), 391-409.
Holds that the notorious California requirement that
convicted sex offenders maintain registration with the
police for life is unconstitutional.

4213. BRADFORD, WILLIAM. **An Enquiry How Far the Punish-
        ment of Death is Necessary in Pennsylvania.** Lon-
        don: J. Johnson, 1795. 80 pp.
Following Montesquieu and Beccaria, supports the abolition
of the death penalty for the "crime against nature."
"Laws might have been proper for a tribe of ardent bar-
barians wandering through the sands of Arabia, which are
wholly unfit for an enlightened people of civilized and
gentle manners" (pp. 20-21).

4214. BRAGG, MORGAN STEVENSON. "Victimless Sex Crimes:
        To the Devil, Not the Dungeon," **University of Flor-
        ida Law Review**, 25 (1972), 139-59.
Summarizes the now-classic arguments from the literature
of the 1950s and 1960s to the effect that sodomy should
not be a crime: separation of church and state, violation
of the right to privacy, victimless offense, and the like.

4215. BRINKLEY, ROLAND, et al. **The Laws against Homosex-**
       uality. Huntsville, TX: Institute of Contemporary
       Corrections and the Behavioral Sciences, Sam
       Houston State University, [1971]. 93 pp. (Crimin-
       al Justice Monographs, 2:4)
Surveys historical development and recent legislative
enactments as well as social science research. Supports
reform as embodied in the Model Penal Code.

4216. CALVANI, TERRY. "Homosexuality and the Law--an
       Overview," **New York Law Forum,** 17 (1971), 273-303.
Examines the criminal laws and civil discriminations
against homosexuals, concluding that they originated in
the efforts of theocratic governments of past centuries
to enforce morality by penal sanctions.

4217. CAMAZINE, ALISSE C. "Gay Lib v. University of
       Missouri," **St. Louis University Law Journal,** 22
       (1978-79), 711-20.
The Eighth Circuit Court of Appeals reversed a district
court ruling that denied Gay Lib the right to gain formal
recognition as a student organization on the campus of the
University of Missouri at Columbia. Later the United
States Supreme Court denied certiorari, part of a pattern
of reluctance to take up questions pertaining to homosexuality. See also: Chris Elliott, "Gay Lib v. University
of Missouri: 1st Amendment Rights in the School Environment," **University of Missouri at Kansas City Law Review,**
46 (1978); and Richard E. McCleod, "Denial of Recognition
to Homosexual Group Abridges Freedom of Association,"
Missouri Law Review, 43 (1978), 109-15).

4218. CANTOR, DONALD J. "Deviation and the Criminal
       Law," **Journal of Criminal Law, Criminology, and**
       Police Science, 55 (1964), 441-53.
Maintains that laws regulating sexual behavior are inef-
fective, serving neither a deterrent, a preventative, nor
a rehabilitative function. Calls for vigorous initiative
for change by the bar, the churches, and the medical
profession.

4219. CAPORALE, DOMENICO, and DERYL F. HAMANN. "Sexual
       Psychopathy[,] a Legal Labyrinth of Medicine, Mor-
       als and Mythology," **Nebraska Law Review,** 36 (1957),
       320-53.
Assessing the impact of the 1949 Nebraska Sexual Psychopath Statute, concludes that "the present status of medical and legal knowledge does not provide an adequate
basis for ... departure from the traditional criminal
methods of dealing" with the sex offender.

4220. CARTER, JESSE. "Searches and Seizures in Califor-
       nia," **Mattachine Review,** 2:2 (February 1956), 22-
       24, 29-33.
Problems commonly encountered by homosexuals before the
restraints imposed on the police by the Warren Supreme

Court.

4221. CHAITLIN, ELLEN, and V. ROY LEFCOURT. "Is Gay
      Suspect?" **Lincoln Law Review,** 8 (1973), 24-54.
Concludes that "if homosexuality is immutable, homosexuals
are clearly entitled to suspect class protection. ...
The issue, however, should not hinge on the immutability
of homosexuality. ... The legal burden should fall upon
those who discriminate."

4222. **The Challenge and Progress of Homosexual Law
      Reform.** San Francisco: Council on Religion and the
      Homosexual, Daughters of Bilitis, Society for In-
      dividual Rights, Tavern Guild, 1968. 72 pp.
In its time a landmark statement of the harassment and
exploitation of homosexuals fostered by then-existing
laws.

4223. COHAN, A. S. "Obstacles to Equality: Government
      Responses to the Gay Rights Movement in the United
      ᵤtates," **Political Studies,** 30 (1982), 59-76.
The gay rights movment has not progressed as rapidly or as
successfully as its adherents have wished for four reasons: the unpopularity of homosexuals and lack of sympathy
for their cause; the division of powers and hierarchy of
legal codes within the governmental system; the fragmented character of the movement itself and the absence of
cohesive support from its own constituency; and the
failure of the Supreme Court to accord homosexuals the
same rights it has extended to other minorities.

4224. COHN, STEVEN F., and JAMES E. GALLAGHER. "Gay
      Movements and Legal Change: Some Aspects of the
      Dynamics of a Social Problem," **Social Problems,** 32
      (1984), 72-86.
Examines public opinion and media coverage surrounding
four important events that affected the development of
homosexual rights in Maine between September 1973 and
June 1975.

4225. COHN, STEVEN F., and JAMES E. GALLAGHER. "Crime
      and the Creation of Criminal Law: A Partial Model,"
      British Journal of Law and Society, 4 (1977), 220-
      36.
A study of the struggle for gay rights in Maine inspired
by Berger and Luckman's **Social Construction of Reality.**
The reactions of various segments of the state's population to the clash of fundamentalist and liberal views is
analyzed.

4226. COLEMAN, THOMAS F. "Procedure and Strategy in Gay
      Rights Litigation," **New York University Review of
      Law and Social Change,** 8 (1978-79), 317-23.
Securing gay rights through constitutional litigation
involves much more than merely having a grasp on substantive consititutional principles. The procedures and

strategy used in each case are equally important in laying
the groundwork for a favorable ruling by the United States
Supreme Court.

4227.   COLEMAN, THOMAS F., et al.   **Report of the Commis-
        sion on Personal Privacy, State of California.**
        Sacramento: State of California, 1982.   489 pp.
This massive report, assembled by a Commission appointed
by Governor Brown, provides an almost encyclopedic discussion of privacy in current legal practice and thought,
with a strong emphasis on sexual orientation.

4228.   COLEMAN, THOMAS F.   "To Publish or Not to Pub-
        lish: That is the Question," **SexuaLaw Reporter,**
        no. 26 (1976), 18-20.
Shows that in California many appellate courts habitually
refuse publication of opinions favorable to gay rights.

4229.   "The Constitutionality of Laws Forbidding Private
        Homosexual Conduct," **Michigan Law Review,** 72
        (1974), 1613-37.
There is a tactical reason for advocates of homosexual
rights to eschew novel constitutional theory. Homosexuality is too controversial to expect a court to create
new constitutional law in order to protect it. But by
extending the right of privacy to all forms of heterosexual conduct, the courts have gone so far that the exclusion of homosexuality cannot be justified.

4230.   "Constitutional Protection of Private Sexual Con-
        duct among Consenting Adults: Another Look at
        Sodomy Statutes," **Iowa Law Review,** 62 (1976), 568-
        90.
Consenting male homosexual relations between adults in
private should be protected by a fundamental right of
privacy. None of the hypothetical interests of the
state in preventing private, male homosexual conduct can
be shown to be valid.

4231.   "Constitutional Status of Sexual Orientation: Homo-
        sexuality as a Suspect Classification," **Harvard Law
        Review,** 98 (1985), 1285-1309.
Finding homosexuality to be a suspect classification requires not that a court invalidate every law that discrim-
inates on that basis, but that the court make a finding
of actual harm rather than perceived immorality before
upholding such a classification.

4232.   COURIS, THOMAS F.   "Sexual Freedom for Consenting
        Adults--Why Not?" **Pacific Law Journal,** 2 (1971),
        206-25.
Argues for reform of California's "anachronistic penal
laws" prescribing "deviant sexual behavior" between
adults, reaffirming the conclusion of the Wolfenden
Report.

4233. CRAFT, LAURA R., and MATTHEW A. HODEL. "City of
       Chicago v. Wilson and Constitutional Protection for
       Personal Appearance: Cross-dressing as an Element
       of Sexual Identity," **Hastings Law Journal**, 30
       (1979), 1151-81.
On a decision which invalidated a local ordinance prohibiting an individual from appearing in public dressed as a
member of the opposite sex with an intent to conceal his
or her gender in the specific case of two transsexuals
who were required to wear women's clothing as part of
"psychiatric therapy in preparation for sex-reassignment
operations."

4234. CROMPTON, LOUIS. "Homosexuals and the Death Pen-
       alty in Colonial America," **JH** 1 (1976), 277-93.
Shows that Biblical prohibitions played an important role
even after the American Revolution, when, however, fines
and imprisonment were substituted for the death penalty.

4235. CURRY, HAYDN, and DENNIS CLIFFORD. **A Legal Guide
       for Lesbian and Gay Couples.** Third ed. Reading,
       MA: Addison-Wesley, 1985. ca. 300 pp.
Two attorneys provide a comprehensive guide for lay
readers covering such topics as buying and selling
property, relating to former spouses, child custody and
visitation rights, living-together arrangements, and
estate planning. Includes sample contracts, forms,
agreements and wills.

4236. P. L. D. "Sexual Assaults and Forced Homosexual
       Relationships in Prison: Cruel and Unusual Punish-
       ment," **Albany Law Review**, 36 (1972), 428-38.
Courts have begun to recognize that subjecting prisoners
to forced homosexual relations and sexual assaults does
constitute unusual punishment. The failure of prison
authorities to check such abuses may violate an inmate's
right under the Eighth Amendment to be free from cruel
and unusual punishment.

4237. DELGADO, RICHARD. "Fact, Norm, and Standard of
       Review--The Case of Homosexuality," **University of
       Dayton Law Review**, 10 (1985), 575-98.
Designation of a model of judicial review requires that
the court commit itself to a view of homosexuality and
the part that sexual orientation and behavior play in
the life of the homosexual.

4238. DONNELLY, RICHARD C., JOSEPH GOLDSTEIN, and RICHARD
       D. SCHWARTZ. **Criminal Law: Problems for Decision
       in the Promulgation, Invocation, and Administration
       of a Law of Crimes.** New York: Free Press, 1962.
       1169 pp.
See Chapter 1, Part 3, "Consensual Homosexual Acts between
Adults in Private--a Crime? A Problem for the Legislature" (pp. 123-201). A digest of opinions by lawyers,
sociologists, anthropologists, psychiatrists, and members

of investigative and legislative commissions between 1935 and 1960.

4239. DRUMMOND, ISABEL. **The Sex Paradox.** New York: Putnam's Sons, 1953. 369 pp.
"An analytical survey of sex and the law in the United States today," citing historical and anthropological records. See Chapter 4: "Sodomy, Exhibitionism and Other Acts 'Contrary to Nature'" (esp. pp. 119-29).

4240. DRZAZGA, JOHN. **Sex Crimes.** Springfield, IL: Thomas, 1960. 241 pp.
Chapter 32, "Homosexuality" (pp. 205-16), constitutes a semipornographic survey of "vice" and vice laws throughout history, drawing upon earlier sexological literature for piquant details.

4241. DUNLAP, MARY C. "The Constitutional Rights of Sexual Minorities: A Crisis of the Male/Female Dichotomy," **Hastings Law Journal**, 30 (1979), 1131-49.
Challenges the right of the legal system to impose an absolute dichotomy of male/female sex roles and sexual identities; holds that greater sexual differentiation in fact contains the greater evolutionary potential.

4242. GALLO, JOHN J., et al. "The Consenting Adult Homosexual and the Law: An Empirical Study of Enforcement and Administration in Los Angeles County," **UCLA Law Review**, 13 (1966), 643-832.
Evaluating a massive project of data collection, describes the use of police decoys, observation, routine patrol and harassment, and abatement and licensing controls over establishments frequented by homosexuals. Concludes that adult consensual homosexuality should be of legal concern only in the case of public displays, and then only because they involve an element of public outrage.

4243. GARDNER, MARTIN R. "The Defense of Necessity and the Right to Escape from Prison--a Step towards Incarceration Free from Sexual Assault," **Southern California Law Review**, 49 (1975), 110-52.
On a California case (People v. Lovercamp) in which an appellate court held that an escape from prison motivated by "threatened imminent homosexual asault by other inmates" may be justified if the inmate eschews violence and subsequently places himself in the hands of the proper authorities.

4244. GAY AND LESBIAN ADVOCATES OF BOSTON. **The Attorney's Directory for Lesbian and Gay Rights.** Boston: GLAB, 1983.
A state-by-state listing of attorneys, including information about areas of expertise.

4245. "Gay Students Organization v. Bonner: Expressive

Conduct and the First Amendment Protection," **Maine Law Review**, 26 (1974), 397-414.
Forbidding of a dance on the campus of the University of New Hampshire led to a decision affirming the First Amendment rights of the organization.

4246.   GEIS, GILBERT. **Not the Law's Business? An Examination of Homosexuality, Abortion, Prostitution, Narcotics and Gambling in the United States.** Rockville, MD: National Institute of Mental Health, Center for Studies of Crime and Delinquency, 1972. 262 pp.
Well-reasoned presentation of the case for decriminalization of "victimless crimes." Chapter 2, "Consensual Adult Homosexuality" (pp. 15-52), discusses the damage inflicted on homosexuals, and on society as a whole, by imposing penalties which are clearly counterproductive.

4247.   GEIS, GILBERT, et al. "Reported Decriminalization of Consensual Adult Homosexuality in Seven American States," **JH**, 1 (1976), 419-26.
Reporting results of a mail survey of police officials, prosecuting attorneys, and members of homosexual groups in the seven states that had decriminalized homosexuality between consenting adults, concludes that decriminalization had no effect on the involvement of homosexuals with minors, the use of force by homosexuals, or the amount of private same-sex behavior.

4248.   GITCHOFF, G. THOMAS, and JOSEPH ELLENBOGEN. "Victimless Crimes: The Case against Continued Enforcement," **Journal of Police Science and Adminstration,** 1 (1973), 401-08.
See esp. p. 403.

4249.   GOMEZ, JOSE. "The Public Expression of Lesbian/Gay Personhood as Protected Speech," **Journal of Law and Inequality,** 1 (1983), 121-53.
Includes survey of discussions of applicability of First Amendment protections to homosexual rights.

4250.   GOULD, MEREDITH. "Lesbians and the Law: Where Sexism and Heterosexism Meet," in: Trudy Darty and Sandee Potter (eds.), **Women-Identified Women,** Palo Alto, CA: Mayfield, 1984, pp. 149-62.
While sodomy laws have a penumbral effect on lesbians, their chief problems lie in the area of divorce and custody--and the difficulties that all women face in our social system.

4251.   HAFEN, BRUCE C. "The Constitutional Status of Marriage, Kinship, and Sexual Privacy--Balancing the Individual and Social Interests," **Michigan Law Review,** 81 (1983), 463-574.
Ambitious attempt to synthesize a conservative "pro-family" legal philosophy, with a number of anti-gay-rights

implications. Opposes the "duty" of family tradition to the "liberty" of economic individualism.

4252. HARKAVY, JEFFREY M. "The Defending of Accused Homosexuals: Will Society Accept Their Use of the Battered Wife Defense?" **Glendale Law Review**, 4 (1982), 208-32.
The "battered wife defense" is not available to the homosexual who kills a violent lover in self-defense, because of prejudice among judges and jurors against homosexual "marriage."

4253. HARPER, JAMES. **Homo Laws**. San Diego: Publishers Export Co., 1968. 208 pp.
Pulp compilation illustrative of then-current popular attitudes.

4254. HINDES, THOMAS L. "Morality Enforcement through the Criminal Law and the Modern Doctrine of Substantive Due Process," **University of Pennsylvania Law Review**, 126 (1977), 344-84.
Concludes that "the power of government to levy criminal sanctions should not be used to impose majoritarian moral values on the rest of society," but only to protect persons and property against the "tangibly harmful acts of others."

4255. HOOK, RONALD W. **The Constitutional Right of Privacy: Sodomy Laws**. Minneapolis: Minnesota Civil Liberties Union Foundation, 1981. 13 pp.
To make criminals out of otherwise law-abiding productive citizens merely because of their mode of sexual expression is a "crime in and of itself." Consensual sodomy legislation infringes the privacy of the individual and is oppressive of the personality of those stigmatized as criminals.

4256. HOWARTH, JOAN W. "The Rights of Gay Prisoners: A Challenge to Protective Custody," **Southern California Law Review**, 53 (1980), 1225-76.
Concludes that Constitutional provisions compel reform of current practices of confinement of homosexuals.

4257. ILLINOIS STATE AND CHICAGO BAR ASSOCIATION'S JOINT COMMITTEE TO REVISE THE ILLINOIS CRIMINAL CODE. **Proposed Illinois Revised Criminal Code of 1961.** Chicago: Burdette Smith Co., 1961. 318 pp.
An impressive official study completed and published prior to the implementation of the Wolfenden reforms in Britain.

4258. JEFFERSON, THOMAS. **The Papers of Thomas Jefferson.** Edited by Julian P. Boyd and others. Princeton: Princeton University Press, 1950- .
Advocated castration as a punishment for sodomy (vol. 2, pp. 325, 497).

4259.   JOHNSON, LEE ANN. "Gay Law Students Association
        v. Pacific Telephone and Telegraph Co.--Constitu-
        tional and Statutory Restraints on Employment--Dis-
        crimination against Homosexuals by Public Util-
        ities," **California Law Review**, 68 (1980), 680-715.
Criticizes the decision in favor of the homosexual plain-
tiffs, concluding that "each cause of action rests on
questionable grounds and contains broad implications that
the majority failed to address adequately."

4260.   JULBER, ERIC. "The Law of Mailable Material," **ONE
        Magazine**, 2:8 (October 1954), 4-6.
This article, by ONE's attorney, seemed to goad the U.S.
Postal Service into declaring the issue unmailable. At
length a 1958 per curiam decision was obtained from the
United States Supreme Court, rejecting the government's
claim and establishing full freedom to write and publish
about homosexuality in other than narrowly defined medical, psychological or legal terms.

4261.   KARST, KENNETH. "The Freedom of Intimate Associa-
        tion," **Yale Law Journal**, 89 (1980), 624-92.
The freedom of intimate association extends to homosexual
associations as much as to heterosexual ones. To affirm
that freedom is to extend the area of moral choice and
moral responsibility.

4262.   KATZER, PEGGY R. "Civil Rights--Title VII and
        Section 1985(3)--Discrimination against Homosex-
        uals," **Wayne Law Review**, 26 (1980), 1611-23.
Protection under Title VII or section 1983(3) against
discrimination because of "sex" does not extend to
homosexuals.

4263.   KLING, SAMUEL G. **Sexual Behavior and the Law.** New
        York: Bernard Geis Associates, 1965.
"Homosexual Behavior" (pp. 97-128) offers a broad survey
of major aspects in question-and-answer format.

4264.   KNUTSON, DONALD C. "Homosexuality and the Law: In-
        troduction," JH, 5:1/2 (1979-80), 5-23.
Introduction to a special issue of **Journal of Homosexuality** on the state of American laws and their effect on
homosexuals. The issue has also been published separately
as a book, **Homosexuality and the Law,** by Haworth Press,
New York.

4265.   LAMBDA LEGAL DEFENSE. **AIDS Legal Guide.** New
        York: Lambda Legal Defense, 1984. 100 pp.
A general legal guide by the New York activist group, with
special emphasis on the consequences of the AIDS epidemic.

4266.   LASSON, KENNETH. "Homosexual Rights: The Law in
        Flux and Conflict," **University of Baltimore Law
        Review**, 9 (1979), 47-74.
The law regarding homosexual rights is clearly in a

state of flux, and this uncertainty extends far beyond
the classroom or military cases. In most jurisdictions,
even apart from the criminal sanction, homosexuals may
be legally discriminated against--a situation that seems
to conflict with our claim to be a free society. See
also his: "Civil Liberties for Homosexuals: The Law in
Limbo," **University of Dayton Law Review**, 10 (1985), 645-
79.

4267. **Lesbian Rights Handbook.** San Francisco: Lesbian
      Rights Project, 1980.
Covers unemployment, wills, shared property, crisis
issues, housing, rights of young lesbians, lesbian
businesses, and so forth.

4268. LEVY, MARTIN R., and C. THOMAS HECTUS. "Privacy
      Revisited: The Downfall of Griswold," **University of
      Richmond Law Review**, 12 (1978), 627-46.
In Doe v. Commonwealth's Attorney for City of Richmond,
the Supreme Court summarily affirmed a lower court decision denying homosexuals constitutional protection
of the right to privacy in sexual acts among consenting
adults in the privacy of the home. The court has upheld
freedom of speech in this area while denying freedom of
conduct. The decision erodes the precedential value of
the opinion in Griswold.

4269. LODGE, THOMAS E. "There May Be Harm in Asking:
      Homosexual Solicitations and the Fighting Words
      Doctrine," **Case Western Reserve Law Review**, 30
      (1980), 461-93.
Statutes against homosexual solicitation should be drafted
only to prohibit those solicitations which cause "severe
emotional disturbance," and should require a private
citizen's complaint containing specific allegations of
harassment.

4270. LUDD, STEVEN O. "The Aftermath of Doe v. Common-
      wealth's Attorney: In Search of the Right to Be
      Left Alone," **University of Dayton Law Review**, 10
      (1985), 705-43.
The Supreme Court's summary affirmance has produced wide
variation in state and federal court determinations of
whether private, adult, consensual behavior is constitutionally protected.

4271. MEYER, ROBERT C. "Legal and Social Ambivalence
      Regarding Homosexuality," **JH**, 2:3 (1977), 281-87.
Finds a mixed pattern in progress towards decriminalization and securing of civil rights for homosexuals.

4272. MILLER, H. "An Argument for the Application of
      Equal Protection Heightened Scrutiny to Classifica-
      tions Based on Homosexuality," **Southern California
      Law Review**, 57 (1984), 797-836.
Contends that homosexuals should be granted the advantages

656   HOMOSEXUALITY

of "heightened scrutiny" because they are the subject of
official discrimination. As a status, rather than a
chosen activity, homosexuality is not subject to individual control.

4273. MITCHELL, ROGER S. **The Homosexual and the Law.**
       New York: Arco, 1969. 96 pp.
Reasonably adequate in its day as an introduction for the
lay public.

4274. MOHR, RICHARD. "Gay Rights," **Social Theory and
       Practice,** 8 (1982), 31-41.
Argues that homosexuals should enjoy the protection of the
1964 Civil Rights Act, and that antihomosexual arguments
cast as "good faith discriminations" are examples of
circular reasoning or are self-fulfilling prophecies--
rationalizations of religious prejudice.

4275. MORRIS, KATRINA K. "Gay Law Students As'n v. Pa-
       cific Telephone and Telegraph Co.," **Santa Clara Law
       Review,** 20 (1980), 263-67.
The California Supreme Court concluded that where a state
entity is the employer, homosexuality should not be a
basis for discrimination against any qualified individual.

4276. MULLINS, CHARLES E. "Case Notes: Schools: Fricke
       v. Lynch," **Journal of Family Law,** 19 (1980-81),
       541-44.
On the attempt to prevent Aaron Fricke from bringing a
male date to his high school prom: the court held that
this amounted to abridgement of First Amendment rights.
See also Fricke's own account of the affair: **Reflections
of a Rock Lobster** (Boston: Alyson, 1980).

4277. OAKS, ROBERT. "Perceptions of Homosexuality by
       Justices of the Peace in Colonial Virginia," **JH,** 5
       (1979-80), 35-41.
Unlike other colonies, Virginia did not have its own
sodomy statute, but relied on the English law of 1533.
The powerful justices of the peace had the responsibility of interpreting it.   See also Oaks: "Things Fearful
to Name: Sodomy and Buggery in Seventeenth-century New
England," **Journal of Social History,** 12 (1978), 68-81.

4278. OLIVIERI, ANTONIO, and IRWIN FINKELSTEIN. "Report
       on 'Victimless Crime' in New York State," **New York
       Law Forum,** 18 (1972), 77-120.
The changing attitude of society toward homosexuality has
vastly increased the support for the repeal of the laws
which prohibit it (pp. 114-20).

4279. PAKALKA, WILLIAM R. "Texas Statue Prohibiting
       Sodomy is Unconstitutionally Overbroad in Proscri-
       bing Private Consensual Acts of Married Couples;
       Buchanan v. Batchelor," **Texas Law Review,** 49
       (1971), 400-06.

The sodomy laws should be challenged on other constitutional grounds than privacy: as representing an establishment of religion as prohibited by the First Amendment, and as punishing a person for a particular condition in contravention of the Eighth Amendment.

4280. PALAIS, DOUGLAS M. "Sexual Privacy," **Journal of Criminal Law and Criminology,** 68 (1977), 77-82.
The discrepancy between the Supreme Court's rulings in Griswold and Doe will create even more variation in lower court interpretations of the privacy right, with the constitutionally intolerable result of varying individual constitutional rights in different jurisdictions.

4281. PERETTI, P. O., et al. "Sexual Assaults and Forced Homosexual Relationships in Prison: Cruel and Unusual Punishment," **Albany Law Review,** 36 (1972), 428-38.
Courts have begun to recognize that sexual assaults and forced homosexual relations in prison constitute cruel and unusual punishment. Toleration of these abuses by prison authorities may violate Eighth Amendment rights of prisoners.

4282. PLOSCOWE, MORRIS. **Sex and the Law.** Revised ed. New York: Ace Books, 1962. 288 pp.
Because many sex acts classified as deviant are engaged in by a broad range of the population, heterosexual as well as homosexual, laws against them are virtually unenforceable, and should be abolished for consenting adults.

4283. RAGAN, JAMES ARTHUR. "Substantial Threats of Homosexual Attack May Support the Defence of Duress in a Prosecution for Prison Escape. People v. Harmon ... 220 N. W. 2d 212 (1974)," **American Journal of Criminal Law,** 3 (1975), 331-40.
The decision in this case marks a new view by the courts of forced homosexuality as a coercive experience and as a valid defense issue to a charge of escape from prison.

4284. REESE, SUSAN ELIZABETH. "The Forgotten Sex: Lesbians, Liberation, and the Law," **Willamette Law Journal,** 11 (1975), 354-77.
The legal system alone can never exorcise society's discrimination against lesbians. What is needed is a far-reaching reevaluation of attitudes toward sexuality in general and toward women in particular. The extent to which the lesbian is ignored by the law reflects society's prejudice against homosexuality as well.

4285. RICE, CHARLES E. **Legalizing Homosexual Conduct: The Role of the Supreme Court in the Gay Rights Movement.** Cumberland, VA: Center for Judicial Studies, 1984. 29 pp.
Study by a scholar who has specialized in civil rights

issues in relation to the United States Supreme Court.

4286. RICHARDS, DAVID A. J. "Conscience, Human Rights,
       and the Anarchist Challenge to the Obligation to
       Obey the Law," **Georgia Law Review,** 18 (1984),
       771-89.
The anarchist challenge denies the very belief that the
state has a claim to obedience to the law. Free acceptance is often so problematic and basic injustice so
often in controversy that citizens of a democracy frequently regard themselves as not bound by law or by the
state's view of law.

4287. RICHARDS, DAVID A. J. "Sexual Autonomy and the
       Constitutional Right to Privacy: A Case Study in
       Human Rights and the Unwritten Constitution,"
       Hastings Law Journal, 30 (1979), 957-1018.
Seeks to apply the right of privacy to homosexual activity
among consenting adults by affirming the principle of love
as a civil liberty.

4288. RICHARDS, DAVID A. J. "Unnatural Acts and the
       Constitutional Right to Privacy: A Moral Theory,"
       Fordham Law Review, 45 (1977) 1281-1348.
An examination of moral and philsophical theory can fundamentally clarify the constitutional right to privacy. It
is wholly improper for the state to impose criminal sanctions on certain forms of consensual sexual activity between adults in private.

4289. RICHTER, ROSALYN. **Anti-gay Legislation: An Attempt
       to Sanction Inequality.** New York: Lambda Legal and
       Education Fund, 1982. 210 pp.
The belief that homosexuality per se is immoral lies at
the heart of this anti-gay legislation. It is difficult
to refute the argument that homosexuality is immoral,
since no specific evidence is often introduced to support
it. Attorneys challenging such legislation may have to
argue that homosexuality is not immoral, but in fact
constitutes "a valid and moral lifestyle."

4290. RITTER, GEORGE P. "Property Rights of Same Sex
       Couples: The Outlook after Marvin," **Loyola Univer-
       sity Law Review** (Los Angeles), 12 (1979), 409-23.
Although numerous federal and state courts, as well as
state legislatures, still feel that "questionable standards of morality justify denial of rights" to homosexuals, arguments can be made that the contractual and
equitable remedies in Marvin should extend to couples of
the same sex, particularly in view of the growing recognition that many homosexual couples "lead relatively
stable and conventional life styles."

4291. RIVERA, RHONDA H. "Our Straight-laced Judges: The
       Legal Postion of Homosexual Persons in the United
       States," **Hastings Law Journal,** 30 (1979), 799-955.

Describes "every civil case dealing with homosexuality
available to the author until August 1979." Somewhat
sprawling, but well documented (938 footnotes). This and
the following item should be consulted for references not
included herein.

4292. RIVERA, RHONDA H. "Recent Developments in Sexual
       Preference Law," **Drake Law Review**, 30 (1980), 311-
       46.
Updates the previous article with some overlooked cases,
as well as new cases decided since 1979. Remarks that
"the decisions often seem clearly to be influenced more by
social and religious thought than by legal precedent." A
further update is her: "Queer Law: Sexual Orientation Law
in the Mid-Eighties," **University of Dayton Law Review**, 10
(1985), 459-540.

4293. ROSS, H. LAURENCE (ed.). **Law and Deviance.** Beverly
       Hills, CA: Sage, 1981. 278 pp. (Sage Annual Re-
       views of Studies in Deviance, 5)
Nine papers on the subject of deviance and the use of
the law as an instrument of social control. Only occasional mention of homosexuality in its legal aspects.

4294. SAPHIRE, RICHARD B. "Gay Rights and the Constitu-
       tion: An Essay on Constitutional Theory, Practice,
       and Dronenburg v. Zech," **University of Dayton Law
       Review**, 10 (1985), 767-813.
The decision constitutes one more precedent against a
plaintiff challenging the constitutionality of laws
against sodomy, but also raises fundamental questions
about the role of judicial review.

4295. SCHUR, EDWIN M. **Crimes without Victims--Deviant
       Behavior and Public Policy: Abortion, Homosexual-
       ity, and Drug Addiction.** Englewood Cliffs, NJ:
       Prentice-Hall, 1965. 180 pp.
Since homosexuality involves the willing exchange between
consenting persons of a desired product or service, the
need for reforming the laws prohibiting such behavior is
urgent. Because laws are unenforceable owing to the lack
of a complaining victim, they often give rise to secondary
offenses such as blackmail and police corruption. An influential statement of this point of view.

4296. SCHWARTZ, LOUIS B. "Morals Offenses and the Model
       Penal Code," **Columbia Law Review**, 63 (1963), 669-
       86.
Loitering for purposes of solicitation by homosexual men
is equated with the same activity by female prostitutes.

4297. SHANK, S. ADELE. "Sticks and Stones: Homosexual
       Solicitation and the Fighting Words Doctrine," **Ohio
       State Law Journal**, 41 (1980), 553-74.
The Ohio Supreme Court in the decision in Phipps, upholding the state's same-sex solicitation statute, relied on

an outdated concept of the fighting words doctrine. It
has carved out a substantial exception to First Amendment
protections, and its poorly reasoned decision demonstrates its prejudice against homosexual lifestyles.

4298. SHERWIN, ROBERT VEIT. "Sodomy," in: Ralph Slovenko
       (ed.), **Sexual Behavior and the Law.** Springfield,
       IL: Charles C. Thomas, 1965, pp. 425-33.
Inasmuch as the sex laws of the United States tend to
punish a person's sexual desires rather than the methods
used to fulfill these desires, they may be considered
antisexual. This volume contains several other contributions of interest.

4299. SILVERMAN, HILDA, et al. **Lesbians and Gay Men: The
       Law in Pennsylvania.** Philadelphia: American Civil
       Liberties Foundation of Pennsylvania, 1981. 59 pp.
A model guide for a major state covering criminal law,
privacy, relationships, parenting, employment, housing,
social services, finances, associations, prisons, military
law, immigration and naturalization, and media.

4300. SOLOMON, DONALD M. "The Emergence of Associational
       Rights for Homosexual Persons," **JH,** 5 (1979-80),
       147-55.
Court decisions involving the rights of homosexuals to
meet together for social and political purposes have
begun to acknowledge that such association are to some
extent constitutionally protected.

4301. STANLEY, WILLIAM R. "The Rights of Gay Student
       Organizations," **Journal of College and University
       Law,** 10 (1983-84), 397-418.
Overview of the problem, including successes and failures.

4302. STODDARD, THOMAS B., E. CARRINGTON BOGGAN, et
       al. **The Rights of Gay People.** Revised ed. New
       York: Bantam Books, 1983. 194 pp. (An American
       Civil Liberties Union Handbook)
Comprehensive guide for the lay reader arranged in a
question-and-answer format, and covering such subjects
as free speech, employment, the military, immigration,
the gay family, criminal law, and the rights of transvestites and transsexuals.

4303. TABER, CARLETON H. A. "Consent Not Morality as the
       Proper Limitation on Sexual Privacy," **Hastings
       Constitutional Law Quarterly,** 4 (1977), 637-64.
The Supreme Court has recognized the existence of the
right to decisional privacy, but not delineated the
boundaries of that right. By adopting a standard of
seclusion as against the public, the courts could allow
the state to regulate public manifestations of sexual
conduct, while protecting those who prefer unconventional modes of private sexual fulfillment.

4304. TAYRIEN, MARY LEE. "California 'Consenting Adults'
      Law: The Sex Act in Perspective," **San Diego Law
      Review,** 13 (1976), 439-53.
The California legislature has acknowledged that the
private and voluntary sexual behavior of adults is not
properly the concern of the state. The "consenting
adults" law constitutes a victory for individual freedoms
through the elimination of unwarranted intrusion by the
state into the private sexual lives of adults.

4305. TONG, ROSEMARIE. "Lesbian Perspectives on Women,
      Sex and the Law," in: **Women, Sex and the Law.**
      Totowa, NJ: Rowman and Allenheld, 1984, pp. 175-92.
A survey of lesbian attitudes and political demands in
such areas as sado-masochism, family protection, pornography, heterosexual prostitution, cross-generational sex,
sexual harassment, and rape.

4306. VETRI, DOMENICK. "The Legal Arena: Progress for
      Gay Civil Rights," **JH,** 5 (1979-80), 25-30.
Asserts that contrary to some misperceptions, the homosexual community does not seek special legal protection but
equal treatment without regard to one's sexual orientation.

4307. VON BEITEL, RANDY. "The Criminalization of Private
      Sex Acts: A Jurisprudential Case Study of a
      Decision by the Texas Bar Penal Code Revision
      Committee," **Human Rights,** 6 (1977), 23-73.
On the question of the suitability of a state bar committee to decide upon the criminalization of the private
homosexual acts of consenting adults. If the question
were one of morality, then some moral philsophers should
have been included; if the considerations were empirical,
then some psychologists and sociologists were needed. The
committee failed to include any representatives of the
homosexual community.

4308. WARNER, ARTHUR C. "Non-commercial Sexual Solicita-
      tion: The Case for Judicial Invalidation," **SexuaLaw
      Reporter,** 4:1 (January-March 1978), 1, 10-20.
Originally submitted as an amicus brief in the case of
Pryor v. Municipal Court to the Supreme Court of California. The victory in this case was a landmark in legal
reform in that state.

4309. WARNER, DOUGLAS. "Homophobia, 'Manifest Homosex-
      uality,' and Political Activity: A New Approach to
      Gay Rights and the 'Issue' of Homosexuality,"
      Golden Gate Law Review, 11 (1981), 635-716.
On a California case in which the state Supreme Court
held that homosexual employees of a privately owned
public utility could sue to challenge the employer's
policy of arbitrary discrimination against homosexuals.

4310. WEISBERG, D. KELLY. "Children of the Night: The

Adequacy of Statutory Treatment of Juvenile Prostitution," **American Journal of Criminal Law**, 12
(1984), 1-67.
Based largely on a San Francisco study, evaluates the
workings of the criminal justice system for both male
and female juvenile prostitutes.

4311.   WILKINSON, J. HARVIE, III, and G. EDWARD WHITE.
        "Constitutional Protection for Personal Life-
        styles," **Cornell Law Review**, 62 (1977), 563-625.
Calls for a balanced and sensitive approach to the central dilemma examined in the article. Accomodation
must be reached with the rights of dissident members of
society, but not such as to leave the fabric of conventional society without legal support.

4312.   WILSON, LAWRENCE A., and RAPHAEL SHANNON. "Homo-
        sexual Organizations and the Right of Association,"
        Hastings Law Journal, 30 (1979), 1029-74.
Examines a series of decisions in the area of gay rights,
and concludes that they can best be furthered through the
litigation process when the well-established right of
association is used as the rationale for challenging restrictive actions on the part of the state.

4313.   WOLFF, BENNETT. "Expanding the Right of Sexual
        Privacy," **Loyola Law Review**, 27 (1981), 1279-1300.
On the constitutional challenge to the sodomy laws. By
its summary affirmation in Doe v. Commonwealth's Attorney,
the Supreme Court failed to provide the necessary guidance
to state and federal courts as to the validity of similar
statutes proscribing consensual sodomy. On the other
hand, the New York State Court of Appeals, in its decision
in Onofre, created a new fundamental value for both right
of privacy and equal protection claims.

4314.   ZERINGER, BRIAN D. "Tort Liability of the State
        for Injuries Suffered by Prisoners Due to Assault
        by Other Inmates," **Tulane Law Review**, 51 (1977),
        1300-06.
On a case in which an inmate of the Louisiana State Penitentiary was fatally stabbed while attempting to move a
newly admitted prisoner from a dormitory where the latter
had received threats upon his life. The Louisiana Supreme
Court affirmed the state's liability on the basis of the
failure of prison officials to take reasonable precau-
tions against the attack.

                    H. US SODOMY LAWS

The sodomy laws are generally recognized as the linchpin
on which discrimination against homosexuals, legal and
extralegal, depends. Accordingly, much effort has gone

into studying their origin, nature, and modus operandi to
prepare the way for the dismantling of this legislation.

4315. BADER, LOUIS. "Commonwealth v. Bonadio," **Duquesne
       Law Review**, 19 (1981), 793-800.
On the 1980 Pennsylvania Supreme Court decision that
struck down the state's Deviate Sexual Intercourse
statute. The court held that the statute exceeded the
valid bounds of the state's police power, and violated
the equal protection clauses of the the Federal and state
constitutions. Compare D. M.Barnhart, below.

4316. BARNETT, WALTER, and ARTHUR C. WARNER. **Why Reform
       the Sodomy Laws?** Princeton: National Committee for
       Sexual Civil Liberties, 1971. 24 pp.
This pithy and comprehensive marshalling of the arguments
for reform set the stage for the ensuing decade of progress.

4317. BARNHART, DEBRA MCCLOSKEY. "Commonwealth v. Bonad-
       io: Voluntary Deviate Intercourse--A Comparative
       Analysis," **University of Pittsburgh Law Review**, 43
       (1981), 253-84.
Argues that such changes in the law reflect concurrent
shifts in the concept of the immoral and the unnatural.

4318. COONEY, LESLIE LARKIN. "Constitutional Law--Right
       of Privacy--Sodomy Statutes--Supreme Court Summary
       Affirmance," **Duquesne Law Review**, 15 (1976), 123-
       32.
The Supreme Court's summary affirmance in Doe v. Commonwealth's Attorney leaves the breadth of the right to
privacy uncertain. Virginia and states with like statutes
can continue to criminalize intimate sexual activity between consenting adults.

4319. "Deviate Sexual Behavior under the New Illinois
       Criminal Code," **Washington University Law Quarter-
       ly** (1965), 220-35.
The new Illiniois criminal code attempted to solve the
problems resulting from the existence of an ambiguous
"crime against nature" provision by regrouping the sanctions around four concerns considered to fall within the
scope of legislative activity.

4320. FADELEY, EDWARD N. "Sex Crime in the New Code,"
       Oregon Law Review, 51 (1972), 515-24.
Victimless crimes have been eliminated from the Oregon
Criminal Code, but the age of consent to sexual intercourse has been raised to eighteen without any social or
psychological justification.

4321. FISHER, ROBERT G. "The Sex Offender Provisions of
       the Proposed New Maryland Criminal Code: Should
       Private, Consenting, Homosexual Behavior Be Ex-

cluded?" **Maryland Law Journal**, 30 (1970), 91-113.
The Sodomy and Perverted Practice crimes should be rede-
fined so that private consensual behavior between adults
is no longer prohibited, only homosexual rape and statutory rape (where the victim in a minor).

4322. IGLOW, ROBERT A. "Oral Copulation: A Constitution-
        al Curtain Must Be Drawn," **San Diego Law Review**, 11
        (1974), 523-34.   /
California Penal Code Section 288(a), which prohibits oral
copulation, is unconstitutionally overbroad in that it is
"an attempt by the State to regulate atypical sexual behavior between consenting adults in private and as such
constitutes an unconstitutional infringement on the individual's fundamental right to privacy in matters relating to sex.

4323. JOPLIN, LARRY E. "Criminal Law: One Examination of
        the Oklahoma Laws concerning Sexual Behavior,"
        Oklahoma Law Review, 23 (1970), 459-72.
See esp. pp. 466-70, "The Crime against Nature." If
society were really opposed to adultery and private homosexuality, it would insist that the present laws be rig-
idly upheld. It is unrealistic to "legislate against
sin where a clear consensus is lacking and social change
challenges old values." Retaining unenforceable laws
forbidding private sexual activity brings the law itself
into disrespect.

4324. KATZ, KATHERINE D. "Sexual Morality and the
        Constitution: People v. Onofre," **Albany Law Review**,
        46 (1982), 311-62.
On the landmark New York state decision, which effectively
decriminalized sodomy. As a matter of federal constitutional law, society may not invoke criminal sanctions to
punish sexual conduct deemed immoral by the majority of
the population unless harm to an interest other than
morality is demonstrated.

4325. KETCHAM, CARLETON P., JR. "Criminal Law--Sodomy
        Statute Not Describing Prohibited Conduct but
        Referring Only to 'Crime against Nature' Held
        Unconstitutionally Overbroad," **Cumberland-Samford
        Law Review**, 3 (1972), 525-31.
In a Florida case, Franklin v. State, the Supreme Court of
Florida overturned the "crime against nature" statute on
grounds of vagueness and uncertainty. Though limited in
its holding, Franklin can have a far-reaching effect in
that new laws will, it may hoped, cope with real criminal
activity rather than attempt to enforce a moral code.

4326. LEVINE, LAWRENCE CARL. "Pryor v. Municipal
        Court: California's Narrowing Definitions of
        Solicitation for Public Lewd Conduct," **Hastings Law
        Journal**, 32 (1980-81), 461-98.
Examines the conclusion of California's Supreme Court that

the phrase "lewd or dissolute conduct" [Calif. Penal Code, 647(a)] is unconstitutionally vague. However, Levine warns that the decision may be weakened unless the court soon clarifies its holding.

4327. O'NEILL, TIM. "Doe v. Commonwealth's Attorney: A
       Set-back for the Right of Privacy," **Kentucky Law
       Journal,** 65 (1976-77), 748-63.
The Supreme Court's decision that the Virginia sodomy statute had a rational basis of state interest may lend credence to the continued existence of these statutes as well as limit the right of personal privacy.

4328. RIZZO, JAMES J. "The Constitutionality of Sodomy
       Statutes," **Fordham Law Review,** 45 (1976-77), 553-
       95.
Offers an overview of constitutional arguments against the statutes including void for vagueness, overbreadth, cruel and unusual punishment, right of privacy, and equal protection.

4329. SIMMONS, JOHN F. "Constitutional Law--Sodomy
       Statutes: The Question of Constitutionality,"
       Nebraska Law Review, 50 (1970-71), 567-75.
On the Buchanan decision of the Nebraska Supreme Court, which extended legal protection to married couples, but not to others.

4330. "State Statute Prohibiting Private Consensual
       Sodomy is Constitutional," **Brigham Young University
       Law Review** (1977), 170-88.
On the United States Supreme Court's decision to uphold the Virginia sodomy statute [Doe v. Commonwealth's Attorney (1976)].

                    I. US LAW: COURTS

It is generally recognized that there may be a gap between legal theory and actual practice. Accordingly, it is necessary to examine courtroom procedures with respect to possible prejudice on the part of judges, district attorneys, and other significant figures. A special problem is the risk that some openly homosexual attorneys run of disbarment under the "good moral character" provisions of the bar.

4331. BAGNALL, ROBERT G., PATRICK C. GALLAGHER, and JONI
       L. GOLDSTEIN. "Burdens on Gay Litigants and Bias
       in the Court System: Homosexual Panic, Child
       Custody, and Anonymous Parties," **Harvard Civil
       Rights--Civil Liberties Law Review,** 19 (1984),
       497-559.

Discusses the pleas of homicide defendants that they were
the victims of homosexual rape; restrictions on parental
rights of gays; and the ability of gay litigants to proceed anonymously. Courts are urged to be sensitive to the
special burdens on gays caused by the loss of privacy.

4332.   BLACKFORD, BARBARA. "Good Moral Character and
        Homosexuality," **Journal of the Legal Profession,** 5
        (1980), 139-49.
Concludes that "at least under certain circumstances,
homosexual acts may illustrate to the bar that an attorney
is lacking good moral character." In an attorney honesty
and trustworthiness are essential.

4333.   DRESSLER, JOSHUA. "Judicial Homophobia: Gay
        Rights' Biggest Roadblock," **The Civil Liberties
        Review** (January-February 1979), 19-27.
Shows the persistence of myths and emotional thinking
in the courts.

4334.   FARRELL, RONALD A. "Class Linkages of Legal
        Treatment of Homosexuals," **Criminology,** 9 (1971),
        49-68.
Sociological study of 108 offenders held for court supports the hypothesis that they show a disproportionately large number of offenders from the lower classes,
and that these offenders received more severe treatment
than comparable higher status persons.

4335.   GOLDYN, LAWRENCE. "Gratuitous Language in Appel-
        late Cases Involving Gay People: 'Queer Baiting'
        from the Bench," **Political Behavior,** 3 (1981),
        31-48.
Although gay litigants are frequently the target of abuse,
this practice varies depending on the type of case and the
level of court involved. There is some indication that
the abuse is declining.

4336.   KNUTSON, DONALD. "Representing the Unpopular
        Client ... Gays," **Law Library Journal,** 72 (1979),
        677-79.
Indicates three main problems confronting gay men: access
to adequate legal representation; need for anonymity; and
homophobia in the legal system.

4337.   LUDWIG, FREDERICK J. "Case for Repeal of the Sex
        Corroboration Requirement in New York," **Brooklyn
        Law Review,** 36 (1970), 378-89.
Article by the Chief Assist;ant District Attorney, Queens
County, who claims that the "corroboration requirement has
nullified the prosecution of practically every sex offense
in the current Penal Law."

4338.   ROBERTS, LESLIE A. "Private Homosexual Activity
        and Fitness to Practice Law: Florida Board of Bar
        Examiners in re N.R.S," **Nova Law Journal,** 6 (1981-

82), 519-34.

The Florida Supreme Court denied the Board authority to question an applicant regarding private homosexual conduct.

4339. SHAFFER, DAVID R., and THOMAS CASE. "On the Decision to Testify in One's Own Behalf: Effects of Withheld Evidence, Defendants' Sexual Preference, and Juror Dogmatism on Juridical Decisions, **Journal of Personality and Social Psychology**, 42 (1982), 335-46.

A study of 360 University of Georgia students simulating roles as jurors showed that while high dogmatic jurors were no more punitive to homosexual than heterosexual defendants, jurors low in dogmatism were actually more lenient toward homosexual than heterosexual defendents.

4340. SHERMAN, JEFFREY G. "Undue Influence and the Homosexual Testator," **University of Pittsburgh Law Review**, 42 (1981), 225-67.

Suggests that "a homosexual testator who bequeaths the bulk of his estate to his lover stands in greater risk of having his testamentary plans overturned than does a heterosexual testator who bequeaths the bulk of his estate to a spouse or a lover." The risk may be somewhat reduced through employing the device of adoption or the revocable inter vivos trust.

4340A. WILLIAMS, MARK A. "Homosexuality and the Good Moral Character Requirement," **University of Detroit Journal of Urban Law**, 56 (1978), 123-39.

With respect to the bar, the author argues that "[c]onsensual homosexual conduct practiced discretely in private no more jeopardizes the values protected by the good moral character requirement than does consensual heterosexual conduct practiced discretely in private." Unless this principle is followed, the bar will become the ultimate arbiter of the private morals of its members.

4341. WILLICK, DANIEL H., GRETCHEN GEHLKER, and ANITA M. WATTS. "Social Class as a Factor Affecting Judicial Disposition: Defendants Charged with Criminal Homosexual Acts," **Criminology**, 13 (1975), 55-77.

Published data are reviewed, and it is concluded that evidence from cases involving felonious homosexual acts does not lend much support to the proposition that there is social class bias in judicial disposition of criminal cases.

J. US LAW: EMPLOYMENT

Recent efforts to protect the employment rights of

disadvantaged groups have suggested that similar strategies may be pursued with respect to homosexual employees. This problem arises in particular with teachers.
See also "Teachers," XI.B.

4341A. BENEDICT, JAMES N.   "Homosexuality and the Law--A
       Right to Be Different," **Albany Law Review**, 38
       (1973), 84-104.
Primarily concerned with the status of homosexuals in
positions of public employment, providing an analysis of
some recent cases. Suggests possible grounds upon which
future constitutional challenges to existing discrimination may be founded.

4342. "Burton v. Cascade School District Union High
       School," **Brigham Young University Law Review**
       (1976), 531-48.
On the discharge, in July 1970, of teacher Peggy Burton,
who filed an action under Section 1983 leading to her reinstatement. This note argues that the reinstatement was
a mistake.

4342A. CLARK, PENNY M.   "Homosexual Public Employees:
       Utilizing Section 1983 to Remedy Discrimination,"
       Hastings Constitutional Law Quarterly, 8 (1981),
       255-311.
The increasing role of government agencies renders it
imperative to use Section 1983 as a remedy for discrimination; other options should also be pursued.

4343. CRUMPLER, WILLIAM B.   "Administrative Law--Constit-
       utional Law--Is Government Policy Affecting the
       Employment of Homosexuals Rational?" **North Carolina
       Law Review**, 48 (1970), 912-214.
Hold that discharges should be considered on a case-by-
case basis according to the overall character and performance of the individual.

4343A. DAVIS, ELAINE.   "Homosexuals in Government Employ-
       ment: The Boys in the Bureau," **Seton Hall Law
       Review**, 3 (1971), 89-107.
The Grimm, Gayer, and Ulrich decisions challenging the
right of government agencies to withhold security clearance from homosexuals set a precedent: homosexuals should
certainly also be allowed to hold jobs that do not involve
national security as well. Court tests are needed.

4344. DECKER, PHILIP J.   "Homosexuality and Employment:
       A Case Law Review," **Personnel Journal**, 59 (1980),
       756-60.
Societal factors, including changing attitudes and lifestyles, appear to be influencing the direction of case law
dealing with homosexual employees.

4344A. "Dismissal of Homosexuals from Government Employ-
       ment: The Developing Role of Due Process in Admin-

istration Adjudications," **Georgetown Law Journal,** 58 (1970), 632-45.
Legal background on advances in the courts in the 'sixties, including Norton v. Macy, in which a homosexual man was found to be unlawfully dismissed from his government job.

4345. DRESSLER, JOSHUA. "Survey of School Principals Regarding Alleged Homosexual Teachers in the Classroom: How Likely (Really) Is Discharge?" **University of Dayton Law Review,** 10 (1985), 599-620.
A substantial minority of pricipals favor loss of licence if the teacher is a gay activist in the classroom or outside it. But in practice the treatment of teachers has been more lenient, and retention of a teacher accused of being homosexual rarely causes long-term problems for the administrator.

4345A. FREIMANN, ARLENE. "Acanfora v. Board of Education: New Interpretations on Standing; Section 1983 and Judicial Review of Administrative Determination," **Temple Law Quarterly,** 48 (1975), 384-96.
Complications ensuing from the dismissal of a Pennsylvania teacher.

4346. FRIEDMAN, JOEL. "Constitutional and Statutory Challenges to Discrimination in Employment Based on Sexual Orientation," **Iowa Law Review,** 64 (1978-79), 527-72.
Examines employment practices that discriminate against homosexuals in the light of governmental obligations under the Constitution and the Civil Rights Acts of 1866 and 1964.

4346A. "Government-created Employment Disabilities of the Homosexual," **Harvard Law Review,** 82 (1969), 1738-51.
Challenges the legal rationale used to exclude homosexuals from federal civil service and from private employment. Suggests a program of "graduated liberalization."

4347. "Government Employment and the Homosexual," **St. Johns Law Review,** 45 (1970-71), 303-23.
Reviews recent cases (Morrison, Norton, and Schlegel), indicating that dismissal of homosexuals is counterproductive, inasmuch as it makes it more difficult for them to lead socially useful lives.

4347A. GRAHAM, KATHLEEN M. "Security Clearances for Homosexuals," **Stanford Law Review,** 25 (1972-73), 403-29.
Details the operations of the Industrial Security Clearance Review Office, the agency that processes security clearances and continues to deny them to homosexuals, despite court victories in Ulrich and Gayer.

4348. HANSEN, KENT A. "Gaylord v. Tacoma School District
       No. 10: Homosexual Held Immoral for Purposes of
       Teacher Discharge," **Willamette Law Journal**, 14
       (1977), 101-14.
Reviews the case, including legal background and the
rationale for the decision. See also John H. Lowe,
"Homosexual Teacher Dismissal: A Deviant Dismissal,"
Washington Law Review, 53 (1977), 499-510 (critical of
the court's findings).

4348A. HEDGPETH, JUDITH M. "Employment Discrimination
       Law and the Rights of Gay Persons," **JH**, 5 (1979-
       80), 67-78.
While considerable progress has been achieved in the
struggle against employment discrimination against homosexuals, administrative and judicial protection has generally been sporadic and unreliable.

4349. HOFFMAN, STEPHEN CLARE. "Analysis of Rationales in
       Homosexual Public Employment Cases," **South Dakota
       Law Review**, 23 (1978), 338-57.
Concludes that the most common arguments used against
homosexuals--the prevention of activity contrary to public
mores, the prevention of emotional instability in employees, and the prevention of the spread of homosexuality--do
not seem to stand up under close examination. "[E]ither
the policy of refusing relief to discharged homosexuals
should be abandoned or a firmer basis for its application
should be found."

4349A. "Homosexual Public Employees and the Right to
       Privacy," **Harvard Law Review**, 97 (1984), 1753-56.
The arguments revisited.

4350. JOHNSON, LEE ANN. "Gay Law Students Ass'n v.
       Pac'c Tel' & Tel' Co.: Constitutional and Statutory
       Restraints on Employment Discrimination against
       Homosexuals by Public Utilities," **California Law
       Review**, 68 (1980), 680-715.
The California Supreme Court found three distinct sources
of law that bar a public utility from engaging in arbitrary employment discrimination: the equal protection
clause in the California constitution; section 453(a) of
the Public Utilities Code; and sections 1101 and 1102 of
the Labor Code.

4351. KAMENY, FRANK. "Government Grants Richard Gayer
       Security Clearance," **Vector**, 7:10 (October 1971),
       32-33, 53.
On the advice of Kameny, a gay activist and lay advocate,
Gayer, a civil service employee successfully fought em-
ployment discrimination.

4352. KNUTSON, KIRBIE. "Constitutional Law--Due Pro-
       cess--Dismissal of a Transsexual from a Tenured
       Teaching Position in a Public School," **Wisconsin**

Law Review (1976), 670-89.
In the case of Paula Grossman, a dismissed tenured teacher, the New Jersey Superior Court, Appellate Division,
upheld the dismissal on the grounds that her negative
impact hindered her effectiveness as a teacher.

4353. LAMORTE, MICHAEL W. "Legal Rights and Responsibil-
       ities of Homosexuals in Public Education," **Journal
       of Law and Education,** 4 (1975), 449-67.
Examines reported decisions dealing with hiring, contract
renewal or dismissal, and revocation of teaching certif-
icates. Perceives an emerging pattern that it is incum-
bent on the employer to demonstrate that a dismissed
teacher's homosexuality interferes with his or her actual
performance (the nexus test).

4354. LAVINE, KAREN S. "Free Speech Rights of Homosexual
       Teachers," **Columbia Law Review,** 80 (1980), 1513-34.
Examines the extent to which the First Amendment protects
teachers who discuss the subject of homosexuality in
class.

4355. LEONARD, ARTHUR S. "Employment Discrimination
       against Persons with AIDS," **University of Dayton
       Law Review,** 10 (1985), 681-703.
Innovative use of the existing statutory framework,
focusing on the disease itself, should provide significant protection for many who suffer discrimination because
of the AIDS crisis.

4356. LEVINE, ELLEN. "Legal Rights of Homosexuals in
       Public Employment," **Annual Survey of American Law**
       (1978), 455-91.
Analyzes the leading cases in the fields of teaching and
federal government service, showing use of the nexus test
and First Amendment claims.

4357. MEEKER, JAMES W., et al. "State Law and Local
       Ordinances in California Barring Discrimination on
       the Basis of Sexual Orientation," **University of
       Dayton Law Review,** 10 (1985), 745-65.
Local ordinances are most effective in filling the void
that is currently left by state statutes and the common
law. It remains questionable, however, whether the
protection afforded is of any substance or is primarily
a symbolic gesture.

4358. MYERS, JOHN E. B. "Singer v. U.S. Civil Service
       Commission: Dismissal of Government Employee for
       Advocacy of Homosexuality," **Utah Law Review** (1976),
       172-85.
Singer was dismissed as a clerk typist in federal employ-
ment for "immoral and notoriously disgraceful conduct."
The dismissal was upheld by the Ninth Circuit Court of
Appeals. The article explores the relevant legal prin-
ciples, claiming that "the Singer opinion marks a major

reversal in the current trend of cases."

4359. PEARLDAUGHTER, ANDRA. "Employment Discrimination
      against Lesbians: Municipal Ordinances and Other
      Remedies," **Golden Gate University Law Review,** 8
      (1979), 537-58.
In addition to pursuing existing remedies for the double
discrimination that lesbians may be subjected to, electoral and legislative initiatives are needed.

4360. "Remedial Balancing Decisions and the Rights of
      Homosexual Teachers: A Pyrrhic Victory," **Iowa Law
      Review,** 61 (1976), 1080-98.
Problems of teachers' rights are highlighted by a recent
decision of the Ninth Circuit, Burton v. Cascade School
District Union High School No. 5.

4361. RUBINSTEIN, RONALD A., and PATRICIA B. FRY. **Of a
      Homosexual Teacher: Beneath the Mainstream of
      Constitutional Equalities.** Frederick, MD: Associ-
      ated Faculty Press, 1981. 92 pp.
Also in: **Texas Southern University Law Review,** 6 (1981),
183-275. Reflections based on the disturbing ramifications of the Gaylord case, where a highly competent
teacher was removed because of his homosexual orientation.

4362. SCHOLZ, JEANNE L. "Out of the Closet, Out of a
      Job: Due Process in Teacher Disqualification,"
      Hastings Constitutional Law Quarterly, 6 (1978-79),
      663-717.
Presents the legal-conceptual background and a review of
leading cases. Argues that "any morally based disqual-
ification of teachers for conduct which is private and
consensual, or which is otherwise protectible under the
First Amendment, offends due process because it is patently arbitrary."

4363. SHAFFER, JOHN SCOTT, JR. "The Boundaries of a
      Church's First Amendment Rights as an Employer,"
      Case Western Reserve Law Review, 31 (1981), 363-85.
Focuses on issues raised by a church's discharge of a
homosexual employeee under the Free Exercise clause, the
Establishment Clause, and general constitutional theory.
Concludes that providing certain conditions are met, a
church's dismissal of a homosexual employee may be upheld.

4364. SINISCALCO, GARY R. "Homosexual Discrimination in
      Employment," **Santa Clara Law Review,** 16 (1976),
      495-512.
Analyzes recent legal developments, esp. as regards the
law governing private employment. Studies of adverse
impact in the private sector may elicit beneficial
government prodding.

4365. TEWKSBURY, MICHAEL D. "Gaylord and Singer: Wash-

ington's Place in the Emerging Laws Concerning
Homosexuals," **Gonzaga Law Review,** 14 (1978),
167-96.
Discusses two cases--one involving a teacher, the other
a clerk typist in federal employment, related cases, and
other areas of the law in relation to homosexuality.

4366. WEIN, STUART A., and CYNTHIA LARK REMMERS. "Employment Protection and Gender Dysphoria: Legal
Definitions of Unequal Treatment on the Basis of
Sex and Disability," **Hastings Law Journal,** 30
(1979), 1079-1130.
Argues that "gender dysphoria persons who have already
borne the psychological and social stigma of their condition, should bear no special legal burden because
of a a sexual characteristic having no relation to their
ability to perform and contribute."

4367. WISE, DONNA L. "Challenging Sexual Preference
Discrimination in Private Employment," **Ohio State
Law Journal,** 41 (1980), 501-31.
Argues that in addition to pursuing existing remedies,
as provided by federal civil rights statutes, state
statutes, and the common law, supporters of homosexual
rights need to secure new protective legislation.

                    K. US LAW: IMMIGRATION

Although most legal sanctions against homosexual behavior
are focused in the states, immigration is under federal
jurisdiction. In this field the situation is complicated
and difficult to resolve without remedial legislation to
undo the discriminatory provisions that have been added to
the law ever since homosexuality came to be recognized as
a "mental illness" in the second decade of this century.

4368. BOGATIN, MARC. "Immigration and Nationality Act
and the Exclusion of Homosexuals: Boutelier v. INS
Revisited," 2 (1981), 359-96.
Analyzes the effects of the 1952 McCarran-Walter Act
[section 212(a) (4)], esp. with regard to the interface
of the medical profession and federal administrative
agencies.

4369. FOWLER, PETER N., and LEONARD GRAFF. "Gay Aliens
and Immigration: Resolving the Conflict between
Hill and Longstaff," **University of Dayton Law
Review,** 10 (1985), 621-44.
The Fifth and Ninth Circuits have reached contradictory
conclusions regarding the requirement of a medical certificate in medical exclusion cases. The issue may
be ultimately be resolved by Congressional enactment.

4370. "Homosexual Resident Alien Deportable as a Psycho-
      pathic Personality," **Catholic Lawyer**, 13 (1967),
      82-90.
Concludes that "[w]hile the choice of whom to admit is
rightfully left to Congress, there is little doubt that
changes are needed in the area of deportation." Present
law and practice are contradictory and unpredictable.

4371. "Immigration and Naturalization: Good Moral Charac-
      ter Requirement is a Question of Federal Law,"
      Suffolk Transnational Law Journal, 6 (1982),
      383-94.
On Nemetz v. INS (647 F. 2d 432). See also: "Immigra-
tion--Aliens--The Invalidation of a Homosexual Marriage
for Immigration Purposes," ibid., 7 (1983), 267-78 (on
Adams v. Howerton, 673 F 2d 1036).

4372. LEGGETT, WALTER E. "Immigration and Naturaliza-
      tion--Petition for Naturalization," **Georgia Journal
      of International and Comparative Law**, 6 (1976),
      333-38.
On the Brodie case, concerning an alien who had served
honorably in the United States Army for two years.

4373. POZNANSKI, ROBERT. "The Propriety of Denying
      Entry to Homosexual Aliens: Examining the Public
      Health Service's Authority over Medical Exclu-
      sions," **University of Michigan Journal of Law
      Reform**, 17 (1984), 331-59.
The fate of homosexual aliens wishing to enter, reside
in, or become citizens of the United States remains un-
settled. The resolution of this conflict depends upon
a determinaton of the Public Health Service's role in
the exclusionary process. The writer holds that the INS
should acknowledge the authority of the PHS by complying
with the decision to not exclude aliens on grounds of
homosexuality.

4374. REYNOLDS, WILLIAM T. "The Immigration and Nation-
      ality Act and the Rights of Homosexual Aliens," **JH**,
      5 (1979-80), 79-87.
While prospects for naturalization of openly gay aliens
have improved in recent years, the present statutory and
administrative frameworks are still riddled with exceptions and outdated standards.

4375. ROBERTS, MAURICE A. "Sex and the Immigration
      Laws," **San Diego Law Review**, 14 (1976), 9-41.
Surveying a range of sexual activities, including adultery, homosexuality, prostitution, and sham marriage, the
writer concludes that changes are long overdue.

4376. SEDLAK, ERIC W. "Nemetz v. INS: The Rights of Gay
      Aliens under the Constitutional Requirement of
      Uniformity and Mutable Standards of Moral Turpi-
      tude," **New York University Journal of International**

Law and Politics, 16 (1984), 881-912.
Concerns a petition of naturalization and the issue of
variation in the state laws on homosexuality.

4377. SILVERS, SAMUEL M. "The Exclusion and Expulsion of
Homosexual Aliens," **Columbia Human Rights Law Review**, 15 (1984), 295-332.
Examines recent contradictory decisions against a background that begins in the 1952 McCarran-Walters Act. Concludes that our constitutional ideals require that we
welcome aliens rather than exclude them on arbitrary bases
such as homosexuality.

4378. WINDHAM, MELISSA QUINN. "Aliens--Immigration and
Naturalization Service Policy of Excluding Homosexual Aliens without a Medical Certificate is Invalid. Hill v. United States Immigration and Naturalization Service. 714 F. 2d 1470," **Vanderbilt Journal of Transnational Law**, 16 (1983), 689-709.
On the case of an English visitor who was turned away
at San Francisco. The district court opinion in this case
was exceedingly far-reaching, invalidating the INS policy
that excluded homosexuals without a medical certificate
and, more significantly, broadening judicial review of
exclusion policies. The Ninth Circuit, however, narrowed
the district court's holding to the point that congressional power over exclusion will remain undaunted.

L. US LAW: MARRIAGE

While in practice the (nonlegal) definition of couples
(see XIV.H) has been broadened to include homosexual and
lesbian dyads, the question of whether unions between two
persons of the same sex should receive official sanction
remains uncertain. Even many prohomosexual persons would
say that such a recognition would not be desirable, and it
seems that this is an idea whose time has not yet come--if
indeed it ever will. For problems related to the custody
of children, see XVIII.D.

4379. BUCHANAN, G. SIDNEY. "Same-Sex Marriage: The
Linchpin Issue," **University of Dayton Law Review**,
10 (1985), 541-73.
A modified version of a chapter in the author's book **Morality, Sex and the Constitution: A Christian Perspective
on the Power of Government to Regulate Private Sexual
Conduct between Consenting Adults** (1985). Argues that
recognition of same-sex marriages poses a significant
threat to the values traditionally promoted by opposite-
sex marriage. Buchanan concedes that non-recognition
impinges on the right of privacy.

4380. COBURN, VINCENT P. "Homosexuality and the Invalid-
       ation of Marriage," **Jurist**, 20 (1960), 441-59.
Examines heterosexual marriage in which one partner is
homosexual from the point of view of canon law, esp. with
respect to annulment.

4381. COLE, ROB. "Two Men Ask Minnesota License for
       First Legal U.S. Gay Marriage: Take Advantage of
       Vague Law, Expect Court Case to Follow," **Advocate**,
       no. 35 (June 10-23, 1970), pp. 1, 4.
First widely publicized effort (by Minnesotans James
McConnell and Jack Baker) to obtain a valid marriage cer-
tificate; the effort ultimately failed.

4382. CULLEM, CATHERINE M. "Fundamental Interests and
       the Question of Same-Sex Marriage," **Tulsa Law
       Journal**, 15 (1979), 141-63.
Argues that the individual's fundamental right to enter
the marital relationship is broad enough to encompass
same-sex marriage.

4383. ELLISTON, FREDERICK. "Gay Marriage," in: R. Baker
       and F. Elliston (eds.), **Philosophy and Sex**.
       Buffalo: Prometheus Books, 1984, pp. 146-66.
Philosophical reflections tending to justify legal sanction for homosexual unions.

4384. HANSEN, TED L. "Domestic Relations--Minnesota
       Marriage Statute Does Not Permit Marriage between
       Persons of the Same Sex and Does Not Violate
       Constitutionally Protected Rights," **Drake Law
       Review**, 22 (1972), 206-12.
The negative decision in Baker v. Nelson (Minn. 1971), did
not provide the answer to the question of whether there is
sufficient moral or medical reason to restrict the right
to same-sex marriage.

4385. "Homosexuals' Right to Marry: A Constitutional Test
       and a Legislative Solution," **University of Pennsyl-
       vania Law Review**, 128 (1979), 193-216.
In decisions beginning in the early 1970s, homosexual
couples were repeatedly denied the possibility of marriage. The article explores the issue by a comparative
analysis, arguing that the concept of equal protection
means that marriage restrictions are unconstitutional:
"the state must afford homosexuals the opportunity to
make a marriage commitment."

4386. INGRAM, J. D. "A Constitutional Critique of
       Restrictions on the Right to Marry--Why Can't Fred
       Marry George--or Mary and Alice at the Same Time?"
       Journal of Contemporary Law, 10 (1984), 33-55.
Advances arguments supporting same-sex unions, while con-
ceding that this is not yet an idea whose time has come.

4387. KENNY, WALTER F., REV. "Homosexuality and Nul-

lity--Developing Jurisprudence," **Catholic Lawyer,**
17 (1971), 110-22.
Concludes with respect to ecclesiastical tribunals: "We
now have a basis in jurisprudence for annulling the
marriage of homosexuals and other deviates."

4388. "The Legality of Homosexual Marriage," **Yale Law
Review,** 82 (1973), 573-89.
Concludes that "[t]he stringent requirements of the
proposed Equal Rights Amendment argue strongly for ...
granting marriage licenses to homosexual couples who
satisfy reasonable and non-discriminatory qualifications."

4389. RITTER, GEORGE P. "Property Rights of Same-Sex
Couples: The Outlook after Marvin," **Loyola of Los
Angeles Law Review,** 12 (1979), 409-23.
Arguments can be made that Marvin's [a heterosexual co-
habitation case] contractual and equitable remedies should
extend to couples of the same sex.

4390. SCHMIDT, JOHN R. "Homosexuality and Validity of
Marriage--A Study of Homopsychosexual Inversion,"
Catholic Lawyer, 19 (1973), 84-101 and 169-99; and
21 (1975), 85-121.
Reprinted from **Jurist,** 32 (1972), 381-99 and 494-530. Extensively documented study seeking to combine psychiatric and canon-law perspectives. Homosexual persons may
be so disturbed as to make their condition "fatally det-
rimental to the matrimonial consortium."

4391. SILVERSTEIN, ARTHUR J. "Constitutional Aspects of
the Homosexual's Right to a Marriage License,"
Journal of Family Law, 12 (1973), 607-34.
Concludes that propsects for acceptance of homosexual
marriage are uncertain for they turn upon future societal
developments which are difficult to predict, inasmuch as
the law of equal protection at present provides no clear
guidance.

4392. THOMAS, PAUL K. "Marriage Annulments for Gay Men
and Lesbian Women: New Canonical and Psychological
Insights," **Jurist** 43 (1983), 318-42.
Seeks to go beyond Schmidt, above, and Tobin, below.

4393. TOBIN, WILLIAM J. **Homosexuality and Marriage: A
Canonical Evaluation on the Relationship of Homosexuality to the Validity of Marriage in the Light
of Recent Rotal Jurisprudence.** Rome: Catholic Book
Agency, 1964.
Discusses two bases for annulling a marriage where one
party suffers from "mental illness": (1) his consent is
deficient; (2) he is unfit to undertake, fulfill, and
receive marital rights (**contractus matrimonialis inexis-
tens**).

4394. VEITCH, EDWARD. "Essence of Marriage--A Comment

on the Homosexual Challenge," **Anglo-American Law
Review,** 5 (1976), 41-49.
Concludes, after reviewing several Canadian and US cases,
that "there would appear to be a distinct state advantage
in the recognition of same-sex marriage."

M. US MILITARY LAW

The attempt to extend homosexual rights to the military is
difficult, owing to the fact that military justice does
not recognize many of the civil rights protections that
are enshrined in our general legal situation. In addition, the armed services have fought doggedly to retain
their right to exclude male homosexuals and lesbians from
service, despite the prevalence of the latter in women's
branches of the military.

4395. CANEPA, THERESA J. "Aftermath of Saal v. Midden-
          dorf: Does Homosexuality Preclude Military Fit-
          ness?" **Santa Clara Law Review,** 22 (1982), 491-511.
Navy servicewoman Mary Sal was honorably discharged, but
assigned an enlistment code that made her ineligible
for reenlistment. Although the district court found in
her favor, this was reversed by the US Court of Appeals,
Ninth Circuit.

4396. CARBETTA-SCANDY, KELLY. "The Armed Services Con-
          tinued Degradation and Expulsion of Their Homosex-
          ual Members: Dronenburg v. Zech," **University of
          Cincinnati Law Review,** 54 (1986), 1055-67.
Criticizes the decision of the United States District
Court for the District of Columbia in a Navy case for
inconsistency and insufficiency of judicial reasoning.

4397. DEITER, LAWRENCE R. "Employment Discrimination in
          the Armed Services--An Analysis of Recent Decisions
          Affecting Sexual Preference Discrimination in the
          Military," **Villanova Law Review,** 27 (1981-82), 351-
          73.
Discusses recent cases which "have left the law in a per-
plexing state of uncertainty."

4398. DUBAN, PATRICIA DODGE. "Matlovich v. Secretary of
          the Air Force, 591 F. 2d 852 (D.C. Cir. 1978),"
          Duquesne Law Review, 18 (1979), 151-60.
Reviews the denial of the action filed in the U.S. District Court for the District of Columbia by Sergeant
Leonard Matlovich to restrain the Air Force from discharg-
ing him.

4399. EVERHARD, JOHN A. "Problems Involving the Disposi-
          tion of Homosexuals in the Service," **United States**

Air Force Judge Advocate General's Bulletin, 2
(1960), 20-23.
Traditional interpretation holding that a known homosexual
is a liability to a military organization by lowering
the "moral fiber" of the military community.

4400.   HEILMAN, JOHN. "The Constitutionality of Discharg-
        ing Homosexual Military Personnel," Columbia Human
        Rights Law Review, 12 (1980), 191-204.
After a review of some salient cases, concludes: "The
military's [negative] policy toward homosexuality has
led to extensive litigation. The policy is irrational
to some extent, unnecessary to some extent, and unwise
in toto.

4401.   HIRSCHHORN, JAMES M. "Due Process in Undesirable
        Discharge Proceedings," **University of Chicago Law
        Review,** 41 (1973), 164-89.
Holds that the present regulations governing undesirable
discharges are unsatisfactory inasmuch as they do not
afford service personnel intelligent standards of behavior
and the rights necessary to contest fully the basis for
the discharge action.

4402.   "Homosexuals in the Military," **Fordham Law Review,**
        37 (1969), 465-76.
Discusses some of the problems and inequities of the
military treatment of the homosexual, in the hope that a
reevaluation will lead to a more rational approach.

4403.   HOWARD, ROLAND (pseud.). "The Homosexual's Right
        to Serve," **Mattachine Review,** 8:12 (December 1962),
        4-13.
Argument by a patriotic homophile for access to military
service.

4404.   JONES, WILLIAM K., CLIFFORD DOUGHERTY, and NORMAN
        LYNCH. "The Administrative Discharge--Military
        Justice?" **George Washington University Law Review,**
        33 (1964), 498-528.
Documents the relatively harsh methods of military sep-
aration that became common towards the end of World War
II.

4405.   LERNER, HARRY V. "Effect of Character of Dis-
        charge and Length of Service on Eligibility to
        Veterans' Benefits," **Military Law Review,** 12
        (1961), 121-42.
Discusses loss of benefits to those discharged under
"conditions less than honorable," including Veterans
Administration regulations.

4406.   LODA, GIFFORD. "Homosexual Conduct in the Milit-
        ary: No Faggots in Military Woodpiles," **Arizona
        State Law Journal** (1983), 79-112.
Argues that decisions supporting blanket proscriptions

of homosexual behavior unfairly reject the key issue of
procedural due process. "[W]here the conduct in question
is private and consensual the only appropriate [proce-
dure] is the individualized fitness hearing."

4407. LUNDING, CHRISTOPHER J. "Judicial Review of
      Military Discharges," **Yale Law Journal,** 83 (1973),
      33-74.
General discussion of types of discharge, hearings, consequences, and remedial bases for judicial relief.

4408. LYNCH, NORMAN B. "The Administrative Discharge:
      Changes Needed?" **Maine Law Review,** 22 (1970),
      141-69.
Points out changes in the military administrative discharge process which either do or may cause injustice.
There is a need for adequate protections and due process
of law for service personnel subjected to dismissal
proceedings.

4409. SEIDENBERG, FAITH. "Military Justice is to Justice
      ..." **Criminal Law Bulletin,** 17 (1981), 45-59.
Personal account by a Syracuse NY attorney of a case involving an Air Force second lieutenant illustrating
the arbitrary workings of the military justice system.

4410. WEST, LOUIS, and ALBERT GLASS. "Sexual Behavior
      and Military Law," in: Ralph Slovenko (ed.), **Sexual
      Behavior and the Law.** Springfield, IL: Charles C.
      Thomas, 1965, pp. 250-72.
Asserts that the primary objective of the military should
be the prompt elimination of homosexuals, rather than
harsh management or punitive discharge.

4411. WILLIAMS, COLIN J., and MARTIN S. WEINBERG. "The
      Military: Its Processing of Accused Homosexuals,"
      American Behavioral Scientist, 14 (1970), 203-17.
Reviews the process whereby homosexuals are discharged
from the armed forces, demonstrating how constitutional
rights are infringed. See also their **Homosexuals and the
Military: A Study of Less than Honorable Discharge.** (New
York: Harper and Row, 1971; 221 pp.).

XXI. LAW ENFORCEMENT

A. POLICE

Police surveillance of homosexuals--attested apparently for the first time in 18th-century France (see III.G)--has served to fuel animosity between police and gay people, aggravated in some instances by bigoted attitudes on the part of officers who believed that they had a moral obligation to punish "deviates" because society was failing to penalize them. Particular problems have been the aggressive activities of vice squads, and, especially in North America, police harassment of bars, ostensibly to enforce liquor laws (see XIV.D). Under these circumstances corruption was rife. In recent decades this confrontational relationship has begun to change thanks to better educated, more tolerant officers, the gradual dismantling of legal sanctions, and the admission of openly gay and lesbian officers to the force.

4412. AANDEWIEL, JAN, THEO VAN SOERLAND, and PETER VAN
       WEERT. **Politie en Homoseksualiteit.** Utrecht:
       Homostudies, 1985. 99 pp.
Studies by three Dutch police officers of gay-police relations and of gays and lesbians who are police officers in the Netherlands.

4413. AVERILL, BRETT, and LENNY GITECK. "On the Beat
       with Gay Cops," **Advocate,** no. 317 (May 14, 1981),
       15-17.
Reports from New York City and San Francisco. See also Gitecks's earlier story: "Recruiting Gay Rookies," **Advocate,** no. 276 (September 20, 1979), 20-23; as well as Thom Willenbecher and Scott Anderson, "Police-Gay Relations," **Advocate,** no. 291 (May 1, 1980), 13-15.

4414. BASKETT, EDWARD EUGENE. **Entrapped: An Accused
       Homosexual Looks at American Justice.** Westport,
       CT: Lawrence Hill, 1976. 151 pp.
Personal record of an uphill struggle against discriminatory law enforcement in Long Beach, CA. See also Roy McCoy, **Entrapment** (Los Angeles: Argyle Books, 1965; 160 pp.).

4415. BERNSTEIN, HAL. "When a Cop Comes Out," **Mandate**
       (July 1981), 48-52.
On Steve Horn of Mesa, AZ, who was dismissed, appealing the case without success to the U.S. Supreme Court.

4416. BUSH, LARRY. "Has the FBI Been in Your Closet?" **Ad-
       vocate,** no. 346 (July 8, 1982), 16-20, 24.

The functioning at least since 1954 of a concerted nationwide surveillance and investigation program by the FBI
into the lives of wealthy, prominent closeted homosexuals,
as well as gay civil rights groups, was confirmed by
senior FBI officials and substantiated by FBI documents
acquired under the Freedom of Information Act.

4417. "Clandestine Police Surveillance of Public Toilet
       Booth Held to Be Unreasonable Search," **Columbia Law
       Review,** 63 (1963), 955-61.
Clandestine surveillance of an enclosed public john
booth--a common police practice during the period--was
ruled unreasonable search if there is not probable cause
to believe that a particular illegal act is being committed at the time. See also: Clare W. Kyler, "Camera
Surveillance of Sex Deviates," **Law and Order,** 11 (1963),
16-18, 20; and William F. McKee, "Camera Surveillance of
Sex Deviates: Evidentiary Problems," ibid., 12 (1964), 72-
74.

4418. ELLIOTT, RICHARD H. "Enforcement of Laws Directed
       at Homosexuals: A Typical Metropolitan Approach,"
       Drum, no. 26 (September 1967), 10-13, 26-28.
Documents a pattern of solicitation arrests by the Phil-
adelphia Police Morals Squad. For a detailed picture of
another city during this period, see John J. Gallo et al.,
"The Consenting Adult Homosexual and the Law: An Empirical
Study of Enforcement and Administration in Los Angeles
County," **UCLA Law Review,** 13 (1966), 643-832.

4419. FARRELL, RONALD A. "Class Linkages of Legal Treat-
       ment of Homosexuals," **Criminology,** 9 (May 1971),
       49-68.
Analysis of court case records of 108 homosexual offenders
shows that men from the lower class are disproportionately
involved in such offenses, receiving harsher penalties as
well.

4420. FIAUX, LOUIS. **La police des moeurs en France et
       dans les principaux pays de l'Europe.** Paris: E.
       Dentu, 1888. 1010 pp.
In this massive study of the operation of police vice
squads throughout Europe, see pp. 15, 26, 135-50, 919-23,
which discuss arrests of homosexuals (including false
arrests).

4421. FREIBERG, PETER. "Gays and Police: Old Problems,
       New Hope," **Advocate,** no. 422 (June 11, 1985),
       10-11, 19.
Surveys gay-police relations, esp. gay people as police,
in a number of cities.

4422. FREIBERG, PETER. "Policing Rest-Stop Sex,"
       Advocate, no. 449 (June 24, 1986), 10-11, 22-23.
On the the arrests of 41 Michigan men at their homes,
after allegedly engaging in rest-stop sex.

4423. GROEN, K. **Kamer 13: Hallo hier de zedenpolitie.**
       The Hague: Daamen, 1951. 223 pp.
Memoirs of the chief of the Amsterdam vice squad. See
also his: **Misdaad in de hoofdstad** (The Hague: Daamen,
1955; 192 pp.).

4424. GUYOT, YVES. **La prostitution.** Paris: Charpentier,
       1882. 577 pp.
See pp. 60, 68, 107-08, 110 and 113-14 for police surveillance of homosexuals. See also the English version: **Prostitution under the Regulation System, French and English**
(London: Redway, 1884; 348 pp.).

4425. HONGISTO, RICHARD. "Why Are There No Gay Choir
       Boys? Ask Your Friendly Chief of Police," **Perspec-
       tives,** 12 (1980), 39-42.
San Francisco official explores police-management homophobia. See also: Pam David, and Lois Helmbold, "San
Francisco: Courts and Cops vs. Gays," **Radical America,** 12
(1979), 27-32; and Randy Shilts, "Police Come to Terms
with the Gay Community," **Police Magazine,** 3 (January
1980), 218-31, 34-36.

4426. JACOBS, HAROLD. "Decoy Enforcement of Homosexual
       Laws," **University of Pennsylvania Law Review,** 112
       (1963), 259-84.
While the writer supports continuation of the practice,
he concedes that it poses legal problems.

4427. KEARFUL, JAMES F. "The New Nazism," **ONE Magazine,**
       11:5 (May 1963), 5-11.
Homophile writer's analysis of the links between street
crime, police repression, and the homosexual as scapegoat.

4428. KEPNER, JIM (ed.). **Quotations from Chief Ed.** Los
       Angeles: Gay Radio Collective, 1976. 31 pp.
Collection of anti-gay comments by Chief Ed Davis of Los
Angeles, together with Kepner's commentary on police
activity during the period. Since retiring from the
force Davis has entered the State Assembly, where he has
emerged as a friend of gay people.

4429. KIRKWOOD, JAMES, JR. **American Grotesque.** New
       York: Simon and Schuster, 1970. 669 pp.
Revealing exposure of New Orleans District Attorney's
self-serving gay-baiting in his futile attempt to prove
that Clay Shaw led a conspiracy to kill President Kennedy.

4430. MASSA, ROBERT. "One of New York's Finest," **Village
       Voice** (November 25, 1981), 15, 106.
On the coming out of Sgt. Charles Cochrane, who says: "I
love being a cop and I love being gay and I'm not ashamed
of either." Subsequently, Cochrane and some associates
formed the Gay Officers' Action League (GOAL).

4431. PROTHERO, BARRY. "Police," **Gay News** (London),

no. 204 (November-December 1980), 12-13.
Shows continuing harassment and oppression of gay people
by the British police.

4432. ROSEN, STEVEN A. "Police Harassment of Homosexual
       Women and Men in New York City, 1960-1980,"
       Columbia Human Rights Law Review, 12:2 (1980-81),
       159-90.
Useful retrospective study, particularly for the crackdown
in the 1960s under Mayor Robert Wagner, Jr.

4433. SHERMAN, LAWRENCE W. **Police Corruption.** Garden
       City, NY: Anchor Books, 1974. 346 pp.
In this overview of a perennial problem, see pp. 8,
179-80, 313-14.

4434. TRESCKOW, HANS VON. **Von Fürsten und anderen
       Sterblichen.** Berlin: Fontane, 1922. 240 pp.
Recollections of a Berlin police official concerning the
Krupp and Eulenburg scandals, and the situation of the
homosexual subculture in the Wilhelmine capital.

4435. WILSON, GEORGE P., et al. "State Intervention and
       Victimless Crimes: A Study of Police Attitudes,"
       Journal of Police Science and Administration, 13
       (1985), 22-29.
Questionnaires completed by 88 officers show that the
majority did not consider vice a serious problem, saw no
public mandate to increase current surveillance procedures, and tended to believe that it is futile to
attempt to control victimless crimes.

                      B. PRISONS: MALE

Sodomy laws, primarily directed against male homosexuals,
have caused the incarceration of homosexuals as such. Yet
by far the greatest number of homosexual acts in prison
are committed by those who have led predominately heterosexual lives "outside" and who generally revert to this
behavior pattern on release. The male prison subculture
has preserved a premodern form in which the role of the
active partner (who usually continues to think of himself
as "straight") is sharply distinguished from that of the
passive one, who bears the full stigma attached to the
effeminate homosexual.

4436. ABBOTT, JACK HENRY. **In the Belly of the Beast.**
       New York: Random House, 1981. 166 pp.
Reflections of a "Marxist-Leninist" convict who, in a
well-publicized case, having obtained his release in part
through the intervention of his admirer Norman Mailer,
then committed murder in New York.

4437. ADLEMAN, ROBERT H. **Alias Big Cherry: The Confessions of a Master Criminal.** New York: Dial Press, 1973. 334 pp.
Reminiscences of Sylvan Scolnick, with some indications of prison sex.

4438. AKERS, RONALD L., et al. "Homosexual and Drug Behavior in Prison: A Test of the Functional and Importation Models of the Inmate System," **Social Problems,** 21 (1974), 410-22.
Finds that the amount of drug and homosexual behavior among inmates was more a function of the type of prison than of the social characteristics which they brought with them from the outside.

4439. AMRAIN, KARL. "Beiträge zur Erforschung des Trieblebens," **Anthropophyteia,** 5 (1908), 361-69.
On homosexuality in German prisons. See also his: "Gefangnispoesie," ibid., 9 (1912), 329-32; and Johannes Jaeger, "Hinter Kerkermauern: Autobiographien, Selbstbekentnisse, etc. von Verbrechern," **Archiv für Kriminalanthropologie und Kriminalistik,** 19 (1904), 1-48.

4440. APPERT, BENJAMIN NICOLAS MARIE. **Bagnes, prisons et criminels.** Paris: Guibert, 1836. 4 vols.
Pioneering comprehensive study of conditions in French prisons.

4441. BARTOLLAS, CLEMENS, et al. "The 'Booty Bandit': A Social Role in a Juvenile Institution," **JH,** 1 (1974-75), 203-212.
The booty bandit is a sexual exploiter of weaker males in juvenile correctional institutions. An inmate pecking order defines who becomes exploited. See also their: **Juvenile Victimization: The Institutional Paradox** (New York: Wiley, 1976; 324 pp.).

4442. BARTOLLAS, CLEMENS, and CHRISTOPHER M. SIEVERDES. "The Sexual Victim in a Coeducational Juvenile Correctional Institution," **Prison Journal** (Philadelphia), 58 (1983), 80-90.
In training schools in a southeastern state, sexual victims are usually 14 or 15 years old; they include both males and females, as well as equal proportions of blacks and whites. Sexual exploiters are frequently older black youths.

4443. BARWASSER, KARLHEINZ A. **Schwulenhetz im Knast: eine Dokumentation.** Bielefeld: Pusteblume, 1982. 162 pp.
Problems of gays in West German prisons, by an inmate.

4444. BELLONI, GIULIO. **Eros incatenato.** Milan: Bocca, 1939. 103 pp.
Freudian-influenced study recommending an end to (heterosexual) sexual repression in prison, which is held to

cause homosexual behavior.

4445. BERKMAN, ALEXANDER. **Prison Memoirs of an Anar-
       chist.** New York: Mother Earth, 1912. 512 pp.
Although he was not a participant, Berkman (1870-1936)
perceived prison sex sympathetically (pp. xix, 167-73,
318-24, 348, 433-34, 437-40).

4446. BILLANY, DAN, and DAVID DOWIE. **The Cage.** London:
       Longmans Green, 1949. 190 pp.
Reminiscences of life in Italian prison camps in World
War II.

4447. BLAKE, JAMES. **The Joint.** Garden City, NY: Double-
       day, 1971. 382 pp.
Autobiographical account, considered by some to have literary merit, of prison life (including homosexuality).

4448. BLOCH, HERBERT A. "Social Pressures of Confinement
       toward Sexual Deviation," **Journal of Social
       Therapy,** 1:3 (1955), 112-25.
Contends that personality variables, situational occur-
rences, motivation, and involvement with the inmate peer
culture are the primary factors.

4449. BOCHMANN, HEINRICH VON. "Zum Problem der Homosex-
       ualitat," **Blätter für Gefängniskunde,** 75 (1944),
       34-72.
Nazi-era study dealing with prisoners serving sentences
under articles 175 and 175a (homosexual offenses) of the
Penal Code of the German Reich.

4450. BOLINO, GIUSEPPE, and ALFONSO DE DEO. **Il sesso
       nelle carceri italiane: inchieste e documenti.**
       Milan: Feltrinelli, 1970. 114 pp.
Well-documented sociological study on sex in Italian
prisons; includes personal testimonies.

4451. BOYD, ROBERT N. **Sex behind Bars: A Novella, Short
       Stories, and True Accounts.** San Francisco: Gay
       Sunshine Press, 1984. 237 pp.
The non-fiction parts, evidently based largely on exper-
iences in Western prisons, are eight sections, pp. 9-85.
Note esp. "Prison Slang," pp. 18-27.

4452. BUFFUM, PETER C. **Homosexuality in Prisons.** Wash-
       ington, DC: U. S. Department of Justice, Law En-
       forcement Assistance Administration, 1972. 48 pp.
Overview of current administrative problems, including
racial tensions.

4453. CARDOZO-FREEMAN, INEZ. **The Joint: Language and
       Culture in a Maximum Security Prison.** Springfield,
       IL: Charles Thomas, 1984. 579 pp.
Anthropologist's report of field work as Washington State
Penitentiary at Walla Walla, reporting inmates' views on

interaction, subsistence, sexuality, and territoriality.
Glossary of 800 words and expressions. See also: Ethan
Hoffman, **Concrete Mama: Prison Profiles from Walla Walla**
(Columbia, MO: University of Missouri Press, 1981; 240
pp.)--150 photographs.

4454. CARROLL, LEO. "Humanitarian Reform and Biracial
       Sexual Assault in a Maximum Security Prison," **Urban
       Life**, 5 (1977), 417-37.
Concludes that "the prison ... is an arena within which
the rage of black males at their social and psychological oppression is vented against while males, thereby
reversing the traditional scale of sexual dominance. ...
Humanitarian reforms of the prison social structure facilitate this pattern of assault."

4455. CLEMMER, DONALD. **The Prison Community**. New
       York: Holt, Rinehart and Winston, 1940. 341 pp.
Estimates that 30% of 2,300 adult male prisoners were
involved in some type of sexual deviation and another 10%
were true homosexuals. See also his: "Some Aspects of
Sexual Behavior in the Prison Community," **Proceedings
of the American Correctional Association**, 88 (1958),
377-85.

4456. COTTON, DONALD J., and A. NICHOLAS GROTH. "Sexual
       Assault in Correctional Institutions: Prevention
       and Intervention," in: Irving R. Stuart and Joanna
       G. Greer (eds.), **Victims of Sexual Aggression**. New
       York: Van Nostrand Reinhold, 1984, pp. 127-55.
The seriousness of the problem of male rape in correctional facilities is often neglected, owing to the nature of
prison conditions, inmate codes, and staff attitudes.
Civil litigation regarding institutional liability is
increasing. The paper presents a model for identifying,
treating, and preventing the sexual abuse of inmates.

4457. CROFT-COOKE, RUPERT. **The Verdict of You All**.
       London: Secker and Warburg, 1955. 254 pp.
The author, a well-known British literary figure, tells
of his arrest, trial, and conviction for homosexual
offenses (1953) and of his prison experiences.

4458. DALLA VOLTA, AMEDEO. **Studi di psicologia e
       psichiatria sulle prigioni di guerra**. Florence:
       Ricci, 1919. 55 pp.
Discusses homosexual behavior in prisoner-of-war camps
during World War I, using letters and poetry as evidence.

4459. DAVIS, ALAN J. "Sexual Assaults in the Philadel-
       phia Prison System and Sheriff's Vans," **Trans-
       action**, 6:2 (December 1968), 8-16.
Virtually every slightly-built young man is sexually
approached within hours of his admission to prison.
Blacks tend to victimize blacks, with the aggressors not
regarding themselves as homosexual.

4460. DEVEREUX, GEORGE, and MALCOLM MOOS. "The Social
       Structure of Prisons, and the Organic Tensions,"
       Journal of Criminal Psychopathology, 4 (1942),
       306-24.
From observations of the Alabama penal system, concludes
that the structure of the prison environment itself fos-
ters homosexual behavior.

4461. DRTIL, J. "Sexuální život mužu při dlouhodobé
       vykonavaném trestu odněti svobody," Československá
       Psychiatrie, 65 (1969), 245-50.
Self-inflicted wounds of long-term homosexual prisoners
reflect their anguish at being separated from their
partners.

4462. DUFFY, CLINTON T., and AL HIRSCHBERG. Sex and
       Crime. New York: Doubleday, 1965. 203 pp.
Observations of Duffy, noted warden of San Quentin Prison
in California. See Chapter 4, "The Homosexuals" (pp. 28-
39).

4463. ELIA, BIANCA. Emarginazione e omosessualità negli
       istituti di rieducazione. Milan: Mazzotta, 1974.
       112 pp.
Criticizes correctional institutions as places that foster
deviance, alienation, and violence, wherein homosexuality appears in a dehumanized form.

4464. ENGEL, KATHLEEN, and STANLEY ROTHMAN. On the Rule
       of Violence in Prisons. New York: The Public
       Interest, 1983.
Contends that, as the authority of the officials and
guards weakens, prisons are increasingly being ruled by
bullying inmates, and rape is becoming more common.

4465. FALCHI, PERSIO. Un anno di prigionia in Austria.
       Florence: Libreria della Voce, 1918. 221 pp.
Memoirs of an Italian prisoner of war in Austria during
World War I; for "love behind barbed wire," see pp. 20,
25-27 and esp. 83-90.

4466. FISHMAN, JOSEPH F. Sex in Prison: Revealing Sex
       Conditions in American Prisons. New York: National
       Library Press, 1934. 256 pp.
In its day, a shocking expose, based largely on Pennsylvania jails, with proposals for reform.

4467. GAGNON, JOHN H., and WILLIAM SIMON. "The Social
       Meaning of Prison Homosexuality," Federal Proba-
       tion, 32 (1968), 23-29.
Homosexuality flourishes in prison because it serves as
a way of satisfying needs not met by the institution.
For men, it fulfils affectional needs, validates masculinity, and helps in coping with prison life; for women, it
tends to be integrated into the system of pseudo-families.

4468. GEBHARD, PAUL H., et al. **Sex Offenders: An Analysis of Types.** New York: Harper and Row, 1965.
923 pp.
This comparative study of 14 types of convicted sex
offender includes three homosexual types: offenders
against children aged 12 or under, against minors, and
against adults. Contends that homosexual offenders had
a poor relationship with their parents and had more sex.

4469. GIZA, JERZY S. "Homoseksualizm w środowisku
wieśniów młodocianych," **Przegląd penitencjarny,**
20:4 (1968), 45-60.
Polish criminologist's study of homosexuality in the
environment of young prisoners.

4470. GRECO, MARSHALL C., and JAMES C. WRIGHT. "The
Correctional Institution in the Etiology of Chronic
Homosexuality," **American Journal of Orthopsychiatry,** 14 (1944), 295-307.
Some inmates succumbed to homosexual practices under the
same set of influences--erotic talk, solicitation by
older inmates, and witnessing acts--that left others
unaffected.

4471. HAINES, WILLIAM H. "Homosexuality," **Journal of
Social Therapy,** 1 (1955), 132-36.
Distinguishes three types found in prison: the frank
homosexual (inluding the "wolf" and effeminate inmates);
the feeble-minded, mentally ill or insane inmates, of
whom others take advantage; and the occasional or situational homosexual.

4472. HAYES, BILLY and WILLIAM HOFFER. **Midnight Express.**
New York: Dutton, 1977. 280 pp.
Harrowing story of young American's drug bust and experiences in a Turkish prison; freely translated into a movie
featuring Brad Davis, with the homoerotic element suppressed.

4473. HEALY, WILLIAM. **The Individual Delinquent: A
Text-Book of Diagnosis and Prognosis for All
Concerned in Understanding Offenders.** Boston:
Little, Brown, 1915. 830 pp.
Contends that life in penal institutions is notorious
for inciting to unnatural sexual practices even those
not otherwise inclined to them. Provides a few homosexual case histories (pp. 197-98, 313, 411-12, 584-87,
734-35, 779).

4474. HENRY, GEORGE W., and ALFRED A. GROSS. "The
Homosexual Delinquent," **Mental Hygiene,** 25 (1941),
420-42.
The delinquent homosexual (as opposed to the middle-
class homosexual) is handicapped by a "poor biological
start," inferior housing, limited education, and little
vocational training.

4475. HERNETT, MICHAEL. "Das Geschlechtsleben im Ker-
      ker," **Zeitschrift für Sexualwissenschaft,** 15
      (1928), 305-13.
On sexual activity in Soviet prisons.

4476. HOENE, ROBERT E. **Annotated Bibliography on De-
      linquent Girls and Related Research (1915-1970s).**
      Washington: American Psychological Association,
      1978. 165 pp. (MS 1686)
Emphasizes empirical studies.

4477. HUFFMAN, ARTHUR V. "Problems Precipitated by
      Homosexual Approaches of Youthful First Offend-
      ers," **Journal of Social Therapy,** 7 (1961), 216-22.
Suggests that the existing environment of correctional
institutions favors the development of sexual deviation.
See also his: "Sex Deviation in a Prison Community,"
Journal of Social Therapy, 6:3 (1960), 170-81.

4478. IBRAHIM, AZMY I. "Deviant Behavior in Men's
      Prisons," **Crime and Delinquency,** 20 (1974), 38-44.
Proposes ways of reducing homosexual activity, such as
conjugal visits.

4479. IVES, CHARLES CECIL. **A History of Penal Methods:
      Criminals, Witnesses, Lunatics.** London: S. Paul,
      1914. 409 pp.
The writer, a closeted English scholar, was an advocate of
prison reform; see pp. 292-301.

4480. JACKSON, BRUCE. **In the Life: Versions of the
      Criminal Experience.** New York: Holt, Rinehart and
      Winston, 1972. 412 pp.
"Queens, Punks, and Studs" (pp. 351-412) covers the whole
gamut of homosexual relationships inside men's prisons.
Inmates who would like to be homosexual on the outside,
but are unable to learn "the role" are enabled to do so
by the prison culture, which--when internalized--actually
makes them unfit for life in civil society.

4481. JOHNSON, EDWIN. "The Homosexual in Prison," **Social
      Theory and Practice,** 1:4 (1971), 83-95.
Presents insiders' interpretations of prison homosexuality
as contributing to the maintenance of institutional stability.

4482. KARPMAN, BENJAMIN. "Sex Life in Prison," **Journal
      of Criminal Law and Criminology,** 38 (1948), 475-86.
In their isolation prisoners turn to masturbation and
homosexuality. These practices have long-term effects,
lasting past the prison term.

4483. KERN, WILLIAM, JR. "Petition to the President of
      the U. S.," **ONE Magazine,** 14:4 (April-May 1966),
      7-10.
Appeal from a prisoner then in the Michigan State Peni-

tentiary at Jackson.

4484. LAITE, WILLIAM E., JR. **The United States vs. William Laite.** Washington, DC: Acropolis Books, 1972. 250 pp.
The experiences and observations of a "white collar" offender in a prison in Fort Worth, TX, including witnessing the gang rape of a white adolescent prisoner (pp. 10, 42-45, 110, 123, 126, 181).

4485. LAMOTT, KENNETH. **Chronicles of San Quentin: The Biography of a Prison.** New York: McKay, 1961. 278 pp.
Includes data going back to the 1850s (pp. 12, 144, 200, 249, 268).

4486. LEE, DONALD. "Seduction of the Guilty: Homosexuality in American Prisons," in: Ralph Ginzburg and Warren Boroson (eds.), **The Best of Fact.** New York: Trident Press, 1967, pp. 81-90.
Experiences of the author as an inmate in Western State Penitentiary in Pennsylvania, where young men predominate among the prisoners; having no female partners, they turn to one another.

4487. LEINWAND, GERALD (ed.). **Prisons.** New York: Pocket Books, 1972. 256 pp.
The true homosexuals have an esoteric, isolated community of their own. One prison hospital was controlled by homosexuals, who forced others to submit sexually for medication. See pp. 32, 35, 58, 81, 82, 116, 161, 175, 176, 189, 196, 199, 217.

4488. LEMOS BRITTO, JOSÉ GABRIEL DE. **A questão nas prisões.** Rio de Janeiro: J. Ribeiro dos Santos, 1934. 202 pp.
Sexual problems in Brazilian prisons, with international comparisons. See pp. 113-26.

4489. LEÓN SÁNCHEZ, JOSÉ. **God Was Looking the Other Way.** Boston: Little, Brown, 1973. 271 pp.
Personal account of the Penitentiary of San Lucas in Costa Rica in the early years of the century (translation of **La isla de los hombres solos**). Unsympathetic presentation (pp. 51-54, 211-16).

4490. LEVY, HOWARD, and DAVID MILLER. "Homosexuality," in: **Going to Jail: The Political Prisoner.** New York: Grove Press, 1972, pp. 137-63.
Problems faced by radicals of the Vietnam-protest era.

4491. LINDNER, ROBERT. "Sex in Prison," **Complex,** 6 (1951), 5-20.
Psychoanalytic approach, contending that "latent tendencies" are exposed by the institutional setting--even though most sexual deviants in prison are not homosex-

ual.

4492. LIPTON, HARRY R. "Stress in Correctional Institu-
       tions," **Journal of Social Therapy,** 6 (1960),
       216-23.
Contends that homosexuality is a frequent source for
acute anxiety states--either among those who are undergoing an internal struggle or those who fear loss of a
partner.

4493. LOCKWOOD, DANIEL. **Prison Sexual Violence.** New
       York: Elsevier, 1980. 167 pp.
A study of 45 inmate "aggressors" and 107 "targets" in New
York State male prisons. Sexual aggression is most intense in youth institutions: 46% of prison aggressors
were 19 or younger. The young black male subculture of
violence underlies sexual aggression in prison.

4494. MACARTNEY, WILFRED. **Walls Have Mouths: A Record of
       Ten Years Penal Servitude.** London: Gollancz,
       1936. 440 pp.
Account of his incarceration in Parkhurst Prison; with
comments by Compton Mackenzie.

4495. MCMURTRIE, DOUGLAS C. "Notes on Pederastic Prac-
       tices in Prison," **Chicago Medical Recorder,** 36
       (1914), 15-17.
McMurtrie, a physician in contact with contemporary work
in Germany, was probably the first American researcher
to give sustained attention to prison homosexuality.

4496. MARTIN, JOHN BARTLOW. **Break Down the Walls.** New
       York: Ballantine Books, 1953. 310 pp.
Contends that homosexuality is the most difficult problem
a warden faces, since it causes more quarrels, fights, and
punishment in prison than any other single problem.

4497. MARTINEZ, JOSÉ AGUSTÍN. **Eros encatenado (el
       problema sexual en las prisiones).** Havana: J. Mon-
       tero, 1938. 15 pp.
Criticizes Cuban prison authorities for laxity regarding
homosexual behavior. Needed are hard work, better super-
vison, and "sublimation."

4498. MICKLEY, RICHARD R. **Prison Ministry Handbook.**
       Third ed. Los Angeles: United Fellowship of
       Metropolitan Community Churches, 1980.
Reflects the success of the MCC, esp. in California, in
ministering to prison populations.

4499. MONEY, JOHN, and CAROL BOHMER. "Prison Sexology:
       Two Personal Accounts of Masturbation, Homosexual-
       ity, and Rape," **Journal of Sex Research,** 16 (198),
       258-66.
Presents a typology of prison homosexuality. Recommends
conjugal visits.

4500. MORTON, D. R. "Strategies in Probation: Treating
       Gay Offenders," **Social Casework,** 64 (1983), 33-38.
The improvement in services to gay probationers depends on
the willingness of the probation departments to gather
knowledge on available community resources and to sensi-
tize the probation officers to the needs of their gay
clients.

4501. MOSS, C. SCOTT. "Sexual Assault in a Prison,"
       Psychological Reports, 44 (1979), 823-28.
Suggest that high rates posited for sexual assault in
federal prisons may be exaggerated.

4502. NACCI, PETER L., and THOMAS R. KANE. "The Incid-
       ence of Sex and Sexual Aggression in Federal
       Prisons," **Federal Probation,** 47:4 (December 1983),
       31-36.
Analyzing results of interviews with 330 male inmates,
contends that federal prisons are "relatively free of
problems associated with homosexuality and sexual aggression." This article was followed by their: "Sex and
Sexual Aggression in Federal Prisons," **Federal Probation,**
48:1 (March 1984), 46-53. See also Nacci and Kane, "Inmate Sexual Aggression: Some Evolving Propositions, Empirical Findings, and Mitigating Counter-Forces," **Journal
of Offender Counseling, Services and Rehabilitation,** 9
(1984), 1-20.

4503. NEESE, ROBERT. **Prison Exposures.** Philadelphia:
       Chilton, 1959. 135 pp.
Experiences as an inmate in the Iowa State Prison at Fort
Madison.

4504. NEIER, ARYEH. "Sex and Confinement," **Civil Liber-
       ties Review,** 5:2 (1978), 6-16.
An overview of current knowledge and concerns, including
the special plight of youth and racial aspects.

4505. NELSON, VICTOR F. **Prison Days and Nights.** Boston:
       Little, Brown, 1933. 282 pp.
"Men without Women" (pp. 140-69) attempts to distinguish
between "pseudo-homosexuality" induced by deprivation and
the constitutional homosexuality of the prison "fairies
and gonsils."

4506. NEUMAN, ELIAS. **El problema sexual en las cárcel-
       es.** Buenos Aires: Editorial Criminalia, 1955. 204
       pp.
Offers an Argentine and international perspective.

4507. NORMAN, FRANK. **Bang to Rights.** London: Pan Books,
       1958. 158 pp.
Account of two years in a British prison.

4508. OSBORNE, THOMAS MOTT. **Prisons and Common Sense.**

Philadelphia: J. Lippincott, 1924. 105 pp.
Compares the "problem' of homosexuality in prisons with
that encountered on naval ships at sea (pp. 88-93).

4509. PANTON, JAMES H. "Characteristics Associated with
      Male Homosexuality within a State Correctional
      Population," **Corrections** (Memphis), 2 (1978),
      26-31.
Forty "active homosexual" inmates in North Carolina were
found to exhibit greater difficulties in handling stress,
frustration, and impulse control; they were more alienated
from both staff and other inmates.

4510. PARKER, JACK B., and ROBERT A. PERKINS. "The
      Influence of Type of Institution on Attitudes
      toward the Handling of the Homosexual among
      Inmates," **Offender Rehabilitation**, 2 (1978),
      245-54.
Tn four different types of correctional facility, attitudes of inmates appear to be independent of those of
staff and to be more liberal in the adult institutions.

4511. PERRIER, CHARLES. **Les criminels.** Paris: Masson/
      Maloine, 1900-05. 2 vols.
In this comprehensive study by a French physician, see
vol. 1, pp.. 184-212, 343-45; vol. 2, pp. 195-243.

4512. PLATTNER, KARL. **Eros im Zuchthaus.** Berlin: Mopr-
      Verlag, 1929. 225 pp.
Personal account of eight years' imprisonment. See
esp. pp. 139-48.

4513. PRICE, JOHN. "Homosexuality in a Victorian Male
      Prison," **Mental Health in Australia** (July 1984),
      3-12.
Information collected by participant observation in
Northern Sub-prison, Pentridge, Australia. Distinguishes
three types of prisoners involved in homosexual activity: cats (young ingenues); hocks (jockers); and queens.

4514. RICHMOND, KATY. "Fear of Homsexuality and Modes of
      Rationalisation in Male Prisons," **Australian and
      New Zealand Journal of Sociology**, 14 (1978), 51-57.
In Australia, emotional involvement is the homosexual norm
in female prisons, but the absence of emotion is the
dominant ideology for homosexual encounters among male
prisoners. This taboo tends to make sex-roles more rigid
and to hinder reintegration into society after release.

4515. ROTH, LOREN H. "Territoriality and Homosexuality
      in a Male Prison Population," **American Journal of
      Orthopsychiatry**, 41 (1971), 510-13.
Found that in a large prison population sexual aggressors
were kept in relative isolation, but with access to
"punks."

4516. ROTHENBERG, DAVID. "Prisoners," in Harvey L. Goch-
      ros and Jean S. Gochros (eds.), **The Sexually**
      Oppppressed. New York: Association Press, 1977,
      pp. 225-36.
Views of the director of New York's Fortune Society, a
rehabilitation and reentry group. See also his: "Group
Rip-off: The Prison Rape," **Advocate,** no. 189 (May 5,
1976), 9-11.

4517. SAGARIN, EDWARD. "Prison Homosexuality and Its
      Effects on Post-Prison Sexual Behavior," **Psychi-**
      atry, 39 (1976), 245-57.
Interviews with nine ex-inmates show that some were able
to switch to a homosexual behavior pattern in prison,
while returning to heterosexuality on release. In a few
instances, however, the change to homosexuality persisted
after release.

4518. SALIERNO, GIULIO. **La ripressione sessuale nelle**
      carceri italiane. Rome: Tattilo, 1973. 280 pp.
Homosexuality often appears in prison as a desire for the
humiliation of other inmates.

4519. SCACCO, ANTHONY M., JR. **Rape in Prison.** Spring-
      field, IL: Charles C. Thomas, 1975. 127 pp.
Based on studies in Connecticut state prisons. Emphasizes
the racial aspect ("the scapegoat is almost always
white"), as well as the place of violence in American
life generally.

4520. SCACCO, ANTHONY M., JR. (ed.). **Male Rape: A**
      Casebook of Sexual Aggression. New York: AMS
      Press, 1982. 326 pp.
Collection of 27 papers on sexual victimization, most
reprinted; some commissioned for the volume. Most reflect conditions in total institutions.

4521. SEATON, GEORGE JOHN. **Isle of the Damned: Twenty**
      Years in the Penal Colony of French Guinea [sic].
      New York: Farrar, Straus and Young, 1951. 302 pp.
Autobiography of an Englishman sentenced to the penal
colony in French Guiana. A few references to the **momes**
(catamites) of the inmates (pp. 25-26, 194-95, 267, 301).

4522. SHORE, DAVID A. **Sex-related Issues in Correctional**
      Facilities: A Classified Bibliography. Chicago:
      Playboy Foundation, 1981. 37 pp.
Carefully compiled (but unannotated) list of 203 entries,
mainly reflecting American conditions. The books and
articles cited cover social work, social science, and
correctional points of view, but do not include personal
testimonies of the offenders themselves.

4523. SHORE, DAVID A. "Sexual Abuse and Sexual Education
      in Child-Caring Institutions," **Journal of Social**
      Work and Human Sexuality, 1 (1982), 171-84.

Suggests programs and procedures for reducing sexual
neglect and abuse and enhancing the sexual self-worth of
the inmates. See also: Shore and Harvey L. Gochros,
Sexual Problems of Adolescents in Institutions (Springfield, IL: Charles C. Thomas, 1981; 240 pp.).

4524. SHORT, JAMES F., JR., and IVAN NYE. "Extent of
       Unrecorded Juvenile Delinquency," **Journal of
       Criminal Law, Criminology and Police Science,** 49
       (1958), 296-302.
In a comparison with the general population, the inmate
boys had had homosexual relations about as frequently as
those in regular high schools, while the institutionalized
girls had had them far more frequently.

4525. SLAVSON, SAMUEL R. **Reclaiming the Delinquent:
       Para-Analytic Group Psychotherapy and the Inversion
       Technique.** New York: Free Press, 1965. 766 pp.
"Sex and Homosexuality" (pp. 45-60) contends that the
sexual conflicts of delinquent boys stem from "Oedipal
guilt."

4526. SMITH, CHARLES E. "The Homosexual Offender: A
       Study of 100 Cases," **Journal of Criminal Law,
       Criminology and Police Science,** 44 (1954), 582-92.
Finds that certain types of crimes--car theft, mail
theft, robbery, and forgery--were more common among
homosexual inmates than among the general prison population. See also his: "Some Problems in Dealing with
Homosexuals in the Prison Situation," **Journal of Social
Therapy,** 2 (1956), 37-45.

4527. SOLAN, NELLIE, et al. "Sex," in: Robert J. Minton,
       Jr. (ed.), **Inside Prison American Style.** New
       York: Random House, 1971, pp. 113-22.
Asserts that the present penal system fails to "rehabilitate" those who have decided on a homosexual life.

4528. SRIVASTAVA, S. P. "Social Profile of Homosex-
       uals in an Indian Male Prison," **Eastern Anthropol-
       ogist,** 26 (1973) 313-22.
From a study of 400 inmates in an Uttar Pradesh prison,
concludes that the incidence of homosexuality in Indian
facilities is far lower than the one prevalent in Western
prisons. However, upper-caste inmates dominate the under-
dogs in the prison and exploit them for their sexual gratification. Appears in a longer form as: "Sex Life in an
Indian Male Prison," **Indian Journal of Social Work,** 35
(1974), 21-33. See also: Amal K. Maitra and Dipali
Banerjea, "Homosexual Practices in Institutionalised
Neglected Adolescents: Intra-Family Dynamics and Thematic
Fantasy," **Bulletin of the Council of Social and Psychological Research, Calcutta,** no. 8 (1967), 13-19.

4529. STONE, W. G., and I. HIRLIMAN. **The Hate Factor:
       The Story of the New Mexico Prison Riot.** New

York: Dell, 1982. 272 pp.
Acount of an extremely violent 1980 takeover, in which
homosexuals were among the victims.

4530. SYKES, GRESHAM M. **The Society of Captives: A Study
       of a Maximum Security Prison.** Princeton: Princeton
       University Press, 1958. 144 pp.
Describes the contrasting roles of "wolves," "punks," and
"fags" in a prison in Trenton, NJ, the last two being
regarded as having forfeited their masculinity.

4531. SYLVESTER, S. F., et al. **Prison Homicide.** New
       York: Spectrum Publications, 1977. 126 pp.
Claims that homosexual involvement and interests are the
leading motive for prison homicides.

4532. THOMAS, PIRI. **Seven Long Times.** New York: Prae-
       ger, 1974. 246 pp.
"Nothing Like the Real Thing" (pp. 136-49) presents an
ex-inmate's analysis of the fantasies of the prisoners,
with prison homosexual behavior as an (unsatisfactory)
substitute for heterosexual gratification.

4533. TOCH, HANS. **Living in Prison: The Ecology of
       Survival.** New York: Free Press, 1977. 318 pp.
Contends that rape, while relatively uncommon in most
prisons, is always figuratively present as the ultimate
threat. See pp. 143-44, 147-53, 158-74, 207, 212-17.

4534. VEDDER, CLYDE B., and PATRICIA G. KING. **Problems
       of Homosexuality in Corrections.** Springfield, IL:
       Charles C. Thomas, 1967. 63 pp.
Favors conjugal visits as a way of reducing the incidence
of frustration and homosexual behavior, while recognizing
that a majority of prison administrators oppose this
innovation.

4535. WARD, JACK B. "Homosexual Behavior of the Institu-
       tionalized Delinquent," **Psychiatric Quarterly
       Supplement,** 32 (1958), 301-14.
Contends that much of the homosexual behavior of institutionalized delinquents represents the suymbolic acting out
of problems of dependency and power.

4536. WEISS, CARL, and DAVID JAMES FRIAR. **Terror in the
       Prisons: Homsexual Rape and Why Society Condones
       It.** Indianapolis: Bobbs Merrill, 1974. 247 pp.
Popular, somewhat sensationalized approach.

4537. WILSON, JOSEPH G., and MICHAEL J. PESCOR. **Problems
       in Prison Psychiatry.** Caldwell, ID: Caxton Print-
       ers, 1939. 275 pp.
"The Homosexual Prisoner" (pp. 195-210) is a horrifying
period document. "...[H]e who would excuse homosexuality
is an enemy of the human race." Homosexual prisoners
ought to receive "a reasonable dose of violence   at the

hands of the other prisoners." In the design of the
prison all opportunity for privacy should be eliminated.

4538. WOODEN, KENNETH. **Weeping in the Playtime of
        Others: America's Incarcerated Children.** New
        York: McGraw-Hill, 1976. 264 pp.
On the sexual exploitation of runaway boys by pimps and
chicken queens; also on sexual abuse and rape in correctional institutions. See pp. 12, 50, 79-91, 110-11, 118-
28, 207, 236.

4538A. WOODEN, WAYNE, and JAY PARKER. **Men behind Bars:
        Sexual Exploitation in Prison.** New York: Plenum
        Press, 1982. 264 pp.
Serious ethnographic study of a medium security prison in
California, one of the authors (Parker) having gathered
some of the information while on the "inside." Presents
a more complex model of ethnic and class interaction in
relation to sexual behavior than the bipolar black-white
model that is usually adopted.

                    C. PRISONS: FEMALE

The homosexual subcultures that prevail in women's prisons
differ markedly from those found in men's institutions.
They are less violent, show a less sharp distinction between dominant and dominated individuals, and are positively characterized by the formation of ad hoc kinship
groups ("families").

4539. BLUESTONE, HARVEY, et al. "Homosexuals in Prison,"
        **Corrective Psychiatry and Journal of Social Ther-
        apy,** 12 (1966), 13-24.
Based on interviews in psychiatric clinics of the Women's
House of Detention in New York City, where an estimated
80% to 90% of the inmates have a history of lesbianism.
Asserts that the sado-masochistic nature of many lesbian
relationships is a threat to the security of the prison.

4540. BOUCARD, ROBERT. **Le dessous des prisons des
        femmes: "des documents, des faits": comment ils
        vivent, expient, se pervertissent.** Paris: Editions
        Documentaires, 1930. 255 pp.
Popular expose of conditions in French women's prisons.

4541. BRUUN, KETTIL. "Koulokotijaerjestelmaemme Ja
        Sukupuolisesti Hairahtuneet Tytot," **Sosiologia**
        (Finland), 1 (1965) 3-14.
On youth correction institutions and sexually deviant
girls in Finland.

4542. BURKHART, KATHRYN WATTERSON. **Women in Prison.**

PRISONS: FEMALE 699

Garden City, NY: Doubleday, 1973. 465 pp.
A woman going to prison effectively loses her family on
the outside, hence the pseudo-families on the inside.
Problems have been exaggerated by the focus of many
matrons and staff on real or imagined lesbianism. In an
Iowa prison, women thought to be lesbian must wear a
yellow uniform. See pp. 361-93.

4543. BURNHAM, CREIGHTON BROWN. **Born Innocent.** Engle-
wood Cliffs, NJ: Prentice-Hall, 1958. 293 pp.
Study of delinquent girls in the Oklahoma State Industrial
School for White Girls, Tecumseh.

4544. CARTER, BARBARA. "Reform School Families," **Society,**
11:1 (1973), 36, 39-43.
The informal subculture of reform school girls is one of
make-believe families, homosexual courtship, and adolescent peer-group culture.

4545. CHOISY, MARISE. **A Month among the Girls.** New
York: Pyramid, 1960.
Journalistic expose of life in French women's prisons.
Translation of: **L'amour dans les prisons** (Paris: Mon-
taigne, 1930). See also: Francis Carco, **Prisons de
femmes** (Paris: Editions de France, 1931; 296 pp.).

4546. CLIMENT, CARLOS E., et al. "Epidemiological
Studies of Female Prisoners: IV. Homosexual
Behavior," **Journal of Nervous and Mental Disease,**
164 (1977), 25-29.
Suicidal thoughts, suicide attempts, psychiatric problems
during menstruation, and a history of violent crimes
against persons were found to characterize the lesbian
offender group, while a history of crimes against self
and property, as well as a history of alcoholism, was
common in the nonhomosexual group.

4547. FITZGERALD, WILLIAM A. **Pseudohomosexuality in
Prison and Out: A Study of the Lower Class Black
Lesbian.** New York: City University, 1977. 357
pp. (unpublished Ph. D. dissertation--sociology)
The most salient feature of lower-class black lesbianism--
which also largely influences the incidence of homosexuality in penal institutions--is an adaptational or instrumental response to the deprivation of poverty. The
dissertation addressed the question of whether lesbian
initiation preceded incarceration or took place during the
experience.

4548. FORD, CHARLES A. "Homosexual Practices of Institutionalized Females," **Journal of Abnormal and Social
Psychology,** 23 (1929), 442-48.
Presents data gathered in a correctional institution for
female delinquents, many of them mentally retarded. Homosexual "friendships" are a tradition at the school; entering them is a voluntary matter.

4549. FORD, CHARLES A. "Homosexual Practices of Institu-
       tionalized Females," **Journal of Abnormal and Social
       Psychiatry,** 23 (1929), 442-48.
An early report on types of relationship, inmate communities, and language.

4550. FOSTER, THOMAS W. "Make-Believe Families: A Re-
       sponse of Women and Girls to the Deprivations of
       Imprisonment," **International Journal of Criminology
       and Penology,** 3 (1975), 71-78.
In some instances, the lesbian dyad has been found to be
the nodal point around which the inmate social structure
of the prison revolves, while elsewhere the families
were mostly matricentric, or homosexual marriages were
observed as isolated units, without developing any
kinship satellites.

4551. GIALLOMBARDO, ROSE. **Society of Women: A Study of a
       Women's Prison.** New York: Wiley, 1966. 244 pp.
This classic sociological study covers relationships
between inmates and staff, organizational goals, and the
nature of the prison experience. With social relations
characterized by isolation and an oppressive sense of
time, adjustment often takes the form of a "marriage,"
that is, a homosexual alliance. Integration occurs
through various kinship ties created ad hoc. See also
her: "Social Roles in a Prison for Women," **Social Problems,** 13 (1966), 268-88; and **The Social World of Imprisoned Girls: A Comparative Study of Institutions for
Juvenile Delinquents** (New York: Wiley, 1974; 317 pp.).

4552. HALLECK, SEYMOUR L., and MARVIN HERSKO. "Homosex-
       ual Behavior in a Correctional Institution for
       Adolescent Girls," **American Journal of Orthopsychi-
       atry,** 32 (1962), 911-17.
The majority of girls were drawn into "homosexually tinged
relationships," with different degrees of emotional
involvement. Most had had poor relationships with men
and had found that lesbian involvement provided a chance
to be loved and accepted.

4553. HAMMER, MAX. "Hypersexuality in Reformatory Wom-
       en," **Corrective Psychiatry and Journal of Social
       Therapy,** 15:4 (1969), 20-26.
When women who have drifted into hypersexuality are sent
to correctional institutions where they cannot relieve
their tensions through heterosexual activity, they
frequently turn to homosexuality or masturbation.

4554. HARPER, IDA. "The Role of the 'Fringer' in a State
       Prison for Women," **Social Forces,** 31 (1952), 53-60.
Profiles a "disorganized personality" who engaged in
lesbian activity, itself an acceptable activity within
the prison, but whose intensity made inmates and staff
fearful of her.

4555. HARRIS, SARA. **Hellhole: The Scandalous Story of
the Inmates and Life in the New York City House of
Detention for Women.** New York: E. P. Dutton,
1967. 288 pp.
Popular expose by an investigative reporter with a particular interest in lesbianism. The old Women's House of
Detention was well known to the public because of its
location in the heart of Greenwich Village.

4556. HUMBERT, JEANNE. **Le pourrissoire Saint-Lazare:
choses vues, entendues et vécues.** Paris: Editions
Prima, 1932. 186 pp.
Account of a French women's prison; see esp. Chapter 6.

4557. KATES, ELIZABETH M. "Sexual Problems in Women's
Institutions," **Journal of Social Therapy,** 1
(1955), 187-91.
Recommends the development of a "sexualmetric scale" to
identify potential lesbians.

4558. MITCHELL, ARLENE E. **Informal Inmate Social
Structure in Prisons for Women: A Comparative
Study.** Palo Alto, CA: R & E Research Associates,
1975. 81 pp.
Reprint of dissertation in sociology, University of Washington, 1969. Compares a treatment-oriented prison with a
custody-oriented one. See esp. Chapter 5, "Inmates Involved in Homosexual Behavior" (pp. 35-46).

4559. NORRIS, LINDA. "Comparison of Two Groups in a
Southern State Women's Prison: Homosexual Behavior
versus Non-Homosexual Behavior," **Psychological
Reports,** 34 (1974), 75-78.
Of 376 inmates in one prison, found that 52% were lesbian,
48% not. Among other differences, the lesbians averaged
9.5 years younger.

4560. O'BRIEN, PATRICIA. **The Promise of Punishment:
Prisons in Nineteenth-Century France.** Princeton:
Princeton University Press, 1982. 330 pp.
Contains material on male and female homosexuality, the
latter derived froma cache of **biftons,** lesbian love
letters.

4561. OTIS, MARGARET. "A Perversion Not Commonly Noted,"
Journal of Abnormal Psychology, 8 (1913), 113-16.
An early report of lesbian relations between black and
white girls in a reform school.

4562. PROPPER, ALICE M. **Prison Homosexuality: Myth and
Reality.** Lexington, MA: D. C. Heath, 1981. 239
pp.
Summarizing the available research on prison homosexuality
among adult and juvenile populations of women and men,
argues that the fragmented hypotheses can be subsumed
under the more general concepts of importation and

deprivation. Substantiated with empirical data from
girls in three coed and four all-female institutions.
See also her: "Lesbianism in Female and Coed Correctional Institutions," **JH**, 3 (1978), 265-74; and "Make-Believe Families and Homosexuality among Imprisoned
Girls," **Criminology: An Interdisciplinary Journal**, 20
(1982), 127-38.

4563. SELLING, LOWELL S. "The Pseudo Family," **American
       Journal of Sociology**, 37 (1931), 247-53.
Pseudo-family relationships among girls in correctional
institutions seems to grow up as a natural substitute for
the family which the institution cannot supply. Contends
that these relationships are not overtly lesbian.

4564. TAYLOR, A. J. W. "The Significance of 'Darls' or
       'Special Relationships' for Borstal Girls," **British
       Journal of Criminology**, 5 (1965), 406-18.
On dyadic relationships in British juvenile correctional
facilities (Borstals).

4565. VAN WORMER, KATHERINE. **Sex Role Behavior in a
       Women's Prison, An Ethnological Analysis.** San
       Francisco: R & E Research Associates, 1978. 113 pp.
Found that, in an Alabama prison, while masculinity and
violence of crime were significantly related to the
active (butch) role, it is doubtful whether a true dominance-submission hierarchy existed.

4566. VEDDER, CLYDE B., and DORA B. SOMERVILLE. **The
       Delinquent Girl.** Second ed. Springfield, IL:
       Charles C. Thomas, 1975. 174 pp.
In a correctional school sample 25% of the girls admitted
to having had lesbian relations, as against 3.6% in a
comparable high school sample (p. 87).

4567. WARD, DAVID A., and GENE G. KASSEBAUM. "Homosex-
       uality: A Mode of Adaptation in a Prison for
       Women," **Social Problems**, 12 (1974), 159-77.
Loss of emotional support is perceived as the chief source
of inmates turning to lesbianism. Inmate estimates of the
incidence of lesbianism (much at variance with official
claims) ran as high as 90%. See also their book: **Women's
Prison: Sex and Social Structure** (Chicago: Aldine, 1965;
269 pp.)

XXII. VIOLENCE

A. GENERAL

Viewed in the perspective of functionalist sociology,
violence or the threat of violence serves the dominant
majority as a device to set limits to the aspirations of
deviant groups. Hence it is not surprising that the
increasing visibility of gay people from the late 1960s on
should be accompanied by increasing number of violent
acts against them ("fag bashing"). A quite different
aspect of violence appears in the very rare, but often
sensationalized instances of mass murders committed by
homosexual men. Public reactions to media reports on such
individuals offer an interesting barometer of attitudes.

4568. BAUER, GÜNTER. "Jürgen Bartsch: Ein Bericht über
den vierfachen Knabenmörder," **Archiv für Kriminologie**, 144 (1969), 61-91.
On a German murderer of boys active in the 1960s. See
also the volume recording responses to Rolf Schubel's
film on Bartsch: **Nachruf auf eine "Bestie": Dokumente--
Bilder--Interviews** (Essen: Torso Verlag, 1984; 237 pp.).

4569. BELL, ARTHUR. **Kings Don't Mean a Thing: The John
Knight Murder Case.** New York: William Morrow,
1978. 228 pp.
Account by the late gay Village Voice columnist of the
savage murder of a closeted publisher in Philadelphia on
December 7, 1975, and the ensuing events.

4570. BERGSMA, WIEGO, et al. **Homoseksualiteit en aggres-
sie.** The Hague: De Woelrat, 1983. 110 pp.
Various articles and personal testimonies documenting recent incidents of violence against gay men and lesbians,
chiefly in the Netherlands, together with suggestions for
combatting the trend. See also: **Leren van je vijand ...
Over pot/t/tenrammerij en alternative sankties** (Amsterdam: N.V.I.H.-C.O.C., 1985; 31 pp.).

4571. BOHN, TED R. "Homophobic Violence: Implications
for Social Work Practice," **Journal of Social Work
and Human Sexuality**, 2:2-3 (1983-84), 91-112.
Contends that homophobic violence serves a function in
society by providing scpaegoating and maintenance of the
male sex role.

4572. BOLITHO, WILLIAM. **Murder for Profit.** Garden City,
NY: Garden City Publishing Co., 1926. 332 pp.
Contains the most detailed account of the German mass-mur-
derer Fritz Haarmann in English. See also the German

monographs: Hans Hyan, **Massenmörder Haarmann** (Berlin: Ver-
lag Es werde Licht, 1924; 68 pp.); and Theodor Lessing,
Haarmann: die Geschichte eines Wehrwolfs (Berlin: Die
Schmiede, 1925; 271 pp.).

4573.   BRONGERSMA, EDWARD.   "Aggression against Pedo-
        philes," **International Journal of Law and Psychi-
        atry,** 7 (1984), 79-87.
Argues that pedophilia has been considered a crime only
since the imposition of Christian taboos and that the
difficulties caused by the repression of pedophilia make
people violent in their rejection of pedophiles.

4574.   CALIFIA, PAT.   "Battered Lovers: The Hidden Problem
        of Gay Domestic Violence," **Advocate,** no. 441 (March
        4, 1986), 42-46.
Discussion of a neglected problem, including lesbian battery, which has been denied because admitting its existence would be "politically incorrect."

4575.   CALIFIA, PAT.   "Queer-Bashing," **Advocate,** no. 314
        (April 1981), 20, 22-24.
Contends that the media are being used to turn gays into a
target to relieve the frustrations of Middle America. See
also: Douglas Ireland, "New Homophobia: Open Season on
Gays," **Nation,** 229 (September 15, 1979), 207-10; and
"Rendezvous in the Ramble," **New York** (July 24, 1978),
39-42.

4576.   GADDIS, THOMAS, and JAMES O. LONG. **Killer: A
        Journal of Murder.** New York: Macmillan, 1970.   388
        pp.
Biography of Carl Panzram, who styled himself the "world's
worst murderer."

4577.   GAUTE, J. H. H., and ROBIN ODELL. **The Murderer's
        Who's Who: Outstanding International Cases ... in
        the Last 150 Years.** New York: Methuen, 1979.   269
        pp.
In this omnium gatherum, see pp. 27, 72-73, 101, 102-03,
118, 141, 150-51, 166, 223.

4578.   GIBSON, IAN. **The Death of Lorca.** London: Paladin,
        1974.   222 pp.
Shows how vicious homophobic prejudice presided over the
murder of the great poet Federico García Lorca near Granada in 1936.   See now the revised version of this book
(New York: Penguin Books, 1983).

4579.   HARRY, JOSEPH. "Derivative Deviance: The Cases of
        Extortion, Fag-Bashing, and Shakedown of Gay Men,"
        Criminology, 19 (1982), 546-64.
Sociological analysis linking several related phenomena.

4580.   HINCKLE, WARREN. **Gayslayer.** Reno: Silver Dollar
        Press, 1985.   100 pp.

On Dan White (who committed suicide in 1985), the murderer
of San Francisco Mayor George Moscone and gay Supervisor
Harvey Milk in 1978. See also M. Weiss, below.

4581. HIRSCHFELD, MAGNUS. "Morde an Homosexuellen,"
       **Vierteljahrsbericht des wissenschaftlich-humanitär-
       en Komites,** 2 (1910), 142-94.
Comments by the noted German sexologist on the risk homosexuals run of being murdered.

4582. KIDDER, TRACY. **The Road to Yuba City: A Journey
       into the Juan Corona Murders.** Garden City, NY:
       Doubleday, 1974. 317 pp.
On a still controversial case of mass murder in Northern
California.

4583. KLUGE, P. F., and THOMAS MOORE. "Boys in the
       Bank," **Life,** 73 (September 22, 1972), 64-65, 68-70,
       72, 74.
On the Brooklyn, NY, bank robbery organized by John Wojte-
wicz to obtain money for his lover's sex change operation. This incident was the basis for the film "Dog Day
Afternoon."

4584. LEOPOLD, NATHAN FREUDENTHAL. **Life Plus 99 Years.**
       Garden City, NY: Doubleday, 1958. 381 pp.
Reminiscences of the man who was notorious for the murder,
in concert with his lover Richard Loeb, of a young boy.
Meyer Levin's novel **Compulsion,** and the subsequent film,
were based on this event. See also: Maureen McKerman,
The Amazing Crime and Trial of Leopold and Loeb (New York:
New American Library, 1957; 300 pp.).

4585. MASTERS, BRIAN. **Killing for Company: The Case of
       Dennis Nilson.** London: Cape, 1985. 336 pp.
On a British pedophile-necrophile mass murderer arrested
in 1983. See also J. Lisners, **House of Horrors** (London:
Corgi, 1983).

4586. MELDRIM, JULIAN. **Attacks on Gay People: A Report.**
       Second ed. London: Campaign for Homosexual Equal-
       ity, 1980. 41 pp.
Well-documented report of a problem that became more acute
in the 1970s as gay people became more visible in the
United Kingdom.

4587. MILLER, BRIAN, and LAUD HUMPHREYS. "Lifestyles and
       Violence: Homosexual Victims of Assault and Mur-
       der," **Qualitative Sociology,** 3 (1980), 169-85.
Offers a composite profile of homosexual victims of
assault, showing that they are generally detached from
the gay subcultures--including the S & M world. [Compare
John A. Lee, "The Social Organization of Sexual Risk,"
Alternative Lifestyles, 2 (1979), 69-100].

4588. OLSEN, JACK. **The Man with the Candy: The Story of**

the **Houston Mass Murders.** New York: Simon and
Schuster, 1974. 218 pp.
The story of Dean Corll and his two teenage accomplices,
who violated and murdered at least 27 boys between 1971
and 1973. See also: John K. Gurwell, **Mass Murder in Hous-**
ton (Houston: Cordovan Press, 1974; 160 pp.).

4589. PRESTON, JOHN. "White Candles at the Ramrod," **The**
Witness, 64 (November 1981), 18-19.
On a homophobic shooting spree at a New York City water-
front bar.

4590. REE, FRANK VAN. **De man die een kind doodde: een**
psychiatrische Studie. Amsterdam: Boom Meppel,
1984. 163 pp.
Story of a conflict-ridden pedophile who killed a boy
becuase he was afraid of the consequences of falling in
love with him.

4591. RIORDON, MICHAEL. "The Mirror of Violence," **Body**
Politic (May 1980), 25-28.
On gay men in Toronto organizing for self-defence.

4592. SAGARIN, EDWARD, and DONAL E. MACNAMARA. "The
Homosexual as a Crime Victim," **International**
Journal of Criminology and Penology, 3 (1975),
13-25.
The fast-changing scene in America, in which homosexual
behavior is increasingly visible, may produce a reduc-
ltion of some types of criminal victimization, while
facilitating others, owing to lack of caution among homosexuals.

4593. SAN MIGUEL, CHRISTOPHER, and JIM MILLHAM. "The
Role of Cognitive and Situational Variables in
Aggression toward Homosexuals," **JH,** 2 (1976),
11-27.
Aggressiveness was found to be related to attitudes toward
homosexuality, perceived similarity toward the target
homosexual, and type of prior contact with the target
homosexual.

4594. SPAZIER, DIETER. **Der Tod des Psychiaters.** Frankfurt am Main: Syndikat, 1982. 235 pp.
Concerns a closeted forensic psychiatrist murdered by a
patient who had become his lover and manservant.

4595. SULLIVAN, TERRY, and PETER T. MAIKIN. **Killer**
Clown: The John Wayne Gacy Murders. New York:
Pinnacle Books, 1984. 375 pp.
An Assistant State's Attorney (Illinois) retraces the
investigation that led to the apprehension and conviction of the killer of at least 33 young men and boys.
See also: Tim Cahill and Russ Ewing, **Buried Dreams: In-**
side the Mind of a Serial Killer (New York: Bantam,
1986); and Clifford L. Linedecker, **The Man Who Killed**

Boys (New York: St. Martin's Press, 1980; 222 pp.).

4596. WEINBERG, DAVID. "Blood of a Critic: Gregory
        Battcock's Rise to Stardom and Fall from Grace,"
        Soho News (October 13, 1981), 12-16.
Reconstruction of the lifestyle and brutal murder, in
Puerto Rico, of a noted gay art critic.

4597. WEISS, MIKE. **Double-Play: The San Francisco City
        Hall Killings.** San Francisco: Addison Wesley,
        1984. 400 pp.
Tells the story of the murder of Mayor George Moscone and
Supervisor Harvey Milk by Dan White in 1978. See also:
Randy Shilts, **The Mayor of Castro Street: The Life and
Times of Harvey Milk** (New York: St. Martin's Press, 1982;
388 pp.); and W. Hinckle, above.

4598. WEISSMAN, ERIC. "Kids Who Attack Gays," **Christo-
        pher Street** (August 1978), 9-13.
On teen-age fag-bashers and their motivations.

                    B. HOMOSEXUAL RAPE

Thanks to the women's movement, forcible rape has emerged
as a major area of social concern. As yet, however, relatively little attention has been devoted to the problem
of males raping other males, and the trauma suffered by
victims. See also "Prisons: Male," XXI.B. Cases of women
raping other women are virtually nonexistent.

4599. ANDERSON, CRAIG L. "Males as Sexual Assault Vic-
        tims: Multiple Levels of Trauma," **JH,** 7 (1981-82),
        145-62.
Offers a paradigm consisting of "set-up," "attack," and
"aftermath" phases. Male victims suffer rape trauma
syndrome, as well as various forms of stigmatization and
secondary trauma. Bibliography, pp. 159-62.

4600. BURGESS, ANN WOLBERT, et al. **Sexual Assault of
        Children and Adolescents.** Lexington, MA: Lexington
        Books, 1978. 272 pp.
Directed at professionals who work with victims and
offenders.

4601. GROTH, A. NICHOLAS, and ANN WOLBERT BURGESS. "Male
        Rape: Offenders and Victims," **American Journal of
        Psychiatry,** 137 (1980), 806-10.
Men tend to avoid reporting rape because of (1) societal
beliefs that a man should be able to defend himself; (2)
the victim's fear that his sexual orientation will become
suspect; and (3) the fact that the telling is highly disturbing.

4602. GUNDLACH, RALPH H. "Sexual Molestation and Rape
       Reported by Homosexual and Heterosexual Women," **JH**,
       2 (1977), 367-84.
Some girls, molested as teenagers, became lesbians. Adult
lesbians were less likely to blame themselves than heterosexual women.

4603. JOSEPHSON, GORDON W. "The Male Rape Victim: Evalu-
       ation and Treatment," **Journal of the American
       College of Emergency Physicians**, 8 (1979), 13-15.
While the medical literature offers little guidance in the
evaluation of male victims of sexual assault, the writer
makes some practical suggestions.

4604. KAUFMAN, ARTHUR. "Rape of Men in the Community,"
       in: Irving R. Stuart and Joanne G. Greer (eds.).
       **Victims of Sexual Aggression: Treatment of Chil-
       dren, Women, and Men.** New York: Van Nostrand
       Reinhold, 1984, pp. 156-69.
Analysis of data sheets of fifteen New Mexico victims.
Compared with female victims, the male victims as a
group sustained more physical trauma and were more
likely to be subjected to multiple assaults from several
assailants. See also his: "Male Rape Victims: Nonin-
stitutionalized Assault," **American Journal of Psychiatry**, 137 (1980), 221-23.

4605. MARTIN, ROBERT ("DONALD TUCKER"). "The Account of
       the White House Seven," in: Anthony M. Scacco, Jr.
       (ed.), **Male Rape: A Casebook of Sexual Aggressions.**
       New York: AMS Press, 1982, pp. 30-57.
Reflective first-person account by a gay activist of his
being gang-raped in a Washington prison in 1973 after his
arrest for participating in a non-violent demonstration
inside the White House. He relates further details, together with his ideological analysis of the experience, in
the same volume in "A Punk's Song: View from the Inside"
(pp. 58-79).

4606. PORTER, EUGENE. **Treating the Young Male Victim of
       Sexual Assault: Issues and Intervention Strat-
       egies.** Syracuse, NY: Safer Society Press, 1986.
       96 pp.
Directed at both professionals and laypersons, this
pamphlet provides an understanding of the context in which
male sexual victimization occurs, the ways in which boys
are likely to repsond, and the primary approaches to
their treatment.

4607. SCHIFF, ARTHUR F. "Examination and Treatment of
       the Male Rape Victim," **Southern Medical Journal**, 73
       (1980), 1498-1502.
The number of known male rape victims is on the increase,
and practitioners have need for information on examination
and treatment (described).

C. SUICIDE

As with stigmatized groups generally, it is to be expected that suicide rates would be higher among male homosexuals and lesbians than among the population at large. Owing in part to the fact that the details are often not adequately recorded, it has been difficult to obtain adequate data on the specific character of gay suicide, despite the belief that homosexuals are prone to end their own lives because of the intolerable burdens that society imposes on them.

4608. ANTHEAUME, ANDRÉ, and PARROT (eds.). "Un cas d'inversion sexuelle," **Annales médico-psycholog-iques** (May 1905), 459-72.
Letter of a despondent homosexual who committed suicide. Reprinted in **Masques**, 3 (1979-80, 88-93.

4609. BADEN, HANS JURGEN. **Literatur und Selbstmord.** Stuttgart: Klett, 1965. 229 pp.
In this study of literature and suicide, see pp. 91-146 on the novelist Klaus Mann, who killed himself in 1949.

4610. FONTANIE, PIERRE. "Suicide et homosexualité," **Arcadie, no.** 314 (February 1980), 108-13; no. 315 (March 1980), 176-83.
Review of noted male and female homosexuals who have attempted or actually committed suicide, followed by a critique of contemporary social pressures that aggravate the problem.

4611. HAZLEWOOD, ROBERT K. et al (eds.). **Autoerotic Fatalities.** Lexington, MA: Lexington Books, 1983. 208 pp.
On apparently accidental deaths that are caused by asphyxiation for sexual stimulation; includes several homosexual cases. See also: H. L. Resnik, "Eroticized Repetitive Hangings: A Form of Self-Destructive Behavior," **American Journal of Psychotherapy,** 26 (1972), 4-21.

4612. HENDIN, HERBERT. **Black Suicide.** New York: Basic Books, 1969.
This psychoanalytical work contains a chapter "Suicide and Male Homosexuality." See also his: "Black Suicide," **Archives of General Psychiatry,** 21 (1969), 407-22.

4613. ROFES, ERIC E. **Lesbians, Gay Men and Suicide.** San Francisco: Grey Fox Press, 1983. 162 pp.
Sympathetic study focusing attention on an important problem of gay self-oppression, discussing interactions with blackmail--real or feared--and alcoholism. Contends that social stigmatization places an added burden on the normal stresses of everyday life.

4614. SCHUMANN, HANS-JOACHIM VON. **Homosexualität und**

Selbstmord: Aetiologische und psychotherapeutische
Betrachtungen. Hamburg: Kriminalistik Verlag,
1965. 141 pp.
Antiquated psychiatric study.

4615. SWARTSBURG, MARSHALL, et al. "Dual Suicide in
Homosexuals," Journal of Nervous and Mental
Disease, 155 (1972), 125-30.
Discusses the psychodynamics underlying double suicides
among homosexuals, presenting a case study of an attempt
by two gay men. (Since this article was written, the
AIDS crisis has increased the number of cases.)

4616. SWIGERT, V. L., et al. "Sexual Suicide: Social,
Psychological, and Legal Aspects," Archives of
Sexual Behavior, 5 (1976), 391-401.
Chiefly on homosexual suicide.

XXIII. MEDICAL

A. GENERAL

At the end of the 15th century, Europeans began to be
aware that there were diseases whose principal characteristic was that they are transmitted through sexual contact. For a long time these diseases were known as
"venereal," from Venus, the goddess of love. More recently they have come to be termed "sexually transmitted
diseases" (STDs). The homosexual aspect of STDs before
the last few decades is largely unknown because of the
double taboo surrounding the subject, but the AIDS crisis
(XXIII.C) has thrown a glaring searchlight on the problem.

4617. CORSARO, MARIA, and CAROLE KORZENIOWSKY. **STD: A**
      Commonsense Guide. New York: St. Martin's Press,
      1980. 135 pp.
Practical guide for the lay public of 13 sexually transmitted diseases, now somewhat dated.

4618. EBBESEN, PETER, MADS MELBYE, and ROBERT BIGGAR.
      "Sex Habits, Recent Disease, and Drug Use in Two
      Groups of Danish Homosexuals," **Archives of Sexual**
      Behavior, 13 (1984), 291-300.
Two-hundred fifty-nine Danish homosexuals interviewed with
regard to health; results resemble those for San Francisco
in 1970.

4619. FENWICK, R. D. **The Advocate Guide to Gay Health.**
      Revised ed. Boston: Alyson, 1982. 236 pp.
Information and advice for gay men, now somewhat out of
date. Considerable emphasis on holistic medicine, some
aspects of which are controversial.

4620. FLUKER, J. L. "A 10-Year Study of Homosexually
      Transmitted Infections," **British Journal of**
      Venereal Diseases, 52 (1976), 155-60.
A considerably higher incidence of VD as a result of
homosexual contact has probably always existed than was
formerly realized, and recent years have seen a massive
further increase.

4621. HOLMES, KING K., PER-ANDERS MARDH, et al. (eds).
      Sexually Transmitted Diseases. New York: McGraw-
      Hill, 1983. 1104 pp.
This massive volume offers a truly multifaceted presentation, including social, political, and legal aspects.

4622. JUDSON, FRANKLYN N. "Comparative Prevalence Rates
      of Sexual Transmitted Diseases in Heterosexual and

Homosexual Men," **American Journal of Epidemiology,**
112 (1980), 836-43.
Confirms the substantially higher homosexual rates that
obtained in the late 1970s.

4623.   KASSLER, JEANNE. **Gay Men's Health: A Guide to the
        AID Syndrome and Other Sexually Transmitted Dis-
        eases.** New York: Harper and Row, 1983. 166 pp.
General survey by an M.D. for the lay reader.

4624.   KAZAL, HENRY L., et al. "The Gay Bowel Syndrome:
        Clinicopathological Correlation in 260 Cases,"
        Annals of Clinical and Laboratory Science, 6
        (1976), 184-92.
A group of New York City male homosexuals constituting
about 10% of a proctological practice presented a distinct
pattern of anorectal and colon disease. See also Norman
Sohn and James G. Robilotti, "The Gay Bowel Syndrome,"
American Journal of Gastroenterology, 67 (1977), 478-84.

4625.   LANGSTON, DEBORAH. **Living with Herpes: The Compre-
        hensive and Authoritative Guide to the Causes,
        Symptoms, and Treatment of Herpes Virus Illnesses.**
        Garden City, NY: Doubleday, 1983. 198 pp.
Guide for the lay reader by a Professor at Harvard Medical
School; see esp. pp. 42-45, 158-64.

4626.   LLEWELYN-JONES, DEREK. **Herpes, AIDS and Other
        Sexually Transmitted Diseases.** New York: Faber and
        Faber, 1985. 155 pp.
An up-to-date survey that, without minimizing the seriousness of AIDS, shows its relative rarity.

4627.   MA, PEARL, and DONALD ARMSTRONG (eds.). **The
        Acquired Immune Deficiency Syndrome and Infections
        of Homosexual Men.** Brooklyn, NY: Yorke Medical
        Books, 1984. 442 pp.
Collection of technical papers by medical authorities.

4628.   MARGOLIS, STEPHEN. **Sexually Transmitted Diseases:
        An Annotated, Selective Bibliography.** New York:
        Garland, 1984. 176 pp.
Covers history, disease control modalities, patient edu-
cation/behavior and compliance, information sources, and
epidemiological and medical resources. Emphasis is on
very recent material, with selected references to earlier
studies. For other bibliographies see XXIII.C.

4629.   MORTON, R. S. **Venereal Diseases.** Baltimore: Pen-
        guin Books, 1966. 185 pp.
Mainly a factual account reflecting then-current knowledge, but occasionally descending to moralism regarding
homosexual behavior.

4630.   O'DONNELL, MARY, et al. **Lesbian Health Matters!**
        Santa Cruz, CA: Santa Cruz Women's Health Collec-

tive, 1979. 101 pp.
Lesbian perspectives on such subjects as alternative
fertilization, alcoholism, menopause, and feminist
therapy.

4631. OSTROW, DAVID G., et al. (eds.). **Sexually Transmitted Diseases in Homosexual Men.** New York: Plenum Medical Book Co., 1983. 272 pp.
A comprehensive professional handbook, covering medical
practice, bacterially sexually transmitted diseases,
enterically transmitted diseases, anal disorders, dermato-
logical problems, AIDS, and volatile nitrates ("poppers").

4632. POLLAK, MICHAEL, and LINDINALVA LAURINDO. "1000
homosexuels temoignent," **Le Gai pied,** no. 193
(November 15, 1985), 18-22.
Results of a questionnaire distributed by the gay weekly
show that French gays are seriously concerned about the
health crisis, but not panicky. Some change in sexual
behavior is documented, but "safe sex" has not been generally adopted. A companion article by Frank Arnal (pp.
14-15) reports on an opinion poll conducted among the
French population at large, showing that they reject
alarmism.

4633. SCHILLER, F., and G. KAHLERT. "Homosexualität---
ein aktuelles venereologisches Problem?" **Dermato-
logische Wochenschrift,** no. 42 (1967), 1161-65.
Medical report on increasing numbers of homosexual cases
in East German hospitals at the time of legal reform.

4634. SCHWABER, FERN A., and MICHAEL SHERNOFF (eds.).
Sourcebook on Lesbian/Gay Health Care. New York:
National Gay Health Education Foundation, 1984.
282 pp.
Includes presentations given at the First International
Lesbian and Gay Health Conference (New York, Hunter
College, 1984), a bibliography, and the fourth edition
of the National Lesbian/Gay Health Directory, listing
practitioners and other health professionals.

4635. SCHWULE MEDIZINMANNER. **Sumpffieber: Medizin für
schwule Männer.** Fourth ed. Berlin: Verlag Rosa
Winkel, 1984. 180 + 34 pp.
Handbook on disease and health for gay men. This edition
contains a special AIDS supplement ("AIDS Nachtrag").

4636. SZMUNESS, WOLF, et al. "Hepatitis B Vaccine: Demonstration of Efficacy in a Controlled Clinical
Trial in High-Risk Population," **New England Journal
of Medicine,** 303 (1980), 833-41.
Account by the team that successfully developed and tested
a vaccine for hepatitis B, with the cooperation of the
gay-male community. See also Szmuness et al., "On the
Role of Sexual Behavior in the Spread of Hepatitis B Infection," **Annals of Internal Medicine,** 83 (1975), 489-95.

B. PROFESSIONALS AND PATIENTS

Gay men and lesbians have for long been hesitant to
discuss their sexuality with health care givers, a
reticence that has tended to hamper treatment. Another
form of concealment--all-too-often a necessary one-- is
the closeted sexuality of gay and lesbian doctors and
nurses.

4637. ANDERSON, CARLA LEE. "The Effect of a Workshop on
        Attitudes of Female Nursing Students toward Male
        Homosexuality," **JH**, 7 (1981), 57-69.
Responses of 64 female nursing students indicated that
they held more negative attitudes and stereotyped beliefs
that did a sample of male counselors and psychologists.
After a two-hour workshop attitudes of 37 had changed.

4638. BELL, ALAN P. "The Homosexual as Patient" and "The
        Homosexual as Physician," in: Richard Green (ed.),
        Human Sexuality: A Health Practitioner's Text.
        Baltimore: Williams and Wilkins, 1975, pp. 54-72
        and 74-81.
Inasmuch as homosexuality involves a large number of
divergent experiences, the label affords little predictability. The physician should listen carefully to the
patient's own statements, so as to help enhance his or
her coping strategies.

4639. BERGER, RAYMOND M. "Health Care for Lesbians and
        Gays: What Social Workers Should Know," **Journal of
        Social Work and Human Sexuality,** 1:3 (Spring 1983),
        59-73.
Urges commitment ot the social-work values of self-deter-
mination and nonjudgmental service.

4640. BROWN, HOWARD. **Familiar Faces, Hidden Lives: The
        Story of Homosexual Men in America Today.** New
        York: Harcourt Brace Jovanovich, 1976. 246 pp.
The late New York City activist describes his life and
medical career with asides on the experiences of others.

4641. DARDICK, LARRY, and KATHLEEN E. GRADY. "Openness
        between Gay Persons and Health Professionals,"
        Annals of Internal Medicine, 93 (1980), 115-19.
Health professionals need to avoid not only overt expres
sions of prejudice, but also procedures that prematurely
foreclose the possibility of patients disclosing their
sexual orientation to practitioners.

4642. HARRISON, HOWARD. "Straight Talk from a Gay
        Doctor," **The New Physician,** 26 (April 1977), 34-36.
Psychiatrist relates his own difficulties in coming to
terms with his homosexuality.

4643. HENDERSON, RALPH H. "Improving Sexually Trans-
       mitted Disease Health Services for Gays: A National
       Prospective," **Sexually Transmitted Diseases,** 4:2
       (April-June 1977), 58-62.
Vigorous efforts must be undertaken to combat the society's tendency to punish those who have contracted sexually transmitted diseases (STDs) and homosexuals.

4644. HIRSH, HERMAN. "The Homosexual and the Family
       Doctor," **GP** [General Practitioner], 26:5 (November
       1962), 103-07.
Traditional attitudes that flourished during the period.

4645. "Homosexual Doctors: Their Place and Influence in
       Medicine Today," **Medical World News,** 15:4 (January
       25, 1974), 41-45, 49, 51.
Asserts that the typical homosexual physician is likely to
live in a large city; probably not married; more likely
to specialize in pathology or anaesthesiology or some
other non-patient-contact discipline than pediatrics,
orthopedics, or internal medicine; and living in mortal
terror of being exposed.

4646. HULL, MICHAEL. "Sexual Orientation Discrimination
       in Medical Statistics," **Australian and New Zealand
       Journal of Sociology,** 13 (1977), 146-48.
Argues that officially accepted statistics for the incidence of STDs among homosexuals are questionable.

4647. "I Am a Homosexual Physician," **Medical Opinion,**
       2:1 (January 1973), 49-50, 54-55, 58.
Personal account describing wrongs suffered and difficulties of "coming out."

4648. JOHNSON, SUSAN R., et al. "Factors Influencing
       Lesbian Gynecologic Care: A Preliminary Study,"
       American Journal of Obstetrics and Gynecology, 140
       (May 1, 1981), 20-28.
A study of 117 lesbians showed that these women actively
utilized the health care system, though many chose less
traditional sources. No medical problems specific to
lesbians were identified.

4649. LAWRENCE, JOHN C. "Homosexuals, Hospitalization,
       and the Nurse," **Nursing Forum,** 14 (1975), 304-17.
Students need to be reminded that passing moral judgments
is not a function of nursing and that such judgments
merely impede the ability to give quality care.

4650. MATHEWS, CHRISTOPHER, et al. "Physician Attitudes
       toward Homosexuality," **Western Journal of Medicine,**
       140 (1984), 290-91.
Before AIDS became prominent, 40% of physicians surveyed
reported feeling uncomfortable treating homosexual patients.

4651. MAURER, TOM B.   "Health Care and the Gay Commu-
         nity," **Postgraduate Medicine**, 58 (1975), 127-30.
Health care professionals who are the most rejecting of
homosexuals are usually uncomfortable with sexuality in
general and with some aspect of their own sexuality in
particular.

4652. MESSING, ALICE E., ROBERT SCHOENBERG, and ROGER
         K. STEPHENS. "Confronting Homphobia in Health Care
         Settings: Guidelines for Social Work Practice,"
         Journal of Social Work and Human Sexuality, 2:2/3
         (Winter-Spring 1984), 65-74.
Urges humanistic, nonjudgmental practices and attitudes.

4653. O'DONNELL, MARY. "Lesbian Health Care: Issues and
         Literature," **Science for the People**, 10:3 (May-June
         1978), 8-19.
Lesbian activist's appraisal of shortcomings of the
health-care delivery system.

4654. PATTERSON, JANE, and LYNDA MADARAS. **Woman/Doctor.**
         New York: Avon, 1983. 217 pp.
Patterson, a physician, recounts her struggles against
discrimination as a woman and a lesbian.

4655. PAULY, IRA B., and STEVEN G. GOLDSTEIN. "Phys-
         icians' Attitudes in Treating Male Homosexuals,"
         Medical Aspects of Human Sexuality, 4:12 (1970),
         26-27, 31-32, 36-37, 41, 44-45.
Results of a questionnaire study of 937 Oregon physicians
show that attitudes vary to some extent according to field
of specialization and age.

4656. PETTYJOHN, RODGER D. "Health Care of the Gay
         Individual," **Nursing Forum**, 18 (1979), 366-93.
An overview of the subject of homosexuality for the
health-care practitioner, including a glossary of slang.

4657. POGONCHEFF, ELAINE, and JEANNE BROSSART. "The Gay
         Patient: What Not to Do, What You Should Be Doing,"
         RN, 42:4 (April 1979), 46-52.
If there are problems in treating the homosexual patient,
they probably stem from the attitudes of the staff.

4658. SANDHOLZER, TERRY A. "Physician Attitudes and
         Other Factors Affecting the Incidence of Sexually
         Transmitted Diseases in Homosexual Males," **JH** , 5
         (1980), 325-27.
Previous research indicates that the views of private
physicians are more liberal towards homosexuals and STDs
in homosexual males than might be expected.

4659. TULNER, H. J. **Reis alleen: Memoires van een
         homofiele arts.** Amsterdam: Tiebosch, 1981. 240
         pp.
Memoirs of a Dutch physician (born 1911), including his

work abroad, his marriage, and his homosexuality.

4659A. WALKER, JIM. "Homosexuality in Australia," **New
      Doctor**, 17 (August-October 1980), 28-30.
Problems encountered by homosexual physicians in disclosing their orientation, and uneasiness felt by homosexual
patients in consulting a physician whom they believe to
be heterosexual.

C. THE AIDS CRISIS

The Acquired Immune Deficiency Syndrome (AIDS) first drew
significant attention in the spring of 1981. The chief
groups affected by this extraordinarily lethal disease are
male homosexuals and intravenous drug users. The following section does not pretend to offer any control over the
thousands of professionally medical reports that have been
published--though these can be approached through the bibliographies that have been cited. Instead the coverage
focuses chiefly on the social and political aspects: the
effects of the disease on the life patterns and self-concept of homosexuals, changes in the structure of gay service organizations, and the response of the larger political community.

4660. ALTMAN, DENNIS. **AIDS in the Mind of America.** New
      York: Doubleday, 1986. 228 pp.
Attempts an overview of how the AIDS crisis has altered
attitudes about sex, disease, medicine, and death. While
the final chapter offers an account of what is specifically American about the response, this ambitious study
lacks comparative depth. See also his: "AIDS: The Polit-
icization of an Epidemic," **Socialist Review**, no. 78 (November-December 1984), 93-109.

4661. BATCHELOR, WALTER F. "AIDS: A Public Health and
      Psychological Emergency," **American Psychologist**, 39
      (1984), 1279-84.
The psychological ramifications of AIDS involve the social
stigmas attached to the lifestyles of high-risk groups
and the fear of contracting AIDS held by the general
public.

4662. BAYER, RONALD. "AIDS and the Gay Community: Be-
      tween the Specter and the Promise of Medicine,"
      Social Research, 52 (1985), 581-606.
Fearful of how medical authority might be abused, the
gay community has sought to invoke protections enunciated in the liberal tradition of biomedical ethics.

4663. BAYER, RONALD. "Gays and the Stigma of 'Bad
      Blood,'" **Hastings Center Report**, 13:2 (April 1983),

5-7.
On March 4, 1983, the U.S. Public Health Service recommended that "sexually active homosexual and bisexual men with multiple partners" be prohibited from donating or selling their blood. Success of the ban depends on the cooperation and honesty of gay men.

4664. BAYER, RONALD, CAROL LEVINE, and THOMAS MURRAY. "Guidelines for Confidentiality in Research on AIDS," **IRB: A Review of Human Subjects Research,** 6:6 (November-December 1984), 1-7.
Increasing knowledge about AIDS and the social problems consequent on this knowledge pose new challenges in the area of personal privacy.

4665. BERGEN, INEKE VAN DEN, and REIJER BREED. **Is het waar dat Lefert AIDS heeft?** Amsterdam: Van Gennep, 1985. 84 pp.
Traces the effects of AIDS on a Dutchman, Lefert Scheepert, diagnosed on November 27, 1984, and his friend Reijer Breed.

4666. BERGMANN, THOMAS, HANS JAGER, and FRANK RUEHMANN. **AIDS: was tun?** Berlin: Bruno Gmunder, 1983. 80 pp.
Objective overview for the lay public by West German gay physicians, now somewhat dated.

4667. BERKOWITZ, RICHARD, MICHAEL CALLEN, and RICHARD DWORKIN. **How to Have Sex in an Epidemic: One Approach.** New York: News from the Front, 1983. 40 pp.
Advice on "safer sex," some of it sensible, some problematic.

4668. BLACK, DAVID. **The Plague Years: A Chronicle of AIDS, the Epidemic of Our Times.** New York: Simon & Schuster, 1986. 224 pp.
An expanded version of a series of articles written for **Rolling Stone** magazine; in keeping with this origin, the book is irritating and sometimes unconsidered, but occasionally insightful.

4669. CAHILL, KEVIN M. (ed.). **The AIDS Epidemic.** New York: St Martins Press, 1983. 173 pp.
A first attempt at a comprehensive assessment: thirteen papers, mainly by physicians, presented at a symposium at Lenox Hill Hospital in New York City and covering epidemiology, immunology, the clinical picture, and implications.

4670. CAPUTO, L. "Dual Diagnosis: AIDS and Addiction," **Social Work** (July-August 1985), 361-64.
Offers some light on an understudied phenomenon.

4671. CECCHI, ROBERT L. "Stress: Prodrome to Immune

Deficiency," **Annals of the New York Academy of Sciences**, 437 (1984), 286-89.
Suggests that communities affected by AIDS may be immune-deficient as a result of stress associated with a negative self-image, inability to express feelings and anger, and a lack of community support.

4672. CENTERS FOR DISEASE CONTROL, ATLANTA. "Report on AIDS," **Morbidity and Mortality Weekly Reports** (June 1981ff.).
These continuing weekly reports are the basis for the nationwide statistics on AIDS.

4673. COATES, THOMAS J., LYDIA TEMOSHOK, and JEFFREY MANDEL. "Psychosocial Research is Essential to Understanding and Treating AIDS," **American Psychologist**, 39 (1984), 1309-14.
In terms of the interface between biological and psychological variables, focuses on the psychological consequences of AIDS, psychosocial determinants of health-promoting and health-damaging behaviors, and factors related to disease incidence and progression.

4674. CONTE, J. E., JR., et al. "Infection-Control Guidelines for Patients with the Acquired Immunodeficiency Syndrome," **New England Journal of Medicine**, 309:12 (September 22, 1983), 740-44.
Professional assessment of infection risks and the means of their control, a subject which has occasioned much fear among the lay public.

4675. DE VITA, VINCENT T., S. HELLMAN, and S. A. ROSENBERG. **AIDS: Etiology, Diagnosis, Treatment and Prevention.** New York: J. B. Lippincott, 1985. 352 pp.
A coordinated collection of contributions designed to serve as a textbook for physicians and medical researchers.

4676. EBBESEN, PETER, ROBERT J. BIGGER, and MALS MELBYE. **AIDS: A Basic Guide for Clinicians.** Philadelphia: W. B. Saunders, 1984. 313 pp.
Medical papers by European and North American investigators. Includes bibliography from the [US] National Institute of Allergy.

4677. FERRACINI, RICCARDO (ed.). **AIDS: Che cos'è: le cause, la diffusione, come si previeni, a chi rivolgersi.** Turin: Edizione Gruppo Abele, 1985. 168 pp.
Manual written in nontechnical language, combining material from physicians and activists. Italian and international focus.

4678. FERRARA, ANTHONY J. "My Personal Experience with AIDS," **American Psychologist**, 39 (1984), 1285-87.

720   HOMOSEXUALITY

The author, now deceased, recounts the emotional and
physical problems, including his experience with four
treatment regimens.

4679. FETTNER, ANN GIUDICI, and WILLIAM A. CHECK. **The
       Truth About AIDS: Evolution of an Epidemic.** New
       York: Holt, Rinehart and Winston, 1984. 288 pp.
This overview for the lay public stressing social rather
than medical aspects. includes discussion of fears and
prejudices, rivalries among researchers, and problems in
securing funds. A somewhat revised edition appeared in
1985.

4680. FISHER, JAMES L. "Homosexuality: Kick and Kick-
       back," **Southern Medical Journal**, 77 (1984), 149-50.
Representative specimen of the conservative backlash
trend.

4681. FISHER, RICHARD B. **AIDS: Your Questions Answered.**
       London: Gay Men's Press, 1984. 126 pp.
Popular work in question-and-answer format addressed to
British gay men. See also: Graham Hancock and Enver
Carim, **AIDS: The Deadly Epidemic** (London: Gollancz, 1986;
191 pp.).

4682. FRIEDMAN-KIEN, ALVIN E., and LINDA J. LAUBENSTEIN
       (eds.). **AIDS: The Epidemic of Kaposi's Sarcoma and
       Opportunistic Infections.** New York: Masson, 1984.
       351 pp.
Forty-four papers by physicians and medical investigators;
many charts and photographs; index. The original article
by the dermatologist Moritz Kaposi (1837-1902) was entitled "Idiopathisches multiples Pigmentsarkom der Haut,"
Archiv für Dermatologie und Syphilis, 4 (1872), 265-73.

4683. FURSTENBERG, ANNE-LINDA, and MIRIAM OLSON. "Social
       Work and AIDS," **Social Work in Health Care**, 9:4
       (Summer 1984), 45-62.
General principles of practice are applied to the specif-
ics of dealing with AIDS and with social work tasks
involving patients, families and significant others.

4684. GAROOGIAN, RHODA. **AIDS, 1981-1983: An Annotated
       Bibliography.** Brooklyn: Compubibs, 1984. 92 pp.
About 400 entries, many with descriptive annotations,
arranged semestrally. Excludes "highly clinical references from the medical literature."

4685. GONG, VICTOR (ed.). **Understanding AIDS: A Compre-
       hensive Guide.** New Brunswick, NJ: Rutgers Univer-
       sity Press, 1985. 240 pp.
Papers by medical personnel written for the lay public
covering definitions; the clinical spectrum, implications; treatment; avoiding and coping with AIDS; and
health resources. Bibliography and index.

4686. GREENLY, MICHAEL (ed.). **Chronicle: The Human Side
       of AIDS.** New York: Irvington, 1986. 439 pp.
Assembles input from more than 100 people, to present a
composite picture of the impact of the disease.

4687. HINZ, STEFAN. **AIDS: Die Lust an der Seuche.** Rein-
       bek bei Hamburg: Rowohlt, 1984. 249 pp.
Medical information, together with interviews with people
with AIDS and others in West Germany.

4688. HIRSCH, DAN A., and ROGER W. ENLOW. "The Effects
       of the Acquired Immune Deficiency Syndrome on Gay
       Lifestyles and the Gay Individual," **Journal of the
       American Academy of Sciences,** 437 (1984), 273-82.
AIDS has elicited a spectrum of responses ranging from
panic, fear, and despair to feelings of closeness and
unity that have helped the gay community to organize a
long-term response to the epidemic.

4689. JOSEPH, JILL G., et al. "Coping with the Threat of
       AIDS: An Approach to Psychosocial Assessment,"
       American Psychologist, 39 (1984), 1297-1302.
Focuses on five areas of the psychosocial welfare of gay
males: obtaining qualitative data, developing inventories,
sampling in the gay community, building community networks, and characterizing the AIDS crisis.

4690. KAYAL, PHILIP. "'Morals,' Medicine and the AIDS
       Epidemic," **Journal of Religion and Health,** 24
       (1985), 218-38.
Evidence is given of the connnection between moral-
izing--largely of religious origin--and the response of
the medical establishment, leading to a tendency to
blame the victim.

4691. KRAMER, LARRY. **The Normal Heart.** New York: New
       American Library, 1985. 123 pp.
This play, an eviscerating work that has been frequently
performed, is largely autobiographical, reflecting the
author's passionate, sometimes strident campaign to
educate the public on AIDS. The play is part of a
growing body of drama and fiction reflecting the AIDS
crisis.

4692. LANDBECK, G. (ed.). **AIDS: Opportunistic Infections
       and Hemophilia: Proceedings of the First German
       Round Table Discussion on AIDS and Its Implications
       in Hemophilia.** Stuttgart: Schattauer, 1984. 128
       pp.
Emphasizes a non-homosexual risk group.

4693. LAURENCE, JEFFREY. "The Immune System in AIDS,"
       Scientific American, 253:6 (December 1985), 84-93.
New knowledge of how the AIDS virus alters the growth and
function of T4 lymphocytes may lead to treatments and
ultimately a vaccine.

4694. LAYGUES, HELENE. **SIDA: Temoignage sur la vie et la
       mort de Martin.** Paris: Hachette, 1985. 300 pp.
Narrates the experiences of a French victim of AIDS.

4695. LEIBOWITCH, JACQUES. **A Strange Virus of Unknown
       Origin.** Translated by Richard Howard. New York:
       Ballantine, 1985. 172 pp.
Overview by a French physician and medical researcher, who
posits an African origin for the disease.

4696. LIEBERSON, JONATHAN. "Anatomy of an Epidemic," **New
       York Review of Books** (August 18, 1983), 17-22.
Thoughts on the social implications of AIDS prompted by
ten recent books. See also his: "The Reality of AIDS,"
ibid. (January 16, 1986), pp. 43-48.

4697. LOPEZ, DIEGO J., and GEORGE S. GETZEL. "Helping
       Gay AIDS Patients in Crisis," **Social Casework,** 65
       (1984), 387-94.
From experiences at the Gay Men's Health Crisis (NYC),
outlines seven phases of service to the gay AIDS patient:
engagement and assessment, support of autonomy, explanation, support of the patient and indirect recognition
of death, monitoring of health status, personal support
networks and grief work, and care and advocacy for the
dying patient.

4698. MARTIN, JOHN L., and CAROLE S. VANCE. "Behavioral
       and Psychosocial Factors in AIDS: Methodological
       and Substantive Issues," **American Psychologist,** 39
       (1984), 1303-07.
Argues that dominance of the germ-theory model has led to
research that neglects lifestyle factors.

4699. McKUSICK, LEON, WILLIAM HORSTMAN, and THOMAS
       J. COATES. "AIDS and Sexual Behavior Reported by
       Gay Men in San Francisco," **American Journal of
       Public Health,** 75 (May 1985), 493-96.
Survey of 655 gay men conducted at the University of California at San Francisco shows substantial decrease in
number of sex partners and in "unsafe sex" among men in
low-risk situations. Those in high risk situations evi-
denced little change.

4700. MELDRUM, JULIAN. **A.I.D.S. through the British
       Media.** London: AIDS Action Group, 1984. ca. 64
       pp.
Bibliographical entries through June 1984 with some annotations, and index. Useful in tracing the evolution of
public awareness and emotion in one country.

4701. MILLER, ALAN V. **Gays and Acquired Immune Defici-
       ency Syndrome.** Second ed. Toronto: Canadian Gay
       Archives, 1983. 67 pp. (Canadian Gay Archives
       Publication no. 7)
This invaluable bibliography has about 1000 items, divided

according to medical press; the gay press (often neglected in such lists); and the mainstream press. Items in the Canadian Gay Archives are starred.

4702. MORIN, STEPHEN F., KENNETH A. CHARLES, and ALAN K. MALYON. "The Psychological Impact of AIDS on Gay Men," **American Psychologist**, 39 (1984), 1288-93.
Finds fear of death and dying, guilt, fear of lifestyle exposure, fear of contagion, loss of self-esteem, and a general sense of gloom among counseling clients. Psychologists should adopt a delicate balance of remaining sex-positive while recommending safer sex.

4703. NICHOLS, EVE K. **Mobilizing Against AIDS: The Unfinished Story of a Virus.** Cambridge, MA: Harvard University Press, 1986. 212 pp.
Synthesizes the AIDS session of the 1985 annual meeting of the Institute of Medicine of the National Academy of Sciences.

4704. NICHOLS, STUART E., and DAVID G. OSTROW. **Psychiatric Implications of Acquired Immune Deficiency Syndrome.** Washington, DC: American Psychiatric Press, 1984. 137 pp. (Clinical Insights Monographs)
Thirteen papers on medical aspects, psychiatric treatment, and social responses.

4705. NUNGESSER, LON G. **Epidemic of Courage: Facing AIDS in America.** New York: St. Martin's Press, 1986. 256 pp.
Frank interviews with seven PWAs (persons with AIDS), and with other concerned individuals.

4706. PANEM, SANDRA. "AIDS, Public Policy and Biomedical Research," **Chest,** 85 (1984), 416-22.
Documents the influence of the conservative backlash.

4707. PATTON, CINDY. **Sex and Germs: The Politics of AIDS.** Boston: South End Press, 1985. 250 pp.
Arguing for a more comprehensive understanding of sexuality and the body in political discourse, relates the fear of sexuality to the AIDS climate and the New Right attacks on gay people.

4708. PAUL, GERD, and LORETTA WALZ. **Hilfe und Selbsthilfe in San Francisco.** Berlin: Nissen, 1986. 144 pp.
Contrasts the pragmatic approach to AIDS in San Francisco with the more emotional response in Germany. Uses interview material.

4709. PAYNE, KENNETH W., and STEPHEN J. RISCH. "The Politics of AIDS," **Science for the People,** 16:5 (1984), 17-22.

Argues that an assault on the gay bathhouses is likely to
be the first step in a wide-ranging campaign against gay
institutions and freedoms.

4710. PEABODY, BARBARA. **The Screaming Room**. San Diego:
        Oak Tree, 1986. 254 pp.
A moving and literate account by a mother's ultimately
unsuccessful effort to save her son from death by AIDS.
See also Betty Clare Moffatt, **When Someone You Love Has
AIDS: A Book of Hope for Family and Friends** (Santa Monica:
IBS Press, 1986; 154 pp.).

4711. PURTILO, RUTH, JOSEPH SONNABEND, and DAVID PUR-
        TILO. "Confidentiality, Informed Consent and
        Untoward Social Consequences in Research on a 'New
        Killer Disease' (AIDS)," **Clinical Research**, 31:4
        (October 1983), 464-72.
Discusses some serious consequences for civil liberties.

4712. RELMAN, ARNOLD S., et al. "AIDS: The Emerging
        Ethical Issues," **Hastings Center Report**: Special
        Supplement (August 1985), 1-32.
Includes discussion of screening, epidemiological investigation, clinical care, public health, and media coverage.

4713. ROZENBAUM, WILLY, DIDIER SEUX, and ANNIE KOUCHNER.
        SIDA: Réalités et fantasmes. Paris: Editions
        P.O.L., 1984. 168 pp.
Account for the lay public in France, where despite a
relatively high number of cases, the public remained
remarkably calm. (SIDA = AIDS.)

4714. SCHMIDT, CASPER G. "The Group-Fantasy Origins of
        AIDS," **Journal of Psychohistory**, 12 (Summer 1984),
        37-78.
This eccentric article posits "a psychosocial origin for
AIDS," which is presented as group fantasy of scapegoating, somehow linked to fear of nuclear attack and neo-con-
servative political trends.

4715. SIMKINS, LAWRENCE, and MARK G. EBERHAGE. "Atti-
        tudes toward AIDS, Herpes II, and Toxic Shock
        Syndrome," **Psychological Reports**, 55 (1984),
        779-86.
A questionnaire administered to 232 Kansas City College
students showed that although male homosexuals were concerned about AIDS they did not appear to have lowered
their level of sexual activity.

4716. SLAFF, JAMES I., and JOHN K. BRUBAKER. **The AIDS
        Epidemic**. New York: Warner Books, 1985. 285 pp.
Comprehensive account for the lay (esp. heterosexual)
public. Part I is question-and-answer in format; part
II traces the history of the disease and future outlook,
with references.

4717. STAVER, SARI. "Psychiatrists' Broad Definition of
       'Pre-AIDS' Stirs Debate," **American Medical News**, 27
       (1984), 3-8.
Ideological overtones of the problem of determining the
onset of the disease proper.

4718. TIELMAN, ROB, and FRITS VAN GRIENSVEN. "Sociaal-
       wetenschappelijk AIDS-onderzoek," **Sociologische
       Gids**, 32 (1985), 416-30.
Reports on a psycho-social study of 1000 gay men begun at
Utrecht University which will examine such variables as
the frequency and character of blood-to-blood and sperm-
to-blood contacts, participation in networks, depression, identity, coping behavior, addiction, and lifestyle.

4718A. WINSTEN, JAY A. "Science and the Media: The
       Boundaries of Truth," **Health Affairs** (Spring 1985),
       5-23.
AIDS reporting in the broad context of the problematics
of publicity for medical research, including grandstanding
and sensationalism.

                    D. MEDICAL ARCHAEOLOGY

The history of medical theorizing about the causes of
homosexual behavior is a veritable museum of oddity.
Nonetheless, the story is interesting as a series of
chapters in the history of ideas. Moreover, some of these
notions are still active today as religious moralizing and
folklore, even sometimes as "science." For medical
writers of the 19th and early 20th century who were
specifically concerned with homosexuality, see "Pioneers,"
I.B; see also "Psychiatry," XVII.A-K.

4719. ARON, JEAN-PAUL, and ROGER KEMPF. **Le pénis et la
       démoralisation de l'Occident.** Paris: Grasset,
       1978. 310 pp.
Claims, improbably, that homosexuality was a taboo subject
in France until the time of Dr. Ambroise Tardieu in the
mid-19th century. Reissued unchanged as **La bourgeoisie,
le sexe et l'honneur** (Paris: Editions Complexe, 1984).

4720. AURELIANUS, CAELIUS. **On Acute Diseases & On
       Chronic Diseases.** Translated by I. E. Drabkin.
       Chicago: University of Chicago Press, 1950. 1019
       pp.
Translation of **De morbis acutis** and **De morbis chronicis**;
text and translation on facing pages. These texts, possibly composed in the 5th century of our era, are based on
Greek treatises by Soranus of Ephesus (early 2d century).
See pp. 901-05 for the ancient origin of the sickness
theory of homosexuality. A detailed commentary on the

relevant passages is provided by P. H. Schrijvers, **Eine
medizinische Erklärung der männlichen Homosexualität aus
der Antike** (Amsterdam: B. R. Grüner, 1985; 75 pp.); see
also Giuseppe Roccatagliata and Sandra Isetta, "Celio
Aureliano e il problema dell'omosessualità," **Archivio di
psicologia neurologia e psichiatria** (April-June 1980),
276-81.

4721. BRANDT, ALLAN M. **No Magic Bullet: A Social History
        of Venereal Disease in the United States since
        1880.** New York: Oxford University Press, 1985.
        320 pp.
Traces America's response to sexually transmitted diseases
from Victorian anxieties about syphilis to the current
fears about herpes and AIDS.

4722. BULLOUGH, VERN L. "Homosexuality and the Medical
        Model," **JH**, 1 (1974), 99-110.
Holds that in the 18th and especially the 19th century,
medical concepts about sexual deviation arose to reinforce
traditional religious concepts which were undergoing erosion. For some latter-day US documents of these currents,
see Jonathan Katz (ed.) **Gay American History** (New York:
Crowell, 1976), 129-207.

4723. BURNHAM, JOHN. "Early References to Homosexual
        Communities in American Medical Writings," **Medical
        Aspects of Human Sexuality,** 7 (August 1973), 36,
        40-49.
Claims that only in the early years of the 20th century,
as a result of vice raids, venereal disease, and the
writings of psychiatrists, did the American medical profession slowly learn of the existence of homosexual
communities in major cities.

4724. CASPER, JOHANN LUDWIG. **A Handbook of the Practice
        of Forensic Medicine.** Translated by G. W. Bal-
        four. London: New Sydenham Society, 1859-65. 4
        vols.
In this influential text by a German physician (1796-
1864), see vol. 3, pp. 328-46 on "disputed unnatural
lewdness." Translation of **Handbuch der gerichtlichen
Medicin** (Berlin: Hirschwald, 1856-58), of which a thor-
oughly revised edition was prepared by Carl Liman in
1881 (Berlin: Hirschwald). As the "Casper-Liman" it was
the standard textbook of forensic medicine in German
universities until 1933.

4725. CHARCOT, JEAN-MARTIN, and VALENTIN MAGNAN. "In-
        versions du sens genital et autres perversions
        génitales," **Archives de Neurologie,** nos. 7 and 12
        (January-February and November 1882), 55-60;
        296-322.
Charcot (1825-1893) was a noted French alienist, who influenced Freud and others. He introduced the term **inversion** (coined by Arrigo Tamassia in Italy in 1878) into

French medical discourse.

4726. CHAUNCEY, GEORGE, JR. "From Sexual Inversion to
        Homosexuality: Medicine and the Changing Concep-
        tualization of Female Deviance," **Salmagundi**, no.
        58-59 (1982-83), 114-46.
Scholarly study of how "homoerotic desire and relations"
between women were understood by U.S. medical professionals during the period 1880-1930.

4727. CHEVALIER, JULIEN. **Une maladie de la personnal-
        ité: l'inversion sexuelle: psychophysiologie,
        sociologie, tératologie, aliénation mentale,
        psychologie morbide, anthropologie, médecine
        judiciaire.** Lyon: Storck, 1893. 520 pp.
An expansion of his 1886 medical thesis, this massive
work helped to spread the inversion model of homosexuality.

4728. COMFORT, ALEX. **The Anxiety Makers: Some Curious
        Preoccupations of the Medical Profession.** New
        York: Dell, 1969. 208 pp.
Popular account of medically based scares, esp. the
mania concerning masturbation.

4729. CONRAD, PETER, and JOSEPH W. SCHNEIDER. **Deviants
        and Medicalization: From Badness to Sickness.**
        St. Louis: C. V. Mosley, 1980. 311 pp.
Chapter 7, "Homosexuality from Sickness to Lifestyle"
(pp. 172-214), seeks to chart the transition in Western
civilization from a religious conception of homosexuality as sin to a medico-psychiatric conception, and
(finally) to the notion of homosexuality as an alterna-
tige lifestyle. Useful as a survey, but theoretically
disappointing.

4730. DRINKA, GEORGE FREDERICK. **The Birth of Neurosis:
        Myth, Malady, and the Victorians.** New York: Simon
        & Schuster, 1984. 431 pp.
Concentrates on the typology of neurotic illnesses de-
veloped by physicians and psychiatrists, ca. 1870-1900.
See esp. Chapter 7, "A Proliferation of Perversions, an
Epidemic of Murder" (pp. 152-83). Superficial.

4731. FADERMAN, LILLIAN. "The Morbidification of Love
        Between Women by 19th-Century Sexologists," **JH**, 4
        (1978), 73-98.
Argues that for the past 100 years medical science and
psychology have "moribidified" intense love relationships between women by inventing ills that ostensibly
accompany such affection and by denying the seriousness
of the affection where such ills are not present.

4732. HALLER, JOHN S., and ROBIN M. HALLER. **The Physici-
        an and Sexuality in Victorian America.** Urbana:
        University of Illinois Press, 1974. 331 pp.

Analysis of 19th-century medical writings on sex, with
many useful references.

4733. HENKE, ADOLF CHRISTIAN HEINRICH. **Lehrbuch der
       gerichtlichen Medicin.** Seventh ed. Stuttgart:
       E. F. Walters, 1832. 471 pp.
Seventh considerably revised edition of an influential
handbook of forensic medicine first published in 1812.
See pp. 105-06 on "unnatural copulation," where Henke
claims that physical injury invariably results.

4734. "HIPPOCRATES." **Hippocratic Writings.** Edited by
       G. E. R. Lloyd. Translated by J. Chadwick, W. N.
       Mann, and others. New York: Penguin, 1978. 380
       pp.
See pp. 67 (The Oath) and 160-67 (Airs, Waters and
Places, 22; on the causes of effeminacy among the Scyth-
ians). The Hippocratic corpus was actually composed by a
number of Greek medical writers over several centuries.
For a fuller selection with Greek texts, see **Hippocrates.**
Edited by W. H. S. Jones. (Cambridge, MA: Harvard Univer-
sity Press: Loeb Classical Library, 1923-31; 4 vols.).

4735. HOPFNER, THEODOR. **Das Sexualleben der Griechen und
       Römer.** Prague: J. G. Calve, 1938. First vol.,
       first half (all issued), 455 pp.
This monograph by a professor at the German university in
Prague, on the primary secondary sex characteristics of
the human male and female, is the fullest modern account
of the knowledge of the Greeks and Romans of the physical
aspects of sexuality.

4736. IRELAND, WILLIAM. **The Blot upon the Brain.** Edin-
       burgh: Bell and Bradfute, 1885. 374 pp.
In its day an influential treatise on insanity and "moral
insanity" (including sexual deviation).

4737. JACQUART, DANIELLE, and CLAUDE THOMASSET. **Sexual-
       ité et savoir médical au moyen âge.** Paris: Presses
       Universitaires de France, 1985. 269 pp.
Attempts a synthesis of medieval medical knowledge about
sexuality, esp. as derived from Greek and Arabic sources.
Homosexuality is briefly discussed, pp. 213-28.

4738. JAMES, ROBERT. **A Medical Dictionary.** London: T.
       Osborne, 1743-45. 3 vols.
See articles on Ganymede, malthacos, tribade, etc. A
French edition was prepared by Denis Diderot and others:
Dictionnaire universel de medecine (Paris: Briasson,
1746-48; 6 vols.).

4739. KAAN, HEINRICH. **Psychopathia sexualis.** Leipzig:
       Leopold Voss, 1844. 124 pp.
Said to be the first comprehensive nosology of human sexual behavior. Argues for a universal perception of sexual
pathology as demonstrated by childhood sexual deviancy.

The title was purloined by Richard von Krafft-Ebing for
his famous work of   four decades later.

4740. LANTÉRI-LAURA, GEORGES. **Lecture des perversions:**
       histoire de leur appropriation médicale. Paris:
       Masson, 1979. 160 pp.
Study of the entry of the idea of perversion into medical
discourse, focusing on the 19th century.

4741. LAUMONIER, DE. "La thérapeutique individuelle de
       l'inversion sexuelle," **Revue de l'hypnotisme,** 23
       (1908), 41-42.
This entire issue of the journal is devoted to homosexuality.

4742. LESKY, ERNA. **Die Zeugungs- und Vererbungslehren**
       der Antike und ihr Nachwirken. Mainz: 1950. 201
       pp. (Abhandlungen der Akademie der Wissenschaft und
       Literatur, 19)
Careful study of Greco-Roman theories of procreation, including their role in explaining the etiology of same-sex
behavior.

4743. LYNCH, MICHAEL. "'Here Is Adhesiveness': From
       Friendship to Homosexuality," **Victorian Studies,** 29
       (1985), 67-96.
Traces the concept of "adhesiveness" with reference to
same-sex affection as it was developed by phrenological
circles in Britain and North America in the 19th century.

4744. MONEY, JOHN. **The Destroying Angel: Sex, Fitness**
       and Food in the legacy of Degeneracy Theory, Graham
       Crackers, Kellogg's Corn Flakes, and American
       Health History. Buffalo: Prometheus Books, 1985.
       213 pp.
Attempts to chart, from their beginnings in European
tradition, the origins of antisexualism in American health
care.

4745. MUELLER, JOHANN VALENTIN. **Entwurf einer gericht-**
       lichen Arzneiwissenschaft. Frankfurt am Main: An-
       drea, 1796.
In Chapter 7 ("On Unnatural Indecency, or Sodomy," pp.
131-41), Mueller holds that masturbation leads to homosexual behavior, and that there are really no essential
differences among sexual sins. The sinner's demeanor reveals his practice.

4746. NYE, ROBERT A. **Crime, Madness, and Politics in**
       Modern France: The Medical Concepts of National
       Decline. Princeton: Princeton University Press,
       1985. 368 pp.
Discusses a medical concept of deviance that developed
in France in the second half of the 19th century, when
medical models of cultural crisis linked thinking about
crime, mental illness, prostitution, alcoholism, suicide

and other pathologies to French national decline.

4747. PACHARZINA, KLAUS, and KARIN ALBRECHT-DESIRAT.
"Die Last der Aerzte: Homosexualität als klinisches
Bild von den Anfängen bis heute," in J. S. Hohmann
(ed.), **Der unterdrückte Sexus.** Lollar: Achenbach,
1977, pp. 97-112.
A somewhat turgid survey of medical opinion on homosexuality over the centuries. The main part of the volume, however, reprints some hard-to-find older texts.

4748. REYDELLET, PIERRE. "Pédérastie." In: **Dictionnaire
des sciences médicales.** Paris: Panckoucke, 1819,
vol. 40, pp. 37-45.
An inquiry on the probable causes of homosexuality; influential.

4749. SALLE, EUSEBE DE. "Médecine legale." In: **Encyclo-
pédie des sciences médicales.** Paris: 1835, vol. 9,
chapter 41, pp. 2246-56.
Perhaps the first mention in modern medical literature of
the contrast between acquired and congenital homosexuality.

4750. SCHRENK-NOTZING, ALBERT VON. "Zur suggestiven
Behandlung der konträren Geschlechtsempfindung,"
Centralblatt für Nervenheilkunde und Psychiatrie,
1899, 257-60.
Advocated hypnotism as a cure for inversion. See also
his: **The Use of Hypnotism in Psychopathia Sexualis, with
Especial Reference to Contrary Sexual Instinct.** [German
original 1895] Translated by C. G. Chaddock. (New
York: Institute for Research in Hypnosis Publication
Society, 1956; 320 pp.).

4751. SZASZ, THOMAS. **The Manufacture of Madness: A Com-
Comparative Study of the Inquisition and the Mental
Health Movement.** New York: Harper and Row, 1970.
385 pp.
One of a number of books by a prolific author who has
done much to delegitimize coercive psychiatry. This
volume offers considerable discussion of sodomy in relation to heresy and witchcraft in the late middle ages.

4752. TARCZYLO, THÉODORE. **Sexe et liberté au siècle des
Lumières.** Paris: Presses de la Renaissance, 1983.
311 pp.
Presents some unenlightened medical attitudes in the 18th
century, with special reference to the masturbation phobia
popularized by Dr. Tissot.

4753. WEEKS, JEFFREY. "'Sins and Diseases': Some Notes
on Homosexuality in the Nineteenth Century," **History Workshop,** 1 (1976), 211-19.
Some British data, reviewed by a social-constructionist
historian.

4754. ZACCHIA, PAOLO (PAULUS). **Questiones medico-
        legales.** Revised ed. Frankfurt am Main: Johannes
        Melchior Bencard, 1688. 3 vols.
First edition, Rome and Amsterdam, 1621-35. Zacchia, a
Roman physician at the papal court (1584-1659), is regarded as the founder of the discipline of forensic medicine. In Book IV, quaestio V, he deals with the forensic
signs of the violation of boys.

XXIV.   BIOLOGY

A.   GENERAL

It is tempting, but simplistic to attribute homosexual
behavior simply to biological factors. Yet to exclude
such factors altogether, stigmatizing this kind of study
as "biologism," as is done by some environmentalists and
egalitarians, would be to err in the opposite direction.
It is true that some studies seeking to demonstrate biological foundations of homosexual behavior have been
poorly designed and tendentious, but future work may be
more convincing. See also "Social Sex Roles," XIV.L.

4755. BAKER, SUSAN W. "Biological Influences on Human
        Sex and Gender," **Signs,** 6 (1980), 80-96.
Holds that the bulk of evidence from studies on human
beings does not support the thesis that prenatal environment is responsible for sex object choice in adolescence.

4756. BARLOW, DAVID H. "Plasma Testosterone Levels in
        Male Homosexuality: A Failure to Replicate," **Ar-
        chives of Sexual Behavior,** 3 (1974), 571-75.
Findings fail to confirm the relation, posted by R. Kolod-
ny's group and others, between degree of homosexuality and
plasma testosterone level. See also: L. Birk et al.,
"Serum Testosterone Levels in Homosexual Men," **New England
Journal of Medicine,** 289 (1973), 1236-38.

4757. BEACH, FRANK A. **Hormones and Behavior.** New York:
        Paul B. Hoeber, 1949. 368 pp
Concludes that, in comparison with animals, hormonal
effects are far less influential in man, where they are
overriden by psychological and social factors. This difference accounts for the lack of success of etiological
studies in human homosexuality that attribute it to
biological/constitutional factors.

4758. BIRKE, LYNDA I. A. "Is Homosexuality Hormonally
        Determined?" **JH,** 6:4 (1981), 35-49.
Considers two types of research (1) mesurement of hormone
levels in adult populations; and (2) hypothesis of behavioral determination by prenatal hormones. Concludes that
the underlying theories are generally naive; their popularity is to be explained by the their perceived potential
in "controlling" homosexuality. See also her: "From Sin
to Sickness: Hormonal Theories of Lesbianism," in Ruth
Hubbard et al. (eds.), **Biological Woman--The Convenient
Myth.** (Cambridge, MA: Schenkman, 1982), 71-90.

4759. DOERR, PETER, et al. "Plasma Testosterone,

Estradiol, and Semen Analysis in Male Homosexuals," **Archives of General Psychiatry,** 29 (1973),
829-33.
Contends that elevated plasma estradiol concentrations of
the homosexual group are a biological feature of this
group and may be associated with homosexual behavior. See
also Doerr et al., "Further Studies on Sex Hormones in
Male Homosexuals," ibid., 33 (1976), 611-14.

4760. DÖRNER, GÜNTER, et al. "A Neuroendocrine Predis-
        position for Homosexuality in Men," **Archives of
        Sexual Behavior,** 4 (1975), 1-8.
Reports that, in male rats, androgen deficiency during a
critical hypothalamic organizational period was found to
give rise to a predominantly female-differentiated brain,
homosexual behavior, and demonstration of a positive
estrogen feedback effect. Despite methodological criticisms on various grounds, this East German researcher and
his colleagues have presented their thesis in over a hundred articles and papers. See, e.g., Paul H. Van Dyck, "A
Critique of Dörner's Analysis of Hormonal Data from Bisexual Males," **Journal of Sex Research,** 20 (1984), 412-14.
See also: Anke Ehrhardt et al., "Sexual Orientation
after Prenatal Exposure to Exogenous Estrogen," **Archives
of Sexual Behavior,** 14 (1985), 57-77.

4761. FAUSTO-STERLING, ANNE. **Myths of Gender: Biological
        Theories about Women and Men.** New York: Basic
        Books, 1985. 258 pp.
A feminist scientist argues that there is no unbiased
research in the socially charged area of sex differences, which (she holds) are much less significant than
usually believed.

4762. FRIEDLÄNDER, BENEDICT. "Entwurf zu reizphysiolog-
        ischen Auslese der erotischen Anziehung unter Zu-
        grundelegung vorwiegend homosexuellen Materials,"
        JfsZ, 7 (1905), 387-462.
This study expands the ideas of physiological attrac-
tion--based in part on what would now be termed phero-
mones--adumbrated in his better known book of 1904,
Renaissance des Eros Uranios.

4763. FRIEDMAN, RICHARD C., et al. "Hormones and Sexual
        Orientation in Men," **American Journal of Psychi-
        atry,** 134 (1977), 571-72.
Finds that the mean plasma androstenedione level for
homosexuals was significantly greater than for heterosexuals. See also Friedman and Andrew G. Frantz, "Plasma
Prolactin Levels in Male Homosexuals," **Hormones and Behavior,** 9 (1977), 19-22; and Friedman et al., "Psychological Development and Blood Levels of Sex Steroids in
Male Identical Twins of Divergent Sexual Orientation,"
Journal of Nervous and Mental Disease, 163 (1976), 282-88.

4764. GARTRELL, NANETTE K. "Hormones and Homosexuality,"

in: William Paul et al. (eds.), **Homosexuality:
Social, Psychological and Biological Issues.**
Beverly Hills, CA: Sage, 1982, pp. 169-82.
Examines research with respect to testosterone levels
hypothesized as lower in homosexual men and higher in
lesbian women, and with respect to purported hormonal excesses or deficiencies in the fetus in the uterus. Concludes that the evidence for hormonal theories of homosexuality is weak. See also Gartrell et al., "Plasma Testosterone in Homosexual and Heterosexual Women," **American
Journal of Psychiatry,** 134 (1977), 1117-19.

4765. GLADUE, BRIAN A., et al. "Neuroendocrine Response
to Estrogen and Sexual Orientation," **Science,** 225
(September 9, 1984), 1496-99.
Presents evidence for suggesting that homosexual men
process hormones differently from heterosexual men.

4766. GOLDSCHMIDT, RICHARD. "Die biologischen Grundlagen
der konträren Sexualität und des Hermaphroditismus
beim Menschen," **Archiv für Rassen- und Gesell-
schafts-Biologie,** 12 (1916), 1-14.
On the basis of experiments in breeding intersexes in but-
terflies, the author argues that homosexuality is part of
a continuum of normal variations within homo sapiens. On
him see Leonie K. Piternick (ed.), **Richard Goldschmidt,
Controversial Geneticist and Creative Biologist** (Basel and
Boston: Birkhauser Verlag, 1980; 154 pp.; Experientia
Supplementum, 35), which concludes that his work on sex
determination and intersexuality remains controversial and
in need of further verification.

4767. HODANN, MAX. "Neue Forschungen zur Kenntnis der
hereditarphysiologischen Grundlagen sexueller
Zwischenstufen," **JfsZ,** 15 (1915), 59-68.
Presents then-new research on the hereditary-physiological
basis of sexual intermediate types.

4768. HOULT, THOMAS F. "Human Sexuality in Biological
Perspective: Theoretical and Methodological Considerations," **JH,** 9:2-3 (1983-84), 137-55.
The results of a review of the evidence suggest that
claims for the biological model are questionable inasmuch
as the evidence for the model either extrapolates from
animal studies (and thus is not as such applicable to
human behavior) or is inconclusive, contradictory, and
methodologically deficient. Hoult prefers a social-learn-
ing model.

4769. JAMES, SHEELAH, et al. "Significance of Androgen
Levels in the Aetiology and Treatment of Homosexuality," **Psychological Medicine,** 7 (1977), 427-29.
Finds that androgen levels have no etiological significance in treatment-seeking homosexuals and have no relevance as indicators of treatment outcome.

4770. KINSEY, ALFRED C. "Criteria for Hormonal Explana-
      tion of the Homosexual," **Journal of Clinical
      Endocrinology**, 1 (1941), 424-28.
Weighing previous research, Kinsey seeks to set forth
standards for judging future endocrinological studies.
Contends that it is a mistake to regard homosexuals and
heterosexuals as two distinct types, rather than as points
on a continuum.

4771. KOLODNY, ROBERT C., et al. "Plasma Testosterone
      and Semen Analysis in Male Homosexuals," **New
      England Journal of Medicine**, 285 (1971), 1170-74.
This much discussed study reports finding that testosterone measurements in predominantly or exclusively homosexual men were significantly lower than in heterosexual
controls. Other studies failed to replicate the findings;
cf. e.g. D. H. Barlow, above.

4772. KRELL, L., et al. "Beziehungen zwischen klinisch
      manifester Homosexualität und dem Oestrogenfeed-
      back-Effekt," **Dermatologische Monatschrift**, 165
      (1975), 567-72.
Reports that under experimental conditions homosexual men
have a positive feedback effect in resonse to LH serum,
while heterosexual men do not.

4773. LANG, THEO. **The Difference Between a Man and a
      Woman.** New York: John Day, 1971. 413 pp.
See pp. 19, 52-57, 107-08, 154, 155-61, 222, 329-30, 332,
340. A constitutional biologist treats the problems of
homosexuality, transvestism, and transsexualism with
insight and tolerance.

4774. MACCULLOCH, MALCOLM J. "Biological Aspects of
      Homosexuality," **Journal of Medical Ethics**, 6
      (1980), 133-38.
Contends that the behavior of primary male homosexuals
has as its essential cause a female differentiated
brain. See also MacCulloch and John L. Waddington,
"Neuroendocrine Mechanisms and the Aetiology of Male and
Female Homosexuality," **British Journal of Psychiatry**,
139 (1981), 341-45.

4775. MARGOLIESE, M. SYDNEY. "Homosexuality: A New
      Endocrine Correlate," **Hormones and Behavior**, 1
      (1970), 151-55.
A well-publicized report on testosterone breakdown, which
further research failed to substantiate.

4776. MEYER-BAHLBURG, HEINO F. L. "Sex Hormones and Male
      Homosexuality in Comparative Perspective," **Archives
      of Sexual Behavior**, 6 (1977), 297-325.
Well-informed review of literature and critique of results
of the endocrinological/hormonal approach to the measurement and therapy of male homosexuality. See also his:
"Sex Hormones and Female Homosexuality: A Critical Exam-

ination," ibid., 8 (1979), 101-19.

4777. MONEY, JOHN. "Gender-Transposition Theory and
       Homosexual Genesis," **Journal of Sex and Marital
       Therapy,** 10 (1984), 75-82.
Discusses the implications of prenatal hormonal programming of the sexual brain, as well as postnatal social
programming for gender transposition, in relation to the
genesis of homosexuality.

4778. MONEY, JOHN. "Genetic and Chromosomal Aspects of
       Homosexuality," in: Judd Marmor (ed.), **Homosexual
       Behavior: A Modern Reappraisal.** New York: Basic
       Books, 1980, 59-72.
Reviews the history of "speculative genetics" about homosexuality; statistical genetics; cytogenetics; and
matched-pair studies. With 45 references. See also Money
and Jean Dalery, "Iatrogenic Homosexuality: Gender Identity in Seven 46,XX Chromosomal Females with Hyperadren-
ocortical Hermaphroditism Born with a Penis, Three Reared
as Boys, Four Reared as Girls," **JH,** 1 (1976), 357-71.

4779. NEWMARK, STEPHEN R., et al. "Gonadotropin, Estrad-
       iol, and Testosterone Profiles in Homosexual Men,"
       American Journal of Psychiatry, 136 (1979), 767-71.
Results suggest that there may be subtle differences in
gonadotropin and estradiol secretion in homosexual subjects that can be detected only by repeated sampling.

4780. PERLOFF, WILLIAM H. "Hormones and Homosexuality,"
       in: Judd Marmor (ed.), **Sexual Inversion: The
       Multiple Roots of Homosexuality.** New York: Basic
       Books, 1965, pp. 44-70.
Emphasizes the lack of definite evidence for hormonal
factors in homosexual behavior.

4781. PILLARD, RICHARD C., et al. "Plasma Testosterone
       Levels in Homosexual Men," **Archives of Sexual
       Behavior,** 3 (19740, 453-58.
Testosterone levels were not related to relative masculinity or femininity or to any other psychological variables
measured.

4782. RABOCH, JAN, and KAREL NEDOMA. "Sex Chromatin and
       Sexual Behavior: A Study of 36 Men with Female
       Nuclear Pattern and of 194 Homosexuals," **Psychoso-
       matic Medicine,** 20 (1958), 55-59.
In the adult group of exclusive or nearly exclusive homosexuals, testes of subnormal size were found in only 9 of
the total 194 cases. The finding of female sex chromatin
in homosexual men is likely to be pure coincidence.

4783. RICHARDSON, DIANE. "Theoretical Perspectives on
       Homosexuality," in: John Hart and Diane Richardson
       (eds.), **The Theory and Practice of Homosexuality.**
       Boston: Routledge and Kegan Paul, 1981, pp. 5-37.

Clear presentation for the lay reader of the theoretical
parameters which should govern hypothesis formation and
research in this sphere.

4784. RICKETTS, WENDELL. "Biological Research on Homo-
       sexuality: Ansell's Cow or Occam's Razor?" **JH**,
       10 (1984), 65-93.
Reviews research based on the assumption that homosexuality can be traced to heredity, prenatal brain differentiation, or effects of gonadotropins in adulthood,
finding it inadequate. Useful bibliography (86 references).

4785. RUSE, MICHAEL. "Nature/Nurture: Reflections on
       Approaches to the Study of Homosexuality," **JH**,
       10:3-4 (1984), 141-51.
Cautions against undue fear of biological approaches to
the study of homosexuality, which should not hamper worth-
while research. Urges that both biological and environmental factors be considered in seeking to render a true
picture of homosexuality.

4786. SEABORG, DAVID M. "Sexual Orientation, Behavioral
       Plasticity, and Evolution," **JH**, 10:3-4 (1984), 153-
       58.
Proposes that the species flexibility that allows human
beings to become homosexual may result from the evolution of the capacity to learn, the complexity of the
central nervous system, and behavioral plasticity in general.

4787. TOURNEY, GARFIELD. "Hormones and Homosexuality,"
       in: Judd Marmor (ed.), **Homosexual Behavior: A
       Modern Reappraisal.** New York: Basic Books, 1980,
       pp. 41-58.
Reviews the literature, regarding the state of the ques-
tion at the time of writing as largely inconclusive,
but with some optimism for future progress. Contrast
L. I. A. Birke; and W. Ricketts, above. See also: Tour-
ney and Lon M. Hatfield, "Androgen Metabolism in Schizo-
phrenics, Homosexuals, and Normal Controls," **Biological
Psychiatry**, 6 (1973), 23-36; Tourney et al., "Hormonal
Relationships in Homosexual Men," **American Journal of
Psychiatry**, 132 (1975), 288-90.

4788. WEINBERG, THOMAS F. "Biology, Ideology, and the
       Reification of Developmental Stages in the Study of
       Homosexual Identities," **JH**, 10:3/4 (1984), 77-84.
Discerns several problems stemming from the use of biologically derived models: (1) stages, which are researchers'
constructs rather than reflections of the subjects' perceptions, become reified; (2) moral assumptions embedded
in biologically derived models become incorporated in
sociopsychological theories of identity; and (3) the models tend to be constructed in a monistic, linear fashion,
excluding the consideration of other approaches.

4789. WILSON, WILLIAM P., et al. "Arousal from Sleep of
       Male Homosexuals," **Biological Psychiatry**, 6 (1973),
       81–84.
Homosexual males differed from normal males in being significantly more arousable in Stage 3 and 4 of the sleep
cycle, as are normal females.

                        B. SOCIOBIOLOGY

Through the publications of Edwin O. Wilson and his colleagues at Harvard, sociobiology became a much-discussed
topic in the 1970s. Most of the controversy revolves
around human behavior, since it is generally conceded that
the sociobiological approach has proved valuable in some
animal studies. With regard to human homosexuality,
sociobiology purports to solve the riddle of how this
behavior pattern can accord with the evolutionary theory
of sexual selection focusing on procreation by proposing
models of "inclusive fitness" in which homosexual behavior
is genetically functional.

4790. FUTUYMA, DOUGLAS J., and STEPHEN J. RISCH. "Sexual
       Orientation, Sociobiology, and Evolution," **JH,**
       9:2-3 (1983-84), 157–68.
Concludes that there is no reliable evidence that homosexual and heterosexual orientations are caused by genetic
differences. Evolutionary theory provides no guide to
morality or ethical progress, nor for appropriate social
attitudes toward homosexuality.

4791. GENGLE, DEAN, and NORMAN D. MURPHY. "Why We Are
       Gay: Revolutionary Extinction? An Evolutionary
       Model of the Origin of Sexualities," **Advocate,**
       no. 253 (November 1, 1978), 15–21.
Speculative theoretical model of the psychobiological
components of gender, gender identity, and sexual orientation.

4792. KIRSCH, JOHN, and JAMES RODMAN. "The Natural
       History of Homosexuality," **Yale Scientific Maga-
       zine,** 51:3 (1977), 7–13.
Concise statement of the case for the sociobiological
approach.

4793. MILLER, ALAN V. **The Genetic Imperative: Fact and
       Fantasy in Sociobiology: A Bibliography.** Toronto:
       Canadian Gay Archives, 1979. 107 pp. (CGA Public-
       ations, 2)
In this useful roster, presenting both pro and con publications, see esp. "Gays," pp. 82–83. For representative
papers on general questions posed by the emergence of
this controversial discipline in the 1970s, see Arthur L.

Caplan (ed.), **The Sociobiology Debate: Readings on Ethical and Scientific Issues.** (New York: Harper and Row, 1978; 514 pp.).

4794. RUSE, MICHAEL. **Is Science Sexist? And Other Problems of Biological Science.** Boston: D. Reidel, 1981. 299 pp.
Rebuttal of some current critiques of the biological theory of evolution (neo-Darwinism). See esp. Chapter 10, "Are Homosexuals Sick?" (pp. 245-72). See also his: **Sociobiology: Sense or Nonsense?** (Boston: D. Reidel, 1979; 231 pp.).

4795. SYMONDS, DONALD. **The Evolution of Human Society.** New York: Oxford University Press, 1979. 358 pp.
Primatologist's presentation situating the emergence of the difference between men and women in the long hunting--and-gathering stage of human evolution. See Chapter 9, "Test Cases: Hormones and Homosexuals" (pp. 286-305).

4796. TRIVERS, ROBERT L. "The Evolution of Reciprocal Altruism," **Quarterly Review of Biology,** 46 (1971), 35-57.
Influential study by a Harvard ornithologist and sociobiologist, setting forth a general theory which has been used to explain the "inclusive fitness" of homosexuality.

4797. WEINRICH, JAMES D. **Human Reproductive Strategy: I. Environmental Predictability and Reproductive Strategy; Effects of Social Class and Race. II. Homosexuality and Non-Reproduction; Some Evolutionary Models.** Cambridge, MA: Harvard University, 1976. 231 pp. (unpublished Ph.D. dissertation--biology)
Part 1 mainly concerns heterosexual behavior. Part 2 is a theoretical exposition of the ways in which certain post-Darwinian evolutionary models--esp. Hamilton's kin selection--can be used to understand homosexuality, transvestism, and transsexualism.

4798. WILSON, EDWARD O. **On Human Nature.** Cambridge, MA: Harvard University Press, 1978. 260 pp.
Presentation of sociobiology for the lay reader by the Harvard entomologist who is its best known proponent. See pp. 142-47 for his argument in favor of "a strong possibility that homosexuality is normal in a biological sense."

C. TWIN STUDIES

Twins have for some time interested researchers as an opportunity for testing the inherited nature of specific traits--among them homosexual behavior. To be valid,

however, such studies must be on twins who are both monozygotic (i.e. from a single egg: "identical" twins) and
reared apart. The difficulty of building up a sufficient
pool of such individuals, as well as defects that have
been detected in research designs, have thus far kept
such reports from making any significant impact.

4799.   DAVISON, K., et al. "A Male Monozygotic Twinship
        Discordant for Homosexuality: A Repertory Grid
        Study," **British Journal of Psychiatry,** 118 (1971),
        675-82.
Reports on a pair of 18-year old male identical twins
discordant for overt homosexuality. Subsequently, the
deviant twin was apparently "cured" through aversion
therapy.

4800.   DIAMOND, MILTON. "Sexual Identity, Monozygotic
        Twins Reared in Discordant Sex Roles and a BBC
        Follow-up," **Archives of Sexual Behavior,** 11 (1982),
        181-86.
Controversy over a pair of monozygotic twin boys, of whom
one accidentally had his penis oblated during circumcision. The child was reassigned as a girl. Concludes
that nature rather than nurture determines one's sexual
identity.

4801.   FARBER, SUSAN. **Identical Twins Reared Apart.** New
        York: Basic Books, 1981. 383 pp.
Although this book discusses many striking behavioral
similarities between twins, the evidence presented regarding homosexual behavior is inconclusive (pp. 221-24).

4801.   GEDDA, LUIGI. **Studio dei gemelli.** Rome: Edizioni
        Orizzonte Medico, 1951. 1381 pp.
On pp. 738-39 the author summarizes the work of several
previous investigators on homosexuality in monozygotic
twins. The twins concordant for homosexuality were all
male. There is also a useful 240-page bibliography on
twin studies in general.

4802.   HABEL, H. "Zwillingsuntersuchungen an Homosexuel-
        len," **Zeitschrift für Sexualforschung,** 1 (1950),
        168-80.
Presents five pairs of identical twins concordant for
homosexuality.

4803.   HESTON, L. L., and JAMES SHIELDS. "Homosexuality
        in Twins: A Family Study and a Registry Study,"
        Archives of General Psychiatry, 18 (1968), 149-60.
Considers an unusual family of 14 siblings, including
three pairs of male monozygotic twins, two pairs of which
were homosexual.

4804.   KALLMANN, FRANZ J. "Comparative Twin Study on the
        Genetic Aspects of Male Homosexuality," **Journal of**

Nervous and Mental Disease, 115 (1952), 283-98.
From case histories of 85 twin male homosexuals, found
that monozygotic twins were very similar in their sex
behavior, even when reared apart. See also his: "Twin
and Sibship Study of Overt Male Homosexuality," **American
Journal of Human Genetics,** 4 (1952), 136-46. On the
author, and the political opposition to his approach, see
Elliot S. Gershon, "The Historical Context of Franz Kallmann and Psychiatric Genetics," **Archiv fur Psychiatrie
und Nervenkrankheiten,** 229 (1981), 273-76.

4805. KLINTWORTH, GORDON K. "A Pair of Male Monozygotic
      Twins Discordant for Homosexuality," **Journal of
      Nervous and Mental Disease,** 135 (1962), 113-25.
Study of a pair of 20-year old male twins in South Africa,
one homosexual, the other heterosexual. Holds that
this discordance does not invalidate the hypothesis of
genetic determination of sexual orientation.

4806. LANGE, JOHANNES. **Verbrechen als Schicksal: Studien
      an kriminellen Zwillingen.** Leipzig: Georg Thieme
      Verlag, 1929. 96 pp.
On pp. 73-76 the author describes a pair of monozygotic
male twins discordant for homosexuality, which he assigns
to brain damage suffered in early childhood by the twin
who later became a hustler. The heterosexual twin exhibited no criminal activity.

4807. PERKINS, MURIEL W. "Homosexuality in Female
      Monozygotic Twins," **Behavior Genetics,** 3 (1973),
      387-88.
Describes a set of 45-year old identical female twins
with a history of homosexuality.

4808. PUTERBAUGH, GEOFF. "Born Gay? Hand Preference and
      Sex Preference," **Cabirion,** 10 (1984), 12-18.
Reexamines the research data on twins, concluding that
there is a significant concordance for identical (though
not for fraternal) twins for homosexuality.

4809. RAINER, JOHN D., et al. "Homosexuality and Hetero-
      sexuality in Identical Twins," **Psychosomatic
      Medicine,** 22 (1960), 251-59.
Seeks to discount evidence for concordance of monozygotic
twins for homosexuality.

4810. SANDERS, JACOB. "Homosexuelle Zwillingen," **Genet-
      ica,** 16 (1934), 401-34.
Reports six pairs of monozygotic twins concordant for
homosexuality. A seventh case was discordant but pseudohomosexual, probably the result of earlier epileptic
fits. The author upholds Hirschfeld's theories and
classifications. A summary of the article also appeared
under the title "Homosexueele tweelingen," **Nederlands
Tijdschrift voor Geneeskunde,** 78 (1934), 3346-52.

4811. ZUGER, BERNARD. "Monozygotic Twins Discordant for
       Homosexuality: Report of a Pair and Significance of
       the Phenomenon," **Comprehensive Psychiatry,** 17
       (1976), 661-69
Case study of a pair of male identical twins who showed
differences in gender role behavior from early childhood,
one following an essentially feminine-type pattern and
later becoming homosexual, the other following a masculine
pattern and becoming heterosexual. The difference does
not seem due to familial factors.

                         D. BODY BUILD

A corollary of the "third sex" hypothesis popular in the
early years of this century was the assumption that homosexuals, both male and female, represent an intermediate
body type. While this hypothesis has not been confirmed,
it is not impossible that some evidence may one day be
forthcoming to indicate that homosexual body types show
statistically significantly differences from those of the
rest of the population--though not necessarily in the
direction of intermediacy between male and female.

4812. COPPEN, A. J. "Body Build of Male Homosexuals,"
       British Medical Journal, no. 5164 (1959), 1443-45.
In a study of patients admitted to a London hospital, it
was found that homosexuals could not be distinguished by
body build.

4813. DELLA PORTA, GIOVANNI BATTISTA. **De humana physiog-
       nomia.** Vico Equense, Italy: J. Cacchium, 1586.
       272 pp.
This once influential pseudo-scientific treatise (translated into several languages) compared human character
types physiognomically to animal prototypes.

4814. EVANS, RAY B. "Physical and Biochemical Character-
       istics of Homosexual Men," **Journal of Consulting
       and Clinical Psychology,** 39 (1972), 140-47.
Found that male homosexuals had less subcutaneous fat
and smaller muscle/bone development and were longer in
proportion to bulk.

4815. KENYON, F. E. "Physique and Physical Health of
       Female Homosexuals," **Journal of Neurology, Neuro-
       surgery and Psychiatry,** 31 (1968), 487-89.
Found that lesbians were significantly heavier, with
bigger busts and waists, but less tall than controls,
and with slightly bigger hips.

4816. KRETSCHMER, ERNST. **Korperbau und Character: Unter-
       suchungen zum Konstitutionsproblem und zur Lehre**

von den Temperamenten. Berlin: Springer, 1921.
192 pp.
There is an English translation by W. J. H. Sprott, **Physique and Character: An Investigation of the Nature of
Constitution and of the Theory of Temperament** (New York:
Humanities Press, 1951; 282 pp.). Kretschmer (1888-1964)
was a German psychologist who created an influential, but
still controversial theory correlating character with
body types.

4817. PERKINS, MURIEL WILSON. "Female Homosexuality and
       Body Build," **Archives of Sexual Behavior,** 10
       (1981), 337-45.
Data show lesbians as having narrower hips, increased arm
and leg girths, less subcutaneous fat, and more muscle
than heterosexual women. However, "psychologically
passive" lesbians most closely approach the physiques of
control groups.

4818. SCHLEGEL, WILLHART SIEGMAR. "Die konstitutions-
       biologischen Grundlagen der Homosexualität,"
       **Zeitschrift für menschliche Vererbungs- und
       Konstitutionslehre,** 36 (1961-62), 341-64.
Believes that body types, esp. in the pelvic region, play
a large role in determining the sexual orientation of
males.

4819. WEIL, ARTHUR. "Körpermasse der Homosexuellen als
       Ausdrucksform ihrer speziellen Konstitution,"
       Archiv für Entwicklungsmechanik der Organismen, 49
       (1921), 538-44.
Argues that the body build of homosexuals is intermediate
between the normal male and the normal female body build.
First of a series of such articles by Weil--a former
associate of Magnus Hirschfeld--in various German periodicals.

4820. WORTIS, JOSEPH. "A Note on the Body Build of the
       Male Homosexual," **American Journal of Psychiatry,**
       93 (1937), 1121-25.
Most homosexuals [at that time] preferred to think of
their anomaly as anchored in their constitution, but the
actual evidence for constant or typical intersexual
traits among male homosexuals is wanting.

E. ANIMAL HOMOSEXUALITY

Since classical antiquity the question of homosexual behavior among animals has been much discussed. Those who
denied that animals engage in it generally regarded this
lack as a confirmation of their assumption that homosexuality was "unnatural." Recent zoological studies have
provided abundant evidence for same-sex behavior among

animals, not only in captivity, but also in the wild.   In
some discussions, however, as when opposite-sex mimicry is
termed "transvestism," researchers seem to have yielded to
a seductive, but deceptive anthropomorphism.   Also, since
the decline of such reductionist fashions as "rat psychology," the scientific community has become sceptical of
research programs that derive complex human behaviors from
simple animal models.   The question of animal homosexuality is therefore not a simple one.

4821.   ABELE, LAURENCE G. and SANDRA GILCHRIST.   "Homosex-
         ual Rape and Sexual Selection in Acanthocephalan
         Worms," **Science,** 197 (1977), 81-83.
"Homosexual rape" occurs when an assailant seals the male
victim's genital region with cement, so that the worm is
effectively removed from the reproductive pool.

4822.   AKERS, JEAN S., and CLINTON H. CONAWAY.   "Female
         Sexual Behavior in **Macaca mulatta,**" **Archives of
         Sexual Behavior,** 8 (1979), 63-80.
Documents homosexual activity among adult females in a
heterosexual group of rhesus monkeys, which seemed to be
linked with affection and not with aggression.   See also:
C. R. Carpenter, "Sexual Behavior of Free Ranging Rhesus
Monkeys (Macaca mulatta).   II.   Periodicity of Estrus,
Homosexual, Autoerotic, and Non-Conformist Behavior,"
Journal of Comparitive Psychology, 33 (1942), 143-62.

4823.   ALLEN, JOHN A., and ROBERT BOICE.   "Effects of
         Rearing on Homosexual Behavior in the Male Labor-
         atory Rat," **Psychonomic Science,** 23 (1971), 321-22.
Male interlopers introduced into the individual cages
of adults elicited mounting and thrusting in isolates.

4824.   ARONSON, L. R.   "The Sexual Behavior of Anura,"
         Natural History, 6 (1944), 1-15.
Mechanisms of sexual contact among frogs and toads.

4825.   BEACH, FRANK A.   "Animal Models for Human Sexual-
         ity," in: **Sex Hormones and Behavior** (Ciba Foun-
         dation Symposium, new series, 62).   Amsterdam: Ex-
         cerpta Medica, 1979, pp. 113-43.
Points out that while the existence of homosexual behavior
in nonhuman primates is known, the reasons why it is
initiated are obscure.   Beach offers some suggestions for
clarifying this problem.

4826.   BETZ, H. D.   "Lukian von Samosata und das Neue
         Testament," **Theologische Untersuchungen,** 76 (1961),
         199-201.
Includes discussion of the claim, found in Lucian's
"Gryllos" (second century of our era), that homosexual
behavior is not found among animals.

4827.   BUFFON, GEORGES LOUIS LECLECQ, COUNT DE.   **Histoire**

naturelle générale et particulière avec la description du Cabinet du Roi. Paris: 1749-67. 15 vols.
This epochal work fostered much comparative and developmental work in biology. More specifically, Buffon reported observations of same-sex behavior among birds.

4828. CELLI, GIORGIO. **L'omosessualità negli animali:
l'omosessualita come strumento naturale di difesa
contro la sovrapopulazione.** Milan: Longanesi,
1973. 170 pp.
One of the few works of synthesis in this field, organized
around the idea that homosexuality functions among animals
as a device to limit population growth. See also: Pietro
Ghisleni, "Pervertimenti omosessuali negli animali domes-
titici: proctiti da coito contra natura," **Nuovo Ercolani**
(Turin), 22 (1917), 303-09.

4829. CHEVALIER-SKOLNIKOFF, SUZANNE. "Male-Female,
Female-Female, and Male-Male Sexual Behavior in the
Stumptail Monkey, with Special Attention to the
Female Orgasm," **Archives of Sexual Behavior**, 3
(1974), 95-116.
In a laboratory setting, homosexual encounters were
numerous and always involved sexual inversions (i.e. the
assumption of the coital role assumed by the opposite
sex). Orgasms were observed in females during the homosexual interactions. See also her: "Homosexual Behavior
in Laboratory of Stumptail Monkeys (**Macaca arctoides**):
Forms, Contexts, and Possible Social Functions," ibid.,
5 (1976), 511-27.

4830. COOK, ROBERT. "'Lesbian' Phenotype of **Drosophila
melanogaster?**" **Nature**, 254 (1975), 241-42.
Reports the existence of a behavioral phenotype of this
fly directing rudimentary male courtship behavior towards
other females and toward males.

4831. DENNISTON, R. H. "Ambisexuality in Animals," in:
Judd Marmor (ed.), **Homosexual Behavior: A Modern
Reappraisal.** New York: Basic Books, 1980, pp. 25-
40.
Shows homosexual behavior in a range of animal species.
Suggests that conditioning, rather than hormones or
structure, is of primary importance.

4832. EBERHARD, WILLIAM G. **Sexual Selection and Animal
Genitalia.** Cambridge, MA: Harvard University
Press, 1986. 244 pp.
A pathfinding biological study of considerable indirect
relevance because of its critique of the "lock and key"
notion of the perfect complementarity of male and female
genitalia, an important component of the ideology of the
"naturalness" of heterosexuality.

4833. ECKHOLM, ERIK. "Male Snakes Find Advantage in
Appearing Female," **New York Times** (July 23, 1985),

C1, 3.
Studies of red-sided garter snakes in Canada show that
about 1/7 of them are able to mimic being female by
exuding pheromones, and thus increase their chances of
copulating with true females.

4834. EDWARDS, GEORGE. **Gleanings of Natural History.**
        London: Royal College of Physicians, 1758-64. 3
        vols.
Includes observations by the British ornithologist (1694-
1773) on same-sex behavior among birds (pp. xxi-xxiv).
Text in English and French in parallel columns.

4835. FISCHER, ROBERT B., and RONALD D. NADLER. "Affil-
        iative, Playful, and Homosexual Interactions of
        Adult Female Lowland Gorillas," **Primates,** 19
        (1978), 657-64.
Sexual interactions in four wild-born adult female gor-
illas included partner positioning and thrusting and
usually were accomplished through ventral-ventral genital
approximations.

4836. GADEAU DE KERVILLE, HENRI. **Observations relatives
        a ma note intitulée "Perversion sexuelle chez des
        coléoptères mâles."** Rouen: J. Lecerf, 1896. 12 pp.
The author recognizes "pederastie de gout," or preferential homosexuality among insects. This brochure was reprinted from **Bulletin de la Société entomologique de
France** (1896).

4837. GADPAILLE, WARREN J. "Cross-Species and Cross-
        Cultural Contributions to Understanding Homosexual-
        ity," **Archives of General Psychology,** 37 (1980),
        349-56.
Contends that Homo sapiens is the only species, however,
in which adult preferential or obligatory homosexuality
occurs naturally.

4838. GEIST, VALERIUS. **Mountain Sheep: A Study in
        Behavior and Evolution.** Chicago: University of
        Chicago Press, 1971. 383 pp.
This study by an authority in the field includes data
on observation of male-male sexual mounting in wild
sheep. See also his: **Mountain Sheep and Man in the
Northern Wilds** (Ithaca, NY: Cornell University Press,
1975; 248 pp.).

4839. GROLLET and L. LEPINAY. "L'inversion sexuelle
        chez les animaux," **Revue de l'hypnotisme,** 23
        (1908), 34-37.
On same-sex relations in male apes, bitches, and cows.
Asserts that only occasional, not true homosexuality
occurs in animals.

4840. GROOS, KARL. **Die Spiele der Tiere.** Jena: G. Fisc-
        her, 1896. 359 pp.

Deals primarily with animal play, but summarizes related studies.

4841. GUHL, A. M. "Unisexual Mating in a Flock of Wild
        Leghorn Hens," **Transactions of the Kansas Academy
        of Science**, 5 (1948), 107-11.
Socially high status hens took the male role, but without crowing or waltzing. See also his: "Social Behavior of the Domestic Fowl," **Technical Bulletin of the Agricultural Experiment Station**, 73 (1953), 1-48; as well as: E. B. Hale, "Defects in Sexual Behavior as Factors Affecting Fertility in Turkeys," **Poultry Science**, 34 (1955), 1059-67.

4842. HORAPOLLO. **Hieroglyphica.** Greek text edited by
        Conradus Leemans. Amsterdam: J. Muller, 1835. 446
        pp.
In this work, influential in the Renaissance, by an obscure Egyptian savant who lived possibly in the 5th century of our era, see II, 69 (pp. 88-89), and 95 (p. 101), on the hyena and the two partridges as homosexual. The English version, by George Boas (New York: Pantheon, 1950), is inadequately annotated. There is a related work by the Renaissance scholar Valeriano.

4843. HÜNEMÖRDER, CHRISTIAN. "Studien zur Wirkungsge-
        schichte biologischer Motive in den pseudo-Klemen-
        tinen," **Medizinhistorisches Journal**, 13 (1978),
        15-28.
On the Early Christian folklore of the hare and hyena as sexually aberrant creatures (pp. 17-20).

4844. HUNT, G. L., and M. W. HUNT. "Female Pairing in
        Western Gulls (Larus occidentalis) in Southern
        California," **Science**, 196 (1977), 1466-67.
Widely publicized research on female pairings during nesting.

4845. KARSCH-HAACK, FERDINAND. "Pederastie und Tribadie
        bei den Tieren auf Grund der Literatur," **JFsZ**, 2
        (1900), 126-60.
Surveys Greco-Roman theorizing on homosexual behavior in animals; then presents studies by modern biologists. Still a useful literature review. See, however, two more recent general studies in German: Monika Meyer-Holzapfel, "Homosexualität bei Tieren," **Praxis** (Bern), 5 (1961), 1266-72; and Friedrich Schutz, "Homosexualität bei Tieren," **Studium generale** 19 (1966), 273-85.

4846. KEVLES, BETTYANN. **Females of the Species.** Cam-
        bridge, MA: Harvard University Press, 1986. 270
        pp.
This evolutionary synthesis concentrating on female animals contains some observations on both male and female homosexuality.

4847. LABOULMÈNE, ALEXANDRE. "Examen anatomique de deux
      Melolontha vulgaris trouvés accouplés et paraissant
      du sexe mâle," **Annales de la Société Entomologique
      de France** (1859), 567-70.
Observations of the coupling of two male insects.

4848. MCBRIDE, A. F., and D. O. HEBB. "Behavior of the
      Captive Bottle-Nose Dolphin," **Journal of Compar-
      ative and Physiological Psychology**, 41 (1948),
      111-23.
Observed two kinds of homosexual activity among the
larger male dolphins: external masturbation on the
bodies of smaller males, and attempts at intromission.

4849. MCROBERT, SCOTT, and LAURIE TOMPKINS. "Courtship
      of Young Males is Ubiquitous in **Drosophila melano-
      gaster**," **Behavior Genetics**, 13 (1983A), 517--23.
In this fly, young males that were only a few hours old
stimulated courtship that was indistinguishable from that
elicited by virgin females.

4850. MAPLE, TERRY, et al. "Dominance-Related Ambisex-
      uality in Two Male Rhesus Monkeys (**Macaca mu-
      latta**)," **Journal of Biological Psychology**, 19
      (1977), 25-28.
Homosexual behavior was repeatedly observed in two young
male rhesus monkeys raised with two older female baboons.

4851. MORRIS, DESMOND. "Homosexuality in the Ten-Spined
      Stickleback," **Behaviorism**, 4:4 (1952), 233-61.
Male sexual behavior in experiments in crowding with
fish. See also his: "Reproductive Behavior in the Zebra
Finch with Special Reference to Pseudo-Female Behavior
and Displacement Activities," ibid., 6 (1954), 271-322;
and "The Causation of Pseudo-Female and Pseudo-Male Behavior: A Further Comment," ibid., 8 (1955), 45-56.

4852. NOBLE, RALPH G. "Male Hamsters Display Female
      Sexual Responses," **Hormones and Behavior**, 12
      (1979), 293-98.
Compared to the commonly studied mammalian species, the
male hamster is highly bisexual. However, more intense
stimulation is required to elicit the lordosis response in
contrast with females.

4853. PRESCOTT, R. G. W. "Mounting Behaviour in the
      Female Cat," **Nature**, 228 (December 12, 1970),
      1106-07.
Among female cats mounting behavior occurs at oestrus and
is directed preferentially toward other oestrous cats.

4854. RASMUSSEN, E. WULFF. "Experimental Homosexual
      Behavior in Male Albino Rats," **Acta Psychologica**,
      11 (1955), 303-34.
An attempt to obtain data through conditioning rats that
would help to understand human homosexual behavior.

4855.   SHARMA, R. P.   "Light-Dependent Homosexual Activity
        in Males of a Mutant of Drosphila Monogaster,"
        Experientia, 33 (1977), 171-73.
Cytogenetic and behavioral studies on an x-ray induced
mutant of the fly Drosophila melanogaster revealed light-
dependent homosexual activity in the males of the mutant.

4856.   THOR, D. H.   "Reciprocal Homosexual Mounting
        Behavior in Paired Anosmic Male Rats," **Psycholog-
        ical Reports,** 47 (1980), 349-50.
Four isolate male rats when paired with anosmia treatment
with InSO4 engaged in repeated copulatory mounts with
three partners.

4857.   WARD, INGEBORG L.   "Prenatal Stress Feminizes and
        Demasculinizes the Behavior of Males," **Science,** 175
        (1972), 82-84.
Prenatally stressed rats showed low levels of male copulatory behavior and high rates of female lordotic response.

4858.   WEINRICH, JAMES D.   "Is Homosexuality Biologically
        Normal?"   in: William Paul (ed.), **Homosexuality:
        Social, Psychological and Biological Issues.**   Bev-
        erly Hills, CA: Sage, 1982, pp. 197-208.
Discusses homosexual behavior in animals, pointing out
that it is important to differentiate studies which have
been made in animals in the wild from those derived from
laboratory situations, where behavior patterns may be
modified significantly (and deliberately).   Also examines
the concept of the natural in its biological and general
contexts.

Billings, Dwight B.   4030
Billings, Joseph   1419
Binder, Hans   4031
Binding, Paul   1902
Bingham, Caroline   640
Binns, J. W.   1806
Birchard, Roy   2307
Biren, Joan E.   1684
Birk, Lee   3830, 4756
Birke, Lynda I. A.   475, 2148
Birnbaum, H. Jean   3962
Bishop, George   2962
Bithell, Jethro   1865
Bittle, William E.   3317
Bixler, Ray   3148
Blachford, Gregg   259
Black, David   4668
Black, Donald J.   2877
Black, Kathryn N.   3512
Black, W. W.   4203
Blackburn, Catherine E.   4066
Blackford, Barbara   4332
Blackmon, Mary K.   3867
Blackridgge, Persimmon   3758
Blackstone, William, Sir   4160
Blackwood, Evelyn   1313, 1426
Blaczynski, Alex   3631
Blaffer, Sarah C.   1460
Blaine, Graham B.   2657
Blair, Doniphan   978
Blair, Jerry D.   4212
Blair, Ralph   2308, 2309, 2310, 2658, 3362, 3645, 3567,
   3840
Blake, James   4447
Blake, Roger   1238
Blamires, David   2247
Blanch, Leslie   1903
Blanchard, Ray   3452, 3603
Blanchard, Roy   3434
Blanco, Jose   1946
Blank, Joani   1685, 2604
Blatt, Emily   1179
Bleibtreu-Ehrenberg, Gisela   575, 1314, 1386, 1420, 3942
Bleuel, Hans Peter   766
Bley, Wulf   2806
Blizzard, Peter J.   245
Bloch, Dorothy   3449
Bloch, Herbert A.   4448
Bloch, Iwan   40, 576, 641, 707, 1315, 3203
Bloch, Robert   467
Block, Adam   2102
Blok, Diana   1686
Blom-Cooper, Louis   4161
Blondeau, Nicolas   2447
Bloomfield, Barry Cambray   1906
Blouin, Lenora P.   2015

Brown, Gabrielle   2530
Brown, Holly   1819
Brown, Howard   4640
Brown, Hudson   2507
Brown, Judith C.   861
Brown, Julia S.   1317
Brown, Laura S.   3761
Brown, Linda   2020
Brown, Marvin   239, 3166
Brown, Peter   2085
Brown, Rita Mae   2949
Browne, Angela   3946
Browne, F. W. Stella   2021
Browne, Susan E.   3039
Browning, Don S.   2248
Brownstone, Harvey   3895
Brubaker, John K.   4716
Brucker, Gene   862
Brule, Christian   3205
Brundage, James   581
Bruneau, Jean   1038
Bruneau, Philippe   1574
Brunel, René   1023
Brunnsake, Sture   1575
Bruns, Roger A.   938
Brussard, A. J. A.   2249
Bruun, Kettil   4541
Bruyn, E. B. de   475
Bry, Adelaide   3062
Bryan, William Jennings   2101
Bryant, Anita   2366
Bryant, Clifton   3027
Bryk, Felix   1350
Brzek, Antonin   3465
Buchanan, G. Sidney   4379
Buchen, Irving   1859, 1914
Buckle, Richard   1812
Buckler, John   476
Buckley, Michael J.   2250
Buckley, William F., Jr.   2722
Buffiere, Felix   477
Buffon, Georges Louis Leclecq, Count de   4827
Buffum, Peter C.   4452
Buhrich, Neil   2611, 3167, 3450, 4001
Bulatov, Sergeï Iakovlevich   4144
Bulkin, Elly   2022, 2023, 3262
Bulliet, Clarence Joseph   4002
Bullinga, Marcel   2811, 3206
Bullough, Bonnie   406, 942
Bullough, Vern L.   6, 122, 404, 405, 406, 433, 434, 580,
    581, 942, 943, 1022, 1108, 1884, 2191, 2889, 3207,
    4003, 4015, 4063, 4722
Bunch, Charlotte   373, 1226
Burbidge, Michael   3339
Burchard, Ernst   2980
Burdick, J. Alan   2890, 3632

Groth, A. Nicholas   3962, 4456, 4601
Grotzfeld, Heinz   1043
Groves, Patricia A.   3772
Grube, John   958
Gruen, John   2094
Grumley, Michael   2618
Grunbaum, Adolf   3678
Grygier, Tadeusz   3423
Gubar, Susan   2045, 2046, 4010
Gubel'man, Minei Izrailevich   910
Guérin, Daniel   2768, 2775, 2776, 2863
Guerra, Francisco   1477
Guerri, Domenico   876
Guest, Barbara   2047
Guhl, A. M.   4841
Guild, Naome   3298
Guilmot, P. H.   3773
Guindon, Andre   2190, 2198
Guiraud, Pierre   2433, 2459
Guirdham, Arthur   2349
Gulik, Robert Hans van   1105
Gumperz, J.   1040
Gundersheimer, Werner   877
Gundlach, Ralph H.   3453, 4602
Gunnison, Foster   1249
Gurwell, John K.   4588
Gurwitz, Sharon B.   3522
Gury, Christian   4132
Gusmão, Chrysolito de   4133
Guthman, Edward   1740
Gutierez, Lewis   2833
Gutman, Robert W.   2095
Gutstadt, Joseph P.   3850
Guttag, Bianca   166
Guyon, René   52
Guyot, Yves   4424
Gwenwald, Morgan   2916

Haas, Harold L.   2268
Habel, H.   4802
Haber, Barbara   380
Haber, Lynne   305
Haberlandt, M.   1359
Hachimonjiya Jisho   1155
Hacker, Hanna   2048
Hacker, Helen Mayer   3189, 3271
Hadden, Samuel B.   3808, 3833
Hader, Marvin   2917
Hadermann-Misguich, Lydie   1601
Haeberle, Erwin J.   105, 774, 1250
Hafen, Bruce C.   4251
Hafkamp, Hans   1938
Hafter, Ernst   4134
Hage, Per   1397
Hagstrum, Jean H.   627, 1939
Hahn, Pierre   132, 731

Hailsham, Quintin Hogg, 2nd Viscount   4175
Haines, William H.   4471
Haire, Norman   133, 151
Halasz, Gyula   712
Halberstadt-Freud, H.   2619
Hale, E. B.   4841
Hall, Marny A.   2789, 3774, 3871
Hall, Richard   1827, 1916
Hallbeck, Nils   925
Halleck, Seymour L.   3765, 4552
Haller, John S.   4732
Haller, Robin M.   4732
Hallett, Judith P.   547
Halliday, Caroline   308
Halloran, Joe   2319
Hallpike, C. R.   1360
Halsband, Robert   656
Hamann, Deryl F.   4219
Hamilton, Alexander   1190
Hamilton, Gilbert van Tassel   3151
Hamilton, Wallace   959
Hammelmann, H. A.   4135
Hammer, Max   4553
Hammer, William   1361
Hammersmith, Sue Kiefer   100, 3480
Hammill, Dennis   2739
Hammill, Pete   2739
Hammond, Harmony   1651
Hammond, William A.   1434
Hanckel, Frances   162, 3337
Hanna, Randel   203
Hannon, Gerald   2954, 3045
Hanry, Pierre   1362
Hanscombe, Gillian E.   180, 3872
Hansen, Bent   17
Hansen, Bert   424
Hansen, Edward   3103
Hansen, Gary L.   3523
Hansen, Kent A.   4348
Hansen, Ted L.   4384
Hansen, Waldemar   1044
Hanson, William   2590
Hansson, Johan   926
Hardin, Clay W.   3031
Harding, Carl B.   1251
Hardison, Sam   1652
Hardman, Edward T.   1398
Hardman, Paul D.   418
Hardy, Barbara   3389
Hardy, Robin   1884
Hare, Denise Brown   1630
Hare, E. H.   3466
Harkavy, Jeffrey M.   4252
Harlan, Sparky   3224
Harley, M.   3353
Harper, Ida   4554

Marcuse, Herbert   3707
Marcuse, Max   153
Marcuse Pfeiffer Gallery   1700
Mardh, Per-Anders   4621
Marecek, Jeanne   3620
Maret, Stephen M.   3538
Margoliese, M. Sydney   4775
Margolis, Stephen   4628
Marino, Giambattista   880
Marion, A.-P.   1202
Mariotti, Ettore   885, 3972
Mark, Mary Ellen   1203
Markey, T. L.   605
Markham, Fred   3235
Marks, Elaine   720, 1896
Marks, Jim   3276
Marks, Neil Alan   2395, 2997
Markus, Georg   791, 2715
Marlowe, Christopher   1808, 1818
Marlowe, Kenneth   3236
Marmor, Judd   142, 1321, 1341, 2869, 2876, 3659, 3711,
    4787, 4831
Marnais, Philip   1204
Marone, Silvio   1614
Marot, Gerard   1701
Marotta, Toby   1261
Marrou, Henri-Irenée   541
Marsan, Hugo   2589
Marsault-R., Ralf   2542
Marsden, William   1205
Marshall, Donald S.   1337, 1371
Marshall, John   2543
Marshall, W. L.   3785
Marti, Mario   886
Martin, A. Damien   2222, 3192, 3346
Martin, April   3786
Martin, Clyde E.   111, 112
Martin, Clyde V.   3539
Martin, Del   329
Martin, Enos D.   2278
Martin, John Bartlow   4496
Martin, John L.   4698
Martin, Maurice   1370
Martin, Robert   2679, 4605
Martin, Robert Bernard   1964
Martin, Robert K.   1931, 1965, 1966
Martin, Ruth K.   2278
Martinez, Inez   2019
Martínez, José Augustín   4143, 4497
Martínez Pizarro, Joaquín   605
Martinson, Floyd M.   3950
Marty, Eric   1912
Masini, Mario   887, 1615
Mason, H. A.   2157
Massa, Robert   4430
Massey, Marilyn Chapin   372

Moore, Thomas   4583
Moos, Malcolm   4460
Moraga, Cherrie   3278
Moran, P. A.   3466
Moran, W. L.   449
Moret, Alexandre   450
Morgan, David   378
Morgan, M. Gwyn   543
Morgan, Ted   1970
Morgenthaler, Fritz   1375, 3708
Morin, Jack   2598, 2599
Morin, Jean-Paul   229
Morin, Stephen F.   250, 2681, 3348, 3418, 3419, 3541,
    4702
Morony, John H.   3475
Morreau, J.   1569
Morrione, Thomas J.   3520
Morris, Clarence   1097
Morris, Desmond   4851
Morris, Donald R.   1372
Morris, Julie   162, 3343
Morris, Katrina K.   4275
Morris, Paul   2372
Morris, Philip A.   256
Morris, Vicki   3009
Morrison, Elizabeth G.   3790
Morrison, James K.   3791
Morrison, Kristin   1971
Morse, Stanley   3173
Morson, Tom   3506
Mortimer, Lee   2744
Morton, D. R.   4500
Morton, R. S.   4629
Mosak, Harold H.   3733
Moses, A. Elfin   3384
Moses, Alice   3134
Mosher, Donald L.   3561
Moss, C. Scott   4501
Mosse, George   795
Mossop, Brian   374
Mott, Luiz R. B.   999
Mottram, Eric   1972
Mouffarege, Nicolas A.   1635
Mount, Eric   2223
Moussa, Ahmed M.   454
Movement for a New Society, Gay Theory Work Group   2782
Muchmore, Wes   2590
Mucklow, Bonnie M.   3879
Muecke, Frances   544
Mueller, Johann Valentin   4745
Muensterberger, Werner   1413
Mukerji, Kamal   3597
Muller, Herbert Ernst   4115
Mullins, Charles E.   4276
Munch, Edvard   1645
Munro, Hector   1959

Nelson, Victor F.   4505
Nerf, Swasarnt   1550
Nery, Lamberto C.   1208
Nestle, Joan   2956, 3011
Nestor, Pauline   3082
Neugebauer, Franz Ludwig von   4059
Neuhaus, Holger   2673
Neuman, Elias   4506
Nevid, Jeffrey   3542
Nevis, Joel A.   2440
New South Wales. Department of the Attorney General and of
   Justice   4195
Newman, Graeme   230
Newmark, Stephen R.   4779
Newmeyer, John A.   3326
Newton, David E.   2683, 2684, 3978
Newton, Esther   330, 1803, 2019, 4019
Nibley, Hugh   451
Nicholls, Mark   1948
Nichols, Dennison W.   3979
Nichols, Eve K.   4703
Nichols, F. M.   4162
Nichols, Jack   171, 2957, 2994
Nichols, Margaret   3012
Nichols, Stuart E.   4703
Nicholson, Joe   192
Nicolson, Nigel   1890
Nicosia, Gerald   2003, 3237
Niditch, Susan   2224
Niederman, William   3742
Nielsen, John   3876
Nies, Judith   2743
Nietzsche, Friedrich   2161
Nimmo, H. Arlo   1209
Nin Frias, Alberto   68, 1974
Nip, R. I. A.   821
Nobili, Nella   326
Noble, Ralph G.   4852
Nobler, Hindy   3833
Noel, Thomas J.   2940
Noguera, Gary   1010
Nomadic Sisters   2609
Noonan, John T.   422
Noordam, Dirk Jaap   822
Norman, Frank   4507
Norris, Linda   4559
Norse, Harold   1975
Norske Forbundet av 1948   4146
North American Man/Boy Love Association   1265
Norton, Joseph L.   3387
Norton, Rictor C.   1872, 1976, 2711
Nouveau, Pierre   747
Novati, F.   888
Nuehring, Elane M.   2685, 3120, 3503
Nugent, Robert   2330, 3862
Nungesser, Lon G.   3420, 3521, 3541, 3922, 4705